Readings in Political Philosophy

Readings in Political Philosophy

THEORY AND APPLICATIONS

edited by

Diane Jeske

and

Richard Fumerton

broadview press

LIBRARY AND ARCHIVES CANADA CATALOGUING IN PUBLICATION

   Readings in political philosophy : theory and applications / edited by Diane Jeske and Richard Fumerton.

Includes bibliographical references and index.
ISBN 978-1-55111-765-2

   1. Political science—Philosophy—Textbooks.
I. Fumerton, Richard A., 1949- II. Jeske, Diane, 1967-

JA71.R42 2011   320.01   C2011-905399-3

BROADVIEW PRESS is an independent, international publishing house, incorporated in 1985.

NORTH AMERICA
Post Office Box 1243
Peterborough, Ontario
Canada K9J 7H5

2215 Kenmore Ave.
Buffalo, New York, USA 14207
TEL: (705) 743-8990
FAX: (705) 743-8353

customerservice@broadviewpress.com

UK, EUROPE, CENTRAL ASIA, MIDDLE EAST, AFRICA,
INDIA, AND SOUTHEAST ASIA
Eurospan Group, 3 Henrietta St., London WC2E 8LU
United Kingdom
TEL: 44 (0) 1767 604972
FAX: 44 (0) 1767 601640
eurospan@turpin-distribution.com

AUSTRALIA & NEW ZEALAND
NewSouth Books
c/o TL Distribution
15-23 Helles Avenue, Moorebank, NSW, 2170
TEL: (02) 8778 9999
FAX: (02) 8778 9944
orders@tldistribution.com.au

We welcome comments and suggestions regarding any aspect of our publications—please feel free to contact us at the addresses above or at broadview@broadviewpress.com / www.broadviewpress.com.

Copy-edited by Martin Boyne

Designed and typeset by Em Dash Design

 This book is printed on paper
containing 50% post-consumer fibre.

Printed in Canada

Contents

UNIT II

Rights, Liberty, and the Limits of Government *261*

Contents

UNIT III

Property and the Distribution of Resources   725

UNIT IV

Responses to Injustice   855

Preface

This anthology provides a survey of important issues and concepts in Western political thought, from Plato to the present day. Our aim is to show both the continuity and the development of the issues over time. Therefore, rather than arranging the anthology chronologically, we have organized it topically. Most of the sections begin with highly theoretical discussions of fundamental principles that deal with the issues at hand. But we also demonstrate the importance of such theory by including articles that apply these principles to contemporary issues and also by including court cases and other political documents that illustrate the importance of getting clear about underlying presuppositions. Many political philosophy anthologies fail to include court cases on the grounds that such inclusion would blur the distinction between political philosophy and philosophy of law. It is our view, however, that it is a mistake to make any sharp distinction between many of the issues that arise in the two fields. After all, perhaps the most important application of any political theory finds expression in the construction and development of legal institutions. Our goal is to make students more informed, thoughtful, and reflective thinkers about political issues and their legal and social implications by teaching them how to reason about issues that arise in these fields. We hope to give them an appreciation of political theory by showing them how that theory can help to clarify contemporary debates about important topics.

We precede the readings contained in each unit with a comprehensive introduction designed to give students an overview of the issues addressed in that unit. In addition, these introductions engage in an evaluation of various theories and offer new alternatives not included in the readings. The section introductions offer explicit examples of philosophical reasoning to aid students in their philosophical development. Unlike other anthologies, this one has been designed to promote philosophical thinking and development, rather than simply to encourage an absorption of positions with names attached. The teaching of political philosophy, we believe, needs to emphasize philosophy as much as it does politics. To this end, we provide study questions at the end of each reading. These questions stress the philosophical activities of identifying, constructing, and evaluating arguments.

Political philosophy necessarily involves basic ethical concepts such as right and wrong, legitimate and illegitimate, duty, obligation, reason, justification, etc., so some grasp of basic ethics is needed for any careful study of political philosophy. However, political philosophy courses often do not have ethics as a prerequisite. Therefore, our section introductions provide some of the necessary background, so that students can go into the readings with a broader knowledge base and can place the issues discussed into the larger philosophical and ethical landscape.

We intend the anthology to be useful for undergraduate political philosophy courses at any level. A lower-level course might involve a broad survey, using only a couple of articles from each section, maybe one theoretical and one applied piece. An upper-level course might focus on two or three sections, delving into more depth on selected topics.

We would like to thank a number of people who helped enormously in the design and construction of this anthology. These include our research assistants Heather Libby and Christoffer Lammer-Heindel; our departmental assistant Allison Roggenburg; our copyeditor Martin Boyne; Alex Sager, a previous editor at Broadview whose support for the project was invaluable; and our current editor, Greg Janzen, whose advice and constructive criticism helped bring the project to a successful completion. We also appreciate the suggestions made by a number of anonymous referees.

This text provides a thorough overview of the central issues in political philosophy. Political philosophy is best understood, we believe, as a branch of *ethics*. Ethics deals with questions about our reasons for action, our moral obligations, what is in our best interest, what constitutes a virtuous character, and what is good or bad, right or wrong. Political philosophy deals with these questions as well, but it does so as they arise in the context of a state or society. So, for example, political philosophy addresses questions such as the following: What reasons would we have to create a state if we did not have one? What reasons, if any, do we have to obey the laws of an already existing state? Is living in a state and obeying its laws always, or ever, in our best interest? What constitutes a good state? Which sorts of legislation is it right or wrong of the state to enact and enforce? To what extent, if any, should the state attempt to make its citizens virtuous?

It is obvious, then, that one cannot adequately deal with the central questions of political philosophy without some prior attempt to deal with the central questions of ethics. If, for example, we do not know what, in general, constitutes a right or a wrong action, we will be unable to assess the rightness or wrongness of a group of legislators enacting and enforcing laws regulating, say, gay marriage, the production and consumption of pornography, affirmative action in university admissions, or the admission of women to the bar. Debates in political philosophy usually reflect underlying disagreement about the answers to ethical questions, and we need to understand that underlying ethical disagreement if we are to understand the political debate.

As an example, let us consider one of the most famous debates in the history of Western political philosophy, that between Thomas Hobbes and John Locke. Hobbes claims that a legitimate state is one in which the sovereign has nearly unlimited power: the sovereign has the authority to seize and distribute property as he sees fit, the discretion to order and enforce punishments, including capital punishment, according to his own judgment, and so on. Locke, on the other hand, insists that a government that failed to preserve citizens' claims to property and to preserve their lives if they had not committed one of a previously specified range of offenses would be illegitimate. Why did Hobbes and Locke differ so sharply about what constitutes a legitimate state?

Their political differences were the result of a radical disagreement about the nature and source of morality. Locke believed that God is the source of all moral claims and obligations, and, thus, even in a state of nature—a condition without any civil government (without, in Hobbes's words, "a power sufficient to overawe them all")—we have moral obligations to preserve not only our own but all human life. Because the preservation of human life requires, Locke believed, exclusive claims to resources such as food and shelter, every human being has a moral obligation to respect the property claims, or 'rights,' of other human beings. These 'rights,' or claims to resources, continue to place constraints on others even in the state; in fact, the entire purpose of the state is the protection of moral rights to our lives and property.

Locke's *Second Treatise of Government* is clearly, at least in part, a response to Hobbes's *Leviathan*, in which Hobbes offers a very different picture of the nature of morality. Hobbes's state of nature is a condition in which no one has any moral claims or obligations. In the state of nature, I "own" what I can get my hands on and keep others' hands off of. As soon as you manage to lead one of my sheep away from my herd, that sheep is now yours—at least until I succeed in retrieving it or in killing you. Given that there are no moral claims or 'rights' in the state of nature, there are no such claims to place constraints on the state. For Hobbes, the purpose of the state is to keep us out of the hell that is the state of nature, so the sovereign is given virtually unlimited power so that he can keep all of us in line and prevent our return to that state of nature. Talk of pre-existing 'rights' is, for the most part, destructive, and so it should be suppressed by the sovereign.

The debate between Hobbes and Locke presents a very stark example of how different understandings of morality lead to different understandings of the nature of the best or the legitimate state. Their conflict over the nature of morality led them to give different answers to questions about the nature of our reasons to obey the state, the limits on legitimate legislation, the extent of the liberty of citizens, and the appropriate distribution of property, punishment, revolution, and war.

All of these issues are addressed in this text, and we have divided up the readings from figures such as Hobbes and Locke so that their views on, for example, political obligation can be found in the unit on that particular topic. Most political philosophy texts include long selections from the important figures in the field, and instructors then need to find the relevant portions for each topic. Our approach has the virtue of allowing instructors to use just those portions of the texts of major figures that they need,

given the topics they intend to cover in their classes, or, alternatively, to assign all of the readings from a given figure (requiring students only to flip a few more pages in order to do so). Our organization of the text reflects our understanding of the field of political philosophy as a branch of ethics rather than as a sub-field of intellectual history. Figures such as Locke and Hobbes are given their due, we believe, only when it is clearly shown that they were ethicists with coherent, wide-ranging theories that they extended to the political realm. They continue to lay claim to our interest because they provide intriguing and challenging answers to the central questions in the field. We hope that the following text, then, not only introduces students to political philosophy itself, but also allows them to see the nature of the broader ethical debates that underlie the subject.

The title of this text emphasizes theory *and application*. Throughout the text we have therefore included legal cases that are usually not found in political philosophy texts. We believe that these cases provide an ideal way for students to see the impact of ethical and political philosophy upon real lives. For example, in *Bradwell v. Illinois*, students can see the concrete consequences for Myra Bradwell (and all other women in the state of Illinois at the time) of a judge's views about what constitutes the virtuous life for a woman. *Bowers v. Harwick* demonstrates how views about the ethics of various kinds of sexual practices influence the creation and enforcement of law. These cases provide wonderful opportunities for students to engage with theoretical issues in a real-life context with real-world consequences.

Organization and Issues

UNIT I: The State of Nature and the Nature of the State: Understanding Political Obligation

The first unit of the text addresses fundamental questions about reasons in political philosophy: What reasons, if any, do we have to create and enter a state? And what reasons, if any, do we have to obey the laws of the state in which we find ourselves?

The first question—about our reasons to enter a state—is vividly addressed by the so-called *social contract theories*. Originally presented by Glaucon in Plato's *Republic*, social contract theory attempts to defend a claim about our reasons to create and enter a state by imagining what life would be like in the state of nature, a condition without a political authority. The various difficulties encountered in the state of nature—at their extreme, these difficulties are understood by Hobbes as a "state of war of every man against every man"—give us reasons to create and become members of a state, at least according to the social contract theorists. As we have already seen with Hobbes and Locke, ethical assumptions—about the nature of self-interest, the nature of morality, and the relationship between self-interest and morality—are usually made starkly clear in their discussions of the state of nature.

Most of us are born into already existent states, not into a state of nature. Even if there were people once in a state of nature who voluntarily contracted to enter civil society, how could their contracting together bind later generations? The second section of this unit addresses this question: do people like us have reasons to obey the laws of the state, and, if so, what are the grounds of those reasons? Various answers to this question have been given: obeying the law is in our best interest; obedience to the law brings about the best long-term consequences for everyone concerned; we have consented to obey the law even if we did not "sign" the original contract; we have a duty to do our part in sustaining fair cooperative endeavors such as the state; and we have obligations to fellow citizens that are like our obligations to friends, family members, and colleagues. Again, one's background moral assumptions will play a large role in determining which, if any, of these accounts is plausible, because each account relies on various assumptions about the range and types of moral duties that human agents can or do have.

UNIT II: Rights, Liberty, and the Limits of Government
The Western political tradition since the Enlightenment has centrally invoked the concept of a 'right':

the American Revolution was fought in order to protect the colonists' rights to life, liberty, and the pursuit of happiness; the French Revolution was supposed to be guided by a commitment to the rights of man; and the United Nations takes as fundamental a list of human rights that it is dedicated to protecting. But what is it for a person to have a right to something? Jeremy Bentham, reflecting upon the aims and results of the French Revolution, famously described talk of rights as "nonsense upon stilts" that does far more harm than good. Bentham was, not coincidentally, a utilitarian—i.e., he held a moral theory that regards right action as action that produces the most good possible. So for Bentham, no action types—such as denying citizens the ability to speak or to practice their religions—are wrong from the outset: everything depends on whether such actions will maximize value. Other philosophers such as Robert Nozick take claims about rights as basic in their theories and regard individual rights as placing constraints on the government's legitimate ability to promote the general welfare.

Questions about rights—what are they, do we have any, and, if so, which do we have—are naturally connected to questions about liberty; after all, if someone is asked what rights they have, they will probably answer that they have at least 'a right to liberty (or freedom).' Does it make sense to suppose that we have a right to liberty? What would be involved in having such a right? What implications would such a right have for the government's ability to promote the morality of its citizens? We devote an entire sub-unit (*Free Speech* in Unit IIE) to the issue of censorship, because it has been a site of contestation with respect to the limits of government, particularly the government's ability to attempt to make its citizens good people.

Political philosophy shares an important feature in common with political practice: until very recently its practitioners have been almost exclusively male. Given this fact, it is sad but, perhaps, not surprising that women have typically been relegated to subordinate roles, both in theory and in reality. Therefore, the issue of the role of women in the state and the state's function in regulating familial relationships such as marriage provides a good arena for testing and applying more theoretical claims (see Unit IIE). Is it permissible for the state to bar women from certain professions? Does the state have the right to deny homosexual couples the ability to enter into the marriage contract? Ought the state to take positive measures to attempt to bring about gender equity?

UNIT III: Property and the Distribution of Resources

Another topic that provides a good site for the testing and elaboration of political theories is property and its appropriate distribution. 'Property' is a broad term: Locke, for example, claims that our fundamental piece of property is ourselves—our bodies, minds, and abilities. Any resources that an individual might need or want, especially those that she might have an interest in laying exclusive claim to, could, in principle, acquire the status of being property. So we don't want to construe the notion of property so narrowly as to include only such things as material possessions. How can resources such as land come to be exclusively held by an individual? Do people have rights to resources such as land, rights that the state should protect even at the cost of the general welfare? Or should resources be distributed in order to maximize benefits for all members of the state? Political philosophy in the Western tradition has been highly concerned, from antiquity to the present day, with questions about distributive justice, so this unit is divided into two sections, the first devoted to classical theories and the second to contemporary developments of those theories.

UNIT IV: Responses to Injustice

Once one has in hand a theory of what a good state looks like and how its citizens ought to behave, one is ready to confront questions about how to deal with bad states and with citizens who fail to fulfill their obligations. When citizens break the law, what, if anything, justifies punishing them? Is the state ever justified in punishing citizens who have not broken the law? What forms of punishment are legitimate? If citizens or the government have acted wrongly in the past, what sorts of corrective measures, if any, are permissible and/or required now? Such issues have come to the fore in the discussion of various controversial policies regarding affirmative action and proposals for reparations for groups whose members claim to have been wronged. When are citizens justified in attempting to dismantle, or break away from, their current state? When are citizens justified in waging war against other states? Many of these questions lie at the cutting edge of contemporary political debate, and it might be interesting to combine the use of this text with discussion of current events.

The State of Nature and the Nature of the State: Understanding Political Obligation

Introduction

Perhaps the most fundamental questions in political philosophy concern our reasons for living together with others in a state, society, or community, the way in which we accomplish that goal through the establishment of a legitimate state, and the way in which the existence of a legitimate state creates obligations—obligations that citizens have to obey the commands of the governing body of their state, and obligations that governing bodies have to their citizens. As we will see, these questions cannot be divorced from more general questions concerning what people have reason to do, and why they have reason to do it.

Basing Obligation on Self-Interest

Many philosophers have found it useful to contrast the state of people living together in a society governed by law with what is sometimes called the state of nature. This state of nature is thought of by some (e.g., Hobbes; see reading 2) as a situation in which people live by no rules other than those they judge to be conducive to their own well-being—it's a kind of "dog-eat-dog" world in which we survive only by our own wits and strength. We regard other people as potential threats competing with us for the same resources. If they get in our way, we'll take whatever steps seem practical to get them out of our way. Others (e.g., Locke) concede that even in the state of nature there are moral laws discoverable by reason, though there is no man-made law

to resolve inevitable disputes concerning what that moral law requires in particular controversial situations. Some of the philosophers, such as Locke (see reading 3), who talk about this state of nature seem to think of it as an historical description of some period from which people actually emerged. But others, such as Hobbes, clearly intend it to be merely a hypothetical situation—a way in which people *can* exist, and a manner of existence that we want to contrast with living together in society.

Often the point of discussing a state of nature is to emphasize the need either to escape such a state (if one thinks that we actually were at one time in such a state) or to ensure that one never approaches such a state (if one is using it merely as a way of underscoring the function of society as a means of avoiding such states). The "dog-eat-dog" existence in a state of nature is famously described by Hobbes as a state in which our lives are "solitary, poor, nasty, brutish, and short." It is a state that rational people will realize they must escape or avoid. In one classical approach, the reasons we have to avoid a state of nature are reasons of self-interest (Plato's Glaucon in reading 1, Hobbes, and Gauthier in reading 5). Indeed, the presupposition of the theories these philosophers develop about our reasons to construct and obey law is what we might call the *strong rationality thesis of egoism*. Let us say that a person acts egoistically when that person has as his or her sole ultimate goal or end in acting his or her own well-being (where well-being is sometimes construed as pleasure and the avoidance of pain, but also is sometimes construed more broadly to include benefits to oneself that go beyond pleasure and avoidance of pain). The strong rationality thesis, then, is the claim that all and only egoistic action is *rational*.

In addition to, or perhaps instead of, a rationality claim, some philosophers have embraced the thesis of *psychological egoism*—the claim that everyone always acts egoistically. In some versions, the thesis is the very strong claim that it is a kind of law of human nature that people act egoistically. If this is true, the impossibility of acting any other way might render moot the question of whether one ought to act egoistically. Many have found plausible the claim (most famously associated with Kant) that "ought implies can" (or more plausibly, perhaps, "ought implies genuine choice"). It makes no sense to recommend a course of action that it is absolutely impossible to take.

Assuming that rationality from an egoistic perspective dictates that we escape the state of nature, the question then becomes how to achieve this goal. The difficulty is particularly acute on the assumption that we are not going to stop being self-interested. The very self-interest that drives us to escape the state of nature will presumably still be at play when we live within a society. Hobbes seems to think that the key to escaping the state of nature lies in an agreement or contract by which we create a sovereign with unlimited power and a sharp sword to enforce agreements (including the very agreement by which the sovereign was created). By creating the danger of punishment for violating agreements that allow for cooperation (and all that we can accomplish through such cooperation), we create reasons of self-interest that we would otherwise lack in a state of nature. Hobbes is often thought of as defending one form of a so-called *social contract theory*. Although developed in far less detail, the same idea is put forth by Glaucon, who speculates that society comes about through agreements that people make to live by various rules—the rules that we call morality. As Glaucon describes them, these rules are a kind of reluctant

compromise forged by self-interested people who would like to dominate others but who realize that the best they can probably achieve is agreements aimed at achieving mutual constraint.

Hobbes's recourse to a sovereign who administers sure and swift punishment may seem too drastic to those of us raised to reject any form of totalitarian government. After all, we might ask, why wouldn't rational persons keep agreements, even in a state of nature, in order to gain a reputation for being trustworthy, thereby also securing for themselves the future cooperation of others? Hobbes, it seems, would respond that we, in our comfortable situations, are not vividly imagining the horrors of the state of nature and that state's tendency to brew distrust and suspicion. All it takes is one bad apple to ruin the bushel: as long as there are some persons either too short-sighted or too vainglorious to desire genuine cooperation, the rest of us will need to be on our guard. How can I be sure that you are not one of the duplicitous few who seek to triumph over me while appearing to be sincerely interested in cooperation? As long as that possibility remains, I need to focus on gaining as much power, and therefore protection, as I can, even if that involves breaking covenants. The presence of the sovereign is supposed to send a clear and unmistakable signal to the duplicitous—"Don't even think about trying it!"—and to the rest of us—"Go ahead, cooperate, I've got your back."

Ironically, perhaps, Hobbes himself raises one of the most powerful objections to the idea that we can create a society (a leviathan) replete with reasons to obey the law relying on nothing but raw self-interest. He has the famous "fool" ask why rational self-interested people won't be constantly prepared to break laws (or contracts or agreements), even with a sovereign in place when they can reasonably conclude that the reward is huge and risk minimal. In *The Republic*, Glaucon in effect asks the "fool's question" of Socrates, invoking an exotic hypothesis involving the "Ring of Gyges"—a mythical ring that allows its owner to become invisible. Would the owner of such a ring, a ring that allows one to escape punishment, have any reason to walk the straight and narrow path of morality and law?

Hobbes, it is pretty clear, would likely respond in this fashion: when you get yourself a ring like Gyges had, then we'll talk again. For now, Hobbes is concerned with the reasons that we ordinary human beings have, and, he believes, no one of us is sufficiently superior that it is rational for us to take on the entire commonwealth at the risk of death. We also need to remember that Hobbes is not imagining a criminal justice system with rights for the accused, appeals processes, and constitutional bans on cruel and unusual punishment. Given the power of the sovereign and of her government, any ordinary human being would have good reason not to risk getting into the sovereign's clutches.

We said that Hobbes is usually thought of as one of the most famous social contract theorists—a political philosopher who sought to understand political obligation, the glue that binds us together in a society, in terms of contracts or agreements. But according to one way of thinking about Hobbes, the contract or agreement that creates the sovereign is merely a means to achieve an end—the existence of someone or some group with the power and will to impose and enforce law. It is not the contracting *per se* that creates any special reasons; it is, rather, the threat of punishment from a sovereign. If we could snap our fingers and create a sovereign with the will and power to create laws that allow and force us to cooperate, that would do just as well. There is another type of social contract theorist, however, who understands the role of contracts and agreements in quite a different way.

Modeling Political Obligation on Contractual Obligation

As one is thinking about why citizens have an obligation to obey the laws of their state, laws with which they might disagree, one might try to understand the relevant obligations in terms of some other familiar sort of reason or obligation. So, for example, a political philosopher might suppose that if anything is relatively unproblematic, it is that we obligate ourselves through explicit promises, contracts, and agreements. One might then wonder if we could construe political obligations as being like the obligations we create through promising, contracting, or making agreements. On this approach we are no longer necessarily assuming that people are purely self-interested. Nor need we let the strong rationality thesis of egoism dictate the sorts of reasons people have to act in certain ways. Indeed, it might be supposed, we often have moral obligations to keep our promises and abide by our agreements, even when it is obvious that is it *not* in our self-interest to do so. Locke supposes that even in the state of nature, there are moral laws, or laws of nature, that govern our interactions with each other. For Locke the source of these laws is God: we are each God's property, and so we are not free to use each other however we see fit in order to advance our egoistic ends. Each of us has 'rights' against the others that place constraints on their liberty. The only way that we can be deprived of these rights is through our voluntary consent.

For Locke this feature of rights is very important when we consider the creation of a government. In Locke's state of nature, each of us has the right to punish those who break the law of nature: God gave us those laws to allow us to live in peace with one another, and thus, Locke insists, He must also have given us the right to enforce those laws, i.e., to ensure that they are effective. But human bias will inevitably lead us to over-punish those who have wronged us, to retaliate against what we perceive as unjust punishment of ourselves and our loved ones, and to make mistakes in determining who deserves punishment. Therefore, we need an impartial administrator of justice—the state—to prevent conflict from escalating. But for the state to have exclusive powers to punish, we must all cede our right to punish, and we must do so voluntarily—we must contract with one another to come out of the state of nature.

So, unlike Hobbes, a "true" social contract theorist such as Locke will construe the state as something that comes into existence as a result of individuals making agreements or contracts to which those individuals are morally bound, and without which the state is illegitimate. The precise terms of an "ideal" contract are a matter of dispute, of course, among social contract theorists, and there is nothing, in principle, to stop a philosopher from arguing that there may be significant differences between perfectly legitimate contracts. For example, in one society people might contract to obey the laws of democratically elected leaders, while in another society people might contract to obey the laws of a leader who is given the discretion to choose subsequent leaders. Like other contracts or agreements, one might also insist that the obligations created by the relevant contracts are merely what philosophers sometimes call *prima facie*—obligations that are initially presumed to hold but where the presumption might be overridden by other considerations. So just as my promise to help you dig a hole this weekend might be voided by my discovery that you are planning to bury a murder victim, so my contract to obey the laws passed by a certain sort of government might also be voided by my discovery that the government has passed grotesquely immoral laws (see Locke, reading 89). Locke insists that the legitimacy of the government depends *both* on the consent of the governed and on the government's abiding by the moral laws that bind us all.

One might, of course, raise questions about the paradigm of obligation on which the contract theorist relies. Philosophers who argue that the morally right thing to do is whatever alternative will bring about the best consequences—such philosophers are called *act consequentialists*—will presumably argue that one ought to keep promises or agreements only when doing so has the best consequences. But even if one grants that contracts do create the kind of obligation the social contract theorist is looking for, there is another obvious objection to the social contract theorist's approach to understanding the source of political obligation. Who, precisely, is supposed to have entered into these social contractual agreements, and when was this supposed to have happened? To be sure, when

a country such as the US is literally being created, there are sometimes constitutional conventions where explicit agreements are hammered out, and the people present might even literally sign a document indicating their assent. Even then, however, in the case of the US Constitution, the ratifiers represented only a tiny percentage of the population. Most of us, by contrast, are simply born into an existing society. We find ourselves living in a land ruled by a certain kind of government that chose various laws that it enforces. How could we possibly be bound by an agreement made by people who have been dead for centuries? How can it be the case that someone else has the moral authority to cede my rights?

Sophisticated contract theorists since Locke have been aware that they need an answer to the question, and many follow Locke by turning to the idea of implicit contract or agreement. While we never "signed on the dotted line," we implicitly accept the terms of the contract when we retain our citizenship and reap all of the advantages of living in a civilized society. Explicit consent involves performing some action—signing our name, saying "Yes," swearing an oath—to indicate assent, while implicit consent involves refraining from some action—not signing our name on the opt-out form, not saying "No," not showing up—to indicate assent. Locke claims that we implicitly consent to our governments when we refrain from the action that would indicate dissent—leaving the country. Our staying is the sign that we agree to abide by the rules.

At this point, critics will often complain that there are all kinds of conditions that must be met by explicit or implicit contracts for those contracts to be binding. If I sign a document agreeing to give you my house, for example, but do so while you are holding a gun to my head, no-one would assume that I have either a legal or a moral obligation to give you the house. When the contract theorist argues that our failure to leave the states in which we are born shows that we have implicitly committed ourselves to giving allegiance to its constitution and whatever government rules in accordance with that constitution, the supposition is surely that in some full-blooded sense we are free to leave. While such freedom obviously doesn't exist in countries such as North Korea, one might suppose that it does in countries such as the United States and Canada. Nothing prevents our citizens from renouncing their citizenship and emigrating to some other state—at least nothing in the form of laws or armies. But, as Hume argues (see reading 8), there may be other very real pressures on people to stay where they are. The economically disadvantaged, in particular, will hardly find it easy to pick up stakes and move, no matter how much they dislike their present situation. We need some way of determining when such pressures start looking like that gun pointed at the person who "agrees" to act in the way the gunman desires.

Fair Play

If one gives up on the idea of modeling political obligation on contractual obligation, one might turn to other paradigms in a search to understand the reasons we have to give our allegiance to our government and its laws. Nozick (see reading 12) discusses a so-called principle of fair play (discussed by Arneson in reading 13). If I accept benefits that result from a scheme of cooperation that 1) is mutually beneficial, 2) is just, 3) produces benefits only if all or most people cooperate, 4) requires sacrifice where 5) there is the possibility of being a free rider (someone who gets the advantages without making the sacrifice), then I have an obligation to cooperate (do my part) to maintain the scheme. The idea is that in a society like ours, there exists, in effect, a scheme of cooperation that is mutually beneficial—the willingness to adjudicate moral disputes by appeal to law established by just, democratically constituted institutions. As Hobbes's fool points out, one can "free ride" and violate law when it is to one's advantage, but this would violate the principle of fair play.

The principle of fair play is, however, hardly uncontroversial. It seems to rely vaguely on the idea that if one receives a benefit, one "owes" something to the person or people who conferred the benefit

upon one. But as Nozick argues, why should that be so? Suppose a secret admirer of mine mows my lawn while I'm at work, and then demands something in return—perhaps a date. If I didn't ask for the help, why should I feel any sort of obligation? And the same might seem to hold true of "schemes of cooperation" of which I want no part. The farmers in my county meet and decide to share the costs of using insecticides to get rid of a serious pest problem. I refuse to attend the meeting at which the decision was made, making it as clear as I can that I want no part of any such plan. If the rest go ahead without me, do I really have any responsibility to kick in my share of the cost—even if I do indeed benefit from the scheme in which I did not want to participate? These examples might suggest that it makes an important difference if I agree to participate in at least the process by which the scheme is instituted. But if that does make the critical difference, then the principle of fair play might no longer be a genuine alternative to the contract theories discussed above.

Associative Obligations

One might try to bolster the principle of fair play with its prohibition against free riding by focusing on yet another paradigm of obligation—the obligations that many think we have toward our intimates (friends, lovers, and family, for example). At least some philosophers think that in virtue of your being a friend of mine, for example, I have reasons to come to help and care for you that I don't have to strangers. If my friend needs to borrow money for an operation, I have more of a reason to help that friend than I would have to help a complete stranger making a similar request. Depending on how precisely one characterizes friendship, one might think that there is a relation that citizens bear to each other that bears at least a "family resemblance" to friendship. If friendship, for example, is created in part by shared interests and values, there might be a sense in which people raised in the same culture, say American culture, are "close" to each other in a way analogous to the closeness of friends. And perhaps such closeness generates a kind of reason analogous to the reason friends have to promote the welfare of those with whom one feels the "tie." Returning to something like the principle of fair play, then, if I see myself benefiting from the sacrifice of a friend, one might suppose that I have a reason to reciprocate in some fashion even if I didn't seek the benefit. And if my fellow citizens are at least a little bit like friends, then perhaps there would be something wrong with benefiting from "co-operative schemes" that involve their sacrifice without doing my fair share.

Of course all of this is extremely vague. How close am I to my fellow citizens—particularly those whose views and policies I don't respect? How much like a friend is someone who just happens to be born into the same society? And furthermore, how different is the situation in which I receive unsolicited benefits from a friend rather than a stranger with respect to my incurring an obligation to return the favor? One might even suppose that it is in the very nature of friendship that one shouldn't insist that there is an obligation on the part of one's friends to defray the cost of one's spontaneous, unsolicited act of generosity.

The Utilitarian Argument

Hume (reading 8) seems to suggest that one needn't and shouldn't try to model political obligation on anything other than a common-sense principle that one ought to do what is best, all things considered. Highly suspicious of the idea that we have all implicitly bound ourselves by some contract or agreement, Hume suggests that we simply find ourselves born into a society with a given power structure and laws that are enforced by that power structure. By and large, we'll correctly conclude that we are better off "going along" with the law of the land. As Hobbes points out, we'll enjoy the advantages of living cooperatively in a community, and we'll avoid the sanctions risked when we violate the law. We need look no further than these considerations to find the reason philosophers seek for obeying the law and giving their allegiance to the state in which they are raised. Of course, if one is unlucky enough to be born into a vicious society in which acquiescence to law or allegiance to the government will be rewarded with nothing but danger and misery, then all bets are off as to what one ought to do. But for most of us lucky enough to live in Western democracies, it is clear that it is in most people's best interest not to "rock the boat."

A.
Classical Social Contract Theory and Contemporary Developments

1

Plato, selection from
The Republic (c. 380 BCE)

The ancient Greek philosopher Plato (429–347 BCE) was, along with his teacher Socrates and student Aristotle, one of the principal founders of the Western philosophical tradition. *The Republic* is widely considered Plato's *magnum opus*, touching on all areas of philosophical inquiry and bringing together many of the ideas and theories explored in his other writings. *The Republic*, like most of Plato's other works, is written as a conversation or dialogue between a number of people, of whom Socrates is the principal character and narrator. In this selection Glaucon presents three stories that suggest (contrary to Socrates' claims) that justice is "irksome." Or in other words, *if* it is good, it is only good as a means.

SOURCE

Plato, *The Republic of Plato*. (Third Edition), Volume 1. Benjamin Jawett, translator. The Clarendon Press at Oxford University Press. First published 1908; reprinted 1927.

This selection opens with Socrates narrating the conclusion of a conversation with Thrasymachus; he goes on to narrate a conversation between Glaucon and himself.

"As an epicure snatches a taste of every dish which is successively brought to table, he not having allowed himself time to enjoy the one before, so have I gone from one subject to another without having discovered what I sought at first, the nature of justice. I left that enquiry and turned away to consider whether justice is virtue and wisdom or evil and folly; and when there arose a further question about the comparative advantages of justice and injustice, I could not refrain from passing on to that. And the result of the whole discussion has been that I know nothing at all. For I know not what justice is, and therefore I am not likely to know whether it is or is not a virtue, nor can I say whether the just man is happy or unhappy."

With these words I was thinking that I had made an end of the discussion; but the end, in truth, proved to be only a beginning. For Glaucon, who is always the most pugnacious of men, was dissatisfied at Thrasymachus' retirement; he wanted to have the battle out. So he said to me: "Socrates, do you wish really to persuade us, or only to seem to have persuaded us, that to be just is always better than to be unjust?"

"I should wish really to persuade you," I replied, "if I could."

"Then you certainly have not succeeded. Let me ask you now:—How would you arrange goods— are there not some which we welcome for their own sakes, and independently of their consequences, as, for example, harmless pleasures and enjoyments, which delight us at the time, although nothing follows from them?"

"I agree in thinking that there is such a class," I replied.

"Is there not also a second class of goods, such as knowledge, sight, health, which are desirable not only in themselves, but also for their results?"

"Certainly," I said.

"And would you not recognize a third class, such as gymnastic, and the care of the sick, and the physician's art; also the various ways of money-making—these do us good but we regard them as disagreeable; and no one would choose them for their own sakes, but only for the sake of some reward or result which flows from them?"

"There is," I said, "this third class also. But why do you ask?"

"Because I want to know in which of the three classes you would place justice?"

"In the highest class," I replied, "among those goods which he who would be happy desires both for their own sake and for the sake of their results."

"Then the many are of another mind; they think that justice is to be reckoned in the troublesome class, among goods which are to be pursued for the sake of rewards and of reputation, but in themselves are disagreeable and rather to be avoided."

"I know," I said, "that this is their manner of thinking, and that this was the thesis which Thrasymachus was maintaining just now, when he censured justice and praised injustice. But I am too stupid to be convinced by him."

"I wish," he said, "that you would hear me as well as him, and then I shall see whether you and I agree. For Thrasymachus seems to me, like a snake, to have been charmed by your voice sooner than he ought to have been; but to my mind the nature of justice and injustice have not yet been made clear. Setting aside their rewards and results, I want to know what they are in themselves, and how they inwardly work in the soul. If you please, then, I will revive the argument of Thrasymachus. And first I will speak of the nature and origin of justice according to the common view of them. Secondly, I will show that all men who practice justice do so against their will, of necessity, but not as a good. And thirdly, I will argue that there is reason in this view, for the life of the unjust is after all better far than the life of the just—if what they say is true, Socrates, since I myself am not of their opinion. But still I acknowledge that I am perplexed when I hear the voices of Thrasymachus and myriads of others dinning in my ears; and, on the other hand, I have never yet heard the superiority of justice to injustice maintained by any one in a satisfactory way. I want to hear justice praised in respect of itself; then I shall be satisfied, and you are the person from whom I think that I am most likely to hear this; and therefore I will praise the unjust life to the utmost of my power, and my manner of speaking will indicate the manner in which I desire to hear you too praising justice and censuring injustice. Will you say whether you approve of my proposal?"

"Indeed I do; nor can I imagine any theme about which a man of sense would oftener wish to converse."

"I am delighted," he replied, "to hear you say so, and shall begin by speaking, as I proposed, of the nature and origin of justice."

"They say," [he continued,] "that to do injustice is, by nature, good; to suffer injustice, evil; but that the evil is greater than the good. And so when men have both done and suffered injustice and have had experience of both, not being able to avoid the one and obtain the other, they think that they had better agree among themselves to have neither; hence there arise laws and mutual covenants; and that which is ordained by law is termed by them lawful and just. This they affirm to be the origin and nature of justice;—it is a mean or compromise, between the best of all, which is to do injustice and not be punished, and the worst of all, which is to suffer injustice without the power of retaliation; and justice, being at a middle point between the two, is tolerated not as a good, but as the lesser evil, and honoured by reason of the inability of men to do injustice. For no man who is worthy to be called a man would ever submit to such an agreement if he were able to resist; he would be mad if he did. Such is the received account, Socrates, of the nature and origin of justice.

"Now that those who practice justice do so involuntarily and because they have not the power to be unjust will best appear if we imagine something of this kind: having given both to the just and the unjust power to do what they will, let us watch and see whither desire will lead them; then we shall discover in the very act the just and unjust man to be proceeding along the same road, following their interest, which all natures deem to be their good, and are only diverted into the path of justice by the force of law. The liberty which we are supposing may be most completely given to them in the form of such a power as is said to have been possessed by Gyges the ancestor of Croesus the Lydian. According to the tradition, Gyges was a shepherd in the service of the king of Lydia; there was a great storm, and an earthquake made an opening in the earth at the place where he was feeding his flock. Amazed at the sight, he descended into the opening, where, among other marvels, he beheld a hollow brazen horse, having doors, at which he stooping and looking in saw a dead body of stature, as appeared to him, more than human, and having nothing on but a gold ring; this he took from the finger of the dead and reascended. Now the shepherds met together, according to custom, that they might send their monthly report about the flocks to the king; into their assembly he came having the ring on his finger, and as he was sitting among them he chanced to turn the collet[1] of the ring inside his hand, when instantly he became invisible to the rest of the company and they began to speak of him as if he were no longer present. He was astonished at this, and again touching the ring he turned the collet outwards and reappeared; he made several trials of the ring, and always with the same result—when he turned the collet inwards he became invisible, when outwards he reappeared.

Whereupon he contrived to be chosen one of the messengers who were sent to the court; where as soon as he arrived he seduced the queen, and with her help conspired against the king and slew him, and took the kingdom. Suppose now that there were two such magic rings, and the just put on one of them and the unjust the other; no man can be imagined to be of such an iron nature that he would stand fast in justice. No man would keep his hands off what was not his own when he could safely take what he liked out of the market, or go into houses and lie with any one at his pleasure, or kill or release from prison whom he would, and in all respects be like a god among men. Then the actions of the just would be as the actions of the unjust; they would both come at last to the same point. And this we may truly affirm to be a great proof that a man is just, not willingly or because he thinks that justice is any good to him individually, but of necessity, for wherever any one thinks that he can safely be unjust, there he is unjust. For all men believe in their hearts that injustice is far more profitable to the individual than justice, and he who argues as I have been supposing, will say that they are right. If you could imagine any one obtaining this power of becoming invisible, and never doing any wrong or touching what was another's, he would be thought by the lookers-on to be a most wretched idiot, although they would praise him to one another's faces, and keep up appearances with one another from a fear that they too might suffer injustice. Enough of this.

"Now, if we are to form a real judgment of the life of the just and unjust, we must isolate them; there is no other way; and how is the isolation to be effected? I answer: Let the unjust man be entirely unjust, and the just man entirely just; nothing is to be taken away from either of them, and both are to be perfectly furnished for the work of their respective lives. First, let the unjust be like other distinguished masters of craft; like the skilful pilot or physician, who knows intuitively his own powers and keeps within their limits, and who, if he fails at any point, is able to recover himself. So let the unjust make his unjust attempts in the

---

[1] [A base that turns.]

right way, and lie hidden if he means to be great in his injustice (he who is found out is nobody): for the highest reach of injustice is: to be deemed just when you are not. Therefore I say that in the perfectly unjust man we must assume the most perfect injustice; there is to be no deduction, but we must allow him, while doing the most unjust acts, to have acquired the greatest reputation for justice. If he have taken a false step he must be able to recover himself; he must be one who can speak with effect, if any of his deeds come to light, and who can force his way where force is required.... And at his side let us place the just man in his nobleness and simplicity, wishing, as Aeschylus says, to be and not to seem good. There must be no seeming, for if he seem to be just he will be honoured and rewarded, and then we shall not know whether he is just for the sake of justice or for the sake of honours and rewards; therefore, let him be clothed in justice only, and have no other covering; and he must be imagined in a state of life the opposite of the former. Let him be the best of men, and let him be thought the worst; then he will have been put to the proof; and we shall see whether he will be affected by the fear of infamy and its consequences. And let him continue thus to the hour of death; being just and seeming to be unjust. When both have reached the uttermost extreme, the one of justice and the other of injustice, let judgment be given which of them is the happier of the two."

"Heavens! my dear Glaucon," I said, "how energetically you polish them up for the decision, first one and then the other, as if they were two statues."

"I do my best," he said. "And now that we know what they are like there is no difficulty in tracing out the sort of life which awaits either of them. This I will proceed to describe; but as you may think the description a little too coarse, I ask you to suppose, Socrates, that the words which follow are not mine.—Let me put them into the mouths of the eulogists of injustice: They will tell you that the just man who is thought unjust will be scourged, racked, bound—will have his eyes burnt out; and, at last, after suffering every kind of evil, he will be impaled: Then he will understand that he ought

to seem only, and not to be, just; the words of Aeschylus may be more truly spoken of the unjust than of the just. For the unjust is pursuing a reality; he does not live with a view to appearances—he wants to be really unjust and not to seem only:—

His mind has a soil deep and fertile,
Out of which spring his prudent counsels.

"In the first place, he is thought just, and therefore bears rule in the city; he can marry whom he will, and give in marriage to whom he will; also he can trade and deal where he likes, and always to his own advantage, because he has no misgivings about injustice and at every contest, whether in public or private, he gets the better of his antagonists, and gains at their expense, and is rich, and out of his gains he can benefit his friends, and harm his enemies; moreover, he can offer sacrifices, and dedicate gifts to the gods abundantly and magnificently, and can honour the gods or any man whom he wants to honour in a far better style than the just, and therefore he is likely to be dearer than they are to the gods. And thus, Socrates, gods and men are said to unite in making the life of the unjust better than the life of the just."

DISCUSSION QUESTIONS

1. In Glaucon's view, what benefits do citizens enjoy living under the rule of law? Could these benefits be secured without establishing a ruling power? Why or why not?

2. What assumptions does Glaucon make about human psychology? Do you agree that no-one could resist using the ring to engage in unjust activities? Would it be *rational* for a person possessing the ring to resist engaging in unjust activities? Why or why not?

3. Glaucon's social contract theory is presented as a response to the question, "What is justice." What, then, *is* his analysis of justice?

2

Thomas Hobbes, selection from *Leviathan* (1651)

The seventeenth-century English philosopher Thomas Hobbes was born in 1588. During the English Civil War, fearing backlash from anti-royalists, he went into a self-imposed exile in France from 1640 to 1651. Hobbes was known for his materialist views, especially as they informed his moral and theological views. He died in 1679. In this selection, Hobbes offers his view of the condition of mankind in the state of nature and suggests how it is that we can justify leaving a state of nature for a commonwealth. The selection is part of a much larger work, *Leviathan*, the first two parts of which try to formulate Hobbes's understanding of human nature and the conditions that would allow people with that nature to cooperate in such a way as to maximize their power to promote their self-interest.

SOURCE

Hobbes, Thomas. *Leviathan*, 2nd ed. George Routledge and Sons, 1886.

Of the Natural Condition of Mankind as Concerning Their Felicity and Misery

Nature hath made men so equal in the faculties of body and mind as that, though there be found one man sometimes manifestly stronger in body or of quicker mind than another, yet when all is reckoned together the difference between man and man is not so considerable as that one man can thereupon claim to himself any benefit to which another may not pretend as well as he. For as to the strength of body, the weakest has strength enough to kill the strongest, either by secret machination or by confederacy with others that are in the same danger with himself.

And as to the faculties of the mind, setting aside the arts grounded upon words, and especially that skill of proceeding upon general and infallible rules, called science, which very few have and but in few things, as being not a native faculty born with us, nor attained, as prudence, while we look after somewhat else, I find yet a greater equality amongst men than that of strength. For prudence is but experience, which equal time equally bestows on all men in those things they equally apply themselves unto. That which may perhaps make such equality incredible is but a vain conceit of one's own wisdom, which almost all men think they have in a greater degree than the vulgar; that is, than all men but themselves, and a few others, whom by fame, or for concurring with themselves, they approve.

For such is the nature of men that howsoever they may acknowledge many others to be more witty, or more eloquent or more learned, yet they will hardly believe there be many so wise as themselves; for they see their own wit at hand, and other men's at a distance. But this proveth rather that men are in that point equal, than unequal. For there is not ordinarily a greater sign of the equal distribution of anything than that every man is contented with his share.

From this equality of ability ariseth equality of hope in the attaining of our ends. And therefore if any two men desire the same thing, which nevertheless they cannot both enjoy, they become enemies; and in the way to their end (which is principally their own conservation, and sometimes their delectation only) endeavour to destroy or subdue one another. And from hence it comes to pass that where an invader hath no more to fear than another man's single power, if one plant, sow, build, or possess a convenient seat, others may probably be expected to come prepared with forces united to dispossess and deprive him, not only of the fruit of his labour, but also of his life or liberty. And the invader again is in the like danger of another.

And from this diffidence of one another, there is no way for any man to secure himself so reasonable as anticipation; that is, by force, or wiles, to master the persons of all men he can so long till he see no other power great enough to endanger him: and this is no more than his own conservation requireth, and is generally allowed. Also, because there be some that, taking pleasure in contemplating their own power in the acts of conquest, which they pursue farther than their security requires, if others, that otherwise would be glad to be at ease within modest bounds, should not by invasion increase their power, they would not be able, long time, by standing only on their defence, to subsist. And by consequence, such augmentation of dominion over men being necessary to a man's conservation, it ought to be allowed him.

Again, men have no pleasure (but on the contrary a great deal of grief) in keeping company where there is no power able to overawe them all.

For every man looketh that his companion should value him at the same rate he sets upon himself, and upon all signs of contempt or undervaluing naturally endeavours, as far as he dares (which amongst them that have no common power to keep them in quiet is far enough to make them destroy each other), to extort a greater value from his contemners, by damage; and from others, by the example.

So that in the nature of man, we find three principal causes of quarrel. First, competition; secondly, diffidence; thirdly, glory.

The first maketh men invade for gain; the second, for safety; and the third, for reputation. The first use violence, to make themselves masters of other men's persons, wives, children, and cattle; the second, to defend them; the third, for trifles, as a word, a smile, a different opinion, and any other sign of undervalue, either direct in their persons or by reflection in their kindred, their friends, their nation, their profession, or their name.

Hereby it is manifest that during the time men live without a common power to keep them all in awe, they are in that condition which is called war; and such a war as is of every man against every man. For war consisteth not in battle only, or the act of fighting, but in a tract of time, wherein the will to contend by battle is sufficiently known: and therefore the notion of time is to be considered in the nature of war, as it is in the nature of weather. For as the nature of foul weather lieth not in a shower or two of rain, but in an inclination thereto of many days together: so the nature of war consisteth not in actual fighting, but in the known disposition thereto during all the time there is no assurance to the contrary. All other time is peace.

Whatsoever therefore is consequent to a time of war, where every man is enemy to every man, the same consequent to the time wherein men live without other security than what their own strength and their own invention shall furnish them withal. In such condition there is no place for industry, because the fruit thereof is uncertain: and consequently no culture of the earth; no navigation, nor use of the commodities that may be imported by sea; no commodious building; no instruments of moving and removing such things as require much force; no knowledge of the face of the earth; no account of time; no arts; no letters; no society; and which is worst of all, continual fear, and danger of violent death; and the life of man, solitary, poor, nasty, brutish, and short.

It may seem strange to some man that has not well weighed these things that Nature should thus dissociate and render men apt to invade and destroy one another: and he may therefore, not trusting to this inference, made from the passions, desire perhaps to have the same confirmed by experience. Let him therefore consider with himself: when taking a journey, he arms himself and seeks to go well accompanied; when going to sleep, he locks his doors; when even in his house he locks his chests; and this when he knows there be laws and public officers, armed, to revenge all injuries shall be done him; what opinion he has of his fellow subjects, when he rides armed; of his fellow citizens, when he locks his doors; and of his children, and servants, when he locks his chests. Does he not there as much accuse mankind by his actions as I do by my words? But neither of us accuse man's nature in it. The desires, and other passions of man, are in themselves no sin. No more are the actions that proceed from those passions till they know a law that forbids them; which till laws be made they cannot know, nor can any law be made till they have agreed upon the person that shall make it.

It may peradventure be thought there was never such a time nor condition of war as this; and I believe it was never generally so, over all the world: but there are many places where they live so now. For the savage people in many places of America, except the government of small families, the concord whereof dependeth on natural lust, have no government at all, and live at this day in that brutish manner, as I said before. Howsoever, it may be perceived what manner of life there would be, where there were no common power to fear, by the manner of life which men that have formerly lived under a peaceful government use to degenerate into a civil war.

But though there had never been any time wherein particular men were in a condition of war one against another, yet in all times kings and persons of sovereign authority, because of their independency, are in continual jealousies, and in the state and posture of gladiators, having their weapons pointing, and their eyes fixed on one another; that is, their forts, garrisons, and guns upon the frontiers of their kingdoms, and continual spies upon their neighbours, which is a posture of war. But because they uphold thereby the industry of their subjects, there does not follow from it that misery which accompanies the liberty of particular men.

To this war of every man against every man, this also is consequent; that nothing can be unjust. The notions of right and wrong, justice and injustice, have there no place. Where there is no common power, there is no law; where no law, no injustice. Force and fraud are in war the two cardinal virtues. Justice and injustice are none of the faculties neither of the body nor mind. If they were, they might be in a man that were alone in the world, as well as his senses and passions. They are qualities that relate to men in society, not in solitude. It is consequent also to the same condition that there be no propriety, no dominion, no mine and thine distinct; but only that to be every man's that he can get, and for so long as he can keep it. And thus much for the ill condition which man by mere nature is actually placed in; though with a possibility to come out of it, consisting partly in the passions, partly in his reason.

The passions that incline men to peace are: fear of death; desire of such things as are necessary to commodious living; and a hope by their industry to obtain them. And reason suggesteth convenient articles of peace upon which men may be drawn to agreement. These articles are they which otherwise are called the laws of nature, whereof I shall speak more particularly in the two following chapters.

Of the First and Second Natural Laws, and of Contracts

The right of nature, which writers commonly call *jus naturale*, is the liberty each man hath to use his own power as he will himself for the preservation of his own nature; that is to say, of his own life; and consequently, of doing anything which, in his own judgement and reason, he shall conceive to be the aptest means thereunto.

By liberty is understood, according to the proper signification of the word, the absence of external impediments; which impediments may oft take away part of a man's power to do what he would, but cannot hinder him from using the power left him according as his judgement and reason shall dictate to him.

A law of nature, *lex naturalis*, is a precept, or general rule, found out by reason, by which a man is forbidden to do that which is destructive of his life, or taketh away the means of preserving the same, and to omit that by which he thinketh it may be best preserved. For though they that speak of this subject use to confound *jus* and *lex*, right and law, yet they ought to be distinguished, because right consisteth in liberty to do, or to forbear; whereas law determineth and bindeth to one of them: so that law and right differ as much as obligation and liberty, which in one and the same matter are inconsistent.

And because the condition of man (as hath been declared in the precedent chapter) is a condition of war of every one against every one, in which case every one is governed by his own reason, and there is nothing he can make use of that may not be a help unto him in preserving his life against his enemies; it followeth that in such a condition every man has a right to every thing, even to one another's body. And therefore, as long as this natural right of every man to every thing endureth, there can be no security to any man, how strong or wise soever he be, of living out the time which nature ordinarily alloweth men to live. And consequently it is a precept, or general rule of reason: that every man ought to endeavour peace, as far as he has hope of obtaining it; and when he cannot obtain it, that he may seek and use all helps and advantages of war. The first branch of which rule containeth the first and fundamental law of nature, which is: to seek peace and follow it. The second, the sum of the right of nature, which is: by all means we can to defend ourselves.

From this fundamental law of nature, by which men are commanded to endeavour peace, is derived this second law: that a man be willing, when others are so too, as far forth as for peace and defence of himself he shall think it necessary, to lay down this right to all things; and be contented with so much liberty against other men as he would allow other men against himself. For as long as every man holdeth this right, of doing anything he liketh; so long are all men in the condition of war. But if other men will not lay down their right, as well as he, then there is no reason for anyone to divest himself of his: for that were to expose himself to prey, which no man is bound to, rather than to dispose himself to peace. This is that law of the gospel: Whatsoever you require that others should do to you, that do ye to them....

To lay down a man's right to anything is to divest himself of the liberty of hindering another of the benefit of his own right to the same. For he that renounceth or passeth away his right giveth not to any other man a right which he had not before, because there is nothing to which every man had not right by nature, but only standeth out of his way that he may enjoy his own original right without hindrance from him, not without hindrance from another. So that the effect which redoundeth to one man by another man's defect of right is but so much diminution of impediments to the use of his own right original.

Right is laid aside, either by simply renouncing it, or by transferring it to another. By simply renouncing, when he cares not to whom the benefit thereof redoundeth. By transferring, when he intendeth the benefit thereof to some certain person or persons. And when a man hath in either manner abandoned or granted away his right, then is he said to be obliged, or bound, not to hinder those to whom such right is granted, or abandoned, from the benefit of it: and that he ought, and it is duty, not to make void that voluntary act of his own: and that such hindrance is injustice, and injury, as being *sine jure*; the right being before renounced or transferred. So that injury or injustice, in the controversies of the world, is somewhat like to that which in the disputations of scholars is called absurdity. For as it is there called an absurdity to contradict what one maintained in the beginning; so in the world it is called injustice, and injury voluntarily to undo that which from the beginning he had voluntarily done. The way by which a man either simply renounceth or transferreth his right is a declaration, or signification, by some voluntary and sufficient sign, or signs, that he doth so renounce or transfer, or hath so renounced or transferred the same, to him that accepteth it. And these signs are either words only, or actions only; or, as it happeneth most often, both words and actions. And the same are the bonds, by which men are bound and obliged: bonds that have their strength, not from their own nature (for nothing is more easily broken than a man's word), but from fear of some evil consequence upon the rupture.

Whensoever a man transferreth his right, or renounceth it, it is either in consideration of some right reciprocally transferred to himself, or for some other good he hopeth for thereby. For it is a voluntary act: and of the voluntary acts of every man, the object is some good to himself. And therefore there be some rights which no man can be understood by any words, or other signs, to have abandoned or transferred. As first a man cannot lay down the right of resisting them that assault him by force to take away his life, because he cannot be understood to aim thereby at any good to himself. The same may be said of wounds, and chains, and imprisonment, both because there is no benefit consequent to such patience, as there is to the patience of suffering another to be wounded or imprisoned, as also because a man cannot tell when he seeth men proceed against him by violence whether they intend his death or not. And lastly the motive and end for which this renouncing and transferring of right is introduced is nothing else but the security

of a man's person, in his life, and in the means of so preserving life as not to be weary of it. And therefore if a man by words, or other signs, seem to despoil himself of the end for which those signs were intended, he is not to be understood as if he meant it, or that it was his will, but that he was ignorant of how such words and actions were to be interpreted.

The mutual transferring of right is that which men call contract.

There is difference between transferring of right to the thing, the thing, and transferring or tradition, that is, delivery of the thing itself. For the thing may be delivered together with the translation of the right, as in buying and selling with ready money, or exchange of goods or lands, and it may be delivered some time after.

Again, one of the contractors may deliver the thing contracted for on his part, and leave the other to perform his part at some determinate time after, and in the meantime be trusted; and then the contract on his part is called pact, or covenant: or both parts may contract now to perform hereafter, in which cases he that is to perform in time to come, being trusted, his performance is called keeping of promise, or faith, and the failing of performance, if it be voluntary, violation of faith.

When the transferring of right is not mutual, but one of the parties transferreth in hope to gain thereby friendship or service from another, or from his friends; or in hope to gain the reputation of charity, or magnanimity; or to deliver his mind from the pain of compassion; or in hope of reward in heaven; this is not contract, but gift, free gift, grace: which words signify one and the same thing.

Signs of contract are either express or by inference. Express are words spoken with understanding of what they signify: and such words are either of the time present or past; as, I give, I grant, I have given, I have granted, I will that this be yours: or of the future; as, I will give, I will grant, which words of the future are called promise.

Signs by inference are sometimes the consequence of words; sometimes the consequence of silence; sometimes the consequence of actions; sometimes the consequence of forbearing an action: and generally a sign by inference, of any contract, is whatsoever sufficiently argues the will of the contractor.

Words alone, if they be of the time to come, and contain a bare promise, are an insufficient sign of a free gift and therefore not obligatory. For if they be of the time to come, as, tomorrow I will give, they are a sign I have not given yet, and consequently that my right is not transferred, but remaineth till I transfer it by some other act. But if the words be of the time present, or past, as, I have given, or do give to be delivered tomorrow, then is my tomorrow's right given away today; and that by the virtue of the words, though there were no other argument of my will. And there is a great difference in the signification of these words, *volo hoc tuum esse cras*, and *cras dabo*; that is, between I will that this be thine tomorrow, and, I will give it thee tomorrow: for the word I will, in the former manner of speech, signifies an act of the will present; but in the latter, it signifies a promise of an act of the will to come: and therefore the former words, being of the present, transfer a future right; the latter, that be of the future, transfer nothing. But if there be other signs of the will to transfer a right besides words; then, though the gift be free, yet may the right be understood to pass by words of the future: as if a man propound a prize to him that comes first to the end of a race, the gift is free; and though the words be of the future, yet the right passeth: for if he would not have his words so be understood, he should not have let them run.

In contracts the right passeth, not only where the words are of the time present or past, but also where they are of the future, because all contract is mutual translation, or change of right; and therefore he that promiseth only, because he hath already received the benefit for which he promiseth, is to be understood as if he intended the right should pass: for unless he had been content to have his words so understood, the other would not have performed his part first. And for that cause, in buying, and selling, and other acts of contract, a promise is equivalent to a covenant, and therefore obligatory.

He that performeth first in the case of a contract is said to merit that which he is to receive by the performance of the other, and he hath it as due. Also when a prize is propounded to many, which is to be given to him only that winneth, or money is thrown amongst many to be enjoyed by them that catch it; though this be a free gift, yet so to win, or so to catch, is to merit, and to have it as due. For the right is transferred in the propounding of the prize, and in throwing down the money, though it be not determined to whom, but by the event of the contention. But there is between these two sorts of merit this difference, that in contract I merit by virtue of my own power and the contractor's need, but in this case of free gift I am enabled to merit only by the benignity of the giver: in contract I merit at the contractor's hand that he should depart with his right; in this case of gift, I merit not that the giver should part with his right, but that when he has parted with it, it should be mine rather than another's. And this I think to be the meaning of that distinction of the Schools between *meritum congrui* and *meritum condigni*.[1] For God Almighty, having promised paradise to those men, hoodwinked with carnal desires, that can walk through this world according to the precepts and limits prescribed by him, they say he that shall so walk shall merit paradise *ex congruo*. But because no man can demand a right to it by his own righteousness, or any other power in himself, but by the free grace of God only, they say no man can merit paradise *ex condigno*. This, I say, I think is the meaning of that distinction; but because disputers do not agree upon the signification of their own terms of art longer than it serves their turn, I will not affirm anything of their meaning: only this I say; when a gift is given indefinitely, as a prize to be contended for, he that winneth meriteth, and may claim the prize as due.

If a covenant be made wherein neither of the parties perform presently, but trust one another,

---

[1] [The distinction between deserving something as a matter of merit where the withholding of the benefit is no injustice and deserving something as a matter of right where the withholding is an injustice.]

in the condition of mere nature (which is a condition of war of every man against every man) upon any reasonable suspicion, it is void: but if there be a common power set over them both, with right and force sufficient to compel performance, it is not void. For he that performeth first has no assurance the other will perform after, because the bonds of words are too weak to bridle men's ambition, avarice, anger, and other passions, without the fear of some coercive power; which in the condition of mere nature, where all men are equal, and judges of the justness of their own fears, cannot possibly be supposed. And therefore he which performeth first does but betray himself to his enemy, contrary to the right he can never abandon of defending his life and means of living.

But in a civil estate, where there is a power set up to constrain those that would otherwise violate their faith, that fear is no more reasonable; and for that cause, he which by the covenant is to perform first is obliged so to do.

The cause of fear, which maketh such a covenant invalid, must be always something arising after the covenant made, as some new fact or other sign of the will not to perform, else it cannot make the covenant void. For that which could not hinder a man from promising ought not to be admitted as a hindrance of performing.

He that transferreth any right transferreth the means of enjoying it, as far as lieth in his power. As he that selleth land is understood to transfer the herbage and whatsoever grows upon it; nor can he that sells a mill turn away the stream that drives it. And they that give to a man the right of government in sovereignty are understood to give him the right of levying money to maintain soldiers, and of appointing magistrates for the administration of justice.

To make covenants with brute beasts is impossible, because not understanding our speech, they understand not, nor accept of any translation of right, nor can translate any right to another: and without mutual acceptation, there is no covenant.

To make covenant with God is impossible but by mediation of such as God speaketh to, either by revelation supernatural or by His lieutenants that govern under Him and in His name: for otherwise we know not whether our covenants be accepted or not. And therefore they that vow anything contrary to any law of nature, vow in vain, as being a thing unjust to pay such vow. And if it be a thing commanded by the law of nature, it is not the vow, but the law that binds them.

The matter or subject of a covenant is always something that falleth under deliberation, for to covenant is an act of the will; that is to say, an act, and the last act, of deliberation; and is therefore always understood to be something to come, and which is judged possible for him that covenanteth to perform.

And therefore, to promise that which is known to be impossible is no covenant. But if that prove impossible afterwards, which before was thought possible, the covenant is valid and bindeth, though not to the thing itself, yet to the value; or, if that also be impossible, to the unfeigned endeavour of performing as much as is possible, for to more no man can be obliged.

Men are freed of their covenants two ways; by performing, or by being forgiven. For performance is the natural end of obligation, and forgiveness the restitution of liberty, as being a retransferring of that right in which the obligation consisted.

Covenants entered into by fear, in the condition of mere nature, are obligatory. For example, if I covenant to pay a ransom, or service for my life, to an enemy, I am bound by it. For it is a contract, wherein one receiveth the benefit of life; the other is to receive money, or service for it, and consequently, where no other law (as in the condition of mere nature) forbiddeth the performance, the covenant is valid. Therefore prisoners of war, if trusted with the payment of their ransom, are obliged to pay it: and if a weaker prince make a disadvantageous peace with a stronger, for fear, he is bound to keep it; unless (as hath been said before) there ariseth some new and just cause of fear to renew the war. And even in Commonwealths, if I be forced to redeem myself from a thief by promising him money, I am bound to pay it, till the civil law discharge me. For whatsoever

I may lawfully do without obligation, the same I may lawfully covenant to do through fear: and what I lawfully covenant, I cannot lawfully break.

A former covenant makes void a later. For a man that hath passed away his right to one man today hath it not to pass tomorrow to another: and therefore the later promise passeth no right, but is null.

A covenant not to defend myself from force, by force, is always void. For (as I have shown before) no man can transfer or lay down his right to save himself from death, wounds, and imprisonment, the avoiding whereof is the only end of laying down any right; and therefore the promise of not resisting force, in no covenant transferreth any right, nor is obliging. For though a man may covenant thus, unless I do so, or so, kill me; he cannot covenant thus, unless I do so, or so, I will not resist you when you come to kill me. For man by nature chooseth the lesser evil, which is danger of death in resisting, rather than the greater, which is certain and present death in not resisting. And this is granted to be true by all men, in that they lead criminals to execution, and prison, with armed men, notwithstanding that such criminals have consented to the law by which they are condemned.

A covenant to accuse oneself, without assurance of pardon, is likewise invalid. For in the condition of nature where every man is judge, there is no place for accusation: and in the civil state the accusation is followed with punishment, which, being force, a man is not obliged not to resist. The same is also true of the accusation of those by whose condemnation a man falls into misery; as of a father, wife, or benefactor. For the testimony of such an accuser, if it be not willingly given, is presumed to be corrupted by nature, and therefore not to be received: and where a man's testimony is not to be credited, he is not bound to give it. Also accusations upon torture are not to be reputed as testimonies. For torture is to be used but as means of conjecture, and light, in the further examination and search of truth: and what is in that case confessed tendeth to the ease of him that is tortured, not to the informing of the torturers, and therefore ought not to have the credit of a sufficient testimony: for whether he deliver himself by true or false accusation, he does it by the right of preserving his own life.

The force of words being (as I have formerly noted) too weak to hold men to the performance of their covenants, there are in man's nature but two imaginable helps to strengthen it. And those are either a fear of the consequence of breaking their word, or a glory or pride in appearing not to need to break it. This latter is a generosity too rarely found to be presumed on, especially in the pursuers of wealth, command, or sensual pleasure, which are the greatest part of mankind. The passion to be reckoned upon is fear; whereof there be two very general objects: one, the power of spirits invisible; the other, the power of those men they shall therein offend. Of these two, though the former be the greater power, yet the fear of the latter is commonly the greater fear. The fear of the former is in every man his own religion, which hath place in the nature of man before civil society. The latter hath not so; at least not place enough to keep men to their promises, because in the condition of mere nature, the inequality of power is not discerned, but by the event of battle. So that before the time of civil society, or in the interruption thereof by war, there is nothing can strengthen a covenant of peace agreed on against the temptations of avarice, ambition, lust, or other strong desire, but the fear of that invisible power which they every one worship as God, and fear as a revenger of their perfidy. All therefore that can be done between two men not subject to civil power is to put one another to swear by the God he feareth: which swearing, or oath, is a form of speech, added to a promise, by which he that promiseth signifieth that unless he perform he renounceth the mercy of his God, or calleth to him for vengeance on himself. Such was the heathen form, Let Jupiter kill me else, as I kill this beast. So is our form, I shall do thus, and thus, so help me God. And this, with the rites and ceremonies which every one useth in his own religion, that the fear of breaking faith might be the greater.

By this it appears that an oath taken according to any other form, or rite, than his that sweareth is in vain and no oath, and that there is no swearing by anything which the swearer thinks not God. For though men have sometimes used to swear by their kings, for fear, or flattery; yet they would have it thereby understood they attributed to them divine honour. And that swearing unnecessarily by God is but profaning of his name: and swearing by other things, as men do in common discourse, is not swearing, but an impious custom, gotten by too much vehemence of talking.

It appears also that the oath adds nothing to the obligation. For a covenant, if lawful, binds in the sight of God, without the oath, as much as with it; if unlawful, bindeth not at all, though it be confirmed with an oath.

Of Other Laws of Nature

From that law of nature by which we are obliged to transfer to another such rights as, being retained, hinder the peace of mankind, there followeth a third; which is this: that men perform their covenants made; without which covenants are in vain, and but empty words; and the right of all men to all things remaining, we are still in the condition of war.

And in this law of nature consisteth the fountain and original of justice. For where no covenant hath preceded, there hath no right been transferred, and every man has right to everything and consequently, no action can be unjust. But when a covenant is made, then to break it is unjust and the definition of injustice is no other than the not performance of covenant. And whatsoever is not unjust is just.

But because covenants of mutual trust, where there is a fear of not performance on either part (as hath been said in the former chapter), are invalid, though the original of justice be the making of covenants, yet injustice actually there can be none till the cause of such fear be taken away; which, while men are in the natural condition of war, cannot be done. Therefore before the names of just and unjust can have place, there must be some coercive power to compel men equally to the performance of their covenants, by the terror of some punishment greater than the benefit they expect by the breach of their covenant, and to make good that

propriety which by mutual contract men acquire in recompense of the universal right they abandon: and such power there is none before the erection of a Commonwealth. And this is also to be gathered out of the ordinary definition of justice in the Schools, for they say that justice is the constant will of giving to every man his own. And therefore where there is no own, that is, no propriety, there is no injustice; and where there is no coercive power erected, that is, where there is no Commonwealth, there is no propriety, all men having right to all things: therefore where there is no Commonwealth, there nothing is unjust. So that the nature of justice consisteth in keeping of valid covenants, but the validity of covenants begins not but with the constitution of a civil power sufficient to compel men to keep them: and then it is also that propriety begins.

The fool hath said in his heart, there is no such thing as justice, and sometimes also with his tongue, seriously alleging that every man's conservation and contentment being committed to his own care, there could be no reason why every man might not do what he thought conduced thereunto: and therefore also to make, or not make; keep, or not keep, covenants was not against reason when it conduced to one's benefit. He does not therein deny that there be covenants; and that they are sometimes broken, sometimes kept; and that such breach of them may be called injustice, and the observance of them justice: but he questioneth whether injustice, taking away the fear of God (for the same fool hath said in his heart there is no God), not sometimes stand with that reason which dictateth to every man his own good; and particularly then, when it conduceth to such a benefit as shall put a man in a condition to neglect not only the dispraise and revilings, but also the power of other men. The kingdom of God is gotten by violence: but what if it could be gotten by unjust violence? Were it against reason so to get it, when it is impossible to receive hurt by it? And if it be not against reason, it is not against justice: or else justice is not to be approved for good. From such reasoning as this, successful wickedness hath obtained the name of virtue: and some that in all other things have disallowed the violation of faith, yet have allowed it when it is for the getting of a kingdom. And the heathen that believed that Saturn was deposed by his son Jupiter believed nevertheless the same Jupiter to be the avenger of injustice, somewhat like to a piece of law in Coke's Commentaries on Littleton;[1] where he says if the right heir of the crown be attainted of treason, yet the crown shall descend to him, and *eo instante* the attainder be void: from which instances a man will be very prone to infer that when the heir apparent of a kingdom shall kill him that is in possession, though his father, you may call it injustice, or by what other name you will; yet it can never be against reason, seeing all the voluntary actions of men tend to the benefit of themselves; and those actions are most reasonable that conduce most to their ends. This specious reasoning is nevertheless false.

For the question is not of promises mutual, where there is no security of performance on either side, as when there is no civil power erected over the parties promising; for such promises are no covenants: but either where one of the parties has performed already, or where there is a power to make him perform, there is the question whether it be against reason; that is, against the benefit of the other to perform, or not. And I say it is not against reason. For the manifestation whereof we are to consider; first, that when a man doth a thing, which notwithstanding anything can be foreseen and reckoned on tendeth to his own destruction, howsoever some accident, which he could not expect, arriving may turn it to his benefit; yet such events do not make it reasonably or wisely done. Secondly, that in a condition of war, wherein every man to every man, for want of a common power to keep them all in awe, is an enemy, there is no man can hope by his own strength, or wit, to himself from destruction without the help of confederates; where every one expects the same defence by the confederation that

any one else does: and therefore he which declares he thinks it reason to deceive those that help him can in reason expect no other means of safety than what can be had from his own single power. He, therefore, that breaketh his covenant, and consequently declareth that he thinks he may with reason do so, cannot be received into any society that unite themselves for peace and defence but by the error of them that receive him; nor when he is received be retained in it without seeing the danger of their error; which errors a man cannot reasonably reckon upon as the means of his security: and therefore if he be left, or cast out of society, he perisheth; and if he live in society, it is by the errors of other men, which he could not foresee nor reckon upon, and consequently against the reason of his preservation; and so, as all men that contribute not to his destruction forbear him only out of ignorance of what is good for themselves.

As for the instance of gaining the secure and perpetual felicity of heaven by any way, it is frivolous; there being but one way imaginable, and that is not breaking, but keeping of covenant.

And for the other instance of attaining sovereignty by rebellion; it is manifest that, though the event follow, yet because it cannot reasonably be expected, but rather the contrary, and because by gaining it so, others are taught to gain the same in like manner, the attempt thereof is against reason. Justice therefore, that is to say, keeping of covenant, is a rule of reason by which we are forbidden to do anything destructive to our life, and consequently a law of nature.

There be some that proceed further and will not have the law of nature to be those rules which conduce to the preservation of man's life on earth, but to the attaining of an eternal felicity after death; to which they think the breach of covenant may conduce, and consequently be just and reasonable; such are they that think it a work of merit to kill, or depose, or rebel against the sovereign power constituted over them by their own consent. But because there is no natural knowledge of man's estate after death, much less of the reward that is then to be given to breach of faith, but only a belief grounded

---

[1] [Edward Coke (1552–1634) was an English jurist famous for his commentaries on the common law. The text referred to here was a standard resource for those studying the law.]

upon other men's saying that they know it supernaturally or that they know those that knew them that knew others that knew it supernaturally, breach of faith cannot be called a precept of reason or nature.

Others, that allow for a law of nature the keeping of faith, do nevertheless make exception of certain persons; as heretics, and such as use not to perform their covenant to others; and this also is against reason. For if any fault of a man be sufficient to discharge our covenant made, the same ought in reason to have been sufficient to have hindered the making of it.

The names of just and unjust when they are attributed to men, signify one thing, and when they are attributed to actions, another. When they are attributed to men, they signify conformity, or inconformity of manners, to reason. But when they are attributed to action they signify the conformity, or inconformity to reason, not of manners, or manner of life, but of particular actions. A just man therefore is he that taketh all the care he can that his actions may be all just; and an unjust man is he that neglecteth it. And such men are more often in our language styled by the names of righteous and unrighteous than just and unjust though the meaning be the same. Therefore a righteous man does not lose that title by one or a few unjust actions that proceed from sudden passion, or mistake of things or persons, nor does an unrighteous man lose his character for such actions as he does, or forbears to do, for fear: because his will is not framed by the justice, but by the apparent benefit of what he is to do. That which gives to human actions the relish of justice is a certain nobleness or gallantness of courage, rarely found, by which a man scorns to be beholding for the contentment of his life to fraud, or breach of promise. This justice of the manners is that which is meant where justice is called a virtue; and injustice, a vice.

But the justice of actions denominates men, not just, but guiltless: and the injustice of the same (which is also called injury) gives them but the name of guilty.

Again, the injustice of manners is the disposition or aptitude to do injury, and is injustice before

it proceed to act, and without supposing any individual person injured. But the injustice of an action (that is to say, injury) supposeth an individual person injured; namely him to whom the covenant was made: and therefore many times the injury is received by one man when the damage redoundeth to another. As when the master commandeth his servant to give money to stranger; if it be not done, the injury is done to the master, whom he had before covenanted to obey; but the damage redoundeth to the stranger, to whom he had no obligation, and therefore could not injure him. And so also in Commonwealths private men may remit to one another their debts, but not robberies or other violences, whereby they are endamaged; because the detaining of debt is an injury to themselves, but robbery and violence are injuries to the person of the Commonwealth.

Whatsoever is done to a man, conformable to his own will signified to the doer, is not injury to him. For if he that doeth it hath not passed away his original right to do what he please by some antecedent covenant, there is no breach of covenant, and therefore no injury done him. And if he have, then his will to have it done, being signified, is a release of that covenant, and so again there is no injury done him.

Justice of actions is by writers divided into commutative and distributive: and the former they say consisteth in proportion arithmetical; the latter in proportion geometrical. Commutative, therefore, they place in the equality of value of the things contracted for; and distributive, in the distribution of equal benefit to men of equal merit. As if it were injustice to sell dearer than we buy, or to give more to a man than he merits. The value of all things contracted for is measured by the appetite of the contractors, and therefore the just value is that which they be contented to give. And merit (besides that which is by covenant, where the performance on one part meriteth the performance of the other part, and falls under justice commutative, not distributive) is not due by justice, but is rewarded of grace only. And therefore this distinction, in the sense wherein it useth to be expounded, is not right. To speak properly, commutative justice is the justice of a contractor; that is, a performance of covenant in buying and selling, hiring and letting to hire, lending and borrowing, exchanging, bartering, and other acts of contract.

And distributive justice, the justice of an arbitrator; that is to say, the act of defining what is just. Wherein, being trusted by them that make him arbitrator, if he perform his trust, he is said to distribute to every man his own: and this is indeed just distribution, and may be called, though improperly, distributive justice, but more properly equity, which also is a law of nature, as shall be shown in due place.

As justice dependeth on antecedent covenant; so does gratitude depend on antecedent grace; that is to say, antecedent free gift; and is the fourth law of nature, which may be conceived in this form: that a man which receiveth benefit from another of mere grace endeavour that he which giveth it have no reasonable cause to repent him of his good will. For no man giveth but with intention of good to himself, because gift is voluntary; and of all voluntary acts, the object is to every man his own good; of which if men see they shall be frustrated, there will be no beginning of benevolence or trust, nor consequently of mutual help, nor of reconciliation of one man to another; and therefore they are to remain still in the condition of war, which is contrary to the first and fundamental law of nature which commandeth men to seek peace. The breach of this law is called ingratitude, and hath the same relation to grace that injustice hath to obligation by covenant.

A fifth law of nature is complaisance; that is to say, that every man strive to accommodate himself to the rest. For the understanding whereof we may consider that there is in men's aptness to society a diversity of nature, rising from their diversity of affections, not unlike to that we see in stones brought together for building of an edifice. For as that stone which by the asperity and irregularity of figure takes more room from others than itself fills, and for hardness cannot be easily made plain, and thereby hindereth the building, is by the builders cast away as unprofitable and troublesome: so also, a man that by asperity of nature will strive to retain those things which to himself are superfluous, and to others necessary, and for the stubbornness of his passions cannot be corrected, is to be left or cast out of society as cumbersome thereunto. For seeing every man, not only by right, but also by necessity of nature, is supposed to endeavour all he can to obtain that which is necessary for his conservation, he that shall oppose himself against it for things superfluous is guilty of the war that thereupon is to follow, and therefore doth that which is contrary to the fundamental law of nature, which commandeth to seek peace. The observers of this law may be called sociable (the Latins call them *commodi*); the contrary, stubborn, insociable, forward, intractable.

A sixth law of nature is this: that upon caution of the future time, a man ought to pardon the offences past of them that, repenting, desire it. For pardon is nothing but granting of peace; which though granted to them that persevere in their hostility, be not peace, but fear; yet not granted to them that give caution of the future time is sign of an aversion to peace, and therefore contrary to the law of nature.

A seventh is: that in revenges (that is, retribution of evil for evil), men look not at the greatness of the evil past, but the greatness of the good to follow. Whereby we are forbidden to inflict punishment with any other design than for correction of the offender, or direction of others. For this law is consequent to the next before it, that commandeth pardon upon security of the future time. Besides, revenge without respect to the example and profit to come is a triumph, or glorying in the hurt of another, tending to no end (for the end is always somewhat to come); and glorying to no end is vainglory, and contrary to reason; and to hurt without reason tendeth to the introduction of war, which is against the law of nature, and is commonly styled by the name of cruelty.

And because all signs of hatred, or contempt, provoke to fight; insomuch as most men choose rather to hazard their life than not to be revenged, we may in the eighth place, for a law of nature, set down this precept: that no man by deed, word, countenance, or gesture, declare hatred or contempt of another. The breach of which law is commonly called contumely.

The question who is the better man has no place in the condition of mere nature, where (as has been shown before) all men are equal. The inequality that now is has been introduced by the laws civil. I know that Aristotle in the first book of his Politics, for a foundation of his doctrine, maketh men by nature, some more worthy to command, meaning the wiser sort, such as he thought himself to be for his philosophy; others to serve, meaning those that had strong bodies, but were not philosophers as he; as master and servant were not introduced by consent of men, but by difference of wit: which is not only against reason, but also against experience. For there are very few so foolish that had not rather govern themselves than be governed by others: nor when the wise, in their own conceit, contend by force with them who distrust their own wisdom, do they always, or often, or almost at any time, get the victory. If nature therefore have made men equal, that equality is to be acknowledged: or if nature have made men unequal, yet because men that think themselves equal will not enter into conditions of peace, but upon equal terms, such equality must be admitted. And therefore for the ninth law of nature, I put this: that every man acknowledge another for his equal by nature. The breach of this precept is pride.

On this law dependeth another: that at the entrance into conditions of peace, no man require to reserve to himself any right which he is not content should be reserved to every one of the rest. As it is necessary for all men that seek peace to lay down certain rights of nature; that is to say, not to have liberty to do all they list, so is it necessary for man's life to retain some: as right to govern their own bodies; enjoy air, water, motion, ways to go from place to place; and all things else without which a man cannot live, or not live well. If in this case, at the making of peace, men require for themselves that which they would not have to be

granted to others, they do contrary to the precedent law that commandeth the acknowledgement of natural equality, and therefore also against the law of nature. The observers of this law are those we call modest, and the breakers arrogant men. The Greeks call the violation of this law *pleonexia*; that is, a desire of more than their share.

Also, if a man he trusted to judge between man and man, it is a precept of the law of nature that he deal equally between them. For without that, the controversies of men cannot be determined but by war. He therefore that is partial in judgement, doth what in him lies to deter men from the use of judges and arbitrators, and consequently, against the fundamental law of nature, is the cause of war.

The observance of this law, from the equal distribution to each man of that which in reason belonged to him, is called equity, and (as I have said before) distributive justice: the violation, acception of persons, *prosopolepsia*.

And from this followeth another law: that such things as cannot be divided be enjoyed in common, if it can be; and if the quantity of the thing permit, without stint; otherwise proportionably to the number of them that have right. For otherwise the distribution is unequal, and contrary to equity.

But some things there be that can neither be divided nor enjoyed in common. Then, the law of nature which prescribeth equity requireth: that the entire right, or else (making the use alternate) the first possession, be determined by lot. For equal distribution is of the law of nature; and other means of equal distribution cannot be imagined.

Of lots there be two sorts, arbitrary and natural. Arbitrary is that which is agreed on by the competitors; natural is either primogeniture (which the Greek calls *kleronomia*, which signifies, given by lot), or first seizure.

And therefore those things which cannot be enjoyed in common, nor divided, ought to be adjudged to the first possessor; and in some cases to the first born, as acquired by lot.

It is also a law of nature: that all men that mediate peace he allowed safe conduct. For the law that commandeth peace, as the end, commandeth intercession, as the means; and to intercession the means is safe conduct.

And because, though men be never so willing to observe these laws, there may nevertheless arise questions concerning a man's action; first, whether it were done, or not done; secondly, if done, whether against the law, or not against the law; the former whereof is called a question of fact, the latter a question of right; therefore unless the parties to the question covenant mutually to stand to the sentence of another, they are as far from peace as ever. This other, to whose sentence they submit, is called an arbitrator. And therefore it is of the law of nature that they that are at controversy submit their right to the judgement of an arbitrator.

And seeing every man is presumed to do all things in order to his own benefit, no man is a fit arbitrator in his own cause: and if he were never so fit, yet equity allowing to each party equal benefit, if one be admitted to be judge, the other is to be admitted also; and so the controversy, that is, the cause of war, remains, against the law of nature.

For the same reason no man in any cause ought to be received for arbitrator to whom greater profit, or honour, or pleasure apparently ariseth out of the victory of one party than of the other: for he hath taken, though an unavoidable bribe, yet a bribe; and no man can be obliged to trust him. And thus also the controversy and the condition of war remaineth, contrary to the law of nature.

And in a controversy of fact, the judge being to give no more credit to one than to the other, if there be no other arguments, must give credit to a third; or to a third and fourth; or more: for else the question is undecided, and left to force, contrary to the law of nature.

These are the laws of nature, dictating peace, for a means of the conservation of men in multitudes; and which only concern the doctrine of civil society. There be other things tending to the destruction of particular men; as drunkenness, and all other parts of intemperance, which may therefore also be reckoned amongst those things which the law of nature hath forbidden, but are not necessary to be mentioned, nor are pertinent enough to this place.

And though this may seem too subtle a deduction of the laws of nature to be taken notice of by all men, whereof the most part are too busy in getting food, and the rest too negligent to understand; yet to leave all men inexcusable, they have been contracted into one easy sum, intelligible even to the meanest capacity; and that is: Do not that to another which thou wouldest not have done to thyself, which showeth him that he has no more to do in learning the laws of nature but, when weighing the actions of other men with his own they seem too heavy, to put them into the other part of the balance, and his own into their place, that his own passions and self-love may add nothing to the weight; and then there is none of these laws of nature that will not appear unto him very reasonable.

The laws of nature oblige *in foro interno*; that is to say, they bind to a desire they should take place: but *in foro externo*; that is, to the putting them in act, not always. For he that should be modest and tractable, and perform all he promises in such time and place where no man else should do so, should but make himself a prey to others, and procure his own certain ruin, contrary to the ground of all laws of nature which tend to nature's preservation. And again, he that having sufficient security that others shall observe the same laws towards him, observes them not himself, seeketh not peace, but war, and consequently the destruction of his nature by violence.

And whatsoever laws bind in *foro interno* may be broken, not only by a fact contrary to the law, but also by a fact according to it, in case a man think it contrary. For though his action in this case be according to the law, yet his purpose was against the law; which, where the obligation is in *foro interno*, is a breach.

The laws of nature are immutable and eternal; for injustice, ingratitude, arrogance, pride, iniquity, acception of persons, and the rest can never be made lawful. For it can never be that war shall preserve life, and peace destroy it.

The same laws, because they oblige only to a desire and endeavour, mean an unfeigned and constant endeavour, are easy to be observed. For in that they require nothing but endeavour, he that endeavoureth their performance fulfilleth them; and he that fulfilleth the law is just.

And the science of them is the true and only moral philosophy. For moral philosophy is nothing else but the science of what is good and evil in the conversation and society of mankind. Good and evil are names that signify our appetites and aversions, which in different tempers, customs, and doctrines of men are different: and diverse men differ not only in their judgement on the senses of what is pleasant and unpleasant to the taste, smell, hearing, touch, and sight; but also of what is conformable or disagreeable to reason in the actions of common life. Nay, the same man, in diverse times, differs from himself; and one time praiseth, that is, calleth good, what another time he dispraiseth, and calleth evil: from whence arise disputes, controversies, and at last war. And therefore so long as a man is in the condition of mere nature, which is a condition of war, private appetite is the measure of good and evil: and consequently all men agree on this, that peace is good, and therefore also the way or means of peace, which (as I have shown before) are justice, gratitude, modesty, equity, mercy, and the rest of the laws of nature, are good; that is to say, moral virtues; and their contrary vices, evil. Now the science of virtue and vice is moral philosophy; and therefore the true doctrine of the laws of nature is the true moral philosophy. But the writers of moral philosophy, though they acknowledge the same virtues and vices; yet, not seeing wherein consisted their goodness, nor that they come to be praised as the means of peaceable, sociable, and comfortable living, place them in a mediocrity of passions: as if not the cause, but the degree of daring, made fortitude; or not the cause, but the quantity of a gift, made liberality.

These dictates of reason men used to call by the name of laws, but improperly: for they are but conclusions or theorems concerning what conduceth to the conservation and defence of themselves; whereas law, properly, is the word of him that by right hath command over others. But yet if we consider the same theorems as delivered in the word of God that by right commandeth all things, then are they properly called laws.

Of the Liberty of Subjects

Liberty, or freedom, signifieth properly the absence of opposition (by opposition, I mean external impediments of motion); and may be applied no less to irrational and inanimate creatures than to rational. For whatsoever is so tied, or environed, as it cannot move but within a certain space, which space is determined by the opposition of some external body, we say it hath not liberty to go further. And so of all living creatures, whilst they are imprisoned, or restrained with walls or chains; and of the water whilst it is kept in by banks or vessels that otherwise would spread itself into a larger space; we use to say they are not at liberty to move in such manner as without those external impediments they would. But when the impediment of motion is in the constitution of the thing itself, we use not to say it wants the liberty, but the power, to move; as when a stone lieth still, or a man is fastened to his bed by sickness.

And according to this proper and generally received meaning of the word, a freeman is he that, in those things which by his strength and wit he is able to do, is not hindered to do what he has a will to. But when the words free and liberty are applied to anything but bodies, they are abused; for that which is not subject to motion is not subject to impediment: and therefore, when it is said, for example, the way is free, no liberty of the way is signified, but of those that walk in it without stop. And when we say a gift is free, there is not meant any liberty of the gift, but of the giver, that was not bound by any law or covenant to give it. So when we speak freely, it is not the liberty of voice, or pronunciation, but of the man, whom no law hath obliged to speak otherwise than he did. Lastly, from the use of the words free will, no liberty can be inferred of the will, desire, or inclination, but the liberty of the man; which consisteth in this, that he finds no stop in doing what he has the will, desire, or inclination to do.

Fear and liberty are consistent: as when a man throweth his goods into the sea for fear the ship should sink, he doth it nevertheless very willingly, and may refuse to do it if he will; it is therefore the action of one that was free: so a man sometimes pays his debt, only for fear of imprisonment, which, because no body hindered him from detaining, was the action of a man at liberty. And generally all actions which men do in Commonwealths, for fear of the law, are actions which the doers had liberty to omit.

Liberty and necessity are consistent: as in the water that hath not only liberty, but a necessity of descending by the channel; so, likewise in the actions which men voluntarily do, which, because they proceed from their will, proceed from liberty, and yet because every act of man's will and every desire and inclination proceedeth from some cause, and that from another cause, in a continual chain (whose first link is in the hand of God, the first of all causes), proceed from necessity. So that to him that could see the connexion of those causes, the necessity of all men's voluntary actions would appear manifest. And therefore God, that seeth and disposeth all things, seeth also that the liberty of man in doing what he will is accompanied with the necessity of doing that which God will and no more, nor less. For though men may do many things which God does not command, nor is therefore author of them; yet they can have no passion, nor appetite to anything, of which appetite God's will is not the cause. And did not His will assure the necessity of man's will, and consequently of all that on man's will dependeth, the liberty of men would be a contradiction and impediment to the omnipotence and liberty of God. And this shall suffice, as to the matter in hand, of that natural liberty, which only is properly called liberty.

But as men, for the attaining of peace and conservation of themselves thereby, have made an artificial man, which we call a Commonwealth; so also have they made artificial chains, called civil laws, which they themselves, by mutual covenants, have fastened at one end to the lips of that man, or assembly, to whom they have given the sovereign power, and at the other to their own ears. These bonds, in their own nature but weak, may nevertheless be made to hold, by the danger, though not by the difficulty of breaking them.

In relation to these bonds only it is that I am to speak now of the liberty of subjects. For seeing there is no Commonwealth in the world wherein there be rules enough set down for the regulating of all the actions and words of men (as being a thing impossible): it followeth necessarily that in all kinds of actions, by the laws pretermitted, men have the liberty of doing what their own reasons shall suggest for the most profitable to themselves. For if we take liberty in the proper sense, for corporal liberty; that is to say, freedom from chains and prison, it were very absurd for men to clamour as they do for the liberty they so manifestly enjoy. Again, if we take liberty for an exemption from laws, it is no less absurd for men to demand as they do that liberty by which all other men may be masters of their lives. And yet as absurd as it is, this is it they demand, not knowing that the laws are of no power to protect them without a sword in the hands of a man, or men, to cause those laws to be put in execution. The liberty of a subject lieth therefore only in those things which, in regulating their actions, the sovereign hath pretermitted: such as is the liberty to buy, and sell, and otherwise contract with one another; to choose their own abode, their own diet, their own trade of life, and institute their children as they themselves think fit; and the like.

Nevertheless we are not to understand that by such liberty the sovereign power of life and death is either abolished or limited. For it has been already shown that nothing the sovereign representative can do to a subject, on what pretence soever, can properly be called injustice or injury; because every subject is author of every act the sovereign doth, so that he never wanteth right to any thing, otherwise than as he himself is the subject of God, and bound thereby to observe the laws of nature. And therefore it may and doth often happen in Commonwealths that a subject may be put to death by the command of the sovereign power, and yet neither do the other wrong; as when Jephthah caused his daughter to be sacrificed: in which, and the like cases, he that so dieth had liberty to do the action, for which he is nevertheless, without injury, put to death. And the same holdeth also in a sovereign prince that putteth to death an innocent subject. For though the action be against the law of nature, as being contrary to equity (as was the killing of Uriah by David); yet it was not an injury to Uriah, but to God. Not to Uriah, because the right to do what he pleased was given him by Uriah himself; and yet to God, because David was God's subject and prohibited all iniquity by the law of nature. Which distinction, David himself, when he repented the fact, evidently confirmed, saying, "To thee only have I sinned." In the same manner, the people of Athens, when they banished the most potent of their Commonwealth for ten years, thought they committed no injustice; and yet they never questioned what crime he had done, but what hurt he would do: nay, they commanded the banishment of they knew not whom; and every citizen bringing his oyster shell into the market place, written with the name of him he desired should be banished, without actually accusing him sometimes banished an Aristides, for his reputation of justice; and sometimes a scurrilous jester, as Hyperbolus, to make a jest of it. And yet a man cannot say the sovereign people of Athens wanted right to banish them; or an Athenian the liberty to jest, or to be just.

The liberty whereof there is so frequent and honourable mention in the histories and philosophy of the ancient Greeks and Romans, and in the writings and discourse of those that from them have received all their learning in the politics, is not the liberty of particular men, but the liberty of the Commonwealth: which is the same with that which every man then should have, if there were no civil laws nor Commonwealth at all. And the effects of it also be the same. For as amongst masterless men, there is perpetual war of every man against his neighbour; no inheritance to transmit to the son, nor to expect from the father; no propriety of goods or lands; no security; but a full and absolute liberty in every particular man: so in states and Commonwealths not dependent on one another, every Commonwealth, not every man, has

an absolute liberty to do what it shall judge, that is to say, what that man or assembly that representeth it shall judge, most conducing to their benefit. But withal, they live in the condition of a perpetual war, and upon the confines of battle, with their frontiers armed, and cannons planted against their neighbours round about. The Athenians and Romans were free; that is, free Commonwealths: not that any particular men had the liberty to resist their own representative, but that their representative had the liberty to resist, or invade, other people. There is written on the turrets of the city of Luca in great characters at this day, the word *libertas*; yet no man can thence infer that a particular man has more liberty or immunity from the service of the Commonwealth there than in Constantinople. Whether a Commonwealth be monarchical or popular, the freedom is still the same.

But it is an easy thing for men to be deceived by the specious name of liberty; and, for want of judgement to distinguish, mistake that for their private inheritance and birthright which is the right of the public only. And when the same error is confirmed by the authority of men in reputation for their writings on this subject, it is no wonder if it produce sedition and change of government. In these western parts of the world we are made to receive our opinions concerning the institution and rights of Commonwealths from Aristotle, Cicero, and other men, Greeks and Romans, that, living under popular states, derived those rights, not from the principles of nature, but transcribed them into their books out of the practice of their own Commonwealths, which were popular; as the grammarians describe the rules of language out of the practice of the time; or the rules of poetry out of the poems of Homer and Virgil. And because the Athenians were taught (to keep them from desire of changing their government) that they were freemen, and all that lived under monarchy were slaves; therefore Aristotle puts it down in his Politics, "In democracy, liberty is to be supposed: for it is commonly held that no man is free in any other government."[1] And as Aristotle,

[1] [Aristotle, *Politics*, Bk VI.]

so Cicero and other writers have grounded their civil doctrine on the opinions of the Romans, who were taught to hate monarchy: at first, by them that, having deposed their sovereign, shared amongst them the sovereignty of Rome; and afterwards by their successors. And by reading of these Greek and Latin authors, men from their childhood have gotten a habit, under a false show of liberty, of favouring tumults, and of licentious controlling the actions of their sovereigns; and again of controlling those controllers; with the effusion of so much blood, as I think I may truly say there was never anything so dearly bought as these western parts have bought the learning of the Greek and Latin tongues.

To come now to the particulars of the true liberty of a subject; that is to say, what are the things which, though commanded by the sovereign, he may nevertheless without injustice refuse to do; we are to consider what rights we pass away when we make a Commonwealth; or, which is all one, what liberty we deny ourselves by owning all the actions, without exception, of the man or assembly we make our sovereign. For in the act of our submission consisteth both our obligation and our liberty; which must therefore be inferred by arguments taken from thence; there being no obligation on any man which ariseth not from some act of his own; for all men equally are by nature free. And because such arguments must either be drawn from the express words, "I authorise all his actions," or from the intention of him that submitteth himself to his power (which intention is to be understood by the end for which he so submitteth), the obligation and liberty of the subject is to be derived either from those words, or others equivalent, or else from the end of the institution of sovereignty; namely, the peace of the subjects within themselves, and their defence against a common enemy.

First therefore, seeing sovereignty by institution is by covenant of every one to every one; and sovereignty by acquisition, by covenants of the vanquished to the victor, or child to the parent; it is manifest that every subject has liberty in all those things the right whereof cannot by covenant be transferred. I have shown before, in the fourteenth Chapter, that covenants not to defend a man's own body are void. Therefore,

If the sovereign command a man, though justly condemned, to kill, wound, or maim himself; or not to resist those that assault him; or to abstain from the use of food, air, medicine, or any other thing without which he cannot live; yet hath that man the liberty to disobey.

If a man be interrogated by the sovereign, or his authority, concerning a crime done by himself, he is not bound (without assurance of pardon) to confess it; because no man, as I have shown in the same chapter, can be obliged by covenant to accuse himself.

Again, the consent of a subject to sovereign power is contained in these words, "I authorise, or take upon me, all his actions"; in which there is no restriction at all of his own former natural liberty: for by allowing him to kill me, I am not bound to kill myself when he commands me. It is one thing to say, "Kill me, or my fellow, if you please"; another thing to say, "I will kill myself, or my fellow." It followeth, therefore, that

No man is bound by the words themselves, either to kill himself or any other man; and consequently, that the obligation a man may sometimes have, upon the command of the sovereign, to execute any dangerous or dishonourable office, dependeth not on the words of our submission, but on the intention; which is to be understood by the end thereof. When therefore our refusal to obey frustrates the end for which the sovereignty was ordained, then there is no liberty to refuse; otherwise, there is.

Upon this ground a man that is commanded as a soldier to fight against the enemy, though his sovereign have right enough to punish his refusal with death, may nevertheless in many cases refuse, without injustice; as when he substituteth a sufficient soldier in his place: for in this case he deserteth not the service of the Commonwealth. And there is allowance to be made for natural timorousness, not only to women (of whom no such dangerous duty is expected), but also to men of feminine courage. When armies fight, there is on one side, or both, a running away; yet when they do it not out of treachery, but fear, they are not esteemed to do it unjustly, but dishonourably. For the same reason, to avoid battle is not injustice, but cowardice. But he that enrolleth himself a soldier, or taketh impressed money, taketh away the excuse of a timorous nature, and is obliged, not only to go to the battle, but also not to run from it without his captain's leave. And when the defence of the Commonwealth requireth at once the help of all that are able to bear arms, every one is obliged; because otherwise the institution of the Commonwealth, which they have not the purpose or courage to preserve, was in vain.

To resist the sword of the Commonwealth in defence of another man, guilty or innocent, no man hath liberty; because such liberty takes away from the sovereign the means of protecting us, and is therefore destructive of the very essence of government. But in case a great many men together have already resisted the sovereign power unjustly, or committed some capital crime for which every one of them expecteth death, whether have they not the liberty then to join together, and assist, and defend one another? Certainly they have: for they but defend their lives, which the guilty man may as well do as the innocent. There was indeed injustice in the first breach of their duty: their bearing of arms subsequent to it, though it be to maintain what they have done, is no new unjust act. And if it be only to defend their persons, it is not unjust at all. But the offer of pardon taketh from them to whom it is offered the plea of self-defence, and maketh their perseverance in assisting or defending the rest unlawful.

As for other liberties, they depend on the silence of the law. In cases where the sovereign has prescribed no rule, there the subject hath the liberty to do, or forbear, according to his own discretion. And therefore such liberty is in some places more, and in some less; and in some times more, in other times less, according as they that have the sovereignty shall think most convenient. As for example, there was a time when in England a man might enter into his own land, and dispossess such as wrongfully possessed it, by force. But in after times that liberty of forcible entry was taken away by a statute made by the king in Parliament. And in some places of the world men have the liberty of many wives: in other places, such liberty is not allowed.

If a subject have a controversy with his sovereign of debt, or of right of possession of lands or goods, or concerning any service required at his hands, or concerning any penalty, corporal or pecuniary, grounded on a precedent law, he hath the same liberty to sue for his right as if it were against a subject, and before such judges as are appointed by the sovereign. For seeing the sovereign demandeth by force of a former law, and not by virtue of his power, he declareth thereby that he requireth no more than shall appear to be due by that law. The suit therefore is not contrary to the will of the sovereign, and consequently the subject hath the liberty to demand the hearing of his cause, and sentence according to that law. But if he demand or take anything by pretence of his power, there lieth, in that case, no action of law: for all that is done by him in virtue of his power is done by the authority of every subject, and consequently, he that brings an action against the sovereign brings it against himself.

If a monarch, or sovereign assembly, grant a liberty to all or any of his subjects, which grant standing, he is disabled to provide for their safety; the grant is void, unless he directly renounce or transfer the sovereignty to another. For in that he might openly (if it had been his will), and in plain terms, have renounced or transferred it and did not, it is to be understood it was not his will, but that the grant proceeded from ignorance of the repugnancy between such a liberty and the sovereign power: and therefore the sovereignty is still retained, and consequently all those powers which are necessary to the exercising thereof; such as are the power of war and peace, of judicature, of appointing officers and counsellors, of levying money, and the rest named in the eighteenth Chapter.

The obligation of subjects to the sovereign is understood to last as long, and no longer, than the power lasteth by which he is able to protect them. For the right men have by nature to protect themselves, when none else can protect them, can by no covenant be relinquished. The sovereignty is the soul of the Commonwealth; which, once departed from the body, the members do no more receive their motion from it. The end of obedience is protection; which, wheresoever a man seeth it, either in his own or in another's sword, nature applieth his obedience to it, and his endeavour to maintain it. And though sovereignty, in the intention of them that make it, be immortal; yet is it in its own nature, not only subject to violent death by foreign war, but also through the ignorance and passions of men it hath in it, from the very institution, many seeds of a natural mortality, by intestine discord.

If a subject be taken prisoner in war, or his person or his means of life be within the guards of the enemy, and hath his life and corporal liberty given him on condition to be subject to the victor, he hath liberty to accept the condition; and, having accepted it, is the subject of him that took him; because he had no other way to preserve himself. The case is the same if he be detained on the same terms in a foreign country. But if a man be held in prison, or bonds, or is not trusted with the liberty of his body, he cannot be understood to be bound by covenant to subjection, and therefore may, if he can, make his escape by any means whatsoever.

If a monarch shall relinquish the sovereignty, both for himself and his heirs, his subjects return to the absolute liberty of nature; because, though nature may declare who are his sons, and who are the nearest of his kin, yet it dependeth on his own will, as hath been said in the precedent chapter, who shall be his heir. If therefore he will have no heir, there is no sovereignty, nor subjection. The case is the same if he die without known kindred, and without declaration of his heir. For then there can no heir be known, and consequently no subjection be due.

If the sovereign banish his subject, during the banishment he is not subject. But he that is sent on a message, or hath leave to travel, is still subject; but it is by contract between sovereigns, not by virtue of the covenant of subjection. For whosoever entereth into another's dominion is subject to all the laws thereof, unless he have a privilege by the amity of the sovereigns, or by special licence.

If a monarch subdued by war render himself subject to the victor, his subjects are delivered from their former obligation, and become obliged to the victor. But if he be held prisoner, or have not the liberty of his own body, he is not understood to have given away the right of sovereignty; and therefore his subjects are obliged to yield obedience to the magistrates formerly placed, governing not in their own name, but in his. For, his right remaining, the question is only of the administration; that is to say, of the magistrates and officers; which if he have not means to name, he is supposed to approve those which he himself had formerly appointed.

DISCUSSION QUESTIONS

1. In Hobbes's view, why does a state of nature always turn into a war of all against all? Do you agree with Hobbes in thinking that people would not peacefully resolve their difficulties? Explain.

2. What are the three "principal causes of quarrel" among people? Explain these in your own words. What goals or aims are at issue? Given these motivations, could we expect ideally rational people to successfully engage in long-term mutual cooperation? Why or why not? Discuss.

3. Given Hobbes's understanding of the state of nature and human psychology, why might we suppose that an absolute sovereign must be brought into power? How could such a sovereign ensure peace?

4. Would it be rational for a person to merely lay down her "right to all things" in the state of nature? In other words, would it be rational for a person to lay down her rights if she were the *only* one to do so? How could she be assured that others would not take advantage of her act of renunciation? In what sort of circumstances *would* it be rational to divest oneself of one's natural rights?

5. Recall Glaucon's story of the ring of Gyges (from reading 1, above). How do you think Hobbes would respond to the following question: "Would it be rational for a person possessing the ring of Gyges to act without regard for the laws or civil authority?" Defend your claim.

6. Hobbes's political theory is premised on the notion that humans are egoistic—i.e., that people always act from motives of self-interest. If this is the case, why then does Hobbes claim that the "fool" ought to obey the law even when he is sure that his crime would not be found out?

7. On what grounds might a sovereign decide that he ought not to pass a statute or law? For example, what sorts of considerations might prevent a sovereign from levying an extremely burdensome tax on his subjects?

8. Do the subjects of Hobbes's ideal state have any rights? If so, what are they and what is the justification behind these rights?

9. It is often objected that no rational or sane person would voluntarily contract into a state such as the one that Hobbes has described. What do you think is Hobbes's best line of defense against this criticism? Do you think it succeeds? Why or why not?

3

John Locke, selection from *Second Treatise of Government* (1689)

John Locke (1632–1704) was an English physician and Enlightenment-era philosopher. He is well known for his contributions to the social-contract tradition in political philosophy and for his advocacy of religious tolerance and freedom. In this selection, Locke considers the justification for political authority. The social contract theory that he develops differs in important respects from that of Hobbes.

SOURCE

Locke, John. *Two Treatises of Government*. Whitmore and Fenn, reprinted 1821.

3.   Political power, then, I take to be a RIGHT of making laws with penalties of death, and consequently all less penalties, for the regulating and preserving of property, and of employing the force of the community, in the execution of such laws, and in the defence of the common-wealth from foreign injury; and all this only for the public good.

Of the State of Nature

4.   To understand political power right, and derive it from its original, we must consider, what state all men are naturally in, and that is, a state of perfect freedom to order their actions, and dispose of their possessions and persons, as they think fit, within the bounds of the law of nature, without asking leave, or depending upon the will of any other man.

A state also of equality, wherein all the power and jurisdiction is reciprocal, no one having more than another; there being nothing more evident, than that creatures of the same species and rank, promiscuously born to all the same advantages of nature, and the use of the same faculties, should also be equal one amongst another without subordination or subjection, unless the lord and master of them all should, by any manifest declaration of his will, set one above another, and confer on him, by an evident and clear appointment, an undoubted right to dominion and sovereignty.

5.   This equality of men by nature, the judicious Hooker[1] looks upon as so evident in itself, and beyond all question, that he makes it the foundation of that obligation to mutual love amongst men, on which he builds the duties they owe one another, and from whence he derives the great maxims of justice and charity. His words are,

> The like natural inducement hath brought men to know that it is no less their duty, to love others than themselves; for seeing those things which are equal, must needs all have one measure; if I cannot but wish to receive good, even as much at every man's hands, as any man can wish unto his own soul, how should I look to have any part of my desire herein satisfied, unless myself be careful to satisfy the like desire, which is undoubtedly in other men, being of one and the same nature? To have any thing offered them repugnant to this desire, must needs in all respects grieve them as much as me; so that if I do harm, I must look to suffer, there being no reason that others should shew greater measure of love to me, than they have by me shewed unto them: my desire therefore to be loved of my equals in nature as much as possible may be, imposeth upon me a natural duty of bearing to them-ward fully the like affection; from which relation of equality between ourselves and them that are as ourselves, what several rules and canons natural reason hath drawn, for direction of life, no man is ignorant. (*Ecclesiastical Polity*, lib. I)

6.   But though this be a state of liberty, yet it is not a state of licence: though man in that state have an uncontrollable liberty to dispose of his person or possessions, yet he has not liberty to destroy himself, or so much as any creature in his possession, but where some nobler use than its bare preservation calls for it. The state of nature has a law of nature to govern it, which obliges every one: and reason, which is that law, teaches all mankind, who will but consult it, that being all equal and independent, no one ought to harm another in his life, health, liberty, or possessions: for men being all the workmanship of one omnipotent, and infinitely wise maker; all the servants of one sovereign master, sent into the world by his order, and about his business; they are his property, whose workmanship they are, made to last during his, not one another's pleasure: and being furnished with like faculties, sharing all in one community of nature, there cannot be supposed any such subordination among us, that may authorize us to destroy one another, as if we were made for one another's uses, as the inferior ranks of creatures are for ours. Every one, as he is bound to preserve himself, and not to quit his station wilfully, so by the like reason, when his own preservation comes not in competition, ought he, as much as he can, to preserve the rest of mankind, and may not, unless it be to do justice on an offender, take away, or impair the life, or what tends to the preservation of the life, the liberty, health, limb, or goods of another.

7.   And that all men may be restrained from invading others rights, and from doing hurt to one another, and the law of nature be observed, which willeth the peace and preservation of all mankind, the execution of the law of nature is, in that state, put into every man's hands, whereby every one has a right to punish the transgressors of that law to such a degree, as may hinder its violation: for the law of nature would, as all other laws that concern men in this world, be in vain, if there were no body that in the state of nature had a power to execute that law, and thereby preserve the innocent and restrain offenders. And if any one in the state of nature may punish another for any evil he has done, every one may do so: for in that state of perfect equality, where naturally there is no superiority or jurisdiction of one over another, what any may do in prosecution of that law, every one must needs have a right to do.

---

[1] [Richard Hooker (1554–1600) was a prominent Anglican theologian and political theorist.]

8.   And thus, in the state of nature, one man comes by a power over another; but yet no absolute or arbitrary power, to use a criminal, when he has got him in his hands, according to the passionate heats, or boundless extravagancy of his own will; but only to retribute to him, so far as calm reason and conscience dictate, what is proportionate to his transgression, which is so much as may serve for reparation and restraint: for these two are the only reasons, why one man may lawfully do harm to another, which is that we call *punishment*. In transgressing the law of nature, the offender declares himself to live by another rule than that of reason and common equity, which is that measure God has set to the actions of men, for their mutual security; and so he becomes dangerous to mankind, the tye, which is to secure them from injury and violence, being slighted and broken by him. Which being a trespass against the whole species, and the peace and safety of it, provided for by the law of nature, every man upon this score, by the right he hath to preserve mankind in general, may restrain, or where it is necessary, destroy things noxious to them, and so may bring such evil on any one, who hath transgressed that law, as may make him repent the doing of it, and thereby deter him, and by his example others, from doing the like mischief. And in the case, and upon this ground, every man hath a right to punish the offender, and be executioner of the law of nature.

9.   I doubt not but this will seem a very strange doctrine to some men: but before they condemn it, I desire them to resolve me, by what right any prince or state can put to death, or punish an alien, for any crime he commits in their country. It is certain their laws, by virtue of any sanction they receive from the promulgated will of the legislative, reach not a stranger: they speak not to him, nor, if they did, is he bound to hearken to them. The legislative authority, by which they are in force over the subjects of that commonwealth, hath no power over him. Those who have the supreme power of making laws in England, France or Holland, are to an Indian, but like the rest of the world, men

without authority: and therefore, if by the law of nature every man hath not a power to punish offences against it, as he soberly judges the case to require, I see not how the magistrates of any community can punish an alien of another country; since, in reference to him, they can have no more power than what every man naturally may have over another.

10. Besides the crime which consists in violating the law, and varying from the right rule of reason, whereby a man so far becomes degenerate, and declares himself to quit the principles of human nature, and to be a noxious creature, there is commonly injury done to some person or other, and some other man receives damage by his transgression: in which case he who hath received any damage, has, besides the right of punishment common to him with other men, a particular right to seek reparation from him that has done it: and any other person, who finds it just, may also join with him that is injured, and assist him in recovering from the offender so much as may make satisfaction for the harm he has suffered.

11. From these two distinct rights, the one of punishing the crime for restraint, and preventing the like offence, which right of punishing is in every body; the other of taking reparation, which belongs only to the injured party, comes it to pass that the magistrate, who by being magistrate hath the common right of punishing put into his hands, can often, where the public good demands not the execution of the law, remit the punishment of criminal offences by his own authority, but yet cannot remit the satisfaction due to any private man for the damage he has received. That, he who has suffered the damage has a right to demand in his own name, and he alone can remit: the damnified person has this power of appropriating to himself the goods or service of the offender, by right of self-preservation, as every man has a power to punish the crime, to prevent its being committed again, by the right he has of preserving all mankind, and doing all reasonable things he can in order to that

end: and thus it is, that every man, in the state of nature, has a power to kill a murderer, both to deter others from doing the like injury, which no reparation can compensate, by the example of the punishment that attends it from every body, and also to secure men from the attempts of a criminal, who having renounced reason, the common rule and measure God hath given to mankind, hath, by the unjust violence and slaughter he hath committed upon one, declared war against all mankind, and therefore may be destroyed as a lion or a tyger, one of those wild savage beasts, with whom men can have no society nor security: and upon this is grounded that great law of nature, "Who so sheddeth man's blood, by man shall his blood be shed." And Cain was so fully convinced, that every one had a right to destroy such a criminal, that after the murder of his brother, he cries out, "Every one that findeth me, shall slay me"; so plain was it writ in the hearts of all mankind.

12. By the same reason may a man in the state of nature punish the lesser breaches of that law. It will perhaps be demanded, with death? I answer, each transgression may be punished to that degree, and with so much severity, as will suffice to make it an ill bargain to the offender, give him cause to repent, and terrify others from doing the like. Every offence, that can be committed in the state of nature, may in the state of nature be also punished equally, and as far forth as it may, in a commonwealth: for though it would be besides my present purpose, to enter here into the particulars of the law of nature, or its measures of punishment; yet, it is certain there is such a law, and that too, as intelligible and plain to a rational creature, and a studier of that law, as the positive laws of commonwealths; nay, possibly plainer; as much as reason is easier to be understood, than the fancies and intricate contrivances of men, following contrary and hidden interests put into words; for so truly are a great part of the municipal laws of countries, which are only so far right, as they are founded on the law of nature, by which they are to be regulated and interpreted.

13. To this strange doctrine, viz. that in the state of nature every one has the executive power of the law of nature, I doubt not but it will be objected, that it is unreasonable for men to be judges in their own cases, that self love will make men partial to themselves and their friends: and on the other side, that ill nature, passion and revenge will carry them too far in punishing others; and hence nothing but confusion and disorder will follow, and that therefore God hath certainly appointed government to restrain the partiality and violence of men. I easily grant, that civil government is the proper remedy for the inconveniencies of the state of nature, which must certainly be great, where men may be judges in their own case, since it is easy to be imagined, that he who was so unjust as to do his brother an injury, will scarce be so just as to condemn himself for it: but I shall desire those who make this objection, to remember, that absolute monarchs are but men; and if government is to be the remedy of those evils, which necessarily follow from men's being judges in their own cases, and the state of nature is therefore not to be endured, I desire to know what kind of government that is, and how much better it is than the state of nature, where one man, commanding a multitude, has the liberty to be judge in his own case, and may do to all his subjects whatever he pleases, without the least liberty to any one to question or control those who execute his pleasure and in whatsoever he doth, whether led by reason, mistake or passion, must be submitted to. Much better it is in the state of nature, wherein men are not bound to submit to the unjust will of another. And if he that judges, judges amiss in his own, or any other case, he is answerable for it to the rest of mankind.

14. 'Tis often asked as a mighty objection, where are, or ever were there any men in such a state of nature? To which it may suffice as an answer at present, that since all princes and rulers of independent governments all through the world, are in a state of nature, it is plain the world never was, nor ever will be, without numbers of men in that state. I have named all governors of independent

communities, whether they are, or are not, in league with others: for it is not every compact that puts an end to the state of nature between men, but only this one of agreeing together mutually to enter into one community, and make one body politic; other promises, and compacts, men may make one with another, and yet still be in the state of nature. The promises and bargains for truck, &c. between the two men in the desert island, mentioned by Garcilasso de la Vega, in his history of Peru;[1] or between a Swiss and an Indian, in the woods of America, are binding to them, though they are perfectly in a state of nature, in reference to one another: for truth and keeping of faith belongs to men, as men, and not as members of society.

15. To those that say, there were never any men in the state of nature, I will not only oppose the authority of the judicious Hooker (*Ecclesiastical Polity*, lib. I, sect. 10), where he says,

> The laws which have been hitherto mentioned, i.e., the laws of nature, do bind men absolutely, even as they are men, although they have never any settled fellowship, never any solemn agreement amongst themselves what to do, or not to do: but forasmuch as we are not by ourselves sufficient to furnish ourselves with competent store of things, needful for such a life as our nature doth desire, a life fit for the dignity of man; therefore to supply those defects and imperfections which are in us, as living single and solely by ourselves, we are naturally induced to seek communion and fellowship with others: this was the cause of men's uniting themselves at first in politic societies.

But I moreover affirm, that all men are naturally in that state, and remain so, till by their own consents they make themselves members of some politic society; and I doubt not in the sequel of this discourse, to make it very clear.

Of the State of War

16. The state of war is a state of enmity and destruction: and therefore declaring by word or action, not a passionate and hasty, but a sedate settled design upon another man's life, puts him in a state of war with him against whom he has declared such an intention, and so has exposed his life to the other's power to be taken away by him, or any one that joins with him in his defence, and espouses his quarrel; it being reasonable and just, I should have a right to destroy that which threatens me with destruction: for, by the fundamental law of nature, man being to be preserved as much as possible, when all cannot be preserved, the safety of the innocent is to be preferred: and one may destroy a man who makes war upon him, or has discovered an enmity to his being, for the same reason that he may kill a wolf or a lion; because such men are not under the ties of the common law of reason, have no other rule, but that of force and violence, and so may be treated as beasts of prey, those dangerous and noxious creatures, that will be sure to destroy him whenever he falls into their power.

17. And hence it is, that he who attempts to get another man into his absolute power, does thereby put himself into a state of war with him; it being to be understood as a declaration of a design upon his life: for I have reason to conclude, that he who would get me into his power without my consent, would use me as he pleased when he had got me there, and destroy me too when he had a fancy to it; for no body can desire to have me in his absolute power, unless it be to compel me by force to that which is against the right of my freedom, i.e., make me a slave. To be free from such force is the only security of my preservation; and reason bids me look on him, as an enemy to my preservation, who would take away that freedom which is the fence to it; so that he who makes an attempt to enslave me, thereby puts himself into a state of

---

[1] [Garcilaso de la Vega (1501–36) was a historian who was well known for his writings on Inca history and culture.]

war with me. He that, in the state of nature, would take away the freedom that belongs to any one in that state, must necessarily be supposed to have a foundation of all the rest; as he that in the state of society, would take away the freedom belonging to those of that society or commonwealth, must be supposed to design to take away from them every thing else, and so be looked on as in a state of war.

18. This makes it lawful for a man to kill a thief, who has not in the least hurt him, nor declared any design upon his life, any farther than, by the use of force, so to get him in his power, as to take away his money, or what he pleases, from him; because using force, where he has no right, to get me into his power, let his pretence be what it will, I have no reason to suppose, that he, who would take away my liberty, would not, when he had me in his power, take away every thing else. And therefore it is lawful for me to treat him as one who has put himself into a state of war with me, i.e., kill him if I can; for to that hazard does he justly expose himself, whoever introduces a state of war, and is aggressor in it.

19. And here we have the plain difference between the state of nature and the state of war, which however some men have confounded, are as far distant, as a state of peace, good will, mutual assistance and preservation, and a state of enmity, malice, violence and mutual destruction, are one from another. Men living together according to reason, without a common superior on earth, with authority to judge between them, is properly the state of nature. But force, or a declared design of force, upon the person of another, where there is no common superior on earth to appeal to for relief, is the state of war: and it is the want of such an appeal gives a man the right of war even against an aggressor, tho' he be in society and a fellow subject. Thus a thief, whom I cannot harm, but by appeal to the law, for having stolen all that I am worth, I may kill, when he sets on me to rob me but of my horse or coat; because the law, which was made for my preservation, where it cannot interpose to secure my life

from present force, which, if lost, is capable of no reparation, permits me my own defence, and the right of war, a liberty to kill the aggressor, because the aggressor allows not time to appeal to our common judge, nor the decision of the law, for remedy in a case where the mischief may be irreparable. Want of a common judge with authority, puts all men in a state of nature: force without right, upon a man's person, makes a state of war, both where there is, and is not, a common judge.

20. But when the actual force is over, the state of war ceases between those that are in society, and are equally on both sides subjected to the fair determination of the law; because then there lies open the remedy of appeal for the past injury, and to prevent future harm: but where no such appeal is, as in the state of nature, for want of positive laws, and judges with authority to appeal to, the state of war once begun, continues, with a right to the innocent party to destroy the other whenever he can, until the aggressor offers peace, and desires reconciliation on such terms as may repair any wrongs he has already done, and secure the innocent for the future; nay, where an appeal to the law, and constituted judges, lies open, but the remedy is denied by a manifest perverting of justice, and a barefaced wresting of the laws to protect or indemnify the violence or injuries of some men, or party of men, there it is hard to imagine any thing but a state of war: for wherever violence is used, and injury done, though by hands appointed to administer justice, it is still violence and injury, however coloured with the name, pretences, or forms of law, the end whereof being to protect and redress the innocent, by an unbiassed application of it, to all who are under it; wherever that is not *bona fide* done, war is made upon the sufferers, who having no appeal on earth to right them, they are left to the only remedy in such cases, an appeal to heaven.

21. To avoid this state of war (wherein there is no appeal but to heaven, and wherein every the least difference is apt to end, where there is no authority

to decide between the contenders) is one great reason of men's putting themselves into society, and quitting the state of nature: for where there is an authority, a power on earth, from which relief can be had by appeal, there the continuance of the state of war is excluded, and the controversy is decided by that power. Had there been any such court, any superior jurisdiction on earth, to determine the right between Jephtha and the Ammonites, they had never come to a state of war: but we see he was forced to appeal to heaven. "The Lord the Judge," says he, "be judge this day between the children of Israel and the children of Ammon" (Judges 11:27), and then prosecuting, and relying on his appeal, he leads out his army to battle: and therefore in such controversies, where the question is put, "Who shall be judge?" it cannot be meant, "Who shall decide the controversy?"; every one knows what Jephtha here tells us, that the Lord the Judge shall judge. Where there is no judge on earth, the appeal lies to God in heaven. That question then cannot mean, "Who shall judge, whether another hath put himself in a state of war with me, and whether I may, as Jephtha did, appeal to heaven in it?" Of that I myself can only be judge in my own conscience, as I will answer it, at the great day, to the supreme judge of all men.

[...]

Of the Beginning of Political Societies

95. Men being, as has been said, by nature, all free, equal, and independent, no one can be put out of this estate, and subjected to the political power of another, without his own consent. The only way whereby any one divests himself of his natural liberty, and puts on the bonds of civil society, is by agreeing with other men to join and unite into a community for their comfortable, safe, and peaceable living one amongst another, in a secure enjoyment of their properties, and a greater security against any, that are not of it. This any number of men may do, because it injures not the freedom of the rest; they are left as they were in the liberty of the state of nature. When any number of men have so consented to make one community or government, they are thereby presently incorporated, and make one body politic, wherein the majority have a right to act and conclude the rest.

96. For when any number of men have, by the consent of every individual, made a community, they have thereby made that community one body, with a power to act as one body, which is only by the will and determination of the majority: for that which acts any community, being only the consent of the individuals of it, and it being necessary to that which is one body to move one way; it is necessary the body should move that way whither the greater force carries it, which is the consent of the majority: or else it is impossible it should act or continue one body, one community, which the consent of every individual that united into it, agreed that it should; and so every one is bound by that consent to be concluded by the majority. And therefore we see, that in assemblies, empowered to act by positive laws, where no number is set by that positive law which empowers them, the act of the majority passes for the act of the whole, and of course determines, as having, by the law of nature and reason, the power of the whole.

97. And thus every man, by consenting with others to make one body politic under one government, puts himself under an obligation, to every one of that society, to submit to the determination of the majority, and to be concluded by it; or else this original compact, whereby he with others incorporates into one society, would signify nothing, and be no compact, if he be left free, and under no other ties than he was in before in the state of nature. For what appearance would there be of any compact? what new engagement if he were no farther tied by any decrees of the society, than he himself thought fit, and did actually consent to? This would be still as great a liberty, as he himself had before his compact, or any one else in the state of nature hath, who may submit himself, and consent to any acts of it if he thinks fit.

98. For if the consent of the majority shall not, in reason, be received as the act of the whole, and conclude every individual; nothing but the consent of every individual can make any thing to be the act of the whole: but such a consent is next to impossible ever to be had, if we consider the infirmities of health, and avocations of business, which in a number, though much less than that of a commonwealth, will necessarily keep many away from the public assembly. To which if we add the variety of opinions, and contrariety of interests, which unavoidably happen in all collections of men, the coming into society upon such terms would be only like Cato's coming into the theatre, only to go out again. Such a constitution as this would make the mighty Leviathan of a shorter duration, than the feeblest creatures, and not let it outlast the day it was born in: which cannot be supposed, till we can think, that rational creatures should desire and constitute societies only to be dissolved: for where the majority cannot conclude the rest, there they cannot act as one body, and consequently will be immediately dissolved again.

99. Whosoever therefore out of a state of nature unite into a community, must be understood to give up all the power, necessary to the ends for which they unite into society, to the majority of the community, unless they expressly agreed in any number greater than the majority. And this is done by barely agreeing to unite into one political society, which is all the compact that is, or needs be, between the individuals, that enter into, or make up a commonwealth. And thus that, which begins and actually constitutes any political society, is nothing but the consent of any number of freemen capable of a majority to unite and incorporate into such a society. And this is that, and that only, which did, or could give beginning to any lawful government in the world.

100. To this I find two objections made. *First,* that there are no instances to be found in story, of a company of men independent, and equal one amongst another, that met together, and in this way began and set up a government.

Secondly, 'tis impossible of right, that men should do so, because all men being born under government, they are to submit to that, and are not at liberty to begin a new one.

101. To the first there is this to answer, That it is not at all to be wondered, that history gives us but a very little account of men, that lived together in the state of nature. The inconveniences of that condition, and the love and want of society, no sooner brought any number of them together, but they presently united and incorporated, if they designed to continue together. And if we may not suppose men ever to have been in the state of nature, because we hear not much of them in such a state, we may as well suppose the armies of Salmanasser or Xerxes were never children, because we hear little of them, till they were men, and imbodied in armies. Government is every where antecedent to records, and letters seldom come in amongst a people till a long continuation of civil society has, by other more necessary arts, provided for their safety, ease, and plenty: and then they begin to look after the history of their founders, and search into their original, when they have outlived the memory of it: for it is with commonwealths as with particular persons, they are commonly ignorant of their own births and infancies: and if they know any thing of their original, they are beholden for it, to the accidental records that others have kept of it. And those that we have, of the beginning of any polities in the world, excepting that of the Jews, where God himself immediately interposed, and which favours not at all paternal dominion, are all either plain instances of such a beginning as I have mentioned, or at least have manifest footsteps of it.

102. He must shew a strange inclination to deny evident matter of fact, when it agrees not with his hypothesis, who will not allow, that shew a strange inclination to deny evident matter of fact, when it agrees not with his hypothesis, who will not allow, that the beginning of Rome and Venice were by the uniting together of several men free and independent one of another, amongst whom there was no

natural superiority or subjection. And if Josephus Acosta's[1] word may be taken, he tells us, that in many parts of America there was no government at all. "There are great and apparent conjectures," says he, "that these men," speaking of those of Peru, "for a long time had neither kings nor commonwealths, but lived in troops, as they do this day in Florida, the Cheriquanas, those of Brazil, and many other nations, which have no certain kings, but as occasion is offered, in peace or war, they choose their captains as they please" (lib. I, c. 25). If it be said, that every man there was born subject to his father, or the head of his family; that the subjection due from a child to a father took not away his freedom of uniting into what political society he thought fit, has been already proved. But be that as it will, these men, it is evident, were actually free; and whatever superiority some politicians now would place in any of them, they themselves claimed it not, but by consent were all equal, till by the same consent they set rulers over themselves. So that their politic societies all began from a voluntary union, and the mutual agreement of men freely acting in the choice of their governors, and forms of government.

103. And I hope those who went away from Sparta with Palantus, mentioned by Justin (lib. 3, c. 4),[2] will be allowed to have been freemen independent one of another, and to have set up a government over themselves, by their own consent. Thus I have given several examples, out of history, of people free and in the state of nature, that being met together incorporated and began a commonwealth. And if the want of such instances be an argument to prove that government were not, nor could not be so begun, I suppose the contenders for paternal empire were better let it alone, than urge it against natural liberty: for if they can give so many instances, out of history, of governments begun upon paternal right, I think (though at best an argument from what has been, to what should of right be, has no great force) one might, without any great danger, yield them the cause. But if I might advise them in the case, they would do well not to search too much into the original of governments, as they have begun de facto, lest they should find, at the foundation of most of them, something very little favourable to the design they promote, and such a power as they contend for.

104. But to conclude, reason being plain on our side, that men are naturally free, and the examples of history shewing, that the governments of the world, that were begun in peace, had their beginning laid on that foundation, and were made by the consent of the people; there can be little room for doubt, either where the right is, or what has been the opinion, or practice of mankind, about the first erecting of governments.

105. I will not deny, that if we look back as far as history will direct us, towards the original of commonwealths, we shall generally find them under the government and administration of one man. And I am also apt to believe, that where a family was numerous enough to subsist by itself, and continued entire together, without mixing with others, as it often happens, where there is much land, and few people, the government commonly began in the father: for the father having, by the law of nature, the same power with every man else to punish, as he thought fit, any offences against that law, might thereby punish his transgressing children, even when they were men, and out of their pupilage; and they were very likely to submit to his punishment, and all join with him against the offender, in their turns, giving him thereby power to execute his sentence against any transgression, and so in effect make him the law-maker, and governor over all that remained in conjunction with his family. He was fittest to be trusted; paternal affection secured their property and interest under his care; and the custom of obeying him, in their

---

[1] [A sixteenth-century Jesuit whose history of the Indies was well known.]

[2] [Justin (100–165 CE) was an early Christian martyr who wrote a well-known apology for the Christian faith. Palantus was the freely chosen leader of a group of Spartans who left the city-state to form their own community.]

childhood, made it easier to submit to him, rather than to any other. If therefore they must have one to rule them, as government is hardly to be avoided amongst men that live together; who so likely to be the man as he that was their common father; unless negligence, cruelty, or any other defect of mind or body made him unfit for it? But when either the father died, and left his next heir, for want of age, wisdom, courage, or any other qualities, less fit for rule; or where several families met, and consented to continue together; there, it is not to be doubted, but they used their natural freedom, to set up him, whom they judged the ablest, and most likely, to rule well over them. Conformable hereunto we find the people of America, who (living out of the reach of the conquering swords, and spreading domination of the two great empires of Peru and Mexico) enjoyed their own natural freedom, though, *caeteris paribus*, they commonly prefer the heir of their deceased king; yet if they find him any way weak, or uncapable, they pass him by, and set up the stoutest and bravest man for their ruler.

106. Thus, though looking back as far as records give us any account of peopling the world, and the history of nations, we commonly find the government to be in one hand; yet it destroys not that which I affirm, viz. that the beginning of politic society depends upon the consent of the individuals, to join into, and make one society; who, when they are thus incorporated, might set up what form of government they thought fit. But this having given occasion to men to mistake, and think, that by nature government was monarchical, and belonged to the father, it may not be amiss here to consider, why people in the beginning generally pitched upon this form, which though perhaps the father's preeminency might, in the first institution of some commonwealths, give a rise to, and place in the beginning, the power in one hand; yet it is plain that the reason, that continued the form of government in a single person, was not any regard, or respect to paternal authority; since all petty monarchies, that is, almost all monarchies, near their original, have been commonly, at least upon occasion, elective.

107. First then, in the beginning of things, the father's government of the childhood of those sprung from him, having accustomed them to the rule of one man, and taught them that where it was exercised with care and skill, with affection and love to those under it, it was sufficient to procure and preserve to men all the political happiness they sought for in society. It was no wonder that they should pitch upon, and naturally run into that form of government, which from their infancy they had been all accustomed to; and which, by experience, they had found both easy and safe. To which, if we add, that monarchy being simple, and most obvious to men, whom neither experience had instructed in forms of government, nor the ambition or insolence of empire had taught to beware of the encroachments of prerogative, or the inconveniences of absolute power, which monarchy in succession was apt to lay claim to, and bring upon them, it was not at all strange, that they should not much trouble themselves to think of methods of restraining any exorbitances of those to whom they had given the authority over them, and of balancing the power of government, by placing several parts of it in different hands. They had neither felt the oppression of tyrannical dominion, nor did the fashion of the age, nor their possessions, or way of living, (which afforded little matter for covetousness or ambition) give them any reason to apprehend or provide against it; and therefore it is no wonder they put themselves into such a frame of government, as was not only, as I said, most obvious and simple, but also best suited to their present state and condition; which stood more in need of defence against foreign invasions and injuries, than of multiplicity of laws. The equality of a simple poor way of living, confining their desires within the narrow bounds of each man's small property, made few controversies, and so no need of many laws to decide them, or variety of officers to superintend the process, or look after the execution of justice, where there were but few trespasses, and few offenders. Since then those, who like one another so well as to join into society, cannot but be supposed to have some acquaintance and friendship together,

and some trust one in another; they could not but have greater apprehensions of others, than of one another: and therefore their first care and thought cannot but be supposed to be, how to secure themselves against foreign force. It was natural for them to put themselves under a frame of government which might best serve to that end, and chuse the wisest and bravest man to conduct them in their wars, and lead them out against their enemies, and in this chiefly be their ruler.

108. Thus we see, that the kings of the Indians in America, which is still a pattern of the first ages in Asia and Europe, whilst the inhabitants were too few for the country, and want of people and money gave men no temptation to enlarge their possessions of land, or contest for wider extent of ground, are little more than generals of their armies; and though they command absolutely in war, yet at home and in time of peace they exercise very little dominion, and have but a very moderate sovereignty, the resolutions of peace and war being ordinarily either in the people, or in a council. Tho' the war itself, which admits not of plurality of governors, naturally devolves the command into the king's sole authority.

109. And thus in Israel itself, the chief business of their judges, and first kings, seems to have been to be captains in war, and leaders of their armies; which (besides what is signified by going out and in before the people, which was, to march forth to war, and home again in the heads of their forces) appears plainly in the story of Jephtha. The Ammonites making war upon Israel, the Gileadites in fear send to Jephtha, a bastard of their family whom they had cast off, and article with him, if he will assist them against the Ammonites, to make him their ruler; which they do in these words, "And the people made him head and captain over them" (Judges 11:11), which was, as it seems, all one as to be judge. "And he judged Israel" (Judges 12:7), that is, was their captain-general six years. So when Jotham upbraids the Shechemites with the obligation they had to Gideon, who had been their judge and ruler, he tells them, "He fought for you, and

adventured his life far, and delivered you out of the hands of Midian" (Judges 11:17). Nothing mentioned of him but what he did as a general: and indeed that is all is found in his history, or in any of the rest of the judges. And Abimelech particularly is called king, though at most he was but their general. And when, being weary of the ill conduct of Samuel's sons, the children of Israel desired a king, "like all the nations to judge them, and to go out before them, and to fight their battles" (1 Samuel 8:20). God granting their desire, says to Samuel, "I will send thee a man, and thou shalt anoint him to be captain over my people Israel, that he may save my people out of the hands of the Philistines" (c. 9:16). As if the only business of a king had been to lead out their armies, and fight in their defence; and accordingly at his inauguration pouring a vial of oil upon him, declares to Saul, that "the Lord had anointed him to be captain over his inheritance" (c. 10:1). And therefore those, who after Saul's being solemnly chosen and saluted king by the tribes at Mispah, were unwilling to have him their king, made no other objection but this, "How shall this man save us?" (v. 27), as if they should have said, "This man is unfit to be our king, not having skill and conduct enough in war, to be able to defend us." And when God resolved to transfer the government to David, it is in these words, "But now thy kingdom shall not continue: the Lord hath sought him a man after his own heart, and the Lord hath commanded him to be captain over his people" (c. 13:14). As if the whole kingly authority were nothing else but to be their general: and therefore the tribes who had stuck to Saul's family, and opposed David's reign, when they came to Hebron with terms of submission to him, they tell him, amongst other arguments they had to submit to him as to their king, that he was in effect their king in Saul's time, and therefore they had no reason but to receive him as their king now. "Also (say they) in time past, when Saul was king over us, thou wast he that reddest out and broughtest in Israel, and the Lord said unto thee, 'Thou shalt feed my people Israel, and thou shalt be a captain over Israel' [1 Chron. 11:2]."

110. Thus, whether a family by degrees grew up into a commonwealth, and the fatherly authority being continued on to the elder son, every one in his turn growing up under it, tacitly submitted to it, and the easiness and equality of it not offending any one, every one acquiesced, till time seemed to have confirmed it, and settled a right of succession by prescription: or whether several families, or the descendants of several families, whom chance, neighbourhood, or business brought together, uniting into society, the need of a general, whose conduct might defend them against their enemies in war, and the great confidence the innocence and sincerity of that poor but virtuous age, (such as are almost all those which begin governments, that ever come to last in the world) gave men one of another, made the first beginners of commonwealths generally put the rule into one man's hand, without any other express limitation or restraint, but what the nature of the thing, and the end of government required: which ever of those it was that at first put the rule into the hands of a single person, certain it is no body was entrusted with it but for the public good and safety, and to those ends, in the infancies of commonwealths, those who had it commonly used it. And unless they had done so, young societies could not have subsisted; without such nursing fathers tender and careful of the public weal, all governments would have sunk under the weakness and infirmities of their infancy, and the prince and the people had soon perished together.

111. But though the golden age (before vain ambition, and *amor sceleratus habendi*, evil concupiscence, had corrupted men's minds into a mistake of true power and honour) had more virtue, and consequently better governors, as well as less vicious subjects, and there was then no stretching prerogative on the one side, to oppress the people; nor consequently on the other, any dispute about privilege, to lessen or restrain the power of the magistrate, and so no contest betwixt rulers and people about governors or government: yet, when ambition and luxury in future ages would retain and increase the power, without doing the business for which it was given; and aided by flattery, taught princes to have distinct and separate interests from their people, men found it necessary to examine more carefully the original and rights of government; and to find out ways to restrain the exorbitances, and prevent the abuses of that power, which they having entrusted in another's hands only for their own good, they found was made use of to hurt them.

112. Thus we may see how probable it is, that people that were naturally free, and by their own consent either submitted to the government of their father, or united together out of different families to make a government, should generally put the rule into one man's hands, and chuse to be under the conduct of a single person, without so much as by express conditions limiting or regulating his power, which they thought safe enough in his honesty and prudence; though they never dreamed of monarchy being *iure divino*, which we never heard of among mankind, till it was revealed to us by the divinity of this last age; nor ever allowed paternal power to have a right to dominion, or to be the foundation of all government. And thus much may suffice to shew, that as far as we have any light from history, we have reason to conclude, that all peaceful beginnings of government have been laid in the consent of the people. I say peaceful, because I shall have occasion in another place to speak of conquest, which some esteem a way of beginning of governments.

The other objection I find urged against the beginning of polities, in the way I have mentioned, is this, viz.:

113. That all men being born under government, some or other, it is impossible any of them should ever be free, and at liberty to unite together, and begin a new one, or ever be able to erect a lawful government.

If this argument be good; I ask, how came so many lawful monarchies into the world? for if any body, upon this supposition, can shew me any one man in any age of the world free to begin a lawful monarchy, I will be bound to shew him ten other free men at liberty, at the same time to unite and begin a new government under a regal, or any other form; it being demonstration, that if any one, born under the dominion of another, may be so free as to have a right to command others in a new and distinct empire, every one that is born under the dominion of another may be so free too, and may become a ruler, or subject, of a distinct separate government. And so by this their own principle, either all men, however born, are free, or else there is but one lawful prince, one lawful government in the world. And then they have nothing to do, but barely to shew us which that is; which when they have done, I doubt not but all mankind will easily agree to pay obedience to him.

114. Though it be a sufficient answer to their objection, to shew that it involves them in the same difficulties that it doth those they use it against; yet I shall endeavour to discover the weakness of this argument a little farther.

"All men," say they, "are born under government, and therefore they cannot be at liberty to begin a new one. Every one is born a subject to his father, or his prince, and is therefore under the perpetual tie of subjection and allegiance." It is plain mankind never owned nor considered any such natural subjection that they were born in, to one or to the other that tied them, without their own consents, to a subjection to them and their heirs.

115. For there are no examples so frequent in history, both sacred and profane, as those of men withdrawing themselves, and their obedience, from the jurisdiction they were born under, and the family or community they were bred up in, and setting up new governments in other places; from whence sprang all that number of petty commonwealths in the beginning of ages, and which always multiplied, as long as there was room enough, till the stronger, or more fortunate, swallowed the weaker; and those great ones again breaking to pieces, dissolved into lesser dominions. All which are so many testimonies against paternal sovereignty, and plainly prove, that it was not the natural right of the father descending to his heirs, that made governments in the beginning, since it was impossible, upon that ground, there should have been so many little kingdoms; all must have been but only one universal monarchy, if men had not been at liberty to separate themselves from their families, and the government, be it what it will, that was set up in it, and go and make distinct commonwealths and other governments, as they thought fit.

116. This has been the practice of the world from its first beginning to this day; nor is it now any more hindrance to the freedom of mankind, that they are born under constituted and ancient polities, that have established laws, and set forms of government, than if they were born in the woods, amongst the unconfined inhabitants, that run loose in them: for those, who would persuade us, that by being born under any government, we are naturally subjects to it, and have no more any title or pretence to the freedom of the state of nature, have no other reason (bating that of paternal power, which we have already answered) to produce for it, but only, because our fathers or progenitors passed away their natural liberty, and thereby bound up themselves and their posterity to a perpetual subjection to the government, which they themselves submitted to. It is true, that whatever engagements or promises any one has made for himself, he is under the obligation of them, but cannot, by any compact whatsoever, bind his children or posterity: for his son, when a man, being altogether as free as the father, any act of the father can no more give away the liberty of the son, than it can of any body else: he may indeed annex such conditions to the land, he enjoyed as a subject of any commonwealth, as may oblige his son to be of that community, if he will enjoy those possessions which were his father's; because that estate being his father's property, he may dispose, or settle it, as he pleases.

117. And this has generally given the occasion to mistake in this matter; because commonwealths not

permitting any part of their dominions to be dismembered, nor to be enjoyed by any but those of their community, the son cannot ordinarily enjoy the possessions of his father, but under the same terms his father did, by becoming a member of the society; whereby he puts himself presently under the government he finds there established, as much as any other subject of that commonwealth. And thus the consent of freemen, born under government, which only makes them members of it, being given separately in their turns, as each comes to be of age, and not in a multitude together; people take no notice of it, and thinking it not done at all, or not necessary, conclude they are naturally subjects as they are men.

118. But, 'tis plain, governments themselves understand it otherwise; they claim no power over the son, because of that they had over the father; nor look on children as being their subjects, by their fathers being so. If a subject of England have a child, by an English woman in France, whose subject is he? Not the king of England's; for he must have leave to be admitted to the privileges of it: nor the king of France's; for how then has his father a liberty to bring him away, and breed him as he pleases? and who ever was judged as a traytor or deserter, if he left, or warred against a country, for being barely born in it of parents that were aliens there? It is plain then, by the practice of governments themselves, as well as by the law of right reason, that a child is born a subject of no country or government. He is under his father's tuition and authority, till he comes to age of discretion; and then he is a freeman, at liberty what government he will put himself under, what body politic he will unite himself to: for if an Englishman's son, born in France, be at liberty, and may do so, it is evident there is no tie upon him by his father's being a subject of this kingdom; nor is he bound up by any compact of his ancestors. And why then hath not his son, by the same reason, the same liberty, though he be born any where else? Since the power that a father hath naturally over his children, is the same, where-ever they be born, and the ties of natural obligations, are not bounded by the positive limits of kingdoms and commonwealths.

119. Every man being, as has been shewed, naturally free, and nothing being able to put him into subjection to any earthly power, but only his own consent; it is to be considered, what shall be understood to be a sufficient declaration of a man's consent, to make him subject to the laws of any government. There is a common distinction of an express and a tacit consent, which will concern our present case. No body doubts but an express consent, of any man entering into any society, makes him a perfect member of that society, a subject of that government. The difficulty is, what ought to be looked upon as a tacit consent, and how far it binds, i.e., how far any one shall be looked on to have consented, and thereby submitted to any government, where he has made no expressions of it at all. And to this I say, that every man, that hath any possessions, or enjoyment, of any part of the dominions of any government, doth thereby give his tacit consent, and is as far forth obliged to obedience to the laws of that government, during such enjoyment, as any one under it; whether this his possession be of land, to him and his heirs for ever, or a lodging only for a week; or whether it be barely travelling freely on the highway; and in effect, it reaches as far as the very being of any one within the territories of that government.

120. To understand this the better, it is fit to consider, that every man, when he at first incorporates himself into any commonwealth, he, by his uniting himself thereunto, annexed also, and submits to the community, those possessions, which he has, or shall acquire, that do not already belong to any other government: for it would be a direct contradiction, for any one to enter into society with others for the securing and regulating of property; and yet to suppose his land, whose property is to be regulated by the laws of the society, should be exempt from the jurisdiction of that government, to which he himself, the proprietor of the land, is a subject. By the same act therefore, whereby any

one unites his person, which was before free, to any commonwealth, by the same he unites his possessions, which were before free, to it also; and they become, both of them, person and possession, subject to the government and dominion of that commonwealth, as long as it hath a being. Whoever therefore, from thenceforth, by inheritance, purchase, permission, or otherways, enjoys any part of the land, so annexed to, and under the government of that commonwealth, must take it with the condition it is under; that is, of submitting to the government of the commonwealth, under whose jurisdiction it is, as far forth as any subject of it.

121. But since the government has a direct jurisdiction only over the land, and reaches the possessor of it, (before he has actually incorporated himself in the society) only as he dwells upon, and enjoys that; the obligation any one is under, by virtue of such enjoyment, to submit to the government, begins and ends with the enjoyment; so that whenever the owner, who has given nothing but such a tacit consent to the government, will, by donation, sale, or otherwise, quit the said possession, he is at liberty to go and incorporate himself into any other commonwealth; or to agree with others to begin a new one, *in vacuis locis*, in any part of the world, they can find free and unpossessed: whereas he, that has once, by actual agreement, and any express declaration, given his consent to be of any commonwealth, is perpetually and indispensably obliged to be, and remain unalterably a

subject to it, and can never be again in the liberty of the state of nature; unless, by any calamity, the government he was under comes to be dissolved; or else by some public act cuts him off from being any longer a member of it.

122. But submitting to the laws of any country, living quietly, and enjoying privileges and protection under them, makes not a man a member of that society: this is only a local protection and homage due to and from all those, who, not being in a state of war, come within the territories belonging to any government, to all parts whereof the force of its laws extends. But this no more makes a man a member of that society, a perpetual subject of that commonwealth, than it would make a man a subject to another, in whose family he found it convenient to abide for some time; though, whilst he continued in it, he were obliged to comply with the laws, and submit to the government he found there. And thus we see, that foreigners, by living all their lives under another government, and enjoying the privileges and protection of it, though they are bound, even in conscience, to submit to its administration, as far forth as any denison; yet do not thereby come to be subjects or members of that commonwealth. Nothing can make any man so, but his actually entering into it by positive engagement, and express promise and compact. This is that, which I think, concerning the beginning of political societies, and that consent which makes any one a member of any commonwealth.

DISCUSSION QUESTIONS

1. What distinction does Locke mean to draw when he claims that the state of nature is a state of complete freedom but *not* a state of license? Contrast Locke's view with that of Hobbes.

2. Do you think Locke shares Hobbes's view that the state of nature is both pre-political *and* pre-moral? That is, does Locke agree with Hobbes that there is no such thing as justice in the state of nature? Support your response with points from the readings.

3. How does the state of nature regress into a state of war? Discuss whether you agree or disagree with Locke on this matter.

4. Why would rational people choose to abandon the state of nature in Locke's view? Discuss the role that punishment for breaches of the law of the nature plays in such a choice.

5. How does Locke's understanding of the way in which a common authority provides for escape from a state of war differ from Hobbes's?

6. According to Locke, what gives government its authority? How is this obtained? Critically evaluate Locke's position.

7. Why does Locke think that remaining in a state signifies that one consents to the authority of that state? What reasons does he muster in favor of this claim?

8. It is often said that if one does not vote in an election, one ought not to complain about the outcome. Discuss this notion in light of the reading. Do you think that participation in an election might count as tacit consent to the authority of the electoral process? Why or why not? Who has the supposed "right" to complain: those who vote or those who abstain?

9. The adoption of the Constitution of the United States might be considered a clear case in which a group of people explicitly consented to a political regime. In what sense does the consent of the country's forefathers transfer from their generation to the present? How can we make sense of this?

10. What might we say in response to the notion that people "vote with their feet" (i.e., that they tacitly consent to the existing political authority by continuing to live in the country)? What sorts of factors or circumstances might render this sort of consent null and void?

4

Jean-Jacques Rousseau, selection from *The Social Contract* (1762)

Jean-Jacques Rousseau (1712–78) was a French philosopher who was born in Geneva, Switzerland. In his *Discourse on Inequality* (1754), Rousseau claims that social structures and pressures have a corrupting influence on individuals and result in deep inequalities. In *The Social Contract*, from which this selection is drawn, Rousseau considers how a government of the right sort can prevent such corruption.

SOURCE

Rousseau, Jean-Jacques. *The Social Contract & Discourses (Everyman's Library Edition; Series No. 660)*. Trans. G.D.H. Cole (E. Rhys, series editor). EP Dutton & Co. First issued 1913; reprinted 1920.

I mean to inquire if, in the civil order, there can be any sure and legitimate rule of administration, men being taken as they are and laws as they might be. In this inquiry I shall endeavour always to unite what right sanctions with what is prescribed by interest, in order that justice and utility may in no case be divided.

I enter upon my task without proving the importance of the subject. I shall be asked if I am a prince or a legislator, to write on politics. I answer that I am neither, and that is why I do so. If I were a prince or a legislator, I should not waste time in saying what wants doing; I should do it, or hold my peace.

As I was born a citizen of a free State, and a member of the Sovereign, I feel that, however feeble the influence my voice can have on public affairs, the right of voting on them makes it my duty to study them: and I am happy, when I reflect upon governments, to find my inquiries always furnish me with new reasons for loving that of my own country.

Subject of the First Book

Man is born free; and everywhere he is in chains. One thinks himself the master of others, and still remains a greater slave than they. How did this change come about? I do not know. What can make it legitimate? That question I think I can answer.

If I took into account only force, and the effects derived from it, I should say: "As long as a people is compelled to obey, and obeys, it does well; as soon as it can shake off the yoke, and shakes it off, it does still better; for, regaining its liberty by the same right as took it away, either it is justified in resuming it, or there was no justification for those who took it away." But the social order is a sacred right which is the basis of all other rights. Nevertheless, this right does not come from nature, and must therefore be founded on conventions. Before coming to that, I have to prove what I have just asserted.

The First Societies

The most ancient of all societies, and the only one that is natural, is the family: and even so the children remain attached to the father only so long as they need him for their preservation. As soon as this need ceases, the natural bond is dissolved. The children, released from the obedience they owed to the father, and the father, released from the care he owed his children, return equally to independence. If they remain united, they continue so no longer naturally, but voluntarily; and the family itself is then maintained only by convention.

This common liberty results from the nature of man. His first law is to provide for his own preservation, his first cares are those which he owes to himself; and, as soon as he reaches years of discretion, he is the sole judge of the proper means of preserving himself, and consequently becomes his own master.

The family then may be called the first model of political societies: the ruler corresponds to the father, and the people to the children; and all, being born free and equal, alienate their liberty only for their own advantage. The whole difference is that, in the family, the love of the father for his children repays him for the care he takes of them, while, in the State, the pleasure of commanding takes the place of the love which the chief cannot have for the peoples under him.

Grotius[1] denies that all human power is established in favour of the governed, and quotes slavery as an example. His usual method of reasoning is constantly to establish right by fact. It would be possible to employ a more logical method, but none could be more favourable to tyrants.

It is then, according to Grotius, doubtful whether the human race belongs to a hundred men, or that hundred men to the human race: and, throughout his book, he seems to incline to the former alternative, which is also the view of Hobbes. On this showing, the human species is divided into so many herds of cattle, each with its ruler, who keeps guard over them for the purpose of devouring them.

As a shepherd is of a nature superior to that of his flock, the shepherds of men, i.e., their rulers, are of a nature superior to that of the peoples under them. Thus, Philo[2] tells us, the Emperor Caligula reasoned, concluding equally well either that kings were gods, or that men were beasts.

The reasoning of Caligula agrees with that of Hobbes and Grotius. Aristotle, before any of them, had said that men are by no means equal naturally, but that some are born for slavery, and others for dominion.

Aristotle was right; but he took the effect for the cause. Nothing can be more certain than that every man born in slavery is born for slavery. Slaves lose everything in their chains, even the desire of escaping from them: they love their servitude, as the comrades of Ulysses loved their brutish condition. If then there are slaves by nature, it is because there have been slaves against nature. Force made the first slaves, and their cowardice perpetuated the condition.

I have said nothing of King Adam, or Emperor Noah, father of the three great monarchs who shared out the universe, like the children of Saturn, whom some scholars have recognised in them. I trust to getting due thanks for my moderation; for, being a direct descendant of one of these princes, perhaps of the eldest branch, how do I know that a verification of titles might not leave me the legitimate king of the human race? In any case, there can

---

[1] [Hugo Grotius (1583–1645) was a Dutch legal theorist who is regarded as the father of the theory of international law.]

[2] [Philo (20 BCE–50 CE) was a Hellenistic Jewish philosopher.]

be no doubt that Adam was sovereign of the world, as Robinson Crusoe was of his island, as long as he was its only inhabitant; and this empire had the advantage that the monarch, safe on his throne, had no rebellions, wars, or conspirators to fear.

The Right of the Strongest

The strongest is never strong enough to be always the master, unless he transforms strength into right, and obedience into duty. Hence the right of the strongest, which, though to all seeming meant ironically, is really laid down as a fundamental principle. But are we never to have an explanation of this phrase? Force is a physical power, and I fail to see what moral effect it can have. To yield to force is an act of necessity, not of will—at the most, an act of prudence. In what sense can it be a duty?

Suppose for a moment that this so-called "right" exists. I maintain that the sole result is a mass of inexplicable nonsense. For, if force creates right, the effect changes with the cause: every force that is greater than the first succeeds to its right. As soon as it is possible to disobey with impunity, disobedience is legitimate; and, the strongest being always in the right, the only thing that matters is to act so as to become the strongest. But what kind of right is that which perishes when force fails? If we must obey perforce, there is no need to obey because we ought; and if we are not forced to obey, we are under no obligation to do so. Clearly, the word "right" adds nothing to force: in this connection, it means absolutely nothing.

Obey the powers that be. If this means yield to force, it is a good precept, but superfluous: I can answer for its never being violated. All power comes from God, I admit; but so does all sickness: does that mean that we are forbidden to call in the doctor? A brigand surprises me at the edge of a wood: must I not merely surrender my purse on compulsion; but, even if I could withhold it, am I in conscience bound to give it up? For certainly the pistol he holds is also a power.

Let us then admit that force does not create right, and that we are obliged to obey only legitimate powers. In that case, my original question recurs.

Slavery

Since no man has a natural authority over his fellow, and force creates no right, we must conclude that conventions form the basis of all legitimate authority among men.

If an individual, says Grotius, can alienate his liberty and make himself the slave of a master, why could not a whole people do the same and make itself subject to a king? There are in this passage plenty of ambiguous words which would need explaining; but let us confine ourselves to the word *alienate*. To alienate is to give or to sell. Now, a man who becomes the slave of another does not give himself; he sells himself, at the least for his subsistence: but for what does a people sell itself? A king is so far from furnishing his subjects with their subsistence that he gets his own only from them; and, according to Rabelais,[1] kings do not live on nothing. Do subjects then give their persons on condition that the king takes their goods also? I fail to see what they have left to preserve.

It will be said that the despot assures his subjects civil tranquillity. Granted; but what do they gain, if the wars his ambition brings down upon them, his insatiable avidity, and the vexatious conduct of his ministers press harder on them than their own dissensions would have done? What do they gain, if the very tranquillity they enjoy is one of their miseries? Tranquillity is found also in dungeons; but is that enough to make them desirable places to live in? The Greeks imprisoned in the cave of the Cyclops lived there very tranquilly, while they were awaiting their turn to be devoured.

To say that a man gives himself gratuitously, is to say what is absurd and inconceivable; such an act is null and illegitimate, from the mere fact that he who does it is out of his mind. To say the same of

---

[1] [François Rabelais (1494–1553) was a French writer, doctor, and humanist.]

a whole people is to suppose a people of madmen; and madness creates no right.

Even if each man could alienate himself, he could not alienate his children: they are born men and free; their liberty belongs to them, and no one but they has the right to dispose of it. Before they come to years of discretion, the father can, in their name, lay down conditions for their preservation and well-being, but he cannot give them irrevocably and without conditions: such a gift is contrary to the ends of nature, and exceeds the rights of paternity. It would therefore be necessary, in order to legitimise an arbitrary government, that in every generation the people should be in a position to accept or reject it; but, were this so, the government would be no longer arbitrary.

To renounce liberty is to renounce being a man, to surrender the rights of humanity and even its duties. For him who renounces everything no indemnity is possible. Such a renunciation is incompatible with man's nature; to remove all liberty from his will is to remove all morality from his acts. Finally, it is an empty and contradictory convention that sets up, on the one side, absolute authority, and, on the other, unlimited obedience. Is it not clear that we can be under no obligation to a person from whom we have the right to exact everything? Does not this condition alone, in the absence of equivalence or exchange, in itself involve the nullity of the act? For what right can my slave have against me, when all that he has belongs to me, and, his right being mine, this right of mine against myself is a phrase devoid of meaning?

Grotius and the rest find in war another origin for the so-called right of slavery. The victor having, as they hold, the right of killing the vanquished, the latter can buy back his life at the price of his liberty; and this convention is the more legitimate because it is to the advantage of both parties.

But it is clear that this supposed right to kill the conquered is by no means deducible from the state of war. Men, from the mere fact that, while they are living in their primitive independence, they have no mutual relations stable enough to constitute either the state of peace or the state of war, cannot be naturally enemies. War is constituted by a relation between things, and not between persons; and, as the state of war cannot arise out of simple personal relations, but only out of real relations, private war, or war of man with man, can exist neither in the state of nature, where there is no constant property, nor in the social state, where everything is under the authority of the laws.

Individual combats, duels and encounters, are acts which cannot constitute a state; while the private wars, authorised by the Establishments of Louis IX, King of France, and suspended by the Peace of God, are abuses of feudalism, in itself an absurd system if ever there was one, and contrary to the principles of natural right and to all good polity.

War then is a relation, not between man and man, but between State and State, and individuals are enemies only accidentally, not as men, nor even as citizens, but as soldiers; not as members of their country, but as its defenders. Finally, each State can have for enemies only other States, and not men; for between things disparate in nature there can be no real relation.

Furthermore, this principle is in conformity with the established rules of all times and the constant practice of all civilised peoples. Declarations of war are intimations less to powers than to their subjects. The foreigner, whether king, individual, or people, who robs, kills or detains the subjects, without declaring war on the prince, is not an enemy, but a brigand. Even in real war, a just prince, while laying hands, in the enemy's country, on all that belongs to the public, respects the lives and goods of individuals: he respects rights on which his own are founded. The object of the war being the destruction of the hostile State, the other side has a right to kill its defenders, while they are bearing arms; but as soon as they lay them down and surrender, they cease to be enemies or instruments of the enemy, and become once more merely men, whose life no one has any right to take. Sometimes it is possible to kill the State without killing a single one of its members; and war gives no right which is not necessary to the gaining of its object. These principles are not those of Grotius: they are not based on the authority of poets, but derived from the nature of reality and based on reason.

The right of conquest has no foundation other than the right of the strongest. If war does not give the conqueror the right to massacre the conquered peoples, the right to enslave them cannot be based upon a right which does not exist. No one has a right to kill an enemy except when he cannot make him a slave, and the right to enslave him cannot therefore be derived from the right to kill him. It is accordingly an unfair exchange to make him buy at the price of his liberty his life, over which the victor holds no right. Is it not clear that there is a vicious circle in founding the right of life and death on the right of slavery, and the right of slavery on the right of life and death?

Even if we assume this terrible right to kill everybody, I maintain that a slave made in war, or a conquered people, is under no obligation to a master, except to obey him as far as he is compelled to do so. By taking an equivalent for his life, the victor has not done him a favour; instead of killing him without profit, he has killed him usefully. So far then is he from acquiring over him any authority in addition to that of force, that the state of war continues to subsist between them: their mutual relation is the effect of it, and the usage of the right of war does not imply a treaty of peace. A convention has indeed been made; but this convention, so far from destroying the state of war, presupposes its continuance.

So, from whatever aspect we regard the question, the right of slavery is null and void, not only as being illegitimate, but also because it is absurd and meaningless. The words slave and right contradict each other, and are mutually exclusive. It will always be equally foolish for a man to say to a man or to a people: "I make with you a convention wholly at your expense and wholly to my advantage; I shall keep it as long as I like, and you will keep it as long as I like."

That We Must Always Go Back to a First Convention

Even if I granted all that I have been refuting, the friends of despotism would be no better off. There will always be a great difference between subduing a multitude and ruling a society. Even if scattered individuals were successively enslaved by one man, however numerous they might be, I still see no more than a master and his slaves, and certainly not a people and its ruler; I see what may be termed an aggregation, but not an association; there is as yet neither public good nor body politic. The man in question, even if he has enslaved half the world, is still only an individual; his interest, apart from that of others, is still a purely private interest. If this same man comes to die, his empire, after him, remains scattered and without unity, as an oak falls and dissolves into a heap of ashes when the fire has consumed it.

A people, says Grotius, can give itself to a king. Then, according to Grotius, a people is a people before it gives itself. The gift is itself a civil act, and implies public deliberation. It would be better, before examining the act by which a people gives itself to a king, to examine that by which it has become a people; for this act, being necessarily prior to the other, is the true foundation of society.

Indeed, if there were no prior convention, where, unless the election were unanimous, would be the obligation on the minority to submit to the choice of the majority? How have a hundred men who wish for a master the right to vote on behalf of ten who do not? The law of majority voting is itself something established by convention, and presupposes unanimity, on one occasion at least.

The Social Compact

I suppose men to have reached the point at which the obstacles in the way of their preservation in the state of nature show their power of resistance to be greater than the resources at the disposal of each individual for his maintenance in that state. That primitive condition can then subsist no longer; and the human race would perish unless it changed its manner of existence.

But, as men cannot engender new forces, but only unite and direct existing ones, they have no other means of preserving themselves than the formation, by aggregation, of a sum of forces great enough to overcome the resistance. These they have to bring into play by means of a single motive power, and cause to act in concert.

This sum of forces can arise only where several persons come together: but, as the force and liberty of each man are the chief instruments of his self-preservation, how can he pledge them without harming his own interests, and neglecting the care he owes to himself? This difficulty, in its bearing on my present subject, may be stated in the following terms:

"The problem is to find a form of association which will defend and protect with the whole common force the person and goods of each associate, and in which each, while uniting himself with all, may still obey himself alone, and remain as free as before." This is the fundamental problem of which the Social Contract provides the solution.

The clauses of this contract are so determined by the nature of the act that the slightest modification would make them vain and ineffective; so that, although they have perhaps never been formally set forth, they are everywhere the same and everywhere tacitly admitted and recognised, until, on the violation of the social compact, each regains his original rights and resumes his natural liberty, while losing the conventional liberty in favour of which he renounced it.

These clauses, properly understood, may be reduced to one—the total alienation of each associate, together with all his rights, to the whole community; for, in the first place, as each gives himself absolutely, the conditions are the same for all; and, this being so, no one has any interest in making them burdensome to others.

Moreover, the alienation being without reserve, the union is as perfect as it can be, and no associate has anything more to demand: for, if the individuals retained certain rights, as there would be no common superior to decide between them and the public, each, being on one point his own judge, would ask to be so on all; the state of nature would thus continue, and the association would necessarily become inoperative or tyrannical.

Finally, each man, in giving himself to all, gives himself to nobody; and as there is no associate over whom he does not acquire the same right as he yields others over himself, he gains an equivalent for everything he loses, and an increase of force for the preservation of what he has.

If then we discard from the social compact what is not of its essence, we shall find that it reduces itself to the following terms:

"Each of us puts his person and all his power in common under the supreme direction of the general will, and, in our corporate capacity, we receive each member as an indivisible part of the whole."

At once, in place of the individual personality of each contracting party, this act of association creates a moral and collective body, composed of as many members as the assembly contains votes, and receiving from this act its unity, its common identity, its life and its will. This public person, so formed by the union of all other persons formerly took the name of *city*, and now takes that of *Republic* or *body politic*; it is called by its members *State* when passive, *Sovereign* when active, and *Power* when compared with others like itself. Those who are associated in it take collectively the name of *people*, and severally are called *citizens*, as sharing in the sovereign power, and *subjects*, as being under the laws of the State. But these terms are often confused and taken one for another: it is enough to know how to distinguish them when they are being used with precision.

The Sovereign

This formula shows us that the act of association comprises a mutual undertaking between the public and the individuals, and that each individual, in making a contract, as we may say, with himself, is bound in a double capacity; as a member of the Sovereign he is bound to the individuals, and as a member of the State to the Sovereign. But the maxim of civil right, that no one is bound by undertakings made to himself, does not apply in this case; for there is a great difference between incurring an obligation to yourself and incurring one to a whole of which you form a part.

Attention must further be called to the fact that public deliberation, while competent to bind all the subjects to the Sovereign, because of the two different capacities in which each of them may be regarded, cannot, for the opposite reason, bind the Sovereign to itself; and that it is consequently against the nature of the body politic for the Sovereign to impose on itself a law which it cannot infringe. Being able to regard itself in only one capacity, it is in the position of an individual who makes a contract with himself; and this makes it clear that there neither is nor can be any kind of fundamental law binding on the body of the people—not even the social contract itself. This does not mean that the body politic cannot enter into undertakings with others, provided the contract is not infringed by them; for in relation to what is external to it, it becomes a simple being, an individual.

But the body politic or the Sovereign, drawing its being wholly from the sanctity of the contract, can never bind itself, even to an outsider, to do anything derogatory to the original act, for instance, to alienate any part of itself, or to submit to another Sovereign. Violation of the act by which it exists would be self-annihilation; and that which is itself nothing can create nothing.

As soon as this multitude is so united in one body, it is impossible to offend against one of the members without attacking the body, and still more to offend against the body without the members resenting it. Duty and interest therefore equally oblige the two contracting parties to give each other help; and the same men should seek to combine, in their double capacity, all the advantages dependent upon that capacity.

Again, the Sovereign, being formed wholly of the individuals who compose it, neither has nor can have any interest contrary to theirs; and consequently the sovereign power need give no guarantee to its subjects, because it is impossible for the body to wish to hurt all its members. We shall also see later on that it cannot hurt any in particular. The Sovereign, merely by virtue of what it is, is always what it should be.

This, however, is not the case with the relation of the subjects to the Sovereign, which, despite the common interest, would have no security that they would fulfil their undertakings, unless it found means to assure itself of their fidelity.

In fact, each individual, as a man, may have a particular will contrary or dissimilar to the general will which he has as a citizen. His particular interest may speak to him quite differently from the common interest: his absolute and naturally independent existence may make him look upon what he owes to the common cause as a gratuitous contribution, the loss of which will do less harm to others than the payment of it is burdensome to himself; and, regarding the moral person which constitutes the State as a *persona ficta*, because not a man, he may wish to enjoy the rights of citizenship without being ready to fulfil the duties of a subject. The continuance of such an injustice could not but prove the undoing of the body politic.

In order then that the social compact may not be an empty formula, it tacitly includes the undertaking, which alone can give force to the rest, that whoever refuses to obey the general will shall be compelled to do so by the whole body. This means nothing less than that he will be forced to be free; for this is the condition which, by giving each citizen to his country, secures him against all personal dependence. In this lies the key to the working of the political machine; this alone legitimises civil undertakings, which, without it, would be absurd, tyrannical, and liable to the most frightful abuses.

The Civil State

The passage from the state of nature to the civil state produces a very remarkable change in man, by substituting justice for instinct in his conduct, and giving his actions the morality they had formerly lacked. Then only, when the voice of duty takes the place of physical impulses and right of appetite, does man, who so far had considered only himself, find that he is forced to act on different principles, and to consult his reason before listening to his inclinations. Although, in this state, he deprives himself of some advantages which he got from nature, he gains in return others so great, his faculties are so stimulated and developed, his ideas so extended, his feelings so ennobled, and his whole soul so uplifted, that, did not the abuses of this new condition often degrade him below that which he left, he would be bound to bless continually the happy moment which took him from it for ever, and, instead of a stupid and unimaginative animal, made him an intelligent being and a man.

Let us draw up the whole account in terms easily commensurable. What man loses by the social contract is his natural liberty and an unlimited right to everything he tries to get and succeeds in getting; what he gains is civil liberty and the proprietorship of all he possesses. If we are to avoid mistake in weighing one against the other, we must clearly distinguish natural liberty, which is bounded only by the strength of the individual, from civil liberty, which is limited by the general will; and possession, which is merely the effect of force or the right of the first occupier, from property, which can be founded only on a positive title.

We might, over and above all this, add, to what man acquires in the civil state, moral liberty, which alone makes him truly master of himself; for the mere impulse of appetite is slavery, while obedience to a law which we prescribe to ourselves is liberty. But I have already said too much on this head, and the philosophical meaning of the word liberty does not now concern us.

DISCUSSION QUESTIONS

1. In Rousseau's view, what makes a state "legitimate"? What is entailed by this notion of legitimacy?

2. What does Rousseau mean by saying that a policy is in accord with the general will?

3. Is a policy that is in accord with the general will always in an individual's interest? Why or why not?

4. Rousseau explains that submission to the general will is in the interest of each person. Given what he says, how is it that one can submit to this and retain one's freedom?

5. Discuss what you to take to be the relevant similarities and differences between Rousseau's vision of a state of nature and that of Glaucon (i.e., Plato), Hobbes, and Locke.

5

David Gauthier, selection from *Morals by Agreement* (1986)

David Gauthier (b. 1932) is professor emeritus in the Philosophy Department at the University of Pittsburgh. He is perhaps best known for his defense of a neo-Hobbesian social-contract theory of morality. In what follows, Gauthier presents a theory of morals as being part of a more general theory of rational choice. He argues that among our principles of rational choice are principles that constrain the pursuit of our own interest impartially.

SOURCE

Gauthier, David. *Morals by Agreement.* Oxford University Press, 1986. Reprinted by permission of Oxford University Press, Inc.

Overview of a Theory

1 What theory of morals can ever serve any useful purpose, unless it can show that all the duties it recommends are also the true interest of each individual?[1] David Hume, who asked this question, seems mistaken; such a theory would be too useful. Were duty no more than interest, morals would be superfluous. Why appeal to right or wrong, to good or evil, to obligation or to duty, if instead we may appeal to desire or aversion, to benefit or cost, to interest or to advantage? An appeal to morals takes its point from the failure of these latter considerations as sufficient guides to what we ought to do. The unphilosophical poet Ogden Nash grasped the assumptions underlying our moral language more clearly than the philosopher Hume when he wrote:

> O Duty!
> Why hast thou not the visage of a sweetie or
> a cutie?[2]

We may lament duty's stern visage but we may not deny it. For it is only as we believe that some

---

[1] See David Hume, *An Enquiry concerning the Principle of Morals,* sect. ix, pt. ii, in L.A. Selby-Bigge (ed.), *Enquiries concerning Human Understanding and concerning the Principles of Morals,* 3rd edn. (Oxford, 1975), p. 280.
[2] Ogden Nash, "Kind of an Ode to Duty," *I Wouldn't Have Missed It: Selected Poems of Ogden Nash* (Boston, 1975), p. 141.

appeals do, alas, override interest or advantage that morality becomes our concern.

But if the language of morals is not that of interest, it is surely that of reason. What theory of morals, we might better ask, can ever serve any useful purpose, unless it can show that all the duties it recommends are also truly endorsed in each individual's reason? If moral appeals are entitled to some practical effect, some influence on our behaviour, it is not because they whisper invitingly to our desires, but because they convince our intellect. Suppose we should find, as Hume himself believes, that reason is impotent in the sphere of action apart from its role in deciding matters of fact.[1] Or suppose we should find that reason is no more than the handmaiden of interest, so that in overriding advantage a moral appeal must also contradict reason. In either case we should conclude that the moral enterprise, as traditionally conceived, is impossible.

To say that our moral language assumes a connection with reason is not to argue for the rationality of our moral views, or of any alternative to them. Moral language may rest on a false assumption.[2] If moral duties are rationally grounded, then the emotivists, who suppose that moral appeals are no more than persuasive, and the egoists, who suppose that rational appeals are limited by self-interest, are mistaken.[3] But are moral duties rationally grounded? This we shall seek to prove, showing that reason has a practical role related to but transcending individual interest, so that principles of action that prescribe duties overriding advantage may be rationally justified. We shall defend the traditional conception of morality as a rational constraint on the pursuit of individual interest.

Yet Hume's mistake in insisting that moral duties must be the true interest of each individual conceals a fundamental insight. Practical reason is linked to interest, or, as we shall come to say, to individual utility, and rational constraints on the pursuit of interest have themselves a foundation in the interest they constrain. Duty over-rides advantage, but the acceptance of duty is truly advantageous. We shall find this seeming paradox embedded in the very structure of interaction. As we come to understand this structure, we shall recognize the need for restraining each person's pursuit of her own utility, and we shall examine its implications for both our principles of action and our conception of practical rationality. Our enquiry will lead us to the rational basis for a morality, not of absolute standards, but of agreed constraints.

2.1 We shall develop a theory of morals. Our concern is to provide a justificatory framework for moral behaviour and principles, not an explanatory framework. Thus we shall develop a normative theory. A complete philosophy of morals would need to explain, and perhaps to defend, the idea of a normative theory. We shall not do this. But we shall exemplify normative theory by sketching the theory of rational choice. Indeed, we shall do more. We shall develop a theory of morals as part of the theory of rational choice. We shall argue that the rational principles for making choices, or decisions among possible actions, include some that constrain the actor pursuing his own interest in an impartial way. These we identify as moral principles.

The study of choice begins from the stipulation of clear conceptions of value and rationality in a form applicable to choice situations.[4] The theory then analyses the structure of these situations so that, for each type of structure distinguished,

---

[1] See David Hume, *A Treatise of Human Nature*, bk. ii, pt. iii, sect. iii, ed. L.A. Selby-Bigge (Oxford, 1888), pp. 413–18.

[2] Thus one might propose an error theory of moral language; for an idea of an error theory, see J.L. Mackie, *Ethics: Inventing Right and Wrong* (Harmondsworth, Middx., 1977), ch. 1, esp. pp. 35, 48–49.

[3] The idea that moral appeals are persuasive is developed by C.L. Stevenson; see *Ethics and Language* (New Haven, 1944), esp. chs. vi, ix.

[4] Our sketch of rational choice owes much to J.C. Harsanyi; see "Advances in Understanding Rational Behavior," *Essays on Ethics, Social Behavior, and Scientific Explanation* (Dordrecht, 1976), pp. 89–98, and "Morality and the theory of rational behavior," in A. Sen and B. Williams (eds.), *Utilitarianism and Beyond* (Cambridge, 1982), pp. 42–44.

the conception of rationality may be elaborated into a set of determinate conditions on the choice among possible actions. These conditions are then expressed as precise principles of rational behaviour, serving both for prescription and for critical assessment. Derivatively, the principles also have an explanatory role in so far as persons actually act rationally.

The simplest, most familiar, and historically primary part of this study constitutes the core of classical and neo-classical economic theory, which examines rational behaviour in those situations in which the actor knows with certainty the outcome of each of his possible actions. The economist does of course offer to explain behaviour, and much of the interest of her theory depends on its having explanatory applications, but her explanations use a model of ideal interaction which includes the rationality of the actors among its assumptions. Thus economic explanation is set within a normative context. And the role of economics in formulating and evaluating policy alternatives should leave us in no doubt about the deeply prescriptive and critical character of the science.

The economist formulates a simple, maximizing conception of practical rationality, which we shall examine in Chapter II.[1] But the assumption that the outcome of each possible choice can be known with certainty seriously limits the scope of economic analysis and the applicability of its account of reason. Bayesian decision theory relaxes this assumption, examining situations with choices involving risk or uncertainty. The decision theorist is led to extend the economist's account of reason, while preserving its fundamental identification of rationality with maximization.

Both economics and decision theory are limited in their analysis of interaction, since both consider outcomes only in relation to the choices of a single actor, treating the choices of others as aspects of that actor's circumstances. The theory of games overcomes this limitation, analysing outcomes in relation to sets of choices, one for each of the persons involved in bringing about the outcome. It considers the choices of an actor who decides on the basis of expectations about the choices of others, themselves deciding on the basis of expectations about his choice. Since situations involving a single actor may be treated as limiting cases of interaction, game theory aims at an account of rational behaviour in its full generality. Unsurprisingly, achievements are related inversely to aims; as a study of rational behaviour under certainty economic theory is essentially complete, whereas game theory is still being developed. The theory of rational choice is an ongoing enterprise, extending a basic understanding of value and rationality to the formulation of principles of rational behaviour in an ever wider range of situations.

2.2 Rational choice provides an exemplar of normative theory. One might suppose that moral theory and choice theory are related only in possessing similar structures. But as we have said, we shall develop moral theory as part of choice theory. Those acquainted with recent work in moral philosophy may find this a familiar enterprise; John Rawls has insisted that the theory of justice is "perhaps the most significant part, of the theory of rational choice," and John Harsanyi explicitly treats ethics as part of the theory of rational behaviour.[2] But these claims are stronger than their results warrant. Neither Rawls nor Harsanyi develops the deep connection between morals and rational choice that we shall defend. A brief comparison will bring our enterprise into sharper focus.

Our claim is that in certain situations involving interaction with others, an individual chooses rationally only in so far as he constrains his pursuit of his own interest or advantage to conform to principles expressing the impartiality characteristic of morality. To choose rationally, one must choose morally. This is a strong claim. Morality, we shall argue, can be generated as a rational constraint

_____

[1] [This does not appear in this volume.]

[2] J. Rawls, *A Theory of Justice* (Cambridge, Mass., 1971), p. 16; Harsanyi, "Morality and the theory of rational behavior," p. 42.

from the non-moral premisses of rational choice. Neither Rawls nor Harsanyi makes such a claim. Neither Rawls nor Harsanyi treats moral principles as a subset of rational principles for choice.

Rawls argues that the principles of justice are the objects of a rational choice—the choice that any person would make, were he called upon to select the basic principles of his society from behind a "veil of ignorance" concealing any knowledge of his own identity.[1] The principles so chosen are not directly related to the making of individual choices.[2] Derivatively, acceptance of them must have implications for individual behaviour, but Rawls never claims that these include rational constraints on individual choices. They may be, in Rawls's terminology, reasonable constraints, but what is reasonable is itself a morally substantive matter beyond the bounds of rational choice.[3]

Rawls's idea, that principles of justice are the objects of a rational choice, is indeed one that we shall incorporate into our own theory, although we shall represent the choice as a bargain, or agreement, among persons who need not be unaware of their identities. But this parallel between our theory and Rawls's must not obscure the basic difference; we claim to generate morality as a set of rational principles for choice. We are committed to showing why an individual, reasoning from non-moral premises, would accept the constraints of morality on his choices.

Harsanyi's theory may seem to differ from Rawls's only in its account of the principles that a person would choose from behind a veil of ignorance; Rawls supposes that persons would choose the well-known two principles of justice, whereas Harsanyi supposes that persons would choose principles of average rule-utilitarianism.[4] But Harsanyi's argument is in some respects closer to our own; he is concerned with principles for moral choice, and with the rational way of arriving at such principles. However, Harsanyi's principles are strictly hypothetical; they govern rational choice from an impartial standpoint or given impartial preferences, and so they are principles only for someone who wants to choose morally or impartially.[5] But Harsanyi does not claim, as we do, that there are situations in which an individual must choose morally in order to choose rationally. For Harsanyi there is a rational way of choosing morally but no rational requirement to choose morally. And so again there is a basic difference between our theory and his.

Putting now to one side the views of Rawls and Harsanyi—views to which we shall often return in later chapters—we may summarise the import of the differences we have sketched. Our theory must generate, strictly as rational principles for choice, and so without introducing prior moral assumptions, constraints on the pursuit of individual interest or advantage that, being impartial, satisfy the traditional understanding of morality. We do not assume that there must be such impartial and rational constraints. We do not even assume that there must be rational constraints, whether impartial or not. We claim to demonstrate that there are rational constraints, and that these constraints are impartial. We then identify morality with these demonstrated constraints, but whether their content corresponds to that of conventional moral principles is a further question, which we shall not examine in detail. No doubt there will be differences, perhaps significant, between the impartial and rational constraints supported by our argument, and the morality learned from parents and peers, priests and teachers. But our concern is to validate the conception of morality as a set of rational, impartial constraints on the pursuit of individual interest, not to defend any

---

[1] See Rawls, p. 12.

[2] See ibid., p. 11; "the principles ... are to assign basic rights and duties and to determine the division of social benefits." Principles for individuals are distinguished from the principles of justice; see p. 108.

[3] See Rawls's distinction of "the Reasonable" and "the Rational," in "Kantian Constructivism in Moral Theory," *Journal of Philosophy* 77 (1980): 528–30.

[4] See Rawls, *A Theory of Justice*, pp. 14–15, and Harsanyi, "Morality and the theory of rational behavior," pp. 44–46, 56–60.

[5] See Harsanyi, "Morality and the theory of rational behavior," p. 62.

particular moral code. And our concern, once again, is to do this without incorporating into the premisses of our argument any of the moral conceptions that emerge in our conclusions.

2.3 To seek to establish the rationality of moral constraints is not in itself a novel enterprise, and its antecedents are more venerable than the endeavour to develop moral theory as part of the theory of rational choice. But those who have engaged in it have typically appealed to a conception of practical rationality, deriving from Kant, quite different from ours.[1] In effect, their understanding of reason already includes the moral dimension of impartiality that we seek to generate.

Let us suppose it agreed that there is a connection between reason and interest—or advantage, benefit, preference, satisfaction, or individual utility, since the differences among these, important in other contexts, do not affect the present discussion. Let it further be agreed that in so far as the interests of others are not affected, a person acts rationally if and only if she seeks her greatest interest or benefit. This might be denied by some, but we wish here to isolate the essential difference between the opposed conceptions of practical rationality. And this appears when we consider rational action in which the interests of others are involved. Proponents of the *maximizing* conception of rationality, which we endorse, insist that essentially nothing is changed, the rational person still seeks the greatest satisfaction of her own interests. On the other hand, proponents of what we shall call the *universalistic* conception of rationality insist that what makes it rational to satisfy an interest does not depend on whose interest it is. Thus the rational person seeks to satisfy all interests. Whether she is a utilitarian, aiming at the greatest happiness of the greatest number, or whether she takes into independent consideration the fair distribution of

benefit among persons, is of no importance to the present discussion.

To avoid possible misunderstanding, note that neither conception of rationality requires that practical reasons be self-interested. On the maximizing conception it is not interests in the self, that take oneself as object, but interests of the self, held by oneself as subject that provide the basis for rational choice and action. On the universalistic conception it is not interests in anyone, that take any person as object, but interests of anyone, held by some person as subject, that provide the basis for rational choice and action. If I have a direct interest in your welfare, then on either conception I have reason to promote your welfare. But your interest in your welfare affords me such reason only given the universalistic conception.

Morality, we have insisted, is traditionally understood to involve an impartial constraint on the pursuit of individual interest. The justification of such a constraint poses no problem to the proponents of universalistic rationality. The rational requirement that all interests be satisfied to the fullest extent possible directly constrains each person in the pursuit of her own interests. The precise formulation of the constraint will of course depend on the way in which interests are to be satisfied, but the basic rationale is sufficiently clear.

The main task of our moral theory—the generation of moral constraints as rational—is thus easily accomplished by proponents of the universalistic conception of practical reason. For them the relation between reason and morals is clear. Their task is to defend their conception of rationality, since the maximizing and universalistic conceptions do not rest on equal footings. The maximizing conception possesses the virtue, among conceptions, of weakness. Any consideration affording one a reason for acting on the maximizing conception, also affords one such a reason on the universalistic conception. But the converse does not hold. On the universalistic conception all persons have in effect the same basis for rational choice—the interests of all—and this assumption, of the impersonality or impartiality of reason, demands defence.

[1] This conception of practical rationality appears with particular clarity in T. Nagel, *The Possibility of Altruism* (Oxford, 1970), esp. ch. x. It can also be found in the moral theory of R.M. Hare; see *Moral Thinking* (Oxford, 1981), esp. chs. 5 and 6.

Furthermore, and perhaps of greater importance, the maximizing conception of rationality is almost universally accepted and employed in the social sciences.[1] As we have noted, it lies at the core of economic theory, and is generalized in decision and game theory. Its lesser prominence in political, sociological, and psychological theory reflects more the lesser concern with rationality among many practitioners of those disciplines, than adherence to an alternative conception. Social scientists may no doubt be mistaken, but we take the onus of proof to fall on those who would defend universalistic rationality.

In developing moral theory within rational choice we thus embrace the weaker and more widely accepted of the two conceptions of rationality that we have distinguished. Of course, we must not suppose that the moral principles we generate will be identical with those that would be derived on the universalistic conception. Its proponents may insist that their account of the connection between reason and morals is correct, even if they come to agree that a form of morality may be grounded in maximizing rationality. But we may suggest, without here defending our suggestion, that few persons would embrace the universalistic conception of practical reason did they not think it necessary to the defence of any form of rational morality. Hence the most effective rebuttal of their position may be, not to seek to undermine their elaborate and ingenious arguments, but to construct an alternative account of a rational morality grounded in the weaker assumptions of the theory of rational choice.

3.1 Morals by agreement begin from an initial presumption against morality, as a constraint on each person's pursuit of his own interest. A person is conceived as an independent centre of activity, endeavouring to direct his capacities and resources to the fulfillment of his interests. He considers what he

can do, but initially draws no distinction between what he may and may not do. How then does he come to acknowledge the distinction? How does a person come to recognize a moral dimension to choice, if morality is not initially present?

Morals by agreement offer a contractarian rationale for distinguishing what one may and may not do. Moral principles are introduced as the objects of fully voluntary *ex ante* agreement among rational persons. Such agreement is hypothetical, in supposing a pre-moral context for the adoption of moral rules and practices. But the parties to agreement are real, determinate individuals, distinguished by their capacities, situations, and concerns. In so far as they would agree to constraints on their choices, restraining their pursuit of their own interests, they acknowledge a distinction between what they may and may not do. As rational persons understanding the structure of their interaction, they recognize a place for mutual constraint, and so for a moral dimension in their affairs.

That there is a contractarian rationale for morality must of course be shown. That is the task of our theory. Here our immediate concern is to relate the idea of such a rationale to the introduction of fundamental moral distinctions. This is not a magical process. Morality does not emerge as the rabbit from the empty hat. Rather, as we shall argue, it emerges quite simply from the application of the maximizing conception of rationality to certain structures of interaction. Agreed mutual constraint is the rational response to these structures. Reason overrides the presumption against morality.

The genuinely problematic element in a contractarian theory is not the introduction of the idea of morality, but the step from hypothetical agreement to actual moral constraint. Suppose that each person recognizes himself as one of the parties to agreement. The principles forming the object of agreement are those that he would have accepted *ex ante* in bargaining with his fellows, had he found himself among them in a context initially devoid of moral constraint. Why need he accept, *ex post* in his actual situation, these principles as constrain-

---

[1] See Harsanyi, "Advances in Understanding Rational Behavior," p. 89; also J. Elster, *Ulysses and the Sirens: Studies in rationality and irrationality* (Cambridge, 1979); "The 'rational-choice' approach to human behavior is without much doubt the best available model ...," p. 112.

ing his choices? A theory of morals by agreement must answer this question.

Historically, moral contractarianism seems to have originated among the Greek Sophists. Glaucon sketched a contractarian account of the origin of justice in Plato's *Republic* but significantly, he offered this view for Socrates to refute, not to defend.[1] Our theory of morals falls in an unpopular tradition, as the identity of its greatest advocate, Thomas Hobbes, will confirm. Hobbes transformed the laws of nature, which lay at the core of Stoic and medieval Christian moral thought, into precepts of reason that require each person, acting in his own interest, to give up some portion of the liberty with which he seeks his own survival and well-being, provided others do likewise.[2] But this agreement gives rise to actual constraint only through the efficacy of the political sovereign; from the standpoint of moral theory, the crucial step requires the intervention of a *deus ex machina*. Nevertheless, in Hobbes we find the true ancestor of the theory of morality that we shall present. Only recently has his position begun to acquire a significant following. G.R. Grice has developed an explicitly contractarian theory, and Kurt Baier has acknowledged the Hobbesian roots of his central thesis, that "The very *raison d'être* of a morality is to yield reasons which overrule the reasons of self-interest in those cases when everyone's following self-interest would be harmful to everyone."[3]

To the conceptual underpinning that may be found in Hobbes, Grice, and Baier, we seek to add the rigour of rational choice. Of course the resulting moral theory need not be one that they would endorse. But the appeal to rational choice enables us to state, with new clarity and precision, why rational persons would agree *ex ante* to constraining

principles, what general characteristics these principles must have as objects of rational agreement, and why rational persons would comply *ex post* with the agreed constraints.

3.2 A useful vantage point for appreciating the rationale of constraint results from juxtaposing two ideas formulated by John Rawls. A contractarian views society as "a cooperative venture for mutual advantage" among persons "conceived as not taking an interest in one another's interests."[4] The contractarian does not claim that all actual societies are cooperative ventures; he need not claim that all afford the expectation of mutual advantage. Rather, he supposes that it is in general possible for a society, analysed as a set of institutions, practices, and relationships, to afford each person greater benefit than she could expect in a non-social "state of nature," and that only such a society could command the willing allegiance of every rational individual. The contractarian need not claim that actual persons take no interest in their fellows; indeed, we suppose that some degree of sociability is characteristic of human beings. But the contractarian sees sociability as enriching human life; for him, it becomes a source of exploitation if it induces persons to acquiesce in institutions and practices that but for their fellow-feelings would be costly to them. Feminist thought has surely made this, perhaps the core form of human exploitation, clear to us. Thus the contractarian insists that a society could not command the willing allegiance of a rational person if, without appealing to her feelings for others, it afforded her no expectation of net benefit.

If social institutions and practices can benefit all, then some set of social arrangements should be acceptable to all as a cooperative venture. Each person's concern to fulfill her own interests should ensure her willingness to join her fellows in a venture assuring her an expectation of increased fulfillment. She may of course reject some proposed venture as insufficiently advantageous to her when she considers both the distribution of benefits that it affords,

---

[1] See Plato, *Republic*, 358b–359b.
[2] Thomas Hobbes, *Leviathan* (London, 1651), ch. 14, pp. 64–65.
[3] See G.R. Grice, *The Grounds of Moral Judgment* (Cambridge, 1967), and K. Baier, *The Moral Point of View: A Rational Basis of Ethics* (Ithaca, NY, 1958); the quotation is from p. 309.

[4] Rawls, *A Theory of Justice*, pp. 4, 13.

and the availability of alternatives. Affording mutual advantage is a necessary condition for the acceptability of a set of social arrangements as a cooperative venture, not a sufficient condition. But we suppose that some set affording mutual advantage will also be mutually acceptable; a contractarian theory must set out conditions for sufficiency.

The rationale for agreement on society as a cooperative venture may seem unproblematic. The step from hypothetical agreement *ex ante* on a set of social arrangements to *ex post* adherence to those arrangements may seem straightforward. If one would willingly have joined the venture, why would one not now continue with it? Why is there need for constraint?

The institutions and practices of society play a coordinative role. Let us say, without attempting a precise definition, that a practice is coordinative if each person prefers to conform to it provided (most) others do, but prefers not to conform to it provided (most) others do not.[1] And let us say that a practice is beneficially coordinative if each person prefers that others conform to it rather than conform to no practice, and does not (strongly) prefer that others conform to some alternative practice. Hume's example, of two persons rowing a boat that neither can row alone, is a very simple example of a beneficially coordinative practice.[2] Each prefers to row if the other rows, and not to row if the other does not. And each prefers the other to row than to act in some alternative way.

It is worth noting that a coordinative practice need not be beneficial. Among peaceable persons, who regard weapons only as instruments of defence, each may prefer to be armed provided (most) others are, and not armed provided (most) others are not. Being armed is a coordinative practice but not a beneficial one; each prefers others not to be armed.

The coordinative advantages of society are not to be underestimated. But not all beneficial social practices are coordinative. Let us say that a practice is beneficial if each person prefers that (almost) everyone conform to it rather than that (most) persons conform to no practice, and does not (strongly) prefer that (almost) everyone conform to some alternative practice. Yet it may be the case that each person prefers not to conform to the practice if (most) others do. In a community in which tax funds are spent reasonably wisely, each person may prefer that almost everyone pay taxes rather than not, and yet may prefer not to pay taxes herself whatever others do. For the payments each person makes contribute negligibly to the benefits she receives. In such a community persons will pay taxes voluntarily only if each accepts some constraint on her pursuit of individual interest; otherwise, each will pay taxes only if coerced, whether by public opinion or by public authority.

The rationale for agreement on society as a cooperative venture may still seem unproblematic. But the step from hypothetical agreement *ex ante* on a set of social arrangements to *ex post* adherence may no longer seem straightforward. We see why one might willingly join the venture, yet not willingly continue with it. Each joins in the hope of benefiting from the adherence of others, but fails to adhere in the hope of benefiting from her own defection.

In the next two chapters we shall offer an account of value, rationality, and interaction, that will give us a precise formulation of the issue just identified. Prior to reflection, we might suppose that were each person to choose her best course of action, the outcome would be mutually as advantageous as possible. As we fill in our tax forms we may be reminded, *inter alia*, that individual benefit and mutual advantage frequently prove at odds. Our theory develops the implications of this reminder, beginning by locating the conflict between individual benefit and mutual advantage within the framework of rational choice.

3.3 Although a successful contractarian theory defeats the presumption against morality arising from its conception of rational, independent individuals, yet it should take the presumption seriously.

---

[1] The discussion here is related to my characterization of a convention in "David Hume, Contractarian," *Philosophical Review* 88 (1979): 5–8.
[2] See Hume, *Treatise*, iii. ii. ii, p. 490.

The first conception central to our theory is therefore that of a morally free zone, a context within which the constraints of morality would have no place.[1] The free zone proves to be that habitat familiar to economists, the perfectly competitive market. Such a market is of course an idealization; how far it can be realized in human society is an empirical question beyond the scope of our enquiry. Our argument is that in a perfectly competitive market, mutual advantage is assured by the unconstrained activity of each individual in pursuit of her own greatest satisfaction, so that there is no place, rationally, for constraint. Furthermore, since in the market each person enjoys the same freedom in her choices and actions that she would have in isolation from her fellows, and since the market outcome reflects the exercise of each person's freedom, there is no basis for finding any partiality in the market's operations. Thus there is also no place, morally, for constraint. The market exemplifies an ideal of interaction among persons who, taking no interest in each other's interests, need only follow the dictates of their own individual interests to participate effectively in a venture for mutual advantage. We do not speak of a cooperative venture, reserving that label for enterprises that lack the natural harmony of each with all assured by the structure of market interaction.

The perfectly competitive market is thus a foil against which morality appears more clearly. Were the world such a market, morals would be unnecessary. But this is not to denigrate the value of morality, which makes possible an artificial harmony where natural harmony is not to be had. Market and morals share the noncoercive reconciliation of individual interest with mutual benefit.

Where mutual benefit requires individual constraint, this reconciliation is achieved through rational agreement. As we have noted, a necessary condition of such agreement is that its outcome be mutually advantageous; our task is to provide

a sufficient condition. This problem is addressed in a part of the theory of games, the theory of rational bargaining, and divides into two issues. The first is the bargaining problem proper, which in its general form is to select a specific outcome, given a range of mutually advantageous possibilities and an initial bargaining position. The second is then to determine the initial bargaining position. Treatment of these issues has yet to reach consensus, so that we shall develop our own theory of bargaining.

Solving the bargaining problem yields a principle that governs both the process and the content of rational agreement. We shall address this in Chapter V,[2] where we introduce a measure of each person's stake in a bargain—the difference between the least he might accept in place of no agreement, and the most he might receive in place of being excluded by others from agreement. And we shall argue that the equal rationality of the bargainers leads to the requirement that the greatest concession, measured as a proportion of the conceder's stake, be as small as possible. We formulate this as the principle of minimax relative concession. And this is equivalent to the requirement that the least relative benefit, measured again as a proportion of one's stake, be as great as possible. So we formulate an equivalent principle of maximin relative benefit, which we claim captures the ideas of fairness and impartiality in a bargaining situation, and so serves as the basis of justice. Minimax relative concession, or maximin relative benefit, is thus the second conception central to our theory.

If society is to be a cooperative venture for mutual advantage, then its institutions and practices must satisfy, or nearly satisfy, this principle. For if our theory of bargaining is correct, then minimax relative concession governs the *ex ante* agreement that underlies a fair and rational cooperative venture. But in so far as the social arrangements constrain our actual *ex post* choices, the question of compliance demands attention. Let it be ever so rational to agree to practices that ensure maximin relative benefit; yet is it not also rational to ignore

---

[1] ... [See] my earlier discussion in "No Need for Morality: The Case of the Competitive Market," *Philosophic Exchange* 3.3 (1982): 41–54.

[2] [This does not appear in this volume.]

these practices should it serve one's interest to do so? Is it rational to internalize moral principles in one's choices, or only to acquiesce in them in so far as one's interests are held in check by external, coercive constraints? The weakness of traditional contractarian theory has been its inability to show the rationality of compliance.

Here we introduce the third conception central to our theory, constrained maximization. We distinguish the person who is disposed straightforwardly to maximize her satisfaction, or fulfil her interest, in the particular choices she makes, from the person who is disposed to comply with mutually advantageous moral constraints, provided he expects similar compliance from others. The latter is a constrained maximizer. And constrained maximizers, interacting one with another, enjoy opportunities for cooperation which others lack. Of course, constrained maximizers sometimes lose by being disposed to compliance, for they may act cooperatively in the mistaken expectation of reciprocity from others who instead benefit at their expense. Nevertheless, we shall show that, under plausible conditions, the net advantage that constrained maximizers reap from cooperation exceeds the exploitative benefits that others may expect. From this we conclude that it is rational to be disposed to constrain maximizing behaviour by internalizing moral principles to govern one's choices. The contractarian is able to show that it is irrational to admit appeals to interest against compliance with those duties founded on mutual advantage.

But compliance is rationally grounded only within the framework of a fully cooperative venture, in which each participant willingly interacts with her fellows. And this leads us back to the second issue addressed in bargaining theory—the initial bargaining position. If persons are willingly to comply with the agreement that determines what each takes from the bargaining table, then they must find initially acceptable what each brings to the table. And if what some bring to the table includes the fruits of prior interaction forced on their fellows, then this initial acceptability will be lacking. If you seize the products of my labour and then say

"Let's make a deal," I may be compelled to accept, but I will not voluntarily comply.

We are therefore led to constrain the initial bargaining position, through a proviso that prohibits bettering one's position through interaction worsening the position of another. No person should be worse off in the initial bargaining position than she would be in a non-social context of no interaction. The proviso thus constrains the base from which each person's stake in agreement, and so her relative concession and benefit, are measured. We shall show that it induces a structure of personal and property rights, which are basic to rationally and morally acceptable social arrangements.

The proviso is the fourth of the core conceptions of our theory. Although a part of morals by agreement, it is not the product of rational agreement. Rather, it is a condition that must be accepted by each person for such agreement to be possible. Among beings, however rational, who may not hope to engage one another in a cooperative venture for mutual advantage, the proviso would have no force. Our theory denies any place to rational constraint, and so to morality, outside the context of mutual benefit. A contractarian account of morals has no place for duties that are strictly redistributive in their effects, transferring but not increasing benefits, or duties that do not assume reciprocity from other persons. Such duties would be neither rationally based, nor supported by considerations of impartiality.

To the four core conceptions whose role we have sketched, we add a fifth—the Archimedean point, from which an individual can move the moral world.[1] To confer this moral power, the Archimedean point must be one of assured impartiality—the position sought by John Rawls behind the "veil of ignorance." We shall conclude the exposition of our moral theory in Chapter VIII[2] by relating the choice of a person occupying the Archimedean point to the other core ideas. We

---

[1] For the idea of an Archimedean point, see Rawls, *A Theory of Justice*, pp. 260–65.

[2] [This does not appear in this volume.]

shall show that Archimedean choice is properly conceived, not as a limiting case of individual decision under uncertainty, but rather as a limiting case of bargaining. And we shall then show how each of our core ideas—the proviso against bettering oneself through worsening others, the morally free zone afforded by the perfectly competitive market, the principle of minimax relative concession, and the disposition to constrained maximization—may be related, directly or indirectly, to Archimedean choice. In embracing these other conceptions central to our theory, the Archimedean point reveals the coherence of morals by agreement.

4   A contractarian theory of morals, developed as part of the theory of rational choice, has evident strengths. It enables us to demonstrate the rationality of impartial constraints on the pursuit of individual interest to persons who may take no interest in others' interests. Morality is thus given a sure grounding in a weak and widely accepted conception of practical rationality. No alternative account of morality accomplishes this. Those who claim that moral principles are objects of rational choice in special circumstances fail to establish the rationality of actual compliance with these principles. Those who claim to establish the rationality of such compliance appeal to a strong and controversial conception of reason that seems to incorporate prior moral suppositions. No alternative account generates morals, as a rational constraint on choice and action, from a non-moral, or morally neutral, base.

But the strengths of a contractarian theory may seem to be accompanied by grave weaknesses. We have already noted that for a contractarian, morality requires a context of mutual benefit. John Locke held that "an Hobbist ... will not easily admit a great many plain duties of morality."[1] And this may seem equally to apply to the Hobbist's modern-day successor. Our theory does not assume any fundamental concern with impartiality, but only a concern derivative from the benefits of agreement, and

those benefits are determined by the effects that each person can have on the interests of her fellows. Only beings whose physical and mental capacities are either roughly equal or mutually complementary can expect to find cooperation beneficial to all. Humans benefit from their interaction with horses, but they do not cooperate with horses and may not benefit them. Among unequals, one party may benefit most by coercing the other, and on our theory would have no reason to refrain. We may condemn all coercive relationships, but only within the context of mutual benefit can our condemnation appeal to a rationally grounded morality.

Moral relationships among the participants in a cooperative venture for mutual advantage have a firm basis in the rationality of the participants. And it has been plausible to represent the society that has emerged in western Europe and America in recent centuries as such a venture. For Western society has discovered how to harness the efforts of the individual, working for his own good, in the cause of ever-increasing mutual benefit. Not only an explosion in the quantity of material goods and in the numbers of persons, but, more important, an unprecedented rise in the average life span, and a previously unimaginable broadening of the range of occupations and activities effectively accessible to most individuals on the basis of their desires and talents, have resulted from this discovery.[2] With personal gain linked to social advance, the individual has been progressively freed from the coercive bonds, mediated through custom and education, law and religion that have characterized earlier societies. But in unleashing the individual, perhaps too much credit has been given to the efficacy of market-like institutions, and too little attention paid to the need for cooperative interaction requiring limited but real constraint. Morals by agreement then express the real concern each of

---

[1] Locke MS, quoted in J. Dunn, *The Political Thought of John Locke* (Cambridge, 1969), pp. 218–19.

[2] For the increase in average life span, see N. Eberstadt, "The Health Crisis in the U.S.S.R.," *New York Review of Books* 28. 2 (1981): 23. For the broadening in the range of accessible occupations, note that "As late as 1815 three-quarters of its [Europe's] population were employed on the land ...," *The Times Concise Atlas of World History*, ed. G. Barraclough (London, 1982), p. 82.

us has in maintaining the conditions in which society can be a cooperative venture.

But if Locke's criticism of the scope of contractarian morality has been bypassed by circumstances that have enabled persons to regard one another as contributing partners to a joint enterprise, changed circumstances may bring it once more to the fore. From a technology that made it possible for an ever-increasing proportion of persons to increase the average level of well-being, our society is passing to a technology, best exemplified by developments in medicine, that make possible an ever-increasing transfer of benefits to persons who decrease that average. Such persons are not party to the moral relationships grounded by a contractarian theory.

Beyond concern about the scope of moral relationships is the question of their place in an ideal human life. Glaucon asked Socrates to refute a contractarian account of justice, because he believed that such an account must treat justice as instrumentally valuable for persons who are mutually dependent, but intrinsically disvaluable, so that it "seems to belong to the form of drudgery."[1] Co-operation is a second-best form of interaction, requiring concessions and constraints that each person would prefer to avoid. Indeed, each has the secret hope that she can be successfully unjust, and easily falls prey to that most dangerous vanity that persuades her that she is truly superior to her fellows, and so can safely ignore their interests in pursuing her own. As Glaucon said, he who "is truly a man" would reject moral constraints.[2]

A contractarian theory does not contradict this view, since it leaves altogether open the content of human desires, but equally it does not require it. May we not rather suppose that human beings depend for their fulfillment on a network of social relationships whose very structure constantly tempts them to misuse it? The constraints of morality then serve to regulate valued social relationships that fail to be self-regulating. They constrain us in the interests of a shared ideal of sociability.

Co-operation may then seem a second-best form of interaction, not because it runs counter to our desires, but because each person would prefer a natural harmony in which she could fulfill herself without constraint. But a natural harmony could exist only if our preferences and capabilities dovetailed in ways that would preclude their free development. Natural harmony would require a higher level of artifice, a shaping of our natures in ways that, at least until genetic engineering is perfected, are not possible, and were they possible, would surely not be desirable. If human individuality is to bloom, then we must expect some degree of conflict among the aims and interests of persons rather than natural harmony. Market and morals tame this conflict, reconciling individuality with mutual benefit.

We shall consider, in the last chapters of our enquiry, what can be said for this interpretation of the place of moral relationships in human life. To do so we shall remark on speculative matters that lead beyond and beneath the theory of rational choice. And we may find ourselves with an alternative reading of what we present as a theory of morals.[3] We seek to forge a link between the rationality of individual maximization and the morality of impartial constraint. Suppose that we have indeed found such a link. How shall we interpret this finding? Are our conceptions of rationality and morality, and so of the contractarian link between them, as we should like them to be, fixed points in the development of the conceptual framework that enables us to formulate permanent practical truths? Or are we contributing to the history of ideas of a particular society, in which peculiar circumstances have fostered an ideology of individuality and interaction that coheres with morals by agreement? Are we telling a story about ideas that will seem as strange to our descendants, as the Form of the Good and the Unmoved Mover do to us?

---

[1] *Republic*, 358a, trans. A. Bloom (New York, 1968), p. 36.
[2] Ibid., 359b, p. 37.

[3] The thoughts in this paragraph have been influenced by R. Rorty; see esp. "Method and Morality," in N. Haan, R.N. Bellah, P. Rabinow, and W.M. Sullivan (eds.), *Social Sciences as Moral Inquiry* (New York, 1983), pp. 155–76.

DISCUSSION QUESTIONS

1. Gauthier argues that among our rational principles for making choices are what we can call moral principles. What does Gauthier take to be the defining characteristic of moral principles? How are they a subset of rational principles?

2. Do you think that it is always rational to act morally? Can you think of an exception where you think it would be irrational to perform the moral action? What do you think should take priority in such situations: rationality or morality? Defend your answer. Compare the way that Gauthier would answer these questions with the way that Glaucon and/or Hobbes would.

3. Gauthier writes "[d]uty overrides advantage, but the acceptance of duty is truly advantageous." Throughout the course of his argument, how does Gauthier attempt to explain away this seeming paradox? Do you think he is successful? Why or why not?

4. Explain the difference between a maximizing conception of rationality and a universalistic conception. Which does Gauthier accept, and what role does it play in his theory of choice?

5. Explain how Gauthier thinks that mutual benefit among participants underlies rational agreement. If this is the case, then how can the moral responsibilities that we think we might have toward, for example, the elderly or the handicapped be justified or rationally accepted?

6

Robert Nozick, selections from *Anarchy, State, and Utopia* (1977)

Robert Nozick (1938–2002) was a professor of philosophy at Harvard University. He worked in several philosophical areas, including epistemology and political philosophy. He is perhaps best known for his book *Anarchy, State, and Utopia*, from which the following excerpt has been taken. In his book, Nozick provides a libertarian response to John Rawls's *A Theory of Justice*. In this selection, Nozick discusses the state of nature and explains how he thinks individuals may move from mutual-protection associations to a dominant protective association. He identifies the necessary features of a state and explains how a state can be arranged so as to protect the rights of its citizens.

SOURCE

Nozick, Robert. *Anarchy, State, and Utopia*. Copyright © 1977 by Robert Nozick. Reprinted by permission of Basic Books, a member of the Perseus Books Group.

Individuals in Locke's state of nature are in "a state of perfect freedom to order their actions and dispose of their possessions and persons as they think fit within the bounds of the law of nature, without asking leave or dependency upon the will of any other man" (sect. 4).[1] The bounds of the law of nature require that "no one ought to harm another in his life, health, liberty, or possessions" (sect. 6). Some persons transgress these bounds, "invading others' rights and ... doing hurt to one another," and in response people may defend themselves or others against such invaders of rights (chap. 3). The injured party and his agents may recover from the offender "so much as may make satisfaction for the harm he has suffered" (sect. 10); "everyone has a right to punish the transgressors of that law to such a degree as may hinder its violation" (sect. 7); each person may, and may only "retribute to [a criminal] so far as calm reason and conscience dictate, what is proportionate to his transgression, which is so much as may serve for reparation and restraint" (sect. 8).

There are "inconveniences of the state of nature" for which, says Locke, "I easily grant that civil government is the proper remedy" (sect. 13). To understand precisely what civil government remedies we must do more than repeat Locke's list of the inconveniences of the state of nature. We also must consider

---

[1] John Locke, *Two Treatises of Government*, 2nd ed., ed. Peter Laslett (New York: Cambridge University Press, 1967). Unless otherwise specified, all references are to the *Second Treatise*.

what arrangements might be made within a state of nature to deal with these inconveniences—to avoid them or to make them less likely to arise or to make them less serious on the occasions when they do arise. Only after the full resources of the state of nature are brought into play, namely all those voluntary arrangements and agreements persons might reach acting within their rights, and only after the effects of these are estimated, will we be in a position to see how serious are the inconveniences that yet remain to be remedied by the state, and to estimate whether the remedy is worse than the disease.

In a state of nature, the understood natural law may not provide for every contingency in a proper fashion (see sections 159 and 160 where Locke makes this point about legal systems, but contrast section 124), and men who judge in their own case will always give themselves the benefit of the doubt and assume that they are in the right. They will overestimate the amount of harm or damage they have suffered, and passions will lead them to attempt to punish others more than proportionately and to exact excessive compensation (sects. 13, 124, 125). Thus private and personal enforcement of one's rights (including those rights that are violated when one is excessively punished) leads to feuds, to an endless series of acts of retaliation and exactions of compensation. And there is no firm way to *settle* such a dispute, to *end* it and to have both parties know it is ended. Even if one party *says* he'll stop his acts of retaliation, the other can rest secure only if he knows the first still does not feel entitled to gain recompense or to exact retribution, and therefore entitled to try when a promising occasion presents itself. Any method a single individual might use in an attempt irrevocably to bind himself into ending his part in a feud would offer insufficient assurance to the other party; tacit agreements to stop also would be unstable. Such feelings of being mutually wronged can occur even with the clearest right and with joint agreement on the facts of each person's conduct; all the more is there opportunity for such retaliatory battle when the facts or the rights are to some extent unclear. Also, in a state of nature a person may lack the power

to enforce his rights; he may be unable to punish or exact compensation from a stronger adversary who has violated them (sects. 123, 126).

Protective Associations

How might one deal with these troubles within a state of nature? Let us begin with the last. In a state of nature an individual may himself enforce his rights, defend himself, exact compensation, and punish (or at least try his best to do so). Others may join with him in his defense, at his call. They may join with him to repulse an attacker or to go after an aggressor because they are public spirited, or because they are his friends, or because he has helped them in the past, or because they wish him to help them in the future, or in exchange for something. Groups of individuals may form mutual-protection associations: all will answer the call of any member for defense or for the enforcement of his rights. In union there is strength. Two inconveniences attend such simple mutual-protection associations: (1) everyone is always on call to serve a protective function (and how shall it be decided who shall answer the call for those protective functions that do not require the services of all members?); and (2) any member may call out his associates by saying his rights are being, or have been, violated. Protective associations will not want to be at the beck and call of their cantankerous or paranoid members, not to mention those of their members who might attempt, under the guise of self-defense, to use the association to violate the rights of others. Difficulties will also arise if two different members of the same association are in dispute, each calling upon his fellow members to come to his aid.

A mutual-protection association might attempt to deal with conflict among its own members by a policy of nonintervention. But this policy would bring discord within the association and might lead to the formation of subgroups who might fight among themselves and thus cause the breakup of the association. This policy would also encourage potential aggressors to join as many mutual-protection associations as possible in order to gain immunity from retaliatory or defensive action, thus placing a great burden on the adequacy of the initial screening procedure of the association. Thus protective associations (almost all of those that will survive which people will join) will not follow a policy of nonintervention; they will use some procedure to determine how to act when some members claim that other members have violated their rights. Many arbitrary procedures can be imagined (for example, act on the side of that member who complains first), but most persons will want to join associations that follow some procedure to find out which claimant is correct. When a member of the association is in conflict with nonmembers, the association also will want to determine in some fashion who is in the right, if only to avoid constant and costly involvement in each member's quarrels, whether just or unjust. The inconvenience of everyone's being on call, whatever their activity at the moment or inclinations or comparative advantage, can be handled in the usual manner by division of labor and exchange. Some people will be *hired* to perform protective functions, and some entrepreneurs will go into the business of selling protective services. Different sorts of protective policies would be offered, at different prices, for those who may desire more extensive or elaborate protection.

An individual might make more particular arrangements or commitments short of turning over to a private protective agency all functions of detection, apprehension, judicial determination of guilt, punishment, and exaction of compensation. Mindful of the dangers of being the judge in his own case, he might turn the decision as to whether he has indeed been wronged, and to what extent, to some other neutral or less involved party. In order for the occurrence of the social effect of justice's being seen to be done, such a party would have to be generally respected and thought to be neutral and upright. Both parties to a dispute may so attempt to safeguard themselves against the appearance of partiality, and both might even agree upon the *same* person as the judge between them, and agree to abide by his decision. (Or there might be a specified process through which one of the parties

dissatisfied with the decision could appeal it.) But, for obvious reasons, there will be strong tendencies for the above-mentioned functions to converge in the same agent or agency.

People sometimes now do take their disputes outside of the state's legal system to other judges or courts they have chosen, for example, to religious courts. If all parties to a dispute find some activities of the state or its legal system so repellent that they want nothing to do with it, they might agree to forms of arbitration or judgment outside the apparatus of the state. People tend to forget the possibilities of acting independently of the state. (Similarly, persons who want to be paternalistically regulated forget the possibilities of contracting into particular limitations on their own behavior or appointing a given paternalistic supervisory board over themselves. Instead, they swallow the exact pattern of restrictions a legislature happens to pass. Is there really someone who, searching for a group of wise and sensitive persons to regulate him for his own good, would choose that group of people who constitute the membership of both houses of Congress?) Diverse forms of judicial adjudication, differing from the particular package the state provides, certainly could be developed. Nor do the costs of developing and choosing these account for people's use of the state form. For it would be easy to have a large number of preset packages which parties could select. Presumably what drives people to use the state's system of justice is the issue of ultimate enforcement. Only the state can enforce a judgment against the will of one of the parties. For the state does not *allow* anyone else to enforce another system's judgment. So in any dispute in which both parties cannot agree upon a method of settlement, or in any dispute in which one party does not trust another to abide by the decision (if the other contracts to forfeit something of enormous value if he doesn't abide by the decision, by what agency is *that* contract to be enforced?), the parties who wish their claims put into effect will have no recourse permitted by the state's legal system other than to use that very legal system. This may present persons greatly opposed to a given state system with particularly poignant and painful choices. (If the state's legal system enforces the results of certain arbitration procedures, people may come to agree—supposing they abide by this agreement—without any actual direct contact with what they perceive to be officers or institutions of the state. But this holds as well if they sign a contract that is enforced only by the state.)

Will protective agencies *require* that their clients renounce exercising their right of private retaliation if they have been wronged by nonclients of the agency? Such retaliation may well lead to counterretaliation by another agency or individual, and a protective agency would not *wish at that late stage* to get drawn into the messy affair by having to defend its client against the counterretaliation. Protective agencies would refuse to protect against counterretaliation unless they had first given permission for the retaliation. (Though might they not merely charge much more for the more extensive protection policy that provides such coverage?) The protective agencies need not even require that, as part of his agreement with the agency, a client renounce, by contract, his right of private enforcement of justice against its *other clients*. The agency need only refuse a client C, who privately enforces his rights against other clients, any protection against counterretaliation upon him by these other clients. This is similar to what occurs if C acts against a nonclient. The additional fact that C acts upon a client of the agency means that the agency will act toward C as it would toward any nonclient who privately enforced his rights upon any one of its clients [see *How May the Dominant Agency Act*, below]. This reduces intra-agency private enforcement of rights to minuscule levels.

The Dominant Protective Association

Initially, several different protective associations or companies will offer their services in the same geographical area. What will occur when there is a conflict between clients of different agencies? Things are relatively simple if the agencies reach the same decision about the disposition of the case. (Though each might want to exact the penalty.) But what happens if they reach different decisions as to the merits of the case, and one agency attempts to protect its client while the other is attempting to punish him or make him pay compensation? Only three possibilities are worth considering:

1.   In such situations the forces of the two agencies do battle. One of the agencies always wins such battles. Since the clients of the losing agency are ill protected in conflicts with clients of the winning agency, they leave their agency to do business with the winner.

2.   One agency has its power centered in one geographical area, the other in another. Each wins the battles fought close to its center of power, with some gradient being established. People who deal with one agency but live under the power of the other either move closer to their own agency's home headquarters or shift their patronage to the other protective agency. (The border is about as conflictful as one between states.)

In neither of these two cases does there remain very much geographical interspersal. Only one protective agency operates over a given geographical area.

3.   The two agencies fight evenly and often. They win and lose about equally, and their interspersed members have frequent dealings and disputes with each other. Or perhaps without fighting or after only a few skirmishes the agencies realize that such battling will occur continually in the absence of preventive measures. In any case, to avoid frequent, costly, and wasteful battles the two agencies, perhaps through their executives, agree to resolve peacefully those cases about which they reach differing judgments. They agree to set up, and abide by the decisions of, some third judge or court to which they can turn when their respective judgments differ. (Or they might establish rules determining which agency has jurisdiction under which circumstances.) Thus emerges a system of appeals courts and agreed upon rules about jurisdiction

and the conflict of laws. Though different agencies operate, there is one unified federal judicial system of which they all are components.

In each of these cases, almost all the persons in a geographical area are under some common system that judges between their competing claims and *enforces* their rights. Out of anarchy, pressed by spontaneous groupings, mutual-protection associations, division of labor, market pressures, economies of scale, and rational self-interest there arises something very much resembling a minimal state or a group of geographically distinct minimal states. Why is this market different from all other markets? Why would a virtual monopoly arise in this market without the government intervention that elsewhere creates and maintains it? The worth of the product purchased, protection against others, is *relative*: it depends upon how strong the others are. Yet unlike other goods that are comparatively evaluated, maximal competing protective services cannot coexist; the nature of the service brings different agencies not only into competition for customers' patronage, but also into violent conflict with each other. Also, since the worth of the less than maximal product declines disproportionately with the number who purchase the maximal product, customers will not stably settle for the lesser good, and competing companies are caught in a declining spiral. Hence the three possibilities we have listed.

Our story above assumes that each of the agencies attempts in good faith to act within the limits of Locke's law of nature. But one "protective association" might aggress against other persons. Relative to Locke's law of nature, it would be an outlaw agency. What actual counterweights would there be to its power? (What actual counterweights are there to the power of a state?) Other agencies might unite to act against it. People might refuse to deal with the outlaw agency's clients, boycotting them to reduce the probability of the agency's intervening in their own affairs. This might make it more difficult for the outlaw agency to get clients; but this boycott will seem an effective tool only on very optimistic

assumptions about what cannot be kept secret, and about the costs to an individual of partial boycott as compared to the benefits of receiving the more extensive coverage offered by an "outlaw" agency. If the "outlaw" agency simply is an *open* aggressor, pillaging, plundering, and extorting under no plausible claim of justice, it will have a harder time than states. For the state's claim to legitimacy induces its citizens to believe they have some duty to obey its edicts, pay its taxes, fight its battles, and so on; and so some persons cooperate with it voluntarily. An openly aggressive agency could not depend upon, and would not receive, any such voluntary cooperation, since persons would view themselves simply as its victims rather than as its citizens.
[...]

Is the Dominant Protective Association a State?

… Writers in the tradition of Max Weber treat having a monopoly on the use of force in a geographical area, a monopoly incompatible with private enforcement of rights, as crucial to the existence of a state. As Marshall Cohen points out in an unpublished essay, a state may exist without *actually* monopolizing the use of force it has not authorized others to use; within the boundaries of a state there may exist groups such as the Mafia, the KKK, White Citizens Councils, striking unionists, and Weathermen that also use force. *Claiming* such a monopoly is not sufficient (if *you* claimed it you would not become the state), nor is being its sole claimant a necessary condition. Nor need everyone grant the legitimacy of the state's claim to such monopoly, either because as pacifists they think no one has the right to use force, or because as revolutionaries they believe that a given state lacks this right, or because they believe they are entitled to join in and help out no matter what the state says. Formulating sufficient conditions for the existence of the state thus turns out to be a difficult and messy task.

For our purposes here we need focus only upon a necessary condition that the system of private protective agencies (or any component agency within it) apparently does not satisfy. A state claims a monopoly on deciding who may use force when; it says that only it may decide who may use force and under what conditions; it reserves to itself the sole right to pass on the legitimacy and permissibility of any use of force within its boundaries; furthermore it claims the right to punish all those who violate its claimed monopoly. The monopoly may be violated in two ways: (1) a person may use force though unauthorized by the state to do so, or (2) though not themselves using force a group or person may set themselves up as an alternative authority (and perhaps even claim to be the sole legitimate one) to decide when and by whom the use of force is proper and legitimate. It is unclear whether a state must claim the right to punish the second sort of violator, and doubtful whether any state actually would refrain from punishing a significant group of them within its boundaries. I glide over the issue of what sort of "may," "legitimacy," and "permissibility" is in question. Moral permissibility isn't a matter of decision, and the state need not be so egomaniacal as to claim the sole right to decide moral questions. To speak of legal permissibility would require, to avoid circularity, that an account of a legal system be offered that doesn't use the notion of the state.

We may proceed, for our purposes, by saying that a necessary condition for the existence of a state is that it (some person or organization) announce that, to the best of its ability (taking into account costs of doing so, the feasibility, the more important alternative things it should be doing, and so forth), it will punish everyone whom it discovers to have used force without its express permission. (This permission may be a particular permission or may be granted via some general regulation or authorization.) This still won't quite do: the state may reserve the right to forgive someone, *ex post facto*; in order to punish they may have not only to discover the "unauthorized" use of force but also prove via a certain specified procedure of proof that it occurred, and so forth. But it enables us to proceed. The protective agencies, it seems, do not make such an announcement, either individually or collectively. *Nor does it seem morally legitimate for them to do so.* So the system of private protective associations, if they perform no morally illegitimate action, appears to lack any monopoly element and so appears not to constitute or contain a state. To examine the question of the monopoly element, we shall have to consider the situation of some group of persons (or some one person) living within a system of private protective agencies who refuse to join any protective society; who insist on judging for themselves whether their rights have been violated, and (if they so judge) on personally enforcing their rights by punishing and/or exacting compensation from those who infringed them.

The second reason for thinking the system described is not a state is that, under it (apart from spillover effects) only those paying for protection get protected; furthermore, differing degrees of protection may be purchased. External economies again to the side, no one pays for the protection of others except as they choose to; no one is required to purchase or contribute to the purchasing of protection for others. Protection and enforcement of people's rights is treated as an economic good to be provided by the market, as are other important goods such as food and clothing. However, under the usual conception of a state, each person living within (or even sometimes traveling outside) its geographical boundaries gets (or at least, is entitled to get) its protection. Unless some private party donated sufficient funds to cover the costs of such protection (to pay for detectives, police to bring criminals into custody, courts, and prisons), or unless the state found some service it could charge for that would cover these costs, one would expect that a state which offered protection so broadly would be redistributive. It would be a state in which some persons paid more so that others could be protected. And indeed the most minimal state seriously discussed by the mainstream of political theorists, the night-watchman state of classical liberal theory, appears to be redistributive in this fashion. Yet how can a protection agency, a business, charge some to provide its product to others? (We ignore things like some partially paying for others because it is too costly for the agency to refine its classification of, and charges to, customers to mirror the costs of the services to them.)

[...]

How May the Dominant Agency Act?

What then may a dominant protective association forbid other individuals to do? The dominant protective association may reserve for itself the right to judge any procedure of justice to be applied to its clients. It may announce, and act on the announcement, that it will punish anyone who uses on one of its clients a procedure that it finds to be unreliable or unfair. It will punish anyone who uses on one of its clients a procedure that it already knows to be unreliable or unfair, and it will defend its clients against the application of such a procedure. May it announce that it will punish anyone who uses on one of its clients a procedure that it has not, at the time of punishment, already approved as reliable and fair? May it set itself up as having to pass, in advance, on any procedure to be used on one of its clients, so that anyone using on one of its clients any procedure that has not already received the protective association's seal of approval will be punished? Clearly, individuals themselves do not have this right. To say that an individual may punish anyone who applies to him a procedure of justice that has not met his approval would be to say that a criminal who refuses to approve anyone's procedure of justice could legitimately punish anyone who attempted to punish him. It might be thought that a protective association legitimately can do this, for it would not be partial to its clients in this manner. But there is no guarantee of this impartiality. Nor have we seen any way that such a new right might arise from the combining of individuals' preexisting rights. We must conclude that protective associations do not have this right, including the sole dominant one.

Every individual does have the right that information sufficient to show that a procedure of justice about to be applied to him is reliable and fair (or no less so than other procedures in use) be made publicly available or made available to him. He has the right to be shown that he is being handled by some reliable and fair system. In the absence of such a showing he may defend himself and resist the imposition of the relatively unknown system. When the information is made publicly available or made available to him, he is in a position to know about the reliability and fairness of the procedure. He examines this information, and if he finds the system within the bounds of reliability and fairness he must submit to it; finding it unreliable and unfair he may resist. His submission means that he refrains from punishing another for using this system. He may resist the imposition of its particular decision though, on the grounds that he is innocent. If he chooses not to, he need not participate in the process whereby the system determines his guilt or innocence. Since it has not yet been established that he is guilty, he may not be aggressed against and forced to participate. However, prudence might suggest to him that his chances of being found innocent are increased if he cooperates in the offering of some defense.

The principle is that a person may resist, in self-defense, if others try to apply to him an unreliable or unfair procedure of justice. In applying this principle, an individual will resist those systems which after all conscientious consideration he finds to be unfair or unreliable. An individual may empower his protective agency to exercise for him his rights to resist the imposition of any procedure which has not made its reliability and fairness known, and to resist any procedure that is unfair or unreliable. [Earlier] we described briefly the processes that would lead to the dominance of one protective association in a given area, or to a dominant federation of protective associations using rules to peacefully adjudicate disputes among themselves. This dominant protective association will prohibit anyone from applying to its members any procedure about which insufficient information is available as to its reliability and fairness. It also will prohibit anyone from applying to its members an unreliable or unfair procedure; which means, since *they* are applying the principle and have the muscle to do so, that others are prohibited from applying to the protective association's members any procedure the protective association deems unfair or unreliable. Leaving aside the chances of evading the system's operation, anyone violating this prohibition will be punished. The protective association will publish a list of those procedures it deems fair and reliable (and perhaps of those it deems otherwise); and it would take a brave soul indeed to proceed to apply a known procedure not yet on its approved list. Since an association's clients will expect it to do all it can to discourage unreliable procedures, the protective association will keep its list up-to-date, covering all publicly known procedures.

It might be claimed that our assumption that procedural rights exist makes our argument too easy. Does a person who *did* violate another's rights himself have a right that this fact be determined by a fair and reliable procedure? It is true that an unreliable procedure will too often find an innocent person guilty. But does applying such an unreliable procedure to a *guilty* person violate any right of his? May he, in self-defense, resist the imposition of such a procedure upon himself? But what would he be defending himself against? Too high a probability of a punishment he deserves? These questions are important ones for our argument. If a guilty person may not defend himself against such procedures and also may not punish someone else for using them upon him, then may his protective agency defend him against the procedures or punish someone afterwards for having used them upon him, independently of whether or not (and therefore even if) he turns out to be guilty? One would have thought the agency's only rights of action are those its clients transfer to it. But if a guilty client has no such right, he cannot transfer it to the agency.

The agency does not, of course, *know* that its client is guilty, whereas the client himself does know (let us suppose) of his own guilt. But does this difference in knowledge make the requisite difference? Isn't the ignorant agency required to investigate the question of its client's guilt, instead of proceeding on the assumption of his innocence? The difference in epistemic situation between agency and client *can* make the following difference. The agency may under some circumstances defend its client against the imposition of a penalty while promptly proceeding to investigate the question of his guilt. If the agency knows that the punishing party has used a reliable procedure, it accepts its verdict of guilty, and it cannot intervene on the assumption that its client is, or well might be, innocent. If the agency deems the procedure unreliable or doesn't know how reliable it is, it need not presume its client guilty and it may investigate the matter itself. If upon investigation it determines that its client is guilty, it allows him to be punished. This protection of its client against the actual imposition of the penalty is relatively straightforward, except for the question of whether the agency must compensate the prospective punishers for any costs imposed upon them by having to delay while the protective agency determines to its satisfaction its own client's guilt. It would seem that the protective agency does have to pay compensation to users of relatively unreliable procedures for any disadvantages caused by the enforced delay; and to the users of procedures of unknown reliability it must pay full compensation if the procedures are reliable, otherwise compensation for disadvantages. (Who bears the burden of proof in the question of the reliability of the procedures?) Since the agency may recover this amount (forcibly) from its client who asserted his innocence, this will be something of a deterrent to false pleas of innocence.

The agency's temporary protection and defense against the infliction of the penalty is relatively straightforward. Less straightforward is the protective agency's appropriate action after a penalty has been inflicted. If the punisher's procedure was a reliable one, the agency does not act against the punisher. But may the agency punish someone who punishes its client, acting on the basis of an unreliable procedure? May it punish that person independently of whether or not its client *is* guilty? Or must it investigate, using its own reliable procedure, to determine his guilt or innocence, punishing his punishers *only* if it determines its client innocent?

(Or is it: if it fails to find him guilty?) By what right could the protective agency announce that it will punish anyone using an unreliable procedure who punishes its clients, independently of the guilt or innocence of the clients?

The person who uses an unreliable procedure, acting upon its result, imposes risks upon others, whether or not his procedure misfires in a case. Someone playing Russian roulette upon another does the same thing if when he pulls the trigger the gun does not fire. The protective agency may treat the unreliable enforcer of justice as it treats any performer of a risky action. [There are] a range of possible responses to a risky action, which [are] appropriate in different sorts of circumstances: prohibition, compensation to those whose boundaries are crossed, and compensation to all those who undergo a risk of a boundary crossing. The unreliable enforcer of justice might either perform actions others are fearful of, or not; and either might be done to obtain compensation for some previous wrong, or to exact retribution. A person who uses an unreliable procedure of enforcing justice and is led to perform some *unfeared* action will not be punished afterwards. If it turns out that the person on whom he acted was guilty and that the compensation taken was appropriate, the situation will be left as is. If the person on whom he acted turns out to be innocent, the unreliable enforcer of justice may be forced fully to compensate him for the action.

On the other hand, the unreliable enforcer of justice may be forbidden to impose those consequences that would be feared if expected. Why? If done frequently enough so as to create general fear, such unreliable enforcement may be forbidden in order to avoid the general uncompensated-for fear. Even if done rarely, the unreliable enforcer may be punished for imposing this feared consequence upon an innocent person. But if the unreliable enforcer acts rarely and creates no general fear, why may he be punished for imposing a feared consequence *upon a person who is guilty*? A system of punishing unreliable punishers for their punishment of guilty persons would help deter them from using their unreliable system upon anyone and therefore from using it upon innocent people. But not everything that would aid in such deterrence may be inflicted. The question is whether it would be legitimate in this case to punish after the fact the unreliable punisher of someone who turned out to be guilty.

No one has a right to use a relatively unreliable procedure in order to decide whether to punish another. Using such a system, he is in no position to know that the other deserves punishment; hence he has no right to punish him. But how can we say this? If the other has committed a crime, doesn't *everyone* in a state of nature have a right to punish him? And therefore doesn't someone who doesn't know that this other person has committed the crime? Here, it seems to me, we face a terminological issue about how to merge epistemic considerations with rights. Shall we say that someone doesn't have a right to do certain things unless he knows certain facts, or shall we say that he does have a right but he does wrong in exercising it unless he knows certain facts? It may be neater to decide it one way, but we can still say all we wish in the other mode; there is a simple translation between the two modes of discourse. We shall pick the latter mode of speech; if anything, this makes our argument look *less* compelling. If we assume that anyone has a right to take something that a thief has stolen, then under this latter terminology someone who takes a stolen object from a thief, without knowing it had been stolen, had a right to take the object; but since he didn't know he had this right, *his* taking the object was wrong and impermissible. Even though no right of the first thief is violated, the second didn't know this and so acted wrongly and impermissibly.

Having taken this terminological fork, we might propose an epistemic principle of border crossing: If doing act A would violate Q's rights unless condition C obtained, then someone who does not know that C obtains may not do A. Since we may assume that all know that inflicting a punishment upon someone violates his rights unless he is guilty of an offense, we may make do with the weaker principle: If someone knows that doing act *A* would violate *Q*'s rights unless condition *C* obtained, he may not do *A* if he does not know that *C* obtains. Weaker still, but sufficient for our purposes, is: If someone *knows* that doing act *A* would violate *Q*'s rights unless condition *C* obtained, he may not do *A* if he has not ascertained that *C* obtains through being in the best feasible position for ascertaining this. (This weakening of the consequent also avoids various problems connected with epistemological skepticism.) Anyone may punish a violator of this prohibition. More precisely, anyone has the right so to punish a violator; people may do so only if they themselves don't run afoul of the prohibition, that is, only if they themselves have ascertained that another violated the prohibition, being in the best position to have ascertained this.

On this view, what a person may do is *not* limited only by the rights of others. An unreliable punisher violates no right of the guilty person; but still he may not punish him. This extra space is created by epistemic considerations. (It would be a fertile area for investigation, if one could avoid drowning in the morass of considerations about "subjective-ought" and "objective-ought.") Note that on this construal, a person does not have a right that he be punished only by use of a relatively reliable procedure. (Even though he may, if he so chooses, give another permission to use a less reliable procedure on him.) On this view, many procedural rights stem not from rights of the person acted upon, but rather from moral considerations about the person or persons doing the acting.

It is not clear to me that this is the proper focus. Perhaps the person acted upon does have such procedural rights against the user of an unreliable procedure. (But what is a *guilty* person's complaint against an unreliable procedure? That it is too likely to mispunish him? Would we have the user of an unreliable procedure compensate the guilty person he punished, for violating his right?) We have seen that our argument for a protective agency's punishing the wielder of the unreliable procedure for inflicting a penalty upon its client would go much more smoothly were this so. The client merely would authorize his agency to act to enforce his procedural right. For the purposes of our subargument here, we have shown that our conclusion stands, even without the facilitating assumption of procedural rights. (We do not mean to imply that there aren't such rights.) In either case, a protective agency may punish a wielder of an unreliable or unfair procedure who (against the client's will) has punished one of its clients, independently of whether or not its client actually is guilty and therefore even if its client is guilty.

The De Facto Monopoly

The tradition of theorizing about the state we discussed [earlier] has a state claiming a monopoly on the use of force. Has any monopoly element yet entered our account of the dominant protective agency? *Everyone* may defend himself against unknown or unreliable procedures and may punish those who use or attempt to use such procedures against him. As its client's agent, the protective association has the right to do this for its clients. It grants that every individual, including those *not* affiliated with the association, has this right. So far, no monopoly is claimed. To be sure, there is a universal element in the content of the claim: the right to pass on *anyone's* procedure. But it does not claim to be the sole possessor of this right; everyone has it. Since no claim is made that there is some right which it and only it has, no monopoly is claimed. With regard to its own clients, however, it applies and enforces these rights which it grants that everyone has. It deems its own procedures reliable and fair. There will be a strong tendency for it to deem all other procedures, or even the "same" procedures run by others, either unreliable or unfair. But we need not suppose it excludes *every* other procedure. Everyone has the right to defend against procedures that are in fact not, or not known to be, both reliable and fair. Since the dominant protective association judges its own procedures to be both reliable and fair, and believes this to be generally known, it will not allow anyone to defend against *them*; that is, it will punish anyone who does so. The dominant protective association will act freely on its own understanding of the situation, whereas no one else will be able to do so with impunity. Although no monopoly is claimed, the dominant agency does occupy a unique position by virtue of its power. It, and it alone, enforces prohibitions on others' procedures of justice, as it sees fit. It does not claim the right to prohibit others arbitrarily; it claims only the right to prohibit anyone's using actually defective procedures on its clients. But when it sees itself as acting against actually defective procedures, others may see it as acting against what it thinks are defective procedures. It alone will act freely against what it thinks are defective procedures, whatever anyone else thinks. As the most powerful applier of principles which it grants everyone the right to apply *correctly*, it enforces its will, which, from the inside, it thinks is correct. From its strength stems its actual position as the ultimate enforcer and the ultimate judge with regard to its own clients. Claiming only the universal right to act correctly, it acts correctly by its own lights. It alone is in a position to act solely by its own lights.

Does this unique position constitute a monopoly? There is no right the dominant protective association claims uniquely to possess. But its strength leads it to be the unique agent acting across the board to enforce a particular right. It is not merely that it *happens* to be the only exerciser of a right it grants that all possess; the nature of the right is such that once a dominant power emerges, it alone will actually exercise that right. For the right includes the right to stop others from wrongfully exercising the right, and only the dominant power will be able to exercise this right against all others. Here, if anywhere, is the place for applying some notion of a *de facto* monopoly: a monopoly that is not *de jure* because it is not the result of some unique grant of exclusive right while others are excluded from exercising a similar privilege. Other protective agencies, to be sure, can enter the market and attempt to wean customers away from the dominant protective agency. They can attempt to replace it as the dominant one. But being the already dominant

protective agency gives an agency a significant market advantage in the competition for clients. The dominant agency can offer its customers a guarantee that no other agencies can match: "Only those procedures *we* deem appropriate will be used on our customers."

The dominant protective agency's domain does *not* extend to quarrels of nonclients *among themselves*. If one independent is about to use his procedure of justice upon another independent, then presumably the protective association would have no right to intervene. It would have the right we all do to intervene to aid an unwilling victim whose rights are threatened. But since it may not intervene on paternalistic grounds, the protective association would have no proper business interfering if both independents were satisfied with *their* procedure of justice. This does not show that the dominant protective association is not a state. A state, too, could abstain from disputes where all concerned parties chose to opt out of the state's apparatus. (Though it is more difficult for people to opt out of the state in a limited way, by choosing some other procedure for settling a particular quarrel of theirs. For that procedure's settlement, and their reactions to it, might involve areas that not all parties concerned have removed voluntarily from the state's concern.) And shouldn't (and mustn't) each state allow that option to its citizens?

Protecting Others

If the protective agency deems the independents' procedures for enforcing their own rights insufficiently reliable or fair when applied to its clients, it will prohibit the independents from such self-help enforcement. The grounds for this prohibition are that the self-help enforcement imposes risks of danger on its clients. Since the prohibition makes it impossible for the independents credibly to threaten to punish clients who violate their rights, it makes them unable to protect themselves from harm and seriously disadvantages the independents in their daily activities and life. Yet it is perfectly possible that the independents' activities including self-help enforcement could proceed without anyone's rights being violated (leaving aside the question of procedural rights). [In] these circumstances those persons promulgating and benefiting from the prohibition must compensate those disadvantaged by it. The clients of the protective agency, then, must compensate the independents for the disadvantages imposed upon them by being prohibited self-help enforcement of their own rights against the agency's clients. Undoubtedly, the least expensive way to compensate the independents would be to *supply* them with protective services to cover those situations of conflict with the paying customers of the protective agency. This will be less expensive than leaving them unprotected against violations of their rights (by not punishing any client who does so) and then attempting to pay them afterwards to cover their losses through having (and being in a position in which they were exposed to having) their rights violated. If it were *not* less expensive, then instead of buying protective services, people would save their money and use it to cover their losses, perhaps by jointly pooling their money in an insurance scheme.

Must the members of the protective agency *pay* for protective services (vis-à-vis its clients) for the independents? Can they insist that the independents purchase the services themselves? After all, using self-help procedures would not have been without costs for the independent. The principle of compensation does not require those who prohibit an epileptic from driving to pay his full cost of taxis, chauffeurs, and so on. If the epileptic were allowed to run his own automobile, this too would have its costs: money for the car, insurance, gasoline, repair bills, and aggravation. In compensating for disadvantages imposed, the prohibitors need pay only an amount sufficient to compensate for the disadvantages of the prohibition *minus* an amount representing the costs the prohibited party would have borne were it not for the prohibition. The prohibitors needn't pay the complete costs of taxis; they must pay only the amount which when combined with the costs to the prohibited party of running his own private automobile is sufficient for taxis.

They may find it less expensive to compensate in kind for the disadvantages they impose than to supply monetary compensation; they may engage in some activity that removes or partially lessens the disadvantages, compensating in money only for the net disadvantages remaining.

If the prohibitor pays to the person prohibited monetary compensation equal to an amount that covers the disadvantages imposed *minus* the costs of the activity where it is permitted, this amount may be insufficient to enable the prohibited party to overcome the disadvantages. If his costs in performing the prohibited action would have been monetary, he can combine the compensation payment with this money unspent and purchase the equivalent service. But if his costs would not have been directly monetary but involve energy, time, and the like, as in the case of the independent's self-help enforcement of rights, then this monetary payment of the difference will not by itself enable the prohibited party to overcome the disadvantage by purchasing the equivalent of what he is prohibited. If the independent has other financial resources he can use without disadvantaging himself, then this payment of the difference will suffice to leave the prohibited party undisadvantaged. But *if* the independent has no such other financial resources, a protective agency may *not* pay him an amount *less* than the cost of its least expensive protective policy, and so leave him only the alternatives of being defenseless against the wrongs of its clients or having to work in the cash market to earn sufficient funds to total the premium on a policy. For this financially pressed prohibited individual, the agency must make up the difference between the *monetary* costs to him of the unprohibited activity and the amount necessary to purchase an overcoming or counterbalancing of the disadvantage imposed. The prohibitor must completely supply enough, in money or in kind, to overcome the disadvantages. No compensation need be provided to someone who would not be disadvantaged by buying protection for himself. For those of scanter resources, to whom the unprohibited activity had no monetary costs, the agency must provide the difference between the resources they can spare without disadvantage and the cost of protection. For someone for whom it had some monetary costs, the prohibitor must supply the additional monetary amount (over and above what they can spare without disadvantage) necessary to overcome the disadvantages. If the prohibitors compensate in kind, they may *charge* the financially pressed prohibited party for this, up to the monetary costs to him of his unprohibited activity provided this amount is not greater than the price of the good. As the only effective supplier, the dominant protective agency must offer in compensation the difference between its own fee and monetary costs to this prohibited party of self-help enforcement. It almost always will receive this amount back in partial payment for the purchase of a protection policy. It goes without saying that these dealings and prohibitions apply only to those using unreliable or unfair enforcement procedures.

Thus the dominant protective agency must supply the independents—that is, everyone it prohibits from self-help enforcement against its clients on the grounds that their procedures of enforcement are unreliable or unfair—with protective services against its clients; it may have to provide some persons services for a fee that is less than the price of these services. These persons may, of course, choose to refuse to pay the fee and so do without these compensatory services. If the dominant protective agency provides protective services in this way for independents, won't this lead people to leave the agency in order to receive its services without paying? Not to any great extent, since compensation is paid only to those who would be disadvantaged by purchasing protection for themselves, and only in the amount that will equal the cost of an unfancy policy when added to the sum of the monetary costs of self-help protection plus whatever amount the person comfortably could pay. Furthermore, the agency protects these independents it compensates only against its own paying clients on whom the independents are forbidden to use self-help enforcement. The more free riders there are, the more desirable it is to be a client always protected by the agency. This factor, along with the others, reduces the number of free riders and to move the equilibrium toward almost universal participation.

DISCUSSION QUESTIONS

1. Explain how, in the state of nature, individuals move from mutual-protection associations to a dominant protective association.

2. What are the two features of a state that Nozick discusses? Does the dominant protective association have these features? Explain.

3. Nozick claims that the dominant protective association can become a state without violating anyone's rights. Explain and evaluate his argument for this claim.

7

John Rawls, selection from *A Theory of Justice* (1971)

John Rawls (1921–2002) was a leading American political philosopher whose political philosophy has been described as "political liberalism." In his most famous work, *A Theory of Justice*, Rawls outlines and defends an account of what he takes to be the legitimate use of political power in a democracy, wherein the notion of "justice as fairness" plays a central role. In the following selection, Rawls presents his theory of justice, a theory that relies heavily on his conception of a hypothetical "original" position in which the parties, who lack certain knowledge about themselves, choose the principles that will govern their society.

SOURCE

Rawls, John. Excerpts from *A Theory of Justice* by John Rawls, pp. 3–22; 65–67; 69–75; 78–80; 82–83; 111–14; 150–56. Cambridge, Mass.: The Belknap Press of Harvard University Press, Copyright © 1971, 1999 by the President and Fellows of Harvard College. Reprinted by permission of the publisher.

1. The Role of Justice

Justice is the first virtue of social institutions, as truth is of systems of thought. A theory however elegant and economical must be rejected or revised if it is untrue; likewise laws and institutions no matter how efficient and well-arranged must be reformed or abolished if they are unjust.

Each person possesses an inviolability founded on justice that even the welfare of society as a whole cannot override. For this reason justice denies that the loss of freedom for some is made right by a greater good shared by others. It does not allow that the sacrifices imposed on a few are outweighed by the larger sum of advantages enjoyed by many. Therefore in a just society the liberties of equal citizenship are taken as settled; the rights secured by justice are not subject to political bargaining or to the calculus of social interests. The only thing that permits us to acquiesce in an erroneous theory is the lack of a better one; analogously, an injustice is tolerable only when it is necessary to avoid an even greater injustice. Being first virtues of human activities, truth and justice are uncompromising.

These propositions seem to express our intuitive conviction of the primacy of justice. No doubt they are expressed too strongly. In any event I wish to inquire whether these contentions or others similar to them are sound, and if so how they can be accounted for. To this end it is necessary to work out a theory of justice in the light of which these assertions can be interpreted and assessed. I shall begin by considering the role of the principles of justice. Let us assume, to fix ideas, that a society is a more or less self-sufficient association of persons who in their relations to one another recognize certain rules of conduct as binding and who for the most part act in accordance with them. Suppose further that these rules specify a system of cooperation designed to advance the good of those taking part in it. Then, although a society is a cooperative venture for mutual advantage, it is typically marked by a conflict as well as by an identity of interests. There is an identity of interests since social cooperation makes possible a better life for all than any would have if each were to live solely by his own efforts. There is a conflict of interests since persons are not indifferent as to how the greater benefits produced by their collaboration are distributed, for in order to pursue their ends they each prefer a larger to a lesser share. A set of principles is required for choosing among the various social arrangements which determine this division of advantages and for underwriting an agreement on the proper distributive shares. These principles are the principles of social justice: they provide a way of assigning rights and duties in the basic institutions of society and they define the appropriate distribution of the benefits and burdens of social cooperation.

Now let us say that a society is well-ordered when it is not only designed to advance the good of its members but when it is also effectively regulated by a public conception of justice. That is, it is a society in which (1) everyone accepts and knows that the others accept the same principles of justice, and (2) the basic social institutions generally satisfy and are generally known to satisfy these principles. In this case while men may put forth excessive demands on one another, they nevertheless acknowledge a common point of view from which their claims may be adjudicated. If men's inclination to self-interest makes their vigilance against one another necessary, their public sense of justice makes their secure association together possible. Among individuals with disparate aims and purposes a shared conception of justice establishes the bonds of civic friendship; the general desire for justice limits the pursuit of other ends. One may think of a public conception of justice as constituting the fundamental charter of a well-ordered human association.

Existing societies are of course seldom well-ordered in this sense, for what is just and unjust is usually in dispute. Men disagree about which principles should define the basic terms of their association. Yet we may still say, despite this disagreement, that they each have a conception of justice. That is, they understand the need for, and they are prepared to affirm, a characteristic set of principles for assigning basic rights and duties and for determining what they take to be the proper distribution of the benefits and burdens of social cooperation. Thus it seems natural to think of the concept of justice as distinct from the various conceptions of justice and as being specified by the role which these different sets of principles, these different conceptions, have in common.[1] Those who hold different conceptions of justice can, then, still agree that institutions are just when no arbitrary distinctions are made between persons in the assigning of basic rights and duties and when the rules determine a proper balance between competing claims to the advantages of social life. Men can agree to this description of just institutions since the notions of an arbitrary distinction and of a proper balance, which are included in the concept of justice, are left open for each to interpret according to the principles of justice that he accepts. These principles single out which similarities and differences among persons are relevant in determining rights and duties and they specify which division of advantages is appropriate. Clearly this distinction between the concept and the various conceptions of justice settles no important questions. It simply helps to identify the role of the principles of social justice.

Some measure of agreement in conceptions of justice is, however, not the only prerequisite for a viable human community. There are other

---

[1] Here I follow H.L.A. Hart, *The Concept of Law* (Oxford: The Clarendon Press, 1961), pp. 155–59.

fundamental social problems, in particular those of coordination, efficiency, and stability. Thus the plans of individuals need to be fitted together so that their activities are compatible with one another and they can all be carried through without anyone's legitimate expectations being severely disappointed. Moreover, the execution of these plans should lead to the achievement of social ends in ways that are efficient and consistent with justice. And finally, the scheme of social cooperation must be stable: it must be more or less regularly complied with and its basic rules willingly acted upon; and when infractions occur, stabilizing forces should exist that prevent further violations and tend to restore the arrangement. Now it is evident that these three problems are connected with that of justice. In the absence of a certain measure of agreement on what is just and unjust, it is clearly more difficult for individuals to coordinate their plans efficiently in order to insure that mutually beneficial arrangements are maintained. Distrust and resentment corrode the ties of civility, and suspicion and hostility tempt men to act in ways they would otherwise avoid. So while the distinctive role of conceptions of justice is to specify basic rights and duties and to determine the appropriate distributive shares, the way in which a conception does this is bound to affect the problems of efficiency, coordination, and stability. We cannot, in general, assess a conception of justice by its distributive role alone, however useful this role may be in identifying the concept of justice. We must take into account its wider connections; for even though justice has a certain priority, being the most important virtue of institutions, it is still true that, other things equal, one conception of justice is preferable to another when its broader consequences are more desirable.

2. The Subject of Justice

Many different kinds of things are said to be just and unjust: not only laws, institutions, and social systems, but also particular actions of many kinds, including decisions, judgments, and imputations. We also call the attitudes and dispositions of persons, and persons themselves, just and unjust. Our topic, however, is that of social justice. For us the primary subject of justice is the basic structure of society, or more exactly, the way in which the major social institutions distribute fundamental rights and duties and determine the division of advantages from social cooperation. By major institutions I understand the political constitution and the principal economic and social arrangements. Thus the legal protection of freedom of thought and liberty of conscience, competitive markets, private property in the means of production, and the monogamous family are examples of major social institutions. Taken together as one scheme, the major institutions define men's rights and duties and influence their life prospects, what they can expect to be and how well they can hope to do. The basic structure is the primary subject of justice because its effects are so profound and present from the start. The intuitive notion here is that this structure contains various social positions and that men born into different positions have different expectations of life determined, in part, by the political system as well as by economic and social circumstances. In this way the institutions of society favor certain starting places over others. These are especially deep inequalities. Not only are they pervasive, but they affect men's initial chances in life; yet they cannot possibly be justified by an appeal to the notions of merit or desert. It is these inequalities, presumably inevitable in the basic structure of any society, to which the principles of social justice must in the first instance apply. These principles, then, regulate the choice of a political constitution and the main elements of the economic and social system. The justice of a social scheme depends essentially on how fundamental rights and duties are assigned and on the economic opportunities and social conditions in the various sectors of society.

The scope of our inquiry is limited in two ways. First of all, I am concerned with a special case of the problem of justice. I shall not consider the justice of institutions and social practices generally, nor except in passing the justice of the law of nations and of relations between states. Therefore, if one supposes that the concept of justice applies whenever there is an allotment of something rationally regarded as advantageous or disadvantageous, then we are interested in only one instance of its application. There is no reason to suppose ahead of time that the principles satisfactory for the basic structure hold for all cases. These principles may not work for the rules and practices of private associations or for those of less comprehensive social groups. They may be irrelevant for the various informal conventions and customs of everyday life; they may not elucidate the justice, or perhaps better, the fairness of voluntary cooperative arrangements or procedures for making contractual agreements. The conditions for the law of nations may require different principles arrived at in a somewhat different way. I shall be satisfied if it is possible to formulate a reasonable conception of justice for the basic structure of society conceived for the time being as a closed system isolated from other societies. The significance of this special case is obvious and needs no explanation. It is natural to conjecture that once we have a sound theory for this case, the remaining problems of justice will prove more tractable in the light of it. With suitable modifications such a theory should provide the key for some of these other questions.

The other limitation on our discussion is that for the most part I examine the principles of justice that would regulate a well-ordered society. Everyone is presumed to act justly and to do his part in upholding just institutions. Though justice may be, as Hume remarked, the cautious, jealous virtue, we can still ask what a perfectly just society would be like.[1] Thus I consider primarily what I call strict compliance as opposed to partial compliance theory. The latter studies the principles that govern how we are to deal with injustice. It comprises such topics as the theory of punishment, the doctrine of just war, and the justification of the various ways of opposing unjust regimes, ranging from civil dis-

obedience and conscientious objection to militant resistance and revolution. Also included here are questions of compensatory justice and of weighing one form of institutional injustice against another. Obviously the problems of partial compliance theory are the pressing and urgent matters. These are the things that we are faced with in everyday life. The reason for beginning with ideal theory is that it provides, I believe, the only basis for the systematic grasp of these more pressing problems. The discussion of civil disobedience, for example, depends upon it. At least, I shall assume that a deeper understanding can be gained in no other way, and that the nature and aims of a perfectly just society is the fundamental part of the theory of justice.

Now admittedly the concept of the basic structure is somewhat vague. It is not always clear which institutions or features thereof should be included. But it would be premature to worry about this matter here. I shall proceed by discussing principles which do apply to what is certainly a part of the basic structure as intuitively understood; I shall then try to extend the application of these principles so that they cover what would appear to be the main elements of this structure. Perhaps these principles will turn out to be perfectly general, although this is unlikely. It is sufficient that they apply to the most important cases of social justice. The point to keep in mind is that a conception of justice for the basic structure is worth having for its own sake. It should not be dismissed because its principles are not everywhere satisfactory.

A conception of social justice, then, is to be regarded as providing in the first instance a standard whereby the distributive aspects of the basic structure of society are to be assessed. This standard, however, is not to be confused with the principles defining the other virtues, for the basic structure, and social arrangements generally, may be efficient or inefficient, liberal or illiberal, and many other things, as well as just or unjust. A complete conception defining principles for all the virtues of the basic structure, together with their respective weights when they conflict, is more than a conception of justice; it is a social ideal. The principles of

---

[1] *An Enquiry Concerning the Principles of Morals*, sec. III, p. I, par. 3, ed. L.A. Selby-Bigge, 2nd edition (Oxford, 1902), p. 184.

justice are but a part, although perhaps the most important part, of such a conception. A social ideal in turn is connected with a conception of society, a vision of the way in which the aims and purposes of social cooperation are to be understood. The various conceptions of justice are the outgrowth of different notions of society against the background of opposing views of the natural necessities and opportunities of human life. Fully to understand a conception of justice we must make explicit the conception of social cooperation from which it derives. But in doing this we should not lose sight of the special role of the principles of justice or of the primary subject to which they apply.

In these preliminary remarks I have distinguished the concept of justice as meaning a proper balance between competing claims from a conception of justice as a set of related principles for identifying the relevant considerations which determine this balance. I have also characterized justice as but one part of a social ideal, although the theory I shall propose no doubt extends its everyday sense. This theory is not offered as a description of ordinary meanings but as an account of certain distributive principles for the basic structure of society. I assume that any reasonably complete ethical theory must include principles for this fundamental problem and that these principles, whatever they are, constitute its doctrine of justice. The concept of justice I take to be defined, then, by the role of its principles in assigning rights and duties and in defining the appropriate division of social advantages. A conception of justice is an interpretation of this role.

Now this approach may not seem to tally with tradition. I believe, though, that it does. The more specific sense that Aristotle gives to justice, and from which the most familiar formulations derive, is that of refraining from *pleonexia*, that is, from gaining some advantage for oneself by seizing what belongs to another, his property, his reward, his office, and the like, or by denying a person that which is due to him, the fulfillment of a promise, the repayment of a debt, the showing of proper

respect, and so on.[1] It is evident that this definition is framed to apply to actions, and persons are thought to be just insofar as they have, as one of the permanent elements of their character, a steady and effective desire to act justly.

Aristotle's definition clearly presupposes, however, an account of what properly belongs to a person and of what is due to him. Now such entitlements are, I believe, very often derived from social institutions and the legitimate expectations to which they give rise. There is no reason to think that Aristotle would disagree with this, and certainly he has a conception of social justice to account for these claims. The definition I adopt is designed to apply directly to the most important case, the justice of the basic structure. There is no conflict with the traditional notion.

3. The Main Idea of the Theory of Justice

My aim is to present a conception of justice which generalizes and carries to a higher level of abstraction the familiar theory of the social contract as found, say, in Locke, Rousseau, and Kant. In order to do this we are not to think of the original contract as one to enter a particular society or to set up a particular form of government. Rather, the guiding idea is that the principles of justice for the basic structure of society are the object of the original agreement. They are the principles that free and rational persons concerned to further their own interests would accept in an initial position of equality as defining the fundamental terms of their association. These principles are to regulate all further agreements; they specify the kinds of social cooperation that can be entered into and the forms of government that can be established. This way of

---

[1] *Nicomachean Ethics*, 1129b–1130b5. I have followed the interpretation of Gregory Vlastos, "Justice and Happiness in *The Republic*," in Gregory Vlastos (ed.), *Plato: A Collection of Critical Essays* (Garden City, NY: Doubleday and Company, 1971), vol. 2, pp. 70f. For a discussion of Aristotle on justice, see W.F.R. Hardie, *Aristotle's Ethical Theory* (Oxford: The Clarendon Press, 1968), ch. X.

regarding the principles of justice I shall call justice as fairness.

Thus we are to imagine that those who engage in social cooperation choose together, in one joint act, the principles which are to assign basic rights and duties and to determine the division of social benefits. Men are to decide in advance how they are to regulate their claims against one another and what is to be the foundation charter of their society. Just as each person must decide by rational reflection what constitutes his good, that is, the system of ends which it is rational for him to pursue, so a group of persons must decide once and for all what is to count among them as just and unjust. The choice which rational men would make in this hypothetical situation of equal liberty, assuming for the present that this choice problem has a solution, determines the principles of justice.

In justice as fairness the original position of equality corresponds to the state of nature in the traditional theory of the social contract. This original position is not, of course, thought of as an actual historical state of affairs, much less as a primitive condition of culture. It is understood as a purely hypothetical situation characterized so as to lead to a certain conception of justice. Among the essential features of this situation is that no one knows his place in society, his class position or social status, nor does any one know his fortune in the distribution of natural assets and abilities, his intelligence, strength, and the like. I shall even assume that the parties do not know their conceptions of the good or their special psychological propensities. The principles of justice are chosen behind a veil of ignorance. This ensures that no one is advantaged or disadvantaged in the choice of principles by the outcome of natural chance or the contingency of social circumstances. Since all are similarly situated and no one is able to design principles to favor his particular condition, the principles of justice are the result of a fair agreement or bargain. For given the circumstances of the original position, the symmetry of everyone's relations to each other, this initial situation is fair between individuals as moral persons, that is, as rational beings with their own ends and capable, I shall assume, of a sense of justice. The original position is, one might say, the appropriate initial status quo, and thus the fundamental agreements reached in it are fair. This explains the propriety of the name "justice as fairness": it conveys the idea that the principles of justice are agreed to in an initial situation that is fair. The name does not mean that the concepts of justice and fairness are the same, any more than the phrase "poetry as metaphor" means that the concepts of poetry and metaphor are the same.

Justice as fairness begins, as I have said, with one of the most general of all choices which persons might make together, namely, with the choice of the first principles of a conception of justice which is to regulate all subsequent criticism and reform of institutions. Then, having chosen a conception of justice, we can suppose that they are to choose a constitution and a legislature to enact laws, and so on, all in accordance with the principles of justice initially agreed upon. Our social situation is just if it is such that by this sequence of hypothetical agreements we would have contracted into the general system of rules which defines it. Moreover, assuming that the original position does determine a set of principles (that is, that a particular conception of justice would be chosen), it will then be true that whenever social institutions satisfy these principles those engaged in them can say to one another that they are cooperating on terms to which they would agree if they were free and equal persons whose relations with respect to one another were fair. They could all view their arrangements as meeting the stipulations which they would acknowledge in an initial situation that embodies widely accepted and reasonable constraints on the choice of principles. The general recognition of this fact would provide the basis for a public acceptance of the corresponding principles of justice. No society can, of course, be a scheme of cooperation which men enter voluntarily in a literal sense; each person finds himself placed at birth in some particular position in some particular society, and the nature of this position materially affects his life prospects. Yet a society satisfying the principles of justice as fairness comes as close as a society can to being a voluntary scheme, for it meets the principles which free and equal persons would assent to under circumstances that are fair. In this sense its members are autonomous and the obligations they recognize self-imposed.

One feature of justice as fairness is to think of the parties in the initial situation as rational and mutually disinterested. This does not mean that the parties are egoists, that is, individuals with only certain kinds of interests, say in wealth, prestige, and domination. But they are conceived as not taking an interest in one another's interests. They are to presume that even their spiritual aims may be opposed, in the way that the aims of those of different religions may be opposed. Moreover, the concept of rationality must be interpreted as far as possible in the narrow sense, standard in economic theory, of taking the most effective means to given ends. I shall modify this concept to some extent, as explained later, but one must try to avoid introducing into it any controversial ethical elements. The initial situation must be characterized by stipulations that are widely accepted.

In working out the conception of justice as fairness one main task clearly is to determine which principles of justice would be chosen in the original position. To do this we must describe this situation in some detail and formulate with care the problem of choice which it presents. These matters I shall take up in the immediately succeeding chapters. It may be observed, however, that once the principles of justice are thought of as arising from an original agreement in a situation of equality, it is an open question whether the principle of utility would be acknowledged. Offhand it hardly seems likely that persons who view themselves as equals, entitled to press their claims upon one another, would agree to a principle which may require lesser life prospects for some simply for the sake of a greater sum of advantages enjoyed by others. Since each desires to protect his interests, his capacity to advance his conception of the good, no one has a reason to acquiesce in an enduring loss for himself in order to bring about a greater net balance of satisfaction.

In the absence of strong and lasting benevolent impulses, a rational man would not accept a basic structure merely because it maximized the algebraic sum of advantages irrespective of its permanent effects on his own basic rights and interests. Thus it seems that the principle of utility is incompatible with the conception of social cooperation among equals for mutual advantage. It appears to be inconsistent with the idea of reciprocity implicit in the notion of a well-ordered society. Or, at any rate, so I shall argue.

I shall maintain instead that the persons in the initial situation would choose two rather different principles: the first requires equality in the assignment of basic rights and duties, while the second holds that social and economic inequalities, for example inequalities of wealth and authority, are just only if they result in compensating benefits for everyone, and in particular for the least advantaged members of society. These principles rule out justifying institutions on the grounds that the hardships of some are offset by a greater good in the aggregate. It may be expedient but it is not just that some should have less in order that others may prosper. But there is no injustice in the greater benefits earned by a few provided that the situation of persons not so fortunate is thereby improved. The intuitive idea is that since everyone's well-being depends upon a scheme of cooperation without which no one could have a satisfactory life, the division of advantages should be such as to draw forth the willing cooperation of everyone taking part in it, including those less well situated. The two principles mentioned seem to be a fair basis on which those better endowed, or more fortunate in their social position, neither of which we can be said to deserve, could expect the willing cooperation of others when some workable scheme is a necessary condition of the welfare of all. Once we decide to look for a conception of justice that prevents the use of the accidents of natural endowment and the contingencies of social circumstance as counters in a quest for political and economic advantage, we are led to these principles. They express the result of leaving aside those aspects of the social world that seem arbitrary from a moral point of view.

The problem of the choice of principles, however, is extremely difficult. I do not expect the answer I shall suggest to be convincing to everyone. It is, therefore, worth noting from the outset that justice as fairness, like other contract views, consists of two parts: (1) an interpretation of the initial situation and of the problem of choice posed there, and (2) a set of principles which, it is argued, would be agreed to. One may accept the first part of the theory (or some variant thereof), but not the other, and conversely. The concept of the initial contractual situation may seem reasonable although the particular principles proposed are rejected. To be sure, I want to maintain that the most appropriate conception of this situation does lead to principles of justice contrary to utilitarianism and perfectionism, and therefore that the contract doctrine provides an alternative to these views. Still, one may dispute this contention even though one grants that the contractarian method is a useful way of studying ethical theories and of setting forth their underlying assumptions.

Justice as fairness is an example of what I have called a contract theory. Now there may be an objection to the term "contract" and related expressions, but I think it will serve reasonably well. Many words have misleading connotations which at first are likely to confuse. The terms "utility" and "utilitarianism" are surely no exception. They too have unfortunate suggestions which hostile critics have been willing to exploit; yet they are clear enough for those prepared to study utilitarian doctrine. The same should be true of the term "contract" applied to moral theories. As I have mentioned, to understand it one has to keep in mind that it implies a certain level of abstraction. In particular, the content of the relevant agreement is not to enter a given society or to adopt a given form of government, but to accept certain moral principles. Moreover, the undertakings referred to are purely hypothetical: a contract view holds that certain principles would be accepted in a well-defined initial situation.

The merit of the contract terminology is that it conveys the idea that principles of justice may be conceived as principles that would be chosen by rational persons, and that in this way conceptions of justice may be explained and justified. The theory of justice is a part, perhaps the most significant part, of the theory of rational choice. Furthermore, principles of justice deal with conflicting claims upon the advantages won by social cooperation; they apply to the relations among several persons or groups. The word "contract" suggests this plurality as well as the condition that the appropriate division of advantages must be in accordance with principles acceptable to all parties. The condition of publicity for principles of justice is also connoted by the contract phraseology. Thus, if these principles are the outcome of an agreement, citizens have a knowledge of the principles that others follow. It is characteristic of contract theories to stress the public nature of political principles. Finally there is the long tradition of the contract doctrine. Expressing the tie with this line of thought helps to define ideas and accords with natural piety. There are then several advantages in the use of the term "contract." With due precautions taken, it should not be misleading.

A final remark. Justice as fairness is not a complete contract theory. For it is clear that the contractarian idea can be extended to the choice of more or less an entire ethical system, that is, to a system including principles for all the virtues and not only for justice. Now for the most part I shall consider only principles of justice and others closely related to them; I make no attempt to discuss the virtues in a systematic way. Obviously if justice as fairness succeeds reasonably well, a next step would be to study the more general view suggested by the name "rightness as fairness." But even this wider theory fails to embrace all moral relationships, since it would seem to include only our relations with other persons and to leave out of account how we are to conduct ourselves toward animals and the rest of nature. I do not contend that the contract notion offers a way to approach these questions which are certainly of the first importance; and I shall have to put them aside. We must recognize the limited scope of justice as fairness and of the general type of view that it exemplifies. How far its conclusions must be revised once these other matters are understood cannot be decided in advance.

4. The Original Position and Justification

I have said that the original position is the appropriate initial status quo which insures that the fundamental agreements reached in it are fair. This fact yields the name "justice as fairness." It is clear, then, that I want to say that one conception of justice is more reasonable than another, or justifiable with respect to it, if rational persons in the initial situation would choose its principles over those of the other for the role of justice. Conceptions of justice are to be ranked by their acceptability to persons so circumstanced. Understood in this way the question of justification is settled by working out a problem of deliberation: we have to ascertain which principles it would be rational to adopt given the contractual situation. This connects the theory of justice with the theory of rational choice.

If this view of the problem of justification is to succeed, we must, of course, describe in some detail the nature of this choice problem. A problem of rational decision has a definite answer only if we know the beliefs and interests of the parties, their relations with respect to one another, the alternatives between which they are to choose, the procedure whereby they make up their minds, and so on. As the circumstances are presented in different ways, correspondingly different principles are accepted. The concept of the original position, as I shall refer to it, is that of the most philosophically favored interpretation of this initial choice situation for the purposes of a theory of justice.

But how are we to decide what is the most favored interpretation? I assume, for one thing, that there is a broad measure of agreement that principles of justice should be chosen under certain conditions. To justify a particular description of the initial situation one shows that it incorporates these commonly shared presumptions. One argues from widely accepted but weak premises to more specific conclusions. Each of the presumptions should by itself be natural and plausible; some of them may seem innocuous or even trivial. The aim of the contract approach is to establish that taken together they impose significant bounds on acceptable principles of justice. The ideal outcome would be that these conditions determine a unique set of principles; but I shall be satisfied if they suffice to rank the main traditional conceptions of social justice.

One should not be misled, then, by the somewhat unusual conditions which characterize the original position. The idea here is simply to make vivid to ourselves the restrictions that it seems reasonable to impose on arguments for principles of justice, and therefore on these principles themselves. Thus it seems reasonable and generally acceptable that no one should be advantaged or disadvantaged by natural fortune or social circumstances in the choice of principles. It also seems widely agreed that it should be impossible to tailor principles to the circumstances of one's own case. We should insure further that particular inclinations and aspirations, and persons' conceptions of their good do not affect the principles adopted. The aim is to rule out those principles that it would be rational to propose for acceptance, however little the chance of success, only if one knew certain things that are irrelevant from the standpoint of justice. For example, if a man knew that he was wealthy, he might find it rational to advance the principle that various taxes for welfare measures be counted unjust; if he knew that he was poor, he would most likely propose the contrary principle. To represent the desired restrictions one imagines a situation in which everyone is deprived of this sort of information. One excludes the knowledge of those contingencies which sets men at odds and allows them to be guided by their prejudices. In this manner the veil of ignorance is arrived at in a natural way. This concept should cause no difficulty if we keep in mind the constraints on arguments that it is meant to express. At any time we can enter the original position, so to speak, simply by following a certain procedure, namely, by arguing for principles of justice in accordance with these restrictions.

It seems reasonable to suppose that the parties in the original position are equal. That is, all have the same rights in the procedure for choosing principles; each can make proposals, submit reasons for their acceptance, and so on. Obviously the purpose of these conditions is to represent equality between human beings as moral persons, as creatures having a conception of their good and capable of a sense of justice. The basis of equality is taken to be similarity in these two respects. Systems of ends are not ranked in value; and each man is presumed to have the requisite ability to understand and to act upon whatever principles are adopted. Together with the veil of ignorance, these conditions define the principles of justice as those which rational persons concerned to advance their interests would consent to as equals when none are known to be advantaged or disadvantaged by social and natural contingencies.

There is, however, another side to justifying a particular description of the original position. This is to see if the principles which would be chosen match our considered convictions of justice or extend them in an acceptable way. We can note whether applying these principles would lead us to make the same judgments about the basic structure of society which we now make intuitively and in which we have the greatest confidence; or whether, in cases where our present judgments are in doubt and given with hesitation, these principles offer a resolution which we can affirm on reflection. There are questions which we feel sure must be answered in a certain way. For example, we are confident that religious intolerance and racial discrimination are unjust. We think that we have examined these things with care and have reached what we believe is an impartial judgment not likely to be distorted by an excessive attention to our own interests. These convictions are provisional fixed points which we presume any conception of justice must fit. But we have much less assurance as to what is the correct distribution of wealth and authority. Here we may be looking for a way to remove our doubts. We

can check an interpretation of the initial situation, then, by the capacity of its principles to accommodate our firmest convictions and to provide guidance where guidance is needed.

In searching for the most favored description of this situation we work from both ends. We begin by describing it so that it represents generally shared and preferably weak conditions. We then see if these conditions are strong enough to yield a significant set of principles. If not, we look for further premises equally reasonable. But if so, and these principles match our considered convictions of justice, then so far well and good. But presumably there will be discrepancies. In this case we have a choice. We can either modify the account of the initial situation or we can revise our existing judgments, for even the judgments we take provisionally as fixed points are liable to revision. By going back and forth, sometimes altering the conditions of the contractual circumstances, at others withdrawing our judgments and conforming them to principle, I assume that eventually we shall find a description of the initial situation that both expresses reasonable conditions and yields principles which match our considered judgments duly pruned and adjusted. This state of affairs I refer to as reflective equilibrium. It is an equilibrium because at last our principles and judgments coincide; and it is reflective since we know to what principles our judgments conform and the premises of their derivation. At the moment everything is in order. But this equilibrium is not necessarily stable. It is liable to be upset by further examination of the conditions which should be imposed on the contractual situation and by particular cases which may lead us to revise our judgments. Yet for the time being we have done what we can to render coherent and to justify our convictions of social justice. We have reached a conception of the original position.

I shall not, of course, actually work through this process. Still, we may think of the interpretation of the original position that I shall present as the result of such a hypothetical course of reflection. It represents the attempt to accommodate within one scheme both reasonable philosophical conditions on principles as well as our considered judgments of justice. In arriving at the favored interpretation of the initial situation there is no point at which an appeal is made to self-evidence in the traditional sense either of general conceptions or particular convictions. I do not claim for the principles of justice proposed that they are necessary truths or derivable from such truths. A conception of justice cannot be deduced from self-evident premises or conditions on principles; instead, its justification is a matter of the mutual support of many considerations, of everything fitting together into one coherent view.

A final comment. We shall want to say that certain principles of justice are justified because they would be agreed to in an initial situation of equality. I have emphasized that this original position is purely hypothetical. It is natural to ask why, if this agreement is never actually entered into, we should take any interest in these principles, moral or otherwise. The answer is that the conditions embodied in the description of the original position are ones that we do in fact accept. Or if we do not, then perhaps we can be persuaded to do so by philosophical reflection. Each aspect of the contractual situation can be given supporting grounds. Thus what we shall do is to collect together into one conception a number of conditions on principles that we are ready upon due consideration to recognize as reasonable. These constraints express what we are prepared to regard as limits on fair terms of social cooperation. One way to look at the idea of the original position, therefore, is to see it as an expository device which sums up the meaning of these conditions and helps us to extract their consequences. On the other hand, this conception is also an intuitive notion that suggests its own elaboration, so that led on by it we are drawn to define more clearly the standpoint from which we can best interpret moral relationships. We need a conception that enables us to envision our objective from afar: the intuitive notion of the original position is to do this for us.

DISCUSSION QUESTIONS

1. Why does Rawls think that "justice as fairness" is an appropriate title for his theory?

2. What role does the original position play in Rawls's theory of justice? How does he characterize the original position, and in what ways does he justify his particular description of the original position?

3. Rawls writes, "There is, however, another side to justifying a particular description of the original position. This is to see if the principles which would be chosen match our considered convictions of justice or extend them in an acceptable way." Explain what you take Rawls to mean by this, making sure to define and use the term *reflective equilibrium* in your answer.

B.
Critiques of
Contract Theory

8

David Hume, "Of the Original Contract" (1752)

David Hume (1711–76) was a Scottish philosopher and historian. Although his philosophical work had only a minimal impact during his lifetime, he is now widely considered one of the most important philosophers in the Empiricist tradition. In this selection, Hume criticizes the notion that political authority is grounded in the consent of the governed.

SOURCE

Hume, David. "Of the Original Contract." In *The Philosophical Works of David Hume*, vol. III (Essay XII). Little, Brown and Company, 1854.

As no party, in the present age, can well support itself without a philosophical or speculative system of principles annexed to its political or practical one, we accordingly find, that each of the factions into which this nation is divided has reared up a fabric of the former kind, in order to protect and cover that scheme of actions which it pursues. The people being commonly very rude builders, especially in this speculative way, and more especially still when actuated by party-zeal, it is natural to imagine that their workmanship must be a little unshapely, and discover evident marks of that violence and hurry in which it was raised. The one party, by tracing up government to the DEITY, endeavoured to render it so sacred and inviolate, that it must be little less than sacrilege, however tyrannical it may become, to touch or invade it in the smallest article. The other party, by founding government altogether on the consent of the PEOPLE, suppose that there is a kind of *original contract*, by which the subjects have tacitly reserved the power of resisting their sovereign, whenever they find themselves aggrieved by that authority, with which they have, for certain purposes, voluntarily intrusted him. These are the speculative principles of the two parties, and these, too, are the practical consequences deduced from them.

I shall venture to affirm, *That both these systems of speculative principles are just; though not in the sense intended by the parties*: and, *That both the schemes of practical consequences are prudent; though not in the extremes to which each party, in opposition to the other, has commonly endeavoured to carry them.*

That the DEITY is the ultimate author of all government, will never be denied by any, who admit a general providence, and allow, that all events in the universe are conducted by an uniform plan, and directed to wise purposes. As it is impossible for the human race to subsist, at least in any comfortable or secure state, without the protection of government, this institution must certainly have been intended by that beneficent Being, who means the good of all his creatures: and as it has universally, in fact, taken place, in all countries, and all ages, we may conclude, with still greater certainty, that it was intended by that omniscient Being who can never be deceived by any event or operation. But since he gave rise to it, not by any particular or miraculous interposition, but by his concealed and universal efficacy, a sovereign cannot, properly speaking, be called his vicegerent in any other sense than every power or force, being derived from him, may be said to act by his commission. Whatever actually happens is comprehended in the general plan or intention of Providence; nor has the greatest and most lawful prince any more reason, upon that account, to plead a peculiar sacredness or inviolable authority, than an inferior magistrate, or even an usurper, or even a robber and a pirate. The same Divine Superintendent, who, for wise purposes, invested a TITUS or a TRAJAN with authority, did also, for purposes no doubt equally wise, though unknown, bestow power on a BORGIA or an ANGRIA.[1] The same causes, which gave rise to the sovereign power in every state, established likewise every petty jurisdiction in it, and every limited authority. A constable, therefore, no less than a king, acts by a divine commission, and possesses an indefeasible right.

---

[1] [Titus Flavius and Trajan were Roman emperors who ruled from 79–81 CE and 98–117 CE, respectively. The House of Borgia was a notorious noble family that sought and sometimes succeeded in holding power in Italy in the fifteenth and sixteenth centuries. Kanhoji Angria (1669–1729) was a pirate who terrorized British ships in the Indian Ocean.]

When we consider how nearly equal all men are in their bodily force, and even in their mental powers and faculties, till cultivated by education, we must necessarily allow, that nothing but their own consent could, at first, associate them together, and subject them to any authority. The people, if we trace government to its first origin in the woods and deserts, are the source of all power and jurisdiction, and voluntarily, for the sake of peace and order, abandoned their native liberty, and received laws from their equal and companion. The conditions upon which they were willing to submit, were either expressed, or were so clear and obvious, that it might well be esteemed superfluous to express them. If this, then, be meant by the *original contract*, it cannot be denied, that all government is, at first, founded on a contract, and that the most ancient rude combinations of mankind were formed chiefly by that principle. In vain are we asked in what records this charter of our liberties is registered. It was not written on parchment, nor yet on leaves or barks of trees. It preceded the use of writing, and all the other civilised arts of life. But we trace it plainly in the nature of man, and in the equality, or something approaching equality, which we find in all the individuals of that species. The force, which now prevails, and which is founded on fleets and armies, is plainly political, and derived from authority, the effect of established government. A man's natural force consists only in the vigour of his limbs, and the firmness of his courage; which could never subject multitudes to the command of one. Nothing but their own consent, and their sense of the advantages resulting from peace and order, could have had that influence.

Yet even this consent was long very imperfect, and could not be the basis of a regular administration. The chieftain, who had probably acquired his influence during the continuance of war, ruled more by persuasion than command; and till he could employ force to reduce the refractory and disobedient, the society could scarcely be said to have attained a state of civil government. No compact or agreement, it is evident, was expressly formed for general submission; an idea far beyond the comprehension of savages: each exertion of authority in the chieftain must have been particular, and called forth by the present exigencies of the case: the sensible utility, resulting from his interposition, made these exertions become daily more frequent; and their frequency gradually produced an habitual, and, if you please to call it so, a voluntary, and therefore precarious, acquiescence in the people.

But philosophers, who have embraced a party (if that be not a contradiction in terms), are not contented with these concessions. They assert, not only that government in its earliest infancy arose from consent, or rather the voluntary acquiescence of the people; but also that, even at present, when it has attained its full maturity, it rests on no other foundation. They affirm, that all men are still born equal, and owe allegiance to no prince or government, unless bound by the obligation and sanction of a *promise*. And as no man, without some equivalent, would forego the advantages of his native liberty, and subject himself to the will of another, this promise is always understood to be conditional, and imposes on him no obligation, unless he meet with justice and protection from his sovereign. These advantages the sovereign promises him in return; and if he fail in the execution, he has broken, on his part, the articles of engagement, and has thereby freed his subject from all obligations to allegiance. Such, according to these philosophers, is the foundation of authority in every government, and such the right of resistance possessed by every subject.

But would these reasoners look abroad into the world, they would meet with nothing that, in the least, corresponds to their ideas, or can warrant so refined and philosophical a system. On the contrary, we find every where princes who claim their subjects as their property, and assert their independent right of sovereignty, from conquest or succession. We find also every where subjects who acknowledge this right in their prince, and suppose themselves born under obligations of obedience to a certain sovereign, as much as under the ties of reverence and duty to certain parents. These connexions are always conceived to be equally independent of our consent, in PERSIA and CHINA; in FRANCE and SPAIN; and even in HOLLAND and ENGLAND, wherever the doctrines above-mentioned have not been carefully inculcated. Obedience or subjection becomes so familiar, that most men never make any inquiry about its origin or cause, more than about the principle of gravity, resistance, or the most universal laws of nature. Or if curiosity ever move them; as soon as they learn that they themselves and their ancestors have, for several ages, or from time immemorial, been subject to such a form of government or such a family, they immediately acquiesce, and acknowledge their obligation to allegiance. Were you to preach, in most parts of the world, that political connexions are founded altogether on voluntary consent or a mutual promise, the magistrate would soon imprison you as seditious for loosening the ties of obedience; if your friends did not before shut you up as delirious, for advancing such absurdities. It is strange that an act of the mind, which every individual is supposed to have formed, and after he came to the use of reason too, otherwise it could have no authority; that this act, I say, should be so much unknown to all of them, that over the face of the whole earth, there scarcely remain any traces or memory of it.

But the contract, on which government is founded, is said to be the *original contract*; and consequently may be supposed too old to fall under the knowledge of the present generation. If the agreement, by which savage men first associated and conjoined their force, be here meant, this is acknowledged to be real; but being so ancient, and being obliterated by a thousand changes of government and princes, it cannot now be supposed to retain any authority. If we would say any thing to the purpose, we must assert that every particular government which is lawful, and which imposes any duty of allegiance on the subject, was, at first, founded on consent and a voluntary compact. But, besides that this supposes the consent of the fathers to bind the children, even to the most remote generations (which republican writers will never allow), besides this, I say, it is not justified by history or experience in any age or country of the world.

Almost all the governments which exist at present, or of which there remains any record in story, have been founded originally, either on usurpation or conquest, or both, without any presence of a fair consent or voluntary subjection of the people. When an artful and bold man is placed at the head of an army or faction, it is often easy for him, by employing, sometimes violence, sometimes false pretences, to establish his dominion over a people a hundred times more numerous than his partisans. He allows no such open communication, that his enemies can know, with certainty, their number or force. He gives them no leisure to assemble together in a body to oppose him. Even all those who are the instruments of his usurpation may wish his fall; but their ignorance of each other's intention keeps them in awe, and is the sole cause of his security. By such arts as these many governments have been established; and this is all the *original contract* which they have to boast of.

The face of the earth is continually changing, by the increase of small kingdoms into great empires, by the dissolution of great empires into smaller kingdoms, by the planting of colonies, by the migration of tribes. Is there any thing discoverable in all these events but force and violence? Where is the mutual agreement or voluntary association so much talked of?

Even the smoothest way by which a nation may receive a foreign master, by marriage or a will, is not extremely honourable for the people; but supposes them to be disposed of, like a dowry or a legacy, according to the pleasure or interest of their rulers.

But where no force interposes, and election takes place; what is this election so highly vaunted? It is either the combination of a few great men, who decide for the whole, and will allow of no opposition; or it is the fury of a multitude, that follow a seditious ringleader, who is not known, perhaps, to a dozen among them, and who owes his advancement merely to his own impudence, or to the momentary caprice of his fellows.

Are these disorderly elections, which are rare too, of such mighty authority as to be the only lawful foundation of all government and allegiance?

In reality, there is not a more terrible event than a total dissolution of government, which gives liberty to the multitude, and makes the determination or choice of a new establishment depend upon a number, which nearly approaches to that of the body of the people: for it never comes entirely to the whole body of them. Every wise man then wishes to see, at the head of a powerful and obedient army, a general who may speedily seize the prize, and give to the people a master which they are so unfit to choose for themselves. So little correspondent is fact and reality to those philosophical notions.

Let not the establishment at the *Revolution*[1] deceive us, or make us so much in love with a philosophical origin to government, as to imagine all others monstrous and irregular. Even that event was far from corresponding to these refined ideas. It was only the succession, and that only in the regal part of the government, which was then changed: and it was only the majority of seven hundred, who determined that change for near ten millions. I doubt not, indeed, but the bulk of those ten millions acquiesced willingly in the determination: but was the matter left, in the least, to their choice? Was it not justly supposed to be, from that moment, decided, and every man punished, who refused to submit to the new sovereign? How otherwise could the matter have ever been brought to any issue or conclusion?

The republic of ATHENS was, I believe, the most extensive democracy that we read of in history: yet if we make the requisite allowances for the women, the slaves, and the strangers, we shall find, that that establishment was not at first made, nor any law ever voted, by a tenth part of those who were bound to pay obedience to it; not to mention the islands and foreign dominions, which the ATHENIANS claimed as theirs by right of conquest. And as it is well known that popular assemblies in that city were always full of licence and disorder, not withstanding the institutions and laws by which they were checked; how much more disorderly must they prove, where they form not the established constitution, but meet tumultuously on the dissolution

---

[1] [Hume is here referring to the Glorious Revolution (1688) in which William of Orange and his wife Mary acceded to the throne of England.]

of the ancient government, in order to give rise to a new one? How chimerical must it be to talk of a choice in such circumstances?

The ACHÆANS enjoyed the freest and most perfect democracy of all antiquity; yet they employed force to oblige some cities to enter into their league, as we learn from POLYBIUS.[1]

HARRY the IVth and HARRY the VIIth of ENGLAND, had really no title to the throne but a parliamentary election; yet they never would acknowledge it, lest they should thereby weaken their authority. Strange, if the only real foundation of all authority be consent and promise?

It is in vain to say, that all governments are, or should be, at first, founded on popular consent, as much as the necessity of human affairs will admit. This favours entirely my pretension. I maintain, that human affairs will never admit of this consent, seldom of the appearance of it; but that conquest or usurpation, that is, in plain terms, force, by dissolving the ancient governments, is the origin of almost all the new ones which were ever established in the world. And that in the few cases where consent may seem to have taken place, it was commonly so irregular, so confined, or so much intermixed either with fraud or violence, that it cannot have any great authority.

My intention here is not to exclude the consent of the people from being one just foundation of government where it has place. It is surely the best and most sacred of any. I only pretend, that it has very seldom had place in any degree, and never almost in its full extent; and that, therefore, some other foundation of government must also be admitted.

Were all men possessed of so inflexible a regard to justice, that, of themselves, they would totally abstain from the properties of others; they had for ever remained in a state of absolute liberty, without subjection to any magistrate or political society: but this is a state of perfection, of which human nature is justly deemed incapable. Again, were all men possessed of so perfect an understanding as always to

know their own interests, no form of government had ever been submitted to but what was established on consent, and was fully canvassed by every member of the society: but this state of perfection is likewise much superior to human nature. Reason, history, and experience shew us, that all political societies have had an origin much less accurate and regular; and were one to choose a period of time when the people's consent was the least regarded in public transactions, it would be precisely on the establishment of a new government. In a settled constitution their inclinations are often consulted; but during the fury of revolutions, conquests, and public convulsions, military force or political craft usually decides the controversy.

When a new government is established, by whatever means, the people are commonly dissatisfied with it, and pay obedience more from fear and necessity, than from any idea of allegiance or of moral obligation. The prince is watchful and jealous, and must carefully guard against every beginning or appearance of insurrection. Time, by degrees, removes all these difficulties, and accustoms the nation to regard, as their lawful or native princes, that family which at first they considered as usurpers or foreign conquerors. In order to found this opinion, they have no recourse to any notion of voluntary consent or promise, which, they know, never was, in this case, either expected or demanded. The original establishment was formed by violence, and submitted to from necessity. The subsequent administration is also supported by power, and acquiesced in by the people, not as a matter of choice, but of obligation. They imagine not that their consent gives their prince a title: but they willingly consent, because they think, that, from long possession, he has acquired a title, independent of their choice or inclination.

Should it be said, that, by living under the dominion of a prince which one might leave, every individual has given a *tacit* consent to his authority, and promised him obedience; it may be answered, that such an implied consent can only have place where a man imagines that the matter depends on his choice. But where he thinks (as all mankind do

[1] [A Greek historian (200–118 BCE).]

who are born under established governments) that, by his birth, he owes allegiance to a certain prince or certain form of government; it would be absurd to infer a consent or choice, which he expressly, in this case, renounces and disclaims.

Can we seriously say, that a poor peasant or artisan has a free choice to leave his country, when he knows no foreign language or manners, and lives, from day to day, by the small wages which he acquires? We may as well assert that a man, by remaining in a vessel, freely consents to the dominion of the master; though he was carried on board while asleep, and must leap into the ocean and perish, the moment he leaves her.

What if the prince forbid his subjects to quit his dominions; as in TIBERIUS's time, it was regarded as a crime in a Roman knight that he had attempted to fly to the PARTHIANS, in order to escape the tyranny of that emperor? Or as the ancient MUSCOVITES prohibited all travelling under pain of death? And did a prince observe, that many of his subjects were seized with the frenzy of migrating to foreign countries, he would, doubtless, with great reason and justice, restrain them, in order to prevent the depopulation of his own kingdom. Would he forfeit the allegiance of all his subjects by so wise and reasonable a law? Yet the freedom of their choice is surely, in that case, ravished from them.

A company of men, who should leave their native country, in order to people some uninhabited region, might dream of recovering their native freedom; but they would soon find, that their prince still laid claim to them, and called them his subjects, even in their new settlement. And in this he would but act conformably to the common ideas of mankind.

The truest *tacit* consent of this kind that is ever observed, is when a foreigner settles in any country, and is beforehand acquainted with the prince, and government, and laws, to which he must submit: yet is his allegiance, though more voluntary, much less expected or depended on, than that of a natural born subject. On the contrary, his native prince still asserts a claim to him. And if he punish not the renegade, where he seizes him in war with

his new prince's commission; this clemency is not founded on the municipal law, which in all countries condemns the prisoner; but on the consent of princes, who have agreed to this indulgence, in order to prevent reprisals.

Did one generation of men go off the stage at once, and another succeed, as is the case with silkworms and butterflies, the new race, if they had sense enough to choose their government, which surely is never the case with men, might voluntarily, and by general consent, establish their own form of civil polity, without any regard to the laws or precedents which prevailed among their ancestors. But as human society is in perpetual flux, one man every hour going out of the world, another coming into it, it is necessary, in order to preserve stability in government, that the new brood should conform themselves to the established constitution, and nearly follow the path which their fathers, treading in the footsteps of theirs, had marked out to them. Some innovations must necessarily have place in every human institution; and it is happy where the enlightened genius of the age give these a direction to the side of reason, liberty, and justice: but violent innovations no individual is entitled to make: they are even dangerous to be attempted by the legislature: more ill than good is ever to be expected from them: and if history affords examples to the contrary, they are not to be drawn into precedent, and are only to be regarded as proofs, that the science of politics affords few rules, which will not admit of some exception, and which may not sometimes be controlled by fortune and accident. The violent innovations in the reign of HENRY VIII proceeded from an imperious monarch, seconded by the appearance of legislative authority: those in the reign of CHARLES I were derived from faction and fanaticism; and both of them have proved happy in the issue. But even the former were long the source of many disorders, and still more dangers; and if the measures of allegiance were to be taken from the latter, a total anarchy must have place in human society, and a final period at once be put to every government.

Suppose that an usurper, after having banished his lawful prince and royal family, should establish his dominion for ten or a dozen years in any country, and should preserve so exact a discipline in his troops, and so regular a disposition in his garrisons that no insurrection had ever been raised, or even murmur heard against his administration: can it be asserted that the people, who in their hearts abhor his treason, have tacitly consented to his authority, and promised him allegiance, merely because, from necessity, they live under his dominion? Suppose again their native prince restored, by means of an army, which he levies in foreign countries: they receive him with joy and exultation, and shew plainly with what reluctance they had submitted to any other yoke. I may now ask, upon what foundation the prince's title stands? Not on popular consent surely: for though the people willingly acquiesce in his authority, they never imagine that their consent made him sovereign. They consent; because they apprehend him to be already by birth, their lawful sovereign. And as to that tacit consent, which may now be inferred from their living under his dominion, this is no more than what they formerly gave to the tyrant and usurper.

When we assert, that all lawful government arises from the consent of the people, we certainly do them a great deal more honour than they deserve, or even expect and desire from us. After the ROMAN dominions became too unwieldy for the republic to govern them, the people over the whole known world were extremely grateful to AUGUSTUS for that authority which, by violence, he had established over them; and they shewed an equal disposition to submit to the successor whom he left them by his last will and testament. It was afterwards their misfortune, that there never was, in one family, any long regular succession; but that their line of princes was continually broken, either by private assassinations or public rebellions. The *prætorian* bands, on the failure of every family, set up one emperor; the legions in the East a second; those in GERMANY, perhaps a third; and the sword alone could decide the controversy. The condition of the people in that mighty monarchy was to be lamented, not because the choice of the emperor was never left to them, for that was impracticable, but because they never fell under any

succession of masters who might regularly follow each other. As to the violence, and wars, and bloodshed, occasioned by every new settlement, these were not blameable because they were inevitable.

The house of LANCASTER ruled in this island about sixty years; yet the partisans of the white rose seemed daily to multiply in ENGLAND. The present establishment has taken place during a still longer period. Have all views of right in another family been utterly extinguished, even though scarce any man now alive had arrived at the years of discretion when it was expelled, or could have consented to its dominion, or have promised it allegiance?—a sufficient indication, surely, of the general sentiment of mankind on this head. For we blame not the partisans of the abdicated family merely on account of the long time during which they have preserved their imaginary loyalty. We blame them for adhering to a family which we affirm has been justly expelled, and which, from the moment the new settlement took place, had forfeited all title to authority.

But would we have a more regular, at least a more philosophical, refutation of this principle of an original contract, or popular consent, perhaps the following observations may suffice.

All *moral* duties may be divided into two kinds. The *first* are those to which men are impelled by a natural instinct or immediate propensity which operates on them, independent of all ideas of obligation, and of all views either to public or private utility. Of this nature are love of children, gratitude to benefactors, pity to the unfortunate. When we reflect on the advantage which results to society from such humane instincts, we pay them the just tribute of moral approbation and esteem: but the person actuated by them feels their power and influence antecedent to any such reflection.

The *second* kind of moral duties are such as are not supported by any original instinct of nature, but are performed entirely from a sense of obligation, when we consider the necessities of human society, and the impossibility of supporting it, if these duties were neglected. It is thus *justice*, or a regard to the property of others, *fidelity*, or the observance of promises, become obligatory, and acquire an authority over mankind. For as it is evident that every man loves himself better than any other person, he is naturally impelled to extend his acquisitions as much as possible; and nothing can restrain him in this propensity but reflection and experience, by which he learns the pernicious effects of that license, and the total dissolution of society which must ensue from it. His original inclination, therefore, or instinct, is here checked and restrained by a subsequent judgment or observation.

The case is precisely the same with the political or civil duty of *allegiance* as with the natural duties of justice and fidelity. Our primary instincts lead us either to indulge ourselves in unlimited freedom, or to seek dominion over others; and it is reflection only which engages us to sacrifice such strong passions to the interests of peace and public order. A small degree of experience and observation suffices to teach us, that society cannot possibly be maintained without the authority of magistrates, and that this authority must soon fall into contempt where exact obedience is not paid to it. The observation of these general and obvious interests is the source of all allegiance, and of that moral obligation which we attribute to it.

What necessity, therefore, is there to found the duty of *allegiance* or obedience to magistrates on that of *fidelity* or a regard to promises, and to suppose, that it is the consent of each individual which subjects him to government, when it appears that both allegiance and fidelity stand precisely on the same foundation, and are both submitted to by mankind, on account of the apparent interests and necessities of human society? We are bound to obey our sovereign, it is said, because we have given a tacit promise to that purpose. But why are we bound to observe our promise? It must here be asserted, that the commerce and intercourse of mankind, which are of such mighty advantage, can have no security where men pay no regard to their engagements. In like manner, may it be said that men could not live at all in society, at least in a civilized society, without laws, and magistrates, and judges, to prevent the encroachments of the strong upon the weak, of the violent upon the just and equitable. The obligation

to allegiance being of like force and authority with the obligation to fidelity, we gain nothing by resolving the one into the other. The general interests or necessities of society are sufficient to establish both.

If the reason be asked of that obedience, which we are bound to pay to government, I readily answer, *Because society could not otherwise subsist*; and this answer is clear and intelligible to all mankind. Your answer is, *Because we should keep our word*. But besides, that no body, till trained in a philosophical system, can either comprehend or relish this answer; besides this, I say, you find yourself embarrassed when it is asked, *Why we are bound to keep our word?* Nor can you give any answer but what would, immediately, without any circuit, have accounted for our obligation to allegiance.

But *to whom is allegiance due? And who is our lawful sovereign?* This question is often the most difficult of any, and liable to infinite discussions. When people are so happy that they can answer, *Our present sovereign, who inherits, in a direct line, from ancestors that have governed us for many ages*, this answer admits of no reply, even though historians, in tracing up to the remotest antiquity the origin of that royal family, may find, as commonly happens, that its first authority was derived from usurpation and violence. It is confessed that private justice, or the abstinence from the properties of others, is a most cardinal virtue. Yet reason tells us that there is no property in durable objects, such as lands or houses, when carefully examined in passing from hand to hand, but must, in some period, have been founded on fraud and injustice. The necessities of human society, neither in private nor public life, will allow of such an accurate inquiry; and there is no virtue or moral duty but what may, with facility, be refined away, if we indulge a false philosophy in sifting and scrutinizing it, by every captious rule of logic, in every light or position in which it may be placed.

The questions with regard to private property have filled infinite volumes of law and philosophy, if in both we add the commentators to the original text; and in the end, we may safely pronounce, that many of the rules there established are uncertain, ambiguous, and arbitrary. The like opinion may be formed with regard to the succession and rights of princes, and forms of government. Several cases no doubt occur, especially in the infancy of any constitution, which admit of no determination from the laws of justice and equity; and our historian RAPIN[1] pretends, that the controversy between EDWARD the Third and PHILIP DE VALOIS was of this nature, and could be decided only by an appeal to heaven, that is, by war and violence.

Who shall tell me, whether GERMANICUS or DRUSUS ought to have succeeded to TIBERIUS, had he died while they were both alive, without naming any of them for his successor? Ought the right of adoption to be received as equivalent to that of blood, in a nation where it had the same effect in private families, and had already, in two instances, taken place in the public? Ought GERMANICUS to be esteemed the elder son, because he was born before DRUSUS; or the younger, because he was adopted after the birth of his brother? Ought the right of the elder to be regarded in a nation, where he had no advantage in the succession of private families? Ought the ROMAN empire at that time to be deemed hereditary, because of two examples; or ought it, even so early, to be regarded as belonging to the stronger, or to the present possessor, as being founded on so recent an usurpation?

COMMODUS mounted the throne after a pretty long succession of excellent emperors, who had acquired their title, not by birth, or public election, but by the fictitious rite of adoption. That bloody debauchee being murdered by a conspiracy, suddenly formed between his wench and her gallant, who happened at that time to be *Prætorian Præfect*; these immediately deliberated about choosing a master to human kind, to speak in the style of those ages; and they cast their eyes on PERTINAX. Before the tyrant's death was known, the *Præfect* went secretly to that senator, who, on the appearance of the soldiers, imagined that his execution had been ordered by COMMODUS. He was immediately saluted emperor by the officer and his attendants, cheerfully proclaimed by the populace, unwillingly submitted to by the guards, formally recognized by the senate, and passively received by the provinces and armies of the empire.

The discontent of the *Prætorian* bands broke out in a sudden sedition, which occasioned the murder of that excellent prince; and the world being now without a master, and without government, the guards thought proper to set the empire formally to sale. JULIAN, the purchaser, was proclaimed by the soldiers, recognized by the senate, and submitted to by the people; and must also have been submitted to by the provinces, had not the envy of the legions begotten opposition and resistance. PESCENNIUS NIGER in SYRIA elected himself emperor, gained the tumultuary consent of his army, and was attended with the secret good-will of the senate and people of ROME. ALBINUS in BRITAIN found an equal right to set up his claim; but SEVERUS, who governed PANNONIA, prevailed in the end above both of them. That able politician and warrior, finding his own birth and dignity too much inferior to the imperial crown, professed, at first, an intention only of revenging the death of PERTINAX. He marched as general into ITALY, defeated JULIAN, and, without our being able to fix any precise commencement even of the soldiers' consent, he was from necessity acknowledged emperor by the senate and people, and fully established in his violent authority, by subduing NIGER and ALBINUS.

[...]

Frequent instances of a like nature occur in the history of the emperors; in that of ALEXANDER'S successors; and of many other countries: nor can any thing be more unhappy than a despotic government of this kind; where the succession is disjointed and irregular, and must be determined, on every vacancy, by force or election. In a free government, the matter is often unavoidable, and is also much less dangerous. The interests of liberty may there frequently lead the people, in their own defence, to alter the succession of the crown. And the constitution, being compounded of parts, may still maintain a sufficient stability, by resting on the

---

[1] [René Rapin (1621–87) was a French Jesuit and writer. The controversy alluded to here concerned the succession to the French throne.]

aristocratical or democratical members, though the monarchical be altered, from time to time, in order to accommodate it to the former.

In an absolute government, when there is no legal prince who has a title to the throne, it may safely be determined to belong to the first occupant. Instances of this kind are but too frequent, especially in the eastern monarchies. When any race of princes expires, the will or destination of the last sovereign will be regarded as a title. Thus the edict of LOUIS the XIVth, who called the bastard princes to the succession in case of the failure of all the legitimate princes, would, in such an event, have some authority. Thus the will of CHARLES the Second disposed of the whole SPANISH monarchy. The cession of the ancient proprietor, especially when joined to conquest, is likewise deemed a good title. The general obligation, which binds us to government, is the interest and necessities of society; and this obligation is very strong. The determination of it to this or that particular prince, or form of government, is frequently more uncertain and dubious. Present possession has considerable authority in these cases, and greater than in private property; because of the disorders which attend all revolutions and changes of government.

We shall only observe, before we conclude, that though an appeal to general opinion may justly, in the speculative sciences of metaphysics, natural philosophy, or astronomy, be deemed unfair and inconclusive, yet in all questions with regard to morals, as well as criticism, there is really no other standard, by which any controversy can ever be decided. And nothing is a clearer proof, that a theory of this kind is erroneous, than to find, that it leads to paradoxes repugnant to the common sentiments of mankind, and to the practice and opinion of all nations and all ages. The doctrine, which founds all lawful government on an *original contract*, or consent of the people, is plainly of this kind; nor has the most noted of its partisans, in prosecution of it, scrupled to affirm, *that absolute monarchy is inconsistent with civil society, and so can be no form of civil government at all; and that the supreme power in a state cannot take from any man, by taxes and impositions, any part of*

his property, without his own consent or that of his representatives. What authority any moral reasoning can have, which leads into opinions so wide of the general practice of mankind, in every place but this single kingdom, it is easy to determine.

The only passage I meet with in antiquity, where the obligation of obedience to government is ascribed to a promise, is in PLATO'S *Crito*; where SOCRATES refuses to escape from prison, because he had tacitly promised to obey the laws. Thus he builds a *Tory* consequence of passive obedience on a *Whig* foundation of the original contract.

New discoveries are not to be expected in these matters. If scarce any man, till very lately, ever imagined that government was founded on compact, it is certain that it cannot, in general, have any such foundation....

DISCUSSION QUESTIONS

1. What reasons does Hume offer for thinking that no contract or agreement could have allowed for general submission to authority?

2. What considerations does Hume bring to bear on the issue of conditional consent? That is, why does Hume think we should be skeptical of such theories?

3. Ultimately, in Hume's opinion, why are we obligated to obey the government? Does his response to this question retain its force when given as a response to the question, "Why should *I* obey the government?" In formulating an answer to this question, consider the Fool's Objection from the selection by Hobbes, or the Ring of Gyges myth from the selection by Plato.

4. What point does Hume mean to make in using the example of the poor peasant or artisan? How do you think Locke would respond to this example?

9

A. John Simmons, selection from *Moral Principles and Political Obligations* (1979)

SOURCE

Simmons, A. John. *Moral Principles and Political Obligations*. Copyright © 1979 by Princeton University Press. Reprinted by permission of Princeton University Press.

IV.ii. Tacit Consent

Since the earliest consent theories it has of course been recognized that "express consent" is not a suitably general ground for political obligation. The paucity of express consentors is painfully apparent. Most of us have never been faced with a situation where express consent to a government's authority was even appropriate, let alone actually performed such an act. And while I think that most of us agree that express consent is a ground of political obligation (and certainly this is my view), the real battleground for consent theory is generally admitted to be the notion of tacit consent. It is on this leg that consent theory must lean most heavily if it is to succeed.

Thomas Hobbes noted that "signs of contract are either express or by inference,"[1] but he had little clear to say about this distinction. Discussions of tacit consent since that time have generally added only confusions to Hobbes's lack of clarity. Certainly Locke's discussion of tacit consent has puzzled many political philosophers by stretching the notion of consent far beyond the breaking point. But we must not be led by these confusions to believe that there is no such thing as tacit consent. On the contrary, genuine instances of tacit consent, at least in nonpolitical contexts, are relatively frequent.

[1] Hobbes, *Leviathan*, chap. 14.

Consider: Chairman Jones stands at the close of the company's board meeting and announces, "There will be a meeting of the board at which attendance will be mandatory next Tuesday at 8:00, rather than at our usual Thursday time. Any objections?" The board members remain silent. In remaining silent and inactive, they have all tacitly consented to the chairman's proposal to make a schedule change (assuming, of course, that none of the members is asleep, or failed to hear, etc.). As a result, they have given the chairman the right (which he does not normally have) to reschedule the meeting, and they have undertaken the obligation to attend at the new time.

Now this example should allow us to elaborate more constructively on the conditions necessary for tacit consent. First, consent here is called "tacit" not because it has a different sort of significance than express consent, nor because it, e.g., binds less completely (as Locke seems to have thought). Consent is called tacit when it is given by remaining silent and inactive; it is not express, explicit, directly and distinctly expressed by action, but rather is expressed by the failure to do certain things. But tacit consent is nonetheless given or expressed. Silence after a call for objections can be just as much an expression of consent as shouting "aye" after a call for ayes and nays. Calling consent tacit, then, points only to the special mode of its expression.

But under what conditions can silence be taken as a sign of consent? At least three spring quickly to mind.[1] (1) The situation must be such that it is perfectly clear that consent is appropriate and that the individual is aware of this. This includes the requirement that the potential consentor be awake and aware of what is happening. (2) There must be a definite period of reasonable duration when objections or expressions of dissent are invited or clearly appropriate, and the acceptable means of expressing this dissent must be understood by or made known to the potential consentor. (3) The

point at which expressions of dissent are no longer acceptable must be obvious or made clear in some way to the potential consentor. These three conditions seem to jointly guarantee that the potential consentor's silence is *significant*. For they show that the silence does not result simply from (1) a failure to grasp the nature of the situation, (2) a lack of understanding of proper procedures, or (3) a misunderstanding about how long one has to decide whether or not to dissent. If any one of the conditions is not satisfied, then silence may indicate a breakdown in communication of one of these kinds. In that case, silence could not be taken as a sign of consent.

Our example of the board meeting meets these three conditions, although the time period specified in condition 3 is fairly informally and loosely set. In addition, of course, the example seems to meet the more general conditions for the possibility of consent of any sort. But while in most circumstances these conditions are, I think, sufficient, I want to suggest two additional conditions which will be important to the political applications of theory of tacit consent: (4) the means acceptable for indicating dissent must be reasonable and reasonably easily performed; and (5) the consequences of dissent cannot be extremely detrimental to the potential consentor. The violation of either condition 4 or 5 will mean that silence cannot be taken as a sign of consent, even though the other conditions for consent and tacit consent are satisfied.

We can easily imagine situations which would fail to satisfy our new conditions 4 and 5. For instance, if Chairman Jones had, in our previous example, said, "Anyone with an objection to my proposal will kindly so indicate by lopping off his arm at the elbow," both conditions would be violated, as they would be if dissent could only be expressed by resignation and the forfeit of company benefits, etc. Less dramatically, perhaps, condition 4 alone would be violated if board meeting traditions demanded that dissent could only be indicated by turning a perfect back handspring. And if the invariable consequence of objecting at a board meeting was dismissal and imprisonment (Chairman Jones

---

[1] Some of the following remarks are suggested by J.F.M. Hunter's remarks in "The Logic of Social Contracts," *Dialogue* 5 (June 1966).

happens also to be the local magistrate), our condition 5 would not be satisfied.

In any of these cases, silence cannot be taken as a sign of consent. As with all of the previous conditions, it is not possible to draw lines very clearly here; but if, say, the obstacles to consent were only the board members' nervousness about talking to Chairman Jones, or the fear that he might not give them a lift to the train station after the meeting, the situation would pretty clearly not violate conditions 4 and 5.

Of our two new conditions, condition 4, at least, seems unobjectionable. It guarantees that the failure to dissent is not due to an inability to dissent. But condition 5 may be more controversial. For it may seem that where the potential consentor remains silent because of fear or coercion, genuine consent is still given, but is simply a case of genuine consent which is not *binding*. I am not really sure how we could choose between calling a coerced act of consent "genuine but nonbinding" and saying that it is "not really consent at all." Ordinary language, for instance, seems to favor neither option over the other. I have chosen the latter description in order to emphasize the fact that we understand consent to involve a choice freely made (where this "freedom" includes freedom from the immediate threat of dire consequences). But both options agree that coerced consent generates no *obligations*. And because we are concerned here with a consent theory account of political *obligation*, how we choose to handle coerced consent is of little moment to our present task. I will insist, then, on the satisfaction of conditions 1 through 5 inclusive, in order for silence to be taken as a sign of consent. Of course, these conditions need not be satisfied if the consentor somehow *confirms* that the significance of his silence is meant to be the giving of tacit consent. But such confirmations are rarely available and more rarely sought in the specific context with which we will be dealing, namely, that setting in which tacit consent might be given to a government's authority.

I have no doubt, of course, that the expression "tacit consent" is sometimes used in ways that do not conform to the account of tacit consent sketched above; my intention was not primarily to catalog all of the ordinary uses of the expression. Rather, I have tried to present what seems to me to be the only ordinary notion of tacit consent that can be useful to the consent theorist. This account stresses particularly the intentionality of even tacit consent. Only if tacit consent is treated, as I have treated it here, as a *deliberate* undertaking can the real force of consent theory be preserved. For consent theory's account of political obligation is appealing only if consent remains a clear ground of obligation, and if the method of consent protects the individual from becoming politically bound unknowingly or against his will. And it seems clear that these essential features of a consent theory cannot be preserved if we allow that tacit consent can be given unintentionally.

IV.iii. Locke and the Failure of Tacit Consent

Now that we have a reasonably clear notion of tacit consent as a tool, we can approach Locke's account of tacit consent somewhat more confidently. Locke's famous discussion of tacit consent begins as follows: "The difficulty is, what ought to be looked upon as a tacit consent, and how far it binds, i.e., how far any one shall be looked on to have consented, and thereby submitted to any government, where he has made no expressions of it at all."[1] It seems that tacit consent need not really be expressed in the strict sense at all for Locke. Tacit consent can be understood or inferred by the observer, quite independent of the consentor's intentions or awareness that he is consenting. This is borne out by Locke's answer to his question: "And to this I say that every man, that hath any possession, or enjoyment, of any part of the dominions of any government, doth thereby give his tacit consent, and is as far forth obliged to obedience to the laws of that government...."[2]

Now I have already suggested that tacit consent should not be taken by the consent theorist to be an "unexpressed" consent; calling consent tacit on

---

[1] Locke, *Second Treatise of Government*, sec. 119.
[2] Ibid.

my account specifies its mode of expression, not its lack of expression. But this is not the only thing which makes Locke's account of consent seem suspicious. For Locke, owning land in the state, lodging in a house in the state, traveling on a highway in the state, all are ways in which one gives his consent. In fact, signs of consent go "as far as the very being of any one within the territories of that government."[1] Now, it is important to understand that Locke is not just saying that these are ways in which one might give his consent without putting it into words; that, of course, would be quite unobjectionable since nearly any act can, given suitable background conditions including the right sorts of conventions, be one whereby a man expresses his consent. Locke is saying rather that, in modern states at least, these acts necessarily constitute the giving of tacit consent. In other words, such acts are always signs of consent, regardless of the intentions of the actor or his special circumstances.

It is easy to see that this sort of "consent" violates (within modern states) nearly all of the general conditions necessary for an act to be an act of giving consent, tacit or otherwise. Most importantly, of course, Locke's suggestion that binding consent can be given unintentionally is a patent absurdity. The weakness of Locke's notion of consent has even led some to question Locke's traditionally accepted status as a consent theorist (indeed, as the classic consent theorist). The most interesting feature of Hanna Pitkin's "Obligation and Consent" is precisely such a questioning of Locke's devotion to personal consent as the ground of political obligation. I want to summarize her argument briefly, since analyzing it will lead us, I think, to a consideration of one of the fundamental confusions about tacit consent that has plagued discussions of this topic.

Pitkin argues that in widening his definition of consent so as "to make it almost unrecognizable," Locke seems to make a citizen's consent virtually automatic. "Why," she asks, "all the stress on consent if it is to include everything we do?"[2] Among

other things, this forces us to conclude that residence within the territory of the worst sort of tyranny would constitute consent to it, which conclusion seems far indeed from Locke's intentions. But, of course, Locke holds that we cannot become bound to such a government even if we try.[3] How then can he reconcile this position with his claim that residence always constitutes consent? Pitkin answers that Locke intends tacit consent to be understood as a special consent given only to "the terms of the original contract which the founders of the commonwealth made."[4] In this manner, residing in or using roads within the territories of a government that is tyrannical or is otherwise acting ultra vires does not constitute tacit consent to the rule of that government. Only when the government acts within its assigned limits do these acts constitute consent.

Regardless of the merits of this argument as an exercise in Locke scholarship, the conclusion Pitkin draws is an interesting one. She maintains that, insofar as consent is virtually automatic in Locke, Locke did not really take personal consent seriously as a ground of political obligation. Rather, she interprets Locke as holding that "you are obligated to obey because of certain characteristics of the government—that it is acting within the bounds of a trusteeship based on an original contract."[5] Further, since she reads Locke as holding that "the terms of the original contract are ... self-evident truths," Locke can be understood as claiming that our obligations in fact arise from the government's conformity to the only possible terms of a not necessarily actual (i.e., possibly hypothetical) contract.

The interesting aspect of this conclusion is the way in which it ties Locke to two contemporary methods for approaching these political problems. First, it brings Locke closer to what is often called a theory of "hypothetical contract," whereby the quality of government is determined in reference to the limits which would be placed on it by rational and self-interested original contractors. This sort of theory has its most mature formulation in John

---

[1] Ibid.
[2] Hanna Pitkin, "Obligation and Consent—I," *American Political Science Review* 59 (December 1965): 995.

[3] Locke, *Second Treatise of Government*, sec. 23
[4] "Obligation and Consent—I," p. 995.
[5] Ibid., p. 996.

Rawls's *A Theory of Justice*. Second, Pitkin makes Locke appear more like contemporary writers who de-emphasize individuals' histories in a theory of political obligation, to stress instead the quality of the government as the source from which our political obligations arise.

This reading of Locke is obviously inconsistent with the radical individualism and voluntarism so evident throughout the *Second Treatise*. But my belief that Pitkin's reading is mistaken is based on more than a desire to preserve intact the Lockean spirit. I think that the oddity of Pitkin's interpretation can be explained by pointing to a single mistake which she makes in understanding Locke's position. The mistake is made when Pitkin concludes that the obligation to obey the government must derive from the quality of the government in question. This conclusion is essentially drawn from two sound premises: first, residence for Locke always constitutes consent; and second, for Locke we are bound to obey good governments but not bad ones. Pitkin concludes that consent must be essentially irrelevant to our political bonds in Locke's theory, for it seems inconsistent to hold all of the following: (1) By residing within their territories, we give our consent even to bad governments; (2) we are not obligated to bad governments; and (3) consent is the ground of political obligation. To preserve consistency in Locke, Pitkin sacrifices (3); but she seems to ignore the possibility that consent might be only a necessary, rather than a sufficient, condition for the generation of political obligations. Let me clarify this observation by again describing a parallel case involving promises.

I make two promises to a friend—one to help him commit murder most foul, the other to give him half my yearly income. It is usually maintained, and it is certainly my belief, that while both promises are real promises, the latter obligates me while the former does not. But following reasoning similar to Pitkin's, we ought to conclude from this that the obligation I am under to keep this latter promise arises solely from the morally commendable (or at least not morally prohibited) quality of the promised act. But this conclusion would be false. The

obligation arises solely from my having promised. The moral quality of the act merely prevents one of the promises (the one to commit murder) from obligating me. But in no way is the morally acceptable quality of the other promised act the *ground* of my obligation to perform it.

Similarly, we might hold that consent to the authority of a tyrannical government does not bind one, just as a promise to act immorally does not bind one. And while I have suggested earlier that I think that consent to a tyranny can sometimes bind one, Locke's position, I maintain, is exactly that described above. Locke holds that our consent only binds us when it is given to good governments. But consent is still the sole ground of the obligation. The quality of the government is, for Locke, merely a feature relevant to the binding force of the consent. This he makes quite clear, I think, in Chapter IV: "For a man, not having the power over his own life, cannot, by compact, or his own consent, enslave himself to any one, nor put himself under the absolute, arbitrary power of another...."[1]

Here Locke asserts that while a man may consent to an arbitrary government's rule, he is never bound to that government, for becoming so bound would involve disposing of rights which he does not possess. This suggests to me that Locke's doctrine of personal consent can with perfect consistency be joined to the claims that residence in any state constitutes consent and that we are only bound to good governments. All that is needed is the additional premise that consent is not always sufficient to obligate. In overlooking Locke's use of this premise, Pitkin has been led to misinterpret Locke's account of political obligation, emphasizing the quality of the government over the consensual act.

I do not, of course, deny that in saying that a man who gives his tacit consent is "as far forth obliged to obedience," Locke appears to make consent sufficient for obligation. I suggest, however, that we understand him here to be thinking specifically of good governments, or, at worst, to be suffering from momentary carelessness. For when he begins seriously to

[1] Locke, *Second Treatise of Government*, sec. 23.

consider tyrannical and arbitrary forms of government later in the *Second Treatise*, Locke frequently repeats his claim that we cannot bind ourselves to such governments by any means, compact included,[1] although we can certainly consent to such governments. Consent in Locke, then, cannot be sufficient always to generate obligations.

My suggestion is that we can believe Locke when he asserts that he holds personal consent to be the sole ground of political obligation. His claims on this point seem to be consistent, if perhaps mistaken. Still, one cannot help but be suspicious, as Pitkin certainly was, of a consent theory in which consent seems to fade into whatever is necessary to obligate everyone living under a good government. And these suspicions may again lead us to believe that Locke was really only halfhearted in his insistence on personal consent as the source of our political bonds.

I would like to suggest, however, that these suspicions can be allayed somewhat by understanding Locke as having become muddled about a distinction that has been similarly missed by many political theorists down to the present day. That distinction is between acts which are "signs of consent" and acts which "imply consent." In calling an act a "sign of consent," I mean that because of the context in which the act was performed, including the appropriate conventions (linguistic or otherwise), the act counts as an expression of the actor's intention to consent; thus, all genuine consensual acts are the givings of "signs of consent." But in saying that an act "implies consent," we mean neither that the actor intended to consent nor that the act would normally be taken as an attempt to consent. There are three ways in which an act might be said to "imply consent" in the sense I have in mind.

1. An act may be such that it leads us to conclude that the actor was in an appropriate frame of mind to, or had attitudes which would lead him to, consent if suitable conditions arose. This conclusion may be expressed by the conditional: if he

had been asked to (or if an appropriate situation had otherwise arisen), he would have consented.

2. An act may be such that it "commits" the actor to consenting. By this I mean that the act would be pointless or hopelessly stupid unless the actor was fully prepared to consent; the act commits the actor "rationally" to giving his consent. Thus, for example, discoursing at great length on how a man would be an idiot not to consent to be governed by the government would, under normal circumstances, imply consent to be so governed, in sense 2 (as well, perhaps, as in sense 1).

3. An act may be such that it binds the actor morally to the same performance to which he would be bound if he had in fact consented. I may do something which is not itself an act of consent, but which nonetheless binds me as if I had consented; after performing the act, it would be wrong (ceteris paribus) for me not to do those things which my actual consent would have bound me to do. Consider a simple case like joining a game of baseball. Many writers have held that although in joining the game I do nothing which could be construed as giving my consent (tacit or otherwise) to be governed by the umpire's decisions, nonetheless, by participating in the activity, I may become bound to be so governed, just as I would be if I had in fact consented. The analysis of the ground of this moral bond, however, would appeal to something other than the performance of a deliberate undertaking, focusing instead on, e.g., the receipt of benefits from or the taking advantage of some established scheme.

All of these three are types of acts which I will say "imply consent," though none of them is normally a "sign of consent." Each is closely related to genuine consent in some way without in fact being consent. I believe that in his peculiar notion of tacit consent Locke has actually, but unknowingly, developed a notion of acts which may very well "imply consent" in sense 3. Tacit consent is for Locke, remember, a consent which is not expressed but which is given in the performance of certain acts; in particular, Locke specifies the "enjoyments" of certain benefits granted by the state as being the sorts of acts in which we are interested. These "enjoyments" are seen by Locke to

---

[1] Ibid., secs. 135, 137, 149, 171, 172.

"imply consent" in the sense that it would be morally wrong for us to accept these enjoyments while refusing to accept the government's authority. When we enjoy the public highways, owning land, police protection, etc., our "acts of enjoyment," though not expressions of our consent, nonetheless are thought by Locke to "imply" our consent by binding us to obedience as if we had in fact consented.

This may seem at first a very implausible position, for it appears to make the generation of very important obligations hang on the performance of very unimportant "acts of enjoyment," such as traveling on public highways. But at least this much can be said in Locke's defense: he was clearly aware that the various enjoyments he mentions do not come packaged separately. When one owns land or travels the highways in a state, one does not *just* enjoy those simple benefits. More importantly, one enjoys the benefits of the rule of law, police protection, protection by the armed forces, etc. And because these benefits are unavoidable for anyone within the government's effective domain, Locke recognizes that "the very being of any one within the territories" of the government will serve quite as well as any of the more specific "enjoyments" he mentions; one receives this important package of the benefits of government simply by being within "the parts whereof the force of its law extends."[1] Thus, the political obligations of "tacit consentors" may not arise from such insignificant enjoyments as it might at first have seemed.

But of course my chief purpose here is to examine Locke's *analysis* of this ground of political obligation, and it is in this analysis that the most obvious problems arise. For in his dedication to personal consent as the sole ground of political obligation, Locke confusedly labels the enjoyments of the benefits of government as a special sort of consensual act—"tacit" consent. But we have seen that while Locke's "enjoyments" might "imply consent," and might therefore have "something to do with" personal consent, they are not "signs of consent." Such enjoyments are not normally deliberate

undertakings. In trying to rob consent of its intentionality, Locke succeeds only in undermining the appeal of his own consent theory, with its dedication to the thesis that only through deliberate undertakings can we become politically bound.

My suggestion is that none of Locke's "consent-implying enjoyments" is in fact a genuine consensual act. In analyzing any obligations which might arise from such enjoyments, we do not appeal to a principle of consent. Rather, such obligations would arise, if at all, because of considerations of fairness or gratitude. Locke's primary error, then, seems to lie in his confusion of consent with other grounds which may be sufficient to generate obligations, grounds which may at best be called "consent-implying."

But if Locke was confused about this distinction between "signs of consent" and "consent-implying" acts, he is certainly not alone. Political theorists have remained confused on the same point for the nearly three hundred years since Locke's groundbreaking confusion. Over and over it is claimed that voting in an election, running for political office, applying for a passport, etc. are signs of consent to the political institutions of the state which bind the actor accordingly. Alexander Meiklejohn[2] and Alan Gewirth[3] both seem to argue in this way. But perhaps the best contemporary example of this confusion surfaces in the second edition of J.P. Plamenatz's *Consent, Freedom, and Political Obligation*. Plamenatz, after avoiding many of these confusions in the body of his book, observes in his apologetic "Postscript to the Second Edition" that certain acts "signify" consent without being simple "expressions" of consent. He is concerned particularly with voting:

> If Smith were in fact elected, it would be odd
> to say of anyone who had voted for him that
> he did not consent to his holding office....

[1] Ibid., sec. 122.

[2] Meiklejohn, *Free Speech and Its Relation to Self-Government* (Harper & Bros., 1948), pp. 14, 11.
[3] Alan Gewirth, "Political Justice," in R.B. Brandt (ed.), *Social Justice* (Prentice-Hall, 1962), p. 129.

Where there is an established process of election to an office, then, provided the election is free, anyone who takes part in the process consents to the authority of whoever is elected to the office.[1]

And beyond just voting, people can be properly said to consent to a political system simply "by taking part in its processes."[2]

But if my account of consent has been correct, all of these observations must be mistaken. For while political participation may "imply consent" (or might *under special arrangements* be a sign of consent), it is not under current arrangements in most states a sign of consent. One may, and probably the average man does, register and vote with only minimal awareness that one is participating at all, and with no intention whatsoever of consenting to anything. Talk of consent in such situations can be no more than metaphorical.

It is easy to be misled, as Plamenatz probably was, by what I will call the "attitudinal" sense of "consent"; "consent" in this sense is merely having an attitude of approval or dedication. And certainly it would be odd (though not inconceivable) if a man who ran for public office did not "consent" to the political system in this attitudinal sense, or if the man who voted for him did not "consent" to his holding office. Voting, after all, is normally at least in part a sign of approval. But this sense of "consent" is quite irrelevant to our present discussion, where we are concerned exclusively with consent in the "occurrence" sense, i.e., with consent as an act which may generate obligations. An attitude of approval or dedication is completely irrelevant to the rights and obligations of the citizen who has it. When a man consents, he has consented and may be bound accordingly, regardless of how he feels about what he has consented to. It is my belief that confusions about this attitudinal–occurrence

distinction, conjoined with similar failures to distinguish signs of consent from consent-implying acts, are responsible for most of the mistakes made in discussions of consent theory from Locke down to contemporary writers.

All of this has been leading, of course, to the conclusion that tacit consent must meet the same fate as express consent concerning its suitability as a general ground of political obligation. For it seems clear that very few of us have ever tacitly consented to the government's authority in the sense developed in this essay; the situations appropriate for such consent simply do not arise frequently. Without major alterations in modern political processes and conventions, consent theory's big gun turns out to be of woefully small caliber. While consent, be it tacit or express, may still be the firmest ground of political obligation (in that people who have consented probably have fewer doubts about their obligations than others), it must be admitted that in most modern states consent will only bind the smallest minority of citizens to obedience. Only attempts to expand the notion of tacit consent beyond proper limits will allow consent to appear to be a suitably general ground of political obligation.

And while we have admitted that Locke does attempt such an illegitimate expansion, we can, from another vantage point, see that Locke was not completely confused in this attempt. For Locke's unconscious transition to "consent-implying" acts as grounds of obligation includes the important (though unstated) recognition that deliberate undertakings, such as promises or consensual acts, may not be necessary for the generation of political obligations; other sorts of acts may serve as well, in spite of their not being genuine acts of consent. This recognition, however, cannot form a part of a consent theory, with its insistence on consent as the sole ground of political obligation.

But it is nonetheless an important insight. The "enjoyments" of benefits of government (which Locke mistakenly classifies as acts of tacit consenting) may very well generate political obligations, as Locke believed. These obligations would not, however, fall under principles of fidelity or

---

[1] J.P. Plamenatz, *Consent, Freedom, and Political Obligation*, 2nd ed. (Oxford University Press, 1960), pp. 168, 170.

[2] Ibid., p. 171.

consent. There are, of course, other sorts of obligations than those generated by consent, and Locke seems to rely on them while, as a consent theorist, officially denying their existence. Thus, some of Locke's consent-implying enjoyments might in fact bind us to political communities under a "principle of fair play," as developed by Hart[1] and Rawls;[2] or they might be thought to bind us under a principle of gratitude, as Plamenatz at one point suggests,[3] or under some other kind of principle of repayment. If so, then Locke's intuitions about obligation, and those of more recent consent theorists, may be essentially sound. Their mistakes may lie primarily in confusing obligation-generating acts with consensual acts,[4] and in overlooking the fact that the consent-implying status of an act is substantially irrelevant to the obligation it generates. Consent theory, then, while it surely fails to give a suitably general account of our political obligations, seems to point the way toward other avenues of inquiry which may prove more rewarding. We will turn our attention in Chapter V [of *Moral Principles and Political Obligations*] to one of these "avenues" (the principle of fair play) and in Chapter VII to the other (the principle of gratitude).

IV.iv. Tacit Consent and Residence

I have, to this point, said relatively little about a problem of tacit consent that lies at the heart of most contemporary works in consent theory. This is the problem of "tacit consent through residence." Locke, as we have observed, believed that residence was a sign of tacit consent. Similarly, Rousseau maintains that "when the State is instituted, residence constitutes consent: to dwell within its territory is to submit to the Sovereign."[5] And more recently, W.D. Ross has written that an "implicit promise to obey" is involved in permanent residence in a state.[6] We have, of course, argued that residence cannot reasonably be thought to constitute genuine consent (given, at least, the current state of political conventions). For it to do so, continued residence would have to be (among other things) a lack of response to a clearly presented "choice situation" allowing for consent or dissent. And clearly, no such choice is ever made available to most of us.

But Socrates has "the Laws" tell us in the *Crito* that Athens systematically did present such a "choice situation" to its people:

> We openly proclaim this principle, that any Athenian, on attaining to manhood and seeing for himself the political organization of the state and us its laws, is permitted, if he is not satisfied with us, to take his property and go away wherever he likes. If any of you chooses to go to one of our colonies, supposing that he should not be satisfied with us and the state, or to emigrate to any other country, not one of the laws hinders or prevents him from going away wherever he likes, without any loss of property. On the other hand, if any one of you stands his ground when he can see how we administer justice and the rest of our public organization, we hold that by doing so he has in fact undertaken to do anything that we tell him.[7]

Socrates, in this remarkably modern dialogue, develops a claim of tacit consent through residence which is much more plausible than the Locke-Rousseau conception (which does not have the benefit of such a choice situation). Our question becomes, then, is it possible through suitable alterations in our political processes to make residence a genuine sign of

[1] Hart, "Are There Any Natural Rights?" [reprinted in this volume, reading 24].
[2] John Rawls, "Legal Obligation and the Duty of Fair Play," in S. Hook (ed.), *Law and Philosophy* (New York University Press, 1964).
[3] Plamenatz, *Consent, Freedom, and Political Obligation*, p. 24.
[4] Hart seems to have this point in mind in "Are There Any Natural Rights?"
[5] Rousseau, *Social Contract*, IV.ii.
[6] Ross, *The Right and the Good*, p. 27.
[7] Plato, *Crito*, 51d-e.

tacit consent? The answer to this question should be of great importance to contemporary consent theorists like Joseph Tussman and Michael Walzer; for obviously, if one believes that consent is the only ground of political obligation, and that a government's legitimacy depends on the consent of its citizens, then the very possibility of legitimate government and widespread political obligation will turn on the possibility of instituting such a choice situation, to draw out the consent of the masses. But there are also other reasons for believing that a situation in which residence constituted consent would be a desirable one. For in that case, each citizen would know that he had consented to the government's authority, and one aspect of his doubts about how he ought to behave in matters political would be eliminated. Further, not only might the presentation of a choice situation heighten awareness of membership in a community, but presumably a general knowledge that such awareness was shared by one's fellow citizens would reap further benefits of trust and cooperation.

I mention these points only to emphasize the fact that the possibility of making residence a genuine sign of consent is not an idle issue. Now one very well-known argument concludes that mere residence could never be a sign of consent, and this conclusion presumably applies even to states which *do* formalize a choice between residence and emigration. This argument was first suggested by Hume, and has been used frequently since that time.[1] The argument runs as follows: residence can never constitute tacit consent to the government's rule, because it is always possible for self-professed revolutionaries, spies, anarchists, gangsters, and outlaws to reside within a state. But to suggest that such men consent, even tacitly, to the rule of a government they actively oppose seems ludicrous.

As popular as this argument has been, it seems to me to be obviously not to the point. Why exactly

does it seem ludicrous that an outlaw should be thought to consent to the government? Presumably, it is because he actively works against and clearly disapproves of the government. But if this is the reason, then the argument makes consent into an attitude rather than an act. That this is so can be seen in the fact that even if an outlaw *had* consented, it would seem just as odd to say that he consents to the government. The force of the argument derives from the apparent assumption that one who opposes the government cannot possibly have consented to it, no matter what he has done. But this assumption is clearly false. While it may be true that outlaws and spies do not "consent" in the "attitudinal sense" mentioned earlier (IV.iii), such "attitudinal consent" is irrelevant to the problems of political obligation and genuine consent. And even if the argument were that an outlaw would never, in a sane moment, consent (in the occurrence sense) sincerely, it could succeed only if we saw sincerity as essential to the success of an act of consent. But, of course, just as we can make binding promises with no intention of keeping them, we can perfectly well consent with no intention of allowing the exercise of the right we accord to another in consenting. The existence of outlaws, then, does not seem to endanger the attempt to show that residence could constitute consent, given suitable alterations in political conventions. For we must remember that in discussing the relation of consent to political obligation we are concerned only with the occurrence sense of consent.

We can, then, return to our original question: could a formal choice situation, like the one described by Socrates, make continued residence a sign of consent? Joseph Tussman has answered this question in the affirmative. As long as the situation makes it clear that one who remains a resident is aware of the significance of so remaining, and as long as there remains a genuine alternative to giving one's tacit consent, then residence will be a sign of consent. We should not be concerned, Tussman argues, that the alternative to consent, namely emigration, is such an unpleasant alternative. For "to say that consenting to the status of a member is involuntary because the alternative is

---

[1] See, e.g., Plamenatz, *Consent, Freedom, and Political Obligation*, p. 7, and Gough, *John Locke's Political Philosophy*, 2nd ed. (Oxford University Press, 1973), p. 70.

not as pleasant or convenient is simply to confuse convenience with necessity"; the unpleasantness of emigration "does not rob a deliberate choice of its voluntary character."[1]

A formal choice procedure, then, seems to satisfy the demands that consent be knowingly given and voluntary. Similarly, such a procedure could easily be structured to satisfy our first three conditions for giving consent through silence—a clear choice situation, a period where dissent is invited, and a limit to time for allowable dissent. But it is not so clear that our conditions 4 and 5 will be satisfied by such a procedure. These conditions state that silence or inactivity cannot be taken as a sign of consent if the means of indicating dissent are unreasonable or very difficult to perform or if the consequences of dissent are extremely detrimental to the consentor. Emigration is a difficult course which might well have disastrous consequences. Of course, even if conditions 4 and 5 were not met, we might still want to call the act of remaining in residence a "voluntary act"; but it is not clear that mere voluntariness is sufficient to make such an act a sign of consent, as Tussman apparently believes. One cannot but feel somewhat inclined to agree with Hume on this point:

> Can we seriously say, that a poor peasant or partizan has a free choice to leave his country, when he knows no foreign language or manners, and lives from day to day, by the small wages which he acquires. We may as well assert that a man, by remaining in a vessel, freely consents to the dominion of the master; though he was carried on board while asleep, and must leap into the ocean, and perish, the moment he leaves her.[2]

Does a man choose freely to remain in prison because he has a knife with which he can wound himself seriously enough to be removed to a hospital? These are strong metaphors, but it is easy to respond that our choice procedure can make provisions for dealing with such difficult cases. It might include, for instance, provisions for assisting the poor and oppressed (who would most desire and be least able to leave) in emigrating.

Would these sorts of provisions finally render continued residence a sign of tacit consent? There is one other problem which suggests that even with such provisions our choice procedure could not satisfy conditions 4 and 5 for tacit consent; and this problem cannot be circumvented by simply adding new provisions to the choice procedure. The problem is that it is precisely the most valuable "possessions" a man has that are often tied necessarily to his country of residence and cannot be taken from it. Most men will treasure home, family, and friends above all things. But these goods are not moveable property and cannot simply be packed on the boat with one's books and television set. Even if a man's home is in a tyrannical state, home can still be the most important thing in his life. And this places a very heavy weight on the side of continued residence. Emigration cannot be thought of as merely unpleasant or inconvenient for most of us; it may very well constitute a "disaster," if only a small one. And if that is true, it may well be that emigration routinely has consequences sufficiently unpleasant to make any formal political choice procedures fail our condition 5. In that case, we would be justified in concluding that no such procedure could ever allow us to take continued residence as a sign of tacit consent to the government's authority. The challenge, then, seems to remain open to the modern-day consent theorist to show us how government by consent can be made a reality. In any event, however, the more plausible alternative is to turn our attention from consent to other possible grounds of political obligation.

[1] Joseph Tussman, *Obligation and the Body Politic* (Oxford University Press, 1968), p. 38.
[2] David Hume, "Of the Original Contract" [reprinted in this volume, reading 8].

DISCUSSION QUESTIONS

1. Simmons claims that very few people ever actually perform an act of explicit or express consent to a government's authority. Do you agree with him?

2. Why might it matter that one was presented with a choice in terms of whether one is subject to a political authority?

3. Simmons ultimately claims that a choice procedure (such as the one mentioned by Socrates in the *Crito*) would not guarantee that one's silence or inactivity would count as an instance of implicit or tacit consent. What is his argument?

4. Simmons claims that actions such as voting do not count as expressions of consent. Why does he think this? Do you agree or disagree?

10

Carole Pateman, "Contract, the Individual, and Slavery" (1988)

Carole Pateman is a Distinguished Professor in the Department of Political Science at the University of California, Los Angeles. She is also an Honorary Professor at the School of European Studies, Cardiff University. In what follows, Pateman examines several traditional social contract theories and discusses the various ways in which they view women and their roles within society.

SOURCE

Pateman, Carole. Excerpts from *The Sexual Contract* by Carole Pateman. Copyright © 1988 by Carole Pateman. All rights reserved. Used with the permission of Stanford University Press, www.sup.org.

The classic social contract theorists assumed that individual attributes and social conditions always made it reasonable for an individual to give an affirmative answer to the fundamental question whether a relationship of subordination should be created through contract. The point of the story of the social contract is that, in the state of nature, freedom is so insecure that it is reasonable for individuals to subordinate themselves to the civil law of the state, or in Rousseau's version, to be subject to themselves collectively, in a participatory political association. The pictures of the state of nature and the stories of the social contract found in the classic texts vary widely, but despite their differences on many important issues, the classic contract theorists have a crucial feature in common. They all tell patriarchal stories.

Contract doctrine entails that there is only one, conventional, origin of political right, yet, except in Hobbes's theory where both sexes are pictured as naturally free and equal, the contract theorists also insist that men's right over women has a natural basis. Men alone have the attributes of free and equal "individuals." Relations of subordination between *men* must, if they are to be legitimate, originate in contract. Women are born into subjection. The classic writers were well aware of the significance of the assumptions of contract doctrine for the relation between the sexes. They could take nothing for granted when the premise of their arguments was potentially so subversive of all authority relations, including conjugal relations. The classic pictures of the state of nature take into account that human beings are sexually differentiated. Even in Hobbes's radically individualist version of the natural condition the sexes are distinguished. In contemporary discussions of the state of nature, however, this feature of human life is usually disregarded. The fact that "individuals" are all of the same sex is never mentioned; attention is focused instead on different conceptions of the masculine "individual."

The naturally free and equal (masculine) individuals who people the pages of the social contract theorists are a disparate collection indeed. They cover the spectrum from Rousseau's social beings to Hobbes's entities reduced to matter in motion, or, more recently, James Buchanan's reduction of individuals to preference and production functions; John Rawls manages to introduce both ends of the spectrum into his version of the contract story. Rousseau criticized his fellow social contract theorists for presenting individuals in the state of nature as lacking all social characteristics, and his criticism has been repeated many times. The attempt to set out the purely natural attributes of individuals is inevitably doomed to fail; all that is left if the attempt is consistent enough is a merely physiological, biological or reasoning entity, not a human being. In order to make their natural beings recognizable, social contract theorists smuggle social characteristics into the natural condition, or their readers supply what is missing. The form of the state or political association that a theorist wishes to justify also influences the "natural" characteristics that he gives to individuals; as Rawls stated recently, the aim of arguing from an original position, Rawls's equivalent to the state of nature, "is to get the desired solution."[1] What is not often recognized, however, is that the "desired solution" includes the sexual contract and men's patriarchal right over women.

Despite disagreement over what counts as a "natural" characteristic, features so designated are held to be common to all human beings. Yet almost all the classic writers held that natural capacities and attributes were sexually differentiated. Contemporary contract theorists implicitly follow their example, but this goes unnoticed because they subsume feminine beings under the apparently universal, sexually neuter category of the "individual." In the most recent rewriting of the social contract story, sexual relations have dropped from view because sexually differentiated individuals have disappeared. In *A Theory of Justice*, the parties in the original position are purely reasoning entities. Rawls follows Kant on this point, and Kant's view of the original contract differs from that of the other classic contract theorists, although (as I shall indicate in chapter 6 [of *The Sexual Contract*]) in some other respects his arguments resemble theirs. Kant does not offer a story about the origins of political right or suggest that, even hypothetically, an original agreement was once made. Kant is not dealing in this kind of political fiction. For Kant, the original contract is "merely an *idea* of reason,"[2] an idea necessary for an understanding of actual political institutions. Similarly, Rawls writes in his most recent discussion that his own argument "tries to draw solely upon basic intuitive ideas that are embedded in the political institutions of a constitutional democratic regime and the public traditions of their interpretation." As an idea of reason, rather than a political fiction, the original contract helps "us work out what we now think."[3] If Rawls is to show how free and equal parties, suitably situated, would agree to principles that are (pretty near to) those implicit in existing institutions, the appropriate idea of reason is required. The problem about political right faced by the classic contract theorists has disappeared. Rawls's task is to find a picture of an original position that will confirm "our" intuitions about existing institutions, which include patriarchal relations of subordination.

[1] J. Rawls, *A Theory of Justice* (Cambridge, MA: Harvard University Press, 1971), p. 141.

[2] I. Kant, *Political Writings*, ed. H. Reiss (Cambridge: Cambridge University Press, 1970), p. 79.

[3] J. Rawls, "Justice as Fairness: Political not Metaphysical," *Philosophy and Public Affairs* 14.3 (1985): 225, 238.

Rawls claims that his parties in their original position are completely ignorant of any "particular facts" about themselves.[1] The parties are free citizens, and Rawls states that their freedom is a "moral power to form, to revise, and rationally to pursue a conception of the good," which involves a view of themselves as sources of valid claims and as responsible for their ends. If citizens change their idea of the good, this has no effect on their "public identity," that is, their juridical standing as civil individuals or citizens. Rawls also states that the original position is a "device of representation."[2] But representation is hardly required. As reasoning entities (as Sandel has noticed), the parties are indistinguishable one from another. One party can "represent" all the rest. In effect, there is only one individual in the original position behind Rawls's "veil of ignorance."[3] Rawls can, therefore, state that "we can view the choice [contract] in the original position from the standpoint of one person selected at random."[4]

Rawls's parties merely reason and make their choice—or the one party does this as the representative of them all—and so their bodies can be dispensed with. The representative is sexless. The disembodied party who makes the choice cannot know one vital "particular fact," namely, its sex. Rawls's original position is a logical construction in the most complete sense; it is a realm of pure reason with nothing human in it—except that Rawls, of course, like Kant before him, inevitably introduces real, embodied male and female beings in the course of his argument. Before ignorance of "particular facts" is postulated, Rawls has already claimed that parties have "descendants" (for whom they are concerned), and Rawls states that he will generally view the parties as "heads of families."[5] He merely takes it for granted that he can, at one and the same time, postulate disembodied parties devoid of all

substantive characteristics, and assume that sexual difference exists, sexual intercourse takes place, children are born and families formed. Rawls's participants in the original contract are, simultaneously, mere reasoning entities, and "heads of families," or men who represent their wives.

Rawls's original position is a logical abstraction of such rigor that nothing happens there. In contrast, the various states of nature pictured by the classic social contract theorists are full of life. They portray the state of nature as a condition that extends over more than one generation. Men and women come together, engage in sexual relations and women give birth. The circumstances under which they do so, whether conjugal relations exist and whether families are formed, depends on the extent to which the state of nature is portrayed as a social condition. I shall begin with Hobbes, the first contractarian, and his picture of the asocial war of all against all. Hobbes stands at one theoretical pole of contract doctrine and his radical individualism exerts a powerful attraction for contemporary contract theorists. However, several of Hobbes's most important arguments had to be rejected before modern patriarchal theory could be constructed.

For Hobbes, all political power was absolute power, and there was no difference between conquest and contract. Subsequent contract theorists drew a sharp distinction between free agreement and enforced submission and argued that civil political power was limited, constrained by the terms of the original contract, even though the state retained the power of life and death over citizens. Hobbes also saw all contractual relations, including sexual relations, as political, but a fundamental assumption of modern political theory is that sexual relations are not political. Hobbes was too revealing about the civil order to become a founding father of modern patriarchy. As I have already mentioned, Hobbes differs from the other classic contract theorists in his assumption that there is no natural mastery in the state of nature, not even of men over women; natural individual attributes and capacities are distributed irrespective of sex. There is

---

[1] Rawls, *Theory of Justice*, pp. 137–38.
[2] Rawls, "Justice as Fairness," pp. 241, 236.
[3] M. Sandel, *Liberalism and the Limits of Justice* (Cambridge: Cambridge University Press, 1982), p. 131.
[4] Rawls, *Theory of Justice*, p. 139.
[5] Ibid., p. 128.

no difference between men and women in their strength or prudence, and all individuals are isolated and mutually wary of each other. It follows that sexual relations can take place only under two circumstances; either a man and woman mutually agree (contract) to have sexual intercourse, or a man, through some stratagem, is able to overpower a woman and take her by force, though she also has the capacity to retaliate and kill him.

Classic patriarchalism rested on the argument that political right originated naturally in fatherhood. Sons were born subject to their fathers, and political right was paternal right. Hobbes insists that all examples of political right are conventional and that, in the state of nature, political right is maternal not paternal. An infant, necessarily, has two parents ("as to the generation, God hath ordained to man a helper"),[1] but both parents cannot have dominion over the child because no one can obey two masters. In the natural condition the mother, not the father, has political right over the child; "every woman that bears children, becomes both a *mother* and a *lord*."[2] At birth, the infant is in the mother's power. She makes the decision whether to expose or to nourish the child. If she decides to "breed him," the condition on which she does so is that, "being grown to full age he become not her enemy";[3] that is to say, the infant must contract to obey her. The postulated agreement of the infant is one example of Hobbes's identification of enforced submission with voluntary agreement, one example of his assimilation of conquest and consent. Submission to overwhelming power in return for protection, whether the power is that of the conqueror's sword or the mother's power over her newly born infant, is always a valid sign of agreement for Hobbes: "preservation of life being the end, for which one man becomes sub-

ject to another, every man [or infant] is supposed to promise obedience, to him [or her], in whose power it is to save, or destroy him."[4] The mother's political right over her child thus originates in contract, and gives her the power of an absolute lord or monarch.

The mother's political power follows from the fact that in Hobbes's state of nature "there are no matrimonial laws."[5] Marriage does not exist because marriage is a long-term arrangement, and long-term sexual relationships, like other such relationships, are virtually impossible to establish and maintain in Hobbes's natural condition. His individuals are purely self-interested and, therefore, will always break an agreement, or refuse to play their part in a contract, if it appears in their interest to do so. To enter into a contract or to signify agreement to do so is to leave oneself open to betrayal. Hobbes's natural state suffers from an endemic problem of keeping contracts, of "performing second." The only contract that can be entered into safely is one in which agreement and performance take place at the same time. No problem arises if there is a simultaneous exchange of property, including property in the person, as in a single act of coitus. If a child is born as a consequence of the act, the birth occurs a long time later, so the child belongs to the mother. A woman can contract away her right over her child to the father, but there is no reason, given women's natural equality with men, why women should always do this, especially since there is no way of establishing paternity with any certainty. In the absence of matrimonial laws, as Hobbes notes, proof of fatherhood rests on the testimony of the mother.

Hobbes's criticism of the natural basis of father-right suggests that there is only one form of political right in the state of nature: mother-right. There can, it seems, be no dominion of one adult over another because individuals of both sexes are strong enough and have wit enough to kill each other. No one has sufficient reason to enter into a contract

---

[1] T. Hobbes, *Leviathan*, in *The English Works of Thomas Hobbes of Malmesbury* (hereafter *EW*) (Aalen: Scientia Verlag Aalen, 1966), vol. III, ch. XX, p. 186.
[2] T. Hobbes, *Philosophical Rudiments Concerning Government and Society* (the English version of *De Cive*), *EW*, vol. II, ch. IX, p. 116.
[3] Ibid., ch. IX, p. 116.

[4] Hobbes, *Leviathan*, ch. XX, p. 188.
[5] Ibid., p. 187.

for protection. But is this so clear? Even if marriage does not exist, are there families in the natural state? Hobbes has been seen, by Hinton for example, as a patriarchalist not an antipatriarchalist (on the question of paternal right). Hobbes's was "the strongest patriarchalism because it was based on consent," and he took "patriarchalism for granted and insert[ed] the act of consent."[1] Hinton refers to Hobbes's mention of a "patrimonial kingdom" and to some passages where Hobbes appears to fall back on the traditional patriarchal story of families growing into kingdoms ("cities and kingdoms ... are but greater families").[2] The criterion for a "family-kingdom" is that the family becomes strong enough to protect itself against enemies. Hobbes writes that the family,

> if it grow by multiplication of children, either by generation, or adoption; or of servants, either by generation, conquest, or voluntary submission, to be so great and numerous, as in probability it may protect itself, then is that family called a *patrimonial kingdom*, or monarchy by acquisition, wherein the sovereignty is in one man, as it is in a monarch made by *political institution*. So that whatsoever rights be in the one, the same also be in the other.[3]

Hobbes also writes of "an *hereditary kingdom*" which differs from a monarchy by institution— that is to say, one established by convention or contract—only in that it is "acquired by force."[4]

To see Hobbes as a patriarchalist is to ignore two questions: first, how have fathers gained their power in the state of nature when Hobbes has taken such pains to show that political right is mother-right?; second, why is political right in the family based on force? Certainly, Hobbes is not a patriar-chalist in the same sense as Sir Robert Filmer, who claims that paternal right is natural, deriving from procreative capacity or generation, not conquest. Hobbes turns Filmer's social bonds into their opposite: Filmer saw families and kingdoms as homologous and bound together through the natural procreative power of the father; Hobbes saw families and kingdoms as homologous, but as bound together through contract (force). For Hobbes, the powers of a mother in the natural state were of exactly the same kind as those of family heads and sovereigns. Perhaps Hobbes is merely inconsistent when he introduces families into the state of nature. But since he is so ruthlessly consistent in everything else—which is why he is so instructive in a variety of ways about contract theory—this seems an odd lapse. The argument that Hobbes is a patriarchalist rests on the patriarchal view that patriarchy is paternal and familial. If we cease to read Hobbes patriarchally it becomes apparent that his patriarchalism is conjugal not paternal and that there is something very odd about Hobbes's "family" in the natural condition.

The "natural" characteristics with which Hobbes endows his individuals mean that long-term relationships are very unlikely in his state of nature. However, Hobbes states in *Leviathan* that in the war of all against all, "there is no man who can hope by his own strength, or wit, to defend himself from destruction, without the help of confederates."[5] But how can such a protective confederation be formed in the natural condition when there is an acute problem of keeping agreements? The answer is that confederations are formed by conquest, and, once formed, are called "families." Hobbes's "family" is very peculiar and has nothing in common with the families in Filmer's pages, the family as found in the writings of the other classic social contract theorists, or as conventionally understood today. Consider Hobbes's definition of a "family." In *Leviathan* he states that a family "consists of a man and his children; or of a man and his servants; or of a man, and his children, and servants together; wherein the

---

[1] R.W.K. Hinton, "Husbands, Fathers and Conquerors," *Political Studies* XVI.1 (1968): 62, 57.

[2] Hobbes, *Leviathan*, ch. XVII, p. 154.

[3] T. Hobbes, *De Corpore Politico, or The Elements of Law, EW,* vol. IV, ch. IV, pp. 158–59; italics in original.

[4] Hobbes, *Philosophical Rudiments*, ch. IV, p. 122.

[5] Hobbes, *Leviathan*, ch. XV, p. 133.

father or master is the sovereign."[1] In *De Cive* we find, "a *father* with his *sons* and *servants*, grown into a civil person by virtue of his paternal jurisdiction, is called a *family*."[2] Only in *Elements of Law* does he write that "the father or mother of the family is sovereign of the same."[3] But the sovereign is very unlikely to be the mother, given Hobbes's references to "man" and "father" and the necessity of securing patriarchal right in civil society.

If one male individual manages to conquer another in the state of nature, the conqueror will have obtained a servant. Hobbes assumes that no one would wilfully give up his life, so, with the conqueror's sword at his breast, the defeated man will make a (valid) contract to obey his victor. Hobbes defines dominion or political right acquired through force as "the dominion of the master over his servant."[4] Conqueror and conquered then constitute "a little body politic, which consisteth of two persons, the one sovereign, which is called the *master*, or lord; the other subject, which is called the *servant*."[5] Another way of putting the point is that the master and servant are a confederation against the rest, or, according to Hobbes's definition, they are a "family." Suppose, however, that a male individual manages to conquer a female individual. To protect her life she will enter into a contract of subjection—and so she, too, becomes the servant of a master, and a "family" has again been formed, held together by the "paternal jurisdiction" of the master, which is to say, his sword, now turned into contract. Hobbes's language is misleading here; the jurisdiction of the master is not "paternal" in the case of either servant. In an earlier discussion, together with Teresa Brennan, of the disappearance of the wife and mother in Hobbes's definition of the family, we rejected the idea that her status was that of a ser-

vant.[6] I now think that we were too hasty. If a man is able to defeat a woman in the state of nature and form a little body politic or a "family," and if that "family" is able to defend itself and grow, the conquered woman is subsumed under the status of "servant." All servants are subject to the political right of the master. The master is then also master of the woman servant's children; he is master of everything that his servant owns. A master's power over all the members of his "family" is an absolute power.

In the state of nature, free and equal individuals can become subordinates through conquest—which Hobbes calls contract. But in the state of nature there are no "wives." Marriage, and thus husbands and wives, appear only in civil society where the civil law includes the law of matrimony. Hobbes assumes that, in civil society, the subjection of women to men is secured through contract; not an enforced "contract" this time, but a marriage contract. Men have no need forcibly to overpower women when the civil law upholds their patriarchal political right through the marriage contract. Hobbes states that in civil society the husband has dominion "because for the most part commonwealths have been erected by the fathers, not by the mothers of families."[7] Or again, "in all cities, … constituted of *fathers*, not *mothers*, governing their families, the domestical command belongs to the man; and such a contract, if it be made according to the civil laws, is called matrimony."[8]

There are two implicit assumptions at work here. First, that husbands are civil masters because men ("fathers") have made the original social contract that brings civil law into being. The men who make the original pact ensure that patriarchal political right is secured in civil society. Second, there is only one way in which women, who have the same status as free and equal individuals in the state of nature as men, can be excluded from participation in the social contract. And they must be excluded if the

[1] Ibid., ch. XX, p. 191.
[2] Hobbes, *Philosophical Rudiments,* ch. IX, p. 121.
[3] Hobbes, *De Corpore Politico,* ch. IV, p. 158.
[4] Hobbes, *Leviathan,* ch. XX, p. 189.
[5] Hobbes, *De Corpore Politico,* ch. III, pp. 149–50; italics in original.

[6] T. Brennan and C. Pateman, "'Mere Auxiliaries to the Commonwealth': Women and the Origins of Liberalism," *Political Studies* XXVII.2 (1979): 189–90.
[7] Hobbes, *Leviathan,* ch. XV, p. 187.
[8] Hobbes, *Philosophical Rudiments*, ch. IX, p. 118.

contract is to be sealed; rational, free and equal women would not agree to a pact that subordinated women to men in civil society. The assumption must necessarily be made that, by the time the social contract is made, all the women in the natural condition have been conquered by men and are now their subjects (servants). If any men have also been subjected and are in servitude, then they, too, will be excluded from the social contract. Only men who stand to each other as free and equal masters of "families" will take part.

A story can be constructed that is (almost) consistent with Hobbes's general assumption about individuals, to show why it might come about that men are able to conquer women in the natural condition. In order to combat and turn upside-down the argument that political right followed naturally from the father's generative powers, Hobbes had to argue that mother-right, not paternal right, existed in the natural condition and that mother-right originated in contract. So the story might run that, at first, women are able to ensure that sexual relations are consensual. When a woman becomes a mother and decides to raise her child, her position changes; she is put at a slight disadvantage against men, since now she has her infant to defend too. A man is then able to defeat the woman he had initially to treat with as an equal (so he obtains a "family"). The problem with the story is that, logically, given Hobbes's assumption that all individuals are completely self-interested, there seems no reason why any woman (or man) would contract to become a lord over an infant. Infants would endanger the person who had right over them by giving openings to their enemies in the war of all against all. Thus, all stories of original social contracts and civil society are nonsense because the individuals in the state of nature would be the last generation. The problem of accounting for the survival of infants is part of a general problem in contractarianism, and I shall return to the wider questions in chapter 6 [of *The Sexual Contract*]. One might speculate that a thinker of Hobbes's brilliance could have been aware of a difficulty here and was thus prompted to make his remark that, in the state of nature, we should think of individuals as springing up like mushrooms, a comment that Filmer dealt with scornfully and swiftly.

[…]

The matter is more straightforward in the state of nature pictured by Locke. Women are excluded from the status of "individual" in the natural condition. Locke assumes that marriage and the family exist in the natural state and he also argues that the attributes of individuals are sexually differentiated; only men naturally have the characteristics of free and equal beings. Women are naturally subordinate to men and the order of nature is reflected in the structure of conjugal relations. At first sight, however, Locke can appear to be a true anti-patriarchalist—Hinton claims that he "countered the patriarchalist case almost too effectively"—and he has even been seen as an embryonic feminist.[1] Locke points out more than once that the Fifth Commandment does not refer only to the father of a family. A mother, too, exercises authority over children; the authority is parental not paternal. More strikingly, Locke suggests that a wife can own property in her own right, and he even introduces the possibility of divorce, of a dissoluble marriage contract. When "Procreation and Education are secured and Inheritance taken care for," then separation of husband and wife is a possibility; "there being no necessity in the nature of the thing, nor to the ends of it, that it should always be for Life." He goes on to say that the liberty that a wife has "in many cases" to leave her husband illustrates that a husband does not have the power of an absolute monarch.[2]

In civil society, no one enjoys an absolute political right, unconstrained by the civil law. The question is not whether a husband is an absolute ruler, but whether he is a ruler at all, and, if he always

---

[1] Hinton, "Husbands, Fathers and Conquerors," p. 66; and M.A. Butler, "Early Liberal Roots of Feminism: John Locke and the Attack on Patriarchy," *American Political Science Review* 72.1 (1978): 135–50.
[2] J. Locke, *Two Treatises of Government*, 2nd ed., ed. P. Laslett (Cambridge: Cambridge University Press, 1967), II, §183, II, §81–82.

has a limited (civil) right over his wife, how that comes about. Locke's answer is that conjugal power originates in nature. When arguing with Sir Robert Filmer about Adam and Eve, Locke disagrees about the character of Adam's power over Eve, not that his power exists. The battle is not over the legitimacy of a husband's conjugal right but over what to call it. Locke insists that Adam was not an absolute monarch, so that Eve's subjection was nothing more "but that Subjection [wives] should ordinarily be in to their Husbands." We know that wives should be subject, Locke writes, because "generally the Laws of mankind and customs of Nations have ordered it so; *and there is, I grant, a Foundation in Nature for it*."[1] The foundation in nature that ensures that the will of the husband and not that of the wife prevails is that the husband is "the abler and the stronger."[2] Women, that is to say, are not free and equal "individuals" but natural subjects. Once a man and a woman become husband and wife and decisions have to be made, the right to decide, or "the last Determination, i.e., the Rule," has to be placed with one or the other (even though Locke's argument against Filmer and Hobbes is designed to show why the rule of one man is incompatible with "civil" life). Locke states that "it naturally falls to the Man's share" to govern over their "common Interest and Property," although a husband's writ runs no further than that.[3]

None of this disturbs Locke's picture of the state of nature as a condition "wherein all the Power and Jurisdiction is reciprocal, … without Subordination or Subjection." When he states that he will consider "what State all Men are naturally in," in order to arrive at a proper understanding of the character of (civil) political power, "men" should be read literally.[4] The natural subjection of women, which entails their exclusion from the category of "individual,"

is irrelevant to Locke's investigation. The subjection of women (wives) to men (husbands) is not an example of political domination and subordination. Locke has already made this clear, both in his argument with Filmer over Adam and Eve in the *First Treatise*, and in his opening statement in chapter I of the *Second Treatise* before he begins his discussion of the state of nature in chapter II. He writes that the power of a father, a master, a lord and a husband are all different from that of a magistrate, who is a properly political ruler with the power of life and death over his subjects. In the *First Treatise*, Locke claims that Eve's subjection

can be no other Subjection than what every Wife owes her Husband … [Adam's] can be only a Conjugal Power, not Political, the Power that every Husband hath to order the things of private Concernment in his Family, as Proprietor of the Goods and Lands there, and to have his Will take place before that of his wife in all things of their common Concernment; but not a Political Power of Life and Death over her, much less over anybody else.[5]

[…]

Perhaps the most obvious puzzle concerns the status of conjugal or sex-right; why, since Hobbes, has it so rarely been seen as an example of political power? In civil society all absolute power is illegitimate (uncivil), so the fact that a husband's right over his wife is not absolute is not sufficient to render his role non-political. On the other hand, a distinguishing feature of civil society is that only the government of the state is held to provide an example of political right. Civil subordination in other "private" social arenas, whether the economy or the domestic sphere, where subordination is constituted through contract, is declared to be non-political.

---

[1] Ibid., I, §47.
[2] Ibid., §82.
[3] Ibid.
[4] Ibid., §4.

---

[5] Ibid., I, §48.

DISCUSSION QUESTIONS

1. Pateman claims that "the classic contract theorists ... all tell patriarchal stories." Explain what she means. Evaluate her claim, being sure to discuss in detail the theory of at least one of the "classic contract theorists."

2. Explain Pateman's critique of Rawls's contract theory. Do you think that her critique is successful? Why or why not? If so, could Rawls's theory be modified in such a way as to avoid Pateman's critique? Explain.

3. According to Pateman, for Hobbes, in the state of nature "political right is maternal not paternal." Explain and assess her reading of Hobbes.

4. Compare and contrast the role of women in the theories of Locke and Hobbes, as presented by Pateman.

11

Charles W. Mills, "Race and the Social Contract Tradition" (2000)

Charles W. Mills is the John Evans Professor of Moral and Intellectual Philosophy at Northwestern University. Mills's work has been in the broad area of social and political philosophy, though he has written extensively on issues of class, gender, and race. In this selection, Mills discusses traditional contractarian theories and argues that what he calls the "domination" or "exclusionary" contract model can be both descriptively and normatively useful, particularly as it relates to issues of race and gender.[1]

Mills, Charles W. "Race and the Social Contract Tradition," *Social Identities: Journal for the Study of Race, Nation and Culture* 6 (2000): 441–62. Reprinted by permission of Taylor & Francis Ltd.

The social contract tradition has historically been viewed somewhat ambivalently by political progressives and radicals seeking a descriptive framework for modelling class, gender and racial domination, or a prescriptive tool for bringing about their elimination. Marx himself had little to say about social contract theory, which by his time, as a result of utilitarian and historicist critiques, had long since fallen into disrepute since its heyday from 1650 to 1800! But many of his critical remarks about liberalism in general are of particular applicability to contractarianism, and have often been repeated by progressives in the subsequent century and a half. Thus, from the perspective of a left and materialist Hegelianism, it would be pointed out to begin with that the idea of a literal contract is ahistorical, simply untrue to the anthropological facts of human evolution. There is never a "state of nature," but always human beings in social groups of greater or lesser complexity. Correspondingly, the idea of a contract is misleadingly asocial, predicated on a methodological starting-point of "pre-social" individuals whose putatively innate (but actually socially created) characteristics are taken to generate patterns of human interrelation which are then, reversing things, read back into the natural. Moreover, the atomic individualism characteristic

---

[1] For a general history of the tradition, see Lessnoff (1986), and for Marxist critiques in particular, Wilde (1994, pp. 164–74).

of liberalism finds here its clearest statement, in that society is represented as being brought into existence by, and composed of, an aggregate of equi-powerful individual decision-makers. Finally, insofar as the contract classically emphasises the centrality of individual will and consent, it voluntarises and represents as the result of free and universal consensual agreement relations and structures of domination about which most people have no real choice, and which actually oppress the majority of the population.

A lengthy indictment, then, and no surprise that as a depiction, even stylised and abstract, of the actual origins of society and government, contract theory is usually seen by the left as bourgeois mystification. However, the remarkable revival of contractarianism stimulated by John Rawls's *A Theory of Justice* (1971) moved some progressives to rethink their aprioristic dismissal, especially since contemporary contractarianism is purely hypothetical in character, thereby seeming to render irrelevant or sidestep some of the standard criticisms of the past. No longer a literal representation of the origins of society, the state, or political obligation, the contract is now just a heuristic device, a thought-experiment for mobilising our intuitions about justice. As such, it has been found useful by at least some Marxists, who have argued that if we admit a knowledge of the workings of class society behind the veil, we would prescribe an egalitarianism far more radical than Rawls's own (see, for example, Peffer, 1990). Feminism covers a wide range of approaches, and some of those feminists sympathetic to liberalism, most notably Susan Moller Okin (1989), have pursued a similar constructive engagement with contractarianism, using Rawls to go beyond Rawls. (Others, however, more impressed by the force of the radical critique, have argued for the principled rejection of contractarianism, either on grounds similar to the original Marxist objections or for distinctively feminist reasons, for example the implications of object-relations theory; see Coole, 1994,

pp. 191–210.[1]) Racial minorities continue to be underrepresented in political science and, even more so, in philosophy and political philosophy. But most of those black philosophers who do work on normative issues, for example Bernard Boxill and Howard McGary, accept a liberal, democratic normative framework for which some form of contractarianism would be congenial (see, for example, Boxill, 1984, and McGary, 1999).

In this paper, I want to make more explicit than I did in my book, *The Racial Contract* (Mills, 1997), the strategic and theoretical value of a retention and development of the contract idea by progressive theorists. Moreover, I mean the "contract"—albeit in a scare-quotes sense—not merely in its normative but also in its descriptive role. The highpoint of revived contractarianism may be past, as exemplified by Rawls's own communitarian concessions in his later work, *Political Liberalism* (Rawls, 1993). But contractarianism obviously remains one of the central strands in the Western political tradition, and will continue to have some influence as long as political theory is taught. I will argue for the conceptual usefulness to political theory—as both a descriptive model and a normative take-off point—of what I will call the "domination" or "exclusionary" contract that can be seen as common to my own work, Carole Pateman's, and the Rousseauean original (the bogus contract of the *Discourse* on *Inequality*; Rousseau, 1984; Mills, 1997; Pateman, 1988). I will focus specifically on race, but many of my points will be valid for gender also.

Let me begin by quickly running through some of the myriad uses of the idea of the contract. There

---

[1] Carole Pateman, author of *The Sexual Contract*, is often seen as the most prominent proponent of the position that contractarianism is necessarily theoretically tainted by its origins in masculinist thought, so that no real feminist retrieval is possible. However, in her panel contribution, "The Sexual and Racial Contracts at the End of the Twentieth Century," she said that this was a misinterpretation of her views, since in *The Sexual Contract* she was "concerned about the logic of a very specific and peculiar form of contract; namely, contracts about property in the person" (p. 2).

are contrasts, distinctions, and sub-distinctions of all kinds: modal status, scope, area, purpose. The protean character of the contract is in fact so striking that two editors of a recent book on contract theory, David Boucher and Paul Kelly, argue against the common assumption "that there is a single unified tradition or a single model or definition of the contract." Instead there are different traditions, different ends, and different kinds of contract (Boucher and Kelly, 1994). It is this very versatility that I will take as authorising the adaptation of the contract to radical ends.

First, there is the familiar (though I will later argue over-simple) contrast between the literal/actual contract and the hypothetical contract, what could be regarded as its modal status. Then there is the contrast between the descriptive/factual contract, as in some sense a representation of actuality, the way things were/are, and the prescriptive/normative contract, as a representation of the way things should be. Fine-tuned distinctions within these contracts are also possible, and have been made. Otto Gierke drew a famous demarcation between the contract to establish society, the *Gesellschaftsvertrag* (the social contract proper), and the contract to establish the state, the *Herrschaftsvertrag* (the political contract). Somewhat relatedly, Boucher and Kelly (1994) demarcate the moral, civil, and constitutional contracts. Within the political contract, Jean Hampton suggests that we need to distinguish the alienation contract that one finds in Hobbes, in which the people surrender their power to the sovereign, from the agency contract that one finds in Locke, in which power is only loaned out (Hampton, 1986, p. 3).

To this familiar list, I want to add some further contrasts that have been implicit in the literature rather than being explicitly flagged as such. I suggest that the contracts of Rousseau, Pateman, and myself can all usefully be gathered under the heading of the demystificatory domination or exclusionary contract, that is distinguished from the mainstream consensual or inclusivist contract. There are two main alternative purposes for positing and theorising a domination contract. The first would be

to argue that the apparatus of contractarianism is necessarily flawed, and should be repudiated altogether. The second would be to use the contract as a device for mapping and making vivid the full extent of social subordination, not to argue for the contract's abandonment but to demonstrate how sweeping would be the changes necessary for the reconstruction of the ideal contract.

The descriptive/normative contrast is sometimes taken to be co-extensive with the actual/hypothetical contrast, but this is mistaken. The descriptive contract does not have to be the literal contract to be in some sense a representation of the way things actually happened because the descriptive contract can be subdivided at least three ways: (i) the literal, historical contract; (ii) the hypothetical, idealised reconstruction contract; and (iii) the useful model contract.

The first of these is perhaps best represented by Locke, though some theorists have argued that in his work there are actually two sets of explanations, so that in a sense he hedged his bets (see Waldron, 1994, pp. 51–72). But at least one explanation seems to rely on a literal contract, the existence of which can be empirically demonstrated. The hypothetical reconstruction contract is best exemplified by Rousseau in his *Discourse on Inequality*. Here Rousseau gives a detailed account of the human degradation produced by the development of class society, and then concludes: "such was, *or must have been*, the origin of society and of laws," and later, "I have tried to set out the origin and progress of inequality, the establishment and the abuse of political societies, *to the extent that these things can be deduced from the nature of man by the light of reason alone*" (Rousseau, 1984, pp. 122, 137; my emphases).

So this is a more cautious formulation than the claim of actuality: the contract as an aprioristic reconstruction of what seems to have happened. However, it is the third sense that is crucial for us: the contract as a useful model, as a way of thinking about things, with claims neither to literal nor hypothetical (in the sense of possible) representation of the past. This employment has long been recognised by theorists who are quite clear that there never was an actual contract. It is exemplified by Ernest Barker's judgment that "Even if there had never been a contract, men actually behaved 'as if' there had been such a thing" (Barker, 1947, 1960, p. vii). Similarly, in an *Encyclopaedia of Philosophy* entry from 30 years ago, Peter Laslett comments on the "explanatory value" of the contract:

> If the collectivity is understood as embody-ing agreement, it does not necessarily follow that any such agreement between parties ever actually took place in historical time.... A contractarian political theory, therefore, can be entirely hypothetical, analyzing state and society as if agreement must always be pre-sumed.... In this hypothetical form the con-tract theory is still of importance to political philosophy. (Laslett, 1967, p. 466) (Note that this use of "hypothetical" is different from the second sense.)

Jean Hampton, more recently, has argued that:

> Philosophers hate to admit it, but sometimes they work from pictures rather than ideas.... [T]he contract imagery has struck many as enormously promising.... I will argue that social contract theorists have intended simul-taneously to describe the nature of political societies, and to prescribe a new and more defensible form of such societies.... [T]heir invocation of a social contract among the people as the source of the state is, in part, an attempt to make one modest factual state-ment, namely, that authoritative political societies are human creations.... The contrac-tarian's term of "social contract" is mislead-ing in so far as it suggests that people either tacitly or explicitly exchange promises with one another to create or support certain gov-ernmental structures. We do no such thing.... Certain institutions, practices and rules become conventionally entrenched (in a vari-ety of ways) in a social system, and in so far as the people continue to support them, these conventions continue to prevail, and thus comprise the political and legal system in the country.... [S]ocial contract arguments for the state can be interpreted so as to provide plausible descriptions of political societies as conventionally generated, human creations— far more plausible, indeed, than rival divine rights arguments or natural subjugation the-ories. (Hampton, 1993, pp. 379–83)

Following Hampton, I want to suggest that con-tract in this sense can still be useful for us, and that—suitably reconceived—it can even be prof-itably adapted by radicals. As Hampton empha-sises, the contract provides an iconography, a set of images, that is immensely powerful and appeal-ing, in large measure because it makes most salient, in simplified and abstract form, the modern idea of society and all its various institutions and practices (the state, the legal system) as human creations. Similarly, Pateman begins *The Sexual Contract* with the observation that "Telling stories of all kinds is the major way that human beings have endeav-oured to make sense of themselves and their social world. The most famous and influential political story of modern times is found in the writings of the social contract theorists" (Pateman, 1988, p. 1). Thus at the basic level of a conceptual frame-work, a picture, a story, it provides an overarching optic for thinking about the socio-political that is immediately graspable and that captures some cen-tral truths about it.

Now one of the tasks of political philosophy is precisely to provide competing abstract pictures of the polity. Sometimes this task is assigned to politi-cal theory rather than political philosophy, the latter being deemed to focus appropriately only on nor-mative questions.[1] But, following Hampton here

---

[1] See, for example, Goodin and Pettit (1993, p. 1): "Political theory sometimes connotes empirical as well as normative thought, thought that bears primarily on how to explain rather than on how to evaluate.... Political phi-losophy, in contrast, is unequivocally concerned with mat-ters of evaluation."

also, I think that it is more useful to operate with a broader conception of political philosophy, one which deals with factual as well as normative matters, though at a higher level of abstraction than political science. In this broader, integrated sense—dealing with the way the world is as well as the way it should be—political philosophy seeks "not any surface description of particular political societies" but their "deep structures," both "the foundations of states and their ethical justification" (Hampton, 1997, pp. xlii–xv). So in this sense, political philosophies make general claims about how societies come into existence, how they are typically structured, how the state and the legal system work, how cognition and normative evaluation characteristically function, how the polity should be morally assessed, etc. In Marxism, for example, we have a distinctive analysis in terms of the causal centrality of economic reproduction, the division of society after the hunting and gathering stage into classes, the role of the state as an organ of class power, the pernicious influence of "ideology," and so forth. And these views are obviously radically different from Plato's claims about innate human inequality and the need for a cognitive elite, or Hobbes's claims about the situational logic that generates human conflict between roughly equal self-seeking individuals.

I take it to be uncontroversial that for progressives of the modern period the central fact about society—the fact that they want to be captured in these simple overarching pictures of how the socio-political works—is the reality of group domination. Where mainstream liberal theorists have tended to focus narrowly on the electoral realm, radicals have typically operated with a broader conception of the political that extends to the extra-parliamentary. They have recognised and brought to light structures of group domination that are unjust, that arise out of social processes rather than being natural, and that shape the character of society as a whole, both the fundamental institutions and general human interaction and group psychology. If we consider the "big three" of class, gender and race, this picture is obviously true of Marxism,

most second-wave feminism, and, though the texts may be less familiar here, true also of the radical black oppositional and Pan-Africanist traditions. So whereas mainstream contractarians are operating with a factual picture that makes equality and consent normative, progressives are insistent that actually inequality and domination are the norm. The retention of the contract by progressives can then be seen as an effective strategy for undermining the influence of the (misleading) mainstream theoretical picture by using its own terms and, in an act of conceptual judo, overthrowing it on its own theoretical terrain.

The simple central innovation is to posit a group domination contract which is exclusionary rather than genuinely inclusive, and then rethink everything from that perspective. (I do not, of course, mean "excluded" from the polity in the sense of being left in the state of nature, but rather included as an unequal.) In Rousseau, it is a class contract which the rich con the poor into accepting, so that "all ran towards their chains believing that they were securing their liberty" (Rousseau, 1984, p. 122). In Pateman and myself, it is a sexual and a racial contract. But the basic idea is to utilise what Hampton sees as central to contractarianism—the shaping role of human causality—and then to show how this is both retained and necessarily transformed in a polity where human causality is group-centred rather than dispersed among equi-powerful individuals. By bringing in groups as the key players rather than individuals, it is then possible to recuperate the insights of radical oppositional theory within a framework still in some sense "contractarian." So if the traditional contract was a valuable polemical tool against Sir Robert Filmer and the patriarchal school, and later conservatives like Burke and De Maistre, with their claims about natural obligation and subordination, the radical contract can be a valuable polemical tool against those who see gender and racial domination as natural.

The key moves are already laid out, if somewhat schematically, in Rousseau. To begin with, it is, of course, a contract that emerges not from the state of nature, but from an earlier state of society.

So it is explicitly historical in outlook, seeking to locate the emergence of class society, or patriarchy, or white supremacy, in specific historical processes. Correspondingly, it is emphatically social, recognising that the negative traits of the social order, and of human beings themselves, are a product of society rather than projecting them back into the natural, and thus endorsing standard Enlightenment social meliorism as against explanatory recourse to divine will, original sin, biological limitation, etc. Since it is a contract of group domination, it is holistic, anti-atomistic in nature, being explicitly predicated on human collectivities, dominating and dominated. The division and transformation of the human population into certain kinds of entities (for example, "males" and "females," "whites" and "blacks") can now readily be accommodated within the contractarian framework, as can the inculcation of corresponding psychologies. The emphasis of current progressive theory on the "constructed" nature of gender and race thus fits perfectly with the idea of a contract as a set of intersubjective agreements. Finally, while it does see human causality as central, it is antivoluntaristic in outlook, recognising pre-existing structures of power as determinative (though these structures are not reified and fetishised, but clearly identified as the congealing of previous human causality), and, as a theory of group domination in which one group imposes its will on the subordinate group, placing explanatory emphasis upon coercion and the likely ideologically generated character of the latter's "consent."

Nevertheless, the obvious question at this point might be: why bother? If you have to work so hard to qualify and modify the original contract to recuperate these insights, why not just move on to the terrain of some other theory in the first place? And in fact, can it really be said that there is anything left of contractarianism after so many modifications?

The answer to the last question would be, as noted, that there is a precedent in the classical tradition itself, in Rousseau. Moreover, in medieval versions of contract theory the contractors were not always individuals, but other kinds of entities—corporations or cities, for example. So the idea of a group contract is not itself strange to the tradition, though a group domination contract is admittedly less familiar. But if Hampton is correct that the central insight of contractarianism is the human-created character of the sociopolitical order, then the concept of a group domination contract does preserve that insight, while developing it against a more sociologically informed and realistic picture of actual modern polities. The versatility of the contract idea makes possible an appropriation that at first seems radically anti-contractarian—until one realises that the atomistic factual assumptions of mainstream contractarianism are not definitive of the tradition, and can (and should) be detached from it, being utterly false to sociopolitical reality.

As to the point of the exercise: here, of course, individual calculations of costs and benefits will vary, and some may argue that more is lost by moving on to this theoretical terrain than is gained by it. My own feeling, as argued, is that a critique that engages contract in its own terms and shows, given the factual record, how inadequate its prescriptions typically are, is likely to be more polemically effective than one which simply dismisses it altogether. In other words, there are certain strategic benefits to be gained by accepting and working within a very mainstream and highly respectable (what could be more respectable?) framework. Contractarianism may have passed the zenith of its recent influence, but it is still very important. Moreover, these texts—Hobbes, Locke, Rousseau, Kant—will be taught as part of the canon, and thus continue to influence students and theorists, as long as political philosophy still exists as a subject. So books like *The Sexual Contract* and *The Racial Contract* can form a natural oppositional section of a standard curriculum on Western political thought. "You want to talk contract? Fine, then let's talk about the actual contract ...".

But there are also theoretical advantages on the normative front. Before turning to this, however, I want to say something specifically about race.

What has come to be called "critical race theory" began in legal theory, as a response to racial minorities' dissatisfaction with the critical legal studies movement (see, for example, Delgado, 1995, and Crenshaw et al., 1995).[1] So this was, so to speak, a critique of the crits, the claim that their analysis of the deficiencies and silences of main-stream legal theory did not pay sufficient attention to race. However, the term has begun to be used much more widely, referring to theory in a num-ber of different disciplines—cultural studies, soci-ology, film theory, philosophy—that operates with race as a central prism of analysis. It is this focus rather than any unified methodology that distin-guishes the approach. Just as feminist theory these days is more appropriately referred to in the plu-ral than the singular—feminisms—so critical race theory is really a meta-theoretical umbrella cover-ing a wide variety of approaches: deconstruction-ist, Foucauldian, Marxist, even liberal.

If there is a key point, a common theoretical denominator, it is the simultaneous recognition of the centrality of race and the unreality of race, its socio-political rather than biological character. The cliché that has come to express this insight is that race is not natural but "constructed." So race is made, unmade, and remade; race is a product of human activity, both personal and institutional, rather than DNA; race is learned, rehearsed, and performed. People's race is contingent, the result of being socially categorised one way rather than another, and as such people can change race by moving from one country to another or even by having the racial rules change in their own coun-try. But this volatility should not be taken to imply the unqualified unreality of race. Rather, as criti-cal race theorists are quick to emphasise, race is both constructed and real, embedded in legal deci-sions, social mores, networks of belief, folkways, institutions, structures of economic privilege and disadvantage. The reality is a social reality—per-haps better, a socio-political reality—but within this

sphere, it is real enough. Moreover, it is a reality that is structured through and through by relations of domination. Subordinated groups do to a cer-tain extent modify their "racial" identities, but for the most part, this is reactive: the identity has been imposed on them. The modern world is a world created by European expansionism—settlement, slavery, colonialism—and as such it is fundamen-tally shaped by the fact of white over non-white domination.

Now it is a striking fact about Western political theory that this domination has until recently hardly been theoretically registered and condemned as such. In the preface to his recent book on European imperialism, Mark Cocker summarises the account that follows as the story of how a handful of small, highly advanced and well-populated nation-states at the western extremity of Eurasia embarked on a mission of territorial conquest. And how in little more than 400 years they had brought within their political orbit most of the diverse peoples across five continents (Cocker, 1998, p. xiii).

But over the course of these same centuries, Western narratives have not told this story as a tale of political oppression. Either it has not been represented as political at all, but part of the natural order (a backdrop to the political) —the working out of God's will, or of a European predestinar-ianism, or the evolutionary process of inevitable racial triumph over the inferior races (or all three) —or it has been represented as political and justi-fiable, for example, the victory of civilisation over barbarism. As with male domination of women, the domination of whites over non-whites has his-torically been naturalised and/or justified. Whether through an exclusionary focus on the white popu-lation, or, in more recent years, with the decline of the acceptability of racism, an obfuscatory assimi-lation of the political experience of people of colour to the categories of the white experience, the dis-tinctive reality of racial oppression as a political system has been ignored and marginalised.

How can this silencing be overcome? I have argued elsewhere that one simple strategy would be to follow the feminist example with "patriarchy"

---

[1] Of course, it should be pointed out that critical analyses of the social order from a racial perspective long predate such work. Whether we would want to term these writings critical race theory *avant la lettre* would depend in part on how crucial we take the assumption of the non-biologi-cal character of race to be.

and press "white supremacy" into service to register, at the level of abstraction appropriate to political philosophy, this structure of domination (Mills, 1998, especially Chapters 4, 5, 6). So "white supremacy" would take its place in the pantheon of other general concepts of political theory, like "aristocracy," "democracy," "absolutism," "fascism," "socialism," etc. This would be one way to facilitate the extension of critical race theory into political philosophy. One could speak both broadly of a global white supremacy, referring to European domination of the planet as a whole, and, more narrowly, to white supremacy in particular nations. The contemporary employment of the term is usually purely ideational, referring to the beliefs and attitudes of white extremist groups (the Ku Klux Klan, Aryan Nations, World Church of the Creator, skinheads, etc.). My recommended use, by contrast, is a revival of the original sense of the term—the systemic privileging (independently of their beliefs) of the white population, as manifested in social, economic, and (formal) political structures. "White supremacy" would then constitute an overarching abstract political concept that would correct for the evasions and silences on race of mainstream political theory.

These evasions are especially remarkable, and especially culpable, in American political theory, since (non-apologist) historians of race have long pointed out the peculiar centrality of race to the formation of the United States in particular. Thus Pulitzer Prize–winning historian Leon Litwack's recent exhaustive account of Jim Crow begins with the matter-of-fact statement that "America was founded on white supremacy and the notion of black inferiority and black unfreedom" (Litwack, 1998, p. xvi). Similarly, in his pioneering study of two decades ago, George Fredrickson points out that

> The phrase "white supremacy" applies with particular force to the historical experience of two nations—South Africa and the United States.... More than the other multiracial societies resulting from the "expansion of Europe" ... South Africa and the United

> States ... have manifested over long periods of time a tendency to push the principle of differentiation by race to its logical outcome—a kind of *Herrenvolk* society in which people of color ... are treated as permanent aliens or outsiders. (Fredrickson, 1981, pp. xi–xii)

More recently, Matthew Frye Jacobson has tracked the evolution of American "whiteness" over "three great epochs" (1790–1840s, 1840s–1920s, 1920s–present), emphasising however that throughout these changes,

> White privilege in various forms has been a constant in American political culture since colonial times.... [Racism] is a theory of who is who, of who belongs and who does not, of who deserves what and who is capable of what.... [I]t is not just that various white immigrant groups' economic successes came at the expense of nonwhites, but that they owe their now stabilized and broadly recognized whiteness *itself* in part to these nonwhite groups.... Racism now appears not anomalous to the working of American democracy, but fundamental to it. (Jacobson, 1998, pp. 4–12)

So historians have long recognised the centrality and significance to the American experience of white racism and white supremacy. Yet, as Rogers Smith's recent magisterial work, Civic Ideals, has shown, the obvious political implications of these historical truths have not been admitted by the most important theorists of American political culture (Smith, 1997).[1] Instead, they have been "ignored, minimized, or dismissed." The mainstream conception, as purveyed by such distinguished theorists as Alexis de Tocqueville, Gunnar Myrdal, and Louis Hartz, has been the "anomaly" view of racism, in

---

[1] My own focus here will be on race, but it should be noted that the scope of Smith's book is much broader, covering sexist and nativist exclusion as well.

which racial exclusion and domination have been a marginal feature of the country's political history. For non-whites,

> their places and roles in American society have never been captured by the categories analysts stress in characterising American politics. They have instead been "lower races," "savages" and "unassimilables," slaves and servants, aliens and denizens, "unnatural" criminals and second-class citizens. (Smith, 1997, p. 18)

Thus in opposition to the mainstream "anomaly" view, Smith puts forward what he calls the "multiple traditions" view, which gives proper weight to the massive historical role of inegalitarian ideologies of racial ascription in American political culture. In a parallel, if not as detailed, treatment of the state in particular, Desmond King documents how, far from being neutral, the US Federal government has functioned as "a powerful institution upholding arrangements privileging Whites and discriminating against Blacks." In Federal government agencies, prisons, the armed services, and access to federally guaranteed mortgages, blacks suffered systemic discrimination backed by the power of the state. Yet, strangely enough, this fact has "been disregarded by most historians of the American Federal government and by students of US politics and government" (King, 1995, pp. vii, 17). Taking this claim to a deeper level, Anthony Marx has argued that we need to see the state as not only discriminating by race, but itself contributing to the making of race:

> Citizenship is a key institutional mechanism for establishing boundaries of inclusion or exclusion in the nation-state.... But by specifying to whom citizenship applies, states also define those outside the community of citizens, who then live within the state as objects of domination.... Nationhood was institutionalized on the basis of race; the political production of race and the political production of nationhood were linked.

Thus, in contrast to the standard narratives, he suggests that we need to think in terms of an alternative "historical pattern of nation-state building through exclusion" (Marx, 1998, pp. 5, 25).

Finally, in legal theory, as mentioned at the start, critical race theorists have for some time now been mapping the ways in which the law is not merely deeply implicated in racial discrimination but in the codification and crystallisation of race itself—how, for example, one became "white by law" (Delgado, 1995; Crenshaw et al., 1995; Higginbotham, 1978, 1996; Haney Lopez, 1996).

So there is an emerging body of work which demonstrates in a number of socio-political spheres the pervasiveness of white domination, and which points toward the need for rethinking standard global conceptualisations of the polity. And the silences and evasions in American political science on the question of race certainly have their counterparts in the more rarefied realm of political philosophy. Most white political philosophers have worked with a contractarianism whose factual presuppositions obfuscate or deny the centrality of white racism and white domination to US history. In their exclusion of race, in their denial of the importance of racial group identity and racial group interests, in their ignoring of systemic white privilege, the tacit assumptions of contemporary contractarianism reproduce at a more abstract level and in more exacerbated form the misrepresentations of mainstream political science. And this is manifested most clearly, of course, in the fact that the normative prescriptions of contemporary white contractarians say so little about redressing racial injustice. White supremacy is not seen in the first place (factual picture), so there is no need to prescribe remedies for ending it (normative picture).

The value of formally articulating a group domination contract, then, is to provide a device for making vivid, within the framework of contractarianism, the actual historical record, and thus counteracting the misleading and mystified historical picture most white contractarians have. To begin with, racial domination is made central, as in fact it has been. But this domination is not seen as in any way innate or natural, but explicitly historicised. The idea of a "contract" fits very nicely with what was earlier emphasised to be one of the central points of critical race theory, the "constructed" character of race. So race should be thought of not as biological, but as an intersubjectivist phenomenon, where, however, the parties are not equals, but some have greater power than others. This captures the idea of race—"whiteness" and "nonwhiteness"—as a created identity imposed on non-whites by whites. Whiteness is a system of domination and exclusion brought into existence by mutual (ingroup) agreement. The political character of race is thus made theoretically central: race is politically created and is a form of political domination. Just as the orthodox social contract was meant to challenge notions of natural "human" (that is, white male) intra-group subordination, so the unorthodox racial contract challenges notions of natural racial subordination. And correspondingly, rather than any recourse to race as a primordial identity, its social character is conceptually recognised. It is not that whites pre-exist the contract, but rather that they come into existence as white through the contract. Issues of group psychology can then be handled through understanding people's positioning in the racial system. One is not dealing with atomic individuals but with people whose identities are significantly constituted by these relations of group domination. The communitarian insight of the embeddedness of the self in culture and tradition can thus be theoretically registered without the usual corresponding implication that these selves can gain no reflexive critical distance on their constitution, and cannot seek their own transformation.

Correspondingly, the group domination contract also obviously does a better job of modelling the real-life workings of the formal juridico-political apparatus of the polity: the legal system and the state. In the idealised mainstream contract, the norm is equal treatment before the law, enforced by a Kantian *Rechtsstaat* whose role is to protect the rights of the equal moral individuals whose moral parity triumphantly brings to a close the epoch of ascriptive hierarchy. But this picture obviously bears no correspondence to the actual historical record of the experience of people of colour, whose expropriation, enslavement, and colonisation have all been facilitated through discriminatory legal systems enforced by a non-neutral state.

In addition—at what could be regarded as the meta-theoretical level—this alternative approach provides a far more sophisticated and illuminating epistemological framework for thinking about issues of social cognition, factual and moral.

Factually, in keeping with its Enlightenment origins, the (modern) mainstream contract generally assumes social transparency, a world that can be fairly easily apprehended if one makes the requisite effort and does not allow one's perceptions to be pulled the wrong way by self-interest. In radical theory, by contrast, starting with Marxism, the emphasis is rather on the opacity of the social world, and the difficulty of attaining the social truth because of the influence of hegemonic ideologies, the group-structuring of experience, the misleading "appearance" of the social order, and the influence of group (rather than self-) interest. These epistemological claims fit somewhat uncomfortably on the terrain of the mainstream contract, which posits equal individuals in a non-exploitative, non-hierarchical social order. But they are obviously easily recuperated in the domination contract, which posits differential group power, structural domination, conflicting group interests, and the possibility of systemic mystification. The study of the workings of gender and racial ideologies, and the motivation for their acceptance, are thus readily accommodated within this framework. Feminists have done much valuable work in uncovering the distorting influence of sexist lenses in numerous areas of social investigation. But because of the underrepresentation of people of colour in the academy, the exposure of the "white mythologies" generated by European expansionism, the analysis of what Mark Cocker calls the "complex language of projection and inversion [that] has exonerated Europeans for five centuries" has not progressed as far:

For in order to maintain tribal peoples and their descendants at the brutal margin of European civilisation it was necessary to reassemble, almost on a daily basis, the fabric of untruths which justified their institutionalised inferiority.... The ubiquity and magnitude of these falsehoods were so great that eventually anything could be laid before a European audience and might be believed. (Young, 1990; Cocker, 1998, pp.20–21)

Normative questions are also better understood once one realises that liberal ideology and mainstream morality were also necessarily shaped by this exclusionary contract. Rogers Smith points out that even some seemingly radical critics, such as Derrick Bell and Barbara Fields, attribute racism merely to interest-driven "deviations" from abstract liberal principles. In other words, there has been insufficient theoretical appreciation of the role of racism as itself an ideology of ascriptive hierarchy that is integral to American political culture (Smith, 1997, pp. 26–30). Smith's own approach, as earlier noted, is to argue for "multiple traditions," inclusivist and exclusivist. An earlier approach, similar but subtly different, is to claim the existence of a "symbiosis" between liberalism and racism.[1] But the basic point is that whether as a competing ideological strain or as an integral symbiotic component of the ostensibly universalist creed, these inegalitarian belief-systems are there from the start. By its very structure, the orthodox social contract downplays the theoretical significance of such claims, since it is assuming inclusiveness and egalitarianism as the norm. Everybody who counts is a "person," and there is no inquiry into who does count. The domination contract, by contrast, makes exclusion conceptually central, which corresponds to the actual historical record. Instead of taking "person" as gender- and race-neutral, it makes explicit that maleness and whiteness were prerequisites for full personhood. (My own book does this for race

by formally demarcating "persons" from "sub-persons.") So from the modern period, exclusionary norms distinguish "men" (as male), from "women" and "men" (as white), from "savages" and "barbarians." The sexual and racial contracts thus put front and centre what is obfuscated and marginalised by the orthodox social contract: that personhood could only really be taken for granted by white males, and that the classic human rights declarations of the eighteenth century are really proclaiming equal rights just for them. So though motivation by privileged group interest undoubtedly plays a contributory role in sustaining belief in sexism and racism, the point is that the moral and political ideologies themselves are two-tiered, with women and non-whites occupying a different and inferior status—sub-persons rather than full persons. I have conceptualised this in terms of what I call a "*Herrenvolk* ethics" and a "racial liberalism" (see Mills, 1998, Chapters 7 and 8). Again, the great virtue of this approach is that the exclusions—which are normative, not marginal or anomalous—are formally registered in the conceptual apparatus itself, requiring that they be admitted and confronted by mainstream political theorists.

Overall, then, it is clear that the domination contract maps the actual socio-political reality of recent global history far better than the egalitarian mainstream contract. The domination contract is thus pedagogically useful in providing a more accurate conceptual framework for students (and professors also!) to operate with. To return one last time to Hampton's claim: we work from basic pictures of how things are. Part of the difficulty in getting a genuine dialogue going between whites and blacks on race is that their overarching pictures of social reality are so different, their foundational assumptions so divergent, that they end up talking past each other. Most whites, cognitively handicapped by racial privilege and crucial silences in their education, have an anomaly view of racism; most blacks have a symbiosis or multiple traditions view. Insofar as contractarianism continues to be taught, the way it is taught is congruent with the anomaly view. Race is ostensibly absent, the polity is represented

[1] See Hochschild (1984, Chapter 1), for a discussion of the "anomaly" and "symbiosis" positions on American racism.

as basically egalitarian, and structural subordination is nowhere to be found. The use of the domination contract provides in simple and accessible form a competing model, a counter-model, that is far truer to the actual historical record. It models racial domination and white supremacy within the same framework that mainstream theory utilises, thus enabling an effective challenge to be mounted to orthodox conceptions.

Finally, I want to turn to the normative contract. With the exception of Kant, for whom the contract is merely "an idea of reason," the classical use of contract unites the descriptive and the prescriptive, though in different ways. For Hobbes and Locke, society and government's coming into existence through consensual agreement implies that people are obligated to obey the government and abide by the moral code chosen. So here the descriptive contract serves to ratify and give a normative backing to the existing polity. In Rousseau's radical domination contract, on the other hand, the descriptive and the normative are brought together for the purposes of condemnation rather than ratification. The descriptive contract here serves to demystify, to provide a general abstract picture of the polity as unjust rather than just, characterised by domination and exploitation rather than egalitarianism and equity.

Two moves are then possible. One can conclude that the contract model itself is necessarily flawed, that contract always produces domination and subordination. As mentioned at the start, most commentators have taken this to be Carole Pateman's move (see, for example, Boucher and Kelly, 1994, pp. 27–28). But even if it isn't, one can easily see why frustration with mainstream political theory might tempt one in that direction. If contractarianism accommodates to oppression so readily, all the while proclaiming its democratic credentials, might the problem not lie in the apparatus itself? So the theoretical point of the exercise would have been to argue for the principled jettisoning of contract itself.

The other approach rejects this conclusion, and insists that the contract itself is flexible enough to

be put to progressive ends once the actual history has been acknowledged. This is Rousseau's move—seven years after the *Discourse on Inequality,* he publishes *The Social Contract.* So from the fact that the actual contract was a bogus contract, it does not follow that an idealised reconstructed contract is not possible. And this is the move I would endorse myself. The point of mapping out the domination contract is then to elucidate both the mechanisms of injustice (what actually happened and what continues to happen) and to expose the justificatory ideological belief-systems, factual and moral, that have obfuscated and rationalised that injustice. Using the contract for both the descriptive/demystified situation and the prescriptive/ideal situation has the advantage of presenting the problems of social justice in a unified and integrated conceptual framework. The actual contract set things up like this—but that was wrong—so here's what has to be corrected for. So this approach would be a kind of synthesis of Pateman and Okin.

The debate over the possibility of appropriating contractarianism obviously shades over into the more general controversy about the extent to which liberalism can be turned to progressive ends. (Think, for example, of the second-wave feminist debates between liberal, Marxist, and radical feminists.)

As my pro-contractarian argument so far should indicate, I want to endorse liberalism. But this is, so to speak, a hybrid liberalism, detached from what are sometimes taken to be its necessary theoretical presuppositions.

What is "liberalism"? I suggest that if we think of liberalism as a political philosophy, then we need to distinguish different things. First, there is liberalism as a set of value commitments, for example to the individual's freedom, self-realisation, rights-protection, and so on. Then there is liberalism as predicated on a particular social ontology, classically portrayed as an ontology of atomic individuals. Finally, it is sometimes thought that liberalism is married to a certain theory of history, for example, a Whig progressivism.

Now what I am suggesting is that there are no strong logical entailments between these different components, so that the value commitments can be analytically separated from the social ontology and the theory of history. The liberalism I want to endorse, then, is the normative component. (If this is too minimalist to count as "liberalism," so be it.) I want to link this normative component with an alternative social ontology and an alternative account of recent global history, as summarised in the racial contract, to produce a liberalism informed by the racial facts. The fact that existing liberalism has largely been racial, in its avoidance and denial of the reality of racial domination, or the actual accommodation to it, does not mean that a reconstructed non-racial liberalism is impossible. Slavery, segregation, the denial of equal opportunity, racial exploitation in general—these would all be condemned by a non-racial liberalism. So one does not have to rely on any distinctively "black" (pre-colonial African? African-American?) values and norms, as some Afrocentrists have claimed in their condemnation of "white/Eurocentric" theory.

There are interesting contrasts with Marxist theory here. Marxism is often seen as anti-moralist, but to the extent that a Marxist normative critique can be reconstructed, it has been viewed by many as essentially parasitic on liberal individualist norms. In other words, there are no distinctively socialist values—the strength of the Marxist critique relies less on an alternative axiology than on a contrasting factual picture, which implies the non-achievability for the majority of genuine equality, freedom, and self-realisation under alienated and alienating class society. But the plausibility of this picture hinges on highly controversial factual/theoretical claims about the extraction of surplus value, the narrowing of proletarian choice by economic constraints, etc. Racial exploitation, by contrast, unlike class exploitation, is wrong by straightforward liberal standards, so that the argument goes through far more easily.

The ideal normative contract, then, would be aimed at undoing the nonideal racial contract, in all its exploitative manifestations. And the virtue of the preliminary mapping of the racial contract would be to show how far-reaching these manifestations are. Discussions of race in mainstream ethical theory have usually focussed narrowly on affirmative action, in keeping with the mainstream anomaly view of racism. The racial contract, as a domination contract, challenges this view and provides a synoptic alternative picture of the polity: not just individual transactions, but the historic functioning of the state and legal system, the workings of the economy, the development of particular moral psychologies and moral codes. If we see the racial contract as establishing the racial polity, white supremacy, then the task of the ideal contract should be how to dismantle white supremacy and realise racial justice. So a much more extensive range of issues can be encompassed than is standardly discussed in the mainstream ethics text. Our attention is directed broadly to the functioning of the racial polity as a whole, the structures and mechanisms by which entrenched racial injustice is perpetuated. One would look at white supremacy as a political system of domination in its multiple dimensions. So it is not merely a matter of ending discrimination, but of ending the unfair advantage that comes from past discrimination, for example, that whites have ten times more wealth, that white schools are superior because the tax base is higher, and so forth. In other words, one will be looking not merely at the present and recent past but at the more distant past also. The question of reparations would thus need to be put back on the agenda. What one wants to eliminate is continuing unjust white advantage, the advantage that comes as a result of the history of racial exploitation.

In such a discussion, both the "politics of redistribution" and the "politics of recognition" would be involved, insofar as subordinated races have suffered both economic exploitation and systematic social stigmatisation (see Fraser, 1997, Chapter 1). The political figures standardly invoked in these debates are usually in the left and communitarian traditions, Marx and Hegel. But in keeping with the endorsement throughout of a contractarian framework, I want to conclude by showing how much mileage can still be gotten out of those two most respectable and bourgeois theorists of the liberal contractarian tradition, John Locke and Immanuel Kant. This will underline my point that once the actual historical record and the actual social ontology are taken into account, conventional liberal values can themselves do most of the work of rectificatory justice. It will also underline my point that the real problem lies not in the norms but in the factual picture tacitly embedded in the orthodox contract and assumed by most mainstream contractarians. All we need to do is to work out the implications for seemingly stodgy mainstream ethics and liberal theory of the radically different factual picture provided by the domination contract.

Consider, for example, Lockean rights to self-ownership, private property, and the legitimate appropriation of the world, so ideologically foundational to a nation conceived of as a polity of proprietors. The actual normative logic of application of these key terms has been a racial logic, as one would expect of the racial liberalism of the domination contract. Thus Matthew Frye Jacobson points out that race has been central to American conceptions of property (who can own property and who can be property, for example), and property in its turn is central to republican notions of self-possession and the "stake in society" necessary for democratic participation.

Inevitably, then, political liberties are affected also:

[W]hiteness was tacitly but irretrievably written into republican ideology as well ... [The new democratic order would require of its participants a remarkable degree of *self-possession*—a condition already denied literally to Africans in slavery and figuratively to all "non-white" or "heathen" peoples in prevailing conceptions of human capacity.... "Fitness for self-government" [was] a racial attribute whose outer property was whiteness. (Jacobson, 1998, pp. 21, 26, 42; emphasis in original)

So the implications of the original qualified, or nonexistent, self-ownership of non-whites ramify into the broader socio-political sphere. Whiteness is not merely economic but civil advantage. Cheryl Harris has argued that in such an intellectual framework, whiteness itself becomes property, and that once this is understood the pattern of enduring white privilege over more than a century of postbellum civil rights legislation ceases to be puzzling and becomes a logical outcome of the differential entitlements of the white population (Harris, 1993).

But this racial liberalism is not inextricably immanent in the concepts themselves. If we theorise from the perspective of a reconstructed, idealised version of Locke's theory, in which "men" or "persons" are genuinely racially inclusive terms, it is obvious that African slavery is wrong, since the captured Africans were clearly not taken in a just war, and in any case nothing is supposed to be able to justify the enslavement of wives and children.[1] Moreover, Native American expropriation is also wrong, since agriculture recognisable by European standards was practised over large sections of the continent. And obviously the outright theft of bullion, as in Mexico and Peru, is wrong. Now Locke emphasises that the victims of crimes against their property have a right to reparations against the perpetrators:

he who hath received any damage, has besides the right of punishment common to him with other Men, a particular Right to seek *Reparation* from him that has done it ... so much as may make satisfaction for the harm he has suffer'd. (Locke, 1690, 1988, p.273; italics in original)

And presumably this also extends to the heirs of those involved, since otherwise later generations will continue to benefit from the ill-gotten gains of their ancestors, or be unfairly disadvantaged by the

---

[1] In opposition to most commentators who see Locke as either racist or hypocritically inconsistent in the *Second Treatise*, William Uzgalis has recently argued that the work is in part meant as a condemnation of the slavery in which he was once an investor. See Uzgalis (1998, pp. 49–77).

property crimes against their ancestors. Moreover, discrimination against blacks did not end with slavery, but continued under Jim Crow, and in more subtle forms is still manifest today (for details of Jim Crow, see Litwack, 1998). So whites have benefited massively from a set of differential entitlements predicated on the sub-personhood of the non-white population: whiteness has been "property" (see, for example, Oliver and Shapiro, 1995). But inasmuch as non-whites are not sub-persons, this differential entitlement has been illegitimate, a systematic violation of natural law. It follows, then, that a significant proportion at least of this "property" has in effect been stolen, and is an illegitimate appropriation of the world. Simply on orthodox Lockean proprietarian grounds, then, blacks and Native Americans have extensive claims to reparations against Europeans to restore property levels to where they should have been.[1] And note that no distinctive African or African American or Native American (or Marxist, if they exist) sets of values are being appealed to here. The radicalness of the conclusion, its dramatic redistributivist challenge to conventional wisdom, comes not from a startling new axiology, but from a demystified look at the actual factual record. Hence the value of the descriptive contract—in its domination version—in condensing and making vivid these facts.

Or consider Kant's (idealised) views on personhood,[2] which might seem by now to be liberal banalities with the explosive qualities of wet spaghetti. Once one takes seriously a social ontology of races rather than colourless (i.e., white) atomic individuals, then the actuality that has to be recognised is that notions of respect for personhood

have been systematically raced. The historical reality has been one in which whites have thought of themselves as the master race and regarded all other races as inferior, indeed often as barely, or not at all, human. Edward Said describes an imperialist cultural discourse "relegating and confining the non-European to a secondary racial, cultural, ontological status," in which, with only seeming paradox, "this secondariness is ... essential to the primariness of the Europeans" (Said, 1993, p. 59). Persons and sub-persons are dialectically interrelated, in that white personhood is achieved through maintaining the sub-personhood of non-whites. So respect has been tied to whiteness, while non-whites have suffered a "disrespect," a "dissin'," that is not a matter of contingent individual bigotry, but part of the moral economy. Now the role of the Kantian Rechtsstaat is not to promote happiness, but to secure a moral environment in which the right is prior to the good, and the enabling conditions for the citizens to maintain their dignity and autonomy are guaranteed. So if citizenship and personhood have overtly or tacitly been defined as white, the role of the state becomes the maintenance of the official subpersonhood of non-whites: the *Rechtsstaat* needs to function as the *Rassensstaat*. And this has in fact been the reality, in the United States and elsewhere, that official, effectively state-sanctioned moral attitudes have been embedded in social policy, education, national narratives, technologies of memorialisation, etc. The polity has been so structured that non-whites have been viewed through official lenses as sub-persons rather than persons, unworthy of respect.

Correcting for this history thus requires that we think of "respect" in a framework that recognises its supra-individual and racial aspects. Michelle Moody-Adams has argued that we need to broaden our usually individualistic conceptions of respect and self-respect to accommodate their actual social dimension: if one is a member of a stigmatised group, it will be much harder for one to attain the basic self-respect that whites take for granted (Moody-Adams, 1996, pp. 251–66). But if

---

[1] Admittedly, this is not an easy matter to calculate, and there are many complications arising from the fact that the original parties, perpetrators and victims, are no longer alive. But the point is that the discussion does not even get to this point; indeed, there is no discussion—the matter is closed *a priori*.

[2] The qualification is necessary because Kant's anthropological writings outline a detailed racial hierarchy which makes it questionable that nonwhites could actually have been full "persons" for him: see Eze (1995).

non-whites really are full persons, then the existence of this actual moral economy represents a flagrant violation of (idealised) Kantian principles. Justice therefore demands that the situation be redressed to end the inferior caste status of subordinated races, and obviously this will require public policy measures to reconstitute societal structures so that whites no longer get differential recognition. National narratives need to be rethought, educational syllabi revamped, the stories of the racially subordinated officially recognised, etc. Again, we see how surprisingly radical conclusions can be extracted from the writings of establishment figures once the actual historical record and the actual social ontology are acknowledged.

In fact, the radicalness of the prerequisites for the full undoing of the racial contract is ultimately manifested in nothing less than the reshaping of ourselves as human beings. Especially in its Rousseauean version, contract is about the constitution and reconstitution of people, their transformation from one kind of entity to another (Rousseau, 1968, Book I, Chapter 8). Since the domination contract involves the creation of an oppressive social ontology, an ontology of persons and sub-persons, undoing it requires a metamorphosis of the self as well as social structures. And ultimately the aim would be to eliminate whiteness itself. The collective around the journal Race Traitor seeks the abolition of the white race, not physically of course, but as a group systemically privileged by racial hierarchy (see Ignatiev and Garvey, 1996). Whites would have to learn to rethink and relinquish their whiteness, understanding the basis of oppression on which it has rested, and the ways in which it is tied up with non-white inferiority. Thus the end of white supremacy will require not merely material changes in opportunity structures and institutional arrangements, but deep psychological and "metaphysical" changes in whites themselves.

In conclusion, then. The virtue of working within a contractarian framework is its congruence with mainstream political discourse: its centring, normatively, of liberal individualist values and, factually, of claims about the shaping role of human causality and will. Actual societies have been characterised by structures of domination of various kinds, so that in reality the will has not been a mythical general will but the will of powerful groups imposed on others, with most human beings not being recognised as full persons and liberal values realised only for a minority. A group domination contract registers this historical reality, and, while inevitably over-simplifying in various ways, provides a demystified alternative picture. Thus it can help people better grasp the actual historical record of the polity, which has been one of exclusion and oppression. And in this way it can make possible a normative debate on achieving social justice less egregiously uninformed by the social facts.

References

Barker, E. (1947, 1960) "Introduction." In *Social Contract: Essays by Locke, Hume, and Rousseau*. Oxford: Oxford University Press.

Boucher, D., and P. Kelly (1994) "Overview." In D. Boucher and P. Kelly (eds.), *The Social Contract from Hobbes to Rawls*. New York: Routledge.

Boxill, B. (1984/1992) *Blacks and Social Justice*. Rev. ed. Lanham, MD: Rowman and Littlefield.

Cocker, M. (1998) *Rivers of Blood, Rivers of Gold: Europe's Conflict with Tribal Peoples*. London: Jonathan Cape.

Coole, D. (1994) "Women, Gender and Contract: Feminist Interpretations." In D. Boucher and P. Kelly (eds.), *The Social Contract from Hobbes to Rawls*. New York: Routledge.

Crenshaw, K., N. Gotanda, G. Peller, and K. Thomas (eds.) (1995) *Critical Race Theory: The Key Writings That Formed the Movement*. New York: New Press.

Delgado, R. (ed.) (1995) *Critical Race Theory: The Cutting Edge*. Philadelphia: Temple University Press.

Eze, E. (1995) "The Colour of Reason: The Idea of 'Race' in Kant's Anthropology." In K.M.

Faull (ed.), *Anthropology and the German Enlightenment: Perspectives on Humanity*. Lewisburg, PA: Bucknell University Press.

Fraser, N. (1997) *Justice Interruptus: Critical Reflections on the "Postsocialist" Condition*. New York: Routledge.

Fredrickson, G. (1981) *White Supremacy: A Comparative Study in American and South African History*. New York: Oxford University Press.

Goodin, R.E., and P. Pettit (1993) "Introduction." In R.E. Goodin and P. Pettit (eds.), *A Companion to Contemporary Political Philosophy*. Cambridge: Blackwell Reference.

Hampton, J. (1986) *Hobbes and the Social Contract Tradition*. New York: Cambridge University Press.

—. (1993) "Contract and Consent." In R.E. Goodin and P. Pettit (eds.), *A Companion to Contemporary Political Philosophy*. Cambridge: Blackwell Reference.

—. (1997) *Political Philosophy*. Boulder, CO: Westview Press.

Haney Lopez, I.F. (1996) *White by Law: The Legal Construction of Race*. New York: New York University Press.

Harris, C. (1993) "Whiteness as Property." *Harvard Law Review* 106: 1709–91.

Higginbotham, A.L., Jr. (1978) *In the Matter of Color: Race and the American Legal Process: The Colonial Period*. New York: Oxford University Press.

—. (1996) *Shades of Freedom: Racial Politics and Presumptions of the American Legal Process*. New York: Oxford University Press.

Hochschild, J. (1984) *The New American Dilemma: Liberal Democracy and School Desegregation*. New Haven: Yale University Press.

Ignatiev, N., and J. Garvey (eds.) (1996) *Race Traitor*. New York: Routledge.

Jacobson, M. (1998) *Whiteness of a Different Color: European Immigrants and the Alchemy of Race*. Cambridge, MA: Harvard University Press.

King, D. (1995) *Separate and Unequal: Black Americans and the US Federal Government*. Oxford: Clarendon Press.

Laslett, P. (1967) "Social Contract." In P. Edwards (ed.), *The Encyclopedia of Philosophy*. Vol. 7.

New York: Macmillan Publishing Co. and The Free Press.

Lessnoff, M. (1986) *Social Contract*. Atlantic Highlands, NJ: Humanities Press International.

Litwack, L.F. (1998) *Trouble in Mind: Black Southerners in the Age of Jim Crow*. New York: Alfred A. Knopf.

Locke, J. (1690, 1988) *Two Treatises of Government*. Cambridge: Cambridge University Press.

Marx, A.W. (1998) *Making Race and Nation: A Comparison of the United States, South Africa, and Brazil*. New York: Cambridge University Press.

McGary, H. (1999) *Race and Social Justice*. Malden, MA: Blackwell.

Mills, C.W. (1997) *The Racial Contract*. Ithaca: Cornell University Press.

—. (1998) *Blackness Visible: Essays on Philosophy and Race*. Ithaca: Cornell University Press.

Moller Okin, S. (1989) *Justice, Gender, and the Family*. New York: Basic Books.

Moody-Adams, M.M. (1996) "Race, Class, and the Social Construction of Self-Respect." In J. Pittman (ed.), *African-American Perspectives and Philosophical Traditions*. New York: Routledge.

Oliver, M.L., and T.M. Shapiro (1995) *Black Wealth/White Wealth: A New Perspective on Racial Inequality*. New York: Routledge.

Pateman, C. (1988) *The Sexual Contract*. Stanford: Stanford University Press.

Peffer, R.G. (1990) *Marxism, Morality, and Social Justice*. Princeton: Princeton University Press.

Rawls, J. (1971) *A Theory of Justice*. Cambridge, MA: Harvard University Press.

—. (1993) *Political Liberalism*. New York: Columbia University Press.

Rousseau, J.-J. (1968) *The Social Contract*. Trans. M. Cranston. London: Penguin.

—. (1984) *Discourse on the Origins and Foundations of Inequality among Men*. Trans. Maurice Cranston. London: Penguin.

Said, E. (1993) *Culture and Imperialism*. New York: Knopf.

Smith, R.M. (1997) *Civic Ideals: Conflicting Visions of Citizenship in US History*. New Haven: Yale University Press.

Uzgalis, W. (1998) "'The Same Tyrannical Principle': Locke's Legacy on Slavery." In T. Lott (ed.), *Subjugation and Bondage: Critical Essays on Slavery and Social Philosophy*. Lanham, MD: Rowman and Littlefield.

Waldron, J. (1994) "John Locke: Social Contract versus Political Anthropology." In D. Boucher and P. Kelly (eds.), *The Social Contract from Hobbes to Rawls*. New York: Routledge.

Wilde, L. (1994) "Marx against the Social Contract." In D. Boucher and P. Kelly (eds.), *The Social Contract from Hobbes to Rawls*. New York: Routledge.

Young, R. (1990) *White Mythologies: Writing History and the West*. London: Routledge.

DISCUSSION QUESTIONS

1. Mills makes two distinctions: (i) the distinction between the literal/actual contract and the hypothetical contract, and (ii) the distinction between the descriptive/factual contract and the prescriptive/normative contract. Explain these distinctions by classifying the theories of some contractarians (e.g., Hobbes, Locke, Rousseau, Rawls).

2. Explain Mills's distinction between the domination (exclusionary) contract and the consensual (inclusivist) contract. Why does Mills think that appeal to the domination contract is useful?

3. Mills claims that [m]ost white political philosophers have worked with a contractarianism whose factual presuppositions obfuscate or deny the centrality of white racism and white domination to US history. Assess his claim. Do you think that his claim, if true, undermines traditional contract theories at the fundamental level?

4. Why does Mills think that the domination contract helps us to make sense of facts about the nature of whiteness and the role of white supremacy in US society? Assess his claims.

5. What role does Mills see for ideal contract, given that he has posited a domination contract? Do you think that the move that Mills makes here is available to traditional contract theorists? Why or why not?

C.
Alternatives to
Contract Theory

12

FAIR PLAY

Robert Nozick, selection from *Anarchy, State, and Utopia* (1977)

In this selection, Nozick argues that the "principle of fairness"—versions of which have been defended by Herbert Hart and John Rawls—ought to be rejected. On Nozick, see reading 6 above.

"The Principle of Fairness"

A principle suggested by Herbert Hart, which (following John Rawls) we shall call the *principle of fairness*, would be of service here if it were adequate. This principle holds that when a number of persons engage in a just, mutually advantageous, cooperative venture according to rules and thus restrain their liberty in ways necessary to yield advantages for all, those who have submitted to these restrictions have a right to similar acquiescence on the part of those who have benefited from their submission.[1] Acceptance of benefits (even when this is not a giving of express or tacit undertaking to cooperate) is enough, according to this principle, to bind one. If one adds to the principle of fairness the claim that the others to whom the obligations are owed or their agents may *enforce* the obligations arising under this principle (including the obligation to limit one's actions), then groups of people in a state of nature who agree to a procedure to pick those to engage in certain acts will have legitimate rights to prohibit "free riders." Such a right may be crucial to the viability of such agreements. We should scrutinize such a powerful right very carefully, especially as it seems to make *unanimous* consent to coercive government in a state of nature *unnecessary*! Yet

---

[1] H.L.A. Hart, "Are There Any Natural Rights?" *Philosophical Review*, 1955 [reprinted in this volume, reading 24]; John Rawls, *A Theory of Justice* (Cambridge: Harvard University Press, 1971), sect. 18....

a further reason to examine it is its plausibility as a counterexample to my claim that no new rights "emerge" at the group level, that individuals in combination cannot create new rights which are not the sum of pre-existing ones. A right to enforce others' obligation to limit their conduct in specified ways might stem from some special feature of the obligation or might be thought to follow from some general principle that all obligations owed to others may be enforced. In the absence of argument for the special enforcement-justifying nature of the obligation supposedly arising under the principle of fairness, I shall consider first the principle of the enforceability of all obligations and then turn to the adequacy of the principle of fairness itself. If either of these principles is rejected, the right to enforce the cooperation of others in these situations totters. I shall argue that *both* of these principles must be rejected.

Herbert Hart's argument for the existence of a natural right[1] depends upon particularizing the principle of the enforceability of all obligations: someone's being under a special obligation to you to do *A* (which might have arisen, for example, by their promising to you that they would do *A*) gives you, not only the right that they do *A*, but also the right to force them to do *A*. Only against a background in which people may not force you to do *A* or other actions you may promise to do can we understand, says Hart, the *point* and purpose of special obligations. Since special obligations do have a point and purpose, Hart continues, there is a natural right not to be forced to do something unless certain specified conditions pertain; this natural right is built into the background against which special obligations exist.

This well-known argument of Hart's is puzzling. I may release someone from an obligation not to force me to do *A*. ("I now release you from the obligation not to force me to do *A*. You now are free to force me to do *A*.") Yet so releasing them does *not* create in me an obligation to them to do *A*. Since Hart supposes that my being under an

obligation to someone to do *A* gives him (entails that he has) the right to force me to do *A*, and since we have seen the converse does not hold, we may consider that component of being under an obligation to someone to do something over and above his having the right to force you to do it. (May we suppose there is this distinguishable component without facing the charge of "logical atomism"?) An alternative view which rejects Hart's inclusion of the right to force in the notion of being owed an obligation might hold that this additional component is the *whole* of the content of being obligated to someone to do something. If I don't do it, then (all things being equal) I'm doing something wrong; control over the situation is in his hands; he has the power to release me from the obligation unless he's promised to someone else that he won't, and so on. Perhaps all this looks too *ephemeral* without the additional presence of rights of enforcement. Yet rights of enforcement are themselves merely *rights;* that is, permissions to do something and obligations on others not to interfere. True, one has the right to enforce these further obligations, but it is not clear that including *rights* of enforcing really shores up the whole structure if one assumes it to be insubstantial to begin with. Perhaps one must merely take the moral realm seriously and think one component amounts to something even without a connection to enforcement. (Of course, this is not to say that this component *never* is connected with enforcement!) On this view, we can explain the point of obligations without bringing in rights of enforcement and hence without supposing a general background of obligation not to force from which this stands out. (Of course, even though Hart's argument does not demonstrate the existence of such an obligation not to force, it may exist nevertheless.)

Apart from these general considerations against the principle of the enforceability of all special obligations, puzzle cases can be produced. For example, if I promise to you that I will not murder someone, this does not *give* you the right to force me not to, for you already have this right, though it does create a particular obligation *to you*. Or, if I

---

[1] Hart, "Are There Any Natural Rights?"

cautiously insist that you first promise to me that you won't force me to do *A* before I will make my promise to you to do *A*, and I do receive this promise from you first, it would be implausible to say that in promising I give you the right to force me to do *A*. (Though consider the situation which results if I am so foolish as to release you unilaterally from your promise to me.)

If there were cogency to Hart's claim that only against a background of required nonforcing can we understand the point of special rights, then there would seem to be equal cogency to the claim that only against a background of *permitted* forcing can we understand the point of *general* rights. For according to Hart, a person has a general right to do *A* if and only if for all persons *P* and *Q*, *Q* may not interfere with *P*'s doing *A* or force him not to do *A*, unless *P* has acted to give *Q* a special right to do this. But not every act can be substituted for "*A*"; people have general rights to do *only* particular types of action. So, one might argue, if there is to be a point to having general rights, to having rights to do a particular type of act *A*, to others' being under an obligation not to force you not to do *A*, then it must be against a contrasting background, in which there is no obligation on people to refrain from forcing you to do, or not to do, things, that is, against a background in which, for actions generally, people do *not* have a general right to do them. If Hart can argue to a presumption against forcing from there being a point to particular rights, then it seems he can equally well argue to the absence of such a presumption from there being a point to general rights.

An argument for an enforceable obligation has two stages: the first leads to the existence of the obligation, and the second, to its enforceability. Having disposed of the second stage (at least insofar as it is supposed generally to follow from the first), let us turn to the supposed obligation to cooperate in the joint decisions of others to limit their activities. The principle of fairness, as we stated it following Hart and Rawls, is objectionable and unacceptable. Suppose some of the people in your neighborhood (there are 364 other adults) have found a public address system and decide to institute a system of public entertainment. They post a list of names, one for each day, yours among them. On his assigned day (one can easily switch days) a person is to run the public address system, play records over it, give news bulletins, tell amusing stories he has heard, and so on. After 138 days on which each person has done his part, your day arrives. Are you obligated to take your turn? You *have* benefited *from* it, occasionally opening your window to listen, enjoying some music or chuckling at someone's funny story. The other people *have* put themselves out. But must you answer the call when it is your turn to do so? As it stands, surely not. Though you benefit from the arrangement, you may know all along that 364 days of entertainment supplied by others will not be worth your giving up *one* day. You would rather not have any of it and not give up a day than have it all and spend one of your days at it. Given these preferences, how can it be that you are required to participate when your scheduled time comes? It would be nice to have philosophy readings on the radio to which one could tune in at any time, perhaps late at night when tired. But it may not be nice enough for you to want to give up one whole day of your *own* as a reader on the program. Whatever *you* want, can others create an obligation for you to do so by going ahead and starting the program themselves? In this case you can choose to forgo the benefit by not turning on the radio; in other cases the benefits may be unavoidable. If each day a different person on your street sweeps the entire street, must you do so when your time comes? Even if you don't care that much about a clean street? Must you imagine dirt as you traverse the street, so as not to benefit as a free rider? Must you refrain from turning on the radio to hear the philosophy readings? Must you mow your front lawn as often as your neighbors mow theirs?

At the very least one wants to build into the principle of fairness the condition that the benefits to a person from the actions of the others are greater than the costs to him of doing his share. How are we to imagine this? Is the condition satisfied if you do enjoy the daily broadcasts over the PA system in your neighborhood but would prefer a day off hiking, rather than hearing these broadcasts all year? For you to be obligated to give up your day to broadcast mustn't it be true, at least, that there is nothing you could do with a day (with that day, with the increment in any other day by shifting some activities to that day) which you would prefer to hearing broadcasts for the year? If the only way to get the broadcasts was to spend the day participating in the arrangement, in order for the condition that the benefits outweigh the costs to be satisfied, you would have to be willing to spend it on the broadcasts rather than to gain *any* other available thing.

If the principle of fairness were modified so as to contain this very strong condition, it still would be objectionable. The benefits might only barely be worth the costs to you of doing your share, yet others might benefit from *this* institution much more than you do; they all treasure listening to the public broadcasts. As the person least benefited by the practice, are you obligated to do an equal amount for it? Or perhaps you would prefer that all cooperated in *another* venture, limiting their conduct and making sacrifices for *it*. It is true, *given* that they are not following your plan (and thus limiting what other options are available to you), that the benefits of their venture *are* worth to you the costs of your cooperation. However, you do not wish to cooperate, as part of your plan to focus their attention on your alternative proposal which they have ignored or not given, in your view at least, its proper due. (You want them, for example, to read the Talmud on the radio instead of the philosophy they are reading.) By lending the institution (their institution) the support of your cooperating in it, you will only make it harder to change or alter.

On the face of it, enforcing the principle of fairness is objectionable. You may not decide to give me something, for example a book, and then grab money from me to pay for it, even if I have nothing better to spend the money on. You have, if anything, even less reason to demand payment if your activity that gives me the book also benefits you; suppose that your best way of getting exercise is by throwing books into people's houses, or that some other activity of yours thrusts books into people's houses as an unavoidable side effect. Nor are things changed if your inability to collect money or payments for the books which unavoidably spill over into others' houses makes it inadvisable or too expensive for you to carry on the activity with this side effect. One cannot, whatever one's purposes, just act so as to give people benefits and then demand (or seize) payment. Nor can a group of persons do this. If you may not charge and collect for benefits you bestow without prior agreement, you certainly may not do so for benefits whose bestowal costs you nothing, and most certainly people need not repay you for costless-to-provide benefits which yet *others* provided them. So the fact that we partially are "social products" in that we benefit from current patterns and forms created by the multitudinous actions of a long string of long-forgotten people, forms which include institutions, ways of doing things, and language (whose social nature may involve our current use depending upon Wittgensteinian matching of the speech of others), does not create in us a general floating debt which the current society can collect and use as it will.

Perhaps a modified principle of fairness can be stated which would be free from these and similar difficulties. What seems certain is that any such principle, if possible, would be so complex and involuted that one could not combine it with a special principle legitimating *enforcement* within a state of nature of the obligations that have arisen under it. Hence, even if the principle could be formulated so that it was no longer open to objection, it would not serve to obviate the need for other persons' *consenting* to cooperate and limit their own activities.

DISCUSSION QUESTIONS

1. Nozick argues that the principle of fairness must be rejected. What is his argument in support of this claim? How does he use the example of the neighborhood PA system to illustrate problems with this principle?

2. Nozick claims that in order to make the principle of fair play begin to look plausible, we would have to add the condition "that the benefits to a person from the actions of the ot..........hers are greater than the costs to him of doing his share." Why does Nozick think that it is necessary to incorporate such a condition? Are you in agreement? In spite of Nozick's claim about the necessity of adding such a condition to the principle of fair play, he nonetheless maintains that the principle would still be objectionable; why does he say this?

3. Nozick is doubtful that it is possible to offer a modified principle of fairness that would be free of any difficulties. Try to offer a revised principle of fair play which is not subject to the same sorts of criticisms as offered by Nozick against the earlier versions of the principle.

13

FAIR PLAY

Richard Arneson, "The Principle of Fairness and Free-Rider Problems" (1982)

Richard Arneson is a Distinguished Professor in the Philosophy Department at the University of California, San Diego. He teaches ethics and social and political philosophy, and has written extensively on these topics. In the following piece, Arneson challenges the "principle of fairness" offered by H.L.A. Hart, acceptance of which is meant to demonstrate that individual members of a society have reciprocal obligations to one another. Arneson then offers his own revised version of the principle of fairness. This reading responds in part to the selection from Nozick (reading 12).

SOURCE

Arneson, Richard. "The Principle of Fairness and Free-Rider Problems." *Ethics*, Vol. 92, No. 4, July 1982.

In a celebrated essay, H.L.A. Hart briefly calls attention to a situation he calls "mutual restriction" and claims that "political obligation is intelligible" only once it is understood exactly how this situation gives rise to obligation.[1] To clarify this matter Hart proposes a principle of mutual restriction: "… when a number of persons conduct any joint enterprise according to rules and thus restrict their liberty, those who have submitted to these restrictions when required have a right to a similar submission from those who have benefited by their submission." According to Hart, the rights of the rule followers here entail a corresponding obligation on the part of the beneficiaries. This principle has been taken over by John Rawls, renamed the "principle of fairness," and reformulated as follows: "… when a number of persons engage in a just, mutually advantageous, cooperative venture according to rules and thus restrain their liberty in ways necessary to yield advantages for all, those who have submitted to these restrictions have a right to similar acquiescence on the part of those who have benefited from their submission."[2] One of the more promising

---

[1] H.L.A. Hart, "Are There Any Natural Rights?" *Philosophical Review* 64 (1955): 175–91; see esp. p. 185. [Reprinted in this volume, reading 24.]

[2] John Rawls, *A Theory of Justice* (Cambridge, MA: Harvard University Press, 1971), pp. 108–14. The formulation quoted in the text follows the suggested phrasing of Robert Nozick, *Anarchy, State, and Utopia* (New York: Basic Books, 1974), p. 90. [Selection reprinted in this volume, reading 12.]

minor achievements of Robert Nozick's *Anarchy, State, and Utopia* is its vigorous polemic against this principle. Nozick writes, "The principle of fairness, as we stated it following Hart and Rawls, is objectionable and unacceptable."[1] As we shall see, some of Nozick's criticisms are well taken, but they appear to motivate revision of the principle rather than its abandonment. Nozick, however, leaps from his criticisms to the conclusion that no reformulation of the principle of fairness would obviate the need for actual individual consent to social requirements before those requirements can rightly be deemed obligations binding on that individual and enforceable by others. Others have endorsed Nozick's leap.[2] Since Hart at any rate proposed the principle in order to correct the tendency of the social contract theorists to assimilate all sources of obligation to voluntary consent of the sort found in promise making, Nozick's conclusion jettisons the project of explaining and justifying political obligation by tracing its origin to mutuality of restriction.

The present article salvages this project. Section I explores Nozick's criticisms to see if the principle of fairness can be revised to accommodate them. Section II argues that a principle that Nozick cannot disavow without disavowing central commitments of his political philosophy requires acceptance of a revised principle of fairness. Section III raises the issue whether those of us who are not attracted to Nozick's style of libertarianism or committed to its principles must nonetheless acknowledge that there are strong reasons for accepting a principle of fairness very much along the lines Hart has mentioned.

I

It will be useful to state in summary form the main objections to which the principle of fairness as quoted above appears to be liable:

1. The principle incorrectly allows that if some persons organize a cooperative scheme that demands a certain contribution from each beneficiary of the scheme, each beneficiary is obligated to make this assigned contribution, even if the cost to him of making the contribution (including the opportunity cost) exceeds the benefit he gains from the scheme.

2. The principle incorrectly allows that an ongoing cooperative scheme that distributes benefits unevenly among individuals can impose on individuals an obligation to make an equal contribution toward the scheme, even though one beneficiary benefits greatly from the scheme while another receives benefits that barely exceed the cost of his contribution.

3. The principle incorrectly allows that a person may be obligated to contribute to a particular scheme, even though he has disinterested, conscientious reasons for opposing the scheme and is working to gain recognition for a substitute scheme.

4. It is not in general true that one acquires the right to coerce somebody by bestowing some benefit on him and then demanding reciprocal payment. "You may not decide to give me something, for example a book, and then grab money from me to pay for it, even if I have nothing better to spend the money on," Nozick observes. "You have, if anything, even less reason to demand payment if your activity that gives me the book also benefits you; suppose that your best way of getting exercise is by throwing books into people's houses, or that some other activity of yours thrusts books into people's houses as an unavoidable side effect.... One cannot, whatever one's purposes, just act so as to give people benefits and then demand (or seize) payment. Nor can a group of persons do this."[3]

This list is a motley. One might quibble that the term "just" inserted into Rawls's formulation of the principle rules out at least objections 1–3. More fundamentally, 1–3 do not seem to strike at the core idea of the principle but only against the principle construed as generating reasons for

[1] Nozick, p. 93.
[2] Frank Miller and Rolf Sartorius, "Population Policy and Public Goods," *Philosophy and Public Affairs* 8 (1979): 148–74; see esp. pp. 165–67; A. John Simmons, "The Principle of Fair Play," *Philosophy and Public Affairs* 8 (1979): 307–37.
[3] Nozick, p. 95.

ascribing obligations that no counterconsideration could ever override. In contrast, objection 4 urges that satisfaction of the terms of the principle of fairness gives no reason at all to hold that a person is under an obligation as specified by the principle. In what follows I concentrate my attention on 4. I simply assume that 1 through 3 are roughly correct; and, when I attempt a revised statement of the principle of fairness, the revisions accommodate these points.

Taking a cue from Nozick's mention of a book as a benefit whose distribution one might regulate by the principle of fairness, we concede straightaway that the principle is plausible only if its application is restricted to particular types of benefits. There is a distinction between gift and exchange which the unrevised principle threatens to collapse. Consider a neighborhood gift-giving association. According to the rules of the association, whenever a resident of the neighborhood has a birthday the other residents are all bound to contribute toward the purchase of a nice present for him. The members of the association cite Hart's principle when a justification is demanded for their forcing residents of the neighborhood to comply with the rules of the organization. But by showering me with gifts you do not succeed in creating an obligation on my part to lavish gifts on you or your friends in return. The members of a neighborhood gift-giving club who initially include me on their list of recipients can simply cross my name off the list, excluding me from future gifts, when I fail to contribute my assigned share to the birthday celebrations of others. The others are free to carry on the scheme without my participation. In such circumstances the idea of mutuality of restriction has no proper application.

Some, but not all, benefits are appropriately regulated by the principle of fairness. Which ones? A start here is to distinguish private from public goods. For a given group of persons, a good is public according to the degree to which it exhibits three features: (1) a unit of the good consumed by one person leaves none the less available for others (jointness), (2) if anyone is consuming the good it is unfeasible to prevent anybody else from consuming the good

(nonexcludability), and (3) all members of the group must consume the same quantity of it. The logical relations among the three features are that 3 entails 2 but 2 does not entail 3, and 1 and 2 are quite independent of one another. A television broadcast signal that can be received by any TV set, when TV sets are as common as mud, exhibits 1 but not 2 or 3. A scrambled television signal that can be received only by a TV set equipped with a special unscrambling device, not easily copied, exhibits 1 and 2 but not 3. National defense for those residing in a geographically unified nation is a stock example of a good for which 1, 2, and 3 all hold to a high degree. It will prove handy to introduce two more labels: we will say a good characterized by 2 is a collective good, and a good characterized by 3 will be referred to as a pure public good.

Notice that, once a pure public good is supplied to a group of persons, there cannot really be any voluntary acceptance or enjoyment of the benefit by individual consumers. One cannot voluntarily accept a good one cannot voluntarily reject. A person can choose not to watch a television program broadcast over the airwaves, but he cannot opt out of the security that a system of national defense provides—at least not in the present state of warfare technology. Of course, a person made uncomfortable by his enjoyment of national security could choose to emigrate to a remote land with no provision for national security, but declining to shoulder the immense costs of emigration does not render one's acceptance of national security truly voluntary.[1] It is also true that people form plans and projects whose success is contingent upon the continued supply of pure public goods such as national defense or safety from epidemic disease, but forming such projects and relying on the continued supply of pure public goods do not count as voluntary acceptance either.

The Hart and Rawls formulations of the principle of fairness assert that those who submit to the

---

[1] For the sense of "voluntary" invoked here, see H.L.A. Hart and A.M. Honoré, *Causation in the Law* (Oxford: Clarendon Press, 1959), pp. 38–41.

rules of cooperative enterprises have a right to similar submission from those who have benefited from their cooperation. In these formulations, the wording does not settle whether a person can qualify as benefiting from a cooperative enterprise without having voluntarily accepted those benefits. In explicating the principle, Rawls does make it plain that he understands "benefited" to mean "voluntarily benefited," but his reason is a matter of definition: he restricts the term "obligation" to refer only to moral requirements that arise from voluntary action undertaken by the person who thereby binds himself. Hart leaves the matter undecided. Textual exegesis aside, it is clear that the principle of fairness cannot fulfill the philosophical ambitions assigned to it by Hart unless it is interpreted as regulating schemes that distribute pure public goods. Hart announced that his principle can help elucidate the character of a range of obligations, including political obligation, which the social contract theorists had tried unsuccessfully to assimilate to the class of obligations deliberately undertaken via promises and contracts. Several of the goods standardly supplied by state authority—for example, military defense, police protection, and the rule of law—are such that all citizens within a given territory must consume pretty much the same amount of them. For practical purposes, significant variety in consumption levels is ruled out. Yet it is in virtue of providing such goods that governments acquire legitimate authority over their citizens; neither Hobbes nor Locke would say a citizen is obligated to obey a government that fails to establish minimal conditions of personal security. Hence any principle such as Hart's that is offered to explain the nature of political obligation, if it is to be interpreted sympathetically, must be taken as intended to apply to those paradigm cases of political obligation.

Further examples will trace out in more detail the limited, tenuous connection between voluntary acceptance of benefits and the generation of obligations under the principle of fairness. Recall the neighborhood gift-giving association. Presented with a gift from the associated neighbors, one has the option to accept or reject. But voluntary receipt

of such gifts from the association, even as mediated by its rules, does not generate obligations in the recipient. Even if the rules are common knowledge, and they state unequivocally that acceptance of a gift is tantamount to pledging that one will contribute to future gifts for others, one can always cancel the implied pledge by announcing beforehand that one's acceptance of a gift in this case is *not* to be understood as tacit acceptance of an obligation. Once again the key feature seems to be excludability. In these circumstances the members of the gift-giving association are still free to exclude this open noncontributor from the benefits. If they do choose to give him a gift anyway, they are doing just that: bestowing a gift and not imposing an obligation.

There are also cases in which nonexcludability prevails and yet voluntary acceptance of benefits does not incur obligation. Consider a case in which a cooperative scheme supplies a collective good—perhaps a plane is hired to write pleasant sayings in the sky—but the scheme is ill-advised (i.e., total costs are greater than total benefits) or significantly unfair in its distribution of the burdens of cooperation. In either of these circumstances, the scheme does not generate genuine obligation. The individual consumer can decide whether or not to enjoy the good here supplied; he can avert his eyes and refrain from peeking at the skywriting (to simplify, let us stipulate that this aversion of eyes involves no inconvenience). Yet it is plausible to hold that in these circumstances the consumer is at liberty to enjoy the collective good without placing himself under obligation to those who ill-advisedly or unfairly supply it. Enjoying the skywriting boosts one's own happiness by a jot and lowers no one else's. If consumption of collective benefits from ill-advised and unfair schemes generated individual obligation to contribute to the scheme, then persons who are simply trying to minimize the losses in happiness from a botched project would willy-nilly generate obligations in themselves to continue support of the scheme.

Where nonexcludability prevails, the scheme is worth its costs, and the division of burdens is fair, yet the good supplied is not a pure public good, voluntary acceptance of the benefits of the scheme by the individual will generally be sufficient to place him under obligation.

So far I have urged several claims about how features of public goods affect our understanding of the scope of the principle of fairness. Where pure public goods are supplied, voluntary acceptance of benefits is impossible and so unnecessary to generate obligations according to the principle of fairness. Mere receipt of benefits may suffice to obligate. Where goods are characterized by jointness, but it is feasible to single out any desired person and exclude him from consumption, even voluntary acceptance of benefits may be insufficient to obligate. Where exclusion of anybody from consumption is unfeasible but individuals may choose whether to engage in consumption—that is to say, where the benefits of cooperation are collective but not pure public—voluntary acceptance of benefits is generally sufficient to generate obligation, provided the cooperative scheme is fair and not ill-advised. So far this is all just counterassertion against Nozick's assertion. My strategy has been to render the principle of fairness less controversial by revising it so that dubious implications no longer follow from it. This retrenching permits a response to Nozick's challenges quoted under 4 above: while it is not in general true that bestowing a benefit on somebody places the beneficiary under an obligation, the circumstance that collective goods are in the offing creates a special situation. A group of individuals cooperating to supply a collective good cannot supply themselves without allowing all other individuals for whom the good is collective to consume some of the good if they choose. If the cooperators may not enforce collection of a charge amounting to a fair price from all consumers, they must either add private incentives to the scheme so that each beneficiary is induced to contribute his fair share of its cost, or forgo the collective benefit altogether, or allow free riders to enjoy the benefit of the scheme without helping defray its cost. The first of these alternatives is often unfeasible and the latter two are often morally repugnant.

Public goods are ubiquitous, but in many cases the benefits they supply are small change that is insufficient to justify imposition of coercion. A handsomely dressed man or woman walking down the street supplies a public good to those in the vicinity who relish the sight of a fashionable pedestrian. But cooperatively organized fashionable dressers cannot claim the right to enforce a charge against ogling pedestrians, because the value supplied is less than the disvalue of enforced collection of costs. When I was very young my mother and I, along with other neighbors, gathered near the local railroad tracks to watch the midmorning freight train roll by, but we would have scoffed at the idea of the railroad charging us for this sight. Neither the people watchers nor the freight watchers in these examples are free riders.

Free-rider conduct as I shall understand it emerges when the following conditions hold:

a) A number of persons have established an ongoing cooperative scheme supplying a benefit B that is collective with respect to the members of a group G.

b) For each member of G the benefits of B are greater than the cost to him of contributing a fair share of the costs of supplying B (including the cost of such coercion as may be required to sustain the scheme).

c) The actual ongoing scheme distributes the cost of supplying B to all beneficiaries in a manner such that the payment requested of each individual beneficiary is fair. In particular, no beneficiary who has a disinterested motive for not contributing to the scheme for supplying B is required to contribute.

d) It is unfeasible that the cooperative scheme be arranged so that private benefits are supplied to each beneficiary of B in sufficient quantity to induce all beneficiaries to contribute their fair share of the costs of the scheme.

e) Each member of G finds his assigned fair share of the costs of supplying B to be burdensome or to involve disutility.

f) The choice by any individual member of G whether to contribute to the cooperative scheme supplying B or not is independent of the choice of every other member. That is, no member's choice is made under the expectation that it will influence any other member's choice.

g) No single member of G will derive such great benefits from B that it is to his advantage to contribute the entire cost of supplying B in the absence of contributions by others. Nor will any coalition of a few members of G find it possible to divide the costs of B among the members of the coalition so that each member of the coalition will find the benefits of B to him outweigh the cost to him of contributing toward the supply of B according to the terms of the coalition. A large number of persons must contribute toward the supply of B if the benefits each receives are to overbalance the cost of each one's contribution.

When conditions *a-g* hold, each person who benefits from the cooperative scheme supplying B can correctly reason as follows: either other persons will contribute sufficient amounts to assure continued provision of B, or they will not. In either case, the individual is better off if he does not contribute. (The razor-edge possibility that the individual's personal contribution might make the difference between success and failure of the scheme has a probability so low that it can be ignored in the individual's calculation of what to do.) If this reasoning induces an individual not to contribute, he counts as a free rider.

Free-rider reasoning contrasts with two other closely related rationales for individual refusal to contribute to mutual-benefit schemes supplying collective benefits. The *nervous cooperator* desires to contribute his assigned fair share of the costs of supplying B, provided that enough other persons also contribute to keep the scheme viable. He fears that other individuals will fail to contribute to the required extent, that the scheme will collapse, and that B will not be supplied regardless of his own contribution. Accordingly he declines to contribute. The *reluctant cooperator* desires to contribute his assigned fair share of the costs of supplying B, provided that all others (or almost all others) also contribute their fair share. He fears that in fact it will not be the case that all or almost all individuals will contribute their assigned fair share. In this

situation, if he contributes he will be assisting the provision of the fruits of cooperation to people who do not contribute their fair share. Accordingly, he declines to contribute. The nervous cooperator does not want to waste resources in support of a lost cause, and the reluctant cooperator is unwilling to allow himself to be, as he thinks, exploited by free riders. What crucially distinguishes the nervous cooperator and the reluctant cooperator from the free rider is that the desire to benefit from the cooperative behavior of others without paying one's fair share of cooperation forms no part of the motivation which induces the former two types to refuse to contribute, while just this desire does loom large in the reasoning of the free rider. While the conduct of each of these types may threaten the stability of cooperative enterprises, the nervous and reluctant cooperators do not seem blameworthy.

Where free-rider conduct is possible, there obligations arise, under the principle of fairness, prohibiting such conduct. Borrowing pertinent provisions from *a* to *g* above, we may state a revised principle of fairness: where a scheme of cooperation is established that supplies a collective benefit that is worth its cost to each recipient, where the burdens of cooperation are fairly divided, where it is unfeasible to attract voluntary compliance to the scheme via supplementary private benefits, and where the collective benefit is either voluntarily accepted or such that voluntary acceptance of it is impossible, those who contribute their assigned fair share of the costs of the scheme have a right, against the remaining beneficiaries, that they should also pay their fair share. A moral obligation to contribute attaches to all beneficiaries in these circumstances, and it is legitimate to employ minimal coercion as needed to secure compliance with this obligation (so long as the cost of coercion does not tip the balance of costs and benefits adversely). This revised formulation preserves the root insight that accepting or even simply receiving the benefits of a cooperative scheme can sometimes obligate an individual to contribute to the support of the scheme, even though the individual has not actually consented to it. The principle of fairness thus streamlines social contract theory by eliminating that theory's awkward dependence on dubious accounts of tacit consent.

II

I have alluded to a gap in Nozick's argument between his objections to the unrevised principle of fairness and his conclusion that patching the principle to meet these obligations is impossible short of acknowledging that an individual must actually consent to a cooperative scheme before he incurs obligations under it. In this section, I will argue that repairing this gap will strain Nozick's system to the point of tearing his fundamental doctrine of private ownership.

Imagine a Lockean state of nature in which neighbors are living peaceably prior to the emergence of private ownership. No government regulates their dealings with one another. Each neighbor is deemed to have the right to use the surrounding land freely, but the exercise of this right occasions frustration, since what one individual sows, another may reap. One day Smith has the novel idea of claiming a chunk of land as his private property. He explains that this act of appropriation gives him exclusive right to use the land and to transfer this same exclusive right to others if he chooses. Smith further holds that, like other rights, the right to property carries with it a right to enforcement: a right to coerce others not to trespass on what is now his land, not to damage it, not to interfere in certain ways with his use of it. In justification of his assertion of a right to property, Smith notes that his appropriation on balance leaves no person worse off than he was previously under the system of free use, since the improvements he intends to install on the land will indirectly benefit the community as well as himself and will in effect compensate each person for the loss of the old—and little valued— right of free use.[1]

On another day a large number of neighbors band together and institute a mutual-benefit scheme, say, a police patrol. They set up a fair plan for apportioning the costs of this scheme among all its beneficiaries, who compose a larger class than the organizing cooperators. Some persons offer their assigned contributions to the scheme. Others do not. The organizing cooperators institute a system of penalties for failure to pay one's assigned dues, these penalties being coercively enforced. In justification of their action, they point out that the scheme is beneficial to all affected by it, even taking into account the assigned costs including the costs of enforcement. They further point out that the coercion is not arbitrarily imposed but is necessary to secure the valuable cooperative scheme, since reliance on voluntary contribution renders the scheme extremely fragile and occasions resentment against the noncontributors. To those beneficiaries of the mutual-benefit scheme who complain that they are being coerced to share its cost despite the fact that they never consented to this imposition of coercion, the organizing cooperators point out that neither did they actually consent to neighbor Smith's appropriation of land as his private property, nor did they consent to the coercion required to sustain this appropriation. Yet private property backed by coercion is now widely thought to be acceptable. Consider a person, Jones, who is newly threatened by coercion at the hands of Smith and at the hands of the organizing cooperators. The question then arises, is there any plausible justification available to a modern follower of Locke, such as Nozick, that will discriminate between these instances of coercion, holding coercion-buttressing private-ownership rights to be morally acceptable but the coercion-supporting mutual-benefit rights to be morally unacceptable?

In the one case Jones is supposedly obligated not to trespass on privately owned land, and in the other case he is supposedly obligated to contribute toward the cost of a cooperative scheme. A possible asymmetry here might be thought to lie in the fact that, whereas Jones is obligated to perform some "positive" act to help the cooperative scheme, he is obligated to refrain from action with regard to Smith's property. The truth of this might be subject to doubt. But even waiving suspicion about the truth of this claim, I doubt much can be made of

---

[1] See Nozick, pp. 174–82, esp. p. 174.

it. Suppose Jones formerly tramped to work across what is now Smith's land, so the "negative" act of avoiding trespass requires extra steps, and the inconvenience might be equal to the inconvenience of contributing one's dues to the co-op scheme. At any rate, considerations of greater or lesser inconvenience will not draw a sharp and fixed line, between acceptable and unacceptable coercion, of the sort Nozick requires.

Jones might reflect that, when Smith claims a chunk of land as his property, he implicitly cedes to Jones the right to claim similar chunks of land as his property. Similarly, the organizers of the mutual-benefit scheme might point out that, in claiming the right to institute a cooperative scheme and to require all beneficiaries (with certain exceptions) to contribute, they implicitly grant to Jones the right to band with others and do likewise. In neither the private-property case nor the collective-benefits case need anybody be claiming rights of a sort he is in principle unwilling to concede to others. Also, in both cases, the acts of the first takers of the right to some degree pre-empt the possibilities of later similar acts. Once Smith stakes out a claim, there is that much less land left to appropriate, and given that there is a fairly small list of collective benefits that are noncontroversially benefits to all, worth their cost, the acts of the initial cooperators limit the alternatives of later would-be cooperators.

Although a private-ownership system has great advantages compared with a free-use system, many of these advantages are due to very general features of a Lockean ownership system that are shared with other possible ownership systems. For example, it is convenient to have a more clear specification of who has the right to use the land at any given moment than a free-use system can provide. But a system in which people lease land from the community for set periods of time would also possess this advantage.[1] Or one might have a semiprivate-ownership

system, in which private-property rights are limited by welfare rights of the indigent and disabled to a share in the produce of the land as improved by private initiative. And so on. What justifies the specific choice of Lockean-style ownership? Pondering this question, Allan Gibbard has proposed a principle I will call the *self-benefit principle*: "The principle behind the choice of the Lockean rule seems to be something like this: moral rules should be so constructed that, if the rules are obeyed, the acts of each person benefit or harm only himself, except as he himself chooses to confer or exchange the benefits of his acts."[2]

This principle must be construed as a counsel of perfection, an ideal which we are enjoined to satisfy as far as lies within our power, rather than as a strict requirement. For if interpreted as a strict requirement, it will not justify Lockean appropriation. One person's act of appropriating previously unclaimed land as private property *does* slightly damage the position of other persons who (*a*) formerly were at liberty to use the land and (*b*) had the option of appropriating it themselves. According to Nozick's version of Lockean appropriation, *a* must be counterbalanced by the utilities flowing from private ownership, if appropriation is to issue in genuine property rights, but *b* need not be. Also, under a private-ownership system it often happens that what a person does with his property spreads external benefits on others. These are benefits to others for which for some reason payment cannot be extracted from those others. At most, Lockean private ownership very roughly approximates satisfaction of the self-benefit principle.

The idea, then, must be that Lockean property rules satisfy the self-benefit principle to a greater degree than alternative appropriation rules or than a system of free use and no permitted appropriation at all. In what follows, I assume this claim to be true. I do not argue for it. Nor do I offer any extended argument to the effect that it is in fact the self-benefit principle that gives the most convincing

---

[1] J.S. Mill mentions this possibility in *Principles of Political Economy*, in *Collected Works* (Toronto: University of Toronto Press, 1965), 2:227.

[2] Allan Gibbard, "Natural Property Rights," *Noûs* 10 (1976): 77–88; see esp. p. 84.

rationale of Lockean private ownership. Toward the end of this section, I indicate evidence in Locke's text that he had something like the self-benefit principle in mind. I claim that, insofar as the self-benefit principle serves to justify a Lockean principle of private ownership, it serves equally to justify a revised version of the principle of fairness. If I am right about this, anybody who wants to reject the principle of fairness while retaining a commitment to private ownership must supply an alternate justification driving a wedge between the rights of owners and the rights of cooperators. I suspect such an alternate justification is not to be had.

How does the self-benefit principle bear on the justification, within a Lockean or Nozickean framework, of the revised principle of fairness? First, let us suppose that cooperative schemes supplying collective benefits must make their way by voluntary contributions or not at all. Consider such a scheme in which the beneficiaries may be divided into those who cooperate to share the costs and those who choose not to cooperate. Here the cooperators must willy-nilly confer benefits on the noncooperators even though they do not voluntarily choose to confer benefits in this fashion. The greater the number of beneficiaries who are not also cooperators in any given cooperative scheme, the greater is the nonvoluntary conferral of benefits. This violates the self-benefit principle. One could deny that there is a nonvoluntary transfer of benefits, but one would be mistaken. Suppose we said: nobody is forcing the cooperators to initiate their scheme and confer collective benefits on everybody. They do it voluntarily. That this is wrong becomes plain when we notice that the same may be said about the diffusion of benefits in a free-use system. Nobody forces Smith to plant crops which, in the absence of private ownership, Jones and others are at liberty to harvest or to trample for fun. Under free use, Smith is free to choose to plant or not to plant, but he has not got the option of planting and excluding others from the benefits of his labors. Similarly without the protection of the principle of fairness, the cooperators can choose to initiate a mutual-benefit scheme or not, but, given the nature of collective goods, they are not at liberty to initiate a scheme and limit the benefits to those who are willing to contribute to their costs. Simplifying somewhat, let us assume that the initial cooperators and those who would voluntarily contribute a fair share of the cost of the scheme under a noncoercive arrangement willingly confer the benefits of their actions on all those who pay their fair share of the scheme.

Permitting cooperators to coerce beneficiaries into contributing their fair share remedies the above situation to some extent. If the revised principle of fairness[1] is adopted and enforced, it is no longer the case that cooperators must bestow the benefits of their activity on others against their will. Also, the persons we identified as nervous and reluctant cooperators will welcome the coercion that forces all beneficiaries to pay their fair share of the costs. Nervous and reluctant cooperators are desirous of contributing their fair share provided certain guarantees are met. Enforcement of the revised principle of fairness provides these guarantees, so nervous and reluctant cooperators will not find themselves in the position of being required to confer benefits on others against their choice. The would-be free riders now dragooned into contributing to the cooperative scheme will, of course, have a different story to tell. They would prefer to reap the benefits of the scheme without contributing to it. Under the principle of fairness, their actions are orchestrated to benefit others against their will. The situation of the free riders, however, seems to be parallel to the situation of those who chafe at the restrictions of private property and wish to garner for themselves the benefits of the labor and abstinence of others. Private-ownership rules force such individuals to respect the property of others, and these actions and forbearances may also be said to be a residue, within a system justified by broad appeal to the principle of self-benefit, of actions that confer benefits on others against the will of the doers. Given this close parallel between would-be free riders and covetous nonowners, we can see the

---

[1] Or something close to it. I am appealing to the general outline, not the detail.

self-benefit principle to be imperfectly but closely approximated under private ownership and under the revised principle of fairness.

Further reflection on the rationale of Lockean private property strengthens the parallel case for the revised principle of fairness. Of somebody who covets the parcel of land another has improved by his labor, when there is enough and as good land remaining unappropriated, Locke says "'tis plain he desired the benefit of another's Pains, which he had no right to."[1] The point of Lockean property rules is to frustrate such desires and to "guarantee to individuals" the "fruits of their own labour and abstinence."[2] This norm would seem to have straightforward application to the desires of would-be free riders to benefit from cooperative schemes without paying a fair share of the costs. The revised principle of fairness encapsulates the moral conviction that it is legitimate to frustrate the desire to benefit from the pains of others when one has no right to the fruit of their pains.

The fact that, in many instances, collective benefits are such that consumption by one individual does not lessen the amount of the good available for the consumption of others may seem to complicate, and threaten, the analogy between mutual-benefit schemes and private ownership. If the covetous non-property owners succeed in devouring the benefits of others' pains, it may be said, there will be that much less left for owners, but the situation is different in many cases of free-rider activity. Why restrict individuals from consuming a good if their consumption does not harm anybody else?

To answer this query, we note that in many cases private ownership of goods gives owners control over goods that, once produced, are costless to supply to others across a relevant range of consumption. Suppose I stage a small circus for my family

in our front yard, and a curious crowd gathers. The sight of this minicircus is such that, for the crowd of persons anxious to watch, one person's consumption is nonrival with another's. Yet in this situation, my private ownership of my land permits me to make a fast buck by moving the family circus to the backyard or inside a tent and charging admission. Somebody who attempted to sneak into the tent without paying would be, in a sense, desirous of the benefits of another's pains, namely, mine, in designing the circus. The sneak is not, in this situation, taking benefits so that less is left for others to consume, but he does seek benefits while striving to evade the payment of a fair equivalent for those benefits. There is, then, a sense of *seeking the benefit of another's pains* which applies with equal propriety to free-rider activity under conditions of joint consumption and to those who chafe under the restrictions of private ownership where goods privately controlled exhibit jointness.

To repeat a point made earlier, instituting a private-ownership system does not fully achieve satisfaction of the self-benefit principle. Under private ownership, neighbors clustered near the edge of my property may enjoy the sweet-smelling smoke wafting from a fire I build on my land. The paint I apply to the exterior of my house may please my neighbor's aesthetic sensibilities and raise the property value of their houses. And so on. But the self-benefit principle justifies private property insofar as the latter does conform to it, and insofar as no feasible system does better on this score; and the self-benefit principle justifies the revised principle of fairness for like reasons.

Recall Nozick's objections to the enforcement of the principle of fairness. They are equally objections to the enforcement of private ownership. "You may not decide to give me something, for example a book, and then grab money from me to pay for it, even if I have nothing better to spend the money on. You have, if anything, even less reason to demand payment if your activity that gives me the book also benefits you; suppose that your best way of getting exercise is by throwing books into people's houses, or that some activity of yours thrusts books

[1] John Locke, *Two Treatises of Government,* ed. Peter Laslett (Cambridge: Cambridge University Press, 1963), "Of Property," par. 34, p. 333. Cf. Lawrence Becker, "The Labor Theory of Property Acquisition," *Journal of Philosophy* 83 (1976): 653–64.
[2] These phrases are quoted from J.S. Mill, perceptive critic of Locke, in *Principles of Political Economy,* 2:208.

into people's houses as an unavoidable side effect."[1] Similarly, why is it legitimate for you to restrict my liberty, excluding me from the use of chunks of the earth, on the ground that your private appropriation of those chunks indirectly benefits me by providing me with economic opportunities or the like? I never requested those benefits or consented to the accompanying restriction of my liberty. In these circumstances, what justifies private appropriation? If the appeal is to a self-benefit principle incorporating the conviction that property rules should not permit individuals to enjoy the benefits of the labor of others without their consent, that appeal will justify the revised principle of fairness as much as the principle of private ownership.

III

The foregoing may seem to be of limited interest. I have claimed that the self-benefit principle, which must be Nozick's background principle that marks off his line of defense of private ownership, will equally serve to defend the revised principle of fairness. This may commit Nozick to the defense of fair cooperative schemes supplying collective benefits, but the argument relies on the self-benefit principle, which many will reject. Some reasons for this rejection are worth mention, for they may help to orient us toward a less controversial rationale for the principle of fairness. Many people of liberal and socialist persuasion believe that, in emergency situations, people who are so situated that, with modest expenditure of effort and at modest risk to themselves, they can avert great harms that threaten others are under strict obligations to tender such Good Samaritan aid. These Good Samaritan obligations may be seen as strict obligations of charity so long as it is remembered that they may be owed to particular persons or groups who have a corresponding right against particular persons who happen to be well situated to help. Many people also believe that able or naturally gifted economic agents are under strict moral obligations to contribute to the welfare of the less able or less naturally gifted. The exact

amount of such obligations that is owed as a matter of strict obligation is subject to dispute, but anyone who accepts that the better endowed are under any obligation to contribute to the welfare of the less well endowed is registering disagreement with the self-benefit principle. I wish to abstract from these disagreements by supposing that some clearly specified principles of Good Samaritanism and of welfare obligations are widely accepted. Society has arrived at a consensus about the extent to which its members disagree with Locke.

Consider this revision of the self-benefit principle: moral rules should be so constructed that if they are obeyed, each person's acts benefit or harm only himself except as he either (a) chooses to confer or exchange the benefits of his acts or (b) is acting in fulfillment of an obligation of strict charity. This liberal revision of the self-benefit principle will considerably affect our understanding of the principle of fairness. For one thing, since to the obligations of the able there correspond rights of the non-able, it will no longer be possible to give unequivocal sanction to the Lockean criticism that any person desirous of the benefits of another's pains is blameworthy. The non-able will be entitled to the benefits of some of the pains of the able, and emergency victims will be entitled to the benefits of some of the pains of those who are in a position to give aid. This result may well leave us wondering whether the modern liberal outlook is not fundamentally at odds with the Lockean conservative idea that each individual is entitled to the fruits of his own labor and abstinence. Does the liberal self-benefit principle mix oil and water?

How much room remains under the liberal self-benefit principle for Lockean feelings to hold sway will depend on the stringency of the liberal principles of charity. At the extreme, requirement b could hold that the more fortunate ought always to give as much help as possible to the less fortunate, which would render a otiose, but nobody believes the requirements of charity are so severe as that. If charitable obligations are limited, then the liberal self-benefit principle expresses a compromise in which the Lockean rule is tempered but

---

[1] Nozick, p. 95. Cf. Becker, pp. 659–60.

not melted away. This compromise still supports the principle of fairness, provided that some adjustment is made for liberal requirements of charity. I can think of two ways in which this adjustment might readily be forthcoming. One would be to restrict the application of the principle of fairness to situations in which requirements of charity are not in question. If a cooperative scheme is in operation, and we are tracking down the obligations it generates, we ask whether the benefits supplied by the cooperators to noncontributors are owed to these noncontributors as strict requirements of charity. If not, the principle of fairness applies. (On the other hand, quite apart from the cooperative scheme, the noncontributors may already strictly owe charity to the persons who happen to be the contributors; and here the requirements of charity may reinforce the requirements of the principle of fairness.)

Another way to adjust the principle of fairness to bring its requirements into line with liberal principles of charity would be to stipulate that the fair division of burdens and benefits which is prerequisite to the generation of obligations under the principle of fairness must incorporate requirements of charity. Insofar as the able or well-off members of society strictly owe charity to the less able or well-off, a fair division of benefits and burdens in public goods schemes adjusts for these requirements. Liberal and Lockean conceptions of the self-benefit principle will surface in controversy as to what constitutes a fair division of the burdens and benefits of cooperation. The point on which I wish to insist is that, even where substantial disputes persist as to the appropriate contribution of the able and the non-able to cooperative schemes, it is noncontroversial that those who scramble to attain an altogether parasitic relation to cooperative schemes are legitimate objects of coercion. There is a distinction between quibbling about the amount of dues one owes and balking entirely at the idea of paying one's dues. The balker exhibits the classic free-rider mentality. For the less able or less well-off, desiring some of the benefits of others' pains may be rendered acceptable by liberal extensions of welfare rights, but desiring the benefits of others'

pains without being willing to reciprocate the benefit at all brings one afoul of the principle of fairness backed by the liberal self-benefit principle.

Here we may note Hart's comment that, in the situations of mutuality of restriction, the moral obligation to obey the rules is owed to "the co-operating members of the society, and they have the correlative moral right to obedience."[1] This comment, along with Rawls's expansion of it, has stimulated the idea that the principle of fairness is meant to apply only in situations where one can discern cooperation in some fairly fullblooded sense of that term, and where the beneficiaries who are obligated must accept the benefits of cooperation in some way that extends beyond mere receipt of benefits. Miller and Sartorius insist that voluntary acceptance is required if the principle of fairness is to give rise to obligations, and they comment, "The principle is surely unacceptable if it permits some to foist obligations upon others by providing benefits not freely chosen and forcing participation in whatever scheme of social cooperation is required to produce them."[2] Simmons suggests that *accepting a benefit* must involve "either (1) trying to get (and succeeding in getting) the benefit, or (2) taking the benefit willingly and knowingly."[3] In the important case of pure public goods, there can be no question of trying to get, so we are reduced to 2. Simmons gives this elaboration of what it is to accept pure public goods willingly and knowingly: (i) We cannot regard the benefit as "having been forced upon us against our will." (ii) We cannot think "the benefits are not worth the price we must pay for them." (iii) "And taking these benefits 'knowingly' seems to involve an understanding of the status of those benefits relative to the party providing them."

These subjective requirements are stringent, and once he has imposed them, it is easy for Simmons to show that obligations arise under the principle of fairness much less frequently than is commonly thought, and that the principle of fairness will cer-

---

[1] Hart, p. 185.
[2] Miller and Sartorius, p. 166.
[3] Simmons, p. 327.

tainly not account for the central range of political obligation it was invoked to explain.

But the subjective requirements i-iii are too stringent. A situation that otherwise issues in an obligation on the part of Jones to contribute to a mutual-benefit scheme will not fail to generate obligation just because Jones does not fully understand that the rule-following behavior of individuals under the mutual-benefit scheme supplies the good in question. Suppose Jones thinks that national defense is manna from heaven. Individuals have some obligation to acquaint themselves with morally pertinent facts of their situation. If Jones's ignorance is excusable, he is entitled to a description of the facts of the matter upon being presented with a bill for cooperative benefits. If Jones has a deeply entrenched belief grossly at variance with the facts, and this counts as negligent or culpable ignorance, his obligation stands. Just having bizarre beliefs about the origins of the collective benefits one enjoys does not relieve one of the obligation to pay one's fair share.

Similar remarks apply to ii, the requirement that one must believe that the costs one is required to pay are fair and in proportion to the benefits one receives. Consider somebody who is racially prejudiced and believes, for no good reason, that it is unfair that the ratio of benefits to costs flowing from cooperation should be the same for whites and blacks. Or consider someone who is disgruntled with what he takes to be the disproportion between the benefits he receives and the contributions he must make compared with others, but who has never bothered to check this imagined perception even against such factual evidence as is readily available just by perusing a daily newspaper. And similarly for i: at a minimum there must be some reasonable basis for skeptical beliefs if they are to block obligations from arising under the principle of fairness.

I think Simmons goes wrong in supposing that a spirit of developed cooperation must pervade a mutual-benefit scheme, extending to all affected by it, before the principle of fairness properly generates obligations. It is obvious that a spirit of cooperation cannot fill persons who do not fully recognize the cooperative nature of the enterprise in which they are required to participate. But a spirit of camaraderie or solidarity is not essential. When Hart says the obligation is owed to the cooperating members, he is pointing to the ongoing character of the scheme, whereby the rule-following and benefit-providing behavior of some continually generates reciprocal obligations in others. Under cooperation, the individual shares in a collective benefit from which there is no way of excluding him (and from which he is unable to exclude himself in the case of pure public goods). If the benefit is uncontroversially a benefit for all, if the division of its costs is fair, the individual beneficiary of an ongoing scheme is required to pay his dues. These conditions themselves are stringent and suffice to guarantee that the principle of fairness will not be an engine of justification of endless regimentation. Querying the relevance of the principle of fairness to actual situations of political obligation, Simmons says, "I do not think that any of us can honestly say that we regard our political lives as a process of working together and making necessary sacrifices for the purpose of improving the common lot."[1] I think one can wax overly skeptical about this possibility. Especially given the contentiousness of the collective goods disbursed and the manifest injustices of their financing, citizens in modern states seem to me to manage to sustain perhaps more of a sense of common collective purpose than is warranted. In any event, the core idea of the principle of fairness is even more prosaic than is conjured up by the idea of common sacrifices to improve the common lot. The basic idea is even simpler and more Lockean—namely, we owe a fair return for services rendered to those who supply the services. The moral intuition here is at bottom the same intuition that it is right to pay the grocer for our groceries or to pay rent for the use of land improved by the landowner, only because of the fact that collective goods come in large nondivisible chunks, coercive provision of such goods is necessary.

---

[1] Ibid., p. 336.

DISCUSSION QUESTIONS

1. Explain the four objections that Arneson presents to Hart's version of the principle of fairness.

2. Explain the following distinctions: private vs. public good, collective vs. pure public good. Explain why Arneson limits the application of the principle of fairness to pure public goods.

3. Compare and contrast the free rider, the nervous cooperator, and the reluctant cooperator. Explain Arneson's revised principle of fairness.

14

ASSOCIATIVE OBLIGATIONS

Samuel Scheffler, "Relationships and Responsibilities" (1997)

Samuel Scheffler is University Professor at the New York University School of Law. Prior to joining the faculty at NYU, he was the Class of 1941 World War II Memorial Professor of Philosophy and Law at the University of California, Berkeley. In this selection, Scheffler considers the relative merits of reductionist and nonreductionist accounts of special responsibilities. In the next reading (15) Diane Jeske provides a response to Scheffler's arguments.

SOURCE

Scheffler, Samuel. "Relationships and Responsibilities." *Philosophy and Public Affairs*, Volume 26, Issue 3, July 1997.

How do we come to have responsibilities to some people that we do not have to others? In our everyday lives, many different kinds of considerations are invoked to explain these "special" responsibilities. Often we cite some kind of interaction that we have had with the person to whom we bear the responsibility. Perhaps we made this person a promise, or entered into an agreement with him. Or perhaps we feel indebted to him because of something he once did for us. Or, again, perhaps we once harmed him in some way, and as a result we feel a responsibility to make reparation to him. In all of these cases, there is either something we have done or something the "beneficiary" of the responsibility has done that is cited as the source of that responsibility.

Not all of our explanations take this form, however. Sometimes we account for special responsibilities not by citing any specific interaction between us and the beneficiary, but rather by citing the nature of our relationship to that person. We have special duties to a person, we may say, because she is our sister, or our friend, or our neighbor. Many different types of relationship are invoked in this way. Perhaps the person is not a relative but a colleague, not a friend but a teammate, not a neighbor but a client. Sometimes the relationship may consist only in the fact that we are both members of a certain kind of group. We may belong to the same community, for example, or be citizens of the same country, or be part of the same nation or people. In some of these cases, we may never have met or had any interaction with the person who is seen as the beneficiary of the responsibility. We may nevertheless be convinced that our shared group membership suffices to generate such a responsibility. Of course, claims of special responsibility can be controversial, especially in cases of this kind. While some people feel strongly that they have special responsibilities to the other members of their national or cultural group, for example, other people feel just as strongly that they do not. Nevertheless, it is a familiar fact that such ties are often seen as a source of special responsibilities. Indeed, we would be hard pressed to find any type of human relationship to which people have attached value or significance but which has never been seen as generating such responsibilities. It seems that whenever people value an interpersonal relationship they are apt to see it as a source of special duties or obligations.[1]

However, although it is clear that we do in fact cite our relationships to other people in explaining why we have special responsibilities to them, many philosophers have been reluctant to take these citations at face value. Instead, they have supposed that the responsibilities we perceive as arising out of special relationships actually arise out of discrete interactions that occur in the context of those relationships. Thus, for example, some special responsibilities, like the mutual responsibilities of spouses, may be said to arise out of promises or commitments that the participants have made to each other. Others, like the responsibilities of children to their parents, may be seen as arising from the provision of benefits to one party by the other. And in cases like those mentioned earlier, in which two people are both members of some group but have not themselves interacted in any way, it may be denied that

the people do in fact have any special responsibilities to each other. As already noted, claims of special responsibility tend to be controversial in such cases anyway, and it may be thought an advantage of this position that it sees grounds for skepticism precisely in the cases that are most controversial.

Clearly, the view that duties arising out of special relationships can always be reduced to duties arising out of discrete interactions is compatible with the view that the relevant interactions, and hence the relevant duties, may be of fundamentally different kinds. Indeed, to some philosophers it seems clear that the relationships that have been seen as generating special responsibilities are so heterogeneous that the responsibilities in question cannot possibly have but a single ground. Nevertheless, one of the greatest pressures toward a reductionist position has come from those who believe that all genuine special responsibilities must be based on consent or on some other voluntary act. These voluntarists, as we may call them, are not hostile to the idea of special responsibilities as such. However, they reject the notion that one can find oneself with such responsibilities without having done anything at all to incur them. Different voluntarists disagree about the types of voluntary act that are capable of generating special responsibilities. Some insist that such responsibilities can only arise from explicit agreements or undertakings. Others believe that one can incur special responsibilities just by voluntarily entering into a relationship with someone, and that no explicit agreement to bear the responsibilities is required. Still others believe that one's acceptance of the benefits of participation in a relationship can generate responsibilities even if one's entry into the relationship was not itself voluntary. Obviously, then, voluntarists will sometimes disagree among themselves about the specific responsibilities of particular people. And different versions of voluntarism will be more or less revisionist with respect to our ordinary moral beliefs, depending on which types of voluntary act they deem capable of generating special responsibilities. For example, voluntarists who believe that special responsibilities can only be incurred through an explicit undertaking

---

[1] In this paragraph and at other points in the next few pages, I draw on my discussions of special responsibilities in the following papers: "Individual Responsibility in a Global Age," *Social Philosophy and Policy* 12 (1995): 219–36; "Families, Nations, and Strangers," in *The Lindley Lecture Series* (Lawrence: University of Kansas, 1995); "Liberalism, Nationalism, and Egalitarianism," in Robert McKim and Jeff McMahan (eds.), *The Morality of Nationalism* (New York: Oxford University Press, 1997).

or the voluntary establishment of a relationship may deny that children have such responsibilities to their parents. But those who think that the voluntary acceptance of benefits can also generate special responsibilities may disagree, at least insofar as they think it makes sense to regard children as voluntarily accepting benefits from their parents. What all voluntarists do agree about, however, is that the mere fact that one stands in a certain relationship to another person cannot by itself give one a special responsibility to that person. In order to have such a responsibility, one must have performed some voluntary act that constitutes the ground of the responsibility.

Voluntarists are sensitive to the fact that special responsibilities can be costly and difficult to discharge, and thus quite burdensome for those who bear them. It would be unfair, they believe, if people could be saddled with such burdens against their wills, and so it would be unfair if special responsibilities could be ascribed to people who had done nothing voluntarily to incur them. In effect, then, voluntarists see a form of reductionism about special responsibilities as necessary if our assignments of such responsibilities are to be fair to those who bear them. Voluntarism is an influential view, and many people find the voluntarist objection to unreduced special responsibilities quite congenial. At the same time, however, there is another objection that may also be directed against such responsibilities. According to this objection, the problem with special responsibilities is not that they may be unfairly burdensome for those who bear them, but rather that they may confer unfair advantages on their bearers. And for the purposes of this objection, it does not matter whether the source of those responsibilities is understood voluntaristically or not.

Suppose that you have recently become my friend and that I have therefore acquired special responsibilities to you. Clearly, these responsibilities work to your advantage, inasmuch as I now have a duty to do things for you that I would not previously have been required to do. At the same time, there are at least two different ways in which my responsibilities to you work to the disadvantage of those people with whom I have no special relationship. First, in the absence of my responsibilities to you, I might have done certain things for them even though I had no duty to do so. Now, however, discharging my responsibilities to you must take priority over doing any of those things for them. Second, there may also be situations in which my responsibilities to you take priority over the responsibilities that I have to them simply as human beings. For example, there may be times when I must help you rather than helping them, if I cannot do both, even though I would have been required to help them but for the fact that you too need help. Thus, in both of these ways, my special responsibilities to you may work to the disadvantage of other people. In one respect, moreover, they may also work to my own disadvantage, since, as the voluntarist objection points out, such responsibilities can be quite burdensome. At the same time, however, my responsibilities to you may also confer some very important advantages on me. For, insofar as I am required to give your interests priority over the interests of other people, I am, in effect, called upon to act in ways that will contribute to the flourishing of our friendship rather than attending to the needs of other people. So my responsibilities to you may work to my net advantage as well as to yours, while working to the disadvantage of people with whom I have no special relationship. Furthermore, if you and I have become friends, then, presumably, not only have I acquired special responsibilities to you but you have acquired such responsibilities to me. And, just as my responsibilities to you may work both to your advantage and to mine, while working to the disadvantage of other people, so too your responsibilities to me may work both to my advantage and to yours, while working to the disadvantage of others.

Now the objection that I have in mind challenges this entire way of allocating benefits and burdens, on the ground that it provides you and me with unfair advantages while unfairly disadvantaging other people. Why exactly, this "distributive objection" asks, should our friendship give rise to a distribution of responsibility that is favorable to us and unfavorable to other people? After all, it may be said, the effect of such a distribution is to reward the very people who have already achieved a rewarding personal relationship, while penalizing those who have not. In addition to enjoying the benefits of our friendship itself, in other words, you and I receive increased claims to each other's assistance, while other people, who never received the original benefits, find that their claims to assistance from us have now become weaker.[1] The distributive objection urges that the fairness of this allocation must be judged against the background of the existing distribution of benefits and burdens of all kinds. Providing additional advantages to people who have already benefited from participation in rewarding relationships will be unjustifiable, according to the distributive objection, whenever the provision of these advantages works to the detriment of people who are needier, whether they are needier because they are not themselves participants in rewarding relationships or because they are significantly worse off in other ways. And it makes no difference, so far as this objection is concerned, whether special responsibilities are thought of as voluntarily incurred or not. Either way, the distributive objection insists that unless the benefits and burdens of special responsibilities are integrated into an overall distribution that is fair, such responsibilities will amount to little more than what one writer has called a "pernicious"[2] form of "prejudice in favor of people who stand in some special relation to US."[3]

It may be protested that it is misleading to represent special responsibilities as providing additional rewards to people who have already secured the advantages of participation in a rewarding relationship. Part of what makes a relationship rewarding, it may be said, is that there are special responsibilities associated with it. So any rewards that special responsibilities may confer on the participants in such relationships are inseparable from the other rewards of participation. This reply raises a variety of issues that I have discussed elsewhere[4] but which cannot be dealt with adequately here. For present purposes, suffice it to say that the reply is unlikely, by itself, to persuade proponents of the distributive objection. They are likely to question whether special responsibilities, as opposed, say, to the de facto willingness of the participants to give special weight to each other's interests, are genuinely necessary for the achievement of a rewarding relationship. They are also likely to argue that, even if it is true that special responsibilities help to make rewarding relationships possible, this only confirms the fundamental point of the objection, which is that such responsibilities work to the advantage of the participants in rewarding relationships and to the disadvantage of nonparticipants. Thus, they are likely to conclude, it remains important that, so far as possible, these advantages and disadvantages should be integrated into an overall distribution of benefits and burdens that is fair.

As we have seen, the voluntarist objection asserts that the source of our special responsibilities must lie in our own voluntary acts. Otherwise, it claims, such responsibilities would be unfairly burdensome for those who bear them. Thus, according to this objection, fairness to the bearers of special responsibilities requires a version of reductionism with respect to such responsibilities. The distributive objection, on the other hand, challenges the fairness of special responsibilities whether or not their source is thought of as lying in the voluntary acts of those who bear them. And its claim is that such responsibilities, far from imposing unfair burdens on the people who bear them, may instead provide those people with unfair advantages. If a

[1] If it is ultimately to be convincing, the distributive objection will need to provide a fuller accounting of the various advantages and disadvantages that special responsibilities may confer both on the participants in interpersonal relationships and on nonparticipants. I consider the implications of such an accounting in "The Conflict Between Justice and Responsibility," in L. Brilmayer and I. Shapiro (eds.), *Nomos XLI: Global Justice* (forthcoming). [New York: New York University Press, 1999; pp. 86–106.]
[2] Robert Goodin, *Protecting the Vulnerable* (Chicago: University of Chicago Press, 1985), p. 1.
[3] Ibid., p. 6.

[4] In "Families, Nations, and Strangers," Section IV.

nonreductionist account of special responsibilities is to be convincing, it will need to address both of these objections.[1]

In this essay, I will sketch the rudiments of a nonreductionist account. My discussion will remain schematic, inasmuch as I will be concerned with the abstract structure of a nonreductionist position rather than with a detailed accounting of the specific responsibilities that such a position would assign people. Nevertheless, I hope that my sketch may suggest a new way of understanding nonreductionist claims of special responsibility and that, in so doing, it may make nonreductionism seem less implausible than it is often thought to be. In any event, I believe that the type of position I will describe merits careful consideration. As is no doubt evident, questions about the status of special responsibilities bear directly on a number of the liveliest controversies in contemporary moral and political philosophy. For example, such questions are central to the debate within moral philosophy between consequentialism and deontology. They are equally central to the debates within political philosophy between liberalism and communitarianism, and between nationalism and cosmopolitanism. Thus the way that we think about special responsibilities may have far-reaching implications, and it would be a mistake to dismiss nonreductionism without attempting to understand it sympathetically.

Nonreductionists are impressed by the fact that we often cite our relationships to people rather than particular interactions with them as the source of our special responsibilities. They believe that our perception of things is basically correct; the source of such responsibilities often does lie in the relationships themselves rather than in particular interactions between the participants. A nonreductionist might begin to elaborate this position as follows. Other people can make claims on me, and their needs can provide me with reasons for

action, whether or not I have any special relationship to them. If a stranger is suffering and I am in a position to help, without undue cost to myself, then I may well have a reason to do so. This much is true simply in virtue of our common humanity. However, if I have a special, valued relationship with someone, and if the value I attach to the relationship is not purely instrumental in character—if, in other words, I do not value it solely as a means to some independently specified end—then I regard the person with whom I have the relationship as capable of making additional claims on me, beyond those that people in general can make. For to attach noninstrumental value to my relationship with a particular person just is, in part, to see that person as a source of special claims in virtue of the relationship between us. It is, in other words, to be disposed, in contexts which vary depending on the nature of the relationship, to see that person's needs, interests, and desires as, in themselves, providing me with presumptively decisive reasons for action, reasons that I would not have had in the absence of the relationship. By "presumptively decisive reasons" I mean reasons which, although they are capable in principle of being outweighed or overridden, nevertheless present themselves as considerations upon which I must act. If there are no circumstances in which I would see a person's needs or interests as giving me such reasons, then, according to the nonreductionist, it makes no sense to assert that I attach (noninstrumental) value to my relationship with that person. But this is tantamount to saying that I cannot value my relationships (noninstrumentally) without seeing them as sources of special responsibilities.[2]

If it is true that one cannot value one's relationship to another person (noninstrumentally) without

_____

[1] I have discussed both objections at greater length in "Families, Nations, and Strangers" and in "Liberalism, Nationalism, and Egalitarianism." I have discussed the distributive objection most extensively in "The Conflict Between Justice and Responsibility."

[2] The nonreductionist recognizes, of course, that it is possible for me to regard relationships in which I am not a participant as valuable. The nonreductionist's claim, however, is that valuing one's own relationship to another person is different, not because one is bound to see such a relationship as more valuable than other relationships of the same type, but rather because one is bound to see it as a source of reasons for action of a distinctive kind.

seeing it, in effect, as a source of special responsibilities, then it hardly seems mysterious that such a wide and apparently heterogeneous assortment of relationships have been seen as giving rise to such responsibilities. Nor, given that different people value relationships of different kinds, does it seem mysterious that some claims of special responsibility remain highly controversial. For if one disapproves of a certain kind of relationship, or of the tendency to invest relationships of that kind with significance, then one is likely to greet claims of special responsibility arising out of such relationships with skepticism. Thus, to take three very different examples, although the members of street gangs, fraternities, and nations often attach considerable importance to their membership in those groups, and although, in consequence, they often have a strong sense of responsibility to their fellow members, someone who disapproves of such groups, or of the tendency to invest them with significance, may be unwilling to accept these claims of responsibility. On the other hand, someone who values his own participation in a relationship of a certain kind is likely to ascribe special responsibilities to the other participants in such relationships, even when they themselves do not value those relationships or acknowledge responsibilities arising out of them. Thus, on the nonreductionist view, differences in the kinds of relationships that people value lead naturally to disagreements about the assignment of special responsibility.

The nonreductionist position as thus far described takes us only so far. It asserts that relationships and not merely interactions are among the sources of special responsibilities, and it claims that people who value their relationships invariably see them as giving rise to such responsibilities. As so far described, however, the position says nothing about the conditions under which relationships actually do give rise to special responsibilities. Now there is, of course, no reason to expect that all nonreductionists will give the same answer to this question, any more than there is reason to expect that all reductionists will identify the same types of interactions as the sources of special responsibilities. In

this essay, however, I wish to explore the specific suggestion that one's relationships to other people give rise to special responsibilities to those people when they are relationships that one has reason to value.[1] For ease of exposition, I will refer to this view simply as "nonreductionism," but we should remember that this is just an expository device, and that other versions of nonreductionism are possible.

Several features of the formulation I have given require comment and clarification. First, the term "value," as it occurs in that formulation and in subsequent discussion, should be taken to mean "value noninstrumentally," and the term "reason" should be taken to mean "net reason." In other words, if a person only has reason to value a relationship instrumentally, then the principle I have stated does not treat that relationship as a source of special responsibilities. And if a person has some reason to value a relationship but more reason not to, then again the principle does not treat it as generating such responsibilities. Furthermore, although the formulation I have given does not presuppose any particular conception of the kinds of reasons that people can have for valuing their relationships, reasons that are reflexively instrumental, in the sense that they derive from the instrumental advantages of valuing a relationship noninstrumentally, are to be understood as excluded. In other words, if attaching noninstrumental value to a certain relationship would itself be an effective means of achieving some independently desirable goal, the principle I have stated does not treat that as a reason of the responsibility-generating kind.

Second, there is a perfectly good sense of "relationship" in which every human being stands in some relationship to every other human being. However, as far as the view that I am presenting is concerned, only socially salient connections among people count as "relations" or "relationships"—two terms that I use interchangeably. Thus, for example,

---

[1] On some views, membership in a group may give one special responsibilities to the group that transcend any responsibilities one has to the individual members. The view I am exploring is agnostic on this question.

if you happen to have the same number of letters in your last name as John Travolta does, that does not mean that you have a relationship with him. Nor does the fact that you admire Travolta suffice to establish the existence of a relationship in the relevant sense, for the fact that one person has a belief about or attitude toward another does not constitute a social tie between them. On the other hand, two members of a socially recognized group do have a relationship in the relevant sense, even if they have never met, and if they value their membership in that group they may also value their relations to the other members. Thus, the fact that you are a member of the John Travolta Fan Club means that you have a relation to each of the other club members, and if you value your membership you may also value those relations.

Third, valuing my relationship with another person, in the sense that matters for nonreductionism, means valuing the relation of each of us to the other. So if, for example, I value my status as the Brutal Tyrant's leading opponent but not his status as my despised adversary, then I do not value our relationship in the sense that the nonreductionist principle treats as relevant. Similar remarks apply, mutatis mutandis, to having reason to value a relationship.

Fourth, nonreductionism as I have formulated it is not committed to a fixed view either of the strength or of the content of special responsibilities. It is compatible with the view that such responsibilities can be outweighed by other considerations. It is also compatible with the view that the strength of one's responsibilities depends on the nature of the relationships that give rise to them, and on the degree of value that one has reason to attach to those relationships. As far as the content of the responsibilities is concerned, we may assume that this too depends on the nature of the relationships in question, but that, at the most abstract level, it always involves a duty to give priority of various kinds, in suitable contexts, to certain of the interests of those to whom the responsibilities are owed.

Fifth, the nonreductionist principle states a sufficient condition for special responsibilities, not a necessary condition. Thus the principle does not

purport to identify the source of all such responsibilities. In particular, it does not deny that promises and other kinds of discrete interactions can also give rise to special responsibilities. It merely claims to identify conditions under which interpersonal relations give rise to responsibilities that need not be fully accounted for in reductionist terms.

Sixth, nonreductionism makes it possible to claim both that people sometimes have special responsibilities that they think they lack, and that they sometimes lack special responsibilities that they think they have. For it is possible to think both that people can fail to value relationships that they have reason to value, and that they can succeed in valuing relationships that they have no reason to value. We may think, for example, that a neglectful father has reason to value his relations to the children he ignores, or that an abused wife lacks any reason to value her relation to the husband she cannot bring herself to leave. Similarly, we may feel that an ambitious young woman has good reasons to value her relationship with the devoted immigrant parents of whom she is ashamed, and little reason to value her relationship with the vain and self-absorbed classmate whose attention she prizes and whose approval she craves.[1]

Finally, however, our ability to sustain claims of this kind is clearly dependent on a conception of reasons, and, more specifically, on a conception of the conditions under which people may be said to have reasons to value their relations to others. The more closely a person's reasons are seen as linked to his existing desires and motivations, the less scope there will be for distinguishing between the relationships that he has reason to value and the relationships that he actually does value. On the other hand, the less closely reasons are thought of as tied to existing desires, the more room there will be to

---

[1] Of course, since the nonreductionist principle does articulate only a sufficient and not a necessary condition for special responsibilities, the fact that one has no reason to value one's relationship to a particular person does not by itself show that one has no special responsibilities whatsoever to that person—only that one has no responsibilities arising under the nonreductionist principle.

draw such distinctions. As I have indicated, non-reductionism does not itself put forward a conception of reasons. Its claim, rather, is that many judgments of special responsibility are dependent on the ascription to people of reasons for valuing their relations to others, so that any substantive conception of such responsibilities is hostage to some conception of reasons.[1]

Nonreductionism of the kind I have described makes possible the following simple defense of unreduced special responsibilities. We human beings are social creatures, and creatures with values. Among the things that we value are our relations with each other. But to value one's relationship with another person is to see it as a source of reasons for action of a distinctive kind. It is, in effect, to see oneself as having special responsibilities to the person with whom one has the relationship. Thus, insofar as we have good reasons to value our interpersonal relations, we have good reasons to see ourselves as having special responsibilities. And, accordingly, skepticism about such responsibilities will be justified only if we are prepared to deny that we have good reasons to value our relationships.

It may seem that this argument is fallacious. For consider: even if I have reason to promise that I will meet you for lunch on Tuesday, and even though I would be obligated to meet you if I were so to promise, it does not follow that, here and now, I actually have such an obligation. On the contrary, I acquire the obligation only if I make the promise. Similarly, it may seem, even if I have reason

to value my relationship with you, and even if I would acquire special responsibilities to you if I did value our relationship, it does not follow that, here and now, I actually have such responsibilities. On the contrary, I acquire the responsibilities only if I value the relationship. However, the nonreductionist will resist this analogy. In the promising case, I have reason to perform an act which, if performed, will generate an obligation. But the nonreductionist's claim about special responsibilities is different. The claim is not that, in having reason to value our relationship, I have reason to perform an act which, if performed, will generate responsibilities. The claim is rather that, to value our relationship is, in part, to see myself as having such responsibilities, so that if, here and now, I have reason to value our relationship, then what I have reason to do, here and now, is to see myself as having such responsibilities. In the promising case, the promise generates the obligation, and no obligation arises in the absence of the promise. But the existence of a relationship that one has reason to value is itself the source of special responsibilities, and those responsibilities arise whether or not the participants actually value the relationship. Or so the nonreductionist claims.

Even if the disanalogy with the promising case is conceded, it may nevertheless be said that the nonreductionist argument stops short of establishing that we really do have special responsibilities. As we have seen, the nonreductionist claims that, insofar as we have reason to value our interpersonal relationships, we also have reason to see ourselves as having such responsibilities. But, it may be said, even if we have reason to see ourselves as having such responsibilities, that is compatible with our not actually having them. This seems to me misleading, however. If the nonreductionist argument establishes that we have good reason to see ourselves as having special responsibilities, then that is how we should see ourselves. There is no substantive difference, in this context, between the conclusion that we do have special responsibilities and the conclusion that, all things considered, we have good reasons for thinking that we do.

---

[1] This means that it would be possible for a reductionist to argue that people's reasons for valuing their relations to others derive exclusively from discrete interactions that occur in the context of those relations. Even if this argument were accepted, however, it would remain the case that, according to the principle under consideration, the source of the relevant responsibilities lies in the relationships rather than the interactions. Furthermore, it may not be possible without loss of plausibility to translate reductionism about special responsibilities into reductionism about people's reasons for valuing their relationships. For some of the types of interaction that have been seen as generating such responsibilities do not seem plausibly construed as generating reasons for valuing relationships.

Some may worry that the nonreductionist principle as I have formulated it focuses too much attention on the bearers of special responsibilities and too little on the beneficiaries. Sometimes, it may be said, the source of a special responsibility does not lie in the fact that the relationship is one that the bearer has reason to value, but rather in the vulnerability created by the beneficiary's trust in or dependence on the bearer. However, this suggestion is not incompatible with the principle I have articulated. For that principle purports to identify only a sufficient condition, and not a necessary condition, for a relationship to give rise to special responsibilities. Thus it no more precludes the possibility that relations of trust and vulnerability may also give rise to such responsibilities than the principle that one ought to keep one's promises precludes the possibility that there are other kinds of obligations as well.

How, then, might a nonreductionist respond to the voluntarist and distributive objections? The voluntarist objection, we may recall, points out that special responsibilities may constitute significant burdens for those who bear them, and asserts that it would be unfair if such responsibilities could be ascribed to individuals who had done nothing voluntarily to incur them. The first thing that nonreductionists may say in response to this objection is that, in addition to our special responsibilities, there are other moral norms that govern our treatment of people in general. These moral norms, they may point out, apply to us whether or not we have agreed to them. For example, one cannot justify one's infliction of harm on a person by saying that one never agreed not to harm people. There are, in other words, general moral responsibilities that can be ascribed to us without our having voluntarily incurred them. And although these general responsibilities, like special responsibilities, may be costly or burdensome, we do not ordinarily regard their imposition as unfair. So why, nonreductionists may ask, should special responsibilities be any different? If voluntarists do not require that general responsibilities be voluntarily incurred, how can they insist that special responsibilities must be? The voluntarist may reply that special responsibilities, unless voluntarily incurred, give other people undue control over one's life. If certain people can make claims on you without your having done anything to legitimate those claims, then, the voluntarist may argue, those people enjoy an unreasonable degree of authority over the way you live. However, since general moral norms also enable people to make claims on individuals who have done nothing to legitimate those claims, nonreductionists will again want to know why special responsibilities that have not been voluntarily incurred should be objectionable in a way that general responsibilities are not.

One reason for the voluntarist's concern about special responsibilities may be as follows. Our most significant social roles and relations determine, to a considerable extent, the ways that we are seen by others and the ways that we see ourselves. They help to determine what might be called our social identities. To the extent that we choose our roles and relations, and decide how much significance they shall have in our lives, we shape our own identities. But to the extent that these things are fixed independently of our choices, our identities are beyond our control. What disturbs the voluntarist about special responsibilities may be this: if our relations to other people can generate responsibilities to those people independently of our choices, then, to that extent, the significance of our social relations is not up to us to determine. And if the significance of such relations is not up to us to determine, then we may be locked into a social identity we did not choose. This suggests that special responsibilities may be troubling to the voluntarist, in a way that general responsibilities are not, because special responsibilities may seem to threaten our capacity for self-determination—our capacity to determine who, in social terms, we are. On this interpretation, it is not wrong to suggest that the voluntarist views special responsibilities, unless voluntarily incurred, as giving other people undue control over our lives. However, the problem is not simply that others may be able to make unwelcome claims on our time and resources. That much would be true even if we had only general responsibilities. The more fundamental problem is that other people may be able to shape our identities in ways that run counter to our wishes.

Seen in this light, the voluntarist's position has obvious appeal. The ability to have our social identities influenced by our choices is something about which most of us care deeply, and which seems to us an important prerequisite for the forms of human flourishing to which we aspire. We regard societies in which one's social identity is rigidly fixed, as a matter of law or social practice, by features of one's birth or breeding over which one has no control, as societies that are inhospitable to human freedom. This does not mean that we are committed to repudiating whatever communal or traditional affiliations may have been conferred upon us at birth. It only means that we want the salience in our lives of such affiliations to be influenced by our own wishes and decisions, rather than being determined by the dictates of the society at large. This is, of course, one reason why liberals insist that the legal status of citizens should be insensitive to facts about their race or religion or social class.

And yet, despite the value that we attach to having our social identities influenced by our choices, and despite the particular importance of protecting this value against political interference, it is clear that the capacity to determine one's identity has its limits. Each of us is born into a web of social relations, and our social world lays claim to us long before we can attain reflective distance from it or begin making choices about our place in it. We acquire personal relations and social affiliations of a formative kind before we are able to conceive of them as such or to contemplate altering them. Thus there is obviously no question, nor can the voluntarist seriously think that there is, of our being able actually to choose all of the relations in which we stand to other people. What the voluntarist can hope to claim is only that the significance of those relations is entirely up to us. However, this claim too is unsustainable. For better or worse, the influence on our personal histories of unchosen social relations—to parents and siblings, families and communities, nations and peoples—is not something that we determine by ourselves. Whether

we like it or not, such relations help to define the contours of our lives, and influence the ways that we are seen both by ourselves and by others. Even those who sever or repudiate such ties—insofar as it is possible to do so—can never escape their influence or deprive them of all significance, for to have repudiated a personal tie is not the same as never having had it, and one does not nullify social bonds by rejecting them. One is, in other words, forever the person who has rejected or repudiated those bonds; one cannot make oneself into a person who lacked them from the outset. Thus, while some people travel enormous social distances in their lives, and while the possibility of so doing is something that we have every reason to cherish, the idea that the significance of our personal ties and social affiliations is wholly dependent on our wills—that we are the supreme gatekeepers of our own identities—can only be regarded as a fantasy. So if, as the nonreductionist believes, our relations to other people can generate responsibilities to them independently of our choices, then it is true that, in an important respect, the significance of our social relations is not fully under our control; but since the significance of those relations is in any case not fully under our control, this by itself does not rob us of any form of self-determination to which we may reasonably aspire.

In the end, then, the nonreductionist's response to the voluntarist objection is to insist that, although the significance of choice and consent in moral contexts is undeniable, nevertheless, the moral import of our relationships to other people does not derive solely from our own decisions. Nor, the nonreductionist may add, need we fear that this is tantamount to conceding the legitimacy of systems of caste or hierarchy, or that it leaves the individual at the mercy of oppressive social arrangements. For the relationships that generate responsibilities for an individual are those relationships that the individual has reason to value. No claims at all arise from relations that are degrading or demeaning, or which serve to undermine rather than to enhance human flourishing. In other words, the alternative to an exaggerated voluntarism is not an exaggerated communitarianism or historicism. In recognizing that the significance of our social relationships does not stem exclusively from our choices, we do not consign ourselves to a form of social bondage. In surrendering the fantasy that our own wills are the source of all our special responsibilities, we do not leave ourselves defenseless against the contingencies of the social world.

Yet even if these remarks constitute an effective response to the voluntarist objection, they may seem only to highlight the nonreductionist's vulnerability to the distributive objection. For, if relationships that are destructive of an individual's well-being do not, in general, give that individual special responsibilities, then presumably the relationships that do give him special responsibilities either enhance or at least do not erode his well-being. But, as we have seen, special responsibilities may themselves work to the advantage of the participants in special relationships, and to the disadvantage of nonparticipants. And, it may be asked, why should a relationship that enhances the well-being of the participants give rise to a distribution of moral responsibility that further advances their interests, while working against the interests of nonparticipants? How can the nonreductionist respond to the charge that, unless the benefits and burdens of special responsibilities are integrated into an overall distribution that is fair, such responsibilities will themselves provide unfair advantages to the participants in interpersonal relations, while unfairly penalizing nonparticipants?

The nonreductionist may begin by reiterating that, as long as people attach value to their interpersonal relations, they will inevitably see themselves as having special responsibilities. And as long as they have good reasons for attaching value to those relations, we must allow that they also have good reasons to see themselves as having such responsibilities. There may, of course, be room for general skepticism about people's reasons for valuing their interpersonal relations. But it seems unlikely that proponents of the distributive objection can afford to be skeptics of this sort. For the distributive objection is animated by a concern for fairness

in the allocation of benefits and burdens, and if, as the skeptic asserts, people never have reason to value their social relations, then it is unclear why considerations of fairness should weigh with them at all. Rather than providing grounds for the rejection of special responsibilities in particular, general skepticism about our reasons for valuing personal relations seems potentially subversive of morality as a whole.

Provided that the distributive objection is not taken to support a wholesale repudiation of special responsibilities, however, nonreductionists may concede that it makes a legitimate point. There are important respects in which special responsibilities may work to the advantage of the participants in personal relationships, and to the disadvantage of other people. These facts seem undeniable once they are called to our attention. That we sometimes lose sight of them is due in large measure to the influence of voluntarism, which focuses exclusively on the respects in which special responsibilities can be burdensome for the people who bear them, and sees the task of legitimating such responsibilities solely as a matter of justifying those burdens. Once we face the facts to which the distributive objection calls attention, however, we must agree that there is another side to special responsibilities: that they may also provide significant advantages for the participants in interpersonal relations and significant disadvantages for nonparticipants. Insofar as the distributive objection insists only on the desirability of integrating these advantages and disadvantages into an overall distribution of benefits and burdens that is fair, nonreductionists have no reason to disagree.

Indeed, once the distributive objection is understood in this way, it may be seen as illustrating a more general point, with which nonreductionists also have no reason to disagree. The general point is that special responsibilities need to be set within the context of our overall moral outlook and constrained in suitable ways by other pertinent values. On a nonreductionist view, such constraints may, in principle, operate in at least three different ways. Some may affect the content of special responsibilities, by setting limits to the circumstances in which, and the extent to which, people are required to give priority to the interests of those to whom they have such responsibilities. Other constraints may affect the strength of special responsibilities, by supplying countervailing considerations that are capable of outweighing or overriding those responsibilities in various contexts. Still other constraints may affect people's reasons for valuing their relationships. Perhaps, for example, people have no (net) reason to value relationships which themselves offend against important moral values or principles, so that such relationships do not generate special responsibilities even if people do in fact value them.[1]

The upshot is that, although nonreductionism insists that unreduced special responsibilities must be part of any adequate moral scheme, it is not hostile to the idea that there are a variety of other moral values, including the values underlying the distributive objection—by which such responsibilities must be constrained and with which they must be integrated if they are to be fully satisfactory. For example, there is nothing to prevent the nonreductionist from agreeing that considerations of distributive fairness serve to limit both the strength and the content of people's special responsibilities. Of course, the mere fact that nonreductionism is open to such possibilities does not suffice to show that a single moral outlook will be capable of accommodating special responsibilities while fully satisfying the values underlying the distributive objection. In fact, I believe that there is a deep and persistent tension between these two features of our moral thought, and nothing in the nonreductionist

position guarantees that we will be able simultaneously to accommodate both features to our own satisfaction.[2]

Although this is a serious problem, however, it is no more of a problem for nonreductionist accounts of special responsibilities than it is for reductionist accounts. In fact, it is a problem for any view that takes special responsibilities seriously, while remaining sensitive to the values underlying the distributive objection. Any such view, and indeed any view that recognizes a diversity of moral values and principles, needs to ask how far that diversity can be accommodated within a unified moral outlook. Too often it is simply taken for granted either that a unified outlook must in principle be available or that any tension at all among our values means that there is no possibility of jointly accommodating them. Neither assumption seems to me to be warranted. Instead, it seems to me a substantive question, the answer to which remains open, to what extent the diverse moral values that we recognize can be jointly accommodated within a unified scheme of thought and practice.

Pending an answer to that question, nonreductionism appears to have the following advantages as an account of special responsibilities. To begin with, it has the virtue of cohering better than do reductionist accounts with our actual practice, which is to cite relationships as well as interactions as sources of special responsibilities. It also has the advantage of being able to explain, in simple and straightforward terms, why it is that people have seen such a diverse and apparently heterogeneous assortment of relationships as giving rise to such responsibilities. Furthermore, nonreductionism makes it possible to agree that our ordinary practices of ascribing special responsibilities to the participants in significant relationships are broadly correct. Like those ordinary practices themselves, however, it also leaves room for the criticism of particular ascriptions of responsibility. Admittedly, the content of the nonreductionist

[1] Might it be said, by someone sympathetic to the distributive objection, that relationships that run afoul of that objection violate this last type of constraint, and thus do not give rise to special responsibilities after all? This is unpersuasive because the distributive objection is not an objection to a class of relationships. In other words, it does not allege that certain relationships offend against important moral values. Instead, it claims only that considerations of distributive fairness prevent some relationships, which may be entirely unobjectionable in themselves, from giving rise to special responsibilities. But the constraint in question applies only to relationships that themselves offend against important moral values.

[2] See, generally, Thomas Nagel, *Equality and Partiality* (New York: Oxford University Press, 1991).

principle depends on some conception of the kinds of reasons people have for valuing their relations to others. Thus, given this principle, disagreements about reasons will inevitably lead to disagreements about the circumstances under which special responsibilities should be ascribed to people. Even this may seem like an advantage, however. For there are many disagreements about the ascription of such responsibilities that do seem plausibly understood as reflecting a more fundamental disagreement about the reasons people have for valuing their relationships. To the extent that this is so, nonreductionism locates controversies about the ascription of special responsibilities in the right place, and provides an illuminating explanation of them. Finally, nonreductionism is sensitive to the concerns underlying the voluntarist and distributive objections, yet it provides reasons for insisting that neither objection supports the complete repudiation of unreduced special responsibilities.

Let me close by returning to a point that I made earlier. The nonreductionist position I have outlined, if it can be persuasively developed, may have implications for a number of important controversies in moral and political philosophy. Inasmuch as it offers a defense of special responsibilities that is nonconsequentialist in character, for example, it points to a possible defense of at least some sorts of "agent-centered restrictions."[1] Similarly, I believe, it suggests some constraints that any adequate formulation of cosmopolitanism may need to respect. Detailed discussion of these implications, however, must await another occasion.

---

[1] See [Samuel Scheffler,] *The Rejection of Consequentialism* (Oxford: Clarendon Press, 1994 [rev. ed.]), esp. Chap. Four.

DISCUSSION QUESTIONS

1. Scheffler raises an objection to special responsibilities which turns on the possibility that they may provide those who possess them (or are beneficiaries of them) with unfair advantages, while burdening those who are not a party to the relationship within which the special responsibilities arise. Explain this objection. What are the relevant benefits and burdens? In what sense might the allocation of benefits and burdens be unfair or unjust? Do you find this objection compelling? Why or why not?

2. What does Scheffler mean when he speaks of "nonreductionism" with respect to special obligations? On what grounds does he object to reductionism?

3. According to Scheffler, under what circumstances does a relationship between people give rise to special obligations on the part of the individuals involved in the relationship? Briefly list some of the people with whom you interact on a daily basis. In Scheffler's view, for whom among those on the list do you have special responsibilities? How would you describe the character of these special responsibilities?

4. How does Scheffler respond to the "fairness" objection (see question 1)? In what sense is his (nonreductionist) response to this objection different than the response that would likely be given by a reductionist?

15

ASSOCIATIVE OBLIGATIONS
Diane Jeske, "Special Relationships and the Problem of Political Obligations" (2001)

Diane Jeske (b. 1967) is a professor in the Philosophy Department at the University of Iowa. She specializes in ethical theory and political philosophy and has written on the nature of obligations among intimates, the nature of friendship, and utilitarianism versus deontology. Her recent research explores the topic of evil. In this piece, which responds directly to Scheffler's article above, Jeske argues that attempts to model the nature of special political obligations on accounts of intimate relationships will fail.

SOURCE

Jeske, Diane. "Special Relationships and the Problem of Political Obligations." *Social Theory and Practice* Volume 27, Number 1, 2001, pp. 19–44. Reprinted by permission of the publisher.

1. Introduction

Beyond those natural duties that each of us owes to all our fellow human beings, ordinary moral thought has always acknowledged that we have obligations to those persons to whom we stand in special relationships. Two types of special relationships have been fairly uncontroversially taken to ground special obligations: promissory or contractual relationships, and intimate relationships between, for example, friends and family members. Naturally, then, in their attempts to ground special political obligations, political philosophers have often taken one of these two types of special relationships as their model for the type of relationship that grounds special obligations between compatriots.

In the history of liberal political thought, the model of promissory or contractual relationships has been the dominant model for special political relationships. The place of consent theory in liberal thought can largely be explained by implicit or explicit acceptance of *voluntarism*, the thesis that special obligations, over and above natural duties, can only be acquired as a result of some voluntary action or actions that the agent knows or ought to know generates such special obligations. If one has given one's consent, made a promise or a contract to perform certain actions, such as obeying the laws of one's country, then one's being bound to perform those actions is clearly compatible with voluntarism: the agent has chosen to do more for certain specified persons than natural duty requires of her and she ought to know that her promising binds her to perform those actions for those persons. But, while consent theorists have struggled valiantly to interpret various types of actions as expressions of citizens' consent to obey the laws of their countries, it has become increasingly obvious that the vast majority of citizens of any modern state have never agreed to do any such thing.

In recent years, then, philosophers have begun to turn to the second type of special relationship as both providing a model for special political relationships and suggesting motivation for the rejection of voluntarism. After all, these philosophers argue, we do not choose our parents or our siblings, yet surely we have special obligations to our family members. Thus, by exploring the grounds of special obligations in intimate relationships, we might find a grounding for special political obligations, in spite of the unchosen nature of our relationships to our compatriots.

I will argue that any attempt to provide a unified account of both obligations arising from intimate relationships and political obligations will fail. Others have also denied the plausibility of any such account, but have, in so doing, misunderstood the real difficulty with attempting to assimilate political contexts to intimate contexts.[1] Such accounts inevitably distort the very notion of a relationship, and thereby distort the nature of the intimate contexts. Appreciating the nature of intimate relationships will lead us to see that we can offer a voluntarist account of special obligations to intimates. Once we do that, however, any hopes of modeling political relationships on intimate relationships must be abandoned.

2. Special Obligations: Contractual and Associative

We need to begin by considering the nature of special obligations. First, as I said above, such obligations are to be distinguished from natural duties, that is, duties owed by each person to all other persons simply in virtue of some feature shared by all persons (rationality and sentience are two favorites for filling this role). Second, I will understand special obligations as obligations that are not derived from and therefore cannot be reduced to those more general duties owed to all persons.[2] Thus, for example, a utilitarian account of genuinely special obligations is not possible: utilitarians can only hope to show the benefits of, for example, persons having dispositions to act in patterns that would accord with what such obligations would dictate.

Special obligations are often understood as arising from special relationships that include on the one hand straightforwardly promissory or contractual relationships and, on the other, those relationships in which we stand to our "associates," that is, our friends, family members, colleagues, and so on. These latter special obligations are sometimes labeled "associative obligations;"[3] thus, those who use relationships to "associates" as the model for political relations are attempting to show that special political obligations are associative rather than contractual obligations. So associative obligations are typically understood as distinct from contractual obligations because the latter are a matter of choice while the former are not. A. John Simmons, for example, sees those who claim that political obligations are associative obligations as rejecting voluntarism, while, of course, traditional consent theory, which views political obligations as contractual obligations, is entirely friendly to and has often probably been, at least in part, motivated by voluntarism.[4]

---

[1] See, most importantly, A. John Simmons, "Associative Political Obligations," *Ethics* 106 (1996): 247–73.

[2] For a discussion of attempts to derive special political obligations from "general moral principles," see Andrew Mason, "Special Obligations to Compatriots," *Ethics* 107 (1997): 429–37. Mason clearly understands special obligations in terms of their content rather than their grounds, so he considers whether they can be derived from natural duties an open question.

[3] This term is Ronald Dworkin's. See his *Law's Empire* (Cambridge, MA: Harvard University Press, 1986), pp. 195 ff.

[4] Simmons, "Associative Political Obligations," pp. 248–49.

Simmons goes on to characterize an associative obligation as "a special moral requirement, attached to a social role or position (including that of membership in a group), whose content is determined by what local practice specifies as required for those who fill that role or position."[1] He equates associative obligations, then, with obligations of role or position: one's obligations to loved ones arise from one's occupation of the role of friend or lover or daughter. Similarly, Ronald Dworkin, one of the first philosophers to suggest that political obligations are associative obligations, understands associative obligations as "responsibilities under social practices that define groups and attach special responsibilities to membership ... when certain other conditions are met or sustained."[2] Thus, if political obligations are associative, they arise from the occupation of the role of citizen (or permanent resident). I will argue that this equation of associative obligations with obligations of role or position trivializes the sorts of relationships that ground genuinely associative obligations in contrast with obligations of mere role or position.[3]

So I will not begin with any understanding of associative obligations as obligations of role, nor with any assumptions about the ways in which associative obligations differ from contractual obligations. I put only two constraints on an account of associative obligations: (1) it must account for the paradigm-associative obligations, that is, our obligations to our intimates (friends, family members); (2) it must ground those obligations by an appeal (at the fundamental level) to some feature of the special relationship that obtains between the obligor and the obligee. Whatever feature is appealed to may be relevantly analogous to one that also characterizes promissory and contractual relationships,

thus allowing a unitary account of associative obligations and contractual obligations. And of course such a feature may also be present in political relationships. I will argue, however, that while the former claim is true, the latter is not.

3. The Problem of Political Obligations

In the last section, I differentiated between natural duties and special obligations, including contractual and associative obligations. Any adequate account of political obligations must place them in the category of special obligations because, as Simmons says, they must satisfy what he calls "the particularity requirement":

> Political obligations are felt to be obligations of obedience and support owed to one particular government or community (our own), above all others. Citizens' obligations are special ties, involving loyalty or commitment to the political community in which they were born or in which they reside. More general moral duties with possible political content, such as duties to promote justice, equality, or utility, cannot explain (or justify, or be) our political obligations, for such duties do not necessarily tie us either to one particular community or to our own community.[4]

Thus, political obligations must be special obligations. Are they contractual or associative? They seem to be obviously not contractual, as the failure of consent theory attests. We (at least most of us) have not chosen our political affiliations. Thus, if political obligations are to be valid for more than a small sector of any given political community, they are not, on the whole, contractual in nature. The fact that we have not chosen our political affiliations supports the claim that any account of special political obligations must be an *antivoluntarist* account. Thus, if political obligations are to be understood as associative, we must offer an

---

[1] Ibid., p. 253.
[2] Dworkin, *Law's Empire*, p. 198.
[3] For a recent defense of associative obligations understood as obligations of role, see Michael Hardimon, "Role Obligations," *The Journal of Philosophy* 91 (1994): 333–63. For a response to Hardimon, see my "Families, Friends, and Special Obligations," *Canadian Journal of Philosophy* 28 (1998): 527–56.

[4] Simmons, "Associative Political Obligations," p. 250.

account of associative obligations that is antivoluntarist in nature, so as to be able to effectively contrast associative obligations with contractual obligations.

So the claim that political obligations are associative would set the following constraints upon an account of associative obligations: (1) the account of associative obligations must be antivoluntarist in nature. But it also would commit one to the acceptance of what Samuel Scheffler calls "*nonreductionism*" about special obligations: (2) the grounds of special obligations must "lie in the relationships themselves rather than in particular interactions between the participants."[1] What the nonreductionist as characterized by Scheffler is denying is that in order to be "associates" in a morally relevant sense, persons must directly causally interact with one another and have knowledge of one another as individuals. Persons do interact with one another in these ways in intimate relationships, but they just as clearly do not interact in these ways in political relationships in modern states. Thus, if political obligations are to be grounded in the same way as the paradigm-associative obligations, then the latter must be grounded by something other than the direct, personal interaction between the parties to the relationship. Nonreductionists, then, must understand "relationship" in a very broad sense.

I will argue that neither constraint (1) nor constraint (2) is plausible as a constraint on an account of associative obligations; that is, I will argue that we should accept voluntarism and reject nonreductionism. Thus, we should reject the claim that political obligations are associative obligations. In section 4 I will suggest why voluntarism is initially attractive, and why I think that intimate relationships can generate special obligations without violating the voluntarist requirement. I will then examine a couple of nonreductionist, antivoluntarist accounts of special obligations, intended to

extend to the political case, and show that neither provides any reason to depart from voluntarism and accept nonreductionism.

4. Voluntarism and Intimacy

In order to see what lies behind the concerns of the voluntarist, we can begin by reiterating that each of us has various natural duties to other persons. Depending on our moral theory, these duties will be more or less extensive and more or less stringent, with utilitarianism being the most demanding. These natural duties, as I have said, are justified by reference to some intrinsic feature of persons such as their rationality or sentience. These features of other persons provide reasons for moral constraints upon the pursuit of our own good. Given that every person has such morally relevant features, *every* other person is *prima facie* morally required to refrain from harming her and to aid her (when causally and epistemically positioned so as to be able to do so). So an important aspect of natural duties is that they are grounded (fundamentally) by some intrinsic feature of the obligee without reference to the obligor or the obligor's relationship to the obligee.

But, as I said in section 2, any account of genuinely special obligations must ground such obligations (fundamentally) on some feature of a special relationship between the obligor and the obligee. So it will *not* be the case that special obligations are such that, leaving aside differences in causal and epistemic positions, each person will have the same set of such obligations. Some people will have more than others, while some (in rare cases) will have none at all. Now we can see why voluntarists are concerned about special obligations. Natural duties represent what is required in order to treat others in the manner in which moral persons ought to be treated. How, then, can we justify a distribution of further duties over and above the natural duties? Further, how can we justify an unequal distribution of such duties? What justifies these further, differentially distributed constraints upon our pursuit of our own good?

---

[1] Samuel Scheffler, "Relationships and Responsibilities," *Philosophy and Public Affairs* 26 (1997): 189–209, at 195–96. [Reprinted in this volume, reading 14.]

This way of presenting the issues makes it clear, I think, why contractual and promissory obligations need not trouble the voluntarist. Contracts and promises represent deliberate, intentional acts of stepping forward and volunteering to perform certain actions for other persons. In Simmons's words, contracts and promises are "voluntary acts which [are] ... the deliberate undertaking of an obligation."[1] If the voluntarist worry about special obligations is that they differentially distribute extra moral work and thereby limit persons' abilities to pursue their own projects, plans, and commitments, the fact that promises and contracts are just voluntary assumptions of commitments serves to dispel the worry with respect to promissory and contractual obligations. The agent can have no legitimate moral complaint given that she has performed an action or actions that she knew or ought to have known was the deliberate voluntary undertaking of an obligation over and above her natural duties.

The case of associative obligations, however, seems to be another issue entirely. As I have indicated, any adequate account of associative obligations must ground them in the special relationship between the obligor and the obligee, and must also accommodate our paradigm cases of such obligations, those to friends and family. But even if we could offer an account of obligations of friendship as voluntarily assumed, it seems difficult to imagine offering such an account of familial obligations. For example, my associative obligations to my mother, if based upon the mere fact that she is my mother, would certainly not be voluntarily assumed: I never chose my mother (or my father, brother, stepfather, etc.). How, then, can associative obligations meet the voluntarist challenge?

The difficulty arises, I think, because we make a serious mistake about what makes familial relationships morally significant, a mistake that is evidenced in the sharp distinction we often draw between those relationships and our relations to our friends. Initially it might seem right to suppose that while we choose our friends we do not choose our family members. But do we "choose" our friends? The difficulty is that "choice" is highly ambiguous. Surely I do not choose my friends in anything like the way in which I choose a new sweater from a catalog or a pasta dish from the menu. I cannot simply decide, upon meeting Richard, "He shall be my friend." Making a friend involves a temporally extended series of actions: it is not a discrete choice like choosing the linguine or, more importantly, making a promise. And when we look back at our histories with our friends, we will probably be unable to locate any discrete mental event that we can identify as having chosen so-and-so as a friend.

In order to see why choosing a friend is a unique sort of choice, we need to consider the nature of friendship. Friendship is, necessarily, a relationship of intimacy between two persons. Genuine intimacy involves reciprocal understanding and a mutual revealing of character. For Tracy and me to be emotionally intimate is for us to have achieved mutual awareness of and responsiveness to each other's character and selfunderstanding. Both parties to the friendship must intentionally aim at these states of awareness and response for it to be the case that they are genuinely intimate with one another rather than just very knowledgeable about each other. So we can consider any intimate relationship to be a joint project on the part of the parties to the relationship, a project chosen and sustained through a series of actions.

But why suppose that the existence of such a joint project generates special obligations between the parties to the project? I suggest that the joint project that we call friendship differs both from joint projects based upon explicit or implicit contracts, and, insofar as it is a *joint* project, from other types of autonomous "choices" that an agent might make. In rule-governed associations such as clubs or philosophy departments, one's joining is clearly an act of consent, and that act of consent grounds one's obligations to the other members. On the other hand, when I make a choice to vacation in Boston or to

[1] A. John Simmons, *Moral Principles and Political Obligations* (Princeton: Princeton University Press, 1979), p. 57.

have a career in philosophy, I acquire no obligations to other persons simply as a result of this choice (although of course I may acquire obligations in acting on those choices).

Friendship is importantly different from joining a club or choosing to vacation in Boston. As I have said, it differs from the latter in its being a *joint* project, one that essentially involves another person, and it differs from the former in its involving some *particular* other person. In order for me to have a friendship with Tracy, Tracy must have a friendship with me. If I act in ways detrimental to my friendship with Tracy, I necessarily act in ways that are detrimental to another person's project, namely Tracy's friendship with me. I have voluntarily chosen (albeit over time) and developed a project that engages not only my will and autonomy but that of someone else as well, and this engagement of another's will is not merely a by-product of my choices but necessary to my choices being what they are. Thus, my joint project of friendship with Tracy generates obligations to care for Tracy and to sustain our project.

I want to make it clear that by appealing to the fact that friendship is a joint project in order to ground obligations to friends, I am not appealing to the expectations of the other party to the friendship to ground those obligations.[1] The presence of expectations in the other party is neither necessary nor sufficient to create obligations. I may have a highly anxiety-prone friend who constantly expects her friends to tire of her and seek out more interesting people. Nonetheless, this lack of raised expectations does not defeat the claim that I have special obligations to my neurotic friend. Also, some people may misread certain kindnesses and gestures as constituting a friendship, and thus, even though such persons may have expectations with respect to the people who have shown them kindness, it

is not the case that the latter have special obligations with respect to them. Just as with promising, it is the actions of the obligor, not any causal effects on the obligee, that generate obligations: if I have done my part in creating an intimacy with Tracy, then I have created certain special obligations for myself.[2] Also, it is objective intimacy, not mere feelings of being close to someone, that grounds special obligations: just as people may misread certain gestures of kindness, they may misunderstand how intimate they are with another person.

I am arguing, then, that it is the intimate relationship that is the joint project of friendship that grounds duties of friendship apart from expectations or mere feelings of closeness. Now the natural move for a voluntarist at this point is, of course, to say that the undertaking of the project of friendship is an act of consent to do certain things for the other party to the friendship. So making a friend is like joining a club or taking a job, despite the fact that the latter need not be commitments to any particular persons but rather to any and all persons who fit the description of member. I do think that many acts constitutive of friendship are *consent-implying acts*: it is reasonable to infer from their performance that the agent would consent if asked, and it might be unclear why anyone would perform such acts if she were not willing to consent. But such facts are not sufficient for it to be the case that the agent's acts are actually signs of consent.[3] It is true that the achievement of intimacy is voluntary and allows room for withdrawal or dissent. But that does not make it an instance of consenting or promise-making. Obligations of consent are grounded in the "personal performance of a voluntary act which is the deliberate undertaking of an obligation."[4] Individuals ought to know the joint nature of friendship but it does not seem

---

[1] In "Filial Morality," *The Journal of Philosophy* 83 (1986): 439–56, Christina Hoff Sommers offers an account of obligations to parents, based upon an account of promising offered by A.I. Melden, that grounds those obligations on expectations. I critique Sommers's account in "Families, Friends, and Special Obligations," pp. 535–36.

[2] I have been helped in thinking about this issue through formulating my comments on Michael Cholbi's 2000 American Philosophical Association Pacific Division contribution, "Promising and Scanlon's Profligate Pal."
[3] I borrow this distinction from Simmons, *Moral Principles*, p. 99.
[4] Simmons, *Moral Principles*, p. 57.

right to say that the acts constitutive of friendship are "deliberate undertakings of obligations." When I listen patiently to Tracy's recounting of her stresses and relate my anxieties and frustrations to her, I am caring for her, not assuming an obligation as I do when I promise to talk to her on the weekend. We do not want to read consent into every action that generates obligations.

I have argued that our intimate relationships with our friends ground our obligations to them. It might seem, however, that this account will not do as a general account of associative obligations. While it does meet one of the constraints that I placed on any such account—that is, it grounds obligations by a fundamental appeal to the special relationship between the obligor and the obligee— it seems to have difficulty with the other constraint: accommodating paradigm cases. Our paradigm cases involve obligations to family members, and we often think that we have such obligations to persons with whom we are not emotionally intimate. Does it seem right to conclude that we have no special obligations to, for example, family members from whom we have grown apart?

Persons have many different sorts of duties and obligations, so we need to be clear about *why* a person is bound to perform certain actions. Consider an adult brother and sister, Bart and Lisa, who have never been emotionally intimate. They meet only at family holiday gatherings. We need to distinguish between (a) their actual obligations to one another and (b) their *felt* obligations. Given societal expectations about persons who occupy certain familial roles, Bart and Lisa are likely to think that they have obligations to one another in virtue of the brother-sister relationship. But I'm unclear about why we should suppose that they actually have such obligations. It is true that we might regard Bart and Lisa as appropriate objects of moral criticism. I think, however, that such criticism is justified only if they have failed to avail themselves of a good opportunity to develop an intimate relationship. After all, family situations are often very conducive to the development of intimacy, and intimacy is objectively valuable. Siblings raised together

have unique resources for understanding and sympathizing with one another. Parents have excellent resources with respect to their children. Adult children ought to recognize how much an effort toward intimacy would mean to the people who have raised and nurtured them. So, in many familial contexts, lack of intimacy is a sign of moral thoughtlessness, laziness, or self-absorption, and such traits deserve moral censure. And, given our causal and epistemic relations to family, we usually have abundant utilitarian reasons to respond to them with benevolence and concern.

These claims together, I think, provide a much more attractive account of the anomalous cases of family where there is no intimacy than does an account that grounds special familial obligations on mere occupation of a role where that role is in part constituted by blood ties. I recognize that most people would appeal to roles or biology in order to ground these obligations. But I think that an adequate account of associative obligations needs to accommodate the paradigm cases only in holding that we do have such obligations to friends and family—it need not agree with the most common understanding of why we have those obligations. And, again, my account appeals to an objective notion of intimacy. So people may come to lack certain feelings with respect to each other, but that does not mean that there is no longer an intimate relationship. These issues become complicated in real relationships, so it is no defect in a theory if it does not provide hard and fast criteria for when two persons are intimate or for when a person is justified in withdrawing from an intimate joint project.

The account of associative obligations that I have offered is both voluntarist and reductionist: specific voluntary interactions with another person ground the obligations, and reflection on these actions will reveal to the individual the joint nature of friendship and, thus, her obligations to her friend. So commitment to voluntarism does not require us to view associative obligations as contractual, but simply to see that the former have important features in common with the latter. Thus, we can accommodate the paradigm cases of associative obligations without rejecting voluntarism or reductionism. But then there seems little, if any, hope of viewing special political obligations as associative. So I will now consider how some recent antivoluntarist, nonreductionist accounts fare.

5. Special Obligations and Histories of Doing Good

Thomas Hurka offers an account of "national partiality" that is modeled on a similar defense of partiality toward friends, lovers, and family members.[1] If I love my friend, he claims, it is true that I love her in part for various qualities that she has such as her sense of humor, her wit and intelligence, her generosity, and so on. But I do not love her *only* because of such qualities, as is evidenced by the fact that I would not abandon her "the moment someone else came along with the same properties to a higher degree." Rather, I love my friend, "as an individual," which "involves loving the person for certain historical qualities, ones deriving from his or her participation with one in a shared history." However, partiality between intimates is justified or grounded by the relationship that obtains between such intimates if and only if that relationship is one of benefiting each other, jointly benefiting some third party or parties, or one of "shared suffering," but is not justified when it involves a "history of doing evil": "Some activities and states of people, most notably their doing good or suffering evil, call for a positive, caring, or associative response.... One should, in general, care more about people who have shared with one in activities and states that call for a caring response."[2] So

once people have a certain type of history with one another, they are justified in showing a differential concern for one another.

Hurka then extends this account in order to justify partiality between compatriots (or, as he prefers, "conationals"). Compatriots participate in a political system that produces significant goods for its members, goods significant enough to be comparable to those produced by intimates for one another. Of course, compatriots do not interact in a direct manner; thus, Hurka claims, "less partiality is justified toward one's conationals than toward one's family members [for example]."[3] But, still, a significant degree of partiality towards compatriots is justified.

Hurka's language of "participating together in shared histories" seems to suggest that his account is voluntarist, although it is clearly not. After all, how often do people choose to suffer evil at all, let alone with some other person? And, of course, citizens have little choice but to participate in political structures that result in goods for themselves and for their compatriots. However, Hurka's appeal to the basis of partiality between friends puts the following challenge to the voluntarist: if it is correct to claim that histories of doing good or sharing evil are the basis of associative obligations between intimates, then why not claim that such histories ground associative obligations between compatriots?

Hurka's account of associative obligations is nonreductionist in that it appeals to "relationships" in a very broad sense rather than to particular interactions between persons. My participation in political structures through paying my taxes, voting, obeying the law, and so on, links me directly to only a very small proportion of the population of the United States (or even of my state of residence). My joint participation in American political structures with Joe Schmoe of Texas really just amounts to our both performing certain types of actions (such as paying our taxes and voting).

[1] Thomas Hurka, "The Justification of National Partiality," in Robert McKim and Jeff McMahan (eds.), *The Morality of Nationalism* (New York: Oxford University Press, 1997), pp. 139–57. Hurka talks about the justification of partiality, but seems to be defending requirements of partiality, given his talk of what is appropriate or called for.
[2] Hurka, "The Justification of National Partiality," pp. 150–52.
[3] Ibid., p. 155.

I suggest that both the antivoluntarist aspect and the nonreductionist aspect of Hurka's account are troubling. Political obligations are restrictions over and above what is required by natural duty. But we do not choose to participate with others in political structures that produce goods for us and our compatriots. If the production of such goods were in fact required by natural duty, the coercion might be permissible, but it is unclear why it would ground further obligations of partiality. If anything, I should now, in accord with natural duty, help to produce these goods for persons living in countries in which such goods are not provided to citizens. If the good that our political structures produce is not required by natural duty, how can my having already been forced to do more than natural duty requires impose even further obligations upon me?

Hurka can again point to the case of friends or family members: we tend to think that if we have a history of doing good or suffering evil together, then we ought to be partial to one another. The explanation for this cannot be just that persons' doing good or suffering evil "calls for" a caring response, as Hurka suggests,[1] because then we would owe special attention to all persons who have done good or suffered evil, not just to those who have done these things with *us*. Hurka admits that he is assuming the agent-relative aspect of his account, but it is precisely the agent-relativity of special obligations that needs justification.

Also, the analogy with intimate relationships only goes so far. Intimates, when they produce good together, interact in a very direct manner, whereas compatriots do not. Hurka appeals to this disanalogy in order to accommodate the commonsense judgment that obligations to intimates are stronger than obligations to compatriots: the explanation for this fact, he says, is that the more direct interaction there is, the stronger the obligations. Once Hurka has made this concession, however, we can wonder what within his account licenses such an appeal to directness of interaction. I think that he has simply made a tacit admission that partiality is not solely grounded on "histories of doing good," but also on further features of such "histories," such as directness of interaction. But, I have argued, we can understand how direct causal interaction generates obligations within the scope of a voluntarist theory. And, given the implausible implications of the nonvoluntarist aspect of Hurka's theory, we have good reason to abandon his appeal to the other feature of "histories," that of being histories of doing good or of suffering evil together.

My arguments are unlikely to have entirely dissipated the attraction of Hurka's view. Consider Hurka's own example of two persons who were prisoners in a Nazi concentration camp,[2] and imagine further that these persons never interacted directly at the camp but meet each other after the end of the war. If one of them needs financial assistance, the other will regard herself as being *specially* obligated to help. Such felt obligations are also present between compatriots: I do feel that I owe more to Joe Schmoe of Texas than I do to Fred Schmed of Canada, all else being equal. So it might be suggested either that (i) any account of associative obligations must respect such strong felt obligations, and people feel that they owe obligations to persons with whom they have done good or suffered evil, or (ii) perhaps associative obligations are generated by those very feelings present in contexts where persons have done good or suffered evil together; on such an account, we could accommodate the whole gamut of special obligations from friends to compatriots.[3]

But such feelings are present in many contexts in which we do not want to admit that both parties to the relationship have special obligations towards one another, contexts in which what we can think of as "false intimacy" is present. Consider, for example, the relationship between a kidnap victim and her captor, or that between a battered woman and her abusive partner. Of course, we could then put the further constraint on the generation of special

---

[1] Ibid., p. 152.

[2] Ibid., p. 151.
[3] I am grateful to Richard Fumerton for suggesting this view to me.

obligations, that they only arise in relationships of doing good or of suffering evil together. But, then we have denied the force of the feelings that we have been trying to respect.

I do not want to deny that feelings of empathy or shared histories of doing good or suffering evil have a role to play in generating associative obligations. Intimacy simply is not possible if persons do not have empathy and a certain expressed concern for one another, so such feelings are necessary conditions, given the nature of human beings, of genuine intimacy. Similarly, a past of shared evil can draw people together and help them achieve intimacy. But given the ways in which people can be coerced into doing good or suffering evil together and thereby end up having certain feelings towards one another, I want to resist saying that such are sufficient conditions for the presence of associative obligations.

6. Valuable Relationships as Sources of Reasons

Samuel Scheffler offers an account of what he calls "special responsibilities" that is consciously antivoluntarist and nonreductionist. (I borrow the term "nonreductionist" from Scheffler.) He wants to defend an antivoluntarist account of special obligations arising from "relationships" construed in a sense broad enough to include being the daughter of, colleague of, compatriot of, co-member of a club with, and so on.

Scheffler points out that people often value such relationships. Valuing such a relationship involves seeing it as a source of special obligations, that is, being disposed to view the other party to the relationship as "providing … [one] with presumptively decisive reasons for action, reasons that … [one] would not have had in the absence of the relationship"; in fact, "I cannot value my relationships (noninstrumentally) without seeing them as sources of special responsibilities."[1] Disagreements as to which relationships generate special obligations

result, then, from differences in the types of relationships that persons value.

Scheffler claims that relationships give rise to special obligations only when persons have reason to value the relationships. Thus, if someone actually values a relationship that she has no reason to value (consider a battered woman's valuing of her relationship to her abusive partner), then that relationship is not the source of special obligations. Further, it is important that Scheffler means by "value" and "reason," "value noninstrumentally" and "net reason," respectively.[2] Relationships give rise to special obligations only when persons have an all-things-considered reason to value intrinsically the relationship—whatever features of the relationship that provide reason against valuing it must be outweighed by those features of the relationship that provide reason for valuing it.

As I have already indicated, Scheffler understands "relationship" to include more than just "discrete interactions." He understands any "socially salient connections among people" to be relationships.[3] Our sharing the common property of humanity does not count as a socially salient connection, while being members of the John Travolta Fan Club does, even if we have never met. It seems clear from the little that Scheffler does say about what relationships are that they can vary from culture to culture and from time to time, because what is a "social tie" or "socially salient" will surely vary. We can even imagine science-fiction contexts in which our common humanity *does* count as a social tie.

Now we can present Scheffler's argument:

(1) We have good reason to value (noninstrumentally) certain relationships with other persons.

(2) To value (noninstrumentally) relationships with others is, in part, to see those relationships as a source of reasons, that is, as a source of special obligations.

(3) Therefore, we have good reason to see ourselves as having special obligations.

---

[1] Scheffler, "Relationships and Responsibilities," p. 196.

[2] Ibid., pp. 197, 198.
[3] Ibid., p. 198.

Scheffler concludes by remarking that "skepticism about such [special] responsibilities [or obligations] will be justified only if we are prepared to deny that we have good reasons to value our relationships."[1] Thus, because being compatriots is surely a socially salient connection among people, and one that many would claim that we have reason to value noninstrumentally, we have special obligations to our compatriots.

Scheffler's nonreductionism and antivoluntarism are overt. Unlike Hurka, however, Scheffler is concerned to respond to the voluntarist's challenge. He first claims that the "voluntarist objection … points out that special responsibilities may constitute significant burdens for those who bear them, and asserts that it would be unfair if such responsibilities could be ascribed to individuals who had done nothing voluntarily to incur them."[2] Scheffler claims that this objection does not differentiate special responsibilities from natural duties, given that the latter are also unchosen and may constitute significant burdens. But, as I have pointed out, special responsibilities such as those owed to compatriots are, unlike natural duties, supposed to arise because of some contingent feature of persons, namely, their standing in a certain relationship to the agent. This contingent feature of persons is created by other persons: it is mere happenstance that I was born in this country rather than some other, and that persons have created the social landscape in which agents are conceived of as citizens or residents of one political entity rather than another. Thus, the constraints imposed upon us by special obligations to compatriots cry out for further justification in a way that natural duties do not.

Scheffler does recognize this further voluntarist worry. As he points out, the more that we are forced into various relationships by existent social structures, the less space we have to choose and develop our own commitments and thus to determine the shape of our lives and our selves. If others have chosen our relationships for us, why should

we suppose that they, as a result, have the power to impose obligations upon us? Scheffler responds:

> We acquire personal relations and social affiliations of a formative kind before we are able to conceive of them as such or to contemplate altering them. Thus there is obviously no question … of our being able to choose all of the relations in which we stand to other people. What the voluntarist can hope to claim is only that the significance of those relations is entirely up to us. However, this claim too is unsustainable. For better or worse, the influence on our personal histories of unchosen social relations—to parents and siblings, families and communities, nations and peoples—is not something that we determine by ourselves. Whether we like it or not, such relations help to define the contours of our lives, and influence the ways that we are seen both by ourselves and by others.[3]

There is no denying the causal claims that Scheffler is making here. That I am my father's daughter, that I am an American, that I am my stepfather's stepdaughter—all of these facts about me have had an unalterable influence, both positive and negative, in forming my self-conception and identity. But it is unclear why these undeniable causal claims ground any normative claims about obligations. If I have been placed, without my consent, in situations that lead me to view myself in a certain light or to have certain subjective values, why suppose that, as a result, I acquire special obligations?

It might be said that the causal facts that Scheffler has enumerated can be used to point out a flaw in voluntarist accounts of associative obligations such as my own. It might be said that even given the fact that I have presented intimate relationships as temporally extended "choices," I have still portrayed them as less spontaneous and unselfconsciously developed than they really are. After all, we often become friends with people

---

[1] Ibid., pp. 200–01.
[2] Ibid., p. 202.

[3] Ibid., p. 204.

after being thrust into situations with them: consider colleagues, college roommates, and neighbors, to name just a few. And people often realize that they are friends with someone in such a way that it seems like a discovery about themselves, rather than a choice that they have made.[1] Thus, it might be argued, it is the fact of the existent relationship, not how it developed, that seems morally significant, and the voluntarist is unable to accept this apparent moral truth.

It is important, however, to see that even given this potential response to my view, there is a serious disanalogy between friendship and political relationships. It is certainly true that I am thrust into the relationships of colleague, roommate, or neighbor, often without my consent (or even against my will). But it is significant that, in ordinary discourse, we make distinctions between mere neighbors, mere roommates, or mere colleagues, and *friends*. I have colleagues and neighbors and have had roommates with whom I am not or was not friends. Thus, in being thrust into the former relationships I was not thereby thrust into the latter relationship. Neighbors can refrain from becoming intimate with one another; that is, they have control over whether they become friends. Of course, the gradual process of becoming intimate is such that persons, if they do not reflect upon their actions, may suddenly realize that they are friends with someone. Nonetheless, unreflective choices are still choices. And we do not want to make a sharp distinction between the nature of an existent relationship and the way in which a relationship came about: the character of a relationship is, in large part, determined by its history.

Now consider the political context. We are thrust into the "relationship" of compatriot, just as we are thrust into the relationship of neighbor or roommate. But in the political context, it is supposedly that very relationship into which we are thrust that generates obligations. Some citizens may be more committed than others, may have an active concern for their compatriots—some even make public statements promising certain types of civic action. So there is some room for a distinction between mere compatriots and what we might call genuine "patriots." But the latter are, in the end, those who have given some form of consent, and we are already familiar with the claim that very few citizens have done that. So Scheffler is right to point out that many "social relations" are unchosen—those between family members and those between compatriots for instance. But genuinely intimate relationships are never unchosen. Thus, we still need reason to broaden our conception of the type of relationship that grounds obligations beyond genuinely intimate relationships to include all "socially salient connections."

So let us now focus on the notion of "relationship" that Scheffler is using. He is claiming that to value noninstrumentally certain sorts of relationships is to see them as a source of special obligations, and such relationships are a source of special obligations if one has reason to value them noninstrumentally. I will leave aside the question of whether I have reason to value my relationships to my compatriots noninstrumentally rather than instrumentally, and focus instead on what sort of "relationship" I have to my compatriots and what it would be to value such a relationship at all. Consider my "relationship" to Joe Schmoe of Texas. I am unaware of Joe Schmoe as an individual—all I know is that I have compatriots living in Texas. Thus, I would be completely unaffected if Joe Schmoe were to die, or be replaced by Fred Schmed.[2] So how can it be claimed that I value my relationship to Joe Schmoe?

The difficulty stems from the fact that Joe Schmoe would be an American if I did not exist and I would be an American if Joe Schmoe did not exist. And each of us would value our being an

---

[1] See [Michael] Sandel, *Liberalism and the Limits of Justice* [(Cambridge: Cambridge University Press, 1998)], especially the conclusion.

[2] If we were considering Michael Jordan of Illinois rather than Joe Schmoe of Texas, none of these claims would be true. But we are looking for a defense of obligations to compatriots as such, not to compatriots who are superstar basketball players.

American just as much if the other did not exist; after all, we are unaware of each other's existence. So "being my compatriot" is relevantly different from "being my friend": Joe Schmoe and I are compatriots in virtue of our both occupying a role or having a certain property, and each of us could occupy that role or have that property regardless of what is true of the other person. But the fact that Fred Schmed and I are friends is such that it could not obtain if Fred Schmed and I did not share a certain history with one another and have certain attitudes towards one another. My obligations to Fred derive from the fact that Fred and I stand in the friendship relation, and supposedly, according to Scheffler's account, my obligations to Joe derive from the fact that Joe and I stand in the compatriot relation. But the fact that Joe and I are compatriots is a fact that is constituted by Joe's having certain properties that are not relational properties involving me and my having certain properties that are not relational properties involving Joe; in other words, our relationship is the result of each of us having properties that we could have whether or not the other person even existed. Such is not the case, however, with respect to the fact that Fred and I are friends: the properties that each of us has upon which the friendship relation between us depends for its existence are ones that we could not have if the other person did not exist. The fact that Joe and I are compatriots is, then, analogous to the fact that Jane and I are kind people, not to the fact that Fred and I are friends.

Scheffler's use of the term "relationship" masks an important difference between political relations and intimate relationships: what I have been suggesting is that the former are not relationships in any substantive sense. Our common citizenship constitutes a relationship between Joe and me only in the weak sense that our common kindness constitutes a relationship between Jane and me. Scheffler might say that an important distinction between those two relationships is that the former is a "socially salient connection," a "social tie," whereas the latter is not. As I have already pointed out, we can imagine circumstances in which common kindness is socially salient, but let us grant to Scheffler that our world is such that common citizenship but not common kindness is a socially salient connection. Why should such social salience make a difference? Such salience is the result of how others, perhaps our culture as a whole, view certain facts about Joe and me. But why should that make a difference to the generation of special obligations? I might value the "relationship" that I stand in to kind people, and I have reason to value it; after all, that relationship just consists in my and others' having the property of being kind. I value being a member of the group of kind people.[1] But now, the same sort of "relationship" in conjunction with social recognition supposedly generates special obligations. Why?

The example of kindness calls into question Scheffler's second premise in his argument: (2) To value (noninstrumentally) relationships with others is, in part, to see those relationships as a source of reasons, that is, as a source of special obligations. I can value (noninstrumentally) my membership in the group of kind people without viewing it as a source of special obligations. Is Scheffler claiming that I cannot value (noninstrumentally) my membership in socially recognized groups without seeing it as a source of special obligations? Again, it is simply unclear what work the notion of social recognition can do here. The apparent cogency of Scheffler's argument derives from his masking of the relevant differences between relationships such as friendship and those between, for example, compatriots. In the former, the parties have intentional attitudes toward and ties to the other party as the specific individual that she is—such is not the case in the latter sort of relationship. Scheffler says that "to value one's relationship with another person is … to see oneself as having special responsibilities to the person with whom one has the relationship."[2] What I am stressing is that when I value my relationship with Fred I see myself as having special obligations to Fred, but if I value my relationship to compatriots, I do not thereby see myself as having

---

[1] Scheffler, "Relationships and Responsibilities," p. 198.
[2] Ibid., p. 200.

special obligations to Joe. But that undermines the claim that I have a relationship with Joe in any real sense of the term "relationship."

Scheffler's nonreductionism, then, leans too heavily with too little justification upon the notion of "social salience."[1] I have also suggested that he, like Hurka, has no good reason for abandoning voluntarism.

7. Reconsidering Voluntarism and Reductionism

The failures of the accounts offered by Hurka and Scheffler point to some general problems for any unified account of associative obligations to intimates and special obligations to compatriots. Intimacy is such that it is always, when genuine, chosen; thus, obligations arising from intimate relationships can conform to the voluntarist requirement. If we could not accommodate obligations to intimates within the scope of a voluntarist theory, I, unlike some voluntarists, I suspect, would, at the very least, reconsider my commitment to voluntarism. But the voluntarist worry seems peculiarly pressing in the case of political relationships, as I have tried to show, particularly in my response to Hurka. So, given that we can, as I have argued, accommodate obligations to intimates without abandoning voluntarism, we should be wary of accounts that reject voluntarism in order to accommodate special political obligations as associative obligations: a requirement that seems peculiarly appropriate for political obligations is being given up in order to assimilate those obligations to a type of obligation that can meet the requirement. At the very least, this is a questionable method of proceeding.

The only way to get around this objection, I think, is to argue that my voluntarist account of obligations to intimates is wrong-headed. After all, it might be said, the voluntarist is concerned about the burdens over and above natural duty that

special obligations represent for the moral agent. In the context of loving relationships, it might be claimed, such obligations do not represent burdens—if the agent sees them as burdens, she is not responding to her intimate with the sort of loving care warranted by the relationship. One must be willing to give to someone one genuinely loves, so rather than being burdens, special obligations should represent natural ways of caring for and responding to the needs of another person.

But we have to make the distinction between how people view their obligations and the nature of those obligations. In many loving relationships, people do want to do more for their loved ones than natural duty requires of them; in fact, such desires are plausibly seen as partly constitutive of love. Nonetheless, in acting on such desires, persons do often sacrifice their own good, even if they want to make the sacrifice. More importantly, however, such a response to my account of associative obligations is unlikely to help the defender of political obligations as associative obligations. We do not love our compatriots, and we are unlikely to view sacrifices we make for them as anything other than that. No matter what sentiments people have toward compatriots, they continue to complain about paying their taxes. So any friend of a unified account of obligations to intimates and political obligations had better not put too much weight on the loving responses present in the case of intimates.

Most importantly, examining Hurka's and Scheffler's accounts brings out the problems with nonreductionism. In order to assimilate political relations to intimate relationships, the notion of a relationship has to be weakened to an extraordinary degree. Thus, all of the features of intimate relationships that seem morally significant—the mutual emotions and attitudes of the parties to each other as individuals, the personal interaction, the mutual knowledge and understanding of each other's character—must be ignored in the grounding of associative obligations. Instead, we are forced to appeal to impersonal features of the "relationship," such as that of doing good or suffering evil

[1] Given Scheffler's use of the notion of social salience, the occupation of alternative roles, such as that of gay or lesbian partner, would not generate special obligations.

"together" (where "together" does not imply any direct interaction), or of giving reason to value.

What is most troubling about nonreductionism in conjunction with antivoluntarism is that one's being in a relationship is a fact determined more by social attitudes and practices than by one's own choices (see my discussion of Scheffler). Further, given the very broad notion of "relationship" employed by nonreductionists such as Scheffler and Hurka, I cannot examine my own actions in order to determine whether and to whom I have special obligations. According to a reductionist, it is an essential feature of the actions that I perform that ground special obligations that they constitute certain types of interactions with, say, Fred Schmed. But, on nonreductionist accounts, the actions that I perform that allegedly ground obligations are ones that do not, in any way, essentially involve the particular other to whom I owe the obligations. I could pay my taxes, vote, and so on, whether or not Joe Schmoe even exists. But I cannot sympathize with Fred if Fred does not exist. Of course, it cannot be the case that Joe and I *both* vote unless Joe exists, but, again, that claim is more analogous to the claim that Jane and I cannot *both* be kind people unless Jane exists than to the claim that Fred and I cannot care about each other unless Fred exists.

Rather than acceptance of voluntarism being a betrayal of our moral experience in the intimate context, I have argued, an understanding of genuine intimacy commits us to voluntarism. But then we are also committed to viewing the direct interactions between intimates as being what grounds associative obligations. Of course, a voluntarist reductionist account of associative obligations cannot accommodate special political obligations. But voluntarism is particularly compelling in the political case, and, if the relationships that ground associative obligations are to include political relations, the notion of a relationship has to be stretched beyond recognition. Those who wish to defend special political obligations must give up on trying to conceive of them as associative obligations. It might just be time to stop trying to claim that special political obligations are really special obligations.

DISCUSSION QUESTIONS

1. Explain the constraints that Jeske places on an adequate account of associative obligations. What does she mean by "associative obligation"?

2. Explain Hurka's defense of partiality. Explain and evaluate Jeske's arguments against Hurka's defense.

3. Explain Scheffler's defense of "special responsibilities." Why does Jeske think that Scheffler's account is not successful as a defense of special political obligations? Evaluate her argument.

D.
Applications

16

Thomas Jefferson, et al., "The Declaration of Independence" (1776)

Thomas Jefferson (1743–1826) was the third president of the United States, the founder of the University of Virginia, and the primary author of the Declaration of Independence. Jefferson penned the Declaration in June 1776. On July 2, the Continental Congress voted to declare independence from Britain, and on July 4 it voted to adopt the Declaration. By August, copies of the Declaration had reached Britain.

SOURCE

Jefferson, Thomas, et al, "The Declaration of Independence." The National Archives. http://www.archives.gov/exhibits/charters/declaration.html (accessed June 6, 2010).

In Congress, July 4, 1776.

The unanimous Declaration of the thirteen united States of America,

When in the Course of human events, it becomes necessary for one people to dissolve the political bands which have connected them with another, and to assume among the powers of the earth, the separate and equal station to which the Laws of Nature and of Nature's God entitle them, a decent respect to the opinions of mankind requires that they should declare the causes which impel them to the separation.

We hold these truths to be self-evident, that all men are created equal, that they are endowed by their Creator with certain unalienable Rights, that among these are Life, Liberty and the pursuit of Happiness.—That to secure these rights, Governments are instituted among Men, deriving their just powers from the consent of the governed,—That whenever any Form of Government becomes destructive of these ends, it is the Right of the People to alter or to abolish it, and to institute new Government, laying its foundation on such principles and organizing its powers in such form, as to them shall seem most likely to effect their Safety and Happiness. Prudence, indeed, will dictate that Governments long established should not be changed for light and transient causes; and accordingly all experience hath shewn, that mankind are more disposed to suffer, while evils are sufferable, than to right themselves by abolishing the forms to which they are accustomed. But when a long train of abuses and usurpations, pursuing invariably the same Object evinces a design to reduce them under absolute Despotism, it is their right, it is their duty, to throw off such Government, and to provide new Guards for their future security.—Such has been the patient sufferance of these Colonies; and such is now the necessity which constrains them to alter their former Systems of Government. The history of the present King of Great Britain is a history of repeated injuries and usurpations, all having in direct object the establishment of an absolute Tyranny over these States. To prove this, let Facts be submitted to a candid world.

He has refused his Assent to Laws, the most wholesome and necessary for the public good.

He has forbidden his Governors to pass Laws of immediate and pressing importance, unless suspended in their operation till his Assent should be obtained; and when so suspended, he has utterly neglected to attend to them.

He has refused to pass other Laws for the accommodation of large districts of people, unless those people would relinquish the right of Representation in the Legislature, a right inestimable to them and formidable to tyrants only.

He has called together legislative bodies at places unusual, uncomfortable, and distant from the depository of their public Records, for the sole purpose of fatiguing them into compliance with his measures.

He has dissolved Representative Houses repeatedly, for opposing with manly firmness his invasions on the rights of the people.

He has refused for a long time, after such dissolutions, to cause others to be elected; whereby the Legislative powers, incapable of Annihilation, have returned to the People at large for their exercise; the State remaining in the mean time exposed to all the dangers of invasion from without, and convulsions within.

He has endeavoured to prevent the population of these States; for that purpose obstructing the Laws for Naturalization of Foreigners; refusing to pass others to encourage their migrations hither, and raising the conditions of new Appropriations of Lands.

He has obstructed the Administration of Justice, by refusing his Assent to Laws for establishing Judiciary powers.

He has made Judges dependent on his Will alone, for the tenure of their offices, and the amount and payment of their salaries.

He has erected a multitude of New Offices, and sent hither swarms of Officers to harrass our people, and eat out their substance.

He has kept among us, in times of peace, Standing Armies without the Consent of our legislatures.

He has affected to render the Military independent of and superior to the Civil power.

He has combined with others to subject us to a jurisdiction foreign to our constitution, and unacknowledged by our laws; giving his Assent to their Acts of pretended Legislation:

For Quartering large bodies of armed troops among us:

For protecting them, by a mock Trial, from punishment for any Murders which they should commit on the Inhabitants of these States:

For cutting off our Trade with all parts of the world:

For imposing Taxes on us without our Consent:

For depriving us in many cases, of the benefits of Trial by Jury:

For transporting us beyond Seas to be tried for pretended offences:

For abolishing the free System of English Laws in a neighbouring Province, establishing therein an Arbitrary government, and enlarging its Boundaries so as to render it at once an example and fit instrument for introducing the same absolute rule into these Colonies:

For taking away our Charters, abolishing our most valuable Laws, and altering fundamentally the Forms of our Governments:

For suspending our own Legislatures, and declaring themselves invested with power to legislate for us in all cases whatsoever.

He has abdicated Government here, by declaring us out of his Protection and waging War against us.

He has plundered our seas, ravaged our Coasts, burnt our towns, and destroyed the lives of our people.

He is at this time transporting large Armies of foreign Mercenaries to compleat the works of death, desolation and tyranny, already begun with circumstances of Cruelty & perfidy scarcely paralleled in the most barbarous ages, and totally unworthy the Head of a civilized nation.

He has constrained our fellow Citizens taken Captive on the high Seas to bear Arms against their Country, to become the executioners of their friends and Brethren, or to fall themselves by their Hands.

He has excited domestic insurrections amongst us, and has endeavoured to bring on the inhabitants of our frontiers, the merciless Indian Savages, whose known rule of warfare, is an undistinguished destruction of all ages, sexes and conditions.

In every stage of these Oppressions We have Petitioned for Redress in the most humble terms: Our repeated Petitions have been answered only by repeated injury. A Prince whose character is thus marked by every act which may define a Tyrant, is unfit to be the ruler of a free people.

Nor have We been wanting in attentions to our British brethren. We have warned them from time to time of attempts by their legislature to extend an unwarrantable jurisdiction over us. We have reminded them of the circumstances of our emigration and settlement here. We have appealed to their native justice and magnanimity, and we have conjured them by the ties of our common kindred to disavow these usurpations, which, would inevitably interrupt our connections and correspondence. They too have been deaf to the voice of justice and of consanguinity. We must, therefore, acquiesce in the necessity, which denounces our Separation, and hold them, as we hold the rest of mankind, Enemies in War, in Peace Friends.

We, therefore, the Representatives of the united States of America, in General Congress, Assembled, appealing to the Supreme Judge of the world for the rectitude of our intentions, do, in the Name, and by Authority of the good People of these Colonies, solemnly publish and declare, That these United Colonies are, and of Right ought to be Free and Independent States; that they are Absolved from all Allegiance to the British Crown, and that all political connection between them and the State of Great Britain, is and ought to be totally dissolved; and that as Free and Independent States, they have full Power to levy War, conclude Peace, contract Alliances, establish Commerce, and to do all other Acts and Things which Independent States may of right do. And for the support of this Declaration, with a firm reliance on the protection of divine Providence, we mutually pledge to each other our Lives, our Fortunes and our sacred Honor.

DISCUSSION QUESTIONS

1. How would Hobbes and Locke assess Jefferson's opening remarks?

2. Do you think the representatives of the colonies who authored the Declaration would identify themselves as contract theorists? Explain your response, drawing on the previous readings in this unit.

3. In support of their case, the authors of the Declaration cite a list of grievances toward the King of Great Britain. Do you feel that such actions as performed by the King towards his subjects provided them with reason for revolt? Have the authors adequately supported their case for independence? How might some of the political theorists featured earlier in this unit assess the King's behavior and the colonists' reactions?

17

Martin Luther King, Jr., "Letter from Birmingham Jail" (1963)

Martin Luther King, Jr. (1929–68) was a Christian minister, civil rights leader, and social activist. As the leader of the Southern Christian Leadership Conference, King organized or participated in numerous acts of protest and demonstrations. In 1964 he was the recipient of the Nobel Peace Prize. He was assassinated on 4 April 1968, while visiting Memphis, Tennessee, in support of striking garbage workers.

The following letter was written by King in 1963 while he was jailed for his involvement in a non-violent protest in Birmingham, Alabama. The letter is a response to a group of white clergy members who had called the protest untimely and unwise, encouraging King and other civil rights leaders to fight against injustice in the courts, rather than in the streets.

SOURCE

16 April 1963

My Dear Fellow Clergymen:

While confined here in the Birmingham city jail, I came across your recent statement calling my present activities "unwise and untimely." Seldom do I pause to answer criticism of my work and ideas. If I sought to answer all the criticisms that cross my desk, my secretaries would have little time for anything other than such correspondence in the course of the day, and I would have no time for constructive work. But since I feel that you are men of genuine good will and that your criticisms are sincerely set forth, I want to try to answer your statement in what I hope will be patient and reasonable terms.

I think I should indicate why I am here in Birmingham, since you have been influenced by the view which argues against "outsiders coming in." I have the honor of serving as president of the Southern Christian Leadership Conference, an organization operating in every southern state, with headquarters in Atlanta, Georgia. We have some eighty five affiliated organizations across the South, and one of them is the Alabama Christian Movement for Human Rights. Frequently we share staff, educational and financial resources with our affiliates. Several months ago the affiliate here in Birmingham asked us to be on call to engage in a nonviolent direct action program if such were deemed necessary. We readily consented, and when the hour came we lived up to our promise. So I, along with several members of my staff, am here because I was invited here. I am here because I have organizational ties here.

But more basically, I am in Birmingham because injustice is here. Just as the prophets of the eighth century B.C. left their villages and carried their "thus saith the Lord" far beyond the boundaries of their home towns, and just as the Apostle Paul left his village of Tarsus and carried the gospel of Jesus Christ to the far corners of the Greco Roman world, so am I compelled to carry the gospel of freedom beyond my own home town. Like Paul, I must constantly respond to the Macedonian call for aid.

Moreover, I am cognizant of the interrelatedness of all communities and states. I cannot sit idly by in Atlanta and not be concerned about what happens in Birmingham. Injustice anywhere is a threat to justice everywhere. We are caught in an inescapable network of mutuality, tied in a single garment of destiny. Whatever affects one directly, affects all indirectly. Never again can we afford to live with the narrow, provincial "outside agitator" idea. Anyone who lives inside the United States can never be considered an outsider anywhere within its bounds.

You deplore the demonstrations taking place in Birmingham. But your statement, I am sorry to say, fails to express a similar concern for the conditions that brought about the demonstrations. I am sure that none of you would want to rest content with the superficial kind of social analysis that deals merely with effects and does not grapple with underlying causes. It is unfortunate that demonstrations are taking place in Birmingham, but it is even more unfortunate that the city's white power structure left the Negro community with no alternative.

In any nonviolent campaign there are four basic steps: collection of the facts to determine whether injustices exist; negotiation; self purification; and direct action. We have gone through all these steps in Birmingham. There can be no gainsaying the fact that racial injustice engulfs this community. Birmingham is probably the most thoroughly segregated city in the United States. Its ugly record of brutality is widely known. Negroes

have experienced grossly unjust treatment in the courts. There have been more unsolved bombings of Negro homes and churches in Birmingham than in any other city in the nation. These are the hard, brutal facts of the case. On the basis of these conditions, Negro leaders sought to negotiate with the city fathers. But the latter consistently refused to engage in good faith negotiation.

Then, last September, came the opportunity to talk with leaders of Birmingham's economic community. In the course of the negotiations, certain promises were made by the merchants—for example, to remove the stores' humiliating racial signs. On the basis of these promises, the Reverend Fred Shuttlesworth and the leaders of the Alabama Christian Movement for Human Rights agreed to a moratorium on all demonstrations. As the weeks and months went by, we realized that we were the victims of a broken promise. A few signs, briefly removed, returned; the others remained. As in so many past experiences, our hopes had been blasted, and the shadow of deep disappointment settled upon us. We had no alternative except to prepare for direct action, whereby we would present our very bodies as a means of laying our case before the conscience of the local and the national community. Mindful of the difficulties involved, we decided to undertake a process of self purification. We began a series of workshops on nonviolence, and we repeatedly asked ourselves: "Are you able to accept blows without retaliating?" "Are you able to endure the ordeal of jail?" We decided to schedule our direct action program for the Easter season, realizing that except for Christmas, this is the main shopping period of the year. Knowing that a strong economic-withdrawal program would be the by product of direct action, we felt that this would be the best time to bring pressure to bear on the merchants for the needed change.

Then it occurred to us that Birmingham's mayoral election was coming up in March, and we speedily decided to postpone action until after election day. When we discovered that the Commissioner of Public Safety, Eugene "Bull" Connor, had piled up enough votes to be in the run off, we decided again to postpone action until the day after the run off so that the demonstrations could not be used to cloud the issues. Like many others, we waited to see Mr. Connor defeated, and to this end we endured postponement after postponement. Having aided in this community need, we felt that our direct action program could be delayed no longer.

You may well ask: "Why direct action? Why sit ins, marches and so forth? Isn't negotiation a better path?" You are quite right in calling for negotiation. Indeed, this is the very purpose of direct action. Nonviolent direct action seeks to create such a crisis and foster such a tension that a community which has constantly refused to negotiate is forced to confront the issue. It seeks so to dramatize the issue that it can no longer be ignored. My citing the creation of tension as part of the work of the nonviolent resister may sound rather shocking. But I must confess that I am not afraid of the word "tension." I have earnestly opposed violent tension, but there is a type of constructive, nonviolent tension which is necessary for growth. Just as Socrates felt that it was necessary to create a tension in the mind so that individuals could rise from the bondage of myths and half truths to the unfettered realm of creative analysis and objective appraisal, so must we see the need for nonviolent gadflies to create the kind of tension in society that will help men rise from the dark depths of prejudice and racism to the majestic heights of understanding and brotherhood. The purpose of our direct action program is to create a situation so crisis packed that it will inevitably open the door to negotiation. I therefore concur with you in your call for negotiation. Too long has our beloved Southland been bogged down in a tragic effort to live in monologue rather than dialogue.

One of the basic points in your statement is that the action that I and my associates have taken in Birmingham is untimely. Some have asked: "Why didn't you give the new city administration time to act?" The only answer that I can give to this query is that the new Birmingham administration must be prodded about as much as the outgoing one, before it will act. We are sadly mistaken if we feel that the election of Albert Boutwell as mayor will bring the millennium to Birmingham. While Mr. Boutwell is a much more gentle person than Mr. Connor, they are both segregationists, dedicated to maintenance of the status quo. I have hope that Mr. Boutwell will be reasonable enough to see the futility of massive resistance to desegregation. But he will not see this without pressure from devotees of civil rights. My friends, I must say to you that we have not made a single gain in civil rights without determined legal and nonviolent pressure. Lamentably, it is an historical fact that privileged groups seldom give up their privileges voluntarily. Individuals may see the moral light and voluntarily give up their unjust posture; but, as Reinhold Niebuhr[1] has reminded us, groups tend to be more immoral than individuals.

We know through painful experience that freedom is never voluntarily given by the oppressor; it must be demanded by the oppressed. Frankly, I have yet to engage in a direct action campaign that was "well timed" in the view of those who have not suffered unduly from the disease of segregation. For years now I have heard the word "Wait!" It rings in the ear of every Negro with piercing familiarity. This "Wait" has almost always meant "Never." We must come to see, with one of our distinguished jurists, that "justice too long delayed is justice denied."

We have waited for more than 340 years for our constitutional and God given rights. The nations of Asia and Africa are moving with jetlike speed toward gaining political independence, but we still creep at horse and buggy pace toward gaining a cup of coffee at a lunch counter. Perhaps it is easy for those who have never felt the stinging darts of segregation to say, "Wait." But when you have seen vicious mobs lynch your mothers and fathers at will and drown your sisters and brothers at whim; when you have seen hate filled policemen curse, kick and even kill your black brothers and sisters; when you see the vast majority of your twenty million Negro brothers smothering in an airtight cage of poverty in the midst

---

[1] [Karl Paul Reinhold Neibuhr (1892–1971) was a well-known American theologian and public intellectual.]

of an affluent society; when you suddenly find your tongue twisted and your speech stammering as you seek to explain to your six year old daughter why she can't go to the public amusement park that has just been advertised on television, and see tears welling up in her eyes when she is told that Funtown is closed to colored children, and see ominous clouds of inferiority beginning to form in her little mental sky, and see her beginning to distort her personality by developing an unconscious bitterness toward white people; when you have to concoct an answer for a five year old son who is asking: "Daddy, why do white people treat colored people so mean?"; when you take a cross county drive and find it necessary to sleep night after night in the uncomfortable corners of your automobile because no motel will accept you; when you are humiliated day in and day out by nagging signs reading "white" and "colored"; when your first name becomes "nigger," your middle name becomes "boy" (however old you are) and your last name becomes "John," and your wife and mother are never given the respected title "Mrs."; when you are harried by day and haunted by night by the fact that you are a Negro, living constantly at tiptoe stance, never quite knowing what to expect next, and are plagued with inner fears and outer resentments; when you are forever fighting a degenerating sense of "nobodiness"—then you will understand why we find it difficult to wait. There comes a time when the cup of endurance runs over, and men are no longer willing to be plunged into the abyss of despair. I hope, sirs, you can understand our legitimate and unavoidable impatience. You express a great deal of anxiety over our willingness to break laws. This is certainly a legitimate concern. Since we so diligently urge people to obey the Supreme Court's decision of 1954 outlawing segregation in the public schools, at first glance it may seem rather paradoxical for us consciously to break laws. One may well ask: "How can you advocate breaking some laws and obeying others?" The answer lies in the fact that there are two types of laws: just and unjust. I would be the first to advocate obeying just laws. One has not only a legal but a moral responsibility to obey just laws. Conversely,

one has a moral responsibility to disobey unjust laws. I would agree with St. Augustine that "an unjust law is no law at all."

Now, what is the difference between the two? How does one determine whether a law is just or unjust? A just law is a man made code that squares with the moral law or the law of God. An unjust law is a code that is out of harmony with the moral law. To put it in the terms of St. Thomas Aquinas: An unjust law is a human law that is not rooted in eternal law and natural law. Any law that uplifts human personality is just. Any law that degrades human personality is unjust. All segregation statutes are unjust because segregation distorts the soul and damages the personality. It gives the segregator a false sense of superiority and the segregated a false sense of inferiority. Segregation, to use the terminology of the Jewish philosopher Martin Buber, substitutes an "I it" relationship for an "I thou" relationship and ends up relegating persons to the status of things. Hence segregation is not only politically, economically and sociologically unsound, it is morally wrong and sinful. Paul Tillich[1] has said that sin is separation. Is not segregation an existential expression of man's tragic separation, his awful estrangement, his terrible sinfulness? Thus it is that I can urge men to obey the 1954 decision of the Supreme Court, for it is morally right; and I can urge them to disobey segregation ordinances, for they are morally wrong.

Let us consider a more concrete example of just and unjust laws. An unjust law is a code that a numerical or power majority group compels a minority group to obey but does not make binding on itself. This is difference made legal. By the same token, a just law is a code that a majority compels a minority to follow and that it is willing to follow itself. This is sameness made legal. Let me give another explanation. A law is unjust if it is inflicted on a minority that, as a result of being denied the right to vote, had no part in enacting or devising the law. Who can say that the legislature of Alabama

---

[1] [Paul Tillich (1886–1965) was a German-American theologian and existentialist religious philosopher.]

which set up that state's segregation laws was democratically elected? Throughout Alabama all sorts of devious methods are used to prevent Negroes from becoming registered voters, and there are some counties in which, even though Negroes constitute a majority of the population, not a single Negro is registered. Can any law enacted under such circumstances be considered democratically structured?

Sometimes a law is just on its face and unjust in its application. For instance, I have been arrested on a charge of parading without a permit. Now, there is nothing wrong in having an ordinance which requires a permit for a parade. But such an ordinance becomes unjust when it is used to maintain segregation and to deny citizens the First-Amendment privilege of peaceful assembly and protest.

I hope you are able to see the distinction I am trying to point out. In no sense do I advocate evading or defying the law, as would the rabid segregationist. That would lead to anarchy. One who breaks an unjust law must do so openly, lovingly, and with a willingness to accept the penalty. I submit that an individual who breaks a law that conscience tells him is unjust, and who willingly accepts the penalty of imprisonment in order to arouse the conscience of the community over its injustice, is in reality expressing the highest respect for law.

Of course, there is nothing new about this kind of civil disobedience. It was evidenced sublimely in the refusal of Shadrach, Meshach and Abednego to obey the laws of Nebuchadnezzar, on the ground that a higher moral law was at stake. It was practiced superbly by the early Christians, who were willing to face hungry lions and the excruciating pain of chopping blocks rather than submit to certain unjust laws of the Roman Empire. To a degree, academic freedom is a reality today because Socrates practiced civil disobedience. In our own nation, the Boston Tea Party represented a massive act of civil disobedience.

We should never forget that everything Adolf Hitler did in Germany was "legal" and everything the Hungarian freedom fighters did in Hungary was "illegal." It was "illegal" to aid and comfort a Jew in Hitler's Germany. Even so, I am sure that, had I lived in Germany at the time, I would have aided and comforted my Jewish brothers. If today I lived in a Communist country where certain principles dear to the Christian faith are suppressed, I would openly advocate disobeying that country's antireligious laws.

I must make two honest confessions to you, my Christian and Jewish brothers. First, I must confess that over the past few years I have been gravely disappointed with the white moderate. I have almost reached the regrettable conclusion that the Negro's great stumbling block in his stride toward freedom is not the White Citizen's Counciler or the Ku Klux Klanner, but the white moderate, who is more devoted to "order" than to justice; who prefers a negative peace which is the absence of tension to a positive peace which is the presence of justice; who constantly says: "I agree with you in the goal you seek, but I cannot agree with your methods of direct action"; who paternalistically believes he can set the timetable for another man's freedom; who lives by a mythical concept of time and who constantly advises the Negro to wait for a "more convenient season." Shallow understanding from people of good will is more frustrating than absolute misunderstanding from people of ill will. Lukewarm acceptance is much more bewildering than outright rejection.

I had hoped that the white moderate would understand that law and order exist for the purpose of establishing justice and that when they fail in this purpose they become the dangerously structured dams that block the flow of social progress. I had hoped that the white moderate would understand that the present tension in the South is a necessary phase of the transition from an obnoxious negative peace, in which the Negro passively accepted his unjust plight, to a substantive and positive peace, in which all men will respect the dignity and worth of human personality. Actually, we who engage in nonviolent direct action are not the creators of tension. We merely bring to the surface the hidden tension that is already alive. We bring it out in the open, where it can be seen and dealt with.

Like a boil that can never be cured so long as it is covered up but must be opened with all its ugliness to the natural medicines of air and light, injustice must be exposed, with all the tension its exposure creates, to the light of human conscience and the air of national opinion before it can be cured.

In your statement you assert that our actions, even though peaceful, must be condemned because they precipitate violence. But is this a logical assertion? Isn't this like condemning a robbed man because his possession of money precipitated the evil act of robbery? Isn't this like condemning Socrates because his unswerving commitment to truth and his philosophical inquiries precipitated the act by the misguided populace in which they made him drink hemlock? Isn't this like condemning Jesus because his unique God consciousness and never ceasing devotion to God's will precipitated the evil act of crucifixion? We must come to see that, as the federal courts have consistently affirmed, it is wrong to urge an individual to cease his efforts to gain his basic constitutional rights because the quest may precipitate violence. Society must protect the robbed and punish the robber. I had also hoped that the white moderate would reject the myth concerning time in relation to the struggle for freedom. I have just received a letter from a white brother in Texas. He writes: "All Christians know that the colored people will receive equal rights eventually, but it is possible that you are in too great a religious hurry. It has taken Christianity almost two thousand years to accomplish what it has. The teachings of Christ take time to come to earth." Such an attitude stems from a tragic misconception of time, from the strangely irrational notion that there is something in the very flow of time that will inevitably cure all ills. Actually, time itself is neutral; it can be used either destructively or constructively. More and more I feel that the people of ill will have used time much more effectively than have the people of good will. We will have to repent in this generation not merely for the hateful words and actions of the bad people but for the appalling silence of the good people. Human progress never rolls in on wheels of inevitability;

it comes through the tireless efforts of men willing to be co-workers with God, and without this hard work, time itself becomes an ally of the forces of social stagnation. We must use time creatively, in the knowledge that the time is always ripe to do right. Now is the time to make real the promise of democracy and transform our pending national elegy into a creative psalm of brotherhood. Now is the time to lift our national policy from the quicksand of racial injustice to the solid rock of human dignity.

You speak of our activity in Birmingham as extreme. At first I was rather disappointed that fellow clergymen would see my nonviolent efforts as those of an extremist. I began thinking about the fact that I stand in the middle of two opposing forces in the Negro community. One is a force of complacency, made up in part of Negroes who, as a result of long years of oppression, are so drained of self respect and a sense of "somebodiness" that they have adjusted to segregation; and in part of a few middle-class Negroes who, because of a degree of academic and economic security and because in some ways they profit by segregation, have become insensitive to the problems of the masses. The other force is one of bitterness and hatred, and it comes perilously close to advocating violence. It is expressed in the various black nationalist groups that are springing up across the nation, the largest and best known being Elijah Muhammad's Muslim movement. Nourished by the Negro's frustration over the continued existence of racial discrimination, this movement is made up of people who have lost faith in America, who have absolutely repudiated Christianity, and who have concluded that the white man is an incorrigible "devil."

I have tried to stand between these two forces, saying that we need emulate neither the "do nothingism" of the complacent nor the hatred and despair of the black nationalist. For there is the more excellent way of love and nonviolent protest. I am grateful to God that, through the influence of the Negro church, the way of nonviolence became an integral part of our struggle. If this philosophy had not emerged, by now many streets of the South would, I am convinced, be flowing with blood. And I am further convinced that if our white brothers dismiss as "rabble rousers" and "outside agitators" those of us who employ nonviolent direct action, and if they refuse to support our nonviolent efforts, millions of Negroes will, out of frustration and despair, seek solace and security in black nationalist ideologies—a development that would inevitably lead to a frightening racial nightmare.

Oppressed people cannot remain oppressed forever. The yearning for freedom eventually manifests itself, and that is what has happened to the American Negro. Something within has reminded him of his birthright of freedom, and something without has reminded him that it can be gained. Consciously or unconsciously, he has been caught up by the Zeitgeist, and with his black brothers of Africa and his brown and yellow brothers of Asia, South America and the Caribbean, the United States Negro is moving with a sense of great urgency toward the promised land of racial justice. If one recognizes this vital urge that has engulfed the Negro community, one should readily understand why public demonstrations are taking place. The Negro has many pent up resentments and latent frustrations, and he must release them. So let him march; let him make prayer pilgrimages to the city hall; let him go on freedom rides—and try to understand why he must do so. If his repressed emotions are not released in nonviolent ways, they will seek expression through violence; this is not a threat but a fact of history. So I have not said to my people: "Get rid of your discontent." Rather, I have tried to say that this normal and healthy discontent can be channeled into the creative outlet of nonviolent direct action. And now this approach is being termed extremist. But though I was initially disappointed at being categorized as an extremist, as I continued to think about the matter I gradually gained a measure of satisfaction from the label. Was not Jesus an extremist for love: "Love your enemies, bless them that curse you, do good to them that hate you, and pray for them which despitefully use you, and persecute you." Was not Amos an extremist for justice: "Let justice roll down like waters and righteousness like an ever flowing stream." Was not

Paul an extremist for the Christian gospel: "I bear in my body the marks of the Lord Jesus." Was not Martin Luther an extremist: "Here I stand; I cannot do otherwise, so help me God." And John Bunyan: "I will stay in jail to the end of my days before I make a butchery of my conscience." And Abraham Lincoln: "This nation cannot survive half slave and half free." And Thomas Jefferson: "We hold these truths to be self evident, that all men are created equal …" So the question is not whether we will be extremists, but what kind of extremists we will be. Will we be extremists for hate or for love? Will we be extremists for the preservation of injustice or for the extension of justice? In that dramatic scene on Calvary's hill three men were crucified. We must never forget that all three were crucified for the same crime—the crime of extremism. Two were extremists for immorality, and thus fell below their environment. The other, Jesus Christ, was an extremist for love, truth and goodness, and thereby rose above his environment. Perhaps the South, the nation and the world are in dire need of creative extremists.

I had hoped that the white moderate would see this need. Perhaps I was too optimistic; perhaps I expected too much. I suppose I should have realized that few members of the oppressor race can understand the deep groans and passionate yearnings of the oppressed race, and still fewer have the vision to see that injustice must be rooted out by strong, persistent and determined action. I am thankful, however, that some of our white brothers in the South have grasped the meaning of this social revolution and committed themselves to it. They are still all too few in quantity, but they are big in quality. Some—such as Ralph McGill, Lillian Smith, Harry Golden, James McBride Dabbs, Ann Braden and Sarah Patton Boyle—have written about our struggle in eloquent and prophetic terms. Others have marched with us down nameless streets of the South. They have languished in filthy, roach infested jails, suffering the abuse and brutality of policemen who view them as "dirty nigger-lovers." Unlike so many of their moderate brothers and sisters, they have recognized the urgency of the moment and sensed the need for powerful "action" antidotes to combat the disease of segregation. Let me take note of my other major disappointment. I have been so greatly disappointed with the white church and its leadership. Of course, there are some notable exceptions. I am not unmindful of the fact that each of you has taken some significant stands on this issue. I commend you, Reverend Stallings,[1] for your Christian stand on this past Sunday, in welcoming Negroes to your worship service on a non-segregated basis. I commend the Catholic leaders of this state for integrating Spring Hill College several years ago.

But despite these notable exceptions, I must honestly reiterate that I have been disappointed with the church. I do not say this as one of those negative critics who can always find something wrong with the church. I say this as a minister of the gospel, who loves the church; who was nurtured in its bosom; who has been sustained by its spiritual blessings and who will remain true to it as long as the cord of life shall lengthen.

When I was suddenly catapulted into the leadership of the bus protest in Montgomery, Alabama, a few years ago, I felt we would be supported by the white church. I felt that the white ministers, priests and rabbis of the South would be among our strongest allies. Instead, some have been outright opponents, refusing to understand the freedom movement and misrepresenting its leaders; all too many others have been more cautious than courageous and have remained silent behind the anesthetizing security of stained glass windows.

In spite of my shattered dreams, I came to Birmingham with the hope that the white religious leadership of this community would see the justice of our cause and, with deep moral concern, would serve as the channel through which our just grievances could reach the power structure. I had hoped that each of you would understand. But again I have been disappointed.

I have heard numerous southern religious leaders admonish their worshipers to comply with a desegregation decision because it is the law, but I have longed to hear white ministers declare: "Follow this decree because integration is morally right and because the Negro is your brother." In the midst of blatant injustices inflicted upon the Negro, I have watched white churchmen stand on the sideline and mouth pious irrelevancies and sanctimonious trivialities. In the midst of a mighty struggle to rid our nation of racial and economic injustice, I have heard many ministers say: "Those are social issues, with which the gospel has no real concern." And I have watched many churches commit themselves to a completely other worldly religion which makes a strange, un-Biblical distinction between body and soul, between the sacred and the secular.

I have traveled the length and breadth of Alabama, Mississippi and all the other southern states. On sweltering summer days and crisp autumn mornings I have looked at the South's beautiful churches with their lofty spires pointing heavenward. I have beheld the impressive outlines of her massive religious education buildings. Over and over I have found myself asking: "What kind of people worship here? Who is their God? Where were their voices when the lips of Governor Barnett dripped with words of interposition and nullification? Where were they when Governor Wallace gave a clarion call for defiance and hatred? Where were their voices of support when bruised and weary Negro men and women decided to rise from the dark dungeons of complacency to the bright hills of creative protest?"

Yes, these questions are still in my mind. In deep disappointment I have wept over the laxity of the church. But be assured that my tears have been tears of love. There can be no deep disappointment where there is not deep love. Yes, I love the church. How could I do otherwise? I am in the rather unique position of being the son, the grandson and the great grandson of preachers. Yes, I see the church as the body of Christ. But, oh! How we have blemished and scarred that body through social neglect and through fear of being nonconformists.

_____

[1] [Earl Stallings (1916–2005) was an American Baptist minister who was active in the civil rights movement.]

There was a time when the church was very powerful—in the time when the early Christians rejoiced at being deemed worthy to suffer for what they believed. In those days the church was not merely a thermometer that recorded the ideas and principles of popular opinion; it was a thermostat that transformed the mores of society. Whenever the early Christians entered a town, the people in power became disturbed and immediately sought to convict the Christians for being "disturbers of the peace" and "outside agitators." But the Christians pressed on, in the conviction that they were "a colony of heaven," called to obey God rather than man. Small in number, they were big in commitment. They were too God-intoxicated to be "astronomically intimidated." By their effort and example they brought an end to such ancient evils as infanticide and gladiatorial contests. Things are different now. So often the contemporary church is a weak, ineffectual voice with an uncertain sound. So often it is an archdefender of the status quo. Far from being disturbed by the presence of the church, the power structure of the average community is consoled by the church's silent—and often even vocal—sanction of things as they are.

But the judgment of God is upon the church as never before. If today's church does not recapture the sacrificial spirit of the early church, it will lose its authenticity, forfeit the loyalty of millions, and be dismissed as an irrelevant social club with no meaning for the twentieth century. Every day I meet young people whose disappointment with the church has turned into outright disgust.

Perhaps I have once again been too optimistic. Is organized religion too inextricably bound to the status quo to save our nation and the world? Perhaps I must turn my faith to the inner spiritual church, the church within the church, as the true ekklesia and the hope of the world. But again I am thankful to God that some noble souls from the ranks of organized religion have broken loose from the paralyzing chains of conformity and joined us as active partners in the struggle for freedom. They have left their secure congregations and walked the streets of Albany, Georgia, with us. They have

gone down the highways of the South on tortuous rides for freedom. Yes, they have gone to jail with us. Some have been dismissed from their churches, have lost the support of their bishops and fellow ministers. But they have acted in the faith that right defeated is stronger than evil triumphant. Their witness has been the spiritual salt that has preserved the true meaning of the gospel in these troubled times. They have carved a tunnel of hope through the dark mountain of disappointment. I hope the church as a whole will meet the challenge of this decisive hour. But even if the church does not come to the aid of justice, I have no despair about the future. I have no fear about the outcome of our struggle in Birmingham, even if our motives are at present misunderstood. We will reach the goal of freedom in Birmingham and all over the nation, because the goal of America is freedom. Abused and scorned though we may be, our destiny is tied up with America's destiny. Before the pilgrims landed at Plymouth, we were here. Before the pen of Jefferson etched the majestic words of the Declaration of Independence across the pages of history, we were here. For more than two centuries our forebears labored in this country without wages; they made cotton king; they built the homes of their masters while suffering gross injustice and shameful humiliation—and yet out of a bottomless vitality they continued to thrive and develop. If the inexpressible cruelties of slavery could not stop us, the opposition we now face will surely fail. We will win our freedom because the sacred heritage of our nation and the eternal will of God are embodied in our echoing demands. Before closing I feel impelled to mention one other point in your statement that has troubled me profoundly. You warmly commended the Birmingham police force for keeping "order" and "preventing violence." I doubt that you would have so warmly commended the police force if you had seen its dogs sinking their teeth into unarmed, nonviolent Negroes. I doubt that you would so quickly commend the policemen if you were to observe their ugly and inhumane treatment of Negroes here in the city jail; if you were to watch them push and curse old Negro women and young Negro girls; if you were to see them slap and kick old Negro men and young boys; if you were to observe them, as they did on two occasions, refuse to give us food because we wanted to sing our grace together. I cannot join you in your praise of the Birmingham police department.

It is true that the police have exercised a degree of discipline in handling the demonstrators. In this sense they have conducted themselves rather "non-violently" in public. But for what purpose? To preserve the evil system of segregation. Over the past few years I have consistently preached that nonviolence demands that the means we use must be as pure as the ends we seek. I have tried to make clear that it is wrong to use immoral means to attain moral ends. But now I must affirm that it is just as wrong, or perhaps even more so, to use moral means to preserve immoral ends. Perhaps Mr. Connor and his policemen have been rather nonviolent in public, as was Chief Pritchett in Albany, Georgia, but they have used the moral means of nonviolence to maintain the immoral end of racial injustice. As T.S. Eliot has said: "The last temptation is the greatest treason: To do the right deed for the wrong reason."

I wish you had commended the Negro sit-inners and demonstrators of Birmingham for their sublime courage, their willingness to suffer and their amazing discipline in the midst of great provocation. One day the South will recognize its real heroes. They will be the James Merediths,[1] with the noble sense of purpose that enables them to face jeering and hostile mobs, and with the agonizing loneliness that characterizes the life of the pioneer. They will be old, oppressed, battered Negro women, symbolized in a seventy two year old woman in Montgomery, Alabama, who rose up with a sense of dignity and with her people decided not to ride segregated buses, and who responded with ungrammatical profundity to one who inquired about her weariness: "My feets is tired, but my soul is at rest." They will be the young high school and college students, the young ministers of the gospel and a host of their elders, courageously and nonviolently sitting in at lunch counters and willingly going to jail for conscience' sake. One day the South will know that when these disinherited children of God sat down at lunch counters, they were in reality standing up for what is best in the American dream and for the most sacred values in our Judaeo Christian heritage, thereby bringing our nation back to those great wells of democracy which were dug deep by the founding fathers in their formulation of the Constitution and the Declaration of Independence.

Never before have I written so long a letter. I'm afraid it is much too long to take your precious time. I can assure you that it would have been much shorter if I had been writing from a comfortable desk, but what else can one do when he is alone in a narrow jail cell, other than write long letters, think long thoughts and pray long prayers?

If I have said anything in this letter that overstates the truth and indicates an unreasonable impatience, I beg you to forgive me. If I have said anything that understates the truth and indicates my having a patience that allows me to settle for anything less than brotherhood, I beg God to forgive me.

I hope this letter finds you strong in the faith. I also hope that circumstances will soon make it possible for me to meet each of you, not as an integrationist or a civil-rights leader but as a fellow clergyman and a Christian brother. Let us all hope that the dark clouds of racial prejudice will soon pass away and the deep fog of misunderstanding will be lifted from our fear drenched communities, and in some not too distant tomorrow the radiant stars of love and brotherhood will shine over our great nation with all their scintillating beauty.

Yours for the cause of Peace and Brotherhood, Martin Luther King, Jr.

---

[1] [James Meredith (b. 1933) was the first African-American student at the University of Mississippi.]

DISCUSSION QUESTIONS

1. King writes, "Injustice anywhere is a threat to justice everywhere." What do you think he means by this?

2. Citing the theologian Reinhold Niebuhr, King mentions that "groups tend to be more immoral than individuals." Do you think this is true? If so, why? If not, why do King and Niebuhr think this is the case? In what respect do you disagree with them?

3. According to King, under what circumstances is it permissible to break a law? Do you think King would advocate breaking a putatively *just* law for the purposes of drawing attention to an *unjust* law? For example, would trespassing or vandalism be acceptable if doing so would draw attention to an immoral or unjust activity?

4. King advocates breaking segregation statutes while maintaining that states ought to obey the Supreme Court's ruling that segregation is unconstitutional. How does he reconcile this tension between asking people to obey one law and asking them to disobey another?

5. How do you think Plato, Hobbes, Locke, Rousseau, Gauthier, Hume, and Simmons would each react to King's position regarding obedience and disobedience? Which among them would agree with King's position, and which would disagree?

18

Henry David Thoreau, "Resistance to Civil Government" (1849)

Henry David Thoreau (1817–62) was a poet, abolitionist, and naturalist. He is often considered to be among the principal figures (along with Ralph Waldo Emerson and Walt Whitman) in the American transcendentalist movement. In this essay, Thoreau takes issue with the presumption in favor of obedience to civil authorities.

SOURCE

Thoreau, Henry David. "Resistance to Civil Government." In *Aesthetic Papers*, pp. 189–211. Ed. E.P. Peabody. G.P. Putnam, 1849.

I heartily accept the motto, "That government is best which governs least"; and I should like to see it acted up to more rapidly and systematically. Carried out, it finally amounts to this, which also I believe—"That government is best which governs not at all"; and when men are prepared for it, that will be the kind of government which they will have. Government is at best but an expedient; but most governments are usually, and all governments are sometimes, inexpedient. The objections which have been brought against a standing army, and they are many and weighty, and deserve to prevail, may also at last be brought against a standing government. The standing army is only an arm of the standing government. The government itself, which is only the mode which the people have chosen to execute their will, is equally liable to be abused and perverted before the people can act through it. Witness the present Mexican war, the work of comparatively a few individuals using the standing government as their tool; for in the outset, the people would not have consented to this measure.

This American government—what is it but a tradition, though a recent one, endeavoring to transmit itself unimpaired to posterity, but each instant losing some of its integrity? It has not the vitality and force of a single living man; for a single man can bend it to his will. It is a sort of wooden gun to the people themselves. But it is not the less necessary for this; for the people must have some complicated machinery or other, and hear its din, to satisfy that idea of government which they have. Governments show thus how successfully men can be imposed upon, even impose on themselves, for their own advantage. It is excellent, we must all allow. Yet this government never of itself furthered any enterprise, but by the alacrity with which it got out of its way. *It* does not keep the country free. *It* does not settle the West. *It* does not educate. The character inherent in the American people has done all that has been accomplished; and it would have done somewhat more, if the government had not sometimes got in its way. For government is an expedient, by which men would fain succeed in letting one another alone; and, as has been said, when it is most expedient, the governed are most let alone by it. Trade and commerce, if they were not made of india-rubber, would never manage to bounce over obstacles which legislators are continually putting in their way; and if one were to judge these men wholly by the effects of their actions and not partly by their intentions, they would deserve to be classed and punished with those mischievious [sic] persons who put obstructions on the railroads.

But, to speak practically and as a citizen, unlike those who call themselves no-government men, I ask for, not at once no government, but *at once* a better government. Let every man make known what kind of government would command his respect, and that will be one step toward obtaining it.

After all, the practical reason why, when the power is once in the hands of the people, a majority are permitted, and for a long period continue, to rule is not because they are most likely to be in the right, nor because this seems fairest to the minority, but because they are physically the strongest. But a government in which the majority rule in all cases can not be based on justice, even as far as men understand it. Can there not be a government in which the majorities do not virtually decide right and wrong, but conscience?—in which majorities decide only those questions to which the rule of expediency is applicable? Must the citizen ever for a moment, or in the least degree, resign his conscience to the legislator? Why has every man a conscience then? I think that we should be men first, and subjects afterward. It is not desirable to cultivate a respect for the law, so much as for the right. The only obligation which I have a right to assume is to do at any time what I think right. It is truly enough said that a corporation has no conscience; but a corporation of conscientious men is a corporation *with* a conscience. Law never made men a whit more just; and, by means of their respect for it, even the well-disposed are daily made the agents of injustice. A common and natural result of an undue respect for the law is, that you may see a file of soldiers, colonel, captain, corporal, privates, powder-monkeys, and all, marching in admirable order over hill and dale to the wars, against their wills, ay, against their common sense and consciences, which makes it very steep marching indeed, and produces a palpitation of the heart. They have no doubt that it is a damnable business in which they are concerned; they are all peaceably inclined. Now, what are they? Men at all? or small movable forts and magazines, at the service of some unscrupulous man in power? Visit the Navy Yard, and behold a marine, such a man as an American government can make, or such as it can make a man with its black arts—a mere shadow and reminiscence of humanity, a man laid out alive and standing, and already, as one may say, buried under arms with funeral accompaniment, though it may be,

"Not a drum was heard, not a funeral note,
    As his corse to the rampart we hurried;
Not a soldier discharged his farewell shot
    O'er the grave where our hero was buried."[1]

The mass of men serve the state thus, not as men mainly, but as machines, with their bodies. They are the standing army, and the militia, jailers, constables, posse comitatus, etc. In most cases there is no free exercise whatever of the judgement or of the moral sense; but they put themselves on a level with wood and earth and stones; and wooden men can perhaps be manufactured that will serve the purpose as well. Such command no more respect than men

---

[1] From "The Burial of Sir John Moore at Corunna" by Charles Wolfe (1791–1823).

of straw or a lump of dirt. They have the same sort of worth only as horses and dogs. Yet such as these even are commonly esteemed good citizens. Others—as most legislators, politicians, lawyers, ministers, and office-holders—serve the state chiefly with their heads; and, as they rarely make any moral distinctions, they are as likely to serve the devil, without intending it, as God. A very few—as heroes, patriots, martyrs, reformers in the great sense, and *men*—serve the state with their consciences also, and so necessarily resist it for the most part; and they are commonly treated as enemies by it. A wise man will only be useful as a man, and will not submit to be "clay," and "stop a hole to keep the wind away," but leave that office to his dust at least:

> "I am too high born to be propertied,
> To be a second at control,
> Or useful serving-man and instrument
> To any sovereign state throughout the world."[1]

He who gives himself entirely to his fellow men appears to them useless and selfish; but he who gives himself partially to them is pronounced a benefactor and philanthropist.

How does it become a man to behave toward the American government today? I answer, that he cannot without disgrace be associated with it. I cannot for an instant recognize that political organization as *my* government which is the *slave's* government also.

All men recognize the right of revolution; that is, the right to refuse allegiance to, and to resist, the government, when its tyranny or its inefficiency are great and unendurable. But almost all say that such is not the case now. But such was the case, they think, in the Revolution of '75. If one were to tell me that this was a bad government because it taxed certain foreign commodities brought to its ports, it is most probable that I should not make an ado about it, for I can do without them. All machines have their friction; and possibly this does enough good to counter-balance the evil. At any rate, it is a great evil to make a stir about it. But when the friction comes to have its machine, and oppression and robbery are organized, I say, let us not have such a machine any longer. In other words, when a sixth of the population of a nation which has undertaken to be the refuge of liberty are slaves, and a whole country is unjustly overrun and conquered by a foreign army, and subjected to military law, I think that it is not too soon for honest men to rebel and revolutionize. What makes this duty the more urgent is the fact that the country so overrun is not our own, but ours is the invading army.

[William] Paley, a common authority with many on moral questions, in his chapter on the "Duty of Submission to Civil Government," resolves all civil obligation into expediency; and he proceeds to say that "so long as the interest of the whole society requires it, that it, so long as the established government cannot be resisted or changed without public inconveniencey, it is the will of God … that the established government be obeyed—and no longer. This principle being admitted, the justice of every particular case of resistance is reduced to a computation of the quantity of the danger and grievance on the one side, and of the probability and expense of redressing it on the other." Of this, he says, every man shall judge for himself. But Paley appears never to have contemplated those cases to which the rule of expediency does not apply, in which a people, as well as an individual, must do justice, cost what it may. If I have unjustly wrested a plank from a drowning man, I must restore it to him though I drown myself. This, according to Paley, would be inconvenient. But he that would save his life, in such a case, shall lose it. This people must cease to hold slaves, and to make war on Mexico, though it cost them their existence as a people.

In their practice, nations agree with Paley; but does anyone think that Massachusetts does exactly what is right at the present crisis?[2]

---

[1] [From Shakespeare's *King John*, Act V, scene ii.]

[2] [Apart from the war with Mexico, Thoreau might be referring to the Massachusetts law that required citizens to turn over escaped slaves for return to their Southern owners.]

"A drab of state, a cloth-o'-silver slut,
To have her train borne up, and her soul trail
in the dirt."[1]

Practically speaking, the opponents to a reform in Massachusetts are not a hundred thousand politicians at the South, but a hundred thousand merchants and farmers here, who are more interested in commerce and agriculture than they are in humanity, and are not prepared to do justice to the slave and to Mexico, *cost what it may*. I quarrel not with far-off foes, but with those who, near at home, cooperate with, and do the bidding of, those far away, and without whom the latter would be harmless. We are accustomed to say, that the mass of men are unprepared; but improvement is slow, because the few are not as materially wiser or better than the many. It is not so important that many should be good as you, as that there be some absolute goodness somewhere; for that will leaven the whole lump. There are thousands who are *in opinion* opposed to slavery and to the war, who yet in effect do nothing to put an end to them; who, esteeming themselves children of Washington and Franklin, sit down with their hands in their pockets, and say that they know not what to do, and do nothing; who even postpone the question of freedom to the question of free trade, and quietly read the prices-current along with the latest advices from Mexico, after dinner, and, it may be, fall asleep over them both. What is the price-current of an honest man and patriot today? They hesitate, and they regret, and sometimes they petition; but they do nothing in earnest and with effect. They will wait, well disposed, for others to remedy the evil, that they may no longer have it to regret. At most, they give up only a cheap vote, and a feeble countenance and Godspeed, to the right, as it goes by them. There are nine hundred and ninety-nine patrons of virtue to one virtuous man. But it is easier to deal with the real possessor of a thing than with the temporary guardian of it.

---

[1] [From Cyril Tourneau's *The Revenger's Tragedy*, Act IV, scene 4.]

All voting is a sort of gaming, like checkers or backgammon, with a slight moral tinge to it, a playing with right and wrong, with moral questions; and betting naturally accompanies it. The character of the voters is not staked. I cast my vote, perchance, as I think right; but I am not vitally concerned that that right should prevail. I am willing to leave it to the majority. Its obligation, therefore, never exceeds that of expediency. Even voting *for the right* is *doing* nothing for it. It is only expressing to men feebly your desire that it should prevail. A wise man will not leave the right to the mercy of chance, nor wish it to prevail through the power of the majority. There is but little virtue in the action of masses of men. When the majority shall at length vote for the abolition of slavery, it will be because they are indifferent to slavery, or because there is but little slavery left to be abolished by their vote. *They* will then be the only slaves. Only *his* vote can hasten the abolition of slavery who asserts his own freedom by his vote.

I hear of a convention to be held at Baltimore, or elsewhere, for the selection of a candidate for the Presidency, made up chiefly of editors, and men who are politicians by profession; but I think, what is it to any independent, intelligent, and respectable man what decision they may come to? Shall we not have the advantage of this wisdom and honesty, nevertheless? Can we not count upon some independent votes? Are there not many individuals in the country who do not attend conventions? But no: I find that the respectable man, so called, has immediately drifted from his position, and despairs of his country, when his country has more reasons to despair of him. He forthwith adopts one of the candidates thus selected as the only *available* one, thus proving that he is himself *available* for any purposes of the demagogue. His vote is of no more worth than that of any unprincipled foreigner or hireling native, who may have been bought. O for a man who is a *man*, and, and my neighbor says, has a bone in his back which you cannot pass your hand through! Our statistics are at fault: the population has been returned too large. How many *men* are there to a square thousand miles in the country? Hardly one. Does not America offer any inducement for men to settle here? The American has dwindled into an Odd Fellow—one who may be known by the development of his organ of gregariousness, and a manifest lack of intellect and cheerful self-reliance; whose first and chief concern, on coming into the world, is to see that the almshouses are in good repair; and, before yet he has lawfully donned the virile garb, to collect a fund to the support of the widows and orphans that may be; who, in short, ventures to live only by the aid of the Mutual Insurance company, which has promised to bury him decently.

It is not a man's duty, as a matter of course, to devote himself to the eradication of any, even to most enormous, wrong; he may still properly have other concerns to engage him; but it is his duty, at least, to wash his hands of it, and, if he gives it no thought longer, not to give it practically his support. If I devote myself to other pursuits and contemplations, I must first see, at least, that I do not pursue them sitting upon another man's shoulders. I must get off him first, that he may pursue his contemplations too. See what gross inconsistency is tolerated. I have heard some of my townsmen say, "I should like to have them order me out to help put down an insurrection of the slaves, or to march to Mexico—see if I would go"; and yet these very men have each, directly by their allegiance, and so indirectly, at least, by their money, furnished a substitute. The soldier is applauded who refuses to serve in an unjust war by those who do not refuse to sustain the unjust government which makes the war; is applauded by those whose own act and authority he disregards and sets at naught; as if the state were penitent to that degree that it hired one to scourge it while it sinned, but not to that degree that it left off sinning for a moment. Thus, under the name of Order and Civil Government, we are all made at last to pay homage to and support our own meanness. After the first blush of sin comes its indifference; and from immoral it becomes, as it were, *un*moral, and not quite unnecessary to that life which we have made.

The broadest and most prevalent error requires the most disinterested virtue to sustain it. The slight reproach to which the virtue of patriotism is commonly liable, the noble are most likely to incur. Those who, while they disapprove of the character and measures of a government, yield to it their allegiance and support are undoubtedly its most conscientious supporters, and so frequently the most serious obstacles to reform. Some are petitioning the State to dissolve the Union, to disregard the requisitions of the President. Why do they not dissolve it themselves—the union between themselves and the State—and refuse to pay their quota into its treasury? Do not they stand in the same relation to the State that the State does to the Union? And have not the same reasons prevented the State from resisting the Union which have prevented them from resisting the State?

How can a man be satisfied to entertain an opinion merely, and enjoy *it*? Is there any enjoyment in it, if his opinion is that he is aggrieved? If you are cheated out of a single dollar by your neighbor, you do not rest satisfied with knowing you are cheated, or with saying that you are cheated, or even with petitioning him to pay you your due; but you take effectual steps at once to obtain the full amount, and see to it that you are never cheated again. Action from principle, the perception and the performance of right, changes things and relations; it is essentially revolutionary, and does not consist wholly with anything which was. It not only divided States and churches, it divides families; ay, it divides the *individual*, separating the diabolical in him from the divine.

Unjust laws exist: shall we be content to obey them, or shall we endeavor to amend them, and obey them until we have succeeded, or shall we transgress them at once? Men, generally, under such a government as this, think that they ought to wait until they have persuaded the majority to alter them. They think that, if they should resist, the remedy would be worse than the evil. But it is the fault of the government itself that the remedy is worse than the evil. It makes it worse. Why is it not more apt to anticipate and provide for reform?

Why does it not cherish its wise minority? Why does it cry and resist before it is hurt? Why does it not encourage its citizens to put out its faults, and do better than it would have them? Why does it always crucify Christ and excommunicate Copernicus and Luther, and pronounce Washington and Franklin rebels?

One would think, that a deliberate and practical denial of its authority was the only offense never contemplated by its government; else, why has it not assigned its definite, its suitable and proportionate, penalty? If a man who has no property refuses but once to earn nine shillings for the State, he is put in prison for a period unlimited by any law that I know, and determined only by the discretion of those who put him there; but if he should steal ninety times nine shillings from the State, he is soon permitted to go at large again.

If the injustice is part of the necessary friction of the machine of government, let it go, let it go: perchance it will wear smooth—certainly the machine will wear out. If the injustice has a spring, or a pulley, or a rope, or a crank, exclusively for itself, then perhaps you may consider whether the remedy will not be worse than the evil; but if it is of such a nature that it requires you to be the agent of injustice to another, then I say, break the law. Let your life be a counter-friction to stop the machine. What I have to do is to see, at any rate, that I do not lend myself to the wrong which I condemn.

As for adopting the ways which the State has provided for remedying the evil, I know not of such ways. They take too much time, and a man's life will be gone. I have other affairs to attend to. I came into this world, not chiefly to make this a good place to live in, but to live in it, be it good or bad. A man has not everything to do, but something; and because he cannot do everything, it is not necessary that he should be petitioning the Governor or the Legislature any more than it is theirs to petition me; and if they should not hear my petition, what should I do then? But in this case the State has provided no way: its very Constitution is the evil. This may seem to be harsh and stubborn and unconciliatory; but it is to treat with the utmost kindness and consideration the only spirit that can appreciate or deserves it. So is all change for the better, like birth and death, which convulse the body.

I do not hesitate to say, that those who call themselves Abolitionists should at once effectually withdraw their support, both in person and property, from the government of Massachusetts, and not wait till they constitute a majority of one, before they suffer the right to prevail through them. I think that it is enough if they have God on their side, without waiting for that other one. Moreover, any man more right than his neighbors constitutes a majority of one already.

I meet this American government, or its representative, the State government, directly, and face to face, once a year—no more—in the person of its tax-gatherer; this is the only mode in which a man situated as I am necessarily meets it; and it then says distinctly, Recognize me; and the simplest, the most effectual, and, in the present posture of affairs, the indispensablest mode of treating with it on this head, of expressing your little satisfaction with and love for it, is to deny it then. My civil neighbor, the tax-gatherer, is the very man I have to deal with—for it is, after all, with men and not with parchment that I quarrel—and he has voluntarily chosen to be an agent of the government. How shall he ever know well what he is and does as an officer of the government, or as a man, until he is obliged to consider whether he will treat me, his neighbor, for whom he has respect, as a neighbor and well-disposed man, or as a maniac and disturber of the peace, and see if he can get over this obstruction to his neighborliness without a ruder and more impetuous thought or speech corresponding with his action. I know this well, that if one thousand, if one hundred, if ten men whom I could name—if ten *honest* men only—ay, if *one* HONEST man, in this State of Massachusetts, *ceasing to hold slaves*, were actually to withdraw from this co-partnership, and be locked up in the county jail therefor, it would be the abolition of slavery in America. For it matters not how small the beginning may seem to be: what is once well done is done forever. But we love better to talk about it: that we say is our mission.

Reform keeps many scores of newspapers in its service, but not one man. If my esteemed neighbor, the State's ambassador, who will devote his days to the settlement of the question of human rights in the Council Chamber, instead of being threatened with the prisons of Carolina, were to sit down the prisoner of Massachusetts, that State which is so anxious to foist the sin of slavery upon her sister— though at present she can discover only an act of inhospitality to be the ground of a quarrel with her—the Legislature would not wholly waive the subject of the following winter.

Under a government which imprisons unjustly, the true place for a just man is also a prison. The proper place today, the only place which Massachusetts has provided for her freer and less despondent spirits, is in her prisons, to be put out and locked out of the State by her own act, as they have already put themselves out by their principles. It is there that the fugitive slave, and the Mexican prisoner on parole, and the Indian come to plead the wrongs of his race should find them; on that separate but more free and honorable ground, where the State places those who are not *with* her, but *against* her—the only house in a slave State in which a free man can abide with honor. If any think that their influence would be lost there, and their voices no longer afflict the ear of the State, that they would not be as an enemy within its walls, they do not know by how much truth is stronger than error, nor how much more eloquently and effectively he can combat injustice who has experienced a little in his own person. Cast your whole vote, not a strip of paper merely, but your whole influence. A minority is powerless while it conforms to the majority; it is not even a minority then; but it is irresistible when it clogs by its whole weight. If the alternative is to keep all just men in prison, or give up war and slavery, the State will not hesitate which to choose. If a thousand men were not to pay their tax bills this year, that would not be a violent and bloody measure, as it would be to pay them, and enable the State to commit violence and shed innocent blood. This is, in fact, the definition of a peaceable revolution, if any such is possible. If the tax-gatherer, or any other public officer, asks me, as one has done, "But what shall I do?" my answer is, "If you really wish to do anything, resign your office." When the subject has refused allegiance, and the officer has resigned from office, then the revolution is accomplished. But even suppose blood shed when the conscience is wounded? Through this wound a man's real manhood and immortality flow out, and he bleeds to an everlasting death. I see this blood flowing now.

I have contemplated the imprisonment of the offender, rather than the seizure of his goods— though both will serve the same purpose—because they who assert the purest right, and consequently are most dangerous to a corrupt State, commonly have not spent much time in accumulating property. To such the State renders comparatively small service, and a slight tax is wont to appear exorbitant, particularly if they are obliged to earn it by special labor with their hands. If there were one who lived wholly without the use of money, the State itself would hesitate to demand it of him. But the rich man—not to make any invidious comparison—is always sold to the institution which makes him rich. Absolutely speaking, the more money, the less virtue; for money comes between a man and his objects, and obtains them for him; it was certainly no great virtue to obtain it. It puts to rest many questions which he would otherwise be taxed to answer; while the only new question which it puts is the hard but superfluous one, how to spend it. Thus his moral ground is taken from under his feet. The opportunities of living are diminished in proportion as what are called the "means" are increased. The best thing a man can do for his culture when he is rich is to endeavor to carry out those schemes which he entertained when he was poor. Christ answered the Herodians according to their condition. "Show me the tribute-money," said he—and one took a penny out of his pocket—if you use money which has the image of Caesar on it, and which he has made current and valuable, that is, *if you are men of the State*, and gladly enjoy the advantages of Caesar's government, then pay him back some of his own when he demands it. "Render therefore to Caesar that which is Caesar's and to God those things which are God's"—leaving them no wiser than before as to which was which; for they did not wish to know.

When I converse with the freest of my neighbors, I perceive that, whatever they may say about the magnitude and seriousness of the question, and their regard for the public tranquillity, the long and the short of the matter is, that they cannot spare the protection of the existing government, and they dread the consequences to their property and families of disobedience to it. For my own part, I should not like to think that I ever rely on the protection of the State. But, if I deny the authority of the State when it presents its tax bill, it will soon take and waste all my property, and so harass me and my children without end. This is hard. This makes it impossible for a man to live honestly, and at the same time comfortably, in outward respects. It will not be worth the while to accumulate property; that would be sure to go again. You must hire or squat somewhere, and raise but a small crop, and eat that soon. You must live within yourself, and depend upon yourself always tucked up and ready for a start, and not have many affairs. A man may grow rich in Turkey even, if he will be in all respects a good subject of the Turkish government. Confucius said: "If a state is governed by the principles of reason, poverty and misery are subjects of shame; if a state is not governed by the principles of reason, riches and honors are subjects of shame." No: until I want the protection of Massachusetts to be extended to me in some distant Southern port, where my liberty is endangered, or until I am bent solely on building up an estate at home by peaceful enterprise, I can afford to refuse allegiance to Massachusetts, and her right to my property and life. It costs me less in every sense to incur the penalty of disobedience to the State than it would to obey. I should feel as if I were worth less in that case.

Some years ago, the State met me in behalf of the Church, and commanded me to pay a certain sum toward the support of a clergyman whose preaching my father attended, but never I myself. "Pay," it said, "or be locked up in the jail." I declined to pay. But, unfortunately, another man saw fit to pay it. I did not see why the schoolmaster should be taxed to support the priest, and not the priest the schoolmaster; for I was not the State's schoolmaster, but I supported myself by voluntary subscription. I did not see why the lyceum should not present its tax bill, and have the State to back its demand, as well as the Church. However, at the request of the selectmen, I condescended to make some such statement as this in writing: "Know all men by these presents, that I, Henry Thoreau, do not wish to be regarded as a member of any society which I have not joined." This I gave to the town clerk; and he has it. The State, having thus learned that I did not wish to be regarded as a member of that church, has never made a like demand on me since; though it said that it must adhere to its original presumption that time. If I had known how to name them, I should then have signed off in detail from all the societies which I never signed on to; but I did not know where to find such a complete list.

I have paid no poll tax for six years. I was put into a jail once on this account, for one night; and, as I stood considering the walls of solid stone, two or three feet thick, the door of wood and iron, a foot thick, and the iron grating which strained the light, I could not help being struck with the foolishness of that institution which treated me as if I were mere flesh and blood and bones, to be locked up. I wondered that it should have concluded at length that this was the best use it could put me to, and had never thought to avail itself of my services in some way. I saw that, if there was a wall of stone between me and my townsmen, there was a still more difficult one to climb or break through before they could get to be as free as I was. I did not for a moment feel confined, and the walls seemed a great waste of stone and mortar. I felt as if I alone of all my townsmen had paid my tax. They plainly did not know how to treat me, but behaved like persons who are underbred. In every threat and in every compliment there was a blunder; for they thought that my chief desire was to stand the other side of that stone wall. I could not but smile to see how industriously they locked the door on my meditations, which followed them out again without let or hindrance, and *they* were really all that was dangerous. As they could not reach me, they had resolved to punish my body; just as boys, if they cannot come at some person against whom they have a spite, will abuse his dog. I saw that the State was half-witted, that it was timid as a lone woman with her silver spoons, and that it did not know its friends from its foes, and I lost all my remaining respect for it, and pitied it.

Thus the state never intentionally confronts a man's sense, intellectual or moral, but only his body, his senses. It is not armed with superior wit or honesty, but with superior physical strength. I was not born to be forced. I will breathe after my own fashion. Let us see who is the strongest. What force has a multitude? They only can force me who obey a higher law than I. They force me to become like themselves. I do not hear of *men* being *forced* to live this way or that by masses of men. What sort of life were that to live? When I meet a government which says to me, "Your money or your life," why should I be in haste to give it my money? It may be in a great strait, and not know what to do: I cannot help that. It must help itself; do as I do. It is not worth the while to snivel about it. I am not responsible for the successful working of the machinery of society. I am not the son of the engineer. I perceive that, when an acorn and a chestnut fall side by side, the one does not remain inert to make way for the other, but both obey their own laws, and spring and grow and flourish as best they can, till one, perchance, overshadows and destroys the other. If a plant cannot live according to nature, it dies; and so a man.

The night in prison was novel and interesting enough. The prisoners in their shirtsleeves were enjoying a chat and the evening air in the doorway, when I entered. But the jailer said, "Come, boys, it is time to lock up"; and so they dispersed, and I heard the sound of their steps returning into the hollow apartments. My room-mate was introduced to me by the jailer as "a first-rate fellow and clever man." When the door was locked, he showed me where to hang my hat, and how he managed matters there. The rooms were whitewashed once a month; and this one, at least, was the whitest, most simply furnished, and probably neatest apartment in town. He naturally wanted to know where I came from, and what brought me there; and, when I had told him, I asked him in my turn how he came there, presuming him to be an honest man, of course; and as the world goes, I believe he was. "Why," said he, "they accuse me of burning a barn; but I never did it." As near as I could discover, he had probably gone to bed in a barn when drunk, and smoked his pipe there; and so a barn was burnt. He had the reputation of being a clever man, had been there some three months waiting for his trial to come on, and would have to wait as much longer; but he was quite domesticated and contented, since he got his board for nothing, and thought that he was well treated.

He occupied one window, and I the other; and I saw that if one stayed there long, his principal business would be to look out the window. I had soon read all the tracts that were left there, and examined where former prisoners had broken out, and where a grate had been sawed off, and heard the history of the various occupants of that room; for I found that even there there was a history and a gossip which never circulated beyond the walls of the jail. Probably this is the only house in the town where verses are composed, which are afterward printed in a circular form, but not published. I was shown quite a long list of young men who had been detected in an attempt to escape, who avenged themselves by singing them.

I pumped my fellow-prisoner as dry as I could, for fear I should never see him again; but at length he showed me which was my bed, and left me to blow out the lamp.

It was like travelling into a far country, such as I had never expected to behold, to lie there for one night. It seemed to me that I never had heard the town clock strike before, nor the evening sounds of the village; for we slept with the windows open, which were inside the grating. It was to see my native village in the light of the Middle Ages, and our Concord was turned into a Rhine stream, and visions of knights and castles passed before me. They were the voices of old burghers that I heard in the streets. I was an involuntary spectator and auditor of whatever was done and said in the kitchen of the adjacent village inn—a wholly new and rare experience to me. It was a closer view of my native town. I was fairly inside of it. I never had seen its institutions before. This is one of its peculiar institutions; for it is a shire town. I began to comprehend what its inhabitants were about.

In the morning, our breakfasts were put through the hole in the door, in small oblong-square tin pans, made to fit, and holding a pint of chocolate, with brown bread, and an iron spoon. When they called for the vessels again, I was green enough to return what bread I had left, but my comrade seized it, and said that I should lay that up for lunch or dinner. Soon after he was let out to work at haying in a neighboring field, whither he went every day, and would not be back till noon; so he bade me good day, saying that he doubted if he should see me again.

When I came out of prison—for some one interfered, and paid that tax—I did not perceive that great changes had taken place on the common, such as he observed who went in a youth and emerged a gray-headed man; and yet a change had to my eyes come over the scene—the town, and State, and country, greater than any that mere time could effect. I saw yet more distinctly the State in which I lived. I saw to what extent the people among whom I lived could be trusted as good neighbors and friends; that their friendship was for summer weather only; that they did not greatly propose to do right; that they were a distinct race from me by their prejudices and superstitions, as the Chinamen and Malays are; that in their sacrifices to humanity they ran no risks, not even to their property; that after all they were not so noble but they treated the thief as he had treated them, and hoped, by a certain outward observance and a few prayers, and by walking in a particular straight though useless path from time to time, to save their souls. This may be to judge my neighbors harshly; for I believe that

many of them are not aware that they have such an institution as the jail in their village.

It was formerly the custom in our village, when a poor debtor came out of jail, for his acquaintances to salute him, looking through their fingers, which were crossed to represent the jail window, "How do ye do?" My neighbors did not thus salute me, but first looked at me, and then at one another, as if I had returned from a long journey. I was put into jail as I was going to the shoemaker's to get a shoe which was mended. When I was let out the next morning, I proceeded to finish my errand, and, having put on my mended shoe, joined a huckleberry party, who were impatient to put themselves under my conduct; and in half an hour—for the horse was soon tackled—was in the midst of a huckleberry field, on one of our highest hills, two miles off, and then the State was nowhere to be seen.

This is the whole history of "My Prisons."

I have never declined paying the highway tax, because I am as desirous of being a good neighbor as I am of being a bad subject; and as for supporting schools, I am doing my part to educate my fellow countrymen now. It is for no particular item in the tax bill that I refuse to pay it. I simply wish to refuse allegiance to the State, to withdraw and stand aloof from it effectually. I do not care to trace the course of my dollar, if I could, till it buys a man a musket to shoot one with—the dollar is innocent—but I am concerned to trace the effects of my allegiance. In fact, I quietly declare war with the State, after my fashion, though I will still make use and get what advantages of her I can, as is usual in such cases.

If others pay the tax which is demanded of me, from a sympathy with the State, they do but what they have already done in their own case, or rather they abet injustice to a greater extent than the State requires. If they pay the tax from a mistaken interest in the individual taxed, to save his property, or prevent his going to jail, it is because they have not considered wisely how far they let their private feelings interfere with the public good.

This, then, is my position at present. But one cannot be too much on his guard in such a case, lest his actions be biased by obstinacy or an undue regard for the opinions of men. Let him see that he does only what belongs to himself and to the hour.

I think sometimes, Why, this people mean well; they are only ignorant; they would do better if they knew how: why give your neighbors this pain to treat you as they are not inclined to? But I think again, This is no reason why I should do as they do, or permit others to suffer much greater pain of a different kind. Again, I sometimes say to myself, When many millions of men, without heat, without ill will, without personal feelings of any kind, demand of you a few shillings only, without the possibility, such is their constitution, of retracting or altering their present demand, and without the possibility, on your side, of appeal to any other millions, why expose yourself to this overwhelming brute force? You do not resist cold and hunger, the winds and the waves, thus obstinately; you quietly submit to a thousand similar necessities. You do not put your head into the fire. But just in proportion as I regard this as not wholly a brute force, but partly a human force, and consider that I have relations to those millions as to so many millions of men, and not of mere brute or inanimate things, I see that appeal is possible, first and instantaneously, from them to the Maker of them, and, secondly, from them to themselves. But if I put my head deliberately into the fire, there is no appeal to fire or to the Maker for fire, and I have only myself to blame. If I could convince myself that I have any right to be satisfied with men as they are, and to treat them accordingly, and not according, in some respects, to my requisitions and expectations of what they and I ought to be, then, like a good Mussulman and fatalist, I should endeavor to be satisfied with things as they are, and say it is the will of God. And, above all, there is this difference between resisting this and a purely brute or natural force, that I can resist this with some effect; but I cannot expect, like Orpheus, to change the nature of the rocks and trees and beasts.

I do not wish to quarrel with any man or nation. I do not wish to split hairs, to make fine distinctions, or set myself up as better than my neighbors.

I seek rather, I may say, even an excuse for conforming to the laws of the land. I am but too ready to conform to them. Indeed, I have reason to suspect myself on this head; and each year, as the tax-gatherer comes round, I find myself disposed to review the acts and position of the general and State governments, and the spirit of the people to discover a pretext for conformity.

> "We must affect our country as our parents,
> And if at any time we alienate
> Our love or industry from doing it honor,
> We must respect effects and teach the soul
> Matter of conscience and religion,
> And not desire of rule or benefit."[1]

I believe that the State will soon be able to take all my work of this sort out of my hands, and then I shall be no better patriot than my fellow-countrymen. Seen from a lower point of view, the Constitution, with all its faults, is very good; the law and the courts are very respectable; even this State and this American government are, in many respects, very admirable, and rare things, to be thankful for, such as a great many have described them; seen from a higher still, and the highest, who shall say what they are, or that they are worth looking at or thinking of at all?

However, the government does not concern me much, and I shall bestow the fewest possible thoughts on it. It is not many moments that I live under a government, even in this world. If a man is thought-free, fancy-free, imagination-free, that which *is not* never for a long time appearing *to be* to him, unwise rulers or reformers cannot fatally interrupt him.

I know that most men think differently from myself; but those whose lives are by profession devoted to the study of these or kindred subjects content me as little as any. Statesmen and legislators, standing so completely within the institution, never distinctly and nakedly behold it. They speak of moving society, but have no resting-place without

---

[1] [From George Peele (1556–96), *The Battle of Alcazar*.]

it. They may be men of a certain experience and discrimination, and have no doubt invented ingenious and even useful systems, for which we sincerely thank them; but all their wit and usefulness lie within certain not very wide limits. They are wont to forget that the world is not governed by policy and expediency. Webster never goes behind government, and so cannot speak with authority about it. His words are wisdom to those legislators who contemplate no essential reform in the existing government; but for thinkers, and those who legislate for all time, he never once glances at the subject. I know of those whose serene and wise speculations on this theme would soon reveal the limits of his mind's range and hospitality. Yet, compared with the cheap professions of most reformers, and the still cheaper wisdom and eloquence of politicians in general, his are almost the only sensible and valuable words, and we thank Heaven for him. Comparatively, he is always strong, original, and, above all, practical. Still, his quality is not wisdom, but prudence. The lawyer's truth is not Truth, but consistency or a consistent expediency. Truth is always in harmony with herself, and is not concerned chiefly to reveal the justice that may consist with wrong-doing. He well deserves to be called, as he has been called, the Defender of the Constitution. There are really no blows to be given him but defensive ones. He is not a leader, but a follower. His leaders are the men of '87. "I have never made an effort," he says, "and never propose to make an effort; I have never countenanced an effort, and never mean to countenance an effort, to disturb the arrangement as originally made, by which various States came into the Union." Still thinking of the sanction which the Constitution gives to slavery, he says, "Because it was part of the original compact—let it stand." Notwithstanding his special acuteness and ability, he is unable to take a fact out of its merely political relations, and behold it as it lies absolutely to be disposed of by the intellect—what, for instance, it behooves a man to do here in American today with regard to slavery—but ventures, or is driven, to make some such desperate answer to the following, while professing

to speak absolutely, and as a private man—from which what new and singular of social duties might be inferred? "The manner," says he, "in which the governments of the States where slavery exists are to regulate it is for their own consideration, under the responsibility to their constituents, to the general laws of propriety, humanity, and justice, and to God. Associations formed elsewhere, springing from a feeling of humanity, or any other cause, have nothing whatever to do with it. They have never received any encouragement from me and they never will."

They who know of no purer sources of truth, who have traced up its stream no higher, stand, and wisely stand, by the Bible and the Constitution, and drink at it there with reverence and humanity; but they who behold where it comes trickling into this lake or that pool, gird up their loins once more, and continue their pilgrimage toward its fountainhead.

No man with a genius for legislation has appeared in America. They are rare in the history of the world. There are orators, politicians, and eloquent men, by the thousand; but the speaker has not yet opened his mouth to speak who is capable of settling the much-vexed questions of the day. We love eloquence for its own sake, and not for any truth which it may utter, or any heroism it may inspire. Our legislators have not yet learned the comparative value of free trade and of freedom, of union, and of rectitude, to a nation. They have no genius or talent for comparatively humble questions of taxation and finance, commerce and manufactures and agriculture. If we were left solely to the wordy wit of legislators in Congress for our guidance, uncorrected by the seasonable experience and the effectual complaints of the people, America would not long retain her rank among the nations. For eighteen hundred years, though perchance I have no right to say it, the New Testament has been written; yet where is the legislator who has wisdom and practical talent enough to avail himself of the light which it sheds on the science of legislation.

The authority of government, even such as I am willing to submit to—for I will cheerfully obey those who know and can do better than I, and in many things even those who neither know nor can do so well—is still an impure one: to be strictly just, it must have the sanction and consent of the governed. It can have no pure right over my person and property but what I concede to it. The progress from an absolute to a limited monarchy, from a limited monarchy to a democracy, is a progress toward a true respect for the individual. Even the Chinese philosopher was wise enough to regard the individual as the basis of the empire. Is a democracy, such as we know it, the last improvement possible in government? Is it not possible to take a step further towards recognizing and organizing the rights of man? There will never be a really free and enlightened State until the State comes to recognize the individual as a higher and independent power, from which all its own power and authority are derived, and treats him accordingly. I please myself with imagining a State at last which can afford to be just to all men, and to treat the individual with respect as a neighbor; which even would not think it inconsistent with its own repose if a few were to live aloof from it, not meddling with it, nor embraced by it, who fulfilled all the duties of neighbors and fellow men. A State which bore this kind of fruit, and suffered it to drop off as fast as it ripened, would prepare the way for a still more perfect and glorious State, which I have also imagined, but not yet anywhere seen.

DISCUSSION QUESTIONS

1. Thoreau writes, "I think we should be men first, and subjects afterwards…. Law never made men a whit more just; and by means of their respect for it, even the well-disposed are daily made the agents of injustice." Explain what he seems to mean by this.

2. Do you think Thoreau would view modern federal governments (such as the United States' or Canada's) as expedient or inexpedient? Explain.

3. Compare and contrast Thoreau's view of civil disobedience to Martin Luther King, Jr.'s. Is either committed to views which the other would find objectionable? Do you think Jefferson and the other signers of the Declaration of Independence would agree with Thoreau's views?

19

United Nations Declaration on the Rights of Indigenous Peoples (2007)

The United Nations Organization was founded in 1945, after World War II, to facilitate international relations among nations, promote global development, foster dialogue concerning human rights, and promote world peace. The Declaration on the Rights of Indigenous Peoples was adopted by the UN General Assembly in 2007. Although it is not legally binding under international law, it attempts to articulate both individually and collectively held rights of indigenous or aboriginal peoples.

SOURCE

General Assembly of the United Nations. The Universal Declaration of Human Rights. Accessed June 6, 2010 from http://www.un.org/en/documents/udhr/index.shtml.

Adopted by General Assembly Resolution 61/295 on 13 September 2007

The General Assembly,
Guided by the purposes and principles of the Charter of the United Nations, and good faith in the fulfilment of the obligations assumed by States in accordance with the Charter,

Affirming that indigenous peoples are equal to all other peoples, while recognizing the right of all peoples to be different, to consider themselves different, and to be respected as such,

Affirming also that all peoples contribute to the diversity and richness of civilizations and cultures, which constitute the common heritage of humankind,

Affirming further that all doctrines, policies and practices based on or advocating superiority of peoples or individuals on the basis of national origin or racial, religious, ethnic or cultural differences are racist, scientifically false, legally invalid, morally condemnable and socially unjust,

Reaffirming that indigenous peoples, in the exercise of their rights, should be free from discrimination of any kind,

Concerned that indigenous peoples have suffered from historic injustices as a result of, inter alia, their colonization and dispossession of their lands, territories and resources, thus preventing them from exercising, in particular, their right to development in accordance with their own needs and interests,

Recognizing the urgent need to respect and promote the inherent rights of indigenous peoples which derive from their political, economic and social structures and from their cultures, spiritual traditions, histories and philosophies, especially their rights to their lands, territories and resources,

Recognizing also the urgent need to respect and promote the rights of indigenous peoples affirmed in treaties, agreements and other constructive arrangements with States,

Welcoming the fact that indigenous peoples are organizing themselves for political, economic, social and cultural enhancement and in order to bring to an end all forms of discrimination and oppression wherever they occur,

Convinced that control by indigenous peoples over developments affecting them and their lands, territories and resources will enable them to maintain and strengthen their institutions, cultures and traditions, and to promote their development in accordance with their aspirations and needs,

Recognizing that respect for indigenous knowledge, cultures and traditional practices contributes to sustainable and equitable development and proper management of the environment,

Emphasizing the contribution of the demilitarization of the lands and territories of indigenous peoples to peace, economic and social progress and development, understanding and friendly relations among nations and peoples of the world,

Recognizing in particular the right of indigenous families and communities to retain shared responsibility for the upbringing, training, education and well-being of their children, consistent with the rights of the child,

Considering that the rights affirmed in treaties, agreements and other constructive arrangements between States and indigenous peoples are, in some situations, matters of international concern, interest, responsibility and character,

Considering also that treaties, agreements and other constructive arrangements, and the relationship they represent, are the basis for a strengthened partnership between indigenous peoples and States,

Acknowledging that the Charter of the United Nations, the International Covenant on Economic, Social and Cultural Rights and the International Covenant on Civil and Political Rights, as well as the Vienna Declaration and Programme of Action, affirm the fundamental importance of the right to self-determination of all peoples, by virtue of which they freely determine their political status and freely pursue their economic, social and cultural development,

Bearing in mind that nothing in this Declaration may be used to deny any peoples their right to self-determination, exercised in conformity with international law,

Convinced that the recognition of the rights of indigenous peoples in this Declaration will enhance harmonious and cooperative relations between the State and indigenous peoples, based on principles of justice, democracy, respect for human rights, non-discrimination and good faith,

Encouraging States to comply with and effectively implement all their obligations as they apply to indigenous peoples under international instruments, in particular those related to human rights, in consultation and cooperation with the peoples concerned,

Emphasizing that the United Nations has an important and continuing role to play in promoting and protecting the rights of indigenous peoples,

Believing that this Declaration is a further important step forward for the recognition, promotion and protection of the rights and freedoms of indigenous peoples and in the development of relevant activities of the United Nations system in this field,

Recognizing and reaffirming that indigenous individuals are entitled without discrimination to all human rights recognized in international law, and that indigenous peoples possess collective rights which are indispensable for their existence, well-being and integral development as peoples,

Recognizing that the situation of indigenous peoples varies from region to region and from country to country and that the significance of national and regional particularities and various historical and cultural backgrounds should be taken into consideration,

Solemnly proclaims the following United Nations Declaration on the Rights of Indigenous Peoples as a standard of achievement to be pursued in a spirit of partnership and mutual respect:

Article 1
Indigenous peoples have the right to the full enjoyment, as a collective or as individuals, of all human rights and fundamental freedoms as recognized in the Charter of the United Nations, the Universal Declaration of Human Rights and international human rights law.

Article 2
Indigenous peoples and individuals are free and equal to all other peoples and individuals and have the right to be free from any kind of discrimination, in the exercise of their rights, in particular that based on their indigenous origin or identity.

Article 3
Indigenous peoples have the right to self-determination. By virtue of that right they freely determine their political status and freely pursue their economic, social and cultural development.

Article 4
Indigenous peoples, in exercising their right to self-determination, have the right to autonomy or self-government in matters relating to their internal and local affairs, as well as ways and means for financing their autonomous functions.

Article 5
Indigenous peoples have the right to maintain and strengthen their distinct political, legal, economic, social and cultural institutions, while retaining their right to participate fully, if they so choose, in the political, economic, social and cultural life of the State.

Article 6
Every indigenous individual has the right to a nationality.

Article 7
1. Indigenous individuals have the rights to life, physical and mental integrity, liberty and security of person.
2. Indigenous peoples have the collective right to live in freedom, peace and security as distinct peoples and shall not be subjected to any act of genocide or any other act of violence, including forcibly removing children of the group to another group.

Article 8
1. Indigenous peoples and individuals have the right not to be subjected to forced assimilation or destruction of their culture.
2. States shall provide effective mechanisms for prevention of, and redress for:
(a) Any action which has the aim or effect of depriving them of their integrity as distinct peoples, or of their cultural values or ethnic identities;

(b) Any action which has the aim or effect of dispossessing them of their lands, territories or resources;
(c) Any form of forced population transfer which has the aim or effect of violating or undermining any of their rights;
(d) Any form of forced assimilation or integration;
(e) Any form of propaganda designed to promote or incite racial or ethnic discrimination directed against them.

Article 9

Indigenous peoples and individuals have the right to belong to an indigenous community or nation, in accordance with the traditions and customs of the community or nation concerned. No discrimination of any kind may arise from the exercise of such a right.

Article 10

Indigenous peoples shall not be forcibly removed from their lands or territories. No relocation shall take place without the free, prior and informed consent of the indigenous peoples concerned and after agreement on just and fair compensation and, where possible, with the option of return.

Article 11

1. Indigenous peoples have the right to practise and revitalize their cultural traditions and customs. This includes the right to maintain, protect and develop the past, present and future manifestations of their cultures, such as archaeological and historical sites, artefacts, designs, ceremonies, technologies and visual and performing arts and literature.
2. States shall provide redress through effective mechanisms, which may include restitution, developed in conjunction with indigenous peoples, with respect to their cultural, intellectual, religious and spiritual property taken without their free, prior and informed consent or in violation of their laws, traditions and customs.

Article 12

1. Indigenous peoples have the right to manifest, practise, develop and teach their spiritual and religious traditions, customs and ceremonies; the right to maintain, protect, and have access in privacy to their religious and cultural sites; the right to the use and control of their ceremonial objects; and the right to the repatriation of their human remains.
2. States shall seek to enable the access and/or repatriation of ceremonial objects and human remains in their possession through fair, transparent and effective mechanisms developed in conjunction with indigenous peoples concerned.

Article 13

1. Indigenous peoples have the right to revitalize, use, develop and transmit to future generations their histories, languages, oral traditions, philosophies, writing systems and literatures, and to designate and retain their own names for communities, places and persons.
2. States shall take effective measures to ensure that this right is protected and also to ensure that indigenous peoples can understand and be understood in political, legal and administrative proceedings, where necessary through the provision of interpretation or by other appropriate means.

Article 14

1. Indigenous peoples have the right to establish and control their educational systems and institutions providing education in their own languages, in a manner appropriate to their cultural methods of teaching and learning.
2. Indigenous individuals, particularly children, have the right to all levels and forms of education of the State without discrimination.
3. States shall, in conjunction with indigenous peoples, take effective measures, in order for indigenous individuals, particularly children, including those living outside their communities, to have access, when possible, to an education in their own culture and provided in their own language.

Article 15

1. Indigenous peoples have the right to the dignity and diversity of their cultures, traditions, histories and aspirations which shall be appropriately reflected in education and public information.

2. States shall take effective measures, in consultation and cooperation with the indigenous peoples concerned, to combat prejudice and eliminate discrimination and to promote tolerance, understanding and good relations among indigenous peoples and all other segments of society.

Article 16

1. Indigenous peoples have the right to establish their own media in their own languages and to have access to all forms of non-indigenous media without discrimination.

2. States shall take effective measures to ensure that State-owned media duly reflect indigenous cultural diversity. States, without prejudice to ensuring full freedom of expression, should encourage privately owned media to adequately reflect indigenous cultural diversity.

Article 17

1. Indigenous individuals and peoples have the right to enjoy fully all rights established under applicable international and domestic labour law.

2. States shall in consultation and cooperation with indigenous peoples take specific measures to protect indigenous children from economic exploitation and from performing any work that is likely to be hazardous or to interfere with the child's education, or to be harmful to the child's health or physical, mental, spiritual, moral or social development, taking into account their special vulnerability and the importance of education for their empowerment.

3. Indigenous individuals have the right not to be subjected to any discriminatory conditions of labour and, inter alia, employment or salary.

Article 18

Indigenous peoples have the right to participate in decision-making in matters which would affect their rights, through representatives chosen by themselves in accordance with their own procedures, as well as to maintain and develop their own indigenous decision-making institutions.

Article 19

States shall consult and cooperate in good faith with the indigenous peoples concerned through their own representative institutions in order to obtain their free, prior and informed consent before adopting and implementing legislative or administrative measures that may affect them.

Article 20

1. Indigenous peoples have the right to maintain and develop their political, economic and social systems or institutions, to be secure in the enjoyment of their own means of subsistence and development, and to engage freely in all their traditional and other economic activities.

2. Indigenous peoples deprived of their means of subsistence and development are entitled to just and fair redress.

Article 21

1. Indigenous peoples have the right, without discrimination, to the improvement of their economic and social conditions, including, inter alia, in the areas of education, employment, vocational training and retraining, housing, sanitation, health and social security.

2. States shall take effective measures and, where appropriate, special measures to ensure continuing improvement of their economic and social conditions. Particular attention shall be paid to the rights and special needs of indigenous elders, women, youth, children and persons with disabilities.

Article 22

1. Particular attention shall be paid to the rights and special needs of indigenous elders, women, youth, children and persons with disabilities in the implementation of this Declaration.

2. States shall take measures, in conjunction with indigenous peoples, to ensure that indigenous women and children enjoy the full protection

and guarantees against all forms of violence and discrimination.

Article 23
Indigenous peoples have the right to determine and develop priorities and strategies for exercising their right to development. In particular, indigenous peoples have the right to be actively involved in developing and determining health, housing and other economic and social programmes affecting them and, as far as possible, to administer such programmes through their own institutions.

Article 24
1. Indigenous peoples have the right to their traditional medicines and to maintain their health practices, including the conservation of their vital medicinal plants, animals and minerals. Indigenous individuals also have the right to access, without any discrimination, to all social and health services.
2. Indigenous individuals have an equal right to the enjoyment of the highest attainable standard of physical and mental health. States shall take the necessary steps with a view to achieving progressively the full realization of this right.

Article 25
Indigenous peoples have the right to maintain and strengthen their distinctive spiritual relationship with their traditionally owned or otherwise occupied and used lands, territories, waters and coastal seas and other resources and to uphold their responsibilities to future generations in this regard.

Article 26
1. Indigenous peoples have the right to the lands, territories and resources which they have traditionally owned, occupied or otherwise used or acquired.
2. Indigenous peoples have the right to own, use, develop and control the lands, territories and resources that they possess by reason of traditional ownership or other traditional occupation or use, as well as those which they have otherwise acquired.
3. States shall give legal recognition and protection to these lands, territories and resources. Such recognition shall be conducted with due respect to the customs, traditions and land tenure systems of the indigenous peoples concerned.

Article 27
States shall establish and implement, in conjunction with indigenous peoples concerned, a fair, independent, impartial, open and transparent process, giving due recognition to indigenous peoples' laws, traditions, customs and land tenure systems, to recognize and adjudicate the rights of indigenous peoples pertaining to their lands, territories and resources, including those which were traditionally owned or otherwise occupied or used. Indigenous peoples shall have the right to participate in this process.

Article 28
1. Indigenous peoples have the right to redress, by means that can include restitution or, when this is not possible, just, fair and equitable compensation, for the lands, territories and resources which they have traditionally owned or otherwise occupied or used, and which have been confiscated, taken, occupied, used or damaged without their free, prior and informed consent.
2. Unless otherwise freely agreed upon by the peoples concerned, compensation shall take the form of lands, territories and resources equal in quality, size and legal status or of monetary compensation or other appropriate redress.

Article 29
1. Indigenous peoples have the right to the conservation and protection of the environment and the productive capacity of their lands or territories and resources. States shall establish and implement assistance programmes for indigenous peoples for such conservation and protection, without discrimination.
2. States shall take effective measures to ensure that no storage or disposal of hazardous materials shall take place in the lands or territories of indigenous peoples without their free, prior and informed consent.

3. States shall also take effective measures to ensure, as needed, that programmes for monitoring, maintaining and restoring the health of indigenous peoples, as developed and implemented by the peoples affected by such materials, are duly implemented.

Article 30
1. Military activities shall not take place in the lands or territories of indigenous peoples, unless justified by a relevant public interest or otherwise freely agreed with or requested by the indigenous peoples concerned.
2. States shall undertake effective consultations with the indigenous peoples concerned, through appropriate procedures and in particular through their representative institutions, prior to using their lands or territories for military activities.

Article 31
1. Indigenous peoples have the right to maintain, control, protect and develop their cultural heritage, traditional knowledge and traditional cultural expressions, as well as the manifestations of their sciences, technologies and cultures, including human and genetic resources, seeds, medicines, knowledge of the properties of fauna and flora, oral traditions, literatures, designs, sports and traditional games and visual and performing arts. They also have the right to maintain, control, protect and develop their intellectual property over such cultural heritage, traditional knowledge, and traditional cultural expressions.
2. In conjunction with indigenous peoples, States shall take effective measures to recognize and protect the exercise of these rights.

Article 32
1. Indigenous peoples have the right to determine and develop priorities and strategies for the development or use of their lands or territories and other resources.
2. States shall consult and cooperate in good faith with the indigenous peoples concerned through their own representative institutions in order to obtain their free and informed consent prior to the approval of any project affecting their lands or territories and other resources, particularly in connection with the development, utilization or exploitation of mineral, water or other resources.
3. States shall provide effective mechanisms for just and fair redress for any such activities, and appropriate measures shall be taken to mitigate adverse environmental, economic, social, cultural or spiritual impact.

Article 33
1. Indigenous peoples have the right to determine their own identity or membership in accordance with their customs and traditions. This does not impair the right of indigenous individuals to obtain citizenship of the States in which they live.
2. Indigenous peoples have the right to determine the structures and to select the membership of their institutions in accordance with their own procedures.

Article 34
Indigenous peoples have the right to promote, develop and maintain their institutional structures and their distinctive customs, spirituality, traditions, procedures, practices and, in the cases where they exist, juridical systems or customs, in accordance with international human rights standards.

Article 35
Indigenous peoples have the right to determine the responsibilities of individuals to their communities.

Article 36
1. Indigenous peoples, in particular those divided by international borders, have the right to maintain and develop contacts, relations and cooperation, including activities for spiritual, cultural, political, economic and social purposes, with their own members as well as other peoples across borders.
2. States, in consultation and cooperation with indigenous peoples, shall take effective measures to facilitate the exercise and ensure the implementation of this right.

Article 37

1. Indigenous peoples have the right to the recognition, observance and enforcement of treaties, agreements and other constructive arrangements concluded with States or their successors and to have States honour and respect such treaties, agreements and other constructive arrangements.

2. Nothing in this Declaration may be interpreted as diminishing or eliminating the rights of indigenous peoples contained in treaties, agreements and other constructive arrangements.

Article 38

States in consultation and cooperation with indigenous peoples, shall take the appropriate measures, including legislative measures, to achieve the ends of this Declaration.

Article 39

Indigenous peoples have the right to have access to financial and technical assistance from States and through international cooperation, for the enjoyment of the rights contained in this Declaration.

Article 40

Indigenous peoples have the right to access to and prompt decision through just and fair procedures for the resolution of conflicts and disputes with States or other parties, as well as to effective remedies for all infringements of their individual and collective rights. Such a decision shall give due consideration to the customs, traditions, rules and legal systems of the indigenous peoples concerned and international human rights.

Article 41

The organs and specialized agencies of the United Nations system and other intergovernmental organizations shall contribute to the full realization of the provisions of this Declaration through the mobilization, inter alia, of financial cooperation and technical assistance. Ways and means of ensuring participation of indigenous peoples on issues affecting them shall be established.

Article 42

The United Nations, its bodies, including the Permanent Forum on Indigenous Issues, and specialized agencies, including at the country level, and States shall promote respect for and full application of the provisions of this Declaration and follow up the effectiveness of this Declaration.

Article 43

The rights recognized herein constitute the minimum standards for the survival, dignity and well-being of the indigenous peoples of the world.

Article 44

All the rights and freedoms recognized herein are equally guaranteed to male and female indigenous individuals.

Article 45

Nothing in this Declaration may be construed as diminishing or extinguishing the rights indigenous peoples have now or may acquire in the future.

Article 46

1. Nothing in this Declaration may be interpreted as implying for any State, people, group or person any right to engage in any activity or to perform any act contrary to the Charter of the United Nations or construed as authorizing or encouraging any action which would dismember or impair, totally or in part, the territorial integrity or political unity of sovereign and independent States.

2. In the exercise of the rights enunciated in the present Declaration, human rights and fundamental freedoms of all shall be respected. The exercise of the rights set forth in this Declaration shall be subject only to such limitations as are determined by law and in accordance with international human rights obligations. Any such limitations shall be non-discriminatory and strictly necessary solely for the purpose of securing due recognition and respect for the rights and freedoms of others and for meeting the just and most compelling requirements of a democratic society.

3. The provisions set forth in this Declaration shall be interpreted in accordance with the principles of justice, democracy, respect for human rights, equality, non-discrimination, good governance and good faith.

DISCUSSION QUESTIONS

1. Does this Declaration extend *special* rights to indigenous peoples, or do non-indigenous people also possess these rights? Explain your answer, citing specific examples from the Declaration. If (at least) some of the rights mentioned are only possessed by indigenous people, what justifies extending these special rights to them? If all people (indigenous and non-indigenous alike) possess the rights mentioned, what is the purpose of the Declaration?

2. What do you take to be the basic or fundamental rights expressed in the Declaration? Choose two or three of these basic rights and provide an argument for each, showing that they are, indeed, rights which properly give rise to (or have as corollaries) obligations on the part of the State or other people. (You might want to consider the arguments and strategies developed by the political theorists featured earlier in this unit.)

20

H.L.A. Hart, selection from *The Concept of Law* (1961)

Herbert Hart (1907–92) was professor of jurisprudence at Oxford University and principal of Brasenose College, Oxford. His work, *The Concept of Law,* is the best-known statement of a positivist theory of law, i.e., a theory that rejects the claim that there is a necessary connection between the concept of a law and moral justifiability. In this selection, Hart considers some reasons to doubt that "international laws" are genuinely *laws*.

SOURCE

Hart, H.L.A. *The Concept of Law*. Oxford University Press, 1961. Reprinted by permission of Oxford University Press, Inc.

Sources of Doubt

The idea of a union of primary and secondary rules to which so important a place has been assigned in this book may be regarded as a mean between juristic extremes. For legal theory has sought the key to the understanding of law sometimes in the simple idea of an order backed by threats and sometimes in the complex idea of morality. With both of these law has certainly many affinities and connexions; yet, as we have seen, there is a perennial danger of exaggerating these and of obscuring the special features which distinguish law from other means of social control. It is a virtue of the idea which we have taken as central that it permits us to see the multiple relationships between law, coercion, and morality for what they are, and to consider afresh in what, if any, sense these are necessary.

Though the idea of the union of primary and secondary rules has these virtues, and though it would accord with usage to treat the existence of this characteristic union of rules as a sufficient condition for the application of the expression "legal system," we have not claimed that the word "law" must be defined in its terms. It is because we make no such claim to identify or regulate in this way the use of words like "law" or "legal," that this book is offered as an elucidation of the *concept* of law, rather than a definition of "law" which might naturally be expected to provide a rule or rules for the use of these expressions. Consistently with this aim, we investigated, in the last chapter [of *The Concept of Law*], the claim made in the German cases, that the title of valid law should be withheld from certain rules on account of their moral iniquity, even though they belonged to an existing system of primary and secondary rules. In the end we rejected this claim; but we did so, not because it conflicted with the view that rules belonging to such a system must be called "law," nor because it conflicted with the weight of usage. Instead we criticized the attempt to narrow the class of valid laws by the extrusion of what was morally iniquitous, on the ground that to do this did not advance or clarify either theoretical inquiries or moral deliberation. For these purposes, the broader concept which is consistent with so much usage and which would permit us to regard rules however morally iniquitous as law, proved on examination to be adequate.

International law presents us with the converse case. For, though it is consistent with the usage of the last 150 years to use the expression "law" here, the absence of an international legislature, courts with compulsory jurisdiction, and centrally organized sanctions have inspired misgivings, at any rate in the breasts of legal theorists. The absence of these institutions means that the rules for states resemble that simple form of social structure, consisting only of primary rules of obligation, which, when we find it among societies of individuals, we are accustomed to contrast with a developed legal system. It is indeed arguable, as we shall show, that international law not only lacks the secondary rules of change and adjudication which provide for legislature and courts, but also a unifying rule of recognition specifying "sources" of law and providing general criteria for the identification of its rules. These differences are indeed striking and the question "Is international law really law?" can hardly be put aside. But in this case also, we shall neither dismiss the doubts, which many feel, with a simple reminder of the existing usage; nor shall we simply confirm them on the footing that the existence of a union of primary and secondary rules is a necessary as well as a sufficient condition for the proper use of the expression "legal system." Instead we shall

inquire into the detailed character of the doubts which have been felt, and, as in the German case, we shall ask whether the common wider usage that speaks of "international law" is likely to obstruct any practical or theoretical aim.

Though we shall devote to it only a single chapter, some writers have proposed an even shorter treatment for this question concerning the character of international law. To them it has seemed that the question "Is international law really law?" has only arisen or survived, because a trivial question about the meaning of words has been mistaken for a serious question about the nature of things: since the facts which differentiate international law from municipal law are clear and well known, the only question to be settled is whether we should observe the existing convention or depart from it; and this is a matter for each person to settle for himself. But this short way with the question is surely too short. It is true that among the reasons which have led theorists to hesitate over the extension of the word "law" to international law, a too simple, and indeed absurd view, of what justifies the application of the same word to many different things has played some part. The variety of types of principle which commonly guide the extension of general classifying terms has too often been ignored in jurisprudence. Nonetheless, the sources of doubt about international law are deeper, and more interesting than these mistaken views about the use of words. Moreover, the two alternatives offered by this short way with the question ("Shall we observe the existing convention or shall we depart from it?") are not exhaustive; for, besides them, there is the alternative of making explicit and examining the principles that have in fact guided the existing usage.

The short way suggested would indeed be appropriate if we were dealing with a proper name. If someone were to ask whether the place called "London" is *really* London, all we could do would be to remind him of the convention and leave him to abide by it or choose another name to suit his taste. It would be absurd, in such a case, to ask on what principle London was so called and whether this principle was acceptable. This would be absurd because, whereas the allotment of proper names rests *only* on an *ad hoc* convention, the extension of the general terms of any serious discipline is never without its principle or rationale, though it may not be obvious what that is. When as, in the present case, the extension is queried by those who in effect say, "We know that it is called law, but is it really law?", what is demanded—no doubt obscurely— is that the principle be made explicit and its credentials inspected.

We shall consider two principal sources of doubt concerning the legal character of international law and, with them, the steps which theorists have taken to meet these doubts. Both forms of doubt arise from an adverse comparison of international law with municipal law, which is taken as the clear, standard example of what law is. The first has its roots deep in the conception of law as fundamentally a matter of orders backed by threats and contrasts the character of the *rules* of international law with those of municipal law. The second form of doubt springs from the obscure belief that states are fundamentally incapable of being the subjects of legal obligation, and contrasts the character of the *subjects* of international law with those of municipal law.

Obligations and Sanction

The doubts which we shall consider are often expressed in the opening chapters of books on international law in the form of the question "How can international law be binding?" Yet there is something very confusing in this favorite form of question; and before we can deal with it we must face a prior question to which the answer is by no means clear. This prior question is: what is meant by saying of a whole system of law that it is "binding"? The statement that a particular rule of a system is binding on a particular person is one familiar to lawyers and tolerably clear in meaning. We may paraphrase it by the assertion that the rule in question is a valid rule, and under it the person in question has some obligation or duty. Besides this, there are some situations in which more general statements of

this form are made. We may be doubtful in certain circumstances whether one legal system or another applies to a particular person. Such doubts may arise in the conflict of laws or in public international law. We may ask, in the former case, whether French or English law is binding on a particular person as regards a particular transaction, and in the latter case we may ask whether the inhabitants of, for example, enemy-occupied Belgium, were bound by what the exiled government claimed was Belgian law or by the ordinances of the occupying power. But in both these cases, the questions are questions of law which arise within some system of law (municipal or international) and are settled by reference to the rules or principles of that system. They do not call in question the general character of the rules, but only their scope or applicability in given circumstances to particular persons or transactions. Plainly the question, "Is international law binding?" and its congeners, "How can international law be binding?" or "What makes international law binding?", are questions of a different order. They express a doubt not about the applicability, but about the general legal status of international law: this doubt would be more candidly expressed in the form "Can such rules as these be meaningfully and truthfully said ever to give rise to obligations?" As the discussions in the books show, one source of doubt on this point is simply the absence from the system of centrally organized sanctions. This is one point of adverse comparison with municipal law, the rules of which are taken to be unquestionably "binding" and to be paradigms of legal obligation. From this stage the further argument is simple: if for this reason the rules of international law are not "binding," it is surely indefensible to take seriously their classification as law; for however tolerant the modes of common speech may be, this is too great a difference to be overlooked. All speculation about the nature of law begins from the assumption that its existence at least makes certain conduct obligatory.

In considering this argument we shall give it the benefit of every doubt concerning the facts of the international system. We shall take it that neither Article 16 of the Covenant of the League of Nations nor Chapter VII of the United Nations Charter introduced into international law anything which can be equated with the sanctions of municipal law. In spite of the Korean war and of whatever moral may be drawn from the Suez incident, we shall suppose that, whenever their use is of importance, the law-enforcement provisions of the Charter are likely to be paralyzed by the veto and must be said to exist only on paper.

To argue that international law is not binding because of its lack of organized sanctions is tacitly to accept the analysis of obligation contained in the theory that law is essentially a matter of orders, backed by threats. This theory, as we have seen, identifies "having an obligation" or "being bound" with "likely to suffer the sanction or punishment threatened for disobedience." Yet, as we have argued, this identification distorts the role played in all legal thought and discourse of the ideas of obligation and duty. Even in municipal law, where there are effective organized sanctions, we must distinguish, for the variety of reasons given in Chapter III [of *The Concept of Law*], the meaning of the external predictive statement "I (you) are likely to suffer for disobedience," from the internal normative statement "I (you) have an obligation to act thus," which assesses a particular person's situation from the point of view of rules accepted as guiding standards of behavior. It is true that not all rules give rise to obligations or duties; and it is also true that the rules which do so generally call for some sacrifice of private interests, and are generally supported by serious demands for conformity and insistent criticism of deviations. Yet once we free ourselves from the predictive analysis and its parent conception of law as essentially an order backed by threats, there seems no good reason for limiting the normative idea of obligation to rules supported by organized sanctions.

We must, however, consider another form of the argument, more plausible because it is not committed to definition of obligation in terms of the likelihood of threatened sanctions. The skeptic may point out that there are in a municipal system, as we have ourselves stressed, certain provisions which

are justifiably called necessary; among these are primary rules of obligation prohibiting the free use of violence, and rules providing for the official use of force as a sanction for these and other rules. If such rules and organized sanctions supporting them are in this sense necessary for municipal law, are they not equally so for international law? That they are may be maintained without insisting that this follows from the very meaning of words like "binding" or "obligation."

The answer to the argument in this form is to be found in those elementary truths about human beings and their environment which constitute the enduring psychological and physical setting of municipal law. In societies of individuals, approximately equal in physical strength and vulnerability, physical sanctions are both necessary and possible. They are required in order that those who would voluntarily submit to the restraints of law shall not be mere victims of malefactors who would, in the absence of such sanctions, reap the advantages of respect for law on the part of others, without respecting it themselves. Among individuals living in close proximity to each other, opportunities for injuring others, by guile, if not by open attack, are so great, and the chances of escape so considerable, that no mere natural deterrents could in any but the simplest forms of society be adequate to restrain those too wicked, too stupid or too weak to obey the law. Yet, because of the same fact of approximate equality and the patent advantages of submission to a system of restraints, no combination of malefactors is likely to exceed in strength those who would voluntarily cooperate in its maintenance. In these circumstances, which constitute the background of municipal law, sanctions may successfully be used against malefactors with relatively small risks, and the threat of them will add much to whatever natural deterrents there may be. But, just because the simple truisms which hold good for individuals do not hold good for states, and the factual background to international law is so different from that of municipal law, there is neither a similar necessity for sanctions (desirable though it may be that international law should be supported by them) nor a similar prospect of their safe and efficacious use.

This is so because aggression between states is very unlike that between individuals. The use of violence between states must be public, and though there is no international police force, there can be very little certainty that it will remain a matter between aggressor and victim, as a murder or theft, in the absence of a police force, might. To initiate a war is, even for the strongest power, to risk much for an outcome which is rarely predictable with reasonable confidence. On the other hand, because of the inequality of states, there can be no standing assurance that the combined strength of those on the side of international order is likely to preponderate over the powers tempted to aggression. Hence the organization and use of sanctions may involve fearful risks and the threat of them adds little to the natural deterrents. Against this background of fact, international law has developed in a form different from that of municipal law. In a population of a modern state, if there were no organized repression and punishment of crime, violence and theft would be hourly expected; but for states, long years of peace have intervened between disastrous wars. These years of peace are only rationally to be expected, given the risks and stakes of war and the mutual needs of states; but they are worth regulating by rules which differ from those of municipal law in (among other things) not providing for their enforcement by any central organ. Yet what rules require is thought and spoken of as obligatory; there is general pressure for conformity to the rules; claims and admissions are based on them and their breach is held to justify not only insistent demands for compensation, but reprisals and countermeasures. When the rules are disregarded, it is not on the footing that they are not binding; instead efforts are made to conceal the facts. It may of course be said that such rules are efficacious only so far as they concern issues over which states are unwilling to fight. This may be so, and may reflect adversely on the importance of the system and its value to humanity. Yet that even so much may be secured shows that no simple

deduction can be made from the necessity of organized sanctions to municipal law, in its setting of physical and psychological facts, to the conclusion that without them international law, in its very different setting, imposes no obligations, is not "binding," and so not worth the title of "law."

Obligation and the Sovereignty of States

Great Britain, Belgium, Greece, and Soviet Russia have rights and obligations under international law and so are among its subjects. They are random examples of states which the layman would think of as independent and the lawyer would recognize as "sovereign." One of the most persistent sources of perplexity about the obligatory character of international law has been the difficulty felt in accepting or explaining the fact that a state which is sovereign may also be "bound" by, or have an obligation under, international law. This form of skepticism is, in a sense, more extreme than the objection that international law is not binding because it lacks sanctions. For whereas that would be met if one day international law were reinforced by a system of sanctions, the present objection is based on a radical inconsistency, said or felt to exist, in the conception of a state which is at once sovereign and subject to law.

Examination of this objection involves a scrutiny of the notion of sovereignty, applied not to a legislature or to some other element or person *within* a state, but to a state itself. Whenever the word "sovereign" appears in jurisprudence, there is a tendency to associate with it the idea of a person above the law whose word is law for his inferiors or subjects. We have seen in the early chapters of this book [of *The Concept of Law*] how bad a guide this seductive notion is to the structure of a municipal legal system; but it has been an even more potent source of confusion in the theory of international law. It is, of course, *possible* to think of a state along such lines, as if it were a species of Superman—a Being inherently lawless but the source of law for its subjects. From the sixteenth century onwards, the symbolical identification of state and monarch ("*L'état c'est moi*") may have encouraged this idea which has been the dubious inspiration of much political as well as legal theory. But it is important for the understanding of international law to shake off these associations. The expression "a state" is not the name of some person or thing inherently or "by nature" outside the law; it is a way of referring to two facts: first, that a population inhabiting a territory lives under that form of ordered government provided by a legal system with its characteristic structure of legislature, courts, and primary rules; and secondly, that the government enjoys a vaguely defined degree of independence.

The word "state" has certainly its own large area of vagueness but what has been said will suffice to display its central meaning. States such as Great Britain or Brazil, the United States or Italy, again to take random examples, possess a very large measure of independence from both legal and factual control by any authorities or persons outside their borders, and would rank as "sovereign states" in international law. On the other hand, individual states which are members of a federal union, such as the United States, are subject in many different ways to the authority and control of the federal government and constitution. Yet the independence which even these federated states retain is large if we compare it with the position, say, of an English county, of which the word "state" would not be used at all. A county may have a local council discharging, for its area, some of the functions of a legislature, but its meager powers are subordinate to those of Parliament and, except in certain minor respects, the area of the county is subject to the same laws and government as the rest of the country.

Between these extremes there are many different types and degrees of dependence (and so of independence) between territorial units which possess an ordered government. Colonies, protectorates, suzerainties, trust territories, confederations, present fascinating problems of classification from this point of view. In most cases the dependence of one unit on another is expressed in legal forms, so that what is law in the territory of the dependent unit

will, at least on certain issues, ultimately depend on law-making operations in the other.

In some cases, however, the legal system of the dependent territory may not reflect its dependence because it is merely formally independent and the territory is in fact governed, through puppets, from outside; or it may be so because the dependent territory has a real autonomy over its internal but not its external affairs, and its dependence on another country in external affairs does not require expression as part of its domestic law. Dependence of one territorial unit on another in these various ways is not, however, the only form in which its independence may be limited. The limiting factor may be not the power or authority of another such unit, but an international authority affecting units which are alike independent of each other. It is possible to imagine many different forms of international authority and correspondingly many different limitations on the independence of states. The possibilities include, among many others, a world legislature on the model of the British Parliament, possessing legally unlimited powers to regulate the internal and external affairs of all; a federal legislature on the model of Congress, with legal competence only over specified matters or one limited by guarantees of specific rights of the constituent units; a regime in which the only form of legal control consists of rules generally accepted as applicable to all; and finally a regime in which the only form of obligation recognized is contractual or self-imposed, so that a state's independence is legally limited only by its own act.

It is salutary to consider this range of possibilities because merely to realize that there are many possible forms and degrees of dependence and independence, is a step towards answering the claim that because states are sovereign they "*cannot*" be subject to or bound by international law or "*can*" only be bound by some specific form of international law. For the word "sovereign" means here no more than "independent"; and, like the latter, is negative in force: a sovereign state is one *not* subject to certain types of control, and its sovereignty is that area of conduct in which it is autonomous. Some measure of autonomy is imported, as we have seen, by the very meaning of the word state but the contention that this "*must*" be unlimited or "*can*" only be limited by certain types of obligations is at best the assertion of a claim that states ought to be free of all other restraints, and at worst is an unreasoned dogma. For if in fact we find that there exists among states a given form of international authority, the sovereignty of states is to that extent limited, and it has just that extent which the rules allow. Hence, we can only know which states are sovereign, and what the extent of their sovereignty is, when we know what the rules are; just as we can only know whether an Englishman or an American is free and the extent of his freedom when we know what English or American law is. The rules of international law are indeed vague and conflicting on many points, so that doubt about the area of independence left to states is far greater than that concerning the extent of a citizen's freedom under municipal law. Nonetheless, these difficulties do not validate the *a priori* argument which attempts to deduce the general character of international law from an absolute sovereignty, which is assumed, without reference to international law, to belong to states.

It is worth observing that an uncritical use of the idea of sovereignty has spread similar confusion in the theory both of municipal and international law, and demands in both a similar corrective. Under its influence, we are led to believe that there must in every municipal legal system be a sovereign legislator subject to no legal limitations; just as we are led to believe that international law must be of a certain character because states are sovereign and incapable of legal limitation save by themselves. In both cases, belief in the necessary existence of the legally unlimited sovereign prejudges a question which we can only answer when we examine the actual rules. The question for municipal law is: what is the extent of the supreme legislative authority recognized in this system? For international law it is: what is the maximum area of autonomy which the rules allow to states?

Thus the simplest answer to the present objection is that it inverts the order in which questions must be considered. There is no way of knowing what sovereignty states have, till we know what the forms of international law are and whether or not they are mere empty forms. Much juristic debate has been confused because this principle has been ignored, and it is profitable to consider in its light those theories of international law which are known as "voluntarist" or theories of "auto-limitation." These attempted to reconcile the (absolute) sovereignty of states with the existence of binding rules of international law, by treating all international obligations as self-imposed like the obligation which arises from a promise. Such theories are in fact the counterpart in international law of the social contract theories of political science. The latter sought to explain the facts that individuals, "naturally" free and independent, were yet bound by municipal law, by treating the obligation to obey the law as one arising from a contract which those bound had made with each other, and in some cases with their rulers. We shall not consider here the well-known objections to this theory when taken literally, nor its value when taken merely as an illuminating analogy. Instead we shall draw from its history a threefold argument against the voluntarist theories of international law.

First, these theories fail completely to explain how it is known that states "*can*" only be bound by self-imposed obligations, or why this view of their sovereignty should be accepted, in advance of any examination of the actual character of international law. Is there anything more to support it besides the fact that it has often been repeated? Secondly, there is something incoherent in the argument designed to show that states, because of their sovereignty, *can* only be subject to or bound by rules which they have imposed upon themselves. In some very extreme forms of "auto-limitation" theory, a state's agreement or treaty engagements are treated as mere declarations of its proposed future conduct, and failure to perform is not considered to be a breach of any obligation. This, though very much at variance with the facts, has at least the merit of consistency: it is the simple theory that the absolute sovereignty of states is inconsistent with obligation of any kind, so that, like Parliament, a state cannot bind itself. The less extreme view that a state may impose obligations on itself by promise, agreement, or treaty is not, however, consistent with the theory that states are subject only to rules which they have thus imposed on themselves. For, in order that words, spoken or written, should in certain circumstances function as a promise, agreement, or treaty, and so give rise to obligations and confer rights which others may claim, *rules* must already exist prescribing that a state is bound to do whatever it undertakes by appropriate words to do. Such rules presupposed in the very notion of a self-imposed obligation obviously cannot derive *their* obligatory status from a self-imposed obligation to obey them.

It is true that every specific *action* which a given state was bound to do might in theory derive its obligatory character from a promise; none the less this could only be the case if the *rule* that promises, &c., create obligations is applicable to the state independently of any promise. In any society, whether composed of individuals or states, what is necessary and sufficient, in order that the words of a promise, agreement, or treaty should give rise to obligations, is that rules providing for this and specifying a procedure for these self-binding operations should be generally, though they need not be universally, acknowledged. Where they are acknowledged the individual or state who wittingly uses these procedures is bound thereby, whether he or it chooses to be bound or not. Hence, even this most voluntary form of social obligation involves some rules which are binding independently of the choice of the party bound by them, and this, in the case of states, is inconsistent with the supposition that their sovereignty demands freedom from all such rules.

Thirdly there are the facts. We must distinguish the *a priori* claim just criticized, that states can only be bound by self-imposed obligations, from the claim that though they could be bound in other ways under a different system, in fact no other form of obligation for states exists under the present rules of international law. It is, of course, possible that the system might be one of this wholly consensual

form, and both assertions and repudiations of this view of its character are to be found in the writings of jurists, in the opinions of judges, even of international courts, and in the declarations of states. Only a dispassionate survey of the actual practice of states can show whether this view is correct or not. It is true that modern international law is very largely treaty law, and elaborate attempts have been made to show that rules which appear to be binding on states without their prior consent do in fact rest on consent, though this may have been given only "tacitly" or has to be "inferred." Though not all are fictions, some at least of these attempts to reduce to one the forms of international obligation excite the same suspicion as the notion of a "tacit command" which, as we have seen, was designed to perform a similar, though more obviously spurious, simplification of municipal law.

A detailed scrutiny of the claim that all international obligation arises from the consent of the party bound, cannot be undertaken here, but two clear and important exceptions to this doctrine must be noticed. The first is the case of a new state. It has never been doubted that when a new, independent state emerges into existence, as did Iraq in 1932, and Israel in 1948, it is bound by the general obligations of international law including, among others, the rules that give binding force to treaties. Here the attempt to rest the new state's international obligations on a "tacit" or "inferred" consent seems wholly threadbare. The second case is that of a state acquiring territory or undergoing some other change, which brings with it, for the first time, the incidence of obligations under rules which previously it had no opportunity either to observe or break, and to which it had no occasion to give or withhold consent. If a state, previously without access to the sea, acquires maritime territory, it is clear that this is enough to make it subject to all the rules of international law relating to the territorial waters and the high seas. Besides these, there are more debatable cases, mainly relating to the effect on non-parties of general or multilateral treaties; but these two important exceptions are enough to justify the suspicion that the general theory that all international obligation is self-imposed has been inspired by too much abstract dogma and too little respect for the facts.

International Law and Morality

… Sometimes the insistence that the rules governing the relations between states are only moral rules is inspired by the old dogmatism, that any form of social structure that is not reducible to orders backed by threats can only be a form of "morality." It is, of course, possible to use the word "morality" in this very comprehensive way; so used, it provides a conceptual wastepaper basket into which will go the rules of games, clubs, etiquette, the fundamental provisions of constitutional law and international law, together with rules and principles which we ordinarily think of as moral ones, such as the common prohibitions of cruelty, dishonesty, or lying. The objection to this procedure is that between what is thus classed together as "morality" there are such important differences of both form and social function, that no conceivable purpose, practical or theoretical, could be served by so crude a classification. Within the category of morality thus artificially widened, we should have to mark out afresh the old distinctions which it blurs.

In the particular case of international law there are a number of different reasons for resisting the classification of its rules as "morality." The first is that states often reproach each other for immoral conduct or praise themselves or other for living up to the standard of international morality. No doubt *one* of the virtues which states may show or fail to show is that of abiding by international law, but that does not mean that the law is morality. In fact the appraisal of states' conduct in terms of morality is recognizably different from the formulation of claims, demands, and the acknowledgment of rights and obligations under the rules of international law. In Chapter V [of *The Concept of Law*] we listed certain features which might be taken as defining characteristics of social morality: among them was the distinctive form of moral pressure by which moral rules are primarily supported. This consists not of appeals to fear or threats of retaliation or demands for compensation, but of appeals to conscience, made in the expectation that once the person addressed is reminded of the moral principle at stake, he may be led by guilt or shame to respect it and make amends.

Claims under international law are not couched in such terms, though of course, as in municipal law, they may be joined with a moral appeal. What predominate in the arguments, often technical, which states address to each other over disputed matters in international law, are references to precedents, treaties and juristic writings; often no mention is made of moral right or wrong, good or bad. Hence the claim that the Peking [Beijing] Government has or has not a right under international law to expel the Nationalist forces from Formosa [Taiwan] is very different from the question of whether this is fair, just, or a morally good or bad thing to do, and is backed by characteristically different arguments. No doubt in the relations between states there are halfway houses between what is clearly law and what is clearly morality, analogous to the standards of politeness and courtesy recognized in private life. Such is the sphere of international "comity" exemplified in the privilege extended to diplomatic envoys of receiving goods intended for personal use free of duty.

A more important ground of distinction is the following. The rules of international law, like those of municipal law, are often morally quite indifferent. A rule may exist because it is convenient or necessary to have some clear fixed rule about the subjects with which it is concerned, but not because any moral importance is attached to the particular rule. It may well be but one of a large number of possible rules, any one of which would have done equally well. Hence legal rules, municipal and international, commonly contain much specific detail, and draw arbitrary distinctions, which would be unintelligible as elements in moral rules or principles. It is true that we must not be dogmatic about the possible content of social morality…. The morality of a social group may contain much by way of injunction which may appear absurd or superstitious when viewed in the light of modern knowledge. So it is possible, though difficult, to imagine that men with general beliefs very different from ours, might come to attach *moral* importance to driving on the left instead of the right of the road or could come to feel moral guilt if they broke a promise witnessed by two witnesses, but no such guilt if it was witnessed by one. Though such strange moralities are possible, it yet remains true that a morality cannot (logically) contain rules which are generally held by those who subscribe to them to be in no way preferable to alternatives and of no intrinsic importance. Law, however, though it also contains much that is of moral importance, can and does contain just such rules, and the arbitrary distinctions, formalities, and highly specific detail which would be most difficult to understand as part of morality, are consequently natural and easily comprehensible features of law. For one of the typical functions of law, unlike morality, is to introduce just these elements in order to maximize certainty and predictability and to facilitate the proof or assessments of claims. Regard for forms and detail carried to excess, has earned for law the reproaches of "formalism" and "legalism"; yet it is important to remember that these vices are exaggerations of some of the law's distinctive qualities.

It is for this reason that just as we expect a municipal legal system, but not morality, to tell us how many witnesses a validly executed will must have, so we expect international law, but not morality, to tell us such things as the number of days a belligerent vessel may stay for refueling or repairs in a neutral port; the width of territorial waters; the methods to be used in their measurement. All these things are necessary and desirable provisions for *legal rules* to make, but so long as the sense is retained that such rules may equally well take any of several forms, or are important only as one among many possible means to specific ends, they remain distinct from rules which have the status in individual or social life characteristic of morality. Of course not all the rules of international law

are of this formal, or arbitrary, or morally neutral kind. The point is only that legal rules *can* and moral rules *cannot* be of this kind.

The difference in character between international law and anything which we naturally think of as morality has another aspect. Though the effect of a law requiring or proscribing certain practices might ultimately be to bring about changes in the morality of a group, the notion of a legislature making or repealing moral rules is ... an absurd one. A legislature cannot introduce a new rule and give it the status of a moral rule by its *fiat*, just as it cannot, by the same means, give a rule the status of a tradition, though the reasons why this is so may not be the same in the two cases. Accordingly morality does not merely lack or happen not to have a legislature; the very idea of change by human legislative *fiat* is repugnant to the idea of morality. This is so because we conceive of morality as the ultimate standard by which human actions (legislative or otherwise) are evaluated. The contrast with international law is clear. There is nothing in the nature or function of international law which is similarly inconsistent with the idea that the rules might be subject to legislative change; the lack of a legislature is just a lack which many think of as a defect one day to be repaired.

Finally we must notice a parallel in the theory of international law between the argument ... that even if particular rules of municipal law may conflict with morality, none the less the system as a whole must rest on a generally diffused conviction that there is a moral obligation to obey its rules, though this may be overridden in special exceptional cases. It has often been said in the discussion of the "foundations" of international law, that in the last resort, the rules of international law *must* rest on the conviction of states that there is a moral obligation to obey them; yet, if this means more than that the obligations which they recognize are not enforceable by officially organized sanctions, there seems no reason to accept it. Of course it is possible to think of circumstances which would certainly justify our saying that a state considered some course of conduct required by international law morally obligatory, and acted for that reason. It might, for example, continue to perform the obligations of an onerous treaty because of the manifest harm to humanity that would follow if confidence in treaties was severely shaken, or because of the sense that it was only fair to shoulder the irksome burdens of a code from which it, in its turn, had profited in the past when the burden fell on others. Precisely whose motives, thoughts and feelings on such matters of moral conviction are to be attributed to the state is a question which need not detain us here.

But though there *may* be such a sense of moral obligation it is difficult to see why or in what sense it *must* exist as a condition of the existence of international law. It is clear that in the practice of states certain rules are regularly respected even at the cost of certain sacrifices; claims are formulated by reference to them; breaches of the rules expose the offender to serious criticism and are held to justify claims for compensation or retaliation. These, surely, are all the elements required to support the statement that there exist among states rules imposing obligations upon them. The proof that "binding" rules in any society exist, is simply that they are thought of, spoken of, and function as such. What more is required by way of "foundations" and why, if more is required, must it be a foundation of moral obligation? It is, of course, true that rules could not exist or function in the relations between states unless a preponderant majority accepted the rules and voluntarily cooperated in maintaining them. It is true also that the pressure exercised on those who break or threaten to break the rules is often relatively weak, and has usually been decentralized or unorganized. But as in the case of individuals, who voluntarily accept the far more strongly coercive system of municipal law, the motives for voluntarily supporting such a system may be extremely diverse. It may well be that any form of legal order is at its healthiest when there is a generally diffused sense that it is morally obligatory to conform to it. Nonetheless, adherence to law may not be motivated by it, but by calculations of long-term interest, or by the wish to continue

a tradition or by disinterested concern for others. There seems no good reason for identifying any of these as a necessary condition of the existence of law either among individuals or states.

Analogies of Form and Content

To the innocent eye, the formal structure of international law lacking a legislature, courts with compulsory jurisdiction and officially organized sanctions, appears very different from that of municipal law. It resembles, ... in form though not at all in content, a simple regime of primary or customary law. Yet some theorists, in their anxiety to defend against the skeptic the title of international law to be called "law," have succumbed to the temptation to minimize these formal differences, and to exaggerate the analogies which can be found in international law to legislation or other desirable formal features of municipal law. Thus, it has been claimed that war, ending with a treaty whereby the defeated power cedes territory, or assumes obligations, or accepts some diminished form of independence, is essentially a legislative act; for, like legislation, it is an imposed legal change. Few would now be impressed by this analogy, or think that it helped to show that international law had an equal title with municipal law to be called "law"; for one of the salient differences between municipal and international law is that the former usually does not, and the latter does, recognize the validity of agreements extorted by violence.

A variety of other, more respectable analogies have been stressed by those who consider the title of "law" to depend on them. The fact that in almost all cases the judgment of the International Court and its predecessor, the Permanent Court of International Justice, have been duly carried out by the parties, has often been emphasized as if this somehow offset the fact that, in contrast with municipal courts, no state can be brought before these international tribunals without its prior consent. Analogies have also been found between the use of force, legally regulated and officially administered, as a sanction in municipal law and "decentralized sanctions," i.e., the resort to war or forceful retaliation by a state which claims that its rights under international law have been violated by another. That there is some analogy is plain; but its significance must be assessed in the light of the equally plain fact that, whereas a municipal court has a compulsory jurisdiction to investigate the rights and wrongs of "self help," and to punish a wrongful resort to it, no international court has a similar jurisdiction.

Some of these dubious analogies may be considered to have been much strengthened by the obligations which states have assumed under the United Nations Charter. But, again, any assessment of their strength is worth little if it ignores the extent to which the law-enforcement provisions of the Charter, admirable on paper, have been paralyzed by the veto and the ideological divisions and alliances of the great powers. The reply, sometimes made, that the law-enforcement provisions of municipal law *might* also be paralyzed by a general strike is scarcely convincing; for in our comparison between municipal law and international law we are concerned with what exists in fact, and here the facts are undeniably different.

There is, however, one suggested formal analogy between international and municipal law which deserves some scrutiny here. Kelsen[1] and many modern theorists insist that, like municipal law, international law possesses and indeed must possess a "basic norm," or what we have termed a rule of recognition, by reference to which the validity of the other rules of the system is assessed, and in virtue of which the rules constitute a single system. The opposed view is that this analogy of structure is false: international law simply consists of a *set* of separate primary rules of obligation which are not united in this manner. It is, in the usual terminology of international lawyers, a set of customary rules of which the rule giving binding force to treaties is one. It is notorious that those who have embarked on the task have found very great difficulties in formulating the "basic norm" of international law.

Candidates for this position include the principle *pacta sunt servanda*.[2] This has, however, been abandoned by most theorists, since it seems incompatible with the fact that not all obligations under international law arise from "*pacta*," however widely that term is construed. So it has been replaced by something less familiar: the so-called rule that "States should behave as they customarily behave." We shall not discuss the merits of these and other rival formulations of the basic norm of international law; instead we shall question the assumption that it must contain such an element. Here the first and perhaps the last question to ask is: why should we make this *a priori* assumption (for that is what it is) and so prejudge the actual character of the rules of international law? For it is surely conceivable (and perhaps has often been the case) that a society may live by rules imposing obligations on its members as "binding," even though they are regarded simply as a set of separate rules, not unified by or deriving their validity from any more basic rule. It is plain that the mere existence of rules does not involve the existence of such a basic rule. In most modern societies there are rules of etiquette, and, though we do not think of them as imposing obligations, we may well talk of such rules as existing; yet we would not look for, nor could we find, a basic rule of etiquette from which the validity of the separate rules was derivable.

Such rules do not form a system but a mere set, and, of course, the inconveniences of this form of social control, where matters more important than those of etiquette are at stake, are considerable. They have already been described in Chapter V [of *The Concept of Law*]. Yet if rules are in fact accepted as standards of conduct, and supported with appropriate forms of social pressure distinctive of obligatory rules, nothing more is required to show that they are binding rules, even though, in this simple form of social structure, we have not something which we do have in municipal law: namely a way of demonstrating the validity

---

[1] [Hans Kelsen (1881–1973) was an Austrian jurist and legal theorist.]

[2] [Latin for "agreements must be kept," often regarded as a fundamental principle of civil and international law.]

of individual rules by reference to some ultimate rule of the system.

There are of course a number of questions which we can ask about rules which constitute not a system but a simple set. We can, for example, ask questions about their historical origin, or questions concerning the causal influences that have fostered the growth of the rules. We can also ask questions about the value of the rules to those who live by them, and whether they regard themselves as morally bound to obey them or obey from some other motive. But we cannot ask in the simpler case one kind of question which we can ask concerning the rules of a system enriched, as municipal law is, by a basic norm or secondary rule of recognition. In the simpler case we cannot ask: "From what ultimate provision of the system do the separate rules derive their validity or 'binding force'?" For there is no such provision and need be none. It is, therefore, a mistake to suppose that a basic rule or rule of recognition is a generally necessary condition of the existence of rules of obligation or "binding" rules. This is not a necessity, but a luxury, found in advanced social systems whose members not merely come to accept separate rules piecemeal, but are committed to the acceptance in advance of general classes of rule, marked out by general criteria of validity. In the simpler form of society we must wait and see whether a rule gets accepted as a rule or not; in a system with a basic rule of recognition we can say before a rule is actually made, that it *will* be valid *if* it conforms to the requirements of the rule of recognition.

The same point may be presented in a different form. When such a rule of recognition is added to the simple set of separate rules, it not only brings with it the advantages of system and ease of identification, but it makes possible for the first time a new form of statement. These are internal statements about the validity of the rules; for we can now ask in a new sense, "What provision of the system makes this rule binding?" or, in Kelsen's language, "What, within the system, is the reason of its validity?" The answers to these new questions are provided by the basic rule of recognition.

But though, in the simpler structure, the validity of the rules cannot thus be demonstrated by reference to any more basic rule, this does not mean that there is some question about the rules or their binding force or validity which is left unexplained. It is not the case that there is some mystery as to why the rules in such a simple social structure are binding, which a basic rule, if only we could find it, would resolve. The rules of the simple structure are, like the basic rule of the more advanced systems, binding if they are accepted and function as such. These simple truths about different forms of social structure can, however, easily be obscured by the obstinate search for unity and system where these desirable elements are not in fact to be found.

There is indeed something comic in the efforts made to fashion a basic rule for the most simple forms of social structure which exist without one. It is as if we were to insist that a naked savage *must* really be dressed in some invisible variety of modern dress. Unfortunately, there is also here a standing possibility of confusion. We may be persuaded to treat as a basic rule, something which is an empty repetition of the mere fact that the society concerned (whether of individuals or states) observes certain standards of conduct as obligatory rules. This is surely the status of the strange basic norm which has been suggested for international law: "States should behave as they have customarily behaved." For it says nothing more than that those who accept certain rules must also observe a rule that the rules ought to be observed. This is a mere useless reduplication of the fact that a set of rules are accepted by states as binding rules.

Again once we emancipate ourselves from the assumption that international law must contain a basic rule, the question to be faced is one of fact. What is the actual character of the rules as they function in the relations between states? Different interpretations of the phenomena to be observed are of course possible; but it is submitted that there is no basic rule providing general criteria of validity for the rules of international law, and that the rules which are in fact operative constitute not a system but a set of rules, among which are the rules providing for the binding force of treaties. It is true that, on many important matters, the relations between states are regulated by multilateral treaties, and it is sometimes argued that these may bind states that are not parties. If this were generally recognized, such treaties would in fact be legislative enactments and international law would have distinct criteria of validity for its rules. A basic rule of recognition could then be formulated which would represent an actual feature of the system and would be more than an empty restatement of the fact that a set of rules are in fact observed by states at present in a state of transition towards acceptance of this and other forms which would bring it nearer in structure to a municipal system. If, and when, this transition is completed, the formal analogies, which at present seem thin and even delusive, would acquire substance, and the skeptic's last doubts about the legal "quality" of international law may then be laid to rest. Till this stage is reached the analogies are surely those of function and content, not of form. Those of function emerge most clearly when we reflect on the ways in which international law differs from morality…. The analogies of content consist in the range of principles, concepts, and methods which are common to both municipal and international law, and make the lawyers' technique freely transferable from the one to the other. Bentham, the inventor of the expression "international law," defended it simply by saying that it was "sufficiently analogous"[1] to municipal

law. To this, two comments are perhaps worth adding. First that the analogy is one of content not of form: secondly that, in this analogy of content, no other social rules are so close to municipal law as those of international law.

---

[1] Jeremy Bentham, *Principles of Morals and Legislation*, XVII, 25, n. 1.

DISCUSSION QUESTIONS

1. Spend a few minutes reflecting on the previous reading (the United Nations Declaration on the Rights of Indigenous Peoples). Do you think that the U.N.'s declaration is binding on all states? If a state failed to recognize the rights and duties explicitly or implicitly mentioned in the declaration, would that state be violating the law? How would Hart answer these questions? Explain.

2. What is a "voluntarist" conception of international law? Does Hart accept the voluntarist position? Explain.

3. Hart draws a distinction between morality and law. What is this distinction and how does it inform his discussion of international law? On his view, does international law rest upon a moral foundation? If so, what is this moral foundation? If not, what are the foundations of international law?

Rights, Liberty, and the Limits of Government

Introduction

There is surely a consensus among most political thinkers that a truly legitimate state must have the proper respect for human freedom. When careless, some talk as if there were no more to a legitimate government than a government elected democratically, or a government whose policies are in accord with the will of the majority. But most will agree that there can be, in de Toqueville's wonderful expression, a tyranny of the majority. The framers of the US Constitution, for example, were acutely aware of the danger that majorities might try to illegitimately impose their will in restricting freedom, and sought through the Bill of Rights to limit even majority-sanctioned societal control over the individual. John Stuart Mill predicted that issues concerning freedom would be among the great controversies of the future. We live in that future to which Mill referred and are, therefore, ideally suited to assess the accuracy of his prediction. And it seems prescient. Whether we are arguing about relatively mundane matters concerning seatbelt laws or the right to smoke cigarettes in public places, or arguing about fundamental issues concerning the legalization of drugs, the right of women to choose to abort a fetus, right-to-work laws, the right to marry the partner (or partners) of one's choice, or censorship of literature, movies, or the web, the extent of legitimate government reach seems at the heart of the issues. As Mill argued, it would be nice to have some principled way of deciding when society through its government can and cannot legitimately attempt to regulate the behavior of individuals. Just as almost everyone agrees that there are areas of an individual's life that ought to be off limits to societal regulation, so also virtually everyone agrees that for society to survive and serve its function there must be limits to freedom. The question is how and where to draw the line.

One approach to the issue, an approach we've encountered elsewhere, is that of the act consequentialist. Using this approach, we decide questions of whether we should prevent someone from doing as he or she chooses in the same way that we would decide any other ethical question. We ask what would maximize value (ignoring, for the sake of simplicity, distinctions we discussed in the Introduction to Unit I between consequentialisms that emphasize actual, probable, or possible consequences). If *allowing* freedom in some cases will make the world a better place, then we should opt in favor of freedom. If *restricting* freedom will in the long run make the world a better place, then we should sacrifice the freedom in question for the greater good. Many other philosophers, however, want to couch the debate in the language of rights: people have a right to behave in certain ways without fear of interference from the state, and that right cannot be trumped by means/ends calculations involving value. It is a matter of some debate whether act consequentialists can find any room within their ethical theory for any meaningful concept of a right understood as something that trumps consequentialist considerations (see reading 26 by Jeske and Fumerton, and reading 31 by Sumner).

One of the most famous efforts to put forth what *looks* like a rights-based approach to determining the limits of legitimate state interference with the individual is Mill's *On Liberty* (see readings 33 and 37). The irony is that in another work, *Utilitarianism* (see readings 23 and 28), Mill appears to defend a robust consequentialism (hedonistic utilitarianism—the view that the right thing to do is whatever maximizes happiness). There has been a great deal of discussion as to whether Mill can reconcile the central tenets of his two most famous works. In *On Liberty*, Mill puts forth the famous Harm Principle, which states that one must allow people (who have reached the age of reason) to act as they please unless their behavior harms another person against that person's will. While the principle might seem initially straightforward, there are a host of issues that immediately arise concerning its interpretation (both exegetical and, more interestingly perhaps, philosophical, insofar as we are concerned with developing a plausible version of the principle). The interpretive difficulties concern both the question of what kind of connection must exist between an action and a harm before the harm can be "laid at the feet" of the actor, and the even more fundamental question concerning just what constitutes a harm.

Before even addressing the above questions, however, it is important to note that the Harm Principle does not even seem to live up to its billing as "the" principle that will allow us to decide when we should limit someone's freedom. As stated, the Harm Principle seems to state only a necessary, not a sufficient condition for legitimate interference with an individual's autonomy. It tells us that we may interfere *only* if the actor is harming another person against his or her will. It does not tell us that when we discover the relevant harm, we *should* act so as to prevent it. If there is any doubt concerning the interpretation of Mill, it should be removed when he states unequivocally (*On Liberty*, Chapter V) that "… it must by no means be supposed, because damage, or probability of damage, to the interests of others can alone justify the interference of society, that

therefore it always does justify such interference." So even if we accept some version of the Harm Principle, it seems that we will need some other principle to decide when we ought to restrict freedom.

In the passage quoted above, Mill introduces a concept that is usually absent in his discussion of the Harm Principle—the concept of probability. The implication is that we can legitimately stop you from doing something on a given occasion if you are acting in a way that makes *probable* harm to another—we don't need to wait for the harm to occur. And such a qualification is surely plausible. But it also opens the door to still further revisions. If we can stop people from doing what will probably harm others, then surely we can legitimately stop people from doing what needlessly *increases* the probability of harm to others. For example, most of us think that it is legitimate to pass laws preventing people from driving cars while even slightly over the legal limit for intoxication. The probability that such people will cause bodily harm or property damage is actually rather low. But as a society we see no need to increase the risk to others by allowing such behavior. As we qualify the Harm Principle in this way, it becomes more and more difficult to think of real-life controversial behavior that will be protected by the Harm Principle. Every time one drives a car, for example, one increases the probability of harm to others. The increase might not be "needless," of course, but now everything hinges on the critical notion of when there are good reasons to allow the behavior despite its risk to others. This concern that the Harm Principle, even if true, might have limited application is exacerbated by Mill's own admission that one can harm others not only through action but through failure to act (failure to benefit). Mill states that making people answerable for failure to aid should be the exception rather than the rule, though his cryptic remarks provide no elaboration. In any event, once one allows that one can harm others through inaction, it is entirely unclear what sphere of an individual's life will get protection from the Harm Principle. While sunning oneself on the hammock in one's backyard, there are, after all, countless actions one fails to take, all of which would aid other people in various ways.

Instead of working on my tan, I could be helping the homeless, volunteering at an animal shelter, raising money for worthy causes, and so on.

The above concerns leave open the interpretation of harm. But any defender of the Harm Principle will need to settle the question of what constitutes harm. It seems fairly obvious that if one acts so as to inflict physical injury on another, the resulting injury will count as harm. It is probably almost as obvious that if one destroys the property of another, the resulting property damage counts as harm. One sort of very difficult case, however, involves what one might call psychological harm. If your neighbor makes vicious threats or obscene phone calls, does the distress caused constitute a kind of harm? If your neighbor paints his house purple with orange polka dots, and decorates his front lawn with realistic animal heads from which spurt fake blood, has that neighbor harmed you in virtue of the aesthetic disgust you feel when looking at the grotesque scene? Most cities have all sorts of zoning laws that will, in fact, place severe restrictions on what we can do to our property.

Mill himself sends mixed signals. He seems to think that the disgust Muslims feel at the sight of pork eaters, or the distress Catholics might feel at the thought of people practicing other religions, does not count as harm in the sense relevant to the application of the Harm Principle. But he also unequivocally endorses "public decency" laws, where it would be difficult to identify the relevant harm that such laws are supposed to prevent other than pointing to aesthetic considerations. And whatever Mill himself thought, it is difficult to remain steadfast in the defense of a liberty "to disgust" others as the imagined behavior becomes more and more obscene (see reading 39 by Feinberg). To deal with such matters, one might try to develop a consistent distinction of some sort between public and private behavior. Perhaps legitimate public-decency laws will prevent people from acting in offensive ways only on public land. Such land is, after all, jointly owned, and we need some mechanism for determining what we will allow on the land we jointly own. Whether the defender of freedom will be content with a majority exercising

onerous requirements of behavior on public land, while allowing people to act as they please in the privacy of their own homes, is debatable. And as the aesthetic considerations discussed earlier suggest, it won't be easy to settle the question of what constitutes privacy. The light and sound that reflect off your property onto mine have, after all, a kind of effect on me, and the extent to which I find them offensive might make your behavior public even if it affects in the first instance only your own property.

Most of the examples of harm we've discussed above involve, directly or indirectly, states that might be construed as painful (even psychological disgust can be construed as a kind of suffering). Still others interested in defending some version of a Harm Principle will argue that we need to broaden the concept of harm enough that it includes any setback to the interests of another. Interests in turn can be defined subjectively (perhaps in terms of a person's goals or desires) or objectively (in terms of what is good independently of anyone's attitudes toward that which is good). The broader one's conception of interests on this view, the harder it will be to find application for the Harm Principle. And as one turns to an objectivist conception of interest, the more one must address head on the question of when one may legitimately attempt to legislate morality, even when the moral views one imposes are rejected by those upon whom the views are forced.

Interestingly enough, many of Mill's positive arguments for freedom (freedom of thought and expression, and freedom of lifestyle) don't focus on the question of whether the behavior he wants to protect harms others. Rather, his consequentialist leanings seem to come to the fore, and he stresses instead the good that will accrue to society from allowing freedom—a good that will outweigh any bad consequences that may occur. When defending freedom of expression, for example, Mill points out that true beliefs are clarified and strengthened by exposure to alternative views. Furthermore, he suggests that we unnecessarily risk suppressing truth or partial truth when we censure. He doesn't argue, however, that no-one ever gets hurt by allowing freedom of expression. And it is probably a good thing that he doesn't, given the unfortunate hateful behavior that has so often been caused throughout history by hateful speech.

Much of the discussion in the Applications section involves particular controversies concerning freedom. In almost of all the controversies, one can identify at least some bad consequences that result from choosing the side of freedom, and at least some bad consequences that result from choosing to restrict freedom. In evaluating particular debates concerning the legitimacy of restricting a given freedom, it is important to uncover the underlying structure of the relevant arguments. Is the author arguing as a consequentialist, or is the author explicitly or implicitly putting forth some rights-based principle that is supposed to take precedence over consequentialist considerations?

Both of the topics in the Applications section (Free Speech; and Sex, Freedom, and Marriage) illustrate how prescient Mill was in worrying about the tyranny of the majority. As our societies have become more diverse, more and more groups have attempted to show that the apparently universal freedoms that we in the Western democracies have historically endorsed might in fact only be freedoms for the dominant group(s) while simultaneously functioning as tools for limiting the freedom and equality of the minority group(s). This is particularly so in the cases of speech and of sexuality and intimate relationships more generally.

In the section on free speech, we have selected hate speech and obscenity/pornography as our focus. Western democracies such as the United States and Canada have long-standing commitments to freedom of speech. But, as has long been recognized, it is not always easy to draw a clear distinction between speech and action; for example, if I whip a crowd into a frenzy, thereby starting a riot, it is true that what I have done counts as speech, but it also counts as incitement to violence. American jurisprudence has long held that it is permissible to curtail speech when it presents a "clear and present danger." We may all agree that shouting "Fire!" in a crowded theater presents a clear and present danger, but few cases are as straightforward as that.

Consider, for example, hate speech, i.e., speech that demeans members of a group on the basis of religion, race, ethnicity, sexuality, or gender. We know that sustained, high levels of such speech can play a significant role in creating conditions of oppression, exploitation, and even systematic mass murder—we need only read the history of anti-Semitic propaganda in Nazi Germany for one example. And there is no doubt that members of minority groups can feel offended or devalued as the result of such speech. Does it contribute to the continued oppression of minority groups such as African Americans? If so, how do we balance the value of free speech against that of equality and equal opportunity? In reading the cases, you will see that the United States and Canada have taken different legal approaches to hate speech. Ask yourself, as you read and compare these free speech cases, the following questions: Which of the theoretical approaches supports the Canadian approach to free speech and which supports the American approach? Which do you find more philosophically defensible?

In recent years, some feminists have argued that pornography functions as a form of hate speech, given that it tends to present women as objects whose primary function is to provide men with sexual gratification. These feminists have argued that the legal notion of obscenity does not address *moral* issues because obscenity is always defined in terms of community standards. But if those community standards are primarily determined and controlled by men, obscenity law will mask the harms inherent in pornography, which in some pieces of legislation (see reading 49, *American Booksellers Association v. Hudnut*) is defined as a way of oppressing women.

The feminist claim that various legal concepts have been developed and interpreted from a male perspective can be taken into the realm of political philosophy as a whole. Until very late in the twentieth century, political philosophy, like philosophy in general, was a discipline written by men and largely directed at men as its intended audience. Women played a role in political philosophy only as subject material—the role of women in the political community was a subject of debate amongst men. It was generally assumed, at least until the nineteenth century, that women's role was in the home, the so-called "private" realm. Thus, women were routinely denied status as members of the political community.

The supposed naturalness of women remaining in their homes and tending to the comfort of their husbands and children functioned as an axiom in a case that came before the United States Supreme Court in 1872. Myra Bradwell was denied a license to practice law in the state of Illinois, and in *Bradwell v. Illinois* (see reading 51), she appealed to the Supreme Court of the United States to overturn the decision of the Illinois Supreme Court supporting the decision to deny her a license to practice law. Unfortunately, the United States Supreme Court came to the same conclusion as had the Illinois Court. In his concurring decision, Justice Bradley asserted that

> The paramount destiny and mission of woman are to fulfil [sic] the noble and benign offices of wife and mother. This is the law of the Creator. And the rules of civil society … must be adapted to the general constitution of things, and cannot be based upon exceptional cases.

Justice Bradley is arguing that women's nature suits them to a certain domestic role, and that it is perfectly legitimate for the state to legislate so as to insure that women perform their function of creating and maintaining a domestic sphere for the comfort of men and children. The mere fact, then, of one's biological sex is taken to justify one's exclusion from various professions and opportunities.

John Stuart Mill, in his *The Subjection of Women* (see reading 52), responds to just these sorts of objections to permitting women access to the public sphere. Mill asks why it is necessary to use coercion in order to keep women in the sphere of life to which they are supposedly best suited. More importantly, however, Mill argues that no one is now in a position to know what women are suited for, because women's nature has been formed according to the wishes and dictates of men. Give

women free reign to develop their capacities and talents, and both men and women will benefit. If women are really best suited for taking care of the family, then competition will weed them out of the public sphere and they will gravitate to those activities at which they naturally excel.

But is the lowering of barriers sufficient to make up for years of discrimination and stereotyping? Some feminist political thinkers, such as Susan Moller Okin (see reading 55), have argued that entrenched assumptions about women's child-care responsibilities have prevented them from achieving success in the public realm. Okin urges that work and school be redesigned to accommodate the emerging and prevalent dual-career family. But the changes advocated by Okin seem to privilege the worker with children, and many women choose to remain childless. Will such women be forced to bear an unjust burden in the workplace? If so, will this pressure act to encourage women to continue to play their traditional roles as child-bearers and caregivers?

Okin, then, shares with many of the male writers of political theory a concern with the traditional two-parent, heterosexual nuclear family. In recent years, however, much political debate has focused on the issue of non-traditional families, in particular on the issue of gay and lesbian marriage. Should persons of the same sex be allowed to enter into the civil contract of marriage, with all of its attendant privileges? Andrew Sullivan (see reading 56) offers an argument in support of gay marriage from the perspective of a political conservative (among whom, in general, gay marriage is anathema). Such debates force us to ask questions about the function of marriage in general, and, in particular, of the state's protection of that form of contract. If we allow gay marriage, are we forced to allow polygamous marriage? Should we in any case allow polygamous marriage? Or perhaps we should abolish the institution of civil marriage entirely. Why do we have such an institution, and does it continue to serve the purposes for which it was created?

A.
The Nature
of Rights

21

The United Nations Declaration of Human Rights (1948)

The Universal Declaration of Human Rights was adopted by the UN General Assembly in 1948 in Paris. It articulates a list of rights to which all human beings are supposedly entitled. It is not legally binding under international law, though it has been influential in shaping both national and international laws and has served as the foundation for further treaties. On the UN in general, see reading 19 above.

SOURCE

General Assembly of the United Nations. The Universal Declaration of Human Rights. Accessed June 6, 2010 from http://www.un.org/en/documents/udhr/index.shtml.

Preamble

Whereas recognition of the inherent dignity and of the equal and inalienable rights of all members of the human family is the foundation of freedom, justice and peace in the world,

Whereas disregard and contempt for human rights have resulted in barbarous acts which have outraged the conscience of mankind, and the advent of a world in which human beings shall enjoy freedom of speech and belief and freedom from fear and want has been proclaimed as the highest aspiration of the common people,

Whereas it is essential, if man is not to be compelled to have recourse, as a last resort, to rebellion against tyranny and oppression, that human rights should be protected by the rule of law,

Whereas it is essential to promote the development of friendly relations between nations,

Whereas the peoples of the United Nations have in the Charter reaffirmed their faith in fundamental human rights, in the dignity and worth of the human person and in the equal rights of men and women and have determined to promote social progress and better standards of life in larger freedom,

Whereas Member States have pledged themselves to achieve, in co-operation with the United Nations, the promotion of universal respect for and observance of human rights and fundamental freedoms,

Whereas a common understanding of these rights and freedoms is of the greatest importance for the full realization of this pledge,

Now, Therefore THE GENERAL ASSEMBLY proclaims THIS UNIVERSAL DECLARATION OF HUMAN RIGHTS as a common standard of achievement for all peoples and all nations, to the end that every individual and every organ of society, keeping this Declaration constantly in mind, shall strive by teaching and education to promote respect for these rights and freedoms and by progressive measures, national and international, to secure their universal and effective recognition and observance, both among the peoples of Member States themselves and among the peoples of territories under their jurisdiction.

Article 1
All human beings are born free and equal in dignity and rights. They are endowed with reason and conscience and should act towards one another in a spirit of brotherhood.

Article 2
Everyone is entitled to all the rights and freedoms set forth in this Declaration, without distinction of any kind, such as race, colour, sex, language, religion, political or other opinion, national or social origin, property, birth or other status. Furthermore, no distinction shall be made on the basis of the political, jurisdictional or international status of the country or territory to which a person belongs, whether it be independent, trust, non-self-governing or under any other limitation of sovereignty.

Article 3
Everyone has the right to life, liberty and security of person.

Article 4
No one shall be held in slavery or servitude; slavery and the slave trade shall be prohibited in all their forms.

Article 5
No one shall be subjected to torture or to cruel, inhuman or degrading treatment or punishment.

Article 6
Everyone has the right to recognition everywhere as a person before the law.

Article 7
All are equal before the law and are entitled without any discrimination to equal protection of the law. All are entitled to equal protection against any discrimination in violation of this Declaration and against any incitement to such discrimination.

Article 8
Everyone has the right to an effective remedy by the competent national tribunals for acts violating the fundamental rights granted him by the constitution or by law.

Article 9
No one shall be subjected to arbitrary arrest, detention or exile.

Article 10
Everyone is entitled in full equality to a fair and public hearing by an independent and impartial tribunal, in the determination of his rights and obligations and of any criminal charge against him.

Article 11
(1) Everyone charged with a penal offence has the right to be presumed innocent until proved guilty according to law in a public trial at which he has had all the guarantees necessary for his defence.
(2) No one shall be held guilty of any penal offence on account of any act or omission which did not constitute a penal offence, under national or international law, at the time when it was committed. Nor shall a heavier penalty be imposed than the one that was applicable at the time the penal offence was committed.

Article 12
No one shall be subjected to arbitrary interference with his privacy, family, home or correspondence, nor to attacks upon his honour and reputation. Everyone has the right to the protection of the law against such interference or attacks.

Article 13
(1) Everyone has the right to freedom of movement and residence within the borders of each state.
(2) Everyone has the right to leave any country, including his own, and to return to his country.

Article 14
(1) Everyone has the right to seek and to enjoy in other countries asylum from persecution.
(2) This right may not be invoked in the case of prosecutions genuinely arising from non-political crimes or from acts contrary to the purposes and principles of the United Nations.

Article 15
(1) Everyone has the right to a nationality.
(2) No one shall be arbitrarily deprived of his nationality nor denied the right to change his nationality.

Article 16
(1) Men and women of full age, without any limitation due to race, nationality or religion, have the right to marry and to found a family. They are entitled to equal rights as to marriage, during marriage and at its dissolution.
(2) Marriage shall be entered into only with the free and full consent of the intending spouses.
(3) The family is the natural and fundamental group unit of society and is entitled to protection by society and the State.

Article 17
(1) Everyone has the right to own property alone as well as in association with others.
(2) No one shall be arbitrarily deprived of his property.

Article 18
Everyone has the right to freedom of thought, conscience and religion; this right includes freedom to change his religion or belief, and freedom, either alone or in community with others and in public or private, to manifest his religion or belief in teaching, practice, worship and observance.

Article 19
Everyone has the right to freedom of opinion and expression; this right includes freedom to hold opinions without interference and to seek, receive and impart information and ideas through any media and regardless of frontiers.

Article 20
(1) Everyone has the right to freedom of peaceful assembly and association.
(2) No one may be compelled to belong to an association.

Article 21
(1) Everyone has the right to take part in the government of his country, directly or through freely chosen representatives.
(2) Everyone has the right of equal access to public service in his country.
(3) The will of the people shall be the basis of the authority of government; this will shall be expressed in periodic and genuine elections which shall be by universal and equal suffrage and shall be held by secret vote or by equivalent free voting procedures.

Article 22
Everyone, as a member of society, has the right to social security and is entitled to realization, through national effort and international co-operation and in accordance with the organization and resources of each State, of the economic, social and cultural rights indispensable for his dignity and the free development of his personality.

Article 23
(1) Everyone has the right to work, to free choice of employment, to just and favourable conditions of work and to protection against unemployment.
(2) Everyone, without any discrimination, has the right to equal pay for equal work.
(3) Everyone who works has the right to just and favourable remuneration ensuring for himself and his family an existence worthy of human dignity, and supplemented, if necessary, by other means of social protection.
(4) Everyone has the right to form and to join trade unions for the protection of his interests.

Article 24
Everyone has the right to rest and leisure, including reasonable limitation of working hours and periodic holidays with pay.

Article 25
(1) Everyone has the right to a standard of living adequate for the health and well-being of himself and of his family, including food, clothing, housing and medical care and necessary social services, and the right to security in the event of unemployment, sickness, disability, widowhood, old age or other lack of livelihood in circumstances beyond his control.
(2) Motherhood and childhood are entitled to special care and assistance. All children, whether born in or out of wedlock, shall enjoy the same social protection.

Article 26
(1) Everyone has the right to education. Education shall be free, at least in the elementary and fundamental stages. Elementary education shall be compulsory. Technical and professional education shall be made generally available and higher education shall be equally accessible to all on the basis of merit.
(2) Education shall be directed to the full development of the human personality and to the strengthening of respect for human rights and fundamental freedoms. It shall promote understanding, tolerance and friendship among all nations, racial or religious groups, and shall further the activities of the United Nations for the maintenance of peace.
(3) Parents have a prior right to choose the kind of education that shall be given to their children.

Article 27
(1) Everyone has the right freely to participate in the cultural life of the community, to enjoy the arts and to share in scientific advancement and its benefits.
(2) Everyone has the right to the protection of the moral and material interests resulting from any scientific, literary or artistic production of which he is the author.

Article 28
Everyone is entitled to a social and international order in which the rights and freedoms set forth in this Declaration can be fully realized.

Article 29
(1) Everyone has duties to the community in which alone the free and full development of his personality is possible.
(2) In the exercise of his rights and freedoms, everyone shall be subject only to such limitations as are determined by law solely for the purpose of securing due recognition and respect for the rights and freedoms of others and of meeting the just requirements of morality, public order and the general welfare in a democratic society.
(3) These rights and freedoms may in no case be exercised contrary to the purposes and principles of the United Nations.

Article 30
Nothing in this Declaration may be interpreted as implying for any State, group or person any right to engage in any activity or to perform any act aimed at the destruction of any of the rights and freedoms set forth herein.

DISCUSSION QUESTIONS

1. What rights (if any) do you think we naturally have? If you think that we do not have rights, what rights do you think other people generally claim we have? How would you describe the nature of such rights? That is, in virtue of what do we have them, and how do they function? Make a list of these rights and then compare it with the rights listed in the UN Declaration of Human Rights. Discuss any discrepancies between the lists.

2. Do you take issue with any of the rights listed in the UN Declaration? If so, which ones? Do you note any potential conflicts between the rights established in the articles of the Declaration? If so, discuss.

3. Can any of the rights mentioned in the Declaration be forfeited? What would it mean to forfeit a right? Under what conditions could one forfeit one's right(s)?

4. Are there any rights put forth in the Declaration that may be practically unattainable for certain governments, given existing social or economic conditions? If so, would we say of these governments that they are unjust, since they cannot realize certain of these rights? Discuss.

22

Jeremy Bentham, selection from "Anarchical Fallacies" (written between 1791 and 1795, published 1816)

Jeremy Bentham (1748–1832) was a British moral and legal philosopher and political reformer. He is known as an early defender of utilitarianism and a fierce critic of the natural law tradition. In this selection he criticizes the notion of natural rights, describing attributions of inalienable rights as "nonsense upon stilts."

SOURCE
Bentham, Jeremy. "Anarchical Fallacies." In *The Works of Jeremy Bentham*, Vol. II. Ed. J. Bowring. William Tait, 1843.

Preliminary Observations

The Declaration of Rights—I mean the paper published under that name by the French National Assembly in 1791—assumes for its subject-matter a field of disquisition as unbounded in point of extent as it is important in its nature. But the more ample the extent given to any proposition or string of propositions, the more difficult it is to keep the import of it confined without deviation, within the bounds of truth and reason. If in the smallest corners of the field it ranges over, it fail of coinciding with the line of rigid rectitude, no sooner is the aberration pointed out, than (inasmuch as there is no medium between truth and falsehood) its pretensions to the appellation of truism are gone, and whoever looks upon it must recognise it to be false and erroneous,—and if, as here, political conduct be the theme, so far as the error extends and fails of being detected, pernicious.

In a work of such extreme importance with a view to practice, and which throughout keeps practice so closely and immediately and professedly in view, a single error may be attended with the most fatal consequences. The more extensive the propositions, the more consummate will be the knowledge, the more exquisite the skill, indispensably requisite to confine them in all points within the pale of truth. The most consummate ability in the whole nation could not have been too much for the task—one may venture to say, it would not have been equal to it. But that, in the sanctioning of each proposition, the most consummate ability should happen to be vested in the heads of the sorry majority in whose hands the plenitude of power happened on that same occasion to be vested, is an event against which the chances are almost as infinity to one.

Here, then, is a radical and all-pervading error—the attempting to give to a work on such a subject the sanction of government; especially of such a government—a government composed of members so numerous, so unequal in talent, as well as discordant in inclinations and affections. Had it been the work of a single hand, and that a private one, and in that character given to the world, every good effect would have been produced by it that could be produced by it when published as the work of government, without any of the bad effects which in case of the smallest error must result from it when given as the work of government.

The revolution which threw the government into the hands of the penners and adopters of this declaration, having been the effect of insurrection, the grand object evidently is to justify the cause. But by justifying it, they invite it: in justifying past insurrections they plant and cultivate a propensity to perpetual insurrection in time future; they sow the seeds of anarchy broadcast: in justifying the demolition of existing authorities, they undermine all future ones, their own consequently in the number. Shallow and reckless vanity! They imitate in their conduct the author of that fabled law, according to which the assassination of the prince upon the throne gave to the assassin a title to succeed him. "People, behold your rights! If a single article of them be violated, insurrection is not your right only, but the most sacred of your duties." Such is the constant language, for such is the professed object of this source and model of all laws—this self-consecrated oracle of all nations....

The great enemies of public peace are the selfish and dissocial passions—necessary as they are—the one to the very existence of each individual, the other to his security. On the part of these affections, a deficiency in point of strength is never to be apprehended: all that is to be apprehended in respect of them, is to be apprehended on the side of their excess. Society is held together only by the sacrifices that men can be induced to make of the gratifications they demand: to obtain these sacrifices is the great difficulty, the great task of government. What has been the object, the perpetual and palpable object, of this declaration of pretended rights? To add as much force as possible to these passions, already but too strong,—to burst the cords that hold them in,—to say to the selfish passions, there—everywhere—is your prey!—to the angry passions, there—everywhere—is your enemy.

Such is the morality of this celebrated manifesto, rendered famous by the same qualities that gave celebrity to the incendiary of the Ephesian temple.

The logic of it is of a piece with its morality—a perpetual vein of nonsense, flowing from a perpetual abuse of words—words having a variety of meanings, where words with single meanings were equally at hand—the same words used in a variety of meanings in the same page—words used in meanings not their own, where proper words were equally at hand—words and propositions of the most unbounded signification, turned loose without any of those exceptions or modifications which are so necessary on every occasion to reduce their import within the compass, not only of right reason, but even of the design in hand, of whatever nature it may be—the same inaccuracy, the same inattention in the penning of this cluster of truths on which the fate of nations was to hang, as if it had been an oriental tale, or an allegory for a magazine—stale epigrams, instead of necessary distinctions—figurative expressions preferred to simple ones,—sentimental conceits, as trite as they are unmeaning, preferred to apt and precise expressions—frippery ornament preferred to the majestic simplicity of good sound sense—and the acts of the senate loaded and disfigured by the tinsel of the playhouse.

[...]

Article II

The end in view of every political association is the preservation of the natural and imprescriptible rights of man. These rights are liberty, property, security, and resistance to oppression.

Sentence 1. The end in view of every political association, is the preservation of the natural and imprescriptible rights of man.

More confusion—more nonsense—and the nonsense, as usual, dangerous nonsense. The words can scarcely be said to have a meaning: but if they have, or rather if they had a meaning, these would be the propositions either asserted or implied:

1. That there are such things as rights anterior to the establishment of governments: for natural, as applied to rights, if it mean anything, is meant to stand in opposition to *legal*—to such rights as are acknowledged to owe their existence to government, and are consequently posterior in their date to the establishment of government.

2. That these rights *can not* be abrogated by government: for *can not* is implied in the form of the word imprescriptible, and the sense it wears when so applied, is the cut-throat sense above explained.

3. That the governments that exist derive their origin from formal associations or what are now called *conventions*: associations entered into by a partnership contract, with all the members for partners—entered into at a day prefixed, for a predetermined purpose, the formation of a new government where there was none before (for as to formal meetings holden under the control of an existing government, they are evidently out of question here) in which it seems again to be implied in the way of inference, though a necessary and an unavoidable inference, that all governments (that is, self-called governments, knots of persons exercising the powers of government) that have had any other origin than an association of the above description, are illegal, that is, no governments at all; resistance to them and subversion of them, lawful and commendable; and so on.

Such are the notions implied in this first part of the article. How stands the truth of things? That there are no such things as natural rights—no such things as rights anterior to the establishment of government—no such things as natural rights opposed

to, in contradistinction to, legal: that the expression is merely figurative; that when used, in the moment you attempt to give it a literal meaning it leads to error, and to that sort of error that leads to mischief—to the extremity of mischief.

We know what it is for men to live without government—and living without government, to live without rights: we know what it is for men to live without government, for we see instances of such a way of life—we see it in many savage nations, or rather races of mankind; for instance, among the savages of New South Wales, whose way of living is so well known to us: no habit of obedience, and thence no government—no government, and thence no laws—no laws, and thence no such things as rights—no security—no property: liberty, as against regular control, the control of laws and government—perfect; but as against all irregular control, the mandates of stronger individuals, none. In this state, at a time earlier than the commencement of history—in this same state, judging from analogy, we the inhabitants of the part of the globe we call Europe, were;—no government, consequently no rights: no rights, consequently no property—no legal security—no legal liberty: security not more than belongs to beasts—forecast and sense of insecurity keener—consequently in point of happiness below the level of the brutal race.

In proportion to the want of happiness resulting from the want of rights, a reason exists for wishing that there were such things as rights. But reasons for wishing there were such things as rights, are not rights; a reason for wishing that a certain right were established, is not that right—want is not supply—hunger is not bread.

That which has no existence cannot be destroyed—that which cannot be destroyed cannot require anything to preserve it from destruction. *Natural rights* is simple nonsense: natural and imprescriptible rights, rhetorical nonsense,—nonsense upon stilts. But this rhetorical nonsense ends in the old strain of mischievous nonsense for immediately a list of these pretended natural rights is given, and those are so expressed as to present to view legal rights. And of these rights, whatever they are, there is not, it seems, any one of which any government *can*, upon any occasion whatever, abrogate the smallest particle.

So much for terrorist language. What is the language of reason and plain sense upon the same subject? That in proportion as it is *right* or *proper*, i.e., advantageous to the society in question, that this or that right—a right to this or that effect—should be established and maintained, in that same proportion it is *wrong* that it should be abrogated: but that as there is no *right*, which ought not to be maintained so long as it is upon the whole advantageous to the society that it should be maintained, so there is no right which, when the abolition of it is advantageous to society, should not be abolished. To know whether it would be more for the advantage of society that this or that right should be maintained or abolished, the time at which the question about maintaining or abolishing is proposed, must be given, and the circumstances under which it is proposed to maintain or abolish it; the right itself must be specifically described, not jumbled with an undistinguishable heap of others, under any such vague general terms as property, liberty, and the like.

One thing, in the midst of all this confusions is but too plain. They know not of what they are talking under the name of natural rights, and yet they would have them imprescriptible—proof against all the power of the laws—pregnant with occasions summoning the members of the community to rise up in resistance against the laws. What, then, was their object in declaring the existence of imprescriptible rights, and without specifying a single one by any such mark as it could be known by? This and no other—to excite and keep up a spirit of resistance to all laws—a spirit of insurrection against all governments—against the governments of all other nations instantly—against the government of their own nation—against the government they themselves were pretending to establish—even that, as soon as their own reign should be at an end. In us is the perfection of virtue and wisdom: in all mankind besides, the extremity of wickedness and folly. Our will shall consequently reign without control,

and for ever: reign now we are living—reign after we are dead.

All nations—all future ages—shall be, for they are predestined to be, our Slaves.

Future governments will not have honesty enough to be trusted with the determination of what rights shall be maintained, what abrogated—what laws kept in force, what repealed. Future subjects (I should say future citizens, for French government does not admit of subjects) will not have wit enough to be trusted with the choice whether to submit to the determination of the government of their time, or to resist it. Governments, citizens— all to the end of time—all must be kept in chains.

Such are their maxims—such their premises— for it is by such premises only that the doctrine of imprescriptible rights and unrepealable laws can be supported.

What is the real source of these imprescriptible rights—these unrepealable laws? Power turned blind by looking from its own height: self-conceit and tyranny exalted into insanity. No man was to have any other man for a servant, yet all men are forever to be their slaves. Making laws with imposture in their mouths, under pretence of declaring them—giving for laws anything that came uppermost, and these unrepealable ones, on pretence of finding them ready made. Made by what? Not by a God—they allow of none; but by their goddess, Nature.

The origination of governments from a contract is a pure fiction, or in other words, a falsehood. It never has been known to be true in any instance; the allegation of it does mischief, by involving the subject in error and confusion, and is neither necessary nor useful to any good purpose.

All governments that we have any account of have been gradually established by habit, after having been formed by force; unless in the instance of governments formed by individuals who have been emancipated, or have emancipated themselves, from governments already formed, the governments under which they were born—a rare case, and from which nothing follows with regard to the rest. What signifies it how governments are formed? Is it the less proper—the less conducive to the happiness of society—that the happiness of society should be the one object kept in view by the members of the government in all their measures? Is it the less the interest of men to be happy—less to be wished that they may be so—less the moral duty of their governors to make them so, as far as they can, at Mogadore than at Philadelphia.

Hence is it, but from government, that contracts derive their binding force? Contracts came from government, not government from contracts. It is from the habit of enforcing contracts, and seeing them enforced that governments are chiefly indebted for whatever disposition they have to observe them.

Sentence 2. These rights [these imprescriptible as well as natural rights,] are liberty, property, security, and resistance to oppression.

Observe the extent of these pretended rights, each of them belonging to every man, and all of them without bounds. Unbounded liberty; that is, amongst other things, the liberty of doing or not doing on every occasion whatever each man pleases: unbounded property; that is, the right of doing with everything around him (with every *thing* at least, if not with every person) whatsoever he pleases; communicating that right to anybody and withholding it from anybody—Unbounded security; that is, security for such his liberty, for such his property and for his person, against every defalcation that can be called for on any account in respect of any of them: Unbounded resistance to oppression; that is, unbounded exercise of the faculty of guarding himself against whatever unpleasant circumstance may present itself to his imagination or his passions under that name. Nature, say some of the interpreters of the pretended law of nature—nature gave to each man a right to everything; which is, in effect, but another way of saying—nature has given no such right to anybody; for in regard to most rights, it is as true that what is every man's right is no man's right, as that what is every man's business is no man's business. Nature gave—gave to every man a right to everything—be it so—true; and hence the necessity of human government and

human laws, to give to every man his own right, without which no right whatsoever would amount to anything. Nature gave every man a right to everything before the existence of laws, and in default of laws. This nominal universality and real nonentity of right, set up provisionally by nature in default of laws, the French oracle lays hold of, and perpetuates it under the law and in spite of laws. These anarchical rights which nature had set out with, democratic art attempts to rivet down, and declares indefeasible.

Unbounded liberty—I must still say unbounded liberty—for though the next article but one returns to the charge, and gives such a definition of liberty as seems intended to set bounds to it, yet in effect the limitation amounts to nothing; and when, as here, no warning is given of any exception in the texture of the general rule, every exception which turns up is, not a confirmation but a contradiction of the rule: liberty, without any preannounced or intelligent bounds; and as to the other rights, they remain unbounded to the end: rights of man composed of a system of contradictions and impossibilities.

In vain would it be said, that though no bounds are here assigned to any of these rights, yet it is to be understood as taken for granted and tacitly admitted and assumed, that they are to have bounds; viz. such bounds as it is understood will be set them by the laws. Vain, I say, would be this apology; for the supposition would be contradictory to the express declaration of the article itself, and would defeat the very object which the whole declaration has in view. It would be self-contradictory, because these rights are, in the same breath in which their existence is declared, declared to be imprescriptible; and imprescriptible, or as we in England should say, indefeasible, means nothing unless it exclude the interference of the laws.

It would be not only inconsistent with itself, but inconsistent with the declared and sole object of the declaration, if it did not exclude the interference of the laws. It is against the laws themselves, and the laws only, that this declaration is levelled. It is for the hands of the legislator and all legislators, and none but legislators, that the shackles it provides are intended—it is against the apprehended encroachments of legislators that the rights in question, the liberty and property, and so forth, are intended to be made secure—it is to such encroachments, and damages, and dangers, that whatever security it professes to give has respect. Precious security for unbounded rights against legislators, if the extent of those rights in every direction were purposely left to depend upon the will and pleasure of those very legislators!

Nonsensical or nugatory, and in both cases mischievous, such is the alternative.

So much for all these pretended indefeasible rights in the lump: their inconsistency with each other, as well as the inconsistency of them in the character of indefeasible rights with the existence of government and all peaceable society, will appear still more plainly when we examine them one by one.

1. *Liberty*, then, is imprescriptible—incapable of being taken away—out of the power of any government ever to take away liberty—that is, every branch of liberty—every individual exercise of liberty; for no line is drawn—no distinction—no exception made. What these instructors as well as governors of mankind appear not to know, is, that all rights are made at the expense of liberty—all laws by which rights are created or confirmed. No right without a correspondent obligation. Liberty, as against the coercion of the law, may, it is true, be given by the simple removal of the obligation by which that coercion was applied—by the simple repeal of the coercing law. But as against the coercion applicable by individual to individual, no liberty can be given to one man but in proportion as it is taken from another. All coercive laws, therefore (that is, all laws but constitutional laws and laws repealing or modifying coercive laws,) and in particular all laws creative of liberty are, as far as they go, abrogative of liberty. Not here and there a law only—not this or that possible law, but almost all laws, are therefore repugnant to these natural and imprescriptible rights, consequently null and void, calling for resistance and insurrection, and so on, as before.

Laws creative of rights of property are also struck at by the same anathema. How is property given? By restraining liberty; that is, by taking it away so far as is necessary for the purpose. How is your house made yours? By debarring every one else from the liberty of entering it without your leave.

2. *Property.* Property stands second on the list—proprietary rights are in the number of the natural and imprescriptible rights of man—of the rights which a man is not indebted for to the laws, and which cannot be taken from him by the laws. Men—that is, every man (for a general expression given without exception is an universal one) has a right to property, to proprietary rights, a *right which* cannot be taken away from him by the laws. To proprietary rights. Good: but in relation to what subject? for as to proprietary rights—without a subject to which they are referable—without a subject in or in relation to which they can be exercised—they will hardly be of much value, they will hardly be worth taking care of, with so much solemnity. In vain would all the laws in the world have ascertained that I have a right to something. If this be all they have done for me—if there be no specific subject in relation to which my proprietary rights are established, I must either take what I want without right, or starve. As there is no such subject specified with relation to each man, or to any man (indeed how could there be?) the necessary inference (taking the passage literally) is, that every man has all manner of proprietary rights with relation to every subject of property without exception: in a word, that every man has a right to every thing. Unfortunately, in most matters of property, what is every man's right is no man's right; so that the effect of this part of the oracle, if observed, would be, not to establish property, but to extinguish it—to render it impossible ever to be revived: and this is one of the rights declared to be imprescriptible.

It will probably be acknowledged, that according to this construction, the clause in question is equally ruinous and absurd—and hence the inference may be, that this was not the construction—this was not the meaning in view. But by the same rule, every possible construction which the words employed can admit of, might be proved not to have been the meaning in view nor is this clause a whit more absurd or ruinous than all that goes before it, and a great deal of what comes after it. And, in short, if this be not the meaning of it, what is? Give it a sense—give it any sense whatever,—it is mischievous—to save it from that imputation, there is but one course to take, which is to acknowledge it to be nonsense.

Thus much could be clear, if anything were clear in it, that according to this clause, whatever proprietary rights, whatever property a man once has, no matter how, being imprescriptible, can never be taken away from him by any law: or of what use or meaning is the clause? So that the moment it is acknowledged in relation to any article, that such article is my property, no matter how or when it became so, that moment it is acknowledged that it can never be taken away from me: therefore, for example, all laws and all judgments, whereby anything is taken away from me without my free consent—all taxes, for example, and all fines—are void, and, as such call for resistance and insurrection, and so forth, as before.

3. *Security*. Security stands the third on the list of these natural and imprescriptible rights which laws did not give, and which laws are not in any degree to be suffered to take away. Under the head of security, liberty might have been included, so likewise property: since security for liberty, or the enjoyment of liberty, may be spoken of as a branch of security—security for property, or the enjoyment of proprietary rights, as another. Security for person is the branch that seems here to have been understood—security for each man's person, as against all those hurtful or disagreeable impressions (exclusive of those which consist in the mere disturbance of the enjoyment of liberty,) by which a man is affected in his person; loss of life—loss of limbs—loss of the use of limbs—wounds, bruises, and the like. All laws are null and void then, which on any account or in any manner seek to expose the person of any man to any risk—which appoint capital or other corporal punishment—which expose a man to personal hazard in the service of the military power against foreign enemies, or in that of the judicial power against delinquents—all laws which, to preserve the country from pestilence, authorise the immediate execution of a suspected person, in the event of his transgressing certain bounds

4. *Resistance to oppression*. Fourth and last in the list of natural and imprescriptible rights, resistance to oppression—meaning, I suppose, the right to resist oppression. What is oppression? Power misapplied to the prejudice of some individual. What is it that a man has in view when he speaks of oppression? Some exertion of power which he looks upon as misapplied to the prejudice of some individual—to the producing on the part of such individual some sufferings to which (whether as forbidden by the laws or otherwise) we conceive he ought not to have been subjected. But against everything that can come under the name of oppression, provision has been already made, in the manner we have seen, by the recognition of the three preceding rights; since no oppression can fall upon a man which is not all infringement of his rights in relation to liberty, rights in relation to property, or rights in relation to security, as above described. Where, then, is the difference?—to what purpose this fourth clause after the three first? To this purpose: the mischief they seek to prevent, the rights they seek to establish are the same; the difference lies in the nature of the remedy endeavoured to be applied. To present the mischief in question, the endeavour of the three former clauses is, to tie the hand of the legislator and his subordinates, by the fear of nullity, and the remote apprehension of general resistance and insurrection. The aim of this fourth clause is to raise the hand of the individual concerned to prevent the apprehended infraction of his rights at the moment when he looks upon it as about to take place.

Whenever you are about to be oppressed, you have a right to resist oppression: whenever you conceive yourself to be oppressed, conceive yourself to have a right to make resistance, and act accordingly. In proportion as a law of any kind—any act of power, supreme or subordinate, legislative, administrative, or judicial, is unpleasant to a man, especially if, in consideration of such unpleasantness, his opinion is, that such act of power ought not to have been exercised, he of course looks upon it as oppression: as often as anything of this sort happens to a man—as often as anything happens to a man to inflame his passions—this article, for fear his passions should not be sufficiently inflamed of themselves, sets itself to work to blow the flame, and urges him to resistance. Submit not to any decree or other act of power, of the justice of which you are not yourself perfectly convinced. If a constable call upon you to serve in the militia, shoot the constable and not the enemy—if the commander of a press-gang trouble you, push him into the sea—if a bailiff, throw him out of the window. If a judge sentences you to be imprisoned or put to death, have a dagger ready, and take a stroke first at the judge.

DISCUSSION QUESTIONS

1. Bentham criticizes the notion of natural rights, saying that they are "nonsense upon stilts." Explain what you think he means.

2. What analysis of rights does Bentham offer? Evaluate and critically discuss his position.

3. When attacking the notion that we have natural property rights, Bentham comes to the conclusion that "every man has a right to every thing," and that in most matters, "what is every man's right is no man's right…" How does he reach this conclusion, and what exactly do you think he means by it? Critically evaluate his argument.

23

John Stuart Mill, selection from *Utilitarianism* (1863)

John Stuart Mill (1806–73) was a British thinker, writing in the areas of general philosophy, moral and political philosophy, and economics. His consequentialist moral theory—utilitarianism—derived much from the previous work of Jeremy Bentham (see reading 22 above). Mill developed and defended his own version of utilitarianism to significant acclaim and lasting effect. In the following selection, Mill provides an analysis of the terms "justice" and "rights," arguing that these concepts can be accommodated by utilitarianism.

SOURCE

Mill, John Stuart. *Utilitarianism* (13th Edition). The University of Chicago Press. Reprinted 1906.

On the Connection between Justice and Utility

In all ages of speculation, one of the strongest obstacles to the reception of the doctrine that Utility or Happiness is the criterion of right and wrong, has been drawn from the idea of *justice*. The powerful sentiment, and apparently clear perception, which that word recalls with a rapidity and certainty resembling an instinct, have seemed to the majority of thinkers to point to an inherent quality in things; to show that the just must have an existence in nature as something absolute, generically distinct from every variety of the expedient, and, in idea, opposed to it, though (as is commonly acknowledged) never, in the long run, disjoined from it in fact.

In the case of this, as of our other moral sentiments, there is no necessary connection between the question of its origin, and that of its binding force. That a feeling is bestowed on us by nature, does not necessarily legitimate all its promptings. The feeling of justice might be a peculiar instinct, and might yet require, like our other instincts, to be controlled and enlightened by a higher reason. If we have intellectual instincts, leading us to judge in a particular way, as well as animal instincts that prompt us to act in a particular way, there is no necessity that the former should be more infallible in their sphere than the latter in theirs: it may as well happen that wrong judgments are occasionally suggested by those, as wrong actions by these. But though it is one thing to believe that we have natural feelings of justice, and another to acknowledge them as an ultimate criterion of conduct, these two opinions are very closely connected in point of fact. Mankind are always predisposed to believe that any subjective feeling, not otherwise accounted for, is a revelation of some objective reality. Our present object is to determine whether the reality, to which the feeling of justice corresponds, is one which needs any such special revelation; whether the justice or injustice of an action is a thing intrinsically peculiar, and distinct from all its other qualities, or only a combination of certain of those qualities, presented under a peculiar aspect. For the purpose of this inquiry it is practically important to consider whether the feeling itself, of justice and injustice, is *sui generis* like our sensations of colour and taste, or a derivative feeling, formed by a combination of others. And this it is the more essential to examine, as people are in general willing enough to allow, that objectively the dictates of justice coincide with a part of the field of general expediency; but inasmuch as the subjective mental feeling of justice is different from that which commonly attaches to simple expediency, and, except in the extreme cases of the latter, is far more imperative in its demands, people find it difficult to see, in justice, only a particular kind or branch of general utility, and think that its superior binding force requires a totally different origin.

To throw light upon this question, it is necessary to attempt to ascertain what is the distinguishing character of justice, or of injustice: what is the quality, or whether there is any quality, attributed in common to all modes of conduct designated as unjust (for justice, like many other moral attributes, is best defined by its opposite), and distinguishing them from such modes of conduct as are disapproved, but without having that particular epithet of disapprobation applied to them. If in everything which men are accustomed to characterise as just or unjust, some one common attribute or collection of attributes is always present, we may judge whether this particular attribute or combination of attributes would be capable of gathering round it a

sentiment of that peculiar character and intensity by virtue of the general laws of our emotional constitution, or whether the sentiment is inexplicable, and requires to be regarded as a special provision of Nature. If we find the former to be the case, we shall, in resolving this question, have resolved also the main problem: if the latter, we shall have to seek for some other mode of investigating it.

To find the common attributes of a variety of objects, it is necessary to begin by surveying the objects themselves in the concrete. Let us therefore advert successively to the various modes of action, and arrangements of human affairs, which are classed, by universal or widely spread opinion, as Just or as Unjust. The things well known to excite the sentiments associated with those names are of a very multifarious character. I shall pass them rapidly in review, without studying any particular arrangement.

In the first place, it is mostly considered unjust to deprive any one of his personal liberty, his property, or any other thing which belongs to him by law. Here, therefore, is one instance of the application of the terms just and unjust in a perfectly definite sense, namely, that it is just to respect, unjust to violate, the *legal rights* of any one. But this judgment admits of several exceptions, arising from the other forms in which the notions of justice and injustice present themselves. For example, the person who suffers the deprivation may (as the phrase is) have *forfeited* the rights which he is so deprived of: a case to which we shall return presently. But also,

Secondly, the legal rights of which he is deprived, may be rights which *ought* not to have belonged to him; in other words, the law which confers on him these rights, may be a bad law. When it is so, or when (which is the same thing for our purpose) it is supposed to be so, opinions will differ as to the justice or injustice of infringing it. Some maintain that no law, however bad, ought to be disobeyed by an individual citizen; that his opposition to it, if shown at all, should only be shown in endeavouring to get it altered by competent authority. This opinion (which condemns many of the most illustrious benefactors of mankind, and would often protect pernicious institutions against the only weapons which, in the state of things existing at the time, have any chance of succeeding against them) is defended, by those who hold it, on grounds of expediency; principally on that of the importance, to the common interest of mankind, of maintaining inviolate the sentiment of submission to law. Other persons, again, hold the directly contrary opinion, that any law, judged to be bad, may blamelessly be disobeyed, even though it be not judged to be unjust, but only inexpedient; while others would confine the license of disobedience to the case of unjust laws: but again, some say, that all laws which are inexpedient are unjust; since every law imposes some restriction on the natural liberty of mankind, which restriction is an injustice, unless legitimated by tending to their good. Among these diversities of opinion, it seems to be universally admitted that there may be unjust laws, and that law, consequently, is not the ultimate criterion of justice, but may give to one person a benefit, or impose on another an evil, which justice condemns. When, however, a law is thought to be unjust, it seems always to be regarded as being so in the same way in which a breach of law is unjust, namely, by infringing somebody's right; which, as it cannot in this case be a legal right, receives a different appellation, and is called a moral right. We may say, therefore, that a second case of injustice consists in taking or withholding from any person that to which he has a *moral right*.

Thirdly, it is universally considered just that each person should obtain that (whether good or evil) which he *deserves*, and unjust that he should obtain a good, or be made to undergo an evil, which he does not deserve. This is, perhaps, the clearest and most emphatic form in which the idea of justice is conceived by the general mind. As it involves the notion of desert, the question arises, what constitutes desert? Speaking in a general way, a person is understood to deserve good if he does right, evil if he does wrong; and in a more particular sense, to deserve good from those to whom he does or has done good, and evil from those to whom he does or has done evil. The precept of returning good for evil has never been regarded as a case of the fulfilment of justice, but as one in which the claims of justice are waived, in obedience to other considerations.

Fourthly, it is confessedly unjust to *break faith* with any one: to violate an engagement, either express or implied, or disappoint expectations raised by our conduct, at least if we have raised those expectations knowingly and voluntarily. Like the other obligations of justice already spoken of, this one is not regarded as absolute, but as capable of being overruled by a stronger obligation of justice on the other side; or by such conduct on the part of the person concerned as is deemed to absolve us from our obligation to him, and to constitute a *forfeiture* of the benefit which he has been led to expect.

Fifthly, it is, by universal admission, inconsistent with justice to be *partial*; to show favour or preference to one person over another, in matters to which favour and preference do not properly apply. Impartiality, however, does not seem to be regarded as a duty in itself, but rather as instrumental to some other duty; for it is admitted that favour and preference are not always censurable, and indeed the cases in which they are condemned are rather the exception than the rule. A person would be more likely to be blamed than applauded for giving his family or friends no superiority in good offices over strangers, when he could do so without violating any other duty; and no one thinks it unjust to seek one person in preference to another as a friend, connection, or companion. Impartiality where rights are concerned is of course obligatory, but this is involved in the more general obligation of giving to every one his right. A tribunal, for example, must be impartial, because it is bound to award, without regard to any other consideration, a disputed object to the one of two parties who has the right to it. There are other cases in which impartiality means, being solely influenced by desert; as with those who, in the capacity of judges, preceptors, or parents, administer reward and punishment as such. There are cases, again, in which it means, being solely influenced by consideration for the public interest; as in making a selection among candidates for a government employment. Impartiality, in short, as an obligation of justice, may be said to mean, being exclusively influenced by the considerations which it is supposed ought to influence the particular case in hand; and resisting the solicitation of any motives which prompt to conduct different from what those considerations would dictate.

Nearly allied to the idea of impartiality is that of *equality*; which often enters as a component part both into the conception of justice and into the practice of it, and, in the eyes of many persons, constitutes its essence. But in this, still more than in any other case, the notion of justice varies in different persons, and always conforms in its variations to their notion of utility. Each person maintains that equality is the dictate of justice, except where he thinks that expediency requires inequality. The justice of giving equal protection to the rights of all, is maintained by those who support the most outrageous inequality in the rights themselves. Even in slave countries it is theoretically admitted that the rights of the slave, such as they are, ought to be as sacred as those of the master; and that a tribunal which fails to enforce them with equal strictness is wanting in justice; while, at the same time, institutions which leave to the slave scarcely any rights to enforce, are not deemed unjust, because they are not deemed inexpedient. Those who think that utility requires distinctions of rank, do not consider it unjust that riches and social privileges should be unequally dispensed; but those who think this inequality inexpedient, think it unjust also. Whoever thinks that government is necessary, sees no injustice in as much inequality as is constituted by giving to the magistrate powers not granted to other people. Even among those who hold levelling doctrines, there are as many questions of justice as there are differences of opinion about expediency. Some Communists consider it unjust that the produce of the labour of the community should be shared on any other principle than that of exact equality; others think it just that those should receive most whose wants are greatest; while others hold that those who work harder, or who produce more, or whose services are more valuable to the community, may justly claim a larger quota in the division of the produce. And the sense of natural justice may be plausibly appealed to in behalf of every one of these opinions.

Among so many diverse applications of the term "justice," which yet is not regarded as ambiguous, it is a matter of some difficulty to seize the mental link which holds them together, and on which the moral sentiment adhering to the term essentially depends. Perhaps, in this embarrassment, some help may be derived from the history of the word, as indicated by its etymology.

In most, if not in all, languages, the etymology of the word which corresponds to "just," points distinctly to an origin connected with the ordinances of law. *Justum* [in Latin] is a form of *jussum*, that which has been ordered. *Dikaion* [in Greek] comes directly from *dikē*, a suit at law. *Recht* [in German], from which came right and righteous, is synonymous with law. The courts of justice, the administration of justice, are the courts and the administration of law. *La justice*, in French, is the established term for judicature. I am not committing the fallacy imputed with some show of truth to Horne Tooke,[1] of assuming that a word must still continue to mean what it originally meant. Etymology is slight evidence of what the idea now signified is, but the very best evidence of how it sprang up. There can, I think, be no doubt that the *idée mère*, the primitive element, in the formation of the notion of justice, was conformity to law. It constituted the entire idea among the Hebrews, up to the birth of Christianity; as might be expected in the case of a people whose laws attempted to embrace all subjects on which precepts were required, and who believed those laws to be a direct emanation from the Supreme Being. But other nations, and in particular the Greeks and Romans, who knew that their laws had been made originally, and still continued to be made, by men, were not afraid to admit that those men might make bad laws; might do, by

---

[1] [John Horne Tooke (1736–1812) was a British politician and philologist.]

law, the same things, and from the same motives, which if done by individuals without the sanction of law, would be called unjust. And hence the sentiment of injustice came to be attached, not to all violations of law, but only to violations of such laws as ought to exist, including such as *ought* to exist, but do not; and to laws themselves, if supposed to be contrary to what ought to be law. In this manner the idea of law and of its injunctions was still predominant in the notion of justice, even when the laws actually in force ceased to be accepted as the standard of it.

It is true that mankind consider the idea of justice and its obligations as applicable to many things which neither are, nor is it desired that they should be, regulated by law. Nobody desires that laws should interfere with the whole detail of private life; yet every one allows that in all daily conduct a person may and does show himself to be either just or unjust. But even here, the idea of the breach of what ought to be law, still lingers in a modified shape. It would always give us pleasure, and chime in with our feelings of fitness, that acts which we deem unjust should be punished, though we do not always think it expedient that this should be done by the tribunals. We forego that gratification on account of incidental inconveniences. We should be glad to see just conduct enforced and injustice repressed, even in the minutest details, if we were not, with reason, afraid of trusting the magistrate with so unlimited an amount of power over individuals. When we think that a person is bound in justice to do a thing, it is an ordinary form of language to say, that he ought to be compelled to do it. We should be gratified to see the obligation enforced by anybody who had the power. If we see that its enforcement by law would be inexpedient, we lament the impossibility, we consider the impunity given to injustice as an evil, and strive to make amends for it by bringing a strong expression of our own and the public disapprobation to bear upon the offender. Thus the idea of legal constraint is still the generating idea of the notion of justice, though undergoing several transformations before that notion, as it exists in an advanced state of society, becomes complete.

The above is, I think, a true account, as far as it goes, of the origin and progressive growth of the idea of justice. But we must observe, that it contains, as yet, nothing to distinguish that obligation from moral obligation in general. For the truth is, that the idea of penal sanction, which is the essence of law, enters not only into the conception of injustice, but into that of any kind of wrong. We do not call anything wrong, unless we mean to imply that a person ought to be punished in some way or other for doing it; if not by law, by the opinion of his fellow-creatures; if not by opinion, by the reproaches of his own conscience. This seems the real turning point of the distinction between morality and simple expediency. It is a part of the notion of Duty in every one of its forms, that a person may rightfully be compelled to fulfil it. Duty is a thing which may be *exacted* from a person, as one exacts a debt. Unless we think that it may be exacted from him, we do not call it his duty. Reasons of prudence, or the interest of other people, may militate against actually exacting it; but the person himself, it is clearly understood, would not be entitled to complain. There are other things, on the contrary, which we wish that people should do, which we like or admire them for doing, perhaps dislike or despise them for not doing, but yet admit that they are not bound to do; it is not a case of moral obligation; we do not blame them, that is, we do not think that they are proper objects of punishment. How we come by these ideas of deserving and not deserving punishment, will appear, perhaps, in the sequel; but I think there is no doubt that this distinction lies at the bottom of the notions of right and wrong; that we call any conduct wrong, or employ, instead, some other term of dislike or disparagement, according as we think that the person ought, or ought not, to be punished for it; and we say, it would be right, to do so and so, or merely that it would be desirable or laudable, according as we would wish to see the person whom it concerns, compelled, or only persuaded and exhorted, to act in that manner.

This, therefore, being the characteristic difference which marks off, not justice, but morality in general, from the remaining provinces of expediency and worthiness; the character is still to be sought which distinguishes justice from other branches of morality. Now it is known that ethical writers divide moral duties into two classes, denoted by the ill-chosen expressions, duties of perfect and of imperfect obligation; the latter being those in which, though the act is obligatory, the particular occasions of performing it are left to our choice— as in the case of charity or beneficence, which we are indeed bound to practise, but not towards any definite person, nor at any prescribed time. In the more precise language of philosophic jurists, duties of perfect obligation are those duties in virtue of which a correlative *right* resides in some person or persons; duties of imperfect obligation are those moral obligations which do not give birth to any right. I think it will be found that this distinction exactly coincides with that which exists between justice and the other obligations of morality. In our survey of the various popular acceptations of justice, the term appeared generally to involve the idea of a personal right—a claim on the part of one or more individuals, like that which the law gives when it confers a proprietary or other legal right. Whether the injustice consists in depriving a person of a possession, or in breaking faith with him, or in treating him worse than he deserves, or worse than other people who have no greater claims, in each case the supposition implies two things—a wrong done, and some assignable person who is wronged. Injustice may also be done by treating a person better than others; but the wrong in this case is to his competitors, who are also assignable persons.

It seems to me that this feature in the case—a right in some person, correlative to the moral obligation—constitutes the specific difference between justice, and generosity or beneficence. Justice implies something which it is not only right to do, and wrong not to do, but which some individual person can claim from us as his moral right. No one has a moral right to our generosity or beneficence, because we are not morally bound to practise those virtues towards any given individual. And it will be found with respect to this, as to every correct

definition, that the instances which seem to conflict with it are those which most confirm it. For if a moralist attempts, as some have done, to make out that mankind generally, though not any given individual, have a right to all the good we can do them, he at once, by that thesis, includes generosity and beneficence within the category of justice. He is obliged to say, that our utmost exertions are *due* to our fellow creatures, thus assimilating them to a debt; or that nothing less can be a sufficient *return* for what society does for us, thus classing the case as one of gratitude; both of which are acknowledged cases of justice. Wherever there is right, the case is one of justice, and not of the virtue of beneficence: and whoever does not place the distinction between justice and morality in general, where we have now placed it, will be found to make no distinction between them at all, but to merge all morality in justice.

Having thus endeavoured to determine the distinctive elements which enter into the composition of the idea of justice, we are ready to enter on the inquiry, whether the feeling, which accompanies the idea, is attached to it by a special dispensation of nature, or whether it could have grown up, by any known laws, out of the idea itself; and in particular, whether it can have originated in considerations of general expediency.

I conceive that the sentiment itself does not arise from anything which would commonly, or correctly, be termed an idea of expediency; but that though the sentiment does not, whatever is moral in it does.

We have seen that the two essential ingredients in the sentiment of justice are, the desire to punish a person who has done harm, and the knowledge or belief that there is some definite individual or individuals to whom harm has been done.

Now it appears to me, that the desire to punish a person who has done harm to some individual is a spontaneous outgrowth from two sentiments, both in the highest degree natural, and which either are or resemble instincts; the impulse of self-defence, and the feeling of sympathy.

It is natural to resent, and to repel or retaliate, any harm done or attempted against ourselves, or against those with whom we sympathise. The origin of this sentiment it is not necessary here to discuss. Whether it be an instinct or a result of intelligence, it is, we know, common to all animal nature; for every animal tries to hurt those who have hurt, or who it thinks are about to hurt, itself or its young. Human beings, on this point, only differ from other animals in two particulars. First, in being capable of sympathising, not solely with their offspring, or, like some of the more noble animals, with some superior animal who is kind to them, but with all human, and even with all sentient, beings. Secondly, in having a more developed intelligence, which gives a wider range to the whole of their sentiments, whether self-regarding or sympathetic. By virtue of his superior intelligence, even apart from his superior range of sympathy, a human being is capable of apprehending a community of interest between himself and the human society of which he forms a part, such that any conduct which threatens the security of the society generally, is threatening to his own, and calls forth his instinct (if instinct it be) of self-defence. The same superiority of intelligence joined to the power of sympathising with human beings generally, enables him to attach himself to the collective idea of his tribe, his country, or mankind, in such a manner that any act hurtful to them, raises his instinct of sympathy, and urges him to resistance.

The sentiment of justice, in that one of its elements which consists of the desire to punish, is thus, I conceive, the natural feeling of retaliation or vengeance, rendered by intellect and sympathy applicable to those injuries, that is, to those hurts, which wound us through, or in common with, society at large. This sentiment, in itself, has nothing moral in it; what is moral is, the exclusive subordination of it to the social sympathies, so as to wait on and obey their call. For the natural feeling would make us resent indiscriminately whatever any one does that is disagreeable to us; but when moralised by the social feeling, it only acts in the directions conformable to the general good: just persons resenting a hurt to society, though not otherwise a hurt to themselves, and not resenting a hurt to themselves, however painful, unless it be of the kind which society has a common interest with them in the repression of.

It is no objection against this doctrine to say, that when we feel our sentiment of justice outraged, we are not thinking of society at large, or of any collective interest, but only of the individual case. It is common enough certainly, though the reverse of commendable, to feel resentment merely because we have suffered pain; but a person whose resentment is really a moral feeling, that is, who considers whether an act is blamable before he allows himself to resent it—such a person, though he may not say expressly to himself that he is standing up for the interest of society, certainly does feel that he is asserting a rule which is for the benefit of others as well as for his own. If he is not feeling this—if he is regarding the act solely as it affects him individually—he is not consciously just; he is not concerning himself about the justice of his actions. This is admitted even by anti-utilitarian moralists. When Kant ... propounds as the fundamental principle of morals, "So act, that thy rule of conduct might be adopted as a law by all rational beings," he virtually acknowledges that the interest of mankind collectively, or at least of mankind indiscriminately, must be in the mind of the agent when conscientiously deciding on the morality of the act. Otherwise he uses words without a meaning: for, that a rule even of utter selfishness could not *possibly* be adopted by all rational beings—that there is any insuperable obstacle in the nature of things to its adoption— cannot be even plausibly maintained. To give any meaning to Kant's principle, the sense put upon it must be, that we ought to shape our conduct by a rule which all rational beings might adopt *with benefit to their collective interest.*

To recapitulate: the idea of justice supposes two things; a rule of conduct, and a sentiment which sanctions the rule. The first must be supposed common to all mankind, and intended for their good. The other (the sentiment) is a desire that punishment may be suffered by those who infringe the rule. There is involved, in addition, the conception of some definite person who suffers by the infringement; whose rights (to use the expression appropriated to the case) are violated by it. And the sentiment of justice appears to me to be, the animal desire to repel or retaliate a hurt or damage to oneself, or to those with whom one sympathises, widened so as to include all persons, by the human capacity of enlarged sympathy, and the human conception of intelligent self-interest. From the latter elements, the feeling derives its morality; from the former, its peculiar impressiveness, and energy of self-assertion.

I have, throughout, treated the idea of a *right* residing in the injured person, and violated by the injury, not as a separate element in the composition of the idea and sentiment, but as one of the forms in which the other two elements clothe themselves. These elements are: a hurt to some assignable person or persons on the one hand, and a demand for punishment on the other. An examination of our own minds, I think, will show, that these two things include all that we mean when we speak of violation of a right. When we call anything a person's right, we mean that he has a valid claim on society to protect him in the possession of it, either by the force of law, or by that of education and opinion. If he has what we consider a sufficient claim, on whatever account, to have something guaranteed to him by society, we say that he has a right to it. If we desire to prove that anything does not belong to him by right, we think this done as soon as it is admitted that society ought not to take measures for securing it to him, but should leave him to chance, or to his own exertions. Thus, a person is said to have a right to what he can earn in fair professional competition; because society ought not to allow any other person to hinder him from endeavouring to earn in that manner as much as he can. But he has not a right to three hundred a year, though he may happen to be earning it; because society is not called on to provide that he shall earn that sum. On the contrary, if he owns ten thousand pounds three per cent stock, he *has* a right to three hundred a year; because society has come under an obligation to provide him with an income of that amount.

To have a right, then, is, I conceive, to have something which society ought to defend me in the possession of. If the objector goes on to ask, why it ought? I can give him no other reason than general utility. If that expression does not seem to convey a sufficient feeling of the strength of the obligation, nor to account for the peculiar energy of the feeling, it is because there goes to the composition of the sentiment, not a rational only, but also an animal element, the thirst for retaliation; and this thirst derives its intensity, as well as its moral justification, from the extraordinarily important and impressive kind of utility which is concerned. The interest involved is that of security, to every one's feelings the most vital of all interests. All other earthly benefits are needed by one person, not needed by another; and many of them can, if necessary, be cheerfully foregone, or replaced by something else; but security no human being can possibly do without; on it we depend for all our immunity from evil, and for the whole value of all and every good, beyond the passing moment; since nothing but the gratification of the instant could be of any worth to us, if we could be deprived of anything the next instant by whoever was momentarily stronger than ourselves. Now this most indispensable of all necessaries, after physical nutriment, cannot be had, unless the machinery for providing it is kept unintermittedly in active play. Our notion, therefore, of the claim we have on our fellow-creatures to join in making safe for us the very groundwork of our existence, gathers feelings around it so much more intense than those concerned in any of the more common cases of utility, that the difference in degree (as is often the case in psychology) becomes a real difference in kind. The claim assumes that character of absoluteness, that apparent infinity, and incommensurability with all other considerations, which constitute the distinction between the feeling of right and wrong and that of ordinary expediency and inexpediency. The feelings concerned are so powerful, and we count so positively on finding a responsive feeling in others (all being alike interested), that *ought* and *should* grow into *must*, and recognised indispensability becomes a moral necessity, analogous to physical, and often not inferior to it in binding force exhorted.

If the preceding analysis, or something resembling it, be not the correct account of the notion of justice; if justice be totally independent of utility, and be a standard *per se*, which the mind can recognise by simple introspection of itself; it is hard to understand why that internal oracle is so ambiguous, and why so many things appear either just or unjust, according to the light in which they are regarded.

We are continually informed that utility is an uncertain standard, which every different person interprets differently, and that there is no safety but in the immutable, ineffaceable, and unmistakable dictates of justice, which carry their evidence in themselves, and are independent of the fluctuations of opinion. One would suppose from this that on questions of justice there could be no controversy; that if we take that for our rule, its application to any given case could leave us in as little doubt as a mathematical demonstration. So far is this from being the fact, that there is as much difference of opinion, and as much discussion, about what is just, as about what is useful to society. Not only have different nations and individuals different notions of justice, but in the mind of one and the same individual, justice is not some one rule, principle, or maxim, but many, which do not always coincide in their dictates, and in choosing between which, he is guided either by some extraneous standard, or by his own personal predilections.

For instance, there are some who say, that it is unjust to punish any one for the sake of example to others; that punishment is just, only when intended for the good of the sufferer himself. Others maintain the extreme reverse, contending that to punish persons who have attained years of discretion, for their own benefit, is despotism and injustice, since if the matter at issue is solely their own good, no one has a right to control their own judgment of it; but that they may justly be punished to prevent evil to others, this being the exercise of the legitimate right of self-defence. Mr. Owen,[1] again, affirms that it is unjust to punish at all; for the criminal did not make his own character; his education, and the circumstances which surrounded him, have made him a criminal, and for these he is not responsible. All these opinions are extremely plausible; and so long as the question is argued as one of justice simply, without going down to the principles which lie under justice and are the source of its authority, I am unable to see how any of these reasoners can be refuted. For in truth every one of the three builds upon rules of justice confessedly true. The first appeals to the acknowledged injustice of singling out an individual, and making a sacrifice, without his consent, for other people's benefit. The second relies on the acknowledged justice of self-defence, and the admitted injustice of forcing one person to conform to another's notions of what constitutes his good. The Owenite invokes the admitted principle that it is unjust to punish any one for what he cannot help. Each is triumphant so long as he is not compelled to take into consideration any other maxims of justice than the one he has selected; but as soon as their several maxims are brought face to face, each disputant seems to have exactly as much to say for himself as the others. No one of them can carry out his own notion of justice without trampling upon another equally binding.

These are difficulties; they have always been felt to be such; and many devices have been invented to turn rather than to overcome them. As a refuge from the last of the three, men imagined what they called the freedom of the will; fancying that they could not justify punishing a man whose will is in a thoroughly hateful state, unless it be supposed to have come into that state through no influence of anterior circumstances. To escape from the other difficulties, a favourite contrivance has been the fiction of a contract, whereby at some unknown

---

[1] [Robert Owen (1771–1858) was a British social theorist who advocated communitarian living. He and his followers founded several communitarian societies in both Britain and the United States.]

period all the members of society engaged to obey the laws, and consented to be punished for any disobedience to them, thereby giving to their legislators the right, which it is assumed they would not otherwise have had, of punishing them, either for their own good or for that of society. This happy thought was considered to get rid of the whole difficulty, and to legitimate the infliction of punishment, in virtue of another received maxim of justice, *Volenti non fit injuria*—that is not unjust which is done with the consent of the person who is supposed to be hurt by it. I need hardly remark, that even if the consent were not a mere fiction, this maxim is not superior in authority to the others which it is brought in to supersede. It is, on the contrary, an instructive specimen of the loose and irregular manner in which supposed principles of justice grow up. This particular one evidently came into use as a help to the coarse exigencies of courts of law, which are sometimes obliged to be content with very uncertain presumptions, on account of the greater evils which would often arise from any attempt on their part to cut finer. But even courts of law are not able to adhere consistently to the maxim, for they allow voluntary engagements to be set aside on the ground of fraud, and sometimes on that of mere mistake or misinformation.

Again, when the legitimacy of inflicting punishment is admitted, how many conflicting conceptions of justice come to light in discussing the proper apportionment of punishments to offences. No rule on the subject recommends itself so strongly to the primitive and spontaneous sentiment of justice, as the *lex talionis*, an eye for an eye and a tooth for a tooth. Though this principle of the Jewish and of the Mahommedan law has been generally abandoned in Europe as a practical maxim, there is, I suspect, in most minds, a secret hankering after it; and when retribution accidentally falls on an offender in that precise shape, the general feeling of satisfaction evinced bears witness how natural is the sentiment to which this repayment in kind is acceptable. With many, the test of justice in penal infliction is that the punishment should be proportioned to the offence; meaning that it should be

exactly measured by the moral guilt of the culprit (whatever be their standard for measuring moral guilt)—the consideration, what amount of punishment is necessary to deter from the offence, having nothing to do with the question of justice, in their estimation: while there are others to whom that consideration is all in all; who maintain that it is not just, at least for man, to inflict on a fellow creature, whatever may be his offences, any amount of suffering beyond the least that will suffice to prevent him from repeating, and others from imitating, his misconduct.

To take another example from a subject already once referred to. In a cooperative industrial association, is it just or not that talent or skill should give a title to superior remuneration? On the negative side of the question it is argued, that whoever does the best he can, deserves equally well, and ought not in justice to be put in a position of inferiority for no fault of his own; that superior abilities have already advantages more than enough, in the admiration they excite, the personal influence they command, and the internal sources of satisfaction attending them, without adding to these a superior share of the world's goods; and that society is bound in justice rather to make compensation to the less favoured, for this unmerited inequality of advantages, than to aggravate it. On the contrary side it is contended, that society receives more from the more efficient labourer; that his services being more useful, society owes him a larger return for them; that a greater share of the joint result is actually his work, and not to allow his claim to it is a kind of robbery; that if he is only to receive as much as others, he can only be justly required to produce as much, and to give a smaller amount of time and exertion, proportioned to his superior efficiency. Who shall decide between these appeals to conflicting principles of justice? Justice has in this case two sides to it, which it is impossible to bring into harmony, and the two disputants have chosen opposite sides; the one looks to what it is just that the individual should receive, the other to what it is just that the community should give. Each, from his own point of view, is unanswerable; and any choice between them, on grounds of justice, must be perfectly arbitrary. Social utility alone can decide the preference.

How many, again, and how irreconcilable, are the standards of justice to which reference is made in discussing the repartition of taxation. One opinion is, that payment to the State should be in numerical proportion to pecuniary means. Others think that justice dictates what they term graduated taxation; taking a higher percentage from those who have more to spare. In point of natural justice a strong case might be made for disregarding means altogether, and taking the same absolute sum (whenever it could be got) from every one: as the subscribers to a mess, or to a club, all pay the same sum for the same privileges, whether they can all equally afford it or not. Since the protection (it might be said) of law and government is afforded to, and is equally required by all, there is no injustice in making all buy it at the same price. It is reckoned justice, not injustice, that a dealer should charge to all customers the same price for the same article, not a price varying according to their means of payment. This doctrine, as applied to taxation, finds no advocates, because it conflicts so strongly with man's feelings of humanity and of social expediency; but the principle of justice which it invokes is as true and as binding as those which can be appealed to against it. Accordingly it exerts a tacit influence on the line of defence employed for other modes of assessing taxation. People feel obliged to argue that the State does more for the rich than for the poor, as a justification for its taking more from them: though this is in reality not true, for the rich would be far better able to protect themselves, in the absence of law or government, than the poor, and indeed would probably be successful in converting the poor into their slaves. Others, again, so far defer to the same conception of justice, as to maintain that all should pay an equal capitation tax for the protection of their persons (these being of equal value to all), and an unequal tax for the protection of their property, which is unequal. To this others reply, that the all of one man is as valuable to him as the all of another. From these confusions there is no other mode of extrication than the utilitarian.

Is, then, the difference between the just and the expedient a merely imaginary distinction? Have mankind been under a delusion in thinking that justice is a more sacred thing than policy, and that the latter ought only to be listened to after the former has been satisfied? By no means. The exposition we have given of the nature and origin of the sentiment, recognises a real distinction; and no one of those who profess the most sublime contempt for the consequences of actions as an element in their morality, attaches more importance to the distinction than I do. While I dispute the pretensions of any theory which sets up an imaginary standard of justice not grounded on utility, I account the justice which is grounded on utility to be the chief part, and incomparably the most sacred and binding part, of all morality. Justice is a name for certain classes of moral rules, which concern the essentials of human well-being more nearly, and are therefore of more absolute obligation, than any other rules for the guidance of life; and the notion which we have found to be of the essence of the idea of justice, that of a right residing in an individual implies and testifies to this more binding obligation.

The moral rules which forbid mankind to hurt one another (in which we must never forget to include wrongful interference with each other's freedom) are more vital to human well-being than any maxims, however important, which only point out the best mode of managing some department of human affairs. They have also the peculiarity, that they are the main element in determining the whole of the social feelings of mankind. It is their observance which alone preserves peace among human beings: if obedience to them were not the rule, and disobedience the exception, every one would see in every one else an enemy, against whom he must be perpetually guarding himself. What is hardly less important, these are the precepts which mankind have the strongest and the most direct inducements for impressing upon one another. By merely giving to each other prudential instruction or exhortation, they may gain, or think they gain, nothing: in inculcating on each other the duty of positive beneficence they have an unmistakable interest, but far less in

degree: a person may possibly not need the benefits of others; but he always needs that they should
not do him hurt. Thus the moralities which protect every individual from being harmed by others,
either directly or by being hindered in his freedom
of pursuing his own good, are at once those which
he himself has most at heart, and those which he
has the strongest interest in publishing and enforcing by word and deed. It is by a person's observance of these that his fitness to exist as one of the
fellowship of human beings is tested and decided;
for on that depends his being a nuisance or not to
those with whom he is in contact. Now it is these
moralities primarily which compose the obligations
of justice. The most marked cases of injustice, and
those which give the tone to the feeling of repugnance which characterises the sentiment, are acts of
wrongful aggression, or wrongful exercise of power
over some one; the next are those which consist in
wrongfully withholding from him something which
is his due; in both cases, inflicting on him a positive hurt, either in the form of direct suffering, or
of the privation of some good which he had reasonable ground, either of a physical or of a social
kind, for counting upon.

The same powerful motives which command the
observance of these primary moralities, enjoin the
punishment of those who violate them; and as the
impulses of self-defence, of defence of others, and of
vengeance, are all called forth against such persons,
retribution, or evil for evil, becomes closely connected with the sentiment of justice, and is universally included in the idea. Good for good is also one
of the dictates of justice; and this, though its social
utility is evident, and though it carries with it a natural human feeling, has not at first sight that obvious connection with hurt or injury, which, existing
in the most elementary cases of just and unjust, is
the source of the characteristic intensity of the sentiment. But the connection, though less obvious, is
not less real. He who accepts benefits, and denies
a return of them when needed, inflicts a real hurt,
by disappointing one of the most natural and reasonable of expectations, and one which he must at
least tacitly have encouraged, otherwise the benefits

would seldom have been conferred. The important
rank, among human evils and wrongs, of the disappointment of expectation, is shown in the fact that
it constitutes the principal criminality of two such
highly immoral acts as a breach of friendship and a
breach of promise. Few hurts which human beings
can sustain are greater, and none wound more, than
when that on which they habitually and with full
assurance relied, fails them in the hour of need; and
few wrongs are greater than this mere withholding of good; none excite more resentment, either in
the person suffering, or in a sympathising spectator. The principle, therefore, of giving to each what
they deserve, that is, good for good as well as evil
for evil, is not only included within the idea of justice as we have defined it, but is a proper object of
that intensity of sentiment, which places the just,
in human estimation, above the simply expedient.

Most of the maxims of justice current in the
world, and commonly appealed to in its transactions, are simply instrumental to carrying into effect
the principles of justice which we have now spoken of. That a person is only responsible for what
he has done voluntarily, or could voluntarily have
avoided; that it is unjust to condemn any person
unheard; that the punishment ought to be proportioned to the offence, and the like, are maxims
intended to prevent the just principle of evil for evil
from being perverted to the infliction of evil without that justification. The greater part of these common maxims have come into use from the practice
of courts of justice, which have been naturally led
to a more complete recognition and elaboration
than was likely to suggest itself to others, of the
rules necessary to enable them to fulfil their double function, of inflicting punishment when due,
and of awarding to each person his right.

That first of judicial virtues, impartiality, is an
obligation of justice, partly for the reason last mentioned; as being a necessary condition of the fulfilment of the other obligations of justice. But this
is not the only source of the exalted rank, among
human obligations, of those maxims of equality and
impartiality, which, both in popular estimation and
in that of the most enlightened, are included among

the precepts of justice. In one point of view, they may be considered as corollaries from the principles already laid down. If it is a duty to do to each according to his deserts, returning good for good as well as repressing evil by evil, it necessarily follows that we should treat all equally well (when no higher duty forbids) who have deserved equally well of us, and that society should treat all equally well who have deserved equally well of it, that is, who have deserved equally well absolutely. This is the highest abstract standard of social and distributive justice; towards which all institutions, and the efforts of all virtuous citizens, should be made in the utmost possible degree to converge.

But this great moral duty rests upon a still deeper foundation, being a direct emanation from the first principle of morals, and not a mere logical corollary from secondary or derivative doctrines. It is involved in the very meaning of Utility, or the Greatest Happiness Principle. That principle is a mere form of words without rational signification, unless one person's happiness, supposed equal in degree (with the proper allowance made for kind), is counted for exactly as much as another's. Those conditions being supplied, Bentham's dictum, "everybody to count for one, nobody for more than one," might be written under the principle of utility as an explanatory commentary. The equal claim of everybody to happiness in the estimation of the moralist and the legislator, involves an equal claim to all the means of happiness, except in so far as the inevitable conditions of human life, and the general interest, in which that of every individual is included, set limits to the maxim; and those limits ought to be strictly construed. As every other maxim of justice, so this is by no means applied or held applicable universally; on the contrary, as I have already remarked, it bends to every person's ideas of social expediency. But in whatever case it is deemed applicable at all, it is held to be the dictate of justice. All persons are deemed to have a *right* to equality of treatment, except when some recognised social expediency requires the reverse. And hence all social inequalities which have ceased to be considered expedient, assume the character not of simple inexpediency, but of injustice, and appear so tyrannical, that people are apt to wonder how they ever could have been tolerated; forgetful that they themselves perhaps tolerate other inequalities under an equally mistaken notion of expediency, the correction of which would make that which they approve seem quite as monstrous as what they have at last learnt to condemn. The entire history of social improvement has been a series of transitions, by which one custom or institution after another, from being a supposed primary necessity of social existence, has passed into the rank of a universally stigmatised injustice and tyranny. So it has been with the distinctions of slaves and freemen, nobles and serfs, patricians and plebeians; and so it will be, and in part already is, with the aristocracies of colour, race, and sex.

It appears from what has been said, that justice is a name for certain moral requirements, which, regarded collectively, stand higher in the scale of social utility, and are therefore of more paramount obligation, than any others; though particular cases may occur in which some other social duty is so important, as to overrule any one of the general maxims of justice. Thus, to save a life, it may not only be allowable, but a duty, to steal, or take by force, the necessary food or medicine, or to kidnap, and compel to officiate, the only qualified medical practitioner. In such cases, as we do not call anything justice which is not a virtue, we usually say, not that justice must give way to some other moral principle, but that what is just in ordinary cases is, by reason of that other principle, not just in the particular case. By this useful accommodation of language, the character of indefeasibility attributed to justice is kept up, and we are saved from the necessity of maintaining that there can be laudable injustice.

The considerations which have now been adduced resolve, I conceive, the only real difficulty in the utilitarian theory of morals. It has always been evident that all cases of justice are also cases of expediency: the difference is in the peculiar sentiment which attaches to the former, as contradistinguished from the latter. If this characteristic sentiment has been sufficiently accounted for; if there is no necessity to assume for it any peculiarity of origin; if it is simply the natural feeling of resentment, moralised by being made coextensive with the demands of social good; and if this feeling not only does but ought to exist in all the classes of cases to which the idea of justice corresponds; that idea no longer presents itself as a stumbling-block to the utilitarian ethics.

Justice remains the appropriate name for certain social utilities which are vastly more important, and therefore more absolute and imperative, than any others are as a class (though not more so than others may be in particular cases); and which, therefore, ought to be, as well as naturally are, guarded by a sentiment not only different in degree, but also in kind; distinguished from the milder feeling which attaches to the mere idea of promoting human pleasure or convenience, at once by the more definite nature of its commands, and by the sterner character of its sanctions.

DISCUSSION QUESTIONS

1. In this selection Mill offers what he takes to be the two "essential ingredients" in our idea (or "sentiment," as he calls it) of justice. What are these ingredients? Do you agree with Mill's evaluation? Why or why not?

2. What is Mill's final analysis of the terms "justice" and "rights"? How do these analyses fit into his broader utilitarian commitments? Critically evaluate his analysis.

3. According to Mill, are rights defeasible? Explain your answer.

4. Does Mill think it is ever permissible to violate the rules of justice? Given his utilitarianism, is it possible for Mill to consistently answer "No" to this question? Why or why not?

24

H.L.A. Hart, "Are There Any Natural Rights?" (1955)

In this selection, Hart discusses the concept of a natural right, arguing that the claim that we possess moral rights implies that we have a natural right to be free. On Hart, see reading 20 above.

SOURCE

Hart, H.L.A. "Are There Any Natural Rights?" *Philosophical Review*, Volume 64, Number 2, April 1955. Published by Duke University Press.

I shall advance the thesis[1] that if there are any moral rights at all, it follows that there is at least one natural right, the equal right of all men to be free. By saying that there is this right, I mean that in the absence of certain special conditions which are consistent with the right being an equal right, any adult human being capable of choice (1) has the right to forbearance on the part of all others from the use of coercion or restraint against him save to hinder coercion or restraint and (2) is at liberty to do (i.e., is under no obligation to abstain from) any action which is not one coercing or restraining or designed to injure other persons.

I have two reasons for describing the equal right of all men to be free as a *natural* right; both of them were always emphasized by the classical theorists of natural rights, (1) This right is one which all men have if they are capable of choice; they have it *qua* men and not only if they are members of some society or stand in some special relation to each other. (2) This right is not created or conferred by men's voluntary action; other moral rights are. Of course, it is quite obvious that my thesis is not as ambitious as the traditional theories of natural rights; for although on my view all men are *equally* entitled to be free in the sense explained, no man has an absolute or unconditional right to do or not

---

[1] I was first stimulated to think along these lines by Mr. Stuart Hampshire, and I have reached by different routes a conclusion similar to his.

to do any particular thing or to be treated in any particular way; coercion or restraint of any action may be justified in special conditions consistent with the general principle. So my argument will not show that men have any right (save the equal right of all to be free) which is "absolute," "indefeasible," or "imprescriptible." This may for many reduce the importance of my contention, but I think that the principle that all men have an equal right to be free, meager as it may seem, is probably all that the political philosophers of the liberal tradition need have claimed to support any program of action even if they have claimed more. But my contention that there is this one natural right may appear unsatisfying in another respect; it is only the conditional assertion that *if* there are any moral rights then there must be this one natural right. Perhaps few would now deny, as some have, that there are moral rights … But it is still important to remember that there may be codes of conduct quite properly termed moral codes (though we can of course say they are "imperfect") which do not employ the notion of *a* right, and there is nothing contradictory or otherwise absurd in a code or morality consisting wholly of prescriptions or in a code which prescribed only what should be done for the realization of happiness or some ideal of personal perfection. Human actions in such systems would be evaluated or criticized as compliances with prescriptions or as *good* or *bad*, *right* or *wrong*, *wise* or *foolish*, *fitting* or *unfitting*, but no one in such a system would have, exercise, or claim rights, or violate or infringe them. So those who lived by such systems could not of course be committed to the recognition of the equal right of all to be free; nor, I think (and this is one respect in which the notion of a right differs from other moral notions), could any parallel argument be constructed to show that, from the bare fact that actions were recognized as ones which ought or ought not to be done, as right, wrong, good or bad, it followed that some specific kind of conduct fell under these categories.

I

(A) Lawyers have for their own purposes carried the dissection of the notion of a legal right some distance, and some of their results[1] are of value in the elucidation of statements of the form "X has a right to …" outside legal contexts. There is of course no simple identification to be made between moral and legal rights, but there is an intimate connection between the two, and this itself is one feature which distinguishes a moral right from other fundamental moral concepts. It is not merely that as a matter of fact men speak of their moral rights mainly when advocating their incorporation in a legal system, but that the concept of a right belongs to that branch of morality which is specifically concerned to determine when one person's freedom may be limited by another's and so to determine what actions may appropriately be made the subject of coercive legal rules … We must distinguish from the rest of morality those principles regulating the proper distribution of human freedom which alone make it morally legitimate for one human being to determine by his choice how another should act; and a certain specific moral value is secured … if human relationships are conducted in accordance with these principles even though coercion has to be used to secure this, for only if these principles are regarded will freedom be distributed among human beings as it should be. And it is I think a very important feature of a moral right that the possessor of it is conceived as having a moral justification for limiting the freedom of another and that he has this justification not because the action he is entitled to require of another has some moral quality but simply because in the circumstances a certain distribution of human freedom will be maintained if he by his choice is allowed to determine how that other shall act.

(B) I can best exhibit this feature of a moral right by reconsidering the question whether moral rights and "duties" are correlative. The contention

---

[1] As W.D. Lamont has seen: cf. his *Principles of Moral Judgment* (Oxford, 1946); for the jurists, cf. Hohfeld's *Fundamental Legal Conceptions* (New Haven, 1923).

that they are means, presumably, that every statement of the form "X has a right to …" entails and
is entailed by "Y has a duty (not) to …" and at this
stage we must not assume that the values of the
name-variables "X" and "Y" must be different persons. Now there is certainly one sense of "a right"
(which I have already mentioned) such that it does
not follow from X's having a right that X or someone else has any duty. Jurists have isolated rights in
this sense and have referred to them as "liberties"
just to distinguish them from rights in the centrally
important sense of "right" which has "duty" as a
correlative. The former sense of "right" is needed
to describe those areas of social life where competition is at least morally unobjectionable. Two people walking along both see a ten-dollar bill in the
road twenty yards away, and there is no clue as to
the owner. Neither of the two are under a "duty"
to allow the other to pick it up; each has in this
sense a right to pick it up. Of course there may be
many things which each has a "duty" not to do in
the course of the race to the spot—neither may kill
or wound the other—and corresponding to these
"duties" there are rights to forbearances. The moral
propriety of all economic competition implies this
minimum sense of "a right" in which to say that
"X has a right to" means merely that X is under
no "duty" not to. Hobbes saw that the expression
"a right" could have this sense but he was wrong
if he thought that there is no sense in which it does
follow from X's having a right that Y has a duty or
at any rate an obligation.

(C) More important for our purpose is the question whether for all moral "duties" there are correlative moral rights, because those who have given
an affirmative answer to this question have usually
assumed without adequate scrutiny that to have a
right is simply to be capable of benefiting by the
performance of a "duty"; whereas in fact this is not
a sufficient condition (and probably not a necessary condition) of having a right. Thus animals and
babies who stand to benefit by our performance of
our "duty" not to ill-treat them are said *therefore*
to have rights to proper treatment. The full consequence of this reasoning is not usually followed out;

most have shrunk from saying that we have rights
against ourselves because we stand to benefit from
our performance of our "duty" to keep ourselves
alive or develop our talents. But the moral situation
which arises from a promise (where the legal-sound-
ing terminology of rights and obligations is most
appropriate) illustrates most clearly that the notion
of having a right and that of benefiting by the performance of a "duty" are not identical. X promises
Y in return for some favor that he will look after Y's
aged mother in his absence. Rights arise out of this
transaction, but it is surely Y to whom the promise
has been made and not his mother who *has* or *possesses* these rights. Certainly Y's mother is a person
concerning whom X has an obligation and a person who will benefit by its performance, but the
person *to whom* he has an obligation to look after
her is Y. This is something *due to* or *owed* to Y, so
it is Y, not his mother, whose right X will disregard
and to whom X will have done *wrong* if he fails to
keep his promise, though the mother may be physically injured. And it is Y who has a moral *claim*
upon X, is *entitled* to have his mother looked after,
and who can *waive* the claim and *release* Y from
the obligation. Y is, in other words, morally in a
position to determine by his choice how X shall act
and in this way to limit X's freedom of choice; and
it is this fact, not the fact that he stands to benefit,
that makes it appropriate to say that he has *a right*.
Of course often the person to whom a promise has
been made will be the only person who stands to
benefit by its performance, but this does not justify
the identification of "having a right" with "benefiting by the performance of a duty." It is important
for the whole logic of rights that, while the person
who stands to benefit by the performance of a duty
is discovered by considering what will happen if the
duty is not performed, the person who has a right (to
whom performance is *owed* or *due*) is discovered by
examining the transaction or antecedent situation
or relations of the parties out of which the "duty"
arises. These considerations should incline us not
to extend to animals and babies whom it is wrong
to ill-treat the notion of a right to proper treatment,
for the moral situation can be simply and adequately

described here by saying that it is wrong or that we ought not to ill-treat them or, in the philosopher's generalized sense of "duty," that we have a duty not to ill-treat them. If common usage sanctions talk of the rights of animals or babies it makes an idle use of the expression "a right," which will confuse the situation with other different moral situations where the expression "a right" has a specific force and cannot be replaced by the other moral expressions which I have mentioned. Perhaps some clarity on this matter is to be gained by considering the force of the preposition "to" in the expression "having a duty to Y" or "being under an obligation to Y" (where "Y" is the name of a person); for it is significantly different from the meaning of "to" in "doing something to Y" or "doing harm to Y," where it indicates the person affected by some action. In the first pair of expressions, "to" obviously does not have this force, but indicates the person to whom the person morally bound is bound. This is an intelligible development of the figure of a bond (*vinculum juris: obligare*);[1] the precise figure is not that of two persons bound by a chain, but of *one* person bound, the other end of the chain lying in the hands of another to use if he chooses.[2] So it appears absurd to speak of having duties or owing obligations to ourselves—of course we may have "duties" not to do harm to ourselves, but what could be meant (once the distinction between these different meanings of "to" has been grasped) by insisting that we have duties or obligations to ourselves not to do harm to ourselves?

[...]

II

So far I have sought to establish that to have a right entails having a moral justification for limiting the freedom of another person and for determining how he should act; it is now important to see that the moral justification must be of a special kind if it is to constitute a right, and this will emerge most clearly from an examination of the circumstances in which rights are asserted with the typical expression "I have a right to ..." It is I think the case that this form of words is used in two main types of situations: (A) when the claimant has some special justification for interference with another's freedom which other persons do not have ("*I* have a right to be paid what you promised for my services"); (B) when the claimant is concerned to resist or object to some interference by another person as having no justification ("*I* have a right to say what I think").

(A) *Special rights.* When rights arise out of special transactions between individuals or out of some special relationship in which they stand to each other, both the persons who have the right and those who have the corresponding obligation are limited to the parties to the special transaction or relationship. I call such rights special rights to distinguish them from those moral rights which are thought of as rights against (i.e., as imposing obligations upon) everyone, such as those that are asserted when some unjustified interference is made or threatened as in (B) above.

(i) The most obvious cases of special rights are those that arise from promises. By promising to do or not to do something, we voluntarily incur obligations and create or confer rights on those to whom we promise; we alter the existing moral independence of the parties' freedom of choice in relation to some action and create a new moral relationship between them, so that it becomes morally legitimate for the person to whom the promise is given to determine how the promisor shall act. The promisee has a temporary authority or sovereignty in relation to some specific matter over the other's will which we express by saying that the promisor is under an obligation *to* the promisee to do what he has promised. To some philosophers the notion that moral phenomena—rights and duties or obligations—can be brought into existence by the voluntary action of individuals has appeared utterly mysterious; but this I think has been so because they have not clearly seen how special the moral

---

[1] [This Latin phrase refers to a civil obligation such that the person to whom the obligation is owed has the right of enforcing it in a court of law.]

[2] Cf. A.H. Campbell, *The Structure of Stair's Institutes* (Glasgow, 1954), p. 31.

notions of a right and an obligation are, nor how peculiarly they are connected with the distribution of freedom of choice; it would indeed be mysterious if we could make actions morally good or bad by voluntary choice. The simplest case of promising illustrates two points characteristic of all special rights: (1) the right and obligation arise not because the promised action has itself any particular moral quality, but just because of the voluntary transaction between the parties; (2) the identity of the parties concerned is vital—only *this* person (the promisee) has the moral justification for determining how the promisor shall act. It is *his* right; only in relation to him is the promisor's freedom of choice diminished, so that if he chooses to release the promisor no one else can complain.

(ii) But a promise is not the only kind of transaction whereby rights are conferred. They may be *accorded* by a person consenting or authorizing another to interfere in matters which but for this consent or authorization he would be free to determine for himself. If I consent to your taking precautions for my health or happiness or authorize you to look after my interests, then you have a right which others have not, and I cannot complain of your interference if it is within the sphere of your authority. This is what is meant by a person surrendering his rights to another; and again the typical characteristics of a right are present in this situation: the person authorized has the right to interfere not because of its intrinsic character but because *these* persons have stood in *this* relationship. No one else (not similarly authorized) has any *right* to interfere in theory even if the person authorized does not exercise his right.

(iii) Special rights are not only those created by the deliberate choice of the party on whom the obligation falls, as they are when they are accorded or spring from promises, and not all obligations to other persons are deliberately incurred, though I think it is true of all special rights that they arise from previous voluntary actions. A third very important source of special rights and obligations which we recognize in many spheres of life is what may be termed mutuality of restrictions, and I think

political obligation is intelligible only if we see what precisely this is and how it differs from the other right-creating transactions (consent, promising) to which philosophers have assimilated it. In its bare schematic outline it is this: when a number of persons conduct any joint enterprise according to rules and thus restrict their liberty, those who have submitted to these restrictions when required have a right to a similar submission from those who have benefited by their submission. The rules may provide that officials should have authority to enforce obedience and make further rules, and this will create a structure of legal rights and duties, but the moral obligation to obey the rules in such circumstances is *due to* the cooperating members of the society, and they have the correlative moral right to obedience. In social situations of this sort (of which political society is the most complex example) the obligation to obey the rules is something distinct from whatever other moral reasons there may be for obedience in terms of good consequences (e.g., the prevention of suffering); the obligation is due to the cooperating members of the society as such and not because they are human beings on whom it would be wrong to inflict suffering. The utilitarian explanation of political obligation fails to take account of this feature of the situation both in its simple version that the obligation exists because and only if the direct consequences of a particular act of disobedience are worse than obedience, and also in its more sophisticated version that the obligation exists even when this is not so, if disobedience increases the probability that the law in question or other laws will be disobeyed on other occasions when the direct consequences of obedience are better than those of disobedience.

Of course to say that there is such a moral obligation upon those who have benefited by the submission of other members of society to restrictive rules to obey these rules in their turn does not entail either that this is the only kind of moral reason for obedience or that there can be no cases where disobedience will be morally justified. There is no contradiction or other impropriety in saying "I have an obligation to do X, someone has a right to ask me to, but I now see I ought not to do it." It will in painful situations sometimes be the lesser of two moral evils to disregard what really are people's rights and not perform our obligations to them. This seems to me particularly obvious from the case of promises: I may promise to do something and thereby incur an obligation just because that is one way in which obligations (to be distinguished from other forms of moral reasons for acting) are created; reflection may show that it would in the circumstances be wrong to keep this promise because of the suffering it might cause, and we can express this by saying "*I ought not* to do it though *I have an obligation to him* to do it" just because the italicized expressions are not synonyms but come from different dimensions of morality. The attempt to explain this situation by saying that our real obligation here is to avoid the suffering and that there is only a prima facie obligation to keep the promise seems to me to confuse two quite different kinds of moral reason, and in practice such a terminology obscures the precise character of what is at stake when "for some greater good" we infringe people's rights or do not perform our obligations to them.

The social-contract theorists rightly fastened on the fact that the obligation to obey the law is not merely a special case of benevolence (direct or indirect), but something which arises between members of a particular political society out of their mutual relationship. Their mistake was to identify *this* right-creating situation of mutual restrictions with the paradigm case of promising; there are of course important similarities, and these are just the points which all special rights have in common, viz., that they arise out of special relationships between human beings and not out of the character of the action to be done or its effects.

(iv) There remains a type of situation which may be thought of as creating rights and obligations: where the parties have a special natural relationship, as in the case of parent and child. The parent's moral right to obedience from his child would I suppose now be thought to terminate when the child reaches the age "of discretion," but the case is worth mentioning because some political

philosophies have had recourse to analogies with this case as an explanation of political obligation, and also because even this case has some of the features we have distinguished in special rights, viz., the right arises out of the special relationship of the parties (though it is in this case a natural relationship) and not out of the character of the actions to the performance of which there is a right.

(v) To be distinguished from special rights, of course, are special liberties, where, exceptionally, one person is *exempted* from obligations to which most are subject but does not thereby acquire a *right* to which there is a correlative obligation. If you catch me reading your brother's diary, you say, "You have no right to read it." I say, "I have a right to read it—your brother said I might unless he told me not to, and he has not told me not to." Here I have been specially *licensed* by your brother who had a right to require me not to read his diary, so I am exempted from the moral obligation not to read it, but your brother is under no obligation to let me go on reading it. Cases where *rights*, not liberties, are accorded to manage or interfere with another person's affairs are those where the license is not revocable at will by the person according the right.

(B) *General rights.* In contrast with special rights, which constitute a justification peculiar to the holder of the right for interfering with another's freedom, are general rights, which are asserted defensively, when some unjustified interference is anticipated or threatened, in order to point out that the interference is unjustified. "I have the right to say what I think." "I have the right to worship as I please." Such rights share two important characteristics with special rights. (1) To have them is to have a moral justification for determining how another shall act, viz., that he shall not interfere. (2) The moral justification does not arise from the character of the particular action to the performance of which the claimant has a right; what justifies the claim is simply—there being no special relation between him and those who are threatening to interfere to justify that interference—that this is a particular exemplification of the equal right to be free. But there are of course striking differences between such defensive general rights and special rights. (1) General rights do not arise out of any special relationship or transaction between men. (2) They are not rights which are peculiar to those who have them but are rights which all men capable of choice have in the absence of those special conditions which give rise to special rights. (3) General rights have as correlatives obligations not to interfere to which everyone else is subject and not merely the parties to some special relationship or transaction, though of course they will often be asserted when some particular persons threaten to interfere as a moral objection to that interference. To assert a general right is to claim in relation to some particular action the equal right of all men to be free in the absence of any of those special conditions which constitute a special right to limit another's freedom; to assert a special right is to assert in relation to some particular action a right constituted by such special conditions to limit another's freedom. The assertion of general rights directly invokes the principle that all men equally have the right to be free; the assertion of a special right (as I attempt to show in Section III) invokes it indirectly.

III

It is, I hope, clear that unless it is recognized that interference with another's freedom requires a moral justification, the notion of a right could have no place in morals; for to assert a right is to assert that there is such a justification. The characteristic function in moral discourse of those sentences in which the meaning of the expression "a right" is to be found— "I have a right to…," "You have no right to…," "What right have you to…?"—is to bring to bear on interferences with another's freedom, or on claims to interfere, a type of moral evaluation or criticism specially appropriate to interference with freedom and characteristically different from the moral criticism of actions made with the use of expressions like "right," "wrong," "good," and "bad." And this is only one of many different types of moral ground for saying "You ought …" or "You ought not …" The use of the expression "What right have you to…?" shows this more clearly, perhaps, than the others;

for we use it, just at the point where interference is actual or threatened, to call for the moral title of the person addressed to interfere; and we do this often without any suggestion at all that what he proposes to do is otherwise wrong and sometimes with the implication that the same interference on the part of another person would be unobjectionable.

But though our use in moral discourse of "a right" does presuppose the recognition that interference with another's freedom requires a moral justification, this would not itself suffice to establish, except in a sense easily trivialized, that in the recognition of moral rights there is implied the recognition that all men have a right to equal freedom; for unless there is some restriction inherent in the meaning of "a right" on the type of moral justification for interference which can constitute a right, the principle could be made wholly vacuous. It would, for example, be possible to adopt the principle and then assert that some characteristic or behavior of some human beings (that they are improvident, or atheists, or Jews, or Negroes) constitutes a moral justification for interfering with their freedom; *any* differences between men could, so far as my argument has yet gone, be treated as a moral justification for interference and so constitute a right, so that the equal right of all men to be free would be compatible with gross inequality. It may well be that the expression "moral" itself imports some restriction on what can constitute a moral justification for interference which would avoid this consequence, but I cannot myself yet show that this is so. It is, on the other hand, clear to me that the moral justification for interference which is to constitute a *right* to interfere (as distinct from merely making it morally good or desirable to interfere) is restricted to certain special conditions and that this is inherent in the meaning of "a right" (unless this is used so loosely that it could be replaced by the other moral expressions mentioned). Claims to interfere with another's freedom based on the general character of the activities interfered with (e.g., the folly or cruelty of "native" practices) or the general character of the parties ("We are Germans; they are Jews") even when well founded are not matters of moral right or obligation. Submission in such cases even where proper is not *due to* or *owed to* the individuals who interfere; it would be equally proper whoever of the same class of persons interfered. Hence other elements in our moral vocabulary suffice to describe this case, and it is confusing here to talk of rights. We saw in Section II that the types of justification for interference involved in special rights was independent of the character of the action to the performance of which there was a right but depended upon certain previous transactions and relations between individuals (such as promises, consent, authorization, submission to mutual restrictions). Two questions here suggest themselves: (1) On what intelligible principle could these bare forms of promising, consenting, submission to mutual restrictions, be either necessary or sufficient, irrespective of their content, to justify interference with another's freedom? (2) What characteristics have these types of transaction or relationship in common? The answer to both these questions is I think this: If we justify interference on such grounds as we give when we claim a moral right, we are in fact indirectly invoking as our justification the principle that all men have an equal right to be free. For we are in fact saying in the case of promises and consents or authorizations that this claim to interfere with another's freedom is justified because he has, in exercise of his equal right to be free, freely chosen to create this claim; and in the case of mutual restrictions we are in fact saying that this claim to interfere with another's freedom is justified because it is fair; and it is fair because only so will there be an equal distribution of restrictions and so of freedom among this group of men. So in the case of special rights as well as of general rights, recognition of them implies the recognition of the equal right of all men to be free.

DISCUSSION QUESTIONS

1. Why, in Hart's view, is the "equal right of all men to be free" a *natural* right?

2. Hart claims, "all people—in virtue of being people—have a right to be free." Explain what he means. In doing so, avoid using the terms "right" or "rights."

25

Robert Nozick, selection from *Anarchy, State, and Utopia* (1977)

In this selection, Nozick provides an analysis of the notion of "rights." Nozick claims that rights constrain our ability to promote the good. In fact, rights cannot be violated even if by doing so we could thereby prevent a greater number of future rights violations. On Nozick, see reading 6 above.

SOURCE

Nozick, Robert. *Anarchy, State, and Utopia.* Copyright © 1977 by Robert Nozick. Reprinted by permission of Basic Books, a member of the Perseus Books Group.

Moral Constraints and Moral Goals

This question assumes that a moral concern can function only as a moral *goal*, as an end state for some activities to achieve as their result. It may, indeed, seem to be a necessary truth that "right," "ought," "should," and so on, are to be explained in terms of what is, or is intended to be, productive of the greatest good, with all goals built into the good. Thus it is often thought that what is wrong with utilitarianism (which *is* of this form) is its too narrow conception of good. Utilitarianism doesn't, it is said, properly take rights and their nonviolation into account; it instead leaves them a derivative status. Many of the counterexample cases to utilitarianism fit under this objection, for example, punishing an innocent man to save a neighborhood from a vengeful rampage. But a theory may include in a primary way the nonviolation of rights, yet include it in the wrong place and the wrong manner. For suppose some condition about minimizing the total (weighted) amount of violations of rights is built into the desirable end state to be achieved. We then would have something like a "utilitarianism of rights"; violations of rights (to be *minimized*) merely would replace the total happiness as the relevant end state in the utilitarian structure. (Note that we do not hold the nonviolation of our rights as our sole greatest good or even rank it first lexicographically to exclude trade-offs, if there is some desirable society we would choose to inhabit even though in it some rights of ours sometimes are violated, rather than move to a desert island where we could survive alone.) This still would require us to violate someone's rights when doing so minimizes the total (weighted) amount of the violation of rights in the society. For example, violating someone's rights might deflect others from *their* intended action of gravely violating rights, or might remove their motive for doing so, or might divert their attention, and so on. A mob rampaging through a part of town killing and burning will violate the rights of those living there. Therefore, someone might try to justify his punishing another *he* knows to be innocent of a crime that enraged a mob, on the grounds that punishing this innocent person would help to avoid even greater violations of rights by others, and so would lead to a minimum weighted score for rights violations in the society.

In contrast to incorporating rights into the end state to be achieved, one might place them as side constraints upon the actions to be done: don't violate constraints C. The rights of others determine the constraints upon your actions. (A *goal-directed* view with constraints added would be: among those acts available to you that don't violate constraints C, act so as to maximize goal G. Here, the rights of others would constrain your goal-directed behavior. I do not mean to imply that the correct moral view includes mandatory goals that must be pursued, even within the constraints.) This view differs from one that tries to build the side constraints C *into* the goal G. The side-constraint view forbids you to violate these moral constraints in the pursuit of your goals; whereas the view whose objective is to minimize the violation of these rights allows you to violate the rights (the constraints) in order to lessen their total violation in the society.

The claim that the proponent of the ultraminimal state is inconsistent, we now can see, assumes that he is a "utilitarian of rights." It assumes that his goal is, for example, to minimize the weighted amount of the violation of rights in the society, and that he should pursue this goal even through means that themselves violate people's rights. Instead, he may place the nonviolation of rights as a constraint upon action, rather than (or in addition to) building it into the end state to be realized. The position held by this proponent of the ultraminimal state will be a consistent one if his conception of rights holds that your being *forced* to contribute to another's welfare violates your rights, whereas someone else's not providing you with things you need greatly, including things essential to the protection of your rights, does not *itself* violate your rights, even though it avoids making it more difficult for someone else to violate them. (That conception will be consistent provided it does not construe the monopoly element of the ultraminimal state as itself a violation of rights.) That it is a consistent position does not, of course, show that it is an acceptable one.

Why Side Constraints?

Isn't it *irrational* to accept a side constraint C, rather than a view that directs minimizing the violations of C? (The latter view treats C as a condition rather than a constraint.) If nonviolation of C is so important, shouldn't that be the goal? How can a concern for the nonviolation of C lead to the refusal to violate C even when this would prevent other more extensive violations of C? What is the rationale for placing the nonviolation of rights as a side constraint upon action instead of including it solely as a goal of one's actions?

Side constraints upon action reflect the underlying Kantian principle that individuals are ends and not merely means; they may not be sacrificed or used for the achieving of other ends without their consent. Individuals are inviolable. More should be said to illuminate this talk of ends and means. Consider a prime example of a means, a tool. There is no side constraint on how we may use a tool, other than the moral constraints on how we may use it upon others. There are procedures to be followed to preserve it for future use ("don't leave it out in the rain"), and there are more and less efficient ways of using it. But there is no limit on what we may do to it to best achieve our goals. Now imagine that there was an overrideable constraint C on some tool's use. For example, the tool might have been lent to you only on the condition that C not be violated unless the gain from doing so was above a certain specified amount, or unless it was necessary to achieve a certain specified goal. Here the object is not *completely* your tool, for use according to your wish or whim. But it is a tool nevertheless, even with regard to the overrideable constraint. If we add constraints on its use that may not be overridden, then the object may not be used as a tool *in those ways. In those respects*, it is not a tool at all. Can one add enough constraints so that an object cannot be used as a tool at all, in *any* respect?

Can behavior toward a person be constrained so that he is not to be used for any end except as he chooses? This is an impossibly stringent condition if it requires everyone who provides us with a good to approve positively of every use to which we wish to put it. Even the requirement that he merely should not object to any use we plan would seriously curtail bilateral exchange, not to mention sequences of such exchanges. It is sufficient that the other party stands to gain enough from the exchange so that he is willing to go through with it, even though he objects to one or more of the uses to which you shall put the good. Under such conditions, the other party is not being used solely as a means, in that respect. Another party, however, who would not choose to interact with you if he knew of the uses to which you *intend* to put his actions or good, *is* being used as a means, even if he receives enough to choose (in his ignorance) to interact with you. ("All along, you were just *using* me" can be said by someone who chose to interact only because he was ignorant of another's goals and of the uses to which he himself would be put.) Is it morally incumbent upon someone to reveal his intended uses of an interaction if he has good reason to believe the other would refuse to interact if he knew? Is he *using* the other person, if he does not reveal this? And what of the cases where the other does not choose to be of use at all? In getting pleasure from seeing an attractive person go by, does one use the other solely as a means? Does someone so use an object of sexual fantasies? These and related questions raise very interesting issues for moral philosophy; but not, I think, for political philosophy.

Political philosophy is concerned only with *certain* ways that persons may not use others; primarily, physically aggressing against them. A specific side constraint upon action toward others expresses the fact that others may not be used in the specific ways the side constraint excludes. Side constraints express the inviolability of others, in the ways they specify. These modes of inviolability are expressed by the following injunction: "Don't use people in specified ways." An end-state view, on the other hand, would express the view that people are ends and not merely means (if it chooses to express this view at all), by a different injunction: "Minimize the use in specified ways of persons as means." Following this precept itself may involve using someone as a means in one of the ways specified. Had Kant held this view, he would have given the second formula of the categorical imperative as, "So act as to minimize the use of humanity simply as a means," rather than the one he actually used: "Act in such a way that you always treat humanity, whether in your own person or in the person of any other, never simply as a means, but always at the same time as an end."[1]

Side constraints express the inviolability of other persons. But why may not one violate persons for the greater social good? Individually, we each sometimes choose to undergo some pain or sacrifice for a greater benefit or to avoid a greater harm: we go to the dentist to avoid worse suffering later; we do some unpleasant work for its results; some persons diet to improve their health or looks; some save money to support themselves when they are older. In each case, some cost is borne for the sake of the greater overall good. Why not, *similarly*, hold that some persons have to bear some costs that benefit other persons more for the sake of the overall social good? But there is no *social entity* with a good that undergoes some sacrifice for its own good. There

---

[1] [Immanuel Kant,] *Groundwork of the Metaphysic of Morals*, trans. H.J. Paton, *The Moral Law* (London: Hutchinson, 1956), p. 96.

are only individual people, different individual people, with their own individual lives. Using one of these people for the benefit of others, uses him and benefits the others. Nothing more. What happens is that something is done to him for the sake of others. Talk of an overall social good covers this up. (Intentionally?) To use a person in this way does not sufficiently respect and take account of the fact that he is a separate person, that his is the only life he has. *He* does not get some overbalancing good from his sacrifice, and no one is entitled to force this upon him—least of all a state or government that claims his allegiance (as other individuals do not) and that therefore scrupulously must be *neutral* between its citizens.

Libertarian Constraints

The moral side constraints upon what we may do, I claim, reflect the fact of our separate existences. They reflect the fact that no moral balancing act can take place among us; there is no moral outweighing of one of our lives by others so as to lead to a greater overall *social* good. There is no justified sacrifice of some of us for others. This root idea, namely, that there are different individuals with separate lives and so no one may be sacrificed for others, underlies the existence of moral side constraints, but it also, I believe, leads to a libertarian side constraint that prohibits aggression against another.

The stronger the force of an end-state maximizing view, the more powerful must be the root idea capable of resisting it that underlies the existence of moral side constraints. Hence the more seriously must be taken the existence of distinct individuals who are not resources for others. An underlying notion sufficiently powerful to support moral side constraints against the powerful intuitive force of the end-state maximizing view will suffice to derive a libertarian constraint on aggression against another. Anyone who rejects *that particular* side constraint has three alternatives: (1) he must reject *all* side constraints; (2) he must produce a different explanation of why there are moral side constraints rather than simply a goal-directed

maximizing structure, an explanation that doesn't itself entail the libertarian side constraint; or (3) he must accept the strongly put root idea about the separateness of individuals and yet claim that initiating aggression against another is compatible with this root idea. Thus we have a promising sketch of an argument from moral form to moral content: the form of morality includes F (moral side constraints); the best explanation of morality's being F is *p* (a strong statement of the distinctness of individuals); and from *p* follows a particular moral content, namely, the libertarian constraint. The particular moral content gotten by this argument, which focuses upon the fact that there are distinct individuals each with his *own* life to lead, will not be the *full* libertarian constraint. It will prohibit sacrificing one person to benefit another. Further steps would be needed to reach a prohibition on paternalistic aggression: using or threatening force for the benefit of the person against whom it is wielded. For this, one must focus upon the fact that there are distinct individuals, each with his own life *to lead*.

A nonaggression principle is often held to be an appropriate principle to govern relations among nations. What difference is there supposed to be between sovereign individuals and sovereign nations that makes aggression permissible among individuals? Why may individuals jointly, through their government, do to someone what no nation may do to another? If anything, there is a stronger case for nonaggression among individuals; unlike nations, they do not contain as parts individuals that others legitimately might intervene to protect or defend.

I shall not pursue here the details of a principle that prohibits physical aggression, except to note that it does not prohibit the use of force in defense against another party who is a threat, even though he is innocent and deserves no retribution. An *innocent* threat is someone who innocently is a causal agent in a process such that he would be an aggressor had he chosen to become such an agent. If someone picks up a third party and throws him at you down at the bottom of a deep well, the third party is innocent and a threat; had he chosen to launch himself at you in that trajectory he would be an aggressor. Even though the falling person would survive his fall onto you, may you use your ray gun to disintegrate the falling body before it crushes and kills you? Libertarian prohibitions are usually formulated so as to forbid using violence on innocent persons. But innocent threats, I think, are another matter to which different principles must apply. Thus, a full theory in this area also must formulate the *different* constraints on response to innocent threats. Further complications concern *innocent shields of threats*, those innocent persons who themselves are nonthreats but who are so situated that they will be damaged by the only means available for stopping the threat. Innocent persons strapped onto the front of the tanks of aggressors so that the tanks cannot be hit without also hitting them are innocent shields of threats. (Some uses of force on people to get at an aggressor do not act upon innocent shields of threats; for example, an aggressor's innocent child who is tortured in order to get the aggressor to stop wasn't *shielding* the parent.) May one knowingly injure innocent shields? *If* one may attack an aggressor and injure an innocent shield, may the innocent shield fight back in self-defense (supposing that he cannot move against or fight the aggressor)? Do we get two persons battling each other in self-defense? Similarly, if you use force against an innocent threat to you, do you thereby become an innocent threat to him, so that he may now justifiably use additional force against you (supposing that he can do this, yet cannot prevent his original threateningness)? I tiptoe around these incredibly difficult issues here, merely noting that a view that says it makes nonaggression central must resolve them explicitly at some point.

What Are Constraints Based Upon?

Such questions do not press upon us as practical problems (yet?), but they force us to consider fundamental issues about the foundations of our moral views: first, is our moral view a side-constraint view, or a view of a more complicated hierarchical structure; and second, in virtue of precisely what characteristics of persons are there moral constraints on how they may treat each other or be treated? We also want to understand *why* these characteristics connect with these constraints. (And, perhaps, we want these characteristics not to be had by animals; or not had by them in as high a degree.) It would appear that a person's characteristics, by virtue of which others are constrained in their treatment of him, must themselves be valuable characteristics. How else are we to understand why something so valuable emerges from them? (This natural assumption is worth further scrutiny.)

The traditional proposals for the important individuating characteristic connected with moral constraints are the following: sentient and self-conscious; rational (capable of using abstract concepts, not tied to responses to immediate stimuli); possessing free will; being a moral agent capable of guiding its behavior by moral principles and capable of engaging in mutual limitation of conduct; having a soul. Let us ignore questions about how these notions are precisely to be understood, and whether the characteristics are possessed, and possessed uniquely, by man, and instead seek their connection with moral constraints on others. Leaving aside the last on the list, each of them seems insufficient to forge the requisite connection. Why is the fact that a being is very smart or foresightful or has an I.Q. above a certain threshold a reason to limit specially how we treat it? Would beings even more intelligent than we have the right not to limit themselves with regard to us? Or, what is the significance of any purported crucial threshold? If a being is capable of choosing autonomously among alternatives, is there some reason to *let it* do so? Are autonomous choices intrinsically good? If a being could make only once an autonomous choice, say between flavors of ice cream on a particular occasion, and would forget immediately afterwards, would there be strong reasons to allow it to choose? That a being can agree with others to mutual rule-governed limitations on conduct shows that it *can* observe limits. But it does not show which limits should be observed toward it ("no abstaining from murdering it"?), or why any limits should be observed at all.

An intervening variable M is needed for which the listed traits are individually necessary, *perhaps* jointly sufficient (at least we should be able to see what needs to be added to obtain M), and which has a perspicuous and convincing connection to moral constraints on behavior toward someone with M. Also, in the light of M, we should be in a position to see why others have concentrated on the traits of rationality, free will, and moral agency. This will be easier if these traits are not merely necessary conditions for M but also are important components of M or important means to M.

But haven't we been unfair in treating rationality, free will, and moral agency individually and separately? In conjunction, don't they add up to something whose significance is clear: a being able to formulate long-term plans for its life, able to consider and decide on the basis of abstract principles or considerations it formulates to itself and hence not merely the plaything of immediate stimuli, a being that limits its own behavior in accordance with some principles or picture it has of what an appropriate life is for itself and others, and so on. However, this exceeds the three listed traits. We can distinguish theoretically between long-term planning and an overall conception of a life that guides particular decisions, and the three traits that are their basis. For a being could possess these three traits and yet also have built into it some particular barrier that prevents it from operating in terms of an overall conception of its life and what it is to add up to. So let us add, as an additional feature, the ability to regulate and guide its life in accordance with some overall conception it chooses to accept. Such an overall conception, and knowing how we are doing in terms of it, is important to the kind of goals we formulate for ourselves and the kind of beings we are. Think how different we would be (and how differently it would be legitimate to treat us) if we all were amnesiacs, forgetting each evening as we slept the happenings of the preceding day. Even if by accident someone were to pick up each day where he left off the previous day, living in accordance with a coherent conception an aware individual might have chosen, he still

would not be leading the other's sort of life. His life would parallel the other life, but it would not be integrated in the same way.

What is the moral importance of this additional ability to form a picture of one's whole life (or at least of significant chunks of it) and to act in terms of some overall conception of the life one wishes to lead? Why not interfere with someone else's shaping of his own life? (And what of those not actively shaping their lives, but drifting with the forces that play upon them?) One might note that anyone might come up with the pattern of life you would wish to adopt. Since one cannot predict in advance that someone won't, it is in your self-interest to allow another to pursue his conception of his life as he sees it; you may learn (to emulate or avoid or modify) from his example. This prudential argument seems insufficient.

I conjecture that the answer is connected with that elusive and difficult notion: the meaning of life. A person's shaping his life in accordance with some overall plan is his way of giving meaning to his life; only a being with the capacity to so shape his life can have or strive for meaningful life. But even supposing that we could elaborate and clarify this notion satisfactorily, we would face many difficult questions. Is the capacity so to shape a life itself the capacity to have (or strive for?) a life with meaning, or is something else required? (For ethics, might the content of the attribute of having a soul simply be that the being strives, or is capable of striving, to give meaning to its life?) Why are there constraints on how we may treat beings shaping their lives? Are certain modes of treatment incompatible with their having meaningful lives? And even if so, why not destroy meaningful lives? Or, why not replace "happiness" with "meaningfulness" within utilitarian theory, and maximize the total "meaningfulness" score of the persons of the world? Or does the notion of the meaningfulness of a life enter into ethics in a different fashion? This notion, we should note, has the right "feel" as something that might help to bridge an "is-ought" gap; it appropriately seems to straddle the two. Suppose, for example, that one could show that if a person acted in certain ways his life would be meaningless. Would this be a hypothetical or a categorical imperative? Would one need to answer the further question: "But why shouldn't my life be meaningless?" Or, suppose that acting in a certain way toward others was itself a way of granting that one's own life (and those very actions) was meaningless. Mightn't this, resembling a pragmatic contradiction, lead at least to a status 2 conclusion of side constraints in behavior to all other human beings? I hope to grapple with these and related issues on another occasion.

DISCUSSION QUESTIONS

1. How might we understand Nozick's use of the term "rights"? That is to say, what does Nozick mean when he says, for example, "The rights of others determine the constraints upon your action"? How might we paraphrase this sentence in such a way that we can drop the word "rights" and substitute an equivalent word or phrase?

2. Consider what might be called the "Separateness of Persons" argument. Why might the fact that an individual is a "separate person" come to bear on how others can appropriately treat or make demands of him/her?

3. Recall that Bentham (in "Anarchical Fallacies," reading 22) wrote, "Society is held together only by the sacrifices that men can be induced to make of the gratifications they demand." He goes on to say that the task of government is to obtain or extract the needed sacrifices. Bearing this in mind, how might Bentham respond to Nozick's "Separateness of Persons" argument?

26

Diane Jeske and Richard Fumerton, "The Right and Wrong Ways to Think about Rights and Wrongs" (2010; written for this volume)

On Jeske, see reading 15 above. Richard Fumerton (b. 1949) is the F. Wendell Miller Professor of Philosophy at the University of Iowa. His books include *Reason and Morality: A Defense of the Egocentric Perspective*; *Metaepistemology and Skepticism*; and *Realism and the Correspondence Theory of Truth*. His research interests include epistemology, metaphysics, and value theory. In this piece, Jeske and Fumerton make important distinctions about various notions of rights and discuss the senses in which deontologists and utilitarians can accommodate talk of rights within their ethical theories.

Natural rights is simple nonsense: natural and imprescriptible rights, rhetorical nonsense—nonsense upon stilts.

–Jeremy Bentham

There is no doubt that we are addicted to talk about rights. In the context of political debate, people talk about our right to free speech, our right to bear firearms, our right to adequate health care, our right to choose abortion, our right to life, liberty and the pursuit of happiness. But there is no consensus on how to understand all this talk of rights. Indeed, on some views about the meaning of fundamental ethical expressions, talk of rights is nothing more than a needlessly confusing distraction.

Setting the Terms of the Debate

The first step in clearly defining a controversy about rights is to make a distinction between talk of legal rights and talk of moral rights. While there are scholars who insist that, necessarily, moral truths partly determine what the law is (or determine how to interpret the law),[1] on the face of it such views

---

[1] Of course, if one has good legislators, they will keep an eye on morality when they do their business of making laws. So at least sometimes, moral truths will play a role in determining what the law is. The stronger and more interesting claim, that *necessarily* moral truths play such a role, is what we find to be implausible: too many bad people throughout history have gotten work as legislators.

aren't very plausible. The ordinary concept of law allows that a given nation might be governed by very bad laws indeed. If one allows that there can be evil laws, then the fact that one has a legal right to do something seems to have nothing much to do with the question of whether one has a moral right to do it (and, similarly, that one lacks a legal right has nothing much to do with whether one lacks a moral right). So in Nazi Germany, for example, the state had a legal right to imprison Jews for having sexual relations with people of the "Aryan" race. It surely had no moral right to behave in such an atrocious manner. (And Jews had no legal rights whatsoever, but, surely, they had exactly the same moral rights as any "Aryan.") To say that someone has a legal right in country Y to do X is roughly to say that there is no law in country Y that prohibits a person from doing X. To say that someone has a legal right to get something (say a tax return) is to say that the law requires someone (in this case the government) to provide something to that person. As we'll see, these two sorts of legal rights are analogous to two kinds of moral rights that we will discuss below.

The characterization of moral rights is more difficult than the characterization of legal rights. To pave the way for the subsequent discussion it will be useful to talk a bit about differences between meta-ethical views—views about the meaning of ethical expressions. One way to distinguish different meta-ethical views concerns which ethical terms are taken to be fundamental by the competing views. Before considering the differences between views, however, we need to distinguish ethical expressions from other terms. One way, not entirely satisfactory, is to begin with a *list*. Ethical judgments are expressed using terms like "good/bad," "right/wrong," "duty," "obligation," "virtue/vice," and the like. Once we have a list with which we are relatively comfortable, we might go on to identify as derivatively ethical any term whose meaning must be explained in part by reference to one of the terms on our list. So, for example, the term "murder" might not seem the most obvious candidate for an ethical expression, but if "murder" means something like "killing

that is morally wrong," then "murder" will count as a moral expression. Other examples might be "cruel," and even "rude."

A difficulty with the above approach is that some of the terms on the list occur in radically different contexts, and it is a matter of considerable controversy whether all of the contexts involve moral claims, or even anything very much like a moral claim. So, for example, we talk about good people and good outcomes, but we also talk about good knives, good toasters, good arguments, good assassins, and good liars. There may be an intimate connection between the use of the term "good" in "good assassin" and the use of the term "good" in "good person," but the connection, if any, is not clear.

Still, let's suppose that we have some intuitive understanding of when we are dealing with an ethical claim. As noted, we can begin to distinguish ethical views by looking at which ethical terms play a fundamental conceptual role in the theory. So, for example, the most straightforward, and surely tempting, ethical theory claims that the most fundamental ethical concept is that of being intrinsically good (where the intrinsic goodness of something does not accrue to the thing that is good in virtue of good consequences that flow from it). According to the crudest version of act consequentialism, when faced with alternative actions, the right thing to do is that alternative that "maximizes" intrinsic value. Intuitively, states that are intrinsically good and bad can be thought of as falling on a scale. One might think of representing the degree to which something is intrinsically good using positive integers, and the degree to which something is intrinsically bad using negative integers. More precisely, then, the view that we might call *actual consequence act consequentialism* says that the right action is that action X such that the sum of the positive and negative intrinsic value that would result from X (thought of as the addition of the positive and negative numbers) is greater than the sum of the intrinsic positive and negative value that would result from any alternative to X. More sophisticated versions of the view will insist that one take into account possible consequences, where one adjusts whatever positive or negative intrinsic value attaches to a possible consequence for the probability of its occurring. On one standard approach one adjusts the value by multiplying the value by the probability of the consequence occurring. So if something has enormous intrinsic value (say +1000 on our "scale" of goodness), but has only a 1/1000 chance of occurring, the adjusted value would be +1. On such a view, X is the right action when the sum of the adjusted value that attaches to the consequences of doing X is greater than the sum of the adjusted value that attaches to the possible consequences of taking any alternative to X.

Just as some think that one can define "right action" in terms of "good," so also others think that one can define talk of rights in terms of facts about what it is right or wrong of people to do. On such an approach it is useful to distinguish what one might call *negative* rights from what one might call *positive* rights. You have a negative right to do X when it would be wrong for anyone to prevent you from doing X. So you have a right in this sense to own firearms insofar as it would be wrong for anyone to prevent you from owning a firearm. In contrast, one has a positive right to X, when it is true that it would be wrong for others (perhaps those in a position to do so) to fail to ensure that you get X. In this sense, for example, it would be true that you have a right to medical care only insofar as it would be wrong for anyone appropriately positioned to refuse such aid.

If we are determined to "translate" all this talk of rights into claims about what would be wrong for others to do, we can make still further distinctions. The most ambitious claims about rights insist that rights are in some fundamental sense "absolute." One has an absolute negative right to do X when it would be wrong *no matter what* for anyone to prevent you from doing X. If we understand "ought" judgments as judgments about an agent's all-things-considered reasons for action, then to say that one has an absolute negative right to do X is to say that no one ought to prevent you from doing X. One has an absolute positive right to have X when it would

be wrong *no matter what* for anyone suitably positioned to refrain from providing X for you—anyone suitably positioned ought to provide you with X. A weaker claim would insist only that when you have a negative right to do X it would be *prima facie* wrong for anyone to prevent you from doing X (with a similar qualification added to the characterization of positive rights). It is *prima facie* wrong for someone to do X when it would be wrong, certain other things being equal, for one to do X. Only when those other things are equal, as it were, would that person have an all-things-considered reason not to do X. The question of how precisely to understand this *prima facie* and all-things-considered talk is one to which we shall return.

It is hardly the case that the above distinctions are crystal clear. In our characterization of positive rights we talked about what people suitably positioned ought to do, but it is not obvious who those suitably positioned are. If you have the right to health care and there is no national health-care system, is every wealthy person who can afford to pay your health-care costs morally required to do so? In our characterization of negative rights we talked about how it would be wrong for people to prevent you from acting in certain ways. But what precisely constitutes preventing someone from acting as that person chooses? I can say, for example, that no-one is preventing people in the inner cities of America from leaving the country if they don't like its policies, but if as a result of our social policies they don't have the means to do so, are we, in effect, preventing them through those policies from doing what they have a right to do? But set these problems aside. In what sense can the consequentialist acknowledge the existence of either positive or negative rights?

Consequentialism and Rights

On the face of it, the act consequentialist simply has no room for *absolute* rights of either the positive or negative sort. The rightness or wrongness of actions is a function of actual or possible consequences of those actions. Such consequences vary from situation to situation. The results of lying, for example, are sometimes very bad, but also sometimes very good. There is no *kind* of action that is always right or always wrong no matter what the circumstances.[1] So, for example, no act consequentialist could recognize an absolute right not to be tortured. Whether or not one should torture someone will be a function of the consequences of doing so. It isn't difficult to imagine situations in which enormous evil could be avoided by torturing and in which, therefore, by consequentialist lights it would clearly be the right thing to do.

An act consequentialist can't accommodate absolute rights because there is no kind of action that is always right or wrong (other than the "kind" of action that maximizes value). As Mill pointed out, however, the acknowledgement of a "first principle" in ethics is certainly consistent with recognizing useful secondary rules. The act utilitarian, however, must think of these secondary rules as rough and ready guidelines learned from past experience. One typically does weave "tangled webs" when one practices to deceive, and it's not a bad idea to go through life remembering that fact. If we understand an act's being *prima facie* right or *prima facie* wrong in terms of there being an epistemic presumption of some kind that it is right or wrong (under normal conditions), then we could still perhaps find room for a "watered down" notion of rights translated into these rules of thumb. But it is highly doubtful that any of this will make the friend of "rights" talk happy. Those who claim that we have a moral right to decent health care, for example, are typically not happy to regard that as a rough and ready rule that holds only for societies in which it is not too costly or in which we can't think of better things to do with our collective resources.

There is a form of consequentialism that is much more hospitable to rights talk. It is now commonplace in philosophy to distinguish rule consequentialism from act consequentialism. The crudest form of rule consequentialism is committed to the view that the rightness or wrongness of actions is defined by the correct rules of morality. As we noted above, act consequentialists can certainly emphasize the importance of recognizing summary rules or rules of thumb—rough and ready guidelines for acting when decisions must be made quickly. The rule utilitarian's rules, by contrast, are sometimes described as *constitutive* of morality in the way that the rules of a game are constitutive of the game. Consider, for example, chess. The rules of chess define how the pieces may or may not move. The bishop, for example, can move any number of squares along a diagonal line provided that that its movement is unimpeded by other pieces. If one plays a board game and allows the bishop to move in some other way one is simply not playing chess.

So the rule utilitarian thinks that what is morally required, morally forbidden, or morally permissible is defined by rules that require, forbid, or permit certain kinds of actions. But we are obviously owed an account of what determines the "correct" rules of morality. The rule consequentialist's answer to this question is what makes the view a version of consequentialism. The crudest version of the view defines the correct rule governing a certain kind of action in terms of the consequences of people following the rule. If the consequences of people following the rule under consideration would be better on balance than the consequences of people following any alternative rule, then that is the correct rule. (Like act consequentialists, more sophisticated rule consequentialists can identify instead the relevant hypothetical consequences of people following rules with probable or possible consequences). So if we are wondering whether the correct rule of morality governing regulation of political speech is a rule requiring that no-one ever interfere with such speech, we are wondering whether a world in which people follow that rule is a better world than a world in which people follow some alternative rule.

If one takes seriously the notion of a constitutive rule, there will be kinds of actions that are always required or always prohibited, and one might be

---

[1] At least no kind of action that is non-trivially always right or wrong. The consequentialist is committed to the view that, by definition, actions that maximize (in the relevant sense) value are always right or wrong.

back in business defining absolute rights. You have an absolute right not to be tortured if it is always wrong for others to torture you, for example. But rule consequentialism is hardly without its problems. The first objection claims that any plausible version of rule consequentialism eventually collapses into act consequentialism. Consider, for example, voting. For rule consequentialists the question of whether or not we ought to vote will be answered by the correct rule for voting. If the only two rules were "Always Vote" or "Never Vote," it probably wouldn't be hard to conclude that the world would be better if everyone followed the "Vote" rule. But no-one thinks one should always follow the "Vote" rule. Consider: you are driving your car to the polls. You have left it rather late, and you have only about an hour to get there. About a mile from your destination, you see a young child beside a mangled bicycle—the child is clearly the victim of a hit-and-run driver. The child is seriously hurt, but if you take the time to help the child you will miss your opportunity to vote. Only a moral monster will wave goodbye to the child on the way to the polls.

The rule utilitarian isn't finished, of course. The obvious solution is to modify the "Vote" rule. It was never that plausible in the first place. Why wouldn't one choose instead, for example, the rule "Vote provided that you know something about the issues and the candidates?" Surely a world in which people followed that rule would be better than a world in which people followed the "Vote (even if you are an ignoramus)" rule. So all we need to do is qualify further the rule: "Vote if you are informed unless you can save a life or help someone seriously injured." But you can see what is coming. Instead of the hurt child, you receive a phone call from the hospital. Your dying sister wants desperately to see you before she leaves this world, and you have just enough time to get to the hospital. You will, however, need to forgo your opportunity to vote. Again, almost everyone will conclude that you should do precisely that. So we'll need to modify the rule again: Vote if you are informed unless you can save a life, or help a hurt child, or ease the pain of a dying relative, or…. Or what?

Philosophers have a good imagination and this isn't going to end. In frustration (and to the act consequentialist's glee) the impatient rule consequentialist might try a one-step fix for all of the potential exceptions: Vote unless you can do more good by not voting. The act consequentialist triumphantly proclaims at this point, however, that this is precisely act consequentialism.

It is not entirely clear that rule consequentialism will collapse into act consequentialism. A great deal depends on how one understands precisely one's criteria for an acceptable rule. If the test is how the world would be if people tried to follow the rule, it might be the case that we would actually get better results if we kept our rules simple. But then we'll inevitably face another problem. Simple rules will conflict. The right "simple" rule for telling the truth might be "Always tell the truth." And the right simple rule for keeping promises might be "Always keep a promise." But you might find yourself in a situation in which (perhaps inadvertently) you promised to lie. Leaving the model of the rules of a game, this rule utilitarian might now claim only that the rules define what is *prima facie* right or wrong. But then we will need instructions on how to resolve conflicts between what is *prima facie* right or wrong. Still this version of rule utilitarianism might give some comfort to the friend of "rights" for, as we saw, the weaker version of rights talk might be content to understand rights in terms of *prima facie* obligations to take or refrain from taking various actions.

There is a second objection to rule consequentialism that will, however, not do much to further the debate. Put very crudely, the objector thinks that the whole idea of going through life bent on conforming one's behavior to rules is idiotic. There are good reasons to have laws, and even to have laws that are relatively straightforward. Complex laws are too difficult to follow or to enforce. But there are no good reasons to artificially construct rules to guide one's decisions in life. If we can make the world a better place, then that is precisely what one ought to do, even if it involves violating rough and ready guidelines that we were taught as children. Most of us have suffered at some time or another having to deal with "rule worshippers"—people who blindly follow rules even when reason cries out that the rules be ignored in this particular situation. And the act consequentialist can't help but think that the rule consequentialist is someone who is trying to include in a metaethic this distressing character trait.

Deontology and Rights

So it seems that consequentialism and rights do not make congenial bedfellows. Many moral philosophers have not, however, regarded this as an objection to rights, but, rather, as an objection to consequentialism. The standard mode of argument used to refute consequentialist moral theories has been the appeal to counterexample: a hypothetical case is presented, the consequentialist theory is applied to the case and shown to yield an intuitively unappealing result, and consequentialism is rejected. The following two cases are famous counterexamples that have been appealed to in the battle against consequentialism:

1. *Hanging the Innocent*: Suppose that you are a sheriff in a town torn by racial strife between the As and the Bs. A member of racial group A has been murdered. You have irrefutable evidence that the murderer is herself an A. However, you are very confident that the As will not believe you, and that deadly rioting will result from the arrest of the actual killer. You can easily frame a B for the murder and ensure that the A murderer cannot strike again: you thereby prevent rioting and any future murders by the A killer. The consequentialist seems committed to saying that you as sheriff ought to convict and hang an innocent B, because better consequences will thereby result. But intuition rebels: surely innocent people have a right not to be punished for crimes that they did not commit. So we must, it is said, reject utilitarianism.

2. *Transplant*: Suppose that you are a great transplant surgeon who has five patients, each in need of a different organ. You find a "donor" who is compatible with all of the five needy patients and who has pristine healthy organs. You can easily dispose of this "donor" without arousing suspicion, thereby saving five people at the cost of one. If you do not act, you will allow one to live at the cost of letting five die. The consequentialist calculus seems to tell you that the right action is to kill the one and save the five for a net gain of four. But surely, common sense insists, the healthy "donor" has a right not to be killed for her organs, and, thus, consequentialism must be rejected as a moral theory.

Those who find themselves incapable of "biting the bullet" and saying "hang the innocent person" and "cut up the healthy individual" will say good-bye to consequentialism.

The type of theory often turned to after consideration of cases such as the above is known as a *deontological* moral theory. Deontologists, unlike consequentialists, regard "right" as a fundamental ethical term—whereas consequentialists define "right" by reference to another ethical term, namely "intrinsic good," deontologists hold that the definition of "right" does not involve any other ethical term.[1] This does not imply that the deontologist must hold that right action has nothing to do with the value of consequences, only that the deontologist, unlike the consequentialist, is not committed to regarding right action as a function of nothing other than the value of the consequences of various alternatives.

In fact, deontologists have appealed to rights as "trumps" (Ronald Dworkin) or as "side-constraints" (Robert Nozick) over utility. What they mean is that the legitimate pursuit of intrinsic value (utility) is morally constrained by other considerations, where such considerations are stated in the form of rights. So, for example, in case 2 above, it is being claimed that the "donor" has a "right" not to be killed for her organs; in other words, the consideration that the "donor" is an innocent person

---

[1] Deontologists differ as to whether "good" is also a fundamental ethical term. What they agree about is that "right" is not definable in terms of "good."

who has not consented to being sacrificed "trumps" the consideration that such sacrifice would result in a net gain of four lives. Some deontologists, then, claim that rights function as constraints on the production of value.

But, of course, so far we have only stated the deontologist position, as motivated by an appeal to counterexamples such as 1 and 2 above. The question remains: why suppose that certain considerations constrain the legitimate quest for maximal intrinsic value? There are a couple of answers that immediately pop to mind, but both need to be avoided, for different reasons:

a. In discussing the transplant case, many are tempted to say that it would be wrong to take the "donor's" organs because she has a right not to be killed for such a reason. But what does it amount to to say that the donor has a right not to be killed for her organs? Suppose we respond: it would be wrong to kill her for her organs. Notice that now we have moved in a circle: she has a right not to be killed because it would be wrong to do so, and it would be wrong to kill her because she has a right not to be. We cannot explain the wrongness of killing the donor by appealing to her right not to be killed if to have a right not to be killed just amounts to its being wrong to kill her.

b. We might be tempted to say that it would be wrong to hang the innocent person in case 1 because killing an innocent person is very bad. But any appeal to the badness of killing is going to fail to provide any kind of trump over utility, because it is just one more appeal to utility. After all, if you as sheriff refuse to hang the innocent member of group B, riots will result in which many more innocent people will be killed. So if killing an innocent is bad, why not kill one innocent in order to avoid the even worse situation in which many innocents are killed? In justifying rights as trumps or side-constraints, the deontologist needs to appeal to something other than the badness of rights violations, in order to avoid the result that it seems rational then to violate one right in order to prevent a greater number of rights violations. (This would be the view that Nozick calls a "utilitarianism of rights.")

What this comes to is that any adequate account of rights needs to explain and justify their *agent-relativity*: insofar as S has a right not to be harmed, it would be at least *prima facie* wrong for R to harm S, even if by harming S, R could prevent greater harm (perhaps even to S herself). So rights on the parts of others provide an agent with reason *for her* not to act in certain ways even if by acting in that way she could prevent greater harm or a greater number of such acts in total. The agent-relativity of the reasons generated by rights puzzles consequentialists: why should each of us be so concerned with what *she* does rather than with what the world, in the end, is like? Consequentialists accuse deontologists who focus on rights of having an overly developed worry about their own moral purity at the cost of more badness and less goodness in the world.

But some deontologists will insist that this is a mischaracterization of their view. A prime source for the position of many contemporary rights-based deontological moral views is, of course, Immanuel Kant. Kant claimed that persons have a certain status, what he called "dignity," that makes it inappropriate to treat them as mere means, rather than as ends in themselves. So we are not allowed to use others as a means to save a greater number, as we would do if we hanged the innocent person or cut the donor up to harvest and distribute her organs.

The challenge for the Kantian deontologist is to explain why "dignity" grounds rights rather than being a valuable feature that ought to be maximized. The consequentialist is going to demand an explanation as to why we ought not to kill one in order to save many from being killed—in such a case, someone's dignity will be violated, so why not do what one can to minimize loss of dignity? This is just another way of pointing up the perplexing nature of the agent-relative aspect of rights. This agent-relativity seems especially odd, given that we are supposedly concerned with the nature of the other persons with whom we are dealing, not with our own agency.

Supposing that the deontologist can explain the grounds of rights and why those grounds are better protected by rights than by rules of maximization, we still need to be told whether rights are absolute trumps over utility or are considerations that can be overridden if sufficient intrinsic value is at stake. Ronald Dworkin claims that "[i]f someone has a right to something, then it is wrong for the government to deny it to him even though it would be in the general interest to do so."[1] This statement is that of an absolute right, insofar as Dworkin does not allow for considerations of value ("the general interest") to override rights, no matter how much value is at stake. Nozick and Kant also seemed to understand rights as absolute in this sense.

But, of course, Dworkin's conception of rights as absolute trumps is a very strong conception. Do we really think that the donor has an absolute right not to be killed for her organs? Suppose that we need her organs, because her organs—and *only* her organs—contain a serum that can be used to save all of humanity from a virulent flesh-eating, fatal virus. Would it still be wrong to kill the donor and drain the serum from her organs? I think common sense is now saying, "kill the donor," especially if the donor's life is also at stake. Our understanding of our rights as embodied in the Constitution is also non-absolute—no one really thinks that we have an absolute right to speak our minds or to practice our religion. Much depends on the consequences of our speaking, and the nature of the rituals entailed by our religion. So it seems that common sense understands rights as having thresholds, i.e., as being overridable by considerations of value when those considerations of value get significant enough.

We said above that whether or not the deontologist opts for absolute rights or for rights with thresholds, she needs to offer us some grounds for rights. In other words, we need to be told what it is that makes it wrong for us to hang the innocent man or to kill the healthy donor, if to have a right not to be killed amounts to nothing more than its being wrong to kill you. But there is another option. A deontologist might want to understand "a right" as an irreducible ethical concept, and so not definable in terms of goodness, wrongness, rightness, or any other ethical term. To have a right is to have a *sui generis* property that entails that it is wrong for others to kill one, but it is not reducible to the wrongness of killing. This option will allow us to capture our intuitions without the worry that any grounds of rights that we appeal to will be better protected by a rule of maximization. However, at the same time, it may appear *ad hoc*: whenever we think that it is wrong to do P to S, we can just say that S has a right not to have P done to her. The consequentialist will jump on this as being just a denial of her view dressed up in rights talk.

Conclusion

We have expressed serious reservations about the value and even the intelligibility of rights talk for the consequentialist. The deontologist has a view that at least leaves room for a weak notion of rights. That weak notion, however, is no more plausible than the corresponding weak notion of *prima facie* obligations to do or refrain from acting in certain ways. Their nonconsequentialist understanding of these *prima facie* obligations cries out for an illuminating philosophical analysis.

But if we are skeptical about the central role that rights talk has come to occupy in philosophical discourse, we might feel at least some burden to explain the phenomenon. In our introduction, we commented briefly on the need to distinguish talk of legal rights and obligations from talk of moral rights and obligations. Nothing we have said in our discussion of morality should detract from the clear intelligibility of the concept of legal rights. Clearly, laws are rules. They are rules intended to allow people to coordinate behavior, protect various interests, and, through clear warnings, anticipate consequences of undesirable behavior. As almost everyone realizes, pragmatic considerations dictate

---

[1] Dworkin, "What Rights Do We Have?," in *Taking Rights Seriously* (Cambridge, MA: Harvard University Press, 1977), p.269.

that laws be somewhat crude. No legislature can anticipate every possible situation which might suggest a reasonable deviation from generally stated rules. It would be a serious mistake even to formulate laws that are so complex and sophisticated that they no longer serve their fundamental purpose. Laws need to be simple enough that ordinary people can understand them, and conform their conduct to them. They need to be simple enough to allow successful prosecution before a jury of our peers. Laws look very much like the rule utilitarian's rules or the deontologist's statement of rights. Again, legal rules allow a relatively unproblematic definition of legal rights and obligations. One has a legal right to do X if there is no law prohibiting one from doing X (or imposing compensatory demands for doing X). One is legally obligated to do X if there is a law requiring one to do X. It is not as if things can't still get complicated. Even relatively rational legislatures can end up enacting "black letter" laws that conflict. And outside of the criminal law, the "laws" about which people talk are often common laws derived from judicial decisions and pronouncements that often conflict. But even if such complications force us to something like the notion of a *prima facie* legal prohibition or obligation, it is relatively clear how the account would proceed.

Our speculation is that the historical role of rights talk in morality is rooted in the highly controversial and potentially problematic presupposition that there is a strong similarity between law and morality. Historically, our Judeo-Christian tradition, for example, takes as the paradigm of a moral code something like the Ten Commandments, and these commandments were often referred to as the laws of God. Humans make their laws, and if they are just, they capture, or at least conform to, moral law. The moral law is constituted by another set of rules—the rules laid down by the supreme Legislator. It is no accident that this tradition often refers to a large part of morality as the Natural Law. Even in the twentieth century one still hears people in the continental tradition worrying that the "death of God" means the end of morality. More

often, however, calmer minds conclude that it would be absurd to suppose that a commitment to atheism implied a commitment to amoralism. Indeed, the problem exposed here is as old as the exchange between Socrates and Euthyphro, in which Socrates famously asks whether the gods love something because it is right or something is right because the gods love it. It doesn't take much intellectual curiosity to wonder how God came up with his commandments. It seems to many absurd to suppose that God's dictates were capricious rules arbitrarily commanding obedience. Surely, even God had a reason to tell us not to covet our neighbor's wives and that reason must have had something to do with His realizing that it would be wrong to do so. Unless deontology is correct, there is no reason to suppose that the morality God recognizes is rule-constituted morality. Indeed, God's commandments might be best construed as rough and ready guidelines that serve much the same function as our human-made laws. God may have decided to keep his commandments relatively simple for the same reason that legislators keep their laws relatively simple. (And, indeed, the God who forbade killing seemed to have no difficulty with David killing Goliath, and the Israelites slaughtering whole nations.)

There are other ways of trying to model moral "law" on a legal system. But all of these are just as controversial. So, for example, on some versions of contractarianism, moral laws are agreements hammered out to facilitate social cooperation. They differ from "black-letter" law formulated by legislatures by being implicit. Often the idea is that these moral "agreements" are rules that people would commit themselves to if they were to consider in some idealized way how to regulate behavior. Again, one must wonder whether such views avoid the problem of the *Euthyphro*. One worries that some of these agreements are reached in order to reflect what the participants realize are pre-existing moral truths.

Our purpose here is not to survey and criticize all of these conceptions of morality. It is rather to emphasize the way in which the place of rights in

morality can be seen to presuppose a highly controversial parallel between law and morality. Once one
abandons the view that the parallel exists, one may
be better off abandoning a conception of morality
that centrally involves rights.

DISCUSSION QUESTIONS

1. If there are no absolute rights, as Jeske
   and Fumerton think, what do they offer
   as an explanation for why we often tend
   to talk as if there were?

2. Is there any sense in which Jeske and
   Fumerton concede that a consequentialist
   can allow for the existence of rights?

3. How do deontologists use appeal to rights
   to object to consequentialism? Why do
   Jeske and Fumerton reject this argument?

4. What are the distinctions between *prima
   facie* and absolute rights; legal rights and
   moral rights; positive and negative rights?

5. Do any of Jeske and Fumerton's objections to absolute moral rights apply
   equally to corresponding legal rights?

B.
Utilitarianism and Rights

27

Jeremy Bentham, selection from *The Principles of Morals and Legislation* (1780)

In this selection, Bentham provides an early articulation of the moral and political theory known as utilitarianism. On Bentham, see reading 22 above.

SOURCE

Bentham, Jeremy. *An Introduction to the Principles of Morals and Legislation* (Second Edition). The Clarendon Press. Reprinted 1879.

Of the Principle of Utility

I. Nature has placed mankind under the governance of two sovereign masters, pain and pleasure. It is for them alone to point out what we ought to do, as well as to determine what we shall do. On the one hand the standard of right and wrong, on the other the chain of causes and effects, are fastened to their throne. They govern us in all we do, in all we say, in all we think: every effort we can make to throw off our subjection, will serve but to demonstrate and confirm it. In words a man may pretend to abjure their empire: but in reality he will remain subject to it all the while. The principle of utility recognizes this subjection, and assumes it for the foundation of that system, the object of which is to rear the fabric of felicity by the hands of reason and of law. Systems which attempt to question it, deal in sounds instead of sense, in caprice instead of reason, in darkness instead of light.

But enough of metaphor and declamation: it is not by such means that moral science is to be improved.

II. The principle of utility is the foundation of the present work: it will be proper therefore at the outset to give an explicit and determinate account of what is meant by it. By the principle of utility is meant that principle which approves or disapproves of every action whatsoever, according to the tendency it appears to have to augment or diminish the happiness of the party whose interest is in question: or, what is the same thing in other words to promote or to oppose that happiness. I say of every action whatsoever, and therefore not only of every action of a private individual, but of every measure of government.

III. By utility is meant that property in any object, whereby it tends to produce benefit, advantage, pleasure, good, or happiness, (all this in the present case comes to the same thing) or (what comes again to the same thing) to prevent the happening of mischief, pain, evil, or unhappiness to the party whose interest is considered: if that party be the community in general, then the happiness of the community: if a particular individual, then the happiness of that individual.

IV. The interest of the community is one of the most general expressions that can occur in the phraseology of morals: no wonder that the meaning of it is often lost. When it has a meaning, it is this. The community is a *fictitious* body, composed of the individual persons who are considered as constituting as it were its *members*. The interest of the community then is, what is it?—the sum of the interests of the several members who compose it.

V. It is in vain to talk of the interest of the community, without understanding what is the interest of the individual. A thing is said to promote the interest, or to be *for* the interest, of an individual, when it tends to add to the sum total of his pleasures: or, what comes to the same thing, to diminish the sum total of his pains.

VI. An action then may be said to be conformable to the principle of utility, or, for shortness sake, to utility, (meaning with respect to the community at large) when the tendency it has to augment the happiness of the community is greater than any it has to diminish it.

VII. A measure of government (which is but a particular kind of action, performed by a particular person or persons) may be said to be conformable to or dictated by the principle of utility, when in like manner the tendency which it has to augment the happiness of the community is greater than any which it has to diminish it.

VIII. When an action, or in particular a measure of government, is supposed by a man to be conformable to the principle of utility, it may be convenient, for the purposes of discourse, to imagine a kind of law or dictate, called a law or dictate of utility: and to speak of the action in question, as being conformable to such law or dictate.

IX. A man may be said to be a partizan of the principle of utility, when the approbation or disapprobation he annexes to any action, or to any measure, is determined by and proportioned to the tendency which he conceives it to have to augment or to diminish the happiness of the community: or in other words, to its conformity or unconformity to the laws or dictates of utility.

X. Of an action that is conformable to the principle of utility one may always say either that it is one that ought to be done, or at least that it is not one that ought not to be done. One may say also, that it is right it should be done; at least that it is not wrong it should be done: that it is a right action; at least that it is not a wrong action. When thus interpreted, the words *ought*, and *right* and *wrong* and others of that stamp, have a meaning: when otherwise, they have none.

XI. Has the rectitude of this principle been ever formally contested? It should seem that it had, by those who have not known what they have been meaning. Is it susceptible of any direct proof? It should seem not: for that which is used to prove every thing else, cannot itself be proved: a chain of proofs must have their commencement somewhere. To give such proof is as impossible as it is needless.

XII. Not that there is or ever has been that human creature breathing, however stupid or perverse, who has not on many, perhaps on most occasions of his life, deferred to it. By the natural constitution of the human frame, on most occasions of their lives men in general embrace this principle, without thinking of it: if not for the ordering of their own actions, yet for the trying of their own actions, as well as of those of other men. There have been, at the same time, not many perhaps, even of the most intelligent, who have been disposed to embrace it purely and without reserve. There are even few who have not taken some occasion or other to quarrel with it, either on account of their not understanding always how to apply it, or on account of some prejudice or other which they were afraid to examine into, or could not bear to part with. For such is the stuff that man is made of: in principle and in practice, in a right track and in a wrong one, the rarest of all human qualities is consistency.

XIII. When a man attempts to combat the principle of utility, it is with reasons drawn, without his being aware of it, from that very principle itself. His arguments, if they prove any thing, prove not that the principle is wrong, but that, according to the applications he supposes to be made of it, it is misapplied. Is it possible for a man to move the earth? Yes; but he must first find out another earth to stand upon.

XIV. To disprove the propriety of it by arguments is impossible; but, from the causes that have been mentioned, or from some confused or partial view of it, a man may happen to be disposed not to relish it. Where this is the case, if he thinks the settling of his opinions on such a subject worth the trouble, let him take the following steps, and at length, perhaps, he may come to reconcile himself to it.

1. Let him settle with himself, whether he would wish to discard this principle altogether; if so, let him consider what it is that all his reasonings (in matters of politics especially) can amount to?

2. If he would, let him settle with himself, whether he would judge and act without any principle, or whether there is any other he would judge an act by?

3. If there be, let him examine and satisfy himself whether the principle he thinks he has found is really any separate intelligible principle; or whether it be not a mere principle in words, a kind of phrase, which at bottom expresses neither more nor less than the mere averment of his own unfounded sentiments; that is, what in another person he might be apt to call caprice?

4. If he is inclined to think that his own approbation or disapprobation, annexed to the idea of an act, without any regard to its consequences, is a sufficient foundation for him to judge and act upon, let him ask himself whether his sentiment is to be a standard of right and wrong, with respect to every other man, or whether every man's sentiment has the same privilege of being a standard to itself?

5. In the first case, let him ask himself whether his principle is not despotical, and hostile to all the rest of the human race?

6. In the second case, whether it is not anarchical, and whether at this rate there are not as many different standards of right and wrong as there are men? And whether even to the same man, the same thing, which is right to-day, may not (without the least change in its nature) be wrong to-morrow? And whether the same thing is not right and wrong in the same place at the same time? And in either case, whether all argument is not at an end? And whether, when two men have said, "I like this," and "I don't like it," they can (upon such a principle) have any thing more to say?

7. If he should have said to himself, No: for that the sentiment which he proposes as a standard must be grounded on reflection, let him say on what particulars the reflection is to turn? If on particulars having relation to the utility of the act, then let him say whether this is not deserting his own principle, and borrowing assistance from that very one in opposition to which he sets it up: or if not on those particulars, on what other particulars?

8. If he should be for compounding the matter, and adopting his own principle in part, and the principle of utility in part, let him say how far he will adopt it?

9. When he has settled with himself where he will stop, then let him ask himself how he justifies to himself the adopting it so far? And why he will not adopt it any farther?

10. Admitting any other principle than the principle of utility to be a right principle, a principle that it is right for a man to pursue; admitting (what is not true) that the word right can have a meaning without reference to utility, let him say whether there is any such thing as a motive that a man can have to pursue the dictates of it: if there is, let him say what that motive is, and how it is to be distinguished from those which enforce the dictates of

utility: if not, then lastly let him say what it is this other principle can be good for?

[...]

Value of a Lot of Pleasure or Pain, How to Be Measured

I. Pleasures then, and the avoidance of pains, are the *ends* that the legislator has in view; it behooves him therefore to understand their *value*. Pleasures and pains are the instruments he has to work with: it behooves him therefore to understand their force, which is again, in other words, their value.

II. To a person considered by *himself*, the value of a pleasure or pain considered *by itself*, will be greater or less, according to the four following circumstances:

1. Its *intensity*.
2. Its *duration*.
3. Its *certainty* or *uncertainty*.
4. Its *propinquity* or *remoteness*.

III. These are the circumstances which are to be considered in estimating a pleasure or a pain considered each of them by itself. But when the value of any pleasure or pain is considered for the purpose of estimating the tendency of any *act* by which it is produced, there are two other circumstances to be taken into the account; these are,

5. Its *fecundity*, or the chance it has of being followed by sensations of the *same* kind: that is, pleasures, if it be a pleasure: pains, if it be a pain.

6. Its *purity*, or the chance it has of not being followed by sensations of the *opposite* kind: that is, pains, if it be a pleasure: pleasures, if it be a pain.

These two last, however, are in strictness scarcely to be deemed properties of the pleasure or the pain itself; they are not, therefore, in strictness to be taken into the account of the value of that pleasure or that pain. They are in strictness to be deemed properties only of the act, or other event, by which such pleasure or pain has been produced; and accordingly are only to be taken into the account of the tendency of such act or such event.

IV. To a *number* of persons, with reference to each of whom to the value of a pleasure or a pain is considered, it will be greater or less, according to seven circumstances: to wit, the six preceding ones; viz.

1. Its *intensity*.
2. Its *duration*.
3. Its *certainty* or *uncertainty*.
4. Its *propinquity* or *remoteness*.
5. Its *fecundity*.
6. Its *purity*.

And one other; to wit:

7. Its *extent*; that is, the number of persons to whom it *extends*; or (in other words) who are affected by it.

V. To take an exact account then of the general tendency of any act, by which the interests of a community are affected, proceed as follows. Begin with any one person of those whose interests seem most immediately to be affected by it: and take an account,

1. Of the value of each distinguishable *pleasure* which appears to be produced by it in the *first* instance.

2. Of the value of each *pain* which appears to be produced by it in the *first* instance.

3. Of the value of each pleasure which appears to be produced by it *after* the first. This constitutes the *fecundity* of the first *pleasure* and the *impurity* of the first *pain*.

4. Of the value of each *pain* which appears to be produced by it after the first. This constitutes the *fecundity* of the first *pain*, and the *impurity* of the first pleasure.

5. Sum up all the values of all the *pleasures* on the one side, and those of all the pains on the other. The balance, if it be on the side of pleasure, will give the *good* tendency of the act upon the whole, with respect to the interests of that *individual* person; if on the side of pain, the *bad* tendency of it upon the whole.

6. Take an account of the *number* of persons whose interests appear to be concerned; and repeat the above process with respect to each. *Sum up* the numbers expressive of the degrees of *good* tendency, which the act has, with respect to each individual, in regard to whom the tendency of it is *good* upon

the whole: do this again with respect to each individual, in regard to whom the tendency of it is *good* upon the whole: do this again with respect to each individual, in regard to whom the tendency of it is *bad* upon the whole. Take the *balance* which if on the side of *pleasure*, will give the general *good tendency* of the act, with respect to the total number or community of individuals concerned; if on the side of pain, the general *evil tendency*, with respect to the same community.

VI. It is not to be expected that this process should be strictly pursued previously to every moral judgment, or to every legislative or judicial operation. It may, however, be always kept in view: and as near as the process actually pursued on these occasions approaches to it, so near will such process approach to the character of an exact one.

VII. The same process is alike applicable to pleasure and pain, in whatever shape they appear: and by whatever denomination they are distinguished: to pleasure, whether it be called *good* (which is properly the cause or instrument of pleasure) or *profit* (which is distant pleasure, or the cause or instrument of, distant pleasure,) or *convenience*, or *advantage*, *benefit*, *emolument*, *happiness*, and so forth: to pain, whether it be called *evil*, (which corresponds to *good*) or *mischief*, or *inconvenience*, or *disadvantage*, or *loss*, or *unhappiness*, and so forth.

VIII. Nor is this a novel and unwarranted, any more than it is a useless theory. In all this there is nothing but what the practice of mankind, wheresoever they have a clear view of their own interest, is perfectly conformable to. An article of property, an estate in land, for instance, is valuable, on what account? On account of the pleasures of all kinds which it enables a man to produce, and what comes to the same thing the pains of all kinds which it

enables him to avert. But the value of such an article of property is universally understood to rise or fall according to the length or shortness of the time which a man has in it: the certainty or uncertainty of its coming into possession: and the nearness or remoteness of the time at which, if at all, it is to come into possession. As to the *intensity* of the pleasures which a man may derive from it, this is never thought of, because it depends upon the use which each particular person may come to make of it; which cannot be estimated till the particular pleasures he may come to derive from it, or the particular pains he may come to exclude by means of it, are brought to view. For the same reason, neither does he think of the *fecundity* or *purity* of those pleasures.

Thus much for pleasure and pain, happiness and unhappiness, in *general*. We come now to consider the several particular kinds of pain and pleasure.

DISCUSSION QUESTIONS

1. Explain the principle of utility. Use an example to show how the principle could be used to decide a matter of political policy, e.g., whether to institute capital punishment or to legalize the use of marijuana.

2. Explain how, according to Bentham, pleasures and pains are to be weighed against one another. Use the example that you used in (1) to show how the factors that Bentham discusses would be involved in an actual decision of policy.

28

John Stuart Mill, selection from *Utilitarianism* (1863)

In the following selection, Mill outlines his utilitarian moral and political theory and defends it against several potential objections. On Mill, see reading 23 above.

SOURCE

Mill, John Stuart. *Utilitarianism* (13th Edition). The University of Chicago Press. Reprinted 1906.

What Utilitarianism Is

A passing remark is all that needs be given to the ignorant blunder of supposing that those who stand up for utility as the test of right and wrong, use the term in that restricted and merely colloquial sense in which utility is opposed to pleasure. An apology is due to the philosophical opponents of utilitarianism, for even the momentary appearance of confounding them with any one capable of so absurd a misconception; which is the more extraordinary, inasmuch as the contrary accusation, of referring everything to pleasure, and that too in its grossest form, is another of the common charges against utilitarianism: and, as has been pointedly remarked by an able writer, the same sort of persons, and often the very same persons, denounce the theory "as impracticably dry when the word utility precedes the word pleasure, and as too practicably voluptuous when the word pleasure precedes the word utility." Those who know anything about the matter are aware that every writer, from Epicurus to Bentham, who maintained the theory of utility, meant by it, not something to be contradistinguished from pleasure, but pleasure itself, together with exemption from pain; and instead of opposing the useful to the agreeable or the ornamental, have always declared that the useful means these, among other things. Yet the common herd, including the herd of writers, not only in newspapers and periodicals, but in books of weight and pretension, are perpetually falling into this shallow mistake. Having caught up the word utilitarian, while knowing nothing whatever about it but its sound, they habitually express by it the rejection, or the neglect, of pleasure in some of its forms; of beauty, of ornament, or of amusement. Nor is the term thus ignorantly misapplied solely in disparagement, but occasionally in compliment; as though it implied superiority to frivolity and the mere pleasures of the moment. And this perverted use is the only one in which the word is popularly known, and the one from which the new generation are acquiring their sole notion of its meaning. Those who introduced the word, but who had for many years discontinued it as a distinctive appellation, may well feel themselves called upon to resume it, if by doing so they can hope to contribute anything towards rescuing it from this utter degradation.

The creed which accepts as the foundation of morals, *utility*, or the *greatest happiness principle*, holds that actions are right in proportion as they tend to promote happiness, wrong as they tend to produce the reverse of happiness. By "happiness" is intended pleasure, and the absence of pain; by unhappiness, pain, and the privation of pleasure. To give a clear view of the moral standard set up by the theory, much more requires to be said; in particular, what things it includes in the ideas of pain and pleasure; and to what extent this is left an open question. But these supplementary explanations do not affect the theory of life on which this theory of morality is grounded—namely, that pleasure, and freedom from pain, are the only things desirable as ends; and that all desirable things (which are as numerous in the utilitarian as in any other scheme) are desirable either for the pleasure inherent in themselves, or as means to the promotion of pleasure and the prevention of pain.

Now, such a theory of life excites in many minds, and among them in some of the most estimable in feeling and purpose, inveterate dislike. To suppose that life has (as they express it) no higher end than pleasure—no better and nobler object of desire and pursuit—they designate as utterly mean and grovelling; as a doctrine worthy only of swine, to

whom the followers of Epicurus were, at a very early period, contemptuously likened; and modern holders of the doctrine are occasionally made the subject of equally polite comparisons by its German, French, and English assailants.

When thus attacked, the Epicureans have always answered, that it is not they, but their accusers, who represent human nature in a degrading light; since the accusation supposes human beings to be capable of no pleasures except those of which swine are capable. If this supposition were true, the charge could not be gainsaid, but would then be no longer an imputation; for if the sources of pleasure were precisely the same to human beings and to swine, the rule of life which is good enough for the one would be good enough for the other. The comparison of the Epicurean life to that of beasts is felt as degrading, precisely because a beast's pleasures do not satisfy a human being's conceptions of happiness. Human beings have faculties more elevated than the animal appetites, and when once made conscious of them, do not regard anything as happiness which does not include their gratification. I do not, indeed, consider the Epicureans to have been by any means faultless in drawing out their scheme of consequences from the utilitarian principle. To do this in any sufficient manner, many Stoic, as well as Christian elements require to be included. But there is no known Epicurean theory of life which does not assign to the pleasures of the intellect, of the feelings and imagination, and of the moral sentiments, a much higher value as pleasures than to those of mere sensation. It must be admitted, however, that utilitarian writers in general have placed the superiority of mental over bodily pleasures chiefly in the greater permanency, safety, uncostliness, etc., of the former—that is, in their circumstantial advantages rather than in their intrinsic nature. And on all these points utilitarians have fully proved their case; but they might have taken the other, and, as it may be called, higher ground, with entire consistency. It is quite compatible with the principle of utility to recognise the fact, that some *kinds* of pleasure are more desirable and more valuable than others. It would be absurd that while, in estimating all other things, quality is considered as well as quantity, the estimation of pleasures should be supposed to depend on quantity alone.

If I am asked, what I mean by difference of quality in pleasures, or what makes one pleasure more valuable than another, merely as a pleasure, except its being greater in amount, there is but one possible answer. Of two pleasures, if there be one to which all or almost all who have experience of both give a decided preference, irrespective of any feeling of moral obligation to prefer it, that is the more desirable pleasure. If one of the two is, by those who are competently acquainted with both, placed so far above the other that they prefer it, even though knowing it to be attended with a greater amount of discontent, and would not resign it for any quantity of the other pleasure which their nature is capable of, we are justified in ascribing to the preferred enjoyment a superiority in quality, so far outweighing quantity as to render it, in comparison, of small account.

Now it is an unquestionable fact that those who are equally acquainted with, and equally capable of appreciating and enjoying, both, do give a most marked preference to the manner of existence which employs their higher faculties. Few human creatures would consent to be changed into any of the lower animals, for a promise of the fullest allowance of a beast's pleasures; no intelligent human being would consent to be a fool, no instructed person would be an ignoramus, no person of feeling and conscience would be selfish and base, even though they should be persuaded that the fool, the dunce, or the rascal is better satisfied with his lot than they are with theirs. They would not resign what they possess more than he for the most complete satisfaction of all the desires which they have in common with him. If they ever fancy they would, it is only in cases of unhappiness so extreme, that to escape from it they would exchange their lot for almost any other, however undesirable in their own eyes. A being of higher faculties requires more to make him happy, is capable probably of more acute suffering, and certainly accessible to it at more points,

than one of an inferior type; but in spite of these liabilities, he can never really wish to sink into what he feels to be a lower grade of existence. We may give what explanation we please of this unwillingness; we may attribute it to pride, a name which is given indiscriminately to some of the most and to some of the least estimable feelings of which mankind are capable: we may refer it to the love of liberty and personal independence, an appeal to which was with the Stoics one of the most effective means for the inculcation of it; to the love of power, or to the love of excitement, both of which do really enter into and contribute to it: but its most appropriate appellation is a sense of dignity, which all human beings possess in one form or other, and in some, though by no means in exact, proportion to their higher faculties, and which is so essential a part of the happiness of those in whom it is strong, that nothing which conflicts with it could be, otherwise than momentarily, an object of desire to them.

Whoever supposes that this preference takes place at a sacrifice of happiness—that the superior being, in anything like equal circumstances, is not happier than the inferior—confounds the two very different ideas, of *happiness*, and *content*. It is indisputable that the being whose capacities of enjoyment are low, has the greatest chance of having them fully satisfied; and a highly endowed being will always feel that any happiness which he can look for, as the world is constituted, is imperfect. But he can learn to bear its imperfections, if they are at all bearable; and they will not make him envy the being who is indeed unconscious of the imperfections, but only because he feels not at all the good which those imperfections qualify. It is better to be a human being dissatisfied than a pig satisfied; better to be Socrates dissatisfied than a fool satisfied. And if the fool, or the pig, are of a different opinion, it is because they only know their own side of the question. The other party to the comparison knows both sides.

It may be objected, that many who are capable of the higher pleasures, occasionally, under the influence of temptation, postpone them to the lower. But this is quite compatible with a full appreciation of the intrinsic superiority of the higher. Men often, from infirmity of character, make their election for the nearer good, though they know it to be the less valuable; and this no less when the choice is between two bodily pleasures, than when it is between bodily and mental. They pursue sensual indulgences to the injury of health, though perfectly aware that health is the greater good.

It may be further objected, that many who begin with youthful enthusiasm for everything noble, as they advance in years sink into indolence and selfishness. But I do not believe that those who undergo this very common change, voluntarily choose the lower description of pleasures in preference to the higher. I believe that before they devote themselves exclusively to the one, they have already become incapable of the other. Capacity for the nobler feelings is in most natures a very tender plant, easily killed, not only by hostile influences, but by mere want of sustenance; and in the majority of young persons it speedily dies away if the occupations to which their position in life has devoted them, and the society into which it has thrown them, are not favourable to keeping that higher capacity in exercise. Men lose their high aspirations as they lose their intellectual tastes, because they have not time or opportunity for indulging them; and they addict themselves to inferior pleasures, not because they deliberately prefer them, but because they are either the only ones to which they have access, or the only ones which they are any longer capable of enjoying. It may be questioned whether any one who has remained equally susceptible to both classes of pleasures, ever knowingly and calmly preferred the lower; though many, in all ages, have broken down in an ineffectual attempt to combine both.

From this verdict of the only competent judges, I apprehend there can be no appeal. On a question which is the best worth having of two pleasures, or which of two modes of existence is the most grateful to the feelings, apart from its moral attributes and from its consequences, the judgment of those who are qualified by knowledge of both, or, if they differ, that of the majority among them, must be admitted as final. And there needs be the

less hesitation to accept this judgment respecting the quality of pleasures, since there is no other tribunal to be referred to even on the question of quantity. What means are there of determining which is the acutest of two pains, or the intensest of two pleasurable sensations, except the general suffrage of those who are familiar with both? Neither pains nor pleasures are homogeneous, and pain is always heterogeneous with pleasure. What is there to decide whether a particular pleasure is worth purchasing at the cost of a particular pain, except the feelings and judgment of the experienced? When, therefore, those feelings and judgment declare the pleasures derived from the higher faculties to be preferable *in kind*, apart from the question of intensity, to those of which the animal nature, disjoined from the higher faculties, is susceptible, they are entitled on this subject to the same regard.

I have dwelt on this point, as being a necessary part of a perfectly just conception of utility or happiness, considered as the directive rule of human conduct. But it is by no means an indispensable condition to the acceptance of the utilitarian standard; for that standard is not the agent's own greatest happiness, but the greatest amount of happiness altogether; and if it may possibly be doubted whether a noble character is always the happier for its nobleness, there can be no doubt that it makes other people happier, and that the world in general is immensely a gainer by it. Utilitarianism, therefore, could only attain its end by the general cultivation of nobleness of character, even if each individual were only benefited by the nobleness of others, and his own, so far as happiness is concerned, were a sheer deduction from the benefit. But the bare enunciation of such an absurdity as this last, renders refutation superfluous.

According to the "greatest happiness principle," as above explained, the ultimate end, with reference to and for the sake of which all other things are desirable (whether we are considering our own good or that of other people), is an existence exempt as far as possible from pain, and as rich as possible in enjoyments, both in point of quantity and quality; the test of quality, and the rule for measuring it against quantity, being the preference felt by those who in their opportunities of experience, to which must be added their habits of self-consciousness and self-observation, are best furnished with the means of comparison. This, being, according to the utilitarian opinion, the end of human action, is necessarily also the standard of morality; which may accordingly be defined, the rules and precepts for human conduct, by the observance of which an existence such as has been described might be, to the greatest extent possible, secured to all mankind; and not to them only, but, so far as the nature of things admits, to the whole sentient creation.

Against this doctrine, however, arises another class of objectors, who say that happiness, in any form, cannot be the rational purpose of human life and action; because, in the first place, it is unattainable: and they contemptuously ask, what right hast thou to be happy?—a question which Mr. Carlyle[1] clenches by the addition, What right, a short time ago, hadst thou even *to be*? Next, they say, that men can do *without* happiness; that all noble human beings have felt this, and could not have become noble but by learning the lesson of *Entsagen*, or renunciation; which lesson, thoroughly learnt and submitted to, they affirm to be the beginning and necessary condition of all virtue.

The first of these objections would go to the root of the matter were it well founded; for if no happiness is to be had at all by human beings, the attainment of it cannot be the end of morality, or of any rational conduct. Though, even in that case, something might still be said for the utilitarian theory; since utility includes not solely the pursuit of happiness, but the prevention or mitigation of unhappiness; and if the former aim be chimerical, there will be all the greater scope and more imperative need for the latter, so long at least as mankind think fit to live, and do not take refuge in the simultaneous act of suicide recommended under certain conditions

by Novalis.[2] When, however, it is thus positively asserted to be impossible that human life should be happy, the assertion, if not something like a verbal quibble, is at least an exaggeration. If by happiness be meant a continuity of highly pleasurable excitement, it is evident enough that this is impossible. A state of exalted pleasure lasts only moments, or in some cases, and with some intermissions, hours or days, and is the occasional brilliant flash of enjoyment, not its permanent and steady flame. Of this the philosophers who have taught that happiness is the end of life were as fully aware as those who taunt them. The happiness which they meant was not a life of rapture; but moments of such, in an existence made up of few and transitory pains, many and various pleasures, with a decided predominance of the active over the passive, and having as the foundation of the whole, not to expect more from life than it is capable of bestowing. A life thus composed, to those who have been fortunate enough to obtain it, has always appeared worthy of the name of happiness. And such an existence is even now the lot of many, during some considerable portion of their lives. The present wretched education, and wretched social arrangements, are the only real hindrance to its being attainable by almost all.

The objectors perhaps may doubt whether human beings, if taught to consider happiness as the end of life, would be satisfied with such a moderate share of it. But great numbers of mankind have been satisfied with much less. The main constituents of a satisfied life appear to be two, either of which by itself is often found sufficient for the purpose: tranquillity, and excitement. With much tranquillity, many find that they can be content with very little pleasure: with much excitement, many can reconcile themselves to a considerable quantity of pain. There is assuredly no inherent impossibility in enabling even the mass of mankind to unite both; since the two are so far from being incompatible

---

[1] [Thomas Carlyle (1795–1881) was a Scottish writer and historian.]

[2] [Novalis was the pseudonym of Georg Philipp Friedrich Freiherr von Hardenberg (1772–1801), a German Romantic author.]

that they are in natural alliance, the prolongation of either being a preparation for, and exciting a wish for, the other. It is only those in whom indolence amounts to a vice, that do not desire excitement after an interval of repose: it is only those in whom the need of excitement is a disease, that feel the tranquillity which follows excitement dull and insipid, instead of pleasurable in direct proportion to the excitement which preceded it. When people who are tolerably fortunate in their outward lot do not find in life sufficient enjoyment to make it valuable to them, the cause generally is, caring for nobody but themselves. To those who have neither public nor private affections, the excitements of life are much curtailed, and in any case dwindle in value as the time approaches when all selfish interests must be terminated by death: while those who leave after them objects of personal affection, and especially those who have also cultivated a fellow-feeling with the collective interests of mankind, retain as lively an interest in life on the eve of death as in the vigour of youth and health. Next to selfishness, the principal cause which makes life unsatisfactory is want of mental cultivation. A cultivated mind—I do not mean that of a philosopher, but any mind to which the fountains of knowledge have been opened, and which has been taught, in any tolerable degree, to exercise its faculties—finds sources of inexhaustible interest in all that surrounds it; in the objects of nature, the achievements of art, the imaginations of poetry, the incidents of history, the ways of mankind, past and present, and their prospects in the future. It is possible, indeed, to become indifferent to all this, and that too without having exhausted a thousandth part of it; but only when one has had from the beginning no moral or human interest in these things, and has sought in them only the gratification of curiosity.

Now there is absolutely no reason in the nature of things why an amount of mental culture sufficient to give an intelligent interest in these objects of contemplation, should not be the inheritance of every one born in a civilised country. As little is there an inherent necessity that any human being should be a selfish egotist, devoid of every feeling or care but those which centre in his own miserable individuality. Something far superior to this is sufficiently common even now, to give ample earnest of what the human species may be made. Genuine private affections and a sincere interest in the public good, are possible, though in unequal degrees, to every rightly brought up human being. In a world in which there is so much to interest, so much to enjoy, and so much also to correct and improve, every one who has this moderate amount of moral and intellectual requisites is capable of an existence which may be called enviable; and unless such a person, through bad laws, or subjection to the will of others, is denied the liberty to use the sources of happiness within his reach, he will not fail to find this enviable existence, if he escape the positive evils of life, the great sources of physical and mental suffering—such as indigence, disease, and the unkindness, worthlessness, or premature loss of objects of affection. The main stress of the problem lies, therefore, in the contest with these calamities, from which it is a rare good fortune entirely to escape; which, as things now are, cannot be obviated, and often cannot be in any material degree mitigated. Yet no one whose opinion deserves a moment's consideration can doubt that most of the great positive evils of the world are in themselves removable, and will, if human affairs continue to improve, be in the end reduced within narrow limits. Poverty, in any sense implying suffering, may be completely extinguished by the wisdom of society, combined with the good sense and providence of individuals. Even that most intractable of enemies, disease, may be indefinitely reduced in dimensions by good physical and moral education, and proper control of noxious influences; while the progress of science holds out a promise for the future of still more direct conquests over this detestable foe. And every advance in that direction relieves us from some, not only of the chances which cut short our own lives, but, what concerns us still more, which deprive us of those in whom our happiness is wrapt up. As for vicissitudes of fortune, and other disappointments connected with worldly circumstances, these are principally the effect either of gross imprudence, of ill-regulated desires, or of bad or imperfect social institutions.

All the grand sources, in short, of human suffering are in a great degree, many of them almost entirely, conquerable by human care and effort; and though their removal is grievously slow—though a long succession of generations will perish in the breach before the conquest is completed, and this world becomes all that, if will and knowledge were not wanting, it might easily be made—yet every mind sufficiently intelligent and generous to bear a part, however small and unconspicuous, in the endeavour, will draw a noble enjoyment from the contest itself, which he would not for any bribe in the form of selfish indulgence consent to be without.

And this leads to the true estimation of what is said by the objectors concerning the possibility, and the obligation, of learning to do without happiness. Unquestionably it is possible to do without happiness; it is done involuntarily by nineteen-twentieths of mankind, even in those parts of our present world which are least deep in barbarism; and it often has to be done voluntarily by the hero or the martyr, for the sake of something which he prizes more than his individual happiness. But this something, what is it, unless the happiness of others or some of the requisites of happiness? It is noble to be capable of resigning entirely one's own portion of happiness, or chances of it: but, after all, this self-sacrifice must be for some end; it is not its own end; and if we are told that its end is not happiness, but virtue, which is better than happiness, I ask, would the sacrifice be made if the hero or martyr did not believe that it would earn for others immunity from similar sacrifices? Would it be made if he thought that his renunciation of happiness for himself would produce no fruit for any of his fellow creatures, but to make their lot like his, and place them also in the condition of persons who have renounced happiness? All honour to those who can abnegate for themselves the personal enjoyment of life, when by such renunciation they contribute worthily to increase the amount of happiness in the world; but he who does it, or professes to do it, for any other purpose, is no more

deserving of admiration than the ascetic mounted on his pillar. He may be an inspiriting proof of what men *can* do, but assuredly not an example of what they *should*.

Though it is only in a very imperfect state of the world's arrangements that any one can best serve the happiness of others by the absolute sacrifice of his own, yet so long as the world is in that imperfect state, I fully acknowledge that the readiness to make such a sacrifice is the highest virtue which can be found in man. I will add, that in this condition the world, paradoxical as the assertion may be, the conscious ability to do without happiness gives the best prospect of realising, such happiness as is attainable. For nothing except that consciousness can raise a person above the chances of life, by making him feel that, let fate and fortune do their worst, they have not power to subdue him: which, once felt, frees him from excess of anxiety concerning the evils of life, and enables him, like many a Stoic in the worst times of the Roman Empire, to cultivate in tranquillity the sources of satisfaction accessible to him, without concerning himself about the uncertainty of their duration, any more than about their inevitable end.

Meanwhile, let utilitarians never cease to claim the morality of self-devotion as a possession which belongs by as good a right to them, as either to the Stoic or to the Transcendentalist. The utilitarian morality does recognise in human beings the power of sacrificing their own greatest good for the good of others. It only refuses to admit that the sacrifice is itself a good. A sacrifice which does not increase, or tend to increase, the sum total of happiness, it considers as wasted. The only self-renunciation which it applauds, is devotion to the happiness, or to some of the means of happiness, of others; either of mankind collectively, or of individuals within the limits imposed by the collective interests of mankind.

I must again repeat, what the assailants of utilitarianism seldom have the justice to acknowledge, that the happiness which forms the utilitarian standard of what is right in conduct, is not the agent's own happiness, but that of all concerned.

As between his own happiness and that of others, utilitarianism requires him to be as strictly impartial as a disinterested and benevolent spectator. In the golden rule of Jesus of Nazareth, we read the complete spirit of the ethics of utility. To do as you would be done by, and to love your neighbour as yourself, constitute the ideal perfection of utilitarian morality. As the means of making the nearest approach to this ideal, utility would enjoin, first, that laws and social arrangements should place the happiness, or (as speaking practically it may be called) the interest, of every individual, as nearly as possible in harmony with the interest of the whole; and secondly, that education and opinion, which have so vast a power over human character, should so use that power as to establish in the mind of every individual an indissoluble association between his own happiness and the good of the whole—especially between his own happiness and the practice of such modes of conduct, negative and positive, as regard for the universal happiness prescribes; so that not only he may be unable to conceive the possibility of happiness to himself, consistently with conduct opposed to the general good, but also that a direct impulse to promote the general good may be in every individual one of the habitual motives of action, and the sentiments connected therewith may fill a large and prominent place in every human being's sentient existence. If the impugners of the utilitarian morality represented it to their own minds in this, its true character, I know not what recommendation possessed by any other morality they could possibly affirm to be wanting to it; what more beautiful or more exalted developments of human nature any other ethical system can be supposed to foster, or what springs of action, not accessible to the utilitarian, such systems rely on for giving effect to their mandates.

The objectors to utilitarianism cannot always be charged with representing it in a discreditable light. On the contrary, those among them who entertain anything like a just idea of its disinterested character, sometimes find fault with its standard as being too high for humanity. They say it is exacting too much to require that people shall always act from the inducement of promoting the general interests of society. But this is to mistake the very meaning of a standard of morals, and confound the rule of action with the motive of it. It is the business of ethics to tell us what are our duties, or by what test we may know them; but no system of ethics requires that the sole motive of all we do shall be a feeling of duty; on the contrary, ninety-nine hundredths of all our actions are done from other motives, and rightly so done, if the rule of duty does not condemn them. It is the more unjust to utilitarianism that this particular misapprehension should be made a ground of objection to it, inasmuch as utilitarian moralists have gone beyond almost all others in affirming that the motive has nothing to do with the morality of the action, though much with the worth of the agent. He who saves a fellow creature from drowning does what is morally right, whether his motive be duty, or the hope of being paid for his trouble; he who betrays the friend that trusts him, is guilty of a crime, even if his object be to serve another friend to whom he is under greater obligations.

But to speak only of actions done from the motive of duty, and in direct obedience to principle: it is a misapprehension of the utilitarian mode of thought, to conceive it as implying that people should fix their minds upon so wide a generality as the world, or society at large. The great majority of good actions are intended not for the benefit of the world, but for that of individuals, of which the good of the world is made up; and the thoughts of the most virtuous man need not on these occasions travel beyond the particular persons concerned, except so far as is necessary to assure himself that in benefiting them he is not violating the rights, that is, the legitimate and authorised expectations, of any one else. The multiplication of happiness is, according to the utilitarian ethics, the object of virtue: the occasions on which any person (except one in a thousand) has it in his power to do this on an extended scale, in other words to be a public benefactor, are but exceptional; and on these occasions alone is he called on to consider public utility; in every other case, private utility, the interest or happiness of some few persons, is all he has to attend to. Those alone the influence of whose actions extends to society in general, need concern themselves habitually about so large an object. In the case of abstinences indeed—of things which people forbear to do from moral considerations, though the consequences in the particular case might be beneficial—it would be unworthy of an intelligent agent not to be consciously aware that the action is of a class which, if practised generally, would be generally injurious, and that this is the ground of the obligation to abstain from it. The amount of regard for the public interest implied in this recognition, is no greater than is demanded by every system of morals, for they all enjoin to abstain from whatever is manifestly pernicious to society.

The same considerations dispose of another reproach against the doctrine of utility, founded on a still grosser misconception of the purpose of a standard of morality, and of the very meaning of the words right and wrong. It is often affirmed that utilitarianism renders men cold and unsympathising; that it chills their moral feelings towards individuals; that it makes them regard only the dry and hard consideration of the consequences of actions, not taking into their moral estimate the qualities from which those actions emanate. If the assertion means that they do not allow their judgment respecting the rightness or wrongness of an action to be influenced by their opinion of the qualities of the person who does it, this is a complaint not against utilitarianism, but against having any standard of morality at all; for certainly no known ethical standard decides an action to be good or bad because it is done by a good or a bad man, still less because done by an amiable, a brave, or a benevolent man, or the contrary. These considerations are relevant, not to the estimation of actions, but of persons; and there is nothing in the utilitarian theory inconsistent with the fact that there are other things which interest us in persons besides the rightness and wrongness of their actions. The Stoics, indeed, with the paradoxical misuse of language which was part of their system, and by which they strove to

raise themselves above all concern about anything but virtue, were fond of saying that he who has that has everything; that he, and only he, is rich, is beautiful, is a king. But no claim of this description is made for the virtuous man by the utilitarian doctrine. Utilitarians are quite aware that there are other desirable possessions and qualities besides virtue, and are perfectly willing to allow to all of them their full worth. They are also aware that a right action does not necessarily indicate a virtuous character, and that actions which are blamable, often proceed from qualities entitled to praise. When this is apparent in any particular case, it modifies their estimation, not certainly of the act, but of the agent. I grant that they are, notwithstanding, of opinion, that in the long run the best proof of a good character is good actions; and resolutely refuse to consider any mental disposition as good, of which the predominant tendency is to produce bad conduct. This makes them unpopular with many people; but it is an unpopularity which they must share with every one who regards the distinction between right and wrong in a serious light; and the reproach is not one which a conscientious utilitarian need be anxious to repel.

If no more be meant by the objection than that many utilitarians look on the morality of actions, as measured by the utilitarian standard, with too exclusive a regard, and do not lay sufficient stress upon the other beauties of character which go towards making a human being lovable or admirable, this may be admitted. Utilitarians who have cultivated their moral feelings, but not their sympathies nor their artistic perceptions, do fall into this mistake; and so do all other moralists under the same conditions. What can be said in excuse for other moralists is equally available for them, namely, that, if there is to be any error, it is better that it should be on that side. As a matter of fact, we may affirm that among utilitarians as among adherents of other systems, there is every imaginable degree of rigidity and of laxity in the application of their standard: some are even puritanically rigorous, while others are as indulgent as can possibly be desired by sinner or by sentimentalist. But on the whole, a doctrine which brings prominently forward the interest that mankind have in the repression and prevention of conduct which violates the moral law, is likely to be inferior to no other in turning the sanctions of opinion against such violations. It is true, the question, "What does violate the moral law?" is one on which those who recognise different standards of morality are likely now and then to differ. But difference of opinion on moral questions was not first introduced into the world by utilitarianism, while that doctrine does supply, if not always an easy, at all events a tangible and intelligible mode of deciding such differences.

It may not be superfluous to notice a few more of the common misapprehensions of utilitarian ethics, even those which are so obvious and gross that it might appear impossible for any person of candour and intelligence to fall into them; since persons, even of considerable mental endowments, often give themselves so little trouble to understand the bearings of any opinion against which they entertain a prejudice, and men are in general so little conscious of this voluntary ignorance as a defect, that the vulgarest misunderstandings of ethical doctrines are continually met with in the deliberate writings of persons of the greatest pretensions both to high principle and to philosophy. We not uncommonly hear the doctrine of utility inveighed against as a *godless* doctrine. If it be necessary to say anything at all against so mere an assumption, we may say that the question depends upon what idea we have formed of the moral character of the Deity. If it be a true belief that God desires, above all things, the happiness of his creatures, and that this was his purpose in their creation, utility is not only not a godless doctrine, but more profoundly religious than any other. If it be meant that utilitarianism does not recognise the revealed will of God as the supreme law of morals, I answer, that a utilitarian who believes in the perfect goodness and wisdom of God, necessarily believes that whatever God has thought fit to reveal on the subject of morals, must fulfil the requirements of utility in a supreme degree. But others besides utilitarians have been of opinion that the Christian revelation was intended, and is fitted, to inform the hearts and minds of mankind with a spirit which should enable them to find for themselves what is right, and incline them to do it when found, rather than to tell them, except in a very general way, what it is; and that we need a doctrine of ethics, carefully followed out, to *interpret* to us the will of God. Whether this opinion is correct or not, it is superfluous here to discuss; since whatever aid religion, either natural or revealed, can afford to ethical investigation, is as open to the utilitarian moralist as to any other. He can use it as the testimony of God to the usefulness or hurtfulness of any given course of action, by as good a right as others can use it for the indication of a transcendental law, having no connection with usefulness or with happiness.

Again, utility is often summarily stigmatised as an immoral doctrine by giving it the name of *expediency*, and taking advantage of the popular use of that term to contrast it with *principle*. But the *expedient*, in the sense in which it is opposed to the *right*, generally means that which is expedient for the particular interest of the agent himself; as when a minister sacrifices the interests of his country to keep himself in place. When it means anything better than this, it means that which is expedient for some immediate object, some temporary purpose, but which violates a rule whose observance is expedient in a much higher degree. The expedient, in this sense, instead of being the same thing with the useful, is a branch of the hurtful. Thus, it would often be expedient, for the purpose of getting over some momentary embarrassment, or attaining some object immediately useful to ourselves or others, to tell a lie. But inasmuch as the cultivation in ourselves of a sensitive feeling on the subject of veracity, is one of the most useful, and the enfeeblement of that feeling one of the most hurtful, things to which our conduct can be instrumental; and inasmuch as any, even unintentional, deviation from truth, does that much towards weakening the trustworthiness of human assertion, which is not only the principal support of all present social well-being, but the insufficiency of which does more than any one thing that can be named to keep back civilisation, virtue, everything on which human happiness on the largest scale depends; we feel that the violation, for a present advantage, of a rule of such transcendant expediency, is not expedient, and that he who, for the sake of a convenience to himself or to some other individual, does what depends on him to deprive mankind of the good, and inflict upon them the evil, involved in the greater or less reliance which they can place in each other's word, acts the part of one of their worst enemies. Yet that even this rule, sacred as it is, admits of possible exceptions, is acknowledged by all moralists; the chief of which is when the withholding of some fact (as of information from a malefactor, or of bad news from a person dangerously ill) would save an individual (especially an individual other than oneself) from great and unmerited evil, and when the withholding can only be effected by denial. But in order that the exception may not extend itself beyond the need, and may have the least possible effect in weakening reliance on veracity, it ought to be recognised, and, if possible, its limits defined; and if the principle of utility is good for anything, it must be good for weighing these conflicting utilities against one another, and marking out the region within which one or the other preponderates.

Again, defenders of utility often find themselves called upon to reply to such objections as this—that there is not time, previous to action, for calculating and weighing the effects of any line of conduct on the general happiness. This is exactly as if any one were to say that it is impossible to guide our conduct by Christianity, because there is not time, on every occasion on which anything has to be done, to read through the Old and New Testaments. The answer to the objection is, that there has been ample time, namely, the whole past duration of the human species. During all that time, mankind have been learning by experience the tendencies of actions; on which experience all the prudence, as well as all the morality of life, are dependent. People talk as if the commencement of this course of experience had hitherto been put off, and as if, at the moment when some man feels tempted to meddle with the property or life of another, he had to

begin considering for the first time whether murder and theft are injurious to human happiness. Even then I do not think that he would find the question very puzzling; but, at all events, the matter is now done to his hand.

It is truly a whimsical supposition that, if mankind were agreed in considering utility to be the test of morality, they would remain without any agreement as to what is useful, and would take no measures for having their notions on the subject taught to the young, and enforced by law and opinion. There is no difficulty in proving any ethical standard whatever to work ill, if we suppose universal idiocy to be conjoined with it; but on any hypothesis short of that, mankind must by this time have acquired positive beliefs as to the effects of some actions on their happiness; and the beliefs which have thus come down are the rules of morality for the multitude, and for the philosopher until he has succeeded in finding better. That philosophers might easily do this, even now, on many subjects; that the received code of ethics is by no means of divine right; and that mankind have still much to learn as to the effects of actions on the general happiness, I admit, or rather, earnestly maintain. The corollaries from the principle of utility, like the precepts of every practical art, admit of indefinite improvement, and, in a progressive state of the human mind, their improvement is perpetually going on.

But to consider the rules of morality as improvable, is one thing; to pass over the intermediate generalisations entirely, and endeavour to test each individual action directly by the first principle, is another. It is a strange notion that the acknowledgment of a first principle is inconsistent with the admission of secondary ones. To inform a traveller respecting the place of his ultimate destination, is not to forbid the use of landmarks and directionposts on the way. The proposition that happiness is the end and aim of morality, does not mean that no road ought to be laid down to that goal, or that persons going thither should not be advised to take one direction rather than another. Men really ought to leave off talking a kind of nonsense on this subject, which they would neither talk nor listen to on other matters of practical concernment. Nobody argues that the art of navigation is not founded on astronomy, because sailors cannot wait to calculate the Nautical Almanac. Being rational creatures, they go to sea with it ready calculated; and all rational creatures go out upon the sea of life with their minds made up on the common questions of right and wrong, as well as on many of the far more difficult questions of wise and foolish. And this, as long as foresight is a human quality, it is to be presumed they will continue to do. Whatever we adopt as the fundamental principle of morality, we require subordinate principles to apply it by; the impossibility of doing without them, being common to all systems, can afford no argument against any one in particular; but gravely to argue as if no such secondary principles could be had, and as if mankind had remained till now, and always must remain, without drawing any general conclusions from the experience of human life, is as high a pitch, I think, as absurdity has ever reached in philosophical controversy.

The remainder of the stock arguments against utilitarianism mostly consist in laying to its charge the common infirmities of human nature, and the general difficulties which embarrass conscientious persons in shaping their course through life. We are told that a utilitarian will be apt to make his own particular case an exception to moral rules, and, when under temptation, will see a utility in the breach of a rule, greater than he will see in its observance. But is utility the only creed which is able to furnish us with excuses for evil doing, and means of cheating our own conscience? They are afforded in abundance by all doctrines which recognise as a fact in morals the existence of conflicting considerations; which all doctrines do, that have been believed by sane persons. It is not the fault of any creed, but of the complicated nature of human affairs, that rules of conduct cannot be so framed as to require

no exceptions, and that hardly any kind of action can safely be laid down as either always obligatory or always condemnable. There is no ethical creed which does not temper the rigidity of its laws, by giving a certain latitude, under the moral responsibility of the agent, for accommodation to peculiarities of circumstances; and under every creed, at the opening thus made, self-deception and dishonest casuistry get in. There exists no moral system under which there do not arise unequivocal cases of conflicting obligation. These are the real difficulties, the knotty points both in the theory of ethics, and in the conscientious guidance of personal conduct. They are overcome practically, with greater or with less success, according to the intellect and virtue of the individual; but it can hardly be pretended that any one will be the less qualified for dealing with them, from possessing an ultimate standard to which conflicting rights and duties can be referred. If utility is the ultimate source of moral obligations, utility may be invoked to decide between them when their demands are incompatible. Though the application of the standard may be difficult, it is better than none at all: while in other systems, the moral laws all claiming independent authority, there is no common umpire entitled to interfere between them; their claims to precedence one over another rest on little better than sophistry, and unless determined, as they generally are, by the unacknowledged influence of considerations of utility, afford a free scope for the action of personal desires and partialities. We must remember that only in these cases of conflict between secondary principles is it requisite that first principles should be appealed to. There is no case of moral obligation in which some secondary principle is not involved; and if only one, there can seldom be any real doubt which one it is, in the mind of any person by whom the principle itself is recognised.

DISCUSSION QUESTIONS

1. It might be argued by some that "utility" is something different from "pleasure"; they perhaps may even say that utility is opposed to pleasure. Why does Mill say that this is an "ignorant blunder"?

2. Make a list of several things (or activities) that you take to be pleasurable. Can you divide these activities into different categories? Do you think that any of the pleasures are "better" or "higher" than any of the others? Explain why Mill thinks that there are "higher" and "lower" pleasures.

3. Mill famously writes, "It is better to be a human being dissatisfied than a pig

satisfied; better to be Socrates dissatisfied than a fool satisfied." Explain what you take Mill to be saying here, and explain his argument in support of this claim. What is your critical assessment?

4. What does Mill have to say about the connection between the rightness or wrongness of an action and the motive behind the performance of that action? Do you agree with him? Why or why not?

5. How does Mill respond to the objection which states that there is not time, prior to acting, for us to calculate and weigh the effects of possible actions upon general happiness? Do you believe that his response is adequate? Why or why not?

29

E.F. Carritt, selection from *Ethical and Political Thinking* (1950)

A student of the famous intuitionist Harold Prichard (1871–1947), E.F. Carritt (1876–1964) was perhaps best known for his work in aesthetics. However, he also made significant contributions to both ethical and political philosophy. In the following excerpt from his book, Carritt offers responses to two frequently advanced charges against utilitarianism: that pleasures and pains can allegedly not be weighed quantitatively or qualitatively, and that utilitarianism cannot make room within the theory for the concept of justice.

SOURCE

Carritt, E.F. *Ethical and Political Thinking*, pp. 61–65. Oxford University Press, 1950. Reprinted with the permission of Jonathan Carritt.

1. One criticism frequently brought against utilitarianism seems to me invalid. It is said that pleasures and pains cannot be measured or weighed like proteins or money and therefore cannot be compared, so that I can never tell whether I shall produce an overbalance of pleasure in this way or in that. I cannot weigh the pleasure of a starving man whom I feed on bread against my own in eating strawberries and say that his is twice as great as mine. Such an argument might seem hardly worth serious discussion had it not been used in defence of applying to conduct a theory of abstract economics: "There is no scientific criterion which would enable us to compare or assess the relative importance of needs of different persons ... illegitimate interpersonal comparison,"[1] and "There is no means of testing the magnitude of A's satisfaction as compared with B's."[2]

But this argument, though those who use it are not ready to admit so much, really should apply against any comparison of my own desires and needs. I cannot say that two glasses of beer will give me twice as much pleasure as one, and still less that hearing a concert will give me three times or half

---

[1] Hayek, *Collectivist Economic Planning* [(New York: A.M. Kelley, 1970)], p. 25.

[2] Robbins, *Nature and Significance of Economic Science* [(London: Macmillan and Company, 1932)], pp. 122–24. Cf. Jay, *The Socialist Case* [(London: Faber and Faber, 1947)], ch. 2.

as much: yet I may know very well indeed which will give me *more,* and may act upon the knowledge, since the two things though not measurable are comparable. It is true that, not being measurable, they are less easy to discriminate precisely, where the difference is not great, than physical objects; I may be unable to say whether the smell of roasting coffee or of bacon fried gives me the greater pleasure (mixed with some pain of appetite) even at two successive moments. It is no doubt often easier to read off the luminosity of two very similar surfaces on a pointer than to say which looks brighter, though in the end I have to trust my eyes for the pointer. As we have admitted, the mere existence of other minds is not demonstrable, still less is the intensity of their desires. But if in self-regarding acts I am sometimes prepared to spend my money in the belief that I shall desire tomorrow's bread more than tomorrow's jam, the utilitarian is justified, on his principles, in believing that it is his duty to provide bread for the starving sooner than jam for the well fed.

In fact it would be no commendation of an ethical theory if, on its showing, moral or even beneficent choice were always clear, since in practice we know that it is not. We often wonder if we can do more for the happiness, even the immediate happiness, of our parents or of our children; the former seem more in need of enjoyments, the latter have a keener capacity but a quicker recovery from disappointment. Utilitarianism has no need to stake its case on the possibility of an accurate "hedonistic (or agathistic) calculus." We have a well-founded belief that starvation hurts most people more than a shortage of grapefruit, and no *knowledge how much* more it will hurt even ourselves tomorrow; and it is on such beliefs that we have to act; we can never know either our objective duty or our objective long-run interest.

2. The second objection to the utilitarians is serious and indeed fatal. They make no room for justice. Most of them really admitted this when they found it hard on their principle to allow for the admitted obligation to distribute happiness "fairly," that is either equally or in proportion to desert. This

led them to qualify their definition of duty as "promoting the greatest amount of happiness," by adding "of the greatest number," and to emphasize this by the proviso "every one counts for one and no more." They can hardly have meant by this merely that it did not matter to whom I gave the happiness so long as I produced the most possible, for this they had already implied. They must at least have meant that if I could produce the same amount either in equal shares or in unequal I ought to prefer the former; and this means that I ought to be just as well as generous. The other demand of justice, that we should take account of past merit in our distribution, I think they would have denied, or rather explained away by the argument that to reward beneficence was to encourage such behaviour by example, and therefore a likely way to increase the total of happiness.

3. A third criticism, incurred by some utilitarians[1] in the attempt to accommodate their theory to our moral judgements, was that of inconsistency in considering differences of quality or kind, as well as of amount, among pleasures when determining what we ought to do. It seems clear that people do not feel the same obligation to endow the art of cookery or pot-boiling as that of poetry or music, and this not because they are convinced that the one causes keener and more constant pleasure to a greater number than the other. Yet the recognition of a stronger obligation to promote "higher" or "better" pleasures implies that we think something good, say musical or poetic experience, not merely in proportion to its general pleasantness but by its own nature. The attempt to unite this "qualification of pleasures" with hedonistic utilitarianism is like saying "I care about nothing but money, but I would not come by it dishonestly." The fundamental fact is that we do not think some pleasures, such as that of cruelty, good at all.

4. Though the inconsistency of modifying their theory in these two ways seems to have escaped the notice of most utilitarians, they could not help seeing that they were bound to meet a fourth criticism

----

[1] E.g., J.S. Mill. Bentham more consistently held that "the pleasure of push-pin is as good as the pleasure of poetry."

by giving some account of the universal belief that we have obligations to keep our promises. It is obvious that the payment of money to a rich creditor may not immediately result in so much satisfaction as the keeping of it by a poor debtor or the giving of it to a useful charity, and that yet it may, under most circumstances, be judged a duty and always an obligation. The argument of utilitarians to explain this has usually been as follows: It is true that a particular instance of justice may not directly increase the sum of human happiness but quite the contrary, and yet we often approve such an instance. This is because the *general* practice of such good faith, with the consequent possibility of credit and contract, is supremely conducive to happiness, and therefore so far as any violation of a bargain impairs this confidence, it is, indirectly and in the long run, pernicious.

Such an attempt to bring promise-keeping under the utilitarian formula breaks down because it only applies where the promise and its performance or neglect would be public and therefore serve as an example to others.

Suppose two explorers in the Arctic have only enough food to keep one alive till he can reach the base, and one offers to die if the other will promise to educate his children. No other person can know that such a promise was made, and the breaking or keeping of it cannot influence the future keeping of promises. On the utilitarian theory, then, it's the duty of the returned traveller to act precisely as he ought to have acted if no bargain had been made: to consider how he can spend his money most expediently for the happiness of mankind, and, if he thinks his own child is a genius, to spend it upon him.

Or, to take a different kind of justice, the utilitarian must hold that we are justified in inflicting pain always and only in order to prevent worse pain or bring about greater happiness. This, then, is all we need consider in so-called punishment, which must be purely preventive. But if some kind of very cruel crime becomes common, and none of the criminals can be caught, it might be highly expedient, as an example, to hang an innocent man, if a charge against him could be so framed that he were universally thought guilty; indeed this would only fail to be an ideal instance of utilitarian "punishment" because the victim himself would not have been so likely as a real felon to commit such a crime in the future, in all other respects it would be perfectly deterrent and therefore felicific.

In short, utilitarianism has forgotten rights; it allows no right to a man because he is innocent or because he has worked hard or has been promised or injured, or because he stands in any other special relation to us. It thinks only of duties or rather of a single duty, to dump happiness wherever we most conveniently can. If it speaks of rights at all it could only say all men have one and the same right, namely that all men should try to increase the total happiness. And this is a manifest misuse of language.

DISCUSSION QUESTIONS

1. Refer to Carritt's discussion of the second objection to utilitarianism. Why would it be problematic for a utilitarian to claim that one has an obligation to be just? Would a utilitarian accept Carritt's interpretation of the maxim, "promote the greatest amount of happiness for the greatest number"? Explain.

2. According to Carritt, how would a utilitarian respond to the creditor/debtor problem? Could a utilitarian provide a different response?

30

J.J.C. Smart (with Bernard Williams), selection from *Utilitarianism: For and Against* (1973)

J.J.C. Smart (b.1920) is emeritus professor of philosophy at Monash University in Australia. Smart has contributed to several areas of philosophy, most notably metaphysics, philosophy of science, and ethics. The following selection is taken from Smart's collaboration with Bernard Williams (1929–2003), wherein Williams offers arguments against utilitarianism. Smart, on the other hand, defends a version of act utilitarianism.

SOURCE

Smart, J.J.C. *Utilitarianism: For and Against*, excerpts from Chapters 2, 7, and 10. Copyright © Cambridge University Press. Reprinted with the permission of Cambridge University Press.

Act-Utilitarianism and Rule-Utilitarianism

The system of normative ethics which I am here concerned to defend is, as I have said earlier, *act*-utilitarianism. Act-utilitarianism is to be contrasted with rule-utilitarianism. Act-utilitarianism is the view that the rightness or wrongness of an action is to be judged by the consequences, good or bad, of the action itself. Rule-utilitarianism is the view that the rightness or wrongness of an action is to be judged by the goodness and badness of the consequences of a rule that everyone should perform the action in like circumstances. There are two sub-varieties of rule-utilitarianism according to whether one construes "rule" here as "actual rule" or "possible rule." With the former, one gets a view like that of S.E. Toulmin[1] and with the latter, one like Kant's.[2] That is, if it is permissible to interpret Kant's principle "Act only on that maxim through which you can at the same time will that it should become a universal law" as "Act only on that maxim which you as a humane and benevolent person would like to see established as a universal law." Of course Kant would resist this appeal to human feeling, but it seems necessary in order to interpret his doctrine

---

[1] Stephen Toulmin, *An Examination of the Place of Reason in Ethics* (London: Cambridge University Press, 1950).

[2] Immanuel Kant, *Groundwork of the Metaphysic of Morals*, translated from the German in *The Moral Law*, by H.J. Paton (London: Hutchinson, 1948).

in a plausible way. A subtle version of the Kantian type of rule-utilitarianism is given by R.F. Harrod in his "Utilitarianism Revised."[1]

I have argued elsewhere[2] the objections to rule-utilitarianism as compared with act-utilitarianism.[3] Briefly they boil down to the accusation of rule worship:[4] the rule-utilitarian presumably advocates his principle because he is ultimately concerned with human happiness: why then should he advocate abiding by a rule when he knows that it will not in the present case be most beneficial to abide by it? The reply that in most cases it is most beneficial to abide by the rule seems irrelevant. And so is the reply that it would be better that everybody should abide by the rule than that nobody should. This is to suppose that the only alternative to "everybody does A" is "no one does A." But clearly we have the possibility "some people do A and some don't." Hence to refuse to break a generally beneficial rule in those cases in which it is not most beneficial to obey it seems irrational and to be a case of rule worship.

The type of utilitarianism which I shall advocate will, then, be act-utilitarianism, not rule-utilitarianism.

David Lyons has recently argued that rule-utilitarianism (by which, I think, he means the sort of rule-utilitarianism which I have called the Kantian one) collapses into act-utilitarianism.[5] His reasons are briefly as follows. Suppose that an exception to a rule R produces the best possible consequences. Then this is evidence that the rule R should be modified so as to allow this exception. Thus we get a new rule of the form "do R except in circumstances of the sort C." That is, whatever would lead the act-utilitarian to break a rule would lead the Kantian rule-utilitarian to modify the rule. Thus an adequate rule-utilitarianism would be extensionally equivalent to act-utilitarianism.

Lyons is particularly interested in what he calls "threshold effects." A difficulty for rule-utilitarianism has often appeared to be that of rules like "do not walk on the grass" or "do not fail to vote at an election." In these cases it would seem that it is beneficial if some people, though not too many, break the rule. Lyons points out that we can distinguish the action of doing something (say, walking on the grass) after some largish number of other people have done it, from the action of doing it when few or no people have done it. When these extra circumstances are written into the rule, Lyons holds that the rule will come to enjoin the same actions as would the act-utilitarian principle. However there seems to be one interesting sort of case which requires slightly different treatment. This is the sort of case in which not too many people must do action X, but each person must plan his action in ignorance of what the other person does. That is, what A does depends on what B does, and what B does depends on what A does. Situations possessing this sort of circularity will be discussed below....

I am inclined to think that an adequate rule-utilitarianism would not only be extensionally equivalent to the act-utilitarian principle (i.e., would enjoin the

[1] *Mind* 45 (1936): 137–56.

[2] In my article "Extreme and restricted utilitarianism," *Philosophical Quarterly* 6 (1956): 344–54. This contains bad errors, and a better version of the article will be found in Philippa Foot (ed.), *Theories of Ethics* (London: Oxford University Press, 1967), or Michael D. Bayles (ed.), *Contemporary Utilitarianism* (New York: Doubleday, 1968). In this article I used the terms "extreme" and "restricted," instead of Brandt's more felicitous "act" and "rule," which I now prefer.

[3] For another discussion of what in effect is the same problem see A.K. Stout's excellent paper, "But suppose everyone did the same," *Australasian Journal of Philosophy* 32 (1954): 1–29.

[4] On rule worship see I.M. Crombie, "Social clockwork and utilitarian morality," in D.M. Mackinnon (ed.), *Christian Faith and Communist Faith* (London: Macmillan, 1953). See p. 109.

[5] David Lyons, *The Forms and Limits of Utilitarianism* (London: Oxford University Press, 1965). Rather similar considerations have been put forward by R.M. Hare, *Freedom and Reason* (London: Oxford University Press, 1961), pp. 131–36, and R.B. Brandt, "Toward a credible form of utilitarianism," in H.N. Castaneda and G. Nakhnikian, *Morality and the Language of Conduct* (Detroit: Wayne State University Press, 1963), esp. pp. 119–23.

same set of actions as it) but would in fact consist of one rule only, the act-utilitarian one: "maximize probable benefit." This is because any rule which can be formulated must be able to deal with an indefinite number of unforeseen types of contingency. No rule, short of the act-utilitarian one, can therefore be safely regarded as extensionally equivalent to the act-utilitarian principle unless it is that very principle itself. I therefore suggest that Lyons's type of consideration can be taken even further, and that rule-utilitarianism of the Kantian sort must collapse into act-utilitarianism in an even stronger way: it must become a "one rule" rule-utilitarianism which is identical to act-utilitarianism. In any case, whether this is correct or not, it is with the defense of act-utilitarianism, and not with rule-utilitarianism (supposing that there are viable forms of rule-utilitarianism which may be distinguished from act-utilitarianism) that this monograph is concerned. (Lyons himself rejects utilitarianism.)

The Place of Rules in Act-Utilitarianism

According to the act-utilitarian … the rational way to decide what to do is to decide to perform that one of those alternative actions open to us (including the null-action, the doing of nothing) which is likely to maximize the probable happiness or well-being of humanity as a whole, or more accurately, of all sentient beings.[1] The utilitarian position is here put forward as a criterion of rational choice. It is true that we may choose to habituate ourselves to behave in accordance with certain rules, such as to keep promises, in the belief that behaving in accordance with these rules is generally optimific, and in the knowledge that we most often just do not have time to

work out individual pros and cons. When we act in such an habitual fashion we do not of course deliberate or make a choice. The act-utilitarian will, however, regard these rules as mere rules of thumb, and will use them only as rough guides. Normally he will act in accordance with them when he has no time for considering probable consequences or when the advantages of such a consideration of consequences are likely to be outweighed by the disadvantage of the waste of time involved. He acts in accordance with rules, in short, when there is no time to think, and since he does not think, the actions which he does habitually are not the outcome of moral thinking. When he has to think what to do, then there is a question of deliberation or choice, and it is precisely for such situations that the utilitarian criterion is intended.

It is, moreover, important to realize that there is no inconsistency whatever in an act-utilitarian's schooling himself to act, in normal circumstances, habitually and in accordance with stereotyped rules. He knows that a man about to save a drowning person has no time to consider various possibilities, such as that the drowning person is a dangerous criminal who will cause death and destruction, or that he is suffering from a painful and incapacitating disease from which death would be a merciful release, or that various timid people, watching from the bank, will suffer a heart attack if they see anyone else in the water. No, he knows that it is almost always right to save a drowning man, and in he goes. Again, he knows that we would go mad if we went in detail into the probable consequences of keeping or not keeping every trivial promise: we will do most good and reserve our mental energies for more important matters if we simply habituate ourselves to keep promises in all normal situations. Moreover he may suspect that on some occasions personal bias may prevent him from reasoning in a correct utilitarian fashion. Suppose he is trying to decide between two jobs, one of which is more highly paid than the other, though he has given an informal promise that he will take the lesser paid one. He may well deceive himself by underestimating the effects of breaking the promise (in

---

[1] In the first edition of this monograph I said, "which is likely to bring about the total situation now and in the future which is the best for the happiness of well-being of humanity as a whole, or more accurately, of all sentient beings." This is inaccurate. To probably maximize the benefit is not the same as to maximize the probable benefit. This has been pointed out by David Braybrooke. See p. 35 of his article "The choice between utilitarianisms," *American Philosophical Quarterly* 4 (1967): 28–38.

causing loss of confidence) and by overestimating the good he can do in the highly paid job. He may well feel that if he trusts to the accepted rules he is more likely to act in the way that an unbiased act-utilitarian would recommend than he would be if he tried to evaluate the consequences of his possible actions himself. Indeed [G.E.] Moore argued on act-utilitarian grounds that one should never in concrete cases think as an act-utilitarian.[1]

This, however, is surely to exaggerate both the usefulness of rules and the human mind's propensity to unconscious bias. Nevertheless, right or wrong, this attitude of Moore's has a rational basis and (though his argument from probability considerations is faulty in detail) is not the law worship of the rule-utilitarian, who would say that we ought to keep to a rule that is the most generally optimific, even though we *knew* that obeying it in this particular instance would have bad consequences.

Nor is this utilitarian doctrine incompatible, as M.A. Kaplan[2] has suggested it is, with a recognition of the importance of warm and spontaneous expressions of emotion. Consider a case in which a man sees that his wife is tired, and simply from a spontaneous feeling of affection for her he offers to wash the dishes. Does utilitarianism imply that he should have stopped to calculate the various consequences of his different possible courses of action? Certainly not. This would make married life a misery and the utilitarian knows very well as a rule of thumb that on occasions of this sort it is best to act spontaneously and without calculation. Moreover I have said that act-utilitarianism is meant to give a method of deciding what to do in those cases in which we do indeed decide what to do. On these occasions when we do not act as a result of delib-

eration and choice, that is, when we act spontaneously, no method of decision, whether utilitarian or non-utilitarian, comes into the matter. What does arise for the utilitarian is the question of whether or not he should consciously encourage in himself the tendency to certain types of spontaneous feeling. There are in fact very good utilitarian reasons why we should by all means cultivate in ourselves the tendency to certain types of warm and spontaneous feeling.

Though even the act-utilitarian may on occasion act habitually and in accordance with particular rules, his criterion is, as we have said, *applied* in cases in which he does not act habitually but in which he deliberates and chooses what to do. Now the right action for an agent in given circumstances is, we have said, that action which produces better results than any alternative action. If two or more actions produce equally good results, and if these results are better than the results of any other action open to the agent, then there is no such thing as *the* right action: there are two or more actions which are *a* right action. However this is a very exceptional state of affairs, which may well never in fact occur, and so usually I will speak loosely of the action which is *the* right one. We are now able to specify more clearly what is meant by "alternative action" here. The fact that the utilitarian criterion is meant to apply in situations of deliberation and choice enables us to say that the class of alternative actions which we have in mind when we talk about an action having the best possible results is the class of actions which the agent could have performed if he had tried. For example, it would be better to bring a man back to life than to offer financial assistance to his dependents, but because it is technologically impossible to bring a man back to life, bringing the man back to life is not something we could do if we tried. On the other hand it may well be possible for us to give financial assistance to the dependents, and this then may be the right action. The right action is the action among those which we could do, i.e., those which we *would* do if we chose to, which has the best possible results.

[1] *Principia Ethica*, p. 162.

[2] Morton A. Kaplan, "Some problems of the extreme utilitarian position," *Ethics* 70 (1959–60): 228–32. This is a critique of my earlier article "Extreme and restricted utilitarianism." He also puts forward a game theoretic argument against me, but this seems cogent only against an egoistic utilitarian. Kaplan continued the discussion in his interesting note "Restricted utilitarianism," *Ethics* 71 (1960–61): 301–02.

It is true that the general concept of action is wider than that of deliberate choice. Many actions are performed habitually and without deliberation. But the actions for whose tightness we as agents want a criterion are, in the nature of the case, those done thinkingly and deliberately. An action is at any rate that sort of human performance which it is appropriate to praise, blame, punish or reward, and since it is often appropriate to praise, blame, punish, or reward habitual performances, the concept of action cannot be identified with that of the outcome of deliberation and choice. With habitual actions the only question that arises for an agent is that of whether or not he should strengthen the habit or break himself of it. And individual acts of habit-strengthening or habit-breaking can themselves be deliberate.

The utilitarian criterion, then, is designed to help a person, who could do various things if he chose to do them, to decide which of these things he should do. His utilitarian deliberation is one of the causal antecedents of his action, and it would be pointless if it were not. The utilitarian view is therefore perfectly compatible with determinism. The only sense of "he could have done otherwise" that we require is the sense "he would have done otherwise if he had chosen." Whether the utilitarian view necessitates complete metaphysical determinism is another matter. All that it requires is that deliberation should determine actions in the way that everyone knows it does anyway. If it is argued that any indeterminism in the universe entails that we can never know the outcome of our actions, we can reply that in normal cases these indeterminacies will be so numerous as approximately to cancel one another out, and anyway all that we require for rational action is that some consequence of our actions should be *more probable* than others, and this is something which no indeterminist is likely to deny.

The utilitarian may now conveniently make a terminological recommendation. Let us use the word "rational" as a term of commendation for that action which is, on the evidence available to the agent, *likely* to produce the best results, and to reserve the word "right" as a term of commendation for the action which does *in fact* produce the best results. That is, let us say that what is rational is to try to perform the right action, to try to produce the best results. Or at least this formulation will do where there is an equal probability of achieving each possible set of results. If there is a very low probability of producing very good results, then it is natural to say that the rational agent would perhaps go for other more probable though not quite so good results. For a more accurate formulation we should have to weigh the goodness of the results with their probabilities. However, neglecting this complication, we can say, roughly, that it is rational to perform the action which is on the available evidence the one which will produce the best results. This allows us to say, for example, that the agent did the right thing but irrationally (he was trying to do something else, or was trying to do this very thing but went about it unscientifically), and that he acted rationally but by bad luck did the wrong thing, because the things that seemed probable to him, for the best reasons, just did not happen.

Roughly, then: we shall use "right" and "wrong" to appraise choices on account of their actual success in promoting the general happiness, and we shall use "rational" and "irrational" to appraise them on account of their likely success. As was noted above ... "likely success" must be interpreted in terms of maximizing the probable benefit, not in terms of probably maximizing the benefit. In effect, it is rational to do what you reasonably think to be right, and what will be right is what will maximize the probable benefit. We need, however, to make one qualification to this. A person may unreasonably believe what it would in fact be reasonable to believe. We shall still call such a person's action irrational. If the agent has been unscientific in his calculation of means-ends relationships he may decide that a certain course of action is probably best for human happiness, and it may indeed be so. When he performs this action we may still call his action irrational, because it was pure luck, not sound reasoning, that brought him to his conclusion.

"Rational" and "irrational" and "right" and "wrong" so far have been introduced as terms of appraisal for chosen or deliberate actions only. There is no reason why we should not use the pair of terms "right" and "wrong" more widely so as to appraise even habitual actions. Nevertheless we shall not have much occasion to appraise actions that are not the outcome of choice. What we do need is a pair of terms of appraisal for *agents* and *motives*. I suggest that we use the terms "good" and "bad" for these purposes. A good agent is one who acts more nearly in a generally optimific way than does the average one. A bad agent is one who acts in a less optimific way than the average. A good motive is one which generally results in beneficent actions, and a bad motive is one which generally ends in maleficent actions. Clearly there is no inconsistency in saying that on a particular occasion a good man did a wrong action, that a bad man did a right action, that a right action was done from a bad motive, or that a wrong action was done from a good motive. Many specious arguments against utilitarianism come from obscuring these distinctions. Thus one may be got to admit that an action is "right," meaning no more than that it is done from a good motive and is praiseworthy, and then it is pointed out that the action is not "right" in the sense of being optimific. I do not wish to legislate as to how other people (particularly non-utilitarians) should use words like "right" and "wrong," but in the interests of clarity it is important for me to state how I propose to use them myself: and to try to keep the various distinctions clear.

It should be noted that in making this terminological recommendation I am not trying to smuggle in valuations under the guise of definitions, as Ardon Lyon, in a review of the first edition of this monograph[1] has suggested that I have done. It is merely a recommendation to pre-empt the already evaluative words "rational" and "irrational" for one lot of commendatory or discommendatory jobs, the already evaluative words "right" and "wrong" for another lot of commendatory or discommenda-

tory jobs, and the already evaluative words "good" and "bad" for yet another lot of commendatory or discommendatory jobs.

We can also use "good" and "bad" as terms of commendation or discommendation of actions themselves. In this case to commend or discommend an action is to commend or discommend the motive from which it sprang. This allows us to say that a man performed a bad action but that it was the right one, or that he performed a good action but that it was wrong. For example, a man near Berchtesgaden in 1938 might have jumped into a river and rescued a drowning man, only to find that it was Hitler. He would have done the wrong thing, for he would have saved the world a lot of trouble if he had left Hitler below the surface. On the other hand his motive, the desire to save life, would have been one which we approve of people having: in general, though not in this case, the desire to save life leads to acting rightly. It is worth our while to strengthen such a desire. Not only should we praise the action (thus expressing our approval of it) but we should perhaps even give the man a medal, thus encouraging others to emulate it. Indeed praise itself comes to have some of the social functions of medal giving: we come to like praise for its own sake, and are thus influenced by the possibility of being given it. Praising a person is thus an important action in itself—it has significant effects. A utilitarian must therefore learn to control his acts of praise and dispraise, thus perhaps concealing his approval of an action when he thinks that the expression of such approval might have bad effects, and perhaps even praising actions of which he does not really approve. Consider, for example, the case of an act-utilitarian, fighting in a war, who succeeds in capturing the commander of an enemy submarine. Assuming that it is a just war and that the act-utilitarian is fighting on the right side, the very courage and ability of the submarine commander has a tendency which is the reverse of optimific. Everything that the submarine commander has been doing was (in my proposed sense of the word) wrong. (I do not of course mean that he did anything wrong in the

[1] *Durham University Journal* 55 (1963): 86–87.

technological sense: presumably he knew how to maneuver his ship in the right way.) He has kept his boat cunningly concealed, when it would have been better for humanity if it had been a sitting duck, he has kept the morale of his crew high when it would have been better it they had been cowardly and inefficient, and he has aimed his torpedoes with deadly effect so as to do the maximum harm. Nevertheless, once the enemy commander is captured, or even perhaps before he is captured, our act-utilitarian sailor does the right thing in praising the enemy commander, behaving chivalrously towards him, giving him honor and so on, for he is powerfully influencing his own men to aspire to similar professional courage and efficiency, to the ultimate benefit of mankind.

What I have said in the last paragraph about the occasional utility of praising harmful actions applies, I think, even when the utilitarian is speaking to other utilitarians. It applies even more when, as is more usually the case, the utilitarian is speaking to a predominantly non-utilitarian audience. To take an extreme case, suppose that the utilitarian is speaking to people who live in a society governed by a form of magical taboo ethics. He may consider that though on occasion keeping to the taboos does harm, on the whole the tendency of the taboo ethics is more beneficial than the sort of moral anarchy into which these people might fall if their reverence for their taboos was weakened. While, therefore, he would recognize that the system of taboos which governed these people's conduct was markedly inferior to a utilitarian ethic, nevertheless he might also recognize that these people's cultural background was such that they could not easily be persuaded to adopt a utilitarian ethic. He will, therefore, on act-utilitarian grounds, distribute his praise and blame in such a way as to strengthen, not to weaken, the system of taboo.

In an ordinary society we do not have such an extreme situation. Many people can be got to adopt a utilitarian, or almost utilitarian, way of thought, but many cannot. We may consider whether it may not be better to throw our weight on the side of the prevailing traditional morality, rather than on the side of trying to improve it with the risk of weakening respect for morality altogether. Sometimes the answer to this question will be "yes," and sometimes "no." As Sidgwick said:[1]

> The doctrine that Universal Happiness is the ultimate *standard* must not be understood to imply that Universal Benevolence is ... always the best *motive* of action. For ... it is not necessary that the end which gives the criterion of rightness should always be the end at which we consciously aim: and if experience shows that the general happiness will be more satisfactorily attained if men frequently act from other motives than pure universal philanthropy, it is obvious that these other motives are to be preferred on Utilitarian principles.

In general, we may note, it is always dangerous to influence a person contrary to his conviction of what is right. More harm may be done in weakening his regard for duty than would be saved by preventing the particular action in question. Furthermore, to quote Sidgwick again, "any particular existing moral rule, though not the ideally best even for such beings, as existing men under the existing circumstances, may yet be the best that they can be got to obey."[2] We must also remember that some motives are likely to be present in excess rather than defect: in which case, however necessary they may be, it is not expedient to praise them. It is obviously useful to praise altruism, even though this is not pure generalized benevolence, the treating of oneself as neither more nor less important than anyone else, simply because most people err on the opposite side, from too much self-love and not enough altruism. It is, similarly, inexpedient to praise self-love, important though this is when it is kept in due proportion. In short, to quote Sidgwick once more, "in distributing our praise of human

---

[1] *Methods of Ethics* [(London: Macmillan and Company, 1884)], p. 413.

[2] Ibid., p. 469.

qualities, on utilitarian principles, we have to consider not primarily the usefulness of the quality, but the usefulness of the praise."[1]

Most men, we must never forget, are not act-utilitarians, and do not use the words "good" and "bad," when applied to agents or to motives, quite in the way which has here been recommended. When a man says that another is wicked he may even be saying something of a partly metaphysical or superstitious connotation. He may be saying that there is something like a yellow stain on the other man's soul. Of course he would not think this quite literally. If you asked him whether souls could be coloured, or whether yellow was a particularly abhorrent colour, he would of course laugh at you. His views about sin and wickedness may be left in comfortable obscurity. Nevertheless the things he does say may indeed entail something like the yellow stain view. "Wicked" has thus come to have much more force than the utilitarian "likely to be very harmful" or "probably a menace." To stigmatize a man as wicked is not, as things are, just to make men wary of him, but to make him the object of a peculiar and very powerful abhorrence, over and above the natural abhorrence one has from a dangerous natural object such as a typhoon or an octopus. And it may well be to the act-utilitarian's advantage, qua act-utilitarian, to acquiesce in this way of talking when he is in the company of non-utilitarians. He himself will not believe in yellow stains in souls, or anything like it.... [A] man is the result of heredity and environment. Nevertheless the utilitarian may influence behavior in the way he desires by using "wicked" in a quasi-superstitious way. Similarly a man about to be boiled alive by cannibals may usefully say that an imminent eclipse is a sign of the gods' displeasure at the proposed culinary activities. We have seen that in a completely utilitarian society the utility of praise of an agent's motives does not always go along with the utility of the action. Still more may this be so in a non-utilitarian society.

I cannot stress too often the importance of Sidgwick's distinction between the utility of an action and the utility of praise or blame of it, for many fallacious "refutations" of utilitarianism depend for their plausibility on confusing the two things.

Thus A.N. Prior[2] quotes the nursery rhyme:

> For want of a nail
> > The shoe was lost;
> For want of a shoe
> > The horse was lost;
> For want of a horse
> > The rider was lost;
> For want of a rider
> > The battle was lost;
> For want of a battle
> > The kingdom was lost;
> And all for the want
> > Of a horse-shoe nail.

So it was all the blacksmith's fault! But, says Prior, it is surely hard to place on the smith's shoulders the responsibility for the loss of the kingdom. This is no objection, however, to act-utilitarianism. The utilitarian could quite consistently say that it would be useless to blame the blacksmith, or at any rate to blame him more than for any other more or less trivial case of "bad maintenance." The blacksmith had no reason to believe that the fate of the kingdom would depend on one nail. If you blame him you may make him neurotic and in future even more horses may be badly shod.

Moreover, says Prior, the loss of the kingdom was just as much the fault of someone whose negligence led to there being one fewer cannon in the field. If it had not been for this other piece of negligence the blacksmith's negligence would not have mattered. Whose was the responsibility? The act-utilitarian will quite consistently reply that the notion of the responsibility is a piece of metaphysical nonsense and should be replaced by "Whom would it be useful to

---

[1] Ibid., p. 428.

[2] "The consequences of actions," *Aristotelian Society Supplementary Volume* 30 (1956): 91–99. See p. 95.

blame?" And in the case of such a close battle, no doubt it would be useful to blame quite a lot of people though no one very much. Unlike, for example, the case where a battle was lost on account of the general getting drunk, where considerable blame of one particular person would clearly be useful.

"But wouldn't a man go mad if he really tried to take the whole responsibility of everything upon himself in this way?" asks Prior. Clearly he would. The blacksmith must not mortify himself with morbid thoughts about his carelessness. He must remember that his carelessness was of the sort that is usually trivial, and that a lot of other people were equally careless. The battle was just a very close thing. But this refusal to blame himself, or blame himself very much, is surely consistent with the recognition that his action was in fact very wrong, that much harm would have been prevented if he had acted otherwise. Though if other people, e.g., the man whose fault it was that the extra cannon did not turn up, had acted differently, then the blacksmith's action would have *in fact* not been very wrong, though it would have been no more and no less blameworthy. A very wrong action is usually very blameworthy, but on some occasions, like the present one, a very wrong action can be hardly blameworthy at all. This seems paradoxical at first, but paradox disappears when we remember Sidgwick's distinction between the utility of an action and the utility of praise of it.

The idea that a consistent utilitarian would go mad with worry about the various effects of his actions is perhaps closely connected with a curious argument against utilitarianism to be found in Baier's book *The Moral Point of View*.[1] Baier holds that (act-)utilitarianism must be rejected because it entails that we should never relax, that we should use up every available minute in good works, and we do not ordinarily think that this is so. The utilitarian has two effective replies. The first is that perhaps what we ordinarily think is false. Perhaps a rational investigation would lead us to the conclusion that we

should relax much less than we do. The second reply is that act-utilitarian premises do not entail that we should never relax. Maybe relaxing and doing few good works today increases threefold our capacity to do good works tomorrow. So relaxation and play can be defended even if we ignore, as we should not, their intrinsic pleasures.

I beg the reader, therefore, if ever he is impressed by any alleged refutation of act-utilitarianism, to bear in mind the distinction between the rightness or wrongness of an action and the goodness or badness of the agent, and Sidgwick's correlative and most important distinction between the utility of an action and the utility of praise or blame of it. The neglect of this distinction is one of the commonest causes of fallacious refutations of act-utilitarianism.

It is also necessary to remember that we are here considering utilitarianism as a *normative* system. The fact that it has consequences which conflict with some of our particular moral judgments need not be decisive against it. In science general principles must be tested by reference to particular facts of observation. In ethics we may well take the opposite attitude, and test our particular moral attitudes by reference to more general ones. The utilitarian can contend that since his principle rests on something so simple and natural as generalized benevolence it is more securely founded than our particular feelings, which may be subtly distorted by analogies with similar looking (but in reality totally different) types of case, and by all sorts of hangovers from traditional and uncritical ethical thinking.

If, of course, act-utilitarianism were put forward as a descriptive systematization of how ordinary men, or even we ourselves in our unreflective and uncritical moments, actually think about ethics, then of course it is easy to refute and I have no wish to defend it. Similarly again if it is put forward not as a *descriptive* theory but as an *explanatory* one. John Plamenatz, in his *English Utilitarians*, seems to hold that utilitarianism "is destroyed and no part of it left standing."[2] This is apparently on

---

[1] K.E.M. Baier, *The Moral Point of View* (Ithaca, NY: Cornell University Press, 1958), pp. 203–04.

[2] *The English Utilitarians*, 2nd ed. (Oxford: Blackwell, 1966), p. 145.

the ground that the utilitarian explanation of social institutions will not work: that we cannot explain various institutions as having come about because they lead to the maximum happiness. In this monograph I am not concerned with what our moral customs and institutions in fact are, and still less am I concerned with the question of why they are as they in fact are. I am concerned with a certain view about what they ought to be. The correctness of an ethical doctrine, when it is interpreted as recommendatory, is quite independent of its truth when it is interpreted as descriptive and of its truth when it is interpreted as explanatory. In fact it is precisely because a doctrine is false as description and as explanation that it becomes important as a possible recommendation.

Utilitarianism and Justice

So far, I have done my best to state utilitarianism in a way which is conceptually clear and to rebut many common objections to it. At the time I wrote the earlier edition of this monograph I did so as a pretty single-minded utilitarian myself. It seemed to me then that since the utilitarian principle expressed the attitude of generalized benevolence, anyone who rejected utilitarianism would have to be hard hearted, i.e., to some extent non-benevolent, or else would have to be the prey of conceptual confusion or an unthinking adherent of traditional ways of thought, or perhaps be an adherent of some religious system of ethics, which could be undermined by metaphysical criticism. Admittedly utilitarianism does have consequences which are incompatible with the common moral consciousness, but I tended to take the view "so much the worse for the common moral consciousness." That is, I was inclined to reject the common methodology of testing general ethical principles by seeing how they square with our feelings in particular instances.

After all, one may feel somewhat as follows. What is the purpose of morality? (Answering this question is to make a moral judgment. To think that one could answer the question "What is the purpose of morality?" without making a moral judgment would be to condone the naturalistic fallacy, the fallacy of deducing an "ought" from an "is.") Suppose that we say, as it is surely at least tempting to do, that the purpose of morality is to subserve the general happiness. Then it immediately seems to follow that we ought to reject any putative moral rule, or any particular moral feeling, which conflicts with the utilitarian principle. It is undeniable that we do have anti-utilitarian moral feelings in particular cases, but perhaps they should be discounted as far as possible, as due to our moral conditioning in childhood. (The weakness of this line of thought is that approval of the general principle of utilitarianism may be due to moral conditioning too. And even if benevolence were in some way a "natural," not an "artificial," attitude, this consideration could at best have persuasive force, without any clear rationale. To argue from the naturalness to the correctness of a moral attitude would be to commit the naturalistic fallacy.) Nevertheless in some moods the general principle of utilitarianism may recommend itself to us so much the more than do particular moral precepts, precisely because it is so general. We may therefore feel inclined to reject an ethical methodology which implies that we should test our general principles by our reactions in particular cases. Rather, we may come to feel, we should test our reactions in particular cases by reference to the most general principles. The analogy with science is not a good one, since it is not far off the truth to say that observation statements are more firmly based than the theories they test.[1] But why should our more particular moral feelings be more worthy of notice than our more generalized ones? That there should be a disanalogy between ethics and science is quite plausible if we accept a non-cognitivist theory of meta-ethics.

The utilitarian, then, will test his particular feelings by reference to his general principle, and not the general principle by reference to his particular

---

[1] I say "not far off the truth" because observation statements are to some extent theory laden, and if they are laden with a bad theory we may have to reject them.

feelings. Now while I have some tendency to take this point of view (and if I had not I would not have been impelled to state and defend utilitarianism as a system of normative ethics), I have also some tendency to feel the opposite, that we should sometimes test our general principles by how we feel about particular applications of them. (I am a bit like G.E. Moore in his reply to C.L. Stevenson,[1] where he feels both that he is right and Stevenson wrong and that he is wrong and Stevenson right. My own indecisiveness may be harder to resolve, since in my case it is a matter of feeling, rather than intellect, which is involved.)

It is not difficult to show that utilitarianism could, in certain exceptional circumstances, have some very horrible consequences. In a very lucid and concise discussion note,[2] H.J. McCloskey has considered such a case. Suppose that the sheriff of a small town can prevent serious riots (in which hundreds of people will be killed) only by "framing" and executing (as a scapegoat) an innocent man. In actual cases of this sort the utilitarian will usually be able to agree with our normal moral feelings about such matters. He will be able to point out that there would be some possibility of the sheriff's dishonesty being found out, with consequent weakening of confidence and respect for law and order in the community, the consequences of which would be far worse even than the painful deaths of hundreds of citizens. But as McCloskey is ready to point out, the case can be presented in such a way that these objections do not apply. For example, it can be imagined that the sheriff could have first-rate empirical evidence that he will not be found out. So the objection that the sheriff knows that the man he "frames" will be killed, whereas he has only probable belief that the riot will occur unless he frames the man, is not a sound one. Someone like McCloskey can always strengthen his story to the point that we would just

have to admit that if utilitarianism is correct, then the sheriff must frame the innocent man. (McCloskey also has cogently argued that similar objectionable consequences are also implied by rule-utilitarianism. That is, an unjust system of punishment might be more equal than a just one. Hence even if rule-utilitarianism can clearly be distinguished from act-utilitarianism, a utilitarian will not be able to avoid offensive consequences of his theory by retreating from the "act" form to the "rule" form.) Now though a utilitarian might argue that it is empirically unlikely that some such situation as McCloskey envisages would ever occur, McCloskey will point out that it is *logically* possible that such a situation will arise. If the utilitarian rejects the unjust act (or system) he is clearly giving up his utilitarianism. McCloskey then remarks: "But as far as I know, only J.J.C. Smart among the contemporary utilitarians, is happy to adopt this 'solution.'" Here I must lodge a mild protest. McCloskey's use of the word "happy" surely makes me look a most reprehensible person. Even in my most utilitarian moods I am not happy about this consequence of utilitarianism. Nevertheless, however unhappy about it he may be, the utilitarian must admit that he draws the consequence that he might find himself in circumstances where he ought to be unjust. Let us hope that this is a logical possibility and not a factual one. In hoping thus I am not being inconsistent with utilitarianism, since any injustice causes misery and so can be justified only as the lesser of two evils. The fewer the situations in which the utilitarian is forced to choose the lesser of two evils, the better he will be pleased. One must not think of the utilitarian as the sort of person who you would not trust further than you could kick him. As a matter of untutored sociological observation, I should say that in general utilitarians are more than usually trustworthy people, and that the sort of people who might do you down are rarely utilitarians.

It is also true that we should probably dislike and fear a man who could bring himself to do the right utilitarian act in a case of the sort envisaged by McCloskey. Though the man in this case might have done the right utilitarian act, his act would

---

[1] See P.A. Schilpp (ed.), *The Philosophy of G.E. Moore* (Evanston, IL: Northwestern University Press, 1942), p. 554.

[2] H.J. McCloskey, "A note on utilitarian punishment," *Mind* 72 (1963): 599.

betoken a toughness and lack of squeamishness which would make him a dangerous person. We must remember that people have egoistic tendencies as well as beneficent ones, and should such a person be tempted to act wrongly he could act very wrongly indeed. A utilitarian who remembers the possible moral weakness of men might quite consistently prefer to be the sort of person who would not always be able to bring himself to do the right utilitarian act and to surround himself by people who would be too squeamish to act in a utilitarian manner in such extreme cases.

No, I am not happy to draw the conclusion that McCloskey quite rightly says that the utilitarian must draw. But neither am I happy with the anti-utilitarian conclusion. For if a case really did arise in which injustice was the lesser of two evils (in terms of human happiness and misery), then the anti-utilitarian conclusion is a very unpalatable one too, namely that in some circumstances one must choose the greater misery, perhaps the very much greater misery, such as that of hundreds of people suffering painful deaths.

Still, to be consistent, the utilitarian must accept McCloskey's challenge. Let us hope that the sort of possibility which he envisages will always be no more than a logical possibility and will never become an actuality. At any rate, even though I have suggested that in ethics we should test particular feelings by general attitudes, McCloskey's example makes me somewhat sympathetic to the opposite point of view. Perhaps indeed it is too much to hope that there is any possible ethical system which will appeal to all sides of our nature and to all our moods.[1] It is perfectly possible to have conflicting attitudes within oneself. It is quite conceivable that there is *no* possible ethical theory which

will be conformable with all our attitudes. If the theory is utilitarian, then the possibility that sometimes it would be right to commit injustice will be felt to be acutely unsatisfactory by someone with a normal civilized upbringing. If on the other hand it is not utilitarian but has deontological elements, then it will have the unsatisfactory implication that sometimes avoidable misery (perhaps very great avoidable misery) ought not to be avoided. It might be thought that some compromise theory, on the lines of Sir David Ross's, in which there is some "balancing up" between considerations of utility and those of deontology, might provide an acceptable compromise. The trouble with this, however, is that such a "balancing" may not be possible: one can easily feel pulled sometimes one way and sometimes the other. How can one "balance" a serious injustice, on the one hand, and hundreds of painful deaths, on the other hand? Even if we disregard our purely self-interested attitudes, for the sake of interpersonal discussions, so as to treat ourselves neither more nor less favorably than other people, it is still possible that there is no ethical system which would be satisfactory to all men, or even to one man at different times. It is possible that something similar is the case with science, that no scientific theory (known or unknown) is correct. If so, the world is more chaotic than we believe and hope that it is. But even though the world is not chaotic, men's moral feelings may be. On anthropological grounds it is only too likely that these feelings are to some extent chaotic. Both as children and as adults, we have probably had many different moral conditionings, which can easily be incompatible with one another.

Meanwhile, among possible options, utilitarianism does have its appeal. With its empirical attitude to questions of means and ends it is congenial to the scientific temper and it has flexibility to deal with a changing world. This last consideration is, however, more self-recommendation than justification. For if flexibility is a recommendation, this is because of the utility of flexibility.

---

[1] J.W.N. Watkins considers this matter in his "Negative utilitarianism," *Aristotelian Society Supp. Vol.* 67 (1963): 95–114. It is now apparent to me that my paper "The methods of ethics and the methods of science," *Journal of Philosophy* 62 (1965): 344–49, on which the present section of this monograph is based, gives a misleading impression of Watkins's position in this respect.

DISCUSSION QUESTIONS

1. Explain why Smart rejects rule utilitarianism in favor of act utilitarianism. Distinguish between Lyons's objection to rule utilitarianism and Smart's extension of the objection.

2. Smart characterizes the act utilitarian's rule as "maximize probable benefit." In what circumstances does he think this rule ought to guide one's conduct? In what circumstances may we, as act utilitarians, look to other rules to help guide our conduct? How do you think that Mill would respond to this version of utilitarianism?

3. Explain how Smart distinguishes between the following terms: "rational/irrational," "right/wrong," "good/bad." Do you think that this is a plausible account? Defend your answer.

4. Explain why Smart thinks that the act utilitarian acts rightly when he commends the enemy submarine commander (who, Smart asserts, has acted wrongly). Do you think that Smart's assessment of the situation is plausible? Why or why not?

5. How does Smart make use of Sidgwick's distinction between the utility of an action and the utility of praise or blame of it?

6. Explain the objection to act utilitarianism which asserts that act utilitarianism may require a person to act unjustly. How does Smart respond to this objection?

31

L.W. Sumner,
"Rights" (2000)

L.W. Sumner is an emeritus professor of philosophy at the University of Toronto, as well as being a University Professor Emeritus at the same institution. He is also a Fellow of the Royal Society of Canada. Sumner's primary philosophical work has been in ethics, philosophy of law, and political philosophy. In the following selection, Sumner provides an extensive discussion of the philosophical concept of "rights" and the extent to which various ethical theories can accommodate talk of moral rights.

SOURCE

Sumner, L.W. "Rights," from *The Blackwell Guide to Ethical Theory*, edited by Hugh LaFollette. Copyright © 2000 by Blackwell Publishing Ltd. Reproduced with permission of Blackwell Publishing Ltd.

Of all the moral concepts, rights seem most in tune with the temper of our time. At their best they evoke images of heroic struggles against oppression and discrimination. At their worst they furnish the material for lurid tabloid stories of litigious former spouses and lovers. Whatever the use to which they are put, they are ubiquitous, the global currency of moral/political argument at the end of the millennium. Liberal societies in particular seem replete with conflicts of rights: young against old, ethnic minority against majority, natives against foreigners, rich against poor, women against men, believers against non believers, children against parents, gays against straights, employees against employers, consumers against producers, students against teachers, cyclists against drivers, pedestrians against cyclists, citizens against the police, and everyone against the state.

Love them or hate them, rights are unavoidable and no modern ethical theory seems complete without taking some account of them. It is therefore important to understand them: what they are, what their distinctive function is in our moral/political thinking, how we might distinguish reasonable from unreasonable claims of rights, and how rights might fit into the larger framework of an ethical theory. The aim of this essay is to help promote this understanding.

We can begin by trying to identify the distinctive kind of normative work rights are best equipped to do. Let us say that one part of our moral thinking has to do with the promotion of collective social goals which we deem to be valuable for their own sake: the general welfare, equality of opportunity, the eradication of poverty, bettering the lot of the worst off, or whatever. It is this part of our thinking which is well captured by the broad family of consequentialist ethical theories. On the other hand, we also tend to think that some means societies might use in order to achieve these goals are unjustifiable because they exploit or victimize particular individuals or groups. One way of expressing this thought is to say that these parties have rights which constrain or limit the pursuit of social goals, rights which must (at least sometimes) be respected even though a valuable goal would be better promoted by ignoring or infringing them. Rights then function morally as safeguards for the position of individuals or particular groups in the face of social endeavors; in the image made famous by Ronald Dworkin (1977: xi), they can be invoked as trumps against the pursuit of collective goals. It is this part of our moral thinking which is well captured by deontological theories, and rights therefore seem most at home in such theories.

Rights impose constraints on the pursuit of collective goals. This very general characterization serves to identify in a preliminary way the moral /political function of rights, and also begins to explain their perennial appeal. But it is not yet sufficient to show how rights are distinctive or unique. Duties and obligations impose similar constraints; if I have an obligation to pay my income tax then that is what I must do even though more good would result from my donating the money to Oxfam. So what is the particular way in which rights limit our promotion of valuable states of affairs? And what exactly is the relationship between rights and duties? We need to look more closely at the anatomy of rights.

How Rights Work

A simple example will serve to get us started. Suppose that Bernard has borrowed Alice's laptop computer with the promise to return it by Tuesday,

and Tuesday has arrived. Alice now has the right to have her computer returned by Bernard. Note to begin with that there are three distinct elements to this right. First, it has a *subject*: the holder or bearer of the right (in this case, Alice). Second, it has an *object*: the person against whom the right is held (in this case, Bernard). Third, it has a *content*: what it is the right to do or to have done (in this ease, to have the computer returned). Every right has these three elements, though they may not always be spelled out fully in the specification of the right. The paradigm subjects of rights are persons, though nothing so far prevents them from being attributed as well to other beings, such as children, animals, corporations, collectivities, and so on. The object of a right must be an agent capable of having duties or obligations, since Alice's right that Bernard return her computer on Tuesday correlates with Bernard's obligation to return the computer on Tuesday. Since rights can be held only against agents, the class of objects of rights may be much narrower than the class of subjects. The object of Alice's right is a specific assignable person, since it is Bernard who has borrowed her computer and who is duty-bound to return it. However, the objects of a right may also be an unassignable group; some rights, such as the right not to be assaulted or killed, may hold against everyone in general.

Finally, the content of a right is always some action on the part of either the subject or the object of the right. This fact is obscured by the shorthand way in which we refer to many rights, where it may appear that the content of the right is a thing or state of affairs. We may speak, for instance, of the right to an education or to health care or to life itself. But in all such cases the full specification of the right will reveal the actions which constitute its content: that the state provide subsidized public education or health care, or that others not act in such at way as to endanger life, or whatever. The contents of many rights are intricate and complex actions on the part of (assignable or unassignable) others, which must be fully spelled out before we know exactly what the right amounts to. In the case of Alice's right, the action in question is simple and specific: having her computer returned by Tuesday. Alice therefore has the right that something be done (by the person against whom her right is held). This kind of normative advantage on Alice's part is usually described as a *claim*: Alice has a claim *against Bernard* that he return her computer, which is equivalent to Bernard's duty *to Alice* to return her computer. In general, A's claim against B that B do X is logically equivalent to B's duty toward A to do X: claims and duties are in this way correlative. Claims are always of the form that something be done; the actions which make up their content must be those of another, never those of the right-holder herself. Since the content of Alice's right against Bernard has the form of a claim, we may call it a *claim-right*. Claim-rights constitute one important class of rights, exemplified primarily by contractual rights (held against assignable parties) and by rights to security of the person (held against everyone in general).

However, not all rights are claim-rights. Another example will make this clear. Alice owns her computer, which implies (among other things) that she has the right to use it (when she wants to). This right has the same subject (Alice) as her claim-right, but a different content and a direct object. Its content is once again an action, but this time an action on the part of the right-holder rather than someone else: it is a right *to do* rather than a right *to have done*. The content of the right therefore does not have the form of a claim; it is common instead to refer to it as a *liberty*. To say that Alice has the liberty to use the computer is to say that she is under no obligation not to use it, or that her use of it is permissible. Actually, it is implicitly to say more than this, since Alice's right to use her computer (when she wants to) includes her right not to use it (when she doesn't want to). Alice therefore has two distinct liberties: to use the computer (which means that she has no duty not to use it) and not to use it (which means that she has no duty to use it). We normally treat these as the two sides of one (complex) liberty: to use or not to use the computer, as she wishes. In general, A's liberty to do X (or not) is logically equivalent to the absence

both of A's duty to do X and A's duty not to do X. Alice's ownership right over the computer therefore entails her freedom to choose whether or not to use the computer; how this is to go is up to her. Since the content of her right has the form of a liberty, we may call it a *liberty-right*. Liberty-rights constitute another important class of rights, exemplified primarily by property rights and by rights to various freedoms (of thought, belief, conscience, expression, etc.).

So far we have located a subject and a content for Alice's liberty-right, but not an object. Against whom is this right held? In the case of claim-rights the answer to this question is straightforward: whoever bears the duty which is equivalent to the claim. Because claim-rights specify obligations, and because these obligations are assigned to particular parties (or to everyone in general), claim-rights enable us to easily locate their objects. But Alice's liberty-right to use her computer involves on the face of it no claim (or duty); the liberty in question just consists in the absence of duties on Alice's part. It is therefore not so obviously held *against* anyone. And indeed if we restrict ourselves just to its stipulated content, that is true: it is a right which imposes no duties. However, we know that property rights are typically protected by duties imposed on others: for instance, duties not to interfere with the use or enjoyment of the property in question. By virtue of her property right Alice has more than just the bare unprotected liberty to use (or not use) her computer as she pleases; this liberty is safe-guarded by what H.L.A. Hart (1982: 171–73) has usefully called a "protective perimeter" of duties imposed on others. Bernard therefore (and everyone else) has the duty not to interfere with Alice's use of her computer (by stealing it, damaging it, using it without permission, etc.). We learn therefore the lesson that liberty-rights are not as simple as they seem: they involve a complex bundle of liberties (held by the subject) and duties (imposed on others). The others who bear these duties are the (implicit) objects of the right.

Even claim-rights are not as simple as they seem. Let us return to Alice's right that Bernard return her computer by Tuesday. Alice's claim against Bernard is, as we have seen, logically equivalent to Bernard's duty toward Alice. But suppose that Bernard needs the computer for an additional day and asks to return it on Wednesday instead. Alice can, of course, refuse the request and insist on her performance of Bernard's duty. But she can also agree to it, in which case she waives her right to have the computer returned by Tuesday and releases Bernard from his original obligation. She now has a new right (to have the computer returned by Wednesday) and Bernard has a new correlative obligation. In waiving her original right Alice has exercised a *power* which enables her to alter Bernard's obligation. Indeed, in entering into the agreement about the computer in the first place, both Alice and Bernard have exercised powers which result in the creation of Alice's claim-right against Bernard and Bernard's liberty-right to use Alice's computer. Contractual rights, which constitute one important class of claim-rights, therefore involve more than just claims; they also involve powers (and liberties to exercise those powers, and duties imposed on others not to interfere with those liberties, and immunities against being deprived of the powers, and so on). Even relatively simple-seeming claim-rights are therefore typically quite complex bundles of different elements. The core of the right is still a claim, but this core is surrounded by a periphery made up of other elements (claims, liberties, powers, etc.). This periphery may be quite different for different claim-rights. Contractual rights typically confer on their subjects considerable discretion about the exercise of the right, including the power to waive it or to annul it entirely. Other claim-rights, such as the right not to be harmed or killed, may impose more limits on the subject's liberty (or power) to waive or annul the right. The full specification of a claim-right, including all of its periphery, can therefore be a very complex matter.

The same complexity, and the same relation of core to periphery, can be found in the case of liberty-rights. Alice's liberty-right to use her computer (or not, as she pleases) is not accompanied only by a protective perimeter of duties imposed on others.

It also includes her power to annul her liberty to use the computer, either temporarily (by lending the computer to Bernard) or permanently (by selling it), plus her liberty to exercise this power, plus further duties imposed on others not to interfere with her exercise of this power, plus…. Like claim-rights, liberty rights are typically complex bundles of different elements. The core of the right (what it is a right to) is still a liberty, but it too is surrounded by a periphery made up of other elements (claims, liberties, powers, etc.).

A full exploration of the intricate anatomy of rights can be a complicated affair (see, for instance, Wellman 1985, ch. 2; Sumner 1987, ch. 2). Fortunately, we have revealed enough of this anatomy to be able to answer some of our questions about the distinctive normative function of rights. First, the relationship between rights and duties. Although these two deontological concepts are clearly connected, the connections between them are more complex than they first appear. There is a simple relationship between claims and their correlative duties: A's claim against B that B do X is logically equivalent to B's duty toward A to do X. Exclusive attention to claim-rights might lead one to think that rights are just duties seen, as it were, from the perspective of the patient rather than the agent. But this is not the case. In the first place, not all duties are relational in the sense of being owed to assignable persons. Bernard's duty to return Alice's computer has an obvious object (Alice) but my duty to pay my income tax does not: it is not clear to whom (if anyone) this duty is owed. If there are non-relational duties then they do not correlate with any rights. More importantly, there is more to a right, even a claim-right, than just a claim against some correlative duty-bearer. Claim-rights, like liberty-rights, are typically complex clusters of different kinds of elements (duties, liberties, powers, immunities, etc.). Every such right will include some duties, either in its core or in its periphery (or both). But no right of either kind can just be reduced to a duty, or a set of duties. Rights also contain elements which are not duties, and are not definable in terms of duties. Furthermore, they have a structure, an internal logic, which is distinctively different from that of duties.

This brings us to our other question: how is it that rights impose constraints on our pursuit of goals? The complex structure of rights reveals two answers to this question. First, by containing duties imposed on their objects, rights limit the freedom of others to pursue valuable collective goals; they must (at least sometimes) fulfill their duty even when a worthwhile goal would be better promoted by not doing so. Second, by containing liberties conferred on their subjects, rights secure the freedom of right-holders not to pursue valuable collective goals; they may (at least sometimes) choose to exercise their right even when a worthwhile goal would be better promoted by not doing so. Rights therefore impose restrictions on others (who must not promote the collectively best outcome) and confer prerogatives on their holders (who need not do so). By these means rights define protected spaces in which individuals are able to pursue their own personal projects or have their personal interests safeguarded, free from the demands of larger collective enterprises.

The qualifiers "at least sometimes" in the preceding paragraph deserve some brief attention. They signal that neither the duties which rights impose on others nor the liberties they confer on their holders need be absolute. And this brings us to a fourth dimension of a right (besides its subject, object, and content), namely, its *strength*. The strength of a right is its level of resistance to rival normative considerations, such as the promotion of worthwhile goals. A right will insulate its holder to some extent against the necessity of taking these considerations into account, but it will also typically have a threshold above which they dominate or override the right. Should it turn out, for instance, that Bernard needs Alice's computer in order to arrange relief for a large-scale disaster in Africa, then his duty to return it on time (and her claim that it be returned) may be overridden even if she wants the computer back. Likewise, the same degree of urgency may override her liberty-right to use the computer when she pleases. Rights raise thresholds against considerations of social utility, but these thresholds are

seldom insurmountable. Some particularly important rights (against torture, perhaps, or slavery, or genocide) may be absolute, but most are not.

Why Theories Need Rights

Since the normative role rights are equipped to play seems useful, even necessary, it is not surprising that most ethical theories make some effort to accommodate them. Given the currency of rights talk in moral/political argument, any theory that either ignored or rejected rights completely would risk dismissal as being hopelessly out of step with our ordinary moral thinking. Not all theories, however, are equally comfortable with rights and not all find it equally easy to take them seriously. Rather than make a positive case for a rights-friendly theory, we will proceed by examining three challenges to rights emanating from three different theoretical orientations. If these challenges can be successfully met then we will have better reason for thinking that only an ethical theory which makes room for rights will be worthy of our allegiance.

The first challenge comes from a surprising direction. At the beginning of this essay I noted that rights seem most at home in deontological theories. We should therefore be able to assume that any deontological theory will provide a hospitable environment for rights. But this is not necessarily so. Some such theories, especially those affiliated with the Kantian or the Thomistic natural law traditions, have a decided preference for the language of duties over that of rights (see, for instance, Finnis 1980, ch. 8). Within such theories there is a tendency to treat rights as mere shadows cast by duties, so that any separate treatment of them is redundant. Now we already have the materials at hand for a response to this disparagement of rights, since we know that rights are not reducible to duties. It is true of claims that they are just (relational) duties looked at from the point of view of the patient rather than the agent, but rights are not just claims (even claim-rights are not just claims). So a theory which treats rights as just shadows cast by duties fails to understand their nature.

However, the redundancy thesis espoused by some deontological theories deserves a little more attention than this, since it enables us to say a little more about the distinctive normative role and contribution of rights. Thus far we have said that rights are complex bundles of packages of simpler constituent elements and shown how they function to constrain the pursuit of goals. But we do not yet have an adequate picture of the internal logic or rationale which unifies these diverse elements. For this we need (what we may call) a conception of the nature of rights. Two such conceptions have dominated the literature on rights. The interest (or benefit) conception holds that the point of rights is to protect the interests or welfare of their holders, it is this purpose which unifies the various elements making up a particular right and which explains why those elements are included and not others. Central to the interest conception is the idea of the right-holder as the beneficiary of duties imposed on others, or as the one whose interest provides the justification for imposing such duties (MacCormick 1982, ch. 8; Raz 1986, ch. 7; Lyons 1994, ch.1). By contrast, the choice (or will) conception holds that rights function so as to protect the freedom or autonomy of their holders. Central to this conception is the idea of the right-holder having the freedom to choose among a set of options, and of this freedom being protected by a set of duties imposed on others (Hart 1982, ch. 7; Wellman 1985, ch. 4; Sumner 1987, ch. 2; Steiner 1994, ch. 3). The main difference between the two conceptions lies in the emphasis which the choice conception places on the right-holder's power to alter, waive, annul, or otherwise control the duties imposed by the right; it is the ability to exercise the power which gives the right holder control over the normative relations involved in the right. On the choice conception, but not on the interest conception, every right must involve some such means of control. (The distinction between these two conceptions must not be confused with the distinction between the two basic categories of rights: claim-rights and liberty-rights. Both conceptions can make sense of both kinds of rights.)

Each of these conceptions attempts to explain what rights are fundamentally *for* and each purports to apply across the full range of the kinds of rights we typically take ourselves (and other subjects of rights) to have. As comprehensive accounts of the nature of rights, each has its problems; fortunately, however, we need not decide which to accept. Either will suffice to show why rights are not redundant, even in a theory rich in duties. That rights have a distinctive normative function is clearest on the choice conception, for we have no other concept similarly dedicated to the protection of the freedom or autonomy of agents. We must be careful not to mistake the issue here. It is not whether the concept of a right might be eliminable in principle in favor of other concepts. Since rights are reducible to packages of claims, liberties, powers, etc., we could in principle substitute these simpler concepts for the more complex concept of a right. But the result would not merely be impossibly clumsy; it would also obscure the point or rationale which binds these packages together. The idea of rights as protected choices illuminates that rationale and reveals why the concept of a right has a role to play for which we have no reasonable substitute. The choice conception also makes short work of the redundancy thesis, since it requires that every right include some discretionary powers on the part of the right-holder, which means in turn that rights are not reducible to duties (not even the kinds of relational duties which are equivalent to claims).

Rights might seem in greater danger of redundancy on the interest conception, since they can function to protect interests while conferring no room for discretion or choice on the right-holder. On this conception, therefore, unlike the choice conception, a right could consist in just a claim, which is in turn logically equivalent to a (relational) duty. However, even here it would be a mistake to think that rights could simply be deleted from a theory of duties without loss. For the interest conception also provides an account of the point or rationale of certain kinds of duties—namely, that the justification for their imposition is to be found in a feature not of the agent or duty-bearer but of the patients whom the duty protects. Duties can have different grounds, which may focus primarily either on agent or on patient. The interest conception singles out duties whose rationale consists in protecting the interests of patients. Again it assigns to rights a point which would be lost in a theory which spoke only the language of duties.

Rights therefore can be safeguarded against redundancy in deontological theories. A challenge from the opposite end of the theoretical spectrum focuses on the function of rights as constraints on the pursuit of collective goals. Consequentialist theories see the whole point of morality as consisting in the pursuit of a very abstract goal: bringing about the best overall state of affairs or making the world go as well as possible. Rights, as we have seen, are impediments to achieving this goal, since they both permit their subjects to choose non-optimizing actions and require their objects to do so. We should not be surprised then to find that rights have been regarded with suspicion or even outright hostility by some consequentialists (Frey 1984). The consequentialist camp is internally divided on the issue of whether to make room for moral rights, some consequentialists being friendlier to this project than others (John Stuart Mill, for instance, was much more rights-friendly than Jeremy Bentham). Toward the end of this essay I will explore a consequentialist strategy for not only accommodating rights but providing a foundation for them. Meanwhile, it will suffice to say that we have identified a normative role for rights—as protections of individual interests or autonomy against the demands of collective goals—which seems very appealing and whose absolute exclusion from an ethical theory threatens to condemn that theory to irrelevancy. Most impartial observers, if asked to choose between the unfettered promotion of the impersonally best consequences, on the one hand, and its constraint in order to safeguard individual welfare or freedom, on the other, are likely to opt for the latter. Consequentialists may still choose to take the high road (though I will suggest later that they are mistaken to do so), but few are likely to follow them.

The third challenge to the inclusion of rights in an ethical theory is much more interesting than either of the other two. It emanates from relatively recent developments in feminist ethical theory (see, for example, Hardwig 1990; Sherwin 1992). Feminists have tended to be critical of approaches to ethical issues which are formulated primarily or exclusively in terms of rights. They see the discourse of rights as locking us into a legalistic form of moral thinking in which justice becomes the pre-eminent virtue. Justice may be appropriate in the public sphere, where individuals confront one another as strangers or as fellow citizens, but it is out of place in other contexts, especially in close personal relationships which thrive on values such as trust and loyalty. Rights, in their view, are adapted to a social ontology of isolated individuals indifferent or hostile to one another who need the protection of fenced off private domains—the world of business or politics, perhaps, but not that of family or friendship. Feminists are also suspicious of the kind of autonomy whose protection is the centerpiece of the choice conception of rights and which seems to promote a very masculine ideal of the rugged, self-reliant, self-defining individual with no roots and no intimate ties to others.

There are a number of important themes in this critique which we will do well to distinguish. Consider first the alleged individualism of rights. It is true that persons are usually assumed to be the paradigm holders of rights (we have operated with that assumption so far in this essay). However, there is nothing in the logic of rights which restricts them to individuals. Some rights, such as the right not to be assaulted or killed, belong to individuals simply as such, but others, such as the right to religious holidays or to services in one's native language, can be held by individuals only as members of an ethno-cultural group. Even individual rights, therefore, need not define their holders as abstractions isolated from their social contexts. Furthermore, nothing seems to prevent us from taking a further step and attributing some rights (of self-determination or cultural survival, for example) to ethno-cultural groups as wholes, where the right cannot be decomposed into the separate rights of the several members of the group. What is necessary in order to qualify as a potential right-holder is the possession of some value (interests on the interest conception, autonomy on the choice conception) which the right can function to protect. It is at the very least arguable that groups united by a common culture, language, history, or religion could satisfy the requirement of having either a collective interest or the capacity for collective choice. If so, then such groups could be the subjects of rights which will safeguard their liberties or restrict the ways in which they may be legitimately treated. Furthermore, if groups are capable of collective agency they will also be capable of serving as the objects of rights (the bearers of the duties entailed by the right). Many rights (both claim- and liberty-rights) are held against the world at large, which still standardly means each individual member of that world considered separately. But rights can, in principle at least, also be held against groups considered collectively, and some rights … appear to have this form. Therefore, if the point of the individualism critique is that rights can belong only to individuals or be held only against individuals, it is misconceived.

Neither does it appear to be true that rights presuppose a certain picture of the nature of society or of social relationships. Rights are versatile normative instruments which can be put to many different political uses. It is true that they can serve libertarians well, who dream of a suburban society of self-reliant burghers, surrounded by picket fences of liberty-rights, who have only negative duties of noninterference toward one another. But they are just as adaptable to the purposes of communitarians, socialists, egalitarians, or—dare one say it—feminists. Rights can be invoked to support a cutthroat competitive marketplace, but they can also promote an ideal of social solidarity by making it a requirement of justice that resources be allocated for the support of the needy and disadvantaged, or that discrimination on the basis of race, gender, or sexual orientation be eliminated, or that the vulnerable be protected against exploitation and oppression. Since women have historically been more likely than men to suffer from these social evils, appeals to rights and justice have been the main rhetorical weapons which they have used to better their lot (it is difficult to imagine the pro-choice movement, for instance, without such weapons). Availing themselves of the language of rights has not transformed women into isolated, rugged, masculine individuals; on the contrary, the reproductive rights which they have claimed have been deeply rooted in their identities as sole childbearers and primary childrearers.

The feminist critique, however, has another aspect to it which is more faithful to the social ideology of rights. Rights, as we have seen, impose duties and duties are normative constraints on the freedom of others, constraints whose justification lies in the protection they afford the rights-holder. The language of rights does therefore presuppose a social landscape in which interests tend to conflict and in which these conflicts must be managed in a principled way. Members of a world free of conflict might have no need for the protections afforded by rights. Since the public sphere is manifestly not free of conflict, rights may be conceded an appropriate, though regrettable, role in it, though even here a fixation on rights may lead us to exaggerate conflict and competition and to overlook possibilities for cooperation and reconciliation. But what place could there be for rights in the more intimate setting of a family or friendship? If personal relations are viewed through a sufficiently romantic gauze then they might come to appear frictionless. However, this utopian ideal is not a good fit for the daily lives of most friends, lovers, spouses, parents, and children who must also learn to manage conflicts in their personal attachments. It was a great moral and political step forward when the parties to such relationships began to be conceived as distinct individuals with a standing of their own (a process still incomplete for children, who are too often considered even now to be the property of their parents), rather than as subordinates whose interests were submerged in those of the male head of household. To consider that these parties have rights against one another (not to be verbally, physically, sexually, or emotionally abused, for instance) is to establish certain basic expectations that every relations should be expected to meet. The participants in any healthy, functional relations will routinely treat one another in ways which greatly exceed this basic minimum. But that is no reason to deny that they do have such rights, and that the relationship can sink to such depths that the rights of one or more of the parties to it are being violated. Friendship may mean giving your friend more than she has a right to, but it also means not giving her less.

The valuable lesson we learn from the feminist critique is that rights do not occupy the entire moral landscape. They are specialized normative devices with a particular function, one to which they are very well adapted, but they cannot take the place of other equally important values such as loyalty, trust, and care. Nor are they a substitute for other means by which we judge personal character. If rights protect personal prerogative, then they also protect the prerogative to behave badly—that is, in ways which, while they do not actually violate any duties or rights, are nonetheless mean-minded and selfish (Waldron 1993). Our moral vocabulary needs the resources to describe deficiencies of character which are compatible with the most punctilious respect for rights. Anyone who believes that human interactions require nothing more than minimal regard for the rights of others would make a very unattractive friend or spouse or neighbor—or business associate for that matter. But it is no fault of rights that the indolent or small-minded might find it convenient to think that they exhaust the requirements of virtue, and it is no solution to this problem to expel rights entirely from our moral thinking. Rights have an important, indeed indispensable, job to do within any complete and comprehensive moral theory. What the feminist critique does well to remind us is that they do not and should not stand alone.

Why Rights Need a Theory

We began by noting the extent to which rights have become the common currency of moral/political discourse and we have seen how that currency can be defended against various kinds of theoretical challenge. Ironically, however, the greatest threat to the integrity of rights discourse stems from its very popularity. It is the ability of rights, their talent for turning up on both (or all) sides of every issue, that is simultaneously their most impressive and their most troubling feature. Rival interest groups which converge on little else agree that rights are indispensable weapons in the political arena. To claim a right to something is not just to say that it would be nice to have it or generous of others to provide it: rather, one is entitled to expect or demand it, others are obliged to provide it, it would be unjust of them to deny or withhold it. Once a right has been invoked on one side of an issue it must therefore be countered by a weapon of similar potency on the other. But then if one interest group has built its case on an appeal to rights, none of its competitors can afford not to respond in kind. Like any other weapons, once they have appeared in the public arena rights claims will tend to proliferate and to escalate.

In an arms race it can be better for each side to increase its stock even though the resulting escalation will be worse for all sides. Where military weapons are concerned the increased threat is that of mutual annihilation. Where rhetorical weapons are concerned, what all sides must fear is a backlash of skepticism or cynicism. An argumentative device capable of justifying anything is capable of justifying nothing. When rights claims have once been deployed on all sides of all public issues they may no longer be taken seriously as a means of resolving any of those issues. Indeed, the danger is that they will no longer be taken seriously at all. Just as fiscal inflation reduces the real value of money, the inflation of rights rhetoric threatens to debase the currency.

If we once pause to reflect on the bewildering array of rights invoked in both personal and political morality then we cannot avoid asking ourselves some hard questions. Do all of these rights deserve to be taken seriously? If not, which are genuine and which are spurious? And in cases in which genuine rights conflict, which ones deserve to be taken more seriously? In order to answer questions like these we need a verification procedure for rights claims, or a criterion of authenticity for rights. As we saw earlier, the full specification of any right includes four dimensions: its subject(s), its content, its object(s), and its strength. Ideally, then, we want a criterion capable of confirming or disconfirming each of these elements in any rights claim. Non-ideally, we at least need some resources to sort reasonable from unreasonable claims. But where are we to find them?

This sounds like a job for philosophers. However, not everyone working within the rights paradigm is equally helpful. Some philosophers go about their business by simply assuming a certain set of basic rights and then working out their implications for social and political arrangements. Robert Nozick, for instance, opens his most famous book with the claim that "Individuals have rights, and there are things no person or group may do to them (without violating their rights)" (Nozick 1974: ix). The rights Nozick has in mind here are (nearly absolute) property rights which stand as ethical impediments to social programs employed by the welfare state in pursuit of such goals as equalizing resources or meeting the needs of the disadvantaged. Working from this premise, Nozick devotes much ingenious argumentation to the project of working out just how much more than the bare nightwatchman state might be compatible with respect for individual rights. However, the premise itself—the assumption that individuals have just these rights and no others—is given much less attention. A more recent example of this kind of "top-down" argumentation, also within the libertarian political camp, may be found in the work of Hillel Steiner (1994). Following out the moral/political implications of libertarian premises about rights can be an illuminating process, especially when libertarians themselves disagree about these implications. It can also serve to remind those of us of more egalitarian or social-democratic persuasion what the costs would be of failing to defend a more generous set of fundamental rights. However, ultimately a top-down methodology invites the response that it

is persuasive only to the already converted, serving for the rest of us merely as a theoretically interesting exercise: yes, you have shown us where we can (and cannot) get from here, but why should we start *here*? If we want some means of testing the authenticity of rights claims, then we want this to apply as well to the starting points of moral/political argument, which will determine the destinations we can reach.

Other philosophers have a different way of proceeding with rights which we might call intuitionist or casuistical. The most accomplished and influential practitioner of this methodology has been Judith Jarvis Thomson (1990). Unlike those who elect to work from an assumed set of basic rights, Thomson's aim is to determine which kinds of rights we have. Furthermore, she thinks that there are some general principles which lie behind the kinds of rights we tend to attribute to ourselves and others, and she wants to determine what those principles are (1990: 1). So we seem here much closer to the ideal of a test or criterion of authenticity for rights: some alleged rights will presumably fare well in terms of these principles (whatever they turn out to be), while others will fare badly. The question then becomes one of discovering or revealing these principles. This is where Thomson's intuitionist methodology comes into play. She rests claims about the kinds of rights we have on appeals to our considered moral judgments, appeals of the sort "But surely A ought to do such and such" or "Plainly it would be wrong for B to do so and so." Because she expects general agreement with these judgments, she makes no attempt to show that they are true. Furthermore, as she herself says (1990: 4), she rests argumentative weight on them, by using them to draw conclusions about people's rights. She therefore takes for granted much of the content of our ordinary morality and offers no means of confirming (or disconfirming) it. Her strategy is to argue from some (hopefully uncontroversial) fixed points in our moral thinking to implications for rights which may not (without some careful argument) seem to follow from them. All moral theorizing, she tells us (1990: 33), begins with a body of data, and her data are moral judgments which she expects her readers to accept as moral truths.

What Thomson's procedure shares with the top-down methodology of Nozick and Steiner is that certain things get taken for granted and used to support arguments for other things. However, whereas Nozick and Steiner assume some very general principles about the kinds of rights we have, the judgments Thomson takes for granted are about particular cases. Furthermore, they are not about rights but about what someone ought or ought not to do, or what it would be right or wrong to do; any claims about rights appear only as the conclusions of arguments from such judgments. Her methodology is therefore more "bottom-up" or particularist. It also more closely resembles common-law judicial reasoning which tries to work from relatively fixed points in the law to conclusions about new cases. It is particularly well suited to a certain picture about morality in general, and the territory of rights in particular, which Thomson professes to share (1990: 33): that it does not form a system governed by a small set of very general principles. In her view, therefore, it is impossible to argue to rights from any such set of principles. Rather, again like the common law, the principles must be uncovered through the process of arguing to, and about, rights.

The results which Thomson reaches by means of her intuitionist methodology are very impressive. She is particularly good at trying to work out rigorously what we mean casually when we say such things as that a right can be overridden or forfeited. Furthermore, the kinds of rights she takes to be genuine are, for the most part, familiar features of our (liberal) moral discourse: claims against harm or invasion by others, protected liberties, and so on. However, the argumentative structure she erects is clearly only as secure as its foundations, and those foundations consist of particular moral judgments whose truth is taken for granted. What happens if some of those judgments are disputable, or disputed? Thomson says (1990: 4, 22) that a mistake on her part about any of these judgements would be just as serious as a mistake in her

reasoning from them. Are any of them mistaken? This question we could not settle without working through Thomson's arguments in detail, a task which is inappropriate in this essay. However, just as a matter of autobiography, I will say that my intuitions about the cases Thomson constructs do not always coincide with hers. Wherever that is true then the further courses of her argument once again become merely an interesting exercise for me, on a par with the arguments of Nozick and Steiner. Furthermore, as is common in analytic ethics, many of Thomson's examples are very schematic and stripped of all social and political context. Very often my response is not so much that I agree or disagree with Thomson's assumption about the case in question, but that I want to know more, often much more, before making up my mind either way. But then many of Thomson's "data" remain question marks for me, not so much mistaken as indeterminate.

The intuitionist methodology which Thomson uses to generate a criterion of authenticity for rights is very common in analytic ethics, where appeals are constantly made to "what we believe" or "what we would say" about particular cases. In a certain respect, it is unexceptionable. Since not everything can be called into question at once, we have to assume something in order to be able to argue to any conclusions. The question is: what to assume? Thomson's implicit contention seems to be that our judgments about particular cases are more secure than any general moral principles; they therefore make safer starting points for moral argument. She makes no attempt to argue for this contention, and I can think of no way of proving (or disproving) it. She may well be right, but other methodological possibilities are equally worth exploring. So far we have considered only two: arguments from general principles about rights and arguments to rights from particular moral judgments. It is time to introduce a third: that a criterion of authenticity for rights needs the resources of a general ethical theory.

By an ethical theory I mean a relatively small, coherent set of fundamental normative principles general enough to cover the whole of our moral thinking. Since some, but not all, of that thinking involves rights, the territory of rights will form a particular subdomain in the overall landscape of a theory. The idea then is that the ultimate resource to which we appeal in order to develop a criterion of authenticity for rights is the set of basic principles in a theory. But what kind of theory? Since the options here are virtually infinite, we need to simplify the problem by focusing on a few basic types of theory. Let us assume that every moral theory has a structure or hierarchy of principles, some of which are basic (serving, in effect, as axioms) while others are derivable from them (theorems). Assume further that every such principle gives justificatory priority to a particular category of moral concepts: duties, rights, virtues, the good, etc. Then in general a theory is X-based if its basic principles give priority to concepts from category X. In this way we can classify theories as duty-based, rights-based, virtue-based, and so on. Now let us ask the question which of these types of (foundationalist) theory is most likely to generate an operational criterion for authenticating rights.

Two kinds of theory can, I think, be excluded at the outset. On the face of it, duty-based theories might seem a hospitable environment for rights, since they are deontological right down to their foundations. However, as we noted earlier, duties form a wider category than rights and need not be patient-centered in the way that is characteristic of rights. The most basic principles in a duty-based theory—the ones which tell us what our most general duties are—may therefore refer not to some feature of moral patients (such as their welfare or autonomy) but to some feature of moral agents (such as their rationality or autonomy). Any duty-based theory with this ultimate derivation of our duties will have difficulty accommodating rights in the full sense in which they have a distinctive and ineliminable normative function. Virtue-based theories, which also tend to be agent-centered, may be excluded for the same reason. If a theory derives rights from principles about the virtues (or about the virtue of justice in particular), and if it grounds these principles in turn on an account of the good of the moral agent,

then it too will lack the focus on moral patients that is the peculiar contribution of rights.

The most obvious kind of theory to provide a criterion of authenticity for rights is one which is rights-based. I will pass over the problem of how comprehensive or complete such a theory could be. After all, we know that rights define only one domain of the moral territory and are out of place in others. We might wonder, for instance, how adequate a picture of personal relationships, and of the many values which such relationships can exemplify, a purely rights-based theory could ever generate. I will also pass over the question of what the basic principles of rights in a rights-based theory might look like or how they themselves might be validated. There is a problem with the very idea of a rights-based theory which runs much deeper.

In our earlier exploration of the anatomy of rights we found their constituent elements to be such things as liberties, duties, powers, and immunities. All of these elements share one important characteristic: they are the creatures of rule systems. The parallel cases liberties and powers will suffice to make (or remind us of) the point. A liberty defines what is normatively permissible for an agent—what she may (is allowed to) do. A power defines what is normatively possible for an agent—what she can (is able to) do (by way of altering her own or others' normative relationships). Liberties presuppose a rule system with a triad of deontic modal concepts (required/permitted/prohibited), while powers presuppose a rule system with the triad of alethic modal concepts (necessary/possible/impossible). A rule system with deontic concepts alone is capable of generating rights on the interest conception, while a system with both sets of concepts is necessary for rights on the choice conception. A legal system is the best example of a rule system with both kinds of resources, which is why it is capable of conferring rights on those subject to its jurisdiction. Those rights have legal force as long as the rules which define them, and the system itself, satisfy whatever requirements are deemed to be necessary for legal validity.

But we want a theory to support not legal rights, not any sort of merely conventional rights, but moral rights—the kinds of rights we use to criticize or justify a system of conventional rights. Legal rights presuppose a system of legal rules, so presumably moral rights must presuppose a system of moral rules. In the case of legal rules we can explain the existence of the rule system in terms of some source (a legislature or a court, for instance) which has the authority to make law. But what are the conditions for the existence of a system of moral rules (or laws)? What makes these rules moral, as opposed to conventional, is precisely the fact that they issue from no authority. But then how can we make sense of their existence? By virtue of what are they rules? And what is the source of their authority over us?

A moral theory can, I think, provide intelligible answers to these important questions. But a theory which takes rights (or, for that matter, duties) as basic labors under a special disability since it must provide existence conditions for moral rules without recourse to any deeper principles. It is vulnerable to the accusation of hypothesizing some ghostly moral realm, the analogue of a legal system, in which moral rules somehow exist with no moral legislator. We are asked to assume that these rules are capable of imposing requirements and prohibitions, and conferring abilities and disabilities, without any of the substructure which supports the existence of a legal system. Rights and duties are of course legalistic concepts, imported into ethics from the law. Whenever such borrowing occurs the question may be raised whether the concepts make sense in the absence of the framework within which they originally developed. Now we know that sense can be made of the concept of a moral right, but only if we presuppose the background of a system of moral rules. The issue is whether a theory which treats rights as basic can make any sense of such a rule system. I cannot prove the impossibility of its doing so, but the story it would need to tell about the origin and authority of the system remain deeply mysterious.

Whether or not the foregoing considerations suffice to exclude rights-based theories as the appropriate theoretical setting for rights, there is another option worth exploring. Consequentialist theories utilize the concept of the good as their basic moral category and combine particular instances of the good into an overall goal to be pursued (or optimized). On the face of it, a goal-based ethical theory would seem to be the least likely home for moral rights, since (as we have seen) rights serve as normative constraints on the pursuit of goals. However, appearances here may be deceiving (Sumner 1987, ch. 6). A goal may be pursued in either of two ways: directly, by just aiming at it in every instance, or indirectly, by employing some more complex motivational strategy. While some goals are best pursued directly, others are not. The goal of personal happiness will serve as an example of the latter sort. If everything you do is directly and consciously motivated by the desire to maximize your own happiness, then you will almost certainly frustrate your own aim. Your goal will be much more efficiently pursued by sometimes aiming at other things (personal relationships, for instance) which require some suppression of your self-centered fixation. Now suppose we are talking about a very abstract moral goal such as the general welfare or equality of resources. Would such a goal be best pursued directly or indirectly? If the former, then there will indeed be no room for taking rights seriously, since they must be acknowledged as obstacles to the pursuit of the goal. But there are good reasons for thinking that, like personal happiness, moral goals are best pursued indirectly. These reasons have principally to do with the cognitive and motivation limitations of moral decision-makers, whether they be individuals or social agencies. Left with no guidance save the general exhortation to promote some abstract moral goal, most decision-makers are likely to choose counterproductive means, as the result either of deficient information or of a natural human tendency to interpret situations in one's own favor. If this hypothesis is correct, then the kinds of goals advocated by most consequentialist theories will be best pursued by accepting and internalizing a set of constraints, then respect for (a suitably contoured set of) rights might be required by a goal-based theory. If so, then there will be room within such a theory for rights to play their characteristic normative role, while the theory's basic goal will serve as the criterion for authenticating rights. A right will count as genuine on this view just in case its recognition within some conventional rule system (formal or informal) is (or would be) morally justified, where the standard of justification is promotion of the theory's basic goal.

A goal-based theory imposes an external control on the proliferation of rights: the purpose of rights is to promote some independently defined value such as welfare or autonomy, and rights are to be recognized as legitimate only to the extent that they serve this purpose. The same basic aim will therefore also serve to demarcate the subdomain of rights, by identifying those areas of private or public life where thinking in terms of rights is inappropriate or counterproductive. A goal-based theory also has no problem accounting for the rule system necessary for making sense of rights, since the only rules it requires (or acknowledges) are ordinary conventional ones (legal and nonlegal, institutional and non-institutional, formal and informal). A moral right on this account is a right whose recognition in some such rule system is (or would be) morally justified—no Platonic heaven is necessary of moral rules with no moral legislator.

The most familiar form of consequentialism is of course utilitarianism, which is distinctive by virtue of its welfarist theory of the good and its aggregative procedure for combining individual welfare into a sum to be maximized. But consequentialist theories come in many different shapes with different theories of the good (both monistic and pluralistic) and different procedures (both aggregative and distributive) for defining a collective goal. For our present purposes it matters not which particular form of consequentialism we have in mind, for their common property is the priority they attach to promotion of their favored goal. Trying to fit rights into this kind of collectivist framework may seem a little like trying to square the circle, but once the air of paradox is dispelled the idea has considerable attraction. It is also the working paradigm in much judicial reasoning about rights, which often takes the form of trying to locate the appropriate balance between conflicting rights. If each of the rights in conflict (for instance, freedom of political expression versus equal respect for minorities) is intended to secure some important social goal, then striking the appropriate balance between them means drawing their boundaries in whatever way will promote the optimal tradeoff between these goals. Any such approach is basically consequentialist, since it treats rights as devices for the pursuit of social goals. But it is compatible with, indeed requires, taking (the appropriate set of) rights seriously.

Other kinds of theories, such as some forms of contractualism, may share with consequentialism the virtue of controlling rights externally rather than internally. My aim here has not been to provide an exhaustive inventory of the possible theoretical settings for rights, but rather to make two tentative suggestions. The first is that the strategy of situating rights within a general ethical theory is worth exploring thoroughly before we settle for the more modest methodology of particularist intuitionism. The second is that among such theories those that are goal—rather than rights—based have a better chance both of making sense of rights and of controlling the inflation of rights claims. I have not been able to give either suggestion more than a very cursory defense, but both merit further development.

References

Dworkin, R. *Taking Rights Seriously*. Cambridge, MA: Harvard University Press, 1977.

Finnis, J. *Natural Law and Natural Rights*. Oxford: Clarendon Press, 1980.

Freeden, M. *Rights*. Minneapolis: University of Minnesota Press, 1991.

Frey, R.G. "Act-Utilitarianism, Consequentialism, and Moral Rights." In R.G. Frey (ed.), *Utility and Rights*. Minneapolis: University of Minnesota Press, 1984, pp. 61–85.

Hardwig, J. "Should Women Think in Terms of Rights?" In C. Sunstein (ed.), *Feminism and Political Theory*. Chicago: University of Chicago Press, 1990, pp. 53–67.

Hart, H.L.A. *Essays on Bentham: Studies in Jurisprudence and Political Theory*. Oxford: Clarendon Press, 1982.

Jones, P. *Rights*. Basingstoke: Macmillan, 1994.

Lomasky, L.E. *Persons, Rights, and the Moral Community*. New York and Oxford: Oxford University Press, 1987.

Lyons, D. *Rights, Welfare, and Mill's Moral Theory*. New York and Oxford: Oxford University Press, 1994.

MacCormick, N. *Legal Right and Social Democracy: Essays in Legal and Political Philosophy*. Oxford: Clarendon Press, 1982.

Nozick, R. *Anarchy, State, and Utopia*. New York: Basic Books, 1974.

Raz, J. *The Morality of Freedom*. Oxford: Clarendon Press, 1986.

Sherwin, S. *No Longer Patient: Feminist Ethics and Health Care*. Philadelphia: Temple University Press, 1992.

Steiner, H. *An Essay on* Rights. Oxford: Blackwell, 1994.

Sumner, L.W. *The Moral Foundation of Rights*. Oxford: Clarendon Press, 1987.

Thomson, J.J. *The Realm of Rights*. Cambridge, MA, and London: Harvard University Press, 1990.

Waldron, J. *Liberal Rights: Collected Papers, 1981–1991*. Cambridge and New York: Cambridge University Press, 1993.

Wellman, C. *A Theory of Rights: Persons Under Laws, Institutions, and Morals*. Totawa, NJ: Rowman and Allanheld, 1985.

DISCUSSION QUESTIONS

1. Why does Sumner think that talk of rights cannot simply be reduced to talk of duties?

2. Why does Sumner think that duty-based ethical theories will have a difficult time adequately accommodating rights? Why does he make the same claim about virtue-based ethical theories? How does Sumner think that consequentialist ethical theories can accommodate rights?

3. Explain what Sumner dubs the "feminist challenge" to the inclusion of rights within an ethical theory. How does Sumner respond to this challenge?

C.
Do We Have a Right to Liberty?

32

Thomas Hobbes, selection from *Leviathan* (1651)

In this selection, Hobbes considers the powers and rights of sovereign rulers, arguing that they are virtually unlimited. On Hobbes, see reading 2 above.

SOURCE

Hobbes, Thomas. *Leviathan* (Second Edition). George Routledge and Sons, 1886.

Of the Rights of Sovereigns by Institution

A commonwealth is said to be instituted when a multitude of men do agree, and covenant, every one with every one, that to whatsoever man, or assembly of men, shall be given by the major part the right to present the person of them all, that is to say, to be their representative; every one, as well he that voted for it as he that voted against it, shall authorize all the actions and judgements of that man, or assembly of men, in the same manner as if they were his own, to the end to live peaceably amongst themselves, and be protected against other men.

From this institution of a Commonwealth are derived all the rights and faculties of him, or them, on whom the sovereign power is conferred by the consent of the people assembled.

First, because they covenant, it is to be understood they are not obliged by former covenant to anything repugnant hereunto. And consequently they that have already instituted a Commonwealth, being thereby bound by covenant to own the actions and judgements of one, cannot lawfully make a new covenant amongst themselves to be obedient to any other, in anything whatsoever, without his permission. And therefore, they that are subjects to a monarch cannot without his leave cast off monarchy and return to the confusion of a disunited multitude; nor transfer their person from him that beareth it to another man, other assembly of men: for they are bound, every man to every man, to own and be reputed author of all that he that already is their sovereign shall do and judge fit to be done; so that any one man dissenting, all the rest should break their covenant made to that man, which is injustice: and they have also every man given the sovereignty to him that beareth their person; and therefore if they depose him, they take from him that which is his own, and so again it is injustice. Besides, if he that attempteth to depose his sovereign be killed or punished by him for such attempt, he is author of his own punishment, as being, by the institution, author of all his sovereign shall do; and because it is injustice for a man to do anything for which he may be punished by his own authority, he is also upon that title unjust. And whereas some men have pretended for their disobedience to their sovereign a new covenant, made, not with men but with God, this also is unjust: for there is no covenant with God but by mediation of somebody that representeth God's person, which none doth but God's lieutenant who hath the sovereignty under God. But this pretence of covenant with God is so evident a lie, even in the pretenders' own consciences, that it is not only an act of an unjust, but also of a vile and unmanly disposition.

Secondly, because the right of bearing the person of them all is given to him they make sovereign, by covenant only of one to another, and not of him to any of them, there can happen no breach of covenant on the part of the sovereign; and consequently none of his subjects, by any pretence of forfeiture, can be freed from his subjection. That he which is made sovereign maketh no covenant with his subjects before hand is manifest; because either he must make it with the whole multitude, as one party to the covenant, or he must make a several covenant with every man. With the whole, as one party, it is impossible, because as they are not one person: and if he make so many several covenants as there be men, those covenants after he hath the sovereignty are void; because what act soever can be pretended by any one of them for breach thereof is the act both of himself, and of all the rest, because done in the person, and by the right of every one of them in particular. Besides, if any one or more of them

pretend a breach of the covenant made by the sovereign at his institution, and others or one other of his subjects, or himself alone, pretend there was no such breach, there is in this case no judge to decide the controversy: it returns therefore to the sword again; and every man recovereth the right of protecting himself by his own strength, contrary to the design they had in the institution. It is therefore in vain to grant sovereignty by way of precedent covenant. The opinion that any monarch receiveth his power by covenant, that is to say, on condition, proceedeth from want of understanding this easy truth: that covenants being but words, and breath, have no force to oblige, contain, constrain, or protect any man, but what it has from the public sword; that is, from the untied hands of that man, or assembly of men, that hath the sovereignty, and whose actions are avouched by them all, and performed by the strength of them all, in him united. But when an assembly of men is made sovereign, then no man imagineth any such covenant to have passed in the institution: for no man is so dull as to say, for example, the people of Rome made a covenant with the Romans to hold the sovereignty on such or such conditions; which not performed, the Romans might lawfully depose the Roman people. That men see not the reason to be alike in a monarchy and in a popular government proceedeth from the ambition of some that are kinder to the government of an assembly, whereof they may hope to participate, than of monarchy, which they despair to enjoy.

Thirdly, because the major part hath by consenting voices declared a sovereign, he that dissented must now consent with the rest; that is, be contented to avow all the actions he shall do, or else justly be destroyed by the rest. For if he voluntarily entered into the congregation of them that were assembled, he sufficiently declared thereby his will, and therefore tacitly covenanted, to stand to what the major part should ordain: and therefore if he refuse to stand thereto, or make protestation against any of their decrees, he does contrary to his covenant, and therefore unjustly. And whether he be of the congregation or not, and whether his consent be asked or not, he must either submit to their decrees or be left in the condition of war he was in before; wherein he might without injustice be destroyed by any man whatsoever.

Fourthly, because every subject is by this institution author of all the actions and judgements of the sovereign instituted, it follows that whatsoever he doth, can be no injury to any of his subjects; nor ought he to be by any of them accused of injustice. For he that doth anything by authority from another doth therein no injury to him by whose authority he acteth: but by this institution of a Commonwealth every particular man is author of all the sovereign doth; and consequently he that complaineth of injury from his sovereign complaineth of that whereof he himself is author, and therefore ought not to accuse any man but himself; no, nor himself of injury, because to do injury to oneself is impossible. It is true that they that have sovereign power may commit iniquity, but not injustice or injury in the proper signification.

Fifthly, and consequently to that which was said last, no man that hath sovereign power can justly be put to death, or otherwise in any manner by his subjects punished. For seeing every subject is author of the actions of his sovereign, he punisheth another for the actions committed by himself.

And because the end of this institution is the peace and defence of them all, and whosoever has right to the end has right to the means, it belonged of right to whatsoever man or assembly that hath the sovereignty to be judge both of the means of peace and defence, and also of the hindrances and disturbances of the same; and to do whatsoever he shall think necessary to be done, both beforehand, for the preserving of peace and security, by prevention of discord at home, and hostility from abroad; and when peace and security are lost, for the recovery of the same. And therefore,

Sixthly, it is annexed to the sovereignty to be judge of what opinions and doctrines are averse, and what conducing to peace; and consequently, on what occasions, how far, and what men are to be trusted withal in speaking to multitudes of people; and who shall examine the doctrines of all books before they be published. For the actions of men proceed from their opinions, and in the well governing of opinions consisteth the well governing of men's actions in order to their peace and concord. And though in matter of doctrine nothing to be regarded but the truth, yet this is not repugnant to regulating of the same by peace. For doctrine repugnant to peace can no more be true, than peace and concord can be against the law of nature. It is true that in a Commonwealth, where by the negligence or unskillfulness of governors and teachers false doctrines are by time generally received, the contrary truths may be generally offensive: yet the most sudden and rough bustling in of a new truth that can be does never break the peace, but only sometimes awake the war. For those men that are so remissly governed that they dare take up arms to defend or introduce an opinion are still in war; and their condition, not peace, but only a cessation of arms for fear of one another; and they live, as it were, in the precincts of battle continually. It belonged therefore to him that hath the sovereign power to be judge, or constitute all judges of opinions and doctrines, as a thing necessary to peace; thereby to prevent discord and civil war.

Seventhly, is annexed to the sovereignty the whole power of prescribing the rules whereby every man may know what goods he may enjoy, and what actions he may do, without being molested by any of his fellow subjects: and this is it men call propriety. For before constitution of sovereign power, as hath already been shown, all men had right to all things, which necessarily causeth war: and therefore this propriety, being necessary to peace, and depending on sovereign power, is the act of that power, in order to the public peace. These rules of propriety (or *meum* and *tuum*) and of good, evil, lawful, and unlawful in the actions of subjects are the civil laws; that is to say, the laws of each Commonwealth in particular; though the name of civil law be now restrained to the ancient civil laws of the city of Rome; which being the head of a great part of the world, her laws at that time were in these parts the civil law.

Eighthly, is annexed to the sovereignty the right of judicature; that is to say, of hearing and deciding all controversies which may arise concerning law, either civil or natural, or concerning fact. For without the decision of controversies, there is no protection of one subject against the injuries of another; the laws concerning *meum* and *tuum* are in vain, and to every man remaineth, from the natural and necessary appetite of his own conservation, the right of protecting himself by his private strength, which is the condition of war, and contrary to the end for which every Commonwealth is instituted.

Ninthly, is annexed to the sovereignty the right of making war and peace with other nations and Commonwealths; that is to say, of judging when it is for the public good, and how great forces are to be assembled, armed, and paid for that end, and to levy money upon the subjects to defray the expenses thereof. For the power by which the people are to be defended consisteth in their armies, and the strength of an army in the union of their strength under one command; which command the sovereign instituted, therefore hath, because the command of the militia, without other institution, maketh him that hath it sovereign. And therefore, whosoever is made general of an army, he that hath the sovereign power is always generalissimo.

Tenthly, is annexed to the sovereignty the choosing of all counsellors, ministers, magistrates, and officers, both in peace and war. For seeing the sovereign is charged with the end, which is the common peace and defence, he is understood to have power to use such means as he shall think most fit for his discharge.

Eleventhly, to the sovereign is committed the power of rewarding with riches or honour; and of punishing with corporal or pecuniary punishment, or with ignominy, every subject according to the law he hath formerly made; or if there be no law made, according as he shall judge most to conduce to the encouraging of men to serve the Commonwealth, or deterring of them from doing disservice to the same.

Lastly, considering what values men are naturally apt to set upon themselves, what respect they look for from others, and how little they value other men; from whence continually arise amongst them,

emulation, quarrels, factions, and at last war, to the destroying of one another, and diminution of their strength against a common enemy; it is necessary that there be laws of honour, and a public rate of the worth of such men as have deserved or are able to deserve well of the Commonwealth, and that there be force in the hands of some or other to put those laws in execution. But it hath already been shown that not only the whole militia, or forces of the Commonwealth, but also the judicature of all controversies, is annexed to the sovereignty. To the sovereign therefore it belonged also to give titles of honour, and to appoint what order of place and dignity each man shall hold, and what signs of respect in public or private meetings they shall give to one another.

These are the rights which make the essence of sovereignty, and which are the marks whereby a man may discern in what man, or assembly of men, the sovereign power is placed and resideth. For these are incommunicable and inseparable. The power to coin money, to dispose of the estate and persons of infant heirs, to have pre-emption in markets, and all other statute prerogatives may be transferred by the sovereign, and yet the power to protect his subjects be retained. But if he transfer the militia, he retains the judicature in vain, for want of execution of the laws; or if he grant away the power of raising money, the militia is in vain; or if he give away the government of doctrines, men will be frighted into rebellion with the fear of spirits. And so if we consider any one of the said rights, we shall presently see that the holding of all the rest will produce no effect in the conservation of peace and justice, the end for which all Commonwealths are instituted. And this division is it whereof it is said, a kingdom divided in itself cannot stand: for unless this division precede, division into opposite armies can never happen. If there had not first been an opinion received of the greatest part of England that these powers were divided between the King and the Lords and the House of Commons, the people had never been divided and fallen into this Civil War; first between those that disagreed in politics, and after between the dissenters about the liberty of religion, which have so instructed men in this point of sovereign right that there be few now in England that do not see that these rights are inseparable, and will be so generally acknowledged at the next return of peace; and so continue, till their miseries are forgotten, and no longer, except the vulgar be better taught than they have hitherto been.

And because they are essential and inseparable rights, it follows necessarily that in whatsoever words any of them seem to be granted away, yet if the sovereign power itself be not in direct terms renounced and the name of sovereign no more given by the grantees to him that grants them, the grant is void: for when he has granted all he can, if we grant back the sovereignty, all is restored, as inseparably annexed thereunto.

This great authority being indivisible, and inseparably annexed to the sovereignty, there is little ground for the opinion of them that say of sovereign kings, though they be *singulis majores*, of greater power than every one of their subjects, yet they be *universis minores*, of less power than them all together. For if by all together, they mean not the collective body as one person, then all together and every one signify the same; and the speech is absurd. But if by all together, they understand them as one person (which person the sovereign bears), then the power of all together is the same with the sovereign's power; and so again the speech is absurd: which absurdity they see well enough when the sovereignty is in an assembly of the people; but in a monarch they see it not; and yet the power of sovereignty is the same in whomsoever it be placed.

And as the power, so also the honour of the sovereign, ought to be greater than that of any or all the subjects. For in the sovereignty is the fountain of honour. The dignities of lord, earl, duke, and prince are his creatures. As in the presence of the master, the servants are equal, and without any honour at all; so are the subjects, in the presence of the sovereign. And though they shine some more, some less, when they are out of his sight; yet in his presence, they shine no more than the stars in presence of the sun.

But a man may here object that the condition of subjects is very miserable, as being obnoxious to the lusts and other irregular passions of him or them that have so unlimited a power in their hands. And commonly they that live under a monarch think it the fault of monarchy; and they that live under the government of democracy, or other sovereign assembly, attribute all the inconvenience to that form of Commonwealth; whereas the power in all forms, if they be perfect enough to protect them, is the same: not considering that the estate of man can never be without some incommodity or other; and that the greatest that in any form of government can possibly happen to the people in general is scarce sensible, in respect of the miseries and horrible calamities that accompany a civil war, or that dissolute condition of masterless men without subjection to laws and a coercive power to tie their hands from rapine and revenge: nor considering that the greatest pressure of sovereign governors proceedeth, not from any delight or profit they can expect in the damage or weakening of their subjects, in whose vigour consisteth their own strength and glory, but in the restiveness of themselves that, unwillingly contributing to their own defence, make it necessary for their governors to draw from them what they can in time of peace that they may have means on any emergent occasion, or sudden need, to resist or take advantage on their enemies. For all men are by nature provided of notable multiplying glasses (that is their passions and self-love) through which every little payment appeareth a great grievance, but are destitute of those prospective glasses (namely moral and civil science) to see afar off the miseries that hang over them and cannot without such payments be avoided.

DISCUSSION QUESTIONS

1. What is Hobbes's justification for asserting that the power and rights of the sovereign are virtually unlimited? Do you
   accept his line of reasoning? Why or why
   not?

2. How does Hobbes define the term "justice"? What does Hobbes mean when
   he says that the sovereign cannot act
   unjustly?

3. What do you think Hobbes would have
   to say about the suffragist and civil-rights
   movements in the United States? Would
   such organized movements/protests be
   protected in Hobbes's ideal state? Why or
   why not?

33

John Stuart Mill, selection from *On Liberty* (1859)

In the following selection, Mill discusses the extent to which government may legitimately interfere in the lives of its citizens. In doing so, he presents his famous "Harm Principle." On Mill, see reading 23 above.

SOURCE

Mill, John Stuart. *On Liberty*. Longman, Roberts & Green, 1869.

The subject of this Essay is not the so-called liberty of the will, so unfortunately opposed to the misnamed doctrine of philosophical necessity; but civil, or social liberty: the nature and limits of the power which can be legitimately exercised by society over the individual. A question seldom stated, and hardly ever discussed, in general terms, but which profoundly influences the practical controversies of the age by its latent presence, and is likely soon to make itself recognised as the vital question of the future. It is so far from being new, that, in a certain sense, it has divided mankind, almost from the remotest ages; but in the stage of progress into which the more civilized portions of the species have now entered, it presents itself under new conditions, and requires a different and more fundamental treatment.

The struggle between liberty and authority is the most conspicuous feature in the portions of history with which we are earliest familiar, particularly in that of Greece, Rome, and England. But in old times this contest was between subjects, or some classes of subjects, and the government. By liberty, was meant protection against the tyranny of the political rulers. The rulers were conceived (except in some of the popular governments of Greece) as in a necessarily antagonistic position to the people whom they ruled. They consisted of a governing One, or a governing tribe or caste, who derived their authority from inheritance or conquest, who, at all events, did not hold it at the pleasure of the governed, and whose supremacy men did not venture, perhaps did not desire, to contest, whatever precautions might be taken against its oppressive exercise. Their power was regarded as necessary, but also as highly dangerous; as a weapon which they would attempt to use against their subjects, no less than against external enemies. To prevent the weaker members of the community from being preyed on by innumerable vultures, it was needful that there should be an animal of prey stronger than the rest, commissioned to keep them down. But as the king of the vultures would be no less bent upon preying upon the flock than any of the minor harpies, it was indispensable to be in a perpetual attitude of defence against his beak and claws. The aim, therefore, of patriots was to set limits to the power which the ruler should be suffered to exercise over the community; and this limitation was what they meant by liberty. It was attempted in two ways. First, by obtaining a recognition of certain immunities, called political liberties or rights, which it was to be regarded as a breach of duty in the ruler to infringe, and which, if he did infringe, specific resistance, or general rebellion, was held to be justifiable. A second, and generally a later expedient, was the establishment of constitutional checks, by which the consent of the community, or of a body of some sort, supposed to represent its interests, was made a necessary condition to some of the more important acts of the governing power. To the first of these modes of limitation, the ruling power, in most European countries, was compelled, more or less, to submit. It was not so with the second; and, to attain this, or when already in some degree possessed, to attain it more completely, became everywhere the principal object of the lovers of liberty. And so long as mankind were content to combat one enemy by another, and to be ruled by a master, on condition of being guaranteed more or less efficaciously against his tyranny, they did not carry their aspirations beyond this point.

A time, however, came, in the progress of human affairs, when men ceased to think it a necessity of nature that their governors should be an independent power, opposed in interest to themselves.

It appeared to them much better that the various magistrates of the State should be their tenants or delegates, revocable at their pleasure. In that way alone, it seemed, could they have complete security that the powers of government would never be abused to their disadvantage. By degrees this new demand for elective and temporary rulers became the prominent object of the exertions of the popular party, wherever any such party existed; and superseded, to a considerable extent, the previous efforts to limit the power of rulers. As the struggle proceeded for making the ruling power emanate from the periodical choice of the ruled, some persons began to think that too much importance had been attached to the limitation of the power itself. *That* (it might seem) was a resource against rulers whose interests were habitually opposed to those of the people. What was now wanted was, that the rulers should be identified with the people; that their interest and will should be the interest and will of the nation. The nation did not need to be protected against its own will. There was no fear of its tyrannizing over itself. Let the rulers be effectually responsible to it, promptly removable by it, and it could afford to trust them with power of which it could itself dictate the use to be made. Their power was but the nation's own power, concentrated, and in a form convenient for exercise. This mode of thought, or rather perhaps of feeling, was common among the last generation of European liberalism, in the Continental section of which it still apparently predominates. Those who admit any limit to what a government may do, except in the case of such governments as they think ought not to exist, stand out as brilliant exceptions among the political thinkers of the Continent. A similar tone of sentiment might by this time have been prevalent in our own country, if the circumstances which for a time encouraged it had continued unaltered.

But in political and philosophical theories, as well as in persons, success discloses faults and infirmities which failure might have concealed from observation. The notion that the people have no need to limit their power over themselves, might seem axiomatic, when popular government was a thing only dreamed about, or read of as having existed at some distant period of the past. Neither was that notion necessarily disturbed by such temporary aberrations as those of the French Revolution, the worst of which were the work of an usurping few, and which, in any case, belonged, not to the permanent working of popular institutions, but to a sudden and convulsive outbreak against monarchical and aristocratic despotism. In time, however, a democratic republic came to occupy a large portion of the earth's surface, and made itself felt as one of the most powerful members of the community of nations; and elective and responsible government became subject to the observations and criticisms which wait upon a great existing fact. It was now perceived that such phrases as "self-government," and "the power of the people over themselves," do not express the true state of the case. The "people" who exercise the power are not always the same people with those over whom it is exercised; and the "self-government" spoken of is not the government of each by himself, but of each by all the rest. The will of the people, moreover, practically means the will of the most numerous or the most active *part* of the people; the majority, or those who succeed in making themselves accepted as the majority; the people, consequently, *may* desire to oppress a part of their number; and precautions are as much needed against this as against any other abuse of power. The limitation, therefore, of the power of government over individuals loses none of its importance when the holders of power are regularly accountable to the community, that is, to the strongest party therein. This view of things, recommending itself equally to the intelligence of thinkers and to the inclination of those important classes in European society to whose real or supposed interests democracy is adverse, has had no difficulty in establishing itself; and in political speculations "the tyranny of the majority" is now generally included among the evils against which society requires to be on its guard.

Like other tyrannies, the tyranny of the majority was at first, and is still vulgarly, held in dread, chiefly as operating through the acts of the public authorities. But reflecting persons perceived that when society is itself the tyrant—society collectively, over the separate individuals who compose it—its means of tyrannizing are not restricted to the acts which it may do by the hands of its political functionaries. Society can and does execute its own mandates: and if it issues wrong mandates instead of right, or any mandates at all in things with which it ought not to meddle, it practises a social tyranny more formidable than many kinds of political oppression, since, though not usually upheld by such extreme penalties, it leaves fewer means of escape, penetrating much more deeply into the details of life, and enslaving the soul itself. Protection, therefore, against the tyranny of the magistrate is not enough: there needs protection also against the tyranny of the prevailing opinion and feeling; against the tendency of society to impose, by other means than civil penalties, its own ideas and practices as rules of conduct on those who dissent from them; to fetter the development, and, if possible, prevent the formation, of any individuality not in harmony with its ways, and compel all characters to fashion themselves upon the model of its own. There is a limit to the legitimate interference of collective opinion with individual independence: and to find that limit, and maintain it against encroachment, is as indispensable to a good condition of human affairs, as protection against political despotism.

But though this proposition is not likely to be contested in general terms, the practical question, where to place the limit—how to make the fitting adjustment between individual independence and social control—is a subject on which nearly everything remains to be done. All that makes existence valuable to any one, depends on the enforcement of restraints upon the actions of other people. Some rules of conduct, therefore, must be imposed, by law in the first place, and by opinion on many things which are not fit subjects for the operation of law. What these rules should be is the principal question in human affairs; but if we except a few of the most obvious cases, it is one of those which least progress has been made in resolving. No two ages, and scarcely any two countries, have decided it alike; and the decision of one age or country is a wonder to another. Yet the people of any given age and country no more suspect any difficulty in it, than if it were a subject on which mankind had always been agreed. The rules which obtain among themselves appear to them self-evident and self-justifying. This all but universal illusion is one of the examples of the magical influence of custom, which is not only, as the proverb says, a second nature, but is continually mistaken for the first. The effect of custom, in preventing any misgiving respecting the rules of conduct which mankind impose on one another, is all the more complete because the subject is one on which it is not generally considered necessary that reasons should be given, either by one person to others, or by each to himself. People are accustomed to believe, and have been encouraged in the belief by some who aspire to the character of philosophers, that their feelings, on subjects of this nature, are better than reasons, and render reasons unnecessary. The practical principle which guides them to their opinions on the regulation of human conduct, is the feeling in each person's mind that everybody should be required to act as he, and those with whom he sympathizes, would like them to act. No one, indeed, acknowledges to himself that his standard of judgment is his own liking; but an opinion on a point of conduct, not supported by reasons, can only count as one person's preference; and if the reasons, when given, are a mere appeal to a similar preference felt by other people, it is still only many people's liking instead of one. To an ordinary man, however, his own preference, thus supported, is not only a perfectly satisfactory reason, but the only one he generally has for any of his notions of morality, taste, or propriety, which are not expressly written in his religious creed; and his chief guide in the interpretation even of that. Men's opinions, accordingly, on what is laudable or blameable, are affected by all the multifarious causes which influence their wishes in regard to the conduct of others, and which are as numerous as those which determine their wishes on any other subject. Sometimes their reason—at other times their prejudices or superstitions: often their social affections, not seldom their antisocial ones, their envy or jealousy, their arrogance or contemptuousness: but most commonly, their desires or fears for themselves—their legitimate or illegitimate self-interest. Wherever there is an ascendant class, a large portion of the morality of the country emanates from its class interests, and its feelings of class superiority. The morality between Spartans and Helots, between planters and Negroes, between princes and subjects, between nobles and roturiers,[1] between men and women, has been for the most part the creation of these class interests and feelings: and the sentiments thus generated, react in turn upon the moral feelings of the members of the ascendant class, in their relations among themselves. Where, on the other hand, a class, formerly ascendant, has lost its ascendancy, or where its ascendancy is unpopular, the prevailing moral sentiments frequently bear the impress of an impatient dislike of superiority. Another grand determining principle of the rules of conduct, both in act and forbearance, which have been enforced by law or opinion, has been the servility of mankind towards the supposed preferences or aversions of their temporal masters, or of their gods. This servility, though essentially selfish, is not hypocrisy; it gives rise to perfectly genuine sentiments of abhorrence; it made men burn magicians and heretics. Among so many baser influences, the general and obvious interests of society have of course had a share, and a large one, in the direction of the moral sentiments: less, however, as a matter of reason, and on their own account, than as a consequence of the sympathies and antipathies which grew out of them: and sympathies and antipathies which had little or nothing to do with the interests of society, have made themselves felt in the establishment of moralities with quite as great force.

The likings and dislikings of society, or of some powerful portion of it, are thus the main thing which has practically determined the rules laid down for general observance, under the penalties

---

[1] [Those who are not of noble birth.]

of law or opinion. And in general, those who have been in advance of society in thought and feeling, have left this condition of things unassailed in principle, however they may have come into conflict with it in some of its details. They have occupied themselves rather in inquiring what things society ought to like or dislike, than in questioning whether its likings or dislikings should be a law to individuals. They preferred endeavouring to alter the feelings of mankind on the particular points on which they were themselves heretical, rather than make common cause in defence of freedom, with heretics generally. The only case in which the higher ground has been taken on principle and maintained with consistency, by any but an individual here and there, is that of religious belief: a case instructive in many ways, and not least so as forming a most striking instance of the fallibility of what is called the moral sense; for the *odium theologicum*, in a sincere bigot, is one of the most unequivocal cases of moral feeling. Those who first broke the yoke of what called itself the Universal Church, were in general as little willing to permit difference of religious opinion as that church itself. But when the heat of the conflict was over, without giving a complete victory to any party, and each church or sect was reduced to limit its hopes to retaining possession of the ground it already occupied; minorities, seeing that they had no chance of becoming majorities, were under the necessity of pleading to those whom they could not convert, for permission to differ. It is accordingly on this battle field, almost solely, that the rights of the individual against society have been asserted on broad grounds of principle, and the claim of society to exercise authority over dissentients, openly controverted. The great writers to whom the world owes what religious liberty it possesses, have mostly asserted freedom of conscience as an indefeasible right, and denied absolutely that a human being is accountable to others for his religious belief. Yet so natural to mankind is intolerance in whatever they really care about, that religious freedom has hardly anywhere been practically realized, except where religious indifference, which dislikes to have its peace disturbed by theological quarrels, has added its weight to the scale. In the minds of almost all religious persons, even in the most tolerant countries, the duty of toleration is admitted with tacit reserves. One person will bear with dissent in matters of church government, but not of dogma; another can tolerate everybody, short of a Papist or an Unitarian; another, every one who believes in revealed religion; a few extend their charity a little further, but stop at the belief in a God and in a future state. Wherever the sentiment of the majority is still genuine and intense, it is found to have abated little of its claim to be obeyed.

In England, from the peculiar circumstances of our political history, though the yoke of opinion is perhaps heavier, that of law is lighter, than in most other countries of Europe; and there is considerable jealousy of direct interference, by the legislative or the executive power, with private conduct; not so much from any just regard for the independence of the individual, as from the still subsisting habit of looking on the government as representing an opposite interest to the public. The majority have not yet learnt to feel the power of the government their power, or its opinions their opinions. When they do so, individual liberty will probably be as much exposed to invasion from the government, as it already is from public opinion. But, as yet, there is a considerable amount of feeling ready to be called forth against any attempt of the law to control individuals in things in which they have not hitherto been accustomed to be controlled by it; and this with very little discrimination as to whether the matter is, or is not, within the legitimate sphere of legal control; insomuch that the feeling, highly salutary on the whole, is perhaps quite as often misplaced as well grounded in the particular instances of its application. There is, in fact, no recognised principle by which the propriety or impropriety of government interference is customarily tested. People decide according to their personal preferences. Some, whenever they see any good to be done, or evil to be remedied, would willingly instigate the government to undertake the business; while others prefer to bear almost any amount of social evil, rather than add one to the departments of human interests amenable to governmental control. And men range themselves on one or the other side in any particular case, according to this general direction of their sentiments; or according to the degree of interest which they feel in the particular thing which it is proposed that the government should do, or according to the belief they entertain that the government would, or would not, do it in the manner they prefer; but very rarely on account of any opinion to which they consistently adhere, as to what things are fit to be done by a government. And it seems to me that in consequence of this absence of rule or principle, one side is at present as often wrong as the other; the interference of government is, with about equal frequency, improperly invoked and improperly condemned.

The object of this Essay is to assert one very simple principle, as entitled to govern absolutely the dealings of society with the individual in the way of compulsion and control, whether the means used be physical force in the form of legal penalties, or the moral coercion of public opinion. That principle is, that the sole end for which mankind are warranted, individually or collectively, in interfering with the liberty of action of any of their number, is self-protection. That the only purpose for which power can be rightfully exercised over any member of a civilized community, against his will, is to prevent harm to others. His own good, either physical or moral, is not a sufficient warrant. He cannot rightfully be compelled to do or forbear because it will be better for him to do so, because it will make him happier, because, in the opinions of others, to do so would be wise, or even right. These are good reasons for remonstrating with him, or reasoning with him, or persuading him, or entreating him, but not for compelling him, or visiting him with any evil in case he do otherwise. To justify that, the conduct from which it is desired to deter him, must be calculated to produce evil to some one else. The only part of the conduct of any one, for which he is amenable to society, is that which concerns others. In the part which merely concerns himself, his independence

is, of right, absolute. Over himself, over his own body and mind, the individual is sovereign.

It is, perhaps, hardly necessary to say that this doctrine is meant to apply only to human beings in the maturity of their faculties. We are not speaking of children, or of young persons below the age which the law may fix as that of manhood or womanhood. Those who are still in a state to require being taken care of by others must be protected against their own actions as well as against external injury. For the same reason, we may leave out of consideration those backward states of society in which the race itself may be considered as in its nonage. The early difficulties in the way of spontaneous progress are so great, that there is seldom any choice of means for overcoming them; and a ruler full of the spirit of improvement is warranted in the use of any expedients that will attain an end, perhaps otherwise unattainable. Despotism is a legitimate mode of government in dealing with barbarians, provided the end be their improvement, and the means justified by actually effecting that end. Liberty, as a principle, has no application to any state of things anterior to the time when mankind have become capable of being improved by free and equal discussion. Until then, there is nothing for them but implicit obedience to an Akbar or a Charlemagne, if they are so fortunate as to find one. But as soon as mankind have attained the capacity of being guided to their own improvement by conviction or persuasion (a period long since reached in all nations with whom we need here concern ourselves), compulsion, either in the direct form or in that of pains and penalties for non-compliance, is no longer admissible as a means to their own good, and justifiable only for the security of others.

It is proper to state that I forego any advantage which could be derived to my argument from the idea of abstract right, as a thing independent of utility. I regard utility as the ultimate appeal on all ethical questions; but it must be utility in the largest sense, grounded on the permanent interests of man as a progressive being. Those interests, I contend, authorize the subjection of individual spontaneity to external control, only in respect to those actions of each, which concern the interest of other people. If any one does an act hurtful to others, there is a *prima facie* case for punishing him, by law, or, where legal penalties are not safely applicable, by general disapprobation. There are also many positive acts for the benefit of others, which he may rightfully be compelled to perform; such as, to give evidence in a court of justice; to bear his fair share in the common defence, or in any other joint work necessary to the interest of the society of which he enjoys the protection; and to perform certain acts of individual beneficence, such as saving a fellow-creature's life, or interposing to protect the defenceless against ill-usage, things which whenever it is obviously a man's duty to do, he may rightfully be made responsible to society for not doing. A person may cause evil to others not only by his actions but by his inaction, and in either case he is justly accountable to them for the injury. The latter case, it is true, requires a much more cautious exercise of compulsion than the former. To make any one answerable for doing evil to others, is the rule; to make him answerable for not preventing evil, is, comparatively speaking, the exception. Yet there are many cases clear enough and grave enough to justify that exception. In all things which regard the external relations of the individual, he is *de jure* amenable to those whose interests are concerned, and if need be, to society as their protector. There are often good reasons for not holding him to the responsibility; but these reasons must arise from the special expediencies of the case: either because it is a kind of case in which he is on the whole likely to act better, when left to his own discretion, than when controlled in any way in which society have it in their power to control him; or because the attempt to exercise control would produce other evils, greater than those which it would prevent. When such reasons as these preclude the enforcement of responsibility, the conscience of the agent himself should step into the vacant judgment seat, and protect those interests of others which have no external protection; judging himself all the more rigidly, because the case does not admit of his being made accountable to the judgment of his fellow-creatures.

But there is a sphere of action in which society, as distinguished from the individual, has, if any, only an indirect interest; comprehending all that portion of a person's life and conduct which affects only himself, or if it also affects others, only with their free, voluntary, and undeceived consent and participation. When I say only himself, I mean directly, and in the first instance: for whatever affects himself, may affect others through himself; and the objection which may be grounded on this contingency, will receive consideration in the sequel. This, then, is the appropriate region of human liberty. It comprises, *first*, the inward domain of consciousness; demanding liberty of conscience, in the most comprehensive sense; liberty of thought and feeling; absolute freedom of opinion and sentiment on all subjects, practical or speculative, scientific, moral, or theological. The liberty of expressing and publishing opinions may seem to fall under a different principle, since it belongs to that part of the conduct of an individual which concerns other people; but, being almost of as much importance as the liberty of thought itself, and resting in great part on the same reasons, is practically inseparable from it. *Secondly*, the principle requires liberty of tastes and pursuits; of framing the plan of our life to suit our own character; of doing as we like, subject to such consequences as may follow: without impediment from our fellow-creatures, so long as what we do does not harm them, even though they should think our conduct foolish, perverse, or wrong. *Thirdly*, from this liberty of each individual, follows the liberty, within the same limits, of combination among individuals; freedom to unite, for any purpose not involving harm to others: the persons combining being supposed to be of full age, and not forced or deceived.

No society in which these liberties are not, on the whole, respected, is free, whatever may be its form of government; and none is completely free in which they do not exist absolute and unqualified. The only freedom which deserves the name, is that of pursuing our own good in our own way, so long as we do not attempt to deprive others of theirs, or impede their efforts to obtain it. Each is the proper guardian of his own health, whether bodily, or mental and spiritual. Mankind are greater gainers by suffering each other to live as seems good to themselves, than by compelling each to live as seems good to the rest.

Though this doctrine is anything but new, and, to some persons, may have the air of a truism, there is no doctrine which stands more directly opposed to the general tendency of existing opinion and practice. Society has expended fully as much effort in the attempt (according to its lights) to compel people to conform to its notions of personal, as of social excellence. The ancient commonwealths thought themselves entitled to practise, and the ancient philosophers countenanced, the regulation of every part of private conduct by public authority, on the ground that the State had a deep interest in the whole bodily and mental discipline of every one of its citizens; a mode of thinking which may have been admissible in small republics surrounded by powerful enemies, in constant peril of being subverted by foreign attack or internal commotion, and to which even a short interval of relaxed energy and self-command might so easily be fatal, that they could not afford to wait for the salutary permanent effects of freedom. In the modern world, the greater size of political communities, and above all, the separation between spiritual and temporal authority (which placed the direction of men's consciences in other hands than those which controlled their worldly affairs), prevented so great an interference by law in the details of private life; but the engines of moral repression have been wielded more strenuously against divergence from the reigning opinion in self-regarding, than even in social matters; religion, the most powerful of the elements which have entered into the formation of moral feeling, having almost always been governed either by the ambition of a hierarchy, seeking control over every department of human conduct, or by the spirit of Puritanism. And some of those modern reformers who have placed themselves in strongest opposition to the religions of the past, have been no way behind either churches or sects in their assertion

of the right of spiritual domination: M. Comte,[1] in particular, whose social system, as unfolded in his *Système de Politique Positive*, aims at establishing (though by moral more than by legal appliances) a despotism of society over the individual, surpassing anything contemplated in the political ideal of the most rigid disciplinarian among the ancient philosophers.

Apart from the peculiar tenets of individual thinkers, there is also in the world at large an increasing inclination to stretch unduly the powers of society over the individual, both by the force of opinion and even by that of legislation: and as the tendency of all the changes taking place in the world is to strengthen society, and diminish the power of the individual, this encroachment is not one of the evils which tend spontaneously to disappear, but, on the contrary, to grow more and more formidable. The disposition of mankind, whether as rulers or as fellow-citizens, to impose their own opinions and inclinations as a rule of conduct on others, is so energetically supported by some of the best and by some of the worst feelings incident to human nature, that it is hardly ever kept under restraint by anything but want of power; and as the power is not declining, but growing, unless a strong barrier of moral conviction can be raised against the mischief, we must expect, in the present circumstances of the world, to see it increase.

It will be convenient for the argument, if, instead of at once entering upon the general thesis, we confine ourselves in the first instance to a single branch of it, on which the principle here stated is, if not fully, yet to a certain point, recognised by the current opinions. This one branch is the *liberty of thought*: from which it is impossible to separate the cognate liberty of speaking and of writing. Although these liberties, to some considerable amount, form part of the political morality of all countries which profess religious toleration and free institutions,

---

[1] [Auguste Comte (1798–1857) was a French social theorist who is regarded by many as the founder of the discipline that we now know as sociology.]

the grounds, both philosophical and practical, on which they rest, are perhaps not so familiar to the general mind, nor so thoroughly appreciated by many even of the leaders of opinion, as might have been expected. Those grounds, when rightly understood, are of much wider application than to only one division of the subject, and a thorough consideration of this part of the question will be found the best introduction to the remainder. Those to whom nothing which I am about to say will be new, may therefore, I hope, excuse me, if on a subject which for now three centuries has been so often discussed, I venture on one discussion more.

DISCUSSION QUESTIONS

1. What does Mill take to be the threat of the "tyranny of the majority" in democratic societies? Do you think that this fear is legitimate?

2. What sorts of restrictions do *you* think should be put into place to limit the extent to which a government may interfere in the lives of its citizens? On what grounds do you think these restrictions are/can be justified? How would Mill answer this same question?

3. Mill explains, "That the only purpose for which power can be rightfully exercised over any member of a civilized community, against his will, is to prevent harm to others." What do you think constitutes producing harm? What constitutes *harm*? Consider whether "psychological harm" would fall under the category of harm that Mill has in mind.

4. Do you think that harm can be produced by the *failure* to act? Explain your answer, and comment on Mill's position regarding such a scenario.

34

Isaiah Berlin, selection from "Two Concepts of Liberty"[1] (1958)

Isaiah Berlin (1909–97) was a Russian-born British philosopher and historian known for his defenses of liberalism and value pluralism. The distinction between positive and negative liberty which Berlin introduces in this selection has come to occupy an important place in political theory.

SOURCE

Berlin, Isaiah. From "Two Concepts of Liberty," from *Four Essays on Liberty*, H. Hardy, Ed. Copyright © Isaiah Berlin. 1958, 1969, 1997. Reproduced with permission of Curtis Brown Group Ltd., London, on behalf of the Estate of Isaiah Berlin.

... [P]olitical theory is a branch of moral philosophy, which starts from the discovery, or application, of moral notions in the sphere of political relations. I do not mean, as I think some Idealist philosophers may have believed, that all historical movements or conflicts between human beings are reducible to movements or conflicts of ideas or spiritual forces, nor even that they are effects (or aspects) of them. But I do mean that to understand such movements or conflicts is, above all, to understand the ideas or attitudes to life involved in them, which alone make such movements a part of human history, and not mere natural events. Political words and notions and acts are not intelligible save in the context of the issues that divide the men who use them. Consequently our own attitudes and activities are likely to remain obscure to us, unless we understand the dominant issues of our own world. The greatest of these is the open war that is being fought between two systems of ideas which return different and conflicting answers to what has long been the central question of politics—the question of obedience and coercion. "Why should I (or anyone) obey anyone else?" "Why should I not live as I like?" "Must I obey?" "If I disobey, may I be coerced?" "By whom, and to what degree, and in the name of what, and for the sake of what?"

Upon the answers to the question of the permissible limits of coercion opposed views are held

---

[1] [Original notes have been omitted throughout due to their length.]

in the world today, each claiming the allegiance of very large numbers of men. It seems to me, therefore, that any aspect of this issue is worthy of examination.

I

To coerce a man is to deprive him of freedom—freedom from what? Almost every moralist in human history has praised freedom. Like happiness and goodness, like nature and reality, it is a term whose meaning is so porous that there is little interpretation that it seems able to resist. I do not propose to discuss either the history of this protean word or the more than two hundred senses of it recorded by historians of ideas. I propose to examine no more than two of these senses—but they are central ones, with a great deal of human history behind them, and, I dare say, still to come. The first of these political senses of freedom or liberty (I shall use both words to mean the same), which (following much precedent) I shall call the "negative" sense, is involved in the answer to the question "What is the area within which the subject—a person or group of persons—is or should be left to do or be what he is able to do or be, without interference by other persons?" The second, which I shall call the "positive" sense, is involved in the answer to the question "What, or who, is the source of control or interference that can determine someone to do, or be, this rather than that?" The two questions are clearly different, even though the answers to them may overlap.

The Notion of "Negative" Freedom

I am normally said to be free to the degree to which no man or body of men interferes with my activity. Political liberty in this sense is simply the area within which a man can act unobstructed by others. If I am prevented by others from doing what I could otherwise do, I am to that degree unfree; and if this area is contracted by other men beyond a certain minimum, I can be described as being coerced, or, it may be, enslaved. Coercion is not, however, a term that covers every form of inability. If I say

that I am unable to jump more than ten feet in the air, or cannot read because I am blind, or cannot understand the darker pages of Hegel, it would be eccentric to say that I am to that degree enslaved or coerced. Coercion implies the deliberate interference of other human beings within the area in which I could otherwise act. You lack political liberty or freedom only if you are prevented from attaining a goal by human beings. Mere incapacity to attain a goal is not lack of political freedom. This is brought out by the use of such modern expressions as "economic freedom" and its counterpart, "economic slavery." It is argued, very plausibly, that if a man is too poor to afford something on which there is no legal ban—a loaf of bread, a journey round the world, recourse to the law courts—he is as little free to have it as he would be if it were forbidden him by law. If my poverty were a kind of disease which prevented me from buying bread, or paying for the journey round the world or getting my case heard, as lameness prevents me from running, this inability would not naturally be described as a lack of freedom, least of all political freedom. It is only because I believe that my inability to get a given thing is due to the fact that other human beings have made arrangements whereby I am, whereas others are not, prevented from having enough money with which to pay for it, that I think myself a victim of coercion or slavery. In other words, this use of the term depends on a particular social and economic theory about the causes of my poverty or weakness. If my lack of material means is due to my lack of mental or physical capacity, then I begin to speak of being deprived of freedom (and not simply about poverty) only if I accept the theory. If, in addition, I believe that I am being kept in want by a specific arrangement which I consider unjust or unfair, I speak of economic slavery or oppression. The nature of things does not madden us, only ill will does, said Rousseau. The criterion of oppression is the part that I believe to be played by other human beings, directly or indirectly, with or without the intention of doing so, in frustrating my wishes. By being free in this sense I mean not being interfered with by others. The wider the area of non-interference the wider my freedom.

This is what the classical English political philosophers meant when they used this word. They disagreed about how wide the area could or should be. They supposed that it could not, as things were, be unlimited, because if it were, it would entail a state in which all men could boundlessly interfere with all other men; and this kind of "natural" freedom would lead to social chaos in which men's minimum needs would not be satisfied; or else the liberties of the weak would be suppressed by the strong. Because they perceived that human purposes and activities do not automatically harmonize with one another, and because (whatever their official doctrines) they put high value on other goals, such as justice, or happiness, or culture, or security, or varying degrees of equality, they were prepared to curtail freedom in the interests of other values and, indeed, of freedom itself. For, without this, it was impossible to create the kind of association that they thought desirable. Consequently, it is assumed by these thinkers that the area of men's free action must be limited by law. But equally it is assumed, especially by such libertarians as Locke and Mill in England, and Constant and Tocqueville in France, that there ought to exist a certain minimum area of personal freedom which must on no account be violated; for if it is overstepped, the individual will find himself in an area too narrow for even that minimum development of his natural faculties which alone makes it possible to pursue, and even to conceive, the various ends which men hold good or right or sacred. It follows that a frontier must be drawn between the area of private life and that of public authority. Where it is to be drawn is a matter of argument, indeed of haggling. Men are largely interdependent, and no man's activity is so completely private as never to obstruct the lives of others in any way. "Freedom for the pike is death for the minnows"; the liberty of some must depend on the restraint of others. Freedom for an Oxford don, others have been known to add, is a very different thing from freedom for an Egyptian peasant.

This proposition derives its force from something that is both true and important, but the phrase itself remains a piece of political claptrap. It is true that to offer political rights, or safeguards against intervention by the State, to men who are half-naked, illiterate, underfed and diseased is to mock their condition; they need medical help or education before they can understand, or make use of, an increase in their freedom. What is freedom to those who cannot make use of it? Without adequate conditions for the use of freedom, what is the value of freedom? First things come first: there are situations in which—to use a saying satirically attributed to the nihilists by Dostoevsky—boots are superior to Pushkin; individual freedom is not everyone's primary need. For freedom is not the mere absence of frustration of whatever kind; this would inflate the meaning of the word until it meant too much or too little. The Egyptian peasant needs clothes or medicine before, and more than, personal liberty, but the minimum freedom that he needs today, and the greater degree of freedom that he may need tomorrow, is not some species of freedom peculiar to him, but identical with that of professors, artists and millionaires.

What troubles the consciences of Western liberals is, I think, the belief, not that the freedom that men seek differs according to their social or economic conditions, but that the minority who possess it have gained it by exploiting, or, at least, averting their gaze from, the vast majority who do not. They believe, with good reason, that if individual liberty is an ultimate end for human beings, none should be deprived of it by others; least of all that some should enjoy it at the expense of others. Equality of liberty; not to treat others as I should not wish them to treat me; repayment of my debt to those who alone have made possible my liberty or prosperity or enlightenment; justice, in its simplest and most universal sense—these are the foundations of liberal morality. Liberty is not the only goal of men. I can, like the Russian critic Belinsky,[1] say that if others are to

---

[1] [Vissarion Grigoryevich Belinsky (1811–48) was a Russian literary critic.]

be deprived of it—if my brothers are to remain in poverty, squalor and chains—then I do not want it for myself, I reject it with both hands and infinitely prefer to share their fate. But nothing is gained by a confusion of terms. To avoid glaring inequality or widespread misery I am ready to sacrifice some, or all, of my freedom: I may do so willingly and freely; but it is freedom that I am giving up for the sake of justice or equality or the love of my fellow men. I should be guilt-stricken, and rightly so, if I were not, in some circumstances, ready to make this sacrifice. But a sacrifice is not an increase in what is being sacrificed, namely freedom, however great the moral need or the compensation for it. Everything is what it is: liberty is liberty, not equality or fairness or justice or culture, or human happiness or a quiet conscience. If the liberty of myself or my class or nation depends on the misery of a number of other human beings, the system which promotes this is unjust and immoral. But if I curtail or lose my freedom in order to lessen the shame of such inequality, and do not thereby materially increase the individual liberty of others, an absolute loss of liberty occurs. This may be compensated for by a gain in justice or in happiness or in peace, but the loss remains, and it is a confusion of values to say that although my "liberal," individual freedom may go by the board, some other kind of freedom—"social" or "economic"—is increased. Yet it remains true that the freedom of some must at times be curtailed to secure the freedom of others. Upon what principle should this be done? If freedom is a sacred, untouchable value, there can be no such principle. One or other of these conflicting rules or principles must, at any rate in practice, yield: not always for reasons which can be clearly stated, let alone generalized into rules or universal maxims. Still, a practical compromise has to be found.

Philosophers with an optimistic view of human nature and a belief in the possibility of harmonising human interests, such as Locke or Adam Smith or, in some moods, Mill, believed that social harmony and progress were compatible with reserving a large area for private life over which neither the State nor any other authority must be allowed to trespass. Hobbes, and those who agreed with him, especially conservative or reactionary thinkers, argued that if men were to be prevented from destroying one another and making social life a jungle or a wilderness, greater safeguards must be instituted to keep them in their places; he wished correspondingly to increase the area of centralised control and decrease that of the individual. But both sides agreed that some portion of human existence must remain independent of the sphere of social control. To invade that preserve, however small, would be despotism. The most eloquent of all defenders of freedom and privacy, Benjamin Constant,[1] who had not forgotten the Jacobin dictatorship, declared that at the very least the liberty of religion, opinion, expression, property must be guaranteed against arbitrary invasion. Jefferson, Burke, Paine, Mill compiled different catalogues of individual liberties, but the argument for keeping authority at bay is always substantially the same. We must preserve a minimum area of personal freedom if we are not to "degrade or deny our nature." We cannot remain absolutely free, and must give up some of our liberty to preserve the rest. But total self-surrender is self-defeating. What then must the minimum be? That which a man cannot give up without offending against the essence of his human nature. What is this essence? What are the standards which it entails? This has been, and perhaps always will be, a matter of infinite debate. But whatever the principle in terms of which the area of non-interference is to be drawn, whether it is that of natural law or natural rights, or of utility, or the pronouncements of a categorical imperative, or the sanctity of the social contract, or any other concept with which men have sought to clarify and justify their convictions, liberty in this sense means liberty *from*; absence of interference beyond the shifting, but always recognizable, frontier. "The only freedom which deserves the name, is that of pursuing our own good in our own way," said the most celebrated of its champions. If this is so, is compulsion ever justified? Mill had no doubt that it was. Since justice demands that all individuals be

---

1 [Henri-Benjamin Constant de Rebecque (1767–1830) was a Swiss-born French writer and politician.]

entitled to a minimum of freedom, all other individuals were of necessity to be restrained, if need be by force, from depriving anyone of it. Indeed, the whole function of law was the prevention of just such collisions: the State was reduced to what Lassalle[1] contemptuously described as the functions of a night-watchman or traffic policeman.

What made the protection of individual liberty so sacred to Mill? In his famous essay he declares that, unless the individual is left to live as he wishes in "the part [of his conduct] which merely concerns himself," civilisation cannot advance; the truth will not, for lack of a free market in ideas, come to light; there will be no scope for spontaneity, originality, genius, for mental energy, for moral courage. Society will be crushed by the weight of "collective mediocrity." Whatever is rich and diversified will be crushed by the weight of custom, by men's constant tendency to conformity, which breeds only "withered" capacities, "pinched and hidebound," "cramped and dwarfed" human beings. "Pagan self-assertion" is as worthy as "Christian self-denial." All the errors which a man is likely to commit against advice and warning, are far outweighed by the evil of allowing others to constrain him to what they deem is good. The defence of liberty consists in the "negative" goal of warding off interference. To threaten a man with persecution unless he submits to a life in which he exercises no choices of his goals; to block before him every door but one, no matter how noble the prospect upon which it opens, or how benevolent the motives of those who arrange this, is to sin against the truth that he is a man, a being with a life of his own to live. This is liberty as it has been conceived by liberals in the modern world from the days of Erasmus (some would say of Occam) to our own. Every plea for civil liberties and individual rights, every protest against exploitation and humiliation, against the encroachment of public authority, or the mass hypnosis of custom or organized propaganda, springs from this individualistic, and much disputed, conception of man.

Three facts about this position may be noted. In the first place Mill confuses two distinct notions. One is that all coercion is, in so far as it frustrates human desires, bad as such, although it may have to be applied to prevent other, greater evils; while non-interference, which is the opposite of coercion, is good as such, although it is not the only good. This is the "negative" conception of liberty in its classical form. The other is that men should seek to discover the truth, or to develop a certain type of character of which Mill approved—critical, original, imaginative, independent, non-conforming to the point of eccentricity, and so on—and that truth can be found, and such character can be bred, only in conditions of freedom. Both these are liberal views, but they are not identical, and the connection between them is, at best, empirical. No one would argue that truth or freedom of self-expression could flourish where dogma crushes all thought. But the evidence of history tends to show (as, indeed, was argued by James Stephen in his formidable attack on Mill in his *Liberty, Equality, Fraternity*) that integrity, love of truth and fiery individualism grow at least as often in severely disciplined communities, among, for example, the puritan Calvinists of Scotland or New England, or under military discipline, as in more tolerant or indifferent societies; and if this is so, Mill's argument for liberty as a necessary condition for the growth of human genius falls to the ground. If his two goals proved incompatible, Mill would be faced with a cruel dilemma, quite apart from the further difficulties created by the inconsistency of his doctrines with strict utilitarianism, even in his own humane version of it.

In the second place, the doctrine is comparatively modern. There seems to be scarcely any discussion of individual liberty as a conscious political ideal (as opposed to its actual existence) in the ancient world. Condorcet had already remarked that the notion of individual rights was absent from the legal conceptions of the Romans and Greeks; this seems to hold equally of the Jewish, Chinese and all other ancient civilisations that have since come to light. The domination of this ideal has been the exception rather than the rule, even in the recent

---

[1] [Ferdinand Lassalle (1825–64) was a German-Jewish jurist and socialist.]

history of the West. Nor has liberty in this sense often formed a rallying cry for the great masses of mankind. The desire not to be impinged upon, to be left to oneself, has been a mark of high civilisation on the part of both individuals and communities. The sense of privacy itself, of the area of personal relationships as something sacred in its own right, derives from a conception of freedom which, for all its religious roots, is scarcely older, in its developed state, than the Renaissance or the Reformation. Yet its decline would mark the death of a civilisation, of an entire moral outlook.

The third characteristic of this notion of liberty is of greater importance. It is that liberty in this sense is not incompatible with some kinds of autocracy, or at any rate with the absence of self-government. Liberty in this sense is principally concerned with the area of control, not with its source. Just as a democracy may, in fact, deprive the individual citizen of a great many liberties which he might have in some other form of society, so it is perfectly conceivable that a liberal-minded despot would allow his subjects a large measure of personal freedom. The despot who leaves his subjects a wide area of liberty may be unjust, or encourage the wildest inequalities, care little for order, or virtue, or knowledge; but provided he does not curb their liberty, or at least curbs it less than many other régimes, he meets with Mill's specification. Freedom in this sense is not, at any rate logically, connected with democracy or self-government. Self-government may, on the whole, provide a better guarantee of the preservation of civil liberties than other regimes, and has been defended as such by libertarians. But there is no necessary connection between individual liberty and democratic rule. The answer to the question "Who governs me?" is logically distinct from the question "How far does government interfere with me?" It is in this difference that the great contrast between the two concepts of negative and positive liberty, in the end, consists. For the "positive" sense of liberty comes to light if we try to answer the question, not "What am I free to do or be?", but "By whom am I ruled?" or "Who is to say what I am, and what I am not, to be or do?" The connection between democracy and individual

liberty is a good deal more tenuous than it seemed to many advocates of both. The desire to be governed by myself, or at any rate to participate in the process by which my life is to be controlled, may be as deep a wish as that for a free area for action, and perhaps historically older. But it is not a desire for the same thing. So different is it, indeed, as to have led in the end to the great clash of ideologies that dominates our world. For it is this, the "positive" conception of liberty, not freedom from, but freedom to—to lead one prescribed form of life—which the adherents of the "negative" notion represent as being, at times, no better than a specious disguise for brutal tyranny.

II

The Notion of Positive Freedom

The "positive" sense of the word "liberty" derives from the wish on the part of the individual to be his own master. I wish my life and decisions to depend on myself, not on external forces of whatever kind. I wish to be the instrument of my own, not of other men's, acts of will. I wish to be a subject, not an object; to be moved by reasons, by conscious purposes, which are my own, not by causes which affect me, as it were, from outside. I wish to be somebody, not nobody; a doer—deciding, not being decided for, self-directed and not acted upon by external nature or by other men as if I were a thing, or an animal, or a slave incapable of playing a human role, that is, of conceiving goals and policies of my own and realizing them. This is at least part of what I mean when I say that I am rational, and that it is my reason that distinguishes me as a human being from the rest of the world. I wish, above all, to be conscious of myself as a thinking, willing, active being, bearing responsibility for my choices and able to explain them by reference to my own ideas and purposes. I feel free to the degree that I believe this to be true, and enslaved to the degree that I am made to realize that it is not.

The freedom which consists in being one's own master, and the freedom which consists in not being prevented from choosing as I do by other men, may, on the face of it, seem concepts at no great logical distance from each other—no more than negative and positive ways of saying much the same thing. Yet the "positive" and "negative" notions of freedom historically developed in divergent directions, not always by logically reputable steps, until, in the end, they came into direct conflict with each other.

One way of making this clear is in terms of the independent momentum which the, initially perhaps quite harmless, metaphor of self-mastery acquired. "I am my own master"; "I am slave to no man"; but may I not (as Platonists or Hegelians tend to say) be a slave to nature? Or to my own "unbridled" passions? Are these not so many species of the identical genus "slave"—some political or legal, others moral or spiritual? Have not men had the experience of liberating themselves from spiritual slavery, or slavery to nature, and do they not in the course of it become aware, on the one hand, of a self which dominates, and, on the other, of something in them which is brought to heel? This dominant self is then variously identified with reason, with my "higher nature," with the self which calculates and aims at what will satisfy it in the long run, with my "real," or "ideal," or "autonomous" self, or with my self "at its best"; which is then contrasted with irrational impulse, uncontrolled desires, my "lower" nature, the pursuit of immediate pleasures, my "empirical" or "heteronomous" self, swept by every gust of desire and passion, needing to be rigidly disciplined if it is ever to rise to the full height of its "real" nature. Presently the two selves may be represented as divided by an even larger gap; the real self may be conceived as something wider than the individual (as the term is normally understood), as a social "whole" of which the individual is an element or aspect: a tribe, a race, a Church, a State, the great society of the living and the dead and the yet unborn. This entity is then identified as being the "true" self which, by imposing its collective, or "organic," single will upon its recalcitrant "members," achieves its own, and therefore their, "higher" freedom. The perils of using organic metaphors to justify the coercion of some men by

others in order to raise them to a "higher" level of freedom have often been pointed out. But what gives such plausibility as it has to this kind of language is that we recognise that it is possible, and at times justifiable, to coerce men in the name of some goal (let us say, justice or public health) which they would, if they were more enlightened, themselves pursue, but do not, because they are blind or ignorant or corrupt. This renders it easy for me to conceive of myself as coercing others for their own sake, in their, not my, interest. I am then claiming that I know what they truly need better than they know it themselves. What, at most, this entails is that they would not resist me if they were rational and as wise as I and understood their interests as I do. But I may go on to claim a good deal more than this. I may declare that they are actually aiming at what in their benighted state they consciously resist, because there exists within them an occult entity—their latent rational will, or their "true" purpose—and that this entity, although it is belied by all that they overtly feel and do and say, is their "real" self, of which the poor empirical self in space and time may know nothing or little; and that this inner spirit is the only self that deserves to have its wishes taken into account. Once I take this view, I am in a position to ignore the actual wishes of men or societies, to bully, oppress, torture them in the name, and on behalf, of their "real" selves, in the secure knowledge that whatever is the true goal of man (happiness, performance of duty, wisdom, a just society, self-fulfillment) must be identical with his freedom—the free choice of his "true," albeit often submerged and inarticulate, self.

This paradox has been often exposed. It is one thing to say that I know what is good for X, while he himself does not; and even to ignore his wishes for its—and his—sake; and a very different one to say that he has *eo ipso* chosen it, not indeed consciously, not as he seems in everyday life, but in his role as a rational self which his empirical self may not know—the "real" self which discerns the good, and cannot help choosing it once it is revealed. This monstrous impersonation, which consists in equating what X would choose if he were something he is not, or at least not yet, with what X actually seeks and chooses, is at the heart of all political theories of self-realization. It is one thing to say that I may be coerced for my own good, which I am too blind to see: this may, on occasion, be for my benefit; indeed it may enlarge the scope of my liberty. It is another to say that if it is my good, then I am not being coerced, for I have willed it, whether I know this or not, and am free (or "truly" free) even while my poor earthly body and foolish mind bitterly reject it, and struggle with the greatest desperation against those who seek, however benevolently, to impose it, with the greatest desperation.

This magical transformation, or sleight of hand (for which William James so justly mocked the Hegelians), can no doubt be perpetrated just as easily with the "negative" concept of freedom, where the self that should not be interfered with is no longer the individual with his actual wishes and needs as they are normally conceived, but the "real" man within, identified with the pursuit of some ideal purpose not dreamed of by his empirical self. And, as in the case of the "positively" free self, this entity may be inflated into some super-personal entity—a State, a class, a nation, or the march of history itself, regarded as a more "real" subject of attributes than the empirical self. But the "positive" conception of freedom as self-mastery, with its suggestion of a man divided against himself, has in fact, and as a matter of history, of doctrine and of practice, lent itself more easily to this splitting of personality into two: the transcendent, dominant controller, and the empirical bundle of desires and passions to be disciplined and brought to heel. It is this historical fact that has been influential. This demonstrates (if demonstration of so obvious a truth is needed) that conceptions of freedom directly derive from views of what constitutes a self, a person, a man. Enough manipulation of the definition of man, and freedom can be made to mean whatever the manipulator wishes. Recent history has made it only too clear that the issue is not merely academic.

DISCUSSION QUESTIONS

1. How does Berlin distinguish between the notions of negative and positive freedom?

2. Berlin writes, "I am normally said to be free to the degree to which no man or body of men interferes with my activity. Political liberty in this sense is simply the area within which a man can act unobstructed by others." In what sense do you take Berlin to be using the notion of "interference"? How does he explicate this notion throughout his article?

3. Consider the following: I am paid a wage which allows me to "get by," but which does not allow for the possibility of my taking vacations abroad. Would we want to say that my employer is interfering with my ability to visit Europe? Am I not free (unfree) in an important sense? How would Berlin respond to this scenario?

4. Both Berlin and Mill discuss the issue of whether it is possible for one party to better know the good of (or what is good for) another. What are their respective views on this matter?

35

Milton Friedman, selection from *Capitalism and Freedom* (1962)

Milton Friedman (1912–2006) was the Paul Snowden Russell Distinguished Service Professor Emeritus of Economics at the University of Chicago. Following his retirement from teaching in 1977 until his death, he served as a fellow at the Hoover Institution at Stanford University. He was the recipient of numerous awards, including the 1976 Nobel Prize in economics and the Presidential Medal of Freedom. In this selection, Friedman considers whether the state is justified in interfering with individuals' private lives in order to promote equality, especially equality in income and wealth.

Government as Rule-Maker and Umpire

It is important to distinguish the day-to-day activities of people from the general customary and legal framework within which these take place. The day-to-day activities are like the actions of the participants in a game when they are playing it; the framework, like the rules of the game they play. And just as a good game requires acceptance by the players both of the rules and of the umpire to interpret and enforce them, so a good society requires that its members agree on the general conditions that will govern relations among them, on some means of arbitrating different interpretations of these conditions, and on some device for enforcing compliance with the generally accepted rules. As in games, so also in society, most of the general conditions are the unintended outcome of custom, accepted unthinkingly. At most, we consider explicitly only minor modifications in them, though the cumulative effect of a series of minor modifications may be a drastic alteration in the character of the game or of the society. In both games and society also, no set of rules can prevail unless most participants most of the time conform to them without external sanctions; unless that is, there is a broad underlying social consensus. But we cannot rely on custom or on this consensus alone to interpret and to enforce the rules; we need an umpire. These then are the basic roles of government in a free society: to provide a means whereby we can modify the rules, to mediate differences among us on the meaning of the rules, and to enforce compliance with the rules on the part of those few who would otherwise not play the game.

The need for government in these respects arises because absolute freedom is impossible. However attractive anarchy may be as a philosophy, it is not feasible in a world of imperfect men. Men's freedoms can conflict, and when they do, one man's freedom must be limited to preserve another's—as a Supreme Court Justice once put it, "My freedom to move my fist must be limited by the proximity of your chin."

The major problem in deciding the appropriate activities of government is how to resolve such conflicts among the freedoms of different individuals. In some cases, the answer is easy. There is little difficulty in attaining near unanimity to the proposition that one man's freedom to murder his neighbor must be sacrificed to preserve the freedom of the other man to live. In other cases, the answer is difficult. In the economic area, a major problem arises in respect of the conflict between freedom to combine and freedom to compete. What meaning is to be attributed to "free" as modifying "enterprise"? In the United States, "free" has been understood to mean that anyone is free to set up an enterprise, which means that existing enterprises are not free to keep out competitors except by selling a better product at the same price or the same product at a lower price. In the continental tradition, on the other hand, the meaning has generally been that enterprises are free to do what they want, including the fixing of prices, division of markets, and the adoption of other techniques to keep out potential competitors. Perhaps the most difficult specific problem in this area arises with respect to combinations among laborers, where the problem of freedom to combine and freedom to compete is particularly acute.

A still more basic economic area in which the answer is both difficult and important is the definition of property rights. The notion of property, as it has developed over centuries and as it is embodied in our legal codes, has become so much a part of us that we tend to take it for granted, and fail to recognize the extent to which just what constitutes property and what rights the ownership of property confers are complex social creations rather than self-evident propositions. Does my having title to land, for example, and my freedom to use my property as I wish, permit me to deny to someone else the right to fly over my land in his airplane? Or does his right to use his airplane take precedence? Or does this depend on how high he flies? Or how much noise he makes? Does voluntary exchange require that he pay me for the privilege of flying over my land? Or that I must pay him to refrain from flying over it? The mere mention of royalties, copyrights, patents; shares of stock in corporations; riparian rights, and the like, may perhaps emphasize the role of generally accepted social rules in the very definition of property. It may suggest also that, in many cases, the existence of a well specified and generally accepted definition of property is far more important than just what the definition is.

Another economic area that raises particularly difficult problems is the monetary system. Government responsibility for the monetary system has long been recognized. It is explicitly provided for in the constitutional provision which gives Congress the power "to coin money, regulate the value thereof, and of foreign coin." There is probably no other area of economic activity with respect to which government action has been so uniformly accepted. This habitual and by now almost unthinking acceptance of governmental responsibility makes thorough understanding of the grounds for such responsibility all the more necessary, since it enhances the danger that the scope of government will spread from activities that are, to those that are not, appropriate in a free society, from providing a monetary framework to determining the allocation of resources among individuals....

In summary, the organization of economic activity through voluntary exchange presumes that we have provided, through government, for the maintenance of law and order to prevent coercion of one individual by another, the enforcement of contracts voluntarily entered into, the definition of the meaning of property rights, the interpretation and enforcement of such rights, and the provision of a monetary framework.

Action through Government on Grounds of Technical Monopoly and Neighborhood Effects

The role of government just considered is to do something that the market cannot do for itself, namely, to determine, arbitrate, and enforce the rules of the game. We may also want to do through government some things that might conceivably be done through the market but that technical or similar conditions render it difficult to do in that way. These all reduce to cases in which strictly voluntary exchange is either exceedingly costly or practically impossible. There are two general classes of such cases: monopoly and similar market imperfections, and neighborhood effects.

Exchange is truly voluntary only when nearly equivalent alternatives exist. Monopoly implies the absence of alternatives and thereby inhibits effective freedom of exchange. In practice, monopoly frequently, if not generally, arises from government support or from collusive agreements among individuals. With respect to these, the problem is either to avoid governmental fostering of monopoly or to stimulate the effective enforcement of rules such as those embodied in our anti-trust laws. However, monopoly may also arise because it is technically efficient to have a single producer or enterprise. I venture to suggest that such cases are more limited than is supposed but they unquestionably do arise. A simple example is perhaps the provision of telephone services within a community. I shall refer to such cases as "technical" monopoly.

When technical conditions make a monopoly the natural outcome of competitive market forces, there are only three alternatives that seem available: private monopoly, public monopoly, or public regulation. All three are bad so we must choose among evils. Henry Simons, observing public regulation of monopoly in the United States, found the results so distasteful that he concluded public

monopoly would be a lesser evil. Walter Eucken, a noted German liberal, observing public monopoly in German railroads, found the results so distasteful that he concluded public regulation would be a lesser evil. Having learned from both, I reluctantly conclude that, if tolerable, private monopoly may be the least of the evils.

If society were static so that the conditions which give rise to a technical monopoly were sure to remain, I would have little confidence in this solution. In a rapidly changing society, however, the conditions making for technical monopoly frequently change, and I suspect that both public regulation and public monopoly are likely to be less responsive to such changes in conditions, to be less readily capable of elimination, than private monopoly.

Railroads in the United States are an excellent example. A large degree of monopoly in railroads was perhaps inevitable on technical grounds in the nineteenth century. This was the justification for the Interstate Commerce Commission. But conditions have changed. The emergence of road and air transport has reduced the monopoly element in railroads to negligible proportions. Yet we have not eliminated the ICC. On the contrary, the ICC, which started out as an agency to protect the public from exploitation by the railroads, has become an agency to protect railroads from competition by trucks and other means of transport, and more recently even to protect existing truck companies from competition by new entrants. Similarly, in England, when the railroads were nationalized, trucking was at first brought into the state monopoly. If railroads had never been subjected to regulation in the United States, it is nearly certain that by now transportation, including railroads, would be a highly competitive industry with little or no remaining monopoly elements.

The choice between the evils of private monopoly, public monopoly, and public regulation cannot, however, be made once and for all, independently of the factual circumstances. If the technical monopoly is of a service or commodity that is regarded as essential and if its monopoly power is sizable, even the short-run effects of private unregulated monopoly may not be tolerable, and either public regulation or ownership may be a lesser evil.

Technical monopoly may on occasion justify a *de facto* public monopoly. It cannot by itself justify a public monopoly achieved by making it illegal for anyone else to compete. For example, there is no way to justify our present public monopoly of the post office. It may be argued that the carrying of mail is a technical monopoly and that a government monopoly is the least of evils. Along these lines, one could perhaps justify a government post office but not the present law, which makes it illegal for anybody else to carry mail. If the delivery of mail is a technical monopoly, no one will be able to succeed in competition with the government. If it is not, there is no reason why the government should be engaged in it. The only way to find out is to leave other people free to enter.

The historical reason why we have a post office monopoly is because the Pony Express did such a good job of carrying the mail across the continent that, when the government introduced transcontinental service, it couldn't compete effectively and lost money. The result was a law making it illegal for anybody else to carry the mail. That is why the Adams Express Company is an investment trust today instead of an operating company. I conjecture that if entry into the mail-carrying business were open to all, there would be a large number of firms entering it and this archaic industry would become revolutionized in short order.

A second general class of cases in which strictly voluntary exchange is impossible arises when actions of individuals have effects on other individuals for which it is not feasible to charge or recompense them. This is the problem of "neighborhood effects." An obvious example is the pollution of a stream. The man who pollutes a stream is in effect forcing others to exchange good water for bad. These others might be willing to make the exchange at a price. But it is not feasible for them, acting individually, to avoid the exchange or to enforce appropriate compensation.

A less obvious example is the provision of highways. In this case, it is technically possible to identify and hence charge individuals for their use of the roads and so to have private operation. However, for general access roads, involving many points of entry and exit, the costs of collection would be extremely high if a charge were to be made for the specific services received by each individual, because of the necessity of establishing toll booths or the equivalent at all entrances. The gasoline tax is a much cheaper method of charging individuals roughly in proportion to their use of the roads. This method, however, is one in which the particular payment cannot be identified closely with the particular use. Hence, it is hardly feasible to have private enterprise provide the service and collect the charge without establishing extensive private monopoly.

These considerations do not apply to long-distance turnpikes with high density of traffic and limited access. For these, the costs of collection are small and in many cases are now being paid, and there are often numerous alternatives, so that there is no serious monopoly problem. Hence, there is every reason why these should be privately owned and operated. If so owned and operated, the enterprise running the highway should receive the gasoline taxes paid on account of travel on it.

Parks are an interesting example because they illustrate the difference between cases that can and cases that cannot be justified by neighborhood effects, and because almost everyone at first sight regards the conduct of National Parks as obviously a valid function of government. In fact, however, neighborhood effects may justify a city park; they do not justify a national park, like Yellowstone National Park or the Grand Canyon. What is the fundamental difference between the two? For the city park, it is extremely difficult to identify the people who benefit from it and to charge them for the benefits which they receive. If there is a park in the middle of the city, the houses on all sides get the benefit of the open space, and people who walk through it or by it also benefit. To maintain toll collectors at the gates or to impose annual charges per window overlooking the park would be very expensive and difficult. The entrances to a national park like Yellowstone, on the other hand, are few; most of the people who come stay for a considerable period of time and it is perfectly feasible to set up toll gates and collect admission charges. This is indeed now done, though the charges do not cover the whole costs. If the public wants this kind of an activity enough to pay for it, private enterprises will have every incentive to provide such parks. And, of course, there are many private enterprises of this nature now in existence. I cannot myself conjure up any neighborhood effects or important monopoly effects that would justify governmental activity in this area.

Considerations like those I have treated under the heading of neighborhood effects have been used to rationalize almost every conceivable intervention. In many instances, however, this rationalization is special pleading rather than a legitimate application of the concept of neighborhood effects. Neighborhood effects cut both ways. They can be a reason for limiting the activities of government as well as for expanding them. Neighborhood effects impede voluntary exchange because it is difficult to identify the effects on third parties and to measure their magnitude; but this difficulty is present in governmental activity as well. It is hard to know when neighborhood effects are sufficiently large to justify particular costs in overcoming them and even harder to distribute the costs in an appropriate fashion. Consequently, when government engages in activities to overcome neighborhood effects, it will in part introduce an additional set of neighborhood effects by failing to charge or to compensate individuals properly. Whether the original or the new neighborhood effects are the more serious can only be judged by the facts of the individual case, and even then, only very approximately. Furthermore, the use of government to overcome neighborhood effects itself has an extremely important neighborhood effect which is unrelated to the particular occasion for government action. Every act of government intervention limits the area of individual freedom directly and threatens the preservation of freedom indirectly....

Our principles offer no hard and fast line how far it is appropriate to use government to accomplish jointly what it is difficult or impossible for us to accomplish separately through strictly voluntary exchange. In any particular case of proposed intervention, we must make up a balance sheet, listing separately the advantages and disadvantages. Our principles tell us what items to put on the one side and what items on the other and they give us some basis for attaching importance to the different items. In particular, we shall always want to enter on the liability side of any proposed government intervention, its neighborhood effect in threatening freedom, and give this effect considerable weight. Just how much weight to give to it, as to other items, depends upon the circumstances. If, for example, existing government intervention is minor, we shall attach a smaller weight to the negative effects of additional government intervention. This is an important reason why many earlier liberals, like Henry Simons, writing at a time when government was small by today's standards, were willing to have government undertake activities that today's liberals would not accept now that government has become so overgrown.

Action through Government on Paternalistic Grounds

Freedom is a tenable objective only for responsible individuals. We do not believe in freedom for madmen or children. The necessity of drawing a line between responsible individuals and others is inescapable, yet it means that there is an essential ambiguity in our ultimate objective of freedom. Paternalism is inescapable for those whom we designate as not responsible. The clearest case, perhaps, is that of madmen. We are willing neither to permit them freedom nor to shoot them. It would be nice if we could rely on voluntary activities of individuals to house and care for the madmen. But I think we cannot rule out the possibility that such charitable activities will be inadequate, if only because of the neighborhood effect involved in the fact that I benefit if another man contributes to the care of the insane. For this reason, we may be willing to arrange for their care through government.

Children offer a more difficult case. The ultimate operative unit in our society is the family, not the individual. Yet the acceptance of the family as the unit rests in considerable part on expediency rather than principle. We believe that parents are generally best able to protect their children and to provide for their development into responsible individuals for whom freedom is appropriate. But we do not believe in the freedom of parents to do what they will with other people. The children are responsible individuals in embryo, and a believer in freedom believes in protecting their ultimate rights.

To put this in a different and what may seem a more callous way, children are at one and the same time consumer goods and potentially responsible members of society. The freedom of individuals to use their economic resources as they want includes the freedom to use them to have children—to buy, as it were, the services of children as a particular form of consumption. But once this choice is exercised, the children have a value in and of themselves and have a freedom of their own that is not simply an extension of the freedom of the parents.

The paternalistic ground for governmental activity is in many ways the most troublesome to a liberal; for it involves the acceptance of a principle—that some shall decide for others—which he finds objectionable in most applications and which he rightly regards as a hallmark of his chief intellectual opponents, the proponents of collectivism in one or another of its guises, whether it be communism, socialism, or a welfare state. Yet there is no use pretending that problems are simpler than in fact they are. There is no avoiding the need for some measure of paternalism. As Dicey wrote in 1914 about an act for the protection of mental defectives, "The Mental Deficiency Act is the first step along a path on which no sane man can decline to enter, but which, if too far pursued, will bring statesmen across difficulties hard to meet without considerable interference with individual liberty."[1] There is

no formula that can tell us where to stop. We must rely on our fallible judgment and, having reached a judgment, on our ability to persuade our fellow men that it is a correct judgment, or their ability to persuade us to modify our views. We must put our faith, here as elsewhere, in a consensus reached by imperfect and biased men through free discussion and trial and error.

Conclusion

A government which maintained law and order, defined property rights, served as a means whereby we could modify property rights and other rules of the economic game, adjudicated disputes about the interpretation of the rules, enforced contracts, promoted competition, provided a monetary framework, engaged in activities to counter technical monopolies and to overcome neighborhood effects widely regarded as sufficiently important to justify government intervention, and which supplemented private charity and the private family in protecting the irresponsible, whether madman or child—such a government would clearly have important functions to perform. The consistent liberal is not an anarchist.

Yet it is also true that such a government would have clearly limited functions and would refrain from a host of activities that are now undertaken by federal and state governments in the United States, and their counterparts in other Western countries.... [I]t may help to give a sense of proportion about the role that a liberal would assign government simply to list, in closing this chapter, some activities currently undertaken by government in the U.S., that cannot, so far as I can see, validly be justified in terms of the principles outlined above:

1. Parity price support programs for agriculture.
2. Tariffs on imports or restrictions on exports, such as current oil import quotas, sugar quotas, etc.
3. Governmental control of output, such as through the farm program, or through prorationing of oil as is done by the Texas Railroad Commission.
4. Rent control, such as is still practiced in New York, or more general price and wage controls such as were imposed during and just after World War II.

[1] A.V. Dicey, *Lectures on the Relations between Law and Public Opinion in England during the Nineteenth Century*, 2nd ed. (London: Macmillan & Co., 1914), p. li.

5. Legal minimum wage rates, or legal maximum prices, such as the legal maximum of zero on the rate of interest that can be paid on demand deposits by commercial banks, or the legally fixed maximum rates that can be paid on savings and time deposits.

6. Detailed regulation of industries, such as the regulation of transportation by the Interstate Commerce Commission. This had some justification on technical monopoly grounds when initially introduced for railroads; it has none now for any means of transport. Another example is detailed regulation of banking.

7. A similar example, but one which deserves special mention because of its implicit censorship and violation of free speech, is the control of radio and television by the Federal Communications Commission.

8. Present social security programs, especially the old-age and retirement programs compelling people in effect (a) to spend a specified fraction of their income on the purchase of retirement annuity, and (b) to buy the annuity from a publicly operated enterprise.

9. Licensure provisions in various cities and states which restrict particular enterprises or occupations or professions to people who have a license, where the license is more than a receipt for a tax which anyone who wishes to enter the activity may pay.

10. So-called "public-housing" and the host of other subsidy programs directed at fostering residential construction such as F.H.A. [Federal Housing Authority] and V.A. [Veterans' Administration] guarantee of mortgage, and the like.

11. Conscription to man the military services in peacetime. The appropriate free-market arrangement is volunteer military forces ; which is to say, hiring men to serve. There is no justification for not paying whatever price is necessary to attract the required number of men. Present arrangements are inequitable and arbitrary, seriously interfere with the freedom of young men to shape their lives, and probably are even more costly than the market alternative. (Universal military training to provide a reserve for war time is a different problem and may be justified on liberal grounds.)

12. National parks, as noted above.

13. The legal prohibition on the carrying of mail for profit.

14. Publicly owned and operated toll roads, as noted above.

This list is far from comprehensive.

DISCUSSION QUESTIONS

1. What, according to Friedman, are the legitimate functions of government? Friedman lists 14 illegitimate functions of the US government. Which, if any, of these do you think is a legitimate function of government in general? Explain.

2. How, according to Friedman, do we determine the limits of individual freedom? Is his account of such limits adequate? Why or why not?

3. Why does Friedman think that government interference in cases of technical monopoly and of neighborhood effects is legitimate? Do you think that his position on these issues is consistent with his overall view? Why or why not?

36

Ronald Dworkin, "What Rights Do We Have?" (1977, 1978)

Ronald Dworkin (b.1931) is professor of philosophy and Frank Henry Sommer Professor of Law at New York University, as well as professor of jurisprudence and fellow of University College at Oxford University. In this selection, Dworkin argues that, although we have rights to certain basic *liberties*, we do not have a right to liberty as such.

SOURCE

Dworkin, Ronald. "What Rights Do We Have?" pp. 266–72 of *Taking Rights Seriously* by Ronald Dworkin. Cambridge, Mass.: The Belknap Press of Harvard University Press, Copyright © 1977, 1978 by Ronald Dworkin. Reprinted by permission of the publisher.

I. No Right to Liberty

Do we have a right to liberty?[1] Thomas Jefferson thought so, and since his day the right to liberty has received more play than the competing rights he mentioned to life and the pursuit of happiness. Liberty gave its name to the most influential political movement of the last century, and many of those who now despise liberals do so on the ground that they are not sufficiently libertarian. Of course, almost everyone concedes that the right to liberty is not the only political right, and that therefore claims to freedom must be limited, for example, by restraints that protect the security or property of others. Nevertheless the consensus in favor of some right to liberty is a vast one, though it is, as I shall argue in this chapter, misguided.

The right to liberty is popular all over this political spectrum. The rhetoric of liberty fuels every radical movement from international wars of liberation to campaigns for sexual freedom and women's liberation. But liberty has been even more prominent in conservative service. Even the mild social reorganizations of the anti-trust and unionization movements, and of the early New Deal, were opposed on the grounds that they infringed the right to liberty, and just now efforts to achieve some racial justice in America through techniques like the busing of

---

[1] I use "liberty" in this essay in the sense Isaiah Berlin called "negative." [See reading 34, p. 388, above.]

black and white schoolchildren, and social justice in Britain through constraints in private education are bitterly opposed on that ground.

It has become common, indeed, to describe the great social issues of domestic politics, and in particular the racial issue, as presenting a conflict between the demands of liberty and equality. It may be, it is said, that the poor and the black and the uneducated and the unskilled have an abstract right to equality, but the prosperous and the whites and the educated and the able have a right to liberty as well, and any efforts at social reorganization in aid of the first set of rights must reckon with and respect the second. Everyone except extremists recognizes, therefore, the need to compromise between equality and liberty. Every piece of important social legislation, from tax policy to integration plans, is shaped by the supposed tension between these two goals.

I have this supposed conflict between equality and liberty in mind when I ask whether we have a *right* to liberty, as Jefferson and everyone else has supposed. That is a crucial question. If freedom to choose one's schools, or employees, or neighborhood is simply something that we all want, like air conditioning or lobsters, then we are not entitled to hang on to these freedoms in the face of what we concede to be the rights of others to an equal share of respect and resources. But if we can say, not simply that we want these freedoms, but that we are ourselves entitled to them, then we have established at least a basis for demanding a compromise.

There is now a movement, for example, in favor of a proposed amendment to the constitution of the United States that would guarantee every school child the legal right to attend a "neighborhood school" and thus outlaw busing. The suggestion, that neighborhood schools somehow rank with jury trials as constitutional values, would seem silly but for the sense many Americans have that forcing school children into buses is somehow as much an interference with the fundamental right to liberty as segregated schooling was an insult to equality. But that seems to me absurd; indeed it seems to me absurd to suppose that men and women have any general right to liberty at all, at least as liberty has traditionally been conceived by its champions.

I have in mind the traditional definition of liberty as the absence of constraints placed by a government upon what a man might do if he wants to. Isaiah Berlin, in the most famous modem essay on liberty, put the matter this way: "The sense of freedom, in which I use this term, entails not simply the absence of frustration but the absence of obstacles to possible choices and activities—absence of obstructions on roads along which a man can decide to walk." This conception of liberty as license is neutral amongst the various activities a man might pursue, the various roads he might wish to walk. It diminishes a man's liberty when we prevent him from talking or making love as he wishes, but it also diminishes his liberty when we prevent him from murdering or defaming others. These latter constraints may be justifiable, but only because they are compromises necessary to protect the liberty or security of others, and not because they do not, in themselves, infringe the independent value of liberty. Bentham said that any law whatsoever is an "infraction" of liberty, and though some such infractions might be necessary, it is obscurantist to pretend that they are not infractions after all. In this neutral, all-embracing sense of liberty as license, liberty and equality are plainly in competition. Laws are needed to protect equality, and laws are inevitably compromises of liberty.

Liberals like Berlin are content with this neutral sense of liberty, because it seems to encourage clear thinking. It allows us to identify just what is lost, though perhaps unavoidably, when men accept constraints on their actions for some other goal or value. It would be an intolerable muddle, on this view, to use the concept of liberty or freedom in such a way that we counted a loss of freedom only when men were prevented from doing something that we thought they ought to do. It would allow totalitarian governments to masquerade as liberal, simply by arguing that they prevent men from doing only what is wrong. Worse, it would obscure the most distinctive point of the liberal tradition, which is that interfering with a man's free choice to do what he might want to do is in and of itself an insult to humanity, a wrong that may be justified but can never be wiped away by competing considerations. For a true liberal, any constraint upon freedom is something that a decent government must regret, and keep to the minimum necessary to accommodate the other rights of its constituents.

In spite of this tradition, however, the neutral sense of liberty seems to me to have caused more confusion than it has cured, particularly when it is joined to the popular and inspiring idea that men and women have a right to liberty. For we can maintain that idea only by so watering down the idea of a right that the right to liberty is something hardly worth having at all.

The term "right" is used in politics and philosophy in many different senses.... In order sensibly to ask whether we have a right to liberty in the neutral sense, we must fix on some one meaning of "right." It would not be difficult to find a sense of that term in which we could say with some confidence that men have a right to liberty. We might say, for example, that someone has a right to liberty if it is in his interest to have liberty, that is, if he either wants it or if it would be good for him to have it. In this sense, I would be prepared to concede that citizens have a right to liberty. But in this sense I would also have to concede that they have a right, at least generally, to vanilla ice cream. My concession about liberty, moreover, would have very little value in political debate. I should want to claim, for example, that people have a right to equality in a much stronger sense, that they do not simply want equality but that they are entitled to it, and I would therefore not recognize the claim that some men and women want liberty as requiring any compromise in the efforts that I believe are necessary to give other men and women the equality to which they are entitled.

If the right to liberty is to play the role cut out for it in political debate, therefore, it must be a right in a much stronger sense. [Elsewhere,[1] I have]

---

[1] [See Chapter 7 of *Taking Rights Seriously*, from which this selection has been excerpted.]

defined a strong sense of right that seems to me to capture the claims men mean to make when they appeal to political and moral rights. I do not propose to repeat my analysis here, but only to summarize it in this way. A successful claim of right, in the strong sense I described, has this consequence. If someone has a right to something, then it is wrong for the government to deny it to him even though it would be in the general interest to do so. This sense of a right (which might be called the anti-utilitarian concept of a right) seems to me very close to the sense of right principally used in political and legal writing and argument in recent years. It marks the distinctive concept of an individual right against the State which is the heart, for example, of constitutional theory in the United States.

I do not think that the right to liberty would come to very much, or have much power in political argument, if it relied on any sense of the right any weaker than that. If we settle on this concept of a right, however, then it seems plain that there exists no general right to liberty as such. I have no political right to drive up Lexington Avenue. If the government chooses to make Lexington Avenue one-way down town, it is a sufficient justification that this would be in the general interest, and it would be ridiculous for me to argue that for some reason it would nevertheless be wrong. The vast bulk of the laws which diminish my liberty are justified on utilitarian grounds, as being in the general interest or for the general welfare; if, as Bentham supposes, each of these laws diminishes my liberty, they nevertheless do not take away from me anything that I have a right to have. It will not do, in the one-way street case, to say that although I have a right to drive up Lexington Avenue, nevertheless the government for special reasons is justified in overriding that right. That seems silly because the government needs no special justification—but only *a* justification—for this sort of legislation. So I can have a political right to liberty, such that every act of constraint diminishes or infringes that right, only in such a weak sense of right that the so called right to liberty is not competitive with strong rights, like the right to equality, at all. In any strong sense of right, which would be competitive with the right to equality, there exists no general right to liberty at all.

It may now be said that I have misunderstood the claim that there is a right to liberty. It does not mean to argue, it will be said, that there is a right to all liberty, but simply to important or basic liberties. Every law is, as Bentham said, an infraction of liberty, but we have a right to be protected against only fundamental or serious infractions. If the constraint on liberty is serious or severe enough, then it is indeed true that the government is not entitled to impose that constraint simply because that would be in the general interest; the government is not entitled to constrain liberty of speech, for example, whenever it thinks that would improve the general welfare. So there is, after all, a general right to liberty as such, provided that that right is restricted to important liberties or serious deprivations. This qualification does not affect the political arguments I described earlier, it will be said, because the rights to liberty that stand in the way of full equality are rights to basic liberties like, for example, the right to attend a school of one's choice.

But this qualification raises an issue of great importance for liberal theory, which those who argue for a right to liberty do not face. What does it mean to say that the right to liberty is limited to basic liberties, or that it offers protection only against serious infractions of liberty? That claim might be spelled out in two different ways, with very different theoretical and practical consequences. Let us suppose two cases in which government constrains a citizen from doing what he might want to do: the government prevents him from speaking his mind on political issues; from driving his car uptown on Lexington Avenue. What is the connection between these two cases, and the difference between them, such that though they are both cases in which a citizen is constrained and deprived of liberty, his right to liberty is infringed only in the first, and not in the second?

On the first of the two theories we might consider, the citizen is deprived of the same commodity, namely liberty, in both cases, but the difference is that in the first case the amount of that commodity taken away from him is, for some reason, either greater in amount or greater in its impact than in the second. But that seems bizarre. It is very difficult to think of liberty as a commodity. If we do try to give liberty some operational sense, such that we can measure the relative diminution of liberty occasioned by different sorts of laws or constraints, then the result is unlikely to match our intuitive sense of what are basic liberties and what are not. Suppose, for example, we measure a diminution in liberty by calculating the extent of frustration that it induces. We shall then have to face the fact that laws against theft, and even traffic laws, impose constraints that are felt more keenly by most men than constraints on political speech would be. We might take a different tack, and measure the degree of loss of liberty by the impact that a particular constraint has on future choices. But we should then have to admit that the ordinary criminal code reduces choice for most men more than laws which forbid fringe political activity. So the first theory—that the difference between cases covered and those not covered by our supposed right to liberty is a matter of degree—must fail.

The second theory argues that the difference between the two cases has to do, not with the degree of liberty involved, but with the special character of the liberty involved in the case covered by the right. On this theory, the offense involved in a law that limits free speech is of a different character, and not just different in degree, from a law that prevents a man from driving up Lexington Avenue. That sounds plausible, though as we shall see it is not easy to state what this difference in character comes to, or why it argues for a right in some cases though not in others. My present point, however, is that if the distinction between basic liberties and other liberties is defended in this way, then the notion of a general right to liberty as such has been entirely abandoned. If we have a right to basic liberties not because they are cases in which the commodity of liberty is somehow especially at stake, but because an assault on basic liberties injures us or demeans us in some way that goes beyond its impact on liberty, then what we have a right to is not liberty at all, but to the values or interests or standing that this particular constraint defeats.

This is not simply a question of terminology. The idea of a right to liberty is a misconceived concept that does a disservice to political thought in at least two ways. First, the idea creates a false sense of a necessary conflict between liberty and other values when social regulation, like the busing program, is proposed. Second, the idea provides too easy an answer to the question of why we regard certain kinds of restraints, like the restraint on free speech or the exercise of religion, as especially unjust. The idea of a right to liberty allows us to say that these constraints are unjust because they have a special impact on liberty as such. Once we recognize that this answer is spurious, then we shall have to face the difficult question of what is indeed at stake in these cases. I should like to turn at once to that question. If there is no general right to liberty, then why do citizens in a democracy have rights to any specific kind of liberty, like freedom of speech or religion or political activity? It is no answer to say that if individuals have these rights, then the community will be better off in the long run as a whole. This idea—that individual rights may lead to overall utility—may or may not be true, but it is irrelevant to the defence of rights as such, because when we say that someone has a right to speak his mind freely, in the relevant political sense, we mean that he is entitled to do so even if this would not be in the general interest. If we want to defend individual rights in the sense in which we claim them, then we must try to discover something beyond utility that argues for these rights.

I mentioned one possibility earlier. We might be able to make out a case that individuals suffer some special damage when the traditional rights are invaded. On this argument, there is something about the liberty to speak out on political issues such that if that liberty is denied the individual suffers a special kind of damage which makes it wrong to inflict that damage upon him even though the community as a whole would benefit. This line

of argument will appeal to those who themselves would feel special deprivation at the loss of their political and civil liberties, but it is nevertheless a difficult argument to pursue for two reasons.

First, there are a great many men and women and they undoubtedly form the majority even in democracies like Britain and the United States, who do not exercise political liberties that they have, and who would not count the loss of these liberties as especially grievous. Second, we lack a psychological theory which would justify and explain the idea that the loss of civil liberties, or any particular liberties, involves inevitable or even likely psychological damage. On the contrary, there is now a lively tradition in psychology, led by psychologists like Ronald Laing, who argue that a good deal of mental instability in modern societies may be traced to the demand for too much liberty rather than too little. In their account, the need to choose, which follows from liberty, is an unnecessary source of destructive tension. These theories are not necessarily persuasive, but until we can be confident that they are wrong, we cannot assume that psychology demonstrates the opposite, however appealing that might be on political grounds. If we want to argue for a right to certain liberties, therefore, we must find another ground. We must argue on grounds of political morality that it is wrong to deprive individuals of these liberties, for some reason, apart from direct psychological damage, in spite of the fact that the common interest would be served by doing so. I put the matter this vaguely because there is no reason to assume, in advance, that only one kind of reason would support that moral position. It might be that a just society would recognize a variety of individual rights, some grounded on very different sorts of moral considerations from others. In what remains of this chapter [of *Taking Rights Seriously*] I shall try to describe only one possible ground for rights. It does not follow that men and women in civil society have only the rights that the argument I shall make would support; but it does follow that they have at least these rights, and that is important enough.

DISCUSSION QUESTIONS

1. Explain the distinction between a neutral conception of liberty as license and a conception of liberty that is not neutral. Why does Dworkin think that use of the latter conception of liberty would cause an "intolerable muddle"?

2. Explain the distinction between the weak sense of a right and the strong sense of a right. Why does Dworkin think that the latter is the more important concept?

3. Dworkin assumes that we have a right to certain basic liberties but not a right to liberty. Explain and evaluate his argument for this claim.

4. Why would Dworkin reject the kind of defense of a basic liberty such as freedom of expression that Mill offers in *On Liberty*? Do you think that Dworkin's reasons for rejecting such an account are convincing? Why or why not?

D.
The Enforcement
of Morality

37

John Stuart Mill, selection from *On Liberty* (1859)

In this selection, Mill presents a utilitarian defense of freedom of expression, which in part includes his famous appeal to the marketplace of ideas. This appeal was later taken up in various Supreme Court First Amendment decisions. On Mill, see reading 23 above.

SOURCE

Mill, John Stuart. *On Liberty*. Longman, Roberts & Green, 1869.

Of the Liberty of Thought and Discussion

The time, it is to be hoped, is gone by, when any defence would be necessary of the "liberty of the press" as one of the securities against corrupt or tyrannical government. No argument, we may suppose, can now be needed, against permitting a legislature or an executive, not identified in interest with the people, to prescribe opinions to them, and determine what doctrines or what arguments they shall be allowed to hear.... Let us suppose, therefore, that the government is entirely at one with the people, and never thinks of exerting any power of coercion unless in agreement with what it conceives to be their voice. But I deny the right of the people to exercise such coercion, either by themselves or by their government. The power itself is illegitimate. The best government has no more title to it than the worst. It is as noxious, or more noxious, when exerted in accordance with public opinion, than when in opposition to it. If all mankind minus one, were of one opinion, and only one person were of the contrary opinion, mankind would be no more justified in silencing that one person, than he, if he had the power, would be justified in silencing mankind. Were an opinion a personal possession of no value except to the owner; if to be obstructed in the enjoyment of it were simply a private injury, it would make some difference whether the injury was inflicted only on a few persons or on many. But the peculiar evil of silencing the expression of an opinion is that it is robbing the human race; posterity as well as the existing generation; those who dissent from the opinion, still more than those who hold it. If the opinion is right, they are deprived of the opportunity of exchanging error for truth: if wrong, they lose, what is almost as great a benefit, the clearer perception and livelier impression of truth, produced by its collision with error.

It is necessary to consider separately these two hypotheses, each of which has a distinct branch of the argument corresponding to it. We can never be sure that the opinion we are endeavouring to stifle is a false opinion; and if we were sure, stifling it would be an evil still.

First: the opinion which it is attempted to suppress by authority may possibly be true. Those who desire to suppress it, of course deny its truth; but they are not infallible. They have no authority to decide the question for all mankind, and exclude every other person from the means of judging. To refuse a hearing to an opinion, because they are sure that it is false, is to assume that *their* certainty is the same thing as *absolute* certainty. All silencing of discussion is an assumption of infallibility. Its condemnation may be allowed to rest on this common argument, not the worse for being common.

Unfortunately for the good sense of mankind, the fact of their fallibility is far from carrying the weight in their practical judgment, which is always allowed to it in theory; for while every one well knows himself to be fallible, few think it necessary to take any precautions against their own fallibility, or admit the supposition that any opinion, of which they feel very certain, may be one of the examples of the error to which they acknowledge themselves to be liable. Absolute princes, or others who are accustomed to unlimited deference, usually feel this complete confidence in their own opinions on nearly all subjects. People more happily situated, who sometimes hear their opinions disputed, and are not wholly unused to be set right when they are wrong, place the same unbounded reliance only on such of their opinions as are shared by all who surround them, or to whom they habitually defer: for in proportion to a man's want of confidence in his own solitary judgment, does he usually repose, with implicit trust, on the infallibility of "the world" in general. And the world, to each individual, means the part of it with which he comes in contact; his party, his sect, his church, his class of society: the man may be called, by comparison, almost liberal and large-minded to whom it means anything so comprehensive as his own country or his own age. Nor is his faith in this collective authority at all shaken by his being aware that other ages, countries, sects, churches, classes, and parties have thought, and even now think, the exact reverse. He devolves upon his own world the responsibility of being in the right against the dissentient worlds of other people; and it never troubles him that mere accident has decided which of these numerous worlds is the object of his reliance, and that the same causes which make him a Churchman in London, would have made him a Buddhist or a Confucian in Pekin. Yet it is as evident in itself, as any amount of argument can make it, that ages are no more infallible than individuals; every age having held many opinions which subsequent ages have deemed not only false but absurd; and it is as certain that many opinions, now general, will be rejected by future ages, as it is that many, once general, are rejected by the present.

The objection likely to be made to this argument, would probably take some such form as the following. There is no greater assumption of infallibility in forbidding the propagation of error, than in any other thing which is done by public authority on its own judgment and responsibility. Judgment is given to men that they may use it. Because it may be used erroneously, are men to be told that they ought not to use it at all? To prohibit what they think pernicious, is not claiming exemption from error, but fulfilling the duty incumbent on them, although fallible, of acting on their conscientious conviction. If we were never to act on our opinions, because those opinions may be wrong, we should leave all our interests uncared for, and all our duties unperformed. An objection which applies to all conduct can be no valid objection to any conduct in particular. It is the duty of governments, and of individuals, to form the truest opinions they can; to form them carefully, and never impose them upon others unless they are quite sure of being right. But when they are sure (such reasoners may say), it is not conscientiousness but cowardice to shrink from acting on their opinions, and allow doctrines which they honestly think dangerous to the welfare of mankind, either in this life or in another, to be scattered abroad without restraint, because other people, in less enlightened times, have persecuted opinions now believed to be true. Let us take care, it may be said, not to make the same mistake: but governments and nations have made mistakes in other things, which are not denied to be fit subjects for the exercise of authority: they have laid on bad taxes, made unjust wars. Ought we therefore to lay on no taxes, and, under whatever provocation, make no wars? Men, and governments, must act to the best of their ability. There is no such thing as absolute certainty, but there is assurance sufficient for the purposes of human life. We may, and must, assume our opinion to be true for the guidance of our own conduct: and it is assuming no more when we forbid bad men to pervert society by the propagation of opinions which we regard as false and pernicious.

I answer, that it is assuming very much more. There is the greatest difference between presuming an opinion to be true, because, with every opportunity for contesting it, it has not been refuted, and assuming its truth for the purpose of not permitting its refutation. Complete liberty of contradicting and disproving our opinion, is the very condition which justifies us in assuming its truth for purposes of action; and on no other terms can a being with human faculties have any rational assurance of being right.

When we consider either the history of opinion, or the ordinary conduct of human life, to what is it to be ascribed that the one and the other are no worse than they are? Not certainly to the inherent force of the human understanding; for, on any matter not self-evident, there are ninety-nine persons totally incapable of judging of it, for one who is capable; and the capacity of the hundredth person is only comparative; for the majority of the eminent men of every past generation held many opinions now known to be erroneous, and did or approved numerous things which no one will now justify. Why is it, then, that there is on the whole a preponderance among mankind of rational opinions and rational conduct? If there really is this preponderance—which there must be unless human affairs are, and have always been, in an almost desperate state—it is owing to a quality of the human mind, the source of everything respectable in man either as an intellectual or as a moral being, namely, that his errors are corrigible. He is capable of rectifying his mistakes, by discussion and experience. Not by experience alone. There must be discussion, to show how experience is to be interpreted. Wrong opinions and practices gradually yield to fact and argument: but facts and arguments, to produce any effect on the mind, must be brought before it. Very few facts are able to tell their own story, without comments to bring out their meaning. The whole strength and value, then, of human judgment, depending on the one property, that it can be set right when it is wrong, reliance can be placed on it only when the means of setting it right are kept constantly at hand. In the case of any person whose judgment is really deserving of confidence, how has it become so? Because he has kept his mind open to criticism of his opinions and conduct. Because it has been his practice to listen to all that could be said against him; to profit by as much of it as was just, and expound to himself, and upon occasion to others, the fallacy of what was fallacious. Because he has felt, that the only way in which a human being can make some approach to knowing the whole of a subject, is by hearing what can be said about it by persons of every variety of opinion, and studying all modes in which it can be looked at by every character of mind. No wise man ever acquired his wisdom in any mode but this; nor is it in the nature of human intellect to become wise in any other manner. The steady habit of correcting and completing his own opinion by collating it with those of others, so far from causing doubt and hesitation in carrying it into practice, is the only stable foundation for a just reliance on it: for, being cognisant of all that can, at least obviously, be said against him, and having taken up his position against all gainsayers—knowing that he has sought for objections and difficulties, instead of avoiding them, and has shut out no light which can be thrown upon the subject from any quarter—he has a right to think his judgment better than that of any person, or any multitude, who have not gone through a similar process.

It is not too much to require that what the wisest of mankind, those who are best entitled to trust their own judgment, find necessary to warrant their relying on it, should be submitted to by that miscellaneous collection of a few wise and many foolish individuals, called the public. The most intolerant of churches, the Roman Catholic Church, even at the canonization of a saint, admits, and listens patiently to, a "devil's advocate." The holiest of men, it appears, cannot be admitted to posthumous honours, until all that the devil could say against him is known and weighed. If even the Newtonian philosophy were not permitted to be questioned, mankind could not feel as complete assurance of its truth as they now do. The beliefs which we have most warrant for have no safeguard to rest on, but a standing invitation to the whole world to prove them unfounded. If the challenge is not accepted, or is accepted and the attempt fails, we are far enough from certainty still; but we have done the best that the existing state of human reason admits of; we have neglected nothing that could give the truth a chance of reaching us: if the lists are kept open, we may hope that if there be a better truth, it will be found when the human mind is capable of receiving it; and in the meantime we may rely on having attained such approach to truth, as is possible in our own day. This is the amount of certainty attainable by a fallible being, and this the sole way of attaining it.

Strange it is, that men should admit the validity of the arguments for free discussion, but object to their being "pushed to an extreme"; not seeing that unless the reasons are good for an extreme case, they are not good for any case. Strange that they should imagine that they are not assuming infallibility, when they acknowledge that there should be free discussion on all subjects which can possibly be *doubtful*, but think that some particular principle or doctrine should be forbidden to be questioned because it is so *certain*, that is, because *they are certain* that it is certain. To call any proposition certain, while there is any one who would deny its certainty if permitted, but who is not permitted, is to assume that we ourselves, and those who agree with us, are the judges of certainty, and judges without hearing the other side.

In the present age—which has been described as "destitute of faith, but terrified at scepticism"—in which people feel sure, not so much that their opinions are true, as that they should not know what to do without them—the claims of an opinion to be protected from public attack are rested not so much on its truth, as on its importance to society. There are, it is alleged, certain beliefs, so useful, not to say indispensable to well-being, that it is as much the duty of governments to uphold those beliefs, as to protect any other of the interests of society. In a case of such necessity, and so directly in the line of their duty, something less than infallibility may, it is maintained, warrant, and even bind, governments, to act on their own opinion, confirmed by the general opinion of mankind. It is also often argued, and still oftener thought, that none but bad men would desire to weaken these salutary beliefs; and there can be nothing wrong, it is thought, in restraining bad men, and prohibiting what only such men would wish to practise. This mode of thinking makes the justification of restraints on discussion not a question of the truth of doctrines, but of their usefulness; and flatters itself by that means to escape the responsibility of claiming to be an infallible judge of opinions. But those who thus satisfy themselves do not perceive that the assumption of infallibility is merely shifted from one point to another. The usefulness of an opinion is itself matter of opinion: as disputable, as open to discussion, and requiring discussion as much, as the opinion itself. There is the same need of an infallible judge of opinions to decide an opinion to be noxious, as to decide it to be false, unless the opinion condemned has full opportunity of defending itself. And it will not do to say that the heretic may be allowed to maintain the utility or harmlessness of his opinion, though forbidden to maintain its truth. The truth of an opinion is part of its utility. If we would know whether or not it is desirable that a proposition should be believed, is it possible to exclude the consideration of whether or not it is true? In the opinion, not of bad men, but of the best men, no belief which is contrary to truth can be really useful: and can you prevent such men from urging that plea, when they are charged with culpability for denying some doctrine which they are told is useful, but which they believe to be false? Those who are on the side of received opinions, never fail to take all possible advantage of this plea; you do not find them handling the question of utility as if it could be completely abstracted from that of truth: on the contrary, it is, above all, because their doctrine is the "truth," that the knowledge or the belief of it is held to be so indispensable. There can be no fair discussion of the question of usefulness, when an argument so vital may be employed on one side, but not on the other. And in point of fact, when law or public feeling do not permit the truth of an opinion to be disputed, they are just as little tolerant of a denial of its usefulness. The utmost they allow is an extenuation of its absolute necessity, or of the positive guilt of rejecting it.

In order more fully to illustrate the mischief of denying a hearing to opinions because we, in our own judgment, have condemned them, it will be desirable to fix down the discussion to a concrete case; and I choose, by preference, the cases which are least favourable to me—in which the argument against freedom of opinion, both on the score of truth and on that of utility, is considered the strongest. Let the opinions impugned be the belief in a God and in a future state, or any of the commonly received doctrines of morality. To fight the battle on such ground, gives a great advantage to an unfair antagonist; since he will be sure to say (and many who have no desire to be unfair will say it internally), Are these the doctrines which you

do not deem sufficiently certain to be taken under the protection of law? Is the belief in a God one of the opinions, to feel sure of which, you hold to be assuming infallibility? But I must be permitted to observe, that it is not the feeling sure of a doctrine (be it what it may) which I call an assumption of infallibility. It is the undertaking to decide that question *for others*, without allowing them to hear what can be said on the contrary side. And I denounce and reprobate this pretension not the less, if put forth on the side of my most solemn convictions. However positive any one's persuasion may be, not only of the falsity but of the pernicious consequences—not only of the pernicious consequences, but (to adopt expressions which I altogether condemn) the immorality and impiety of an opinion; yet if, in pursuance of that private judgment, though backed by the public judgment of his country or his contemporaries, he prevents the opinion from being heard in its defence, he assumes infallibility. And so far from the assumption being less objectionable or less dangerous because the opinion is called immoral or impious, this is the case of all others in which it is most fatal. These are exactly the occasions on which the men of one generation commit those dreadful mistakes, which excite the astonishment and horror of posterity. It is among such that we find the instances memorable in history, when the arm of the law has been employed to root out the best men and the noblest doctrines; with deplorable success as to the men, though some of the doctrines have survived to be (as if in mockery) invoked, in defence of similar conduct towards those who dissent from *them*, or from their received interpretation.

Mankind can hardly be too often reminded, that there was once a man named Socrates, between whom and the legal authorities and public opinion of his time, there took place a memorable collision. Born in an age and country abounding in individual greatness, this man has been handed down to us by those who best knew both him and the age, as the most virtuous man in it; while we know him as the head and prototype of all subsequent teachers of virtue, the source equally of the lofty inspiration of Plato and the judicious utilitarian-ism of Aristotle, "*i maëstri di color che sanno*,"[1] the two headsprings of ethical as of all other philoso-phy. This acknowledged master of all the eminent thinkers who have since lived—whose fame, still growing after more than two thousand years, all but outweighs the whole remainder of the names which make his native city illustrious—was put to death by his countrymen, after a judicial convic-tion, for impiety and immorality. Impiety, in deny-ing the gods recognised by the State; indeed his accuser asserted (see the *Apologia*) that he believed in no gods at all. Immorality, in being, by his doc-trines and instructions, a "corrupter of youth." Of these charges the tribunal, there is every ground for believing, honestly found him guilty, and con-demned the man who probably of all then born had deserved best of mankind, to be put to death as a criminal.

To pass from this to the only other instance of judicial iniquity, the mention of which, after the condemnation of Socrates, would not be an anti-cli-max: the event which took place on Calvary rather more than eighteen hundred years ago. The man who left on the memory of those who witnessed his life and conversation, such an impression of his moral grandeur, that eighteen subsequent cen-turies have done homage to him as the Almighty in person, was ignominiously put to death, as what? As a blasphemer. Men did not merely mistake their benefactor; they mistook him for the exact contrary of what he was, and treated him as that prodigy of impiety, which they themselves are now held to be, for their treatment of him. The feelings with which mankind now regard these lamentable transactions, especially the later of the two, ren-der them extremely unjust in their judgment of the unhappy actors. These were, to all appearance, not bad men—not worse than men most commonly are, but rather the contrary; men who possessed in a full, or somewhat more than a full measure, the religious, moral, and patriotic feelings of their time and people: the very kind of men who, in all

times, our own included, have every chance of pass-ing through life blameless and respected. The high-priest who rent his garments when the words were pronounced, which, according to all the ideas of his country, constituted the blackest guilt, was in all probability quite as sincere in his horror and indignation, as the generality of respectable and pious men now are in the religious and moral sen-timents they profess; and most of those who now shudder at his conduct, if they had lived in his time, and been born Jews, would have acted precisely as he did. Orthodox Christians who are tempted to think that those who stoned to death the first mar-tyrs must have been worse men than they them-selves are, ought to remember that one of those persecutors was Saint Paul.

Let us add one more example, the most strik-ing of all, if the impressiveness of an error is mea-sured by the wisdom and virtue of him who falls into it. If ever any one, possessed of power, had grounds for thinking himself the best and most enlightened among his contemporaries, it was the Emperor Marcus Aurelius. Absolute monarch of the whole civilized world, he preserved through life not only the most unblemished justice, but what was less to be expected from his Stoical breeding, the tenderest heart. The few failings which are attrib-uted to him were all on the side of indulgence: while his writings, the highest ethical product of the ancient mind, differ scarcely perceptibly, if they differ at all, from the most characteristic teachings of Christ. This man, a better Christian in all but the dogmatic sense of the word, than almost any of the ostensibly Christian sovereigns who have since reigned, persecuted Christianity. Placed at the summit of all the previous attainments of human-ity, with an open, unfettered intellect, and a char-acter which led him of himself to embody in his moral writings the Christian ideal, he yet failed to see that Christianity was to be a good and not an evil to the world, with his duties to which he was so deeply penetrated. Existing society he knew to be in a deplorable state. But such as it was, he saw, or thought he saw, that it was held together, and pre-vented from being worse, by belief and reverence

---

[1] ["The master of those who know."]

of the received divinities. As a ruler of mankind, he deemed it his duty not to suffer society to fall in pieces; and saw not how, if its existing ties were removed, any others could be formed which could again knit it together. The new religion openly aimed at dissolving these ties: unless, therefore, it was his duty to adopt that religion, it seemed to be his duty to put it down. Inasmuch then as the theology of Christianity did not appear to him true or of divine origin; inasmuch as this strange history of a crucified God was not credible to him, and a system which purported to rest entirely upon a foundation to him so wholly unbelievable, could not be foreseen by him to be that renovating agency which, after all abatements, it has in fact proved to be; the gentlest and most amiable of philosophers and rulers, under a solemn sense of duty, authorized the persecution of Christianity. To my mind this is one of the most tragical facts in all history. It is a bitter thought, how different a thing the Christianity of the world might have been, if the Christian faith had been adopted as the religion of the empire under the auspices of Marcus Aurelius instead of those of Constantine. But it would be equally unjust to him and false to truth, to deny, that no one plea which can be urged for punishing anti-Christian teaching, was wanting to Marcus Aurelius for punishing, as he did, the propagation of Christianity. No Christian more firmly believes that Atheism is false, and tends to the dissolution of society, than Marcus Aurelius believed the same things of Christianity; he who, of all men then living, might have been thought the most capable of appreciating it. Unless any one who approves of punishment for the promulgation of opinions, flatters himself that he is a wiser and better man than Marcus Aurelius—more deeply versed in the wisdom of his time, more elevated in his intellect above it—more earnest in his search for truth, or more single-minded in his devotion to it when found;—let him abstain from that assumption of the joint infallibility of himself and the multitude, which the great Antoninus[1] made with so unfortunate a result....

A theory which maintains that truth may justifiably be persecuted because persecution cannot possibly do it any harm, cannot be charged with being intentionally hostile to the reception of new truths; but we cannot commend the generosity of its dealing with the persons to whom mankind are indebted for them. To discover to the world something which deeply concerns it, and of which it was previously ignorant; to prove to it that it had been mistaken on some vital point of temporal or spiritual interest, is as important a service as a human being can render to his fellow-creatures, and in certain cases, as in those of the early Christians and of the Reformers, those who think with Dr. Johnson[2] believe it to have been the most precious gift which could be bestowed on mankind. That the authors of such splendid benefits should be requited by martyrdom; that their reward should be to be dealt with as the vilest of criminals, is not, upon this theory, a deplorable error and misfortune, for which humanity should mourn in sackcloth and ashes, but the normal and justifiable state of things. The propounder of a new truth, according to this doctrine, should stand, as stood, in the legislation of the Locrians,[3] the proposer of a new law, with a halter round his neck, to be instantly tightened if the public assembly did not, on hearing his reasons, then and there adopt his proposition. People who defend this mode of treating benefactors, cannot be supposed to set much value on the benefit; and I believe this view of the subject is mostly confined to the sort of persons who think that new truths may have been desirable once, but that we have had enough of them now.

But, indeed, the dictum that truth always triumphs over persecution, is one of those pleasant falsehoods which men repeat after one another till they pass into commonplaces, but which all experience refutes. History teems with instances of truth

[1] [Roman emperor from 138–161 CE.]

[2] [Samuel Johnson (1709–84) was a renowned British author who made important contributions to biography, literary criticism, lexicography, and many other literary fields.]

[3] [The Locrians were an ancient Greek tribe.]

put down by persecution. If not suppressed for ever, it may be thrown back for centuries. To speak only of religious opinions: the Reformation broke out at least twenty times before Luther, and was put down. Arnold of Brescia was put down. Fra Dolcino was put down. Savonarola was put down. The Albigeois were put down. The Vaudois were put down. The Lollards were put down. The Hussites were put down.[1] Even after the era of Luther, wherever persecution was persisted in, it was successful. In Spain, Italy, Flanders, the Austrian empire, Protestantism was rooted out; and, most likely, would have been so in England, had Queen Mary lived, or Queen Elizabeth died. Persecution has always succeeded, save where the heretics were too strong a party to be effectually persecuted. No reasonable person can doubt that Christianity might have been extirpated in the Roman Empire. It spread, and became predominant, because the persecutions were only occasional, lasting but a short time, and separated by long intervals of almost undisturbed propagandism. It is a piece of idle sentimentality that truth, merely as truth, has any inherent power denied to error, of prevailing against the dungeon and the stake. Men are not more zealous for truth than they often are for error, and a sufficient application of legal or even of social penalties will generally succeed in stopping the propagation of either. The real advantage which truth has, consists in this, that when an opinion is true, it may be extinguished once, twice, or many times, but in the course of ages there will generally be found persons to rediscover it, until some one of its reappearances falls on a time when from favourable circumstances it escapes persecution until it has made such head as to withstand all subsequent attempts to suppress it.

It will be said, that we do not now put to death the introducers of new opinions: we are not like our fathers who slew the prophets, we even build sepulchres to them. It is true we no longer put heretics to death; and the amount of penal infliction which modern feeling would probably tolerate, even against the most obnoxious opinions, is not sufficient to extirpate them. But let us not flatter ourselves that we are yet free from the stain even of legal persecution. Penalties for opinion, or at least for its expression, still exist by law; and their enforcement is not, even in these times, so unexampled as to make it at all incredible that they may some day be revived in full force. In the year 1857, at the summer assizes of the county of Cornwall, an unfortunate man, said to be of unexceptionable conduct in all relations of life, was sentenced to twenty-one months imprisonment, for uttering, and writing on a gate, some offensive words concerning Christianity. Within a month of the same time, at the Old Bailey, two persons, on two separate occasions, were rejected as jurymen, and one of them grossly insulted by the judge and by one of the counsel, because they honestly declared that they had no theological belief; and a third, a foreigner, for the same reason, was denied justice against a thief. This refusal of redress took place in virtue of the legal doctrine, that no person can be allowed to give evidence in a court of justice, who does not profess belief in a God (any god is sufficient) and in a future state; which is equivalent to declaring such persons to be outlaws, excluded from the protection of the tribunals; who may not only be robbed or assaulted with impunity, if no one but themselves, or persons of similar opinions, be present, but any one else may be robbed or assaulted with impunity, if the proof of the fact depends on their evidence. The assumption on which this is grounded, is that the oath is worthless, of a person who does not believe in a future state; a proposition which betokens much ignorance of history in those who assent to it (since it is historically true that a large proportion of infidels in all ages have been persons of distinguished integrity and honor); and would be maintained by

---

[1] [Arnold of Brescia (1090–1155), Fra Dolcino (1250–1307), and Savonarola (1452–98) were all either monks or preachers who were executed by the Church for their oppositional or heretic views. The Albigeois were the people of the Albi region of France who protected their Cathar population against the Catholic crusade that began in 1208. The Vaudois people of Switzerland opposed the Catholic separatists in the nineteenth century. Both the Lollards and the Hussites were groups that broke with the Catholic Church to follow John Wycliffe (1320–84) and Jan Hus (1369–1415), respectively.]

no one who had the smallest conception how many of the persons in greatest repute with the world, both for virtues and for attainments, are well known, at least to their intimates, to be unbelievers. The rule, besides, is suicidal, and cuts away its own foundation. Under pretence that atheists must be liars, it admits the testimony of all atheists who are willing to lie, and rejects only those who brave the obloquy of publicly confessing a detested creed rather than affirm a falsehood. A rule thus self-convicted of absurdity so far as regards its professed purpose, can be kept in force only as a badge of hatred, a relic of persecution; a persecution, too, having the peculiarity, that the qualification for undergoing it, is the being clearly proved not to deserve it. The rule, and the theory it implies, are hardly less insulting to believers than to infidels. For if he who does not believe in a future state, necessarily lies, it follows that they who do believe are only prevented from lying, if prevented they are, by the fear of hell. We will not do the authors and abettors of the rule the injury of supposing, that the conception which they have formed of Christian virtue is drawn from their own consciousness.

These, indeed, are but rags and remnants of persecution, and may be thought to be not so much an indication of the wish to persecute, as an example of that very frequent infirmity of English minds, which makes them take a preposterous pleasure in the assertion of a bad principle, when they are no longer bad enough to desire to carry it really into practice. But unhappily there is no security in the state of the public mind that the suspension of worse forms of legal persecution, which has lasted for about the space of a generation, will continue. In this age the quiet surface of routine is as often ruffled by attempts to resuscitate past evils, as to introduce new benefits. What is boasted of at the present time as the revival of religion, is always, in narrow and uncultivated minds, at least as much the revival of bigotry; and where there is the strong permanent leaven of intolerance in the feelings of a people, which at all times abides in the middle classes of this country, it needs but little to provoke them into actively persecuting those whom they have never ceased to think

proper objects of persecution. For it is this—it is the opinions men entertain, and the feelings they cherish, respecting those who disown the beliefs they deem important, which makes this country not a place of mental freedom. For a long time past, the chief mischief of the legal penalties is that they strengthen the social stigma. It is that stigma which is really effective, and so effective is it, that the profession of opinions which are under the ban of society is much less common in England, than is, in many other countries, the avowal of those which incur risk of judicial punishment. In respect to all persons but those whose pecuniary circumstances make them independent of the good will of other people, opinion, on this subject, is as efficacious as law; men might as well be imprisoned, as excluded from the means of earning their bread. Those whose bread is already secured, and who desire no favours from men in power, or from bodies of men, or from the public, have nothing to fear from the open avowal of any opinions, but to be ill-thought of and ill-spoken of, and this it ought not to require a very heroic mould to enable them to bear. There is no room for any appeal *ad misericordiam* in behalf of such persons. But though we do not now inflict so much evil on those who think differently from us, as it was formerly our custom to do, it may be that we do ourselves as much evil as ever by our treatment of them. Socrates was put to death, but the Socratic philosophy rose like the sun in heaven, and spread its illumination over the whole intellectual firmament. Christians were cast to the lions, but the Christian church grew up a stately and spreading tree, overtopping the older and less vigorous growths, and stifling them by its shade. Our merely social intolerance kills no one, roots out no opinions, but induces men to disguise them, or to abstain from any active effort for their diffusion. With us, heretical opinions do not perceptibly gain, or even lose, ground in each decade or generation; they never blaze out far and wide, but continue to smoulder in the narrow circles of thinking and studious persons among whom they originate, without ever lighting up the general affairs of mankind with either a true or a deceptive light. And thus is kept up a state of things very satisfactory to some minds, because, without the unpleasant process of fining or imprisoning anybody, it maintains all prevailing opinions outwardly undisturbed, while it does not absolutely interdict the exercise of reason by dissentients afflicted with the malady of thought. A convenient plan for having peace in the intellectual world, and keeping all things going on therein very much as they do already. But the price paid for this sort of intellectual pacification, is the sacrifice of the entire moral courage of the human mind. A state of things in which a large portion of the most active and inquiring intellects find it advisable to keep the general principles and grounds of their convictions within their own breasts, and attempt, in what they address to the public, to fit as much as they can of their own conclusions to premises which they have internally renounced, cannot send forth the open, fearless characters, and logical, consistent intellects who once adorned the thinking world. The sort of men who can be looked for under it, are either mere conformers to commonplace, or time-servers for truth, whose arguments on all great subjects are meant for their hearers, and are not those which have convinced themselves. Those who avoid this alternative, do so by narrowing their thoughts and interest to things which can be spoken of without venturing within the region of principles, that is, to small practical matters, which would come right of themselves, if but the minds of mankind were strengthened and enlarged, and which will never be made effectually right until then: while that which would strengthen and enlarge men's minds, free and daring speculation on the highest subjects, is abandoned.

Those in whose eyes this reticence on the part of heretics is no evil, should consider in the first place, that in consequence of it there is never any fair and thorough discussion of heretical opinions; and that such of them as could not stand such a discussion, though they may be prevented from spreading, do not disappear. But it is not the minds of heretics that are deteriorated most, by the ban placed on all inquiry which does not end in the orthodox conclusions. The greatest harm done is to those who are not heretics, and whose whole mental development is cramped, and their reason cowed, by the fear of heresy. Who can compute what the world loses in the multitude of promising intellects combined with timid characters, who dare not follow out any bold, vigorous, independent train of thought, lest it should land them in something which would admit of being considered irreligious or immoral? Among them we may occasionally see some man of deep conscientiousness, and subtle and refined understanding, who spends a life in sophisticating with an intellect which he cannot silence, and exhausts the resources of ingenuity in attempting to reconcile the promptings of his conscience and reason with orthodoxy, which yet he does not, perhaps, to the end succeed in doing. No one can be a great thinker who does not recognise, that as a thinker it is his first duty to follow his intellect to whatever conclusions it may lead. Truth gains more even by the errors of one who, with due study and preparation, thinks for himself, than by the true opinions of those who only hold them because they do not suffer themselves to think. Not that it is solely, or chiefly, to form great thinkers, that freedom of thinking is required. On the contrary, it is as much and even more indispensable, to enable average human beings to attain the mental stature which they are capable of. There have been, and may again be, great individual thinkers, in a general atmosphere of mental slavery. But there never has been, nor ever will be, in that atmosphere, an intellectually active people. When any people has made a temporary approach to such a character, it has been because the dread of heterodox speculation was for a time suspended. Where there is a tacit convention that principles are not to be disputed; where the discussion of the greatest questions which can occupy humanity is considered to be closed, we cannot hope to find that generally high scale of mental activity which has made some periods of history so remarkable....

Let us now pass to the second division of the argument, and dismissing the supposition that any of the received opinions may be false, let us assume them to be true, and examine into the worth of the manner in which they are likely to be held, when their truth is not freely and openly canvassed.

However unwillingly a person who has a strong opinion may admit the possibility that his opinion may be false, he ought to be moved by the consideration that however true it may be, if it is not fully, frequently, and fearlessly discussed, it will be held as a dead dogma, not a living truth.

There is a class of persons (happily not quite so numerous as formerly) who think it enough if a person assents undoubtingly to what they think true, though he has no knowledge whatever of the grounds of the opinion, and could not make a tenable defence of it against the most superficial objections. Such persons, if they can once get their creed taught from authority, naturally think that no good, and some harm, comes of its being allowed to be questioned. Where their influence prevails, they make it nearly impossible for the received opinion to be rejected wisely and considerately, though it may still be rejected rashly and ignorantly; for to shut out discussion entirely is seldom possible, and when it once gets in, beliefs not grounded on conviction are apt to give way before the slightest semblance of an argument. Waiving, however, this possibility—assuming that the true opinion abides in the mind, but abides as a prejudice, a belief independent of, and proof against, argument—this is not the way in which truth ought to be held by a rational being. This is not knowing the truth. Truth, thus held, is but one superstition the more, accidentally clinging to the words which enunciate a truth.

If the intellect and judgment of mankind ought to be cultivated, a thing which Protestants at least do not deny, on what can these faculties be more appropriately exercised by any one, than on the things which concern him so much that it is considered necessary for him to hold opinions on them? If the cultivation of the understanding consists in one thing more than in another, it is surely in learning the grounds of one's own opinions. Whatever people believe, on subjects on which it is of the first importance to believe rightly, they ought to be able to defend against at least the common objections. But, some one may say, "Let them be *taught* the grounds of their opinions. It does not follow that opinions must be merely parroted because they are never heard controverted. Persons who learn geometry do not simply commit the theorems to memory, but understand and learn likewise the demonstrations; and it would be absurd to say that they remain ignorant of the grounds of geometrical truths, because they never hear any one deny, and attempt to disprove them." Undoubtedly: and such teaching suffices on a subject like mathematics, where there is nothing at all to be said on the wrong side of the question. The peculiarity of the evidence of mathematical truths is that all the argument is on one side. There are no objections, and no answers to objections. But on every subject on which difference of opinion is possible, the truth depends on a balance to be struck between two sets of conflicting reasons. Even in natural philosophy, there is always some other explanation possible of the same facts; some geocentric theory instead of heliocentric, some phlogiston instead of oxygen; and it has to be shown why that other theory cannot be the true one: and until this is shown, and until we know how it is shown, we do not understand the grounds of our opinion. But when we turn to subjects infinitely more complicated, to morals, religion, politics, social relations, and the business of life, three-fourths of the arguments for every disputed opinion consist in dispelling the appearances which favour some opinion different from it. The greatest orator, save one, of antiquity, has left it on record that he always studied his adversary's case with as great, if not with still greater, intensity than even his own. What Cicero practised as the means of forensic success, requires to be imitated by all who study any subject in order to arrive at the truth. He who knows only his own side of the case, knows little of that. His reasons may be good, and no one may have been able to refute them. But if he is equally unable to refute the reasons on the opposite side; if he does not so much as know what they are, he has no ground for preferring either opinion. The rational position for him would be suspension of judgment, and unless he contents himself with that, he is either led by authority, or adopts, like the generality of the world, the side to which he feels most inclination. Nor is it enough that he should hear the arguments of adversaries from his own teachers, presented as they state them, and accompanied by what they offer as refutations. That is not the way to do justice to the arguments, or bring them into real contact with his own mind. He must be able to hear them from persons who actually believe them; who defend them in earnest, and do their very utmost for them. He must know them in their most plausible and persuasive form; he must feel the whole force of the difficulty which the true view of the subject has to encounter and dispose of; else he will never really possess himself of the portion of truth which meets and removes that difficulty. Ninety-nine in a hundred of what are called educated men are in this condition; even of those who can argue fluently for their opinions. Their conclusion may be true, but it might be false for anything they know: they have never thrown themselves into the mental position of those who think differently from them, and considered what such persons may have to say; and consequently they do not, in any proper sense of the word, know the doctrine which they themselves profess. They do not know those parts of it which explain and justify the remainder; the considerations which show that a fact which seemingly conflicts with another is reconcilable with it, or that, of two apparently strong reasons, one and not the other ought to be preferred. All that part of the truth which turns the scale, and decides the judgment of a completely informed mind, they are strangers to; nor is it ever really known, but to those who have attended equally and impartially to both sides, and endeavoured to see the reasons of both in the strongest light. So essential is this discipline to a real understanding of moral and human subjects, that if opponents of all important truths do not exist, it is indispensable to imagine them, and supply them with the strongest arguments which the most skilful devil's advocate can conjure up.

To abate the force of these considerations, an enemy of free discussion may be supposed to say, that there is no necessity for mankind in general to know and understand all that can be said against or for their opinions by philosophers and theologians. That it is not needful for common men to be able to expose all the misstatements or fallacies of an ingenious opponent. That it is enough if there is always somebody capable of answering them, so that nothing likely to mislead uninstructed persons remains unrefuted. That simple minds, having been taught the obvious grounds of the truths inculcated on them, may trust to authority for the rest, and being aware that they have neither knowledge nor talent to resolve every difficulty which can be raised, may repose in the assurance that all those which have been raised have been or can be answered, by those who are specially trained to the task.

Conceding to this view of the subject the utmost that can be claimed for it by those most easily satisfied with the amount of understanding of truth which ought to accompany the belief of it; even so, the argument for free discussion is no way weakened. For even this doctrine acknowledges that mankind ought to have a rational assurance that all objections have been satisfactorily answered; and how are they to be answered if that which requires to be answered is not spoken? Or how can the answer be known to be satisfactory, if the objectors have no opportunity of showing that it is unsatisfactory? If not the public, at least the philosophers and theologians who are to resolve the difficulties, must make themselves familiar with those difficulties in their most puzzling form; and this cannot be accomplished unless they are freely stated, and placed in the most advantageous light which they admit of. The Catholic Church has its own way of dealing with this embarrassing problem. It makes a broad separation between those who can be permitted to receive its doctrines on conviction, and those who must accept them on trust. Neither, indeed, are allowed any choice as to what they will accept; but the clergy, such at least as can be fully confided in, may admissibly and meritoriously make themselves acquainted with the arguments of opponents, in order to answer them, and may, therefore, read heretical books; the laity, not unless by special permission, hard to be obtained. This discipline recognises a knowledge of the enemy's case as beneficial to the teachers, but finds means, consistent with this, of denying it to the rest of the world: thus giving to the élite more mental culture, though not more mental freedom, than it allows to the mass. By this device it succeeds in obtaining the kind of mental superiority which its purposes require; for though culture without freedom never made a large and liberal mind, it can make a clever *nisi prius* advocate of a cause. But in countries professing Protestantism, this resource is denied; since Protestants hold, at least in theory, that the responsibility for the choice of a religion must be borne by each for himself and cannot be thrown off upon teachers. Besides, in the present state of the world, it is practically impossible that writings which are read by the instructed can be kept from the uninstructed. If the teachers of mankind are to be cognisant of all that they ought to know, everything must be free to be written and published without restraint.

If, however, the mischievous operation of the absence of free discussion, when the received opinions are true, were confined to leaving men ignorant of the grounds of those opinions, it might be thought that this, if an intellectual, is no moral evil, and does not affect the worth of the opinions, regarded in their influence on the character. The fact, however, is, that not only the grounds of the opinion are forgotten in the absence of discussion, but too often the meaning of the opinion itself. The words which convey it cease to suggest ideas, or suggest only a small portion of those they were originally employed to communicate. Instead of a vivid conception and a living belief, there remain only a few phrases retained by rote; or, if any part, the shell and husk only of the meaning is retained, the finer essence being lost. The great chapter in human history which this fact occupies and fills cannot be too earnestly studied and meditated on.

It is illustrated in the experience of almost all ethical doctrines and religious creeds. They are all full of meaning and vitality to those who originate them, and to the direct disciples of the originators. Their meaning continues to be felt in undiminished strength, and is perhaps brought out into even fuller consciousness, so long as the struggle lasts to give the doctrine or creed an ascendancy over other creeds. At last it either prevails, and becomes the general opinion, or its progress stops; it keeps possession of the ground it has gained, but ceases to spread further. When either of these results has become apparent, controversy on the subject flags, and gradually dies away. The doctrine has taken its place, if not as a received opinion, as one of the admitted sects or divisions of opinion: those who hold it have generally inherited, not adopted it; and conversion from one of these doctrines to another, being now an exceptional fact, occupies little place in the thoughts of their professors. Instead of being, as at first, constantly on the alert either to defend themselves against the world, or to bring the world over to them, they have subsided into acquiescence, and neither listen, when they can help it, to arguments against their creed, nor trouble dissentients (if there be such) with arguments in its favour. From this time may usually be dated the decline in the living power of the doctrine. We often hear the teachers of all creeds lamenting the difficulty of keeping up in the minds of believers a lively apprehension of the truth which they nominally recognise, so that it may penetrate the feelings, and acquire a real mastery over the conduct. No such difficulty is complained of while the creed is still fighting for its existence: even the weaker combatants then know and feel what they are fighting for, and the difference between it and other doctrines; and in that period of every creed's existence, not a few persons may be found, who have realized its fundamental principles in all the forms of thought, have weighed and considered them in all their important bearings, and have experienced the full effect on the character, which belief in that creed ought to produce in a mind thoroughly imbued with it. But when it has come to be an hereditary creed, and to be received passively, not actively—when the mind is no longer compelled, in the same degree as at first, to exercise its vital powers on the questions which its belief presents to it, there is a progressive tendency to forget all of the belief except the formularies, or to give it a dull and torpid assent, as if accepting it on trust dispensed with the necessity of realizing it in consciousness, or testing it by personal experience; until it almost ceases to connect itself at all with the inner life of the human being. Then are seen the cases, so frequent in this age of the world as almost to form the majority, in which the creed remains as it were outside the mind, incrusting and petrifying it against all other influences addressed to the higher parts of our nature; manifesting its power by not suffering any fresh and living conviction to get in, but itself doing nothing for the mind or heart, except standing sentinel over them to keep them vacant.

To what an extent doctrines intrinsically fitted to make the deepest impression upon the mind may remain in it as dead beliefs, without being ever realized in the imagination, the feelings, or the understanding, is exemplified by the manner in which the majority of believers hold the doctrines of Christianity. By Christianity I here mean what is accounted such by all churches and sects—the maxims and precepts contained in the New Testament. These are considered sacred, and accepted as laws, by all professing Christians. Yet it is scarcely too much to say that not one Christian in a thousand guides or tests his individual conduct by reference to those laws. The standard to which he does refer it, is the custom of his nation, his class, or his religious profession. He has thus, on the one hand, a collection of ethical maxims, which he believes to have been vouchsafed to him by infallible wisdom as rules for his government; and on the other, a set of every-day judgments and practices, which go a certain length with some of those maxims, not so great a length with others, stand in direct opposition to some, and are, on the whole, a compromise between the Christian creed and the interests and suggestions of worldly life. To the first of these standards he gives his homage; to the other his real allegiance. All Christians believe that the blessed are the poor and humble, and those who are ill-used by the world; that it is easier for a camel to pass through the eye of a needle than for a rich man to enter the kingdom of heaven; that they should judge not, lest they be judged; that they should swear not at all; that they should love their neighbour as themselves; that if one take their cloak, they should give him their coat also; that they should take no

thought for the morrow; that if they would be perfect, they should sell all that they have and give it to the poor. They are not insincere when they say that they believe these things. They do believe them, as people believe what they have always heard lauded and never discussed. But in the sense of that living belief which regulates conduct, they believe these doctrines just up to the point to which it is usual to act upon them. The doctrines in their integrity are serviceable to pelt adversaries with; and it is understood that they are to be put forward (when possible) as the reasons for whatever people do that they think laudable. But any one who reminded them that the maxims require an infinity of things which they never even think of doing, would gain nothing but to be classed among those very unpopular characters who affect to be better than other people. The doctrines have no hold on ordinary believers—are not a power in their minds. They have an habitual respect for the sound of them, but no feeling which spreads from the words to the things signified, and forces the mind to take *them* in, and make them conform to the formula. Whenever conduct is concerned, they look round for Mr. A and B to direct them how far to go in obeying Christ.

Now we may be well assured that the case was not thus, but far otherwise, with the early Christians. Had it been thus, Christianity never would have expanded from an obscure sect of the despised Hebrews into the religion of the Roman Empire. When their enemies said, "See how these Christians love one another" (a remark not likely to be made by anybody now), they assuredly had a much livelier feeling of the meaning of their creed than they have ever had since. And to this cause, probably, it is chiefly owing that Christianity now makes so little progress in extending its domain, and after eighteen centuries, is still nearly confined to Europeans and the descendants of Europeans. Even with the strictly religious, who are much in earnest about their doctrines, and attach a greater amount of meaning to many of them than people in general, it commonly happens that the part which is thus comparatively active in their minds is that which was made by Calvin, or Knox, or some such person much nearer in character to themselves. The sayings of Christ coexist passively in their minds, producing hardly any effect beyond what is caused by mere listening to words so amiable and bland. There are many reasons, doubtless, why doctrines which are the badge of a sect retain more of their vitality than those common to all recognised sects, and why more pains are taken by teachers to keep their meaning alive; but one reason certainly is, that the peculiar doctrines are more questioned, and have to be oftener defended against open gainsayers. Both teachers and learners go to sleep at their post, as soon as there is no enemy in the field.

The same thing holds true, generally speaking, of all traditional doctrines—those of prudence and knowledge of life, as well as of morals or religion. All languages and literatures are full of general observations on life, both as to what it is, and how to conduct oneself in it; observations which everybody knows, which everybody repeats, or hears with acquiescence, which are received as truisms, yet of which most people first truly learn the meaning, when experience, generally of a painful kind, has made it a reality to them. How often, when smarting under some unforeseen misfortune or disappointment, does a person call to mind some proverb or common saying, familiar to him all his life, the meaning of which, if he had ever before felt it as he does now, would have saved him from the calamity. There are indeed reasons for this, other than the absence of discussion: there are many truths of which the full meaning *cannot* be realized, until personal experience has brought it home. But much more of the meaning even of these would have been understood, and what was understood would have been far more deeply impressed on the mind, if the man had been accustomed to hear it argued *pro* and *con* by people who did understand it. The fatal tendency of mankind to leave off thinking about a thing when it is no longer doubtful is the cause of half their errors. A contemporary author has well spoken of "the deep slumber of a decided opinion."

But what! (it may be asked) Is the absence of unanimity an indispensable condition of true knowledge? Is it necessary that some part of mankind should persist in error, to enable any to realize the truth? Does a belief cease to be real and vital as soon as it is generally received—and is a proposition never thoroughly understood and felt unless some doubt of it remains? As soon as mankind have unanimously accepted a truth, does the truth perish within them? The highest aim and best result of improved intelligence, it has hitherto been thought, is to unite mankind more and more in the acknowledgment of all important truths: and does the intelligence only last as long as it has not achieved its object? Do the fruits of conquest perish by the very completeness of the victory?

I affirm no such thing. As mankind improve, the number of doctrines which are no longer disputed or doubted will be constantly on the increase: and the well-being of mankind may almost be measured by the number and gravity of the truths which have reached the point of being uncontested. The cessation, on one question after another, of serious controversy, is one of the necessary incidents of the consolidation of opinion; a consolidation as salutary in the case of true opinions, as it is dangerous and noxious when the opinions are erroneous. But though this gradual narrowing of the bounds of diversity of opinion is necessary in both senses of the term, being at once inevitable and indispensable, we are not therefore obliged to conclude that all its consequences must be beneficial. The loss of so important an aid to the intelligent and living apprehension of a truth, as is afforded by the necessity of explaining it to, or defending it against, opponents, though not sufficient to outweigh, is no trifling drawback from, the benefit of its universal recognition. Where this advantage can no longer be had, I confess I should like to see the teachers of mankind endeavouring to provide a substitute for it; some contrivance for making the difficulties of the question as present to the learner's consciousness, as if they were pressed upon him by a dissentient champion, eager for his conversion.

But instead of seeking contrivances for this purpose, they have lost those they formerly had. The Socratic dialectics, so magnificently exemplified in the dialogues of Plato, were a contrivance of this description. They were essentially a negative discussion of the great questions of philosophy and life, directed with consummate skill to the purpose of convincing any one who had merely adopted the commonplaces of received opinion, that he did not understand the subject—that he as yet attached no definite meaning to the doctrines he professed; in order that, becoming aware of his ignorance, he might be put in the way to attain a stable belief, resting on a clear apprehension both of the meaning of doctrines and of their evidence. The school disputations of the middle ages had a somewhat similar object. They were intended to make sure that the pupil understood his own opinion, and (by necessary correlation) the opinion opposed to it, and could enforce the grounds of the one and confute those of the other. These last-mentioned contests had indeed the incurable defect, that the premises appealed to were taken from authority, not from reason; and, as a discipline to the mind, they were in every respect inferior to the powerful dialectics which formed the intellects of the "*Socratici viri*";[1] but the modern mind owes far more to both than it is generally willing to admit, and the present modes of education contain nothing which in the smallest degree supplies the place either of the one or of the other. A person who derives all his instruction from teachers or books, even if he escape the besetting temptation of contenting himself with cram, is under no compulsion to hear both sides; accordingly it is far from a frequent accomplishment, even among thinkers, to know both sides; and the weakest part of what everybody says in defence of his opinion, is what he intends as a reply to antagonists. It is the fashion of the present time to disparage negative logic—that which points out weaknesses in theory or errors in practice, without establishing positive truths. Such negative criticism would indeed be poor enough as an ultimate result; but as a means to attaining any positive knowledge or conviction worthy the name, it cannot be valued too highly; and until people are again systematically

trained to it, there will be few great thinkers, and a low general average of intellect, in any but the mathematical and physical departments of speculation. On any other subject no one's opinions deserve the name of knowledge, except so far as he has either had forced upon him by others, or gone through of himself, the same mental process which would have been required of him in carrying on an active controversy with opponents. That, therefore, which when absent, it is so indispensable, but so difficult, to create, how worse than absurd is it to forego, when spontaneously offering itself! If there are any persons who contest a received opinion, or who will do so if law or opinion will let them, let us thank them for it, open our minds to listen to them, and rejoice that there is some one to do for us what we otherwise ought, if we have any regard for either the certainty or the vitality of our convictions, to do with much greater labour for ourselves.

It still remains to speak of one of the principal causes which make diversity of opinion advantageous, and will continue to do so until mankind shall have entered a stage of intellectual advancement which at present seems at an incalculable distance. We have hitherto considered only two possibilities: that the received opinion may be false, and some other opinion, consequently, true; or that, the received opinion being true, a conflict with the opposite error is essential to a clear apprehension and deep feeling of its truth. But there is a commoner case than either of these; when the conflicting doctrines, instead of being one true and the other false, share the truth between them; and the nonconforming opinion is needed to supply the remainder of the truth, of which the received doctrine embodies only a part. Popular opinions, on subjects not palpable to sense, are often true, but seldom or never the whole truth. They are a part of the truth; sometimes a greater, sometimes a smaller part, but exaggerated, distorted, and disjoined from the truths by which they ought to be accompanied and limited. Heretical opinions, on the other hand, are generally some of these suppressed and neglected truths, bursting the bonds which kept them down, and either seeking reconciliation with

---

[1] ["Socrates' men," or "Socrates' followers."]

the truth contained in the common opinion, or fronting it as enemies, and setting themselves up, with similar exclusiveness, as the whole truth. The latter case is hitherto the most frequent, as, in the human mind, one-sidedness has always been the rule, and many-sidedness the exception. Hence, even in revolutions of opinion, one part of the truth usually sets while another rises. Even progress, which ought to superadd, for the most part only substitutes, one partial and incomplete truth for another; improvement consisting chiefly in this, that the new fragment of truth is more wanted, more adapted to the needs of the time, than that which it displaces. Such being the partial character of prevailing opinions, even when resting on a true foundation, every opinion which embodies somewhat of the portion of truth which the common opinion omits, ought to be considered precious, with whatever amount of error and confusion that truth may be blended. No sober judge of human affairs will feel bound to be indignant because those who force on our notice truths which we should otherwise have overlooked, overlook some of those which we see. Rather, he will think that so long as popular truth is one-sided, it is more desirable than otherwise that unpopular truth should have one-sided asserters too; such being usually the most energetic, and the most likely to compel reluctant attention to the fragment of wisdom which they proclaim as if it were the whole....

In politics, again, it is almost a commonplace, that a party of order or stability, and a party of progress or reform, are both necessary elements of a healthy state of political life; until the one or the other shall have so enlarged its mental grasp as to be a party equally of order and of progress, knowing and distinguishing what is fit to be preserved from what ought to be swept away. Each of these modes of thinking derives its utility from the deficiencies of the other; but it is in a great measure the opposition of the other that keeps each within the limits of reason and sanity. Unless opinions favourable to democracy and to aristocracy, to property and to equality, to cooperation and to competition, to luxury and to abstinence, to sociality and

individuality, to liberty and discipline, and all the other standing antagonisms of practical life, are expressed with equal freedom, and enforced and defended with equal talent and energy, there is no chance of both elements obtaining their due; one scale is sure to go up, and the other down. Truth, in the great practical concerns of life, is so much a question of the reconciling and combining of opposites, that very few have minds sufficiently capacious and impartial to make the adjustment with an approach to correctness, and it has to be made by the rough process of a struggle between combatants fighting under hostile banners. On any of the great open questions just enumerated, if either of the two opinions has a better claim than the other, not merely to be tolerated, but to be encouraged and countenanced, it is the one which happens at the particular time and place to be in a minority. That is the opinion which, for the time being, represents the neglected interests, the side of human well-being which is in danger of obtaining less than its share. I am aware that there is not, in this country, any intolerance of differences of opinion on most of these topics. They are adduced to show, by admitted and multiplied examples, the universality of the fact, that only through diversity of opinion is there, in the existing state of human intellect, a chance of fair play to all sides of the truth. When there are persons to be found, who form an exception to the apparent unanimity of the world on any subject, even if the world is in the right, it is always probable that dissentients have something worth hearing to say for themselves, and that truth would lose something by their silence....

I do not pretend that the most unlimited use of the freedom of enunciating all possible opinions would put an end to the evils of religious or philosophical sectarianism. Every truth which men of narrow capacity are in earnest about, is sure to be asserted, inculcated, and in many ways even acted on, as if no other truth existed in the world, or at all events none that could limit or qualify the first. I acknowledge that the tendency of all opinions to become sectarian is not cured by the freest discussion, but is often heightened and exacerbated thereby; the truth which ought to have been, but was not, seen, being rejected all the more violently because proclaimed by persons regarded as opponents. But it is not on the impassioned partisan, it is on the calmer and more disinterested bystander, that this collision of opinions works its salutary effect. Not the violent conflict between parts of the truth, but the quiet suppression of half of it, is the formidable evil; there is always hope when people are forced to listen to both sides; it is when they attend only to one that errors harden into prejudices, and truth itself ceases to have the effect of truth, by being exaggerated into falsehood. And since there are few mental attributes more rare than that judicial faculty which can sit in intelligent judgment between two sides of a question, of which only one is represented by an advocate before it, truth has no chance but in proportion as every side of it, every opinion which embodies any fraction of the truth, not only finds advocates, but is so advocated as to be listened to.

We have now recognised the necessity to the mental well-being of mankind (on which all their other well-being depends) of freedom of opinion, and freedom of the expression of opinion, on four distinct grounds; which we will now briefly recapitulate.

First, if any opinion is compelled to silence, that opinion may, for aught we can certainly know, be true. To deny this is to assume our own infallibility.

Secondly, though the silenced opinion be an error, it may, and very commonly does, contain a portion of truth; and since the general or prevailing opinion on any subject is rarely or never the whole truth, it is only by the collision of adverse opinions that the remainder of the truth has any chance of being supplied.

Thirdly, even if the received opinion be not only true, but the whole truth; unless it is suffered to be, and actually is, vigorously and earnestly contested, it will, by most of those who receive it, be held in the manner of a prejudice, with little comprehension or feeling of its rational grounds. And not only this, but, fourthly, the meaning of the doctrine itself will be in danger of being lost, or enfeebled, and deprived of its vital effect on the character and conduct: the

dogma becoming a mere formal profession, inefficacious for good, but cumbering the ground, and preventing the growth of any real and heartfelt conviction, from reason or personal experience.

Before quitting the subject of freedom of opinion, it is fit to take some notice of those who say, that the free expression of all opinions should be permitted, on condition that the manner be temperate, and do not pass the bounds of fair discussion. Much might be said on the impossibility of fixing where these supposed bounds are to be placed; for if the test be offence to those whose opinion is attacked, I think experience testifies that this offence is given whenever the attack is telling and powerful, and that every opponent who pushes them hard, and whom they find it difficult to answer, appears to them, if he shows any strong feeling on the subject, an intemperate opponent. But this, though an important consideration in a practical point of view, merges in a more fundamental objection. Undoubtedly the manner of asserting an opinion, even though it be a true one, may be very objectionable, and may justly incur severe censure. But the principal offences of the kind are such as it is mostly impossible, unless by accidental self-betrayal, to bring home to conviction. The gravest of them is, to argue sophistically, to suppress facts or arguments, to misstate the elements of the case, or misrepresent the opposite opinion. But all this, even to the most aggravated degree, is so continually done in perfect good faith, by persons who are not considered, and in many other respects may not deserve to be considered, ignorant or incompetent, that it is rarely possible on adequate grounds conscientiously to stamp the misrepresentation as morally culpable; and still less could law presume to interfere with this kind of controversial misconduct. With regard to what is commonly meant by intemperate discussion, namely invective, sarcasm, personality, and the like, the denunciation of these weapons would deserve more sympathy if it were ever proposed to interdict them equally to both sides; but it is only desired to restrain the employment of them against the prevailing opinion: against the unprevailing they may not only be used without general disapproval, but will be likely to obtain for him who uses them the praise of honest zeal and righteous indignation. Yet whatever mischief arises from their use is greatest when they are employed against the comparatively defenceless; and whatever unfair advantage can be derived by any opinion from this mode of asserting it, accrues almost exclusively to received opinions. The worst offence of this kind which can be committed by a polemic, is to stigmatize those who hold the contrary opinion as bad and immoral men. To calumny of this sort, those who hold any unpopular opinion are peculiarly exposed, because they are in general few and uninfluential, and nobody but themselves feels much interested in seeing justice done them; but this weapon is, from the nature of the case, denied to those who attack a prevailing opinion: they can neither use it with safety to themselves, nor, if they could, would it do anything but recoil on their own cause. In general, opinions contrary to those commonly received can only obtain a hearing by studied moderation of language, and the most cautious avoidance of unnecessary offence, from which they hardly ever deviate even in a slight degree without losing ground: while unmeasured vituperation employed on the side of the prevailing opinion, really does deter people from professing contrary opinions, and from listening to those who profess them. For the interest, therefore, of truth and justice, it is far more important to restrain this employment of vituperative language than the other; and, for example, if it were necessary to choose, there would be much more need to discourage offensive attacks on infidelity, than on religion. It is, however, obvious that law and authority have no business with restraining either, while opinion ought, in every instance, to determine its verdict by the circumstances of the individual case; condemning every one, on whichever side of

the argument he places himself, in whose mode of advocacy either want of candour, or malignity, bigotry or intolerance of feeling manifest themselves; but not inferring these vices from the side which a person takes, though it be the contrary side of the question to our own: and giving merited honour to every one, whatever opinion he may hold, who has calmness to see and honesty to state what his opponents and their opinions really are, exaggerating nothing to their discredit, keeping nothing back which tells, or can be supposed to tell, in their favour. This is the real morality of public discussion: and if often violated, I am happy to think that there are many controversialists who to a great extent observe it, and a still greater number who conscientiously strive towards it.

DISCUSSION QUESTIONS

1. Mill anticipates the following objection to his defense of freedom of expression: some beliefs, true or not, are useful and so must not be challenged. How does Mill respond to this objection? Is his response successful? Why or why not?

2. Mill argues that even if the suppressed opinion were wholly false, it is still wrong to censor it. Explain Mill's argument. Is it a good argument?

3. Explain how Mill appeals to his utilitarianism to defend his view of freedom of expression. Does his defense succeed on utilitarian grounds? Explain.

38

Patrick Devlin, "Morals and the Criminal Law" (1960)

Patrick Devlin (1905–92) was a British jurist who served on the High Court of Justice and the Court of Appeals. After retiring from the Court, Devlin served as a judge for the International Labour Organization. In the following lecture, Devlin criticizes some of the underlying assumptions or principles expressed in the Wolfenden Report of 1957, i.e., that issues of private immorality should not be sanctioned, and, similarly, that popular conceptions of morality should not influence the law.

SOURCE

Devlin, Patrick. "The Enforcement of Morals," from *Proceedings of the British Academy* 45, London, pp. 129–51. Copyright © The British Academy 1960.

The Report of the Committee on Homosexual Offences and Prostitution, generally known as the Wolfenden Report,[1] is recognized to be an excellent study of two very difficult legal and social problems. But it has also a particular claim to the respect of those interested in jurisprudence; it does what law reformers so rarely do: it sets out clearly and carefully what in relation to its subjects it considers the function of the law to be. Statutory additions to the criminal law are too often made on the simple principle that "there ought to be a law against it." The greater part of the law relating to sexual offences is the creation of statute, and it is difficult to ascertain any logical relationship between it and the moral ideas which most of us uphold. Adultery, fornication, and prostitution are not, as the Report[2] points out, criminal offences: homosexuality between males is a criminal offence, but between females it is not. Incest was not an offence until it was declared so by statute only fifty years ago. Does the legislature select these offences haphazardly or are there some principles which can be used to determine what part of the moral law should be embodied in the criminal? There is, for example, being now considered

---

[1] [This report was issued in 1957 by a committee that was charged with making recommendations concerning possible changes in laws criminalizing both prostitution and homosexual conduct. The committee recommended that homosexual conduct between consenting adults no longer be criminal in Britain.]

[2] Para. 14.

a proposal to make A.I.D., that is, the practice of artificial insemination of a woman with the seed of a man who is not her husband, a criminal offence; if, as is usually the case, the woman is married, this is in substance, if not in form, adultery. Ought it to be made punishable when adultery is not? This sort of question is of practical importance, for a law that appears to be arbitrary and illogical, in the end and after the wave of moral indignation that has put it on the statute book subsides, forfeits respect. As a practical question it arises more frequently in the field of sexual morals than in any other, but there is no special answer to be found in that field. The inquiry must be general and fundamental. What is the connexion between crime and sin and to what extent, if at all, should the criminal law of England concern itself with the enforcement of morals and punish sin or immorality as such?

The statements of principle in the Wolfenden Report provide an admirable and modern starting-point for such an inquiry. In the course of my examination of them I shall find matter for criticism. If my criticisms are sound, it must not be imagined that they point to any shortcomings in the Report. Its authors were not, as I am trying to do, composing a paper on the jurisprudence of morality; they were evolving a working formula to use for reaching a number of practical conclusions. I do not intend to express any opinion one way or the other about these; that would be outside the scope of a lecture on jurisprudence. I am concerned only with general principles; the statement of these in the Report illuminates the entry into the subject and I hope that its authors will forgive me if I carry the lamp with me into places where it was not intended to go.

Early in the Report[1] the Committee put forward:

Our own formulation of the function of the criminal law so far as it concerns the subjects of this enquiry. In this field, its function, as we see it, is to preserve public order and decency, to protect the citizen from what is offensive or injurious, and to provide sufficient safeguards against exploitation and corruption of others, particularly those who are specially vulnerable because they are young, weak in body or mind, inexperienced, or in a state of special physical, official or economic dependence.

It is not, in our view, the function of the law to intervene in the private lives of citizens, or to seek to enforce any particular pattern of behaviour, further than is necessary to carry out the purposes we have outlined.

The Committee preface their most important recommendation[2]

that homosexual behaviour between consenting adults in private should no longer be a criminal offence, [by stating the argument[3]] which we believe to be decisive, namely, the importance which society and the law ought to give to individual freedom of choice and action in matters of private morality. Unless a deliberate attempt is to be made by society, acting through the agency of the law, to equate the sphere of crime with that of sin, there must remain a realm of private morality and immorality which is, in brief and crude terms, not the law's business. To say this is not to condone or encourage private immorality.

Similar statements of principle are set out in the chapters of the Report which deal with prostitution. No case can be sustained, the Report says, for attempting to make prostitution itself illegal.[4] The Committee refer to the general reasons already given and add, "We are agreed that private immorality should not be the concern of the criminal law except in the special circumstances therein

---

[1] Para. 13.

[2] Para. 62.

[3] Para. 61.

[4] Para. 224.

mentioned." They quote[1] with approval the report of the Street Offences Committee,[2] which says, "As a general proposition it will be universally accepted that the law is not concerned with private morals or with ethical sanctions." It will be observed that the emphasis is on private immorality. By this is meant immorality which is not offensive or injurious to the public in the ways defined or described in the first passage which I quoted. In other words, no act of immorality should be made a criminal offence unless it is accompanied by some other feature such as indecency, corruption, or exploitation. This is clearly brought out in relation to prostitution: "It is not the duty of the law to concern itself with immorality as such … it should confine itself to those activities which offend against public order and decency or expose the ordinary citizen to what is offensive or injurious."[3]

These statements of principle are naturally restricted to the subject-matter of the Report. But they are made in general terms and there seems to be no reason why, if they are valid, they should not be applied to the criminal law in general. They separate very decisively crime from sin, the divine law from the secular, and the moral from the criminal. They do not signify any lack of support for the law, moral or criminal, and they do not represent an attitude that can be called either religious or irreligious. There are many schools of thought among those who may think that morals are not the law's business. There is first of all the agnostic or freethinker. He does not of course disbelieve in morals, nor in sin if it be given the wider of the two meanings assigned to it in the *Oxford English Dictionary* where it is defined as "transgression against divine law or the principles of morality." He cannot accept the divine law; that does not mean that he might not view with suspicion any departure from moral principles that have for generations been accepted by the society in which he lives; but in the end he judges for himself. Then there is the deeply religious

person who feels that the criminal law is sometimes more of a hindrance than a help in the sphere of morality, and that the reform of the sinner—at any rate when he injures only himself—should be a spiritual rather than a temporal work. Then there is the man who without any strong feeling cannot see why, where there is freedom in religious belief, there should not logically be freedom in morality as well. All these are powerfully allied against the equating of crime with sin.

I must disclose at the outset that I have as a judge an interest in the result of the inquiry which I am seeking to make as a jurisprudent. As a judge who administers the criminal law and who has often to pass sentence in a criminal court, I should feel handicapped in my task if I thought that I was addressing an audience which had no sense of sin or which thought of crime as something quite different. Ought one, for example, in passing sentence upon a female abortionist to treat her simply as if she were an unlicensed midwife? If not, why not? But if so, is all the panoply of the law erected over a set of social regulations? I must admit that I begin with a feeling that a complete separation of crime from sin (I use the term throughout this lecture in the wider meaning) would not be good for the moral law and might be disastrous for the criminal. But can this sort of feeling be justified as a matter of jurisprudence? And if it be a right feeling, how should the relationship between the criminal and the moral law be stated? Is there a good theoretical basis for it, or is it just a practical working alliance, or is it a bit of both? That is the problem which I want to examine, and I shall begin by considering the standpoint of the strict logician. It can be supported by cogent arguments, some of which I believe to be unanswerable and which I put as follows.

Morals and religion are inextricably joined— the moral standards generally accepted in Western civilization being those belonging to Christianity. Outside Christendom other standards derive from other religions. None of these moral codes can claim any validity except by virtue of the religion on which it is based. Old Testament morals differ in some respects from New Testament morals.

---

[1] Para. 227.

[2] Cmd. 3231 (1928).

[3] Para. 257.

Even within Christianity there are differences. Some hold that contraception is an immoral practice and that a man who has carnal knowledge of another woman while his wife is alive is in all circumstances a fornicator; others, including most of the English-speaking world, deny both these propositions. Between the great religions of the world, of which Christianity is only one, there are much wider differences. It may or may not be right for the State to adopt one of these religions as the truth, to found itself upon its doctrines, and to deny to any of its citizens the liberty to practise any other. If it does, it is logical that it should use the secular law wherever it thinks it necessary to enforce the divine. If it does not, it is illogical that it should concern itself with morals as such. But if it leaves matters of religion to private judgement, it should logically leave matters of morals also. A State which refuses to enforce Christian beliefs has lost the right to enforce Christian morals.

If this view is sound, it means that the criminal law cannot justify any of its provisions by reference to the moral law. It cannot say, for example, that murder and theft are prohibited because they are immoral or sinful. The State must justify in some other way the punishments which it imposes on wrongdoers and a function for the criminal law independent of morals must be found. This is not difficult to do. The smooth functioning of society and the preservation of order require that a number of activities should be regulated. The rules that are made for that purpose and are enforced by the criminal law are often designed simply to achieve uniformity and convenience and rarely involve any choice between good and evil. Rules that impose a speed limit or prevent obstruction on the highway have nothing to do with morals. Since so much of the criminal law is composed of rules of this sort, why bring morals into it at all? Why not define the function of the criminal law in simple terms as the preservation of order and decency and the protection of the lives and property of citizens, and elaborate those terms in relation to any particular subject in the way in which it is done in the Wolfenden Report? The criminal law in carrying out these

objects will undoubtedly overlap the moral law. Crimes of violence are morally wrong and they are also offences against good order; therefore they offend against both laws. But this is simply because the two laws in pursuit of different objectives happen to cover the same area. Such is the argument.

Is the argument consistent or inconsistent with the fundamental principles of English criminal law as it exists today? That is the first way of testing it, though by no means a conclusive one. In the field of jurisprudence one is at liberty to overturn even fundamental conceptions if they are theoretically unsound. But to see how the argument fares under the existing law is a good starting-point.

It is true that for many centuries the criminal law was much concerned with keeping the peace and little, if at all, with sexual morals. But it would be wrong to infer from that that it had no moral content or that it would ever have tolerated the idea of a man being left to judge for himself in matters of morals. The criminal law of England has from the very first concerned itself with moral principles. A simple way of testing this point is to consider the attitude which the criminal law adopts towards consent.

Subject to certain exceptions inherent in the nature of particular crimes, the criminal law has never permitted consent of the victim to be used as a defence. In rape, for example, consent negatives an essential element. But consent of the victim is no defence to a charge of murder. It is not a defence to any form of assault that the victim thought his punishment well deserved and submitted to it; to make a good defence the accused must prove that the law gave him the right to chastise and that he exercised it reasonably. Likewise, the victim may not forgive the aggressor and require the prosecution to desist; the right to enter a *nolle prosequi* belongs to the Attorney-General alone.

Now, if the law existed for the protection of the individual, there would be no reason why he should avail himself of it if he did not want it. The reason why a man may not consent to the commission of an offence against himself beforehand or forgive it afterwards is because it is an offence against society. It is not that society is physically injured; that would be impossible. Nor need any individual be shocked, corrupted, or exploited; everything may be done in private. Nor can it be explained on the practical ground that a violent man is a potential danger to others in the community who have therefore a direct interest in his apprehension and punishment as being necessary to their own protection. That would be true of a man whom the victim is prepared to forgive but not of one who gets his consent first; a murderer who acts only upon the consent, and maybe the request, of his victim is no menace to others, but he does threaten one of the great moral principles upon which society is based, that is, the sanctity of human life. There is only one explanation of what has hitherto been accepted as the basis of the criminal law and that is that there are certain standards of behaviour or moral principles which society requires to be observed; and the breach of them is an offence not merely against the person who is injured but against society as a whole.

Thus, if the criminal law were to be reformed so as to eliminate from it everything that was not designed to preserve order and decency or to protect citizens (including the protection of youth from corruption), it would overturn a fundamental principle. It would also end a number of specific crimes. Euthanasia or the killing of another at his own request, suicide, attempted suicide and suicide pacts, duelling, abortion, incest between brother and sister, are all acts which can be done in private and without offence to others and need not involve the corruption or exploitation of others. Many people think that the law on some of these subjects is in need of reform, but no one hitherto has gone so far as to suggest that they should all be left outside the criminal law as matters of private morality. They can be brought within it only as a matter of moral principle. It must be remembered also that although there is much immorality that is not punished by the law, there is none that is condoned by the law. The law will not allow its processes to be used by those engaged in immorality of any sort. For example, a house may not be let for immoral purposes;

the lease is invalid and would not be enforced. But if what goes on inside there is a matter of private morality and not the law's business, why does the law inquire into it at all?

I think it is clear that the criminal law as we know it is based upon moral principle. In a number of crimes its function is simply to enforce a moral principle and nothing else. The law, both criminal and civil, claims to be able to speak about morality and immorality generally. Where does it get its authority to do this and how does it settle the moral principles which it enforces? Undoubtedly, as a matter of history, it derived both from Christian teaching. But I think that the strict logician is right when he says that the law can no longer rely on doctrines in which citizens are entitled to disbelieve. It is necessary therefore to look for some other source.

In jurisprudence, as I have said, everything is thrown open to discussion and, in the belief that they cover the whole field, I have framed three interrogatories addressed to myself to answer:

1. Has society the right to pass judgement at all on matters of morals? Ought there, in other words, to be a public morality, or are morals always a matter for private judgement?

2. If society has the right to pass judgement, has it also the right to use the weapon of the law to enforce it?

3. If so, ought it to use that weapon in all cases or only in some; and if only in some, on what principles should it distinguish?

I shall begin with the first interrogatory and consider what is meant by the right of society to pass a moral judgement, that is, a judgement about what is good and what is evil. The fact that a majority of people may disapprove of a practice does not of itself make it a matter for society as a whole. Nine men out of ten may disapprove of what the tenth man is doing and still say that it is not their business. There is a case for a collective judgement (as distinct from a large number of individual opinions which sensible people may even refrain from pronouncing at all if it is upon somebody else's private affairs) only if society is affected. Without a collective judgement there can be no case at all for intervention. Let me take as an illustration the Englishman's attitude to religion as it is now and as it has been in the past. His attitude now is that a man's religion is his private affair; he may think of another man's religion that it is right or wrong, true or untrue, but not that it is good or bad. In earlier times that was not so; a man was denied the right to practise what was thought of as heresy, and heresy was thought of as destructive of society.

The language used in the passages I have quoted from the Wolfenden Report suggests the view that there ought not to be a collective judgement about immorality *per se*. Is this what is meant by "private morality" and "individual freedom of choice and action"? Some people sincerely believe that homosexuality is neither immoral nor unnatural. Is the "freedom of choice and action" that is offered to the individual, freedom to decide for himself what is moral or immoral, society remaining neutral; or is it freedom to be immoral if he wants to be? The language of the Report may be open to question, but the conclusions at which the Committee arrive answer this question unambiguously. If society is not prepared to say that homosexuality is morally wrong, there would be no basis for a law protecting youth from "corruption" or punishing a man for living on the "immoral" earnings of a homosexual prostitute, as the Report recommends.[1] This attitude the Committee make even clearer when they come to deal with prostitution. In truth, the Report takes it for granted that there is in existence a public morality which condemns homosexuality and prostitution. What the Report seems to mean by private morality might perhaps be better described as private behaviour in matters of morals.

This view—that there is such a thing as public morality—can also be justified by *a priori* argument. What makes a society of any sort is community of ideas, not only political ideas but also ideas about the way its members should behave and govern their lives; these latter ideas are its morals. Every society has a moral structure as well as a political

one: or rather, since that might suggest two independent systems, I should say that the structure of every society is made up both of politics and morals. Take, for example, the institution of marriage. Whether a man should be allowed to take more than one wife is something about which every society has to make up its mind one way or the other. In England we believe in the Christian idea of marriage and therefore adopt monogamy as a moral principle. Consequently the Christian institution of marriage has become the basis of family life and so part of the structure of our society. It is there not because it is Christian. It has got there because it is Christian, but it remains there because it is built into the house in which we live and could not be removed without bringing it down. The great majority of those who live in this country accept it because it is the Christian idea of marriage and for them the only true one. But a non-Christian is bound by it, not because it is part of Christianity but because, rightly or wrongly, it has been adopted by the society in which he lives. It would be useless for him to stage a debate designed to prove that polygamy was theologically more correct and socially preferable; if he wants to live in the house, he must accept it as built in the way in which it is.

We see this more clearly if we think of ideas or institutions that are purely political. Society cannot tolerate rebellion; it will not allow argument about the rightness of the cause. Historians a century later may say that the rebels were right and the Government was wrong and a percipient and conscientious subject of the State may think so at the time. But it is not a matter which can be left to individual judgement.

The institution of marriage is a good example for my purpose because it bridges the division, if there is one, between politics and morals. Marriage is part of the structure of our society and it is also the basis of a moral code which condemns fornication and adultery.

The institution of marriage would be gravely threatened if individual judgements were permitted about the morality of adultery; on these points there must be a public morality. But public morality is

---

[1] Para. 76.

not to be confined to those moral principles which support institutions such as marriage. People do not think of monogamy as something which has to be supported because our society has chosen to organize itself upon it; they think of it as something that is good in itself and offering a good way of life and that it is for that reason that our society has adopted it. I return to the statement that I have already made, that society means a community of ideas; without shared ideas on politics, morals, and ethics no society can exist. Each one of us has ideas about what is good and what is evil; they cannot be kept private from the society in which we live. If men and women try to create a society in which there is no fundamental agreement about good and evil they will fail; if, having based it on common agreement, the agreement goes, the society will disintegrate. For society is not something that is kept together physically; it is held by the invisible bonds of common thought. If the bonds were too far relaxed the members would drift apart. A common morality is part of the bondage. The bondage is part of the price of society; and mankind, which needs society, must pay its price.

Common lawyers used to say that Christianity was part of the law of the land. That was never more than a piece of rhetoric as Lord Sumner said in *Bowman v. The Secular Society*.[1] What lay behind it was the notion which I have been seeking to expound, namely that morals—and up till a century or so ago no one thought it worth distinguishing between religion and morals—were necessary to the temporal order. In 1675 Chief Justice Hale said, "To say that religion is a cheat is to dissolve all those obligations whereby civil society is preserved."[2] In 1797 Mr. Justice Ashurst said of blasphemy that it was "not only an offence against God but against all law and government from its tendency to dissolve all the bonds and obligations of civil society."[3] By 1908 Mr. Justice Phillimore was able to say, "A man is free to think, to speak and to teach what he pleases as to religious matters, but not as to morals."[4]

You may think that I have taken far too long in contending that there is such a thing as public morality, a proposition which most people would readily accept, and may have left myself too little time to discuss the next question which to many minds may cause greater difficulty: to what extent should society use the law to enforce its moral judgements? But I believe that the answer to the first question determines the way in which the second should be approached and may indeed very nearly dictate the answer to the second question. If society has no right to make judgements on morals, the law must find some special justification for entering the field of morality: if homosexuality and prostitution are not in themselves wrong, then the onus is very clearly on the lawgiver who wants to frame a law against certain aspects of them to justify the exceptional treatment. But if society has the right to make a judgement and has it on the basis that a recognized morality is as necessary to society as, say, a recognized government, then society may use the law to preserve morality in the same way as it uses it to safeguard anything else that is essential to its existence. If therefore the first proposition is securely established with all its implications, society has a *prima facie* right to legislate against immorality as such.

The Wolfenden Report, notwithstanding that it seems to admit the right of society to condemn homosexuality and prostitution as immoral, requires special circumstances to be shown to justify the intervention of the law. I think that this is wrong in principle and that any attempt to approach my second interrogatory on these lines is bound to break down. I think that the attempt by the Committee does break down and that this is shown by the fact that it has to define or describe its special circumstances so widely that they can be supported only if it is accepted that the law *is* concerned with immorality as such.

The widest of the special circumstances are described as the provision of "sufficient safeguards

[1] (1917), A.C. 406, at 457.

[2] *R. v. Williams*, 26 St. Tr. 653, at 715.

[3] *Taylor's Case*, I Vent. 293.

[4] *R. v. Boulter*, 72 J.P. 188.

against exploitation and corruption of others, particularly those who are specially vulnerable because they are young, weak in body or mind, inexperienced, or in a state of special physical, official or economic dependence."[1] The corruption of youth is a well-recognized ground for intervention by the State and for the purpose of any legislation the young can easily be defined. But if similar protection were to be extended to every other citizen, there would be no limit to the reach of the law. The "corruption and exploitation of others" is so wide that it could be used to cover any sort of immorality which involves, as most do, the cooperation of another person. Even if the phrase is taken as limited to the categories that are particularized as "specially vulnerable," it is so elastic as to be practically no restriction. This is not merely a matter of words. For if the words used are stretched almost beyond breaking-point, they still are not wide enough to cover the recommendations which the Committee make about prostitution.

Prostitution is not in itself illegal and the Committee do not think that it ought to be made so.[2] If prostitution is private immorality and not the law's business, what concern has the law with the ponce or the brothel-keeper or the householder who permits habitual prostitution? The Report recommends that the laws which make these activities criminal offences should be maintained or strengthened and brings them (so far as it goes into principle; with regard to brothels it says simply that the law rightly frowns on them) under the head of exploitation. There may be cases of exploitation in this trade, as there are or used to be in many others, but in general a ponce exploits a prostitute no more than an impresario exploits an actress. The Report finds that "the great majority of prostitutes are women whose psychological makeup is such that they choose this life because they find in it a style of living which is to them easier, freer and more profitable than would be provided by any other occupation.... In the main the association

between prostitute and ponce is voluntary and operates to mutual advantage."[3] The Committee would agree that this could not be called exploitation in the ordinary sense. They say, "It is in our view an over-simplification to think that those who live on the earnings of prostitution are exploiting the prostitute as such. What they are really exploiting is the whole complex of the relationship between prostitute and customer; they are, in effect, exploiting the human weaknesses which cause the customer to seek the prostitute and the prostitute to meet the demand."[4]

All sexual immorality involves the exploitation of human weaknesses. The prostitute exploits the lust of her customers and the customer the moral weakness of the prostitute. If the exploitation of human weaknesses is considered to create a special circumstance, there is virtually no field of morality which can be defined in such a way as to exclude the law.

I think, therefore, that it is not possible to set theoretical limits to the power of the State to legislate against immorality. It is not possible to settle in advance exceptions to the general rule or to define inflexibly areas of morality into which the law is in no circumstances to be allowed to enter. Society is entitled by means of its laws to protect itself from dangers, whether from within or without. Here again I think that the political parallel is legitimate. The law of treason is directed against aiding the king's enemies and against sedition from within. The justification for this is that established government is necessary for the existence of society and therefore its safety against violent overthrow must be secured. But an established morality is as necessary as good government to the welfare of society. Societies disintegrate from within more frequently than they are broken up by external pressures. There is disintegration when no common morality is observed and history shows that the loosening of moral bonds is often the first stage of disintegration, so that society is justified in taking the same steps to preserve its moral code as it does to preserve its government

[1] Para. 13.
[2] Paras. 224, 285, and 318.
[3] Para. 223.
[4] Para. 306.

UNIT II: D. The Enforcement of Morality

and other essential institutions. The suppression of vice is as much the law's business as the suppression of subversive activities; it is no more possible to define a sphere of private morality than it is to define one of private subversive activity. It is wrong to talk of private morality or of the law not being concerned with immorality as such or to try to set rigid bounds to the part which the law may play in the suppression of vice. There are no theoretical limits to the power of the State to legislate against treason and sedition, and likewise I think there can be no theoretical limits to legislation against immorality. You may argue that if a man's sins affect only himself it cannot be the concern of society. If he chooses to get drunk every night in the privacy of his own home, is any one except himself the worse for it? But suppose a quarter or a half of the population got drunk every night, what sort of society would it be? You cannot set a theoretical limit to the number of people who can get drunk before society is entitled to legislate against drunkenness. The same may be said of gambling. The Royal Commission on Betting, Lotteries, and Gaming took as their test the character of the citizen as a member of society. They said: "Our concern with the ethical significance of gambling is confined to the effect which it may have on the character of the gambler as a member of society. If we were convinced that whatever the degree of gambling this effect must be harmful we should be inclined to think that it was the duty of the state to restrict gambling to the greatest extent practicable."[1]

In what circumstances the State should exercise its power is the third of the interrogatories I have framed. But before I get to it I must raise a point which might have been brought up in any one of the three. How are the moral judgements of society to be ascertained? By leaving it until now, I can ask it in the more limited form that is now sufficient for my purpose. How is the law-maker to ascertain the moral judgements of society? It is surely not enough that they should be reached by the opinion of the majority; it would be too much to require the individual assent of every citizen. English law

has evolved and regularly uses a standard which does not depend on the counting of heads. It is that of the reasonable man. He is not to be confused with the rational man. He is not expected to reason about anything and his judgement may be largely a matter of feeling. It is the viewpoint of the man in the street—or to use an archaism familiar to all lawyers—the man in the Clapham omnibus. He might also be called the right-minded man. For my purpose I should like to call him the man in the jury box, for the moral judgement of society must be something about which any twelve men or women drawn at random might after discussion be expected to be unanimous. This was the standard the judges applied in the days before Parliament was as active as it is now and when they laid down rules of public policy. They did not think of themselves as making law but simply as stating principles which every right-minded person would accept as valid. It is what Pollock called "practical morality," which is based not on theological or philosophical foundations but "in the mass of continuous experience half-consciously or unconsciously accumulated and embodied in the morality of common sense." He called it also "a certain way of thinking on questions of morality which we expect to find in a reasonable civilized man or a reasonable Englishman, taken at random."[2]

Immorality then, for the purpose of the law, is what every right-minded person is presumed to consider to be immoral. Any immorality is capable of affecting society injuriously and in effect to a greater or lesser extent it usually does; this is what gives the law its *locus standi*. It cannot be shut out. But—and this brings me to the third question— the individual has a *locus standi* too; he cannot be expected to surrender to the judgement of society the whole conduct of his life. It is the old and familiar question of striking a balance between the rights and interests of society and those of the individual. This is something which the law is constantly doing in matters large and small. To take a very

---

[1] (1951) Cmd. 8190, para. 159.

[2] *Essays in Jurisprudence and Ethics* (Macmillan, 1882), pp. 2, 78, and 353.

down-to-earth example, let me consider the right of the individual whose house adjoins the highway to have access to it; that means in these days the right to have vehicles stationary in the highway, sometimes for a considerable time if there is a lot of loading or unloading. There are many cases in which the courts have had to balance the private right of access against the public right to use the highway without obstruction. It cannot be done by carving up the highway into public and private areas. It is done by recognizing that each have rights over the whole; that if each were to exercise their rights to the full, they would come into conflict; and therefore that the rights of each must be curtailed so as to ensure as far as possible that the essential needs of each are safeguarded.

I do not think that one can talk sensibly of a public and private morality any more than one can of a public or private highway. Morality is a sphere in which there is a public interest and a private interest, often in conflict, and the problem is to reconcile the two. This does not mean that it is impossible to put forward any general statements about how in our society the balance ought to be struck. Such statements cannot of their nature be rigid or precise; they would not be designed to circumscribe the operation of the lawmaking power but to guide those who have to apply it. While every decision which a court of law makes when it balances the public against the private interest is an *ad hoc* decision, the cases contain statements of principle to which the court should have regard when it reaches its decision. In the same way it is possible to make general statements of principle which it may be thought the legislature should bear in mind when it is considering the enactment of laws enforcing morals.

I believe that most people would agree upon the chief of these elastic principles. There must be toleration of the maximum individual freedom that is consistent with the integrity of society. It cannot be said that this is a principle that runs all through the criminal law. Much of the criminal law that is regulatory in character—the part of it that deals with *malum prohibitum* rather than *malum in se*— is based upon the opposite principle, that is, that the choice of the individual must give way to the convenience of the many. But in all matters of conscience the principle I have stated is generally held to prevail. It is not confined to thought and speech; it extends to action, as is shown by the recognition of the right to conscientious objection in wartime; this example shows also that conscience will be respected even in times of national danger. The principle appears to me to be peculiarly appropriate to all questions of morals. Nothing should be punished by the law that does not lie beyond the limits of tolerance. It is not nearly enough to say that a majority dislike a practice; there must be a real feeling of reprobation. Those who are dissatisfied with the present law on homosexuality often say that the opponents of reform are swayed simply by disgust. If that were so it would be wrong, but I do not think one can ignore disgust if it is deeply felt and not manufactured. Its presence is a good indication that the bounds of toleration are being reached. Not everything is to be tolerated. No society can do without intolerance, indignation, and disgust; they are the forces behind the moral law, and indeed it can be argued that if they or something like them are not present, the feelings of society cannot be weighty enough to deprive the individual of freedom of choice. I suppose that there is hardly anyone nowadays who would not be disgusted by the thought of deliberate cruelty to animals. No one proposes to relegate that or any other form of sadism to the realm of private morality or to allow it to be practised in public or in private. It would be possible no doubt to point out that until a comparatively short while ago nobody thought very much of cruelty to animals and also that pity and kindliness and the unwillingness to inflict pain are virtues more generally esteemed now than they have ever been in the past. But matters of this sort are not determined by rational argument. Every moral judgement, unless it claims a divine source, is simply a feeling that no right-minded man could behave in any other way without admitting that he was doing wrong. It is the power of a common sense and not the power of reason that is behind the judgements of society. But before a society can put a practice beyond the limits of tolerance there must be a deliberate judgement that the practice is injurious to society. There is, for example, a general abhorrence of homosexuality. We should ask ourselves in the first instance whether, looking at it calmly and dispassionately, we regard it as a vice so abominable that its mere presence is an offence. If that is the genuine feeling of the society in which we live, I do not see how society can be denied the right to eradicate it. Our feeling may not be so intense as that. We may feel about it that, if confined, it is tolerable, but that if it spread it might be gravely injurious; it is in this way that most societies look upon fornication, seeing it as a natural weakness which must be kept within bounds but which cannot be rooted out. It becomes then a question of balance, the danger to society in one scale and the extent of the restriction in the other. On this sort of point the value of an investigation by such a body as the Wolfenden Committee and of its conclusions is manifest.

The limits of tolerance shift. This is supplementary to what I have been saying but of sufficient importance in itself to deserve statement as a separate principle which law-makers have to bear in mind. I suppose that moral standards do not shift; so far as they come from divine revelation they do not, and I am willing to assume that the moral judgements made by a society always remain good for that society. But the extent to which society will tolerate—I mean tolerate, not approve—departures from moral standards varies from generation to generation. It may be that over-all tolerance is always increasing. The pressure of the human mind, always seeking greater freedom of thought, is outwards against the bonds of society forcing their gradual relaxation. It may be that history is a tale of contraction and expansion and that all developed societies are on their way to dissolution. I must not speak of things I do not know; and anyway as a practical matter no society is willing to make provision for its own decay. I return therefore to the simple and observable fact that in matters of morals the limits of tolerance shift. Laws, especially those which are based on morals, are less easily moved. It follows as another good working principle that in any new matter of morals

the law should be slow to act. By the next generation the swell of indignation may have abated and the law be left without the strong backing which it needs. But it is then difficult to alter the law without giving the impression that moral judgement is being weakened. This is now one of the factors that is strongly militating against any alteration to the law on homosexuality.

A third elastic principle must be advanced more tentatively. It is that as far as possible privacy should be respected. This is not an idea that has ever been made explicit in the criminal law. Acts or words done or said in public or in private are all brought within its scope without distinction in principle. But there goes with this a strong reluctance on the part of judges and legislators to sanction invasions of privacy in the detection of crime. The police have no more right to trespass than the ordinary citizen has; there is no general right of search; to this extent an Englishman's home is still his castle. The Government is extremely careful in the exercise even of those powers which it claims to be undisputed. Telephone tapping and interference with the mails afford a good illustration of this. A Committee of three Privy Councillors who recently inquired[1] into these activities found that the Home Secretary and his predecessors had already formulated strict rules governing the exercise of these powers and the Committee were able to recommend that they should be continued to be exercised substantially on the same terms. But they reported that the power was "regarded with general disfavour."

This indicates a general sentiment that the right to privacy is something to be put in the balance against the enforcement of the law. Ought the same sort of consideration to play any part in the formation of the law? Clearly only in a very limited number of cases. When the help of the law is invoked by an injured citizen, privacy must be irrelevant; the individual cannot ask that his right to privacy should be measured against injury criminally done to another. But when all who are involved in the deed are consenting parties and the injury is done

---

[1] (1957) Cmd. 283.

to morals, the public interest in the moral order can be balanced against the claims of privacy. The restriction on police powers of investigation goes further than the affording of a parallel; it means that the detection of crime committed in private and when there is no complaint is bound to be rather haphazard and this is an additional reason for moderation. These considerations do not justify the exclusion of all private immorality from the scope of the law. I think that, as I have already suggested, the test of "private behaviour" should be substituted for "private morality" and the influence of the factor should be reduced from that of a definite limitation to that of a matter to be taken into account. Since the gravity of the crime is also a proper consideration, a distinction might well be made in the case of homosexuality between the lesser acts of indecency and the full offence, which on the principles of the Wolfenden Report it would be illogical to do.

The last and the biggest thing to be remembered is that the law is concerned with the minimum and not with the maximum; there is much in the Sermon on the Mount that would be out of place in the Ten Commandments. We all recognize the gap between the moral law and the law of the land. No man is worth much who regulates his conduct with the sole object of escaping punishment, and every worthy society sets for its members standards which are above those of the law. We recognize the existence of such higher standards when we use expressions such as "moral obligation" and "morally bound." The distinction was well put in the judgement of African elders in a family dispute: "We have power to make you divide the crops, for this is our law, and we will see this is done. But we have not power to make you behave like an upright man."[1]

It can only be because this point is so obvious that it is so frequently ignored. Discussion among law-makers, both professional and amateur, is too often limited to what is right or wrong and good or bad for society. There is a failure to keep separate the two questions I have earlier posed: the question of society's right to pass a moral judgement and the question of whether the arm of the law should be used to enforce the judgement. The criminal law is not a statement of how people ought to behave; it is a statement of what will happen to them if they do not behave; good citizens are not expected to come within reach of it or to set their sights by it, and every enactment should be framed accordingly.

The arm of the law is an instrument to be used by society, and the decision about what particular cases it should be used in is essentially a practical one. Since it is an instrument, it is wise before deciding to use it to have regard to the tools with which it can be fitted and to the machinery which operates it. Its tools are fines, imprisonment, or lesser forms of supervision (such as Borstal[2] and probation) and—not to be ignored—the degradation that often follows upon the publication of the crime. Are any of these suited to the job of dealing with sexual immorality? The fact that there is so much immorality which has never been brought within the law shows that there can be no general rule. It is a matter for decision in each case; but in the case of homosexuality the Wolfenden Report rightly has regard to the views of those who are experienced in dealing with this sort of crime and to those of the clergy who are the natural guardians of public morals.

The machinery which sets the criminal law in motion ends with the verdict and the sentence; and a verdict is given either by magistrates or by a jury. As a general rule, whenever a crime is sufficiently serious to justify a maximum punishment of more than three months, the accused has the right to the verdict of a jury. The result is that magistrates administer mostly what I have called the regulatory part of the law. They deal extensively with drunkenness, gambling, and prostitution, which are matters of morals or close to them, but not with any of the graver moral offences. They are more responsive than juries to the ideas of the legislature; it may

---

[1] A case in the Saa-Katengo Kuta at Lialiu, August 1942, quoted in *The Judicial Process among the Barotse of Northern Rhodesia* by Max Gluckman (Manchester University Press, 1955), p. 172.

[2] [A type of prison for youth in Britain.]

not be accidental that the Wolfenden Report, in recommending increased penalties for solicitation, did not go above the limit of three months. Juries tend to dilute the decrees of Parliament with their own ideas of what should be punishable. Their province of course is fact and not law, and I do not mean that they often deliberately disregard the law. But if they think it is too stringent, they sometimes take a very merciful view of the facts. Let me take one example out of many that could be given. It is an offence to have carnal knowledge of a girl under the age of sixteen years. Consent on her part is no defence; if she did not consent, it would of course amount to rape. The law makes special provision for the situation when a boy and girl are near in age. If a man under twenty-four can prove that he had reasonable cause to believe that the girl was over the age of sixteen years, he has a good defence. The law regards the offence as sufficiently serious to make it one that is triable only by a judge at assizes. "Reasonable cause" means not merely that the boy honestly believed that the girl was over sixteen but also that he must have had reasonable grounds for his belief. In theory it ought not to be an easy defence to make out but in fact it is extremely rare for anyone who advances it to be convicted. The fact is that the girl is often as much to blame as the boy. The object of the law, as judges repeatedly tell juries, is to protect young girls against themselves; but juries are not impressed.

The part that the jury plays in the enforcement of the criminal law, the fact that no grave offence against morals is punishable without their verdict, these are of great importance in relation to the statements of principle that I have been making. They turn what might otherwise be pure exhortation to the legislature into something like rules that the law-makers cannot safely ignore. The man in the jury box is not just an expression; he is an active reality. It will not in the long run work to make laws about morality that are not acceptable to him.

This then is how I believe my third interrogatory should be answered—not by the formulation of hard and fast rules, but by a judgement in each case taking into account the sort of factors I have

been mentioning. The line that divides the criminal law from the moral is not determinable by the application of any clear-cut principle. It is like a line that divides land and sea, a coastline of irregularities and indentations. There are gaps and promontories, such as adultery and fornication, which the law has for centuries left substantially untouched. Adultery of the sort that breaks up marriage seems to me to be just as harmful to the social fabric as homosexuality or bigamy. The only ground for putting it outside the criminal law is that a law which made it a crime would be too difficult to enforce; it is too generally regarded as a human weakness not suitably punished by imprisonment. All that the law can do with fornication is to act against its worst manifestations; there is a general abhorrence of the commercialization of vice, and that sentiment gives strength to the law against brothels and immoral earnings. There is no logic to be found in this. The boundary between the criminal law and the moral law is fixed by balancing in the case of each particular crime the pros and cons of legal enforcement in accordance with the sort of considerations I have been outlining. The fact that adultery, fornication, and lesbianism are untouched by the criminal law does not prove that homosexuality ought not to be touched. The error of jurisprudence in the Wolfenden Report is caused by the search for some single principle to explain the division between crime and sin. The Report finds it in the principle that the criminal law exists for the protection of individuals; on this principle fornication in private between consenting adults is outside the law and thus it becomes logically indefensible to bring homosexuality between consenting adults in private within it. But the true principle is that the law exists for the protection of society. It does not discharge its function by protecting the individual from injury, annoyance, corruption, and exploitation; the law must protect also the institutions and the community of ideas, political and moral, without which people cannot live together. Society cannot ignore the morality of the individual any more than it can his loyalty; it flourishes on both and without either it dies.

I have said that the morals which underlie the law must be derived from the sense of right and wrong which resides in the community as a whole; it does not matter whence the community of thought comes, whether from one body of doctrine or another or from the knowledge of good and evil which no man is without. If the reasonable man believes that a practice is immoral and believes also—no matter whether the belief is right or wrong, so be it that it is honest and dispassionate—that no right-minded member of his society could think otherwise, then for the purpose of the law it is immoral. This, you may say, makes immorality a question of fact, what the law would consider as self-evident fact no doubt, but still with no higher authority than any other doctrine of public policy. I think that that is so, and indeed the law does not distinguish between an act that is immoral and one that is contrary to public policy. But the law has never yet had occasion to inquire into the differences between Christian morals and those which every right-minded member of society is expected to hold. The inquiry would, I believe, be academic. Moralists would find differences; indeed they would find them between different branches of the Christian faith on subjects such as divorce and birth-control. But for the purpose of the limited entry which the law makes into the field of morals, there is no practical difference. It seems to me therefore that the free-thinker and the non-Christian can accept, without offence to his convictions, the fact that Christian morals are the basis of the criminal law and that he can recognize, also without taking offence, that without the support of the churches the moral order, which has its origin in and takes its strength from Christian beliefs, would collapse.

This brings me back in the end to a question I posed at the beginning. What is the relationship between crime and sin, between the Church and the Law? I do not think that you can equate crime with sin. The divine law and the secular have been disunited, but they are brought together again by the need which each has for the other. It is not my function to emphasize the Church's need of the secular law; it can be put tersely by saying that you cannot have a ceiling without a floor. I am very clear about the law's need for the Church. I have spoken of the criminal law as dealing with the minimum standards of human conduct and the moral law with the maximum. The instrument of the criminal law is punishment; those of the moral law are teaching, training, and exhortation. If the whole dead weight of sin were ever to be allowed to fall upon the law, it could not take the strain. If at any point there is a lack of clear and convincing moral teaching, the administration of the law suffers. Let me take as an illustration of this the law on abortion. I believe that a great many people nowadays do not understand why abortion is wrong. If it is right to prevent conception, at what point does it become sinful to prevent birth and why? I doubt if anyone who has not had a theological training would give a satisfactory answer to that question. Many people regard abortion as the next step when by accident birth-control has failed; and many more people are deterred from abortion not because they think it sinful or illegal but because of the difficulty which illegality puts in the way of obtaining it. The law is powerless to deal with abortion *per se*; unless a tragedy occurs or a "professional" abortionist is involved— the parallel between the "professional" in abortions and the "professional" in fornication is quite close—it has to leave it alone. Without one or other of these features the crime is rarely detected; and when detected, the plea *ad misericordiam* is often too strong. The "professional" abortionist is usually the unskilled person who for a small reward helps girls in trouble; the man and the girl involved are essential witnesses for the prosecution and therefore go free; the paid abortionist generally receives a very severe sentence, much more severe than that usually given to the paid assistant in immorality, such as the ponce or the brothel keeper. The reason is because unskilled abortion endangers life. In a case in 1949[1] Lord Chief Justice Goddard said, "It is because the unskilful attentions of ignorant people in cases of this kind often result in death that attempts to produce abortion are regarded by the law as very serious offences." This gives the law

----

[1] *R. v. Tate, The Times,* 22 June 1949.

a twist which disassociates it from morality and, I think, to some extent from sound sense. The act is being punished because it is dangerous, and it is dangerous largely because it is illegal and therefore performed only by the unskilled.

The object of what I have said is not to criticize theology or law in relation to abortion. That is a large subject and beyond my present scope. It is to show what happens to the law in matters of morality about which the community as a whole is not deeply imbued with a sense of sin; the law sags under a weight which it is not constructed to bear and may become permanently warped.

I return now to the main thread of my argument and summarize it. Society cannot live without morals. Its morals are those standards of conduct which the reasonable man approves. A rational man, who is also a good man, may have other standards. If he has no standards at all he is not a good man and need not be further considered. If he has standards, they may be very different; he may, for example, not disapprove of homosexuality or abortion. In that case he will not share in the common morality; but

that should not make him deny that it is a social necessity. A rebel may be rational in thinking that he is right but he is irrational if he thinks that society can leave him free to rebel.

A man who concedes that morality is necessary to society must support the use of those instruments without which morality cannot be maintained. The two instruments are those of teaching, which is doctrine, and of enforcement, which is the law. If morals could be taught simply on the basis that they are necessary to society, there would be no social need for religion; it could be left as a purely personal affair. But morality cannot be taught in that way. Loyalty is not taught in that way either. No society has yet solved the problem of how to teach morality without religion. So the law must base itself on Christian morals and to the limit of its ability enforce them, not simply because they are the morals of most of us, nor simply because they are the morals which are taught by the established Church—on these points the law recognizes the right to dissent—but for the compelling reason that without the help of Christian teaching the law will fail.

DISCUSSION QUESTIONS

1. Devlin asserts that "society means a community of ideas; without shared ideas on politics, morals, and ethics no society can exist." Why does Devlin think this? Do you agree?

2. Devlin thinks that a society must have a "fundamental agreement about good and evil" as a cementing bond of sorts. If he is right, what exactly do you think our society agrees on?

3. In Devlin's view, what condition(s) must be satisfied if a society is to legitimately exercise its right to pass judgment on moral

matters? Should we interpret this merely as a necessary condition that must be met, or is it a sufficient condition?

4. Devlin refers to the "reasonable man" as he attempts to explain how the specific moral judgments of a society are to be ascertained. Explain this concept and critically evaluate.

5. How does Devlin define the term "immorality"? Do you find his definition acceptable? Why or why not?

6. Under what circumstances do you think we should not be tolerant of alternative moralities and lifestyles? How do you think Devlin would respond to this question?

39

Joel Feinberg, selection from *Offense to Others* (1988)

Joel Feinberg (1926–2004) was a social and political philosopher who wrote extensively on topics concerning the ways in which government may legitimately interfere in the lives of, or restrict the liberty of, its citizens. In this selection, Feinberg considers whether statutes attempting to prohibit offensive behavior can ever be defensible. Just as various "harm principles" have been suggested as means by which we can justify the restriction of individual liberty with the goal of preventing harm, so too might we wonder whether an "offense principle" can be accepted that would be designed to restrict offensive behavior.

SOURCE

Feinberg, Joel. *Offense to Others: The Moral Limits of the Criminal Law*, Volume 2, by Joel Feinberg et al. Copyright © 1988 by Oxford University Press, Inc. Reprinted by permission of Oxford University Press, Inc.

I. Offensive Nuisances

1. Disclaimers: The Relative Triviality of Mere Offense

Passing annoyance, disappointment, disgust, embarrassment, and various other disliked conditions such as fear, anxiety, and minor ("harmless") aches and pains, are not in themselves necessarily harmful. Consequently, no matter how the harm principle is mediated, it will not certify as legitimate those interferences with the liberty of some citizens that are made for the sole purpose of preventing such unpleasant states in others. For convenience I will use the word "offense" to cover the whole miscellany of universally disliked mental states … and not merely that species of the wider genus that are offensive in a strict and proper sense. If the law is justified, then, in using its coercive methods to protect people from mere offense, it must be by virtue of a separate and distinct legitimizing principle, which we can label "the offense principle" and formulate as follows: *It is always a good reason in support of a proposed criminal prohibition that it would probably be an effective way of preventing serious offense (as opposed to injury or harm) to persons other than the actor, and that it is probably a necessary means to that end* (i.e., there is probably no other means that is equally effective at no greater cost to the other values). The principle asserts, in effect, that the prevention of offensive conduct is properly the state's business.

Like the word "harm," the word "offense" has both a general and a specifically normative sense, the former including in its reference any or all of a miscellany of disliked mental states (disgust, shame, hurt, anxiety, etc.), and the latter referring to those states only when caused by the wrongful (right-violating) conduct of others. Only the latter sense—wrongful offense—is intended in the offense principle as we shall understand it. In this respect there is a parallel with the harm principle. We can also use the verb "to offend" meaning "to cause another to experience a mental state of a universally disliked kind (e.g., disgust, shame). The offense principle then cites the need to prevent some people from *wrongfully offending* (offending and wronging) others as a reason for coercive legislation. Finally, the word "offense" in the strict and proper sense it bears in ordinary language is specific in a different way. Whereas "offense" in the sense of the offense principle specifies an objective condition—the unpleasant mental state must be caused by conduct that really is wrongful— "offense" in the strict sense of ordinary language specifies a subjective condition—the offending act must be taken by the offended person to wrong him whether in fact it does or not. In the strict and narrow sense, I am offended (or "take offense") when (a) I suffer a disliked state, and (b) I attribute that state to the wrongful conduct of another, and (c) I *resent* the other for his role in causing me to be in the state. The sense of grievance against the other or resentment of him for wronging me in this way is a phenomenological component of the unpleasant experience itself, an element that actually re-enforces and magnifies its unpleasantness. If I am disgusted by the sight of a hospital patient's bloody wounds, the experience is one of that miscellany of disliked states I call "offended states of mind in the broad sense," but I can hardly resent the poor fellow for his innocent role in causing me to suffer that state of mind, and indeed there may be nobody to resent, in which case I do not "take offense," which is to say I am not offended in the strict and narrow sense.

The offense principle requires that the disliked state of mind (offense in the broad sense) be produced wrongfully by another party, but not that it be an offense in the strict sense of ordinary language. The victim may not know, or may not care, that another has wrongfully caused his unease, and therefore his unpleasant state of mind will not contain the element of resentment, and thus will not be offense in the strict sense. The offense principle as we shall interpret it then applies to offended states in either the broad or the strict sense—that is either with or without resentment—when these states are in fact wrongfully produced in violation of the offended party's rights. It is necessary that there be a wrong, but not that the victim *feel* wronged. And there will always be a wrong whenever an offended state (in the generic sense) is produced in another without justification or excuse.

Since I shall be defending a highly restricted version of the offense principle in this chapter, I should begin with some important disclaimers. To begin with, *offense is surely a less serious thing than harm*. That comparative value judgment seems to me self-evident, yet not simply true by definition. It is possible to deny it without contradiction if only because offense is not strictly commensurable with harm. It is a misconception to think of offenses as occupying the lower part of the same scale as harms; rather offenses are a different sort of thing altogether, with a scale all of their own. Yet most people after reflection will probably acknowledge that a person is not treated as badly, other things being equal, when he is merely offended as when he is harmed. We may (at most) be inclined to rank extreme offenses as greater wrongs to their victims than trifling harms, but perhaps that is because they may become so offensive as to be actually harmful, in a minor sort of way. (At any rate the comparison of extreme offense with minor harm is the only place controversy could reasonably arise over the relative seriousness of offenses and harms.) Continued extreme offense … can cause harm to a person who becomes emotionally upset over the offense, to the neglect of his real interests. But the offended mental state in itself is not a condition of harm. From the moral point of view, considered in its own nature (apart from possible causal linkages to harmful consequences), it is a relatively trivial thing.

It follows from this evident but unprovable truth that the law should not treat offenses as if they were as serious, by and large, as harms. It should not, for example, attempt to control offensiveness by the criminal law when other modes of regulation can do the job as efficiently and economically. For the control of uncommon and transitory forms of offensiveness, for example, reliance can be placed on individual suits for injunctions, or by court orders initiated by police to cease and desist on pain of penalty, or by licensing procedures that depend on administrative suspension of license as a sanction. These alternatives would not entirely dispense with the need for punishment (which is almost always a disproportionately greater evil to the offender than offended mental states are to his "victims"), but punishment would be reserved as a back-up threat, not inflicted for offending others so much as for defying authority by persisting in prohibited conduct…. It may well be that the ordinary criminal law need not concern itself at all with defining crimes of offensiveness, even though offensiveness is the sort of evil it could in principle be used legitimately to combat. It is more likely, however, that for various practical reasons, reliance on injunctions, administrative orders, and license withdrawals would be insufficient to control all properly prohibitable offensive conduct. In some cases, we can know very well in advance that conduct of a certain kind will offend; that is, we don't have to wait for the particular circumstances to decide the question. Moreover, in some cases there will not be time to get an injunction or administrative hearing. By the time that sort of relief is forthcoming, the annoyance has come and gone, and the offense, such as it is, already committed.

Even if there must be defined crimes with specified penalties for purely offensive conduct, however, the penalties should be light ones: more often fines than imprisonment, but when imprisonment, it should be measured in days rather than months or years. Where crimes are divided into the categories of misdemeanor and felony, purely offensive crimes should always be misdemeanors, never felonies. Where penal codes follow the American Law Institute model[1] in dividing offenses into felonies, misdemeanors, petty misdemeanors, and "violations," harmlessly offensive conduct at its worst should be a petty misdemeanor, but typically only a violation—a status it would share with traffic and parking violations, various illegal sales, and unintentional violations of health or safety codes. When a given crime is both harmful and offensive the punishment can properly be severe, but legislators and judges should make it clear that the severity of the punishment is primarily a function of the harmfulness (or dangerousness) of the criminal act, not a reaction to its offensiveness. The state should punish a very harmful or dangerous but only routinely offensive crime much more severely than a crime that is greatly offensive but harmful or dangerous only to a minor degree.

[…]

3. A Ride on the Bus

There is a limit to the power of abstract reasoning to settle questions of moral legitimacy. The question raised by this chapter is whether there are any human experiences that are harmless in themselves yet so unpleasant that we can rightly demand legal protection from them even at the cost of other persons' liberties. The best way to deal with that question at the start is to engage our imaginations in the inquiry, consider hypothetically the most offensive experiences we can imagine, and then sort them into groups in an effort to isolate the kernel of the offense in each category. Accordingly, this section will consist of a number of vividly sketched imaginary tales, and the reader is asked to project himself into each story and determine as best he can what his reaction would be. In each story the reader should think of himself as a passenger on a normally crowded public bus on his way to work or to some important appointment in circumstances such that if he is forced to leave the bus prematurely, he will not only have to pay another fare to get where he is going, but he will probably be

---

[1] American Law Institute, *Model Penal Code, Proposed Official Draft* (Philadelphia, 1962), Section 1.04.

late, to his own disadvantage. If he is not exactly a captive on the bus, then, he would nevertheless be greatly inconvenienced if he had to leave the bus before it reached his destination. In each story, another passenger, or group of passengers, gets on the bus, and proceeds to cause, by their characteristics or their conduct, great offense to you. The stories form six clusters corresponding to the kind of offense caused.

A. Affronts to the Senses

Story 1. A passenger who obviously hasn't bathed in more than a month sits down next to you. He reeks of a barely tolerable stench. There is hardly room to stand elsewhere on the bus and all other seats are occupied.

Story 2. A passenger wearing a shirt of violently clashing orange and crimson sits down directly in your forward line of vision. You must keep your eyes down to avoid looking at him.

Story 3. A passenger sits down next to you, pulls a slate tablet from his briefcase, and proceeds to scratch his fingernails loudly across the slate, sending a chill up your spine and making your teeth clench. You politely ask him to stop, but he refuses.

Story 4. A passenger elsewhere in the bus turns on a portable radio to maximum volume. The sounds it emits are mostly screeches, whistles, and static, but occasionally some electronically amplified rock and roll music blares through.

B. Disgust and Revulsion

Story 5. This is much like story 1 except that the malodorous passenger in the neighboring seat continually scratches, drools, coughs, farts, and belches.

Story 6. A group of passengers enters the bus and shares a seating compartment with you. They spread a table cloth over their laps and proceed to eat a picnic lunch that consists of live insects, fish heads, and pickled sex organs of lamb, veal, and pork, smothered in garlic and onions. Their table manners leave almost everything to be desired.

Story 7. Things get worse and worse. The itinerant picnickers practice gluttony in the ancient

Roman manner, gorging until satiation and then vomiting on to their table cloth. Their practice, however, is a novel departure from the ancient custom in that they eat their own and one another's vomit along with the remaining food.

Story 8. A coprophagic sequel to story 7.

Story 9. At some point during the trip the passenger at one's side quite openly and nonchalantly changes her sanitary napkin and drops the old one into the aisle.

C. Shock to Moral, Religious, or Patriotic Sensibilities

Story 10. A group of mourners carrying a coffin enters the bus and shares a seating compartment with you. Although they are all dressed in black their demeanor is by no means funereal. In fact they seem more angry than sorrowful, and refer to the deceased as "the old bastard," and "the bloody corpse." At one point they rip open the coffin with hammers and proceed to smash the corpse's face with a series of hard hammer blows.

Story 11. A strapping youth enters the bus and takes a seat directly in your line of vision. He is wearing a T-shirt with a cartoon across his chest of Christ on the cross. Underneath the picture appear the words "Hang in there, baby!"

Story 12. After taking the seat next to you a passenger produces a bundle wrapped in a large American flag. The bundle contains, among other things, his lunch, which he proceeds to eat. Then he spits into the star-spangled corner of the flag and uses it first to clean his mouth and then to blow his nose. Then he uses the main striped part of the flag to shine his shoes.

D. Shame, Embarrassment (Including Vicarious Embarrassment), and Anxiety

Story 13. The passenger who takes the seat directly across from you is entirely naked. On one version of the story, he or she is the same sex as you; on the other version of the story, he or she is the opposite sex.

Story 14. The passenger in the previous story proceeds to masturbate quietly in his or her seat.

Story 15.   A man and woman, more or less fully clothed to start, take two seats directly in front of you, and then begin to kiss, hug, pet, and fondle one another to the accompaniment of loud sighs and groans of pleasure. They continue these activities throughout the trip.

Story 16.   The couple of the previous story, shortly before the bus reaches their destination, engage in acts of mutual masturbation, with quite audible instructions to each other and other sound effects.

Story 17.   A variant of the previous story which climaxes in an act of coitus, somewhat acrobatically performed as required by the crowded circumstances.

Story 18.   The seat directly in front of you is occupied by a youth (of either sex) wearing a T-shirt with a lurid picture of a copulating couple across his or her chest.

Story 19.   A variant of the previous story in which the couple depicted is recognizable (in virtue of conventional representations) as Jesus and Mary.

Story 20.   The couple in stories 15–17 perform a variety of sadomasochistic sex acts with appropriate verbal communications ("Oh, that hurts so sweet! Hit me again! Scratch me! Publicly humiliate me!").

Story 21.   The two seats in front of you are occupied by male homosexuals. They flirt and tease at first, then kiss and hug, and finally perform mutual fellatio to climax.

Story 22.   This time the homosexuals are both female and they perform cunnilingus.

Story 23.   A passenger with a dog takes an aisle seat at your side. He or she keeps the dog calm at first by petting it in a familiar and normal way, but then petting gives way to hugging, and gradually goes beyond the merely affectionate to the unmistakably erotic, culminating finally with oral contact with the canine genitals.

E. Annoyance, Boredom, Frustration

Story 24.   A neighboring passenger keeps a radio at a reasonably low volume, and the sounds it emits are by no means offensive to the senses. Nor is the content of the program offensive to the sensibilities. It is, however, a low quality "talk show" which you find intensely boring, and there is no possible way for you to disengage your attention.

Story 25.   The two seats to your left are occupied by two persons who put on a boring "talk show" of their own. There is no way you can avoid hearing every animated word of their inane conversation, no way your mind can roam to its own thoughts, problems, and reveries.

Story 26.   The passenger at your side is a friendly bloke, garrulous and officious. You quickly tire of his conversation and beg leave to read your newspaper, but he persists in his chatter despite repeated requests to desist. The bus is crowded and there are no other empty seats.

F. Fear, Resentment, Humiliation, Anger (From Empty Threats, Insults, Mockery, Flaunting, or Taunting)

Story 27.   A passenger seated next to you reaches into a military kit and pulls out a "hand grenade" (actually only a realistic toy), and fondles and juggles it throughout the trip to the accompaniment of menacing leers and snorts. Then he pulls out a (rubber) knife and "stabs" himself and others repeatedly to peals of maniacal laughter. He turns out to be harmless enough. His whole intent was to put others in apprehension of harm.

Story 28.   A passenger sits next to you wearing a black armband with a large white swastika on it.

Story 29.   A passenger enters the bus straight from a dispersed street rally. He carries a banner with a large and abusive caricature of the Pope and an anti-Catholic slogan. (You are a loyal and pious Catholic.)

Story 30.   Variants of the above. The banner displays a picture of a black according to some standard offensive stereotype (Step 'n Fetchit, Uncle Tom, etc.) with an insulting caption, or a picture of a sneering, sniveling, hook-nosed Fagin or Shylock, with a scurrilous anti-Jewish caption, or a similar offensive denunciation or lampooning of groups called "Spicks," "Dagos," "Polacks," etc.

Story 31.   Still another variant. A counter-demonstrator leaves a feminist rally to enter the bus. He carries a banner with an offensive caricature of a female and the message, in large red letters: "Keep the bitches barefoot and pregnant."

4. The Modes and Meaning of "Offense"

I have tried to make a number of different points by telling these bloodcurdling tales: that there are at least six distinguishable classes of offended states that can be caused by the blamable conduct of others; that to suffer such experiences, at least in their extreme forms, is an evil; but that to the normal person (like the reader) such experiences, unpleasant as they are, do not cause or constitute harm. It is very important that the reader put himself on the bus and imagine his own reactions, for no amount of abstract argument can convince him otherwise that the represented experiences are in principle of a kind that the state can legitimately make its business to prevent.

[...]

It should be clear at this point that despite the miscellaneous character of "offended states" they have some important characteristics in common. They are at the very least unpleasant to the one who suffers them, though the mode of displeasure varies from case to case. With the exception of irritations to the senses, and only some of these, they are complex states whose unpleasantness is in part a function of the tension between conflicting elements. And, most importantly from the legislative point of view, they are nuisances, making it difficult for one to enjoy one's work or leisure in a locality which one cannot reasonably be expected to leave in the circumstances. In extreme cases, the offending conduct commandeers one's attention from the outside, forcing one to relinquish control of one's inner state, and drop what one was doing in order to cope, when it is greatly inconvenient to do so.

5. The Relation Between Offense and Privacy

In what manner, if any, do the offensive people on the bus violate the privacy of their fellow passengers? The word "privacy" may seem clear enough in ordinary discourse, but its ever more frequent use in law courts and legislatures has caused increasing

bewilderment and controversy. Privacy as a legal category came into American law less than a century ago. Its first appearance was in the law of torts, where it served to protect persons from misappropriation of their names or pictures for commercial purposes, and then was gradually extended to include protection of persons from embarrassing publicity, from being put in a false light by the public attribution of beliefs they do not hold, and most importantly, from unwarranted intrusion into their personal affairs by such means as wire tapping, electronic surveillance, shadowing, and peeping. The moral rights to be free of these various evils are certainly genuine ones, and the evils themselves, genuine evils. These rights, moreover, had not been adequately protected by the common law before the "right to privacy" was invented or discovered. But they have an irreducibly heterogeneous character summarizable in a unitary way only by such an imprecise phrase as "the right to be let alone."

Soon it became popular to designate still other legal protections under the same flexible rubric. The old privilege of confidentiality protecting certain special relationships is now considered a special case of privacy.[1] In torts, the right to privacy came to encompass not only the right not to be known about in certain ways by others, but also the right to avoid "seeing and hearing what others say," apparently on the ground that "it may be as distasteful to suffer the intrusions of a garrulous and unwelcome guest as to discover an eavesdropper or peeper."[2] In constitutional law, the Supreme Court has come to discover a miscellany of "penumbral rights" of privacy against governmental action that impose limits even on otherwise valid legislation, including a right to marital privacy which is violated by a state statute prohibiting the sale of contraceptives even to married couples.[3] The tendency to apply the one concept "privacy" to such a motley collection of rights has alarmed many

---

[1] Paul A. Freund, "Privacy: One Concept or Many?," in J.R. Pennock and J.W. Chapman (eds.), *Nomos XIII: Privacy* (New York: Artherton Press, 1971), p. 102.

[2] Fowler V. Harper and Fleming James, Jr., *The Law of Torts* (Boston: Little, Brown, and Co., 1956), vol. I, p. 681.

[3] *Griswold v. Connecticut*, 381 U.S. 479 (1965).

commentators who fear that so plastic and expansive a concept will obfuscate legal analysis. "Given this disparity of central issues," wrote Paul Freund, "privacy becomes too greedy a legal concept."[1]

Many or most of the disparate legal uses of the idea of privacy, however, can be grouped in one or the other of two families of sense. Elizabeth Beardsley has put the distinction well: "Alleged violations [of privacy] seem to fall into two major categories: conduct by which one person A restricts the power of another person B to determine for himself whether or not he will perform an act X or undergo an experience E, and conduct by which one person A acquires or discloses information about B which B does not wish to have known or disclosed."[2] Beardsley labels the right to privacy violated in the former case, the right to *autonomy*, and that violated in the latter case, the right to *selective disclosure*. Window peeping, secret shadowing or photographing, wire tapping, publishing of intimate conversation, intercepted correspondence, candid photographs, and the like, all violate a person's privacy in the sense that they invade his right not to be observed or known about in certain ways without his consent. Nothing like that kind of wrong is committed by the offensive passengers on the bus against their fellow travelers, so we can put that notion of privacy aside. A typical violation of privacy in the sense of autonomy occurs when unwanted noises obtrude upon one's experience restricting one's power to determine for oneself "whether one will do X, or undergo E, or not." "Noise removes [one's] power to choose effectively between sound and silence, or between one sound and another, as features of [one's] immediate experience."[3] The offensive passengers clearly do violate their neighbors' privacy in this sense (auton-

omy) not only when they are noisy, but also when they are disgusting, shocking, embarrassing, boring, threatening, and enraging, for in each case, they deprive the unwilling spectators of the power to determine for themselves whether or not to undergo a certain experience. No passenger, moreover, would decide, if the choice were left to him, to undergo experiences of these offensively unpleasant kinds. Each must spend the whole bus trip coping with feelings induced in himself from the outside when he would much prefer, presumably, to be doing something else. In being made to experience and be occupied in certain ways by outsiders, and having had no choice in the matter whatever, the captive passengers suffer a violation of their autonomy (assuming that the "boundaries" of the autonomous realm do not shrink to the vanishing point when they enter the public world).

We can agree with Beardsley that "selective disclosure" and "autonomy" are two different kinds of things commonly called "privacy," while insisting that they are not without a common element that explains why the word "privacy" is commonly applied to both. They are, in short, two species of the genus "privacy" rather than two distinct senses of the word "privacy." The root idea in the generic concept of privacy is that of a privileged territory or domain in which an individual person has the exclusive authority of determining whether another may enter, and if so, when and for how long, and under what conditions.... Within this area, the individual person is—pick your metaphor—boss, sovereign, owner. The area includes not only the land and buildings he owns and occupies, but his special relationships with spouse, attorney, or priest, and his own mental states or "inner sanctum." His rightful control over his "inner property" is violated when another learns and/or reveals its secret contents without his consent, for he should be the one who decides what is to be known of them and by whom. His will alone reigns supreme over them. But his sovereignty or ownership is also violated when others obtrude their own sounds, and shapes, and affairs upon his "territory" without his consent, for within the privileged area, he has the sole right to determine

---

[1] Freund, "Privacy," p. 192.

[2] Elizabeth L. Beardsley, "Privacy, Autonomy and Selective Disclosure," in J.R. Pennock and J.W. Chapman (eds.), *Nomos XIII: Privacy* (New York: Artherton Press, 1971), p. 56. Letter variables revised to accord with the convention of this [i.e., Feinberg's] book.

[3] Ibid.

what he is to experience, insofar as these matters are rightfully subject to his control. When he is forced to experience loud or grating sensations, disgusting or enraging activities while on his privileged ground, something like a property right has been violated, and violated in a manner similar to that of "private nuisance." The legislative problem of determining when offensive conduct is a public or criminal nuisance could with equal accuracy be expressed as a problem about determining the extent of personal privacy or autonomy. The former way of describing the matter (in terms of "nuisance") lends itself naturally to talk of balancing (the independent value or reasonableness of the offending conduct against the degree of seriousness of the offense caused) whereas the latter way (in terms of "privacy") lends itself naturally to talk of drawing boundaries between the various private domains of persons, and between the private domain of any given person and the public world. The metaphors are different; the actual modes of reasoning are the same.

II. Mediating the Offense Principle

1. On the Scales: The Seriousness of the Offense
The case for the legitimacy of the criminal law's concern with "mere offensiveness" even in the absence of harm or danger, must in the end rest on the intuitive force of the examples given, most of which have been made as extreme as possible and depicted with uncompromising vividness. Offensiveness produces unpleasant experiences and causes annoying inconveniences, both of which are surely evils, though not as great evils as actual harms. Unlike certain other evils, however, offenses and harms are done to persons. They have determinate victims with genuine grievances and a right to complain against determinate wrongdoers about the way in which they have been treated.... Those facts, it seems to me, constitute as good reasons as one could expect to find for the legitimacy in principle of legal interference, even though in a given case, or even in all given cases, there are stronger countervailing reasons of a practical kind. There are abundant reasons, however, for being

extremely cautious in applying the offense principle. People take offense—perfectly genuine offense—at many socially useful or even necessary activities, from commercial advertisement to inane chatter. Moreover, bigoted prejudices of a very widespread kind (e.g., against interracial couples strolling hand in hand down the main street of a town in the deep South) can lead onlookers to be disgusted and shocked, even "morally" repelled, by perfectly innocent activities, and we should be loath to permit their groundless repugnance to outweigh the innocence of the offending conduct. For these and similar reasons, the offense principle must be formulated in a very precise way, and supplemented by appropriate standards or mediating maxims, so as not to open the door to wholesale and intuitively unwarranted legal interference.

As formulated so far, the offense principle commits us only to the view that when public conduct causes offense to someone, the fact of that offense is relevant to the permissibility of the conduct in question. A relevant consideration, of course, can be outweighed by relevant reasons on the other side, and there always is another side, namely that of the offending actor's own interests. Hence conscientious legislators can no more escape the necessity of balancing conflicting considerations when they consider prohibiting offensive conduct than they can escape interest-balancing in the application of the harm principle. Following the model of nuisance law, they will have to weigh, in each main category and context of offensiveness, the seriousness of the offense caused to unwilling witnesses against the reasonableness of the offender's conduct. The seriousness of the offensiveness would be determined by (1) the intensity and durability of the repugnance produced, and the extent to which repugnance could be anticipated to be the general reaction of strangers to the conduct displayed or represented (conduct offensive only to persons with an abnormal susceptibility to offense would not count as very offensive); (2) the ease with which unwilling witnesses can avoid the offensive displays; and (3) whether or not the witnesses have willingly assumed the risk of being offended either through curiosity or the anticipation of pleasure. (The maxim *Volenti non fit injuria*[1] applies to offense as well as to harm.) We can refer to these norms, in order, as "the extent of offense standard," "the reasonable avoidability standard," and "the *Volenti* standard."

These factors would be weighed as a group against the reasonableness of the offending party's conduct as determined by (1) its personal importance to the actors themselves and its social value generally, remembering always the enormous social utility of unhampered expression (in those cases where expression is involved); (2) the availability of alternative times and places where the conduct in question would cause less offense; (3) the extent, if any, to which the offense is caused with spiteful motives. In addition, the legislature would examine the prior established character of various neighborhoods, and consider establishing licensed zones in areas where the conduct in question is known to be already prevalent, so that people inclined to be offended are not likely to stumble on it to their surprise.
[…]

III. Profound Offense

[…]
7. The Nazis in Skokie
Profound offense is never more worthy of respect than when it results from brandishing the symbols of race hatred and genocide. The attempt of an American Nazi Party to demonstrate in the 60% Jewish community of Skokie, Illinois, in 1977 was a rare pure case of symbolic conduct of just that kind, and has since become a kind of symbol of the category ("Skokie-type cases"). The case became legally complex and difficult, ironically, because of its very purity. Political expression is almost categorically defended by the First Amendment, and no one can validly prevent the public advocacy (in appropriate time, place, and manner) of any political opinions no matter how odious. But the small group of American Nazis planned no political advocacy in Skokie. Their avowed purpose was to march in the village parks without giving speeches and without distributing

literature, but dressed in authentic stormtroopers' uniforms, wearing swastikas, and carrying taunting signs. Free expression of opinion, a pre-emptive constitutional value, was not obviously involved. Rather the point was deliberately and maliciously to affront the sensibilities of the Jews in Skokie (including from 5,000 to 7,000 aged survivors of Nazi death camps), to insult them, lacerate their feelings, and indirectly threaten them. Surely if they had carried banners emblazoned only with the words "Jews are scum," they could not have been described as advocating a political program or entering an "opinion" in "the marketplace of ideas." Only some speech acts are acts of advocacy, or assertions of belief; others are pure menacing insult, no less and no more. The Nazi demonstration was to have been very close to the pure insult extreme.

One of the Holocaust survivors in Skokie had witnessed the death of his mother during the Second World War, when fifty German troopers, presumably attired in brown shirts, boots, and swastika armbands, threw her and fifty other women down a well and buried them alive in gravel. The other survivors had all suffered similar experiences. Now their village was to be the scene of a celebration of Hitler's birthday by jack-booted youths in the same Nazi uniforms. The American Nazis had deliberately sought them out; their "message" was not primarily for non-Jews. Who could blame the anxious residents of Skokie for interpreting that "message" thus: "You escaped us before, you dirty Jew, but we are coming and we will get you"?[2] This seems a much more natural interpretation of the "symbolic behavior" of the uniformed demonstrators than that of the Illinois Supreme Court in 1978, when it struck down the prohibitive injunction of a lower court. Addressing only the somewhat narrower question of whether an injunction against display of the swastika violated First Amendment rights, it wrote: "The display of the swastika, as offensive to the principles of a free nation as the memories it recalls may be, is symbolic political speech intended to convey to the public the beliefs of those who display it." That is

---

[1] ["To a willing person, no injury is done."]

[2] Letter to the editor, *The Nation*, 6 May 1978, from Gilbert Gordon, Senior Attorney to the Village of Skokie.

almost as absurd as saying that a nose thumbing, or a giving of "the finger," or a raspberry jeer is a form of "political speech," or that "Death to the Niggers!" is the expression of a political opinion.

The Nazi demonstration without question would have produced "offended states of mind" of great intensity in almost any Skokie resident forced to witness it. Equally clearly, the offense would be of the profound variety since the planned affront was to values held sacred by those singled out as targets. But since the Nazis announced the demonstration well in advance, it could be easily avoided by all who wished to avoid it, in most cases with but minimal inconvenience. Even those who would have to endure some inconvenience to escape witnessing the spectacle, for example a mother who could not take her children to the park that afternoon, could complain only of a minor nuisance, since with so much notice, nearly as satisfactory alternative arrangements could be made. The main complainants then would be those who stayed at home or at work, and found that physical separation from the witnessed event was no bar to their experiencing intolerably severe emotions. The offense derived from bare knowledge that the demonstration was taking place in Skokie was an experience that could have been shared at the time equally intensely and equally profoundly by a Jew in New York, Los Angeles, or Tel Aviv. That offense would be a complex mental state, compounded of moral indignation and disapproval, resentment (offense in the strict sense), and perhaps some rage or despair. But insofar as the moral elements predominate, there will be little sense of personal grievance involved, and even less of a case, objectively speaking, that the person in question was himself wronged. It is not a necessary truth that we are personally wronged by everything at which we are morally outraged. Insofar as there is a sense of *personal* grievance in the non-witnessing Skokie Jew, it would no doubt be directed at the nuisance he suffered in having to avoid the area of the Village Hall and adjacent public parks. That element in the experience, however, is not "profound."

Despite the intense aversion felt by the offended parties, there was not an exceptionally weighty case for legal interference with the Nazis, given the relative ease by which their malicious and spiteful insults could be avoided. But the scales would tip the other way if their behavior became more frequent, for the constant need to avoid public places at certain times can become a major nuisance quickly. Even more to the point, if the Nazis, at unpredictable intervals, freely mingled with the throngs in shopping malls or on public sidewalks while wearing swastika armbands and stormtrooper uniforms, then they would clearly cross the line of public nuisance. Practically speaking, the best remedies for those nuisances that consist of group affronts are administrative—cease and desist orders, withheld permits, and injunctions, with criminal penalties reserved only as back-up sanctions. But without such measures, the whole public world would become as unpleasant for some as the revolting public bus ... and equally inescapable.

DISCUSSION QUESTIONS

1. Explain Feinberg's Offense Principle and his distinction between offense and harm/injury. Compare and contrast Feinberg's Offense Principle with Mill's Harm Principle.

2. Feinberg discusses two reasons why we need to be careful in using the Offense Principle to make legislation. Explain. Can we legislate against offense while still taking seriously these worries? Explain.

3. Feinberg claims that we need to balance the degree of offensiveness against the interests of the offending party. How does he propose determining the seriousness of the offense and the reasonableness of the offending party's conduct?

4. Compare and contrast Feinberg's discussion of the case of *Village of Skokie v. National Socialist Party of America* with that of the court in that case. (See reading 41, below.)

40

George Sher, "Liberal Neutrality and the Value of Autonomy" (1995)

George Sher is the Herbert S. Autrey Professor of Philosophy at Rice University. Sher's work has been focused in moral psychology and political philosophy. In the following selection, Sher discusses the notion of individual autonomy and explains what he takes to be the proper attitude (and actions) that governments ought to take with respect to their citizens' autonomy.

SOURCE

Sher, George. "Liberal Neutrality and the Value of Autonomy." *Social Philosophy and Policy* 12, Issue 1, 1995, pp. 136–59. Reprinted with the permission of Cambridge University Press.

Many liberals believe that government should not base its decisions on any particular conception of the good life. Many believe, further, that this principle of neutrality is best defended through appeal to some normative principle about autonomy. In this essay, I shall discuss the prospects of mounting one such defense. I say only "one such defense" because neutralists can invoke the demands of autonomy in two quite different ways. They can argue, first, that because autonomy itself has such great value, the state can produce the best results by simply allowing each citizen to shape his own life; or they can argue, second, that even if nonneutral policies would produce the most value, the state remains obligated to eschew them out of *respect* for its citizens' autonomy. Here I shall discuss only the first and more consequentialist of these arguments.

I. Conditions for Autonomy

Because the notion of autonomy is so elusive, there is an obvious risk that any formulation of the argument will be tendentious. Fortunately, the very analysis of autonomy that seems to me most plausible is also the one that offers the argument its best chance of success. To make the case for that analysis, it will be helpful to review a number of alternative approaches. These can usefully be grouped under three main headings.

1. Perhaps the first thing that comes to mind about autonomy is its close connection to freedom.

Indeed, in some discussions, these notions are simply equated. Thomas Hurka, for example, seems to treat them as interchangeable when he writes:

> This, then, is the challenge to the value of autonomy: if free choice is intrinsically good, it should be better to have one good option and nine bad options than just to have one good option. And why should this be so?[1]

Moreover, even when freedom and autonomy are distinguished, they are often (and rightly) taken to be closely linked.

Their linkage complicates our task because the conditions for freedom are themselves complex. As Hurka's remarks suggest, a person's freedom depends in part on the number and quality of his options. But a person may also act unfreely because he lacks the information to evaluate his options or because he lacks the ability to process what information he has. In addition, we deny that people choose freely when their choices are coerced by threats of harm and when they are subject to "alien" internal forces such as compulsion and irresistible impulse.

Given the close connections between freedom and autonomy, it is not surprising that many conditions necessary for freedom have also been taken to be necessary for autonomy. For example, Joseph Raz has written that "autonomy is opposed to a life of coerced choices."[2] Raz also writes that an autonomous person "must have the mental abilities to form intentions of a sufficiently complex kind, and to plan their execution,"[3] and that he must have "an adequate range of options to choose from."[4] But while these claims are not clearly wrong, they are also not all clearly correct. It is not obvious that a person can never autonomously surrender his money to avoid being shot by robbers. It is also not obvious that persons can never autonomously choose from restricted ranges of options or exercise autonomy despite their ignorance of relevant features of their situation. Also, of course, there are hard questions about which proposals are coercive, which internal forces *are* alien, and which ranges of options *are* adequate.

2. Although autonomy may in some respects demand less than freedom, in other respects it demands more. Someone who makes an informed, uncoerced, noncompulsive choice from an adequate range of options may be choosing freely; but his choice is not autonomous if it is the result of certain sorts of past manipulation. For example, persons are thought not to act autonomously when they are motivated by preferences that were shaped by systematic indoctrination or "brainwashing." More subtly, they are often said to be deprived of autonomy by certain forms of *unintended* conditioning. To recall a useful cliché, we would consider someone nonautonomous if, as a result of lengthy past involuntary servitude, he now opted to remain a slave when he might go free. Here again, there are hard questions about which forms of conditioning undermine autonomy; but we need not be able to answer them to say that some forms of conditioning clearly have this effect.

3. Yet even together, freedom and the absence of a history of objectionable conditioning may not exhaust the prerequisites for autonomy. In addition, many believe that agents are not autonomous unless they have subjected their ends to rational scrutiny. Subjecting one's ends to scrutiny involves considering the reasons for and against doing what one prefers, and acting only on the preferences that survive. It also involves trying to modify any preferences that one finds good reason to abandon. As William E. Connolly describes the process,

> [a] person may want to follow a particular career simply because his parents and friends expect him to pursue this path. He might, however, adopt the same goal after deliberately canvassing the expectations others have

---

[1] Thomas Hurka, "Why Value Autonomy?" *Social Theory and Practice* 13.3 (Fall 1987): 363.

[2] Joseph Raz, *The Morality of Freedom* (Oxford: Oxford University Press, 1986), p. 371.

[3] Ibid., p. 372.

[4] Ibid., p. 374.

of him, reassessing his previous tendency to adopt unreflectively the hopes those others have for him as his own, critically exploring the contours of the profession under consideration in the light of his own capacities, strengths, and weaknesses, and comparing the career in question to other alternatives that might be open to a person with his interests, capacities, and opportunities.[1]

Though somewhat more controversial than the others, this critical-reflection requirement, too, is widely accepted. Also like the others, it is in need of further specification—in this case, of the standards that agents should use when thinking critically about their preferences.

Taken together, these three sets of conditions (or some subset of their elements) may indeed be sufficient for autonomy. Yet even if they are, difficult questions remain. Given the diversity of its prerequisites, is autonomy really a single notion? If so, how are its elements related? If not, which form(s) of autonomy are morally important?

II. A Unifying Approach

Despite its apparent fragmentation, I believe that autonomy is a strongly unified notion. In this and the next section, I shall sketch and briefly defend the account that I take to integrate its elements.

That account is a variant of the familiar idea that autonomous persons are self-directing, but it differs from other variants in its understanding of "self-direction." On many readings, this means only that an agent's goals, plans, and decisions originate in his own will. By contrast, on the reading I favor, autonomous agents are self-directing in the more stringent sense of exercising their will *on the basis of good reasons*. A bit less cryptically, I shall argue that we can make the most sense of what most of us believe about autonomy—our disagreement as

well as our agreement—if we adopt the hypothesis that in this context "self-directed activity" means "activity that is motivated by an agent's appreciation of reasons provided by his situation."

The idea that autonomy is responsiveness to reasons is of course not new. A version of this idea is central to Kant's ethical theory, and the idea is presupposed by all who believe that "moral autonomy means doing what is right and good *because* it is right and good."[2] But as the quotation illustrates, the idea is most often confined to discussions of autonomous *moral* decisions. By contrast, I want to generalize it to apply also to nonmoral decisions; I mean it as an analysis of personal as well as moral autonomy. Also, while many Kantians appear to believe that acting autonomously is responding to what is *objectively the strongest* (moral) reason provided by one's situation, I shall allow that persons may act autonomously in response to reasons that are less than the strongest. To defend this account, I shall argue that it explains (1) why autonomy imposes the requirements that it does, (2) why autonomy is morally important, and (3) why so much of what we believe about autonomy is unclear or indeterminate.

Consider, first, the question of how any univocal notion can impose requirements as disparate as (some of) the prerequisites for freedom, the absence of a history of (certain forms of) conditioning, and a critical attitude toward one's own ends. If autonomy is responsiveness to reasons, the answer is straightforward: each requirement rules out a way in which responsiveness to reasons can fail. Thus, the explanation of why autonomous agents must have various cognitive abilities is that otherwise they could not recognize their reasons for acting. The explanation of why they must have control over their impulses is that otherwise they could not respond to whatever reasons they recognize. The explanation

---

[1] William E. Connolly, *The Terms of Political Discourse*, 2nd ed. (Princeton: Princeton University Press, 1983), pp. 150–51.

[2] Amy Gutmann, *Democratic Education* (Princeton: Princeton University Press, 1987), p. 62. For Kant's theory, see Immanuel Kant, *Foundations of the Metaphysics of Morals*, trans. Lewis White Beck (Indianapolis: Bobbs-Merrill, 1959).

of why a history of brainwashing, indoctrination, or oppressive servitude undermines autonomy is that it diminishes one's current ability to respond to reasons. And the explanation of why autonomous agents must subject their ends to critical scrutiny (or at least be open to reasons to initiate such scrutiny) is that otherwise they would be apt to overlook important reasons for acting.

The responsiveness-to-reasons account thus makes at least rough sense of various necessary conditions for autonomy. But it also explains why we may feel ambivalent toward other (alleged) necessary conditions. As we saw, acts performed under threat, such as surrendering one's money to a gunman, are clearly unfree; but they do not always seem nonautonomous. The explanation, we can now see, is that unlike other factors that undermine freedom, a threat does not prevent an agent from responding to reasons. Instead, it restructures the situation that *provides* his reasons. This means that an agent can have, and respond to, a good reason for complying with a threat. Similarly, the explanation of why having few options does not necessarily undermine autonomy is that even someone with few options may have a good reason for choosing one course of action over others.

Consider, second, what the responsiveness-to-reasons account implies about the moral importance of autonomy. If autonomy were simply arbitrary choice, there would be no obvious basis upon which to claim either that it is good to be autonomous or that our legal and political system should protect and foster autonomous choice. Mere self-assertion uninformed by reason appears to have little value. But if autonomy is *reasoned* self-direction—if it consists precisely in recognizing and allowing oneself to be guided by rational considerations—then its normative significance is much easier to grasp. In that case, its value is essentially that of (practical) rationality itself. This, of course, does not explain *why* autonomy is valuable; but since rationality is widely considered one of our most precious attributes, it does place autonomy's value effectively beyond dispute.

Consider, finally, how the responsiveness-to-reasons account illuminates what we find unclear about autonomy. There are, as we saw, a number of unresolved questions: about what sorts of impulses, etc., render agents nonautonomous, about what forms of conditioning lead agents to make nonautonomous choices, and about what standards an agent should use in evaluating his ends. If autonomy is responsiveness to reasons, the existence of these questions is easy to understand. They arise because our basic concept of autonomy is schematic, and hence requires completion by a substantive theory of reasons and how they move us. Because these matters are obscure, the lacunae in our understanding of autonomy are just what we should expect. Moreover—a separate point—while the proposed account does not itself answer the questions, it does at least tell us how to approach them. To find out which impulses and mental incapacities subvert autonomy, it directs us to ask which impulses and incapacities prevent reasons from getting a motivational grip. To find out which forms of conditioning undermine (later) autonomy, it directs us to ask which influences cause us to develop preferences that later resist rational alteration. And to establish the criteria for evaluating one's ends, it directs us to ask which aspects of an agent's situation are relevant to his deliberations.

III. Objections to the Unifying Approach

Given our broader topic, most of these issues are beyond our scope. But before I resume the discussion's main thread, I must consider some objections to the proposed account. There are, it seems, at least two important difficulties.

The first is that agents often make (nonmoral) choices which seem autonomous despite the absence of objective reasons to choose one option over another. When someone must make a moral choice—when, for instance, he must choose between self-interest and fairness, or between promoting the general welfare and keeping a promise—at least one available action always has moral value, so there is always some moral reason to which he can respond.

But when someone must make a *nonmoral* choice—when, for instance, he must choose between marrying and remaining single—the possibility of his recognizing and responding to an objective reason may seem less clear. Against this possibility, one might argue that neither being married nor being single has inherent value, and hence that the agent has no objective reason to choose one over the other. Nor, to vary the example, does there appear to be anything about collecting stamps that makes it objectively better or worse than, say, bird-watching. Because such choices can nonetheless be autonomous, one might conclude that autonomy cannot be responsiveness to reasons.

This conclusion would be too quick, however. One way to resist it is simply to challenge its assumption that the world contains too few objective values to guide all nonmoral choices. Certainly the fact that being married does not *always* have objective value does not entail that it *never* does. And, more generally, the worry about the paucity of nonmoral values may reflect only an unwarranted suspicion of perfectionism (i.e., the view that some aspects of people's lives, such as knowledge and friendship, are intrinsically good, and should be promoted, whether or not they are desired). But while I am sympathetic to this reply, I need not press it here; for there is a much easier way to show that there are always enough reasons to guide nonmoral choices. Even if the world is far less rich in values than I take it to be—indeed, even if *no* outcomes are intrinsically better or worse than any others—an agent's own desires and aversions, as well as his past decisions and psychological make-up, are surely themselves important sources of reasons. Moreover, while a desire is in one sense a subjective state, its existence is no less objective than any other fact. Hence, the easiest way to secure an ample stock of nonmoral reasons is to include an agent's desires, history, capacities, and traits in his reason-generating situation. Once these factors are included, we no longer need fear the inference from "no fact external to X gives X a reason to marry Y" to "X cannot choose to marry Y in response to an objective reason"; for

X's wanting to marry Y will itself provide just such a reason. If X lacks countervailing reasons (and is aware of this), his desire-based decision to marry Y may indeed satisfy the requirements for autonomy. Moreover, in other cases, agents may satisfy those requirements by responding to reasons provided by their second-order desires to be, or not be, specific sorts of persons.

Thus, however we understand nonmoral reasons—whether we take them to stem from perfectionist values, from psychological facts about agents or others, or from some mixture of the two—there plainly are enough of them to guide choice whenever autonomy is possible. Indeed, there probably are few acts that are not supported by one or another reason. But just because of this, the responsiveness-to-reasons account now raises a very different question: namely, to *which* of the many reasons provided by an agent's situation must he respond to qualify as autonomous?[1]

The simplest answer to this second difficulty, of course, is that he must respond to the *strongest* reason provided by his situation. This proposal would forge the tightest possible link between autonomy and practical rationality. It would also account adequately for our intuitions about some cases. For example, we might well doubt the autonomy of someone who refused to undergo lifesaving surgery merely because he feared postoperative pain. Here the explanation may indeed be that self-preservation is much more important than avoiding transient pain, and hence that anyone who declined the operation would not be responding to the strongest reason provided by his situation. But the same proposal that yields this explanation also has many less-welcome implications. Suppose, for example, that a second agent also needs surgery to survive, but unlike the first has no *way* of knowing this. If autonomy were responsiveness to the strongest reason provided by one's situation, then this agent, too, would fail to act autonomously if he chose not

---

[1] I owe my appreciation of the issues discussed in the remainder of this section to the constructive bullying of Derk Pereboom and David Christensen.

to undergo surgery. Yet if someone is unavoidably ignorant of his need for surgery, then his failure to submit to it surely does *not* affect the autonomy of whatever else he does.

To block such counterexamples, we must at least relativize the reasons to which autonomous agents must respond to what they know (or, perhaps, can reasonably be expected to know) about their situations. Yet even when so relativized, the proposal that acting autonomously is responding to one's strongest reason remains problematic. For consider, next, a case in which X not only has a strong desire to marry Y, but also knows that their marriage will fail unless he gives up his career. Suppose, further, that X knows that his talents are modest and that his career is not promising in any event. Knowing all this, X may well have more reason to marry Y than to pursue his career. Yet while X certainly can autonomously choose to marry Y and give up his career, we must concede that he also can autonomously choose the career over the marriage. More generally, we must concede that persons can and often do exercise their autonomy by acting *against* their strongest reasons.

To allow for this, we might try further relativizing the reasons to which autonomous agents must respond. Those reasons, we might now say, depend not only on what agents know about their situations, but also on their beliefs about which aspects of their situations are reasons and how strong these reasons are. We might suppose, in other words, that an agent acts autonomously whenever he acts in response to *whichever reasons appear strongest to him*.

But this proposal will not do either; for while it would account for the intuition that X could autonomously choose either to marry Y or to pursue his career, it would do so at the cost of making the conditions for autonomy so weak that virtually all actions (except, perhaps, some that result from weakness of will) could satisfy them. It would imply, indeed, that even a madman acts autonomously as long as he acts reasonably by his own lights. Worse yet, if acting autonomously were acting merely on what one *regards* as one's strongest

reasons, then one could act autonomously without making any contact at all with one's actual reasons. This would eliminate the very connection between autonomy and practical rationality that promised to explain why autonomy is valuable.

To avoid these difficulties, we must hold fast to the idea that acting autonomously is allowing oneself to be guided by one's actual reasons. The question, though, is how we can both do this and still make the needed concession that an autonomous act need not be supported by the agent's *strongest* reasons.

To work our way toward an answer, let us return to X's decision to pursue his career. That decision, we said, could qualify as autonomous despite the fact that X's reason to pursue his career was less strong than his reason to marry Y. But here it may be relevant that even if X's reason to pursue his career is not his strongest, it remains both reasonably strong and reasonably close to its competitor in strength. Even if we disagree with X's choice, we must admit that, given the central role that careers play in life-plans, there is a good deal to be said for it. In this respect, choosing a career over a marriage is very different from deciding to forgo life-saving surgery merely to avoid postoperative pain.

Could an act's autonomy depend on the *relative* strength of the reasons for performing it? Because we are taking autonomy to be *responsiveness* to reasons, the only reasons whose relative strength can count are those that actually influence the agent. Hence, if we adopt this suggestion, we will have to say that agents can be influenced by reasons that are real but not their strongest. This may at first seem implausible. However, as Raz has noted,

> I may not have a reason to prefer going to medical school to going to law school. But if that is what I do then I do it because I believe that a medical education is important and worthwhile for it will, for example, enable me (1) to serve others, as well as (2) to have a satisfying career, and (3) to live and work in almost any country. 1 to 3 are my reasons, and the fact that I believe that I also have

reasons for choosing a legal career which are no less worthy and important does not undermine the fact that when I choose medicine I choose it for the stated reasons.[1]

Although Raz presents no real argument, I believe these remarks are correct and important. At least when one's alternatives are either equally valuable or incommensurable, the fact that neither is supported by a stronger reason does not imply that neither can be chosen for whatever reason does support it. Even if B would be just as good as A, one's choice of A may still be grounded in what *makes* A good.

But once we have come this far, we can go farther. If a choice can be reason-based despite the existence of *equally good* reasons to do something else, it surely can also be reason-based despite the existence of *better* reasons to do something else. As long as A is supported by reasons, an agent may respond to those reasons despite his awareness of facts that provide even stronger reasons to do B. Of course, in failing to respond to the stronger reasons, the agent will fall short of *full* rationality; but falling short of full rationality is not the same as being irrational. Moreover, if the reasons for A and B are nearly equal in strength, then the choice of A will at least be close to fully rational.

Although these observations are obvious, they are also liberating; for they immediately suggest an alternative to the view that acting autonomously is acting in response to the strongest reasons provided by what one knows. They suggest, instead, that an agent may qualify as autonomous whenever he acts in response to reasons provided by what he knows about his situation that are at least strong *enough*. By retreating just this far, we can retain the link between autonomy and practical rationality while allowing that agents can autonomously choose what is less than best. Of course, to make this suggestion precise, we would need to spell out just when a reason is strong enough. That in turn would require deciding whether what matters is a

reason's absolute strength or its strength in comparison to the agent's other reasons. But whatever we say about this, any defensible threshold seems likely to be exceeded both by X's reason to marry Y and by X's reason to pursue his career. Thus, on any reasonable interpretation, the current proposal will explain why X could make either decision autonomously.

While much more could be said, the conclusion at this point is that neither of the main objections to the responsiveness-to-reasons account is unduly damaging. Moreover, as we saw earlier, that account has the positive virtues of integrating autonomy's elements, explaining its value, and illuminating its obscurities. Even alone, these considerations would add up to a strong case for adopting the account. But in the current context, the case is far stronger. For, as we will soon see, if autonomy is *not* construed as responsiveness to reasons, the argument from its value to neutralism cannot be made even superficially plausible.

IV. Understanding the Value-of-Autonomy Argument

To see *why,* let us now turn to the value-of-autonomy argument itself. At least in broad outline, that argument is very familiar. Bruce Ackerman, who characterizes it as one of "several weighty arguments in support of neutrality,"[2] summarizes it this way:

> Even if you don't think you need to experiment [with different forms of life in order to discover which is best], you may adopt a conception of the good that gives a central place to autonomous deliberation and deny that it is possible to *force* a person to be good. On this view, the intrusion of non-neutral argument into power talk will seem self-defeating at best—since it threatens to divert

---

[1] Raz, *The Morality of Freedom,* p. 304.

[2] Bruce Ackerman, *Social Justice in the Liberal State* (New Haven: Yale University Press, 1980), p. 11.

people from the true means of cultivating a truly good life.[1]

In a similar vein, David A.J. Richards first postulates "a general right of personal autonomy,"[2] but then goes on to write that "[t]he neutrality, in [Ronald] Dworkin's sense, of this right, among a wide number of visions of the good life, arises from its source in the value of autonomy."[3] And while John Stuart Mill tends to present the case against government interference in people's lives as resting on the value of individuality rather than autonomy, similar reasoning can be extracted from various passages in *On Liberty*.[4]

Familiar though it is, however, the idea that governments can always promote the most value by allowing citizens to exercise their own autonomy is extremely puzzling. Perhaps the most obvious problem is that even if autonomy has great value, it hardly follows (and is almost certainly false) that autonomy is the *only* thing with value. Indeed, on the account of autonomy just defended—an agent acts autonomously when he acts in response to reasons provided by his situation—the claim that nothing except autonomy has value *must* be false. It must be false because an agent cannot respond to a reason for pursuing X unless there is a reason for him to pursue X, and there cannot be such a reason unless his pursuing or attaining X either has intrinsic value or has acquired value from the agent's or someone else's desires. Because one cannot respond to a reason unless there is some value which gives rise to that reason, it is inconsistent to hold both

that autonomy is responsiveness to reasons and that autonomy is the only thing with value.

Yet if autonomy is *not* the only thing with value—if it is only one good thing among others—then exactly how can its value justify neutralism? Even if promoting other values invariably undermines autonomy, why must governments always resolve the dilemma in autonomy's favor? If governments or their agents have well-grounded beliefs that citizens' lives are improved by close and committed family relationships, or that the breakdown of public civility is a bad thing, why shouldn't they promote public civility or the family even at the cost of sacrificing some autonomy? Or, again, why shouldn't they sacrifice some autonomy to promote such values as high culture or communal solidarity? There actually are two cases to consider, since either the value of autonomy is commensurable with these other values or it is not. But if the values are not commensurable, then nothing follows about how governments should choose between autonomy and other values; while if they are commensurable, then the conclusion seems to be that governments should *not* promote autonomy if they can do more good by promoting other values. Either way, the inference from the value of autonomy to neutralism appears to fail.[5]

Is there any way to rescue it short of retreating to the untenable view that autonomy is the only thing with value? One possibility, suggested by Ackerman, is that "[i]t is … not necessary for autonomy to be the only good thing; it suffices for it to be the best thing that there is."[6] Here Ackerman's thought appears to be that if autonomy is better than anything else—as he believes it to be—then governments can never reasonably promote other values at its expense. Yet even if autonomy is the best thing there is, the amount of value a government can produce by promoting it may still be smaller than the amount of value that can be produced by promoting more of something less valuable. Thus,

---

[1] Ibid.

[2] David A.J. Richards, "Human Rights and Moral Ideals: An Essay on the Moral Theory of Liberalism," *Social Theory and Practice* 5.3–4 (1980): 474.

[3] Ibid.

[4] Here I have in mind not only some of what Mill says about individuality in chapter 3—see, for example, his remarks about Calvinism (John Stuart Mill, *On Liberty*, ed. Elizabeth Rapaport [Indianapolis: Hackett, 1978], pp. 59ff.)—but also his emphasis in chapter 2 on the importance of understanding the grounds for one's beliefs.

[5] Hurka notices this problem in "Why Value Autonomy?" p. 377.

[6] Ackerman, *Social Justice in the Liberal State*, p. 368.

to rule out the possibility of trade-offs, the value of autonomy must be prior in some stronger sense.

Can a stronger priority claim be made out? Although I know of no neutralist who has squarely addressed this question, one possibility, at least, seems worth exploring. This is the suggestion that autonomy is *internally* connected to the perfectionist values that appear to call for trade-offs that, in our terms, the value of superior ways of life resides not merely in their intrinsic nature, but rather in their being chosen *because of* that nature. On this account, the values of family, culture, community, and the rest will not be competitors with autonomy, but rather will presuppose it; for lives involving close family ties, culture, and community will be valuable only when (or only to the extent that) they are adopted *for the reasons provided by their value.*

Is this suggestion coherent? At first glance, it may seem not to be; for it asserts both that whether a way of life is valuable depends on whether it is autonomously chosen, and that whether a way of life is autonomously chosen depends on whether it has independent value. Given this circularity, we may seem unable to make determinations of either autonomy or value. Yet despite initial appearances, the circularity need not be vicious. To tame it, we need only say, first, that when we call a way of life independently valuable, what we mean is that it would have actual value if it were chosen autonomously, and, second, that choosing it autonomously is choosing it precisely because one recognizes this potentiality. To mark this complication, I shall henceforth speak not simply of responding to value, but of responding to (potential) value.

Like the idea that autonomy is responsiveness to reasons, the idea that only autonomously chosen ways of life have value is not new. Although Lawrence Haworth does not recognize the complication just discussed, he plainly implies that at least some values presuppose autonomy when he writes:

> [W]hat is there to value in a community of shared values when the members of the community are automata? The fact of sharing or

of being mutually devoted to a transcendent or collective good commands respect only to the extent that the members of the community participate autonomously—to the extent that each, by joining with the rest in a collective pursuit, is living his own life, pursuing his (procedurally) own conception of the good.[1]

Will Kymlicka makes the same point in more general terms when he writes that "no life goes better by being led from the outside according to values the person doesn't endorse. My life only goes better if I'm leading it from the inside, according to my beliefs about value."[2] Moreover, the view we are considering—that some ways of life are better than others, but that even the (potentially) best lack value if not chosen for the right reasons—is the exact structural analogue of Kant's famous view that some sorts of actions are morally better than others, but that even the (potentially) best lack moral value if not performed for the right reasons.

This view immediately opens up new possibilities. If only autonomously chosen activities can have value, then any government that tries to increase the value of its citizens' activities at the expense of their autonomy will merely destroy the conditions under which their activities can *be* valuable. Because of this, a person's activities will always lack value when his government has induced him to pursue them nonautonomously; but they will not always lack value when his government has not induced him to pursue them nonautonomously. Under these conditions, one's chances of living a valuable life may indeed be best if one's government interferes least with one's autonomy.

It should now be clear *why* the value-of-autonomy argument must treat autonomy as responsiveness to reasons. We just saw that that argument

---

[1] Lawrence Haworth, *Autonomy: An Essay in Philosophical Psychology and Ethics* (New Haven: Yale University Press, 1986), p. 208. For a similar suggestion, see Hurka, "Why Value Autonomy?" p. 378.
[2] Will Kymlicka, *Liberalism, Community, and Culture* (Oxford: Oxford University Press, 1989), p. 12.

will not succeed if there can be trade-offs between autonomy and other values. We saw, as well, that the only way to rule out such trade-offs is to hold that no activity can have value unless it is chosen on the basis *of* its (potential) value. Since this way of saving the argument equates being chosen autonomously with being chosen on the basis of (potential) value, it in effect presupposes a responsiveness-to-reasons account of autonomy. Of course, the reasons provided by an activity's (potential) value need not exhaust the reasons for engaging in it, so this version of the responsiveness-to-reasons account does not exactly match the one developed above. Still, as long as the current version also requires that the reasons provided by (potential) value exceed a certain level of strength, it can be viewed as an especially stringent variant of the original.

The harder question, of course, is whether it is *true* that only autonomously chosen activities can have value. Certainly that premise is not universally accepted. Against it, some would maintain that there is value even (or especially) in unquestioning obedience to (divine or human) authority. Others would insist that certain specific ways of behaving—for example, premarital chastity and marital fidelity—are best no matter *what* the agent's reasons. Of course, the mere fact of disagreement settles nothing, since it may be the dissenters who are mistaken; but right or wrong, their view does not seem absurd. Thus, the premise that only autonomously chosen activities have value is itself in need of defense.

V. Nonneutral Policies, Autonomous Acts

Fortunately, we need not decide whether it can be defended; for the argument from the value of autonomy—or, as we now might more accurately call it, the argument from autonomy's contribution to value—breaks down decisively at another point. To succeed, that argument must presuppose not merely that only autonomously chosen activities have value, but also that when governments try to induce citizens to choose valuable activities, the resulting choices never *are* autonomous. Yet

whatever we say about the first premise, the second is clearly false.

In the remainder of this essay, I shall argue this point in some detail. First, though, I must specify more precisely what needs to be shown.... [A] government can promote (what it considers) a valuable form of life in at least four ways. It can (1) nonrationally cause its citizens to prefer to live as it thinks good, or (2) offer them incentives to live that way, or (3) create institutions or social forms that make the favored way of life possible or enable it to flourish, or (4) threaten to punish anyone who rejects it. Because the most interesting version of neutralism forbids all four methods of promoting good lives, we could block the current argument for that version merely by showing that *one* of those methods can issue in autonomous choices. But if we showed only this much, we would leave open the possibility of invoking autonomy's contribution to value to establish a weaker version of neutralism. To foreclose this possibility, I shall try to show that *all four* methods of promoting valuable lives can issue in autonomous choices.

Consider, first, policies aimed at nonrationally causing citizens to acquire or retain preferences for (what the policy makers consider) good lives. Although their actual rationales are no doubt mixed, many current policies appear to have this aim among others. These policies encompass the use of "directive" techniques of moral education, including exhortation, reward, punishment, and personal example, to cause students to acquire desirable habits and preferences. They also include employing the techniques of advertising to instill an aversion to drug use and other unwholesome activities; encouraging writers to portray women in nonstereotyped ways; hiring workers who are positive "role models" for persons with low aspirations; making work a condition of public assistance to alter the habits of recipients; and trying to reform criminals by incarcerating them. To simplify the discussion, I shall simply assume that some such policies do nonrationally cause people to acquire new preferences. Granting this, the question is whether those preferences can issue in autonomous choices.

Given our analysis of autonomy, the answer may at first seem to be a clear "no." For suppose a government's policies do nonrationally cause a citizen C to prefer a way of life W; and suppose, further, that C's choice of W is motivated by the preference that is thus caused. Because that preference is, by hypothesis, not a response to any reason for preferring W, C's choice of W must also not be a response to any such reason. However, according to our account of autonomy, an autonomous choice just is a choice that is made in response to a good reason. Hence, it may seem to follow immediately that nonrational conditioning cannot issue in autonomous choices.

I shall explain shortly what I take to be wrong with this argument. First, though, I want briefly to discuss a response that we should not make. We saw earlier that even if neither being married nor being single has any inherent value, the fact that X wants to marry Y can itself give X a good reason to marry Y. We saw, further, that if X does choose to marry Y for this reason, X's choice can indeed be autonomous. But if so, then it may seem that C's choice of W can similarly qualify as autonomous; for even if C's preference for W is not *grounded* in a good reason to adopt W, that preference itself may *provide* C with such a reason. If it does, then C's choice of W will indeed be grounded in a good reason, and hence will be made autonomously, as long as C chooses W in response to the reason that is thus provided.

The problem with this rejoinder is that it ignores the special requirements imposed by the current context. Because our aim is to find out whether C's choice of W can actualize W's (potential) value, our question is not merely whether C's choice of W is autonomous in the sense of being a response to *some* sufficiently strong reason. Instead, it is whether C's choice of W satisfies the more stringent requirement of being a response to a sufficiently strong reason *that is provided by W's potential value.* Of course, the mere fact that C's immediate reason is his preference for W does not show that C is *not* responding to W's (potential) value; for many preferences are themselves grounded in deeper

reasons. But because C's preference for W has by hypothesis been nonrationally instilled, that cannot be the case here. Hence, for present purposes, C's choice of W must indeed be nonautonomous.

This, I think, is (one of) the grain(s) of truth in the widely held view that nonrationally influencing people's preferences undermines their autonomy. But while the point is not insubstantial, it falls far short of establishing that governments cannot induce their citizens to live valuable lives by nonrationally influencing their preferences. To establish that, one would have to show not merely that C's *initial* choice of W is nonautonomous, but also that its lack of autonomy infects *any further* choices to which it leads. Yet even if C does choose W nonautonomously at t_1, his resulting later choice(s) of W may surely have a different status. Precisely by living the life he was nonrationally caused to prefer, C may become increasingly aware of the value-based reasons for living that way. He may come to appreciate W's (potential) value "from the inside." By putting C in a position to do this, his choosing W at t_1 may enable him to respond at t_2 to the reasons provided by W's (potential) value. If at t_2 C does choose W on this basis, then C's nonrational conditioning *will* have led him to choose W in a way that actualizes its (potential) value.

This is far more than a bare logical possibility. We have all known students who were first influenced to take up a subject by a respected teacher, but who later made it their life's work because they recognized its beauty or depth, or because they were challenged by its puzzles. We also know people who at first acted truthfully and fairly to avoid punishment or to please their parents, but who now act in these ways because they recognize the interests of others. In these and many other cases, the agent's behavior eventually acquires whatever value his initial failure to respond to the appropriate reasons may have caused it to lack. Even *if* the later behavior is overdetermined—even if either the original nonrationally acquired preference or the agent's new appreciation of reasons would now be sufficient to motivate it—there is no reason to deny that it *has* value.[1] And the same holds, *mutatis mutandis*, of the behavior of citizens who have come to appreciate the reasons for continuing to live in the ways that they were nonrationally caused to prefer.

Thus, nonrationally induced preferences can indeed lead individuals to make choices that are autonomous enough to actualize the (potential) value of what is chosen. But what, next, of *incentives* to adopt (potentially) valuable ways of life? Although incentives are less widely regarded as threats to autonomy than conditioning, they too provide reasons for choosing that are unconnected to the (potential) value of what is chosen. Hence, choices motivated by incentives must also lack the autonomy that (we are assuming) is alone capable of actualizing (potential) value. Indeed, in one respect, incentives are actually *more* inimical to autonomy than nonrational conditioning; for while preferences instilled by conditioning can generally coexist with the appreciation of (potential) value, incentives are apt to divert attention from the (potential) value of what they make attractive. In this way, incentives can actively prevent agents from responding to (potential) value.

Here again, however, an influence that does not at first lead someone to choose something for the right reasons may in the longer run do precisely that. Like choices based on nonrationally conditioned preferences, choices that are directed at incentives—and hence are unconnected to the (potential) value of what is chosen—may themselves put agents in a position to appreciate that (potential) value "from the inside." If as a result an agent subsequently does respond to an activity's (potential) value, the incentive will indirectly have led him to choose it autonomously. Moreover, while incentives admittedly can divert attention from value-based reasons, they can also cancel the effects of counterincentives that otherwise would themselves divert attention from such reasons. For example,

by subsidizing artistic projects, a government can reduce the need for artists to undertake commercial ventures, and thus can free them to respond to more purely aesthetic considerations.

Our third method of promoting valuable activities—the creation and sustenance of valuable options—may seem even less threatening to autonomy. Unlike its predecessors, this method does not seem even to diminish anyone's *present* ability to respond to value-based reasons. Instead, when governments codify and enforce what they consider potentially valuable types of arrangements—when, for example, they extend official approval and protection to monogamous but not polygamous marriages—they appear only to enrich the array of value-based reasons to which their citizens may respond. Hence, this method of promoting valuable activities may seem entirely unproblematical.

But on closer inspection, the issue is not this simple; for, as Jeremy Waldron has argued, "[t]he decision to favor one type of relationship with a legal framework but not another artificially distorts people's estimate of which sort of relationship is morally preferable."[2] To make this estimate without distortion,

[e]veryone who chooses to live with another and to make a life together has to contemplate the possibility that things may go wrong. The relationship may break up or one of the partners may die, and then property and financial entanglements will have to be sorted out. One of the partners may fall ill.... Even if things do not go wrong, they may be complicated. A child may be born, and questions will then arise about who should take care of it and make decisions about its future....[3]

Thus, to choose monogamy autonomously, one must do so (at least partly) because it generates

[1] For pertinent discussion, see George Sher and William J. Bennett, "Moral Education and Indoctrination," *Journal of Philosophy* 79.11 (November 1982): 665–77.

[2] Jeremy Waldron, "Autonomy and Perfectionism in Raz's *Morality of Freedom*," *Southern California Law Review* 62.3/4 (1989): 1151.

[3] Ibid.

fewer complications than polygamy. However, in sanctioning monogamous but not polygamous marriages, "[t]he government has decided on the basis of its estimate of these factors to distort the matter by making it *even easier* for monogamous couples to sort these problems out than for polygamists."[1] By thus making it more difficult to respond to monogamy's true measure of (potential) value, a government does reduce the chances that its citizens will choose it autonomously.

Although I doubt that monogamy's (potential) value has much to do with the relative ease with which monogamists can "sort out problems," Waldron may be right to say that governments which recognize only monogamous marriages provide what amount to artificial incentives to choose monogamy over polygamy. But even if he is right, this will hardly save the case for neutralism. The reason, of course, is that in that case, the same considerations that showed that *incentives* can induce citizens to respond to (potential) value will also show this about the state's attempts to create new options. Thus, even if this third method of inducing citizens to live good lives is no less threatening to autonomy than the first two, it is at least no more threatening either.

VI. An Objection

I have now discussed three of the four ways in which governments can use their power to promote the good. The fourth way—the use of threats and force—will be considered shortly. However, before I turn to it, I must consider the objection that even if the first three methods sometimes do lead citizens to choose the good autonomously, they do not do so often enough to tip the balance against neutralism.

This objection trades on two concessions that were made earlier. I conceded above that only *some* of the persons who are induced by nonrational conditioning or incentives to adopt (potentially) valuable ways of life will eventually respond to their (potential) value. I conceded, as well, that the

choices that stem more immediately from nonrationally conditioned preferences and incentives are *not* autonomous in the relevant sense. But given these concessions, can't a neutralist still insist that many people's lives will have more value if their government does *not* try to shape their preferences or provide them with incentives? And, hence, isn't the consequentialist case for rejecting neutralism inconclusive at best?

I think, in fact, that this suggestion badly underestimates our ability to make reasonable predictions. While not all incentives or nonrationally induced preferences are equally likely to increase an agent's later responsiveness to (potential) value, we can say a good deal about the conditions under which these effects are likely. Where those conditions are met, there is every reason to believe that the agent's later choices will actualize enough (potential) value to outweigh any earlier losses.

But this is not the main problem with the current suggestion. A further (and in my view more decisive) difficulty is that no government can *avoid* either nonrationally shaping its citizens' preferences or providing them with incentives. Even if governments do not try to produce these effects, they are bound to occur as unintended consequences of many political arrangements—including, importantly, many arrangements that are adopted for quite different reasons. It is, indeed, precisely this sort of fact that has led most who discuss neutralism to interpret it as ruling out, not all political arrangements with value-promoting *effects*, but rather all political decisions whose justifications *appeal to* such effects. By taking neutralism to forbid only the adoption of political arrangements *because* they will issue in preferences or incentives that favor certain ways of life, we can acknowledge that all political arrangements will have such effects without concluding that it is impossible to be a neutralist.

But the same considerations that tell for this interpretation now suggest that if a government knows which ways of living are (potentially) best, it can definitely increase overall value through the judicious use of conditioning and incentives. The

---

[1] Ibid.

reason, in brief, is that if all political arrangements do nonrationally shape preferences and provide incentives, a government will not *further* diminish autonomy simply by producing these effects intentionally. It will only further diminish autonomy if it shapes preferences or provides incentives in ways that undermine responsiveness to reasons more than it would be undermined in any event. Thus, if a government makes no effort to promote value by conditioning preferences and providing incentives, the result will be no gain in autonomy, but only a lessening in the number of citizens who live in the ways that the government considers (potentially) valuable. Since by hypothesis those ways of life *are* (potentially) valuable, this means that fewer citizens will be put in a position to appreciate their (potential) value from the inside, and hence that fewer citizens will eventually respond to it. Thus, the ultimate effect of neutralism will be to prevent at least some citizens from living valuable lives.

VII. Coercion and Autonomy

Far from ruling out all four methods of promoting valuable ways of life, autonomy's contribution to value has been found to be compatible with at least three. But we have yet to consider its bearing on what many regard as the core thesis of neutralism. This, of course, is the thesis that governments should never use force (or threats of force) to promote ways of life which they consider valuable, or to deter behavior which does not harm others but is viewed as ignoble, base, or degraded. A prohibition against such "legal moralism" is sometimes regarded as the sole consequence of the appeal to autonomy's (contribution to) value, and is always regarded as its most important conclusion.

It is not hard to see why. Although threats do not so much undermine responsiveness to reasons as alter the reasons to which agents can respond, threats resemble incentives and conditioned preferences in that none of the choices which they motivate are grounded in the (potential) value of what is chosen. Hence, no such choices can be autonomous in the sense that concerns us. Moreover, in addition to being just as destructive to autonomy as the other methods, the use of force is much easier for governments to avoid. While eliminating one form of conditioning only opens the way for others, and while removing one incentive may only make others more attractive, a government that decriminalizes one class of acts need not compensate by criminalizing another. Although every government needs some criminal justice system, governments may punish their citizens for wider or narrower ranges of activities. Hence, if a government does not pass laws against (what it considers) base, ignoble, or degrading behavior, it will genuinely reduce the number of reasons that compete with the reasons provided by (potential) value.

In view of this, it is not surprising that the second premise of the argument designed to ground neutralism in autonomy's contribution to value (see the beginning of Section V) is most often couched in terms of threats or force.[1] Thus construed, the premise asserts that it is either useless or self-defeating for a government to force its citizens to lead good lives because any activity that is undertaken to avoid punishment is *ex hypothesi* not undertaken because of its (potential) value. Yet while this version of the premise may be less decisively false than its predecessors, it is vulnerable to essentially the same reply: that even if a choice is not itself a response to (potential) value, it may contribute to further choices which *are* responses to (potential) value.

Before I elaborate the reply as it applies to threats and coercion, it may again be helpful to introduce some examples. Many laws forbid or seriously restrict activities that do not harm others in any straightforward way. These activities include, among others: copulating in public places, defecating in public, using profane language on television or radio, selling bodily organs, selling babies, gambling, and using narcotic drugs. Although some of the laws clearly

---

[1] ... [See, for example,] Kymlicka, "Rawls on Teleology and Deontology," *Philosophy and Public Affairs* 17.3 (Summer 1988): 186.

have nonperfectionist aims—human waste endangers health, gambling and narcotics are said to attract organized crime—they also appear to be informed by a widely shared vision of what sorts of lives are decent and worthy. While the notion of decency can easily seem quaint or priggish, I believe it represents a deep and significant evaluative category. I believe, too, that it is a notion that few persons, either in our own age or in others, would altogether wish to discard. And while I have already conceded that anyone who is deterred by laws against the cited activities is not responding to the (potential) value of a decent and worthy life, it is not hard to see how the laws can make eventual responses to that (potential) value more likely.

For, first, if an agent avoids narcotic drugs, he will obviously not become addicted. Thus, even if his choice is not autonomous, it will protect his later capacity to respond to (potential) value—including, but not restricted to, the (potential) value of a drug-free life. If his behavior provides an example to others, or reduces the peer pressure on them, the choice that he made in order to avoid punishment may also help to protect *their* capacity to respond to (potential) value. Similarly, if an agent is in danger of becoming a compulsive gambler, his nonautonomous decision not to gamble may protect his later capacity to respond to (potential) value. By attaching penalties to such autonomy-threatening behavior, the law acknowledges that disvaluable as well as valuable activities can be most attractive "from the inside."

This, however, is not the main point; for while any activity can become a habit, most disvaluable behavior is neither especially addictive nor especially destructive of one's general capacity to respond to value. But even when the general capacity remains intact, repeated exposure to disvaluable activities can reduce one's sensitivity to specific kinds of value or disvalue. Hence, an even more important rationale for laws against disvaluable behavior is that those laws create and sustain the conditions under which such sensitivity can thrive.

This, I think, is the most significant effect of laws that attach penalties to coarse and licentious activities. Where such activities abound, it becomes difficult even to envision, much less to see the appeal of, the richer but more subtle possibilities of a more refined sensibility. But by creating an environment in which (at least outward) decency and civility prevail, the law can inscribe a measure of these qualities in the public culture. Moreover, since there is no clear boundary between the public culture and our inner lives, all citizens can thereby be made acquainted with the texture of decent, civil lives and the possibilities these afford. Assuming that decency and civility really are (potentially) valuable, all citizens will thus be put in a better position to appreciate their (potential) value, and hence to choose them for the right reasons. And, while I think the argument is less promising, a similar case can be made that prohibiting the sale of bodily organs curtails commercialism while increasing responsiveness to the demands of altruism.[1]

Of course, none of this shows (or is intended to show) that governments should criminalize any major part of the behavior that most citizens consider disvaluable. Even if we assume, unrealistically, that the majority's unreflective judgments are usually correct, some disfavored activities—watching and reading pornography are standard examples—may become less rather than more attractive with repetition. These may best be allowed to extinguish or stabilize themselves. Others, such as gambling, become addictive to comparatively few. Still others, such as disapproved sexual behavior, are detectable only through massive invasions of privacy, or are preventable only by laws that are so intrusive as to elicit strong resentment. A person who is forced to curtail his sexual proclivities, or to endure religious prohibitions he does not accept, is more apt to despise than to internalize his society's way of life. Hence, threatening him with punishment is unlikely to increase the value of what he subsequently chooses.

Yet these facts demand not that governments altogether avoid using the criminal law to promote

---

[1] See Richard Titmuss, *The Gift Relationship* (New York: Pantheon, 1971)....

valuable choices, but only that they temper its use with good judgment. They suggest that before any government uses force to encourage the better or suppress the worse, it must ask both how successful the effort is likely to be and whether any expected gains are important enough to warrant overriding the general presumption in favor of liberty and noninterference. If there are no deeper objections, a government that wishes its citizens to live the best possible lives must neither use coercion indiscriminately nor withhold it altogether, but must consider each occasion on its merits.

The interesting question, of course, is whether there *are* deeper objections. I have maintained that if one argues that all departures from neutrality undermine the autonomy that valuable choices require, one makes a consequentialist argument that is defeated by the contributions of nonautonomous choices to autonomous ones. Yet precisely because our target has been a defense of neutralism that appeals to consequences, we may be said to have missed the real point. According to many, the real significance of autonomy is not that it is (or contributes to) a value that should be maximized, but that it is a source of rights or an object of respect. While these suggestions may themselves differ importantly, they agree that what autonomy demands is precisely that we treat each person's assessment of his own situation, and any decisions he bases on it, as decisive *whether or not* we have good grounds for expecting them to bring about a net loss of value. Autonomy thus enters not as a locus, ingredient, or prerequisite of value, but as a constraint on its pursuit.

Clearly this second version of the appeal to autonomy requires separate treatment. To assess it properly, we would have to investigate both the basis of the obligation to respect even wrong decisions, and the exact scope and content of that obligation. I believe that when carefully scrutinized, this argument fares no better than the first; but that is a topic for another occasion. For now, the conclusion is only that the principle of autonomy cannot be grounded in any argument that appeals to autonomy's value.

DISCUSSION QUESTIONS

1. Why does Sher think it is "puzzling" to say that government can promote the most value by allowing citizens to exercise their autonomy?

2. Sher claims that "the value-of-autonomy argument must treat autonomy as responsiveness to reasons." Why does he say this? Do you agree? Why or why not?

3. Sher devotes most of his argument to attacking the idea that actions cannot properly be called autonomous if they have resulted from outside (i.e., governmental) influence. He argues that a government can promote what it takes to be valuable in at least four ways, and then argues that all four of these methods can still leave open the possibility of autonomous action. Identify these four ways and Sher's corresponding arguments. Critically evaluate his position.

4. How does Sher think that laws which allow (or fail to restrict) "disvaluable activities" may undermine our responsiveness to activities of real value? Do you think that Sher is assuming a measure of objectivity with regards to what has actual or potential value? If so, do you think this is problematic? Why or why not?

E.
Applications

41

FREE SPEECH

Village of Skokie v. National Socialist Party of America (1978)

In 1977 the neo-Nazi organization known as the National Socialist Party of America (NSPA) planned a political march to take place in Skokie, Illinois, a Chicago suburb with a sizable population of Holocaust survivors. The city government of Skokie refused permission for the NSPA to assemble in the city, prompting the American Civil Liberties Union to pursue court action on behalf of the NSPA. Among the questions facing the courts was whether the display of the Nazi swastika constituted "fighting words" that could reasonably be assumed to incite violence.

SOURCE
Supreme Court of Illinois 373 N.E. 2d 21 (Ill. 1978).

Plaintiff, the village of Skokie, filed a complaint in the circuit court of Cook County seeking to enjoin defendants, the National Socialist Party of America (the American Nazi Party) and 10 individuals as "officers and members" of the party, from engaging in certain activities while conducting a demonstration within the village. The circuit court issued an order enjoining certain conduct during the planned demonstration. The appellate court modified the injunction order, and, as modified, defendants are enjoined from "intentionally displaying the swastika on or off their persons, in the course of a demonstration, march, or parade." ... We allowed defendants' petition for leave to appeal....

It is alleged in plaintiff's complaint that the "uniform of the National Socialist Party of America consists of the storm trooper uniform of the German Nazi Party embellished with the Nazi swastika"; that the plaintiff village has a population of about 70,000 persons of which approximately 40,500 persons are of "Jewish religion or Jewish ancestry" and of this latter number 5,000 to 7,000 are survivors of German concentration camps; that the defendant organization is "dedicated to the incitation of racial and religious hatred directed principally against individuals of Jewish faith or ancestry and non-Caucasians"; and that its members "have patterned their conduct, their uniform, their slogan and their tactics along the pattern of the German Nazi Party."

Defendants moved to dismiss the complaint. In an affidavit attached to defendants' motion to dismiss, defendant Frank Collin, who testified that he was "party leader," stated that on or about March 20, 1977, he sent officials of the plaintiff village a letter stating that the party members and supporters would hold a peaceable, public assembly in the village on May 1, 1977, to protest the Skokie Park District's requirement that the party procure $350,000 of insurance prior to the party's use of the Skokie public parks for public assemblies. The demonstration was to begin at 3 p.m., last 20 to 30 minutes, and consist of 30 to 50 demonstrators marching in single file, back and forth, in front of the village hall. The marchers were to wear uniforms which include a swastika emblem or armband. They were to carry a party banner containing a swastika emblem and signs containing such statements as "White Free Speech," "Free Speech for the White Man," and "Free Speech for White America." The demonstrators would not distribute handbills, make any derogatory statements directed to any ethnic or religious group, or obstruct traffic. They would cooperate with any reasonable police instructions or requests.

At the hearing on plaintiff's motion for an "emergency injunction" a resident of Skokie testified that he was a survivor of the Nazi holocaust. He further testified that the Jewish community in and around Skokie feels the purpose of the march in the "heart of the Jewish population" is to remind the two million survivors "that we are not through with you" and to show "that the Nazi threat is not over, it can happen again." Another resident of Skokie testified that as the result of defendants' announced intention to march in Skokie, 15 to 18 Jewish organizations, within the village and surrounding area, were called and a counter-demonstration of an estimated 12,000 to 15,000 people was scheduled for the same day. There was opinion evidence that defendants' planned demonstration in Skokie would result in violence.

The circuit court entered an order enjoining defendants from "marching, walking or parading in the uniform of the National Socialist Party of America; marching, walking or parading or otherwise displaying the swastika on or off their person; distributing pamphlets or displaying any materials which incite or promote hatred against persons of Jewish faith or ancestry or hatred against persons of any faith or ancestry, race or religion" within the village of Skokie. The appellate court, as earlier noted, modified the order so that defendants were enjoined only from intentional display of the swastika during the Skokie demonstration.

The appellate court opinion adequately discussed and properly decided those issues arising from the portions of the injunction order which enjoined defendants from marching, walking, or parading, from distributing pamphlets or displaying materials, and from wearing the uniform of the National Socialist Party of America. The only issue remaining before this court is whether the circuit court order enjoining defendants from displaying the swastika violates the First Amendment rights of those defendants.

In defining the constitutional rights of the parties who come before this court, we are, of course, bound by the pronouncements of the United States Supreme Court in its interpretation of the United States Constitution. The decisions of that court, particularly *Cohen v. California* … in our opinion compel us to permit the demonstration as proposed, including display of the swastika.

"It is firmly settled that under our Constitution the public expression of ideas may not be prohibited merely because the ideas are themselves offensive to some of their hearers" … and it is entirely clear that the wearing of distinctive clothing can be symbolic expression of a thought or philosophy. The symbolic expression of thought falls within the free speech clause of the First Amendment … and the plaintiff village has the heavy burden of justifying the imposition of a prior restraint upon defendants' right to freedom of speech…. The village of Skokie seeks to meet this burden by application of the "fighting words" doctrine first enunciated in *Chaplinsky v. New Hampshire*…. That doctrine was designed to permit punishment of extremely hostile personal communication likely to cause immediate physical response, "no words being 'forbidden except such as have a direct tendency to cause acts of violence by the persons to whom, individually, the remark is addressed.'" … In *Cohen* the Supreme Court restated the description of fighting words as "those personally abusive epithets which, when addressed to the ordinary citizen, are, as a matter of common knowledge, inherently likely to provoke violent reaction." … Plaintiff urges, and the appellate court has held, that the exhibition of the Nazi symbol, the swastika, addresses to ordinary citizens a message which is tantamount to fighting words. Plaintiff further asks this court to extend *Chaplinsky*, which upheld a statute punishing the use of such words, and hold that the fighting-words doctrine permits a prior restraint on defendants' symbolic speech. In our judgment we are precluded from doing so.

In *Cohen*, defendant's conviction stemmed from wearing a jacket bearing the words "Fuck the Draft" in a Los Angeles County courthouse corridor. The Supreme Court for reasons we believe applicable here refused to find that the jacket inscription constituted fighting words. That court stated:

The constitutional right of free expression is powerful medicine in a society as diverse and populous as ours. It is designed and intended to remove governmental restraints from the arena of public discussion, putting the decision as to what views shall be voiced largely into the hands of each of us, in the hope that use of such freedom will ultimately produce a more capable citizenry and more perfect polity and in the belief that no other approach would comport with the premise of individual dignity and choice upon which our political system rests.…

To many, the immediate consequence of this freedom may often appear to be only verbal tumult, discord, and even offensive utterance. These are, however, within established limits, in truth necessary side effects of the broader enduring values which the process of open debate permits us to achieve. That the air may at times seem filled with verbal cacophony is, in this sense not a sign of weakness but of strength. We cannot lose sight of the fact that, in what otherwise might seem a trifling and annoying instance of individual distasteful abuse of a privilege, these fundamental societal values are truly implicated … "so long as the means are peaceful, the communication need not meet standards of acceptability." …

Against this perception of the constitutional policies involved we discern certain more particularized considerations that peculiarly call for reversal of this conviction. First, the principle contended for by the State seems inherently boundless. How is one to distinguish this from any other offensive word? Surely the State has no right to cleanse public debate to the point where it is grammatically palatable to the most squeamish among us. Yet no readily ascertainable general principle exists for stopping short of that result were we to affirm the judgment below. For, while the particular four-letter word (emblem) being litigated here is perhaps more distasteful than most others of its genre, it is nevertheless often true that one man's vulgarity is another's lyric. Indeed, we think it is largely because governmental officials cannot make principled distinctions in this area that the Constitution leaves matters of taste and style so largely to the individual.…

Finally, and in the same vein, we cannot indulge the facile assumption that one can forbid particular words without also running a substantial risk of suppressing ideas in the process. Indeed, governments might soon seize upon the censorship of particular words as a convenient guise for banning the expression of unpopular views. We have been able, as noted above, to discern little social benefit that might result from running the risk of opening the door to such grave results.…

The display of the swastika, as offensive to the principles of a free nation as the memories it recalls may be, is symbolic political speech intended to convey to the public the beliefs of those who display it, it does not, in our opinion, fall within the definition of "fighting words," and that doctrine cannot be used here to overcome the heavy presumption against the constitutional validity of a prior restraint.

Nor can we find that the swastika, while not representing fighting words, is nevertheless so offensive and peace threatening to the public that its display can be enjoined. We do not doubt that the sight of this symbol is abhorrent to the Jewish citizens of Skokie, and that the survivors of the Nazi persecutions, tormented by their recollections, may have strong feelings regarding its display. Yet it is entirely clear that this factor does not justify enjoining defendants' speech. The *Cohen* court spoke to this subject:

> Finally, in arguments before this Court much has been made of the claim that Cohen's distasteful mode of expression was thrust upon unwilling or unsuspecting viewers, and that the State might therefore legitimately act as it did in order to protect the sensitive from otherwise unavoidable exposure to appellant's crude form of protest. Of course, the mere presumed presence of unwitting listeners or viewers does not serve automatically to just curtailing all speech capable of giving offense.... While this Court has recognized that government may properly act in many situations to prohibit intrusion into the privacy of the home of unwelcome views and ideas which cannot be totally banned from the public dialogue ... we have at the same time consistently stressed that "we are often 'captives' outside the sanctuary of the home and subject to objectionable speech." The ability of government, consonant with the Constitution, to shut off discourse solely to protect others from hearing it is, in other words, dependent upon a showing that substantial privacy interests are being invaded in an essentially intolerable manner. Any broader view of this authority would effectively empower a

majority to silence dissidents simply as a matter of personal predilections....

Similarly, the Court of Appeals for the Seventh Circuit, in reversing the denial of defendant Collin's application for a permit to speak in Chicago's Marquette Park, noted that courts have consistently refused to ban speech because of the possibility of unlawful conduct by those opposed to the speaker's philosophy.

> Starting with *Terminiello v. City of Chicago*.... and continuing to *Gregory v. City of Chicago*, ... it has become patent that a hostile audience is not a basis for restraining otherwise legal First Amendment activity. As with many of the cases cited herein, if the actual behavior is not sufficient to sustain a conviction under a statute, then certainly the anticipation of such events cannot sustain the burden necessary to justify a prior restraint....

Rockwell v. Morris also involved an American Nazi leader, George Lincoln Rockwell, who challenged a bar to his use of a New York City park to hold a public demonstration where anti-Semitic speeches would be made. Although approximately [2.5] million Jewish New Yorkers were hostile to Rockwell's message, the court ordered that a permit to speak be granted, stating:

> A community need not wait to be subverted by street riots and storm troopers; but, also, it cannot, by its policemen or commissioners, suppress a speaker, in prior restraint, on the basis of news reports, hysteria, or inference that what he did yesterday, he will do today. Thus, too, if the speaker incites others to immediate unlawful action he may be punished—in a proper case, stopped when disorder actually impends; but this is not to be confused with unlawful action from others who seek unlawfully to suppress or punish the speaker.

So, the unpopularity of views, their shocking quality, their obnoxiousness, and even their alarming impact is not enough. Otherwise, the preacher of any strange doctrine could be stopped; the anti-racist himself could be suppressed, if he undertakes to speak in "restricted" areas; and one who asks that public schools be open indiscriminately to all ethnic groups could be lawfully suppressed, if only he choose to speak where persuasion is needed most....

In summary, as we read the controlling Supreme Court opinions, use of the swastika is a symbolic form of free speech entitled to First Amendment protections. Its display on uniforms or banners by those engaged in peaceful demonstrations cannot be totally precluded solely because that display may provoke a violent reaction by those who view it. Particularly is this true where, as here, there has been advance notice by the demonstrators of their plans so that they have become, as the complaint alleges, "common knowledge" and those to whom sight of the swastika banner or uniforms would be offense [sic] are forewarned and need not view them. A speaker who gives prior notice of his message has not compelled a confrontation with those who voluntarily listen.

As to those who happen to be in a position to be involuntarily confronted with the swastika, the following observations from *Erznoznik v. City of Jacksonville* are appropriate:

> The plain, if at all times disquieting, truth is that in our pluralistic society, constantly proliferating new and ingenious forms of expression, "we are inescapably captive audiences for many purposes." ... Much that we encounter offends our esthetic, if not our political and moral, sensibilities. Nevertheless, the Constitution does not permit government to decide which types of otherwise protected speech are sufficiently offensive to require protection for the unwilling listener or viewer. Rather, absent the

narrow circumstances described above [home intrusion or captive audience], the burden normally falls upon the viewer to avoid further bombardment of [his] sensibilities simply by averting [his] eyes....

Thus by placing the burden upon the viewer to avoid further bombardment, the Supreme Court has permitted speakers to justify the initial intrusion into the citizen's sensibilities.

We accordingly, albeit reluctantly, conclude that the display of the swastika cannot be enjoined under the fighting-words exception to free speech, nor can anticipation of a hostile audience justify the prior restraint. Furthermore, *Cohen* and *Erznoznik* direct the citizens of Skokie that it is their burden to avoid the offensive symbol if they can do so without unreasonable inconvenience. Accordingly, we are constrained to reverse that part of the appellate court judgment enjoining the display of the swastika. That judgment is in all other respects affirmed.

DISCUSSION QUESTIONS

1. The court claims that *Cohen v. California* is a precedent for the current case. Explain the facts of *Cohen* and how it provides a precedent for this case.

2. Apply Mill's defense of freedom of expression to the current case: would Mill uphold the decision of the court? Why or why not?

3. Apply Feinberg's Offense Principle to the current case: would you, on the basis of that principle, uphold the decision of the court? Why or why not?

4. The court rejects the claim that the potential of a violent response to a demonstration is reason for preventing the demonstration. How does it defend this claim? Evaluate its defense.

R. v. Keegstra (1990)

R. v. Keegstra is a Supreme Court of Canada decision concerned with issues of freedom of expression. The Court considers whether hate propaganda can be analogized to acts of violence or threats of violence.

The Court likewise considers the alleged types of harm which may result from hate propaganda, and discusses how those concerns ought to be balanced against concerns about the protection of free speech.

SOURCE

R. v. Keegstra (1990) 3 S.C.R. 697.

Her Majesty The Queen   *Appellant*
v.
James Keegstra   *Respondent*

and
The Attorney General of Canada,
the Attorney General for Ontario,
the Attorney General of Quebec,
the Attorney General for New Brunswick,
the Attorney General of Manitoba,
the Canadian Jewish Congress,
the League for Human Rights of B'nai Brith,
Canada, Interamicus, the Women's Legal
Education and Action Fund, and the
Canadian Civil Liberties Association
                                      Interveners

indexed as: r. *v.* keegstra
File No.: 21118.
1989: December 5, 6; 1990: December 13.
Present: Dickson C.J. and Wilson, La Forest,
L'Heureux-Dubé, Sopinka, Gonthier and McLachlin
JJ.
on appeal from the court of appeal for Alberta
[...]

I. Facts

Mr. James Keegstra was a high school teacher in Eckville, Alberta, from the early 1970s until his dismissal in 1982. In 1984 Mr. Keegstra was charged under s. 319(2) (then s. 281.2(2)) of the *Criminal*

Code with unlawfully promoting hatred against an identifiable group by communicating anti-Semitic statements to his students. He was convicted by a jury in a trial before McKenzie J. of the Alberta Court of Queen's Bench.

Mr. Keegstra's teachings attributed various evil qualities to Jews. He thus described Jews to his pupils as "treacherous," "subversive," "sadistic," "money-loving," "power hungry" and "child killers." He taught his classes that Jewish people seek to destroy Christianity and are responsible for depressions, anarchy, chaos, wars and revolution. According to Mr. Keegstra, Jews "created the Holocaust to gain sympathy" and, in contrast to the open and honest Christians, were said to be deceptive, secretive and inherently evil. Mr. Keegstra expected his students to reproduce his teachings in class and on exams. If they failed to do so, their marks suffered.

Prior to his trial, Mr. Keegstra applied to the Court of Queen's Bench in Alberta for an order quashing the charge on a number of grounds, the primary one being that s. 319(2) of the *Criminal Code* unjustifiably infringed his freedom of expression as guaranteed by s. 2(*b*) of the *Charter*.... The application was dismissed by Quigley J., and Mr. Keegstra was thereafter tried and convicted. He then appealed his conviction to the Alberta Court of Appeal, raising the same *Charter* issues. The Court of Appeal unanimously accepted his argument, and it is from this judgment that the Crown appeals. [...]

III. Relevant Statutory and Constitutional Provisions

The relevant legislative and *Charter* provisions are set out below:

Criminal Code

319....

(2) Everyone who, by communicating statements, other than in private conversation, willfully promotes hatred against any identifiable group is guilty of

(*a*) an indictable offence and is liable to imprisonment for a term not exceeding two years; or

(*b*) an offence punishable on summary conviction.

(3) No person shall be convicted of an offence under subsection (2)

(*a*) if he establishes that the statements communicated were true;

(*b*) if, in good faith, he expressed or attempted to establish by argument an opinion on a religious subject;

(*c*) if the statements were relevant to any subject of public interest, the discussion of which was for the public benefit, and if on reasonable grounds he believed them to be true; or

(*d*) if, in good faith, he intended to point out, for the purpose of removal, matters producing or tending to produce feelings of hatred towards an identifiable group in Canada.

[...]

(4) In this section, "identifiable group" means any section of the public distinguished by colour, race, religion or ethnic origin.

Canadian Bill of Rights, R.S.C., 1985, App. III

The Parliament of Canada, affirming that the Canadian Nation is founded upon principles that acknowledge the supremacy of God, the dignity and worth of the human person and the position of the family in a society of free men and free institutions;

Affirming also that men and institutions remain free only when freedom is founded upon respect for moral and spiritual values and the rule of law;

And being desirous of enshrining these principles and the human rights and fundamental freedoms derived from them, in a Bill of Rights which shall reflect the respect of Parliament for its constitutional authority and which shall ensure the protection of these rights and freedoms in Canada:

Therefore Her Majesty, by and with the advice and consent of the Senate and House of Commons of Canada, enacts as follows:

...

1. It is hereby recognized and declared that in Canada there have existed and shall continue to exist without discrimination by reason of race, national origin, colour, religion or sex, the following human rights and fundamental freedoms, namely, ...

(d) freedom of speech;

Canadian Charter of Rights and Freedoms

1. The *Canadian Charter of Rights and Freedoms* guarantees the rights and freedoms set out in it subject only to such reasonable limits prescribed by law as can be demonstrably justified in a free and democratic society.

2. Everyone has the following fundamental freedoms:

[...]

(b) freedom of thought, belief, opinion and expression, including freedom of the press and other media of communication;

[...]

VI. Section 2(b) of the Charter—Freedom of Expression

... I can now address the constitutional questions arising for decision in this appeal. The first of these concerns whether the *Charter* guarantee of freedom of expression is infringed by s. 319(2) of the *Criminal Code*. In other words, does the coverage of s. 2(*b*) extend to the public and wilful promotion of hatred against an identifiable group. Before looking to the specific facts of this appeal, however, I would like to comment upon the nature of the s. 2(*b*) guarantee. Obviously, one's conception of the freedom of expression provides a crucial backdrop to any s. 2(*b*) inquiry; the values promoted by the freedom help not only to define the ambit of s. 2(*b*), but also come to the forefront when discussing how competing interests might co-exist with the freedom under s. 1 of the *Charter*.

[...]

... the reach of s. 2(*b*) is potentially very wide, expression being deserving of constitutional protection if "it serves individual and societal values in a free and democratic society." In subsequent cases, the Court has not lost sight of this broad view of the values underlying the freedom of expression, though the majority decision in *Irwin Toy*[1] perhaps goes further towards stressing as primary the "democratic commitment" said to delineate the protected sphere of liberty (p. 971). Moreover, the Court has attempted to articulate more precisely some of the convictions fueling the freedom of expression, these being summarized in *Irwin Toy* (at p. 976) as follows: (1) seeking and attaining truth is an inherently good activity; (2) participation in social and political decision-making is to be fostered and encouraged; and (3) diversity in forms of individual self-fulfillment and human flourishing ought to be cultivated in a tolerant and welcoming environment for the sake of both those who convey a meaning and those to whom meaning is conveyed. [...]

Irwin Toy can be seen as at once clarifying the relationship between ss. 2(*b*) and 1 in freedom of expression cases and reaffirming and strengthening the large and liberal interpretation given the freedom in s. 2(*b*) by the Court in *Ford*. These aspects of the decision flow largely from a two-step analysis used in determining whether s. 2(*b*) has been infringed, an approach affirmed by this Court in subsequent cases, for example *Reference re ss. 193 and 195.1(1)(c) of the Criminal Code (Man.), supra,* and *Royal College of Dental Surgeons, supra*.

The first step in the *Irwin Toy* analysis involves asking whether the activity of the litigant who alleges an infringement of the freedom of expression falls within the protected s. 2(*b*) sphere. In outlining a broad, inclusive approach to answering this question, the following was said (at p. 968):

"Expression" has both a content and a form, and the two can be inextricably connected.

---

[1] [*Irwin Toy Ltd. v. Quebec* (1989) was an important Supreme Court of Canada case that provided guidelines for interpreting section 2(b) of the Charter. In *Irwin Toy* the Court upheld a law that placed restrictions on advertising aimed at children.]

Activity is expressive if it attempts to convey meaning. That meaning is its content. Freedom of expression was entrenched in our Constitution and is guaranteed in the Quebec *Charter* so as to ensure that everyone can manifest their thoughts, opinions, beliefs, indeed all expressions of the heart and mind, however unpopular, distasteful or contrary to the mainstream. Such protection is, in the words of both the Canadian and Quebec Charters, "fundamental" because in a free, pluralistic and democratic society we prize a diversity of ideas and opinions for their inherent value both to the community and to the individual.

Apart from rare cases where expression is communicated in a physically violent form, the Court thus viewed the fundamental nature of the freedom of expression as ensuring that "if the activity conveys or attempts to convey a meaning, it has expressive content and *prima facie* falls within the scope of the guarantee" (p. 969). In other words, the term "expression" as used in s. 2(*b*) of the *Charter* embraces all content of expression irrespective of the particular meaning or message sought to be conveyed (*Reference re ss. 193 and 195.1(1)(c) of the Criminal Code (Man.), supra,* at p. 1181, *per* Lamer J.).

The second step in the analysis outlined in *Irwin Toy* is to determine whether the purpose of the impugned government action is to restrict freedom of expression. The guarantee of freedom of expression will necessarily be infringed by government action having such a purpose. If, however, it is the effect of the action, rather than the purpose, that restricts an activity, s. 2(*b*) is not brought into play unless it can be demonstrated by the party alleging an infringement that the activity supports rather than undermines the principles and values upon which freedom of expression is based.

Having reviewed the *Irwin Toy* test, it remains to determine whether the impugned legislation in this appeal—s. 319(2) of the *Criminal Code*—infringes the freedom of expression guarantee of s. 2(*b*). Communications which wilfully promote

hatred against an identifiable group without doubt convey a meaning, and are intended to do so by those who make them. Because *Irwin Toy* stresses that the type of meaning conveyed is irrelevant to the question of whether s. 2(*b*) is infringed, that the expression covered by s. 319(2) is invidious and obnoxious is beside the point. It is enough that those who publicly and wilfully promote hatred convey or attempt to convey a meaning, and it must therefore be concluded that the first step of the *Irwin Toy* test is satisfied.

Moving to the second stage of the s. 2(*b*) inquiry, one notes that the prohibition in s. 319(2) aims directly at words—in this appeal, Mr. Keegstra's teachings—that have as their content and objective the promotion of racial or religious hatred. The purpose of s. 319(2) can consequently be formulated as follows: to restrict the content of expression by singling out particular meanings that are not to be conveyed. Section 319(2) therefore overtly seeks to prevent the communication of expression, and hence meets the second requirement of the *Irwin Toy* test.

In my view, through s. 319(2) Parliament seeks to prohibit communications which convey meaning, namely, those communications which are intended to promote hatred against identifiable groups. I thus find s. 319(2) to constitute an infringement of the freedom of expression guaranteed by s. 2(*b*) of the *Charter*. Before moving on to see whether the impugned provision is nonetheless justified under s. 1, however, I wish to canvas two arguments made in favour of the position that communications intended to promote hatred do not fall within the ambit of s. 2(*b*). The first of these arguments concerns an exception mentioned in *Irwin Toy* concerning expression manifested in a violent form....

Beginning with the suggestion that expression covered by s. 319(2) falls within an exception articulated in *Irwin Toy*, it was argued before this Court that the wilful promotion of hatred is an activity the form and consequences of which are analogous to those associated with violence or threats of violence. This argument contends that Supreme Court

of Canada precedent excludes violence and threats of violence from the ambit of s. 2(b), and that the reason for such exclusion must lie in the fact that these forms of expression are inimical to the values supporting freedom of speech. Indeed, in support of this view it was pointed out to us that the Court in *Irwin Toy* stated that "freedom of expression ensures that we can convey our thoughts and feelings in non-violent ways without fear of censure" (p. 970). Accordingly, we were urged to find that hate propaganda of the type caught by s. 319(2), insofar as it imperils the ability of target group members themselves to convey thoughts and feelings in non-violent ways without fear of censure, is analogous to violence and threats of violence and hence does not fall within s. 2(b).
[…]

Turning specifically to the proposition that hate propaganda should be excluded from the coverage of s. 2(b), I begin by stating that the communications restricted by s. 319(2) cannot be considered as violence, which on a reading of *Irwin Toy* I find to refer to expression communicated directly through physical harm. Nor do I find hate propaganda to be analogous to violence, and through this route exclude it from the protection of the guarantee of freedom of expression. As I have explained, the starting proposition in *Irwin Toy* is that all activities conveying or attempting to convey meaning are considered expression for the purposes of s. 2(b); the content of expression is irrelevant in determining the scope of this *Charter* provision. Stated at its highest, an exception has been suggested where meaning is communicated directly via physical violence, the extreme repugnance of this form to free expression values justifying such an extraordinary step. Section 319(2) of the *Criminal Code* prohibits the communication of meaning that is repugnant, but the repugnance stems from the content of the message as opposed to its form. For this reason, I am of the view that hate propaganda is to be categorized as expression so as to bring it within the coverage of s. 2(b).

As for threats of violence, *Irwin Toy* spoke only of restricting s. 2(b) to certain *forms* of expression, stating at p. 970 that,

[w]hile the guarantee of free expression protects all content of expression, certainly violence as a *form* of expression receives no such protection. It is not necessary here to delineate precisely when and on what basis a form of expression chosen to convey a meaning falls outside the sphere of the guarantee. But it is clear, for example, that a murderer or rapist cannot invoke freedom of expression in justification of the form of expression he has chosen. [Emphasis in original.]

While the line between form and content is not always easily drawn, in my opinion threats of violence can only be so classified by reference to the content of their meaning. As such, they do not fall within the exception spoken of in *Irwin Toy*, and their suppression must be justified under s. 1. As I do not find threats of violence to be excluded from the definition of expression envisioned by s. 2(b), it is unnecessary to determine whether the threatening aspects of hate propaganda can be seen as threats of violence, or analogous to such threats, so as to deny it protection under s. 2(b).
[…]

VII. Section 1 Analysis of Section 319(2)

A. General Approach to Section 1

Though the language of s. 1 appears earlier in these reasons, it is appropriate to repeat its words:
1. The *Canadian Charter of Rights and Freedoms* guarantees the rights and freedoms set out in it subject only to such reasonable limits prescribed by law as can be demonstrably justified in a free and democratic society.

In *R. v. Oakes*, [1986] 1 S.C.R. 103, this Court offered a course of analysis to be employed in determining whether a limit on a right or freedom can be demonstrably justified in a free and democratic society. Under the approach in *Oakes*, it must first be established that impugned state action has an objective of pressing and substantial concern in a free and democratic society. Only such an objective is of sufficient stature to warrant overriding a constitutionally protected right or freedom (p. 138). The second feature of the *Oakes* test involves assessing the proportionality between the objective and the impugned measure. The inquiry as to proportionality attempts to guide the balancing of individual and group interests protected in s. 1, and in *Oakes* was broken down into the following three segments (at p. 139):

> First, the measures adopted must be carefully designed to achieve the objective in question. They must not be arbitrary, unfair or based on irrational considerations. In short, they must be rationally connected to the objective. Second, the means, even if rationally connected to the objective in this first sense, should impair "as little as possible" the right or freedom in question…. Third, there must be a proportionality between the *effects* of the measures which are responsible for limiting the *Charter* right or freedom, and the objective which has been identified as of "sufficient importance." [Emphasis in original]

[…]

C. Objective of Section 319(2)

I now turn to the specific requirements of the *Oakes* approach in deciding whether the infringement of s. 2(*b*) occasioned by s. 319(2) is justifiable in a free and democratic society. According to *Oakes*, the first aspect of the s. 1 analysis is to examine the objective of the impugned legislation. Only if the objective relates to concerns which are pressing and substantial in a free and democratic society can the legislative limit on a right or freedom hope to be permissible under the *Charter*. In examining the objective of s. 319(2), I will begin by discussing the harm caused by hate propaganda as identified by the Cohen Committee and subsequent study

groups, and then review in turn the impact upon this objective of international human rights instruments and ss. 15 and 27 of the *Charter*.

(i) Harm Caused by Expression Promoting the Hatred of Identifiable Groups

Looking to the legislation challenged in this appeal, one must ask whether the amount of hate propaganda in Canada causes sufficient harm to justify legislative intervention of some type. The Cohen Committee, speaking in 1965, found that the incidence of hate propaganda in Canada was not insignificant (at p. 24):

> … there exists in Canada a small number of persons and a somewhat larger number of organizations, extremist in outlook and dedicated to the preaching and spreading of hatred and contempt against certain identifiable minority groups in Canada. It is easy to conclude that because the number of persons and organizations is not very large, they should not be taken too seriously. The Committee is of the opinion that this line of analysis is no longer tenable after what is known to have been the result of hate propaganda in other countries, particularly in the 1930's when such material and ideas played a significant role in the creation of a climate of malice, destructive to the central values of Judaic-Christian society, the values of our civilization. The Committee believes, therefore, that the actual and potential danger caused by present hate activities in Canada cannot be measured by statistics alone.

> Even the statistics, however, are not unimpressive, because while activities have centered heavily in Ontario, they nevertheless have extended from Nova Scotia to British Columbia and minority groups in at least eight Provinces have been subjected to these vicious attacks.

In 1984, the House of Commons Special Committee on Participation of Visible Minorities in Canadian Society in its report, entitled *Equality Now!*, observed that increased immigration and periods of economic difficulty "have produced an atmosphere that may be ripe for racially motivated incidents" (p. 69). With regard to the dissemination of hate propaganda, the Special Committee found that the prevalence and scope of such material had risen since the Cohen Committee made its report, stating (at p. 69):

> There has been a recent upsurge in hate pro-paganda. It has been found in virtually every part of Canada. Not only is it anti-semitic and anti-black, as in the 1960s, but it is also now anti-Roman Catholic, anti-East Indian, anti-aboriginal people and anti-French. Some of this material is imported from the United States but much of it is produced in Canada. Most worrisome of all is that in recent years Canada has become a major source of sup-ply of hate propaganda that finds its way to Europe, and especially to West Germany.

As the quotations above indicate, the presence of hate propaganda in Canada is sufficiently substan-tial to warrant concern. Disquiet caused by the exis-tence of such material is not simply the product of its offensiveness, however, but stems from the very real harm which it causes. Essentially, there are two sorts of injury caused by hate propaganda. First, there is harm done to members of the target group. It is indisputable that the emotional damage caused by words may be of grave psychological and social consequence. In the context of sexual harassment, for example, this Court has found that words can in themselves constitute harassment (*Janzen v. Platy Enterprises Ltd.*, [1989] 1 S.C.R. 1252). In a similar manner, words and writings that wilfully promote hatred can constitute a serious attack on persons belonging to a racial or religious group, and in this regard the Cohen Committee noted that these per-sons are humiliated and degraded (p. 214).

In my opinion, a response of humiliation and degradation from an individual targeted by hate propaganda is to be expected. A person's sense of human dignity and belonging to the community at large is closely linked to the concern and respect accorded the groups to which he or she belongs (see I. Berlin, "Two Concepts of Liberty," in *Four Essays on Liberty* [1969], 118, at p. 155). The deri-sion, hostility and abuse encouraged by hate propa-ganda therefore have a severely negative impact on the individual's sense of self-worth and acceptance. This impact may cause target group members to take drastic measures in reaction, perhaps avoid-ing activities which bring them into contact with non-group members or adopting attitudes and pos-tures directed towards blending in with the major-ity. Such consequences bear heavily in a nation that prides itself on tolerance and the fostering of human dignity through, among other things, respect for the many racial, religious and cultural groups in our society.

A second harmful effect of hate propaganda which is of pressing and substantial concern is its influence upon society at large. The Cohen Committee noted that individuals can be persuaded to believe "almost anything" (p. 30) if information or ideas are communicated using the right technique and in the proper circumstances (at p. 8):

> ... we are less confident in the 20th century that the critical faculties of individuals will be brought to bear on the speech and writ-ing which is directed at them. In the 18th and 19th centuries, there was a widespread belief that man was a rational creature, and that if his mind was trained and liberated from superstition by education, he would always distinguish truth from falsehood, good from evil. So Milton, who said "let truth and false-hood grapple: who ever knew truth put to the worse in a free and open encounter."

> We cannot share this faith today in such a simple form. While holding that over the long run, the human mind is repelled by blatant

falsehood and seeks the good, it is too often true, in the short run, that emotion displaces reason and individuals perversely reject the demonstrations of truth put before them and forsake the good they know. The successes of modern advertising, the triumphs of impudent propaganda such as Hitler's, have qualified sharply our belief in the rationality of man. We know that under strain and pressure in times of irritation and frustration, the individual is swayed and even swept away by hysterical, emotional appeals. We act irresponsibly if we ignore the way in which emotion can drive reason from the field.

It is thus not inconceivable that the active dissemination of hate propaganda can attract individuals to its cause, and in the process create serious discord between various cultural groups in society. Moreover, the alteration of views held by the recipients of hate propaganda may occur subtly [sic], and is not always attendant upon conscious acceptance of the communicated ideas. Even if the message of hate propaganda is outwardly rejected, there is evidence that its premise of racial or religious inferiority may persist in a recipient's mind as an idea that holds some truth, an incipient effect not to be entirely discounted....

The threat to the self-dignity of target group members is thus matched by the possibility that prejudiced messages will gain some credence, with the attendant result of discrimination, and perhaps even violence, against minority groups in Canadian society. With these dangers in mind, the Cohen Committee made clear in its conclusions that the presence of hate propaganda existed as a baleful and pernicious element, and hence a serious problem, in Canada (at p. 59):

> The amount of hate propaganda presently being disseminated and its measurable effects probably are not sufficient to justify a description of the problem as one of crisis or near crisis proportions. Nevertheless the problem is a serious one. We believe that,

given a certain set of socio-economic circumstances, such as a deepening of the emotional tensions or the setting in of a severe business recession, public susceptibility might well increase significantly. Moreover, the potential psychological and social damage of hate propaganda, both to a desensitized majority and to sensitive minority target groups, is incalculable. As Mr. Justice Jackson of the United States Supreme Court wrote in *Beauharnais v. Illinois*,[1] such "sinister abuses of our freedom of expression ... can tear apart a society, brutalize its dominant elements, and persecute even to extermination, its minorities."

As noted previously, in articulating concern about hate propaganda and its contribution to racial and religious tension in Canada, the Cohen Committee recommended that Parliament use the *Criminal Code* in order to prohibit wilful, hate-promoting expression and underline Canada's commitment to end prejudice and intolerance.

The close connection between the recommendations of the Cohen Committee and the hate propaganda amendments to the *Criminal Code* made in 1970 indicates that in enacting s. 319(2) Parliament's purpose was to prevent the harm identified by the Committee as being caused by hate-promoting expression. More recent reports have echoed the findings and concerns of the Cohen Committee, lending further support to the substantial nature of the legislative objective....

[...]

(iii) Other Provisions of the Charter

Significant indicia of the strength of the objective behind s. 319(2) are gleaned not only from the international arena, but are also expressly evident

---

[1] [This was a United States Supreme Court Case decided in 1952. In *Beauharnais* the Court upheld as constitutional a law that criminalized certain kinds of negative portrayals of persons identified via their membership in racial or religious groups. The Court regarded the speech as a form of libel and, thus, as unprotected by the First Amendment to the United States Constitution.]

UNIT II: E. Applications

in various provisions of the *Charter* itself. As Wilson J. noted in *Singh v. Minister of Employment and Immigration*, [1985] 1 S.C.R. 177, at p. 218:

> ... it is important to bear in mind that the rights and freedoms set out in the *Charter* are fundamental to the political structure of Canada and are guaranteed by the *Charter* as part of the supreme law of our nation. I think that in determining whether a particular limitation is a reasonable limit prescribed by law which can be "demonstrably justified in a free and democratic society" it is important to remember that the courts are conducting this inquiry in light of a commitment to uphold the rights and freedoms set out in the other sections of the *Charter*.

Most importantly for the purposes of this appeal, ss. 15 and 27 represent a strong commitment to the values of equality and multiculturalism, and hence underline the great importance of Parliament's objective in prohibiting hate propaganda.

Looking first to s. 15, in *R. v. Big M Drug Mart Ltd.*, [1985] 1 S.C.R. 295, I said that "[a] free society is one which aims at equality with respect to the enjoyment of fundamental freedoms and I say this without any reliance upon s. 15 of the *Charter*" (p. 336). Section 15 lends further support to this observation, for the effects of entrenching a guarantee of equality in the *Charter* are not confined to those instances where it can be invoked by an individual against the state. Insofar as it indicates our society's dedication to promoting equality, s. 15 is also relevant in assessing the aims of s. 319(2) of the *Criminal Code* under s. 1. In *Andrews v. Law Society of British Columbia*, [1989] 1 S.C.R. 143, this Court examined the equality guarantee of s. 15, McIntyre J. noting (at p. 171):

> It is clear that the purpose of s. 15 is to ensure equality in the formulation and application of the law. The promotion of equality entails the promotion of a society in which all are secure in the knowledge that they are recognized at law as human beings equally deserving of concern, respect and consideration. It has a large remedial component.

As noted in *Big M Drug Mart*, promoting equality is an undertaking essential to any free and democratic society, and I believe that the words of McIntyre J. support this position. The principles underlying s. 15 of the *Charter* are thus integral to the s. 1 analysis.

In its written submission to the Court, the intervenor L.E.A.F. made the following comment in support of the view that the public and wilful promotion of group hatred is properly understood as a practice of inequality:

> Government sponsored hatred on group grounds would violate section 15 of the *Charter*. Parliament promotes equality and moves against inequality when it prohibits the wilful public promotion of group hatred on these grounds. It follows that government action against group hate, because it promotes social equality as guaranteed by the *Charter*, deserves special constitutional consideration under section 15.

I agree with this statement. In light of the *Charter* commitment to equality, and the reflection of this commitment in the framework of s. 1, the objective of the impugned legislation is enhanced insofar as it seeks to ensure the equality of all individuals in Canadian society. The message of the expressive activity covered by s. 319(2) is that members of identifiable groups are not to be given equal standing in society, and are not human beings equally deserving of concern, respect and consideration. The harms caused by this message run directly counter to the values central to a free and democratic society, and in restricting the promotion of hatred Parliament is therefore seeking to bolster the notion of mutual respect necessary in a nation which venerates the equality of all persons.

Section 15 is not the only *Charter* provision which emphasizes values both important to a free and democratic society and pertinent to the disposition of this appeal under s. 1. Section 27 states that:

27. This Charter shall be interpreted in a manner consistent with the preservation and enhancement of the multicultural heritage of Canadians.

This Court has where possible taken account of s. 27 and its recognition that Canada possesses a multicultural society in which the diversity and richness of various cultural groups is a value to be protected and enhanced. Section 27 has therefore been used in a number of judgments of this Court, both as an aid in interpreting the definition of *Charter* rights and freedoms (see, e.g., *Big M Drug Mart*, *supra*, *per* Dickson J., at pp. 337–38, *Edwards Books*, *supra*, *per* Dickson C.J., at p. 758; and *Andrews v. Law Society of British Columbia*, *supra*, *per* McIntyre J., at p. 171) and as an element in the s. 1 analysis (see, e.g., *Edwards Books*, *per* La Forest J., at p. 804, and Wilson J., at p. 809).

The value expressed in s. 27 cannot be casually dismissed in assessing the validity of s. 319(2) under s. 1, and I am of the belief that s. 27 and the commitment to a multicultural vision of our nation bear notice in emphasizing the acute importance of the objective of eradicating hate propaganda from society. Professor J.E. Magnet has dealt with some of the factors which may be used to inform the meaning of s. 27, and of these I expressly adopt the principle of non-discrimination and the need to prevent attacks on the individual's connection with his or her culture, and hence upon the process of self-development…. Indeed, the sense that an individual can be affected by treatment of a group to which he or she belongs is clearly evident in a number of other *Charter* provisions not yet mentioned, including ss. 16 to 23 (language rights), s. 25 (aboriginal rights), s. 28 (gender equality) and s. 29 (denominational schools).

Hate propaganda seriously threatens both the enthusiasm with which the value of equality is accepted and acted upon by society and the connection of target group members to their community. I thus agree with the sentiments of Cory J.A. who, in writing to uphold s. 319(2) in *R. v. Andrews* (1988), 65 O.R. (2d) 161, said (at p. 181):

Multiculturalism cannot be preserved let alone enhanced if free rein is given to the promotion of hatred against identifiable cultural groups.

When the prohibition of expressive activity that promotes hatred of groups identifiable on the basis of colour, race, religion, or ethnic origin is considered in light of s. 27, the legitimacy and substantial nature of the government objective is therefore considerably strengthened.

(iv) Conclusion Respecting Objective of Section 319(2)

In my opinion, it would be impossible to deny that Parliament's objective in enacting s. 319(2) is of the utmost importance. Parliament has recognized the substantial harm that can flow from hate propaganda, and in trying to prevent the pain suffered by target group members and to reduce racial, ethnic and religious tension in Canada has decided to suppress the wilful promotion of hatred against identifiable groups. The nature of Parliament's objective is supported not only by the work of numerous study groups, but also by our collective historical knowledge of the potentially catastrophic effects of the promotion of hatred (*Jones*, *supra*, *per* La Forest J., at pp. 299–300). Additionally, the international commitment to eradicate hate propaganda and the stress placed upon equality and multiculturalism in the *Charter* strongly buttress the importance of this objective. I consequently find that the first part of the test under s. 1 of the *Charter* is easily satisfied and that a powerfully convincing legislative objective exists such as to justify some limit on freedom of expression.

D. Proportionality

[…]

(i) Relation of the Expression at Stake to Free Expression Values

In discussing the nature of the government objective, I have commented at length upon the way in which the suppression of hate propaganda furthers values basic to a free and democratic society. I have said little, however, regarding the extent to which these same values, including the freedom of expression, are furthered by *permitting* the exposition of such expressive activity. This lacuna is explicable when one realizes that the interpretation of s. 2(*b*) under *Irwin Toy*, *supra* gives protection to a very wide range of expression. Content is irrelevant to this interpretation, the result of a high value being placed upon freedom of expression in the abstract. This approach to s. 2(*b*) often operates to leave unexamined the extent to which the expression *at stake in a particular case* promotes freedom of expression principles. In my opinion, however, the s. 1 analysis of a limit upon s. 2(*b*) cannot ignore the nature of the expressive activity which the state seeks to restrict. While we must guard carefully against judging expression according to its popularity, it is equally destructive of free expression values, as well as the other values which underlie a free and democratic society, to treat all expression as equally crucial to those principles at the core of s. 2(*b*).

In *Rocket v. Royal College of Dental Surgeons of Ontario*, *supra*, McLachlin J. recognized the importance of context in evaluating expressive activity under s. 1, stating with regard to commercial speech (at pp. 246–47):

> While the Canadian approach does not apply special tests to restrictions on commercial expression, our method of analysis does permit a sensitive, case-oriented approach to the determination of their constitutionality. Placing the conflicting values in their factual and social context when performing the s. 1 analysis permits the courts to have regard to special features of the expression in question. As Wilson J. notes in *Edmonton Journal v. Alberta (Attorney General)*, [1989] 2 S.C.R. 1326, not all expression is equally worthy of protection. Nor are all infringements of free expression equally serious. [See also *Reference re ss. 193 and 195.1(1)(c) of the Criminal Code (Man.)*, *per* Dickson C.J., at p. 1135.]

Using this contextual approach, McLachlin J. evaluated the expression jeopardized by government regulation in light of s. 2(*b*) values. She thus went on to consider those interests which argued for restriction only after having assessed the importance of the freedom of expression interest at stake on the facts of the case.

Royal College dealt with provincial limitations upon the freedom of dentists to impart information to patients and potential patients via advertisements. In these circumstances, the Court found that the expression regulated was of a nature that made its curtailment something less than a most serious infringement of the freedom of expression, the limitation affecting neither participation in the political process nor the ability of the individual to achieve spiritual or artistic self-fulfillment. The resulting conclusion was that "restrictions on expression of this kind might be easier to justify than other infringements" (p. 247). At the same time, however, it was recognized that an interest existed in those who wished to make an informed choice as to a dentist, and in so far as access to such information was restricted the infringement of s. 2(*b*) could not be lightly dismissed (p. 247). Moreover, unlike in *Irwin Toy*, the information was not aimed at children, a group hampered in making informed choices, and hence any heightened state interest that might arise in protecting a vulnerable group was absent (p. 248).

Applying the *Royal College* approach to the context of this appeal is a key aspect of the s. 1 analysis. One must ask whether the expression prohibited by s. 319(2) is tenuously connected to the values underlying s. 2(*b*) so as to make the restriction "easier to justify than other infringements." In this regard, let me begin by saying that, in my opinion, there can be no real disagreement about the subject matter of the messages and teachings communicated by the respondent, Mr. Keegstra: it is deeply offensive, hurtful and damaging to target group members, misleading to his listeners, and antithetical to the furtherance of tolerance and understanding in society. Furthermore, as will be clear when I come to discuss in detail the interpretation of s. 319(2), there is no doubt that all expression fitting within the terms of the offence can be similarly described. To say merely that expression is offensive and disturbing, however, fails to address satisfactorily the question of whether, and to what extent, the expressive activity prohibited by s. 319(2) promotes the values underlying the freedom of expression. It is to this difficult and complex question that I now turn.

From the outset, I wish to make clear that in my opinion the expression prohibited by s. 319(2) is not closely linked to the rationale underlying s. 2(*b*). Examining the values identified in *Ford* and *Irwin Toy* as fundamental to the protection of free expression, arguments can be made for the proposition that each of these values is diminished by the suppression of hate propaganda. While none of these arguments is spurious, I am of the opinion that expression intended to promote the hatred of identifiable groups is of limited importance when measured against free expression values.

At the core of freedom of expression lies the need to ensure that truth and the common good are attained, whether in scientific and artistic endeavors or in the process of determining the best course to take in our political affairs. Since truth and the ideal form of political and social organization can rarely, if at all, be identified with absolute certainty, it is difficult to prohibit expression without impeding the free exchange of potentially valuable information. Nevertheless, the argument from truth does not provide convincing support for the protection of hate propaganda. Taken to its extreme, this argument would require us to permit the communication of all expression, it being impossible to know with *absolute* certainty which factual statements are true, or which ideas obtain the greatest good. The problem with this extreme position, however, is that the greater the degree of certainty that a statement is erroneous or mendacious, the less its value in the quest for truth. Indeed, expression can be used to the detriment of our search for truth; the state should not be the sole arbiter of truth, but neither should we overplay the view that rationality will overcome all falsehoods in the unregulated marketplace of ideas. There is very little chance

that statements intended to promote hatred against an identifiable group are true, or that their vision of society will lead to a better world. To portray such statements as crucial to truth and the betterment of the political and social milieu is therefore misguided.

Another component central to the rationale underlying s. 2(*b*) concerns the vital role of free expression as a means of ensuring individuals the ability to gain self-fulfillment by developing and articulating thoughts and ideas as they see fit. It is true that s. 319(2) inhibits this process among those individuals whose expression it limits, and hence arguably works against freedom of expression values. On the other hand, such self-autonomy stems in large part from one's ability to articulate and nurture an identity derived from membership in a cultural or religious group. The message put forth by individuals who fall within the ambit of s. 319(2) represents a most extreme opposition to the idea that members of identifiable groups should enjoy this aspect of the s. 2(*b*) benefit. The extent to which the unhindered promotion of this message furthers free expression values must therefore be tempered insofar as it advocates with inordinate vitriol an intolerance and prejudice which view as execrable the process of individual self-development and human flourishing among all members of society.

Moving on to a third strain of thought said to justify the protection of free expression, one's attention is brought specifically to the political realm. The connection between freedom of expression and the political process is perhaps the linchpin of the s. 2(*b*) guarantee, and the nature of this connection is largely derived from the Canadian commitment to democracy. Freedom of expression is a crucial aspect of the democratic commitment, not merely because it permits the best policies to be chosen from among a wide array of proffered options, but additionally because it helps to ensure that participation in the political process is open to all persons. Such open participation must involve to a substantial degree the notion that all persons are equally deserving of respect and dignity. The state therefore cannot act to hinder or condemn a political view without to some extent harming the openness of Canadian democracy and its associated tenet of equality for all.

The suppression of hate propaganda undeniably muzzles the participation of a few individuals in the democratic process, and hence detracts somewhat from free expression values, but the degree of this limitation is not substantial. I am aware that the use of strong language in political and social debate—indeed, perhaps even language intended to promote hatred—is an unavoidable part of the democratic process. Moreover, I recognize that hate propaganda is expression of a type which would generally be categorized as "political," thus putatively placing it at the very heart of the principle extolling freedom of expression as vital to the democratic process. Nonetheless, expression can work to undermine our commitment to democracy where employed to propagate ideas anathemic to democratic values. Hate propaganda works in just such a way, arguing as it does for a society in which the democratic process is subverted and individuals are denied respect and dignity simply because of racial or religious characteristics. This brand of expressive activity is thus wholly inimical to the democratic aspirations of the free expression guarantee.

Indeed, one may quite plausibly contend that it is through rejecting hate propaganda that the state can best encourage the protection of values central to freedom of expression, while simultaneously demonstrating dislike for the vision forwarded by hate-mongers. In this regard, the reaction to various types of expression by a democratic government may be perceived as meaningful expression on behalf of the vast majority of citizens. I do not wish to be construed as saying that an infringement of s. 2(b) can be justified under s. 1 merely because it is the product of a democratic process; the *Charter* will not permit even the democratically elected legislature to restrict the rights and freedoms crucial to a free and democratic society. What I do wish to emphasize, however, is that one must be careful not to accept blindly that the suppression of expression must always and unremittingly detract from values central to freedom of expression (L.C.

Bollinger, *The Tolerant Society: Freedom of Speech and Extremist Speech in America* ([New York: Oxford University Press,]1986), at pp. 87–93).

I am very reluctant to attach anything but the highest importance to expression relevant to political matters. But given the unparalleled vigour with which hate propaganda repudiates and undermines democratic values, and in particular its condemnation of the view that all citizens need be treated with equal respect and dignity so as to make participation in the political process meaningful, I am unable to see the protection of such expression as integral to the democratic ideal so central to the s. 2(b) rationale. Together with my comments as to the tenuous link between communications covered by s. 319(2) and other values at the core of the free expression guarantee, this conclusion leads me to disagree with the opinion of McLachlin J. that the expression at stake in this appeal mandates the most solicitous degree of constitutional protection. In my view, hate propaganda should not be accorded the greatest of weight in the s. 1 analysis.

As a caveat, it must be emphasized that the protection of extreme statements, even where they attack those principles underlying the freedom of expression, is not completely divorced from the aims of s. 2(b) of the *Charter*. As noted already, suppressing the expression covered by s. 319(2) does to some extent weaken these principles. It can also be argued that it is partly through a clash with extreme and erroneous views that truth and the democratic vision remain vigorous and alive (see Braun, op. cit., at p. 490). In this regard, judicial pronouncements strongly advocating the importance of free expression values might be seen as helping to expose prejudiced statements as valueless even while striking down legislative restrictions that proscribe such expression. Additionally, condoning a democracy's collective decision to protect itself from certain types of expression may lead to a slippery slope on which encroachments on expression central to s. 2(b) values are permitted. To guard against such a result, the protection of communications virulently unsupportive of free expression values may be necessary in order to ensure that expression more compatible with these values is never unjustifiably limited.

None of these arguments is devoid of merit, and each must be taken into account in determining whether an infringement of s. 2(*b*) can be justified under s. 1. It need not be, however, that they apply equally or with the greatest of strength in every instance. As I have said already, I am of the opinion that hate propaganda contributes little to the aspirations of Canadians or Canada in either the quest for truth, the promotion of individual self-development or the protection and fostering of a vibrant democracy where the participation of all individuals is accepted and encouraged. While I cannot conclude that hate propaganda deserves only marginal protection under the s. 1 analysis, I can take cognizance of the fact that limitations upon hate propaganda are directed at a special category of expression which strays some distance from the spirit of s. 2(*b*), and hence conclude that "restrictions on expression of this kind might be easier to justify than other infringements of s. 2(*b*)" (*Royal College, supra*, at p. 247).

DISCUSSION QUESTIONS

1. The court considers the claim that "hate propaganda" "is an activity the form and consequences of which are analogous to those associated with violence or threats of violence." Why does the court reject this claim? Do you agree with the court? Why or why not?

2. What sorts of harm does the court view as the results of hate propaganda? Does the court think that these harms justify restrictions on the freedom of speech? Explain and evaluate the court's claim.

3. The court points to both equality and multiculturalism as values that are undermined by hate propaganda. Explain what these values are, and then evaluate the court's claim that they are undermined by hate propaganda.

4. The court claims that "expression intended to promote the hatred of identifiable groups is of limited importance when measured against free expression values." Explain this claim and the court's argument in support of it. Do you agree with the court? Why or why not?

43

FREE SPEECH

Owens v. Saskatchewan (Human Rights Commission) (2006)

In 1997, Appellant Hugh Owens placed a newspaper advertisement reflecting his religious objections to homosexuality. A human rights board of inquiry found that Owens had violated a portion of *The Saskatchewan Human Rights Code* which prohibits the "publication of statements which expose or tend to expose to hatred, or which ridicule, belittle or otherwise affront the dignity of any person or class of persons on the basis of various prohibited grounds."
The Court of Appeals, however, overturned that decision.

SOURCE
2006 SKCA 41.

Richards J.A.

I. Introduction

Section 14(1)(b) of *The Saskatchewan Human Rights Code*, S.S. 1979, c. S-24.1 prohibits the publication of statements which expose or tend to expose to hatred, or which ridicule, belittle or otherwise affront the dignity of any person or class of persons on the basis of various prohibited grounds. One of those grounds is sexual orientation.

A human rights board of inquiry found that the appellant, Hugh Owens, contravened s. 14(1)(b) by publishing a newspaper advertisement which reflected his Biblically-based views about homosexuality. That result was upheld by the Court of Queen's Bench.

I conclude, for the reasons which follow, that Mr. Owens did not violate s. 14(1)(b) and that his appeal should be allowed.

II. Background

A. The Facts

Mr. Owens saw an advertisement in the Saskatoon *StarPhoenix* in June of 1997 announcing an upcoming gay pride week. He thought that his Christian faith required him to respond to the celebration of what he believes God calls a sin. He contacted *The StarPhoenix* with a view to running his own advertisement during gay pride week in the church pages of the paper.

The StarPhoenix did not respond until eight days later which, as it turned out, was too late to place the ad in the church pages. Mr. Owens then told *The StarPhoenix* to run the ad wherever there was space. It ultimately appeared in the sports section of the newspaper on June 30, 1997.

The advertisement consisted of the citations of four Bible passages, "Romans 1:26; Leviticus 18:22; Leviticus 20:13; 1 Corinthians 6:9–10," set out prominently in bold type. They were accompanied by a reference in smaller print to the New International version of the Bible. The citations were followed by an equal sign and then by two stickmen holding hands. A circle with a line running diagonally from the two o'clock to the eight o'clock position (the "not permitted" symbol) was superimposed on the stickmen. The following words appeared in small print at the bottom of the advertisement: "This message can be purchased in bumper sticker form. Please call [telephone number]."

The passages referred to in the advertisement, as found in the New International version of the Bible, read as follows:

ROMANS 1:26 Because of this, God gave them over to shameful lusts. Even their women exchanged natural relations for unnatural ones. In the same way the men also abandoned natural relations with women and were inflamed with lust for one another. Men committed indecent acts with other men, and received in themselves the due penalty for their perversion. Furthermore, since they did not think it worthwhile to retain the knowledge of God, he gave them over to a depraved mind, to do what ought not to be done. They have become filled with every kind of wickedness, evil, greed and depravity. They are full of envy, murder, strife, deceit and malice. They are gossips, slanderers, God-haters, insolent, arrogant, and boastful; they invent ways of doing evil; they disobey their parents; they are senseless, faithless,

heartless, ruthless. Although they know God's righteous decree that those who do such things deserve death, they not only continue to do these very things but also approve of those who practice them.

LEVITICUS 18:22 Do not lie with a man as one lies with a woman; that is detestable.

LEVITICUS 20:13 If a man lies with a man as one lies with a woman, both of them have done what is detestable. They must be put to death; their blood will be on their own heads.

1 CORINTHIANS 6:9 Do you not know that the wicked will not inherit the kingdom of God? Do not be deceived: Neither the sexually immoral nor idolaters nor adulterers nor male prostitutes nor homosexual offenders…

Mr. Owens planned to follow-up with a second message. It also featured a not permitted sign superimposed on two stickmen holding hands but, rather than containing a reference to the Bible, it stated "You do have a choice friend, his name is Jesus." In his evidence, he explained his thinking as follows:

… Christians and the Christian community are accused and rightly so, many times of being all too judgmental, all to [sic] condemning, and never offering any solutions, never offering any ways of dealing with certain situations. As I said, this message was crafted in two particular bumper stickers. The first one was, as we already know, the advertisement that was placed that dealt with God's declaration concerning homosexual behaviour, and then the second message was the bumper sticker that offered the solution. As a Christian, there is only one solution, and that is God himself and His name just happens to be Jesus Christ.

The StarPhoenix declined to publish the second message given the complaints and protest which had been sparked by Mr. Owens' first advertisement.

The respondents Gens Hellquist, Jason Roy and Jeff Dodds filed complaints with the respondent Saskatchewan Human Rights Commission in August of 1997. They alleged the publication of the advertisement had offended s. 14 of the *Code*. Section 14 reads as follows:

> 14(1) No person shall publish or display, or cause or permit to be published or displayed, on any lands or premises or in a newspaper, through a television or radio broadcasting station or any other broadcasting device, or in any printed matter or publication or by means of any other medium that the person owns, controls, distributes or sells, any representation, including any notice, sign, symbol, emblem, article, statement or other representation:
>
> (a) tending or likely to tend to deprive, abridge or otherwise restrict the enjoyment by any person or class of persons, on the basis of a prohibited ground, of any right to which that person or class of persons is entitled under law; or
>
> (b) that exposes or tends to expose to hatred, ridicules, belittles or otherwise affronts the dignity of any person or class of persons on the basis of a prohibited ground.
>
> (2) Nothing in subsection (1) restricts the right to freedom of expression under the law upon any subject.

Mr. Hellquist, Mr. Roy and Mr. Dodds each stated the particulars of his complaint in the same way:

> I am a gay man. On or about June, 1997, Hugh Owens caused an advertisement to be published in *The StarPhoenix*, a daily newspaper in Saskatchewan. The advertisement contained a message that certain passages of the Bible were authority for the proposition that gay men should not be allowed. The advertisement indicated the message could be purchased in bumper sticker form. I have reasonable grounds to believe, and I do believe, that Hugh Owens has caused this representation to be published or displayed in a newspaper, and that he is distributing the representation, which tends to restrict the enjoyment of rights which I am entitled to under the law and which exposes me to hatred and otherwise affronts my dignity of [sic] because of my sexual orientation, contrary to Section 14 of the *Saskatchewan Human Rights Code*.

The complaints named both Mr. Owens and Sterling Newspapers Company, the operator of *The StarPhoenix*, as respondents. Sterling Newspapers is no longer involved in these proceedings and, as a result, I need make no further reference to it in these reasons. I also note that Mr. Roy did not participate in this appeal and has renounced any claim to the compensation awarded to him.

B. The Board of Inquiry Decision

The complaints filed by Mr. Hellquist, Mr. Roy and Mr. Dodds were referred to a board of inquiry for determination.

The Board of Inquiry heard a considerable amount of evidence. The complainants provided a compelling narrative with respect to the difficulties, threats and dangers faced by gay men. They expressed the anger, hurt and frustration caused to them by the message in the advertisement. Mr. Hellquist believed the advertisement gave licence to people who wanted to discriminate against gay men and a licence to people who were inclined to harass or assault gay men. Mr. Roy said the overall message he received from the ad was that "God instructs us that intimacy between two people of the same gender is inappropriate or some type of religious crime and those who engage in such acts should be put to death." Mr. Dodds saw the advertisement in a very similar way.

The Board of Inquiry also heard evidence from several individuals who were qualified as experts. Dr. Madiha Khayatt testified in general terms about human sexuality, including homosexuality, from a sociological point of view. Reverend Brent Hawkes testified about the history of the Bible, the Bible's commentary on homosexuality and possible interpretations of the Bible passages referred to in Mr. Owens' advertisement. Reverend Canon Clay gave evidence concerning the various degrees of acceptance of homosexuality among different church groups. The Board of Inquiry also heard from individuals who testified as to the approach taken to homosexuality by the Lutheran, Roman Catholic and Jewish faiths.

In its decision, reported at (2001), 40 C.H.R.R. D/197, the Board of Inquiry began by summarizing the evidence which had been presented. It then considered whether the advertisement breached s. 14(1)(b) of the *Code* and concluded that it did. Its finding as to whether the advertisement involved some or all of hate, belittlement, ridicule or an affront to dignity was not stated in a consistent way. The Board first wrote as follows:

Having reviewed all of the evidence, the Board accepts that the universal symbol for forbidden, not allowed or not wanted, consisting of a circle with a slash through it, may itself not communicate hatred. However, when combined with the passages from the Bible, the Board finds that the advertisement would expose or tend to expose homosexuals to hatred or ridicule, or may otherwise affront their dignity on the basis of their sexual orientation. It is a combination of both the symbol and the biblical references which have led to this conclusion.

After referring to case authority in relation to the significance of the not permitted symbol, the Board stated its views somewhat differently by saying:

[28] The use of the circle and slash combined with the passages of the Bible herein make the meaning of the advertisement unmistakeable. It is clear that the advertisement is

intended to make the group depicted appear to be inferior or not wanted at best. When combined with the biblical quotations, the advertisement may result in a far stronger meaning. It is obvious that certain of the biblical quotations suggest more dire consequences and there can be no question that the advertisement can objectively be seen as exposing homosexuals to hatred or ridicule.

The Board then went on to consider whether the advertisement was a permissible exercise of freedom of speech within the meaning of s. 14(2) of the *Code*. After referring to leading case authority, it presented its conclusion in this way:

The Board has concluded that the complainants, Jeff Dodds, Jason Roy, and Gens Hellquist, have been discriminated against with respect to the advertisement placed in the Saskatoon *Star Phoenix* on June 30, 1997, and as a result, were exposed to hatred, ridicule and their dignity was affronted on the basis of their sexual orientation. Based on the evidence given by the complainants, the Board finds that the complainants suffered in respect of their feelings and self-respect as a result of the contravention.

The Board made an order prohibiting Mr. Owens from further publishing or displaying the bumper stickers featured in the advertisement and directed him to pay damages of $1,500 to each of the complainants.

C. The Queen's Bench Decision

Mr. Owens appealed the Board of Inquiry's decision to the Court of Queen's Bench. In dismissing the appeal, the Chambers judge purported to agree with the findings of the Board but was also somewhat inconsistent as to whether the advertisement involved only hatred or whether it also involved ridicule, belittlement and/or an affront to dignity. The relevant passages from that aspect of his decision, reported at (2002), 228 Sask. R. 148, are set out below:

> [21] In my view the Board was correct in concluding that the advertisement can objectively be seen as exposing homosexuals to hatred or ridicule. When the use of the circle and slash is combined with the passages of the Bible, it exposes homosexuals to detestation, vilification, and disgrace. In other words, the Biblical passage which suggest that if a man lies with a man they must be put to death exposes homosexuals to hatred.

> [22] I agree with counsel for the Board that the Board was correct in holding that a reference to statements that call for homosexuals to be put to death in the context of equalizing that with a prohibition against them does expose homosexuals to hatred and affronts to their dignity as contemplated by s. 14(1) of the *Code*.

Having stated his conclusion in those terms, the Chambers judge considered whether the advertisement was protected by the guarantees of freedom of speech or religion. His analysis in that regard consisted of quoting from *Saskatchewan (Human Rights Commission) v. Bell*, [1994] 5 W.W.R. 460 (Sask. C.A.) and then stating:

> [24] In my view, s. 14(1) of the *Code* is a reasonable restriction on the appellant's right to freedom of expression and religion as contemplated by s. 2(a) of the *Charter*. See *Bell*, supra. In *Attis v. Board of Education of District No. 15 et al.*, [*Ross v. New Brunswick School District No. 15*], [1996] 1 S.C.R. 825; 195 N.R. 81; 171 N.B.R. (2d) 321; 437 A.P.R. 321, La Forest J. held that the analysis under s.1 of the *Charter* is the same whether the legislation infringes the respondent's freedom of expression or freedom of religion.

[25] For all the above reasons the appeal is dismissed.

Mr. Owens takes issue with that decision. Two interveners, Canadian Civil Liberties Association and Canadian Religious Freedom Alliance, support his request that the appeal be allowed.

III. Issues

Mr. Owens raised a number of points but there was considerable overlap among them. His essential argument can be reduced to two key contentions. The first is that the Board of Inquiry and the Court of Queen's Bench erred in their characterization of the advertisement. He submits that it does not convey hatred or otherwise offend s. 14(1)(b) of the *Code*. The second is that the Board of Inquiry and the Court of Queen's Bench both failed to give proper consideration to the fact that, in publishing the advertisement, he was exercising his freedom of religion.

[...]

For their part, the respondents, *i.e.*, the Commission and the complainants, argued that the Board of Inquiry properly identified the import of the advertisement. They accept that the advertisement involved the exercise of Mr. Owens' freedom of religion but say his freedom in that regard is not absolute and that the *Code* justifiably limits religious speech which is hateful or otherwise comes within the scope of s. 14(1)(b).

[...]

C. The Meaning and Scope of Section 14(1)(b)

Section 14(1)(b) of the *Code* prohibits the publication or display of any statement or symbol "that exposes or tends to expose to hatred, ridicule, belittles or otherwise affronts the dignity" of any person or class of persons on the basis of a prohibited ground. The task of determining whether Mr. Owens violated the *Code* by publishing the advertisement must begin with a confirmation of the meaning and scope of those statutory terms.

1. Some General Principles

Section 14(1)(b) is aimed directly at expressive activity and hence self-evidently constrains free speech. It also limits constitutionally protected religious interests in that freedom of religion includes the right to disseminate beliefs. Dickson J. confirmed that point in *R. v. Big M Drug Mart Ltd.*, [1985] 1 S.C.R. 295 at p. 336:

> ... The essence of the concept of freedom of religion is the right to entertain such religious beliefs as a person chooses, the right to declare religious beliefs openly and without fear of hindrance or reprisal, and the right to manifest religious belief by worship and practice or by teaching and dissemination.

The *Charter* guarantees both freedom of speech and freedom of religion by providing as follows in ss. 2(a) and (b):

> 2. Everyone has the following fundamental freedoms:
> a) freedom of conscience and religion;
> b) freedom of thought, belief, opinion and expression, including freedom of the press and other media of communication;

Those guarantees can only be limited in ways which are reasonable and demonstrably justifiable within the meaning of s. 1 of the *Charter*. Section 14(1)(b) would, of course, be constitutionally invalid to the extent it is not a reasonable limitation of guaranteed freedoms.

Freedom of expression and freedom of religion are also enshrined in the *Human Rights Code* itself. The Bill of Rights part of the *Code* expressly protects both freedoms. Sections 4 and 5 of the *Code* state:

> 4 Every person and every class of persons shall enjoy the right to freedom of conscience, opinion and belief and freedom of religious association, teaching, practice and worship.

> 5 Every person and every class of persons shall, under the law, enjoy the right to freedom of expression through all means of communication, including, without limiting the generality of the foregoing, the arts, speech, the press or radio, television or any other broadcasting device.

Section 14(2), it will be recalled, specifically says that "Nothing in subsection (1) restricts the right to freedom of expression under the law upon any subject."

All of this means freedom of speech and religion must be carefully considered when interpreting s. 14(1)(b)....

2. The Authorities

With that background, it is appropriate to turn to the authorities which have considered the meaning of s. 14(1)(b). There are two key and controlling cases. The first is *Canada (Human Rights Commission) v. Taylor*, [1990] 3 S.C.R. 892. The second is *Saskatchewan (Human Rights Commission) v. Bell, supra.*

In *Taylor*, the Supreme Court considered the constitutional validity of the hate speech prohibition in s. 13(1) of the *Canadian Human Rights Act*. That provision reads as follows:

> 13. (1) It is a discriminatory practice for a person or a group of persons acting in concert to communicate telephonically or to cause to be so communicated, repeatedly, in whole or in part by means of the facilities of a telecommunication undertaking within the legislative authority of Parliament, any matter that is likely to expose a person or persons to hatred or contempt by reason of the fact that that person or those persons are identifiable on the basis of a prohibited ground of discrimination.

The prohibited grounds of discrimination referred to in the section include (but are not limited to) race, national or ethnic origin, colour and religion.

Mr. Taylor had initiated a telephone service whereby members of the public could dial a telephone number and listen to a recorded message. Some thirteen different messages were played over a two year period but they had a consistent overriding theme involving an attack on Jews. A human rights tribunal determined that Mr. Taylor had violated s. 13(1) of the *Human Rights Act* and, in so doing, it summarized the nature of the messages as follows at p. 903:

> Although many of these messages are difficult to follow, there is a recurring theme. There is a conspiracy which controls and programmes Canadian society; it is difficult to find out the truth about this conspiracy because our books, our schools and our media are controlled by the conspirators. The conspirators cause unemployment and inflation; they weaken us by encouraging perversion, laziness, drug use and race mixing. They become enriched by stealing our property. They have founded communism which is responsible for many of our economic problems such as the postal strike; they continue to control communism and they use it in the furtherance of the conspiracy. The conspirators are Jews.

The Supreme Court narrowly upheld s. 13(1) as being a reasonable limitation on the right of freedom of expression guaranteed by s. 2(b) of the *Charter*. Dickson C.J.C. wrote for the majority. In the central part of his reasons, he referred to a decision of a human rights tribunal which had considered the meaning of "hatred" and "contempt" in s. 13(1) and then went on to summarize his own position as follows at pp. 928–29:

> The approach taken in [the decision of the human rights tribunal] gives full force and recognition to the purpose of the *Canadian Human Rights Act* while remaining consistent with the *Charter*. The reference to "hatred" in the above quotation speaks of

"extreme" ill-will and an emotion which allows for "no redeeming qualities" in the person at whom it is directed. "Contempt" appears to be viewed as similarly extreme, though is felt by the Tribunal to describe more appropriately circumstances where the object of one's feelings is looked down upon. According to the reading of the Tribunal, s. 13(1) thus refers to unusually strong and deep-felt emotions of detestation, calumny and vilification, and I do not find this interpretation to be particularly expansive. To the extent that the section may impose a slightly broader limit upon freedom of expression than does s. 319(2) of the *Criminal Code*, however, I am of the view that the conciliatory bent of a human rights statute renders such a limit more acceptable than would be the case with a criminal provision.
62 In sum, the language employed in s. 13(1) of the *Canadian Human Rights Act* extends only to that expression giving rise to the evil sought to be eradicated and provides a standard of conduct sufficiently precise to prevent the unacceptable chilling of expressive activity. Moreover, as long as the Human Rights Tribunal continues to be well aware of the purpose of s. 13(1) and pays heed to the ardent and extreme nature of feeling described in the phrase "hatred or contempt," there is little danger that subjective opinion as to offensiveness will supplant the proper meaning of the section.

The key to the *Taylor* decision for present purposes is Dickson C.J.C.'s requirement that, in order to pass constitutional muster, s. 13(1) must be read as being aimed only at expression involving feelings of an "ardent and extreme nature" and, in particular, "unusually strong and deep-felt emotions of detestation, calumny and vilification."

I turn then to *Bell,* a decision of this Court. It involved a human rights complaint under s. 14 of the *Code* arising from a situation where Mr. Bell, the owner of a motorcycle shop, had displayed and offered for sale offensive stickers. The stickers carried crude and demeaning caricatures of a Sikh person, an Oriental person and a Black person superimposed with a red circle and a diagonal bar—the not permitted sign. Mr. Bell challenged the constitutional validity of s. 14 on the basis that it offended the guarantee of freedom of expression found in s. 2(b) of the *Charter*.

Not surprisingly, the *Taylor* ruling figured prominently in Sherstobitoff J.A.'s reasons upholding the validity of s. 14. He noted that *Taylor* directly governed the question of whether the "hate" aspect of s. 14(1) could be justified. He also found that the reasoning in *Taylor* applied in relation to those aspects of s. 14 which speak to belittlement, ridicule and affronts to dignity. The most significant passage from his reasons is reproduced below...

> 29 ....Since we have found that the stickers exposed and tended to expose to hatred, there has been a breach of the section, and, ordinarily, that would be an end of the appeal.

> 30 However, s. 14 goes beyond prohibiting material exposing to hatred. It also prohibits material which ridicules, belittles or otherwise affronts the dignity of any group because of race or religion. The appellant argued that these additional grounds for prohibition of publication broadened the section to the extent that the reasoning in *Taylor* should not apply, and that, as a result, s. 14 was not a reasonable limit on the right to freedom of expression.

> 31 The legislation under consideration in *Taylor* prohibited communications which were "likely to expose ... to hatred or contempt." The prohibition in s. 14 against communications which expose or tend to expose to hatred, or which "ridicule, belittle or otherwise affront the dignity" of persons is so similar to that considered in *Taylor* that the words of Dickson C.J.C. at p. 929 apply:

In sum, the language employed in s. 13(1) of the *Canadian Rights Act* extends only to that expression giving rise to the evil sought to be eradicated and provides a standard of conduct sufficiently precise to prevent the unacceptable chilling of expressive activity. Moreover, as long as the Human Rights Tribunal continues to be well aware of the purpose of s. 13(1) and pays heed to the ardent and extreme nature of feeling described in the phrase "hatred or contempt," there is little danger that subjective opinion as to offensiveness will supplant the proper meaning of the section.

32 This reasoning is reinforced by the fact that s. 14 of the *Code* is tempered by interpretative and exemption provisions which were absent in the legislation under consideration in *Taylor*. Subsection (2) of s. 14 provides:

> (2) Nothing in subsection (1) restricts the right to freedom of speech under the law upon any subject.

Section 5 provides:

> 5 Every person and every class of persons shall, under the law, enjoy the right to freedom of expression through all means of communication, including, without limiting the generality of the foregoing, the arts, speech, the press or radio, television or any other broadcasting device.

Such provisions are normal in human rights legislation and Dickson C.J.C. said as follows in reference to such provisions at p. 930:

> Perhaps the so-called exemptions found in many human rights statutes are best seen as indicating to human rights tribunals the necessity of balancing the objective of eradicating discrimination with the

need to protect free expression (see, e.g., *Rasheed v. Bramhill* (1980), 2 C.H.R.R. D/249, at p. D/252).

33 Accordingly, in our view, s. 14 of the *Code* is a reasonable limit on the right to freedom of expression as allowed under s. 1 of the *Charter*. Our reasons for this conclusion are rather perfunctory because the result of this appeal would be the same even if we had concluded that the words "ridicules, belittles or otherwise affronts the dignity of" in s. 14(1)(a) had taken the section beyond the reasoning in *Taylor* which justified the limit as being reasonable.

Thus, while *Bell* upheld s. 14(1)(b) of the *Code* as being a reasonable limit on freedom of expression, it did so on a very particular basis. The Court saw s. 14(1)(b) as operating only in those situations where the "ridicule," "belittlement" or "affront to dignity" in issue met the standard endorsed in *Taylor*. In other words, the Court interpreted the prohibition against ridicule, belittlement and affronts to dignity as extending only to communications of that sort which involve extreme feelings and strong emotions of detestation, calumny and vilification.

No other result, of course, could be justifiable. Much speech which is self-evidently constitutionally protected involves some measure of ridicule, belittlement or an affront to dignity grounded in characteristics like race, religion and so forth. I have in mind, by way of general illustration, the editorial cartoon which satirizes people from a particular country, the magazine piece which criticizes the social policy agenda of a religious group and so forth. Freedom of speech in a healthy and robust democracy must make space for that kind of discourse and the *Code* should not be read as being inconsistent with that imperative. Section 14(1)(b) is concerned only with speech which is genuinely extreme in the sense contemplated by the *Taylor* and *Bell* decisions.

3. Freedom of Religion

Bell concerned the validity of s. 14(1)(b) with reference to freedom of expression as protected by s. 2(b) of the *Charter*. Although he does not directly attack the constitutionality of s. 14(1)(b) itself, Mr. Owens argues that both the Board of Inquiry and the Court of Queen's Bench erred in their deliberations because they failed to give weight or effect to his freedom of religion. In this regard, all parties to this appeal agree and accept that Mr. Owens published the advertisement pursuant to a sincere and *bona fide* conviction forming part of his religious beliefs. As a result, there is no doubt that s. 2(a) of the *Charter* is engaged by the facts of this case and must be examined.

Mr. Owens correctly contends that the Board of Inquiry said nothing about freedom of religion and that the Chambers judge gave it only the briefest of consideration. However, at least insofar as the constitutional validity of s. 14(1)(b) is concerned, the result in *Bell* does not change when freedom of religion is brought into the equation. This is so because the authorities universally recognize that freedom of religion is not absolute. See: *Multani v. Commission scolaire Marguerite-Bourgeoys*, [2006] S.C.J. No. 6; 2006 SCC 6 at para. 30.

As is the case with all other rights and freedoms, religious speech and religious practices which harm others are subject to limitation in ways which are reasonable and justifiable within the meaning of s. 1 of the *Charter*. This is part of the foundation on which our pluralistic society has been constructed. Iacobucci J. recently underlined this point when exploring the allowable limitations on religious freedom in *Syndicat Northcrest v. Amselem*, [2004] 2 S.C.R. 551 at para. 61:

61 In this respect, it should be emphasized that not every action will become summarily unassailable and receive automatic protection under the banner of freedom of religion. No right, including freedom of religion, is absolute: see, e.g., *Big M, supra*; *P. (D.) v. S. (C.)*, [1993] 4 S.C.R. 141, at p. 182; *B. (R.) v. Children's Aid Society of*

Metropolitan Toronto, [1995] 1 S.C.R. 315, at para. 226; *Trinity Western University v. British Columbia College of Teachers*, [2001] 1 S.C.R. 772, 2001 SCC 31, at para. 29. This is so because we live in a society of individuals in which we must always take the rights of others into account. In the words of John Stuart Mill: "The only freedom which deserves the name, is that of pursuing our own good in our own way, so long as we do not attempt to deprive others of theirs, or impede their efforts to obtain it": *On Liberty and Considerations on Representative Government* (1946), at p. 11. In the real world, oftentimes the fundamental rights of individuals will conflict or compete with one another.

The Constitution protects all dimensions of freedom of religion. However, it also accommodates the need to safeguard citizens from harm and to ensure that each of them has non-discriminatory access to education, employment, accommodation and services. In situations where religiously motivated speech involves injury or harm to others, it is necessarily subject to reasonable limitations. As a result, s. 14(1)(b) is a justifiable limit on religiously inspired speech in effectively the same way as it is a justifiable limit on speech generally. See: *Ross v. New Brunswick School District No. 15*, [1996] 1 S.C.R. 825.

4. Applying Section 14(1)(b)

The sensibilities and vulnerabilities of the individuals who are the target of speech which is alleged to breach s. 14(1)(b) should not be disregarded in deciding whether there has been a violation of the *Code*. However, the question of how a particular individual or particular individuals understand a message cannot determine whether it should be found to involve hate, belittlement, ridicule or is an affront to dignity. Injecting that sort of subjectivity into the analysis would make the reach of the section entirely unpredictable and, as a result, would create an unacceptable chilling effect on free speech.

Similarly, the perspective of the person who sends a message cannot control the outcome of the inquiry as to whether the message violates s. 14(1)(b). He or she might have a sense of the meaning of the message which, because of prejudice or otherwise, is wholly inconsistent with its actual effect. Focusing on the subjective views of the person alleged to have offended s. 14(1)(b) thus runs the risk of making that provision inapplicable to even the most offensive and dangerous messages and, consequently, of defeating its purpose.

As a result, it is apparent that s. 14(1)(b) must be applied using an objective approach. The question is whether, when considered objectively by a reasonable person aware of the relevant context and circumstances, the speech in question would be understood as exposing or tending to expose members of the target group to hatred or as ridiculing, belittling or affronting their dignity within the restricted meaning of those terms as prescribed by *Bell*.

C. The Characterization of the Advertisement

Having confirmed the construction of s. 14(1)(b) and the way in which it must be applied, it is now possible to turn to the particulars of Mr. Owens' advertisement and the question of whether he offended the *Code* by publishing it.

There is no doubt that the advertisement is jarring and would have been seen by many as distressing and offensive. That, however, is not the basis on which the *Code* prohibits speech. The overriding question is whether the advertisement was characterized by the intense feelings and strong sense of detestation, calumny and vilification referred to in *Bell*.

That question can be answered only by considering the contents of the advertisement as a whole in light of the circumstances in which it was published. Context is critically important in this regard. The analysis pursuant to s. 14(1)(b) of the *Code* must be performed carefully and always on a case-by-case basis.

For his part, Mr. Owens says the advertisement simply means "God says no to the behaviour of homosexuality" and, as a result, he submits there was no violation of s. 14(1)(b).

1. Context

Part of the context which must inform the meaning of Mr. Owens' advertisement is the long history of discrimination against gay, lesbian, bisexual and trans-identified people in this country and elsewhere. As Cory J. said in *Egan v. Canada*, [1995] 2 S.C.R. 513 at para. 175, gays and lesbians "whether as individuals or couples, form an identifiable minority who have suffered and continue to suffer serious social, political and economic disadvantage." The evidence of the complainants in this case clearly revealed the marginalization and fear which are part of the life many gay men are obliged to live.

At the same time, it is significant that the advertisement in issue here was published in 1997 and, thus, in the middle of an ongoing national debate about how Canadian legal and constitutional regimes should or should not accommodate sexual identities. "Sexual orientation" had been added as a prohibited ground of discrimination under *The Saskatchewan Human Rights Code* only in 1993. Sexual orientation had been found by the Supreme Court of Canada to be an analogous ground of discrimination under s. 15 of the *Charter* just two years before the advertisement was published. See: *Egan v. Canada*, *supra*. Parliament would not pass legislation to make government programs and benefits available on an equal basis to gay and lesbian couples until three years after the advertisement appeared. See: *Modernization of Benefits and Obligations Act*, S.C. 2000, c. 12. When Mr. Owens' message was published the judicial sanctioning of same-sex marriage in Saskatchewan was still seven years in the future and its sanctioning by the Supreme Court of Canada was eight years in the future. See: *W. (N.) v. Canada (Attorney General)* (2004), 246 D.L.R. (4th) 345 (Q.B.); *Reference Re Same-Sex Marriage*, [2004] 3 S.C.R. 698.

This does not mean that a newly won right to be free from discrimination should be accorded less vigorous protection than similar rights based on more historically established grounds such as race and religion. But, for purposes of applying a provision like s. 14(1)(b) of the *Code*, it is important to consider Mr. Owens' advertisement in the context of the time and circumstances in which it was published. That environment featured an active debate and discussion about the place of sexual identity in Canadian society. Indeed, the advertisement at issue here was published in connection with gay pride week—an event promoted by the gay community as a celebration of diversity and used in part as a platform for the advancement of gay rights.

Seen in this broader context, Mr. Owens' advertisement tends to take on the character of a position advanced in a continuing public policy debate rather than the character of a message of hatred or ill will in the sense contemplated by *Bell*. Both the Board of Inquiry and the Chambers judge erred by failing to give any consideration to this wider context.

2. The Detail of the Advertisement

In analyzing the advertisement itself, it is useful to begin by separately considering its two main elements: the not permitted symbol superimposed on the stickmen and the Bible passages.

I begin with the stickmen. They are drawn very simply in the classic style of the genre. The two figures are identical and stand side by side with conjoined hands. They are not, as was the case with the caricatures at issue in *Bell*, depicted in a way which suggests undesirable characteristics such as dangerousness, untrustworthiness, lack of cleanliness, dishonesty or deceit. They are presented in a neutral and straightforward fashion. As a result, there is nothing about the stickmen themselves which might engage s. 14(1)(b) of the *Code*.

The significance of the not permitted sign itself is somewhat more difficult to ascertain. In the proper context, I do not doubt that it can confirm or be an integral part of a hateful message. That was the case in *Bell* where it was superimposed on cruel and demeaning racial caricatures. However, at the same time, the not permitted sign can also be used in ways which do not involve the kind of malevolent feelings described in *Bell* and *Taylor*. The evidence at the Board of Inquiry showed it was employed in a range of circumstances including those which were quite innocuous. Accordingly, in my view, the Board of Inquiry properly concluded that the not permitted symbol "may itself not communicate hatred."

In the result, it is apparent that the part of the advertisement involving the not permitted symbol superimposed on the stickmen does not, in and of itself, satisfy the standard prescribed by *Bell*. The Board of Inquiry and the Chambers judge reached the same conclusion, finding that s. 14(1)(b) of the *Code* was not independently offended by that feature of the advertisement but was offended only by that feature *combined* with the Bible passages.

This leads to the other element of the advertisement, the Bible citations. As an initial point on this limb of the case, Mr. Owens contends that the Board of Inquiry and the Court of Queen's Bench should not have looked beyond the advertisement itself to determine its meaning. In his view, the advertisement should have been evaluated on its face and in isolation from the Biblical text it cites.

I do not accept that proposition. In principle, the effect of s. 14(1)(b) of the *Code* cannot be side-stepped by publishing or distributing what amounts to a direction or invitation to refer to material which offends its terms. That approach would deprive the provision of much of its effect and does not reconcile with the concept that human rights legislation should be given a generous and purposive interpretation. See: *Gould v. Yukon Order of Pioneers, supra* at paras. 119–20; *University of British Columbia v. Berg, supra*, at para. 39.

The advertisement was, in effect, an invitation to consult the referenced Bible passages. That text, of course, is readily available as the Bible enjoys a wider circulation than any other book. Accordingly, therefore, it is necessary to consider the referenced Bible passages themselves in order to determine whether s. 14(1)(b) was offended.

Those passages, as quoted above from the New International version of the Bible, use undeniably strong language. Romans 1:26 indicates that men who commit indecent acts with other men "deserve death." Leviticus 18:22 says it is "detestable" for a man to lie with a man as he would a woman. Leviticus 20:13 says it is "detestable" that a man lie with a man and that those who do so "must be put to death." 1 Corinthians 6:9 says that "homosexual offenders" will not inherit the Kingdom of God.

The Board of Inquiry and the Chambers judge both took these passages at face value, making no allowance for the fact they are ancient and fundamental religious text. In other words, the passages referred to by Mr. Owens were assessed by the Board and the Chambers judge in the same way as one might consider a contemporary poster, notice or publication saying "Homosexuals should be killed." In my view, that was an error.

I do not mean by this to suggest in some blanket way that a foundational religious text itself could never be hateful or otherwise offend s. 14(1)(b) of the *Code* or that it could never be used in a way that offended the *Code*. That broad issue is not before the Court in this case. However, at the same time, it is apparent that a human rights tribunal or court should exercise care in dealing with arguments to the effect that foundational religious writings violate the *Code*. While the courts cannot be drawn into the business of attempting to authoritatively interpret sacred texts such as the Bible, those texts will typically have characteristics which cannot be ignored if they are to be properly assessed in relation to s. 14(1)(b) of the *Code*. That is certainly true in this case.

First, the passages cited by Mr. Owens are self-evidently part of a larger work, the Bible, and would tend to be seen as such by an objective observer. One need not be a Biblical scholar, or even a Christian, to know that the Bible as a whole is the source of more than one sort of message and, more specifically, is the source of messages involving themes of love, tolerance and forgiveness. It contains many passages of that sort: Mark 12:31 "Love your neighbor as yourself"; Matthew 6:14–15 "For if you forgive men when they sin against you, your heavenly Father will also forgive you. But if you do not forgive men their sins, your Father will not forgive your sins"; Matthew 7:1 "Do not judge, or you too will be judged"; Leviticus 19:18 "Do not seek revenge or bear a grudge against one of your people, but love your neighbor as yourself"; Proverbs 10:12 "Hatred stirs up dissension, but love covers over all wrongs." Although, as indicated, the Court cannot authoritatively determine the meaning of sacred writings, it is important to recognize that an objective reader of Mr. Owens' advertisement would see it in the context of the other concepts popularly understood as flowing from the Bible. This would tend to colour the advertisement as something falling below the standard prescribed in *Bell*.

A second point concerning the Bible passages cited by Mr. Owens is that an objective observer would understand that their meaning and relevance for contemporary society can and would be assessed in a variety of ways. Some, like Mr. Owens himself, might see them as definitive revelations to the effect that God is opposed to certain gay sexual practices. Other people might see the passages as meaning the Bible opposes such practices but would consider that same-sex sexual activity is a sin no more heinous than various others identified in the text such as sexual immorality, idolatry, adultery and male prostitution. Others might contest the very meaning of the passages and suggest they refer to pederasty (a relationship between an older male partner and a youth) rather than same-sex relationships as understood in contemporary terms. Still others might acknowledge that the Bible opposes same-sex relationships but would see its dictates as so dated in time and rooted in ancient culture, or as so foreign to their own beliefs, as to be irrelevant. See: R. Scroggs, *The New Testament and Homosexuality,* (Philadelphia: Fortress Press, 1983) at pp. 7–16.

The fact that the passages referred to in the advertisement can be seen in such a variety of ways makes them significantly different than the hypothetical present day message referred to above, *i.e.*, a message that "Homosexuals should be killed." Unlike the Bible text in issue, that sort of statement admits of only one meaning. This characteristic of

the Bible passages also cuts against seeing them as coming within the scope of s. 14(1)(b).

A third point, stressed by Mr. Owens and the interveners supporting him, is that the Bible passages in issue refer to *behaviour* said to be sinful or morally wrong and do not condemn the mere fact of gay men's sexual identity. In most contexts, I would have difficulty placing stock in what is sometimes referred to as the distinction between the "sin" and the "sinner." Sexuality and sexual practices are such intimately central aspects of an individual's identity that it is artificial to suggest that the practices of gays and lesbians in this regard can somehow be separated out from those individuals themselves.

However, in the present circumstances, it is necessary to recognize that many people do make such a distinction and believe on moral or religious grounds that they can disapprove of the same-sex sexual practices without disapproving of gays and lesbians themselves. This fact is at least part of the overall context in which Mr. Owens' advertisement must be considered. Again this tends to shade the content of the advertisement away from it being the sort of message which falls within the scope of s. 14(1)(b) of the *Code*.

As a result, despite its strong language, the Bible text referred to in the advertisement cannot be seen from an objective perspective as involving feeling and emotions that are as categorical or as loaded with the sort of emotion canvassed in *Bell* as the respondents suggest and as the Board of Inquiry and the Court of Queen's Bench found. At least in the context at issue here, the Bible passages must be seen in a different light than a plain assertion made in contemporary times to the effect that "Homosexuality is evil and homosexuals should be killed."

3. The Advertisement as a Whole
I have separately considered the two basic elements of Mr. Owens' advertisement—the stickmen and the Bible passages. It is now necessary to bring those two elements together and assess their global import.

In my view, the core or gravamen of the advertisement is its first element—the Bible passages. As discussed above, in and of themselves and as presented here, they do not violate the *Code*. Given the benign design of the stickmen and the somewhat ambiguous meaning of the not permitted symbol, I do not believe that the second element of the advertisement transforms the advertisement as a whole into a message which meets the *Bell* standard. Indeed, the stickmen element of the advertisement can be seen as understating the literal meaning of the most extreme parts of the Bible text in that it suggests certain kinds of activity are not allowed rather than suggesting that gay men should be killed.

Overall, although bluntly presented and doubtless upsetting to many, the essential message conveyed by the advertisement is not one which involves the ardent emotions and strong sense of detestation, calumny and vilification required by *Bell*.

[...]

V. Conclusion

I conclude that the appeal should be allowed. The publication of the advertisement, properly considered in its full context, did not offend s. 14(1)(b) of the *Code*.

DISCUSSION QUESTIONS

1. Explain and evaluate the standard for reasonable restrictions upon freedom of expression set by *Saskatchewan (Human Rights Commission) v. Bell*. The court claims that this standard was not met in *Owen v. Saskatchewan*. Explain.

2. The Court of Appeals rejected Mr. Owens's claim that the Court of the Queen's Bench "failed to give proper consideration to the fact that he was exercising his freedom of religion" in placing the contested advertisement. Explain and evaluate the argument of the Court of Appeals.

3. What does the court mean when it claims that "...s.14(1)(b) must be applied using an objective approach"? Do you agree? Why or why not?

4. The court claims that the placement of the disputed ad can be seen as Mr. Owens's participation in an "ongoing public policy debate" as opposed to an expression of hatred or ill will. Do you agree? Why or why not?

5. The court claims that, when viewed from an objective perspective, Mr. Owens's reference to the Biblical passages would not be viewed as conveying a message of hatred. Outline and evaluate the court's arguments in support of this claim.

44

FREE SPEECH

Adam Liptak, "Hate Speech or Free Speech? What Much of West Bans Is Protected in U.S." (2008)

The following article compares the United States' approach to free speech protection to that of other countries, including Canada. The article was filed from Vancouver, British Columbia.

SOURCE

Liptak, Adam. "Hate Speech or Free Speech?" From *The New York Times*, June 12, 2008. Copyright © *The New York Times*. All rights reserved. Used by permission and protected by the Copyright Laws of the United States. The printing, copying, redistribution, or retransmission of the Content without express written permission is prohibited.

A couple of years ago, a Canadian magazine published an article arguing that the rise of Islam threatened Western values. The article's tone was mocking and biting, but it said nothing that conservative magazines and blogs in the United States did not say every day without fear of legal reprisal.

Things are different here. The magazine is on trial.

Under Canadian law, there is a serious argument that the article contained hate speech and that its publisher, *Maclean's* magazine, the nation's leading newsweekly, should be forbidden from saying similar things, forced to publish a rebuttal and made to compensate Muslims for injuring their "dignity, feelings and self respect."

The British Columbia Human Rights Tribunal, which held five days of hearings on those questions in Vancouver last week, will soon rule on whether *Maclean's* violated a provincial hate speech law by stirring up animosity toward Muslims.

As spectators lined up for the afternoon session last week, an argument broke out.

"It's hate speech!" yelled one man.

"It's free speech!" yelled another.

In the United States, that debate has been settled. Under the First Amendment, newspapers and magazines can say what they like about minority groups and religions—even false, provocative or hateful things—without legal consequence.

The *Maclean's* article, "The Future Belongs to Islam," was an excerpt from a book by Mark Steyn called *America Alone*. The title was fitting: the United States, in its treatment of hate speech, as in so many areas of the law, takes a distinctive legal path.

"In much of the developed world, one uses racial epithets at one's legal peril, one displays Nazi regalia and the other trappings of ethnic hatred at significant legal risk and one urges discrimination against religious minorities under threat of fine or imprisonment," Frederick Schauer, a professor at the John F. Kennedy School of Government at Harvard, wrote in a recent essay called "The Exceptional First Amendment."

"But in the United States," Schauer continued, "all such speech remains constitutionally protected."

Canada, Britain, France, Germany, the Netherlands, South Africa, Australia and India all have laws or have signed international conventions banning hate speech. Israel and France forbid the sale of Nazi items like swastikas and flags. It is a crime to deny the Holocaust in Canada, Germany and France.

Last week, the actress Brigitte Bardot, an animal rights activist, was fined €15,000, or $23,000, in France for provoking racial hatred by criticizing a Muslim ceremony involving the slaughter of sheep.

By contrast, U.S. courts would not stop the American Nazi Party from marching in Skokie, Illinois, in 1977, though the march was deeply distressing to the many Holocaust survivors there.

Six years later, a state court judge in New York dismissed a libel case brought by several Puerto Rican groups against a business executive who had called food stamps "basically a Puerto Rican program." The First Amendment, Justice Eve Preminger wrote, does not allow even false statements about racial or ethnic groups to be suppressed or punished just because they may increase "the general level of prejudice."

Some prominent legal scholars say the United States should reconsider its position on hate speech.

"It is not clear to me that the Europeans are mistaken," Jeremy Waldron, a legal philosopher, wrote in *The New York Review of Books* last month, "when they say that a liberal democracy must take affirmative responsibility for protecting the atmosphere of mutual respect against certain forms of vicious attack."

Waldron was reviewing *Freedom for the Thought That We Hate: A Biography of the First Amendment* by Anthony Lewis, the former *New York Times* columnist. Lewis has been critical of attempts to use the law to limit hate speech.

But even Lewis, a liberal, wrote in his book that he was inclined to relax some of the most stringent First Amendment protections "in an age when words have inspired acts of mass murder and terrorism." In particular, he called for a re-examination of the Supreme Court's insistence that there is only one justification for making incitement a criminal offense: the likelihood of imminent violence.

The imminence requirement sets a high hurdle. Mere advocacy of violence, terrorism or the overthrow of the government is not enough; the words must be meant to, and be likely to, produce violence or lawlessness right away. A fiery speech urging an angry racist mob immediately to assault a black man in its midst probably qualifies as incitement under the First Amendment. A magazine article—or any publication—aimed at stirring up racial hatred surely does not.

Lewis wrote that there is "genuinely dangerous" speech that does not meet the imminence requirement. "I think we should be able to punish speech that urges terrorist violence to an audience, some of whose members are ready to act on the urging," Lewis wrote. "That is imminence enough."

Harvey Silverglate, a civil liberties lawyer in Boston, disagreed.

"When times are tough," he said, "there seems to be a tendency to say there is too much freedom."

"Free speech matters because it works," Silverglate continued. Scrutiny and debate are more effective ways of combating hate speech than censorship, he said, and all the more so in the post-Sept. 11 era.

"The world didn't suffer because too many people read *Mein Kampf*," Silverglate said. "Sending

Hitler on a speaking tour of the United States would have been quite a good idea."

Silverglate seemed to be echoing the words of Justice Oliver Wendell Holmes, whose 1919 dissent in *Abrams v. United States* eventually formed the basis for modern First Amendment law.

"The best test of truth is the power of the thought to get itself accepted in the competition of the market," Holmes wrote. "I think that we should be eternally vigilant," he added, "against attempts to check the expression of opinions that we loathe and believe to be fraught with death."

The First Amendment is not, of course, absolute. The Supreme Court has said that the government may ban fighting words or threats. Punishments may be enhanced for violent crimes prompted by race hate. And private institutions, including universities and employers, are not subject to the First Amendment, which restricts only government activities.

But merely saying hateful things about minority groups, even with the intent to cause their members distress and to generate contempt and loathing, is protected by the First Amendment.

In 1969, for instance, the Supreme Court unanimously overturned the conviction of a leader of a Ku Klux Klan group under an Ohio statute that banned the advocacy of terrorism. The Klan leader, Clarence Brandenburg, had urged his followers at a rally to "send the Jews back to Israel," to "bury" blacks, though he did not call them that, and to consider "revengeance" against politicians and judges who were unsympathetic to whites.

Only Klan members and journalists were present. Because Brandenburg's words fell short of calling for immediate violence in a setting where such violence was likely, the Supreme Court ruled that he could not be prosecuted for incitement.

In his opening statement in the Canadian magazine case, a lawyer representing the Muslim plaintiffs aggrieved by the *Maclean's* article pleaded with a three-member panel of the tribunal to declare that the article subjected his clients to "hatred and ridicule" and to force the magazine to publish a response.

"You are the only thing between racist, hateful, contemptuous Islamophobic and irresponsible journalism," the lawyer, Faisal Joseph, told the tribunal, "and law-abiding Canadian citizens."

In response, a lawyer for *Maclean's* all but called the proceeding a sham.

"Innocent intent is not a defense," the lawyer, Roger McConchie, said, in a bitter criticism of the British Columbia hate speech law. "Nor is truth. Nor is fair comment on true facts. Publication in the public interest and for the public benefit is not a defense. Opinion expressed in good faith is not a defense. Responsible journalism is not a defense."

Jason Gratl, a lawyer for the British Columbia Civil Liberties Association, which has intervened in the case, was measured in his criticism of the law forbidding hate speech.

"Canadians do not have a cast-iron stomach for offensive speech," Gratl said in a telephone interview. "We don't subscribe to a marketplace of ideas. Americans as a whole are more tough-minded and more prepared for verbal combat."

Many foreign courts have respectfully considered the U.S. approach—and then rejected it.

A 1990 decision from the Canadian Supreme Court, for instance, upheld the criminal conviction of James Keegstra for "unlawfully promoting hatred against an identifiable group by communicating anti-Semitic statements." Keegstra, a teacher, had told his students that Jews are "money loving," "power hungry" and "treacherous."

Writing for the majority, Chief Justice Robert Dickson said there was an issue "crucial to the disposition of this appeal: the relationship between Canadian and American approaches to the constitutional protection of free expression, most notably in the realm of hate propaganda."

Dickson said, "There is much to be learned from First Amendment jurisprudence." But he concluded that "the international commitment to eradicate hate propaganda and, most importantly, the special role given equality and multiculturalism in the Canadian Constitution necessitate a departure from the view, reasonably prevalent in America at present, that the suppression of hate propaganda is incompatible with the guarantee of free expression."

The distinctive U.S. approach to free speech, legal scholars say, has many causes. It is partly rooted in an individualistic view of the world. Fear of allowing the government to decide what speech is acceptable plays a role. So does history.

"It would be really hard to criticize Israel, Austria, Germany and South Africa, given their histories," for laws banning hate speech, said Schauer, the professor at Harvard, in an interview.

In Canada, however, the laws seem to stem from a desire to promote societal harmony. Three time zones east of British Columbia, the Ontario Human Rights Commission—while declining to hear a separate case against *Maclean's*—nonetheless condemned the article.

"In Canada, the right to freedom of expression is not absolute, nor should it be," the commission's statement said. "By portraying Muslims as all sharing the same negative characteristics, including being a threat to 'the West,' this explicit expression of Islamophobia further perpetuates and promotes prejudice toward Muslims and others."

British Columbia human rights law, unlike that in Ontario, does appear to allow claims based on statements published in magazines.

Steyn, the author of the *Maclean's* article, said the court proceeding illustrated some important distinctions. "The problem with so-called hate speech laws is that they're not about facts," he said in a telephone interview. "They're about feelings."

"What we're learning here is really the bedrock difference between the United States and the countries that are in a broad sense its legal cousins," Steyn added. "Western governments are becoming increasingly comfortable with the regulation of opinion. The First Amendment really does distinguish the U.S., not just from Canada but from the rest of the Western world."

DISCUSSION QUESTIONS

1. The article cites Jeremy Waldron as suggesting that "a liberal democracy must take affirmative responsibility for protecting the atmosphere of mutual respect against certain forms of vicious attack." Waldron's argument is not provided; what sort of argument do you think can be developed in support of this claim?

2. The article notes that in the U.S. the only justification for making incitement a criminal offense is when the likelihood of imminent violence is present. Do you think that this requirement allows too much hateful speech to escape criminal prosecution? Do you think that there are forms of speech which, while not meeting the imminence requirement, are nonetheless dangerous? Does this then justify restricting those forms of speech? Explain your answers.

3. Do you think that cultural context is relevant to what sorts of speech ought to be restricted in a given society? For example, do you think that Germany is justified in outlawing, as it does, Holocaust denials? Defend your answer.

4. The civil liberties lawyer Harvey Silverglate is quoted as saying that "[t]he world didn't suffer because too many people read *Mein Kampf....* Sending Hitler on a speaking tour of the United States would have been quite a good idea." What do you think Silverglate means? How do you think Mill would respond to this sentiment? Explain your answer.

45

FREE SPEECH

Texas v. Johnson (1989)

The following United States Supreme Court case deals with issues of offensive behavior and First Amendment protections of expressive conduct. The accused, Gregory Lee Johnson, was arrested for burning an American flag during a protest staged at the 1984 Republican National Convention in Dallas, Texas. A Texas statute in effect at the time outlawed such action, but Johnson argued before the court that the statute was unconstitutional. The court concurred. In the course of its decision, the Court discussed the underlying rationale for the First Amendment.

SOURCE

491 U.S. 397 (U.S. Supreme Court).

During the 1984 Republican National Convention in Dallas, Texas, respondent Johnson participated in a political demonstration to protest the policies of the Reagan administration and some Dallas-based corporations. After a march through the city streets, Johnson burned an American flag while protesters chanted. No one was physically injured or threatened with injury, although several witnesses were seriously offended by the flag burning. Johnson was convicted of desecration of a venerated object in violation of a Texas statute, and a State Court of Appeals affirmed. However, the Texas Court of Criminal Appeals reversed, holding that the State, consistent with the First Amendment, could not punish Johnson for burning the flag in these circumstances. The court first found that Johnson's burning of the flag was expressive conduct protected by the First Amendment. The court concluded that the State could not criminally sanction flag desecration in order to preserve the flag as a symbol of national unity. It also held that the statute did not meet the State's goal of preventing breaches of the peace, since it was not drawn narrowly enough to encompass only those flag burnings that would likely result in a serious disturbance, and since the flag burning in this case did not threaten such a reaction. Further, it stressed that another Texas statute prohibited breaches of the peace and could be used to prevent disturbances without punishing this flag desecration.

Held: Johnson's conviction for flag desecration is inconsistent with the First Amendment.

(a) Under the circumstances, Johnson's burning of the flag constituted expressive conduct, permitting him to invoke the First Amendment. The State conceded that the conduct was expressive. Occurring as it did at the end of a demonstration coinciding with the Republican National Convention, the expressive, overtly political nature of the conduct was both intentional and overwhelmingly apparent.

(b) Texas has not asserted an interest in support of Johnson's conviction that is unrelated to the suppression of expression and would therefore permit application of the test set forth in *United States v. O'Brien*, whereby an important governmental interest in regulating nonspeech can justify incidental limitations on First Amendment freedoms when speech and nonspeech elements are combined in the same course of conduct. An interest in preventing breaches of the peace is not implicated on this record. Expression may not be prohibited on the basis that an audience that takes serious offense to the expression may disturb the peace, since the government cannot assume that every expression of a provocative idea will incite a riot but must look to the actual circumstances surrounding the expression. Johnson's expression of dissatisfaction with the Federal Government's policies also does not fall within the class of "fighting words" likely to be seen as a direct personal insult or an invitation to exchange fisticuffs. This Court's holding does not forbid a State to prevent "imminent lawless action" and, in fact, Texas has a law specifically prohibiting breaches of the peace. Texas' interest in preserving the flag as a symbol of nationhood and national unity is related to expression in this case and, thus, falls outside the *O'Brien* test.

(c) The latter interest does not justify Johnson's conviction. The restriction on Johnson's political expression is content based, since the Texas statute is not aimed at protecting the physical integrity of the flag in all circumstances, but is designed to protect it from intentional and knowing abuse that causes serious offense to others. It is therefore subject to "the most exacting scrutiny." The government may not prohibit the verbal or nonverbal expression of an idea merely because society finds the idea offensive or disagreeable, even where our flag is involved. Nor may a State foster its own view of the flag by prohibiting expressive conduct relating to it, since the government may not permit designated symbols to be used to communicate a limited set of messages. Moreover, this Court will not create an exception to these principles protected by the First Amendment for the American flag alone.

[...]

Justice Brennan delivered the opinion of the Court.

After publicly burning an American flag as a means of political protest, Gregory Lee Johnson was convicted of desecrating a flag in violation of Texas law. This case presents the question whether his conviction is consistent with the First Amendment. We hold that it is not.

I

While the Republican National Convention was taking place in Dallas in 1984, respondent Johnson participated in a political demonstration dubbed the "Republican War Chest Tour." As explained in literature distributed by the demonstrators and in speeches made by them, the purpose of this event was to protest the policies of the Reagan administration and of certain Dallas-based corporations. The demonstrators marched through the Dallas streets, chanting political slogans and stopping at several corporate locations to stage "die-ins" intended to dramatize the consequences of nuclear war. On several occasions they spray-painted the walls of buildings and overturned potted plants, but Johnson himself took no part in such activities. He did, however, accept an American flag handed to him by a fellow protestor who had taken it from a flagpole outside one of the targeted buildings.

The demonstration ended in front of Dallas City Hall, where Johnson unfurled the American flag, doused it with kerosene, and set it on fire. While the flag burned, the protestors chanted: "America, the red, white, and blue, we spit on you." After the demonstrators dispersed, a witness to the flag burning collected the flag's remains and buried them in his backyard. No one was physically injured or threatened with injury, though several witnesses testified that they had been seriously offended by the flag burning.

Of the approximately 100 demonstrators, Johnson alone was charged with a crime. The only criminal offense with which he was charged was the desecration of a venerated object in violation of Tex. Penal Code Ann. 42.09(a)(3) (1989). After a trial, he was convicted, sentenced to one year in prison, and fined $2,000. The Court of Appeals for the Fifth District of Texas at Dallas affirmed Johnson's conviction, but the Texas Court of Criminal Appeals reversed, holding that the State could not, consistent with the First Amendment, punish Johnson for burning the flag in these circumstances.

The Court of Criminal Appeals began by recognizing that Johnson's conduct was symbolic speech protected by the First Amendment: "Given the context of an organized demonstration, speeches, slogans, and the distribution of literature, anyone who observed appellant's act would have understood the message that appellant intended to convey. The act for which appellant was convicted was clearly 'speech' contemplated by the First Amendment." To justify Johnson's conviction for engaging in symbolic speech, the State asserted two interests: preserving the flag as a symbol of national unity and preventing breaches of the peace. The Court of Criminal Appeals held that neither interest supported his conviction.

Acknowledging that this Court had not yet decided whether the Government may criminally sanction flag desecration in order to preserve the flag's symbolic value, the Texas court nevertheless concluded that our decision in *West Virginia Board of Education v. Barnette* suggested that furthering this interest by curtailing speech was impermissible. "Recognizing that the right to differ is the centerpiece of our First Amendment freedoms," the court explained, "a government cannot mandate by fiat a feeling of unity in its citizens. Therefore, that very same government cannot carve out a symbol of unity and prescribe a set of approved messages to be associated with that symbol when it cannot

mandate the status or feeling the symbol purports to represent." Noting that the State had not shown that the flag was in "grave and immediate danger" of being stripped of its symbolic value, the Texas court also decided that the flag's special status was not endangered by Johnson's conduct.

As to the State's goal of preventing breaches of the peace, the court concluded that the flag-desecration statute was not drawn narrowly enough to encompass only those flag burnings that were likely to result in a serious disturbance of the peace. And in fact, the court emphasized, the flag burning in this particular case did not threaten such a reaction. "'Serious offense' occurred," the court admitted, "but there was no breach of peace nor does the record reflect that the situation was potentially explosive. One cannot equate 'serious offense' with incitement to breach the peace." The court also stressed that another Texas statute prohibited breaches of the peace. Citing *Boos v. Barry*, the court decided that [that statute] demonstrated Texas' ability to prevent disturbances of the peace without punishing this flag desecration.

Because it reversed Johnson's conviction on the ground that [the statute] was unconstitutional as applied to him, the state court did not address Johnson's argument that the statute was, on its face, unconstitutionally vague and overbroad. We granted certiorari, 488 U.S. 907 (1988), and now affirm.

II

Johnson was convicted of flag desecration for burning the flag rather than for uttering insulting words. This fact somewhat complicates our consideration of his conviction under the First Amendment. We must first determine whether Johnson's burning of the flag constituted expressive conduct, permitting him to invoke the First Amendment in challenging his conviction. If his conduct was expressive, we next decide whether the State's regulation is related to the suppression of free expression. If the State's regulation is not related to expression, then the less stringent standard we announced in *United States v. O'Brien* for regulations of noncommunicative conduct controls. If it is, then we are outside of *O'Brien*'s test, and we must ask whether this interest justifies Johnson's conviction under a more demanding standard. A third possibility is that the State's asserted interest is simply not implicated on these facts, and in that event the interest drops out of the picture.

The First Amendment literally forbids the abridgment only of "speech," but we have long recognized that its protection does not end at the spoken or written word. While we have rejected "the view that an apparently limitless variety of conduct can be labeled 'speech' whenever the person engaging in the conduct intends thereby to express an idea," we have acknowledged that conduct may be "sufficiently imbued with elements of communication to fall within the scope of the First and Fourteenth Amendments."

In deciding whether particular conduct possesses sufficient communicative elements to bring the First Amendment into play, we have asked whether "[a]n intent to convey a particularized message was present, and [whether] the likelihood was great that the message would be understood by those who viewed it." Hence, we have recognized the expressive nature of students' wearing of black armbands to protest American military involvement in Vietnam; of a sit-in by blacks in a "whites only" area to protest segregation; of the wearing of American military uniforms in a dramatic presentation criticizing American involvement in Vietnam; and of picketing about a wide variety of causes.

Especially pertinent to this case are our decisions recognizing the communicative nature of conduct relating to flags. Attaching a peace sign to the flag, refusing to salute the flag, and displaying a red flag, we have held, all may find shelter under the First Amendment.... That we have had little difficulty identifying an expressive element in conduct relating to flags should not be surprising. The very purpose of a national flag is to serve as a symbol of our country; it is, one might say, "the one visible manifestation of two hundred years of nationhood." Thus, we have observed:

[T]he flag salute is a form of utterance. Symbolism is a primitive but effective way of communicating ideas. The use of an emblem or flag to symbolize some system, idea, institution, or personality, is a short cut from mind to mind. Causes and nations, political parties, lodges and ecclesiastical groups seek to knit the loyalty of their followings to a flag or banner, a color or design.

Pregnant with expressive content, the flag as readily signifies this Nation as does the combination of letters found in "America."

We have not automatically concluded, however, that any action taken with respect to our flag is expressive. Instead, in characterizing such action for First Amendment purposes, we have considered the context in which it occurred. In *Spence*, for example, we emphasized that Spence's taping of a peace sign to his flag was "roughly simultaneous with and concededly triggered by the Cambodian incursion and the Kent State tragedy." The State of Washington had conceded, in fact, that Spence's conduct was a form of communication, and we stated that "the State's concession is inevitable on this record."

The State of Texas conceded for purposes of its oral argument in this case that Johnson's conduct was expressive conduct, and this concession seems ... prudent.... Johnson burned an American flag as part—indeed, as the culmination—of a political demonstration that coincided with the convening of the Republican Party and its renomination of Ronald Reagan for President. The expressive, overtly political nature of this conduct was both intentional and overwhelmingly apparent. At his trial, Johnson explained his reasons for burning the flag as follows: "The American Flag was burned as Ronald Reagan was being renominated as President. And a more powerful statement of symbolic speech, whether you agree with it or not, couldn't have been made at that time. It's quite a just position [juxtaposition]. We had new patriotism and no patriotism." In these circumstances, Johnson's burning of the flag was conduct "sufficiently imbued with elements of communication," to implicate the First Amendment.

III

The government generally has a freer hand in restricting expressive conduct than it has in restricting the written or spoken word. It may not, however, proscribe particular conduct because it has expressive elements. "[W]hat might be termed the more generalized guarantee of freedom of expression makes the communicative nature of conduct an inadequate basis for singling out that conduct for proscription. A law directed at the communicative nature of conduct must, like a law directed at speech itself, be justified by the substantial showing of need that the First Amendment requires." It is, in short, not simply the verbal or nonverbal nature of the expression, but the governmental interest at stake, that helps to determine whether a restriction on that expression is valid.

Thus, although we have recognized that where "'speech' and 'nonspeech' elements are combined in the same course of conduct, a sufficiently important governmental interest in regulating the nonspeech element can justify incidental limitations on First Amendment freedoms," we have limited the applicability of *O'Brien*'s relatively lenient standard to those cases in which "the governmental interest is unrelated to the suppression of free expression." In stating, moreover, that *O'Brien*'s test "in the last analysis is little, if any, different from the standard applied to time, place, or manner restrictions," we have highlighted the requirement that the governmental interest in question be unconnected to expression in order to come under *O'Brien*'s less demanding rule.

In order to decide whether *O'Brien*'s test applies here, therefore, we must decide whether Texas has asserted an interest in support of Johnson's conviction that is unrelated to the suppression of expression. If we find that an interest asserted by the State is simply not implicated on the facts before us, we need not ask whether *O'Brien*'s test applies. The State offers two separate interests to justify this conviction: preventing breaches of the peace and preserving the flag as a symbol of nationhood and national unity. We hold that the first interest is not implicated on this record and that the second is related to the suppression of expression.

A

Texas claims that its interest in preventing breaches of the peace justifies Johnson's conviction for flag desecration. However, no disturbance of the peace actually occurred or threatened to occur because of Johnson's burning of the flag. Although the State stresses the disruptive behavior of the protestors during their march toward City Hall, it admits that "no actual breach of the peace occurred at the time of the flagburning or in response to the flagburning." The State's emphasis on the protestors' disorderly actions prior to arriving at City Hall is not only somewhat surprising given that no charges were brought on the basis of this conduct, but it also fails to show that a disturbance of the peace was a likely reaction to Johnson's conduct. The only evidence offered by the State at trial to show the reaction to Johnson's actions was the testimony of several persons who had been seriously offended by the flag burning.

The State's position, therefore, amounts to a claim that an audience that takes serious offense at particular expression is necessarily likely to disturb the peace and that the expression may be prohibited on this basis. Our precedents do not countenance such a presumption. On the contrary, they recognize that a principal "function of free speech under our system of government is to invite dispute. It may indeed best serve its high purpose when it induces a condition of unrest, creates dissatisfaction with conditions as they are, or even stirs people to anger." It would be odd indeed to conclude both that "if it is the speaker's opinion that gives offense, that consequence is a reason for according it constitutional protection," and that the government may ban the expression of certain disagreeable ideas on the unsupported presumption that their very disagreeableness will provoke violence.

Thus, we have not permitted the government to assume that every expression of a provocative idea will incite a riot, but have instead required careful consideration of the actual circumstances surrounding such expression, asking whether the expression "is directed to inciting or producing imminent lawless action and is likely to incite or produce such action." See *Brandenburg v. Ohio*. To accept Texas' arguments that it need only demonstrate "the potential for a breach of the peace," and that every flag burning necessarily possesses that potential, would be to eviscerate our holding in *Brandenburg*. This we decline to do.

Nor does Johnson's expressive conduct fall within that small class of "fighting words" that are "likely to provoke the average person to retaliation, and thereby cause a breach of the peace." No reasonable onlooker would have regarded Johnson's generalized expression of dissatisfaction with the policies of the Federal Government as a direct personal insult or an invitation to exchange fisticuffs.

We thus conclude that the State's interest in maintaining order is not implicated on these facts. The State need not worry that our holding will disable it from preserving the peace. We do not suggest that the First Amendment forbids a State to prevent "imminent lawless action." And, in fact, Texas already has a statute specifically prohibiting breaches of the peace, which tends to confirm that Texas need not punish this flag desecration in order to keep the peace.

B

The State also asserts an interest in preserving the flag as a symbol of nationhood and national unity. In *Spence*, we acknowledged that the government's interest in preserving the flag's special symbolic value "is directly related to expression in the context of activity" such as affixing a peace symbol to a flag. We are equally persuaded that this interest is related to expression in the case of Johnson's burning of the flag. The State, apparently, is concerned that such conduct will lead people to believe either that the flag does not stand for nationhood and national unity, but instead reflects other, less positive concepts, or that the concepts reflected in the flag do not in fact exist, that is, that we do not enjoy unity as a Nation. These concerns blossom only when a person's treatment of the flag communicates some message, and thus are related "to the suppression of free expression" within the meaning of *O'Brien*. We are thus outside of *O'Brien*'s test altogether.

IV

It remains to consider whether the State's interest in preserving the flag as a symbol of nationhood and national unity justifies Johnson's conviction.

As in *Spence*, "[w]e are confronted with a case of prosecution for the expression of an idea through activity," and "[a]ccordingly, we must examine with particular care the interests advanced by [petitioner] to support its prosecution." Johnson was not, we add, prosecuted for the expression of just any idea; he was prosecuted for his expression of dissatisfaction with the policies of this country, expression situated at the core of our First Amendment values.

Moreover, Johnson was prosecuted because he knew that his politically charged expression would cause "serious offense." If he had burned the flag as a means of disposing of it because it was dirty or torn, he would not have been convicted of flag desecration under this Texas law: federal law designates burning as the preferred means of disposing of a flag "when it is in such condition that it is no longer a fitting emblem for display," and Texas has no quarrel with this means of disposal. The Texas law is thus not aimed at protecting the physical integrity of the flag in all circumstances, but is designed instead to protect it only against impairments that would cause serious offense to others. Texas concedes as much....

Whether Johnson's treatment of the flag violated Texas law thus depended on the likely communicative impact of his expressive conduct. Our decision in *Boos v. Barry*, tells us that this restriction on Johnson's expression is content based. In *Boos*, we considered the constitutionality of a law prohibiting "the display of any sign within 500 feet of a foreign embassy if that sign tends to bring that foreign government into 'public odium' or 'public disrepute.'" Rejecting the argument that the law was content neutral because it was justified by "our international law obligation to shield diplomats from speech that offends their dignity," we held that "[t]he emotive impact of speech on its audience is not a 'secondary effect'" unrelated to the content of the expression itself.

According to the principles announced in *Boos*, Johnson's political expression was restricted because of the content of the message he conveyed. We must therefore subject the State's asserted interest in preserving the special symbolic character of the flag to "the most exacting scrutiny."

Texas argues that its interest in preserving the flag as a symbol of nationhood and national unity survives this close analysis. Quoting extensively from the writings of this Court chronicling the flag's historic and symbolic role in our society, the State emphasizes the "special place" reserved for the flag in our Nation. The State's argument is not that it has an interest simply in maintaining the flag as a symbol of something, no matter what it symbolizes; indeed, if that were the State's position, it would be difficult to see how that interest is endangered by highly symbolic conduct such as Johnson's. Rather, the State's claim is that it has an interest in preserving the flag as a symbol of nationhood and national unity, a symbol with a determinate range of meanings. According to Texas, if one physically treats the flag in a way that would tend to cast doubt on either the idea that nationhood and national unity are the flag's referents or that national unity actually exists, the message conveyed thereby is a harmful one and therefore may be prohibited.

If there is a bedrock principle underlying the First Amendment, it is that the government may not prohibit the expression of an idea simply because society finds the idea itself offensive or disagreeable.

We have not recognized an exception to this principle even where our flag has been involved. In *Street v. New York* we held that a State may not criminally punish a person for uttering words critical of the flag. Rejecting the argument that the conviction could be sustained on the ground that Street had "failed to show the respect for our national symbol which may properly be demanded of every citizen," we concluded that "the constitutionally guaranteed 'freedom to be intellectually ... diverse or even contrary,' and the 'right to differ as to things that touch the heart of the existing order,' encompass the freedom to express publicly one's opinions about our flag, including those opinions which are defiant or contemptuous." Nor may the government, we have held, compel conduct that would evince respect for the flag. "To sustain the compulsory flag salute we are required to say that a Bill of Rights which guards the individual's right to speak his own mind, left it open to public authorities to compel him to utter what is not in his mind."

In holding ... that the Constitution did not leave this course open to the government, Justice Jackson described one of our society's defining principles in words deserving of their frequent repetition: "If there is any fixed star in our constitutional constellation, it is that no official, high or petty, can prescribe what shall be orthodox in politics, nationalism, religion, or other matters of opinion or force citizens to confess by word or act their faith therein." In *Spence*, we held that the same interest asserted by Texas here was insufficient to support a criminal conviction under a flag-misuse statute for the taping of a peace sign to an American flag. "Given the protected character of [Spence's] expression and in light of the fact that no interest the State may have in preserving the physical integrity of a privately owned flag was significantly impaired on these facts," we held, "the conviction must be invalidated." ...

In short, nothing in our precedents suggests that a State may foster its own view of the flag by prohibiting expressive conduct relating to it. To bring its argument outside our precedents, Texas attempts to convince us that even if its interest in preserving the flag's symbolic role does not allow it to prohibit words or some expressive conduct critical of the flag, it does permit it to forbid the outright destruction of the flag. The State's argument cannot depend here on the distinction between written or spoken words and nonverbal conduct. That distinction, we have shown, is of no moment where the nonverbal conduct is expressive, as it is here, and where the regulation of that conduct is related to expression, as it is here. In addition, both *Barnette* and *Spence* involved expressive conduct, not only verbal communication, and both found that conduct protected.

Texas' focus on the precise nature of Johnson's expression, moreover, misses the point of our prior decisions: their enduring lesson, that the government may not prohibit expression simply because it disagrees with its message, is not dependent on the particular mode in which one chooses to express an idea. If we were to hold that a State may forbid flag burning wherever it is likely to endanger the flag's symbolic role, but allow it wherever burning a flag promotes that role—as where, for example, a person ceremoniously burns a dirty flag—we would be saying that when it comes to impairing the flag's physical integrity, the flag itself may be used as a symbol—as a substitute for the written or spoken word or a "short cut from mind to mind"—only in one direction. We would be permitting a State to "prescribe what shall be orthodox" by saying that one may burn the flag to convey one's attitude toward it and its referents only if one does not endanger the flag's representation of nationhood and national unity.

We never before have held that the Government may ensure that a symbol be used to express only one view of that symbol or its referents. Indeed, in *Schacht v. United States*, we invalidated a federal statute permitting an actor portraying a member of one of our Armed Forces to "'wear the uniform of that armed force if the portrayal does not tend to discredit that armed force.'" This proviso, we held, "which leaves Americans free to praise the war in Vietnam but can send persons like Schacht to prison for opposing it, cannot survive in a country which has the First Amendment."

We perceive no basis on which to hold that the principle underlying our decision in Schacht does not apply to this case. To conclude that the government may permit designated symbols to be used to communicate only a limited set of messages would be to enter territory having no discernible or defensible boundaries. Could the government, on this theory, prohibit the burning of state flags? Of copies of the Presidential seal? Of the Constitution? In evaluating these choices under the First Amendment, how would we decide which symbols were sufficiently special to warrant this unique status? To do so, we would be forced to consult our own political preferences, and impose them on the citizenry, in the very way that the First Amendment forbids us to do.

There is, moreover, no indication—either in the text of the Constitution or in our cases interpreting it—that a separate juridical category exists for the American flag alone. Indeed, we would not be surprised to learn that the persons who framed our Constitution and wrote the Amendment that we now construe were not known for their reverence for the Union Jack. The First Amendment does not guarantee that other concepts virtually sacred to our Nation as a whole—such as the principle that discrimination on the basis of race is odious and destructive—will go unquestioned in the marketplace of ideas. See *Brandenburg v. Ohio*, 395 U.S. 444 (1969). We decline, therefore, to create for the flag an exception to the joust of principles protected by the First Amendment.

It is not the State's ends, but its means, to which we object. It cannot be gainsaid that there is a special place reserved for the flag in this Nation, and thus we do not doubt that the government has a legitimate interest in making efforts to "preserv[e] the national flag as an unalloyed symbol of our country." We reject the suggestion, urged at oral argument by counsel for Johnson, that the government lacks "any state interest whatsoever" in regulating the manner in which the flag may be displayed. Congress has, for example, enacted … regulations describing the proper treatment of the flag, and we cast no doubt on the legitimacy of its interest in making such recommendations. To say that the government has an interest in encouraging proper treatment of the flag, however, is not to say that it may criminally punish a person for burning a flag as a means of political protest. "National unity as an end which officials may foster by persuasion and example is not in question. The problem is whether under our Constitution compulsion as here employed is a permissible means for its achievement."

We are fortified in today's conclusion by our conviction that forbidding criminal punishment for conduct such as Johnson's will not endanger the special role played by our flag or the feelings it inspires. To paraphrase Justice Holmes, we submit that nobody can suppose that this one gesture of an unknown man will change our Nation's attitude towards its flag. Indeed, Texas' argument that the burning of an American flag "is an act having a high likelihood to cause a breach of the peace," and its statute's implicit assumption that physical mistreatment of the flag will lead to "serious offense," tend to confirm that the flag's special role is not in danger; if it were, no one would riot or take offense because a flag had been burned.

We are tempted to say, in fact, that the flag's deservedly cherished place in our community will be strengthened, not weakened, by our holding today. Our decision is a reaffirmation of the principles of freedom and inclusiveness that the flag best reflects, and of the conviction that our toleration of criticism such as Johnson's is a sign and source of our strength. Indeed, one of the proudest images of our flag, the one immortalized in our own national anthem, is of the bombardment it survived at Fort McHenry. It is the Nation's resilience, not its rigidity, that Texas sees reflected in the flag—and it is that resilience that we reassert today.

The way to preserve the flag's special role is not to punish those who feel differently about these matters. It is to persuade them that they are wrong. "To courageous, self-reliant men, with confidence in the power of free and fearless reasoning applied through the processes of popular government, no danger flowing from speech can be deemed clear and present, unless the incidence of the evil apprehended is so imminent that it may befall before there is opportunity for full discussion. If there be time to expose through discussion the falsehood and fallacies, to avert the evil by the processes of education, the remedy to be applied is more speech, not enforced silence." And, precisely because it is our flag that is involved, one's response to the flag burner may exploit the uniquely persuasive power of the flag itself. We can imagine no more appropriate response to burning a flag than waving one's own, no better way to counter a flag burner's message than by saluting the flag that burns, no surer means of preserving the dignity even of the flag that burned than by—as one witness here did—according its remains a respectful burial. We do not consecrate the flag by punishing its desecration, for in doing so we dilute the freedom that this cherished emblem represents.

V

Johnson was convicted for engaging in expressive conduct. The State's interest in preventing breaches of the peace does not support his conviction because Johnson's conduct did not threaten to disturb the peace. Nor does the State's interest in preserving the flag as a symbol of nationhood and national unity justify his criminal conviction for engaging in political expression. The judgment of the Texas Court of Criminal Appeals is therefore affirmed.

DISCUSSION QUESTIONS

1. Explain what the court claims is the underlying rationale for the First Amendment. Do you agree with the court's claim about the rationale for the amendment? How would Mill respond to this rationale for freedom of expression?

2. The court cites with approval a claim that "the emotive impact of speech" is not "unrelated to the content of the expression itself." Explain. Do you agree?

3. The court claims that protection of expression "is not dependent on the particular mode in which one chooses to express an idea." Explain. Do you agree?

4. The court claims that Johnson's flag burning was "expressive conduct." What does that term mean? Do you agree with the court's characterization of Johnson's actions? Why or why not?

46

FREE SPEECH
R. v. Butler (1992)

R. v. Butler is a Supreme Court of Canada decision concerning issues of pornography and censorship. In its decision, the Court tackles such questions as whether obscene materials pose a threat to the community, and, if so, whether these potential harms can provide the justificatory grounds for censorship. The Court also considers various tests by which material can be deemed obscene.

SOURCE
R. v. Butler, [1992] 1 S.C.R. 452.

Donald Victor Butler   *Appellant*
v.
Her Majesty The Queen   *Respondent*
(...)
Indexed as: R. *v.* Butler
File No.: 22191.
1991: June 6; 1992: February 27.
Present: Lamer C.J. and La Forest,
L'Heureux-Dubé, Sopinka, Gonthier, Cory,
McLachlin, Stevenson and Iacobucci JJ.
on appeal from the court of appeal for Manitoba
[...]

The accused owned a shop selling and renting "hard core" videotapes and magazines as well as sexual paraphernalia. He was charged with various counts of selling obscene material, possessing obscene material for the purpose of distribution or sale, and exposing obscene material to public view, contrary to s. 159 (now s. 163) of the *Criminal Code*. Section 163(8) of the *Code* provides that "any publication a dominant characteristic of which is the undue exploitation of sex, or of sex and any one or more of ... crime, horror, cruelty and violence, shall be deemed to be obscene." The trial judge concluded that the obscene material was protected by the guarantee of freedom of expression in s. 2(*b*) of the *Canadian Charter of Rights and Freedoms*, and that *prima facie* only those materials which contained scenes involving violence or cruelty intermingled with sexual activity or depicted lack of consent to sexual contact or otherwise could be said to dehumanize men or women in a sexual context were legitimately proscribed under s. 1. He convicted the accused on eight counts relating to eight films and entered acquittals on the remaining charges. The Crown appealed the acquittals. The Court of Appeal, in a majority decision, allowed the appeal and entered convictions with respect to all the counts. The majority concluded that the materials in question fell outside the protection of the *Charter* since they constituted purely physical activity and involved the undue exploitation of sex and the degradation of human sexuality.

Held: The appeal should be allowed and a new trial directed on all charges. Section 163 of the *Criminal Code* infringes s. 2(*b*) of the *Charter* but can be justified under s. 1 of the *Charter*.

Per Lamer C.J. and La Forest, Sopinka, Cory, McLachlin, Stevenson and Iacobucci JJ.: While the constitutional questions as stated concern s. 163 in its entirety, this appeal should be confined to an examination of the constitutional validity of the definition of obscenity in s. 163(8). Section 163(8) provides an exhaustive test of obscenity with respect to publications and objects which exploit sex as a dominant characteristic. In order for a work or material to qualify as "obscene," the exploitation of sex must not only be its dominant characteristic, but such exploitation must be "undue." The courts have attempted to formulate workable tests to determine when the exploitation of sex is "undue." The most important of these is the "community standard of tolerance" test. This test is concerned not with what Canadians would not tolerate being exposed to themselves, but with what they would not tolerate other Canadians being exposed to. There has been a growing recognition in recent cases that material which may be said to exploit sex in a "degrading or dehumanizing" manner will necessarily fail the community standards test, not because it offends against morals but because it is perceived by public opinion to be harmful to society, particularly women. In the appreciation of whether material is degrading or dehumanizing, the appearance of consent is not necessarily determinative. The last step in the analysis of whether the exploitation of sex is undue is the "internal necessities" test or artistic defence. Even material which by itself offends community standards will not be considered "undue" if it is required for the serious treatment of a theme. Thus far the jurisprudence has failed to specify the relationship of these tests to each other.

The courts must determine as best they can what the community would tolerate others being exposed to on the basis of the degree of harm that may flow from such exposure. Harm in this context means that it predisposes persons to act in an anti-social manner, in other words, a manner which society formally recognizes as incompatible with its proper functioning. The stronger the inference of a risk of harm, the lesser the likelihood of tolerance. The portrayal of sex coupled with violence will almost always constitute the undue exploitation of sex. Explicit sex which is degrading or dehumanizing may be undue if the risk of harm is substantial. Explicit sex that is not violent and neither degrading nor dehumanizing is generally tolerated in our society and will not qualify as the undue exploitation of sex unless it employs children in its production. If material is not obscene under this framework, it does not become so by reason of the person to whom it is or may be shown or by reason of the place or manner in which it is shown.

The need to apply the "internal necessities" test arises only if a work contains sexually explicit material that by itself would constitute the undue exploitation of sex. The portrayal of sex must then be viewed in context to determine whether undue exploitation of sex is the main object of the work or whether the portrayal of sex is essential to a wider artistic, literary or other similar purpose. The court must determine whether the sexually explicit material when viewed in the context of the whole work would be tolerated by the community as a whole. Any doubt in this regard must be resolved in favour of freedom of expression.

Section 163 of the *Code* seeks to prohibit certain types of expressive activity and thereby infringes s. 2(*b*) of the *Charter*. Activities cannot be excluded from the scope of the guaranteed freedom on the basis of the content or meaning being conveyed.

The infringement is justifiable under s. 1 of the *Charter*. Section 163(8), as interpreted in prior judgments and supplemented by these reasons, prescribes an intelligible standard. The overriding objective of s. 163 is not moral disapprobation but the avoidance of harm to society, and this is a sufficiently pressing and substantial concern to warrant a restriction on freedom of expression. One does not have to resort to the "shifting purpose" doctrine in order to identify the objective as the avoidance of harm to society. There is a sufficiently rational link between the criminal sanction, which demonstrates our community's disapproval of the dissemination of materials which potentially victimize women and restricts the negative influence which such materials have on changes in attitudes and behaviour, and the objective. While a direct link between obscenity and harm to society may be difficult to establish, it is reasonable to presume that exposure to images bears a causal relationship to changes in attitudes and beliefs. Section 163 of the *Code* minimally impairs freedom of expression. It does not proscribe sexually explicit erotica without violence that is not degrading or dehumanizing, but is designed to catch material that creates a risk of harm to society. Materials which have scientific, artistic or literary merit are not caught by the provision. Since the attempt to provide exhaustive instances of obscenity has been shown to be destined to fail, the only practical alternative is to strive towards a more abstract definition of obscenity which is contextually sensitive. The standard of "undue exploitation" is thus appropriate. Further, it is only the public distribution and exhibition of obscene materials which is in issue here. Given the gravity of the harm, and the threat to the values at stake, there is no alternative equal to the measure chosen by Parliament. Serious social problems such as violence against women require multi-pronged approaches by government; education and legislation are not alternatives but complements in addressing such problems. Finally, the effects of the law do not so severely trench on the protected right that the legislative objective is outweighed by the infringement.

Per L'Heureux-Dubé and Gonthier JJ.: Sopinka J.'s reasons were generally agreed with, subject to the following comments. The subject matter of s. 163 of the *Code*, obscene materials, comprises the dual elements of representation and content, and it is the combination of the two that attracts criminal liability. Obscenity is not limited to the acts prohibited in the *Code*: Parliament ascribed a broader content to it because it involves a representation. Obscenity leads to many ills. Obscene materials convey a distorted image of human sexuality, by making public and open elements of human nature that are usually hidden behind a veil of modesty and privacy. These materials are often evidence of the commission of reprehensible actions in their making, and can induce attitudinal changes which may lead to abuse and harm.

Parliament through s. 163 prohibits, and does not regulate, the circulation of obscene materials. In determining whether they are obscene, the impugned materials must therefore be presumed available to the Canadian public at large, since restrictions on availability are the result of regulatory measures which fall outside the purview of these provisions.

Explicit sex with violence will generally constitute undue exploitation of sex, and explicit sex that is degrading or dehumanizing will be undue if it creates a substantial risk of harm, as outlined by Sopinka J. Explicit sex that is neither violent nor degrading or dehumanizing may also come within the definition of obscene in s. 163(8). While the content of this category of materials is generally perceived as unlikely to cause harm, there are exceptions, such as child pornography. As well, it is quite conceivable that the representation may cause harm, even if its content as such is not seen as harmful. While the actual audience to which the materials are presented is not relevant, the manner of representation can greatly contribute to the deformation of sexuality, through the loss of its humanity, and make it socially harmful. The likelihood of harm, and the tolerance of the community, may vary according to the medium of representation, even if the content stays the same. The overall type or use of the representation may also be relevant. The assessment of the risk of harm here depends on the tolerance of the community. If the community cannot tolerate the risk of harm, then the materials, even though they may offer a non-violent, non-degrading, non-dehumanizing content, will constitute undue exploitation of sex and fall within the definition of obscenity.

Section 163 of the *Code* is aimed at preventing harm to society, a moral objective that is valid under s. 1 of the *Charter*. The avoidance of harm to society is but one instance of a fundamental conception of morality. In order to warrant an override of *Charter* rights the moral claims must be grounded; they must involve concrete problems such as life, harm and well-being, and not merely differences of opinion or taste. A consensus must also exist among the population on these claims. The avoidance of harm caused to society through attitudinal changes certainly qualifies as a fundamental conception of morality. It is well grounded, since the harm takes the form of violations of the principles of human equality and dignity.

[...]

2. Relevant Legislation

Criminal Code, R.S.C., 1985, c. C-46

163. (1) Everyone commits an offence who,

(*a*) makes, prints, publishes, distributes, circulates, or has in his possession for the purpose of publication, distribution or circulation any obscene written matter, picture, model, phonograph record or other thing whatever; or

(*b*) makes, prints, publishes, distributes, sells or has in his possession for the purpose of publication, distribution or circulation a crime comic.

(2) Every one commits an offence who knowingly, without lawful justification or excuse,

(*a*) sells, exposes to public view or has in his possession for such a purpose any obscene written matter, picture, model, phonograph record or other thing whatever;

(*b*) publicly exhibits a disgusting object or an indecent show;

(*c*) offers to sell, advertises or publishes an advertisement of, or has for sale or disposal, any means, instructions, medicine, drug or article intended or represented as a method of causing abortion or miscarriage; or

(*d*) advertises or publishes an advertisement of any means, instructions, medicine, drug or article intended or represented as a method for restoring sexual virility or curing venereal diseases or diseases of the generative organs.

(3) No person shall be convicted of an offence under this section if he establishes that the public good was served by the acts that are alleged to constitute the offence and that the acts alleged did not extend beyond what served the public good.

(4) For the purposes of this section, it is a question of law whether an act served the public good and whether there is evidence that the act alleged went beyond what served the public good, but it is a question of fact whether the acts did or did not extend beyond what served the public good.

(5) For the purposes of this section, the motives of an accused are irrelevant.

(6) Where an accused is charged with an offence under subsection (1), the fact that the accused was ignorant of the nature or presence of the matter, picture, model, phonograph record, crime comic or other thing by means of or in relation to which the offence was committed is not a defence to the charge.

(7) In this section, "crime comic" means a magazine, periodical or book that exclusively or substantially comprises matter depicting pictorially

(*a*) the commission of crimes, real or fictitious; or

(*b*) events connected with the commission of crimes, real or fictitious, whether occurring before or after the commission of the crime.

(8) For the purposes of this Act, any publication a dominant characteristic of which is the undue exploitation of sex, or of sex and any one or more of the following subjects, namely, crime, horror, cruelty and violence, shall be deemed to be obscene.

[...]

(b) Tests of "Undue Exploitation of Sex"

In order for the work or material to qualify as "obscene," the exploitation of sex must not only be its dominant characteristic, but such exploitation must be "undue." In determining when the exploitation of sex will be considered "undue," the courts have attempted to formulate workable tests. The most important of these is the "community standard of tolerance" test.

i) "Community Standard of Tolerance" Test

In *Brodie*, Judson J. accepted the view espoused notably by the Australian and New Zealand courts that obscenity is to be measured against "community standards." He cited, at pp. 705–06, the following passage in the judgment of Fullager J. in *R. v. Close*, [1948] V.L.R. 445, at p. 465:

> There does exist in any community at all times—however the standard may vary from time to time—a general instinctive sense of what is decent and what is indecent, of what is clean and what is dirty, and when the distinction has to be drawn, I do not know that today there is any better tribunal than a jury to draw it…. I am very far from attempting to lay down a model direction, but a judge might perhaps, in the case of a novel, say something like this: "It would not be true to say that any publication dealing with sexual relations is obscene. The relations of the sexes are, of course, legitimate matters for discussion everywhere…. There are certain standards of decency which prevail in the community, and you are really called upon to try this case because you are regarded as representing, and capable of justly applying, those standards. What is obscene is something which offends against those standards."

The community standards test has been the subject of extensive judicial analysis. It is the standards of the community as a whole which must be considered and not the standards of a small segment of that community such as the university community where a film was shown (*R. v. Goldberg*, [1971] 3 O.R. 323 (C.A.)) or a city where a picture was exposed (*R. v. Kiverago* (1973), 11 C.C.C. (2d) 463 (Ont. C.A.)). The standard to be applied is a national one (*R. v. Cameron* (1966), 58 D.L.R. (2d) 486 (Ont. C.A.); *R. v. Duthie Books Ltd.* (1966), 58 D.L.R. (2d) 274 (B.C.C.A.); *R. v. Ariadne Developments Ltd.* (1974), 19 C.C.C. (2d) 49 (N.S.S.C., App. Div.), at p. 59). With respect to expert evidence, it is not necessary and is not a fact which the Crown is obliged to prove as part of its case (*R. v. Sudbury News Service Ltd.* (1978), 18 O.R. (2d) 428 (C.A.); *R. v. Prairie Schooner News Ltd.* (1970), 75 W.W.R. 585 (Man. C.A.); *R. v. Great West News Ltd.*, [1970] 4 C.C.C. 307 (Man. C.A.)). In *R. v. Dominion News & Gifts (1962) Ltd.*, [1963] 2 C.C.C. 103 (Man. C.A.), Freedman J.A. (dissenting) emphasized that the community standards test must necessarily respond to changing mores (at pp. 116–17):

> Community standards must be contemporary. Times change, and ideas change with them. Compared to the Victorian era this is a liberal age in which we live. One manifestation of it is the relative freedom with which the whole question of sex is discussed. In books, magazines, movies, television, and sometimes even in parlour conversation, various aspects of sex are made the subject of comment, with a candour that in an earlier day would have been regarded as indecent and intolerable. We cannot and should not ignore these present-day attitudes when we face the question whether [the subject materials] are obscene according to our criminal law.

Our Court was called upon to elaborate the community standards test in *Towne Cinema Theatres Ltd. v. The Queen*, [1985] 1 S.C.R. 494. Dickson C.J. reviewed the case law and found (at pp. 508–09):

> The cases all emphasize that it is a standard of *tolerance*, not taste, that is relevant. What

matters is not what Canadians think is right for themselves to see. What matters is what Canadians would not abide other Canadians seeing because it would be beyond the contemporary Canadian standard of tolerance to allow them to see it.

Since the standard is tolerance, I think the audience to which the allegedly obscene material is targeted must be relevant. The operative standards are those of the Canadian community as a whole, but since what matters is what other people may see, it is quite conceivable that the Canadian community would tolerate varying degrees of explicitness depending upon the audience and the circumstances. [Emphasis in original.]

Therefore, the community standards test is concerned not with what Canadians would not tolerate being exposed to themselves, but what they would not tolerate *other* Canadians being exposed to. The minority view was that the tolerance level will vary depending on the manner, time and place in which the material is presented as well as the audience to whom it is directed. The majority opinion on this point was expressed by Wilson J. in the following passage, at p. 521:

It is not, in my opinion, open to the courts under s. 159(8) of the *Criminal Code* to characterize a movie as obscene if shown to one constituency but not if shown to another…. In my view, a movie is either obscene under the *Code* based on a national community standard of tolerance or it is not. If it is not, it may still be the subject of provincial regulatory control.

ii) "Degradation or Dehumanization" Test
There has been a growing recognition in recent cases that material which may be said to exploit sex in a "degrading or dehumanizing" manner will necessarily fail the community standards test. Borins Co. Ct. J. expressed this view in *R. v. Doug Rankine Co.* (1983), 9 C.C.C. (3d) 53 (Ont. Co. Ct.), at p. 70:

… films which consist substantially or partially of scenes which portray violence and cruelty in conjunction with sex, particularly where the performance of indignities degrade and dehumanize the people upon whom they are performed, exceed the level of community tolerance.

Subsequent decisions, such as *R. v. Ramsingh* (1984), 14 C.C.C. (3d) 230 (Man. Q.B.) and *R. v. Wagner* (1985), 43 C.R. (3d) 318 (Alta. Q.B.) held that material that "degraded" or "dehumanized" any of the participants would exceed community standards even in the absence of cruelty and violence. In *R. v. Ramsingh, supra,* Ferg J. described in graphic terms the type of material that qualified for this label. He states on p. 239:

They are exploited, portrayed as desiring pleasure from pain, by being humiliated and treated only as an object of male domination sexually, or in cruel or violent bondage. Women are portrayed in these films as pining away their lives waiting for a huge male penis to come along, on the person of a so-called sex therapist, or window washer, supposedly to transport them into complete sexual ecstasy. Or even more false and degrading one is led to believe their raison d'être is to savour semen as a life elixir, or that they secretly desire to be forcefully taken by a male.

Among other things, degrading or dehumanizing materials place women (and sometimes men) in positions of subordination, servile submission or humiliation. They run against the principles of equality and dignity of all human beings. In the appreciation of whether material is degrading or dehumanizing, the appearance of consent is not necessarily determinative. Consent cannot save materials that otherwise contain degrading or dehumanizing scenes. Sometimes the very appearance of consent makes the depicted acts even more degrading or dehumanizing.

This type of material would, apparently, fail the community standards test not because it offends against morals but because it is perceived by public opinion to be harmful to society, particularly to women. While the accuracy of this perception is not susceptible of exact proof, there is a substantial body of opinion that holds that the portrayal of persons being subjected to degrading or dehumanizing sexual treatment results in harm, particularly to women and therefore to society as a whole. See *Wagner, supra*, at p. 336. See also: Attorney General's Commission on Pornography (the "Meese Commission"), *Final Report* (U.S., 1986), vol. 1, at pp. 938-1035; Metro Toronto Task Force on Public Violence Against Women and Children, *Final Report* (1984), at p. 66; *Report of the Joint Select Committee on Video Material* (Australia, 1988), at pp. 185–230; *Pornography: Report of the Ministerial Committee of Inquiry into Pornography* (New Zealand, 1988), at pp. 38–45. It would be reasonable to conclude that there is an appreciable risk of harm to society in the portrayal of such material. The effect of the evidence on public opinion was summed up by Wilson J. in *Towne Cinema, supra*, at p. 524, as follows:

> The most that can be said, I think, is that the public has concluded that exposure to material which degrades the human dimensions of life to a subhuman or merely physical dimension and thereby contributes to a process of moral desensitization must be harmful in some way.

In *Towne Cinema*, Dickson C.J. considered the "degradation" or "dehumanization" test to be the principal indicator of "undueness" without specifying what role the community tolerance test plays in respect of this issue. He did observe, however, that the community might tolerate some forms of exploitation that caused harm that were nevertheless undue. The relevant passages appear at p. 505:

> There are other ways in which exploitation of sex might be "undue." Ours is not a

perfect society and it is unfortunate but true that the community may tolerate publications that cause harm to members of society and therefore to society as a whole. Even if, at certain times, there is a coincidence between what is not tolerated and what is harmful to society, there is no necessary connection between these two concepts. Thus, a legal definition of "undue" must also encompass publications harmful to members of society and, therefore, to society as a whole.

Sex related publications which portray persons in a degrading manner as objects of violence, cruelty or other forms of dehumanizing treatment, may be "undue" for the purpose of s. 159(8). No one should be subject to the degradation and humiliation inherent in publications which link sex with violence, cruelty, and other forms of dehumanizing treatment. It is not likely that at a given moment in a society's history, such publications will be tolerated....

> However, as I have noted above, there is no *necessary* coincidence between the undueness of publications which degrade people by linking violence, cruelty or other forms of dehumanizing treatment with sex, and the community standard of tolerance. Even if certain sex related materials were found to be within the standard of tolerance of the community, it would still be necessary to ensure that they were not "undue" in some other sense, for example in the sense that they portray persons in a degrading manner as objects of violence, cruelty, or other forms of dehumanizing treatment. [Emphasis in original.]

In the reasons of Wilson J. concurring in the result, the line between the mere portrayal of sex and the dehumanization of people is drawn by the "undueness" concept. The community is the arbiter as to what is harmful to it. She states, at p. 524:

As I see it, the essential difficulty with the definition of obscenity is that "undueness" must presumably be assessed in relation to consequences. It is implicit in the definition that at some point the exploitation of sex becomes harmful to the public or at least the public believes that to be so. It is therefore necessary for the protection of the public to put limits on the degree of exploitation and, through the application of the community standard test, the public is made the arbiter of what is harmful to it and what is not. The problem is that we know so little of the consequences we are seeking to avoid. Do obscene movies spawn immoral conduct?

Do they degrade women? Do they promote violence? The most that can be said, I think, is that the public has concluded that exposure to material which degrades the human dimensions of life to a subhuman or merely physical dimension and thereby contributes to a process of moral desensitization must be harmful in some way. It must therefore be controlled when it gets out of hand, when it becomes "undue."

iii) "Internal Necessities Test" or "Artistic Defence"

In determining whether the exploitation of sex is "undue," Judson J. set out the test of "internal necessities" in Brodie, supra, at pp. 704–05:

What I think is aimed at is excessive emphasis on the theme for a base purpose. But I do not think that there is undue exploitation if there is no more emphasis on the theme than is required in the serious treatment of the theme of a novel with honesty and uprightness. That the work under attack is a serious work of fiction is to me beyond question. It has none of the characteristics that are often described in judgments dealing with obscenity—dirt for dirt's sake, the leer of the sensualist, depravity in the mind of an author with an obsession for dirt, pornography, an appeal

to a prurient interest, etc. The section recognizes that the serious-minded author must have freedom in the production of a work of genuine artistic and literary merit and the quality of the work, as the witnesses point out and common sense indicates, must have real relevance in determining not only a dominant characteristic but also whether there is undue exploitation.

As counsel for the Crown pointed out in his oral submissions, the artistic defence is the last step in the analysis of whether the exploitation of sex is undue. Even material which by itself offends community standards will not be considered "undue," if it is required for the serious treatment of a theme. For example, in *R. v. Odeon Morton Theatres Ltd.* (1974), 16 C.C.C. (2d) 185, the majority of the Manitoba Court of Appeal held that the film "Last Tango in Paris" was not obscene within the meaning of the *Code*. To determine whether a dominant characteristic of the film is the undue exploitation of sex, Freedman C.J.M. noted that the courts must have regard to various things—the author's artistic purpose, the manner in which he or she has portrayed and developed the story, the depiction and interplay of character and the creation of visual effect through skilful camera techniques (at p. 194). Freedman C.J.M. stated that the issue of whether the film is obscene must be determined according to contemporary community standards in Canada. Relevant to that determination were several factors: the testimony of experts, the classification of "Restricted" which made the film unavailable to persons under 18 years of age and the fact that the film had passed the scrutiny of the censor boards of several provinces.

Accordingly, the "internal necessities" test, or what has been referred to as the "artistic defence," has been interpreted to assess whether the exploitation of sex has a justifiable role in advancing the plot or the theme, and in considering the work as a whole, does not merely represent "dirt for dirt's sake" but has a legitimate role when measured by the internal necessities of the work itself.

[...]

(b) Objective

The respondent argues that there are several pressing and substantial objectives which justify overriding the freedom to distribute obscene materials. Essentially, these objectives are the avoidance of harm resulting from antisocial attitudinal changes that exposure to obscene material causes and the public interest in maintaining a "decent society." On the other hand, the appellant argues that the objective of s. 163 is to have the state act as "moral custodian" in sexual matters and to impose subjective standards of morality.

The obscenity legislation and jurisprudence prior to the enactment of s. 163 were evidently concerned with prohibiting the "immoral influences" of obscene publications and safeguarding the morals of individuals into whose hands such works could fall. The *Hicklin* philosophy posits that explicit sexual depictions, particularly outside the sanctioned contexts of marriage and procreation, threatened the morals or the fabric of society (Clare Beckton, "Freedom of Expression (s. 2(b))", in Tarnopolsky and Beaudoin (eds.), *The Canadian Charter of Rights and Freedoms: Commentary* (1982), at p. 105). In this sense, its dominant, if not exclusive, purpose was to advance a particular conception of morality. Any deviation from such morality was considered to be inherently undesirable, independently of any harm to society. As Judson J. described the test in *Brodie*, *supra*, at pp. 704–05:

> [The work under attack] has none of the characteristics that are often described in judgments dealing with obscenity — dirt for dirt's sake, the leer of the sensualist, depravity in the mind of an author with an obsession for dirt, pornography, an appeal to a prurient interest, etc.

I agree with Twaddle J.A. of the Court of Appeal that this particular objective is no longer defensible in view of the *Charter*. To impose a certain standard of public and sexual morality, solely because it reflects the conventions of a given community, is inimical to the exercise and enjoyment of individual freedoms, which form the basis of our social contract. D. Dyzenhaus, "Obscenity and the Charter: Autonomy and Equality" (1991), 1 C.R. (4th) 367, at p. 370, refers to this as "legal moralism," of a majority deciding what values should inform individual lives and then coercively imposing those values on minorities. The prevention of "dirt for dirt's sake" is not a legitimate objective which would justify the violation of one of the most fundamental freedoms enshrined in the *Charter*.

On the other hand, I cannot agree with the suggestion of the appellant that Parliament does not have the right to legislate on the basis of some fundamental conception of morality for the purposes of safeguarding the values which are integral to a free and democratic society. As Dyzenhaus, *supra*, at p. 376, writes:

> Moral disapprobation is recognized as an appropriate response when it has its basis in *Charter* values.

As the respondent and many of the interveners have pointed out, much of the criminal law is based on moral conceptions of right and wrong and the mere fact that a law is grounded in morality does not automatically render it illegitimate. In this regard, criminalizing the proliferation of materials which undermine another basic *Charter* right may indeed be a legitimate objective.

In my view, however, the overriding objective of s. 163 is not moral disapprobation but the avoidance of harm to society. In *Towne Cinema*, Dickson C.J. stated, at p. 507:

> It is harm to society from undue exploitation that is aimed at by the section, not simply lapses in propriety or good taste.

The harm was described in the following way in the Report on Pornography by the Standing

Committee on Justice and Legal Affairs (MacGuigan Report) (1978), at p. 18:4:

> The clear and unquestionable danger of this type of material is that it reinforces some unhealthy tendencies in Canadian society. The effect of this type of material is to reinforce male-female stereotypes to the detriment of both sexes. It attempts to make degradation, humiliation, victimization, and violence in human relationships appear normal and acceptable. A society which holds that egalitarianism, non-violence, consensualism, and mutuality are basic to any human interaction, whether sexual or other, is clearly justified in controlling and prohibiting any medium of depiction, description or advocacy which violates these principles.

The appellant argues that to accept the objective of the provision as being related to the harm associated with obscenity would be to adopt the "shifting purpose" doctrine explicitly rejected in *R. v. Big M Drug Mart Ltd.*, [1985] 1 S.C.R. 295. This Court concluded in that case that a finding that the *Lord's Day Act* has a secular purpose was not possible given that its religious purpose, in compelling sabbatical observance, has been long-established and consistently maintained by the courts. The appellant relies on the words of Dickson J. (as he then was), at pp. 335–36:

> ... the theory of a shifting purpose stands in stark contrast to fundamental notions developed in our law concerning the nature of "Parliamentary intention." Purpose is a function of the intent of those who drafted and enacted the legislation at the time, and not of any shifting variable. [...] While the effect of such legislation as the *Lord's Day Act* may be more secular today than it was in 1677 or in 1906, such a finding cannot justify a conclusion that its purpose has similarly changed. In result, therefore, the *Lord's Day Act* must be characterized as it has always been, a law

the primary purpose of which is the compulsion of sabbatical observance.

I do not agree that to identify the objective of the impugned legislation as the prevention of harm to society, one must resort to the "shifting purpose" doctrine. First, the notions of moral corruption and harm to society are not distinct, as the appellant suggests, but are inextricably linked. It is moral corruption of a certain kind which leads to the detrimental effect on society. Second, and more importantly, I am of the view that with the enactment of s. 163, Parliament explicitly sought to address the harms which are linked to certain types of obscene materials. The prohibition of such materials was based on a belief that they had a detrimental impact on individuals exposed to them and consequently on society as a whole. Our understanding of the harms caused by these materials has developed considerably since that time; however this does not detract from the fact that the purpose of this legislation remains, as it was in 1959, the protection of society from harms caused by the exposure to obscene materials. In this regard, I lend support to the analysis of Charron Dist. Ct. J. in *R. v. Fringe Product Inc.*, *supra*, at p. 443:

> Even though one can still find an emphasis on the enforcement of moral standards of decency in relation to expression in sexual matters in the jurisprudence subsequent to the enactment of s-s.(8), it is clear that, by the very words it has chosen, Parliament in 1959 moved beyond such narrow concern and expanded the scope of the legislation to include further concerns with respect to sex combined with crime, horror, cruelty and violence.

It is the harm to society resulting from the undue exploitation of such matters which is aimed by the section. The "harm" conceived by Parliament in 1959 may not have been expressed in the same words as one would today. The court is not limited to a 1959 perspective in the determination of this matter. As noted in *Irwin Toy Ltd. v. Quebec (Attorney-General)*, *supra*, at p. 618:

> In showing that the legislation pursues a pressing and substantial objective, it is not open to the government to assert *post facto* a purpose which did not animate the legislation in the first place.... However, in proving that the original objective remains pressing and substantial, the government surely can and should draw upon the best evidence currently available. The same is true as regards proof that the measure is proportional to its objective.... It is equally possible that a purpose which was not demonstrably pressing and substantial at the time of the legislative enactment becomes demonstrably pressing and substantial with the passing of time and the changing of circumstances.

In 1959, the harm to society caused by the undue exploitation of sex or of sex and other named matters may well have been defined more strictly in terms of public morality, *i.e.*, that such expression offended society's sense of right and wrong. It may well be that if such was the only identifiable harm today that the legislation could not be said to pertain to pressing and substantial concerns thereby warranting an infringement of the right of expression. But that is not so. The harm goes beyond public morality in this narrow sense.

A permissible shift in emphasis was built into the legislation when, as interpreted by the courts, it adopted the community standards test. Community standards as to what is harmful have changed since 1959.

This being the objective, is it pressing and substantial? Does the prevention of the harm associated with the dissemination of certain obscene materials constitute a sufficiently pressing and substantial concern to warrant a restriction on the freedom of expression? In this regard, it should be recalled that in *Keegstra*, *supra*, this Court unanimously accepted that the prevention of the influence of hate propaganda on society at large was a legitimate objective.

Dickson C.J. wrote with respect to the changes in attitudes which exposure to hate propaganda can bring about (at pp. 747–48):

> ... the alteration of views held by the recipients of hate propaganda may occur subtly, and is not always attendant upon conscious acceptance of the communicated ideas. Even if the message of hate propaganda is outwardly rejected, there is evidence that its premise of racial or religious inferiority may persist in a recipient's mind as an idea that holds some truth, an incipient effect not to be entirely discounted....
>
> The threat to the self-dignity of target group members is thus matched by the possibility that prejudiced messages will gain some credence, with the attendant result of discrimination, and perhaps even violence, against minority groups in Canadian society.

This Court has thus recognized that the harm caused by the proliferation of materials which seriously offend the values fundamental to our society is a substantial concern which justifies restricting the otherwise full exercise of the freedom of expression. In my view, the harm sought to be avoided in the case of the dissemination of obscene materials is similar. In the words of Nemetz C.J.B.C. in *R. v. Red Hot Video Ltd.* (1985), 45 C.R. (3d) 36 (B.C.C.A.), there is a growing concern that the exploitation of women and children, depicted in publications and films, can, in certain circumstances, lead to "abject and servile victimization" (at pp. 43–44). As Anderson J.A. also noted in that same case, if true equality between male and female persons is to be achieved, we cannot ignore the threat to equality resulting from exposure to audiences of certain types of violent and degrading material. Materials portraying women as a class as objects for sexual exploitation and abuse have a negative impact on "the individual's sense of self-worth and acceptance."

In reaching the conclusion that legislation pro-scribing obscenity is a valid objective which justi-fies some encroachment on the right to freedom of expression, I am persuaded in part that such legis-lation may be found in most free and democratic societies. As Nemetz C.J.B.C. aptly pointed out in *R. v. Red Hot Video, supra*, for centuries demo-cratic societies have set certain limits to freedom of expression. He cited (at p. 40) the following pas-sage of Dickson J.A. (as he then was) in *R. v. Great West News Ltd., supra*, at p. 309:

> ... all organized societies have sought in one manner or another to suppress obscenity. The right of the state to legislate to protect its moral fibre and well-being has long been recognized, with roots deep in history. It is within this frame that the Courts and Judges must work.

The advent of the *Charter* did not have the effect of dramatically depriving Parliament of a power which it has historically enjoyed. It is also noteworthy that the criminalization of obscenity was considered to be compatible with the *Canadian Bill of Rights*. As Dickson J.A. stated in *R. v. Prairie Schooner News Ltd., supra*, at p. 604:

> Freedom of speech is not unfettered either in criminal law or civil law. The *Canadian Bill of Rights* was intended to protect, and does pro-tect, basic freedoms of vital importance to all Canadians. It does not serve as a shield behind which obscene matter may be disseminated without concern for criminal consequences. The interdiction of the publications which are the subject of the present charges in no way trenches upon the freedom of expression which the *Canadian Bill of Rights* assures.

The enactment of the impugned provision is also consistent with Canada's international obligations (*Agreement for the Suppression of the Circulation of Obscene Publications* and the *Convention for the Suppression of the Circulation of and Traffic in Obscene Publications*).

Finally, it should be noted that the burgeon-ing pornography industry renders the concern even more pressing and substantial than when the impugned provisions were first enacted. I would therefore conclude that the objective of avoiding the harm associated with the dissemination of pornog-raphy in this case is sufficiently pressing and sub-stantial to warrant some restriction on full exercise of the right to freedom of expression. The analy-sis of whether the measure is proportional to the objective must, in my view, be undertaken in light of the conclusion that the objective of the impugned section is valid only in so far as it relates to the harm to society associated with obscene materials. Indeed, the section as interpreted in previous deci-sions and in these reasons is fully consistent with that objective. The objective of maintaining con-ventional standards of propriety, independently of any harm to society, is no longer justified in light of the values of individual liberty which underlie the *Charter*. This, then, being the objective of s. 163, which I have found to be pressing and substantial, I must now determine whether the section is ratio-nally connected and proportional to this objective. As outlined above, s. 163(8) criminalizes the exploi-tation of sex and sex and violence, when, on the basis of the community test, it is undue. The deter-mination of when such exploitation is undue is directly related to the immediacy of a risk of harm to society which is reasonably perceived as arising from its dissemination.

[...]

DISCUSSION QUESTIONS

1. The court claims that obscene materials pose a risk of harm to the community. What are the harms that they regard as potential results of the dissemination of such materials? Evaluate their claims. Do you think that if there is a risk of such harms, such a risk justifies censorship of obscene materials?

2. Explain and evaluate the following tests that are to be used when determining whether some material is obscene: (i) the "community standard of tolerance" test; (ii) the "degradation or dehumanization" test; (iii) the "internal necessities" test, or "artistic defence."

3. The court rejects "legal moralism." Explain what is meant by that term, and how it is relevant to the issues of obscenity.

47

FREE SPEECH
Miller v. California (1973)

Miller v. California was the 1973 US Supreme Court Case that considered whether the sale and distribution of obscene material are protected under the First Amendment's guarantee of free speech. The court concluded that obscenity was *not* so protected and established a three-pronged test, known thereafter as the "Miller test," to identify obscene material.

SOURCE
413 U.S. 15 (U.S. Supreme Court).

Syllabus

SUPREME COURT OF THE UNITED STATES

413 U.S. 15
Miller v. California
APPEAL FROM THE APPELLATE
DEPARTMENT, SUPERIOR COURT OF
CALIFORNIA, COUNTY OF ORANGE
No. 70–73 Argued: January 18–19, 1972—Decided: June 21, 1973

Appellant was convicted of mailing unsolicited sexually explicit material in violation of a California statute that approximately incorporated the obscenity test formulated in *Memoirs v. Massachusetts*, 383 U.S. 413, 418 (plurality opinion). The trial court instructed the jury to evaluate the materials by the contemporary community standards of California. Appellant's conviction was affirmed on appeal. In lieu of the obscenity criteria enunciated by the *Memoirs* plurality, it is held:

1. Obscene material is not protected by the First Amendment. *Roth v. United States*, 354 U.S. 476, reaffirmed. A work may be subject to state regulation where that work, taken as a whole, appeals to the prurient interest in sex; portrays, in a patently offensive way, sexual conduct specifically defined by the applicable state law; and, taken as a whole, does not have serious literary, artistic, political, or scientific value....

2. The basic guidelines for the trier of fact must be: (a) whether "the average person, applying contemporary community standards" would find that the work, taken as a whole, appeals to the prurient interest, *Roth, supra*, at 489, (b) whether the work depicts or describes, in a patently offensive way, sexual conduct specifically defined by the applicable state law, and (c) whether the work, taken as a whole, lacks serious literary, artistic, political, or scientific value. If a state obscenity law is thus limited, First Amendment values are adequately protected by ultimate independent appellate review of constitutional claims when necessary....

3. The test of "utterly without redeeming social value" articulated in *Memoirs, supra*, is rejected as a constitutional standard....

4. The jury may measure the essentially factual issues of prurient appeal and patent offensiveness by the standard that prevails in the forum community, and need not employ a "national standard."...

Vacated and remanded...

BURGER, C.J., delivered the opinion of the Court, in which WHITE, BLACKMUN, POWELL, and REHNQUIST, JJ., joined. DOUGLAS, J., filed a dissenting opinion, post, p. 37. BRENNAN, J., filed a dissenting opinion, in which STEWART and MARSHALL, JJ., joined, post, p. 47.
BURGER, C.J., Opinion of the Court

SUPREME COURT OF THE UNITED STATES

413 U.S. 15
Miller v. California
APPEAL FROM THE APPELLATE DEPARTMENT, SUPERIOR COURT OF CALIFORNIA, COUNTY OF ORANGE
No. 70–73 Argued: January 18–19, 1972—Decided: June 21, 1973

MR. CHIEF JUSTICE BURGER delivered the opinion of the Court.

This is one of a group of "obscenity-pornography" cases being reviewed by the Court in a reexamination of standards enunciated in earlier cases involving what Mr. Justice Harlan called "the intractable obscenity problem." *Interstate Circuit, Inc. v. Dallas*, 390 U.S. 676, 704 (1968) (concurring and dissenting).

Appellant conducted a mass mailing campaign to advertise the sale of illustrated books, euphemistically called "adult" material. After a jury trial, he was convicted of violating California Penal Code § 311.2(a), a misdemeanor, by knowingly distributing obscene matter,[n.1][1] and the Appellate Department, Superior Court of California, County of Orange, summarily affirmed the judgment without opinion. Appellant's conviction was specifically based on his conduct in causing five unsolicited advertising brochures to be sent through the mail in an envelope addressed to a restaurant in Newport Beach, California. The envelope was opened by the manager of the restaurant and his mother. They had not requested the brochures; they complained to the police.

The brochures advertise four books entitled "Intercourse," "Man-Woman," "Sex Orgies Illustrated," and "An Illustrated History of Pornography," and a film entitled "Marital Intercourse." While the brochures contain some descriptive printed material, primarily they consist of pictures and drawings very explicitly depicting men and women in groups of two or more engag-

---

[1] [All other footnotes have been omitted.] 1. At the time of the commission of the alleged offense, which was prior to June 25, 1969, §§ 311.2(a) and 311 of the California Penal Code read in relevant part:

§ 311.2 Sending or bringing into state for sale or distribution; printing, exhibiting, distributing or possessing within state

(a) Every person who knowingly: sends or causes to be sent, or brings or causes to be brought, into this state for sale or distribution, or in this state prepares, publishes, prints, exhibits, distributes, or offers to distribute, or has in his possession with intent to distribute or to exhibit or offer to distribute, any obscene matter is guilty of a misdemeanor....

ing in a variety of sexual activities, with genitals often prominently displayed.

I

This case involves the application of a State's criminal obscenity statute to a situation in which sexually explicit materials have been thrust by aggressive sales action upon unwilling recipients who had in no way indicated any desire to receive such materials. This Court has recognized that the States have a legitimate interest in prohibiting dissemination or exhibition of obscene material when the mode of dissemination carries with it a significant danger of offending the sensibilities of unwilling recipients or of exposure to juveniles. *Stanley v. Georgia*, 394 U.S. 557, 567 (1969); *Ginsberg v. New York*, 390 U.S. 629, 637–643 (1968); *Interstate Circuit, Inc. v. Dallas*, supra, at 690; *Redrup v. New York*, 386 U.S. 767, 769 (1967); *Jacobellis v. Ohio*, 378 U.S. 184, 195 (1964). See *Rabe v. Washington*, 405 U.S. 313, 317 (1972) (BURGER, C.J., concurring); *United States v. Reidel*, 402 U.S. 351, 360–362 (1971) (opinion of MARSHALL, J.); *Joseph Burstyn, Inc. v. Wilson*, 343 U.S. 495, 502 (1952); *Breard v. Alexandria*, 341 U.S. 622, 644–645 (1951); *Kovacs v. Cooper*, 336 U.S. 77, 88–89 (1949); *Prince v. Massachusetts*, 321 U.S. 158, 169–170 (1944). Cf. *Butler v. Michigan*, 32 U.S. 380, 382–383 (1957); *Public Utilities Comm'n v. Pollak*, 343 U.S. 451, 464–465 (1952). It is in this context that we are called on to define the standards which must be used to identify obscene material that a State may regulate without infringing on the First Amendment as applicable to the States through the Fourteenth Amendment.

The dissent of MR. JUSTICE BRENNAN reviews the background of the obscenity problem, but since the Court now undertakes to formulate standards more concrete than those in the past, it is useful for us to focus on two of the landmark cases in the somewhat tortured history of the Court's obscenity decisions. In *Roth v. United States*, 354 U.S. 476 (1957), the Court sustained a conviction under a federal statute punishing the mailing of "obscene, lewd, lascivious or filthy ..." materials.

The key to that holding was the Court's rejection of the claim that obscene materials were protected by the First Amendment. Five Justices joined in the opinion stating:

> All ideas having even the slightest redeeming social importance—unorthodox ideas, controversial ideas, even ideas hateful to the prevailing climate of opinion—have the full protection of the [First Amendment] guaranties, unless excludable because they encroach upon the limited area of more important interests. But implicit in the history of the First Amendment is the rejection of obscenity as utterly without redeeming social importance.... This is the same judgment expressed by this Court in *Chaplinsky v. New Hampshire*, 315 U.S. 568, 571–572:
>
> > ... There are certain well defined and narrowly limited classes of speech, the prevention and punishment of which have never been thought to raise any Constitutional problem. *These include the lewd and obscene.... It has been well observed that such utterances are no essential part of any exposition of ideas, and are of such slight social value as a step to truth that any benefit that may be derived from them is clearly outweighed by the social interest in order and morality....*

[Emphasis by Court in Roth opinion.]

We hold that obscenity is not within the area of constitutionally protected speech or press. 354 U.S. at 48 85 (footnotes omitted).

Nine years later, in *Memoirs v. Massachusetts*, 383 U.S. 413 (1966), the Court veered sharply away from the *Roth* concept and, with only three Justices in the plurality opinion, articulated a new test of obscenity. The plurality held that, under the *Roth* definition, as elaborated in subsequent cases, three elements must coalesce: it must be established that (a) the dominant theme of the material, taken as a whole, appeals to a prurient interest in sex; (b) the material is patently offensive because it affronts contemporary community standards relating to the description or representation of sexual matters; and (c) the material is utterly without redeeming social value. Id. at 418.

The sharpness of the break with *Roth*, represented by the third element of the *Memoirs* test and emphasized by MR. JUSTICE WHITE's dissent, id. at 460–462, was further underscored when the Memoirs plurality went on to state:

> The Supreme Judicial Court erred in holding that a book need not be "unqualifiedly worthless before it can be deemed obscene." A book cannot be proscribed unless it is found to be *utterly* without redeeming social value.
> Id. at 419 (emphasis in original).

While *Roth* presumed "obscenity" to be "utterly without redeeming social importance," *Memoirs* required that to prove obscenity it must be affirmatively established that the material is "utterly without redeeming social value." Thus, even as they repeated the words of *Roth*, the *Memoirs* plurality produced a drastically altered test that called on the prosecution to prove a negative, i.e., that the material was "utterly without redeeming social value"— a burden virtually impossible to discharge under our criminal standards of proof. Such considerations caused Mr. Justice Harlan to wonder if the "utterly without redeeming social value" test had any meaning at all. See *Memoirs v. Massachusetts*, id. at 459 (Harlan, J., dissenting). See also id. at 461 (WHITE, J., dissenting); *United States v. Groner*, 479 F.2d 577, 579–581 (CA5 1973).

Apart from the initial formulation in the *Roth* case, no majority of the Court has at any given time been able to agree on a standard to determine what constitutes obscene, pornographic material subject to regulation under the States' police power. See, e.g., *Redrup v. New York*, 386 U.S. at 770–771. We have seen "a variety of views among the members of the Court unmatched in any other course of constitutional adjudication." *Interstate Circuit, Inc. v. Dallas*, 390 U.S. at 704–705 (Harlan, J., concurring and dissenting) (footnote omitted). This is not remarkable, for in the area of freedom of speech and press the courts must always remain sensitive to any infringement on genuinely serious literary, artistic, political, or scientific expression. This is an area in which there are few eternal verities.

The case we now review was tried on the theory that the California Penal Code § 311 approximately incorporates the three-stage *Memoirs* test, *supra*. But now the *Memoirs* test has been abandoned as unworkable by its author, and no Member of the Court today supports the *Memoirs* formulation.

II

This much has been categorically settled by the Court, that obscene material is unprotected by the First Amendment. *Kois v. Wisconsin*, 408 U.S. 229 (1972); *United States v. Reidel*, 402 U.S. at 354; *Roth v. United States*, *supra*, at 485. "The First and Fourteenth Amendments have never been treated as absolutes [footnote omitted]." *Breard v. Alexandria*, 341 U.S. at 642, and cases cited. See *Times Film Corp. v. Chicago*, 365 U.S. 43, 47–50 (1961); *Joseph Burstyn, Inc. v. Wilson*, 343 U.S. at 502. We acknowledge, however, the inherent dangers of undertaking to regulate any form of expression. State statutes designed to regulate obscene materials must be carefully limited. See *Interstate Circuit, Inc. v. Dallas*, *supra*, at 682–685. As a result, we now confine the permissible scope of such regulation to works which depict or describe sexual conduct. That conduct must be specifically defined by the applicable state law, as written or authoritatively construed. A state offense must also be limited to works which, taken as a whole, appeal to the prurient interest in sex, which portray sexual conduct in a patently offensive way, and which, taken as a whole, do not have serious literary, artistic, political, or scientific value.

The basic guidelines for the trier of fact must be: (a) whether "the average person, applying contemporary community standards" would find that the work, taken as a whole, appeals to the prurient interest, *Kois v. Wisconsin, supra*, at 230, quoting *Roth v. United States, supra*, at 489; (b) whether the work depicts or describes, in a patently offensive way, sexual conduct specifically defined by the applicable state law; and (c) whether the work, taken as a whole, lacks serious literary, artistic, political, or scientific value. We do not adopt as a constitutional standard the "utterly without redeeming social value" test of *Memoirs v. Massachusetts*, 383 U.S. at 419; that concept has never commanded the adherence of more than three Justices at one time. See *supra* at 21. If a state law that regulates obscene material is thus limited, as written or construed, the First Amendment values applicable to the States through the Fourteenth Amendment are adequately protected by the ultimate power of appellate courts to conduct an independent review of constitutional claims when necessary. See *Kois v. Wisconsin, supra*, at 232; *Memoirs v. Massachusetts, supra*, at 459–460 (Harlan, J., dissenting); *Jacobellis v. Ohio*, 378 U.S. at 204 (Harlan, J., dissenting); *New York Times Co. v. Sullivan*, 376 U.S. 254, 284–285 (1964); *Roth v. United States, supra*, at 497–498 (Harlan, J., concurring and dissenting).

We emphasize that it is not our function to propose regulatory schemes for the States. That must await their concrete legislative efforts. It is possible, however, to give a few plain examples of what a state statute could define for regulation under part (b) of the standard announced in this opinion, *supra*:

(a) Patently offensive representations or descriptions of ultimate sexual acts, normal or perverted, actual or simulated.

(b) Patently offensive representations or descriptions of masturbation, excretory functions, and lewd exhibition of the genitals.

Sex and nudity may not be exploited without limit by films or pictures exhibited or sold in places of public accommodation any more than live sex and nudity can be exhibited or sold without limit in such public places. At a minimum, prurient, patently offensive depiction or description of sexual conduct must have serious literary, artistic, political, or scientific value to merit First Amendment protection. See *Kois v. Wisconsin, supra*, at 230–232; *Roth v. United States, supra*, at 487; *Thornhill v. Alabama*, 310 U.S. 88, 101–102 (1940). For example, medical books for the education of physicians and related personnel necessarily use graphic illustrations and descriptions of human anatomy. In resolving the inevitably sensitive questions of fact and law, we must continue to rely on the jury system, accompanied by the safeguards that judges, rules of evidence, presumption of innocence, and other protective features provide, as we do with rape, murder, and a host of other offenses against society and its individual members.

MR. JUSTICE BRENNAN, author of the opinions of the Court, or the plurality opinions, in *Roth v. United States, supra*; *Jacobellis v. Ohio, supra*; *Ginzburg v. United States*, 383 U.S. 463 (1966), *Mishkin v. New York*, 383 U.S. 502 (1966); and *Memoirs v. Massachusetts, supra*, has abandoned his former position and now maintains that no formulation of this Court, the Congress, or the States can adequately distinguish obscene material unprotected by the First Amendment from protected expression, *Paris Adult Theatre I v. Slaton, post*, p. 73 (BRENNAN, J., dissenting). Paradoxically, MR. JUSTICE BRENNAN indicates that suppression of unprotected obscene material is permissible to avoid exposure to unconsenting adults, as in this case, and to juveniles, although he gives no indication of how the division between protected and nonprotected materials may be drawn with greater precision for these purposes than for regulation of commercial exposure to consenting adults only. Nor does he indicate where in the Constitution he finds the authority to distinguish between a willing "adult" one month past the state law age of majority and a willing "juvenile" one month younger.

Under the holdings announced today, no one will be subject to prosecution for the sale or exposure of obscene materials unless these materials depict or describe patently offensive "hard core" sexual conduct specifically defined by the regulating state law, as written or construed. We are satisfied that these specific prerequisites will provide fair notice to a dealer in such materials that his public and commercial activities may bring prosecution. See *Roth v. United States, supra,* at 491–492. Cf. *Ginsberg v. New York,* 390 U.S. at 643. If the inability to define regulated materials with ultimate, god-like precision altogether removes the power of the States or the Congress to regulate, then "hard core" pornography may be exposed without limit to the juvenile, the passerby, and the consenting adult alike, as, indeed, MR. JUSTICE DOUGLAS contends. As to MR. JUSTICE DOUGLAS' position, see *United States v. Thirty-seven Photographs,* 402 U.S. 363, 379–380 (1971) (Black, J., joined by DOUGLAS, J., dissenting); *Ginzburg v. United States, supra,* at 476, 491–492 (Black, J., and DOUGLAS, J., dissenting); *Jacobellis v. Ohio, supra,* at 196 (Black, J., joined by DOUGLAS, J., concurring); *Roth, supra,* at 508–514 (DOUGLAS, J., dissenting). In this belief, however, MR. JUSTICE DOUGLAS now stands alone.

MR. JUSTICE BRENNAN also emphasizes "institutional stress" in justification of his change of view. Noting that "[t]he number of obscenity cases on our docket gives ample testimony to the burden that has been placed upon this Court," he quite rightly remarks that the examination of contested materials "is hardly a source of edification to the members of this Court." *Paris Adult Theatre I v. Slaton, post,* at 92, 93. He also notes, and we agree, that "uncertainty of the standards creates a continuing source of tension between state and federal courts...."

> The problem is ... that one cannot say with certainty that material is obscene until at least five members of this Court, applying inevitably obscure standards, have pronounced it so. Id. at 93, 92.

It is certainly true that the absence, since *Roth,* of a single majority view of this Court as to proper standards for testing obscenity has placed a strain on both state and federal courts. But today, for the first time since *Roth* was decided in 1957, a majority of this Court has agreed on concrete guidelines to isolate "hard core" pornography from expression protected by the First Amendment. Now we may abandon the casual practice of *Redrup v. New York,* 386 U.S. 767 (1967), and attempt to provide positive guidance to federal and state courts alike.

This may not be an easy road, free from difficulty. But no amount of "fatigue" should lead us to adopt a convenient "institutional" rationale—an absolutist, "anything goes" view of the First Amendment—because it will lighten our burdens. "Such an abnegation of judicial supervision in this field would be inconsistent with our duty to uphold the constitutional guarantees." *Jacobellis v. Ohio, supra,* at 187–188 (opinion of BRENNAN, J.). Nor should we remedy "tension between state and federal courts" by arbitrarily depriving the States of a power reserved to them under the Constitution, a power which they have enjoyed and exercised continuously from before the adoption of the First Amendment to this day. See *Roth v. United States, supra,* at 482–485.

Our duty admits of no "substitute for facing up to the tough individual problems of constitutional judgment involved in every obscenity case." [*Roth v. United States, supra,* at 498]; see *Manual Enterprises, Inc. v. Day,* 370 U.S. 478, 488 (opinion of Harlan, J.) [footnote omitted].

Jacobellis v. Ohio, supra, at 188 (opinion of BRENNAN, J.).

III

Under a National Constitution, fundamental First Amendment limitations on the powers of the States do not vary from community to community, but this does not mean that there are, or should or can be, fixed, uniform national standards of precisely what appeals to the "prurient interest" or is "patently offensive." These are essentially questions of fact, and our Nation is simply too big and too diverse for this Court to reasonably expect that such standards could be articulated for all 50 States in a single formulation, even assuming the prerequisite consensus exists. When triers of fact are asked to decide whether "the average person, applying contemporary community standards" would consider certain materials "prurient," it would be unrealistic to require that the answer be based on some abstract formulation. The adversary system, with lay jurors as the usual ultimate factfinders in criminal prosecutions, has historically permitted triers of fact to draw on the standards of their community, guided always by limiting instructions on the law. To require a State to structure obscenity proceedings around evidence of a national "community standard" would be an exercise in futility.

As noted before, this case was tried on the theory that the California obscenity statute sought to incorporate the tripartite test of *Memoirs*. This, a "national" standard of First Amendment protection enumerated by a plurality of this Court, was correctly regarded at the time of trial as limiting state prosecution under the controlling case law. The jury, however, was explicitly instructed that, in determining whether the "dominant theme of the material as a whole ... appeals to the prurient interest," and, in determining whether the material "goes substantially beyond customary limits of candor and affronts contemporary community standards of decency," it was to apply "contemporary community standards of the State of California."

During the trial, both the prosecution and the defense assumed that the relevant "community standards" in making the factual determination of obscenity were those of the State of California, not some hypothetical standard of the entire United States of America. Defense counsel at trial never objected to the testimony of the State's expert on community standards or to the instructions of the trial judge on "state-wide" standards. On appeal to the Appellate Department, Superior Court of California, County of Orange, appellant for the first time contended that application of state, rather than national, standards violated the First and Fourteenth Amendments.

We conclude that neither the State's alleged failure to offer evidence of "national standards," nor the trial court's charge that the jury consider state community standards, were constitutional errors. Nothing in the First Amendment requires that a jury must consider hypothetical and unascertainable "national standards" when attempting to determine whether certain materials are obscene as a matter of fact. Mr. Chief Justice Warren pointedly commented in his dissent in *Jacobellis v. Ohio, supra,* at 200:

> It is my belief that, when the Court said in Roth that obscenity is to be defined by reference to "community standards," it meant community standards—not a national standard, as is sometimes argued. I believe that there is no provable "national standard." ... At all events, this Court has not been able to enunciate one, and it would be unreasonable to expect local courts to divine one.

It is neither realistic nor constitutionally sound to read the First Amendment as requiring that the people of Maine or Mississippi accept public depiction of conduct found tolerable in Las Vegas, or New York City. See *Hoyt v. Minnesota,* 399 U.S. at 524–525 (1970) (BLACKMUN, J., dissenting); *Walker v. Ohio,* 398 U.S. at 434 (1970) (BURGER, C.J., dissenting); id. at 434–435 (Harlan, J., dissenting); *Cain v. Kentucky,* 397 U.S. 319 (1970) (BURGER, C.J., dissenting); id. at 319–320 (Harlan, J., dissenting); *United States v. Groner,* 479 F.2d at 581–583; O'Meara & Shaffer, Obscenity in The Supreme Court: A Note on Jacobellis v. Ohio, 40 Notre Dame Law. 1, 6–7 (1964). See also *Memoirs v. Massachusetts,* 383 U.S. at 458 (Harlan, J., dissenting); *Jacobellis v. Ohio, supra,* at 203–204 (Harlan, J., dissenting); *Roth v. United States, supra,* at 505–506 (Harlan, J., concurring and dissenting). People in different States vary in their tastes and attitudes, and this diversity is not to be strangled by the absolutism of imposed uniformity. As the Court made clear in *Mishkin v. New York,* 383 U.S. at 508–509, the primary concern with requiring a jury to apply the standard of "the average person, applying contemporary community standards" is to be certain that, so far as material is not aimed at a deviant group, it will be judged by its impact on an average person, rather than a particularly susceptible or sensitive person—or indeed a totally insensitive one. See *Roth v. United States*, *supra*, at 489. Cf. the now discredited test in *Regina v. Hicklin*, [1868] L.R. 3 Q.B. 360. We hold that the requirement that the jury evaluate the materials with reference to "contemporary standards of the State of California" serves this protective purpose and is constitutionally adequate.

IV

The dissenting Justices sound the alarm of repression. But, in our view, to equate the free and robust exchange of ideas and political debate with commercial exploitation of obscene material demeans the grand conception of the First Amendment and its high purposes in the historic struggle for freedom. It is a "misuse of the great guarantees of free speech and free press...." *Breard v. Alexandria*, 341 U.S. at 645. The First Amendment protects works which, taken as a whole, have serious literary, artistic, political, or scientific value, regardless of whether the government or a majority of the people approve of the ideas these works represent.

> The protection given speech and press was fashioned to assure unfettered interchange of *ideas* for the bringing about of political and social changes desired by the people,

Roth v. United States, *supra*, at 484 (emphasis added). See *Kois v. Wisconsin*, 408 U.S. at 230–232; *Thornhill v. Alabama*, 310 U.S. at 101–102. But the public portrayal of hard-core sexual conduct for its own sake, and for the ensuing commercial gain, is a different matter.

There is no evidence, empirical or historical, that the stern 19th century American censorship of public distribution and display of material relating to sex, see *Roth v. United States*, *supra*, at 482–485, in any way limited or affected expression of serious literary, artistic, political, or scientific ideas. On the contrary, it is beyond any question that the era following Thomas

Jefferson to Theodore Roosevelt was an "extraordinarily vigorous period" not just in economics and politics, but in belles lettres and in "the outlying fields of social and political philosophies." We do not see the harsh hand of censorship of ideas—good or bad, sound or unsound—and "repression" of political liberty lurking in every state regulation of commercial exploitation of human interest in sex.

MR. JUSTICE BRENNAN finds "it is hard to see how state-ordered regimentation of our minds can ever be forestalled." *Paris Adult Theatre I v. Slaton*, *post*, at 110 (BRENNAN, J., dissenting). These doleful anticipations assume that courts cannot distinguish commerce in ideas, protected by the First Amendment, from commercial exploitation of obscene material. Moreover, state regulation of hard-core pornography so as to make it unavailable to nonadults, a regulation which MR. JUSTICE BRENNAN finds constitutionally permissible, has all the elements of "censorship" for adults; indeed even more rigid enforcement techniques may be called for with such dichotomy of regulation. See *Interstate Circuit, Inc. v. Dallas*, 390 U.S. at 690. One can concede that the "sexual revolution" of recent years may have had useful byproducts in striking layers of prudery from a subject long irrationally kept from needed ventilation. But it does not follow that no regulation of patently offensive "hard core" materials is needed or permissible; civilized people do not allow unregulated access to heroin because it is a derivative of medicinal morphine.

In sum, we (a) reaffirm the *Roth* holding that obscene material is not protected by the First Amendment; (b) hold that such material can be regulated by the States, subject to the specific safeguards enunciated above, without a showing that the material is "utterly without redeeming social value"; and (c) hold that obscenity is to be determined by applying "contemporary community standards," see *Kois v. Wisconsin*, *supra*, at 230, and *Roth v. United States*, *supra*, at 489, not "national standards." The judgment of the Appellate Department of the Superior Court, Orange County, California, is vacated and the case remanded to that court for further proceedings not inconsistent with the First Amendment standards established by this opinion. See *United States v. 12 200-ft. Reels of Film, post*, at 130 n. 7.

Vacated and remanded.

[...]

DOUGLAS, J., Dissenting Opinion

SUPREME COURT OF THE UNITED STATES

413 U.S. 15
Miller v. California
APPEAL FROM THE APPELLATE
DEPARTMENT, SUPERIOR COURT OF
CALIFORNIA, COUNTY OF ORANGE
No. 70–73 Argued: January 18–19, 1972—Decided:
June 21, 1973

MR. JUSTICE DOUGLAS, dissenting.

I
[...]
Today the Court retreats from the earlier formulations of the constitutional test and undertakes to make new definitions. This effort, like the earlier ones, is earnest and well intentioned. The difficulty is that we do not deal with constitutional terms, since "obscenity" is not mentioned in the Constitution or Bill of Rights. And the First Amendment makes no such exception from "the press" which it undertakes to protect nor, as I have said on other occasions, is an exception necessarily implied, for there was no recognized exception to the free press at the time the Bill of Rights was adopted which treated "obscene" publications differently from other types of papers, magazines, and books. So there are no constitutional guidelines for deciding what is and what is not "obscene." The Court is at large because we deal with tastes and standards of literature. What shocks me may be sustenance for my neighbor. What causes one person to boil up in rage over one pamphlet or movie may reflect only his neurosis, not shared by others. We deal here with a regime of censorship which, if adopted, should be done by constitutional amendment after full debate by the people.

Obscenity cases usually generate tremendous emotional outbursts. They have no business being in the courts. If a constitutional amendment authorized censorship, the censor would probably be an administrative agency. Then criminal prosecutions could follow as, if, and when publishers defied the censor and sold their literature. Under that regime, a publisher would know when he was on dangerous ground. Under the present regime—whether the old standards or the new ones are used—the criminal law becomes a trap. A brand new test would put a publisher behind bars under a new law improvised by the courts after the publication. That was done in Ginzburg, and has all the evils of an *ex post facto* law.

My contention is that, until a civil proceeding has placed a tract beyond the pale, no criminal prosecution should be sustained. For no more vivid illustration of vague and uncertain laws could be designed than those we have fashioned. As Mr. Justice Harlan has said:

> The upshot of all this divergence in viewpoint is that anyone who undertakes to examine the Court's decisions since *Roth* which have held particular material obscene or not obscene would find himself in utter bewilderment.

[...]

III
While the right to know is the corollary of the right to speak or publish, no one can be forced by government to listen to disclosure that he finds offensive. That was the basis of my dissent in *Public Utilities Comm'n v. Pollak*, 343 U.S. 451, 467, where I protested against making streetcar passengers a "captive" audience. There is no "captive audience" problem in these obscenity cases. No one is being compelled to look or to listen. Those who enter newsstands or bookstalls may be offended by what they see. But they are not compelled by the State to frequent those places; and it is only state or governmental action against which the First

Amendment, applicable to the States by virtue of the Fourteenth, raises a ban.

The idea that the First Amendment permits government to ban publications that are "offensive" to some people puts an ominous gloss on freedom of the press. That test would make it possible to ban any paper or any journal or magazine in some benighted place. The First Amendment was designed "to invite dispute," to induce "a condition of unrest," to "create dissatisfaction with conditions as they are," and even to stir "people to anger." *Terminiello v. Chicago*, 337 U.S. 1, 4. The idea that the First Amendment permits punishment for ideas that are "offensive" to the particular judge or jury sitting in judgment is astounding. No greater leveler of speech or literature has ever been designed. To give the power to the censor, as we do today, is to make a sharp and radical break with the traditions of a free society. The First Amendment was not fashioned as a vehicle for dispensing tranquilizers to the people. Its prime function was to keep debate open to "offensive" as well as to "staid" people. The tendency throughout history has been to subdue the individual and to exalt the power of government. The use of the standard "offensive" gives authority to government that cuts the very vitals out of the First Amendment. As is intimated by the Court's opinion, the materials before us may be garbage. But so is much of what is said in political campaigns, in the daily press, on TV, or over the radio. By reason of the First Amendment—and solely because of it—speakers and publishers have not been threatened or subdued because their thoughts and ideas may be "offensive" to some. [...]

If there are to be restraints on what is obscene, then a constitutional amendment should be the way of achieving the end. There are societies where religion and mathematics are the only free segments. It would be a dark day for America if that were our destiny. But the people can make it such if they choose to write obscenity into the Constitution and define it.

We deal with highly emotional, not rational, questions. To many, the Song of Solomon is obscene. I do not think we, the judges, were ever given the constitutional power to make definitions of obscenity. If it is to be defined, let the people debate and decide by a constitutional amendment what they want to ban as obscene and what standards they want the legislatures and the courts to apply. Perhaps the people will decide that the path towards a mature, integrated society requires that all ideas competing for acceptance must have no censor. Perhaps they will decide otherwise. Whatever the choice, the courts will have some guidelines. Now we have none except our own predilections.

[...]

DISCUSSION QUESTIONS

1. Why did the court reject the "utterly without redeeming social value" test of *Memoirs v. Massachusetts* as a means for identifying obscene works?

2. The guidelines for identifying obscene material set forth in the court's decision include "whether the average person, applying contemporary community standards would find that the work, taken as a whole, appeals to the prurient interest." Explain and evaluate the court's reasons for rejecting the interpretation of "community standards" to mean "national standards."

3. Can you think of any well-known films that would qualify as being obscene under a strict interpretation of the tripartite test set forth in *Miller v. California*? Do you think that this conclusion is problematic? Explain your answer.

4. Explain and evaluate the court's claim that restriction of material deemed obscene does not conflict with the First Amendment guarantee of free speech.

48

FREE SPEECH

Ronald Dworkin, selection from "Is There a Right to Pornography?" (1981)

In this article, Dworkin addresses the question of whether individuals ought to be allowed to produce, distribute, and view pornography, even if it is granted that such practices are morally wrong. On Dworkin, see reading 36 above.

SOURCE

Dworkin, Ronald. "Is There a Right to Pornography?" *Oxford Journal of Legal Studies*, Volume 1, Issue 2, Summer 1981; pp. 177–212. Reprinted by permission of Oxford University Press.

Goals

The Williams Strategy

It is an old problem for liberal theory how far people should have the right to do the wrong thing. Liberals insist that people have the legal right to say what they wish on matters of political or social controversy. But should they be free to incite racial hatred, for example? British and American law now give different answers to that specific question. The United Kingdom Race Relations law makes it a crime to advocate racial prejudice, but the First Amendment to the United States Constitution forbids Congress or any of the states from adopting any such law.

Pornography in its various forms presents another instance of the same issue. The majority of people in both countries would prefer (or so it seems) substantial censorship, if not outright prohibition, of "sexually explicit" books, magazines, photographs, and films, and this majority includes a considerable number of those who are themselves consumers of whatever pornography is on offer. (It is part of the complex psychology of sex that many of those with a fixed taste for the obscene would strongly prefer that their children, for example, not follow them in that taste.) If we assume that the majority is correct, and that people who publish and consume pornography do the wrong thing, or at least display the wrong sort of character, should they nevertheless have the legal right to do so?

Some lawyers and political philosophers consider the problem of pornography to be only an instance of the first problem I mentioned, the problem of freedom to speak unpopular or wicked thoughts. But we should be suspicious of that claim, because the strongest arguments in favor of allowing *Mein Kampf* to be published hardly seem to apply in favor of the novel *Whips Incorporated* or the film *Sex Kittens*. No one, I think, is denied an equal voice in the political process, however broadly conceived, when he is forbidden to circulate photographs of genitals to the public at large, or denied his right to listen to argument when he is forbidden to consider these photographs at his leisure. If we believe it wrong to censor these forms of pornography, then we should try to find the justification for that opinion elsewhere than in the literature celebrating freedom of speech and press.

We should consider two rather different strategies that might be thought to justify a permissive attitude. The first argues that even if the publication and consumption of pornography is bad for the community as a whole, just considered in itself, the consequences of trying to censor or otherwise suppress pornography would be, in the long run, even worse. I shall call this the "goal-based" strategy. The second argues that even if pornography makes the community worse off, even in the very long run, it is nevertheless wrong to censor or restrict it because this violates the individual moral or political rights of citizens who resent the censorship. I shall call this the "rights-based" strategy.

Which of these strategies, if either, does the 1979 Report of the Committee on Obscenity and Film Censorship[1] (the Williams Report) follow? The Report recommends that the present law on obscenity be revised radically and provides an important distinction as the centerpiece of the new legal scheme it suggests. Certain forms of pornography are to be prohibited altogether. These include live sex shows (actual rather than merely simulated copulation, fellatio, and the like performed live before an audience) and films and photographs produced through the exploitation of children. Other forms of pornography are to be, not prohibited, but restricted in various ways. These restrictions include rules about offensive displays or advertising in public places, limitation of the sale of pornography to special shops, and an elaborate scheme of previewing and licensing of films. I shall later discuss whether these admirably clear recommendations can all be justified in a coherent way. I want first to identify the justification the Report offers.

It sets out and endorses what it calls the harm condition, that "no conduct should be suppressed by law unless it can be shown to harm someone." It notes the popularity of that condition, but rightly adds that either the popularity or the power of the condition evaporates when it is made less ambiguous. Everything turns on what "harm" is taken to be. If "harm" includes only direct physical damage to particular people, or direct damage to their property or financial interests, then the condition is much too strong, since it would condemn a large part of standing British and American law. It would forbid regulating the commercial development of certain parts of cities, or restricting the private use of natural resources like the seashore. Almost everyone would reject the harm condition interpreted in that way. But if "harm" is broadened to include mental distress or annoyance, then the condition becomes much too weak to be of any use in political theory, since any kind of conduct likely to be made criminal in a democracy, at least, is conduct that causes annoyance or distress to someone. Suppose "harm" is taken to exclude mental distress, but to include damage to the general social and cultural environment. Then the harm condition is in itself no help in considering the problem of pornography, because opponents of pornography argue, with some force, that free traffic in obscenity does damage the general cultural environment.

So the harm condition does not in itself recommend a permissive attitude toward pornography, except in a form much too strong to be accepted, and the Report places little weight on that condition. Its argument begins instead in a special

---

[1] Cmnd 7772, HMSO, London, 1979. [Hereafter cited as "Report."]

and attractive theory about the general value of free expression. John Stuart Mill suggested, in *On Liberty*, that society has most chance to discover truth, not only in science but about the best conditions for human flourishing as well, if it tolerates a free marketplace of ideas. The Report rejects Mill's optimistic (not to say complacent) ideas about the conditions most propitious for the discovery of truth. But it nevertheless accepts something close to Mill's position in the following important passage.

> The more basic idea, to which Mill attached the market-place model, remains a correct and profound idea: that we do not know in advance what social, moral or intellectual developments will turn out to be possible, necessary, or desirable for human beings and for their future, and free expression, intellectual and artistic—something which may need to be fostered and protected as well as merely permitted—is essential to human development, as a process which does not merely happen (in some form or another, it will happen anyway) but so far as possible is rationally understood. It is essential to it, moreover, not just as a means to it, but as part of it. Since human beings are not just subject to their history but aspire to be conscious of it, the development of human individuals, of society and of humanity in general, is a process itself properly constituted in part by free expression and the exchange of human communication.[1]

This account of the value of free expression requires some supplement before it can provide a justification for much of contemporary pornography, because the offerings of Soho and Eighth Avenue—close-up glossies and *Beyond the Green Door*—are not patently expressions about desirable human development. The Report finds that supplement in the topology of the slippery slope.[2] It is difficult, if not impossible, to devise a form of words that we can be confident will in practice separate useless trash from potentially valuable contributions. Any form of words will be administered by prosecutors, jurors, and judges with their own prejudices, their own love or fear of the new, and, in the case of prosecutors, their own warm sense of the political advantages of conformity. In any case, writers and publishers, anxious to avoid risk and trouble, will exercise a self-censorship out of abundant caution, and themselves extend the constraint of any words we find. If we recognize the general value of free expression, therefore, we should accept a presumption against censorship or prohibition of any activity when that activity even probably expresses a conviction about how people should live or feel, or opposes established or popular convictions. The presumption need not be absolute. It might be overcome by some showing that the harm the activity threatens is grave, probable, and uncontroversial, for example. But it should nevertheless be a strong presumption in order to protect the long-term goal of securing, in spite of our ignorance, the best conditions that we can for human development.

This general strategy, which I shall sometimes call the "Williams strategy," organizes the more specific arguments and distinctions of the Report. The Committee concedes, for example, the relevance of the question whether an increase in the amount of pornography in circulation in the community is likely to produce more violence or more sexual crimes of any particular sort. If harm of this sort can be demonstrated, then the presumption can be overcome. But the Committee finds no persuasive evidence of this causal influence. The same strategy supports the crucial distinction between outright prohibition and various forms of restriction of

---

[1] Report, p. 55.

[2] Legal purists might object that the argument of the Report here depends not on the slippery slope but on that different weapon, the bright line (or absence of the same). But it is perfectly clear what argument is meant, and I follow the Report's language.

pornography. Restriction does not so severely curtail the contribution that pornography might make to the exchange of ideas and attitudes, though it will change the character of that contribution. So the slippery slope is not so much of a threat when the question is whether some book must be sold only in special shops as it is when the question is whether it can be published at all.

The Williams strategy is a version of the goal-based strategy that I earlier distinguished from the rights-based strategy. It does not define the goal it seeks to promote as the crude Benthamite might, as the outcome that produces the highest surplus of pleasure over pain, or even as a more sophisticated utilitarian would, perhaps as the outcome in which more people have more of what they want to have. The Report speaks instead of human development, and insists that some social, moral, and intellectual developments are more "desirable" than others. We would not go far wrong, I think, to summarize the Report's conception of the best society as the society that is most conducive to human beings' making intelligent decisions about what the best lives for them to lead are, and then flourishing in those lives. The Williams strategy emphasizes, however, an important idea latent in that description. It would be wrong to think of social and political decisions as aimed only at producing the best society at some particular (and therefore arbitrary) future time, so that the acts and forbearances of people now are merely parts of a development to be judged for its instrumental value in producing the best society then. How a society develops is itself an important part of the value of that society, now conceived in a longer perspective that includes the present and the indefinite future as well. In particular, the social development of ideals of human flourishing must be "conscious" and "rationally understood," and "a process itself properly constituted in part by free expression and the exchange of human communication." Human development must be self-development or its value is compromised from the start.

Live Sex

This is in many ways a more attractive picture of the good society than either the crude or the more sophisticated utilitarian can provide. But it is nevertheless a theory (as these less attractive pictures are theories) about what outcomes are good as a whole, rather than a theory about what rights must be recognized even at the cost of accepting less than the best outcome on the whole. I want now to ask whether the Report's attractive goal-based theory justifies its recommendations about pornography. I shall begin with a fairly specific and limited question. Does the Williams strategy support the recommendation that live sex shows be prohibited altogether, rather than simply being restricted in their advertising, or in the location or outside display of the theater in which they take place, or in the age of those who may be admitted? In that way live shows with unfeigned sex are treated more stringently than live shows with simulated sex or films with actual sex. Can the goal-based Williams strategy show why?

We might, by way of preparation for this question, compose a list of possible justifications for treating different forms of pornography differently. I assume that we do not have any good reason to believe that any of the pornography we are now considering does make a positive and valuable contribution to the free exchange of ideas about human flourishing. (The Report considers the claim that some does, and seems to reject it as humbug. It recommends only that we accept the presumption that some pornography might make such a contribution.) So we cannot discriminate between different forms on the basis of our present beliefs that the positive contribution of some is greater than that of others, that the positive contribution of the film *Deep Throat* is greater, for example, than a cabaret re-enactment of the main events of that film. We may, however, be able to justify discrimination between different forms of pornography, conformably with the Williams strategy, in some other way. After all, if we do think that pornography appeals to the less attractive aspects of human personality, we may very well think that the unrestrained publication and consumption of pornography is very much a wrong turn in human nourishing. We may be persuaded, by the Williams strategy, that the damage to human development might be greater still if all pornography were prohibited, because we cannot be sure about our views of human flourishing, because the slippery slope argument warns us that we may prohibit too much, and because in any case any restraint just in itself damages the process of social development because it makes that process less a matter of rational and deliberate choice. But this is very much a question of balancing, and we may be prepared to restrain some form of pornography rather more than other forms, in spite of these competing arguments of the Williams strategy, if (1) we believe that that form does present a special danger of personal harm narrowly conceived, or (2) we believe that that form presents some special danger of cultural pollution that will, we believe, do more damage to the prospects for human flourishing than other forms, or (3) we think that we can be more secure of our footing on the slippery slope in prohibiting that form; that is, that we can draft legislation specifically aimed at that form that will not in practice carry away anything valuable with the dross.

The Report says that live shows are different from films because the former involve the spectator "being in the same space" as "people actually engaged in sexual activity." It is "from this relationship between actual people that arises the peculiar objectionableness that many find is the idea of the live sex show, and the sense that the kind of voyeurism involved is especially degrading to both audience and performers."[1] This last suggestion might be thought ambiguous. It might mean that the justification for prohibiting live sex shows lies in the fact that so many people object to others performing or watching them, that so many others believe that this is degrading. In that case the argument is of the first sort we just distinguished: the harm in question is direct personal harm in the form of the mental suffering or pain of those who know that others are behaving in a degrading way. But the Report cannot consistently appeal to that sort of harm as the justification of a prohibition, because it elsewhere explicitly rejects the idea that that kind of harm can count. "If one accepted, as a basis for coercing one person's actions, the fact that others would be upset even by the thought of his performing those actions, one would be denying any substantive individual liberty at all."[2]

So we should take the other interpretation of the remarks about live sex shows, which is that they should be prohibited not because many people believe that they are degrading, but just because they are degrading. This must then be understood as an appeal to the second sort of justification for restraint: the strong presumption in favor of freedom of expression must yield to prohibition here, because the cultural pollution that would be inflicted by live sex shows, and hence the setback to the achievement of the best conditions for human development, is too great to keep such shows within the presumption of the Williams strategy. This is, however, an extraordinary justification for singling out live sex shows in this way. For the Report emphasizes that live sex shows will in any case be so rare, will appeal to so limited an audience, and will be relatively so expensive, that the impact that they could have on the general environment must be very small whether it is for good or bad. Live shows would be very unlikely to offer more of an overall threat of cultural pollution than the all too lifeless and depressingly obscene photographs and films that the Report allows though restricts, each of which can be duplicated and distributed to millions.

Does the third sort of argument just listed provide a better argument here? Is the slippery slope less of a danger in the case of live sex? The Report does say that "it seems to us, in fact, that the presentation of actual sex on the stage immediately introduces a presumption that the motives no longer have any artistic pretension."[3] But that seems an

---

[1] Report, p. 138.

[2] Report, p. 100.

[3] Report, p. 139.

ill-considered remark. I am not aware of any serious dramatic presentation that uses "actual sex." But that is, apart from obvious casting problems, because it would not now be permitted. Certainly serious dramatic work uses simulated sex, as the Report recognizes, and it can hardly be maintained that a passion for realism on the stage is inconsistent with "artistic pretension." An entire school of dramatic theory argues just the contrary. At one point the Report, apparently as an argument for prohibition, observes that "the live show is a contemporary happening with an unknown future end, which the audience may be capable of influencing or in which they might participate."[1] But that passage might have been lifted from an essay on the aims of Arthauld or Genet or even Brecht or dozens of other ambitious playwrights, and any director who was wholly indifferent to that conception of theater would probably be a boring hack. The slippery slope argument seems especially strong rather than especially weak in the case of live sex on the stage. The continuing flat prohibition of actual copulation undoubtedly limits the drama in its examination of the relation between art and taboo; and the assumption that the consequences of live sex in serious theater are both predictable and very bad betrays, I think, exactly the claim to omniscience that the Williams strategy deplores. It is not my present purpose to suggest that the ban should be relaxed, but only that the strategy of the Report provides no very clear or very effective argument why it should not be.

Why Restrict?

We must not make too much of the Report's difficulties in disposing of live sex shows. Though the Report is an outstanding example of a political argument, it is a political argument nevertheless, both in the sense that it hopes to encourage legislation and in the different sense that it is the joint product of many people with diverse points of view. Perhaps the members of the Committee felt that live sex shows, even in a restricted form,

were intolerable, good arguments or not. But the point is important because it illustrates the great force of the different assumptions embedded in the Williams strategy, and how difficult it is to justify, within that strategy, any exception to the permissive policy it generally recommends.

We might therefore turn to a much more important part of the Report's recommendations, which is the distinction it draws between the restriction and the production of pornography. If the Williams strategy argues against the outright prohibition of pornographic pictures and films, except in very limited cases, can it consistently accept the restrictions the Report commends? The Report offers different arguments proposing to justify the distinction. These arguments fall into groups rather like the different kinds of arguments we considered justifying the special treatment of live sex shows. It argues in favor of the restrictions it urges on the open display and advertising of pornography, for example, (1) that the personal harm caused by such display is much greater than the harm caused by private consumption alone, (2) that the cultural pollution is also greater, and (3) that the slippery slope is less of a danger in the case of restriction because if genuinely valuable material is caught by the restriction it is nevertheless still allowed to enter the exchange of ideas in a sufficiently effective way. We must look at each of these claims, and I shall consider them in reverse order.

The Report argues, in favor of the last claim, that restricting a pornographic publication to a volunteer audience does not defeat the aims of the publication, as distinct perhaps from the aims of its author who may make less money. But this personification takes a rather narrow view of the aims of publication, a view that does not sit comfortably with the Williams strategy. From the standpoint of that strategy, which emphasizes the contribution that expression may make to the reflective search for new possibilities of social and cultural practice, the manner in which pornography is presented to the public may be equally important as its content. Though pornography may not itself be a form of art (the Report speaks instructively to that

---

[1] Report, p. 138.

troublesome issue), the analogy is appropriate here. When Duchamp hung a urinal on the wall of an art gallery, he made a claim about the nature of art—a claim that was to engage critics for many years— that he could not have made by inviting a volunteer audience to view the same object in a public convenience. His medium was certainly his message. If we attend only to the immediate purpose of pornography, and we take that purpose to be the gratification of those who are willing to take trouble and risk embarrassment to secure it, then restricted publication may serve that purpose. But if we are concerned—as the Williams strategy says we must be—with the consequences of publication for the exploration of forms of life, then restricted publication is not simply less publication. It is publication of something different. Restricted publication leaves a certain hypothesis entirely unmade: the hypothesis that sex should enter all levels of public culture on the same standing as soap opera romance or movie trivia, for example, and play the role in day-to-day life that it then would. There may be good reason for not allowing that hypothesis to be presented in the most natural and effective way. But this cannot be the reason now given, that those who are already converted may not complain so long as their own needs are (perhaps inconveniently) met.

Is there more power in the second kind of argument, that even though the danger of cultural pollution is not strong enough to justify prohibition it is nevertheless strong enough to justify restriction? The argument here is contained, I think, in the following comments of the Report:

> One witness whom we saw made it clear that she looked forward to a society in which nothing one saw going on in the park would be more surprising than anything else, except perhaps in the sense of being more improbable. Most of us doubt whether this day will come, or that nothing would have been lost if it did. Still less do we look forward to a world in which sexual activity is not only freely conducted in public and can be viewed, but is offered to be viewed, copulating

parties soliciting the interest of the passer-by. But this is, in effect, what publicly displayed pornography does.... The basic point that pornography involves by its nature some violation of lines between public and private is compounded when the pornography not only exists for private consumption, but is publicly displayed.[1]

The "basic point" of this last sentence suggests that public display threatens to break down the culturally important distinction between public and private activity. But that seems an overstatement. It would be more accurate, I think, to say that public display of pornography trades on that distinction—what it displays would not be shocking or (to those who might find it so) attractive without that distinction—but that it trades on it in a way that might (or might not) rearrange the boundaries, so that people used to (perhaps we should say hardened by) public displays of pictures of copulation would no longer think that such displays were wholly inappropriate to the public space. It does not follow that if the boundaries were rearranged in that way that they would be rearranged further, so that people would take the same attitude to copulation in the open spaces of parks. The Report itself, as we noticed, insists on the special character of live sex just because being "in the same space" as people actually copulating is so different from looking at pictures of such people. But suppose that the public display of photographs would bring the day nearer in which the boundaries were further rearranged so that copulation itself became much more a public activity than now it is. That does not mean that the distinction between public and private, which is certainly of great cultural importance, would itself fall. We have seen great rearrangements of these boundaries even in recent years. People now eat in public streets, kiss and embrace in public, and play naked on at least certain public beaches, and these activities belonged much more firmly to the private space not long

---

[1] Report, pp. 96–97.

ago. The boundaries culture sets on what is public have in other ways contracted in the same period: people are much less likely now than once to pray in public, for example, because the attitude that prayer is a more private than a public activity, limited to the home or special places of worship, has become much more widespread. Surely the dimensions and contours of the public space properly belong to the dialogue through example about the possibilities of human development, the dialogue the Williams strategy wishes to protect. The vitality and character of the basic distinction, the basic idea that there must be a private space, is more threatened by any legally enforced freeze on the boundaries set at any particular time than by allowing the market of expression constantly to re-examine and redraw those boundaries. The Committee says that it would not like to see a world in which the contours of the private were set in the particular way it describes and fears. But that seems exactly the sort of opinion which the Williams strategy argues should be treated with respectful skepticism. It is not plain why it deserves to be enforced through law any more than the opinion of others who dread a world in which their children will be free to fantasize over obscene photographs in private.

What of the first kind of reason that might support the central distinction between prohibition and restriction? This appeals to greater personal harm. The Report argues that if pornography were not restricted in the way it suggests, then the personal harm it would cause would be much greater, or would be of a character that the law should attend to more, than the personal harm that pornography restricted and made essentially a private activity would cause. If this is correct, then it might indeed supply an argument for restriction that does not hold for outright prohibition. If it can be shown that the public display of pornography in the form of advertisements, for example, causes special or great harm to passersby, then even though the presumption of the Williams strategy is strong enough to defeat arguments of prohibition it might fall before the claims for restriction. But what is this special or serious harm that public display might cause? It is not the danger of violent assault or sexual abuse. The Report rejects the evidence offered to it, that even unrestricted pornography would cause an increase in such crimes, as at best inconclusive. The harm is rather of the sort suggested by the word the Report adopts: "offensiveness."

Once again it is worth setting out the clear and concise language of the Report itself:

> Laws against public sex would generally be thought to be consistent with the harm condition, in the sense that if members of the public are upset, distressed, disgusted, outraged or put out by witnessing some class of acts, then that constitutes a respect in which the public performance of those acts harms their interests and gives them a reason to object.... The offensiveness of publicly displayed pornography seems to us ... to be in line with traditionally accepted rules protecting the interest in public decency. Restrictions on the open sale of these publications, and analogous arrangements for films, thus seem to us to be justified.... If one goes all the way down this line, however, one arrives at the situation in which people objected to even knowing that pornography was being read in private; and if one accepted as a basis for coercing one person's actions, the fact that others would be upset even by the thought of his performing these actions, one would be denying any substantive liberty at all. Any offence caused by such shops would clearly be much less vivid, direct and serious than that caused by the display of the publications, and we do not accept that it could outweigh the rights of those who do wish to see this material, or more generally the argument in favour of restricting, rather than suppressing, pornography.[1]

---

[1] Report, pp. 99–100. For the point about denying substantive liberty, in the penultimate sentence, the Report cites H.L.A. Hart, *Law, Liberty, and Morality* (Stanford: Stanford University Press, 1963), pp. 45 ff.

The last sentence, if I understand it correctly, raises one argument distinct from the others, which is that the disgust or other offense likely to be caused to people who are affected just by the knowledge that pornography exists will be "less vivid, direct and serious" than the disgust caused by directly encountering indecent displays. But this seems far from clear, particularly if we take the numbers likely to suffer these different injuries into account. Everything depends, of course, on how much display the market would bear, and where the market would put that display, if pornography were wholly unrestricted. But if we take the present situation in New York City as a useful guide, then only a very small part of the population of Britain would often be forced to encounter displays if they did exist or have to adjust their lives much to avoid them altogether. No doubt a much larger part of the population would be very upset just by the fact that public displays of pornography existed, even though not in their ordinary paths; but this would be an instance of being upset by knowledge of what others were doing, not by the sight of it. Even if my guess is wrong (as it well might be) and the misadventure of actually stumbling on pornography would in fact be a great source of mental distress in a society that permitted pornography without restriction, this is hardly so obvious and so readily predictable as to justify the Report's crucial distinction without a good deal more empirical evidence.

But it is wrong to pursue this point, because the Report plainly places more weight on the preceding point, that the distress of those who are disgusted by the bare knowledge of pornography should not be counted at all in any overall calculation of the personal harm pornography does. But why should it not be counted? The Report says only that if this kind of harm was allowed to count, one would be denying all individual liberty. We might well ask why, if this observation makes sense, it argues only against counting disgust-harm arising from the bare knowledge of what is thought disgusting. Why does it not argue instead against counting any disgust-harm at all, including disgust-harm from actual sighting of the allegedly disgusting act? The point

seems to be that we must stop somewhere short of counting all disgust-harm; but this does not justify the particular stopping point the Report chooses.

But I shall not pursue this issue either, because I cannot make much sense of the Report's initial claim. Of course individual liberty would be very restricted if no one was allowed to do anything that any single other person found offensive. But the suggestion now in question, which the Committee believes would deny "any substantive liberty," is very much weaker than that.[1] The suggestion is only that the disgust that people feel when they learn that others are doing what they regard as offensive should figure along with other kinds of mental and physical distress in the calculation whether the presumption in favor of liberty should be overturned. So the question is whether the harm to those who find offense would outweigh the desire of all those who wish to do what would offend them. If only one or a few people took offense there would be little danger of that. It would be different if a large majority found some activity disgusting. But whether the majority's outrage would then leave much substantive individual liberty would depend on what that majority found outrageous. If the majority found it disgusting that anyone practice a religion other than the established religion, then liberty would be invaded in a way that we have independent reasons for thinking grave. (That is why we speak of a right to religious freedom.) But suppose the majority merely thinks it disgusting if people read or contemplate pornography in private. The slippery slope argument calls our attention to the fact that if the majority is allowed to

---

[1] The Report cites Hart to support its argument here. But Hart's argument seems to consist only in the mistake just identified. "To punish people for causing this form of distress would be tantamount to punishing them simply because others object to what they do; and the only liberty that would coexist with this extension of the utilitarian principle is liberty to do those things to which *no one* seriously objects. Such liberty is plainly quite nugatory." Hart, *Law, Liberty, and Morality,* p. 47 (italics mine). The first of these sentences is a non-sequitur, and provides no argument against the suggestion described in the text.

have its way, individuals might be prevented from reading some things that are valuable for them to read. But even so it would surely overstate the facts to say that if people were not allowed any sexually explicit literature or art at all, they would lose their liberty altogether.

The Report may mean to say something different from this. It may mean that if the suggestion were adopted, that people may not do whatever the majority finds deeply disgusting, even in private, then people would have lost their *right* to liberty—because they may no longer insist that it is always wrong for the majority to restrict them for that reason—even if their actual loss of liberty turns out not to be very great. I agree that some such right is important (even though I would hesitate to call it a right to liberty as such).[1] But whether people have that right, as a matter of principle, is exactly what is now in dispute. Lord Devlin, for example, and presumably Mrs. Whitehouse, Lord Longford,[2] and the other members of the putative "Moral Majority" as well, may be understood as challenging the proposition that they do. In any case, if it is some right to liberty, rather than liberty itself, that is in play here, then the Report has departed from the Williams strategy, unless it can be shown that that right, and not merely a large area of liberty, is essential to reflective social development. The Report does not provide arguments why this is so. In the next section I shall argue that that idea is antagonistic to the Williams strategy's goal-based character. But even if we assume that such a right can be extracted from that strategy, then the question I set aside a moment ago reappears. If the right to liberty is the right not to be limited in one's freedom simply because others are

disgusted by what one proposes to do, why does that right not include the right to do what one wants in public free from the majority's possible offense at actually viewing it? Nothing, I think, in the subjective character of the harm the majority suffers from seeing what it finds disgusting can provide the necessary distinction here. For the offense in question is not just offense to the majority's aesthetic tastes, like the offense people might find in a pink house in Belgravia. The offense is freighted with moral convictions, particularly with convictions about what kinds of sights are indecent rather than only regrettable in the public space, so that people would be offended by a pornographic billboard among the already ugly and cheap displays of Piccadilly or Times Square. The Report does not explain why allowing moral convictions to count in this way, through the offense that people suffer in public displays because of their moral beliefs, does not invade the individual right that is, however, invaded when the majority protects itself from being offended, perhaps more painfully, through its knowledge of what happens behind closed doors.

Why Not Prohibit?

So the Williams strategy does not offer very persuasive grounds for the operating distinction the Report makes fundamental to its recommendations, the distinction between prohibition and restriction. But the situation is, I think, even worse than that, because it is unclear that the strategy even provides a good argument for the generally permissive recommendations of the Report about the use of pornography in private. The strategy adopts an attitude of tolerant skepticism on the question of which "social, moral or intellectual developments" will turn out to be "most desirable" for human flourishing. It urges something like a free market in the expression of ideas about what people should be like and how they should live, not because freedom of expression is a good in itself, but because it enables a variety of hypotheses about the best developments to be formulated and tested in experience. But does this strategy leave sufficient room for the hypothesis that now has (or seems to have) the

---

[1] See the second part of this essay; see also Dworkin, *Taking Rights Seriously* (Cambridge, MA: Harvard University Press, 1978 ed.), ch. 12.

[2] [Lord Patrick Devlin (1905–92) was a British jurist who advocated for public morality. Mary Whitehouse (1910–2001) was a Christian reformer who advocated for "cleaning up" television in Britain. Frances Pakenham, Lord Longford (1905–2001) was a British politician known for his opposition to gay rights.]

widest appeal? This is the hypothesis that humans will develop differently and best, and find the most suitable conditions for their own flourishing, if their law cultivates an ennobling rather than a degrading attitude toward their sexual activity by prohibiting, even in private, practices that are in fact perversions or corruptions of the sexual experience. We cannot be sure that this hypothesis, which I shall call the enforcement hypothesis, is sound. Many of us may believe that it is unsound. But can we be sure of that? The Report sometimes suggests that only those who "think that fundamental human moral truths have been laid down unchangeably for all time, for instance in religious terms"[1] will wish to urge the enforcement hypothesis. But I do not see why that must be so. Those who find the enforcement hypothesis plausible may say that it represents their best judgment, though of course they might be wrong, just as those who reject the hypothesis should concede that they might be wrong.

Suppose we reply that prohibition freezes the market in expression, so that the enforcement hypothesis is the one view that should not be allowed to be tested, because it will then make itself immune to re-examination. Experience hardly supports this claim, at least in democracies. For though the law of obscenity in Great Britain has been relatively repressive since Victorian times, it has become steadily more liberal, on the whole, in practice if not in text, as the result of nonpornographic political debate about pornography, and also as a result of the acts of those who feel strongly enough about the principle, or are greedy enough, to break the law. In any case, this is a compliment that can easily be returned. Perhaps a society dulled by conformity in matters of sexual practice and expression would become a society in which more liberal attitudes are less likely to find a voice or a hearing in politics. But a society weakened by permissiveness is correspondingly a society less likely to attend to the advantages of a public and publicly enforced morality.

This is not an argument that the Williams strategy actually recommends prohibition; but rather

that it should be neutral between prohibition and permissiveness. Skepticism about the most desirable developments for human beings, or about the most desirable conditions for their flourishing, should not rule out a set of conditions that a great many people believe to be the most promising of all. It does recommend an open political process with no substantive part of the criminal law, for example, privileged against change. But that, as I just said, does not argue for present permissiveness any more than present prohibition. Skepticism may perhaps provide an argument for giving the present advantage to one rather than another hypothesis through something like Louis Brandeis' "fifty laboratories" theory. That famous Justice proposed that the different states (and territories) of the United States experiment with different economic and social models so that the best system might emerge by comparison. But no particular country need now, I think, eschew prohibition of pornography for that reason. There is already enough experimentation in the level of permissiveness the Report recommends, if not in more radical alternatives, in other countries.

But I have so far ignored the Williams strategy's insistence that cultural development must be conscious and reflective, must be, that is, self-development. That might be thought to suggest that cultural development should be the product of individuals deciding for themselves what form of life best suits their own condition or, if that seems too grand, what shoe seems to fit; and therefore to rule the enforcement hypothesis out of order from the start. But it is hard to see why the admittedly attractive idea, that society's search for the best conditions for fulfillment must be reflective and self-conscious, demands this particular form of individualism. For in a democracy politics is an appropriate (some would say the appropriate) vehicle through which people strive to determine the circumstances of their situation and to give effect to their own convictions about the conditions of human flourishing. It is only in politics, for example, that people can express in any effective way their sense of justice, or of conservation of the art of the past, or of the design of the space

---

[1] Report, p. 55.

in which they will live and work, or the education their children will, at least for the most part, receive. There are losers in politics, but we cannot say that a society's development of its own culture is unreflective or unconscious or otherwise not self-development just because the convictions of some people do not triumph.

Once we admit that political activity is part of the idea of social self-determination, then we cannot draw, from the idea that human beings should be conscious actors in the process of developing their own culture, any disqualification of the enforcement hypothesis as a theory about human flourishing to be given equal room with other theories. The Report states, as I said earlier, that it follows from this idea that human development is "a process itself properly constituted in part by free expression and the exchange of human communication."[1] But it is suddenly unclear what this means. This inference is unexceptionable, I think, if it means only that free speech as conventionally defined should be protected. But the inference does not hold if it means that people must have a right to privacy that prevents the majority from achieving the cultural environment that it, after full reflection, believes best. Suppose that the community is persuaded such a right exists, and that in consequence it would be wrong to forbid the use of pornography in private. That decision would sharply limit the ability of individuals consciously and reflectively to influence the conditions of their own and their children's development. It would limit their ability to bring about the cultural structure they think best, a structure in which sexual experience generally has dignity and beauty, without which structure their own and their families' sexual experience are likely to have these qualities in less degree. They would not be free to campaign for the enforcement hypothesis in politics on the same basis as others would be free to campaign, for example, for programs of conservation or of state aid to the arts; that is, simply by providing their reasons for believing that enforcement provided the best conditions for human

fulfillment. They would meet the reply that a society that chose enforcement would become, for that reason, a society of automatons led by blind forces rather than a society in charge of its own affairs. But that reply is wrong. If we are concerned only with the power of individuals to influence the conditions in which they must try to thrive, any theory of self-development that forbids the majority the use of politics and the law, even the criminal law, is at least *prima facie* self-defeating.

All this points up the importance of not conflating the argument of the Williams strategy, that people should be in charge of the development of the social conditions in which they try to flourish, rather than the unknowing objects of social forces, with the very different argument that each person, for some other reason, should have some sphere private to himself in which he is solely responsible, answerable only to his own character, about what he does. These two ideas are not (as is sometimes thought) two sides of the same coin, but are antagonistic ideas, because the protection of a private sphere, the recognition of an individual right to privacy of that sort, reduces the power of people generally to put into play their own ideas about the best circumstances for human flourishing. Their power to do this is reduced whether this right is given legal standing, through incorporation in some constitution like that of the United States, or just accepted as part of a moral constitution. The concept of a right to privacy therefore belongs not to the class of goal-based strategies for defending a permissive attitude to pornography, but to the very different class of right-based strategies, because that concept argues that people should have a private sphere even if this damages rather than advances society's long-term goals, and therefore gives most people less rather than more actual control over the design of their environment. The right to privacy cannot be extracted from even the sophisticated Williams version of a goal-based strategy, at least as it now stands.

So the main point remains. The Williams strategy should be as hospitable to the enforcement hypothesis as to the more permissive scheme of the Report.

---

[1] Ibid., quoted above at note [1, p. 544].

I must be careful not to misdescribe this point. I am not arguing (in the spirit of those who make this argument against liberalism) that the strategy is circular or self-contradictory. It is not my point, for example, that the strategy must apply the same skepticism to itself that it applies to theories about the desirable conditions for human development. Any political theory is entitled—indeed obliged—to claim truth for itself, and so to exempt itself from any skepticism it endorses. My point instead depends on distinguishing the content from the consequences of the Williams strategy. Those who favor the outright prohibition of pornography might, I agree, put their position on the same level as, and in flat opposition to, that strategy. They might argue that we can be certain that the best possibility for human development lies in a society that forbids all pornography everywhere, so that we should not allow even political discussion of alternatives. But they *need* not defend prohibition in that way. They might accept the Williams strategy, and appeal to it as warrant for political action aimed at testing their own convictions about the best developments for human flourishing (in which of course they believe though they cannot be certain). If they pitch their argument on this level, it is no answer that if they succeed they make the campaign for opposing views much more difficult or much less effective. For they can answer that any political decision, including the decision that prohibition is wrong in principle, will have exactly that consequence for other views.

Opponents of prohibition would then be remitted to one or another of two substantive arguments the Report recognizes as possible arguments but does not itself make. They may make the heroic claim that a society in which people actually do read pornography in private will for that reason provide more desirable conditions for human excellence. The Report steadily and deliberately avoids that claim. Or they may make the different and perhaps more plausible claim that a society in which people are legally free to read pornography in private, even if some people actually do so, provides better conditions than a society in which no one does because no one can. This claim goes far beyond

the argument of the Williams strategy, that different theories about the best conditions should be free to compete, because it argues that one such theory is better than other theories, not just that it might be. No doubt some members of the Committee do believe this, but the Report offers no grounds. We need a positive argument that freedom of individual choice whether or not to read sadistic novels or study photographs of oral sex is an essential or highly desirable condition for human flourishing. Or at least that it is an undesirable condition that people who want to do these things should be told that they cannot. The general skepticism of the Williams strategy does not even begin to make out such an argument, even as bolstered by the proposition that human development should be self-conscious rather than automatic.

A New Start

I hope it is now clear what fish I am trying to fry. I am not arguing that the Report's conclusions are too conservative, and certainly not that they are too liberal. But only that the goal-based strategy the Report uses is inadequate to support its conclusions. It does not follow from this that no better, more refined goal-based strategy could do so. But we should remember that the Committee included several members of great intellectual and practical ability, and that it had as its chairman a famous philosopher of unusual power and subtlety. It is evident why a goal-based strategy, which promises that things will go better for everyone in the long run if we accept what we do not like now, would seem an attractive premise for a political document. But it does not seem likely that any committee could extract much better arguments from that premise than this committee was able to do.

In any case, my arguments point up a general weakness of goal-based arguments that may be especially evident when these arguments are used to defend a liberal attitude toward pornography, but which is latent even when they are used to defend the protection of other unpopular activities like, for example, bogus or hateful political speech. Most of us feel, for reasons we perhaps cannot fully formulate, that it would be wrong to prevent Communists from defending the Russian invasion of Afghanistan on Hyde Park soapboxes, or neo-Nazis from publishing tracts celebrating Hitler. The goal-based justification of these convictions proposes that even though we might be worse off in the short run by tolerating distasteful political speech, because it distresses us and because there is always some chance that it will prove persuasive to others, there are reasons why we shall nevertheless be better off in the long run—come nearer to fulfilling the goals we ought to set for ourselves—if we do tolerate that speech. This argument has the weakness of providing contingent reasons for convictions that we do not hold contingently. For the story usually told about why free speech is in our long-term interests is not drawn from any deep physical necessity like the laws of motion, or even deep facts about the genetic structure or psychic constitution of human beings; the argument is highly problematical, speculative and in any case marginal. If the story is true, we might say, it is only just true, and no one can have any overwhelming ground for accepting it. But our convictions about free speech are not tentative or halfhearted or marginal. They are not just barely convictions. We can easily construct a goal-based *explanation* of why people like us would develop convictions we thought deep and lasting, even though the advantages to us of having these convictions were both temporary and contingent. But that is beside the present point, which is rather that these explanations do not provide a justification of the meaning these convictions have for us.

This problem in all goal-based justifications of fundamental political convictions is aggravated, in the case of liberal convictions about pornography, because the goal-based story seems not only speculative and marginal, but implausible as well. In the case of free political speech, we might well concede, to the goal-based theory, that each person has an important interest in developing his own independent political convictions, because that is an essential part of his personality, and because his political convictions will be more authentically

his own, more the product of his own personality, the more varied the opinions of others he encounters. We might also concede that political activity in a community is made more vigorous by variety, even by the entry, that is, of wholly despicable points of view. These are decent arguments why both individuals and the community as a whole are at least in certain respects better off when the Nazi has spoken his piece; they are arguments not only for liberty of political expression but also for more political speech rather than less. But the parallel arguments in the case of most pornography seem silly, and very few of those who defend people's right to read pornography in private would actually claim that the community or any individual is better off with more pornography rather than less. So a goal-based argument for pornography must do without what seem the strongest (though still contingent) strands in the goal-based argument for free speech. The Williams strategy ingeniously ignores that defect by providing an argument for tolerance of pornography that, unlike the standard arguments for tolerance of speech, does not suppose that more of what is to be tolerated is better for everyone. But that argument fails, as we have seen, precisely because it does not include that supposition or anything like it. Its claim of skepticism toward the value of pornography (even assisted by the slippery slope) produces nothing stronger than impartial skepticism about the value of prohibiting it.

I want to consider what sort of an argument might be found in the other kind of strategy I mentioned at the outset, the rights-based strategy. Do people have moral or political rights such that it would be wrong to prohibit them from either publishing or reading or contemplating dirty books or pictures or films even if the community would be better off—providing more suitable conditions within which its members might develop—if they did not? Would these rights nevertheless permit the limited sorts of prohibitions that the Report accepts? Would these rights also permit restrictions like those the Report recommends on the public display of pornography that it does not prohibit altogether? I want to take the occasion of the Report, not only to ask these special questions about the proper attitude of the law toward pornography, but also to ask something more general, about what questions like these mean, and how they might even in principle be answered.

Rights

Consider the following suggestion. People have the right not to suffer disadvantage in the distribution of social goods and opportunities, including disadvantage in the liberties permitted to them by the criminal law, just on the ground that their officials or fellow-citizens think that their opinions about the right way for them to lead their own lives are ignoble or wrong. I shall call this (putative) right the right to moral independence, and in this part I shall consider what force this right would have on the law of pornography if it were recognized. In the next part I shall consider what grounds we might have to recognize it.

The right to moral independence is a very abstract right (or, if you prefer, the statement of the right I gave is a very abstract statement of the right) because this statement takes no account of the impact of competing rights. It does not attempt to decide whether the right can always be jointly satisfied for everyone, or how conflicts with other rights, if they arise, are to be settled. These further questions, along with other related questions, are left for more concrete statements of the right. Or (what comes to the same thing) for statements of the more concrete rights that people have in virtue of the abstract right. Nevertheless, the questions I wish to put may usefully be asked even about the abstract statement or the abstract right.

Someone who appeals to the right of moral independence in order to justify a permissive legal regime of obscenity does not suppose that the community will be better off in the long run (according to some description of what makes a community better off like, for example, the description offered in the Williams strategy) if people are free to look at obscene pictures in private. He does not deny this.

His argument is in the conditional mood: even if conditions will not then be so suitable for human flourishing as they might be, for example, nevertheless the right must be respected. But what force does the right then have? When does the government violate that right?

It violates the right, we may say, at least in this case: when the only apparent or plausible justification for a scheme of regulation of pornography includes the hypothesis that the attitudes about sex displayed or nurtured in pornography are demeaning or bestial or otherwise unsuitable to human beings of the best sort, even though this hypothesis may be true. It also violates that right when that justification includes the proposition that most people in the society accept that hypothesis and are therefore pained or disgusted when other members of their own community, for whose lives they understandably feel special responsibility, do read dirty books or look at dirty pictures. The right is therefore a powerful constraint on the regulation of pornography, or at least so it seems, because it prohibits giving weight to exactly the arguments most people think are the best arguments for even a mild and enlightened policy of restriction of obscenity. What room is left, by the apparently powerful right, for the government to do anything at all about pornography?

Suppose it is discovered that the private consumption of pornography does significantly increase the danger of crimes of violence, either generally or specifically crimes of sexual violence. Or suppose that private consumption has some special and deleterious effect on the general economy, by causing great absenteeism from work, for example, as drink or breakfast television is sometimes said to do. Then government would have, in these facts, a justification for the restraint and perhaps even for the prohibition of pornography that does not include the offending hypothesis either directly, by the assumption that the hypothesis is true, or indirectly, in the proposition that many people think it true. After all (as is often pointed out in discussions of obscenity, including the Williams Report), the Bible or Shakespeare might turn out to have these unfortunate consequences, in which case government would have a reason for banning these books that did not require a comparable hypothesis about them.

This possibility raises a slightly more subtle point. Suppose it were discovered that all forms of emotionally powerful literature (including Shakespeare, the Bible, and many forms of pornography) contributed significantly to crime. But the government responded to this discovery selectively, banning most examples of pornography and other literature it considered worthless, but allowing Shakespeare and the Bible nevertheless, on the ground that these were of such literary and cultural value that it was worth the crime they caused to preserve them. Nothing in this selection and discrimination (as so far stated) violates the right to moral independence. The judgment in question—that pornography does not in fact contribute enough of literary value, or that it is not sufficiently informative or imaginative about the different ways in which people might express themselves or find value in their lives, to justify accepting the damage of crime as the cost of its publication—is not the judgment that those who do enjoy pornography have worse character on that account. Any judgment of literary or cultural value will be a judgment about which honest and reasonable people will disagree. But this is true of many other kinds of judgments that government must nevertheless make. The present judgment is no doubt special because it may be used as a screen to hide a different judgment that would offend the right to independence, the judgment that pornography should be treated differently from the Bible because the people who prefer it are worse people. That danger might be sufficiently strong so that a society jealous of the right of moral independence will, for prophylactic reasons, forbid officials to make the literary judgment that would distinguish *Sex Kittens* from *Hamlet* if both were found to provoke crime. That does not touch the present point, that the literary judgment is different, and does not itself threaten the right of independence; and it is worth adding that very few of the people who do

admit to enjoying pornography claim distinct literary merit for it. They claim at most the kind of merit that others, with more conventional ideas about amusement, claim for thrillers.

But this is, in any case, only academic speculation, because there is no reason to suppose a sufficiently direct connection between crime and either *Sex Kittens* or *Hamlet* to provide a ground for banning either one as private entertainment. But what about public display? Can we find a plausible justification for restricting the display of pornography that does not violate the right of moral independence? We can, obviously, construct a certain argument in that direction, as follows. "Many people do not like to encounter genital displays on the way to the grocer. This taste is not, nor does it necessarily reflect, any adverse view of the character of those who do not mind such encounters. Someone who would not like to find pornography in his ordinary paths may not even object to finding it elsewhere. He may simply have tastes and preferences that reject certain combinations in his experience, like someone who likes pink sunsets but not pink houses in Belgravia, who does not object to neon in Leicester Square but would hate it in the Cotswolds. Or he may have a more structured or more consequentialist scheme of preferences about his environment. He may find or believe, for example, that his own delight in other people's bodies is lessened or made less sharp and special if nakedness becomes either too familiar to him or less peculiar to those occasions in which it provides him special pleasure, which may be in museums or his own bedroom or both. Or that sex will come to be different and less valuable for him if he is too often or too forcefully reminded that it has different, more commercial or more sadistic, meaning for others. Or that his goal that his children develop certain similar tastes and opinions will be thwarted by the display or advertising that he opposes. None of these different opinions and complaints *must* be the product of some conviction that those with other opinions and tastes are people of bad character, any more than those who hope that state-supported theater will produce the classics exclusively must think that those who pre-fer experimental theater are less worthy people."

This picture of the motives people might have for not wanting to encounter pornography on the streets is a conceivable picture. But I suspect, as I suggested earlier, that it is far too crude and one-dimensional as a picture of what these motives actually are. The discomfort many people find in encountering blatant nudity on the hoardings is rarely so independent of their moral convictions as these various descriptions suggest. It is at least part of the offense, for many people, that they detest themselves for taking the interest in the proceedings that they do. It is a major part of the offense, for others, that they are so forcefully reminded of what their neighbors are like and, more particularly, of what their neighbors are getting away with. People object to the display of naked men and women in erotic poses, that is, even when these displays occur (as for commercial reasons they inevitably do) in those parts of cities that would be in no sense beau-tiful or enlightening even without the pornography. Even if we took the descriptions of people's motives in the argument I set out at face value, moreover, we should be forced to recognize the substantial influence of moral convictions just in those motives, for someone's sense of what he wants his own atti-tudes toward sex to be, and certainly his sense of what attitudes he hopes to encourage in his chil-dren, are not only influenced by, but constitute, his moral opinions in the broad sense.

We therefore encounter, in people's motives for objecting to the advertising or display of pornog-raphy, at least a mix and interaction of attitudes, beliefs, and tastes that rule out any confident asser-tion that regulation justified by appeal to these motives would not violate the right to moral inde-pendence. We do not know whether, if we could disentangle the different strands of taste, ambition, and belief, so as to winnow out those that express moral condemnation or would not exist but for it, the remaining strands would justify any particular scheme of regulation of display. This is not just a failure of information that would be expensive to obtain. The problem is more conceptual than that:

the vocabulary we use to identify and individuate motives—our own as well as those of others—can-not provide the discrimination we need.

A society anxious to defend the abstract right to moral independence in the face of this complex-ity, has two options at least. It might decide that if popular attitudes toward a minority or a minority practice are mixed in this way, so that the impact of adverse moral convictions can be neither excluded nor measured, then these attitudes should all be deemed to be corrupted by such convictions, and no regulation is permissible. Or it might decide that the case of mixed attitudes is a special kind of case in the administration of the abstract right, so that more concrete statements of what people are enti-tled to have under the right must take the fact of mixed attitudes into account. It might do this, for example, by stipulating, at the more concrete level, that no one should suffer *serious* damage through legal restraint when this can only be justified by the fact that what he proposes to do will frustrate or defeat preferences of others that we have reason to believe are mixed with or are consequences of the conviction that people who act in that way are people of bad character. This second option, which defines a concrete right tailored to the problem of mixed preferences, is not a relaxation or compro-mise of the abstract right, but rather a (no doubt controversial) application of it to that special situ-ation. Which of the two options (or which further option) provides the best response to the problem of mixed motives is part of the more general problem of justification that I postponed to the next section [of this article]. The process of making an abstract right successively more concrete is not simply a pro-cess of deduction or interpretation of the abstract statement but a fresh step in political theory.

If society takes the second option just described in the case of pornography (as I think it should, for reasons I describe later), then its officials must undertake to decide what damage to those who wish to publish or read pornography is serious and what is trivial. Once again reasonable and hon-est officials will disagree about this, but we are trying to discover, not an algorithm for a law of obscenity, but rather whether a plausible concrete conception of a plausible abstract right will yield a sensible scheme of regulation. We should therefore consider the character of the damage that would be inflicted on consumers of pornography by, say, a scheme of zoning that requires that pornographic materials be sold and films shown only in particular areas, a scheme of advertising that prohibits in public places advertisements that would widely be regarded as indecent, and a scheme of labeling so that those entering cinemas or shops whose contents they might find indecent would be warned. There are three main heads of damage that such a regime might inflict on consumers: inconvenience, expense, and embarrassment. Whether the inconvenience is serious will depend on the details of, for example, the zoning. But it should not be considered serious if shoppers for pornography need travel on average only as far as, say, shoppers for stereo equipment or diamonds or secondhand books need travel to find the centers of such trade. How far this scheme of restriction would increase the price of pornography is harder to predict. Perhaps the constraint on advertising would decrease the volume of sales and therefore increase unit costs. But it seems unlikely that this effect would be very great, particularly if the legal ban runs to the character not to the extent of the advertising, and permits, as it should, not only stark "tombstone" notices, but the full range of the depressingly effective techniques through which manufacturers sell soap and video cassette recorders.

Embarrassment raises a more interesting and important question. Some states and countries have required people to identify themselves as belonging to a particular religion or holding certain political convictions just for the sake of that identification, and for the sake of the disadvantage it brings in its train. The Nazis' regime of yellow armbands for Jews, for example, or the registry of members of civil rights groups that some southern states established and the Supreme Court ruled unconstitutional in *NAACP v. Alabama, ex rel. Patterson*.[1]

[1] 357 US 449 (1958).

Since in cases like these identification is required just as a mark of public contempt, or just to provide the social and economic pressure that follows from that contempt, these laws are ruled out by even the abstract form of the right. But the situation is rather different if identification is a by-product rather than the purpose of a scheme of regulation, and is as voluntary as the distinct goals of regulation permit. It would violate the right of moral independence, plainly, if pornography houses were not allowed to use plain-brown-wrapper mail for customers who preferred anonymity, because embarrassment would be the point of that restriction, not a by-product. Also, I think, if the law forbade pornography shops from selling anything but pornography, so that a shy pornographer could not walk out of the shop with a new umbrella as well as a bulge in his coat pocket. But the right of moral independence does not carry with it any government obligation to insure that people may exercise that right in public places without its being known by the public that they do. Perhaps the government would be obliged to take special measures to guard against embarrassment in a society in which people actually were likely to suffer serious economic harm if they were seen leaving a shop carrying the wrong sign.

But that is unlikely to be true about shy pornographers in this country now, who might sensibly be required to bear the social burden of being known to be the kind of people they are.

I conclude that the right to moral independence, if it is a genuine right, requires a permissive legal attitude toward the consumption of pornography in private, but that a certain concrete conception of that right nevertheless permits a scheme of restriction rather like the scheme that the Williams Report recommends. It remains to consider whether that right and that conception can themselves be justified in political theory. But I might first observe that nothing in my conclusion collides with my earlier claim that the Williams strategy, on which the Report relies, cannot support either its permissive attitude or its restrictive scheme. For I did not argue, in support of that claim, that the restrictive scheme would impose great damage on individuals. I said only that the Williams strategy as a whole, which based its arguments not on the interests of pornographers but on the contribution they might make to a beneficial exchange of communication, failed to provide the necessary distinction. Nor do I now appeal to the ideal that is the nerve of that strategy—that the community be free to develop the best conditions for human flourishing—in support of my own conclusions about the law of pornography. I argue rather that, whether or not the instrumental claims of the Williams Report are sound, private liberty is required and public constraint permitted by an appealing conception of an important political right....

DISCUSSION QUESTIONS

1. Explain Dworkin's distinction between goal-based and right-based strategies for justifying a permissive attitude toward pornography. Which kind of strategy would Mill take? Which kind does Dworkin take?

2. Explain what Dworkin calls "the right to moral independence." Under what conditions would a prohibition or restriction of pornography constitute a violation of the right to moral independence?

3. Could a utilitarian accept a right to moral independence? What does Dworkin think? What do you think?

4. Explain the kinds of restrictions on pornography that Dworkin claims could be instituted without violating the right to moral independence. Is the resulting policy an attractive one? Why or why not?

49

American Booksellers Association v. Hudnut (1985)

> *American Booksellers Association v. Hudnut* arose as a challenge to Indianapolis's "Antipornography Civil Rights Ordinance," which defined pornography as a practice that violated women's civil rights. The ordinance thereby allowed those harmed by pornography to seek damages in civil court. A circuit court ruled that the ordinance violated the First Amendment insofar as it attempted to regulate *speech* rather than *conduct*. The matter was taken up on appeal by the United States Court of Appeals for the Seventh Circuit. What follows is that Court's decision.
>
> **SOURCE**
>
> 771 F .2d 323 (7th Circuit, 1985).

Indianapolis enacted an ordinance defining "pornography" as a practice that discriminates against women. "Pornography" is to be redressed through the administrative and judicial methods used for other discrimination. The City's definition of "pornography" is considerably different from "obscenity," which the Supreme Court has held is not protected by the First Amendment.

To be "obscene" under *Miller v. California*, "a publication must, taken as a whole, appeal to the prurient interest, must contain patently offensive depictions or descriptions of specified sexual conduct, and on the whole have no serious literary, artistic, political, or scientific value." *Brockett v. Spokane Arcades, Inc.* Offensiveness must be assessed under the standards of the community. Both offensiveness and an appeal to something other than "normal, healthy sexual desires" are essential elements of "obscenity."

"Pornography" under the ordinance is "the graphic sexually explicit subordination of women, whether in pictures or in words, that also includes one or more of the following":

(1) Women are presented as sexual objects who enjoy pain or humiliation; or
(2) Women are presented as sexual objects who experience sexual pleasure in being raped; or
(3) Women are presented as sexual objects tied up or cut up or mutilated or bruised or

physically hurt, or as dismembered or trun-
cated or fragmented or severed into body
parts; or

(4) Women are presented as being penetrated
by objects or animals; or

(5) Women are presented in scenarios of degradation, injury abasement, torture, shown
as filthy or inferior, bleeding, bruised, or hurt
in a context that makes these conditions sexual; or

(6) Women are presented as sexual objects
for domination, conquest, violation, exploitation, possession, or use, or through pos-
tures or positions of servility or submission
or display.

The statute provides that the "use of men, children,
or transsexuals in the place of women in paragraphs
(1) through (6) above shall also constitute pornography under this section." The ordinance as passed
in April 1984 defined "sexually explicit" to mean
actual or simulated intercourse or the uncovered
exhibition of the genitals, buttocks or anus. An
amendment in June 1984 deleted this provision,
leaving the term undefined.

The Indianapolis ordinance does not refer to the
prurient interest, to offensiveness, or to the standards of the community. It demands attention to
particular depictions, not to the work judged as a
whole. It is irrelevant under the ordinance whether
the work has literary, artistic, political, or scientific value. The City and many *amici* point to these
omissions as virtues. They maintain that pornography influences attitudes, and the statute is a way
to alter the socialization of men and women rather
than to vindicate community standards of offensiveness. And as one of the principal drafters of
the ordinance has asserted, "if a woman is subjected, why should it matter that the work has other
value?" (Catharine A. MacKinnon, "Pornography,
Civil Rights, and Speech," 20 *Harv. Civ. Rts.—Civ.
Lib. L. Rev.* 1, 21 [1985]).

Civil rights groups and feminists have entered
this case as *amici* on both sides. Those supporting
the ordinance say that it will play an important role

in reducing the tendency of men to view women as
sexual objects, a tendency that leads to both unacceptable attitudes and discrimination in the workplace and violence away from it. Those opposing
the ordinance point out that much radical feminist literature is explicit and depicts women in
ways forbidden by the ordinance and that the ordinance would reopen old battles. It is unclear how
Indianapolis would treat works from James Joyce's
Ulysses to Homer's *Iliad*; both depict women as
submissive objects for conquest and domination.

We do not try to balance the arguments for and
against an ordinance such as this. The ordinance
discriminates on the ground of the content of the
speech. Speech treating women in the approved
way—in sexual encounters "premised on equality"—is lawful no matter how sexually explicit.
Speech treating women in the disapproved way—as
submissive in matters sexual or as enjoying humiliation—is unlawful no matter how significant the
literary, artistic, or political qualities of the work
taken as a whole. The state may not ordain preferred viewpoints in this way. The Constitution forbids the state to declare one perspective right and
silence opponents.

I

The ordinance contains four prohibitions. People
may not "traffic" in pornography, "coerce" others
into performing in pornographic works, or "force"
pornography on anyone. Anyone injured by someone who has seen or read pornography has a right
of action against the maker or seller.

Trafficking is defined in § 16–3(g)(4) as the "production, sale, exhibition, or distribution of pornography." The offense excludes exhibition in a public
or educational library, but a "special display" in a
library may be sex discrimination. Section 16–3(g)
(4)(C) provides that the trafficking paragraph "shall
not be construed to make isolated passages or isolated parts actionable."

"Coercion into pornographic performance" is
defined in § 16–3(g)(5) as "coercing, intimidating or
fraudulently inducing any person … into performing for pornography…." The ordinance specifies

that proof of any of the following "shall not constitute a defense: I. That the person is a woman; ... VI. That the person has previously posed for sexually explicit pictures ... with anyone.... VIII. That the person actually consented to a use of the performance that is changed into pornography; ... IX. That the person knew that the purpose of the acts or events in question was to make pornography; ... XI. That the person signed a contract, or made statements affirming a willingness to cooperate in the production of pornography; XII. That no physical force, threats, or weapons were used in the making of the pornography; or XIII. That the person was paid or otherwise compensated."

"Forcing pornography on a person," according to § 16–3(g)(5), is the "forcing of pornography on any woman, man, child, or transsexual in any place of employment, in education, in a home, or in any public place." The statute does not define forcing, but one of its authors states that the definition reaches pornography shown to medical students as part of their education or given to language students for translation.

Section 16–3(g)(7) defines as a prohibited practice the "assault, physical attack, or injury of any woman, man, child, or transsexual in a way that is directly caused by specific pornography."

For purposes of all four offenses, it is generally "not ... a defense that the respondent did not know or intend that the materials were pornography...." But the ordinance provides that damages are unavailable in trafficking cases unless the complainant proves "that the respondent knew or had reason to know that the materials were pornography." It is a complete defense to a trafficking case that all of the materials in question were pornography only by virtue of category of the definition of pornography. In cases of assault caused by pornography, those who seek damages from "a seller, exhibitor or distributor" must show that the defendant knew or had reason to know of the material's status as pornography. By implication, those who seek damages from an author need not show this.

A woman aggrieved by trafficking in pornography may file a complaint "as a woman acting against the subordination of women" with the office of equal opportunity. Section 16–17(b). A man, child, or transsexual also may protest trafficking "but must prove injury in the same way that a woman is injured...." Subsection (a) also provides, however, that "any person claiming to be aggrieved" by trafficking, coercion, forcing, or assault may complain against the "perpetrators." We need not decide whether § 16–17(b) qualifies the right of action in § 16–17(a).

The office investigates and within 30 days makes a recommendation to a panel of the equal opportunity advisory board. The panel then decides whether there is reasonable cause to proceed and may refer the dispute to a conciliation conference or to a complaint adjudication committee for a hearing. The committee uses the same procedures ordinarily associated with civil rights litigation. It may make findings and enter orders, including both orders to cease and desist and orders "to take further affirmative action ... including but not limited to the power to restore complainant's losses...." Either party may appeal the committee's decision to the board, which reviews the record before the committee and may modify its decision.

Under Indiana law an administrative decision takes effect when rendered, unless a court issues a stay. The board's decisions are subject to review in the ordinary course. Judicial review in pornography cases is to be *de novo*, which provides a second complete hearing. When the board finds that a person has engaged in trafficking or that a seller, exhibitor, or distributor is responsible for an assault, it must initiate judicial review of its own decision, and the statute prohibits injunctive relief in these cases in advance of the court's final decision....

The district court held the ordinance unconstitutional. The court concluded that the ordinance regulates speech rather than the conduct involved in making pornography. The regulation of speech could be justified, the court thought, only by a compelling interest in reducing sex discrimination, an interest Indianapolis had not established. The ordinance is also vague and overbroad, the court believed, and establishes a prior restraint of speech.

II

The plaintiffs are a congeries of distributors and readers of books, magazines, and films. The American Booksellers Association comprises about 5,200 bookstores and chains. The Association for American Publishers includes most of the country's publishers. Video Shack, Inc., sells and rents video cassettes in Indianapolis. Kelly Bentley, a resident of Indianapolis, reads books and watches films. There are many more plaintiffs. Collectively the plaintiffs (or their members, whose interests they represent) make, sell, or read just about every kind of material that could be affected by the ordinance, from hard-core films to W.B. Yeats's poem "Leda and the Swan" (from the myth of Zeus in the form of a swan impregnating an apparently subordinate Leda), to the collected works of James Joyce, D.H. Lawrence, and John Cleland.

[...]

III

"If there is any fixed star in our constitutional constellation, it is that no official, high or petty, can prescribe what shall be orthodox in politics, nationalism, religion, or other matters of opinion or force citizens to confess by word or act their faith therein" (*West Virginia State Board of Education v. Barnette*). Under the First Amendment the government must leave to the people the evaluation of ideas. Bald or subtle, an idea is as powerful as the audience allows it to be. A belief may be pernicious—the beliefs of Nazis led to the death of millions, those of the Klan to the repression of millions. A pernicious belief may prevail. Totalitarian governments today rule much of the planet, practicing suppression of billions and spreading dogma that may enslave others. One of the things that separates our society from theirs is our absolute right to propagate opinions that the government finds wrong or even hateful.

The ideas of the Klan may be propagated. Communists may speak freely and run for office. The Nazi Party may march through a city with a large Jewish population. People may criticize the President by misrepresenting his positions, and they have a right to post their misrepresentations on public property. People may seek to repeal laws guaranteeing equal opportunity in employment or to revoke the constitutional amendments granting the vote to blacks and women. They may do this because "above all else, the First Amendment means that government has no power to restrict expression because of its message [or] its ideas...."

Under the ordinance graphic sexually explicit speech is "pornography" or not depending on the perspective the author adopts. Speech that "subordinates" women and also, for example, presents women as enjoying pain, humiliation, or rape, or even simply presents women in "positions of servility or submission or display" is forbidden, no matter how great the literary or political value of the work taken as a whole. Speech that portrays women in positions of equality is lawful, no matter how graphic the sexual content. This is thought control. It establishes an "approved" view of women, of how they may react to sexual encounters, of how the sexes may relate to each other. Those who espouse the approved view may use sexual images; those who do not, may not.

Indianapolis justifies the ordinance on the ground that pornography affects thoughts. Men who see women depicted as subordinate are more likely to treat them so. Pornography is an aspect of dominance. It does not persuade people so much as change them. It works by socializing, by establishing the expected and the permissible. In this view pornography is not an idea; pornography is the injury.

There is much to this perspective. Beliefs are also facts. People often act in accordance with the images and patterns they find around them. People raised in a religion tend to accept the tenets of that religion, often without independent examination. People taught from birth that black people are fit only for slavery rarely rebelled against that creed; beliefs coupled with the self-interest of the masters established a social structure that inflicted great harm while enduring for centuries. Words and images act at the level of the subconscious before they persuade at the level of the conscious. Even the truth has little chance unless a statement fits within the framework of beliefs that may never have been subjected to rational study.

Therefore we accept the premises of this legislation. Depictions of subordination tend to perpetuate subordination. The subordinate status of women in turn leads to affront and lower pay at work, insult and injury at home, battery and rape on the streets. In the language of the legislature, "pornography is central in creating and maintaining sex as a basis of discrimination. Pornography is a systematic practice of exploitation and subordination based on sex which differentially harms women. The bigotry and contempt it produces, with the acts of aggression it fosters, harm women's opportunities for equality and rights [of all kinds]."

Yet this simply demonstrates the power of pornography as speech. All of these unhappy effects depend on mental intermediation. Pornography affects how people see the world, their fellows, and social relations. If pornography is what pornography does, so is other speech. Hitler's orations affected how some Germans saw Jews. Communism is a world view, not simply a Manifesto by Marx and Engels or a set of speeches. Efforts to suppress communist speech in the United States were based on the belief that the public acceptability of such ideas would increase the likelihood of totalitarian government. Religions affect socialization in the most pervasive way. The opinion in *Wisconsin v. Yoder* shows how a religion can dominate an entire approach to life, governing much more than the relation between the sexes. Many people believe that the existence of television, apart from the content of specific programs, leads to intellectual laziness, to a penchant for violence, to many other ills. The Alien and Sedition Acts passed during the administration of John Adams rested on a sincerely held belief that disrespect for the government leads to social collapse and revolution—a belief with support in the history of many nations. Most governments of the world act on this empirical regularity, suppressing critical speech. In the United States, however, the strength of the support for this belief is irrelevant. Seditious libel is protected speech unless the danger is not only grave but also imminent. See *New York Times Co. v. Sullivan.*

Racial bigotry, anti-Semitism, violence on television, reporters' biases—these and many more influence the culture and shape our socialization. None is directly answerable by more speech, unless that speech too finds its place in the popular culture. Yet all is protected as speech, however insidious. Any other answer leaves the government in control of all of the institutions of culture, the great censor and director of which thoughts are good for us.

Sexual responses often are unthinking responses, and the association of sexual arousal with the subordination of women therefore may have a substantial effect. But almost all cultural stimuli provoke unconscious responses. Religious ceremonies condition their participants. Teachers convey messages by selecting what not to cover; the implicit message about what is off limits or unthinkable may be more powerful than the messages for which they present rational argument. Television scripts contain unarticulated assumptions. People may be conditioned in subtle ways. If the fact that speech plays a role in a process of conditioning were enough to permit governmental regulation, that would be the end of freedom of speech.

It is possible to interpret the claim that the pornography is the harm in a different way. Indianapolis emphasizes the injury that models in pornographic films and pictures may suffer. The record contains materials depicting sexual torture, penetration of women by red-hot irons and the like. These concerns have nothing to do with written materials subject to the statute, and physical injury can occur with or without the "subordination" of women. As we discuss in Part IV, a state may make injury in the course of producing a film unlawful independent of the viewpoint expressed in the film.

The more immediate point, however, is that the image of pain is not necessarily pain. In *Body Double*, a suspense film directed by Brian DePalma, a woman who has disrobed and presented a sexually explicit display is murdered by an intruder with a drill. The drill runs through the woman's body. The film is sexually explicit and a murder occurs—yet no one believes that the actress suffered pain or died. In *Barbarella* a character played by Jane

Fonda is at times displayed in sexually explicit ways and at times shown "bleeding, bruised, [and] hurt in a context that makes these conditions sexual"— and again no one believes that Fonda was actually tortured to make the film. In *Carnal Knowledge* a woman grovels to please the sexual whims of a character played by Jack Nicholson; no one believes that there was a real sexual submission, and the Supreme Court held the film protected by the First Amendment. And this works both ways. The description of women's sexual domination of men in *Lysistrata*[1] was not real dominance. Depictions may affect slavery, war, or sexual roles, but a book about slavery is not itself slavery, or a book about death by poison a murder.

Much of Indianapolis's argument rests on the belief that when speech is "unanswerable," and the metaphor that there is a "marketplace of ideas" does not apply, the First Amendment does not apply either. The metaphor is honored; Milton's *Aeropagitica* and John Stewart [sic] Mill's *On Liberty* defend freedom of speech on the ground that the truth will prevail, and many of the most important cases under the First Amendment recite this position. The Framers undoubtedly believed it. As a general matter it is true. But the Constitution does not make the dominance of truth a necessary condition of freedom of speech. To say that it does would be to confuse an outcome of free speech with a necessary condition for the application of the amendment.

A power to limit speech on the ground that truth has not yet prevailed and is not likely to prevail implies the power to declare truth. At some point the government must be able to say (as Indianapolis has said): "We know what the truth is, yet a free exchange of speech has not driven out falsity, so that we must now prohibit falsity." If the government may declare the truth, why wait for the failure of speech? Under the First Amendment, however, there is no such thing as a false idea, so the government may not restrict speech on the ground that in a free exchange truth is not yet dominant.

At any time, some speech is ahead in the game; the more numerous speakers prevail. Supporters of minority candidates may be forever "excluded" from the political process because their candidates never win, because few people believe their positions. This does not mean that freedom of speech has failed.

The Supreme Court has rejected the position that speech must be "effectively answerable" to be protected by the Constitution. For example, in *Buckley v. Valeo* the Court held unconstitutional limitations on expenditures that were neutral with regard to the speakers' opinions and designed to make it easier for one person to answer another's speech. In *Mills v. Alabama* the Court held unconstitutional a statute prohibiting editorials on election day—a statute the state had designed to prevent speech that came too late for answer.... [The] Court has held that the First Amendment protects political stratagems—obtaining legislation through underhanded ploys and outright fraud in *Noerr*, obtaining political and economic ends through boycotts in *Claiborne Hardware*—that may be beyond effective correction through more speech.

We come, finally, to the argument that pornography is "low value" speech, that it is enough like obscenity that Indianapolis may prohibit it. Some cases hold that speech far removed from politics and other subjects at the core of the Framers' concerns may be subjected to special regulation. These cases do not sustain statutes that select among viewpoints, however. In *Pacifica* the FCC sought to keep vile language off the air during certain times. The Court held that it may; but the Court would not have sustained a regulation prohibiting scatological descriptions of Republicans but not scatological descriptions of Democrats, or any other form of selection among viewpoints.

At all events, "pornography" is not low value speech within the meaning of these cases. Indianapolis seeks to prohibit certain speech because it believes this speech influences social relations and politics on a grand scale, that it controls attitudes at home and in the legislature. This precludes a characterization of the speech as low value. True, pornography and obscenity have sex

---

[1] [A play by Aristophanes (450s–380s BCE).]

in common. But Indianapolis left out of its definition any reference to literary, artistic, political, or scientific value. The ordinance applies to graphic sexually explicit subordination in works great and small. The Court sometimes balances the value of speech against the costs of its restriction, but it does this by category of speech and not by the content of particular works....

Any rationale we could imagine in support of this ordinance could not be limited to sex discrimination. Free speech has been on balance an ally of those seeking change. Governments that want stasis start by restricting speech. Culture is a powerful force of continuity; Indianapolis paints pornography as part of the culture of power. Change in any complex system ultimately depends on the ability of outsiders to challenge accepted views and the reigning institutions. Without a strong guarantee of freedom of speech, there is no effective right to challenge what is.

IV

The definition of "pornography" is unconstitutional. No construction or excision of particular terms could save it. The offense of trafficking in pornography necessarily falls with the definition. We express no view on the district court's conclusions that the ordinance is vague and that it establishes a prior restraint. Neither is necessary to our judgment. We also express no view on the argument presented by several *amici* that the ordinance is itself a form of discrimination on account of sex.

Section 8 of the ordinance is a strong severability clause, and Indianapolis asks that we parse the ordinance to save what we can. If a court could do this by surgical excision, this might be possible. But a federal court may not completely reconstruct a local ordinance, and we conclude that nothing short of rewriting could save anything.

The offense of coercion to engage in a pornographic performance, for example, has elements that might be constitutional. Without question a state may prohibit fraud, trickery, or the use of force to induce people to perform—in pornographic films or in any other films. Such a statute may be written without regard to the viewpoint depicted in the work. *New York v. Ferber* suggests that when a state has a strong interest in forbidding the conduct that makes up a film (in *Ferber* sexual acts involving minors), it may restrict or forbid dissemination of the film in order to reinforce the prohibition of the conduct. A state may apply such a rule to non-sexual coercion (although it need not). We suppose that if someone forced a prominent political figure, at gunpoint, to endorse a candidate for office, a state could forbid the commercial sale of the film containing that coerced endorsement. The same principle allows a court to enjoin the publication of stolen trade secrets and award damages for the publication of copyrighted matter without permission.

But the Indianapolis ordinance, unlike our hypothetical statute, is not neutral with respect to viewpoint. The ban on distribution of works containing coerced performances is limited to pornography; coercion is irrelevant if the work is not "pornography," and we have held the definition of "pornography" to be defective root and branch. A legislature might replace "pornography" in § 16–3(g)(4) with "any film containing explicit sex" or some similar expression, but even the broadest severability clause does not permit a federal court to rewrite as opposed to excise. Rewriting is work for the legislature of Indianapolis.

The offense of forcing pornography on unwilling recipients is harder to assess. Many kinds of forcing (such as giving texts to students for translation) may themselves be protected speech. *Rowan v. Post Office* shows that a state may permit people to insulate themselves from categories of speech—in *Rowan* sexual mail—but that the government must leave the decision about what items are forbidden in the hands of the potentially offended recipients. See *Bolger v. Youngs Drug Products Corp.* (the government may not define for itself a category of constitutionally protected but sexual speech that may not be mailed). Exposure to sex is not something the government may prevent, see *Erznoznik v. City of Jacksonville*. We therefore could not save the offense of "forcing" by redefining "pornography" as all sexually-offensive speech or some related category. The statute needs a definition of "forcing" that removes the government from the role of censor. See also *Planned Parenthood Ass'n*, holding that the "captive audience" problem does not permit a government to discriminate on account of the speaker's message.

The section creating remedies for injuries and assaults attributable to pornography also is salvageable in principle, although not by us. The First Amendment does not prohibit redress of all injuries caused by speech. Injury to reputation is redressed through the law of libel, which is constitutional subject to strict limitations. Cases such as *Brandenburg v. Ohio* and NAACP *v. Claiborne Hardware* hold that a state may not penalize speech that does not cause immediate injury. But we do not doubt that if, immediately after the Klan's rally in Brandenburg, a mob had burned to the ground the house of a nearby black person, that person could have recovered damages from the speaker who whipped the crowd into a frenzy. All of the Justices assumed in *Claiborne Hardware* that if the threats in Charles Evers's incendiary speech had been a little less veiled and had led directly to an assault against a person shopping in a store owned by a white merchant, the victim of the assault and even the merchant could have recovered damages from the speaker.

The law of libel has the potential to muzzle the press, which led to *New York Times v. Sullivan*. A law awarding damages for assaults caused by speech also has the power to muzzle the press, and again courts would place careful limits on the scope of the right. Certainly no damages could be awarded unless the harm flowed directly from the speech and there was an element of intent on the part of the speaker, as in *Sullivan* and *Brandenburg*.

Much speech is dangerous. Chemists whose work might help someone build a bomb, political theorists whose papers might start political movements that lead to riots, speakers whose ideas attract violent protesters, all these and more leave loss in their wake. Unless the remedy is very closely confined, it could be more dangerous to speech than all the libel judgments in history. The constitutional requirements for a valid recovery for assault caused by speech might turn out to be too rigorous for any plaintiff to meet. But the Indianapolis ordinance requires the complainant to show that the attack was "directly caused by specific pornography," and it is not beyond the realm of possibility that a state court could construe this limitation in a way that would make the statute constitutional. We are not authorized to prevent the state from trying.

Again, however, the assault statute is tied to "pornography," and we cannot find a sensible way to repair the defect without seizing power that belongs elsewhere. Indianapolis might choose to have no ordinance if it cannot be limited to viewpoint-specific harms, or it might choose to extend the scope to all speech, just as the law of libel applies to all speech. An attempt to repair this ordinance would be nothing but a blind guess.

No amount of struggle with particular words and phrases in this ordinance can leave anything in effect. The district court came to the same conclusion. Its judgment is therefore affirmed.

DISCUSSION QUESTIONS

1. Compare and contrast the criteria of obscenity as given in *Miller v. California* with the criteria of pornography in the Indianapolis statute.

2. The court claims that the Indianapolis statute constitutes "thought control." What do they mean? Why is such control objectionable? Do you agree? How would MacKinnon (see reading 50) respond to this claim of the court's?

3. The court understands pornography as speech. Explain their position. How would MacKinnon critique that position?

4. Apply Dworkin's view to the Indianapolis statute. Would he regard it as violating the right to moral independence? Why or why not?

50

FREE SPEECH

Catharine A. MacKinnon, selection from *Toward a Feminist Theory of the State* (1989)

Catharine A. MacKinnon (b.1946) is the Elizabeth A. Long Professor of Law at the University of Michigan Law School and also serves as the James Barr Ames Visiting Professor of Law at Harvard Law School. MacKinnon is well known for her work on issues of sex equality. She is a co-author of the Indiana anti-pornography ordinance at the center of the case *American Booksellers Association v. Hudnut* (see reading 49 above) and has presented arguments to the Supreme Court of Canada on issues of equality, pornography, and hate speech. More recently, she has represented Bosnian women survivors of Serbian genocidal sexual crimes. In the following selection from her book, MacKinnon argues that pornography is both a form of sex discrimination and a civil rights violation.

SOURCE

MacKinnon, Catharine A. "Pornography: On Morality and Politics," from *Toward a Feminist Theory of the State*, pp. 195–214 (1989) by Catharine A. MacKinnon. Reprinted by permission from *Toward a Feminist Theory of the State* by Catharine A. MacKinnon, Cambridge, Mass.: Harvard University Press, Copyright © 1989 by the President and Fellows of Harvard College.

Possession and use of women through the sexualization of intimate intrusion and access to them is a central feature of women's social definition as inferior and feminine. Visual and verbal intrusion, access, possession, and use are predicated upon and produce physical and psychic intrusion, access, possession, and use. In contemporary industrial society, pornography is an industry that mass produces sexual intrusion on, access to, possession and use of women by and for men for profit. It exploits women's sexual and economic inequality for gain. It sells women to men as and for sex. It is a technologically sophisticated traffic in women.

This understanding of the reality of pornography must contend not only with centuries of celebratory intellectual obfuscation. It must contend with a legal tradition of neutralization through abstraction from the realities of power, a tradition that has authoritatively defined pornography as not about women as such at all, but about sex, hence about morality, and as not about acts or practices, but about ideas. Uncovering gender in this area of law reveals women to be most invisible when most exposed and most silent when used in defense of speech. In both pornography and the law of obscenity, women are seen only as sex and heard only when mouthing a sexual script. When pornography and the law of pornography are investigated together, it becomes clear that pornography is to women's status, hence its critique is to feminism, as its preservation is to male supremacy in its liberal legal guise.

The law of obscenity is the state's approach to addressing the pornography problem, which it construes as an issue of regulation of expression under the First Amendment. Nudity, explicitness, excess of candor, arousal or excitement, prurience, unnaturalness—these qualities raise concerns under obscenity law when sex is depicted or portrayed....Obscenity as such probably does little harm. Pornography contributes causally to attitudes and behaviors of violence and discrimination which define the treatment and status of half the population.

Obscenity law is concerned with morality, meaning good and evil, virtue and vice. The concerns of feminism with power and powerlessness are first political, not moral. From the feminist perspective, obscenity is a moral idea; pornography is a political practice. Obscenity is abstract; pornography is concrete. Obscenity conveys moral condemnation as a predicate to legal condemnation. Pornography identifies apolitical practice that is predicated on power and powerlessness—a practice that is, in fact, legally protected. The two concepts represent two entirely different things.

In accounting for gender inequality as part of the socially constructed relationship between power—the political—on the one hand and knowledge of truth and reality—the epistemological—on the other, the classic description Justice Stewart once offered of the obscenity standard, "I know it when I see it,"[1] becomes even more revealing than it is usually taken to be. Taken as a statement that connects epistemology with power, if one asks, from the point of view of women's experience, does he know what women know when we see what we see, one has to doubt it, given what is on the newsstands. How does his point of view keep what is there, there? To liberal critics, his admission exposed the relativity, the partiality, the insufficient abstractness of the obscenity standard. Not to be emptily universal, to leave your concreteness showing, is a sin among men. Their problem with Justice Stewart's formulation is that it implies that

anything, capriciously, could be suppressed. In fact, almost nothing is. The meaning of what his view permits, as it turns out, is anything but capricious. It is entirely systematic and determinate. His statement is precisely descriptively accurate; its candor is why it has drawn so much criticism. He admitted what courts do epistemologically all the time. In so doing, he both did it and gave it the stature of doctrine (if only dictum). That is, he revealed that the obscenity standard—and it is not unique—is built on what the male standpoint sees. The problem is, so is pornography. In this way, the law of obscenity reproduces the pornographic point of view of women on the level of constitutional jurisprudence.

Pornography, in the feminist view, is a form of forced sex, a practice of sexual politics, an institution of gender inequality. In this perspective, pornography, with the rape and prostitution in which it participates, institutionalizes the sexuality of male supremacy, which fuses the eroticization of dominance and submission with the social construction of male and female. Gender is sexual. Pornography constitutes the meaning of that sexuality. Men treat women as whom they see women as being. Pornography constructs who that is. Men's power over women means that the way men see women defines who women can be. Pornography is that way. In this light, obscenity law can be seen to treat morals from the male point of view, meaning the standpoint of male dominance. The feminist critique of pornography, by contrast, proceeds from women's point of view, meaning the standpoint of the subordination of women to men.

[...]

Obscenity law proposes to control what and how sex can be publicly shown. In practice, its standard centers upon the same features that feminism and pornography both reveal as key to male sexuality: the erect penis and penetration. Historically, obscenity law was vexed by restricting such portrayals while protecting great literature. (Nobody considered protecting women.) Solving this problem by exempting works of perceived value, obscenity restrictions relaxed—some might say collapsed—revealing a significant shift in the last decade. Under

---

[1] *Jacobellis v. Ohio*, 378 U.S. 184, 197 (1964) (Stewart, J. concurring).

the old law, pornography was publicly repudiated yet privately consumed and actualized: do anything to women with impunity in private behind a veil of public denial and civility. Under the new law, in a victory for Freudian derepression, pornography is publicly celebrated. The old private rules have become the new public rules. Women were sex and are still sex. Greater efforts of brutality have become necessary to eroticize the taboo—each taboo being a hierarchy in disguise—since the frontier of the taboo keeps vanishing as one crosses it. Put another way, more and more violence has become necessary to keep the progressively desensitized consumer aroused to the illusion that sex (and he) is daring and dangerous. Making sex with the powerless "not allowed" is a way of keeping "getting it" defined as an act of power, an assertion of hierarchy, which keeps it sexy in a sexual system in which hierarchy is sexy. In addition, pornography has become ubiquitous. Sexual terrorism has become democratized. Pornography has become truly available to women for the first time in history. Among other effects, this central mechanism of sexual subordination, this means of systematizing the definition of women as a sexual class, has now become available to its victims for scrutiny and analysis as an open public system, not just as a private secret abuse. Hopefully, this was a mistake.

[...]

In 1973, obscenity under law came to mean that which "the average person applying contemporary standards, would find that, taken as a whole, appeals to the prurient interest; that [which] depicts or describes, in a patently offensive way, sexual conduct as defined by the applicable state law; and that which, taken as a whole, lacks serious literary, artistic, political, or scientific value." Feminism doubts whether "the average person," gender neutral, exists; has more questions about the content and process of definition of community standards than about deviations from them; wonders why prurience counts but powerlessness does not, why sensibilities are better protected from offense than women are from exploitation; defines sexuality, hence its violation and expropriation,

more broadly than does any state law; and wonders why a body of law which cannot in practice tell rape from intercourse should be entrusted with telling pornography from anything less. In feminist perspective, one notices that although the law of obscenity says that sex on streetcorners is not supposed to be legitimated "by the fact that the persons are simultaneously engaged in a valid political dialogue,"[1] the requirement that the work be considered "as a whole" legitimates something very like that on the level of publications such as *Playboy*,[2] even though experimental evidence is beginning to support what victims have long known: legitimate settings diminish the injury perceived to be done to the women whose trivialization and objectification it contextualizes. Besides, if a woman is subjected, why should it matter that the work has other value? Perhaps what redeems a work's value among men enhances its injury to women. Existing standards of literature, art, science, and politics are, in feminist light, remarkably consonant with pornography's mode, meaning, and message. Finally and foremost, a feminist approach reveals that although the content and dynamic of pornography concerns women—the sexuality of women, women as sexuality—in the same way that the vast majority of "obscenities" refer specifically to women's bodies, women's invisibility has been such that the law of obscenity has never even considered pornography a women's issue.

To appeal to "prurient interest" means to give a man an erection. Men are scared to make it possible for some men to tell other men what they can and cannot have sexual access to, because men have power. Men believe that if you do not let them have theirs, they might not let you have yours. This is why the indefinability of pornography—all the "one man's this is another man's that"—is so central to pornography's definition. It is not because all men are such great liberals, but because those

---

[1] *Paris Adult Theatre I v. Slayton*, 413 U.S. 49, 67 (1973)....

[2] *Penthouse International v. McAuliffe*, 610 F. 2nd 1353 (5th Cir. 1980)....

other men might be able to do to them whatever *they* can do to *them*, which may explain why the liberal principle is what it is.

What this frame on the issue obscures, because the fought-over are invisible, is that the fight over a definition of pornography is a fight among men over the terms of access to women, hence over the best means to guarantee male power as a system. The tacit questions become: Whose sexual practices threaten this system? Are they men whose sexual access can be sacrificed in the interest of maintaining it for the rest? Public sexual access by men to anything other than women is far less likely to be protected speech. This is not to say that male sexual access to anything—children, other men, women with women, objects, animals—is not the real rule. The issue is rather how public, hence how express in law, that system will be.

In this light, the "prurient interest" prong of the obscenity standard has a built-in bind. To find prurience as a fact, someone has to admit sexual arousal by the materials; but male sexual arousal signals the importance of protection. Men put themselves in this position and then wonder why they cannot agree. Sometimes it seems that what is obscene is what does not turn on the Supreme Court, or what revolts them more, which is rare, since revulsion is eroticized. Sometimes it seems that what is obscene is what turns on those men whom the men in power think they can afford to ignore. Sometimes it seems that what is obscene is what makes dominant men see themselves as momentary potential targets of male sexual aggression. Sometimes it seems that anything can be done to a woman, but obscenity is sex that makes male sexuality look bad.

Courts' difficulties in framing workable standards to separate "prurient" from other sexual interest, commercial exploitation from art or advertising, sexual speech from sexual conduct, and obscenity from great literature make the feminist point. These lines have proved elusive in law because they do not exist in life. Commercial sex resembles art because both exploit women's sexuality. The liberal slippery slope is the feminist totality. Politically speaking, whatever obscenity may do,

pornography converges with more conventionally acceptable depictions and descriptions just as rape does with intercourse, because both are acts within the same power relation. Just as it is difficult to distinguish literature or art against a background, a standard, of objectification, it is difficult to discern sexual freedom against a background, a standard, of sexual coercion. This does not mean that it cannot be done. It means that legal standards will be practically unenforceable, will reproduce this problem rather than solve it, until they address its fundamental issue—gender inequality—directly.

To define the pornographic as the "patently offensive" further misconstrues its harm. Pornography is not bad manners or poor choice of audience; obscenity is. Pornography is also not an idea; obscenity is. The legal fiction whereby the obscene is "not speech" has deceived few; it has effectively avoided the need to adjudicate pornography's social etiology. But obscenity law got one thing right: pornography is more actlike than thoughtlike. The fact that pornography, in a feminist view, furthers the idea of the sexual inferiority of women, a political idea, does not make pornography a political idea. That one can express the idea a practice expresses does not make that practice an idea. Pornography is not an idea any more than segregation or lynching are ideas, although both institutionalize the idea of the inferiority of one group to another. The law considers obscenity deviant, antisocial. If it causes harm, it causes antisocial acts, acts against the social order. In a feminist perspective, pornography is the essence of a sexist social order....

The success, therefore the harm, of pornography, is invisible to the male state in its liberal guise and so has been defined out of the customary approach taken to, and the dominant values underlying, the First Amendment. The theory of the First Amendment under which most pornography is protected from governmental restriction proceeds from liberal assumptions that do not apply to the situation of women. First Amendment theory, like virtually all liberal legal theory, presumes the validity of the distinction between public and private: the "role of law [is] to make and guard the line between the sphere of social power, organized in the form of the state, and the arena of private right." On this basis, courts distinguish between obscene billboards ("thrust upon the unwilling viewer") and the private possession of obscenity at home. The problem is that not only the public but also the private is a "sphere of social power" of sexism. On paper and in life, pornography is thrust upon unwilling women in their homes. The distinction between public and private does not cut the same for women as for men. As a result, it is men's right to inflict pornography upon women in private that is protected.

The liberal theory underlying First Amendment law proceeds on the belief that free speech, including pornography, helps discover truth. Censorship, in its view, restricts society to partial truths. *Laissez-faire* might be an adequate theory of the social preconditions for knowledge in a nonhierarchical society. In a society of gender inequality, the speech of the powerful impresses its view upon the world, concealing the truth of powerlessness under a despairing acquiescence that provides the appearance of consent and makes protest inaudible as well as rare. Pornography can invent women because it has the power to make its vision into reality, which then passes, objectively, for truth. So while the First Amendment supports pornography on the belief that consensus and progress are facilitated by allowing all views, however divergent and unorthodox, it fails to notice that pornography (like the racism, including anti-Semitism, of the Nazis and the Klan) is not at all divergent or unorthodox. It is the ruling ideology. Feminism, the dissenting view, is suppressed by pornography. Thus, while defenders of pornography argue that allowing all speech, including pornography, frees the mind to fulfill itself, pornography freely enslaves women's minds and bodies inseparably, normalizing the terror that enforces silence on women's point of view.

In liberalism, speech must never be sacrificed for other social goals. But liberalism has never understood this reality of pornography: the free so-called speech of men silences the free speech of women. It is the same social goal, just other people. This is what a real inequality, a real conflict, a real disparity in social power looks like. First, women do not simply have freedom of speech on a social level. The most basic assumption underlying First Amendment adjudication is that, socially, speech is free. The First Amendment itself says, "Congress shall make no law … abridging the freedom of speech." Free speech exists. The problem for government is to avoid constraining that which, if unconstrained by government, is free. This tends to presuppose that whole segments of the population are not systematically silenced socially, prior to government action. Second, the law of the First Amendment comprehends that freedom of expression, in the abstract, is a system but fails to comprehend that sexism (and racism), in the concrete, are also systems. As a result, it cannot grasp that the speech of some silences the speech of others in a way that is not simply a matter of competition for airtime. That pornography chills women's expression is difficult to demonstrate empirically because silence is not eloquent. Yet on no more of the same kind of evidence, the argument that suppressing pornography might chill legitimate speech has supported its protection.

First Amendment logic has difficulty grasping harm that is not linearly caused in the "John hit Mary" sense. The idea is that words or pictures can be harmful only if they produce harm in a form that is considered an action. Words work in the province of attitudes, actions in the realm of behavior. Words cannot constitute harm in themselves—never mind libel, invasion of privacy, blackmail, bribery, conspiracy, most sexual harassment, and most discrimination. What is saying "yes" in Congress—a word or an act? What is saying "Kill" to a trained guard dog? What is its training? What is saying "You're fired" or "We have enough of your kind around here"? What is a sign that reads "Whites Only"? What is a real estate advertisement that reads "Churches Nearby"? What is a "Help Wanted—Male" ad? What is a letter that states: "Constituent interests dictate that the understudy to my administrative assistant be a man"? What is "Sleep with me and I'll give you an 'A'"? These words, printed or spoken, are so far from legally protecting the cycle of events they actualize that they are regarded as evidence that acts occurred, in some cases as actionable in themselves. Is a woman raped by an attitude or a behavior? Which is sexual arousal? Which is cross burning? The difficulty of the distinction in the abstract has not prevented the law from acting when the consequences were seen to matter. When words are tantamount to acts, they are treated as acts.

[...]

The dominant view is that pornography must cause harm just as car accidents cause harm, or its effects are not cognizable as harm. The trouble with this individuated, atomistic, linear, exclusive, isolated, narrowly tortlike—in a word, positivistic—conception of injury is that the way pornography targets and defines women for abuse and discrimination does not work like this. It does hurt individuals, just not as individuals in a one-at-a-time sense, but as members of the group *women*. Individual harm is caused one woman and not another essentially as one number rather than another is caused in roulette; but on a group basis, the harm is absolutely selective and systematic. Its causality is essentially collective and totalistic and contextual. To reassert atomistic linear causality as a *sine qua non* of injury—you cannot be harmed unless you are harmed through this etiology—is to refuse to respond to the true nature of this specific kind of harm. Such refusals call for explanation. Morton Horowitz has written that the issue of causality in tort law is "one of the pivotal ideas in a system of legal thought that sought to separate private law from politics and to insulate the legal system from the threat of redistribution." Perhaps causality in the law of obscenity is an attempt to privatize the injury pornography does to women in order to insulate the same system from the threat of gender equality.

Women are known to be brutally coerced into pornographic performances. But so far it is only with children, usually male children, that courts see that the speech of pornographers was once someone else's life. Courts and commissions and legislatures and researchers have searched largely in vain for the injury of pornography in the mind of the (male) consumer or in "society," or in empirical correlations between variations in levels of "antisocial" acts and liberalization in obscenity laws. Speech can be regulated "in the interest of unwilling viewers, captive audiences, young children, and beleaguered neighborhoods," but a normal level of sexual force—force that is not seen as force because it is inflicted on women and called sex—has never been a policy issue in the pornography area. Until the last few years experimental research never approached the question of whether pornographic stimuli might support sexual aggression against women or whether violence *per se* might be sexually stimulating or have sexual sequelae. Research is just beginning on the consequences for women of sexual depictions that show consensual dominance and submission. We know the least about the impact of female-only nudity, depictions of specific acts like penetration, or sex that appears mutual in a social context of gender inequality. We know even less about why sex—that is, women—*must*, seemingly, be experienced through a traffic in pictures and words.

[...]

Because obscenity law so evades the reality of pornography, it is difficult to show that the male state, hegemonically liberal whether in the hands of conservatives or of liberals, actually protects pornography. The deception that the state is hostile to sexual derepression and eager to repress pornography, the fantasy that an authoritarian state restricts pornography rather than protects it, lay clearly exposed when the courts were confronted with the real damage pornography does to women's status and treatment as the basis for making it civilly actionable to its victims. The courts accepted the harm but held the pornography more important than those it harms—hence protected it as speech. In *American Booksellers Assn. Inc. v. Hudnut* the Seventh Circuit Court of Appeals held that an ordinance that makes the injuries of pornography actionable as sex inequality is unconstitutional under the First Amendment because it prohibits expression of a point of view.[1]

---

[1] *American Booksellers Assn., Inc. v. Hudnut* [reprinted in this volume; see reading 49].

Acts became ideas and politics became morals as the court transformed coercion, force, assault, and trafficking in subordination into "thought control" and second-class citizenship on the basis of gender into "ideas that can be expressed about sexuality."[1] Obscenity law, which is based upon nothing but value judgments about morality, was presented as the standard for constitutional point-of-viewlessness. The court saw legal intervention against acts (most of which are already crimes) as "point of view" discrimination without doubting the constitutionality of state intervention against obscenity, which has no connection with acts and is expressly defined on the basis of point of view about sex. The court saw civil action by individual women as censorship threatening freedom, yet saw no threat to freedom and no censorship in criminal prosecutions of obscenity. When is a point of view not a point of view? When it is yours—especially when your words, like those of the pornographers, are words in power. In the epistemologically hermetic doublethink of the male point of view, prohibiting advances toward sex equality under law is state neutrality. From the male standpoint, it looks neutral because the state mirrors the inequality of the social world. Under the aegis of this neutrality, state protection of pornography becomes official policy.

The law of pornography thus has the same surface theme and the same underlying theme as pornography itself. Superficially both involve morality: rules made and transgressed for purposes of sexual arousal. Actually, both are about power: the equation between the erotic and the control of women by men, *women* made and transgressed for purposes of sexual arousal. It seems essential to the kick of pornography that it be to some degree against the rules, but never truly unavailable or truly illegitimate. Thus obscenity law, like the law of rape, preserves both the value and the ability to get what it purports to devalue and restrict access to by prohibition. Obscenity law helps keep pornography sexy by putting state power—force, hierarchy—behind its purported prohibition on what men can have

sexual access to. The law of obscenity is to pornography as pornography is to sex: a map that purports to be a mirror, a practice that pretends to represent a practice, a legitimation and authorization and set of directions and guiding controls that project themselves onto social reality, while purporting merely to reflect an image of what is already there. Pornography presents itself as fantasy or illusion or idea, which can be good or bad as it is accurate or inaccurate while it actually, hence accurately, distributes power. Liberal morality cannot deal with illusions that constitute reality because its theory of reality, lacking a substantive critique of the distribution of social power, cannot get behind the empirical word, truth by correspondence. On the surface, both pornography and the law of obscenity are about sex. But it is the status of women that is at stake.

---

[1] 771 F. 2nd at 328.

DISCUSSION QUESTIONS

1. MacKinnon claims that "[f]rom the feminist perspective, obscenity is a moral idea; pornography is a political practice." Explain what she means.

2. Why does MacKinnon reject the decision in *American Booksellers Association v. Hudnut*? Compare and contrast this with the ways in which you think that Dworkin would assess that decision.

3. MacKinnon compares pornography to segregation and lynching. Explain why she does so. Do you think that these are good comparisons? Why or why not?

4. MacKinnon claims that First Amendment jurisprudence presupposes that speech is free. What does she mean and why does she think that this presupposition is both false and harmful to women? Assess her claims.

51

SEX, FREEDOM, AND MARRIAGE

Bradwell v. Illinois (1872)

In 1872, Myra Bradwell was denied a license to practice law in the state of Illinois. Her case was brought before the Illinois United States Supreme Court, where she argued that her right to practice law was protected by the Fourteenth Amendment. The case is notable for many reasons, not the least of which is the insight it gives us into arguments concerned with identifying the alleged proper role of "virtuous" women within society.

SOURCE

83 U.S. 130 (U.S. Supreme Court).

The Plaintiff's Case

Mrs. Myra Bradwell, residing in the State of Illinois, made application to the judges of the Supreme Court of that State for a license to practice law. She accompanied her petition with the usual certificate from an inferior court of her good character, and that on due examination she had been found to possess the requisite qualifications. Pending this application she also filed an affidavit, to the effect "that she was born in the State of Vermont; that she was (had been) a citizen of that State; that she is now a citizen of the United States, and has been for many years past a resident of the city of Chicago, in the State of Illinois." And with this affidavit she also filed a paper asserting that, under the foregoing facts, she was entitled to the license prayed for by virtue of the second section of the fourth article of the Constitution of the United States, and of the fourteenth article of amendment of that instrument. The statute of Illinois on the subject of admissions to the bar, enacts that no person shall be permitted to practice as an attorney or counselor-at-law, or to commence, conduct, or defend any action, suit, or complaint, in which he is not a party concerned, in any court of record within the State, either by using or subscribing his own name or the name of any other person, without having previously obtained a license for that purpose from some two of the justices of the Supreme Court, which license shall constitute the

576

person receiving the same an attorney and counselor-at-law, and shall authorize him to appear
in all the courts of record within the State, and
there to practice as an attorney and counselor-at-
law, according to the laws and customs thereof.

On Mrs. Bradwell's application first coming
before the court, the license was refused, and it was
stated as a sufficient reason that under the decisions
of the Supreme Court of Illinois, the applicant "as
a married woman would be bound neither by her
express contracts nor by those implied contracts
which it is the policy of the law to create between
attorney and client." After the announcement of this
decision, Mrs. Bradwell, admitting that she was a
married woman—though she expressed her belief
that such fact did not appear in the record—filed a
printed argument in which her right to admission,
notwithstanding that fact, was earnestly and ably
maintained. The court thereupon gave an opinion
in writing. Extracts are here given:

> Our statute provides that no person shall
> be permitted to practice as an attorney or
> counsellor at law without having previously
> obtained a license for that purpose from two
> of the justices of the Supreme Court. By the
> second section of the act, it is provided that
> no person shall be entitled to receive a license
> until he shall have obtained a certificate from
> the court of some county of his good moral
> character, and this is the only express limi-
> tation upon the exercise of the power thus
> intrusted to this court. In all other respects it
> is left to our discretion to establish the rules
> by which admission to this office shall be
> determined. But this discretion is not an arbi-
> trary one, and must be held subject to at least
> two limitations. One is, that the court should
> establish such terms of admission as will pro-
> mote the proper administration of justice; the
> second, that it should not admit any persons
> or class of persons who are not intended by
> the legislature to be admitted, even though
> their exclusion is not expressly required by
> the statute.

> The substance of the last limitation is simply
> that this important trust reposed in us should
> be exercised in conformity with the designs
> of the power creating it.

> Whether, in the existing social relations
> between men and women, it would pro-
> mote the proper administration of justice,
> and the general well-being of society, to per-
> mit women to engage in the trial of cases at
> the bar, is a question opening a wide field of
> discussion, upon which it is not necessary for
> us to enter. It is sufficient to say that, in our
> opinion, the other implied limitation upon
> our power, to which we have above referred,
> must operate to prevent our admitting
> women to the office of attorney at law. If we
> were to admit them, we should be exercising
> the authority conferred upon us in a manner
> which, we are fully satisfied, was never con-
> templated by the legislature.

> It is to be remembered that at the time this
> statute was enacted we had, by express pro-
> vision, adopted the common law of England,
> and, with three exceptions, the statutes of
> that country passed prior to the fourth year
> of James the First, so far as they were appli-
> cable to our condition.

> It is to be also remembered that female attor-
> neys at law were unknown in England, and
> a proposition that a woman should enter the
> courts of Westminster Hall in that capacity,
> or as a barrister, would have created hardly
> less astonishment than one that she should
> ascend the bench of bishops, or be elected to
> a seat in the House of Commons.

> It is to be further remembered, that when our
> act was passed, that school of reform which
> claims for women participation in the mak-
> ing and administering of the laws had not
> then arisen, or, if here and there a writer had
> advanced such theories, they were regarded

rather as abstract speculations than as an actual basis for action.

That God designed the sexes to occupy different spheres of action, and that it belonged to men to make, apply, and execute the laws, was regarded as an almost axiomatic truth.

In view of these facts, we are certainly warranted in saying that when the legislature gave to this court the power of granting licenses to practice law, it was with not the slightest expectation that this privilege would be extended to women.

The court having thus denied the application, Mrs. Bradwell brought the case here.... Mr. Matthew Hale Carpenter, for the plaintiff in error:

The question does not involve the right of a female to vote. It presents a narrow matter: Can a female citizen, duly qualified in respect of age, character, and learning, claim, under the fourteenth amendment, the privilege of earning a livelihood by practicing at the bar of a judicial court?

The original Constitution said: "The citizens of each State shall be entitled to all privileges and immunities of citizens in the several States." Under this provision each State could determine for itself what the privileges and immunities of its citizens should be. A citizen emigrating from one State to another carried with him, not the privileges and immunities he enjoyed in his native State, but was entitled, in the State of his adoption, to such privileges and immunities as were enjoyed by the class of citizens to which he belonged by the laws of such adopted State.

But the fourteenth amendment executes itself in every State of the Union. Whatever are the privileges and immunities of a citizen in the State of New York, such citizen, emigrating, carries them with him into any other State of the Union. It utters the will of the United States in every State, and silences

every State constitution, usage, or law which conflicts with it. If to be admitted to the bar, on attaining the age and learning required by law, be one of the privileges of a white citizen in the State of New York, it is equally the privilege of a colored citizen in that State; and if in that State, then in any State. If no State may "make or enforce any law" to abridge the privileges of a citizen, it must follow that the privileges of all citizens are the same.

Does admission to the bar belong to that class of privileges which a State may not abridge, or that class of political rights as to which a State may discriminate between its citizens?

It is evident that there are certain "privileges and immunities" which belong to a citizen of the United States as such; otherwise it would be nonsense for the fourteenth amendment to prohibit a State from abridging them. I concede that the right to vote is not one of those privileges. And the question recurs whether admission to the bar, the proper qualification being possessed, is one of the privileges which a State may not deny.

In Cummings v. Missouri, this court says:

The theory upon which our political institutions rest is, that all men have certain inalienable rights—that among these are life, liberty, and the pursuit of happiness; and that in the pursuit of happiness all avocations, all honors, all positions, are alike open to every one, and that in the protection of these rights all are equal before the law. Any deprivation or suspension of any of these rights for past conduct is punishment, and can be in no otherwise defined.

In *Ex parte* Garland, this court says:

The profession of an attorney and counselor is not like an office created by an act of Congress, which depends for its continuance, its powers, and its emoluments upon the will of its creator, and the possession of which may be burdened with any conditions not prohibited by the Constitution. Attorneys and counselors are not officers of the United States; they are not elected or appointed in the manner prescribed by the Constitution for the election and appointment of such officers. They are officers of the court, admitted as such by its order, upon evidence of their possessing sufficient legal learning and fair private character.... The order of admission is the judgment of the court, that the parties possess the requisite qualifications as attorneys and counselors, and are entitled to appear as such and conduct causes therein. From its entry the parties become officers of the court, and are responsible to it for professional misconduct. They hold their office during good behavior, and can only be deprived of it for misconduct, ascertained and declared by the judgment of the court, after opportunity to be heard has been offered.

It is now settled by numerous cases, that the courts in admitting attorneys to, and in expelling them from, the bar, act judicially, and that such proceedings are subject to review on writ of error or appeal, as the case may be.

From these cases the conclusion is irresistible, that the profession of the law, like the clerical profession and that of medicine, is an avocation open to every citizen of the United States. And while the legislature may prescribe qualifications for entering upon this pursuit, they cannot, under the guise of fixing qualifications, exclude a class of citizens from admission to the bar. The legislature may say at what age candidates shall be admitted; may elevate or depress the standard of learning required. But a qualification, to which a whole class of citizens never can attain, is not a regulation of admission to the bar, but is, as to such citizens, a prohibition. For instance, a State legislature could not, in enumerating the qualifications, require the candidate to be a white citizen. This would be the exclusion of all colored citizens, without regard to age, character, or learning. Yet no sound mind can draw a distinction between such an act and a custom, usage, or law of a State, which denies this privilege to all

female citizens, without regard to age, character, or learning. If the legislature may, under pretence of fixing qualifications, declare that no female citizen shall be permitted to practice law, it may as well declare that no colored citizen shall practice law; for the only provision in the Constitution of the United States which secures to colored male citizens the privilege of admission to the bar, or the pursuit of the other ordinary avocations of life, is the provision that "no State shall make or enforce any law which shall abridge the privileges or immunities of a citizen." And if this provision does protect the colored citizen, then it protects every citizen, black or white, male or female.

Now, Mrs. Bradwell is a citizen of the United States, and of the State of Illinois, residing therein; she has been judicially ascertained to be of full age, and to possess the requisite character and learning.

Still admission to the bar was denied her, not upon the ground that she was not a citizen; not for want of age or qualifications; not because the profession of the law is not one of those avocations which are open to every American citizen as matter of right, upon complying with the reasonable regulations prescribed by the legislature; but first upon the ground that inconvenience would result from permitting her to enjoy her legal rights in this, to wit, that her clients might have difficulty in enforcing the contracts they might make with her, as their attorney, because of her being a married woman; and, finally, on the ground of her sex, merely.

Now, the argument *ab inconvenienti*, which might have been urged with whatever force belongs to it, against adopting the fourteenth amendment in the full scope of its language, is futile to resist its full and proper operation, now that it has been adopted. But that objection is really without force; for Mrs. Bradwell, admitted to the bar, becomes an officer of the court, subject to its summary jurisdiction. Any malpractice or unprofessional conduct towards her client would be punishable by fine, imprisonment, or expulsion from the bar, or by all three. Her clients would, therefore, not be compelled to resort to actions at law against her. The objection arising from her coverture was in fact abandoned, in its more full consideration of the case, by the court itself; and the refusal put upon the fact that the statute of Illinois, interpreted by the light of early days, could not have contemplated the admission of any woman, though unmarried, to the bar. But whatever the statute of Illinois meant, I maintain that the fourteenth amendment opens to every citizen of the United States, male or female, black or white, married or single, the honorable professions as well as the servile employments of life; and that no citizen can be excluded from any one of them. Intelligence, integrity, and honor are the only qualifications that can be prescribed as conditions precedent to an entry upon any honorable pursuit or profitable avocation, and all the privileges and immunities which I vindicate to a colored citizen, I vindicate to our mothers, our sisters, and our daughters. The inequalities of sex will undoubtedly have their influence, and be considered by every client desiring to employ counsel.

There may be cases in which a client's rights can only be rescued by an exercise of the rough qualities possessed by men. There are many causes in which the silver voice of woman would accomplish more than the severity and sternness of man could achieve. Of a bar composed of men and women of equal integrity and learning, women might be more or less frequently retained, as the taste or judgment of clients might dictate. But the broad shield of the Constitution is over them all, and protects each in that measure of success which his or her individual merits may secure.

The Opinion of the Court

… [C]ounsel for the plaintiff in this court truly says that there are certain privileges and immunities which belong to a citizen of the United States as such; otherwise it would be nonsense for the fourteenth amendment to prohibit a State from abridging them, and he proceeds to argue that admission to the bar of a State of a person who possesses the requisite learning and character is one of those which a State may not deny. In this latter proposition we are not able to concur with counsel. We

agree with him that there are privileges and immunities belonging to citizens of the United States, in that relation and character, and that it is these and these alone which a State is forbidden to abridge. But the right to admission to practice in the courts of a State is not one of them. This right in no sense depends on citizenship of the United States. It has not, as far as we know, ever been made in any State, or in any case, to depend on citizenship at all. Certainly many prominent and distinguished lawyers have been admitted to practice, both in the State and Federal courts, who were not citizens of the United States or of any State. But, on whatever basis this right may be placed, so far as it can have any relation to citizenship at all, it would seem that, as to the courts of a State, it would relate to citizenship of the State, and as to Federal courts, it would relate to citizenship of the United States.

The opinion just delivered in the Slaughter-House Cases[1] renders elaborate argument in the present case unnecessary; for, unless we are wholly and radically mistaken in the principles on which those cases are decided, the right to control and regulate the granting of license to practice law in the courts of a State is one of those powers which are not transferred for its protection to the Federal government, and its exercise is in no manner governed or controlled by citizenship of the United States in the party seeking such license.

It is unnecessary to repeat the argument on which the judgment in those cases is founded. It is sufficient to say they are conclusive of the present case.

[The judgment of the Illinois Supreme Court is affirmed.]

Justice Bradley's Concurring Opinion

I concur in the judgment of the court in this case, by which the judgment of the Supreme Court of Illinois is affirmed, but not for the reasons specified

---

[1] [The Slaughter-House cases (83 U.S. 36 [1873]) were landmark cases involving the interpretation of the newly ratified Fourteenth Amendment.]

in the opinion just read. The claim of the plaintiff, who is a married woman, to be admitted to practice as an attorney and counselor-at-law, is based upon the supposed right of every person, man or woman, to engage in any lawful employment for a livelihood. The Supreme Court of Illinois denied the application on the ground that, by the common law, which is the basis of the laws of Illinois, only men were admitted to the bar, and the legislature had not made any change in this respect, but had simply provided that no person should be admitted to practice as attorney or counselor without having previously obtained a license for that purpose from two justices of the Supreme Court, and that no person should receive a license without first obtaining a certificate from the court of some county of his good moral character. In other respects it was left to the discretion of the court to establish the rules by which admission to the profession should be determined. The court, however, regarded itself as bound by at least two limitations. One was that it should establish such terms of admission as would promote the proper administration of justice, and the other that it should not admit any persons, or class of persons, not intended by the legislature to be admitted, even though not expressly excluded by statute. In view of this latter limitation the court felt compelled to deny the application of females to be admitted as members of the bar. Being contrary to the rules of the common law and the usages of Westminster Hall from time immemorial, it could not be supposed that the legislature had intended to adopt any different rule.

The claim that, under the fourteenth amendment of the Constitution, which declares that no State shall make or enforce any law which shall abridge the privileges and immunities of citizens of the United States, the statute law of Illinois, or the common law prevailing in that State, can no longer be set up as a barrier against the right of females to pursue any lawful employment for a livelihood (the practice of law included), assumes that it is one of the privileges and immunities of women as citizens to engage in any and every profession, occupation, or employment in civil life. It certainly cannot be affirmed, as an historical fact, that this has ever been established as one of the fundamental privileges and immunities of the sex. On the contrary, the civil law, as well as nature herself, has always recognized a wide difference in the respective spheres and destinies of man and woman. Man is, or should be, woman's protector and defender. The natural and proper timidity and delicacy which belongs to the female sex evidently unfits it for many of the occupations of civil life. The constitution of the family organization, which is founded in the divine ordinance, as well as in the nature of things, indicates the domestic sphere as that which properly belongs to the domain and functions of womanhood. The harmony, not to say identity, of interest and views which belong, or should belong, to the family institution is repugnant to the idea of a woman adopting a distinct and independent career from that of her husband. So firmly fixed was this sentiment in the founders of the common law that it became a maxim of that system of jurisprudence that a woman had no legal existence separate from her husband, who was regarded as her head and representative in the social state; and, notwithstanding some recent modifications of this civil status, many of the special rules of law flowing from and dependent upon this cardinal principle still exist in full force in most States. One of these is, that a married woman is incapable, without her husband's consent, of making contracts which shall be binding on her or him. This very incapacity was one circumstance which the Supreme Court of Illinois deemed important in rendering a married woman incompetent fully to perform the duties and trusts that belong to the office of an attorney and counselor.

It is true that many women are unmarried and not affected by any of the duties, complications, and incapacities arising out of the married state, but these are exceptions to the general rule. The paramount destiny and mission of woman are to fulfil the noble and benign offices of wife and mother. This is the law of the Creator. And the rules of civil society must be adapted to the general constitution of things, and cannot be based upon exceptional cases.

The humane movements of modern society, which have for their object the multiplication of avenues for woman's advancement, and of occupations adapted to her condition and sex, have my heartiest concurrence. But I am not prepared to say that it is one of her fundamental rights and privileges to be admitted into every office and position, including those which require highly special qualifications and demanding special responsibilities. In the nature of things it is not every citizen of every age, sex, and condition that is qualified for every calling and position. It is the prerogative of the legislator to prescribe regulations founded on nature, reason, and experience for the due admission of qualified persons to professions and callings demanding special skill and confidence. This fairly belongs to the police power of the State; and, in my opinion, in view of the peculiar characteristics, destiny, and mission of woman, it is within the province of the legislature to ordain what offices, positions, and callings shall be filled and discharged by men, and shall receive the benefit of those energies and responsibilities, and that decision and firmness which are presumed to predominate in the sterner sex.

For these reasons I think that the laws of Illinois now complained of are not obnoxious to the charge of abridging any of the privileges and immunities of citizens of the United States.

DISCUSSION QUESTIONS

1. Explain the facts of the case. Explain Carpenter's argument for the plaintiff that she has a constitutional right to be admitted to the Illinois bar.

2. Explain Justice Bradley's view about the role of women in society. How does he use that view to justify the exclusion of women from the practice of law in the state of Illinois? Is it legitimate for legislation to be based on such views about the nature of women (or about the nature of any other class of citizens)?

3. Explain how Mill would respond to Bradley. Evaluate his response.

52

SEX, FREEDOM, AND MARRIAGE

John Stuart Mill, selections from *The Subjection of Women* (1869)

In the following selection, Mill provides an extensive discussion of the role and treatment of women within society. He presents a utilitarian argument against laws that would seek to subordinate women to men. On Mill, see reading 23 above.

SOURCE

Mill, John Stuart. *The Subjection of Women*. Longman, Roberts & Green, 1869.

Chapter I

The object of this Essay is to explain as clearly as I am able, the grounds of an opinion which I have held from the very earliest period when I had formed any opinions at all on social or political matters, and which, instead of being weakened or modified, has been constantly growing stronger by the progress of reflection and the experience of life: That the principle which regulates the existing social relations between the two sexes—the legal subordination of one sex to the other—is wrong in itself, and now one of the chief hindrances to human improvement; and that it ought to be replaced by a principle of perfect equality, admitting no power or privilege on the one side, nor disability on the other.

The very words necessary to express the task I have undertaken, show how arduous it is. But it would be a mistake to suppose that the difficulty of the case must lie in the insufficiency or obscurity of the grounds of reason on which my conviction rests. The difficulty is that which exists in all cases in which there is a mass of feeling to be contended against. So long as an opinion is strongly rooted in the feelings, it gains rather than loses in stability by having a preponderating weight of argument against it. For if it were accepted as a result of argument, the refutation of the argument might shake the solidity of the conviction; but when it rests solely on feeling, the worse it fares in argumentative contest, the more persuaded its adherents are that their feeling must have some deeper ground, which the arguments do not reach; and while the feeling remains, it is always throwing up fresh intrenchments of argument to repair any breach made in the old. And there are so many causes tending to make the feelings connected with this subject the most intense and most deeply-rooted of all those which gather round and protect old institutions and customs, that we need not wonder to find them as yet less undermined and loosened than any of the rest by the progress of the great modern spiritual and social transition; nor suppose that the barbarisms to which men cling longest must be less barbarisms than those which they earlier shake off.

In every respect the burthen is hard on those who attack an almost universal opinion. They must be very fortunate as well as unusually capable if they obtain a hearing at all. They have more difficulty in obtaining a trial, than any other litigants have in getting a verdict. If they do extort a hearing, they are subjected to a set of logical requirements totally different from those exacted from other people. In all other cases, the burthen of proof is supposed to lie with the affirmative. If a person is charged with a murder, it rests with those who accuse him to give proof of his guilt, not with himself to prove his innocence. If there is a difference of opinion about the reality of any alleged historical event, in which the feelings of men in general are not much interested, as the Siege of Troy for example, those who maintain that the event took place are expected to produce their proofs, before those who take the other side can be required to say anything; and at no time are these required to do more than show that the evidence produced by the others is of no value. Again, in practical matters, the burthen of proof is supposed to be with those who are against liberty; who contend for any restriction or prohibition; either any limitation of the general freedom of human action, or any disqualification or disparity of privilege affecting one person or kind of persons, as compared with others. The a priori presumption is in favour of freedom and impartiality. It is held that there should be no restraint not required by the general good,

and that the law should be no respecter of persons, but should treat all alike, save where dissimilarity of treatment is required by positive reasons, either of justice or of policy. But of none of these rules of evidence will the benefit be allowed to those who maintain the opinion I profess. It is useless for me to say that those who maintain the doctrine that men have a right to command and women are under an obligation to obey, or that men are fit for government and women unfit, are on the affirmative side of the question, and that they are bound to show positive evidence for the assertions, or submit to their rejection. It is equally unavailing for me to say that those who deny to women any freedom or privilege rightly allowed to men, having the double presumption against them that they are opposing freedom and recommending partiality, must be held to the strictest proof of their case, and unless their success be such as to exclude all doubt, the judgment ought to go against them. These would be thought good pleas in any common case; but they will not be thought so in this instance. Before I could hope to make any impression, I should be expected not only to answer all that has ever been said by those who take the other side of the question, but to imagine all that could be said by them— to find them in reasons, as well as answer all I find: and besides refuting all arguments for the affirmative, I shall be called upon for invincible positive arguments to prove a negative. And even if I could do all this, and leave the opposite party with a host of unanswered arguments against them, and not a single unrefuted one on their side, I should be thought to have done little; for a cause supported on the one hand by universal usage, and on the other by so great a preponderance of popular sentiment, is supposed to have a presumption in its favour, superior to any conviction which an appeal to reason has power to produce in any intellects but those of a high class.

I do not mention these difficulties to complain of them; first, because it would be useless; they are inseparable from having to contend through people's understandings against the hostility of their feelings and practical tendencies: and truly the understandings of the majority of mankind would need to be much better cultivated than has ever yet been the case, before they can be asked to place such reliance in their own power of estimating arguments, as to give up practical principles in which they have been born and bred and which are the basis of much of the existing order of the world, at the first argumentative attack which they are not capable of logically resisting. I do not therefore quarrel with them for having too little faith in argument, but for having too much faith in custom and the general feeling. It is one of the characteristic prejudices of the reaction of the nineteenth century against the eighteenth, to accord to the unreasoning elements in human nature the infallibility which the eighteenth century is supposed to have ascribed to the reasoning elements. For the apotheosis of Reason we have substituted that of Instinct; and we call everything instinct which we find in ourselves and for which we cannot trace any rational foundation. This idolatry, infinitely more degrading than the other, and the most pernicious of the false worships of the present day, of all of which it is now the main support, will probably hold its ground until it gives way before a sound psychology, laying bare the real root of much that is bowed down to as the intention of Nature and the ordinance of God. As regards the present question, I am willing to accept the unfavourable conditions which the prejudice assigns to me. I consent that established custom, and the general feeling, should be deemed conclusive against me, unless that custom and feeling from age to age can be shown to have owed their existence to other causes than their soundness, and to have derived their power from the worse rather than the better parts of human nature. I am willing that judgment should go against me, unless I can show that my judge has been tampered with. The concession is not so great as it might appear; for to prove this, is by far the easiest portion of my task.

The generality of a practice is in some cases a strong presumption that it is, or at all events once was, conducive to laudable ends. This is the case, when the practice was first adopted, or afterwards kept up, as a means to such ends, and was grounded on experience of the mode in which they could be most effectually attained. If the authority of men over women, when first established, had been the result of a conscientious comparison between different modes of constituting the government of society; if, after trying various other modes of social organization—the government of women over men, equality between the two, and such mixed and divided modes of government as might be invented—it had been decided, on the testimony of experience, that the mode in which women are wholly under the rule of men, having no share at all in public concerns, and each in private being under the legal obligation of obedience to the man with whom she has associated her destiny, was the arrangement most conducive to the happiness and well being of both; its general adoption might then be fairly thought to be some evidence that, at the time when it was adopted, it was the best: though even then the considerations which recommended it may, like so many other primeval social facts of the greatest importance, have subsequently, in the course of ages, ceased to exist. But the state of the case is in every respect the reverse of this. In the first place, the opinion in favour of the present system, which entirely subordinates the weaker sex to the stronger, rests upon theory only; for there never has been trial made of any other: so that experience, in the sense in which it is vulgarly opposed to theory, cannot be pretended to have pronounced any verdict. And in the second place, the adoption of this system of inequality never was the result of deliberation, or forethought, or any social ideas, or any notion whatever of what conduced to the benefit of humanity or the good order of society. It arose simply from the fact that from the very earliest twilight of human society, every woman (owing to the value attached to her by men, combined with her inferiority in muscular strength) was found in a state of bondage to some man. Laws and systems of polity always begin by recognising the relations they find already existing between individuals. They convert what was a mere physical fact into a legal right, give it the sanction of society, and principally aim at the substitution of public and organized means of asserting and protecting these rights, instead of the irregular and lawless conflict of physical strength. Those who had already been compelled to obedience became in this manner legally bound to it. Slavery, from being a mere affair of force between the master and the slave, became regularized and a matter of compact among the masters, who, binding themselves to one another for common protection, guaranteed by their collective strength the private possessions of each, including his slaves. In early times, the great majority of the male sex were slaves, as well as the whole of the female. And many ages elapsed, some of them ages of high cultivation, before any thinker was bold enough to question the rightfulness, and the absolute social necessity, either of the one slavery or of the other. By degrees such thinkers did arise: and (the general progress of society assisting) the slavery of the male sex has, in all the countries of Christian Europe at least (though, in one of them, only within the last few years) been at length abolished, and that of the female sex has been gradually changed into a milder form of dependence. But this dependence, as it exists at present, is not an original institution, taking a fresh start from considerations of justice and social expediency—it is the primitive state of slavery lasting on, through successive mitigations and modifications occasioned by the same causes which have softened the general manners, and brought all human relations more under the control of justice and the influence of humanity. It has not lost the taint of its brutal origin. No presumption in its favour, therefore, can be drawn from the fact of its existence. The only such presumption which it could be supposed to have, must be grounded on its having lasted till now, when so many other things which came down from the same odious source have been done away with. And this, indeed, is what makes it strange to ordinary ears, to hear it asserted that the inequality of rights between men and women has no other source than the law of the strongest.

That this statement should have the effect of a paradox, is in some respects creditable to the progress of civilization, and the improvement of the moral sentiments of mankind. We now live—that is to say, one or two of the most advanced nations of the world now live—in a state in which the law of the strongest seems to be entirely abandoned as the regulating principle of the world's affairs: nobody professes it, and, as regards most of the relations between human beings, nobody is permitted to practise it. When any one succeeds in doing so, it is under cover of some pretext which gives him the semblance of having some general social interest on his side. This being the ostensible state of things, people flatter themselves that the rule of mere force is ended; that the law of the strongest cannot be the reason of existence of anything which has remained in full operation down to the present time. However any of our present institutions may have begun, it can only, they think, have been preserved to this period of advanced civilization by a well-grounded feeling of its adaptation to human nature, and conduciveness to the general good. They do not understand the great vitality and durability of institutions which place right on the side of might; how intensely they are clung to; how the good as well as the bad propensities and sentiments of those who have power in their hands, become identified with retaining it; how slowly these bad institutions give way, one at a time, the weakest first, beginning with those which are least interwoven with the daily habits of life; and how very rarely those who have obtained legal power because they first had physical, have ever lost their hold of it until the physical power had passed over to the other side. Such shifting of the physical force not having taken place in the case of women; this fact, combined with all the peculiar and characteristic features of the particular case, made it certain from the first that this branch of the system of right founded on might, though softened in its most atrocious features at an earlier period than several of the others, would be the very last to disappear. It was inevitable that this one case of a social relation grounded on force, would survive through generations of institutions grounded on equal justice, an almost solitary exception to the general character of their laws and customs; but which, so long as it does not proclaim its own origin, and as discussion has not brought out its true character, is not felt to jar with modern civilization, any more than domestic slavery among the Greeks jarred with their notion of themselves as a free people.

The truth is, that people of the present and the last two or three generations have lost all practical sense of the primitive condition of humanity; and only the few who have studied history accurately, or have much frequented the parts of the world occupied by the living representatives of ages long past, are able to form any mental picture of what society then was. People are not aware how entirely, in former ages, the law of superior strength was the rule of life; how publicly and openly it was avowed, I do not say cynically or shamelessly—for these words imply a feeling that there was something in it to be ashamed of, and no such notion could find a place in the faculties of any person in those ages, except a philosopher or a saint. History gives a cruel experience of human nature, in shewing how exactly the regard due to the life, possessions, and entire earthly happiness of any class of persons, was measured by what they had the power of enforcing; how all who made any resistance to authorities that had arms in their hands, however dreadful might be the provocation, had not only the law of force but all other laws, and all the notions of social obligation against them; and in the eyes of those whom they resisted, were not only guilty of crime, but of the worst of all crimes, deserving the most cruel chastisement which human beings could inflict. The first small vestige of a feeling of obligation in a superior to acknowledge any right in inferiors, began when he had been induced, for convenience, to make some promise to them. Though these promises, even when sanctioned by the most solemn oaths, were for many ages revoked or violated on the most trifling provocation or temptation, it is probable that this, except by persons of still worse than the average morality, was seldom done without some twinges of conscience. The ancient republics, being mostly grounded from the first upon some kind of mutual compact, or at any rate formed by an union of persons not very unequal in strength,

afforded, in consequence, the first instance of a portion of human relations fenced round, and placed under the dominion of another law than that of force. And though the original law of force remained in full operation between them and their slaves, and also (except so far as limited by express compact) between a commonwealth and its subjects, or other independent commonwealths; the banishment of that primitive law even from so narrow a field, commenced the regeneration of human nature, by giving birth to sentiments of which experience soon demonstrated the immense value even for material interests, and which thenceforward only required to be enlarged, not created. Though slaves were no part of the commonwealth, it was in the free states that slaves were first felt to have rights as human beings. The Stoics were, I believe, the first (except so far as the Jewish law constitutes an exception) who taught as a part of morality that men were bound by moral obligations to their slaves. No one, after Christianity became ascendant, could ever again have been a stranger to this belief, in theory; nor, after the rise of the Catholic Church, was it ever without persons to stand up for it. Yet to enforce it was the most arduous task which Christianity ever had to perform. For more than a thousand years the Church kept up the contest, with hardly any perceptible success. It was not for want of power over men's minds. Its power was prodigious. It could make kings and nobles resign their most valued possessions to enrich the Church. It could make thousands, in the prime of life and the height of worldly advantages, shut themselves up in convents to work out their salvation by poverty, fasting, and prayer. It could send hundreds of thousands across land and sea, Europe and Asia, to give their lives for the deliverance of the Holy Sepulchre. It could make kings relinquish wives who were the object of their passionate attachment, because the Church declared that they were within the seventh (by our calculation the fourteenth) degree of relationship. All this it did; but it could not make men fight less with one another, nor tyrannize less cruelly over the serfs, and when they were able, over burgesses. It could not make them renounce either of the applications of force; force militant, or force triumphant. This they could never be induced to do until they were themselves in their turn compelled by superior force. Only by the growing power of kings was an end put to fighting except between kings, or competitors for kingship; only by the growth of a wealthy and warlike bourgeoisie in the fortified towns, and of a plebeian infantry which proved more powerful in the field than the undisciplined chivalry, was the insolent tyranny of the nobles over the bourgeoisie and peasantry brought within some bounds. It was persisted in not only until, but long after, the oppressed had obtained a power enabling them often to take conspicuous vengeance; and on the Continent much of it continued to the time of the French Revolution, though in England the earlier and better organization of the democratic classes put an end to it sooner, by establishing equal laws and free national institutions.

If people are mostly so little aware how completely, during the greater part of the duration of our species, the law of force was the avowed rule of general conduct, any other being only a special and exceptional consequence of peculiar ties—and from how very recent a date it is that the affairs of society in general have been even pretended to be regulated according to any moral law; as little do people remember or consider, how institutions and customs which never had any ground but the law of force, last on into ages and states of general opinion which never would have permitted their first establishment. Less than forty years ago, Englishmen might still by law hold human beings in bondage as saleable property: within the present century they might kidnap them and carry them off, and work them literally to death. This absolutely extreme case of the law of force, condemned by those who can tolerate almost every other form of arbitrary power, and which, of all others, presents features the most revolting to the feelings of all who look at it from an impartial position, was the law of civilized and Christian England within the memory of persons now living: and in one half of Anglo-Saxon America three or four years ago, not only did slavery exist, but the slave trade, and

the breeding of slaves expressly for it, was a general practice between slave states. Yet not only was there a greater strength of sentiment against it, but, in England at least, a less amount either of feeling or of interest in favour of it, than of any other of the customary abuses of force: for its motive was the love of gain, unmixed and undisguised; and those who profited by it were a very small numerical fraction of the country, while the natural feeling of all who were not personally interested in it, was unmitigated abhorrence. So extreme an instance makes it almost superfluous to refer to any other: but consider the long duration of absolute monarchy. In England at present it is the almost universal conviction that military despotism is a case of the law of force, having no other origin or justification. Yet in all the great nations of Europe except England it either still exists, or has only just ceased to exist, and has even now a strong party favourable to it in all ranks of the people, especially among persons of station and consequence. Such is the power of an established system, even when far from universal; when not only in almost every period of history there have been great and well-known examples of the contrary system, but these have almost invariably been afforded by the most illustrious and most prosperous communities. In this case, too, the possessor of the undue power, the person directly interested in it, is only one person, while those who are subject to it and suffer from it are literally all the rest. The yoke is naturally and necessarily humiliating to all persons, except the one who is on the throne, together with, at most, the one who expects to succeed to it. How different are these cases from that of the power of men over women! I am not now prejudging the question of its justifiableness. I am showing how vastly more permanent it could not but be, even if not justifiable, than these other dominations which have nevertheless lasted down to our own time. Whatever gratification of pride there is in the possession of power, and whatever personal interest in its exercise, is in this case not confined to a limited class, but common to the whole male sex. Instead of being, to most of its supporters, a thing desirable chiefly in the abstract, or, like the political ends usually contended for by factions, of little private importance to any but the leaders; it comes home to the person and hearth of every male head of a family, and of every one who looks forward to being so. The clodhopper exercises, or is to exercise, his share of the power equally with the highest nobleman. And the case is that in which the desire of power is the strongest: for every one who desires power, desires it most over those who are nearest to him, with whom his life is passed, with whom he has most concerns in common, and in whom any independence of his authority is oftenest likely to interfere with his individual preferences. If, in the other cases specified, powers manifestly grounded only on force, and having so much less to support them, are so slowly and with so much difficulty got rid of, much more must it be so with this, even if it rests on no better foundation than those. We must consider, too, that the possessors of the power have facilities in this case, greater than in any other, to prevent any uprising against it. Every one of the subjects lives under the very eye, and almost, it may be said, in the hands, of one of the masters—in closer intimacy with him than with any of her fellow-subjects; with no means of combining against him, no power of even locally over-mastering him, and, on the other hand, with the strongest motives for seeking his favour and avoiding to give him offence. In struggles for political emancipation, everybody knows how often its champions are bought off by bribes, or daunted by terrors. In the case of women, each individual of the subject-class is in a chronic state of bribery and intimidation combined. In setting up the standard of resistance, a large number of the leaders, and still more of the followers, must make an almost complete sacrifice of the pleasures or the alleviations of their own individual lot. If ever any system of privilege and enforced subjection had its yoke tightly riveted on the necks of those who are kept down by it, this has. I have not yet shown that it is a wrong system: but every one who is capable of thinking on the subject must see that even if it is, it was certain to outlast all other forms of unjust authority. And when some of the

grossest of the other forms still exist in many civilized countries, and have only recently been got rid of in others, it would be strange if that which is so much the deepest-rooted had yet been perceptibly shaken anywhere. There is more reason to wonder that the protests and testimonies against it should have been so numerous and so weighty as they are.

Some will object, that a comparison cannot fairly be made between the government of the male sex and the forms of unjust power which I have adduced in illustration of it, since these are arbitrary, and the effect of mere usurpation, while it on the contrary is natural. But was there ever any domination which did not appear natural to those who possessed it? There was a time when the division of mankind into two classes, a small one of masters and a numerous one of slaves, appeared, even to the most cultivated minds, to be a natural, and the only natural, condition of the human race. No less an intellect, and one which contributed no less to the progress of human thought, than Aristotle, held this opinion without doubt or misgiving; and rested it on the same premises on which the same assertion in regard to the dominion of men over women is usually based, namely that there are different natures among mankind, free natures, and slave natures; that the Greeks were of a free nature, the barbarian races of Thracians and Asiatics of a slave nature. But why need I go back to Aristotle? Did not the slave-owners of the Southern United States maintain the same doctrine, with all the fanaticism with which men cling to the theories that justify their passions and legitimate their personal interests? Did they not call heaven and earth to witness that the dominion of the white man over the black is natural, that the black race is by nature incapable of freedom, and marked out for slavery? some even going so far as to say that the freedom of manual labourers is an unnatural order of things anywhere. Again, the theorists of absolute monarchy have always affirmed it to be the only natural form of government; issuing from the patriarchal, which was the primitive and spontaneous form of society, framed on the model of the paternal, which is anterior to society itself, and, as they contend, the most natural authority of all.

Nay, for that matter, the law of force itself, to those who could not plead any other, has always seemed the most natural of all grounds for the exercise of authority. Conquering races hold it to be Nature's own dictate that the conquered should obey the conquerors, or, as they euphoniously paraphrase it, that the feebler and more unwarlike races should submit to the braver and manlier. The smallest acquaintance with human life in the Middle Ages, shows how supremely natural the dominion of the feudal nobility over men of low condition appeared to the nobility themselves, and how unnatural the conception seemed, of a person of the inferior class claiming equality with them, or exercising authority over them. It hardly seemed less so to the class held in subjection. The emancipated serfs and burgesses, even in their most vigorous struggles, never made any pretension to a share of authority; they only demanded more or less of limitation to the power of tyrannizing over them. So true is it that unnatural generally means only uncustomary, and that everything which is usual appears natural. The subjection of women to men being a universal custom, any departure from it quite naturally appears unnatural. But how entirely, even in this case, the feeling is dependent on custom, appears by ample experience. Nothing so much astonishes the people of distant parts of the world, when they first learn anything about England, as to be told that it is under a queen: the thing seems to them so unnatural as to be almost incredible. To Englishmen this does not seem in the least degree unnatural, because they are used to it; but they do feel it unnatural that women should be soldiers or members of parliament. In the feudal ages, on the contrary, war and politics were not thought unnatural to women, because not unusual; it seemed natural that women of the privileged classes should be of manly character, inferior in nothing but bodily strength to their husbands and fathers. The independence of women seemed rather less unnatural to the Greeks than to other ancients, on account of the fabulous Amazons (whom they believed to be historical), and the partial example afforded by the Spartan women; who, though no less subordinate by law than in other Greek states,

were more free in fact, and being trained to bodily exercises in the same manner with men, gave ample proof that they were not naturally disqualified for them. There can be little doubt that Spartan experience suggested to Plato, among many other of his doctrines, that of the social and political equality of the two sexes.

But, it will be said, the rule of men over women differs from all these others in not being a rule of force: it is accepted voluntarily; women make no complaint, and are consenting parties to it. In the first place, a great number of women do not accept it. Ever since there have been women able to make their sentiments known by their writings (the only mode of publicity which society permits to them), an increasing number of them have recorded protests against their present social condition: and recently many thousands of them, headed by the most eminent women known to the public, have petitioned Parliament for their admission to the Parliamentary Suffrage. The claim of women to be educated as solidly, and in the same branches of knowledge, as men, is urged with growing intensity, and with a great prospect of success; while the demand for their admission into professions and occupations hitherto closed against them, becomes every year more urgent. Though there are not in this country, as there are in the United States, periodical Conventions and an organized party to agitate for the Rights of Women, there is a numerous and active Society organized and managed by women, for the more limited object of obtaining the political franchise. Nor is it only in our own country and in America that women are beginning to protest, more or less collectively, against the disabilities under which they labour. France, and Italy, and Switzerland, and Russia now afford examples of the same thing. How many more women there are who silently cherish similar aspirations, no one can possibly know; but there are abundant tokens how many would cherish them, were they not so strenuously taught to repress them as contrary to the proprieties of their sex. It must be remembered, also, that no enslaved class ever asked for complete liberty at once. When Simon de Montfort[1] called the deputies of the commons to sit for the first time in Parliament, did any of them dream of demanding that an assembly, elected by their constituents, should make and destroy ministries, and dictate to the king in affairs of state? No such thought entered into the imagination of the most ambitious of them. The nobility had already these pretensions; the commons pretended to nothing but to be exempt from arbitrary taxation, and from the gross individual oppression of the king's officers. It is a political law of nature that those who are under any power of ancient origin, never begin by complaining of the power itself, but only of its oppressive exercise. There is never any want of women who complain of ill usage by their husbands. There would be infinitely more, if complaint were not the greatest of all provocatives to a repetition and increase of the ill usage. It is this which frustrates all attempts to maintain the power but protect the woman against its abuses. In no other case (except that of a child) is the person who has been proved judicially to have suffered an injury, replaced under the physical power of the culprit who inflicted it. Accordingly wives, even in the most extreme and protracted cases of bodily ill usage, hardly ever dare avail themselves of the laws made for their protection: and if, in a moment of irrepressible indignation, or by the interference of neighbours, they are induced to do so, their whole effort afterwards is to disclose as little as they can, and to beg off their tyrant from his merited chastisement.

All causes, social and natural, combine to make it unlikely that women should be collectively rebellious to the power of men. They are so far in a position different from all other subject classes, that their masters require something more from them than actual service. Men do not want solely the obedience of women, they want their sentiments. All men, except the most brutish, desire to have, in the woman most nearly connected with them, not a forced slave but a willing one, not a slave merely, but a favourite. They have therefore put everything in practice to enslave their minds. The masters of all other slaves rely, for maintaining obedience, on fear; either fear of themselves, or religious fears. The masters of women wanted more than simple obedience, and they turned the whole force of education to effect their purpose. All women are brought up from the very earliest years in the belief that their ideal of character is the very opposite to that of men; not self-will, and government by self-control, but submission, and yielding to the control of others. All the moralities tell them that it is the duty of women, and all the current sentimentalities that it is their nature, to live for others; to make complete abnegation of themselves, and to have no life but in their affections. And by their affections are meant the only ones they are allowed to have—those to the men with whom they are connected, or to the children who constitute an additional and indefeasible tie between them and a man. When we put together three things—first, the natural attraction between opposite sexes; secondly, the wife's entire dependence on the husband, every privilege or pleasure she has being either his gift, or depending entirely on his will; and lastly, that the principal object of human pursuit, consideration, and all objects of social ambition, can in general be sought or obtained by her only through him, it would be a miracle if the object of being attractive to men had not become the polar star of feminine education and formation of character. And, this great means of influence over the minds of women having been acquired, an instinct of selfishness made men avail themselves of it to the utmost as a means of holding women in subjection, by representing to them meekness, submissiveness, and resignation of all individual will into the hands of a man, as an essential part of sexual attractiveness. Can it be doubted that any of the other yokes which mankind have succeeded in breaking, would have subsisted till now if the same means had existed, and had been as sedulously used, to bow down their minds to it? If it had been made the object of the life of every young plebeian to find personal favour in the eyes of some patrician, of every young serf

---

[1] [Simon de Montfort (1208–65) was a key force in England's development of an elected parliament.]

with some seigneur; if domestication with him, and a share of his personal affections, had been held out as the prize which they all should look out for, the most gifted and aspiring being able to reckon on the most desirable prizes; and if, when this prize had been obtained, they had been shut out by a wall of brass from all interests not centering in him, all feelings and desires but those which he shared or inculcated; would not serfs and seigneurs, plebeians and patricians, have been as broadly distinguished at this day as men and women are? and would not all but a thinker here and there, have believed the distinction to be a fundamental and unalterable fact in human nature?

The preceding considerations are amply sufficient to show that custom, however universal it may be, affords in this case no presumption, and ought not to create any prejudice, in favour of the arrangements which place women in social and political subjection to men. But I may go farther, and maintain that the course of history, and the tendencies of progressive human society, afford not only no presumption in favour of this system of inequality of rights, but a strong one against it; and that, so far as the whole course of human improvement up to this time, the whole stream of modern tendencies, warrants any inference on the subject, it is, that this relic of the past is discordant with the future, and must necessarily disappear.

For, what is the peculiar character of the modern world—the difference which chiefly distinguishes modern institutions, modern social ideas, modern life itself, from those of times long past? It is, that human beings are no longer born to their place in life, and chained down by an inexorable bond to the place they are born to, but are free to employ their faculties, and such favourable chances as offer, to achieve the lot which may appear to them most desirable. Human society of old was constituted on a very different principle. All were born to a fixed social position, and were mostly kept in it by law, or interdicted from any means by which they could emerge from it. As some men are born white and others black, so some were born slaves and others freemen and citizens; some were born patricians,

others plebeians; some were born feudal nobles, others commoners and roturiers.[1] A slave or serf could never make himself free, nor, except by the will of his master, become so. In most European countries it was not till towards the close of the Middle Ages, and as a consequence of the growth of regal power, that commoners could be ennobled. Even among nobles, the eldest son was born the exclusive heir to the paternal possessions, and a long time elapsed before it was fully established that the father could disinherit him. Among the industrious classes, only those who were born members of a guild, or were admitted into it by its members, could lawfully practise their calling within its local limits; and nobody could practise any calling deemed important, in any but the legal manner—by processes authoritatively prescribed. Manufacturers have stood in the pillory for presuming to carry on their business by new and improved methods. In modern Europe, and most in those parts of it which have participated most largely in all other modern improvements, diametrically opposite doctrines now prevail. Law and government do not undertake to prescribe by whom any social or industrial operation shall or shall not be conducted, or what modes of conducting them shall be lawful. These things are left to the unfettered choice of individuals. Even the laws which required that workmen should serve an apprenticeship, have in this country been repealed: there being ample assurance that in all cases in which an apprenticeship is necessary, its necessity will suffice to enforce it. The old theory was, that the least possible should be left to the choice of the individual agent; that all he had to do should, as far as practicable, be laid down for him by superior wisdom. Left to himself he was sure to go wrong. The modern conviction, the fruit of a thousand years of experience, is, that things in which the individual is the person directly interested, never go right but as they are left to his own discretion; and that any regulation of them by authority, except to protect the rights of others, is sure to be mischievous. This

_____
[1] [Persons of non-noble birth.]

conclusion, slowly arrived at, and not adopted until almost every possible application of the contrary theory had been made with disastrous result, now (in the industrial department) prevails universally in the most advanced countries, almost universally in all that have pretensions to any sort of advancement. It is not that all processes are supposed to be equally good, or all persons to be equally qualified for everything; but that freedom of individual choice is now known to be the only thing which procures the adoption of the best processes, and throws each operation into the hands of those who are best qualified for it. Nobody thinks it necessary to make a law that only a strong-armed man shall be a blacksmith. Freedom and competition suffice to make blacksmiths strong-armed men, because the weak-armed can earn more by engaging in occupations for which they are more fit. In consonance with this doctrine, it is felt to be an overstepping of the proper bounds of authority to fix beforehand, on some general presumption, that certain persons are not fit to do certain things. It is now thoroughly known and admitted that if some such presumptions exist, no such presumption is infallible. Even if it be well grounded in a majority of cases, which it is very likely not to be, there will be a minority of exceptional cases in which it does not hold: and in those it is both an injustice to the individuals, and a detriment to society, to place barriers in the way of their using their faculties for their own benefit and for that of others. In the cases, on the other hand, in which the unfitness is real, the ordinary motives of human conduct will on the whole suffice to prevent the incompetent person from making, or from persisting in, the attempt.

If this general principle of social and economical science is not true; if individuals, with such help as they can derive from the opinion of those who know them, are not better judges than the law and the government, of their own capacities and vocation; the world cannot too soon abandon this principle, and return to the old system of regulations and disabilities. But if the principle is true, we ought to act as if we believed it, and not to ordain that to be born a girl instead of a boy, any more than to be born black instead of white, or a commoner instead of a nobleman, shall decide the person's position through all life—shall interdict people from all the more elevated social positions, and from all, except a few, respectable occupations. Even were we to admit the utmost that is ever pretended as to the superior fitness of men for all the functions now reserved to them, the same argument applies which forbids a legal qualification for members of Parliament. If only once in a dozen years the conditions of eligibility exclude a fit person, there is a real loss, while the exclusion of thousands of unfit persons is no gain; for if the constitution of the electoral body disposes them to choose unfit persons, there are always plenty of such persons to choose from. In all things of any difficulty and importance, those who can do them well are fewer than the need, even with the most unrestricted latitude of choice: and any limitation of the field of selection deprives society of some chances of being served by the competent, without ever saving it from the incompetent.

At present, in the more improved countries, the disabilities of women are the only case, save one, in which laws and institutions take persons at their birth, and ordain that they shall never in all their lives be allowed to compete for certain things. The one exception is that of royalty. Persons still are born to the throne; no one, not of the reigning family, can ever occupy it, and no one even of that family can, by any means but the course of hereditary succession, attain it. All other dignities and social advantages are open to the whole male sex: many indeed are only attainable by wealth, but wealth may be striven for by any one, and is actually obtained by many men of the very humblest origin. The difficulties, to the majority, are indeed insuperable without the aid of fortunate accidents; but no male human being is under any legal ban: neither law nor opinion superadd artificial obstacles to the natural ones. Royalty, as I have said, is excepted: but in this case every one feels it to be an exception—an anomaly in the modern world, in marked opposition to its customs and principles, and to be justified only by extraordinary special expediencies, which, though individuals and nations differ in estimating their weight, unquestionably do in fact exist. But in this exceptional case, in which a high social function is, for important reasons, bestowed on birth instead of being put up to competition, all free nations contrive to adhere in substance to the principle from which they nominally derogate; for they circumscribe this high function by conditions avowedly intended to prevent the person to whom it ostensibly belongs from really performing it; while the person by whom it is performed, the responsible minister, does obtain the post by a competition from which no full-grown citizen of the male sex is legally excluded. The disabilities, therefore, to which women are subject from the mere fact of their birth, are the solitary examples of the kind in modern legislation. In no instance except this, which comprehends half the human race, are the higher social functions closed against any one by a fatality of birth which no exertions, and no change of circumstances, can overcome; for even religious disabilities (besides that in England and in Europe they have practically almost ceased to exist) do not close any career to the disqualified person in case of conversion.

The social subordination of women thus stands out an isolated fact in modern social institutions; a solitary breach of what has become their fundamental law; a single relic of an old world of thought and practice exploded in everything else, but retained in the one thing of most universal interest; as if a gigantic dolmen, or a vast temple of Jupiter Olympus, occupied the site of St. Paul's and received daily worship, while the surrounding Christian churches were only resorted to on fasts and festivals. This entire discrepancy between one social fact and all those which accompany it, and the radical opposition between its nature and the progressive movement which is the boast of the modern world, and which has successively swept away everything else of an analogous character, surely affords, to a conscientious observer of human tendencies, serious matter for reflection. It raises a *primâ facie* presumption on the unfavourable side, far outweighing any which custom and

usage could in such circumstances create on the favourable; and should at least suffice to make this, like the choice between republicanism and royalty, a balanced question.

The least that can be demanded is, that the question should not be considered as prejudged by existing fact and existing opinion, but open to discussion on its merits, as a question of justice and expediency: the decision on this, as on any of the other social arrangements of mankind, depending on what an enlightened estimate of tendencies and consequences may show to be most advantageous to humanity in general, without distinction of sex. And the discussion must be a real discussion, descending to foundations, and not resting satisfied with vague and general assertions. It will not do, for instance, to assert in general terms, that the experience of mankind has pronounced in favour of the existing system. Experience cannot possibly have decided between two courses, so long as there has only been experience of one. If it be said that the doctrine of the equality of the sexes rests only on theory, it must be remembered that the contrary doctrine also has only theory to rest upon. All that is proved in its favour by direct experience, is that mankind have been able to exist under it, and to attain the degree of improvement and prosperity which we now see; but whether that prosperity has been attained sooner, or is now greater, than it would have been under the other system, experience does not say. On the other hand, experience does say, that every step in improvement has been so invariably accompanied by a step made in raising the social position of women, that historians and philosophers have been led to adopt their elevation or debasement as on the whole the surest test and most correct measure of the civilization of a people or an age. Through all the progressive period of human history, the condition of women has been approaching nearer to equality with men. This does not of itself prove that the assimilation must go on to complete equality; but it assuredly affords some presumption that such is the case.

Neither does it avail anything to say that the nature of the two sexes adapts them to their present functions and position, and renders these appropriate to them. Standing on the ground of common sense and the constitution of the human mind, I deny that any one knows, or can know, the nature of the two sexes, as long as they have only been seen in their present relation to one another. If men had ever been found in society without women, or women without men, or if there had been a society of men and women in which the women were not under the control of the men, something might have been positively known about the mental and moral differences which may be inherent in the nature of each. What is now called the nature of women is an eminently artificial thing—the result of forced repression in some directions, unnatural stimulation in others. It may be asserted without scruple, that no other class of dependents have had their character so entirely distorted from its natural proportions by their relation with their masters; for, if conquered and slave races have been, in some respects, more forcibly repressed, whatever in them has not been crushed down by an iron heel has generally been let alone, and if left with any liberty of development, it has developed itself according to its own laws; but in the case of women, a hothouse and stove cultivation has always been carried on of some of the capabilities of their nature, for the benefit and pleasure of their masters. Then, because certain products of the general vital force sprout luxuriantly and reach a great development in this heated atmosphere and under this active nurture and watering, while other shoots from the same root, which are left outside in the wintry air, with ice purposely heaped all round them, have a stunted growth, and some are burnt off with fire and disappear; men, with that inability to recognise their own work which distinguishes the unanalytic mind, indolently believe that the tree grows of itself in the way they have made it grow, and that it would die if one half of it were not kept in a vapour bath and the other half in the snow.

Of all difficulties which impede the progress of thought, and the formation of well-grounded opinions on life and social arrangements, the greatest is now the unspeakable ignorance and inattention of mankind in respect to the influences which form human character. Whatever any portion of the human species now are, or seem to be, such, it is supposed, they have a natural tendency to be: even when the most elementary knowledge of the circumstances in which they have been placed, clearly points out the causes that made them what they are. Because a cottier[1] deeply in arrears to his landlord is not industrious, there are people who think that the Irish are naturally idle. Because constitutions can be overthrown when the authorities appointed to execute them turn their arms against them, there are people who think the French incapable of free government. Because the Greeks cheated the Turks, and the Turks only plundered the Greeks, there are persons who think that the Turks are naturally more sincere: and because women, as is often said, care nothing about politics except their personalities, it is supposed that the general good is naturally less interesting to women than to men. History, which is now so much better understood than formerly, teaches another lesson: if only by showing the extraordinary susceptibility of human nature to external influences, and the extreme variableness of those of its manifestations which are supposed to be most universal and uniform. But in history, as in travelling, men usually see only what they already had in their own minds; and few learn much from history, who do not bring much with them to its study.

Hence, in regard to that most difficult question, what are the natural differences between the two sexes—a subject on which it is impossible in the present state of society to obtain complete and correct knowledge—while almost everybody dogmatizes upon it, almost all neglect and make light of the only means by which any partial insight can be obtained into it. This is, an analytic study of the most important department of psychology, the laws of the influence of circumstances on character. For, however great and apparently ineradicable the moral and intellectual differences between men and women might be, the evidence of their being

---

[1] [A farmer or serf.]

natural differences could only be negative. Those only could be inferred to be natural which could not possibly be artificial—the residuum, after deducting every characteristic of either sex which can admit of being explained from education or external circumstances. The profoundest knowledge of the laws of the formation of character is indispensable to entitle any one to affirm even that there is any difference, much more what the difference is, between the two sexes considered as moral and rational beings; and since no one, as yet, has that knowledge, (for there is hardly any subject which, in proportion to its importance, has been so little studied), no one is thus far entitled to any positive opinion on the subject. Conjectures are all that can at present be made; conjectures more or less probable, according as more or less authorized by such knowledge as we yet have of the laws of psychology, as applied to the formation of character.

Even the preliminary knowledge, what the differences between the sexes now are, apart from all question as to how they are made what they are, is still in the crudest and most incomplete state. Medical practitioners and physiologists have ascertained, to some extent, the differences in bodily constitution; and this is an important element to the psychologist: but hardly any medical practitioner is a psychologist. Respecting the mental characteristics of women; their observations are of no more worth than those of common men. It is a subject on which nothing final can be known, so long as those who alone can really know it, women themselves, have given but little testimony, and that little, mostly suborned. It is easy to know stupid women. Stupidity is much the same all the world over. A stupid person's notions and feelings may confidently be inferred from those which prevail in the circle by which the person is surrounded. Not so with those whose opinions and feelings are an emanation from their own nature and faculties. It is only a man here and there who has any tolerable knowledge of the character even of the women of his own family. I do not mean, of their capabilities; these nobody knows, not even themselves, because most of them have never been called out. I mean their actually existing thoughts and feelings. Many a man thinks he perfectly understands women, because he has had amatory relations with several, perhaps with many of them. If he is a good observer, and his experience extends to quality as well as quantity, he may have learnt something of one narrow department of their nature—an important department, no doubt. But of all the rest of it, few persons are generally more ignorant, because there are few from whom it is so carefully hidden. The most favourable case which a man can generally have for studying the character of a woman, is that of his own wife: for the opportunities are greater, and the cases of complete sympathy not so unspeakably rare. And in fact, this is the source from which any knowledge worth having on the subject has, I believe, generally come. But most men have not had the opportunity of studying in this way more than a single case: accordingly one can, to an almost laughable degree, infer what a man's wife is like, from his opinions about women in general. To make even this one case yield any result, the woman must be worth knowing, and the man not only a competent judge, but of a character so sympathetic in itself, and so well adapted to hers, that he can either read her mind by sympathetic intuition, or has nothing in himself which makes her shy of disclosing it. Hardly anything, I believe, can be more rare than this conjunction. It often happens that there is the most complete unity of feeling and community of interests as to all external things, yet the one has as little admission into the internal life of the other as if they were common acquaintance. Even with true affection, authority on the one side and subordination on the other prevent perfect confidence. Though nothing may be intentionally withheld, much is not shown. In the analogous relation of parent and child, the corresponding phenomenon must have been in the observation of every one. As between father and son, how many are the cases in which the father, in spite of real affection on both sides, obviously to all the world does not know, nor suspect, parts of the son's character familiar to his companions and equals. The truth is, that the position of looking up to another is extremely unpropitious to complete sincerity and openness with him. The fear of losing ground in his opinion or in his feelings is so strong, that even in an upright character, there is an unconscious tendency to show only the best side, or the side which, though not the best, is that which he most likes to see: and it may be confidently said that thorough knowledge of one another hardly ever exists, but between persons who, besides being intimates, are equals. How much more true, then, must all this be, when the one is not only under the authority of the other, but has it inculcated on her as a duty to reckon everything else subordinate to his comfort and pleasure, and to let him neither see nor feel anything coming from her, except what is agreeable to him. All these difficulties stand in the way of a man's obtaining any thorough knowledge even of the one woman whom alone, in general, he has sufficient opportunity of studying. When we further consider that to understand one woman is not necessarily to understand any other woman; that even if he could study many women of one rank, or of one country, he would not thereby understand women of other ranks or countries; and even if he did, they are still only the women of a single period of history; we may safely assert that the knowledge which men can acquire of women, even as they have been and are, without reference to what they might be, is wretchedly imperfect and superficial, and always will be so, until women themselves have told all that they have to tell.

And this time has not come; nor will it come otherwise than gradually. It is but of yesterday that women have either been qualified by literary accomplishments, or permitted by society, to tell anything to the general public. As yet very few of them dare tell anything, which men, on whom their literary success depends, are unwilling to hear. Let us remember in what manner, up to a very recent time, the expression, even by a male author, of uncustomary opinions, or what are deemed eccentric feelings, usually was, and in some degree still is, received; and we may form some faint conception under what impediments a woman, who is brought up to think custom and opinion her sovereign rule, attempts to express in books anything drawn from the depths of her own nature. The greatest woman who has left writings behind her sufficient to give her an eminent rank in the literature of her country, thought it necessary to prefix as a motto to her boldest work, "Un homme peut braver l'opinion; une femme doit s'y soumettre."[1] The greater part of what women write about women is mere sycophancy to men. In the case of unmarried women, much of it seems only intended to increase their chance of a husband. Many, both married and unmarried, overstep the mark, and inculcate a servility beyond what is desired or relished by any man, except the very vulgarest. But this is not so often the case as, even at a quite late period, it still was. Literary women are becoming more freespoken, and more willing to express their real sentiments. Unfortunately, in this country especially, they are themselves such artificial products, that their sentiments are compounded of a small element of individual observation and consciousness, and a very large one of acquired associations. This will be less and less the case, but it will remain true to a great extent, as long as social institutions do not admit the same free development of originality in women which is possible to men. When that time comes, and not before, we shall see, and not merely hear, as much as it is necessary to know of the nature of women, and the adaptation of other things to it.

I have dwelt so much on the difficulties which at present obstruct any real knowledge by men of the true nature of women, because in this as in so many other things "opinio copiæ inter maximas causas inopiæ est;"[2] and there is little chance of reasonable thinking on the matter, while people flatter themselves that they perfectly understand a subject of which most men know absolutely nothing, and of which it is at present impossible that any man, or all men taken together, should have knowledge which can qualify them to lay down the law to women as to what is, or is not, their vocation.

---

[1] ["A man must learn to brave public opinion, a woman to submit" (Madame de Stael [1766–1817]).]
[2] ["Popular opinion is deficient on most matters" (Francis Bacon [1561–1626]).]

Happily, no such knowledge is necessary for any practical purpose connected with the position of women in relation to society and life. For, according to all the principles involved in modern society, the question rests with women themselves—to be decided by their own experience, and by the use of their own faculties. There are no means of finding what either one person or many can do, but by trying—and no means by which any one else can discover for them what it is for their happiness to do or leave undone.

One thing we may be certain of—that what is contrary to women's nature to do, they never will be made to do by simply giving their nature free play. The anxiety of mankind to interfere in behalf of nature, for fear lest nature should not succeed in effecting its purpose, is an altogether unnecessary solicitude. What women by nature cannot do, it is quite superfluous to forbid them from doing. What they can do, but not so well as the men who are their competitors, competition suffices to exclude them from; since nobody asks for protective duties and bounties in favour of women; it is only asked that the present bounties and protective duties in favour of men should be recalled. If women have a greater natural inclination for some things than for others, there is no need of laws or social inculcation to make the majority of them do the former in preference to the latter. Whatever women's services are most wanted for, the free play of competition will hold out the strongest inducements to them to undertake. And, as the words imply, they are most wanted for the things for which they are most fit; by the apportionment of which to them, the collective faculties of the two sexes can be applied on the whole with the greatest sum of valuable result.

The general opinion of men is supposed to be, that the natural vocation of a woman is that of a wife and mother. I say, is supposed to be, because, judging from acts—from the whole of the present constitution of society—one might infer that their opinion was the direct contrary. They might be supposed to think that the alleged natural vocation of women was of all things the most repugnant to their nature; insomuch that if they are free

to do anything else—if any other means of living, or occupation of their time and faculties, is open, which has any chance of appearing desirable to them—there will not be enough of them who will be willing to accept the condition said to be natural to them. If this is the real opinion of men in general, it would be well that it should be spoken out. I should like to hear somebody openly enunciating the doctrine (it is already implied in much that is written on the subject)—"It is necessary to society that women should marry and produce children. They will not do so unless they are compelled. Therefore it is necessary to compel them." The merits of the case would then be clearly defined. It would be exactly that of the slaveholders of South Carolina and Louisiana. "It is necessary that cotton and sugar should be grown. White men cannot produce them. Negroes will not, for any wages which we choose to give. Ergo they must be compelled." An illustration still closer to the point is that of impressment. Sailors must absolutely be had to defend the country. It often happens that they will not voluntarily enlist. Therefore there must be the power of forcing them. How often has this logic been used! and, but for one flaw in it, without doubt it would have been successful up to this day. But it is open to the retort—First pay the sailors the honest value of their labour. When you have made it as well worth their while to serve you, as to work for other employers, you will have no more difficulty than others have in obtaining their services. To this there is no logical answer except "I will not": and as people are now not only ashamed, but are not desirous, to rob the labourer of his hire, impressment is no longer advocated. Those who attempt to force women into marriage by closing all other doors against them, lay themselves open to a similar retort. If they mean what they say, their opinion must evidently be, that men do not render the married condition so desirable to women, as to induce them to accept it for its own recommendations. It is not a sign of one's thinking the boon one offers very attractive, when one allows only Hobson's choice, "that or none." And here, I believe, is the clue to the feelings of those men, who have a real antipathy to the equal freedom of women. I believe they are afraid, not lest women should be unwilling to marry, for I do not think that any one in reality has that apprehension; but lest they should insist that marriage should be on equal conditions; lest all women of spirit and capacity should prefer doing almost anything else, not in their own eyes degrading, rather than marry, when marrying is giving themselves a master, and a master too of all their earthly possessions. And truly, if this consequence were necessarily incident to marriage, I think that the apprehension would be very well founded. I agree in thinking it probable that few women, capable of anything else, would, unless under an irresistible entrainement, rendering them for the time insensible to anything but itself, choose such a lot, when any other means were open to them of filling a conventionally honourable place in life: and if men are determined that the law of marriage shall be a law of despotism, they are quite right, in point of mere policy, in leaving to women only Hobson's choice. But, in that case, all that has been done in the modern world to relax the chain on the minds of women, has been a mistake. They never should have been allowed to receive a literary education. Women who read, much more women who write, are, in the existing constitution of things, a contradiction and a disturbing element: and it was wrong to bring women up with any acquirements but those of an odalisque,[1] or of a domestic servant.

[...]

Chapter IV

There remains a question, not of less importance than those already discussed, and which will be asked the most importunately by those opponents whose conviction is somewhat shaken on the main point. What good are we to expect from the changes proposed in our customs and institutions? Would mankind be at all better off if women were free? If not, why disturb their minds, and attempt to make a social revolution in the name of an abstract right?

It is hardly to be expected that this question will be asked in respect to the change proposed in the condition of women in marriage. The sufferings, immoralities, evils of all sorts, produced in innumerable cases by the subjection of individual women to individual men, are far too terrible to be overlooked. Unthinking or uncandid persons, counting those cases alone which are extreme, or which attain publicity, may say that the evils are exceptional; but no one can be blind to their existence, nor, in many cases, to their intensity. And it is perfectly obvious that the abuse of the power cannot be very much checked while the power remains. It is a power given, or offered, not to good men, or to decently respectable men, but to all men; the most brutal, and the most criminal. There is no check but that of opinion, and such men are in general within the reach of no opinion but that of men like themselves. If such men did not brutally tyrannise over the one human being whom the law compels to bear everything from them, society must already have reached a paradisiacal state. There could be no need any longer of laws to curb men's vicious propensities. Astraea[2] must not only have returned to earth, but the heart of the worst man must have become her temple. The law of servitude in marriage is a monstrous contradiction to all the principles of the modern world, and to all the experience through which those principles have been slowly and painfully worked out. It is the sole case, now that negro slavery has been abolished, in which a human being in the plenitude of every faculty is delivered up to the tender mercies of another human being, in the hope forsooth that this other will use the power solely for the good of the person subjected to it. Marriage is the only actual bondage known to our law. There remain no legal slaves, except the mistress of every house.

It is not, therefore, on this part of the subject, that the question is likely to be asked, *Cui bono*?[3]

---

[1] [A female slave.]

[2] [In Greek mythology Astraea was a daughter of Zeus. She was a personification of justice and was also associated with innocence and purity.]

[3] ["For whose good?"]

We may be told that the evil would outweigh the good, but the reality of the good admits of no dispute. In regard, however, to the larger question, the removal of women's disabilities—their recognition as the equals of men in all that belongs to citizenship—the opening to them of all honourable employments, and of the training and education which qualifies for those employments—there are many persons for whom it is not enough that the inequality has no just or legitimate defence; they require to be told what express advantage would be obtained by abolishing it.

To which let me first answer, the advantage of having the most universal and pervading of all human relations regulated by justice instead of injustice. The vast amount of this gain to human nature, it is hardly possible, by any explanation or illustration, to place in a stronger light than it is placed by the bare statement, to anyone who attaches a moral meaning to words. All the selfish propensities, the self-worship, the unjust self-preference, which exist among mankind, have their source and root in, and derive their principal nourishment from, the present constitution of the relation between men and women. Think what it is to a boy, to grow up to manhood in the belief that without any merit or any exertion of his own, though he may be the most frivolous and empty or the most ignorant and stolid of mankind, by the mere fact of being born a male he is by right the superior of all and every one of an entire half of the human race: including probably some whose real superiority to himself he has daily or hourly occasion to feel; but even if in his whole conduct he habitually follows a woman's guidance, still, if he is a fool, she thinks that of course she is not, and cannot be, equal in ability and judgment to himself; and if he is not a fool, he does worse—he sees that she is superior to him, and believes that, notwithstanding her superiority, he is entitled to command and she is bound to obey. What must be the effect on his character, of this lesson? And men of the cultivated classes are often not aware how deeply it sinks into the immense majority of male minds. For, among right-feeling and wellbred people, the inequality is kept as much as possible out of sight; above all, out of sight of the children. As much obedience is required from boys to their mother as to their father: they are not permitted to domineer over their sisters, nor are they accustomed to see these postponed to them, but the contrary; the compensations of the chivalrous feeling being made prominent, while the servitude which requires them is kept in the background. Well brought-up youths in the higher classes thus often escape the bad influences of the situation in their early years, and only experience them when, arrived at manhood, they fall under the dominion of facts as they really exist. Such people are little aware, when a boy is differently brought up, how early the notion of his inherent superiority to a girl arises in his mind; how it grows with his growth and strengthens with his strength; how it is inoculated by one schoolboy upon another; how early the youth thinks himself superior to his mother, owing her perhaps forbearance, but no real respect; and how sublime and sultan-like a sense of superiority he feels, above all, over the woman whom he honours by admitting her to a partnership of his life. Is it imagined that all this does not pervert the whole manner of existence of the man, both as an individual and as a social being? It is an exact parallel to the feeling of a hereditary king that he is excellent above others by being born a king, or a noble by being born a noble. The relation between husband and wife is very like that between lord and vassal, except that the wife is held to more unlimited obedience than the vassal was. However the vassal's character may have been affected, for better and for worse, by his subordination, who can help seeing that the lord's was affected greatly for the worse? whether he was led to believe that his vassals were really superior to himself, or to feel that he was placed in command over people as good as himself, for no merits or labours of his own, but merely for having, as Figaro says, taken the trouble to be born. The self-worship of the monarch, or of the feudal superior, is matched by the self-worship of the male. Human beings do not grow up from childhood in the possession of unearned distinctions, without pluming themselves upon them. Those whom privileges not acquired by their merit, and which they feel to be disproportioned to it, inspire with additional humility, are always the few, and the best few. The rest are only inspired with pride, and the worst sort of pride, that which values itself upon accidental advantages, not of its own achieving. Above all, when the feeling of being raised above the whole of the other sex is combined with personal authority over one individual among them; the situation, if a school of conscientious and affectionate forbearance to those whose strongest points of character are conscience and affection, is to men of another quality a regularly constituted academy or gymnasium for training them in arrogance and overbearingness; which vices, if curbed by the certainty of resistance in their intercourse with other men, their equals, break out towards all who are in a position to be obliged to tolerate them, and often revenge themselves upon the unfortunate wife for the involuntary restraint which they are obliged to submit to elsewhere.

The example afforded, and the education given to the sentiments, by laying the foundation of domestic existence upon a relation contradictory to the first principles of social justice must, from the very nature of man, have a perverting influence of such magnitude, that it is hardly possible with our present experience to raise our imaginations to the conception of so great a change for the better as would be made by its removal. All that education and civilisation are doing to efface the influences on character of the law of force, and replace them by those of justice, remains merely on the surface, as long as the citadel of the enemy is not attacked. The principle of the modern movement in morals and politics, is that conduct, and conduct alone, entitles to respect: that not what men are, but what they do, constitutes their claim to deference; that, above all, merit, and not birth, is the only rightful claim to power and authority. If no authority, not in its nature temporary, were allowed to one human being over another, society would not be employed in building up propensities with one hand which it has to curb with the

other. The child would really, for the first time in man's existence on earth, be trained in the way he should go, and when he was old there would be a chance that he would not depart from it. But so long as the right of the strong to power over the weak rules in the very heart of society, the attempt to make the equal right of the weak the principle of its outward actions will always be an uphill struggle; for the law of justice, which is also that of Christianity, will never get possession of men's inmost sentiments; they will be working against it, even when bending to it.

The second benefit to be expected from giving to women the free use of their faculties, by leaving them the free choice of their employments, and opening to them the same field of occupation and the same prizes and encouragements as to other human beings, would be that of doubling the mass of mental faculties available for the higher service of humanity. Where there is now one person qualified to benefit mankind and promote the general improvement, as a public teacher, or an administrator of some branch of public or social affairs, there would then be a chance of two. Mental superiority of any kind is at present everywhere so much below the demand; there is such a deficiency of persons competent to do excellently anything which it requires any considerable amount of ability to do; that the loss to the world, by refusing to make use of one half of the whole quantity of talent it possesses, is extremely serious. It is true that this amount of mental power is not totally lost. Much of it is employed, and would in any case be employed, in domestic management, and in the few other occupations open to women; and from the remainder indirect benefit is in many individual cases obtained, through the personal influence of individual women over individual men. But these benefits are partial; their range is extremely circumscribed; and if they must be admitted, on the one hand, as a deduction from the amount of fresh social power that would be acquired by giving freedom to one-half of the whole sum of human intellect, there must be added, on the other, the benefit of the stimulus that would be given to the intellect of men by the competition;

or (to use a more true expression) by the necessity that would be imposed on them of deserving precedency before they could expect to obtain it.

This great accession to the intellectual power of the species, and to the amount of intellect available for the good management of its affairs, would be obtained, partly, through the better and more complete intellectual education of women, which would then improve *pari passu* with that of men. Women in general would be brought up equally capable of understanding business, public affairs, and the higher matters of speculation, with men in the same class of society; and the select few of the one as well as of the other sex, who were qualified not only to comprehend what is done or thought by others, but to think or do something considerable themselves, would meet with the same facilities for improving and training their capacities in the one sex as in the other. In this way, the widening of the sphere of action for women would operate for good, by raising their education to the level of that of men, and making the one participate in all improvements made in the other. But independently of this, the mere breaking down of the barrier would of itself have an educational virtue of the highest worth. The mere getting rid of the idea that all the wider subjects of thought and action, all the things which are of general and not solely of private interest, are men's business, from which women are to be warned off—positively interdicted from most of it, coldly tolerated in the little which is allowed them—the mere consciousness a woman would then have of being a human being like any other, entitled to choose her pursuits, urged or invited by the same inducements as anyone else to interest herself in whatever is interesting to human beings, entitled to exert the share of influence on all human concerns which belongs to an individual opinion, whether she attempted actual participation in them or not—this alone would effect an immense expansion of the faculties of women, as well as enlargement of the range of their moral sentiments.

Besides the addition to the amount of individual talent available for the conduct of human affairs, which certainly are not at present so abundantly provided in that respect that they can afford to dispense with one-half of what nature proffers; the opinion of women would then possess a more beneficial, rather than a greater, influence upon the general mass of human belief and sentiment. I say a more beneficial, rather than a greater influence; for the influence of women over the general tone of opinion has always, or at least from the earliest known period, been very considerable. The influence of mothers on the early character of their sons, and the desire of young men to recommend themselves to young women, have in all recorded times been important agencies in the formation of character, and have determined some of the chief steps in the progress of civilisation. Even in the Homeric age [respect for the Trojan women of the trailing robes][1] is an acknowledged and powerful motive of action in the great Hector. The moral influence of women has had two modes of operation. First, it has been a softening influence. Those who were most liable to be the victims of violence, have naturally tended as much as they could towards limiting its sphere and mitigating its excesses. Those who were not taught to fight, have naturally inclined in favour of any other mode of settling differences rather than that of fighting. In general, those who have been the greatest sufferers by the indulgence of selfish passion, have been the most earnest supporters of any moral law which offered a means of bridling passion. Women were powerfully instrumental in inducing the northern conquerors to adopt the creed of Christianity, a creed so much more favourable to women than any that preceded it. The conversion of the Anglo-Saxons and of the Franks may be said to have been begun by the wives of Ethelbert and Clovis. The other mode in which the effect of women's opinion has been conspicuous, is by giving a powerful stimulus to those qualities in men, which, not being themselves trained in, it was necessary for them that they should find in their protectors. Courage, and the military virtues generally, have at all times been greatly indebted to the desire which men felt of being admired by women: and

---

[1] [This is a translation from an ancient Greek text.]

the stimulus reaches far beyond this one class of eminent qualities, since, by a very natural effect of their position, the best passport to the admiration and favour of women has always been to be thought highly of by men. From the combination of the two kinds of moral influence thus exercised by women, arose the spirit of chivalry: the peculiarity of which is, to aim at combining the highest standard of the warlike qualities with the cultivation of a totally different class of virtues—those of gentleness, generosity, and self-abnegation, towards the non-military and defenseless classes generally, and a special submission and worship directed towards women; who were distinguished from the other defenceless classes by the high rewards which they had it in their power voluntarily to bestow on those who endeavoured to earn their favour, instead of extorting their subjection. Though the practice of chivalry fell even more sadly short of its theoretic standard than practice generally falls below theory, it remains one of the most precious monuments of the moral history of our race; as a remarkable instance of a concerted and organised attempt by a most disorganised and distracted society, to raise up and carry into practice a moral ideal greatly in advance of its social condition and institutions; so much so as to have been completely frustrated in the main object, yet never entirely inefficacious, and which has left a most sensible, and for the most part a highly valuable impress on the ideas and feelings of all subsequent times.

The chivalrous ideal is the acme of the influence of women's sentiments on the moral cultivation of mankind: and if women are to remain in their subordinate situation, it were greatly to be lamented that the chivalrous standard should have passed away, for it is the only one at all capable of mitigating the demoralizing influences of that position. But the changes in the general state of the species rendered inevitable the substitution of a totally different ideal of morality for the chivalrous one. Chivalry was the attempt to infuse moral elements into a state of society in which everything depended for good or evil on individual prowess, under the softening influences of individual delicacy and generosity. In modern societies, all things, even in the military

department of affairs, are decided, not by individual effort, but by the combined operations of numbers; while the main occupation of society has changed from fighting to business, from military to industrial life. The exigencies of the new life are no more exclusive of the virtues of generosity than those of the old, but it no longer entirely depends on them. The main foundations of the moral life of modern times must be justice and prudence; the respect of each for the rights of every other, and the ability of each to take care of himself. Chivalry left without legal check all forms of wrong which reigned unpunished throughout society; it only encouraged a few to do right in preference to wrong, by the direction it gave to the instruments of praise and admiration. But the real dependence of morality must always be upon its penal sanctions—its power to deter from evil. The security of society cannot rest on merely rendering honour to right, a motive so comparatively weak in all but a few, and which on very many does not operate at all. Modern society is able to repress wrong through all departments of life, by a fit exertion of the superior strength which civilisation has given it, and thus to render the existence of the weaker members of society (no longer defenceless but protected by law) tolerable to them, without reliance on the chivalrous feelings of those who are in a position to tyrannise. The beauties and graces of the chivalrous character are still what they were, but the rights of the weak, and the general comfort of human life, now rest on a far surer and steadier support; or rather, they do so in every relation of life except the conjugal.

At present the moral influence of women is no less real, but it is no longer of so marked and definite a character: it has more nearly merged in the general influence of public opinion. Both through the contagion of sympathy, and through the desire of men to shine in the eyes of women, their feelings have great effect in keeping alive what remains of the chivalrous ideal—in fostering the sentiments and continuing the traditions of spirit and generosity. In these points of character, their standard is higher than that of men; in the quality of justice, somewhat lower. As regards the relations of private life it may be said generally, that their influence is, on the whole, encouraging to the softer virtues, discouraging to the sterner: though the statement must be taken with all the modifications dependent on individual character. In the chief of the greater trials to which virtue is subject in the concerns of life—the conflict between interest and principle—the tendency of women's influence—is of a very mixed character. When the principle involved happens to be one of the very few which the course of their religious or moral education has strongly impressed upon themselves, they are potent auxiliaries to virtue: and their husbands and sons are often prompted by them to acts of abnegation which they never would have been capable of without that stimulus. But, with the present education and position of women, the moral principles which have been impressed on them cover but a comparatively small part of the field of virtue, and are, moreover, principally negative; forbidding particular acts, but having little to do with the general direction of the thoughts and purposes. I am afraid it must be said, that disinterestedness in the general conduct of life—the devotion of the energies to purposes which hold out no promise of private advantages to the family—is very seldom encouraged or supported by women's influence. It is small blame to them that they discourage objects of which they have not learnt to see the advantage, and which withdraw their men from them, and from the interests of the family. But the consequence is that women's influence is often anything but favourable to public virtue.

Women have, however, some share of influence in giving the tone to public moralities since their sphere of action has been a little widened, and since a considerable number of them have occupied themselves practically in the promotion of objects reaching beyond their own family and household. The influence of women counts for a great deal in two of the most marked features of modern European life—its aversion to war, and its addiction to philanthropy. Excellent characteristics both; but unhappily, if the influence of women is valuable in the encouragement it gives to these feelings in general, in the particular applications the direction it gives

to them is at least as often mischievous as useful. In the philanthropic department more particularly, the two provinces chiefly cultivated by women are religious proselytism and charity. Religious proselytism at home, is but another word for embittering of religious animosities: abroad, it is usually a blind running at an object, without either knowing or heeding the fatal mischiefs—fatal to the religious object itself as well as to all other desirable objects—which may be produced by the means employed. As for charity, it is a matter in which the immediate effect on the persons directly concerned, and the ultimate consequence to the general good, are apt to be at complete war with one another: while the education given to women—an education of the sentiments rather than of the understanding—and the habit inculcated by their whole life, of looking to immediate effects on persons, and not to remote effects on classes of persons—make them both unable to see, and unwilling to admit, the ultimate evil tendency of any form of charity or philanthropy which commends itself to their sympathetic feelings. The great and continually increasing mass of unenlightened and shortsighted benevolence, which, taking the care of people's lives out of their own hands, and relieving them from the disagreeable consequences of their own acts, saps the very foundations of the self-respect, self-help, and self-control which are the essential conditions both of individual prosperity and of social virtue—this waste of resources and of benevolent feelings in doing harm instead of good, is immensely swelled by women's contributions, and stimulated by their influence. Not that this is a mistake likely to be made by women, where they have actually the practical management of schemes of beneficence. It sometimes happens that women who administer public charities—with that insight into present fact, and especially into the minds and feelings of those with whom they are in immediate contact, in which women generally excel men—recognise in the clearest manner the demoralising influence of the alms given or the help afforded, and could give lessons on the subject to many a male political economist. But women who only give their money, and are not brought face to face with the effects it produces, how can they be expected to foresee them? A woman born to the present lot of women, and content with it, how should she appreciate the value of self-dependence? She is not self-dependent; she is not taught self-dependence; her destiny is to receive everything from others, and why should what is good enough for her be bad for the poor? Her familiar notions of good are of blessings descending from a superior. She forgets that she is not free, and that the poor are; that if what they need is given to them unearned, they cannot be compelled to earn it; that everybody cannot be taken care of by everybody, but there must be some motive to induce people to take care of themselves; and that to be helped to help themselves, if they are physically capable of it, is the only charity which proves to be charity in the end.

These considerations show how usefully the part which women take in the formation of general opinion, would be modified for the better by that more enlarged instruction, and practical conversancy with the things which their opinions influence, that would necessarily arise from their social and political emancipation. But the improvement it would work through the influence they exercise, each in her own family, would be still more remarkable.

It is often said that in the classes most exposed to temptation, a man's wife and children tend to keep him honest and respectable, both by the wife's direct influence, and by the concern he feels for their future welfare. This may be so, and no doubt often is so, with those who are more weak than wicked; and this beneficial influence would be preserved and strengthened under equal laws; it does not depend on the woman's servitude, but is, on the contrary, diminished by the disrespect which the inferior class of men always at heart feel towards those who are subject to their power. But when we ascend higher in the scale, we come among a totally different set of moving forces. The wife's influence tends, as far as it goes, to prevent the husband from falling below the common standard of approbation of the country. It tends quite as strongly to hinder him from rising above it. The wife is the auxiliary of the common public opinion. A man who is married to a woman his inferior in intelligence, finds her a perpetual dead weight, or, worse than a dead weight, a drag, upon every aspiration of his to be better than public opinion requires him to be. It is hardly possible for one who is in these bonds, to attain exalted virtue. If he differs in his opinion from the mass—if he sees truths which have not yet dawned upon them, or if, feeling in his heart truths which they nominally recognise, he would like to act up to those truths more conscientiously than the generality of mankind—to all such thoughts and desires, marriage is the heaviest of drawbacks, unless he be so fortunate as to have a wife as much above the common level as he himself is.

For, in the first place, there is always some sacrifice of personal interest required; either of social consequence, or of pecuniary means; perhaps the risk of even the means of subsistence. These sacrifices and risks he may be willing to encounter for himself; but he will pause before he imposes them on his family. And his family in this case means his wife and daughters; for he always hopes that his sons will feel as he feels himself, and that what he can do without, they will do without, willingly, is the same cause. But his daughters—their marriage may depend upon it: and his wife, who is unable to enter into or understand the objects for which these sacrifices are made—who, if she thought them worth any sacrifice, would think so on trust, and solely for his sake—who could participate in none of the enthusiasm or the self-approbation he himself may feel, while the things which he is disposed to sacrifice are all in all to her; will not the best and most unselfish man hesitate the longest before bringing on her this consequence? If it be not the comforts of life, but only social consideration, that is at stake, the burthen upon his conscience and feelings is still very severe. Whoever has a wife and children has given hostages to Mrs. Grundy.[1] The approbation

---

[1] [A character from Thomas Morton's play *Speed the Plough* (1798). She was considered the paradigm of a slave to conventional propriety.]

of that potentate may be a matter of indifference to him, but it is of great importance to his wife. The man himself may be above opinion, or may find sufficient compensation in the opinion of those of his own way of thinking. But to the women connected with him, he can offer no compensation. The almost invariable tendency of the wife to place her influence in the same scale with social consideration, is sometimes made a reproach to women, and represented as a peculiar trait of feebleness and childishness of character in them: surely with great injustice. Society makes the whole life of a woman, in the easy classes, a continued self sacrifice; it exacts from her an unremitting restraint of the whole of her natural inclinations, and the sole return it makes to her for what often deserves the name of a martyrdom, is consideration. Her consideration is inseparably connected with that of her husband, and after paying the full price for it, she finds that she is to lose it, for no reason of which she can feel the cogency. She has sacrificed her whole life to it, and her husband will not sacrifice to it a whim, a freak, an eccentricity; something not recognised or allowed for by the world, and which the world will agree with her in thinking a folly, if it thinks no worse! The dilemma is hardest upon that very meritorious class of men, who, without possessing talents which qualify them to make a figure among those with whom they agree in opinion, hold their opinion from conviction, and feel bound in honour and conscience to serve it, by making profession of their belief, and giving their time, labour, and means, to anything undertaken in its behalf. The worst case of all is when such men happen to be of a rank and position which of itself neither gives them, nor excludes them from, what is considered the best society; when their admission to it depends mainly on what is thought of them personally—and however unexceptionable their breeding and habits, their being identified with opinions and public conduct unacceptable to those who give the tone to society would operate as an effectual exclusion. Many a woman flatters herself (nine times out of ten quite erroneously) that nothing prevents her and her husband from moving in the highest society of her neighbourhood—society in which others well known to her, and in the same class of life, mix freely—except that her husband is unfortunately a Dissenter, or has the reputation of mingling in low radical politics. That it is, she thinks, which hinders George from getting a commission or a place, Caroline from making an advantageous match, and prevents her and her husband from obtaining invitations, perhaps honours, which, for aught she sees, they are as well entitled to as some folks. With such an influence in every house, either exerted actively, or operating all the more powerfully for not being asserted, is it any wonder that people in general are kept down in that mediocrity of respectability which is becoming a marked characteristic of modern times?

There is another very injurious aspect in which the effect, not of women's disabilities directly, but of the broad line of difference which those disabilities create between the education and character of a woman and that of a man, requires to be considered. Nothing can be more unfavourable to that union of thoughts and inclinations which is the ideal of married life. Intimate society between people radically dissimilar to one another, is an idle dream. Unlikeness may attract, but it is likeness which retains; and in proportion to the likeness is the suitability of the individuals to give each other a happy life. While women are so unlike men, it is not wonderful that selfish men should feel the need of arbitrary power in their own hands, to arrest *in limine* the life-long conflict of inclinations, by deciding every question on the side of their own preference. When people are extremely unlike, there can be no real identity of interest. Very often there is conscientious difference of opinion between married people, on the highest points of duty. Is there any reality in the marriage union where this takes place? Yet it is not uncommon anywhere, when the woman has any earnestness of character; and it is a very general case indeed in Catholic countries, when she is supported in her dissent by the only other authority to which she is taught to bow, the priest. With the usual barefacedness of power not accustomed to find itself disputed, the influence of priests over women is attacked by Protestant and Liberal writers, less for being bad in itself, than because it is a rival authority to the husband, and raises up a revolt against his infallibility. In England, similar differences occasionally exist when an Evangelical wife has allied herself with a husband of a different quality; but in general this source at least of dissension is got rid of, by reducing the minds of women to such a nullity, that they have no opinions but those of Mrs. Grundy, or those which the husband tells them to have. When there is no difference of opinion, differences merely of taste may be sufficient to detract greatly from the happiness of married life. And though it may stimulate the amatory propensities of men, it does not conduce to married happiness, to exaggerate by differences of education whatever may be the native differences of the sexes. If the married pair are well-bred and well-behaved people, they tolerate each other's tastes; but is mutual toleration what people look forward to, when they enter into marriage? These differences of inclination will naturally make their wishes different, if not restrained by affection or duty, as to almost all domestic questions which arise. What a difference there must be in the society which the two persons will wish to frequent, or be frequented by! Each will desire associates who share their own tastes: the persons agreeable to one, will be indifferent or positively disagreeable to the other; yet there can be none who are not common to both, for married people do not now live in different parts of the house and have totally different visiting lists, as in the reign of Louis XV. They cannot help having different wishes as to the bringing up of the children: each will wish to see reproduced in them their own tastes and sentiments: and there is either a compromise, and only a half satisfaction to either, or the wife has to yield—often with bitter suffering; and, with or without intention, her occult influence continues to counterwork the husband's purposes.

It would of course be extreme folly to suppose that these differences of feeling and inclination only exist because women are brought up differently from men, and that there would not be differences of taste under any imaginable circumstances. But there is nothing beyond the mark in saying that the distinction in bringing up immensely aggravates those differences, and renders them wholly inevitable. While women are brought up as they are, a man and a woman will but rarely find in one another real agreement of tastes and wishes as to daily life. They will generally have to give it up as hopeless, and renounce the attempt to have, in the intimate associate of their daily life, that *idem velle, idem nolle*,[1] which is the recognised bond of any society that is really such: or if the man succeeds in obtaining it, he does so by choosing a woman who is so complete a nullity that she has no *velle* or *nolle* at all, and is as ready to comply with one thing as another if anybody tells her to do so. Even this calculation is apt to fail; dullness and want of spirit are not always a guarantee of the submission which is so confidently expected from them. But if they were, is this the ideal of marriage? What, in this case, does the man obtain by it, except an upper servant, a nurse, or a mistress? on the contrary, when each of two persons, instead of being a nothing, is a something; when they are attached to one another, and are not too much unlike to begin with; the constant partaking in the same things, assisted by their sympathy, draws out the latent capacities of each for being interested in the things which were at first interesting only to the other; and works a gradual assimilation of the tastes and characters to one another, partly by the insensible modification of each, but more by a real enriching of the two natures, each acquiring the tastes and capacities of the other in addition to its own. This often happens between two friends of the same sex, who are much associated in their daily life: and it would be a common, if not the commonest, case in marriage, did not the totally different bringing up of the two sexes make it next to an impossibility to form a really well-assorted union. Were this remedied, whatever differences there might still be in individual tastes, there would at least be, as a general rule, complete unity and unanimity as to the

---

[1] [To share the same wishes, whether positive or negative (*velle* = to want; *nolle* = not to want).]

great objects of life. When the two persons both care for great objects, and are a help and encouragement to each other in whatever regards these, the minor matters on which their tastes may differ are not all-important to them; and there is a foundation for solid friendship, of an enduring character, more likely than anything else to make it, through the whole of life, a greater pleasure to each to give pleasure to the other, than to receive it.

I have considered, thus far, the effects on the pleasures and benefits of the marriage union which depend on the mere unlikeness between the wife and the husband: but the evil tendency is prodigiously aggravated when the unlikeness is inferiority. Mere unlikeness, when it only means difference of good qualities, may be more a benefit in the way of mutual improvement, than a drawback from comfort. When each emulates, and desires and endeavours to acquire, the other's peculiar qualities the difference does not produce diversity of interest, but increased identity of it, and makes each still more valuable to the other. But when one is much the inferior of the two in mental ability and cultivation, and is not actively attempting by the other's aid to rise to the other's level, the whole influence of the connexion upon the development of the superior of the two is deteriorating: and still more so in a tolerably happy marriage than in an unhappy one. It is not with impunity that the superior in intellect shuts himself up with an inferior, and elects that inferior for his chosen, and sole completely intimate, associate. Any society which is not improving is deteriorating: and the more so, the closer and more familiar it is. Even a really superior man almost always begins to deteriorate when he is habitually (as the phrase is) king of his company: and in his most habitual company the husband who has a wife inferior to him is always so. While his self-satisfaction is incessantly ministered to on the one hand, on the other he insensibly imbibes the modes of feeling, and of looking at things, which belong to a more vulgar or a more limited mind than his own. This evil differs from many of those which have hitherto been dwelt on, by being an increasing one. The association of men with women in daily life is much closer and more complete than it ever was before. Men's life is more domestic. Formerly, their pleasures and chosen occupations were among men, and in men's company: their wives had but a fragment of their lives. At the present time, the progress of civilisation, and the turn of opinion against the rough amusements and convivial excesses which formerly occupied most men in their hours of relaxation—together with (it must be said) the improved tone of modern feeling as to the reciprocity of duty which binds the husband towards the wife—have thrown the man very much more upon home and its inmates, for his personal and social pleasures: while the kind and degree of improvement which has been made in women's education, has made them in some degree capable of being his companions in ideas and mental taste, while leaving them, in most cases, still hopelessly inferior to him. His desire of mental communion is thus in general satisfied by a communion from which he learns nothing. An unimproving and unstimulating companionship is substituted for (what he might otherwise have been obliged to seek) the society of his equals in powers and his fellows in the higher pursuits. We see, accordingly, that young men of the greatest promise generally cease to improve as soon as they marry, and, not improving, inevitably degenerate. If the wife does not push the husband forward, she always holds him back. He ceases to care for what she does not care for; he no longer desires, and ends by disliking and shunning, society congenial to his former aspirations, and which would now shame his falling-off from them; his higher faculties both of mind and heart cease to be called into activity. And this change coinciding with the new and selfish interests which are created by the family, after a few years he differs in no material respect from those who have never had wishes for anything but the common vanities and the common pecuniary objects.

What marriage may be in the case of two persons of cultivated faculties, identical in opinions and purposes, between whom there exists that best kind of equality, similarity of powers and capacities with reciprocal superiority in them—so that each can enjoy the luxury of looking up to the other, and can have alternately the pleasure of leading and of being led in the path of development—I will not attempt to describe. To those who can conceive it, there is no need; to those who cannot, it would appear the dream of an enthusiast. But I maintain, with the profoundest conviction, that this, and this only, is the ideal of marriage; and that all opinions, customs, and institutions which favour any other notion of it, or turn the conceptions and aspirations connected with it into any other direction, by whatever pretences they may be coloured, are relics of primitive barbarism. The moral regeneration of mankind will only really commence, when the most fundamental of the social relations is placed under the rule of equal justice, and when human beings learn to cultivate their strongest sympathy with an equal in rights and in cultivation.

Thus far, the benefits which it has appeared that the world would gain by ceasing to make sex a disqualification for privileges and a badge of subjection, are social rather than individual; consisting in an increase of the general fund of thinking and acting power, and an improvement in the general conditions of the association of men with women. But it would be a grievous understatement of the case to omit the most direct benefit of all, the unspeakable gain in private happiness to the liberated half of the species; the difference to them between a life of subjection to the will of others, and a life of rational freedom. After the primary necessities of food and raiment, freedom is the first and strongest want of human nature. While mankind are lawless, their desire is for lawless freedom. When they have learnt to understand the meaning of duty and the value of reason, they incline more and more to be guided and restrained by these in the exercise of their freedom; but they do not therefore desire freedom less; they do not become disposed to accept the will of other people as the representative and interpreter of those guiding principles. On the contrary, the communities in which the reason has been most cultivated, and in which the idea of social duty has been most powerful, are those which have most strongly asserted the freedom of action of the individual—the liberty of each to govern his conduct by his own feelings of

duty, and by such laws and social restraints as his own conscience can subscribe to.

He who would rightly appreciate the worth of personal independence as an element of happiness, should consider the value he himself puts upon it as an ingredient of his own. There is no subject on which there is a greater habitual difference of judgment between a man judging for himself, and the same man judging for other people. When he hears others complaining that they are not allowed freedom of action—that their own will has not sufficient influence in the regulation of their affairs—his inclination is, to ask, what are their grievances? what positive damage they sustain? and in what respect they consider their affairs to be mismanaged? and if they fail to make out, in answer to these questions, what appears to him a sufficient case, he turns a deaf ear, and regards their complaint as the fanciful querulousness of people whom nothing reasonable will satisfy. But he has a quite different standard of judgment when he is deciding for himself. Then, the most unexceptionable administration of his interests by a tutor set over him, does not satisfy his feelings: his personal exclusion from the deciding authority appears itself the greatest grievance of all, rendering it superfluous even to enter into the question of mismanagement. It is the same with nations. What citizen of a free country would listen to any offers of good and skilful administration, in return for the abdication of freedom? Even if he could believe that good and skilful administration can exist among a people ruled by a will not their own, would not the consciousness of working out their own destiny under their own moral responsibility be a compensation to his feelings for great rudeness and imperfection in the details of public affairs? Let him rest assured that whatever he feels on this point, women feel in a fully equal degree. Whatever has been said or written, from the time of Herodotus to the present, of the ennobling influence of free government—the nerve and spring which it gives to all the faculties, the larger and higher objects which it presents to the intellect and feelings, the more unselfish public spirit, and calmer and broader views of duty, that it engenders, and the generally loftier platform on which it elevates the individual as a moral, spiritual, and social being—is every particle as true of women as of men. Are these things no important part of individual happiness? Let any man call to mind what he himself felt on emerging from boyhood—from the tutelage and control of even loved and affectionate elders—and entering upon the responsibilities of manhood. Was it not like the physical effect of taking off a heavy weight, or releasing him from obstructive, even if not otherwise painful, bonds? Did he not feel twice as much alive, twice as much a human being, as before? And does he imagine that women have none of these feelings? But it is a striking fact, that the satisfactions and mortifications of personal pride, though all in all to most men when the case is their own, have less allowance made for them in the case of other people, and are less listened to as a ground or a justification of conduct, than any other natural human feelings; perhaps because men compliment them in their own case with the names of so many other qualities, that they are seldom conscious how mighty an influence these feelings exercise in their own lives. No less large and powerful is their part, we may assure ourselves, in the lives and feelings of women. Women are schooled into suppressing them in their most natural and most healthy direction, but the internal principle remains, in a different outward form. An active and energetic mind, if denied liberty, will seek for power: refused the command of itself, it will assert its personality by attempting to control others. To allow to any human beings no existence of their own but what depends on others, is giving far too high a premium on bending others to their purposes. Where liberty cannot be hoped for, and power can, power becomes the grand object of human desire; those to whom others will not leave the undisturbed management of their own affairs, will compensate themselves, if they can, by meddling for their own purposes with the affairs of others. Hence also women's passion for personal beauty, and dress and display; and all the evils that flow from it, in the way of mischievous luxury and social immorality. The love of power

and the love of liberty are in eternal antagonism. Where there is least liberty, the passion for power is the most ardent and unscrupulous. The desire of power over others can only cease to be a depraving agency among mankind, when each of them individually is able to do without it: which can only be where respect for liberty in the personal concerns of each is an established principle.

But it is not only through the sentiment of personal dignity, that the free direction and disposal of their own faculties is a source of individual happiness, and to be fettered and restricted in it, a source of unhappiness, to human beings, and not least to women. There is nothing, after disease, indigence, and guilt, so fatal to the pleasurable enjoyment of life as the want of a worthy outlet for the active faculties. Women who have the cares of a family, and while they have the cares of a family, have this outlet, and it generally suffices for them: but what of the greatly increasing number of women, who have had no opportunity of exercising the vocation which they are mocked by telling them is their proper one? What of the women whose children have been lost to them by death or distance, or have grown up, married, and formed homes of their own? There are abundant examples of men who, after a life engrossed by business, retire with a competency to the enjoyment, as they hope, of rest, but to whom, as they are unable to acquire new interests and excitements that can replace the old, the change to a life of inactivity brings ennui, melancholy, and premature death. Yet no one thinks of the parallel case of so many worthy and devoted women, who, having paid what they are told is their debt to society—having brought up a family blamelessly to manhood and womanhood—having kept a house as long as they had a house needing to be kept—are deserted by the sole occupation for which they have fitted themselves; and remain with undiminished activity but with no employment for it, unless perhaps a daughter or daughter-in-law is willing to abdicate in their favour the discharge of the same functions in her younger household. Surely a hard lot for the old age of those who have worthily discharged, as long as it was given to them to discharge, what the world accounts their only social duty. Of such women, and of those others to whom this duty has not been committed at all—many of whom pine through life with the consciousness of thwarted vocations, and activities which are not suffered to expand—the only resources, speaking generally, are religion and charity. But their religion, though it may be one of feeling, and of ceremonial observance, cannot be a religion of action, unless in the form of charity. For charity many of them are by nature admirably fitted; but to practise it usefully, or even without doing mischief, requires the education, the manifold preparation, the knowledge and the thinking powers, of a skilful administrator. There are few of the administrative functions of government for which a person would not be fit, who is fit to bestow charity usefully. In this as in other cases (pre-eminently in that of the education of children), the duties permitted to women cannot be performed properly, without their being trained for duties which, to the great loss of society, are not permitted to them. And here let me notice the singular way in which the question of women's disabilities is frequently presented to view, by those who find it easier to draw a ludicrous picture of what they do not like, than to answer the arguments for it. When it is suggested that women's executive capacities and prudent counsels might sometimes be found valuable in affairs of State, these lovers of fun hold up to the ridicule of the world, as sitting in Parliament or in the Cabinet, girls in their teens, or young wives of two or three and twenty, transported bodily, exactly as they are, from the drawing-room to the House of Commons. They forget that males are not usually selected at this early age for a seat in Parliament, or for responsible political functions. Common sense would tell them that if such trusts were confided to women, it would be to such as having no special vocation for married life, or preferring another employment of their faculties (as many women even now prefer to marriage some of the few honourable occupations within their reach), have spent the best years of their youth in attempting to qualify themselves for the pursuits in which they desire to engage; or

still more frequently perhaps, widows or wives of forty or fifty, by whom the knowledge of life and faculty of government which they have acquired in their families, could by the aid of appropriate studies be made available on a less contracted scale. There is no country of Europe in which the ablest men have not frequently experienced, and keenly appreciated, the value of the advice and help of clever and experienced women of the world, in the attainment both of private and of public objects; and there are important matters of public administration to which few men are equally competent with such women; among others, the detailed control of expenditure. But what we are now discussing is not the need which society has of the services of women in public business, but the dull and hopeless life to which it so often condemns them, by forbidding them to exercise the practical abilities which many of them are conscious of, in any wider field than one which to some of them never was, and to others is no longer, open. If there is anything vitally important to the happiness of human beings, it is that they should relish their habitual pursuit. This requisite of an enjoyable life is very imperfectly granted, or altogether denied, to a large part of mankind; and by its absence many a life is a failure, which is provided, in appearance, with every requisite of success. But if circumstances which society is not yet skilful enough to overcome, render such failures often for the present inevitable, society need not itself inflict them. The injudiciousness of parents, a youth's own inexperience, or the absence of external opportunities for the congenial vocation, and their presence for an uncongenial, condemn numbers of men to pass their lives in doing one thing reluctantly and ill, when there are other things which they could have done well and happily. But on women this sentence is imposed by actual law, and by customs equivalent to law. What, in unenlightened societies, colour, race, religion, or in the case of a conquered country, nationality, are to some men, sex is to all women; a peremptory exclusion from almost all honourable occupations, but either such as cannot be fulfilled by others, or such as those others do not think worthy of their acceptance. Sufferings arising from causes of this nature usually meet with so little sympathy, that few persons are aware of the great amount of unhappiness even now produced by the feeling of a wasted life. The case will be even more frequent, as increased cultivation creates a greater and greater disproportion between the ideas and faculties—of women, and the scope which society allows to their activity.

When we consider the positive evil caused to the disqualified half of the human race by their disqualification—first in the loss of the most inspiriting and elevating kind of personal enjoyment, and next in the weariness, disappointment, and profound dissatisfaction with life, which are so often the substitute for it; one feels that among all the lessons which men require for carrying on the struggle against the inevitable imperfections of their lot on earth, there is no lesson which they more need, than not to add to the evils which nature inflicts, by their jealous and prejudiced restrictions on one another. Their vain fears only substitute other and worse evils for those which they are idly apprehensive of: while every restraint on the freedom of conduct of any of their human fellow-creatures (otherwise than by making them responsible for any evil actually caused by it), dries up *pro tanto* the principal fountain of human happiness, and leaves the species less rich, to an inappreciable degree, in all that makes life valuable to the individual human being.

DISCUSSION QUESTIONS

1. Why does Mill think that the system involving the subordination of women to men has endured for so long? How does he account for the apparent acquiescence of women to their own subordination?

2. Why does Mill think that any argument that takes some claim about the nature of women as a premise is problematic? Evaluate his claim.

3. Explain why Chapter IV is a utilitarian argument against laws that subordinate women to men. Is it an effective utilitarian argument? Why or why not?

4. How might Mill use his Harm Principle to attempt to undermine a system of subordination? Would an appeal to the Harm Principle be effective? Why or why not?

53

SEX, FREEDOM, AND MARRIAGE
Bowers v. Hardwick[1]
(1986)

In deciding *Bowers*, the Supreme
Court of the United States upheld the
constitutionality of a "sodomy law"
that prohibited oral and anal sex
between consenting adults.
In its decision, the Court decided
to focus on the issue of sodomy
between homosexuals.

SOURCE

478 U.S. 186 (U.S. Supreme Court).

After being charged with violating the Georgia
statute criminalizing sodomy by committing that
act with another adult male in the bedroom of his
home, respondent Hardwick (respondent) brought
suit in Federal District Court, challenging the constitutionality of the statute insofar as it criminalized
consensual sodomy. The court granted the defendants' motion to dismiss for failure to state a claim.
The Court of Appeals reversed and remanded, holding that the Georgia statute violated respondent's
fundamental rights.

Held: The Georgia statute is constitutional.

Opinion of the Court

In August 1982, respondent Hardwick (hereafter
respondent) was charged with violating the Georgia
statute criminalizing sodomy by committing that act
with another adult male in the bedroom of respondent's home. After a preliminary hearing, the District
Attorney decided not to present the matter to the
grand jury unless further evidence developed.

Respondent then brought suit in the Federal
District Court, challenging the constitutionality
of the statute insofar as it criminalized consensual sodomy. He asserted that he was a practicing homosexual, that the Georgia sodomy statute,
as administered by the defendants, placed him in

---

[1] [The original citations have been omitted.]

imminent danger of arrest, and that the statute for several reasons violates the Federal Constitution. The District Court granted the defendants' motion to dismiss for failure to state a claim, relying on *Doe v. Commonwealth's Attorney for the City of Richmond*, which this Court summarily affirmed.

A divided panel of the Court of Appeals for the Eleventh Circuit reversed. The court first held that, because Doe was distinguishable and in any event had been undermined by later decisions, our summary affirmance in that case did not require affirmance of the District Court. Relying on our decisions in *Griswold v. Connecticut* and *Roe v. Wade*, the court went on to hold that the Georgia statute violated respondent's fundamental rights because his homosexual activity is a private and intimate association that is beyond the reach of state regulation by reason of the Ninth Amendment and the Due Process Clause of the Fourteenth Amendment. The case was remanded for trial, at which, to prevail, the State would have to prove that the statute is supported by a compelling interest and is the most narrowly drawn means of achieving that end.

Because other Courts of Appeals have arrived at judgments contrary to that of the Eleventh Circuit in this case, we granted the Attorney General's petition for *certiorari* questioning the holding that the sodomy statute violates the fundamental rights of homosexuals. We agree with petitioner that the Court of Appeals erred, and hence reverse its judgment.

This case does not require a judgment on whether laws against sodomy between consenting adults in general, or between homosexuals in particular, are wise or desirable. It raises no question about the right or propriety of state legislative decisions to repeal their laws that criminalize homosexual sodomy, or of state-court decisions invalidating those laws on state constitutional grounds. The issue presented is whether the Federal Constitution confers a fundamental right upon homosexuals to engage in sodomy and hence invalidates the laws of the many States that still make such conduct illegal and have done so for a very long time. The

case also calls for some judgment about the limits of the Court's role in carrying out its constitutional mandate.

We first register our disagreement with the Court of Appeals and with respondent that the Court's prior cases have construed the Constitution to confer a right of privacy that extends to homosexual sodomy and for all intents and purposes have decided this case. The reach of this line of cases was sketched in *Carey v. Population Services International. Pierce v. Society of Sisters* and *Meyer v. Nebraska* were described as dealing with child rearing and education; *Prince v. Massachusetts* with family relationships; *Skinner v. Oklahoma ex rel. Williamson* with procreation; *Loving v. Virginia* with marriage; *Griswold v. Connecticut* and *Eisenstadt v. Baird* with contraception; and *Roe v. Wade* with abortion. The latter three cases were interpreted as construing the Due Process Clause of the Fourteenth Amendment to confer a fundamental individual right to decide whether or not to beget or bear a child.

Accepting the decisions in these cases and the above description of them, we think it evident that none of the rights announced in those cases bears any resemblance to the claimed constitutional right of homosexuals to engage in acts of sodomy that is asserted in this case. No connection between family, marriage, or procreation on the one hand and homosexual activity on the other has been demonstrated, either by the Court of Appeals or by respondent. Moreover, any claim that these cases nevertheless stand for the proposition that any kind of private sexual conduct between consenting adults is constitutionally insulated from state proscription is unsupportable. Indeed, the Court's opinion in Carey twice asserted that the privacy right, which the Griswold line of cases found to be one of the protections provided by the Due Process Clause, did not reach so far.

Precedent aside, however, respondent would have us announce, as the Court of Appeals did, a fundamental right to engage in homosexual sodomy. This we are quite unwilling to do. It is true that despite the language of the Due Process Clauses of the Fifth and Fourteenth Amendments, which appears to focus only on the processes by which life, liberty, or property is taken, the cases are legion in which those Clauses have been interpreted to have substantive content, subsuming rights that to a great extent are immune from federal or state regulation or proscription. Among such cases are those recognizing rights that have little or no textual support in the constitutional language. *Meyer*, *Prince*, and *Pierce* fall in this category, as do the privacy cases from *Griswold* to *Carey*.

Striving to assure itself and the public that announcing rights not readily identifiable in the Constitution's text involves much more than the imposition of the Justices' own choice of values on the States and the Federal Government, the Court has sought to identify the nature of the rights qualifying for heightened judicial protection. In *Palko v. Connecticut* it was said that this category includes those fundamental liberties that are "implicit in the concept of ordered liberty," such that "neither liberty nor justice would exist if [they] were sacrificed." A different description of fundamental liberties appeared in *Moore v. East Cleveland*, where they are characterized as those liberties that are "deeply rooted in this Nation's history and tradition."

It is obvious to us that neither of these formulations would extend a fundamental right to homosexuals to engage in acts of consensual sodomy. Proscriptions against that conduct have ancient roots. Sodomy was a criminal offense at common law and was forbidden by the laws of the original States when they ratified the Bill of Rights. In 1868, when the Fourteenth Amendment was ratified, all but 5 of the 37 States in the Union had criminal sodomy laws. In fact, until 1961, all 50 States outlawed sodomy, and today, 24 States and the District of Columbia continue to provide criminal penalties for sodomy performed in private and between consenting adults. Against this background, to claim that a right to engage in such conduct is "deeply rooted in this Nation's history and tradition" or "implicit in the concept of ordered liberty" is, at best, facetious.

Nor are we inclined to take a more expansive view of our authority to discover new fundamental rights imbedded in the Due Process Clause. The Court is most vulnerable and comes nearest to illegitimacy when it deals with judge-made constitutional law having little or no cognizable roots in the language or design of the Constitution. That this is so was painfully demonstrated by the face-off between the Executive and the Court in the 1930's, which resulted in the repudiation of much of the substantive gloss that the Court had placed on the Due Process Clauses of the Fifth and Fourteenth Amendments. There should be, therefore, great resistance to expand the substantive reach of those Clauses, particularly if it requires redefining the category of rights deemed to be fundamental. Otherwise, the Judiciary necessarily takes to itself further authority to govern the country without express constitutional authority. The claimed right pressed on us today falls far short of overcoming this resistance.

Respondent, however, asserts that the result should be different where the homosexual conduct occurs in the privacy of the home. He relies on *Stanley v. Georgia*, where the Court held that the First Amendment prevents conviction for possessing and reading obscene material in the privacy of one's home: "If the First Amendment means anything, it means that a State has no business telling a man, sitting alone in his house, what books he may read or what films he may watch."

Stanley did protect conduct that would not have been protected outside the home, and it partially prevented the enforcement of state obscenity laws; but the decision was firmly grounded in the First Amendment. The right pressed upon us here has no similar support in the text of the Constitution, and it does not qualify for recognition under the prevailing principles for construing the Fourteenth Amendment. Its limits are also difficult to discern. Plainly enough, otherwise illegal conduct is not always immunized whenever it occurs in the home. Victimless crimes, such as the possession and use of illegal drugs, do not escape the law where they are committed at home. *Stanley* itself recognized that its holding offered no protection for the possession in the home of drugs, firearms, or stolen goods. And if respondent's submission is limited to the voluntary sexual conduct between consenting adults, it would be difficult, except by fiat, to limit the claimed right to homosexual conduct while leaving exposed to prosecution adultery, incest, and other sexual crimes even though they are committed in the home. We are unwilling to start down that road.

Even if the conduct at issue here is not a fundamental right, respondent asserts that there must be a rational basis for the law and that there is none in this case other than the presumed belief of a majority of the electorate in Georgia that homosexual sodomy is immoral and unacceptable. This is said to be an inadequate rationale to support the law. The law, however, is constantly based on notions of morality, and if all laws representing essentially moral choices are to be invalidated under the Due Process Clause, the courts will be very busy indeed. Even respondent makes no such claim, but insists that majority sentiments about the morality of homosexuality should be declared inadequate. We do not agree, and are unpersuaded that the sodomy laws of some 25 States should be invalidated on this basis.

Accordingly, the judgment of the Court of Appeals is reversed.

Chief Justice Burger's Concurring Opinion

I join the Court's opinion, but I write separately to underscore my view that in constitutional terms there is no such thing as a fundamental right to commit homosexual sodomy.

As the Court notes, the proscriptions against sodomy have very "ancient roots." Decisions of individuals relating to homosexual conduct have been subject to state intervention throughout the history of Western civilization. Condemnation of those practices is firmly rooted in Judeao-Christian moral and ethical standards. Homosexual sodomy was a capital crime under Roman law. During the English Reformation when powers of the ecclesiastical courts were transferred to the King's Courts,

the first English statute criminalizing sodomy was passed. Blackstone described "the infamous crime against nature" as an offense of "deeper malignity" than rape, a heinous act "the very mention of which is a disgrace to human nature," and "a crime not fit to be named." The common law of England, including its prohibition of sodomy, became the received law of Georgia and the other Colonies. In 1816 the Georgia Legislature passed the statute at issue here, and that statute has been continuously in force in one form or another since that time. To hold that the act of homosexual sodomy is somehow protected as a fundamental right would be to cast aside millennia of moral teaching.

This is essentially not a question of personal "preferences" but rather of the legislative authority of the State. I find nothing in the Constitution depriving a State of the power to enact the statute challenged here.

Justice Blackmun's Dissenting Opinion

This case is no more about "a fundamental right to engage in homosexual sodomy," as the Court purports to declare, than *Stanley v. Georgia* was about a fundamental right to watch obscene movies, or *Katz v. United States* was about a fundamental right to place interstate bets from a telephone booth. Rather, this case is about "the most comprehensive of rights and the right most valued by civilized men," namely, "the right to be let alone."

The statute at issue, Ga. Code Ann. 16-6-2 (1984), denies individuals the right to decide for themselves whether to engage in particular forms of private, consensual sexual activity. The Court concludes that 16-6-2 is valid essentially because "the laws of … many States … still make such conduct illegal and have done so for a very long time." But the fact that the moral judgments expressed by statutes like 16-6-2 may be "'natural and familiar … ought not to conclude our judgment upon the question whether statutes embodying them conflict with the Constitution of the United States.'" Like Justice Holmes, I believe that "[i]t is revolting to have no better reason for a rule of law than that so it was laid down in the time of Henry IV. It is still more revolting if the grounds upon which it was laid down have vanished long since, and the rule simply persists from blind imitation of the past." I believe we must analyze respondent Hardwick's claim in the light of the values that underlie the constitutional right to privacy. If that right means anything, it means that, before Georgia can prosecute its citizens for making choices about the most intimate aspects of their lives, it must do more than assert that the choice they have made is an "abominable crime not fit to be named among Christians."

I

In its haste to reverse the Court of Appeals and hold that the Constitution does not "confe[r] a fundamental right upon homosexuals to engage in sodomy," the Court relegates the actual statute being challenged to a footnote and ignores the procedural posture of the case before it. A fair reading of the statute and of the complaint clearly reveals that the majority has distorted the question this case presents.

First, the Court's almost obsessive focus on homosexual activity is particularly hard to justify in light of the broad language Georgia has used. Unlike the Court, the Georgia Legislature has not proceeded on the assumption that homosexuals are so different from other citizens that their lives may be controlled in a way that would not be tolerated if it limited the choices of those other citizens. Rather, Georgia has provided that "[a] person commits the offense of sodomy when he performs or submits to any sexual act involving the sex organs of one person and the mouth or anus of another." The sex or status of the persons who engage in the act is irrelevant as a matter of state law. In fact, to the extent I can discern a legislative purpose for Georgia's 1968 enactment of 16-6-2, that purpose seems to have been to broaden the coverage of the law to reach heterosexual as well as homosexual activity. I therefore see no basis for the Court's decision to treat this case as an "as applied" challenge to 16-6-2, or for Georgia's attempt, both in its brief and at oral argument, to defend 16-6-2 solely on the grounds that it prohibits homosexual

activity. Michael Hardwick's standing may rest in significant part on Georgia's apparent willingness to enforce against homosexuals a law it seems not to have any desire to enforce against heterosexuals. But his claim that 16-6-2 involves an unconstitutional intrusion into his privacy and his right of intimate association does not depend in any way on his sexual orientation.

Second, I disagree with the Court's refusal to consider whether 16-6-2 runs afoul of the Eighth or Ninth Amendments or the Equal Protection Clause of the Fourteenth Amendment. Respondent's complaint expressly invoked the Ninth Amendment, and he relied heavily before this Court on *Griswold v. Connecticut*, which identifies that Amendment as one of the specific constitutional provisions giving "life and substance" to our understanding of privacy. More importantly, the procedural posture of the case requires that we affirm the Court of Appeals' judgment if there is any ground on which respondent may be entitled to relief. This case is before us on petitioner's motion to dismiss for failure to state a claim. It is a well-settled principle of law that "a complaint should not be dismissed merely because a plaintiff's allegations do not support the particular legal theory he advances, for the court is under a duty to examine the complaint to determine if the allegations provide for relief on any possible theory." Thus, even if respondent did not advance claims based on the Eighth or Ninth Amendments, or on the Equal Protection Clause, his complaint should not be dismissed if any of those provisions could entitle him to relief. I need not reach either the Eighth Amendment or the Equal Protection Clause issues because I believe that Hardwick has stated a cognizable claim that 16-6-2 interferes with constitutionally protected interests in privacy and freedom of intimate association. But neither the Eighth Amendment nor the Equal Protection Clause is so clearly irrelevant that a claim resting on either provision should be peremptorily dismissed. The Court's cramped reading of the issue before it makes for a short opinion, but it does little to make for a persuasive one.

II

"Our cases long have recognized that the Constitution embodies a promise that a certain private sphere of individual liberty will be kept largely beyond the reach of government." In construing the right to privacy, the Court has proceeded along two somewhat distinct, albeit complementary, lines. First, it has recognized a privacy interest with reference to certain decisions that are properly for the individual to make. Second, it has recognized a privacy interest with reference to certain places without regard for the particular activities in which the individuals who occupy them are engaged. The case before us implicates both the decisional and the spatial aspects of the right to privacy.

A

The Court concludes today that none of our prior cases dealing with various decisions that individuals are entitled to make free of governmental interference "bears any resemblance to the claimed constitutional right of homosexuals to engage in acts of sodomy that is asserted in this case." While it is true that these cases may be characterized by their connection to protection of the family, the Court's conclusion that they extend no further than this boundary ignores the warning in *Moore v. East Cleveland* against "clos[ing] our eyes to the basic reasons why certain rights associated with the family have been accorded shelter under the Fourteenth Amendment's Due Process Clause." We protect those rights not because they contribute, in some direct and material way, to the general public welfare, but because they form so central a part of an individual's life. "[T]he concept of privacy embodies the 'moral fact that a person belongs to himself and not others nor to society as a whole.'" And so we protect the decision whether to marry precisely because marriage "is an association that promotes a way of life, not causes; a harmony in living, not political faiths; a bilateral loyalty, not commercial or social projects." We protect the decision whether to have a child because parenthood alters so dramatically an individual's self-definition, not because of demographic considerations or the Bible's command to be fruitful and multiply. And we protect the family because it contributes so powerfully to the happiness of individuals, not because of a preference for stereotypical households. The Court recognized in *Roberts* that the "ability independently to define one's identity that is central to any concept of liberty" cannot truly be exercised in a vacuum; we all depend on the "emotional enrichment from close ties with others."

Only the most willful blindness could obscure the fact that sexual intimacy is "a sensitive, key relationship of human existence, central to family life, community welfare, and the development of human personality." The fact that individuals define themselves in a significant way through their intimate sexual relationships with others suggests, in a Nation as diverse as ours, that there may be many "right" ways of conducting those relationships, and that much of the richness of a relationship will come from the freedom an individual has to choose the form and nature of these intensely personal bonds.

In a variety of circumstances we have recognized that a necessary corollary of giving individuals freedom to choose how to conduct their lives is acceptance of the fact that different individuals will make different choices. For example, in holding that the clearly important state interest in public education should give way to a competing claim by the Amish to the effect that extended formal schooling threatened their way of life, the Court declared: "There can be no assumption that today's majority is 'right' and the Amish and others like them are 'wrong.' A way of life that is odd or even erratic but interferes with no rights or interests of others is not to be condemned because it is different." The Court claims that its decision today merely refuses to recognize a fundamental right to engage in homosexual sodomy; what the Court really has refused to recognize is the fundamental interest all individuals have in controlling the nature of their intimate associations with others.

B

The behavior for which Hardwick faces prosecution occurred in his own home, a place to which the Fourth Amendment attaches special significance. The Court's treatment of this aspect of the case is symptomatic of its overall refusal to consider the broad principles that have informed our treatment of privacy in specific cases. Just as the right to privacy is more than the mere aggregation of a number of entitlements to engage in specific behavior, so too, protecting the physical integrity of the home is more than merely a means of protecting specific activities that often take place there. Even when our understanding of the contours of the right to privacy depends on "reference to a 'place,'" "the essence of a Fourth Amendment violation is 'not the breaking of [a person's] doors, and the rummaging of his drawers,' but rather is 'the invasion of his indefensible right of personal security, personal liberty and private property.'"

The Court's interpretation of the pivotal case of *Stanley v. Georgia*, is entirely unconvincing. *Stanley* held that Georgia's undoubted power to punish the public distribution of constitutionally unprotected, obscene material did not permit the State to punish the private possession of such material. According to the majority here, *Stanley* relied entirely on the First Amendment, and thus, it is claimed, sheds no light on cases not involving printed materials. But that is not what *Stanley* said. Rather, the *Stanley* Court anchored its holding in the Fourth Amendment's special protection for the individual in his home:

"'The makers of our Constitution undertook to secure conditions favorable to the pursuit of happiness. They recognized the significance of man's spiritual nature, of his feelings and of his intellect. They knew that only a part of the pain, pleasure and satisfactions of life are to be found in material things. They sought to protect Americans in their beliefs, their thoughts, their emotions and their sensations.'

[...]

"These are the rights that appellant is asserting in the case before us. He is asserting the right to read or observe what he pleases—the right to

satisfy his intellectual and emotional needs in the privacy of his own home." [*Stanley*]

... "If obscene material unprotected by the First Amendment in itself carried with it a 'penumbra' of constitutionally protected privacy, this Court would not have found it necessary to decide Stanley on the narrow basis of the 'privacy of the home,' which was hardly more than a reaffirmation that 'a man's home is his castle'" [*Paris Adult Theatre I. v. Slaton* 413 U.S. 49 (1973)]. "The right of the people to be secure in their ... houses," expressly guaranteed by the Fourth Amendment, is perhaps the most "textual" of the various constitutional provisions that inform our understanding of the right to privacy, and thus I cannot agree with the Court's statement that "[t]he right pressed upon us here has no ... support in the text of the Constitution." Indeed, the right of an individual to conduct intimate relationships in the intimacy of his or her own home seems to me to be the heart of the Constitution's protection of privacy.

III

The Court's failure to comprehend the magnitude of the liberty interests at stake in this case leads it to slight the question whether petitioner, on behalf of the State, has justified Georgia's infringement on these interests. I believe that neither of the two general justifications for 16-6-2 that petitioner has advanced warrants dismissing respondent's challenge for failure to state a claim.

First, petitioner asserts that the acts made criminal by the statute may have serious adverse consequences for "the general public health and welfare," such as spreading communicable diseases or fostering other criminal activity. Inasmuch as this case was dismissed by the District Court on the pleading, it is not surprising that the record before us is barren of any evidence to support petitioner's claim. In light of the state of the record, I see no justification for the Court's attempt to equate the private, consensual sexual activity at issue here with the "possession in the home of drugs, firearms, or stolen goods," to which *Stanley* refused to extend its protection. None of the behavior so mentioned in *Stanley* can properly be viewed as "[v]ictimless": drugs and weapons are inherently dangerous, and for property to be "stolen," someone must have been wrongfully deprived of it. Nothing in the record before the Court provides any justification for finding the activity forbidden by 16-6-2 to be physically dangerous, either to the persons engaged in it or to others.

The core of petitioner's defense of 16-6-2, however, is that respondent and others who engage in the conduct prohibited by 16-6-2 interfere with Georgia's exercise of the "'right of the Nation and of the States to maintain a decent society.'" Essentially, petitioner argues, and the Court agrees, that the fact that the acts described in 16-6-2 "for hundreds of years, if not thousands, have been uniformly condemned as immoral" is a sufficient reason to permit a State to ban them today.

I cannot agree that either the length of time a majority has held its convictions or the passions with which it defends them can withdraw legislation from this Court's security. As Justice Jackson wrote so eloquently for the Court in *West Virginia Board of Education v. Barnette*, "we apply the limitations of the Constitution with no fear that freedom to be intellectually and spiritually diverse or even contrary will disintegrate the social organization.... [F]reedom to differ is not limited to things that do not matter much. That would be a mere shadow of freedom. The test of its substance is the right to differ as to things that touch the heart of the existing order." It is precisely because the issue raised by this case touches the heart of what makes individuals what they are that we should be especially sensitive to the rights of those whose choices upset the majority.

The assertion that "traditional Judeo-Christian values proscribe" the conduct involved, cannot provide an adequate justification for 16-6-2. That certain, but by no means all, religious groups condemn the behavior at issue gives the State no license to impose their judgments on the entire citizenry. The legitimacy of secular legislation depends instead on whether the State can advance some justification for its law beyond its conformity to religious doctrine. Thus, far from buttressing his case,

petitioner's invocation of Leviticus, Romans, St. Thomas Aquinas, and sodomy's heretical status during the Middle Ages undermines his suggestion that 16-6-2 represents a legitimate use of secular coercive power. A State can no more punish private behavior because of religious intolerance than it can punish such behavior because of racial animus. "The Constitution cannot control such prejudices, but neither can it tolerate them. Private biases may be outside the reach of the law, but the law cannot, directly or indirectly, give them effect." No matter how uncomfortable a certain group may make the majority of this Court, we have held that "[m]ere public intolerance or animosity cannot constitutionally justify the deprivation of a person's physical liberty."

Nor can 16-6-2 be justified as a "morally neutral" exercise of Georgia's power to "protect the public environment." Certainly, some private behavior can affect the fabric of society as a whole. Reasonable people may differ about whether particular sexual acts are moral or immoral, but "we have ample evidence for believing that people will not abandon morality, will not think any better of murder, cruelty and dishonesty, merely because some private sexual practice which they abominate is not punished by the law" (H.L.A. Hart, *Immorality and Treason*, reprinted in *The Law as Literature* 220, 225 [L. Blom-Cooper ed. 1961]). Petitioner and the Court fail to see the difference between laws that protect public sensibilities and those that enforce private morality. Statutes banning public sexual activity are entirely consistent with protecting the individual's liberty interest in decisions concerning sexual relations: the same recognition that those decisions are intensely private which justifies protecting them from governmental interference can justify protecting individuals from unwilling exposure to the sexual activities of others. But the mere fact that intimate behavior may be punished when it takes place in public cannot dictate how States can regulate intimate behavior that occurs in intimate places....

This case involves no real interference with the rights of others, for the mere knowledge that other individuals do not adhere to one's value system cannot be a legally cognizable interest, let alone an interest that can justify invading the houses, hearts, and minds of citizens who choose to live their lives differently.

IV

It took but three years for the Court to see the error in its analysis in *Minersville School District v. Gobitis* and to recognize that the threat to national cohesion posed by a refusal to salute the flag was vastly outweighed by the threat to those same values posed by compelling such a salute. I can only hope that here, too, the Court soon will reconsider its analysis and conclude that depriving individuals of the right to choose for themselves how to conduct their intimate relationships poses a far greater threat to the values most deeply rooted in our Nation's history than tolerance of nonconformity could ever do. Because I think the Court today betrays those values, I dissent.

DISCUSSION QUESTIONS

1. Sodomy laws are an attempt by the state to proscribe certain behavior that is believed to be immoral. What are your initial thoughts regarding these laws? Explain either why you think they are legitimate or illegitimate.

2. On what grounds does the court distinguish a citizen's right to view pornographic material (which is taken to be immoral) from a citizen's "right" to engage in sexual acts outlawed by sodomy statutes?

3. What grounds does the court appeal to in ruling that homosexuals do not have a right to engage in sodomy?

4. What characteristics of a putative "right" qualify it as deserving of judicial protection?

54

SEX, FREEDOM, AND MARRIAGE
Lawrence v. Texas (1998)

In September 1998, petitioners John Lawrence and Tyron Garner were arrested and charged with violating Texas's anti-sodomy statute. Upon conviction, their case ultimately reached the US Supreme Court, where they argued that the Texas statute was unconstitutional. The petitioners successfully argued that intimate consensual sexual conduct was a liberty protected by the Due Process Clause of the Fourteenth Amendment.

SOURCE

539 U.S. 558 (U.S. Supreme Court).

Responding to a reported weapons disturbance in a private residence, Houston police entered petitioner Lawrence's apartment and saw him and another adult man, petitioner Garner, engaging in a private, consensual sexual act. Petitioners were arrested and convicted of deviate sexual intercourse in violation of a Texas statute forbidding two persons of the same sex to engage in certain intimate sexual conduct. In affirming, the State Court of Appeals held, *inter alia*, that the statute was not unconstitutional under the Due Process Clause of the Fourteenth Amendment. The court considered *Bowers v. Hardwick* [see reading 53] controlling on that point.

Held: The Texas statute making it a crime for two persons of the same sex to engage in certain intimate sexual conduct violates the Due Process Clause.

Opinion of the Court

Liberty protects the person from unwarranted government intrusions into a dwelling or other private places. In our tradition the State is not omnipresent in the home. And there are other spheres of our lives and existence, outside the home, where the State should not be a dominant presence. Freedom extends beyond spatial bounds. Liberty presumes an autonomy of self that includes freedom of thought, belief, expression, and certain intimate conduct. The instant case involves liberty of the person both in its spatial and more transcendent dimensions.

I

The question before the Court is the validity of a Texas statute making it a crime for two persons of the same sex to engage in certain intimate sexual conduct.

In Houston, Texas, officers of the Harris County Police Department were dispatched to a private residence in response to a reported weapons disturbance. They entered an apartment where one of the petitioners, John Geddes Lawrence, resided. The right of the police to enter does not seem to have been questioned. The officers observed Lawrence and another man, Tyron Garner, engaging in a sexual act. The two petitioners were arrested, held in custody over night, and charged and convicted before a Justice of the Peace.

The complaints described their crime as "deviate sexual intercourse, namely anal sex, with a member of the same sex (man)." It provides: "A person commits an offense if he engages in deviate sexual intercourse with another individual of the same sex." The statute defines "[d]eviate sexual intercourse" as follows:

(A) any contact between any part of the genitals of one person and the mouth or anus of another person; or
(B) the penetration of the genitals or the anus of another person with an object.

The petitioners exercised their right to a trial *de novo* in Harris County Criminal Court. They challenged the statute as a violation of the Equal Protection Clause of the Fourteenth Amendment and of a like provision of the Texas Constitution. Those contentions were rejected. The petitioners, having entered a plea of *nolo contendere*, were each fined $200 and assessed court costs of $141.25.

The Court of Appeals for the Texas Fourteenth District considered the petitioners' federal constitutional arguments under both the Equal Protection and Due Process Clauses of the Fourteenth Amendment. After hearing the case *en banc* the court, in a divided opinion, rejected the constitutional arguments and affirmed the convictions. The majority opinion indicates that the Court of Appeals considered our decision in *Bowers v. Hardwick* to be controlling on the federal due process aspect of the case. *Bowers* then being authoritative, this was proper.

We granted *certiorari*, 537 U.S. 1044 (2002), to consider three questions:

1. Whether Petitioners' criminal convictions under the Texas "Homosexual Conduct" law—which criminalizes sexual intimacy by same-sex couples, but not identical behavior by different-sex couples—violate the Fourteenth Amendment guarantee of equal protection of laws?
2. Whether Petitioners' criminal convictions for adult consensual sexual intimacy in the home violate their vital interests in liberty and privacy protected by the Due Process Clause of the Fourteenth Amendment?
3. Whether *Bowers v. Hardwick*, 478 U.S. 186 (1986), should be overruled?

[...]

II

We conclude the case should be resolved by determining whether the petitioners were free as adults to engage in the private conduct in the exercise of their liberty under the Due Process Clause of the Fourteenth Amendment to the Constitution. For this inquiry we deem it necessary to reconsider the Court's holding in Bowers.

There are broad statements of the substantive reach of liberty under the Due Process Clause in earlier cases, including *Pierce v. Society of Sisters* and *Meyer v. Nebraska*; but the most pertinent beginning point is our decision in *Griswold v. Connecticut*.

In *Griswold* the Court invalidated a state law prohibiting the use of drugs or devices of contraception and counseling or aiding and abetting the use of contraceptives. The Court described the protected interest as a right to privacy and placed emphasis on the marriage relation and the protected space of the marital bedroom.

After *Griswold* it was established that the right to make certain decisions regarding sexual conduct extends beyond the marital relationship. In *Eisenstadt v. Baird*, the Court invalidated a law prohibiting the distribution of contraceptives to unmarried persons. The case was decided under the Equal Protection Clause, but with respect to unmarried persons, the Court went on to state the fundamental proposition that the law impaired the exercise of their personal rights. It quoted from the statement of the Court of Appeals finding the law to be in conflict with fundamental human rights, and it followed with this statement of its own:

"It is true that in *Griswold* the right of privacy in question inhered in the marital relationship…. If the right of privacy means anything, it is the right of the individual, married or single, to be free from unwarranted governmental intrusion into matters so fundamentally affecting a person as the decision whether to bear or beget a child."

The opinions in *Griswold* and *Eisenstadt* were part of the background for the decision in *Roe v. Wade*. As is well known, the case involved a challenge to the Texas law prohibiting abortions, but the laws of other States were affected as well. Although the Court held the woman's rights were not absolute, her right to elect an abortion did have real and substantial protection as an exercise of her liberty under the Due Process Clause. The Court cited cases that protect spatial freedom and cases that go well beyond it. *Roe* recognized the right of a woman to make certain fundamental decisions affecting her destiny and confirmed once more that the protection of liberty under the Due Process Clause has a substantive dimension of fundamental significance in defining the rights of the person.

In *Carey v. Population Services Int'l*, the Court confronted a New York law forbidding sale or distribution of contraceptive devices to persons under 16 years of age. Although there was no single opinion for the Court, the law was invalidated. Both

Eisenstadt and *Carey*, as well as the holding and rationale in *Roe*, confirmed that the reasoning of *Griswold* could not be confined to the protection of rights of married adults. This was the state of the law with respect to some of the most relevant cases when the Court considered *Bowers v. Hardwick*.

The facts in *Bowers* had some similarities to the instant case. A police officer, whose right to enter seems not to have been in question, observed Hardwick, in his own bedroom, engaging in intimate sexual conduct with another adult male. The conduct was in violation of a Georgia statute making it a criminal offense to engage in sodomy. One difference between the two cases is that the Georgia statute prohibited the conduct whether or not the participants were of the same sex, while the Texas statute, as we have seen, applies only to participants of the same sex. Hardwick was not prosecuted, but he brought an action in federal court to declare the state statute invalid. He alleged he was a practicing homosexual and that the criminal prohibition violated rights guaranteed to him by the Constitution. The Court, in an opinion by Justice White, sustained the Georgia law….

The Court began its substantive discussion in *Bowers* as follows: "The issue presented is whether the Federal Constitution confers a fundamental right upon homosexuals to engage in sodomy and hence invalidates the laws of the many States that still make such conduct illegal and have done so for a very long time." That statement, we now conclude, discloses the Court's own failure to appreciate the extent of the liberty at stake. To say that the issue in *Bowers* was simply the right to engage in certain sexual conduct demeans the claim the individual put forward, just as it would demean a married couple were it to be said marriage is simply about the right to have sexual intercourse. The laws involved in *Bowers* and here are, to be sure, statutes that purport to do no more than prohibit a particular sexual act. Their penalties and purposes, though, have more far-reaching consequences, touching upon the most private human conduct, sexual behavior, and in the most private of places, the home. The statutes do seek to control a personal relationship that, whether or not entitled to formal recognition in the law, is within the liberty of persons to choose without being punished as criminals.

This, as a general rule, should counsel against attempts by the State, or a court, to define the meaning of the relationship or to set its boundaries absent injury to a person or abuse of an institution the law protects. It suffices for us to acknowledge that adults may choose to enter upon this relationship in the confines of their homes and their own private lives and still retain their dignity as free persons. When sexuality finds overt expression in intimate conduct with another person, the conduct can be but one element in a personal bond that is more enduring. The liberty protected by the Constitution allows homosexual persons the right to make this choice.

Having misapprehended the claim of liberty there presented to it, and thus stating the claim to be whether there is a fundamental right to engage in consensual sodomy, the *Bowers* Court said: "Proscriptions against that conduct have ancient roots." In academic writings, and in many of the scholarly *amicus* briefs filed to assist the Court in this case, there are fundamental criticisms of the historical premises relied upon by the majority and concurring opinions in *Bowers*. We need not enter this debate in the attempt to reach a definitive historical judgment, but the following considerations counsel against adopting the definitive conclusions upon which Bowers placed such reliance.

At the outset it should be noted that there is no longstanding history in this country of laws directed at homosexual conduct as a distinct matter. Beginning in colonial times there were prohibitions of sodomy derived from the English criminal laws passed in the first instance by the Reformation Parliament of 1533. The English prohibition was understood to include relations between men and women as well as relations between men and men.... Nineteenth-century commentators similarly read American sodomy, buggery, and crime-against-nature statutes as criminalizing certain relations between men and women and between men and

men. The absence of legal prohibitions focusing on homosexual conduct may be explained in part by noting that according to some scholars the concept of the homosexual as a distinct category of person did not emerge until the late 19th century. Thus early American sodomy laws were not directed at homosexuals as such but instead sought to prohibit nonprocreative sexual activity more generally. This does not suggest approval of homosexual conduct. It does tend to show that this particular form of conduct was not thought of as a separate category from like conduct between heterosexual persons.

Laws prohibiting sodomy do not seem to have been enforced against consenting adults acting in private. A substantial number of sodomy prosecutions and convictions for which there are surviving records were for predatory acts against those who could not or did not consent, as in the case of a minor or the victim of an assault. As to these, one purpose for the prohibitions was to ensure there would be no lack of coverage if a predator committed a sexual assault that did not constitute rape as defined by the criminal law. Thus the model sodomy indictments presented in a 19th-century treatise, addressed the predatory acts of an adult man against a minor girl or minor boy. Instead of targeting relations between consenting adults in private, 19th-century sodomy prosecutions typically involved relations between men and minor girls or minor boys, relations between adults involving force, relations between adults implicating disparity in status, or relations between men and animals.

To the extent that there were any prosecutions for the acts in question, 19th-century evidence rules imposed a burden that would make a conviction more difficult to obtain even taking into account the problems always inherent in prosecuting consensual acts committed in private. Under then-prevailing standards, a man could not be convicted of sodomy based upon testimony of a consenting partner, because the partner was considered an accomplice. A partner's testimony, however, was admissible if he or she had not consented to the act or was a minor, and therefore incapable of consent. The rule may explain in part the infrequency

UNIT II: E. Applications

of these prosecutions. In all events that infrequency makes it difficult to say that society approved of a rigorous and systematic punishment of the consensual acts committed in private and by adults. The longstanding criminal prohibition of homosexual sodomy upon which the *Bowers* decision placed such reliance is as consistent with a general condemnation of nonprocreative sex as it is with an established tradition of prosecuting acts because of their homosexual character.

The policy of punishing consenting adults for private acts was not much discussed in the early legal literature. We can infer that one reason for this was the very private nature of the conduct. Despite the absence of prosecutions, there may have been periods in which there was public criticism of homosexuals as such and an insistence that the criminal laws be enforced to discourage their practices. But far from possessing "ancient roots," American laws targeting same-sex couples did not develop until the last third of the 20th century. The reported decisions concerning the prosecution of consensual, homosexual sodomy between adults for the years 1880–1995 are not always clear in the details, but a significant number involved conduct in a public place.

It was not until the 1970's that any State singled out same-sex relations for criminal prosecution, and only nine States have done so. Post-*Bowers* even some of these States did not adhere to the policy of suppressing homosexual conduct. Over the course of the last decades, States with same-sex prohibitions have moved toward abolishing them.

In summary, the historical grounds relied upon in *Bowers* are more complex than the majority opinion and the concurring opinion by Chief Justice Burger indicate. Their historical premises are not without doubt and, at the very least, are overstated.

It must be acknowledged, of course, that the Court in Bowers was making the broader point that for centuries there have been powerful voices to condemn homosexual conduct as immoral. The condemnation has been shaped by religious beliefs, conceptions of right and acceptable behavior, and respect for the traditional family. For many persons these are not trivial concerns but profound and deep convictions accepted as ethical and moral principles to which they aspire and which thus determine the course of their lives. These considerations do not answer the question before us, however. The issue is whether the majority may use the power of the State to enforce these views on the whole society through operation of the criminal law. "Our obligation is to define the liberty of all, not to mandate our own moral code."

Chief Justice Burger joined the opinion for the Court in Bowers and further explained his views as follows: "Decisions of individuals relating to homosexual conduct have been subject to state intervention throughout the history of Western civilization. Condemnation of those practices is firmly rooted in Judeao-Christian moral and ethical standards." As with Justice White's assumptions about history, scholarship casts some doubt on the sweeping nature of the statement by Chief Justice Burger as it pertains to private homosexual conduct between consenting adults. In all events we think that our laws and traditions in the past half century are of most relevance here. These references show an emerging awareness that liberty gives substantial protection to adult persons in deciding how to conduct their private lives in matters pertaining to sex. "[H]istory and tradition are the starting point but not in all cases the ending point of the substantive due process inquiry."

This emerging recognition should have been apparent when Bowers was decided. In 1955 the American Law Institute promulgated the Model Penal Code and made clear that it did not recommend or provide for "criminal penalties for consensual sexual relations conducted in private." It justified its decision on three grounds: (1) The prohibitions undermined respect for the law by penalizing conduct many people engaged in; (2) the statutes regulated private conduct not harmful to others; and (3) the laws were arbitrarily enforced and thus invited the danger of blackmail. In 1961 Illinois changed its laws to conform to the Model Penal Code. Other States soon followed.

In *Bowers* the Court referred to the fact that before 1961 all 50 States had outlawed sodomy, and that at the time of the Court's decision 24 States and the District of Columbia had sodomy laws. Justice Powell pointed out that these prohibitions often were being ignored, however. Georgia, for instance, had not sought to enforce its law for decades.

The sweeping references by Chief Justice Burger to the history of Western civilization and to Judeo-Christian moral and ethical standards did not take account of other authorities pointing in an opposite direction. A committee advising the British Parliament recommended in 1957 repeal of laws punishing homosexual conduct. *The Wolfenden Report: Report of the Committee on Homosexual Offenses and Prostitution* (1963). Parliament enacted the substance of those recommendations 10 years later.

Of even more importance, almost five years before *Bowers* was decided the European Court of Human Rights considered a case with parallels to *Bowers* and to today's case. An adult male resident in Northern Ireland alleged he was a practicing homosexual who desired to engage in consensual homosexual conduct. The laws of Northern Ireland forbade him that right. He alleged that he had been questioned, his home had been searched, and he feared criminal prosecution. The court held that the laws proscribing the conduct were invalid under the European Convention on Human Rights. Authoritative in all countries that are members of the Council of Europe (21 nations then, 45 nations now), the decision is at odds with the premise in *Bowers* that the claim put forward was insubstantial in our Western civilization.

In our own constitutional system the deficiencies in *Bowers* became even more apparent in the years following its announcement. The 25 States with laws prohibiting the relevant conduct referenced in the *Bowers* decision are reduced now to 13, of which 4 enforce their laws only against homosexual conduct. In those States where sodomy is still proscribed, whether for same-sex or heterosexual conduct, there is a pattern of nonenforcement with respect to consenting adults acting in private. The State of Texas admitted in 1994 that as of that date it had not prosecuted anyone under those circumstances.

Two principal cases decided after Bowers cast its holding into even more doubt. In *Planned Parenthood of Southeastern Pa. v. Casey*, the Court reaffirmed the substantive force of the liberty protected by the Due Process Clause. The *Casey* decision again confirmed that our laws and tradition afford constitutional protection to personal decisions relating to marriage, procreation, contraception, family relationships, child rearing, and education. In explaining the respect the Constitution demands for the autonomy of the person in making these choices, we stated as follows:

> These matters, involving the most intimate and personal choices a person may make in a lifetime, choices central to personal dignity and autonomy, are central to the liberty protected by the Fourteenth Amendment. At the heart of liberty is the right to define one's own concept of existence, of meaning, of the universe, and of the mystery of human life. Beliefs about these matters could not define the attributes of personhood were they formed under compulsion of the State.

Persons in a homosexual relationship may seek autonomy for these purposes, just as heterosexual persons do. The decision in *Bowers* would deny them this right.

The second post-*Bowers* case of principal relevance is *Romer v. Evans*. There the Court struck down class-based legislation directed at homosexuals as a violation of the Equal Protection Clause. *Romer* invalidated an amendment to Colorado's constitution which named as a solitary class persons who were homosexuals, lesbians, or bisexual either by "orientation, conduct, practices or relationships," and deprived them of protection under state antidiscrimination laws. We concluded that the provision was "born of animosity toward the class of persons affected" and further that it had no rational relation to a legitimate governmental purpose.

As an alternative argument in this case, counsel for the petitioners and some *amici* contend that *Romer* provides the basis for declaring the Texas statute invalid under the Equal Protection Clause. That is a tenable argument, but we conclude the instant case requires us to address whether *Bowers* itself has continuing validity. Were we to hold the statute invalid under the Equal Protection Clause some might question whether a prohibition would be valid if drawn differently, say, to prohibit the conduct both between same-sex and different-sex participants.

Equality of treatment and the due process right to demand respect for conduct protected by the substantive guarantee of liberty are linked in important respects, and a decision on the latter point advances both interests. If protected conduct is made criminal and the law which does so remains unexamined for its substantive validity, its stigma might remain even if it were not enforceable as drawn for equal protection reasons. When homosexual conduct is made criminal by the law of the State, that declaration in and of itself is an invitation to subject homosexual persons to discrimination both in the public and in the private spheres. The central holding of Bowers has been brought in question by this case, and it should be addressed. Its continuance as precedent demeans the lives of homosexual persons.

The stigma this criminal statute imposes, moreover, is not trivial. The offense, to be sure, is but a class C misdemeanor, a minor offense in the Texas legal system. Still, it remains a criminal offense with all that imports for the dignity of the persons charged. The petitioners will bear on their record the history of their criminal convictions. Just this Term we rejected various challenges to state laws requiring the registration of sex offenders. We are advised that if Texas convicted an adult for private, consensual homosexual conduct under the statute here in question the convicted person would come within the registration laws of a least four States were he or she to be subject to their jurisdiction.

This underscores the consequential nature of the punishment and the state-sponsored condemnation attendant to the criminal prohibition. Furthermore, the Texas criminal conviction carries with it the other collateral consequences always following a conviction, such as notations on job application forms, to mention but one example.

The foundations of *Bowers* have sustained serious erosion from our recent decisions in *Casey* and *Romer*. When our precedent has been thus weakened, criticism from other sources is of greater significance. In the United States, criticism of *Bowers* has been substantial and continuing, disapproving of its reasoning in all respects, not just as to its historical assumptions. The courts of five different States have declined to follow it in interpreting provisions in their own state constitutions parallel to the Due Process Clause of the Fourteenth Amendment.

To the extent *Bowers* relied on values we share with a wider civilization, it should be noted that the reasoning and holding in *Bowers* have been rejected elsewhere. The European Court of Human Rights has followed not *Bowers* but its own decision in *Dudgeon v. United Kingdom*. Other nations, too, have taken action consistent with an affirmation of the protected right of homosexual adults to engage in intimate, consensual conduct. The right the petitioners seek in this case has been accepted as an integral part of human freedom in many other countries. There has been no showing that in this country the governmental interest in circumscribing personal choice is somehow more legitimate or urgent.

The doctrine of *stare decisis* is essential to the respect accorded to the judgments of the Court and to the stability of the law. It is not, however, an inexorable command. In *Casey* we noted that when a Court is asked to overrule a precedent recognizing a constitutional liberty interest, individual or societal reliance on the existence of that liberty cautions with particular strength against reversing course. The holding in *Bowers*, however, has not induced detrimental reliance comparable to some instances where recognized individual rights are involved. Indeed, there has been no individual or societal reliance on *Bowers* of the sort that could counsel against overturning its holding once there are compelling reasons to do so. *Bowers* itself causes uncertainty, for the precedents before and after its issuance contradict its central holding.

The rationale of *Bowers* does not withstand careful analysis. In his dissenting opinion in *Bowers* Justice Stevens came to these conclusions:

> Our prior cases make two propositions abundantly clear. First, the fact that the governing majority in a State has traditionally viewed a particular practice as immoral is not a sufficient reason for upholding a law prohibiting the practice; neither history nor tradition could save a law prohibiting miscegenation from constitutional attack. Second, individual decisions by married persons, concerning the intimacies of their physical relationship, even when not intended to produce offspring, are a form of "liberty" protected by the Due Process Clause of the Fourteenth Amendment. Moreover, this protection extends to intimate choices by unmarried as well as married persons.

Justice Stevens' analysis, in our view, should have been controlling in *Bowers* and should control here.

Bowers was not correct when it was decided, and it is not correct today. It ought not to remain binding precedent. *Bowers v. Hardwick* should be and now is overruled.

The present case does not involve minors. It does not involve persons who might be injured or coerced or who are situated in relationships where consent might not easily be refused. It does not involve public conduct or prostitution. It does not involve whether the government must give formal recognition to any relationship that homosexual persons seek to enter. The case does involve two adults who, with full and mutual consent from each other, engaged in sexual practices common to a homosexual lifestyle. The petitioners are entitled to respect for their private lives. The State cannot demean their existence or control their destiny by making their private sexual conduct a crime. Their right to liberty under the Due Process Clause gives them the full right to engage in their conduct without intervention of the government. "It is a promise of the Constitution that there is a realm of personal liberty which the government may not enter." The Texas statute furthers no legitimate state interest which can justify its intrusion into the personal and private life of the individual.

Had those who drew and ratified the Due Process Clauses of the Fifth Amendment or the Fourteenth Amendment known the components of liberty in its manifold possibilities, they might have been more specific. They did not presume to have this insight. They knew times can blind us to certain truths and later generations can see that laws once thought necessary and proper in fact serve only to oppress. As the Constitution endures, persons in every generation can invoke its principles in their own search for greater freedom.

The judgment of the Court of Appeals for the Texas Fourteenth District is reversed, and the case is remanded for further proceedings not inconsistent with this opinion.

It is so ordered.

DISCUSSION QUESTIONS

1. How does the court distinguish between the issues presented in this case and those presented in *Bowers v. Hardwick*? In other words, what are the legal differences between the two cases?

2. Do you think that considerations of personal dignity should play into deciding whether a supposed moral matter should be legislated? Why or why not? In what ways?

55

SEX, FREEDOM, AND MARRIAGE
Susan Moller Okin, selection from *Justice, Gender, and the Family* (1991)

Susan Moller Okin (1946–2004) was the Marta Sutton Weeks Professor of Ethics in Society at Stanford University. In her book *Justice, Gender, and the Family*, she criticizes traditional familial structures as sources of injustice that manifest and perpetuate gender inequalities.

SOURCE

… [M]ajor contemporary theories of social justice pay little or no attention to the multiple inequalities between the sexes that exist in our society, or to the social construct of gender that gives rise to them. Neither mainstream theorists of social justice nor their critics (with rare exceptions) have paid much attention to the internal inequalities of the family. They have considered the family relevant for one or more of only three reasons. Some have seen the family as an impediment to equal opportunity. But the focus of such discussion has been on class differentials among families, not on sex differentials within them. While the concern that the family limits equality of opportunity is legitimate and serious, theorists who raise it have neglected the issue of gender and therefore ignored important aspects of the problem. Those who discuss the family without paying attention to the inequalities between the sexes are blind to the fact that the gendered family radically limits the equality of opportunity of women and girls of all classes—as well as that of poor and working-class children of both sexes. Nor do they see that the vulnerability of women that results from the patriarchal structure and practices of the family *exacerbates* the problem that the inequality of families poses for children's equality of opportunity. As I shall argue in this chapter, with the increasing prevalence of families headed by a single female, children suffer more and more from the economic vulnerability of women.

Second and third, theorists of justice and their critics have tended either to idealize the family as a social institution for which justice is not an appropriate virtue, or, more rarely, to see it as an important locus for the development of a sense of justice. I have disagreed strongly with those who, focusing on an idealized vision of the family, perceive it as governed by virtues nobler than justice and therefore not needing to be subjected to the tests of justice to which we subject other fundamental social institutions. While I strongly support the *hope* that families will live up to nobler virtues, such as generosity, I contend that in the real world, justice is a virtue of fundamental importance for families, as for other basic social institutions. An important sphere of distribution of many social goods, from the material to the intangible, the family has a history of distributing these goods in far from just ways. It is also, as some who have overlooked its internal justice have acknowledged, a sphere of life that is absolutely crucial to moral development. If justice cannot at least begin to be learned from our day-to-day experience within the family, it seems futile to expect that it can be developed anywhere else. Without just families, how can we expect to have a just society? In particular, if the relationship between a child's parents does not conform to basic standards of justice, how can we expect that child to grow up with a sense of justice?

It is not easy to think about marriage and the family in terms of justice. For one thing, we do not readily associate justice with intimacy, which is one reason some theorists idealize the family. For another, some of the issues that theories of justice are most concerned with, such as differences in standards of living, do not obviously apply among members of a family. Though it is certainly not the case in some countries, in the United States the members of a family, so long as they live together, usually share the same standard of living. As we shall see, however, the question of who earns the family's income, or how the earning of this income is shared, has a great deal to do with the distribution of power and influence within the family, including decisions on how to spend this income. It also affects the distribution of other benefits, including basic security. Here, I present and analyze the facts of contemporary gender-structured marriage in the light of theories about power and vulnerability and the issues of justice they inevitably raise. I argue that marriage and the family, as currently practiced in our society, are unjust institutions. They constitute the pivot of a societal system of gender that renders women vulnerable to dependency, exploitation, and abuse. When we look seriously at the distribution between husbands and wives of such critical social goods as work (paid and unpaid), power, prestige, self-esteem, opportunities for self-development, and both physical and economic security, we find socially constructed inequalities between them, right down the list.

The argument I shall make in this chapter depends to a large extent on contemporary empirical data, but also reflects the insights of two theorists, moral philosopher Robert Goodin and economist Albert O. Hirschman. Neither has used his argument to make a case about the injustice of the gender-structured family, but both establish convincing arguments about power and vulnerability that will be invaluable as we look at the data about contemporary marriage.

Goodin's recent book *Protecting the Vulnerable* discusses the significance of socially caused vulnerability for issues of justice. He argues that, over and above the general moral obligations that we owe to persons in general, "we bear special responsibilities for protecting those who are particularly vulnerable to us."[1] His major aim is to justify the obligations that welfare states place on citizens to contribute to the welfare of their more vulnerable fellow citizens. But his arguments can be employed to shed light on a number of other important social issues and institutions, including marriage and the family. Goodin's theory is particularly applicable to marriage because of its concern not only with the protection of the vulnerable but also with the moral status of vulnerability itself. Obviously, as

---

[1] Robert E. Goodin, *Protecting the Vulnerable: A Reanalysis of Our Social Responsibilities* (Chicago: University of Chicago Press, 1985), p. 109.

he acknowledges, some cases of vulnerability have a large natural component—the vulnerability of infants, for example, although societies differ in how they allocate responsibility for protecting infants. Some instances of vulnerability that may at first appear "natural," such as those caused by illness, are in fact to a greater or lesser extent due to existing social arrangements.[1] And "some of the most important dependencies and vulnerabilities seem to be *almost wholly social in character*."[2] Because asymmetric vulnerabilities create social obligations, which may fail to be fulfilled, and because they open up opportunities for exploitation, Goodin argues that insofar as they are alterable they are morally unacceptable and should be minimized. In this, he cites and follows the example of John Stuart Mill, who complained about the "great error of reformers and philanthropists [who] … nibble at the consequences of unjust power, instead of redressing the injustice itself."[3] As Goodin concludes, in the case of those vulnerabilities that are "created, shaped, or sustained by current social arrangements … [w]hile we should always strive to protect the vulnerable, we should also strive to reduce the latter sort of vulnerabilities insofar as they render the vulnerable liable to exploitation."[4]

One of the tests Goodin employs to distinguish such unacceptable relations of asymmetrical vulnerability from acceptable relations of mutual vulnerability or interdependence is to examine the respective capacities of the two parties to withdraw from the relationship. Even if there is some degree of inequality in a relationship, Goodin says, "as long as the subordinate party can withdraw without severe cost, the superordinate cannot exploit him."[5]

As I shall argue, the differing respective potentials for satisfactory withdrawal from the relationship is one of the major elements making marriage, in its typical contemporary manifestations in the United States, a morally unacceptable relationship of vulnerability.

The idea that the mutuality or asymmetry of a relationship can be measured by the relative capacities of the parties to withdraw from it has been developed extensively by Albert O. Hirschman, in two books written many years apart. In his 1970 book entitled *Exit, Voice and Loyalty*, Hirschman makes a convincing connection between the influence of voice by members within groups or institutions and the feasibility of their exit from them. There is a complex relation, he argues, between voice and exit. On the one hand, if the exit option is readily available, this will "tend to *atrophy the development of the art of voice*." Thus, for example, dissatisfied customers who can easily purchase equivalent goods from another firm are unlikely to expend their energies voicing complaints. On the other hand, the nonexistence or low feasibility of the exit option can impede the effectiveness of voice, since the threat of exit, whether explicit or implicit, is an important means of making one's voice influential. Thus "voice is not only handicapped when exit is possible, but also, though in a quite different way, when it is not." Because of this, for members' influence to be most effective, "there should be the possibility of exit, but exit should not be too easy or too attractive."[6] Hirschman concludes that institutions that deter exit by exacting a very high price for it, thereby rendering implausible the threat of exit, also repress the use and effectiveness of voice. Thus both potential modes of influence for combating deterioration are rendered ineffective.

Because the subjects of Hirschman's attention in *Exit, Voice and Loyalty* are groups with many

---

[1] Ibid., p. 190.

[2] Ibid., p. 191; emphasis added.

[3] John Stuart Mill, *Principles of Political Economy* (London: Parker and Son, 1848), bk. 5, chap. 11, sec. 9; cited by Goodin, *Protecting the Vulnerable*, p. 189.

[4] Goodin, *Protecting the Vulnerable*, p. xi. This succinct statement of the position (argued in his chap. 7) is quoted from Goodin's synopsis.

[5] Ibid., p. 197.

[6] Albert O. Hirschman, *Exit, Voice and Loyalty: Responses to Decline in Firms, Organizations, and States* (Cambridge, MA: Harvard University Press, 1970), pp. 43, 55, 83.

members, his concern is with the power of the members vis-à-vis the institution, rather than with the power of the members relative to one another. But in the case of a two-member institution, such as marriage, special dynamics result from the fact that exit by one partner does not just weaken the institution, but rather results in its dissolution. Whether or not the other party wishes to exit, he or she is effectively expelled by the decision of the other to exit. Because of this, the *relative* potential of the exit option for the two parties is crucial for the relationship's power structure. Hirschman had made this argument, in the context of international relations, in a book published twenty-five years earlier, *National Power and the Structure of Foreign Trade*.[1] There he showed how state A can increase its power and influence by developing trading relations with state B, which is more dependent on the continuance of the trading relationship than A is. While both states gain something from the trade, the gain is far more significant in the one case than in the other. Thus the less dependent state's greater potential for exiting unharmed from the relationship gives it power or influence that can be used (through explicit or implicit threat of withdrawal) to make the more dependent state comply with its wishes. In addition, because of the extent of its dependence on trade with A, state B may alter its economic behavior in such a way that it becomes even more dependent on its trade with A.[2] Power (which may or may not remain latent) is likely to result from dependencies that are entered into voluntarily by parties whose initial resources and options differ, and in such circumstances the asymmetric dependency may well increase in the course of the relationship.

How do these principles apply to marriage? Few people would disagree with the statement that marriage involves, in some respects, especially emotionally, *mutual* vulnerability and dependence. It is, clearly, also a relationship in which some aspects of unequal vulnerability are not determined along sex lines. For example, spouses may vary in the extent of their love for and emotional dependence on each other; it is certainly not the case that wives always love their husbands more than they are loved by them, or vice versa. Nevertheless, as we shall see, in crucial respects gender-structured marriage *involves women in a cycle of socially caused and distinctly asymmetric vulnerability*. The division of labor within marriage (except in rare cases) makes wives far more likely than husbands to be exploited both within the marital relationship and in the world of work outside the home. To a great extent and in numerous ways, contemporary women in our society are *made* vulnerable by marriage itself. They are first set up for vulnerability during their developing years by their personal (and socially reinforced) expectations that they will be the primary caretakers of children, and that in fulfilling this role they will need to try to attract and to keep the economic support of a man, to whose work life they will be expected to give priority. They are rendered vulnerable by the actual division of labor within almost all current marriages. They are disadvantaged at work by the fact that the world of wage work, including the professions, is still largely structured around the assumption that "workers" have wives at home. They are rendered far more vulnerable if they become the primary caretakers of children, and their vulnerability peaks if their marriages dissolve and they become single parents.

Part of the reason that many nonfeminist social theorists have failed to recognize this pattern is that they confuse the socially caused (and therefore avoidable) vulnerability of women with the largely natural (and therefore largely unavoidable) vulnerability of children. This goes along with the usually unargued and certainly unfounded assumption that women are inevitably the primary caretakers of children. But as I shall show, women are made vulnerable, both economically and socially, by the interconnected traditions of female responsibility for rearing children and female subordination

[1] Albert O. Hirschman, *National Power and the Structure of Foreign Trade* (Berkeley: University of California Press, 1945; expanded ed. 1980). See pp. vi–viii of the expanded edition for a summary of the original argument.

[2] Ibid., p. 31.

and dependence, of which both the history and the contemporary practices of marriage form a significant part.

It may be argued that it makes no sense to claim that something as ill defined and variable as "modern marriage" is unjust, since marriages and families take so many forms, and not all marriages result in the dependence and vulnerability of their female members. There is some validity to this objection, and I shall try to counter it by making qualifications and pointing out exceptions to some of the general points I shall make. Part of the peculiarity of contemporary marriage comes from its very lack of definition. The fact that society seems no longer to have any consensual view of the norm and expectations of marriage is particularly apparent from the gulf that exists between the continued *perception* of most men and women that it is still the primary responsibility of husbands to "provide for" their wives by participating in wage work and of wives to perform a range of unpaid "services" for their husbands, and the *fact* that most women, including mothers of small children, are both in the labor force *and* performing the vast majority of household duties. In addition, the persistent perception of the male as provider is irreconcilable with both the prevalence of separation and divorce and the fact that, more and more, women and children are not being provided for after divorce. Between the expectations and the frequent outcome lies an abyss that not only is unjust in itself but radically affects the ways in which people behave within marriage. There is no way to alleviate the continuing inequality of women without more clearly defining and also reforming marriage. It seems evident, both from the disagreements between traditionalists and feminists and from the discrepancy between people's expectations of marriage and what in fact often happens to those who enter into it that there exists no clear current consensus in this society about what marriage is or should be.

Marriage has a long history, and we live in its shadow. It is a clear case of Marx's notion that we make our history "under circumstances directly encountered, given and transmitted from the past."[1] Certainly, gender is central to the way most people think about marriage. A recent, detailed study of thousands of couples, of different types—married and unmarried, heterosexual, gay and lesbian—confirms the importance of gender to our concept of marriage. Philip Blumstein and Pepper Schwartz's findings in *American Couples* demonstrate how not only current family law but the traditional expectations of marriage influence the attitudes, expectations, and behavior of married couples. By contrast, the lack of expectations about gender, and the lack of history of the institution of marriage, allow gay and lesbian couples more freedom in ordering their lives together and more chance to do so in an egalitarian manner. As the study concludes: "First, while the heterosexual model offers more stability and certainty, it inhibits change, innovation, and *choice* regarding roles and task. Second, the heterosexual model, which provides so much efficiency, is predicated on the man's being the dominant partner." The unmarried couples interviewed did not, in general, assume so readily that one partner would be the primary economic provider or that they would pool their income and assets. Homosexual couples, because of the absence of both marriage and the "gender factor," made even fewer such assumptions than did cohabiting heterosexual couples. They were almost unanimous, for example, in refusing to assign to either partner the role of homemaker. By contrast, many of the married respondents still enthusiastically subscribed to the traditional female/male separation of household work from wage work. While the authors also found the more egalitarian, two-paycheck marriage "emerging," they conclude that "the force of the previous tradition still guides the behavior of most modern marriages."[2]

---

[1] Karl Marx, *The Eighteenth Brumaire of Louis Bonaparte*, in *Selected Works* (Moscow: Progress Publishers, 1969), vol. 2, p. 378.

[2] Philip Blumstein and Pepper Schwartz, *American Couples* (New York: Morrow, 1983), pp. 324, 115.

It is important to recollect, in this context, how recently white married women in the United States have begun to work outside the home in significant numbers. Black women have always worked, first as slaves, then mostly—until very recently—as domestic servants. But in 1860, only 15 percent of all women were in the paid labor force and, right up to World War II, wage work for married women was strongly disapproved of. In 1890, only 5 percent of married women were in the labor force, and by 1960 the rate of married women's labor force participation had still reached only 50 percent. Moreover, wage work has a history of extreme segregation by sex that is closely related to the traditional female role within marriage. The largest category of women workers were domestic servants as late as 1950, since which time clerical workers have outnumbered them. Service (mostly no longer domestic) is still very predominantly female work. Even the female dominated professions, such as nursing, grade-school teaching, and library work, have been "pink-collar labor ghettos [which] have historically discouraged high work ambitions that might detract from the pull of home and children." Like saleswomen and clerical workers, these female professionals "tend to arrive early in their 'careers' at a point above which they cannot expect to rise."[1] In sum, married women's wage work has a history of being exceptional, and women's wage work in general has been—as much of it still is—highly segregated and badly paid.

The traditional idea of sex-differentiated marital responsibility, with its provider-husband and domestic-wife roles, continues to be a strong influence on what men and women think and how they behave. Husbands, at least, tend to feel this way even when their wives do work outside the home; and when there is disagreement about whether the wife should work, it is more often the case that she wants to but that he does not want to "let" her. Thirty-four percent of the husbands and 25 percent of the wives surveyed by Blumstein and Schwartz did not think that couples should share the responsibility for earning a living. These percentages rise sharply when children are involved: 64 percent of husbands and 60 percent of wives did not think that the wife should be employed if a couple has small children.[2] Given the emphasis our society places on economic success, belief in the male provider role strongly reinforces the domination of men within marriage. Although, as we shall see, many wives actually work longer hours (counting paid and unpaid work) than their husbands, the fact that a husband's work is predominantly paid gives him not only status and prestige, both within and outside the marriage, but also a greater sense of entitlement. As a consequence, wives experiencing divorce, especially if they have been housewives and mothers throughout marriage, are likely to devalue their own contributions to the marriage and to discount their right to share its assets. "Many divorcing women still see the money their husbands have earned as 'his money.'"[3] In ongoing marriages too, it is not uncommon for husbands to use the fact that they are the primary breadwinners to enforce their views or wishes.[4]

Vulnerability by Anticipation of Marriage

In many respects, marriage is an institution whose tradition weighs upon those who enter into it. The cycle of women's vulnerability begins early, with their anticipation of marriage. Almost all women and men marry, but marriage has earlier and far greater impact on the lives and life choices of women than on those of men.[5] Socialization and the culture in general place more emphasis on marriage

---

[1] Quotations are from Kathleen Gerson, *Hard Choices: How Women Decide About Work, Career, and Motherhood* (Berkeley: University of California Press, 1985), p. 209.

[2] Blumstein and Schwartz, *American Couples*, pp. 52, 118–25, 560n2.

[3] Lenore J. Weitzman, *The Divorce Revolution: The Unexpected Social and Economic Consequences for Women and Children in America* (New York: The Free Press, 1985), pp. 315–16.

[4] Blumstein and Schwartz, *American Couples*, pp. 51–111 passim, esp. pp. 58–59, 82.

[5] [Suzanne M.] Bianchi and [Daphne] Spain, *American Women* [New York: Russell Sage, 1986], p. 2; U.S. Bureau of the Census, *Statistical Abstract of the U.S.: 1986* (Washington, DC: 1987), p. 40.

for girls than for boys and, although people have recently become less negative about remaining single, young women are more likely than young men to regard "having a good marriage and family life" as extremely important to them.[1] This fact, together with their expectation of being the parent primarily responsible for children, clearly affects women's decisions about the extent and field of education and training they will pursue, and their degree of purposiveness about careers. It is important to note that vulnerability by anticipation of marriage affects at least as adversely the futures of many women who do not marry as it affects those who do. This is particularly significant among disadvantaged groups, particularly poor urban black women, whose actual chances of marrying and being economically supported by a man are small (largely because of the high unemployment rate among the available men), but who are further burdened by growing up surrounded by a culture that still identifies femininity with this expectation.

Even though the proportion of young women who plan to be housewives exclusively has declined considerably, women's choices about work are significantly affected from an early age by their expectations about the effects of family life on their work and of work on their family life. As is well known, the participation of women in the labor force, especially women with small children, has continued to rise.[2] But, although a small minority of women are rapidly increasing the previously tiny percentages of women in the elite professions, the vast majority of women who work outside the home are still in low-paying jobs with little or no prospect of advancement. This fact is clearly related to girls' awareness of the complexity they are likely to face in combining work with family life.[3] As the authors of one study conclude: "the occupational aspirations and expectations of adolescents are highly differentiated by sex ... [and this] differentiation follows the pattern of sexual segregation which exists in the occupational structure." They found not only that the high school girls in their large-scale study were much less likely than the boys to aspire to the most prestigious occupations, but that the girls who had such aspirations displayed a much lower degree of confidence than the boys about being able to attain their goals.[4]

As the women Kathleen Gerson recently studied looked back on their girlhood considerations about the future, virtually all of them saw themselves as confronting a choice: *either* domesticity and motherhood *or* career.[5] Given the pervasiveness of sex-role socialization (including the mixed or negative messages that girls are often given about their future work lives), the actual obstacles that our social structures place in the way of working mothers, and the far greater responsibility, both psychological and practical, that is placed on mothers than on fathers for their children's welfare, it is not surprising that these women perceived a conflict between their own work interests and the interests of any children they might have. While many reacted against their own mothers' domestic lives, very few were able to imagine successfully combining motherhood with a career. And those who did generally avoided confronting the dilemmas they would have to face.[6] But most grew up with the belief that "a woman can

---

[1] Bianchi and Spain, *American Women*, p. 9, quoting Arland Thornton and Deborah Freedman, "Changing Attitudes Toward Marriage and Single Life," *Family Planning Perspectives* 14 (November–December 1982): 297–303.

[2] Victor Fuchs, *Women's Quest for Economic Equality* (Cambridge, MA: Harvard University Press, 1988), pp. 11–13, 77–78 (the 51 percent reported on p. 12 appears to be a misprint, since the 1983 figure was 53 percent); David Ellwood, *Poor Support: Poverty in the American Family* (New York: Basic Books, 1988), pp. 47–49.

[3] [Kathleen] Gerson, *Hard Choices*[: *How Women Decide About Work, Career, and Motherhood* (Berkeley: University of California Press, 1985)].

[4] [Margaret Mooney] Marini and [Ellen] Greenberger, "Sex Differences in Occupational Aspirations and Expectations," *Sociology of Work and Occupations* 5.2 (1978): 147–48, 157.

[5] Gerson, *Hard Choices*, esp. pp. 136–38.

[6] In Gerson's sample, only 14 percent of the respondents' own mothers had worked during their preschool years, and 46 percent had mothers who had never worked outside the home until their children left (p. 45). On avoidance of the conflict between wage work and motherhood, see Gerson, *Hard Choices*, pp. 64–65.

have either a career or children, but not both."[1] Not surprisingly, many of them, assuming that they would want to have children, followed educational and work paths that would readily accommodate the demands of being a primary parent. The only way that those who were career-oriented came to believe that they might avoid the difficult choice, and even attempt to combine their work with mothering, was by deciding to be trailblazers, rejecting strongly ingrained beliefs about the incompatibility of the two.

Needless to say, such a choice does not confront boys in their formative years. They assume—reasonably enough, given our traditions and present conditions and beliefs—that what is expected of them as husbands and fathers is that, by developing a solid work life, they will provide the primary financial support of the family. Men's situation can have its own strains, since those who feel trapped at work cannot opt for domesticity and gain as much support for this choice as a woman can. For those who become unemployed, the conflict of their experience with society's view of the male as provider can be particularly stressful. But boys do not experience the dilemma about work and family that girls do as they confront the choices that are crucial to their educations, future work lives and opportunities, and economic security.

When women envisage a future strongly influenced by the demands on them as wives and particularly as mothers, they are likely to embark on traditionally female fields of study and/or occupational paths. The typical route for women is still to finish their education with high school and to marry and have children in their early twenties, though a growing minority are continuing their education, establishing themselves in careers, and marrying later.[2] Some of those who are primarily family-oriented foresee their wage work as temporary or intermittent, while some envisage trying to combine some continued work in the marketplace with traditionally female family responsibilities. But

whether such women enter clerical, sales, or service work, or train for one of the predominantly female professions such as teaching or nursing, they are heading not only for the relatively more flexible hours or greater replaceability that most of these jobs afford but also for low pay, poor working conditions, and, above all, blocked mobility. In 1987, women who worked year-round at full-time jobs earned a median wage of $15,704—71 percent of the $22,204 earned by full-time working men. The fact that women's educational achievement is becoming equal to men's, through the level of master's degrees, is clearly affecting women's *participation* in the work force. But, though it could also potentially affect their earnings relative to men's, it has done so very little up to now, in part because the professional and service occupations that are more than two-thirds female—such as education, humanities, home economics, library science, and health science—are far worse paid than those that are still more than two-thirds male—such as science and engineering. Occupational sex segregation cancels out women's educational advances: in 1985, the average full-time working white woman with a college degree or higher earned $2,000 less than the average white man who had only a high-school diploma; and the average black woman with some college education earned slightly less than the average white man who had only an elementary school education.[3]

Regardless of educational achievement, women are far more likely than men to work in administrative support jobs, as a secretary, typist, or bookkeeper, for example, which in most cases hold no prospects for advancement. Almost 50 percent of employed women worked in this category in 1985, compared with fewer than 6 percent of men.[4] A study of workplaces during the late 1960s and the

[1] Ibid., p. 137.
[2] Bianchi and Spain, *American Women*, chaps. 1 and 4.

[3] *Women in the American Economy*, Current Population Reports, Special Studies, U.S. Department of Commerce, Bureau of the Census (Washington, DC: Government Printing Office, 1986).
[4] *Current Population Reports*, Population Profile of the United States 1984–85, U.S. Department of Commerce, Bureau of the Census.

1970s (*after* the 1963 Equal Pay Act and Title VII of the 1964 Civil Rights Act) found the sex segregation of specific jobs and occupational ladders in both manufacturing and nonmanufacturing firms to be so pervasive that more than 90 percent of women would have had to change jobs in order for women to share equally the same job titles as men. Frequently, workplaces had only one or two job titles that included members of both sexes. On top of all this, recent research has shown that large discrepancies exist between male and female wages for the same job title. While female secretaries earned a median wage of $278 per week in 1985, the median for male secretaries was $365; moreover, in twenty-four other narrowly defined occupations in which females earned less than they would have as secretaries, males earned more in every case than a female secretary. Indeed, some firms designate particular jobs as male and others designate the same jobs as female, and the wage rates differ accordingly. It seems, therefore, that "the wage level for a particular job title in a particular establishment is set *after the employer decides whether those jobs will be filled by women or men*."[1] Barbara Bergmann's detailed study of sex segregation in the workplace leads her to conclude:

> Women are fenced off from a disproportionate share of what we might call "labor-market turf." ... [Thus] the supply and the demand in the markets for men's and women's labor are powerfully affected by discrimination.... The exclusion of women from a big share of all of the jobs in the economy is what creates two labor markets where there should be only one. The discriminatory assignment of jobs to one sex or the other is what sets the level of demand in each market ... [and] force[s] women to have to sell their labor at a low price.[2]

Thus workplace discrimination *per se* is very significant. In addition, as I have suggested, some of the segregation of wage work by sex is attributable to the individual choices that women and men make in the context of their own socialization and with knowledge of the gender structure of the family in particular. M. Rivka Polatnick has recently summarized the situation:

> Not only during the period of childrearing do women become economically or professionally disadvantaged vis-à-vis men; most women's lives have already been constructed in anticipation of that period. "Helpful advice" from family, friends, and guidance counselors, and discriminatory practices in schools and in the job market steer women towards jobs and interests compatible with a future in childrearing.[3]

It is no wonder, then, that most women are, even before marriage, in an economic position that sets them up to become more vulnerable during marriage, and most vulnerable of all if their marriage ends and—unprepared as they are—they find themselves in the position of having to provide for themselves and their children.

Vulnerability within Marriage

Marriage continues the cycle of inequality set in motion by the anticipation of marriage and the related sex segregation of the workplace. Partly because of society's assumptions about gender, but also because women, on entering marriage, tend already to be disadvantaged members of the work force, married women are likely to start out with less leverage in the relationship than their husbands. As I shall show, answers to questions such as whose work life and work needs take priority, and how the unpaid work of the family will be allocated—if they are not simply assumed to be decided along

---

[1] Barbara R. Bergmann, *The Economic Emergence of Women* (New York: Basic Books, 1986), esp. chap. 6 (statistics and quotations are from pp. 121 and 133).

[2] Ibid., pp. 125–26. See also Gerson, *Hard Choices*, p. 220.

[3] M. Rivka Polatnick, "Why Men Don't Rear Children: A Power Analysis," in Joyce Trebilcot (ed.), *Mothering: Essays in Feminist Theory* (Totowa, NJ: Rowman and Allanheld, 1983), p. 28.

the lines of sex difference, but are live issues in the marriage—are likely to be strongly influenced by the differences in earning power between husbands and wives. In many marriages, partly because of discrimination at work and the wage gap between the sexes, wives (despite initial personal ambitions and even when they are full-time wage workers) come to perceive themselves as benefiting from giving priority to their husbands' careers. Hence they have little incentive to question the traditional division of labor in the household. This in turn limits their own commitment to wage work and their incentive and leverage to challenge the gender structure of the workplace. Experiencing frustration and lack of control at work, those who thus turn toward domesticity, while often resenting the lack of respect our society gives to full-time mothers, may see the benefits of domestic life as greater than the costs.[1]

Thus, the inequalities between the sexes in the workplace and at home reinforce and exacerbate each other. It is not necessary to choose between two alternative, competing explanations of the inequalities between men and women in the workplace—the "human capital" approach, which argues that, because of expectations about their family lives, women *choose* to enter lower-paid and more dead-end occupations and specific jobs,[2] and the workplace discrimination explanation, which blames factors largely outside the control of female employees. When the pivotal importance of gender-structured marriage and the expectation of it are acknowledged, these explanations can be seen, rather, as complementary reasons for women's inequality. *A cycle of power relations and decisions pervades both family and workplace, and the inequalities of each reinforce those that already exist in the other.* Only with the recognition of this truth will we be able to begin to confront the changes that need to occur if women are to have a real opportunity to be equal participants in either sphere.

Human capital theorists, in perceiving women's job market attachment as a matter of voluntary choice, appear to miss or virtually to ignore the fact of unequal power within the family. Like normative theorists who idealize the family, they ignore potential conflicts of interest, and consequently issues of justice and power differentials, *within* families. This means that they view the question of whether a wife works solely in terms of the total aggregate costs and benefits for the family unit as a whole.[3] They assume that if a wife's paid work benefits the family more (in terms, say, of aggregate income and leisure) than her working exclusively within the household, her rational choice, and that of her husband, will be that she should get a job; if the reverse is true, she should not. But this simplistic attention to the family's "aggregate good" ignores the fact that a wife, like a husband, may have an independent interest in her own career advancement or desire for human contact, for example, that may give her an incentive to work even if the family as a whole may on that account find its life more difficult. Further, the human capital approach overlooks the fact that such goods as leisure and influence over the expenditure of income are by no means always equally shared within families. It also fails to recognize that the considerable influence that husbands often exert over their wives' decisions on whether to take paid work may be motivated not by a concern for the aggregate welfare of the household but, at least in part, by their desire

[1] Gerson, *Hard Choices*, chap. 5 and pp. 130–31.

[2] Key articles contributing to this argument are Jacob Mincer, "Labor Force Participation of Married Women[: A Study of Labor Supply]," in *Aspects of Labor Economics: A Conference of the Universities—National Bureau Committee for Economic Research* (Princeton: Princeton University Press, 1962); Jacob Mincer and Solomon Polachek, "Family Investment in Human Capital: Earnings of Women," in Theodore W. Schulz (ed.), *Marriage, Family Human Capital, and Fertility* (Chicago: University of Chicago Press, 1974); Jacob Mincer and Haim Ofek, "Interrupted Work Careers: Depreciation and Restoration of Human Capital," *Journal of Human Resources* 17 (Winter 1982)[, pp. 3–24]; Solomon Polachek, "Occupational Self-Selection: A Human Capital Approach to Sex Differences in Occupational Structure," *Review of Economics and Statistics* 63 (February 1981)[, pp. 60–69]. Gary Becker's *A Treatise on the Family* (Cambridge, MA: Harvard University Press, 1981) also belongs within this general mode of thinking.

[3] See, for example, Becker, *A Treatise on the Family*.

to retain the authority and privilege that accrues to them by virtue of being the family's breadwinner. Thus the decisions of married women about their participation in the job market, even when they *are* choices, may not be such simple or voluntary choices as human capital theory seems to imply.

In addition, those who seek to explain women's comparative disadvantage in the labor market by their preference for domestic commitments do not consider whether at least some of the causality may run in the opposite direction. But there is considerable evidence that women's "choices" to become domestically oriented, and even whether to have children, may result at least in part from their frequently blocked situations at work. Kathleen Gerson's study shows that, though they usually did not notice the connection, many of the women in her sample decided to leave wage work and turn to childbearing and domesticity coincidentally with becoming frustrated with the dead-end nature of their jobs. Conversely, she found that some women who had initially thought of themselves as domestically oriented, and who had in many cases chosen traditionally female occupations, reversed these orientations when unusual and unexpected opportunities for work advancement opened up to them.[1]

Even if these problems with the human capital approach did not exist, we would still be faced with the fact that the theory can explain, at most, half of the wage differential between the sexes. In the case of the differential between white men and black women, 70 percent of it is unexplained. At *any* given level of skill, experience, and education, men earn considerably more than women. The basic problem with the human capital approach is that, like much of neoclassical economic theory, it pays too little attention to the multiple constraints placed on people's choices. It pays too little attention to differentials of power between the sexes both in the workplace and in the family. It thus ignores the fact that women's commitment and attachment to the workplace are strongly influenced by a number of factors that are largely beyond their control.

[1] Gerson, *Hard Choices*, chaps. 5 and 6.

As we have seen, a woman's typically less advantaged position in the work force and lower pay may lead her to choices about full-time motherhood and domesticity that she would have been less likely to make had her work life been less dead-ended. They also give her less power in relation to her husband should she want to resist the traditional division of labor in her household and to insist on a more equal sharing of child care and other domestic responsibilities. Those who stress the extent to which both husbands and wives cling to the "male provider/female nurturer" roles as unobjectionable because efficient and economically rational for the family unit need to take a step back and consider the extent to which the continued sex segregation of the work force serves to perpetuate the traditional division of labor within the household, even in the face of women's rising employment.

Housework and the Cycle of Vulnerability

It is no secret that in almost all families women do far more housework and child care than men do. But the distribution of paid and unpaid work within the family has rarely—outside of feminist circles—been considered a significant issue by theorists of justice. Why should it be? If two friends divide a task so that each takes primary responsibility for a different aspect of it, we would be loath to cry "injustice" unless one were obviously coercing the other. But at least three factors make the division of labor within the household a very different situation, and a clear question of justice. First, the uneven distribution of labor within the family is strongly correlated with an innate characteristic, which appears to make it the kind of issue with which theorists of justice have been most concerned. The virtually automatic allocation to one person of more of the paid labor and to the other of more of the unpaid labor would be regarded as decidedly odd in any relationship other than that of a married or cohabiting heterosexual couple. One reason for this is that, as we shall see, it has distinct effects on the distribution of power. While the unequal distribution of paid and unpaid work has different repercussions in different types of marriages, it is always of significance. Second, though it is by no means always absolute, the division of labor in a traditional or quasi-traditional marriage is often quite complete and usually long-standing. It lasts in many cases at least through the lengthy years of child rearing, and is by no means confined to the preschool years. Third, partly as a result of this, and of the structure and demands of most paid work, the household division of labor has a lasting impact on the lives of married women, especially those who become mothers. It affects every sphere of their lives, from the dynamics of their marital relationship to their opportunities in the many spheres of life outside the household. The distribution of labor within the family by sex has deep ramifications for its respective members' material, psychological, physical, and intellectual well-being. One cannot even begin to address the issue of why so many women and children live in poverty in our society, or why women are inadequately represented in the higher echelons of our political and economic institutions, without confronting the division of labor between the sexes within the family. Thus it is not only itself an issue of justice but it is also at the very root of other significant concerns of justice, including equality of opportunity for children of both sexes, but especially for girls, and political justice in the broadest sense.

The justice issues surrounding housework are not simply issues about who does *more* work. However, on average, wives living with their husbands do now work slightly more total hours than their husbands do.[1] In addition, this averaging obscures a great variety of distributions of both quantity and type of work within marriages. For the purposes of this discussion, it will be helpful to separate couples into two major categories: those in which the wife is "predominantly houseworking" (either a full-time housewife or employed part-time) and those in which the wife is "predominantly wage-working" (employed full-time or virtually full-time). Within each category, I shall look at issues such as the distribution of work (paid and unpaid),

income, power, opportunity to choose one's occupation, self-respect and esteem, and availability of exit. As we shall see, wives in each category experience a somewhat different pattern of injustice and vulnerability. But, except in the case of some of the small number of elite couples who make considerable use of paid help, the typical divisions of labor in the family cannot be regarded as just.

Predominantly Houseworking Wives

When a woman is a full-time housewife—as are about two-fifths of married women in the United States who live with their husbands—she does less total work, on average, than her employed husband: 49.3 hours per week, compared with his 63.2. This is also true of couples in which the wife works part-time (defined as fewer than thirty hours per week, including commuting time), though the average difference per week is reduced to eight hours in this case.[2] This is, of course, partly because housework is less burdensome than it was before the days of labor-saving devices and declining fertility. Not surprisingly, however, during the early years of child rearing, a nonemployed wife (or part-time employed wife) is likely to work about the same total number of hours as her employed husband. But the *quantity* of work performed is only one of a number of important variables that must be considered in order for us to assess the justice or injustice of the division of labor in the family, particularly in relation to the issue of the cycle of women's vulnerability.

In terms of the quality of work, there are considerable disadvantages to the role of housewife.[3] One is that much of the work is boring and/or unpleasant. Surveys indicate that most people of both sexes do not like to clean, shop for food, or do laundry, which constitute a high proportion of housework. Cooking rates higher, and child care

[1] Victor Fuchs, *Women's Quest*, pp. 77–78.

[2] Bergmann, *Economic Emergence*, p. 263, table 11–2, using University of Michigan 1975–76 data.
[3] See Bergmann, *Economic Emergence*, chap. 9, "The Job of Housewife."

even higher, with both sexes, than other domestic work.[1] In reality, this separation of tasks is strictly hypothetical, at least for mothers, who are usually cleaning, shopping, doing laundry, and cooking at the same time as taking care of children. Many wage workers, too, do largely tedious and repetitive work. But the housewife-mother's work has additional disadvantages. One is that her hours of work are highly unscheduled; unlike virtually any other worker except the holder of a high political office, she can be called on at any time of the day or night, seven days a week. Another is that she cannot, nearly as easily as most other workers, change jobs. Her family comes to depend on *her* to do all the things she does. Finding substitutes is difficult and expensive, even if the housewife is not discouraged or forbidden by her husband to seek paid work. The skills and experience she has gained are not valued by prospective employers. Also, once a woman has taken on the role of housewife, she finds it extremely difficult, for reasons that will be explored, to shift part of this burden back onto her husband. Being a housewife thus both impairs a woman's ability to support herself and constrains her future choices in life.[2]

Many of the disadvantages of being a housewife spring directly or indirectly from the fact that all her work is unpaid work, whereas more than four-fifths of her husband's total work is paid work. This may at first seem a matter of little importance. If wives, so long as they stay married, usually share their husbands' standards of living for the most part, why should it matter who earns the income? It matters a great deal, for many reasons. In the highly money-oriented society we live in, the housewife's work is devalued. In fact, in spite of the fact that a major part of it consists of the nurturance and socialization of the next generation of citizens, it is frequently not even acknowledged

as work or as productive, either at the personal or at the policy level. This both affects the predominantly houseworking wife's power and influence within the family and means that her social status depends largely upon her husband's, a situation that she may not consider objectionable so long as the marriage lasts, but that is likely to be very painful for her if it does not.[3]

Also, although married couples usually share material well-being, a housewife's or even a part-time working wife's lack of access to much money of her own can create difficulties that range from the mildly irritating through the humiliating to the devastating, especially if she does not enjoy a good relationship with her husband. Money is the subject of most conflict for married couples, although the issue of housework may be overtaking it. Bergmann reports that in an informal survey, she discovered that about 20 percent of the housewife-mothers of her students were in the position of continually having to appeal to their husbands for money. The psychological effects on an adult of economic dependence can be great. As Virginia Woolf pointed out fifty years ago, any man who has difficulty estimating them should simply imagine himself depending on his wife's income.[4] The dark side of economic dependence is also indicated by the fact that, in the serious predivorce situation of having to fight for their future economic well-being, many wives even of well-to-do men do not have access to enough cash to pay for the uncovering and documentation of their husband's assets.

At its (not so uncommon) worst, the economic dependence of wives can seriously affect their day-to-day physical security. As Linda Gordon has recently concluded: "The basis of wife-beating is male dominance—not superior physical strength or violent temperament ... but social, economic, political, and psychological power.... Wife-beating is the chronic battering of a person of inferior power who for that

[1] Ibid., p. 267.

[2] See [Lenore J.] Weitzmann, *The Divorce Revolution* [: *The Unexpected Social and Economic Consequences for Women and Children in America* (New York: The Free Press, 1985)], esp. pp. xi, 35.

[3] See Gerson, *Hard Choices*, pp. 211–12.

[4] Bergmann, *Economic Emergence*, pp. 211–12; Virginia Woolf, *Three Guineas* (London: Harcourt Brace, 1938), p. 110; see also pp. 54–57.

reason cannot effectively resist."[1] Both wife abuse and child abuse are clearly exacerbated by the economic dependence of women on their husbands or cohabiting male partners. Many women, especially full-time housewives with dependent children, have no way of adequately supporting themselves, and are often in practice unable to leave a situation in which they and/or their children are being seriously abused. In addition to increasing the likelihood of the more obvious forms of abuse—physical and sexual assault—the fear of being abandoned, with its economic and other dire consequences, can lead a housewife to tolerate infidelity, to submit to sexual acts she does not enjoy, or experience psychological abuse including virtual desertion.[2] The fact that a predominantly houseworking wife has no money of her own or a small paycheck is not necessarily significant, but it can be very significant, especially at crucial junctures in the marriage.

Finally, as I shall discuss, the earnings differential between husband and housewife can become devastating in its significance for her and for any dependent children in the event of divorce (which in most states can now occur without her consent). This fact, which significantly affects the relative potential of wives and husbands for exit from the marriage, is likely to influence the distribution of power, and in turn paid and unpaid work, *during* the marriage as well.

Predominantly Wage-Working Wives and Housework

Despite the increasing labor force participation of married women, including mothers, "working wives still bear almost all the responsibility for housework." They do less of it than housewives, but "they still do the vast bulk of what needs to be done,"

and the difference is largely to be accounted for not by the increased participation of men, but by lowered standards, the participation of children, purchased services such as restaurant or frozen meals, and, in elite groups, paid household help. Thus, while the distribution of paid labor between the sexes is shifting quite considerably onto women, that of unpaid labor is not shifting much at all, and "the couple that shares household tasks equally remains rare."[3] The differences in total time spent in all "family work" (housework and child care plus yard work, repairs, and so on) vary considerably from one study to another, but it seems that fully employed husbands do, at most, approximately half as much as their fully employed wives, and some studies show a much greater discrepancy.

Bergmann reports that "husbands of wives with full-time jobs averaged about two minutes more housework per day than did husbands in housewife-maintaining families, hardly enough additional time to prepare a soft-boiled egg."[4] Even unemployed husbands do much less housework than wives who work a forty-hour week. Working-class husbands are particularly vocal about not being equal partners in the home, and do little housework. In general, however, a husband's income and job prestige are inversely related to his involvement in household chores, unless his wife is employed in a similarly high-paid and prestigious job. Many husbands who profess belief in sharing household tasks equally actually do far less than their wives, when time spent and chores done are assessed. In many cases, egalitarian attitudes make little or no difference to who actually does the work, and often "the idea of shared responsibility turn[s] out to be a myth."[5]

Some scholars are disinclined to perceive these facts as indicating unequal power or exploitation.

---

[1] Linda Gordon, *Heroes of Their Own Lives* (New York: Viking, 1988), p. 251.

[2] Bergmann, Economic Emergence, pp. 205–06; [Ruth] Sidel, *Women and Children* [*Last: The Plight of Poor Women in Affluent America* (New York: Viking, 1986)], pp. 40–46.

[3] See Bergmann, *Economic Emergence*, chap. 11; Bianchi and Spain, *American Women*, pp. 231–40; Blumstein and Schwartz, *American Couples*, p. 144; and Gerson, *Hard Choices*, p. 170.

[4] Bergmann, *Economic Emergence*, p. 263.

[5] Blumstein and Schwartz, *American Couples*, p. 145.

They prefer to view them as merely embodying adherence to traditional patterns, or to justify them as efficient in terms of the total welfare of the family (the husband's time being too valuable to spend doing housework).[1] There are clear indications, however, that the major reason that husbands and other heterosexual men living with wage-working women are not doing more housework is that *they do not want to, and are able, to a very large extent, to enforce their wills.* How do we know that the unequal allocation of housework is not equally women's choice? First, because most people do not like doing many of the major household chores. Second, because almost half of wage-working wives who do more than 60 percent of the housework say that they would prefer their husbands to do more of it.[2] Third, because husbands with higher salaries and more prestigious jobs than their wives (the vast majority of two-job couples) are in a powerful position to resist their wives' appeal to them to do more at home, and it is husbands with the highest prestige who do the least housework of all. Even when there is little conflict, and husbands and wives seem to agree that the woman should do more of the housework, they are often influenced by the prevailing idea that whoever earns less or has the less prestigious job should do more unpaid labor at home. But since the maldistribution of wages and jobs between the sexes in our society is largely out of women's control, even *seemingly nonconflictual* decisions made on this basis cannot really be considered fully voluntary on the part of wives.[3] Finally, the resistance of most husbands to housework is well documented, as is the fact that the more housework men do, the more it becomes a cause of fighting within couples. Examining factors that caused the breakup of some of the couples in their sample, Blumstein and Schwartz say:

> Among both married and cohabiting couples, housework is a source of conflict.... *[A] woman cannot be perceived as doing less housework than her partner wants her to do without jeopardizing the relationship.* However, a man, who is unlikely to be doing even half the work, can be perceived as doing less than his fair share without affecting the couple's durability. *It is difficult for women to achieve an equal division of housework and still preserve the relationship.*[4]

As a result, in many of the households in which men and women both work full-time—those for which much paid household help or reliance on other purchased services is not a practical option—the unequal distribution of housework between husbands and wives leads to gross inequities in the amount and type of work done by each. "Drudge wives," as Bergmann has recently termed women in such households, do more total work than their husbands, averaging 71.1 hours a week to the husband's 64.9. But of greater overall significance is the fact that a vastly higher proportion of the wife's than of the husband's work is unpaid. She averages 28.1 hours of unpaid "family" work to 43 hours of paid work, whereas he averages only 9.2 hours of family work to 55.8 hours of paid work.[5] One important effect of unequal sharing of housework and other family work within dual working couples is that the amount of time and energy the wife has left to commit to her wage work is considerably more limited than her husband's. It used to be assumed, in the days when the full traditional division of labor in the family prevailed, that any job requiring responsibility and commitment was incompatible with day-to-day responsibilities for home and children. This was why, or so it was argued, men could not, and should not be expected

---

[1] For recent examples, see Becker, *A Treatise on the Family*; and Jonathan Gershuny, *Social Innovation and the Division of Labour* (Oxford: Oxford University Press, 1983), p. 156.

[2] Bergmann, *Economic Emergence*, pp. 267–68 and refs., p. 350n9.

[3] Blumstein and Schwartz, *American Couples*, pp. 139–54, esp. 151–54.

[4] Ibid., p. 312; emphasis added.

[5] Bergmann, *Economic Emergence*, table 11.2, p. 263.

to, share in these tasks. But now many women, whether forced by economic need or refusing to accept the choice between parenthood and career that men have never had to make, are trying to do both. Their chances of success are significantly affected by the fact that, although they are likely to expend significant amounts of time on their homes and children, they must compete at work, not only with men from families like their own, who do significantly less family work than they do, but also with men whose wives are full-time housewives or work only part-time.

Wives and Wage Work

While theorists of justice have largely ignored it, women's double burden and its effects have long been recognized by feminists. Largely because of the unequal distribution of housework and child care, married women's opportunities in the work force are considerably more constrained than men's. As Gerson notes, "the simple fact of [women's] working ... does not by itself entail significant social change." Though women are now less inclined than they were a generation ago to be part-time and sporadic workers, there is a wide gap between the increase in their labor force participation and their labor force attachment and position.[1] Because of their lower level of labor force attachment, their tendency to work part-time and at jobs that in other respects bend to meet the needs of the family, and their propensity to accommodate their own employment to their husbands', women's wages become lower in relation to men's as they get older. Whereas the ratio between an average full-time working woman's earnings and a full-time working man's is 83:100 between the ages of twenty-one to twenty-nine, the wage gap by ages forty-five to sixty-four has increased to 60:100.[2]

The constraints placed on wives as workers are strengthened by the fact that many full-time employers assume, in innumerable ways, that "someone" is at home at least part-time during the day to assume primary responsibility for children. The traditional or quasi-traditional division of labor is clearly assumed in the vast discrepancy between normal full-time working hours and children's school hours and vacations. It is assumed by the high degree of geographical mobility required by many higher-level management positions. It is also implicit in the structure of the professions, in which the greatest demands are placed on workers at the very peak of the child-rearing years. Academia and the law are two clear examples; both tenure and partnership decisions are typically made for a person between the ages of thirty and thirty-five, with obvious discriminatory implications for the professional parent (almost always a woman) who does not have a partner willing to assume the major responsibility for children.

Because the structure of most wage work is inconsistent with the parenting responsibilities chiefly borne by women, far fewer women (especially married women) than men do work full-time. Only 27 percent of all wives in families with children worked full-time year-round in 1984, compared with 77 percent of husbands.[3] Some mothers conclude that, given the demands of their work, the only reasonable answer to the needs of their children is to take time out of the workplace altogether. Others work part-time. But the repercussions of either of these choices, given the current structure and attitudes of the workplace, are often serious and long-lasting. The investment in career assets is by far the most valuable property owned by most couples. To the extent that wives work part-time or intermittently, their own career potential atrophies, and they become deeply dependent on their husbands' career assets. Even when a wife maintains her career, her husband's work needs—in terms of time, freedom from other preoccupations, education and training, and geographical mobility—usually

---

[1] Gerson, *Hard Choices*, pp. 128–29.
[2] U.S. Bureau of the Census 1986 data, cited in the *New York Times*, September 14, 1987, p. A13.

[3] Ellwood, *Poor Support*, table 5.1, p. 33 (tabulated from U.S. Bureau of the Census, Current Population Survey, March 1985).

take priority. This is often the case even with dual-career couples who are similarly qualified and claim to be committed to an egalitarian ideology.[1] In relation to the outside world of employment, therefore, the notion that husbands and wives are equals is myth. Typically, women as workers are disadvantaged by marriage itself, and the more so the longer the duration of the marriage.[2]

Power in the Family

There are very few studies of power within marriage. Of those few, the one most frequently cited until recently—Robert O. Blood, Jr., and Donald M. Wolfe's 1960 *Husbands and Wives*—though informative, is now outdated and unreliable in the way it interprets its own findings.[3] The study in itself is of considerable interest for the question of power and gender, given its influential character, not only because of what it purports to discover but also because these findings are both distorted and blurred by the authors' initial assumption that a moderate degree of male dominance is the desirable norm within families. This assumption leads them to define what their own scale indicates to be moderate male dominance as "relative equalitarianism" in family decision making. When reinterpreted in the absence of this sexist normative assumption, we find that what Blood and Wolfe's study of married life in the 1950s discovered was not, as they claimed, that "the American family has changed its authority pattern from one of patriarchal male dominance to one of equalitarian sharing," but rather that male dominance was still the norm, though its extent varied in accordance with

a number of factors.[4] The most important of these was the discrepancy in income and wage-work success between the husband and the wife.

As Blood and Wolfe report their findings about what variables affect family power, they are again misleading, due to their implicit assumptions. They conclude that the distribution of power, and its ebb and flow during the course of a marriage, vary with the "resources" that each spouse contributes to the family. But they completely fail to notice that the only resources that affect marital power are those—such as income, success, and prestige—that are valued in the world *outside* the marriage. Resources such as domestic services and childbearing and child-rearing capacities, skills, and labor are not only not positively correlated with marital power but are in fact *negatively* correlated with it. While Blood and Wolfe note that the housewife with preschool children is at the least powerful point in her marriage, and that her power decreases as the number of children rises, they do not question why she should be so powerless at a time when she is contributing so much to the family. Because of their unstated sexist assumptions about what constitutes a "resource," they explain her lack of power in terms of her extreme financial dependence on her husband, and fail to perceive her husband as dependent on *her* for any resources at all.[5]

Only recently, with the publication of Blumstein and Schwartz's *American Couples*, have we had a large-scale and more neutral account of the power picture behind decision making by couples. They asked thousands of couples to respond on a scale of 1 to 9 (with 5 defined as "both equally") to the question: "In general, who has more say about important decisions affecting your relationship, you or your partner?" Clearly, what this new study reveals about married couples confirms the major findings that Blood and Wolfe's earlier study discovered but obscured. First, though the number

[1] Barbara Strudler Wallston, Martha A. Foster, and Michael Berger, "I will Follow Him: Myth, Reality, or Forced Choice—Job Seeking Experiences of Dual Career Couples," in Jeff Bryson and Rebecca Bryson (eds.), *Dual Career Couples* (New York: Human Sciences Press, 1978)....

[2] See Weitzman, *The Divorce Revolution*, pp. xi–xviii, chaps. 5, 7, and 11 *passim.*

[3] Robert O. Blood and Donald M. Wolfe, *Husbands and Wives: The Dynamics of Married Living* (New York: The Free Press, 1960).

[4] Ibid., p. 47 and chap. 2.

[5] This is pointed out by Heer, "The Measurement and Bases of Family Power: An Overview," *Marriage and Family Living* 25.2 (1963): 137–38.

of marriages in which spouses consider that they share decision-making power relatively equally has increased considerably, the tendency in others is still distinctly toward male rather than female dominance.[1] Second, it is still clearly the case that the possession by each spouse of resources valued by the *outside* world, especially income and work status, rather than resources valuable primarily within the family, has a significant effect on the distribution of power in the relationship.

Blumstein and Schwartz preface their findings about couples, money, and power by noting that they are not likely to accord with "cherished American beliefs about fairness and how people acquire influence in romantic relationships." Perhaps this is why, as they point out, although "economic factors tend to be involved in every aspect of a couple's life," standard textbooks on marriage and the family are unlikely to devote more than five pages to this subject. Just as political and moral theorists have been extremely reluctant to admit that questions of justice pertain to family life, a similar tendency to idealize—and to conceal dominance—has apparently characterized sociologists of the family until recently, too. But Blumstein and Schwartz's study establishes quite decisively that "in three out of four of the types of couples ... studied [all types except lesbian couples], ... the amount of money a person earns—in comparison with a partner's income—establishes relative power."[2] Given that even the 26 percent of all wives who work full-time earn, on average, only 63 percent as much as the average full-time working husband, and the average wife who works for pay (full- or part-time) earns only 42 percent as much, it is therefore not at all surprising that male dominance is far more common than female dominance in couples who deviate from a relatively egalitarian distribution of power.[3] When women are employed, and especially when their earnings

approach those of their husbands, they are more likely to share decision-making power equally with their husbands and to have greater financial autonomy. In marriages in which the husband earned over $8,000 more than the wife (more than half the marriages in the Blumstein and Schwartz sample), the husband was rated as more powerful (as opposed to an equal sharing of power or to the wife's being more powerful) in 33 percent of cases. In marriages in which the incomes of husband and wife were approximately equal, only 18 percent of the husbands were rated as more powerful. The workplace success of wives, then, helps considerably to equalize the balance of power within their marriages and gains them greater respect from their husbands, who often have little respect for housework. Success at work, moreover, can reduce the expectation that a wife will do the vast bulk of family work.[4] Nevertheless, the full-time employment, and even the equal or greater earnings, of wives do not guarantee them equal power in the family, for the male-provider *ideology* is sometimes powerful enough to counteract these factors.[5]

Given these facts about the way power is distributed in the family, and the facts brought out earlier about the typical contentiousness of the issue of housework, it is not difficult to see how the vulnerability of married women in relation to the world of work and their inequality within the family tend to form part of a vicious cycle. Wives are likely to start out at a disadvantage, because of both the force of the traditions of gender and the fact that they are likely to be already earning less than their husbands at the time of marriage. In many cases, the question of who is responsible for the bulk of the unpaid labor of the household is probably not raised at all, but *assumed*, on the basis of these two factors alone. Because of this "nondecision" factor, studies of marital power that ask only about the respective influence of the partners over *decisions*

---

[1] Blumstein and Schwartz, *American Couples*, figs. 1 and 2 and text, pp. 54, 57.

[2] Ibid., pp. 53, 52.

[3] Bianchi and Spain, *American Women*, p. 212.

[4] Blumstein and Schwartz, *American Couples*, pp. 53–93 passim and 139–44. See also Polatnick, "Why Men Don't Rear Children," esp. pp. 23–25.

[5] Blumstein and Schwartz, *American Couples*, pp. 56–57.

are necessarily incomplete, since they ignore distributions of burdens and benefits that may not be perceived as arising from decisions at all.

However, there *is* often conflict about how much time each partner should devote to wage work and how much to family work. This may include disagreement over the issue of whether the wife should have a job at all, whereas this is almost always taken for granted (a "nondecision") in the case of the husband. Since the partner whose wage work is given priority and who does far less unpaid family work is likely to increase the disparity between his and his spouse's earnings, seniority, and work status, his power in the family will tend to grow accordingly. Hence if, as is likely, he wishes to preserve a traditional or semitraditional division of labor in the family, he is likely to be able to do so. This need not involve constant fighting, with the man always winning; his "man" power and his earning power combined may be so pre-eminent that the issue is never even raised. Either way, his wife is likely to find it difficult to reallocate the family work so as to make him responsible for more of it so that she can take a job or expend more time and energy on the one she has. In addition, the weight of tradition and of her own sex-role socialization will contribute to her powerlessness to effect change.

Vulnerability by Separation or Divorce

The impact of the unequal distribution of benefits and burdens between husbands and wives is hardest and most directly felt by the increasing numbers of women and children whose families are no longer intact. In 1985, 28 percent of ever-married white women and 49 percent of ever-married black women in the United States were separated, divorced, or widowed.[1] Marital disruption through the death of a spouse, divorce, or separation is consistently rated as the most psychologically stressful life event for men and women alike.[2] But in women's lives, the personal disruption caused by these events is frequently exacerbated by the serious social and economic dislocation that accompanies them.

Every year, divorce disrupts the lives of more than three million men, women, and children in the United States.[3] The annual divorce rate per 1,000 married women increased from 9.2 in 1960 to 22.6 in 1981; it has leveled off and even declined slightly during the 1980s. Half of all marriages contracted in the 1970s are projected to end in divorce, and between 50 and 60 percent of the children born in the early 1980s are likely to experience the breakup of their parents' marriage by the age of eighteen. Rates of separation and divorce are much higher for black than for white women: in 1983 there were 126 divorced white women for every 1,000 married women; for black women, the ratio was 297 to 1,000.[4] In 1985, about 23 percent of children under the age of eighteen lived with only one parent—in about 90 percent of cases, the mother. Contrary to popular prejudice, female-maintained families with children consist in only a fairly small percentage of cases of never-married women raising children alone. They are in the vast majority of cases the result of separation or divorce.

Not only has the rate of divorce increased rapidly but the differential in the economic impact of divorce on men and women has also grown. Divorce and its economic effects contribute significantly to the fact that nearly one quarter of all children now live in single-parent households, more than half of them, even after transfer payments, below the poverty level. Moreover, partly because of the increased labor force participation of married women, there has been a growing divergence between female-maintained families and two-par-

[1] U.S. Bureau of the Census, *Current Population Reports: Marital Status and Living Arrangements*, March 1985 (Washington, DC: Government Printing Office).

[2] Weitzman, *The Divorce Revolution*, p. 349 and refs.

[3] Ibid., p. xvii, citing Arland Thornton and Deborah Freedman, "The Changing American Family," *Population Bulletin* 38.4 (1983): 7.

[4] Bianchi and Spain, *American Women*, pp. 21–25.

ent families.[1] These dramatic shifts, with their vast impact on the lives of women and children, must be addressed by any theory of justice that can claim to be about all of us, rather than simply about the male "heads of households" on which theories of justice in the past have focused.

There is now little doubt that, while no-fault divorce does not appear to have caused the increasing rate of divorce, it has considerably affected the economic outcome of divorce for both parties.[2] Many studies have shown that whereas the average economic status of men improves after divorce, that of women and children deteriorates seriously. Nationwide, the per-capita income of divorced women, which was only 62 percent that of divorced men in 1960, decreased to 56 percent by 1980.[3] The most illuminating explanation of this is Lenore Weitzman's recent pathbreaking study, *The Divorce Revolution*. Based on a study of 2,500 randomly selected California court dockets between 1968 and 1977 and lengthy interviews with many lawyers, judges, legal experts, and 228 divorced men and women, the book both documents and explains the differential social and economic impact of current divorce law on men, women, and children. Weitzman presents the striking finding that in the first year after divorce, the avenge standard of living of divorced men, adjusted for household size, increases by 42 percent while that of divorced women falls by 75 percent. "For most women and children," Weitzman concludes,

> divorce means precipitous downward mobility—both economically and socially. The reduction in income brings residential moves and inferior housing, drastically diminished or nonexistent funds for recreation and leisure, and intense pressures due to inadequate

time and money. Financial hardships in turn cause social dislocation and a loss of familiar networks for emotional support and social services, and intensify the psychological stress for women and children alike. On a societal level, divorce increases female and child poverty and creates an ever-widening gap between the economic well-being of divorced men, on the one hand, and their children and former wives on the other.[4]

Weitzman's findings have been treated with disbelief by some, who claim, for example, that California, being a community property state, is atypical, and that these figures could not be projected nationwide without distortion. However, studies done in other states (including common law states and both urban and rural areas) have corroborated Weitzman's central conclusion: that the economic situation of men and that of women and children typically diverge after divorce.

The basic reason for this is that the courts are now treating divorcing men and women more or less as equals. Divorcing men and women are not, of course, equal, both because the two sexes are not treated equally in society and, as we have seen, because typical, gender-structured marriage makes women socially and economically vulnerable. The treatment of unequals as if they were equals has long been recognized as an obvious instance of injustice. In this case, the injustice is particularly egregious because the inequality is to such a large extent the result of the marital relationship itself. Nonetheless, that divorce as it is currently practiced in the United States involves such injustice took years to be revealed. There are various discrete parts of this unjust treatment of unequals as if they were equals, and we must briefly examine each of them.

The first way in which women are unequally situated after divorce is that they almost always continue to take day-to-day responsibility for the

---

[1] Ellwood, *Poor Support*, chap. 5; Sidel, *Women and Children*, p. xvi.

[2] Bianchi and Spain, *American Women*, p. 26, citing numerous studies.

[3] Ibid., pp. 30–32 and refs., 205–07, 216–18; Gerson, *Hard Choices*, pp. 221–22 and refs.

[4] Weitzman, *The Divorce Revolution*, p. 323. See esp. introduction and chaps. 2 and 10.

children. The increased rate of divorce has especially affected couples between the ages of twenty-five and thirty-nine—those most likely to have dependent children. And in approximately 90 percent of cases, children live with mothers rather than fathers after divorce. This is usually the outcome preferred by both parents. Relatively few fathers seek or are awarded sole custody, and in cases of joint custody, which are increasing in frequency, children still tend to live mainly with their mothers. Thus women's post-divorce households tend to be larger than those of men, with correspondingly larger economic needs, and their work lives are much more limited by the needs of their children.[1]

Second, as Weitzman demonstrates, no-fault divorce laws, by depriving women of power they often exerted as the "innocent" and less willing party to the divorce, have greatly reduced their capacity to achieve an equitable division of the couple's tangible assets. Whereas the wife (and children) typically used to be awarded the family home, or more than half of the total tangible assets of the marriage, they are now doing much worse in this respect. In California, the percentage of cases in which the court explicitly ordered that the family home be sold and the proceeds divided rose from about one-tenth of divorces in 1968 to about one-third in 1977. Of this one-third, 66 percent had minor children, who were likely on this account to suffer significantly more than the usual dislocations of divorce. James McLindon's study of divorcing couples in New Haven, Connecticut, confirms this effect of no-fault divorce. In the case of an older housewife, forced sale of the family home can mean the loss of not only her marriage, occupation, and social status, but also her home of many years, all in one blow.[2] Whether what is supposed to be happening is the "equal" division of property, as in the community property states, or the "equitable" division, as in the common law states, what is in fact happening is neither equal nor equitable. This is

partly because even when the division of tangible property is fairly equal, what is in fact most families' principal asset is largely or entirely left out of the equation. This leads us to the third component of injustice in the current practice of divorce.[3]

As we have seen, most married couples give priority to the husband's work life, and wives, when they work for wages, earn on average only a small fraction of the family income, and perform the great bulk of the family's unpaid labor. The most valuable economic asset of a typical marriage is not any tangible piece of property, such as a house (since, if there is one, it is usually heavily mortgaged). In fact, "the average divorcing couple has less than $20,000 in net worth." By far the most important property acquired in the average marriage is its career assets, or human capital, the vast majority of which is likely to be invested in the husband. As Weitzman reports, it takes the average divorced man only about *ten months* to earn as much as the couple's entire net worth.[4] The importance of this marital asset is hard to overestimate, yet it has only recently begun to be treated in some states as marital property for the purposes of divorce settlements. Even if "marital property" as traditionally understood is divided evenly, there can be no equity so long as this crucial piece is left in the hands of the husband alone. Except for the wealthy few who have significant material assets, "support awards that divide income, especially future income, are the most valuable entitlements awarded at divorce."[5] Largely because of the division of labor within marriage, to the extent that divorced women have to fall back on their own earnings, they are much worse off than they were when married, and than their ex-husbands are after divorce. In many cases, full-time work at or around the minimum wage, which may be the best a woman without much job training or experience can earn, is insufficient to pull the household out of poverty. As Bianchi and Spain state, "women's labor market adjustments

[1] Ibid., pp. xiii-xiv and chaps. 8, 9; Blumstein and Schwartz, *American Couples*, pp. 33–34.
[2] [Cited in] Weitzman, *The Divorce Revolution*, pp. 78–79.
[3] Ibid., chap. 4.
[4] Ibid., pp. 53, 60.
[5] Ibid., p. 61; see also pp. 68–69.

to accommodate children, which are often made within a two parent family context and seem economically rational at the time, cause difficulty later when these same women find themselves divorced and in great need of supporting themselves and their children."[1]

For reasons that seem to have been exacerbated by no-fault divorce laws, most separated or divorced women do have to fall back on their own earnings. These earnings—as opposed to spousal support payments or public transfer payments—make up the major portion of the income of female-maintained families. In 1980, they constituted the entire income of almost half such households.[2] The major reason for this is that, loath to recognize that the husband's earning power, and therefore his continuing income, is the most important asset of a marriage, judges have not been dividing it fairly at the time of divorce. As Weitzman summarizes the situation, "Under the new divorce laws, … a woman is now expected to become self-sufficient (and, in many cases, to support her children as well)."[3] Alimony and child support are either not awarded, not adequate, or not paid, in the great majority of cases. For many separated or divorced women, as for most single mothers, the idea of the male provider is nothing but a misleading myth that has negatively affected their own work lives while providing them with nothing at all.

In many divorces, there is inadequate income to support two households, with the paradoxical result that poor women with dependent children are even less likely than others to be awarded child support. But even in the case of families who were comfortably off, judges frequently consider what proportion of his income the husband will need to maintain his own standard of living (and even that of his hypothetical future family) before considering the needs of his wife and children. Instead of thinking in terms of compensating wives for all

the unpaid effort that most have expended on the home and children, judges are thinking in terms of "what she can earn, and what he can pay."[4] On top of this, they are often misled by the fact that many women are now in the labor force into assuming that wives who have spent many years predominantly as mothers and homemakers will suddenly be able to support themselves.[5]

Contrary to popular belief, alimony has always been awarded rarely, only to the ex-wives of middle- and upper-class men—a small minority of the divorcing population. While this situation has not changed, what has changed is the nature of alimony, which under no-fault practices has become in almost all cases a short-term "transitional" award, designed to help divorced women become self-sufficient as rapidly as possible. The burden of proof is now distinctly on the woman to show that she cannot support herself. In Weitzman's sample, only 17 percent, or roughly one-sixth, of divorcing wives were awarded alimony in 1978. The average amount awarded was $350 a month in 1984 dollars, for a median length of twenty-five months. Partly because of the shorter duration of their marriages, the incidence of alimony awards to mothers of preschool children was even lower than the average—only 13 percent. Even in cases in which a husband's high earning capacity has clearly resulted in large part from his wife's financial and/or domestic support during marriage, judges have been extremely reluctant to require him to continue to share it with her in order to allow her to complete a comparable education or training herself. Since about 1985, however, there has been a trend in some states toward reversing time limitations on alimony after long-term traditional marriages.

The phenomenon of shrinking alimony is exacerbated by the paucity of child support. David Ellwood reports that nationwide, as of 1985, 82 percent of divorced custodial mothers of children under twenty-one were awarded child support but only 54 percent received any, and the average received amounted

[1] Bianchi and Spain, *American Women*, p. 243; see also pp. 207–11.

[2] Ibid., p. 206.

[3] Weitzman, *The Divorce Revolution*, p. 143.

[4] Ibid., p. x.

[5] Bianchi and Spain, *American Women*, p. 213.

to $2,538 per year, or just over $200 a month. Separated and never-married women are awarded and receive child support less frequently and in lesser amount.[1] A 1982 Census Bureau survey reported over eight million women raising at least one child without the father in the home. Of these, the court had ordered support in only five million cases. The average annual payment ordered was $2,180 for white women, $2,070 for Hispanic women, and $1,640 for black women. Weitzman's California-based research showed that a divorced man is rarely (and only in the lowest earning groups) ordered to pay more than a third of his net income in *total* support payments to his former wife and children.[2]

The inadequate levels of child support ordered are only part of the problem. A nationwide survey showed that, in 1981, the ordered amounts were paid in full in less than one-half of cases. Approximately one-quarter of mothers awarded support received partial payment, and one-quarter received no payment at all.[3] In general, except in the case of fathers earning more than $50,000, who comply in more than 90 percent of cases, nonpayment of child support bears little relation to the father's income. One of the major problems appears to be the ineffectiveness or lack of enforcement procedures.[4] With the Child Support Enforcement Amendments of 1984, the problem has now been addressed by federal legislation mandating the withholding of payments from the father's paycheck. Even when paid in full, however, the amounts of alimony and child support that are being awarded are grossly unfair, given the unequal situations in which marriage leaves men and women. The effect of judges' tendency to regard the husband's post-divorce income as first and foremost his is that they "rarely require him to help [his for-mer wife and children] sustain a standard of living *half as good as his own*."[5]

Another reason that divorced women are likely to have to rely on their own, often inadequate, earnings is that they are much less likely than their ex-husbands to remarry. The reasons for this are almost all socially created and therefore alterable. In the vast majority of cases, a divorced mother continues to take primary responsibility for the children, but she has lost to a very large extent the financial resources she had within marriage, making her a less attractive marital partner than the typical divorced man. Custody of children is known to be a factor that discourages remarriage. Men who divorce in their thirties and forties are typically noncustodial parents, and are often at the height of their earning power—not an insignificant factor in attracting a subsequent, sometimes much younger wife. Such a couple will not be affected by the social disapproval attached to a woman who marries a much younger man, in the rare case that she does so. Whereas increasing age is not much of an impediment for a man seeking to remarry, it seriously affects a woman's chances which decrease from 56 percent in her thirties to less than 12 percent if she is in her fifties or older when divorced. This is largely, of course, because so much more emphasis is placed on youth and good looks as constituting attractiveness in women than in men. And ironically, success at work, highly correlated with remarriage for men, is inversely correlated for women.

By attempting to treat men and women as equals at the end of marriage, current divorce law neglects not only the obvious fact that women are not the socioeconomic equals of men in our society, but also the highly relevant fact that the experience of gendered marriage and primary parenting greatly exacerbates the inequality that women already bring with them into marriage. To divide the property equally and leave each partner to support himself or herself and to share support of the children might be fair in the case of a marriage in which the paid

---

[1] Ellwood, *Poor Support*, p. 158.

[2] Weitzman, *The Divorce Revolution*, pp. 264–76.

[3] Bianchi and Spain, *American Women*, pp. 212–14; Sidel, *Women and Children*, p. 103.

[4] Weitzman, *The Divorce Revolution*, pp. 295–300, esp. table 25, p. 296.

[5] Ibid., p. 183, emphasis added; see also Ellwood, *Poor Support*, pp. 158–60.

and unpaid labor had been shared equally, and in which neither spouse's work life had taken priority over that of the other. However, as we have seen, such marriages are exceedingly rare. Traditional or quasi-traditional marriages are far more common, even in the case of the many wives who currently work full-time outside the home. A wife who has contributed at least her fair share in a gender-structured marriage, by undertaking virtually all of the unpaid family work while her husband pursues his work life, meanwhile greatly enhancing his actual and prospective earnings, is by no means treated equally if, at the time of divorce, she is almost entirely cut off from the benefits of his enhanced economic position. But in the typical divorce today, this is exactly what happens.

Clearly, the prospects of a divorcing woman, particularly if she is a custodial parent, are in many ways much bleaker than the prospects of a divorcing man. For the many reasons discussed, the economic costs of divorce fall overwhelmingly on women and children, and not on men. Along with these costs go great social and psychological costs, associated with the greater dislocation of their lives and the stress that accompany economic loss. It is highly significant that, unlike men, both women and children experience economic loss as the worst dimension of divorce. Moreover, recent research has shown that, due to the inadequacy in amount and duration of child support, even children of middle-class divorced parents often experience serious and long-term disadvantage and loss of opportunity.

This implies, of course, that social reform could significantly alter the negative impact of divorce on those who suffer most from it. The important lesson is that women's vulnerability within marriage and their disadvantaged position in the case of marital breakdown are intimately linked. Women are made vulnerable by anticipation of gendered marriage, and are made more vulnerable by entering into and living within such marriage. But they are most vulnerable if they marry and have children, but then the marriage fails. Surely women's awareness of this situation has some effects on their behavior and on the distribution of power within marriage itself.

Exit, Threat of Exit, and Power in the Family

At the beginning of this chapter, I summarized Goodin's argument that socially created asymmetric vulnerability is morally unacceptable, and should be minimized. I also referred to Hirschman's arguments about the effects of persons' relative potentials for exit on their power or influence within relationships or groups. Neither of these theorists considers the institution of contemporary marriage an example of such power imbalance. But the evidence presented here suggests that typical, contemporary, gender-structured marriage is an excellent example of socially created vulnerability, partly because the asymmetric dependency of wives on husbands affects their potential for satisfactory exit, and thereby influences the effectiveness of their voice within the marriage.

There has been virtual silence among theorists about the dimension of power in the family that accrues to the spouse who would lose less by exiting from the marriage—a dimension that those who study it seem loath to recognize, partly, no doubt, because it ill accords with society's beliefs about how intimate or romantic relationships are conducted. Three rare scholars who have explicitly applied the notion that potential for exit affects power of voice within marriage are Heer, critiquing Blood and Wolfe's distorted theory of family power, and Bergmann and Fuchs in their recent studies of women's continuing inequality.[1] All three make brief but succinct and lucid arguments that are clearly further validated by the evidence presented here—that marriage is a clear case of asymmetric vulnerability, in which not only power to make decisions but also power to prevent issues from becoming objects of decision is related to the spouses' relative opportunities to exit satisfactorily from the relationship. More typically, marriage is not treated as a situation to which the general theory of the effects of unequal dependency and potential for exit on power applies.

---

[1] Bergmann, *Economic Emergence*, pp. 269–70; Fuchs, *Women's Quest*, pp. 71–76; Heer, "The Measurement and Bases of Family Power: An Overview," p. 138.

Blood asserts, for example, that Heer's "exit" theory is rendered implausible by the fact that "*only* 37 percent" of the couples questioned in a 1939 study of marital success or failure had ever contemplated separation or divorce.[1] Surely this is a remarkably high percentage, especially given the far lower divorce rate then than now.

Of course, the family and other personal relations are special cases of this theory, as of so many others. But the aspects of families that make them different from other institutions such as political parties, schools, and so on, to which theories about the effect of different potentials for exit on power have typically been applied, do not render these theories inapplicable to them. Families are typically held together by strong ties of loyalty, and separation or divorce represents a drastic "solution" to their conflicts. But, particularly now that one in two marriages is expected to end in divorce, it is simply unrealistic to suggest that the threat of exit is absent, especially at times of marital conflict, or that the different abilities of spouses implicitly or explicitly to call on this threat are not likely to affect power and influence in the relationship. Ending a marriage usually causes pain and dislocation for both adults as well as for any children involved. However, the argument presented in this chapter has demonstrated clearly that, in all the ways that are affected by economic deprivation, women and children are likely to suffer considerably more than men from marital dissolution. It is highly probable that most wives, well aware of this fact, take it into consideration in deciding how firm a stand to take on, or even whether to raise, important issues that are likely to be conflictual. We cannot adequately understand the distribution of power in the family without taking this factor into account, and the idea that marriage is a just relationship of mutual vulnerability cannot survive this analysis.

If we are to aim at making the family, our most fundamental social grouping, more just, we must work toward eradicating the socially created vulnerabilities of women that stem from the division of labor and the resultant division of power within it. As I shall argue in the final chapter [in *Justice, Gender, and the Family*], in order to do anything effective about the cycle of women's socially created vulnerability, we must take into account the current lack of clarity in law, public policy, and public opinion about *what marriage is*. Since evidently we do not all agree about what it is or should be, we must think in terms of building family and work institutions that enable people to structure their personal lives in different ways. If they are to avoid injustice to women and children, these institutions must encourage the avoidance of socially created vulnerabilities by facilitating and reinforcing the equal sharing of paid and unpaid work between men and women, and consequently the equalizing of their opportunities and obligations in general. They must also ensure that those who enter into relationships in which there is a division of labor that might render them vulnerable are fully protected against such vulnerability, both within the context of the ongoing relationship and in the event of its dissolution.

DISCUSSION QUESTIONS

1. Okin argues that "gender-structured marriage *involves women in a cycle of socially caused and distinctly asymmetric vulnerability*." Explain what she means.

2. Explain how Okin appeals to the ability to exit marriage in her argument. What does she mean by that phrase? Do you agree with her claims? Why or why not?

3. What sorts of policy proposals might help to address the kinds of vulnerabilities that Okin ascribes to women? Are any such proposals desirable or attractive? Why or why not?

56

SEX, FREEDOM, AND MARRIAGE

Andrew Sullivan, "The Conservative Case" (1995)

Andrew Sullivan (b.1963) is a conservative political commentator. Born in England, he has lived in the United States since 1984. He is the former editor of *The New Republic* and is the author of the well-known blog *The Daily Dish*, which is part of *The Atlantic Online*. As an openly gay man and an advocate of gay marriage, Sullivan has attracted much attention and spawned much controversy within conservative circles.

SOURCE

Sullivan, Andrew. "The Conservative Case," from *Virtually Normal* by Andrew Sullivan. Copyright © 1995 by Andrew Sullivan. Used by permission of Alfred A. Knopf, a division of Random House, Inc.

The most common conservative argument against same-sex marriage is that the public acceptance of homosexuality subverts the stability and self-understanding of the heterosexual family. But here the conservative position undermines itself somewhat. Since most conservatives concede the presence of a number of involuntarily homosexual persons, they must also concede that these persons are already part of "heterosexual" families. They are sons and daughters, brothers and sisters, even mothers and fathers, of heterosexuals. The distinction between "families" and "homosexuals" is, to begin with, empirically false; and the stability of existing families is closely linked to how homosexuals are treated within them. Presumably, it is against the interest of heterosexual families to force homosexuals into roles they are not equipped to play and may disastrously perform. This is not an abstract matter. It is quite common that homosexual fathers and mothers who are encouraged into heterosexual marriages subsequently find the charade and dishonesty too great to bear: spouses are betrayed, children are abandoned, families are broken, and lives are ruined. It is also common that homosexual sons and daughters who are denied the love and support of their families are liable to turn against the institution of the family, to wound and destroy it, out of hurt and rejection. And that parents, inculcated in the kind of disdain of homosexuality conservatives claim is necessary to protect the family, react to the existence of gay children with unconscionable anger and pain, and actually help destroy loving families.

Still, conservatives may concede this and still say that it's worth it. The threat to the stability of the family posed by public disapproval of homosexuality is not as great as the threat posed by public approval. How does this argument work? Largely by saying that the lives saved by preventing wavering straights from becoming gay are more numerous than the lives saved by keeping gay people out of heterosexual relationships and allowing greater tolerance of gay members of families themselves; that the stability of the society is better served by the former than by the latter. Now, recall that conservatives are not attempting to assert absolute moral truths here. They are making an argument about social goods, in this case, social and familial stability. They are saying that a homosexual life is, on the face of it, worse than a heterosexual life, as far as society is concerned. In Harvard psychologist E.L. Pattullo's words,

> Though we acknowledge some influences—social and biological—beyond their control, we do not accept the idea that people of bad character had no choice. Further, we are concerned to maintain a social climate that will steer them in the direction of the good.

The issue here is bad character and the implied association of bad character with the life of homosexuals. Although many conservatives feel loath to articulate what they mean by this life, it's clear what lies behind it. So if they won't articulate it, allow me. They mean by "a homosexual life" one in which emotional commitments are fleeting, promiscuous sex is common, disease is rampant, social ostracism is common, and standards of public decency, propriety, and self-restraint are flaunted [sic]. They mean a way of life that deliberately subverts gender norms in order to unsettle the virtues that make family life possible, ridicules heterosexual life, and commits itself to an ethic of hedonism, loneliness, and deceit. They mean by all this "the other," against which any norm has to be defended

and any cohesive society protected. So it is clear that whatever good might be served by preventing gay people from becoming parents or healing internal wounds within existing families, it is greatly outweighed by the dangers of unleashing this kind of ethic upon the society as a whole.

But the argument, of course, begs a question. Is this kind of life, according to conservatives, what a homosexual life *necessarily* is? Surely not. If homosexuality is often indeed involuntary, as conservatives believe, then homosexuals are not automatically the "other"; they are sprinkled randomly throughout society, into families that are very much like anybody else's, with characters and bodies and minds as varied as the rest of humanity. If all human beings are, as conservatives believe, subject to social inducements to lead better or worse lives, then there is nothing inevitable at all about a homosexual leading a depraved life. In some cases, he might even be a paragon of virtue. Why then is the choice of a waverer to live a homosexual rather than a heterosexual life necessarily a bad one, from the point of view of society? Why does it lead to any necessary social harm at all?

Of course, if you simply define "homosexual" as "depraved," you have an answer; but it's essentially a tautologous one. And if you argue that in our society at this time, homosexual lives simply *are* more depraved, you are also begging a question. There are very few social incentives of the kind conservatives like for homosexuals *not* to be depraved: there's little social or familial support, no institution to encourage fidelity or monogamy, precious little religious or moral outreach to guide homosexuals into more virtuous living. This is not to say that homosexuals are not responsible for their actions, merely that in a large part of homosexual subculture there is much a conservative would predict, when human beings are abandoned with extremely few social incentives for good or socially responsible behavior. But the proper conservative response to this is surely not to infer that this behavior is inevitable, or to use it as a reason to deter others from engaging in a responsible homosexual existence, if that is what they want; but rather to construct social institutions and guidelines to modify and change that behavior for the better. But that is what conservatives resolutely refuse to do.

Why? Maybe for conservatives, there is something inherent even in the most virtuous homosexual life that renders it less desirable than the virtuous heterosexual life, and therefore merits social discouragement to deter the waverers. Let's assume, from a conservative perspective, the best-case scenario for such a waverer: he can choose between a loving, stable, and responsible same-sex relationship and a loving, stable, and responsible opposite-sex relationship. Why should society preference the latter?

The most common response is along the lines of Hadley Arkes, the conservative commentator, who has written on this subject on occasion. It is that the heterosexual relationship is good for men not simply because it forces them to cooperate and share with other human beings on a daily basis but because it forces them into daily contact and partnership with *women*:

> It is not marriage that domesticates men; it is women. Left to themselves, these forked creatures follow a way of life that George Gilder once recounted in its precise, chilling measures: bachelors were twenty-two times more likely than married men to be committed to hospital for mental disease (and ten times more likely to suffer chronic diseases of all lands). Single men had nearly double the mortality rate of married men and three times the mortality rate of single women. Divorced men were three times more likely than divorced women to commit suicide or die by murder, and they were six times more likely to die of heart disease.

I will leave aside the statistical difficulties here: it's perfectly possible that many of the problems Arkes recounts were reasons why the men didn't get married, rather than consequences of their failing to do so. Let's assume, for the sake of argument, that Arkes is right: that marriage to a woman is clearly preferable to being single for an adult man; that such a man is more likely to be emotionally stable, physically healthy, psychologically in balance; and that this is good for the society as a whole. There is in this argument a belief that women are naturally more prone to be stable, nurturing, supportive of stability, fiscally prudent, and family-oriented than men, and that their connection to as many men as possible is therefore clearly a social good. Let's assume also, for the sake of argument, that Arkes is right about that too. It's obvious, according to conservatives, that society should encourage a stable opposite-sex relationship over a stable same-sex relationship.

But the waverer has another option: he can remain single. Should society actually encourage him to do this rather than involve himself in a stable, loving same-sex relationship? Surely, even conservatives who think women are essential to the successful socialization of men would not deny that the discipline of domesticity, of shared duties and lives, of the inevitable give-and-take of cohabitation and love with anyone, even of the same sex, tends to benefit men more than the option of constant, freewheeling, etiolating bachelorhood. But this would mean creating a public moral and social climate which preferred stable gay relationships to gay or straight bachelorhood. And it would require generating a notion of homosexual responsibility that would destroy the delicately balanced conservative politics of private discretion and undiscriminating public disapproval. So conservatives are stuck again: their refusal to embrace responsible public support for virtuous homosexuals runs counter to their entire social agenda.

Arkes's argument also leads to another (however ironic) possibility destabilizing to conservatism's delicate contemporary compromise on the homosexual question: that for a wavering woman, a lesbian relationship might actually be socially *preferable* to a heterosexual relationship. If the issue is not mere domesticity but the presence of women, why would two women not be better than one, for the sake of children's development and social stability? Since lesbianism seems to be more amenable to choice than male homosexuality in most studies and surveys, conservatism's emphasis on social encouragement of certain behaviors over others might be seen as even more relevant here. If conservatism is about the social benefits of feminizing society, there is no reason why it should not be an integral part of the movement for women to liberate themselves completely from men. Of course, I'm being facetious; conservatives would be terrified by all the single males such a society would leave rampaging around. But it's not inconceivable at all from conservative premises that, solely from the point of view of the wavering woman, the ascending priorities would be: remaining single, having a stable, loving opposite-sex relationship, and having a stable, loving same-sex relationship. And there is something deliciously ironic about the sensibility of Hadley Arkes and E.L. Pattullo finding its full fruition in a lesbian collective.

Still, the conservative has another option. He might argue that removing the taboo on homosexuality would unravel an entire fabric of self-understanding in the society at large that could potentially destabilize the whole system of incentives for stable family relationships. He might argue that now, of all times, when families are in an unprecedented state of collapse, is not the occasion for further tinkering with this system; that the pride of heterosexual men and women is at stake; that their self-esteem and self-understanding would be undermined if society saw them as equivalent to homosexuals. In this view, the stigmatization of homosexuals is the necessary corollary to the celebration of traditional family life.

Does this ring true? To begin with, it's not at all clear why, if public disapproval of homosexuals is indeed necessary to keep families together, homosexuals of all people should bear the primary brunt of the task. But it's also not clear why the corollary really works to start with. Those homosexuals who have no choice at all to be homosexual, whom conservatives do not want to be in a heterosexual family in the first place, are clearly no threat to the heterosexual family. Why would accepting that such people exist, encouraging them to live virtuous lives, incorporating their difference into society as a whole, necessarily devalue the traditional family? It is not a zero-sum game. Because they have no choice but to be homosexual, they are not choosing that option over heterosexual marriage; and so they are not sending any social signals that heterosexual family life should be denigrated.

The more difficult case, of course, pertains to Arkes's "waverers." Would allowing them the option of a stable same-sex relationship as a preferable social option to being single really undermine the institution of the family? Is it inconceivable that a society can be subtle in its public indications of what is and what is not socially preferable? Surely, society can offer a hierarchy of choices, which, while preferencing one, does not necessarily denigrate the others, but accords them some degree of calibrated respect. It does this in many other areas. Why not in sexual arrangements?

You see this already in many families with homosexual members. While some parents are disappointed that their son or daughter will not marry someone of the opposite sex, provide grandchildren and sustain the family line for another generation, they still prefer to see that child find someone to love and live with and share his or her life with. That child's siblings, who may be heterosexual, need feel no disapproval attached to their own marriage by the simple fact of their sibling's difference. Why should society as a whole find it an impossible task to share in the same maturity? Even in the most homosexualized culture, conservatives would still expect over eighty percent of couples to be heterosexual: why is their self-esteem likely to be threatened by a paltry twenty percent—especially when, according to conservatives, the homosexual life is so self-evidently inferior?

In fact, it's perfectly possible to combine a celebration of the traditional family with the celebration of a stable homosexual relationship. The one, after all, is modeled on the other. If constructed carefully as a conservative social ideology, the notion of stable gay relationships might even serve to buttress the ethic of heterosexual marriage, by showing how even those excluded from it can wish to model themselves on its shape and structure. This very truth, of course, is why liberationists are so hostile to the entire notion. Rather than liberating society from asphyxiating conventions it actually harnesses one minority group—homosexuals—and enlists them in the conservative structures that liberationists find so inimical. One can indeed see the liberationists' reasons for opposing such a move. But why should conservatives oppose it?

DISCUSSION QUESTION

1. Which of the conservative arguments against gay marriage discussed by Sullivan do you think is the strongest argument? Do you think that Sullivan has a good response to that argument? Explain.

57

SEX, FREEDOM, AND MARRIAGE
Loving v. Virginia[1] (1967)

Loving v. Virginia was the notable civil rights case in which the US Supreme Court decided by that Virginia's anti-miscegenation statute was unconstitutional. Married in 1958 in the District of Columbia, plaintiffs Mildred Loving (of African and American-Indian descent) and Richard Loving were arrested upon returning to their home in Virginia. Virginia's Racial Integrity Act banned marriage between any white person and any non-white person. The Lovings successfully argued that the ban on interracial marriage violated their rights as protected both by the Equal Protection and the Due Process Clauses of the Fourteenth Amendment.

SOURCE
388 U.S. 1 (U.S. Supreme Court).

Syllabus
SUPREME COURT OF THE UNITED STATES
388 U.S. 1
Loving v. Virginia
APPEAL FROM THE SUPREME COURT OF APPEALS OF VIRGINIA
No. 395 Argued: April 10, 1967—Decided: June 12, 1967
Virginia's statutory scheme to prevent marriages between persons solely on the basis of racial classifications held to violate the Equal Protection and Due Process Clauses of the Fourteenth Amendment. [...]

MR. CHIEF JUSTICE WARREN delivered the opinion of the Court.

This case presents a constitutional question never addressed by this Court: whether a statutory scheme adopted by the State of Virginia to prevent marriages between persons solely on the basis of racial classifications violates the Equal Protection and Due Process Clauses of the Fourteenth Amendment. For reasons which seem to us to reflect the central meaning of those constitutional commands, we conclude that these statutes cannot stand consistently with the Fourteenth Amendment.

In June, 1958, two residents of Virginia, Mildred Jeter, a Negro woman, and Richard Loving, a white man, were married in the District of Columbia

---

[1] [Original notes have been omitted.]

pursuant to its laws. Shortly after their marriage, the Lovings returned to Virginia and established their marital abode in Caroline County. At the October Term, 1958, of the Circuit Court of Caroline County, a grand jury issued an indictment charging the Lovings with violating Virginia's ban on interracial marriages. On January 6, 1959, the Lovings pleaded guilty to the charge, and were sentenced to one year in jail; however, the trial judge suspended the sentence for a period of 25 years on the condition that the Lovings leave the State and not return to Virginia together for 25 years. He stated in an opinion that:

> Almighty God created the races white, black, yellow, malay and red, and he placed them on separate continents. And, but for the interference with his arrangement, there would be no cause for such marriage. The fact that he separated the races shows that he did not intend for the races to mix.

After their convictions, the Lovings took up residence in the District of Columbia. On November 6, 1963, they filed a motion in the state trial court to vacate the judgment and set aside the sentence on the ground that the statutes which they had violated were repugnant to the Fourteenth Amendment. The motion not having been decided by October 28, 1964, the Lovings instituted a class action in the United States District Court for the Eastern District of Virginia requesting that a three-judge court be convened to declare the Virginia anti-miscegenation statutes unconstitutional and to enjoin state officials from enforcing their convictions. On January 22, 1965, the state trial judge denied the motion to vacate the sentences, and the Lovings perfected an appeal to the Supreme Court of Appeals of Virginia. On February 11, 1965, the three-judge District Court continued the case to allow the Lovings to present their constitutional claims to the highest state court.

The Supreme Court of Appeals upheld the constitutionality of the anti-miscegenation statutes and, after modifying the sentence, affirmed the convictions. The Lovings appealed this decision, and we noted probable jurisdiction on December 12, 1966, 385 U.S. 986.

The two statutes under which appellants were convicted and sentenced are part of a comprehensive statutory scheme aimed at prohibiting and punishing interracial marriages. The Lovings were convicted of violating § 258 of the Virginia Code:

> *Leaving State to evade law.*—If any white person and colored person shall go out of this State, for the purpose of being married, and with the intention of returning, and be married out of it, and afterwards return to and reside in it, cohabiting as man and wife, they shall be punished as provided in § 20–59, and the marriage shall be governed by the same law as if it had been solemnized in this State. The fact of their cohabitation here as man and wife shall be evidence of their marriage.

Section 259, which defines the penalty for miscegenation, provides:

> *Punishment for marriage.* —If any white person intermarry with a colored person, or any colored person intermarry with a white person, he shall be guilty of a felony and shall be punished by confinement in the penitentiary for not less than one nor more than five years.

Other central provisions in the Virginia statutory scheme are § 20–57, which automatically voids all marriages between "a white person and a colored person" without any judicial proceeding, and §§ 20–54 and 1–14 which, respectively, define "white persons" and "colored persons and Indians" for purposes of the statutory prohibitions. The Lovings have never disputed in the course of this litigation that Mrs. Loving is a "colored person" or that Mr. Loving is a "white person" within the meanings given those terms by the Virginia statutes.

Virginia is now one of 16 States which prohibit and punish marriages on the basis of racial classifications. Penalties for miscegenation arose as an incident to slavery, and have been common in Virginia since the colonial period. The present statutory scheme dates from the adoption of the Racial Integrity Act of 1924, passed during the period of extreme nativism which followed the end of the First World War. The central features of this Act, and current Virginia law, are the absolute prohibition of a "white person" marrying other than another "white person," a prohibition against issuing marriage licenses until the issuing official is satisfied that the applicants' statements as to their race are correct, certificates of "racial composition" to be kept by both local and state registrars, and the carrying forward of earlier prohibitions against racial intermarriage.

I

In upholding the constitutionality of these provisions in the decision below, the Supreme Court of Appeals of Virginia referred to its 1965 decision in *Naim v. Naim,* 197 Va. 80, 87 S.E.2d 749, as stating the reasons supporting the validity of these laws. In *Naim,* the state court concluded that the State's legitimate purposes were "to preserve the racial integrity of its citizens," and to prevent "the corruption of blood," "a mongrel breed of citizens," and "the obliteration of racial pride," obviously an endorsement of the doctrine of White Supremacy. *Id.* at 90, 87 S.E.2d at 756. The court also reasoned that marriage has traditionally been subject to state regulation without federal intervention, and, consequently, the regulation of marriage should be left to exclusive state control by the Tenth Amendment.

While the state court is no doubt correct in asserting that marriage is a social relation subject to the State's police power, *Maynard v. Hill,* 125 U.S. 190 (1888), the State does not contend in its argument before this Court that its powers to regulate marriage are unlimited notwithstanding the commands of the Fourteenth Amendment. Nor could it do so in light of *Meyer v. Nebraska,* 262 U.S. 390 (1923), and *Skinner v. Oklahoma,* 316 U.S. 535 (1942). Instead, the State argues that the meaning of the Equal Protection Clause, as illuminated by the statements of the Framers, is only that state penal laws containing an interracial element

as part of the definition of the offense must apply equally to whites and Negroes in the sense that members of each race are punished to the same degree. Thus, the State contends that, because its miscegenation statutes punish equally both the white and the Negro participants in an interracial marriage, these statutes, despite their reliance on racial classifications, do not constitute an invidious discrimination based upon race. The second argument advanced by the State assumes the validity of its equal application theory. The argument is that, if the Equal Protection Clause does not outlaw miscegenation statutes because of their reliance on racial classifications, the question of constitutionality would thus become whether there was any rational basis for a State to treat interracial marriages differently from other marriages. On this question, the State argues, the scientific evidence is substantially in doubt and, consequently, this Court should defer to the wisdom of the state legislature in adopting its policy of discouraging interracial marriages.

Because we reject the notion that the mere "equal application" of a statute containing racial classifications is enough to remove the classifications from the Fourteenth Amendment's proscription of all invidious racial discriminations, we do not accept the State's contention that these statutes should be upheld if there is any possible basis for concluding that they serve a rational purpose. The mere fact of equal application does not mean that our analysis of these statutes should follow the approach we have taken in cases involving no racial discrimination where the Equal Protection Clause has been arrayed against a statute discriminating between the kinds of advertising which may be displayed on trucks in New York City, *Railway Express Agency, Inc. v. New York,* 336 U.S. 106 (1949), or an exemption in Ohio's *ad valorem* tax for merchandise owned by a nonresident in a storage warehouse, *Allied Stores of Ohio, Inc. v. Bowers,* 358 U.S. 522 (1959). In these cases, involving distinctions not drawn according to race, the Court has merely asked whether there is any rational foundation for the discriminations, and has deferred to the wisdom of the state legislatures. In the case at bar, however, we deal with statutes containing racial classifications, and the fact of equal application does not immunize the statute from the very heavy burden of justification which the Fourteenth Amendment has traditionally required of state statutes drawn according to race.

The State argues that statements in the Thirty-ninth Congress about the time of the passage of the Fourteenth Amendment indicate that the Framers did not intend the Amendment to make unconstitutional state miscegenation laws. Many of the statements alluded to by the State concern the debates over the Freedmen's Bureau Bill, which President Johnson vetoed, and the Civil Rights Act of 1866, 14 Stat. 27, enacted over his veto. While these statements have some relevance to the intention of Congress in submitting the Fourteenth Amendment, it must be understood that they pertained to the passage of specific statutes, and not to the broader, organic purpose of a constitutional amendment. As for the various statements directly concerning the Fourteenth Amendment, we have said in connection with a related problem that, although these historical sources "cast some light" they are not sufficient to resolve the problem; [a]t best, they are inconclusive. The most avid proponents of the post-War Amendments undoubtedly intended them to remove all legal distinctions among "all persons born or naturalized in the United States." Their opponents, just as certainly, were antagonistic to both the letter and the spirit of the Amendments, and wished them to have the most limited effect. [*Brown v. Board of Education,* 347 U.S. 483, 489 (1954). *See also Strauder v. West Virginia,* 100 U.S. 303, 310 (1880).]

We have rejected the proposition that the debates in the Thirty-ninth Congress or in the state legislatures which ratified the Fourteenth Amendment supported the theory advanced by the State, that the requirement of equal protection of the laws is satisfied by penal laws defining offenses based on racial classifications so long as white and Negro participants in the offense were similarly punished. *McLaughlin v. Florida,* 379 U.S. 184 (1964).

The State finds support for its "equal application" theory in the decision of the Court in *Pace*

v. Alabama, 106 U.S. 583 (1883). In that case, the Court upheld a conviction under an Alabama statute forbidding adultery or fornication between a white person and a Negro which imposed a greater penalty than that of a statute proscribing similar conduct by members of the same race. The Court reasoned that the statute could not be said to discriminate against Negroes because the punishment for each participant in the offense was the same. However, as recently as the 1964 Term, in rejecting the reasoning of that case, we stated "*Pace* represents a limited view of the Equal Protection Clause which has not withstood analysis in the subsequent decisions of this Court." *McLaughlin v. Florida, supra,* at 188. As we there demonstrated, the Equal Protection Clause requires the consideration of whether the classifications drawn by any statute constitute an arbitrary and invidious discrimination. The clear and central purpose of the Fourteenth Amendment was to eliminate all official state sources of invidious racial discrimination in the States. *Slaughter-House Cases,* 16 Wall. 36, 71 (1873); *Strauder v. West Virginia,* 100 U.S. 303, 307–308 (1880); *Ex parte Virginia,* 100 U.S. 339, 334–335 (1880); *Shelley v. Kraemer,* 334 U.S. 1 (1948); *Burton v. Wilmington Parking Authority,* 365 U.S. 715 (1961).

There can be no question but that Virginia's miscegenation statutes rest solely upon distinctions drawn according to race. The statutes proscribe generally accepted conduct if engaged in by members of different races. Over the years, this Court has consistently repudiated "[d]istinctions between citizens solely because of their ancestry" as being "odious to a free people whose institutions are founded upon the doctrine of equality." *Hirabayashi v. United States,* 320 U.S. 81, 100 (1943). At the very least, the Equal Protection Clause demands that racial classifications, especially suspect in criminal statutes, be subjected to the "most rigid scrutiny," *Korematsu v. United States,* 323 U.S. 214, 216 (1944), and, if they are ever to be upheld, they must be shown to be necessary to the accomplishment of some permissible state objective, independent of the racial discrimination which it was the object of the Fourteenth Amendment to eliminate. Indeed, two members of this Court have already stated that they cannot conceive of a valid legislative purpose … which makes the color of a person's skin the test of whether his conduct is a criminal offense.

McLaughlin v. Florida, supra, at 198 (STEWART, J., joined by DOUGLAS, J., concurring).

There is patently no legitimate overriding purpose independent of invidious racial discrimination which justifies this classification. The fact that Virginia prohibits only interracial marriages involving white persons demonstrates that the racial classifications must stand on their own justification, as measures designed to maintain White Supremacy. We have consistently denied the constitutionality of measures which restrict the rights of citizens on account of race. There can be no doubt that restricting the freedom to marry solely because of racial classifications violates the central meaning of the Equal Protection Clause.

II

These statutes also deprive the Lovings of liberty without due process of law in violation of the Due Process Clause of the Fourteenth Amendment. The freedom to marry has long been recognized as one of the vital personal rights essential to the orderly pursuit of happiness by free men.

Marriage is one of the "basic civil rights of man," fundamental to our very existence and survival. *Skinner v. Oklahoma,* 316 U.S. 535, 541 (1942).

See also Maynard v. Hill, 125 U.S. 190 (1888). To deny this fundamental freedom on so unsupportable a basis as the racial classifications embodied in these statutes, classifications so directly subversive of the principle of equality at the heart of the Fourteenth Amendment, is surely to deprive all the State's citizens of liberty without due process of law. The Fourteenth Amendment requires that the freedom of choice to marry not be restricted by invidious racial discriminations. Under our Constitution, the freedom to marry, or not marry, a person of another race resides with the individual, and cannot be infringed by the State.

These convictions must be reversed.

It is so ordered.

DISCUSSION QUESTIONS

1. Explain the "equal application" rationale for upholding the legality of statutes criminalizing interracial marriage. Why did the court reject such defenses in *Loving v. Virginia*?

2. How did the court argue that Virginia's anti-miscegenation statute violated the Equal Protection Clause of the Fourteenth Amendment? Evaluate its argument.

58

SEX, FREEDOM, AND MARRIAGE
Selection from *Marriage Cases*, Supreme Court of California (2008)[1]

The following selection from *Marriage Cases* summarizes the arguments and opinions of the Supreme Court of California regarding the issue of the constitutionality of denying homosexual couples the right to marry. The Court argues that homosexuals do have such a right under the Constitution and that the previous "domestic partnership" legislation failed to treat them with equal dignity and respect.

SOURCE

43 Cal. 4th 757 (Supreme Court of California).

[...]
In re **MARRIAGE CASES**.
[Six consolidated appeals.]
[...]

In *Lockyer v. City and County of San Francisco* (2004) 33 Cal.4th 1055 (*Lockyer*), this court concluded that public officials of the City and County of San Francisco acted unlawfully by issuing marriage licenses to same-sex couples in the absence of a judicial determination that the California statutes limiting marriage to a union between a man and a woman are unconstitutional. Our decision in *Lockyer* emphasized, however, that the substantive question of the constitutional validity of the California marriage statutes was not before this court in that proceeding, and that our decision was not intended to reflect any view on that issue. (*Id.* at p. 1069; see also *id.* at p. 1125 (conc. opn. of Moreno, J.); *id.* At pp. 1132–1133 (conc. & dis. opn. of Kennard, J.); *id.* at p. 1133 (conc. & dis. opn. of Werdegar, J.).) The present proceeding, involving the consolidated appeal of six cases that were litigated in the superior court and the Court of Appeal in the wake of this court's decision in *Lockyer*, squarely presents the substantive constitutional question that was not addressed in *Lockyer*.

In considering this question, we note at the outset that the constitutional issue before us differs in

---

[1] [Many of the original notes have been omitted.]

a significant respect from the constitutional issue that has been addressed by a number of other state supreme courts and intermediate appellate courts that recently have had occasion, in interpreting the applicable provisions of their respective state constitutions, to determine the validity of statutory provisions or common law rules limiting marriage to a union of a man and a woman. (See, e.g., *Conaway v. Deane* (Md. 2007) 932 A.2d 571; *Goodridge v. Dept. of Pub. Health* (Mass. 2003) 798 N.E.2d 941; *Lewis v. Harris* (N.J. 2006) 908 A.2d 196; *Hernandez v. Robles* (N.Y. 2006) 855 N.E.2d 1; *Baker v. State* (Vt. 1999) 744 A.2d 864; *Andersen v. King County* (Wn. 2006) 138 P.3d 963; *Standhardt v. Superior Court* (Ariz.Ct.App. 2003) 77 P.3d 451; *Morrison v. Sadler* (Ind.Ct.App. 2005) 821 N.E.2d 15.) These courts, often by a one-vote margin ..., have ruled upon the validity of statutory schemes that contrast with that of California, which in recent years has enacted comprehensive domestic partnership legislation under which a same-sex couple may enter into a legal relationship that affords the couple virtually all of the same substantive legal benefits and privileges, and imposes upon the couple virtually all of the same legal obligations and duties, that California law affords to and imposes upon a married couple. Past California cases explain that the constitutional validity of a challenged statute or statutes must be evaluated by taking into consideration all of the relevant statutory provisions that bear upon how the state treats the affected persons with regard to the subject at issue. (See, e.g., *Brown v. Merlo* (1973) 8 Cal.3d 855, 862.) Accordingly, the legal issue we must resolve is not whether it would be constitutionally permissible under the California Constitution for the state to limit marriage only to opposite-sex couples while denying same-sex couples any opportunity to enter into an official relationship with all or virtually all of the same substantive attributes, but rather whether our state Constitution prohibits the state from establishing a statutory scheme in which both opposite-sex and same-sex couples are granted the right to enter into an officially recognized family relationship that affords all of the

significant legal rights and obligations traditionally associated under state law with the institution of marriage, but under which the union of an opposite-sex couple is officially designated a "marriage" whereas the union of a same-sex couple is officially designated a "domestic partnership." The question we must address is whether, under these circumstances, the failure to designate the official relationship of same-sex couples as marriage violates the California Constitution.

It also is important to understand at the outset that our task in this proceeding is not to decide whether we believe, *as a matter of policy*, that the officially recognized relationship of a same-sex couple *should* be designated a marriage rather than a domestic partnership (or some other term), but instead only to determine whether the difference in the official names of the relationships *violates the California Constitution*. We are aware, of course, that very strongly held differences of opinion exist on the matter of policy, with those persons who support the inclusion of same-sex unions within the definition of marriage maintaining that it is unfair to same-sex couples and potentially detrimental to the fiscal interests of the state and its economic institutions to reserve the designation of marriage solely for opposite-sex couples, and others asserting that it is vitally important to preserve the long-standing and traditional definition of marriage as a union between a man and a woman, even as the state extends comparable rights and responsibilities to committed same-sex couples. Whatever our views as individuals with regard to this question as a matter of policy, we recognize as judges and as a court our responsibility to limit our consideration of the question to a determination of the constitutional validity of the current legislative provisions.

As explained hereafter, the determination whether the current California statutory scheme relating to marriage and to registered domestic partnership is constitutionally valid implicates a number of distinct and significant issues under the California Constitution.

First, we must determine the nature and scope of the "right to marry"—a right that past cases establish as one of the fundamental constitutional rights embodied in the California Constitution. Although, as an historical matter, civil marriage and the rights associated with it traditionally have been afforded only to opposite-sex couples, this court's landmark decision 60 years ago in *Perez v. Sharp* (1948) 32 Cal.2d 711—which found that California's statutory provisions prohibiting interracial marriages were inconsistent with the fundamental constitutional right to marry, notwithstanding the circumstance that statutory prohibitions on interracial marriage had existed since the founding of the state—makes clear that history alone is not invariably an appropriate guide for determining the meaning and scope of this fundamental constitutional guarantee. The decision in *Perez*, although rendered by a deeply divided court, is a judicial opinion whose legitimacy and constitutional soundness are by now universally recognized.

As discussed below, upon review of the numerous California decisions that have examined the underlying bases and significance of the constitutional right to marry (and that illuminate *why* this right has been recognized as one of the basic, inalienable civil rights guaranteed to an individual by the California Constitution), we conclude that, under this state's Constitution, the constitutionally based right to marry properly must be understood to encompass the core set of basic *substantive* legal rights and attributes traditionally associated with marriage that are so integral to an individual's liberty and personal autonomy that they may not be eliminated or abrogated by the Legislature or by the electorate through the statutory initiative process. These core substantive rights include, most fundamentally, the opportunity of an individual to establish—with the person with whom the individual has chosen to share his or her life—an *officially recognized and protected family* possessing mutual rights and responsibilities and entitled to the same respect and dignity accorded a union traditionally designated as marriage. As past cases establish, the substantive right of two adults who share a loving relationship to join together to establish an officially recognized family of their own—and,

if the couple chooses, to raise children within that family—constitutes a vitally important attribute of the fundamental interest in liberty and personal autonomy that the California Constitution secures to all persons for the benefit of both the individual and society.

Furthermore, in contrast to earlier times, our state now recognizes that an individual's capacity to establish a loving and long-term committed relationship with another person and responsibly to care for and raise children does not depend upon the individual's sexual orientation, and, more generally, that an individual's sexual orientation—like a person's race or gender—does not constitute a legitimate basis upon which to deny or withhold legal rights. We therefore conclude that in view of the substance and significance of the fundamental constitutional right to form a family relationship, the California Constitution properly must be interpreted to guarantee this basic civil right to all Californians, whether gay or heterosexual, and to same-sex couples as well as to opposite-sex couples.[1]

In defending the constitutionality of the current statutory scheme, the Attorney General of California maintains that even if the constitutional right to marry under the California Constitution applies to same-sex couples as well as to opposite-sex couples, this right should not be understood as requiring the Legislature to designate a couple's official family relationship by the term "marriage," as opposed to some other nomenclature. The Attorney General, observing that fundamental constitutional rights generally are defined by *substance* rather than by *form*, reasons that so long as the state affords a couple all of the constitutionally protected *substantive* incidents of marriage, the state does not violate the couple's constitutional right to marry simply by assigning their official relationship a *name* other

---

[1] For convenience and economy of language, in this opinion we shall use the term "gay," with reference to an individual, to relate either to a lesbian or to a gay man, and the term "gay couple" to refer to a couple consisting of either two women or two men.

than marriage. Because the Attorney General maintains that California's current domestic partnership legislation affords same-sex couples all of the core substantive rights that plausibly may be guaranteed to an individual or couple as elements of the fundamental state constitutional right to marry, the Attorney General concludes that the current California statutory scheme relating to marriage and domestic partnership does not violate the fundamental constitutional right to marry embodied in the California Constitution.

We need not decide in this case whether the name "marriage" is *invariably* a core element of the state constitutional right to marry so that the state would violate a couple's constitutional right even if—perhaps in order to emphasize and clarify that this civil institution is distinct from the religious institution of marriage—the state were to assign a name other than marriage as the official designation of the formal family relationship for *all* couples. Under the current statutes, the state has not revised the name of the official family relationship for *all* couples, but rather has drawn a distinction between the name for the official family relationship of opposite-sex couples (marriage) and that for same-sex couples (domestic partnership). One of the core elements of the right to establish an officially recognized family that is embodied in the California constitutional right to marry is a couple's right to have their family relationship accorded dignity and respect equal to that accorded other officially recognized families, and assigning a different designation for the family relationship of same-sex couples while reserving the historic designation of "marriage" exclusively for opposite-sex couples poses at least a serious risk of denying the family relationship of same-sex couples such equal dignity and respect. We therefore conclude that although the provisions of the current domestic partnership legislation afford same-sex couples most of the substantive elements embodied in the constitutional right to marry, the current California statutes nonetheless must be viewed as potentially impinging upon a same-sex couple's constitutional right to marry under the California Constitution.

Furthermore, the circumstance that the current California statutes assign a different name for the official family relationship of same-sex couples as contrasted with the name for the official family relationship of opposite-sex couples raises constitutional concerns not only under the state constitutional right to marry, but also under the state constitutional equal protection clause. In analyzing the validity of this differential treatment under the latter clause, we first must determine which standard of review should be applied to the statutory classification here at issue. Although in most instances the deferential "rational basis" standard of review is applicable in determining whether different treatment accorded by a statutory provision violates the state equal protection clause, a more exacting and rigorous standard of review—"strict scrutiny"—is applied when the distinction drawn by a statute rests upon a so-called "suspect classification" or impinges upon a fundamental right. As we shall explain, although we do not agree with the claim advanced by the parties challenging the validity of the current statutory scheme that the applicable statutes properly should be viewed as an instance of discrimination on the basis of the suspect characteristic of sex or gender and should be subjected to strict scrutiny on that ground, we conclude that strict scrutiny nonetheless is applicable here because (1) the statutes in question properly must be understood as classifying or discriminating on the basis of sexual orientation, a characteristic that we conclude represents—like gender, race, and religion—a constitutionally suspect basis upon which to impose differential treatment, and (2) the differential treatment at issue impinges upon a same-sex couple's fundamental interest in having their family relationship accorded the same respect and dignity enjoyed by an opposite-sex couple.

Under the strict scrutiny standard, unlike the rational basis standard, in order to demonstrate the constitutional validity of a challenged statutory classification the state must establish (1) that the state interest intended to be served by the differential treatment not only is a constitutionally legitimate interest, but is a *compelling* state interest, and

(2) that the differential treatment not only is reasonably related to but is *necessary* to serve that compelling state interest. Applying this standard to the statutory classification here at issue, we conclude that the purpose underlying differential treatment of opposite-sex and same-sex couples embodied in California's current marriage statutes—the interest in retaining the traditional and well-established definition of marriage—cannot properly be viewed as a *compelling* state interest for purposes of the equal protection clause, or as *necessary* to serve such an interest. A number of factors lead us to this conclusion. First, the exclusion of same-sex couples from the designation of marriage clearly is not *necessary* in order to afford full protection to all of the rights and benefits that currently are enjoyed by married opposite-sex couples; permitting same-sex couples access to the designation of marriage will not deprive opposite-sex couples of any rights and will not alter the legal framework of the institution of marriage, because same-sex couples who choose to marry will be subject to the same obligations and duties that currently are imposed on married opposite-sex couples. Second, retaining the traditional definition of marriage and affording same-sex couples only a separate and differently named family relationship will, as a realistic matter, impose appreciable harm on same-sex couples and their children, because denying such couples access to the familiar and highly favored designation of marriage is likely to cast doubt on whether the official family relationship of same-sex couples enjoys dignity equal to that of opposite-sex couples. Third, because of the widespread disparagement that gay individuals historically have faced, it is all the more probable that excluding same-sex couples from the legal institution of marriage is likely to be viewed as reflecting an official view that their committed relationships are of lesser stature than the comparable relationships of opposite-sex couples. Finally, retaining the designation of marriage exclusively for opposite-sex couples and providing only a separate and distinct designation for same-sex couples may well have the effect of perpetuating a more general premise—now emphatically rejected by this state—that gay individuals and same-sex couples are in some respects "second-class citizens" who may, under the law, be treated differently from, and less favorably than, heterosexual individuals or opposite-sex couples. Under these circumstances, we cannot find that retention of the traditional definition of marriage constitutes a *compelling* state interest. Accordingly, we conclude that to the extent the current California statutory provisions limit marriage to opposite-sex couples, these statutes are unconstitutional.

[...]

III

We now turn to the significant substantive constitutional issues before us....

[...]

Although California statutes always have limited and continue to limit marriage to opposite-sex couples, as noted at the outset of this opinion California recently has enacted comprehensive domestic partnership legislation that affords same-sex couples the opportunity, by entering into a domestic partnership, to obtain virtually all of the legal benefits, privileges, responsibilities, and duties that California law affords to and imposes upon married couples. The recent comprehensive domestic partnership legislation constitutes the culmination of a gradual expansion of rights that have been made available in this state to same-sex couples who choose to register as domestic partners. We briefly review the history of domestic partnership legislation in California....

[...]

Thus, in sum, the current California statutory provisions generally afford same-sex couples the opportunity to enter into a domestic partnership and thereby obtain virtually all of the benefits and responsibilities afforded by California law to married opposite-sex couples.

While acknowledging that the Domestic Partner Act affords substantial benefits to same-sex couples, plaintiffs repeatedly characterize that legislation as granting same-sex couples only the "material" or "tangible" benefits of marriage. At least in some respects, this characterization inaccurately minimizes the scope and nature of the benefits and responsibilities afforded by California's domestic partnership law. The broad reach of this legislation extends to the extremely wide network of statutory provisions, common law rules, and administrative practices that give substance to the legal institution of civil marriage, including, among many others, various rules and policies concerning parental rights and responsibilities affecting the raising of children, mutual duties of respect, fidelity and support, the fiduciary relationship between partners, the privileged nature of confidential communications between partners, and a partner's authority to make health care decisions when his or her partner is unable to act for himself or herself. These legal rights and responsibilities embody more than merely the "material" or "tangible" financial benefits that are extended by government to married couples. As we explained in *Koebke, supra,* 36 Cal.4th 824, 843: "[T]he decision … to enter into a domestic partnership is more than a change in the legal status of individuals…. [T]he consequence[] of the decision is the creation of a new family unit with all of its implications in terms of personal commitment as well as legal rights and obligations."

The nature and breadth of the rights afforded same-sex couples under the Domestic Partner Act is significant, because under California law the scope of that enactment is directly relevant to the question of the constitutional validity of the provisions in California's marriage statutes limiting marriage to opposite-sex couples. As this court explained in *Brown v. Merlo, supra,* 8 Cal.3d 855, 862: "In determining the scope of the class singled out for special burdens or benefits, a court cannot confine its view to the terms of the specific statute under attack, but must judge the enactment's operation against the background of other legislative, administrative and judicial directives which govern the legal rights of similarly situated persons. As the United States Supreme Court recognized long ago: 'The question of constitutional validity is not to be determined by artificial standards [confining

review 'within the four corners' of a statute]. What is required is that state action, whether through one agency or another, or through one enactment or more than one, shall be consistent with the restrictions of the Federal Constitution.'"

Accordingly, the provisions of both the current marriage statutes and the current domestic partnership statutes must be considered in determining whether the challenged provisions of the marriage statutes violate the constitutional rights of same-sex couples guaranteed by the California Constitution.

IV

Plaintiffs contend that by limiting marriage to opposite-sex couples, California's marriage statutes violate a number of provisions of the California Constitution.[1] In particular, plaintiffs contend that the challenged statutes violate a same-sex couple's fundamental "right to marry" as guaranteed by the privacy, free speech, and due process clauses of the California Constitution (Cal. Const., art. I, §§ 1, 2, 7), and additionally violate the equal protection clause of the California Constitution (Cal. Const., art. I, § 7).[2] Because the question whether the challenged aspect of the marriage statutes violates or impinges upon the fundamental right to marry may be determinative in deciding the appropriate standard of review to be applied in evaluating plaintiffs'

---

[1] Plaintiffs base their constitutional challenge in this case solely upon the provisions of the California Constitution and do not advance any claim under the federal Constitution.

[2] Article I, section 1 provides: "All people are by nature free and independent and have inalienable rights. Among these are enjoying and defending life and *liberty*, acquiring, possessing, and protecting property, and pursuing and obtaining safety, happiness, and *privacy*" (italics added). Article I, section 2, subdivision (a), provides: "Every person may freely speak, write and publish his or her sentiments on all subjects, being responsible for the abuse of this right. A law may not restrain or abridge *liberty of speech or press*" (italics added). Article I, section 7, subdivision (a), provides in relevant part: "A person may not be deprived of life, *liberty*, or property *without due process of law* or denied *equal protection of the laws* …" (italics added).

equal protection challenge, we first address the question whether the challenged statutes independently infringe a fundamental constitutional right guaranteed by the California Constitution.

A

Although our state Constitution does not contain any explicit reference to a "right to marry," past California cases establish beyond question that the right to marry is a fundamental right whose protection is guaranteed to all persons by the California Constitution. (See, e.g., *Conservatorship of Valerie N.*... "The right to marriage and procreation are now recognized as fundamental, constitutionally protected interests.... These rights are aspects of the right of privacy which ... is express in section I of article I of the California Constitution which includes among the inalienable rights possessed by all persons in this state, that of 'privacy'"; *Williams v. Garcetti* (1993) ... "we have ... recognized that '[t]he concept of personal liberties and fundamental human rights entitled to protection against overbroad intrusion or regulation by government ... extends to ... such basic civil liberties and rights not explicitly listed in the Constitution [as] the right "to marry, establish a home and bring up children"'"; *Ortiz v. Los Angeles Police Relief Assn.*... "under the state Constitution, the right to marry and the right of intimate association are virtually synonymous.... [W]e will refer to the privacy right in this case as the right to marry"; *In re Carrafa* (1978) ... "[t]he right to marry is a fundamental constitutional right.") The United States Supreme Court initially discussed the constitutional right to marry as an aspect of the fundamental substantive "liberty" protected by the due process clause of the federal Constitution (see *Meyer v. Nebraska* (1923) 262 U.S. 390, 399), but thereafter in *Griswold v. Connecticut* (1965) 381 U.S. 479 (*Griswold*), the federal high court additionally identified the right to marry as a component of a "right of privacy" protected by the federal Constitution. (*Griswold*, at p. 486.) With California's adoption in 1972 of a constitutional amendment explicitly adding "privacy" to the "inalienable rights" of all Californians protected by article I, section I of the California Constitution—an amendment whose history demonstrates that it was intended, among other purposes, to encompass the federal constitutional right of privacy, "particularly as it developed beginning with *Griswold v. Connecticut* ..." (*Hill v. National Collegiate Athletic Assn.*)—the state constitutional right to marry, while presumably still embodied as a component of the liberty protected by the state due process clause, now also clearly falls within the reach of the constitutional protection afforded to an individual's interest in personal autonomy by California's explicit state constitutional privacy clause. (See, e.g., *Hill v. National Collegiate Athletic Assn.*, ... the interest in personal autonomy protected by the state constitutional privacy clause includes "the freedom to pursue consensual familial relationships"; *Valerie N.*....)[1]

Although all parties in this proceeding agree that the right to marry constitutes a fundamental right protected by the state Constitution, there is considerable disagreement as to the scope and content of this fundamental state constitutional right. The Court of Appeal concluded that because marriage in California (and elsewhere) historically has been limited to opposite-sex couples, the constitutional right to marry under the California Constitution properly should be interpreted to afford only a right to marry a person of the opposite sex, and that the constitutional right that plaintiffs actually are asking the court to recognize is a constitutional "right to same-sex marriage." In the absence of any historical or precedential support for such a right in this state, the Court of Appeal determined that plaintiffs' claim of the denial of a fundamental right under the California Constitution must be rejected.

Plaintiffs challenge the Court of Appeal's characterization of the constitutional right they seek

---

[1] As we recognized in *Hill v. National Collegiate Athletic Assn.*... the privacy interests protected under article I, section I, fall into two categories: autonomy privacy and informational privacy. The right to marry constitutes an aspect of autonomy privacy.

to invoke as the right to same-sex marriage, and on this point we agree with plaintiffs' position. In *Perez v. Sharp*—this court's 1948 decision holding that the California statutory provisions prohibiting interracial marriage were unconstitutional—the court did not characterize the constitutional right that the plaintiffs in that case sought to obtain as "a right to interracial marriage" and did not dismiss the plaintiffs' constitutional challenge on the ground that such marriages never had been permitted in California.[1] Instead, the *Perez* decision focused on the *substance* of the constitutional right at issue—that is, the importance to an individual of the freedom "to join in marriage *with the person of one's choice*"—in determining whether the statute impinged upon the plaintiffs' fundamental constitutional right.... Similarly, in *Valerie N.*—which involved a challenge to a statute limiting the reproductive freedom of a developmentally disabled woman—our court did not analyze the scope of the constitutional right at issue by examining whether developmentally disabled women *historically* had enjoyed a constitutional right of reproductive freedom, but rather considered the substance of that constitutional right in determining whether the right was one that properly should be interpreted as extending to a developmentally disabled woman.... And, in addressing a somewhat analogous point, the United States Supreme Court in *Lawrence v. Texas* (2003) concluded that its prior decision in *Bowers v. Hardwick* (1986) had erred in narrowly characterizing the constitutional right sought to be invoked in that case as the right to engage in intimate *homosexual* conduct, determining instead that the constitutional right there at issue properly should be understood in a broader and more neutral fashion so as to focus upon the substance of the interests that the constitutional right is intended to protect.[2]

The flaw in characterizing the constitutional right at issue as the right to same-sex marriage rather than the right to marry goes beyond mere semantics. It is important both analytically and from the standpoint of fairness to plaintiffs' argument that we recognize they are not seeking to create a new constitutional right—the right to "same-sex marriage"—or to change, modify, or (as some have suggested) "deinstitutionalize" the existing institution of marriage. Instead, plaintiffs contend that, properly interpreted, the state constitutional right to marry affords same-sex couples the same rights and benefits—accompanied by the same mutual responsibilities and obligations—as this constitutional right affords to opposite-sex couples. For this reason, in evaluating the constitutional issue before us, we consider it appropriate to direct our focus to the meaning and substance of the constitutional right to marry, and to avoid the potentially misleading implications inherent in analyzing the issue in terms of "same-sex marriage."

Accordingly, in deciding whether the constitutional right to marry protected by the California Constitution applies to same-sex couples as well as to opposite-sex couples and, further, whether the current California marriage and domestic partnership statutes deny same-sex couples this fundamental constitutional right, we shall examine the nature and substance of the interests protected by the constitutional right to marry. In undertaking this inquiry, we put to the side for the moment the question whether the substantive rights embodied within the constitutional right to marry include the right to have the couple's official relationship

---

[1] The marriage statute enacted in California's first legislative session contained an explicit provision declaring that "[a]ll marriages of white persons with negroes or mulattoes are declared to be illegal and void" (Stats. 1850, ch. 140, § 3, p. 424).

[2] Similarly, in addressing under the federal Constitution the validity of a prison rule that permitted a prisoner to marry only if the superintendent of the prison found there were compelling reasons to permit the marriage, the high court did not characterize the constitutional right at issue as "the right to inmate marriage," but rather considered whether the purposes and attributes of the general fundamental right to marry were applicable in the prison context (*Turner v. Safley* (1987) 482 U.S. 78, 95–96).

designated by the name "marriage" rather than by some other term, such as "domestic partnership."...

In discussing the constitutional right to marry in *Perez v. Sharp* ... then Justice Traynor in the lead opinion quoted the seminal passage from the United States Supreme Court's decision in *Meyer v. Nebraska*.... There the high court, in describing the scope of the "liberty" protected by the due process clause of the federal Constitution, stated that "'[w]ithout doubt, it denotes not merely freedom from bodily restraint, but also the right of the individual to contract, to engage in any of the common occupations of life, to acquire useful knowledge, *to marry, establish a home and bring up children*, to worship God according to the dictates of one's own conscience, *and, generally, to enjoy those privileges long recognized at common law as essential to the orderly pursuit of happiness by free men*'" (*Perez*, quoting *Meyer*). The *Perez* decision continued: "*Marriage is thus something more than a civil contract subject to regulation by the state; it is a fundamental right of free men*" (*Perez*, italics added).

Like *Perez*, subsequent California decisions discussing the nature of marriage and the right to marry have recognized repeatedly the linkage between marriage, establishing a home, and raising children in identifying civil marriage as the means available to an individual to establish, with a loved one of his or her choice, an officially recognized *family* relationship. In *DeBurgh v. DeBurgh* (1952), for example, in explaining "the public interest in the institution of marriage," this court stated: "The family is the basic unit of our society, the center of the personal affections that ennoble and enrich human life. It channels biological drives that might otherwise become socially destructive; it ensures the care and education of children in a stable environment; it establishes continuity from one generation to another; it nurtures and develops the individual initiative that distinguishes a free people. Since the family is the core of our society, the law seeks to foster and preserve marriage."

In *Elden v. Sheldon*, in rejecting the claim that persons in an unmarried cohabitant relationship that allegedly was akin to a marital relationship should be treated similarly to married persons for purposes of bringing an action for negligent infliction of emotional distress, this court explained that "'[m]arriage is accorded [a special] degree of dignity in recognition that "[t]he joining of the man and woman in marriage is at once *the most socially productive and individually fulfilling relationship that one can enjoy in the course of a lifetime*"'" (italics added, quoting *Nieto v. City of Los Angeles*, quoting *Marvin v. Marvin*). The court in *Elden v. Sheldon* further explained: "Our emphasis on the state's interest in promoting the marriage relationship is not based on anachronistic notions of morality. *The policy favoring marriage is 'rooted in the necessity of providing an institutional basis for defining the fundamental relational rights and responsibilities in organized society.'* Formally married couples are granted significant rights and bear important responsibilities toward one another which are not shared by those who cohabit without marriage.... Plaintiff does not suggest a convincing reason why cohabiting unmarried couples, who do not bear such legal obligations toward one another, should be permitted to recover for injuries to their partners to the same extent as those who undertake these responsibilities" (italics added).

[...]

And in *Warfield v. Peninsula Golf & Country Club* (1995), in discussing the types of relationship that fall within the scope of the constitutionally protected right of intimate association (one component of our state constitutional right of privacy), we explained that "the highly personal relationships that are sheltered by this constitutional guaranty are exemplified by '*those that attend the creation and sustenance of a family—marriage*..., childbirth..., the raising and education of children ... and cohabitation with one's relatives....' ... 'Family relationships, by their nature, involve deep attachments and commitments to the necessarily few other individuals with whom one shares not only a special community of thoughts, experiences, and beliefs but also distinctly personal aspects of one's life'" (italics added, quoting *Roberts v. United States Jaycees*

(1984) 468 U.S. 609, 619–620). The constitutional right to marry thus may be understood as constituting a subset of the right of intimate association—a subset possessing its own substantive content and affording a distinct set of constitutional protections and guarantees.

As these and many other California decisions make clear, the right to marry represents the right of an individual to establish a legally recognized family with the person of one's choice, and, as such, is of fundamental significance both to society and to the individual.

Society is served by the institution of civil marriage in many ways. Society, of course, has an overriding interest in the welfare of children, and the role marriage plays in facilitating a stable family setting in which children may be raised by two loving parents unquestionably furthers the welfare of children and society. In addition, the role of the family in educating and socializing children serves society's interest by perpetuating the social and political culture and providing continuing support for society over generations. It is these features that the California authorities have in mind in describing marriage as the "basic unit" or "building block" of society. (See, e.g., *DeBurgh v. DeBurgh, supra*, 39 Cal.2d 858, 863 ["[t]he family is the basic unit of our society"]; *Baker v. Baker* (1859) 13 Cal. 87, 94 ["[t]he public is interested in the marriage relation and the maintenance of its integrity, as it is the foundation of the social system"]; *Elden v. Sheldon, supra*, 46 Cal.3d 267, 281, fn. 1 (dis. opn. of Broussard, J.) [referring to "the well-accepted maxim that marriage serves as the building block of society"]; *Dawn D. v. Superior Court* (1998) 17 Cal.4th 932, 968 (dis. opn. of Chin, J.) ["'the family provides the foundation upon which our society is built and through which its most cherished values are best transmitted'"].) Furthermore, the legal obligations of support that are an integral part of marital and family relationships relieve society of the obligation of caring for individuals who may become incapacitated or who are otherwise unable to support themselves. (See, e.g., *Elisa B. v. Superior Court* (2005) 37 Cal.4th 108, 123.) In view of the public's significant interest in marriage, California decisions have recognized that the Legislature has broad authority in seeking to protect and regulate this relationship by creating incentives to marry and adopting measures to protect the marital relationship. (See, e.g., *McClure v. Donovan* (1949) 33 Cal.2d 717, 728 ["the Legislature has full control of the subject of marriage and may fix the conditions under which the marital state may be created or terminated"].)

Although past California cases emphasize that marriage is an institution in which society as a whole has a vital interest, our decisions at the same time recognize that the legal right and opportunity to enter into such an officially recognized relationship also is of overriding importance to the individual and to the affected couple. As noted above, past California decisions have described marriage as "the most socially productive and individually fulfilling relationship that one can enjoy in the course of a lifetime" (*Marvin v. Marvin, supra*, 18 Cal.3d 660, 684; accord, *Maynard v. Hill, supra*, 125 U.S. 190, 205 [describing marriage as "the most important relation in life"]). The ability of an individual to join in a committed, long-term, officially recognized family relationship with the person of his or her choice is often of crucial significance to the individual's happiness and well-being. The legal commitment to long-term mutual emotional and economic support that is an integral part of an officially recognized marriage relationship provides an individual with the ability to invest in and rely upon a loving relationship with another adult in a way that may be crucial to the individual's development as a person and achievement of his or her full potential.

Further, entry into a formal, officially recognized family relationship provides an individual with the opportunity to become a part of one's partner's family, providing a wider and often critical network of economic and emotional security. (Accord, e.g., *Moore v. City of East Cleveland* (1977) 431 U.S. 494, 504–505 ["Ours is by no means a tradition limited to respect for the bonds uniting the members of the nuclear family…. Out of choice, necessity, or a sense of family responsibility, it has been common for close relatives to draw together and participate in the duties and the satisfactions of a common home.... Especially in times of adversity ... the broader family has tended to come together for mutual sustenance and to maintain or rebuild a secure home life"].) The opportunity of a couple to establish an officially recognized family of their own not only grants access to an extended family but also permits the couple to join the broader family social structure that is a significant feature of community life. Moreover, the opportunity to publicly and officially express one's love for and long-term commitment to another person by establishing a family together with that person also is an important element of self-expression that can give special meaning to one's life. Finally, of course, the ability to have children and raise them with a loved one who can share the joys and challenges of that endeavor is without doubt a most valuable component of one's liberty and personal autonomy. Although persons can have children and raise them outside of marriage, the institution of civil marriage affords official governmental sanction and sanctuary to the family unit, granting a parent the ability to afford his or her children the substantial benefits that flow from a stable two-parent family environment, a ready and public means of establishing to others the legal basis of one's parental relationship to one's children (cf. *Koebke, supra,* 36 Cal.4th 824, 844–845; *Elden v. Sheldon, supra,* 46 Cal.3d 267, 275), and the additional security that comes from the knowledge that his or her parental relationship with a child will be afforded protection by the government against the adverse actions or claims of others....

There are, of course, many persons and couples who choose not to enter into such a relationship and who prefer to live their lives without the formal, officially recognized and sanctioned, long-term legal commitment to another person signified by marriage or an equivalent relationship. Nonetheless, our cases recognize that the *opportunity* to establish an officially recognized family with a loved one and to obtain the substantial benefits such a relationship may offer is of the deepest and utmost importance to any individual and couple who wish to make such a choice.

If civil marriage were an institution whose *only* role was to serve the interests of society, it reasonably could be asserted that the state should have full authority to decide whether to establish or abolish the institution of marriage (and any similar institution, such as domestic partnership). In recognizing, however, that the right to marry is a basic, *constitutionally protected* civil right—"a fundamental right of free men [and women]" (*Perez, supra,* 32 Cal.2d 711, 714)—the governing California cases establish that this right embodies fundamental interests of an individual that are protected from abrogation or elimination by the state. Because our cases make clear that the right to marry is an integral component of an individual's interest in *personal autonomy* protected by the privacy provision of article I, section 1, and of the *liberty* interest protected by the due process clause of article I, section 7, it is apparent under the California Constitution that the right to marry—like the right to establish a home and raise children—has independent *substantive* content, and cannot properly be understood as simply the right to enter into such a relationship *if (but only if)* the Legislature chooses to establish and retain it. (Accord, *Poe v. Ullman* (1961) 367 U.S. 497, 553 (dis. opn. of Harlan, J.) ["the intimacy of husband and wife is necessarily an essential and accepted feature of the institution of marriage, *an institution which the State not only must allow,* but which always and in every age it has fostered and protected" (italics added)].)

One very important aspect of the substantive protection afforded by the California constitutional right to marry is, of course, an individual's right to be free from undue governmental intrusion into (or interference with) integral features of this relationship—that is, the right of marital or familial privacy. (See, e.g., *In re Marriage of Wellman* (1980) 104 Cal.App.3d 992, 996 [manner of raising one's child]; accord, e.g., *Griswold, supra,* 381 U.S. 479 [use of contraception]; *Moore v. City of East Cleveland, supra,* 431 U.S. 494 [cohabitation with extended family].) The substantive protection embodied in the constitutional right to marry, how-ever, goes beyond what is sometimes characterized as simply a "negative" right insulating the couple's relationship from overreaching governmental intrusion or interference, and includes a "positive" right to have the state take at least some affirmative action to acknowledge and support the family unit.

Although the constitutional right to marry clearly does not obligate the state to afford specific tax or other governmental benefits on the basis of a couple's family relationship, the right to marry does obligate the state to take affirmative action to grant official, public recognition to the couple's relationship as a family (*Perez, supra,* 32 Cal.2d 711; *In re Carrafa, supra,* 77 Cal.App.3d 788, 791), as well as to protect the core elements of the family relationship from at least some types of improper interference by others. (Cf. *Sesler v. Montgomery* (1889) 78 Cal. 486, 488–489 [in holding that a confidential conversation between husband and wife, allegedly overheard by an eavesdropper, "does not constitute a publication within the meaning of the law of slander," the court explained that "every sound consideration of public policy, every just regard for the integrity and inviolability of the marriage relation—the most confidential relation known to the law"—dictated that conclusion].) This constitutional right also has the additional affirmative substantive effect of providing assurance to each member of the relationship that the government will enforce the mutual obligations between the partners (and to their children) that are an important aspect of the commitments upon which the relationship rests. (Cf. *In re Marriage of Bonds* (2000) 24 Cal.4th 1, 27–29 [contrasting fiduciary relationship during marriage with relationship prior to marriage].)

In light of the fundamental nature of the substantive rights embodied in the right to marry—and their central importance to an individual's opportunity to live a happy, meaningful, and satisfying life as a full member of society—the California Constitution properly must be interpreted to guarantee this basic civil right to *all* individuals and couples, without regard to their sexual orientation. It is true, of course, that as an historical matter in this state marriage always has been limited to a union between a man and a woman. Tradition alone, however, generally has not been viewed as a sufficient justification for perpetuating, without examination, the restriction or denial of a fundamental *constitutional* right. (Cf. *Perez, supra,* 32 Cal.2d 711, 727; *Sail'er Inn, Inc. v. Kirby* (1971) 5 Cal.3d 1, 17–19 (*Sail'er Inn*).) As this court observed in *People v. Belous, supra,* 71 Cal.2d 954, 967, "[c]onstitutional concepts are not static.... 'In determining what lines are unconstitutionally discriminatory, we have never been confined to historic notions of equality, any more than we have restricted due process to a fixed catalogue of what was at a given time deemed to be the limits of fundamental rights.'" (See, e.g., *In re Antazo* (1970) 3 Cal.3d 100, 109 ["the long-standing recognition of this practice does not foreclose its reassessment in the light of the continued evolution of fundamental precepts of our constitutional system"].)

There can be no question but that, in recent decades, there has been a fundamental and dramatic transformation in this state's understanding and legal treatment of gay individuals and gay couples. California has repudiated past practices and policies that were based on a once common viewpoint that denigrated the general character and morals of gay individuals, and at one time even characterized homosexuality as a mental illness rather than as simply one of the numerous variables of our common and diverse humanity. This state's current policies and conduct regarding homosexuality recognize that gay individuals are entitled to the same legal rights and the same respect and dignity afforded all other individuals and are protected from discrimination on the basis of their sexual orientation, and, more specifically, recognize that gay individuals are fully capable of entering into the kind of loving and enduring committed relationships that may serve as the foundation of a family and of responsibly caring for and raising children.

[...]

... Thus, just as this court recognized in *Perez* that it was not constitutionally permissible to continue to treat racial or ethnic minorities as inferior

(*Perez, supra*, 32 Cal.2d at pp. 720–727), and in *Sail'er Inn* that it was not constitutionally acceptable to continue to treat women as less capable than and unequal to men (*Sail'er Inn, supra*, 5 Cal.3d at pp. 17–20 & fn. 15), we now similarly recognize that an individual's homosexual orientation is not a constitutionally legitimate basis for withholding or restricting the individual's legal rights.

In light of this recognition, sections 1 and 7 of article I of the California Constitution cannot properly be interpreted to withhold from gay individuals the same basic civil right of personal autonomy and liberty (including the right to establish, with the person of one's choice, an officially recognized and sanctioned family) that the California Constitution affords to heterosexual individuals. The privacy and due process provisions of our state Constitution—in declaring that "[a]ll people ... have [the] inalienable right [of] privacy" (art. I, § 1) and that no person may be deprived of "liberty" without due process of law (art. I, § 7)—do not purport to reserve to persons of a particular sexual orientation the substantive protection afforded by those provisions. In light of the evolution of our state's understanding concerning the equal dignity and respect to which all persons are entitled without regard to their sexual orientation, it is not appropriate to interpret these provisions in a way that, as a practical matter, excludes gay individuals from the protective reach of such basic civil rights....

[...]

None of the foregoing decisions—in emphasizing the importance of undertaking a "'careful description' of the asserted fundamental liberty interest" (*Washington v. Glucksberg, supra*, 521 U.S. 702, 721)—suggests, however, that it is appropriate to define a fundamental constitutional right or interest in so narrow a fashion that the basic protections afforded by the right are withheld from a class of persons—composed of individuals sharing a personal characteristic such as a particular sexual orientation—who historically have been denied the benefit of such rights. As noted above, our decision in *Perez, supra*, 32 Cal.2d 711, declining to define narrowly the right to marry, did not consider the fact

that discrimination against interracial marriage was "sanctioned by the state for many years" a reason to reject the plaintiffs' claim in that case. (*Id.*, at p. 727.) Instead the court looked to the essence and substance of the right to marry, a right itself deeply rooted in the history and tradition of our state and nation, to determine whether the challenged statute impinged upon the plaintiffs' constitutional right. For similar reasons, it is apparent that history alone does not provide a justification for interpreting the constitutional right to marry as protecting only one's ability to enter into an officially recognized family relationship with a person of the opposite sex....

Furthermore, unlike the situation presented in several prior decisions of this court in which recognition of a party's claim of a constitutional right necessarily and invariably would have had the effect of reducing or diminishing the rights of other persons (see, e.g., *Johnson v. Calvert* (1993) 5 Cal.4th 84, 92, fn. 8, 100 [noting, in rejecting surrogate mother's claim of a liberty interest in the companionship of a child, that recognition of such an interest would impinge upon the liberty interests of the child's legal parents]; *Dawn D. v. Superior Court, supra*, 17 Cal.4th 932 [rejecting asserted biological father's claim of a liberty interest in establishing relationship with a child whose biological mother was married to another man when the child was conceived and born]), in the present context our recognition that the constitutional right to marry applies to same-sex couples as well as to opposite-sex couples does not diminish any other person's constitutional rights. Opposite-sex couples will continue to enjoy precisely the same constitutional rights they traditionally have possessed, unimpaired by our recognition that this basic civil right is applicable, as well, to gay individuals and same-sex couples.

The Proposition 22 Legal Defense Fund and the Campaign agree that the constitutional right to marry is integrally related to the right of two persons to join together to establish an officially recognized family, but they contend that the only family that possibly can be encompassed by the constitutional right to marry is a family headed by a man and a woman. Pointing out that past cases often have linked marriage and procreation, these parties argue that because only a man and a woman can produce children biologically with one another, the constitutional right to marry necessarily is limited to opposite-sex couples.

This contention is fundamentally flawed for a number of reasons. To begin with, although the legal institution of civil marriage may well have originated in large part to promote a stable relationship for the procreation and raising of children (see, e.g., *Baker v. Baker, supra*, 13 Cal. 87, 103 ["the first purpose of matrimony, by the laws of nature and society, is procreation"]; see generally Blankenhorn, The Future of Marriage (2007) pp. 23–125), and although the right to marry and to procreate often are treated as closely related aspects of the privacy and liberty interests protected by the state and federal Constitutions (see, e.g., *Valerie N., supra*, 40 Cal.3d 143, 161; *Skinner v. Oklahoma* (1942) 316 U.S. 527, 541), the constitutional right to marry never has been viewed as the sole preserve of individuals who are physically capable of having children. Men and women who desire to raise children with a loved one in a recognized family but who are physically unable to conceive a child with their loved one never have been excluded from the right to marry. Although the Proposition 22 Legal Defense Fund and the Campaign assert that the circumstance that marriage has not been limited to those who can bear children can be explained and justified by reference to the state's reluctance to intrude upon the privacy of individuals by inquiring into their fertility, if that were an accurate and adequate explanation for the absence of such a limitation it would follow that in instances in which the state is able to make a determination of an individual's fertility without such an inquiry, it would be constitutionally permissible for the state to preclude an individual who is incapable of bearing children from entering into marriage. There is, however, no authority whatsoever to support the proposition that an individual who is physically incapable of bearing children does not possess a fundamental constitutional right to marry. Such a proposition clearly is untenable. A

person who is physically incapable of bearing children still has the potential to become a parent and raise a child through adoption or through means of assisted reproduction, and the constitutional right to marry ensures the individual the opportunity to raise children in an officially recognized family with the person with whom the individual has chosen to share his or her life. Thus, although an important purpose underlying marriage may be to channel procreation into a stable family relationship, that purpose cannot be viewed as limiting the constitutional right to marry to couples who are capable of biologically producing a child together.

A variant of the contention that the right to marry is limited to couples who are capable of procreation is that the purpose of marriage is to promote "responsible procreation" and that a restriction limiting this right exclusively to opposite-sex couples follows from this purpose. A number of recent state court decisions, applying the rational basis equal protection standard, have relied upon this purpose as a reasonably conceivable justification for a statutory limitation of marriage to opposite-sex couples. These decisions have explained that although same-sex couples can have or obtain children through assisted reproduction or adoption, resort to such methods demonstrates, in the case of a same-sex couple, that parenthood necessarily is an *intended* consequence because each of these two methods requires considerable planning and expense, whereas in the case of an opposite-sex couple a child often is the *unintended* consequence of the couple's sexual intercourse. These courts reason that a state plausibly could conclude that although affording the benefits of marriage to opposite-sex couples is an incentive needed to ensure that *accidental* procreation is channeled into a stable family relationship, a similar incentive is not required for same-sex couples because they cannot produce children accidentally.

Whether or not the state's interest in encouraging responsible procreation properly can be viewed as a reasonably conceivable justification for the statutory limitation of marriage to a man and a woman for purposes of the rational basis equal protection standard, this interest clearly does not provide an appropriate basis for defining or limiting the scope of the constitutional right to marry. None of the past cases discussing the right to marry—and identifying this right as one of the fundamental elements of personal autonomy and liberty protected by our Constitution—contains any suggestion that the constitutional right to marry is possessed only by individuals who are at risk of producing children accidentally, or implies that this constitutional right is not equally important for and guaranteed to responsible individuals who can be counted upon to take appropriate precautions in planning for parenthood. Thus, although the state undeniably has a legitimate interest in promoting "responsible procreation," that interest cannot be viewed as a valid basis for defining or limiting the class of persons who may claim the protection of the fundamental constitutional right to marry.

Furthermore, although promoting and facilitating a stable environment for the procreation and raising of children is unquestionably one of the vitally important purposes underlying the institution of marriage and the constitutional right to marry, past cases make clear that this right is not confined to, or restrictively defined by, that purpose alone. (See, e.g., *Baker v. Baker, supra,* 13 Cal. 87, 103 ["[t]he second purpose of matrimony is the promotion of the happiness of the parties by the society of each other"].) As noted above, our past cases have recognized that the right to marry is the right to enter into a relationship that is "the center of the personal affections that ennoble and enrich human life" (*DeBurgh v. DeBurgh*)—a relationship that is "at once the most socially productive and individually fulfilling relationship that one can enjoy in the course of a lifetime" (*Marvin v. Marvin;* see also *Elden v. Sheldon*). The personal enrichment afforded by the right to marry may be obtained by a couple whether or not they choose to have children, and the right to marry never has been limited to those who plan or desire to have children. Indeed, in *Griswold v. Connecticut*—one of the seminal federal cases striking down a state law as violative of the federal constitutional right of privacy—the high court upheld a married couple's right to use contraception *to prevent procreation,* demonstrating quite clearly that the promotion of procreation is not the sole or defining purpose of marriage. Similarly, in *Turner v. Safley*, the court held that the constitutional right to marry extends to an individual confined in state prison—even a prisoner who has no right to conjugal visits with his would-be spouse—emphasizing that "[m]any important attributes of marriage remain … after taking into account the limitations imposed by prison life … [including the] expressions of emotional support and public commitment [that] are an important and significant aspect of the marital relationship" (482 U.S. at pp. 95–96). Although *Griswold* and *Turner* relate to the right to marry under the federal Constitution, they accurately reflect the scope of the state constitutional right to marry as well. Accordingly, this right cannot properly be defined by or limited to the state's interest in fostering a favorable environment for the procreation and raising of children.

The Proposition 22 Legal Defense Fund and the Campaign also rely upon several academic commentators who maintain that the constitutional right to marry should be viewed as inapplicable to same-sex couples because a contrary interpretation assertedly would sever the link that marriage provides between procreation and child rearing and would "send a message" to the public that it is immaterial to the state whether children are raised by their biological mother and father…. Although we appreciate the genuine concern for the well-being of children underlying that position, we conclude this claim lacks merit. Our recognition that the core substantive rights encompassed by the constitutional right to marry apply to same-sex as well as opposite-sex couples does not imply in any way that it is unimportant or immaterial to the state whether a child is raised by his or her biological mother and father. By recognizing this circumstance we do not alter or diminish either the legal responsibilities that biological parents owe to their children or the substantial incentives that the state provides to a child's biological parents to enter into and raise their child in a stable, long-term committed relationship.[1] Instead, such an interpretation of the constitutional right to marry simply confirms that a stable two-parent family relationship, supported by the state's official recognition and protection, is equally as important for the numerous children in California who are being raised by same-sex couples as for those children being raised by opposite-sex couples (whether they are biological parents or adoptive parents).[2] This interpretation also guarantees individuals who are in a same-sex relationship, and who are raising children, the opportunity to obtain from the state the official recognition and support accorded a family by agreeing to take on the substantial and long-term mutual obligations and responsibilities that are an essential and inseparable part of a family relationship.

Accordingly, we conclude that the right to marry, as embodied in article I, sections 1 and 7 of the California Constitution, guarantees same-sex couples the same substantive constitutional rights as opposite-sex couples to choose one's life partner and enter with that person into a committed, officially recognized, and protected family relationship that enjoys all of the constitutionally based incidents of marriage.[3]

B

The Attorney General, in briefing before this court, argues that even if, as we have concluded, the state constitutional right to marry extends to same-sex couples as well as to opposite-sex couples, the current California statutes do not violate the fundamental rights of same-sex couples, "because all of the personal and dignity interests that have traditionally informed the right to marry have been given to same-sex couples through the Domestic Partner Act." Maintaining that "under the domestic partnership system, the word 'marriage' is all that the state is denying to registered domestic partners," the Attorney General asserts that "[t]he fundamental right to marry can no more be the basis for same-sex couples to compel the state to denominate their committed relationships 'marriage' than it could be the basis for anyone to prevent the state legislature from changing the name of the marital institution

---

[1] As noted in our earlier discussion of the relationship between procreation and marriage, many opposite-sex married couples choose not to have children and many other opposite-sex married couples become parents through adoption or through a variety of assisted-reproduction techniques. If societal acceptance of these marriages (whose numbers surely exceed the number of potential same-sex unions) does not "send a message" that it is immaterial to the state whether children are raised by their biological mother and father—and we conclude there clearly is no such message—it is difficult to understand why the message would be sent by our recognition that same-sex couples possess a constitutional right to marry. (See, e.g., *Baker v. State*.)

[2] According to a report based upon a review of data from the 2000 Census, at the time of that census same-sex couples in California were raising more than 70,000 children. (See Badgett & Sears, *Same-Sex Couples and Same-Sex Couples Raising Children in California: Data from Census 2000* (May 2004) p. 2 <http://www.law.ucla.edu/williamsproj/publications/CaliforniaCouplesReport.pdf> [as of May 15, 2008].) The report also states that the 2000 census data indicates that, as of that date, 33 percent of female same-sex couples and 28.4 percent of all same-sex couples in California were raising children, and further notes that those figures do not include foster children being raised by same-sex couples. (*Id*. at p. 10.)

[3] We emphasize that our conclusion that the constitutional right to marry properly must be interpreted to apply to gay individuals and gay couples does not mean that this constitutional right similarly must be understood to extend to polygamous or incestuous relationships. Past judicial decisions explain why our nation's culture has considered the latter types of relationships inimical to the mutually supportive and healthy family relationships promoted by the constitutional right to marry. [See, e.g., *Reynolds v. United States* (1878); *Davis v. Beason* (1890); *People v. Scott* (2007); *State v. Freeman*; *Smith v. State*.] Although the historic disparagement of and discrimination against gay individuals and gay couples clearly is no longer constitutionally permissible, the state continues to have a strong and adequate justification for refusing to officially sanction polygamous or incestuous relationships because of their potentially detrimental effect on a sound family environment.... Thus, our conclusion that it is improper to interpret the state constitutional right to marry as inapplicable to gay individuals or couples does not affect the constitutional validity of the existing legal prohibitions against polygamy and the marriage of close relatives.

itself to 'civil unions.'" Accordingly, the Attorney General argues that in light of the rights afforded to same-sex couples by the Domestic Partner Act, the current California statutes cannot be found to violate the right of same-sex couples to marry.

We have no occasion in this case to determine whether the state constitutional right to marry necessarily affords all couples the constitutional right to require the state to designate their official family relationship a "marriage," or whether, as the Attorney General suggests, the Legislature would not violate a couple's constitutional right to marry if—perhaps in order to emphasize and clarify that this civil institution is distinct from the religious institution of marriage—it were to assign a name other than marriage as the official designation of the family relationship for *all* couples. The current California statutes, of course, do not assign a name other than marriage for *all* couples, but instead reserve exclusively to opposite-sex couples the traditional designation of marriage, and assign a different designation—domestic partnership—to the only official family relationship available to same-sex couples.

Whether or not the name "marriage," in the abstract, is considered a core element of the state constitutional right to marry, one of the core elements of this fundamental right is the right of same-sex couples to have their official family relationship accorded the same dignity, respect, and stature as that accorded to all other officially recognized family relationships. The current statutes—by drawing a distinction between the name assigned to the family relationship available to opposite-sex couples and the name assigned to the family relationship available to same-sex couples, and by reserving the historic and highly respected designation of marriage exclusively to opposite-sex couples while offering same-sex couples only the new and unfamiliar designation of domestic partnership—pose a serious risk of denying the official family relationship of same-sex couples the equal dignity and respect that is a core element of the constitutional right to marry. As observed by the City at oral argument, this court's conclusion in *Perez, supra,* 32 Cal.2d

711, that the statutory provision barring interracial marriage was unconstitutional, undoubtedly would have been the same even if alternative nomenclature, such as "transracial union," had been made available to interracial couples.

Accordingly, although we agree with the Attorney General that the provisions of the Domestic Partner Act afford same-sex couples most of the substantive attributes to which they are constitutionally entitled under the state constitutional right to marry, we conclude that the current statutory assignment of different designations to the official family relationship of opposite-sex couples and of same-sex couples properly must be viewed as potentially impinging upon the state constitutional right of same-sex couples to marry.

V

The current statutory assignment of different names for the official family relationships of opposite-sex couples on the one hand, and of same-sex couples on the other, raises constitutional concerns not only in the context of the state constitutional right to marry, but also under the state constitutional equal protection clause. Plaintiffs contend that by permitting only opposite-sex couples to enter into a relationship designated as a "marriage," and by designating as a "domestic partnership" the parallel relationship into which same-sex couples may enter, the statutory scheme impermissibly denies same-sex couples the equal protection of the laws, guaranteed by article 1, section 7, of the California Constitution. The relevant California statutes clearly treat opposite-sex and same-sex couples differently in this respect, and the initial question we must consider in addressing the equal protection issue is the standard of review that should be applied in evaluating this distinction.

There are two different standards traditionally applied by California courts in evaluating challenges made to legislation under the equal protection clause. As we recently explained in *Hernandez v. City of Hanford* (2007), "'"[t]he first is the basic and conventional standard for reviewing economic and social welfare legislation in which there is a 'discrimination' or differentiation of treatment between classes or individuals.... [That standard] invests legislation involving such differentiated treatment with a presumption of constitutionality and 'requir[es] merely that distinctions drawn by a challenged statute bear some rational relationship to a conceivable legitimate state purpose.'... [T]he burden of demonstrating the invalidity of a classification under this standard rests squarely upon *the party who assails it*."' This first basic equal protection standard generally is referred to as the 'rational relationship' or 'rational basis' standard" (41 Cal.4th at pp. 298–299).

Our decision in *Hernandez* further explained:

> [T]he second equal protection standard is ""[a] more stringent test [that] is applied ... in cases involving 'suspect classifications' or touching on 'fundamental interests.' Here the courts adopt 'an attitude of active and critical analysis, subjecting the classifications to strict scrutiny.... Under the strict standard applied in such cases, *the state* bears the burden of establishing not only that it has a *compelling* interest which justifies the law but that the distinctions drawn by the law are *necessary* to further its purpose."' ... This second standard generally is referred to as the 'strict scrutiny' standard. (41 Cal.4th at p. 299)

Plaintiffs maintain, on three separate grounds, that strict scrutiny is the standard that should be applied in this case, contending the distinctions drawn by the statutes between opposite-sex and same-sex couples ... (2) discriminate on the basis of sexual orientation, and (3) impinge upon a fundamental right. We discuss each of these ... claims in turn.

[...]

B

Plaintiffs next maintain that even if the applicable California statutes do not discriminate on the basis of sex or gender, they do so on the basis of sexual orientation, and that statutes that discriminate on the basis of sexual orientation should be subject to strict scrutiny under the California Constitution. In response, defendants assert the marriage statutes do not discriminate on the basis of sexual orientation, and, even if they do, discrimination on the basis of sexual orientation should not trigger strict scrutiny.

In arguing that the marriage statutes do not discriminate on the basis of sexual orientation, defendants rely upon the circumstance that these statutes, on their face, do not refer explicitly to sexual orientation and do not prohibit gay individuals from marrying a person of the opposite sex. Defendants contend that under these circumstances, the marriage statutes should not be viewed as directly classifying or discriminating on the basis of sexual orientation but at most should be viewed as having a "disparate impact" on gay persons.

In our view, the statutory provisions restricting marriage to a man and a woman cannot be understood as having merely a disparate impact on gay persons, but instead properly must be viewed as directly classifying and prescribing distinct treatment on the basis of sexual orientation. By limiting marriage to opposite-sex couples, the marriage statutes, realistically viewed, operate clearly and directly to impose different treatment on gay individuals because of their sexual orientation. By definition, gay individuals are persons who are sexually attracted to persons of the same sex and thus, if inclined to enter into a marriage relationship, would choose to marry a person of their own sex or gender. A statute that limits marriage to a union of persons of opposite sexes, thereby placing marriage outside the reach of couples of the same sex, unquestionably imposes different treatment on the basis of sexual orientation. In our view, it is sophistic to suggest that this conclusion is avoidable by reason of the circumstance that the marriage statutes permit a gay man or a lesbian to marry someone of the opposite sex, because making such a choice would require the negation of the person's sexual orientation. Just as a statute that restricted marriage only to couples of the same sex would discriminate against heterosexual persons on the basis of their heterosexual orientation, the current

California statutes realistically must be viewed as discriminating against gay persons on the basis of their homosexual orientation.

Having concluded that the California marriage statutes treat persons differently on the basis of sexual orientation, we must determine whether sexual orientation should be considered a "suspect classification" under the California equal protection clause, so that statutes drawing a distinction on this basis are subject to strict scrutiny. As pointed out by the parties defending the marriage statutes, the great majority of out-of-state decisions that have addressed this issue have concluded that, unlike statutes that impose differential treatment on the basis of an individual's race, sex, religion, or national origin, statutes that treat persons differently because of their sexual orientation should not be viewed as constitutionally suspect and thus should not be subjected to strict scrutiny. The issue is one of first impression in California, however, and for the reasons discussed below we conclude that sexual orientation should be viewed as a suspect classification for purposes of the California Constitution's equal protection clause and that statutes that treat persons differently because of their sexual orientation should be subjected to strict scrutiny under this constitutional provision. [...]

C

Plaintiffs additionally contend that the strict scrutiny standard applies here not only because the statutes in question impose differential treatment between individuals on the basis of the suspect classification of sexual orientation, but also because the classification drawn by the statutes impinges upon a same-sex couple's fundamental, constitutionally protected privacy interest, creating unequal and detrimental consequences for same-sex couples and their children. [O]ne of the core elements embodied in the state constitutional right to marry is the right of an individual and a couple to have their own official family relationship accorded respect and dignity equal to that accorded the family relationship of other couples. Even when the state affords substantive legal rights and benefits to a couple's family relationship that are comparable to the rights and benefits afforded to other couples, the state's assignment of a different name to the couple's relationship poses a risk that the different name itself will have the effect of denying such couple's relationship the equal respect and dignity to which the couple is constitutionally entitled. Plaintiffs contend that in the present context, the different nomenclature prescribed by the current California statutes properly must be understood as having just such a constitutionally suspect effect.

We agree with plaintiffs' contention in this regard. Although in some contexts the establishment of separate institutions or structures to remedy the past denial of rights or benefits has been found to be constitutionally permissible, and although it may be possible to conceive of some circumstances in which assignment of the name "marriage" to one category of family relationship and of a name other than marriage to another category of family relationship would not likely be stigmatizing or raise special constitutional concerns, for a number of reasons we conclude that in the present context, affording same-sex couples access only to the separate institution of domestic partnership, and denying such couples access to the established institution of marriage, properly must be viewed as impinging upon the right of those couples to have their family relationship accorded respect and dignity equal to that accorded the family relationship of opposite-sex couples.

First, because of the long and celebrated history of the term "marriage" and the widespread understanding that this term describes a union unreservedly approved and favored by the community, there clearly is a considerable and undeniable symbolic importance to this designation. Thus, it is apparent that affording access to this designation exclusively to opposite-sex couples, while providing same-sex couples access to only a novel alternative designation, realistically must be viewed as constituting significantly unequal treatment to same-sex couples. In this regard, plaintiffs persuasively invoke by analogy the decisions of the United States Supreme Court finding inadequate a state's creation of a separate law school for Black students rather than granting such students access to the University of Texas Law School (*Sweatt v. Painter* (1950) 339 U.S. 629, 634), and a state's founding of a separate military program for women rather than admitting women to the Virginia Military Institute (*United States v. Virginia* (1996) 518 U.S. 515, 555–556). As plaintiffs maintain, these high court decisions demonstrate that even when the state grants ostensibly equal benefits to a previously excluded class through the creation of a new institution, the intangible symbolic differences that remain often are constitutionally significant.

Second, particularly in light of the historic disparagement of and discrimination against gay persons, there is a very significant risk that retaining a distinction in nomenclature with regard to this most fundamental of relationships whereby the term "marriage" is denied only to same-sex couples inevitably will cause the new parallel institution that has been made available to those couples to be viewed as of a lesser stature than marriage and, in effect, as a mark of second-class citizenship. As the Canada Supreme Court observed in an analogous context: "One factor which may demonstrate that legislation that treats a claimant differently has the effect of demeaning the claimant's dignity is the existence of pre-existing disadvantage, stereotyping, prejudice, or vulnerability experienced by the individual or group at issue.... '... It is logical to conclude that, in most cases, further differential treatment will contribute to the perpetuation or promotion of their unfair social characterization, and will have a more severe impact upon them, since they are already vulnerable.'" (*M. v. H.* [1999] 2 S.C.R. 3, 54–55 [¶ 68].)
[...]

D

As already explained, in circumstances, as here, in which the strict scrutiny standard of review applies, the state bears a heavy burden of justification. In order to satisfy that standard, the state must demonstrate not simply that there is a rational, constitutionally legitimate interest that supports the differential treatment at issue, but instead that the state interest is a *constitutionally compelling* one that justifies the disparate treatment prescribed by the statute in question. (See, e.g., *Darces v. Wood*.) Furthermore, unlike instances in which the rational basis test applies, the state does not meet its burden of justification under the strict scrutiny standard merely by showing that the classification established by the statute is rationally or reasonably related to such a compelling state interest. Instead, the state must demonstrate that the distinctions drawn by the statute (or statutory scheme) are *necessary* to further that interest. (See, e.g., *Ramirez v. Brown*.)

In the present case, the question before us is whether the state has a constitutionally *compelling* interest in reserving the designation of marriage only for opposite-sex couples and excluding same-sex couples from access to that designation, and whether this statutory restriction is *necessary* to serve a compelling state interest. In their briefing before this court, various defendants have advanced different contentions in support of the current statutes, and we discuss each of these arguments.
[...]

In defending the state's proffered interest in retaining the traditional definition of marriage as limited to a union between a man and a woman, the Attorney General and the Governor rely primarily upon the historic and well-established nature of this limitation and the circumstance that the designation of marriage continues to apply only to a relationship between opposite-sex couples in the overwhelming majority of jurisdictions in the United States and around the world. Because, until recently, there has been widespread societal disapproval and disparagement of homosexuality in many cultures, it is hardly surprising that the institution of civil marriage generally has been limited to opposite-sex couples and that many persons have considered the designation of marriage to be appropriately applied only to a relationship of an opposite-sex couple.

Although the understanding of marriage as limited to a union of a man and a woman is undeniably the predominant one, if we have learned anything from the significant evolution in the prevailing societal views and official policies toward members of minority races and toward women over the past half-century, it is that even the most familiar and generally accepted of social practices and traditions often mask an unfairness and inequality that frequently is not recognized or appreciated by those not directly harmed by those practices or traditions. It is instructive to recall in this regard that the traditional, well-established legal rules and practices of our not-so-distant past (1) barred interracial marriage, (2) upheld the routine exclusion of women from many occupations and official duties, and (3) considered the relegation of racial minorities to separate and assertedly equivalent public facilities and institutions as constitutionally equal treatment. As the United States Supreme Court observed in its decision in *Lawrence v. Texas*, the expansive and protective provisions of our constitutions, such as the due process clause, were drafted with the knowledge that "times can blind us to certain truths and later generations can see that laws once thought necessary and proper in fact serve only to oppress." For this reason, the interest in retaining a tradition that excludes an historically disfavored minority group from a status that is extended to all others—even when the tradition is long-standing and widely shared—does not necessarily represent a compelling state interest for purposes of equal protection analysis.

After carefully evaluating the pertinent considerations in the present case, we conclude that the state interest in limiting the designation of marriage exclusively to opposite-sex couples, and in excluding same-sex couples from access to that designation, cannot properly be considered a compelling state interest for equal protection purposes. To begin with, the limitation clearly is not necessary to preserve the rights and benefits of marriage currently enjoyed by opposite-sex couples. Extending access to the designation of marriage to same-sex couples will not deprive any opposite-sex couple or their children of any of the rights and benefits conferred by the marriage statutes, but simply will make the benefit of the marriage designation available to same-sex couples and their children. As Chief Judge Kaye of the New York Court of Appeals succinctly observed in her dissenting opinion in *Hernandez v. Robles*, (dis. opn. of Kaye, C.J.): "There are enough marriage licenses to go around for everyone." Further, permitting same-sex couples access to the designation of marriage will not alter the substantive nature of the legal institution of marriage; same-sex couples who choose to enter into the relationship with that designation will be subject to the same duties and obligations to each other, to their children, and to third parties that the law currently imposes upon opposite-sex couples who marry. Finally, affording same-sex couples the opportunity to obtain the designation of marriage will not impinge upon the religious freedom of any religious organization, official, or any other person; no religion will be required to change its religious policies or practices with regard to same-sex couples, and no religious officiant will be required to solemnize a marriage in contravention of his or her religious beliefs.

While retention of the limitation of marriage to opposite-sex couples is not needed to preserve the rights and benefits of opposite-sex couples, the exclusion of same-sex couples from the designation of marriage works a real and appreciable harm upon same-sex couples and their children. As discussed above, because of the long and celebrated history of the term "marriage" and the widespread understanding that this word describes a family relationship unreservedly sanctioned by the community, the statutory provisions that continue to limit access to this designation exclusively to opposite-sex couples—while providing only a novel, alternative institution for same-sex couples—likely will be viewed as an official statement that the family relationship of same-sex couples is not of comparable stature or equal dignity to the family relationship of opposite-sex couples. Furthermore, because of the historic disparagement of gay persons, the retention of a distinction in nomenclature by which the term "marriage" is withheld only from the family relationship of same-sex couples is all the more likely to cause the new parallel institution that has been established for same-sex couples to be considered a mark of second-class citizenship. Finally, in addition to the potential harm flowing from the lesser stature that is likely to be afforded to the family relationships of same-sex couples by designating them domestic partnerships, there exists a substantial risk that a judicial decision upholding the differential treatment of opposite-sex and same-sex couples would be understood as *validating* a more general proposition that our state by now has repudiated: that it is permissible, under the law, for society to treat gay individuals and same-sex couples differ-

ently from, and less favorably than, heterosexual individuals and opposite-sex couples.

In light of all of these circumstances, we conclude that retention of the traditional definition of marriage does not constitute a state interest sufficiently compelling, under the strict scrutiny equal protection standard, to justify withholding that status from same-sex couples. Accordingly, insofar as the provisions of sections 300 and 308.5 draw a distinction between opposite-sex couples and same-sex couples and exclude the latter from access to the designation of marriage, we conclude these statutes are unconstitutional.

DISCUSSION QUESTIONS

1. Explain and evaluate the court's argument that the constitutional right of same-sex couples to marry would be infringed upon were their union to be labeled a "domestic partnership" as opposed to a "marriage." How does the court address the objection that, given that same-sex couples are guaranteed the same "substantive rights" as heterosexual couples under the Domestic Partner Act, the difference in terminology with regards to their official family relationship ought not to be considered an infringement upon their rights?

2. The court claims that the differential treatment afforded to same-sex couples as a result of the classification of their relationships as "domestic partnerships" is not justified. Specifically, the court argues that the right of same-sex couples to be afforded equal dignity and respect would be violated. Explain and evaluate the court's argument.

3. The court states that "…our cases recognize that the *opportunity* to establish an

officially recognized family with a loved one and to obtain the substantial benefits such a relationship may offer is of the deepest and utmost importance to any individual and couple who wish to make such a choice." Discuss the various benefits that the court identifies as being of such central importance.

4. The court claims that along with a constitutional right to marry comes a "… positive right to have the state take at least some affirmative action to acknowledge and support the family unit." What justification is given for this claim? In what specific ways, if any, do you think the state ought to "support the family unit"?

5. The court addresses arguments which claim that the right to marry ought to be limited to opposite-sex couples. Among those are arguments dealing with tradition, procreation, and child-rearing. Explain those arguments and outline the court's response. Do you think that the court has adequately responded to these counter-arguments against same-sex marriage? Why or why not?

SEX, FREEDOM, AND MARRIAGE
Statement of Proposition 8 (2008)

The following is the text of "Proposition 8," otherwise known as the "California Marriage Protection Act," which was presented to California voters during the state elections of 2008. The measure sought a constitutional amendment which would restrict marriage to heterosexual couples. The measure's passing overturned the California Supreme Court's ruling in *In re Marriage Cases*, which had concluded that same-sex couples have a constitutional right to marry. Proposition 8 was in turn overturned by US District Chief Judge Vaughn R. Walker in 2010. Walker's ruling is being appealed.

SOURCE
California State-Election Ballot 2008.

PROPOSITION 8
This initiative measure is submitted to the people in accordance with the provisions of Article 11, Section 8, of the California Constitution. This initiative measure expressly amends the California Constitution by adding a section thereto; therefore, new provisions proposed to be added are printed in *italic type* to indicate that they are new.

SECTION 1. Title
This measure shall be known and may be cited as the "California Marriage Protection Act."

SECTION 2. Section 7.5 is added to Article 1 of the California Constitution, to read:

SEC. 7.5. Only marriage between a man and a woman is valid or recognized in California.

DISCUSSION QUESTION

1. Should questions of this sort be decided by a referendum? Should a society committed to protecting minority rights be willing to allow majorities to decide these sorts of issues? Defend your answer.

SEX, FREEDOM, AND MARRIAGE
State (Utah) v. Holm[1]
(2006)

The following selection is taken from the 2006 State of Utah Supreme Court Case, *State v. Holm*. The court heard arguments from Rodney Hans Holm, a member of the Fundamentalist Church of Jesus Christ of Latter-day Saints, who had been convicted of bigamy and unlawful sexual conduct as a result of his marriage to then-sixteen-year-old Ruth Stubbs. At the time of the marriage, Holm was already married to Wendy Holm. Ruth bore Holm two children, both of whom were conceived before her eighteenth birthday. Holm argued that his bigamy conviction violated his constitutional guarantee of freedom of religion. The Court's deliberations raised important questions about the state's interest in defining and protecting certain conceptions of marriage.

SOURCE
Supreme Court of Utah, No. 20030847.

State of Utah, Plaintiff and Apellee, v. Rodney Hans Holm, Defendant and Appellant
Filed May 16, 2006
[…]

Durrant, Justice
In this case, we are asked to determine whether Rodney Hans Holm was appropriately convicted for bigamy and unlawful sexual conduct with a minor. Specifically, we are asked to determine whether Holm's behavior violated Utah's bigamy statute and whether that statute is constitutional. We are also asked to decide whether the trial court adequately established its criminal jurisdiction over the unlawful sexual conduct charges and whether the unlawful sexual conduct statute is unconstitutional on equal protection grounds. We conclude that Holm's behavior falls squarely within the realm of behavior criminalized by our State's bigamy statute and that the protections enshrined in the federal constitution, as well as our state constitution, guaranteeing the free exercise of religion and conscience, due process, and freedom of association do not shield Holm's polygamous practices from state prosecution. We further conclude that the trial court appropriately exercised jurisdiction over Holm's unlawful sexual conduct charges and that the unlawful sexual conduct statute is constitutional.

---

[1] [Many of the original notes have been omitted.]

Accordingly, we affirm the defendant's conviction under Utah Code section 76-7-101 for bigamy and under Utah Code section 76-5-401.2 for unlawful sexual conduct with a minor.

Background

Holm was legally married to Suzie Stubbs in 1986. Subsequent to this marriage, Holm, a member of the Fundamentalist Church of Jesus Christ of Latter-day Saints (the "FLDS Church"),[1] participated in a religious marriage ceremony with Wendy Holm. Then, when Rodney Holm was thirty-two, he participated in another religious marriage ceremony with then-sixteen-year-old Ruth Stubbs, Suzie Stubbs's sister. After the ceremony, Ruth moved into Holm's house, where her sister Suzie Stubbs, Wendy Holm, and their children also resided. By the time Ruth turned eighteen, she had conceived two children with Holm, the second of which was born approximately three months after her eighteenth birthday.

Holm was subsequently arrested in Utah and charged with three counts of unlawful sexual conduct with a sixteen- or seventeen-year-old, in violation of Utah Code section 76-5-401.2 (2003), and one count of bigamy, in violation of Utah Code section 76-7-101 (2003)—all third-degree felonies....

At trial, Ruth Stubbs testified that although she knew that the marriage was not a legal civil marriage under the law, she believed that she was married. Stubbs's testimony included a description of the ceremony she had participated in with Holm. Stubbs testified that, at the ceremony, she had answered "I do" to the following question:

Do you, Sister [Stubbs], take Brother [Holm] by the right hand, and give yourself to him

to be his lawful and wedded wife for time and all eternity, with a covenant and promise on your part, that you will fulfil all the laws, rites and ordinances pertaining to this holy bond of matrimony in the new and ever-lasting covenant, doing this in the presence of God, angels, and these witnesses, of your own free will and choice?

Stubbs testified that she had worn a white dress, which she considered a wedding dress; that she and Holm exchanged vows; that Warren Jeffs, a religious leader in the FLDS religion, conducted the ceremony; that other church members and members of Holm's family attended the ceremony; and that photographs were taken of Holm, Stubbs, and their guests who attended the ceremony.

Stubbs also testified about her relationship with Holm after the ceremony. She testified that she had moved in with their children; and that she and Holm had "regularly" engaged in sexual intercourse at the house in Hildale, Utah. Evidence was also introduced at trial that Holm and Stubbs "regarded each other as husband and wife."

At the close of the State's case in chief, Holm moved for reconsideration of his motion to dismiss, arguing that the jury should not be allowed to consider whether he violated the bigamy statute by purporting to marry Stubbs. Specifically, he argued that the "purporting to marry" prong of the bigamy statute applied only to legally recognized marriages. The court again rejected his motion.

During the course of the trial, the court denied Holm's request to present rebuttal evidence in the form of expert testimony concerning FLDS practice and beliefs. This evidence would have included Kenneth D. Driggs's testimony about the deeply held religious belief among FLDS adherents that this type of marriage is "necessary to their personal salvation," the history of polygamy, and the social health of polygamous communities.

The jury returned a guilty verdict on each of the charges, indicating on a special verdict form that Holm was guilty of bigamy both because he "purported to marry Ruth Stubbs" and because

---

[1] The FLDS Church is one of a number of small religious communities in Utah that continue to interpret the early doctrine of the Church of Jesus Christ of Latter-day Saints (the "LDS Church" or "Mormon Church") as supporting the practice of "plural marriage," or polygamy. Though often referred to as "fundamentalist Mormons," these groups have no connection to the LDS Church, which renounced the practice of polygamy in 1890.

he had "cohabited with Ruth Stubbs." The trial court sentenced Holm to up to five years in state prison on each conviction, to be served concurrently, and imposed a $3,000 fine. Both the prison time and the fine were suspended in exchange for three years on probation, one year in the county jail with work release, and two hundred hours of community service.

Holm appealed his conviction on all charges....
[...]

C. Holm's Conviction Does Not Offend the Federal Constitution

Holm claims his conviction runs afoul of the federal constitution in several ways. Specifically, he argues (1) that his conviction was obtained in violation of the federal constitution's guarantee of the free exercise of religion; (2) that his conviction violates his liberty interest protected by the Due Process Clause of the Fourteenth Amendment; (3) that his conviction raises equal protection concerns because the State targets only religiously motivated polygamists with prosecution; (4) that the bigamy statute is facially overbroad because it unduly infringes upon his right of association; and (5) that the term "marry," as used in the bigamy statute and the unlawful sexual conduct with a minor statute, is unconstitutionally vague. We address each of Holm's contentions in turn.

1. The Bigamy Statute Does Not Impermissibly Infringe Holm's Federal Free Exercise Right

Although the United States Supreme Court, in *Reynolds v. United States*, 98 U.S. 145 (1879), upheld the criminal prosecution of a religiously motivated polygamist as nonviolative of the Free Exercise Clause, Holm contends on appeal that his federal free exercise right is unduly infringed upon by his conviction in this case. Holm argues that *Reynolds* is "nothing more than a hollow relic of bygone days of fear, prejudice, and Victorian morality," and that modern free exercise jurisprudence dictates that no criminal penalty can be imposed for engaging in religiously motivated polygamy. This court recently rejected an identical argument in *State v. Green*, 2004 UT 76, ¶¶ 18–19, 99 P.3d 820.

As we pointed out in *Green*, *Reynolds*, despite its age, has never been overruled by the United States Supreme Court and, in fact, has been cited by the Court with approval in several modern free exercise cases, signaling its continuing vitality. See *Green*, 2004 UT 76, ¶ 19 (refusing to depart from the *Reynolds* holding and citing cases indicating the continuing vitality of *Reynolds* as precedent). Moreover, even if Holm's assertion that *Reynolds* is antiquated beyond usefulness is accurate, our opinion in *Green* conducted a thorough analysis, using the most recent standards announced by the United States Supreme Court, of the claim that religiously motivated polygamy is immune from criminal sanction. Id. ¶¶ 20–41. As we noted in *Green*, the United States Supreme Court held in *Employment Division, Department of Human Resources v. Smith*, 494 U.S. 872 (1990), partially superseded by statute, Religious Freedom Restoration Act of 1993, 107 Stat. 1488, as recognized in *Gonzales v. O Centro Espirita Beneficente Uniao Do Vegetal*, 126 S. Ct. 1211 (2006), and Religious Land Use and Institutionalized Persons Act of 2000, 114 Stat. 804, as recognized in *Cutter v. Wilkinson*, 544 U.S. 709 (2005), that a state may, even without furthering a compelling state interest, burden an individual's right to free exercise so long as the burden is imposed by a neutral law of general applicability. Id. at 878–80. The Court has since clarified that a law is not neutral if the intent of that law "is to infringe upon or restrict practices because of their religious motivation." *Church of the Lukumi Babalu Aye, Inc. v. City of Hialeah*, 508 U.S. 520, 533 (1993). In *Green*, we concluded that Utah's bigamy statute is a neutral law of general applicability and that any infringement upon the free exercise of religion occasioned by that law's application is constitutionally permissible. 2004 UT 76, ¶ 33.

Regardless of the wisdom of the United States Supreme Court's current federal free exercise analysis, that analysis is controlling, and this court does not enjoy the freedom to tamper with or modify pronouncements by that Court. In light of those pronouncements and our own case law rejecting the notion that religiously motivated polygamy is protected by the federal Free Exercise Clause, we conclude that Holm cannot avail himself of that clause in his attempt to escape conviction. Having so concluded, we turn to Holm's claim that his conviction violates his individual liberty interest protected by the Due Process Clause of the Fourteenth Amendment.

2. Holm's Conviction Does Not Offend the Due Process Clause of the Fourteenth Amendment

Holm argues that the State of Utah is foreclosed from criminalizing polygamous behavior because the freedom to engage in such behavior is a fundamental liberty interest that can be infringed only for compelling reasons and that the State has failed to identify a sufficiently compelling justification for its criminalization of polygamy. We disagree and conclude that there is no fundamental liberty interest to engage in the type of polygamous behavior at issue in this case.

In arguing that his behavior is constitutionally protected as a fundamental liberty interest, Holm relies primarily on the United States Supreme Court's decision in *Lawrence v. Texas*, 539 U.S. 558 (2003). In that case, the United States Supreme Court struck down a Texas statute criminalizing homosexual sodomy, concluding that private, consensual sexual behavior is protected by the Due Process Clause of the Fourteenth Amendment. See id. at 578. Holm argues that the liberty interest discussed in *Lawrence* is sufficiently broad to shield the type of behavior that he engages in from the intruding hand of the state. Holm misconstrues the breadth of the *Lawrence* opinion.

Despite its use of seemingly sweeping language, the holding in *Lawrence* is actually quite narrow.[1] Specifically, the Court takes pains to limit the opinion's reach to decriminalizing private and intimate acts engaged in by consenting adult gays and lesbians. In fact, the Court went out of its way to exclude from protection conduct that causes "injury to a person or abuse of an institution the law protects." Id. at 567. Further, after announcing its holding, the Court noted the following: "The present case does not involve minors. It does not involve persons who might be injured or coerced or who are situated in relationships where consent might not easily be refused. It does not involve public conduct…." Id. at 578.

In marked contrast to the situation presented to the Court in *Lawrence*, this case implicates the public institution of marriage, an institution the law protects, and also involves a minor. In other words, this case presents the exact conduct identified by the Supreme Court in *Lawrence* as outside the scope of its holding.

First, the behavior at issue in this case is not confined to personal decisions made about sexual activity, but rather raises important questions about the State's ability to regulate marital relationships and prevent the formation and propagation of marital forms that the citizens of the State deem harmful.

> Sexual intercourse … is the most intimate behavior in which the citizenry engages. [*Lawrence*] spoke to this discreet, personal activity. Marriage, on the other hand, includes both public and private conduct. Within the privacy of the home, marriage means essentially whatever the married individuals wish it to mean. Nonetheless, marriage extends beyond the confines of the home to our society.
>
> Joseph Bozzuti, Note, "The Constitutionality of Polygamy Prohibitions After *Lawrence v. Texas*: Is Scalia a Punchline or a Prophet?," 43 *Catholic Law.* 409, 435 (Fall 2004).

---

[1] In fact, numerous litigants have relied upon the *Lawrence* decision to attempt to expand the sphere of behavior protected by the federal constitution. Given the quite limited nature of that case's holding, however, it should come as no surprise that the Lawrence opinion has been distinguished more than forty times since it was issued. See, e.g., *Muth v. Frank*, 412 F.3d 808, 817 (7th Cir. 2005).

("*Lawrence* … did not announce … a [constitutionally protected] fundamental right … to engage in all manner of consensual sexual conduct, specifically in this case, incest."); *United States v. Bach*, 400 F.3d 622, 628–29 (8th Cir. 2005) (holding that Lawrence did not protect an adult from criminal sanction for taking pornographic photos of a sixteen-year-old).

The very "concept of marriage possesses 'undisputed social value.'" *Green*, 2004 UT 76, ¶ 72 (Durrant, J., concurring) (quoting *In re Marriage of Mehren & Dargan*, 13 Cal. Rptr. 3d 522, 523 (Ct. App. 2004). Utah's own constitution enshrines a commitment to prevent polygamous behavior. See Utah Const. art. III, § 1; id. art. XXIV, § 2. That commitment has undergirded this State's establishment of "a vast and convoluted network of … laws … based exclusively upon the practice of monogamy as opposed to plural marriage." *Potter v. Murray City*, 760 F.2d 1065, 1070 (10th Cir. 1985). Our State's commitment to monogamous unions is a recognition that decisions made by individuals as to how to structure even the most personal of relationships are capable of dramatically affecting public life.

The dissent states quite categorically that the State of Utah has no interest in the commencement of an intimate personal relationship so long as the participants do not present their relationship as being state-sanctioned. On the contrary, the formation of relationships that are marital in nature is of great interest to this State, no matter what the participants in or the observers of that relationship venture to name the union. We agree with the dissent's statement that any two people may make private pledges to each other and that these relationships do not receive legal recognition unless a legal adjudication of marriage is sought. See *infra* ¶ 145. That does not, however, prevent the legislature from having a substantial interest in criminalizing such behavior when there is an existing marriage.

As the dissent recognizes, a marriage license significantly alters the bond between two people because the State becomes a third party to the marital contract. *Infra* ¶ 145. It is precisely that third-party contractual relationship that gives the State a substantial interest in prohibiting unlicensed marriages when there is an existing marriage. Without this contractual relationship, the State would be unable to enforce important marital rights and obligations. See *infra* ¶ 102. In situations where there is no existing marriage, the Legislature has developed a mechanism for legally determining that a marriage did in fact exist, even where the couple did not seek legal recognition of that marriage, so that the State may enforce marital obligations such as spousal support or prevent welfare abuse. See Utah Code Ann. § 30-1-4.5 (Supp. 2005). There is no such mechanism for protecting the State's interest in situations where there is an existing marriage because, under any interpretation of the bigamy statute, a party cannot seek a legal adjudication of a second marriage. Thus, the State has a substantial interest in criminalizing such an unlicensed second marriage.

Moreover, marital relationships serve as the building blocks of our society. The State must be able to assert some level of control over those relationships to ensure the smooth operation of laws and further the proliferation of social unions our society deems beneficial while discouraging those deemed harmful. The people of this State have declared monogamy a beneficial marital form and have also declared polygamous relationships harmful. As the Tenth Circuit stated in *Potter*, Utah "is justified, by a compelling interest, in upholding and enforcing its ban on plural marriage to protect the monogamous marriage relationship." 760 F.2d at 1070 (internal quotation marks omitted); see also *Green*, 2004 UT 76, ¶ 72 (Durrant, J., concurring) ("[Utah] has a compelling interest in prohibiting conduct, such as the practice of polygamy, which threatens [monogamous marriage].").

Further, this case features another critical distinction from *Lawrence*; namely, the involvement of a minor. Stubbs was sixteen years old at the time of her betrothal, and evidence adduced at trial indicated that she and Holm regularly engaged in sexual activity. Further, it is not unreasonable to conclude that this case involves behavior that warrants inquiry into the possible existence of injury and the validity of consent. See, e.g., *Green*, 2004 UT 76, ¶ 40 ("The practice of polygamy … often coincides with crimes targeting women and children. Crimes not unusually attendant to the practice of polygamy include incest, sexual assault, statutory rape, and failure to pay child support.") (citing Richard A. Vazquez, Note, "The Practice of Polygamy: Legitimate Free Exercise of Religion or

Legitimate Public Menace? Revisiting *Reynolds* in Light of Modern Constitutional Jurisprudence," 5 *N.Y.U.J. Legis. & Pub. Pol'y* 225, 239–45 (2001)).

Given the above, we conclude that *Lawrence* does not prevent our Legislature from prohibiting polygamous behavior. The distinction between private, intimate sexual conduct between consenting adults and the public nature of polygamists' attempts to extralegally redefine the acceptable parameters of a fundamental social institution like marriage is plain. The contrast between the present case and *Lawrence* is even more dramatic when the minority status of Stubbs is considered. Given the critical differences between the two cases, and the fact that the United States Supreme Court has not extended its polygamous marital arrangements, we conclude that the criminalization of the behavior engaged in by Holm does not run afoul of the personal liberty interests protected by the Fourteenth Amendment. Having so concluded, we now address Holm's contention that our State's bigamy statute violates equal protection guarantees.

3. No Equal Protection Concerns Are Implicated by Utah's Bigamy Statute

Holm claims that his conviction for bigamy is unconstitutional because the bigamy statute unfairly discriminates against individuals who are religiously compelled to practice polygamy. We disagree.

Generally speaking, the Equal Protection Clause of the Fourteenth Amendment mandates that similarly situated individuals be treated in the same manner. See *City of Cleburne v. Cleburne Living Ctr., Inc.*, 473 U.S. 432, 439 (1985). In *Green*, we held that Utah's bigamy statute is facially neutral as to religion; in other words, it delineates no distinction between classes of individuals. 2004 UT 76, ¶ 25. "The statute does not ... mention polygamists or their religion." Id. One could engage in polygamy out of animus for religion and still be considered in violation of the statute. Quite simply, the statute is designed to punish behavior regardless of the motivations giving rise to that behavior.

Furthermore, in *Green*, we concluded that the facially neutral text of the bigamy statute is not merely a smokescreen meant to disguise a discriminatory intent to prosecute only religiously motivated polygamy. Id. ¶ 28. As we noted in *Green*, the last reported decision concerning a bigamy prosecution prior to *Green* involved a man engaging in non-religiously motivated polygamy. Id. Ironically, the defendant in that case argued that the State of Utah selectively prosecutes "'only those bigamists who practice bigamy for other than religious reasons.'" Id. ¶ 28 n.10 (quoting *State v. Geer*, 765 P.2d 1, 3 (Utah Ct. App. 1988)). Although Holm asserts that discriminatory prosecution of bigamy occurs, the record before us is devoid of any meaningful evidence supporting that assertion. In light of our holding in Green that the bigamy statute is facially neutral and that its enactment was not intended to provide a vehicle for discriminatory actions, and in the absence of evidence giving credence to Holm's assertion of unequal treatment, we decline to find Holm's conviction violative of equal protection guarantees.

Having so concluded, we now turn to Holm's assertion that the bigamy statute is unconstitutional because it unduly infringes upon his right of association.

4. Criminalization of Polygamy Does Not Unduly Infringe upon the Right of Association

Holm claims that the State of Utah, by criminalizing polygamous behavior, has unjustifiably restricted his ability to teach his family the principle of plural marriage by way of example. According to Holm, such a restriction violates his right of association protected by the First Amendment of the United States Constitution. We conclude that Holm's right of association is not so broad as to render him immune from criminal sanction for polygamous behavior.

As an initial matter, we point out that the freedom of association protected by the federal constitution has been conceived of as covering two separate but related rights. As the United States Supreme Court acknowledged in *Roberts v. United States Jaycees*, 468 U.S. 609, 617–18 (1984), there are "two distinct senses" of the freedom of asso-

694

ciation, commonly referred to as intrinsic and instrumental association.

Holm argues that Utah's criminalization of polygamous behavior infringes upon his right of association in both senses. We disagree and conclude that Holm's rights to intrinsic and instrumental association have not been unduly restricted.

First, the concept of intrinsic association encompasses certain intimate associations. Id. Under this type of association, the United States Supreme Court has recognized that the freedom to form certain intimate associations is constitutionally protected, stating that "choices to enter into and maintain certain intimate human relationships must be secured against undue intrusion by the State because of the role of such relationships in safeguarding the individual freedom that is central to our constitutional scheme." Id. In this sense, the "freedom of association receives protection as a fundamental element of personal liberty." Id. at 618. When considering claims that a certain governmental action violates the right to intimate association, the United States Supreme Court has essentially conducted a fundamental liberty analysis to determine whether the type of behavior allegedly infringed upon is protected. See id. at 618–19 (citing fundamental rights cases when identifying the characteristics of relationships possibly entitled to associational protection).

Holm's right to intrinsic association has not been unduly infringed upon because, as discussed above, *supra* ¶¶ 53–63, the right to engage in polygamous behavior is not encompassed within the ambit of the individual liberty protections contained in our federal constitution. Consequently, Holm cannot argue that his associational rights prevent the State from interfering with his ability to engage in properly criminalized behavior, as the right of intimate association protects only those associations that further or otherwise support fundamental liberty interests.

Second, instrumental associations include those associations "indispensable" to the "preserv[ation] [of] other individual liberties" including "those activities protected by the First Amendment." Id. at 618. "An individual's freedom to speak, to worship,

and to petition the government for the redress of grievances could not be vigorously protected from interference by the State unless a correlative freedom to engage in group effort toward those ends were not also guaranteed." Id. at 622.

Holm's right to instrumental association has not been infringed. We have already concluded that Utah's prohibition on polygamous behavior does not run afoul of constitutional guarantees protecting the free exercise of religion. Further, we see nothing contained within the language of the bigamy statute that prevents Holm from associating with a group advocating the social and spiritual desirability of a polygamous lifestyle. Although it is true that the bigamy statute prevents Holm from expressing his opinions regarding polygamy by engaging in polygamous behavior, we are not convinced that the State is constrained to tolerate constitutionally prohibited behavior in order to allow individuals to express their dissatisfaction with the criminal status of that behavior.

Accordingly, we conclude that Utah's prohibition against polygamous behavior does not violate Holm's First Amendment right to freedom of association....

[...]

Conclusion

We conclude that Holm was properly convicted of both bigamy and unlawful sexual conduct with a minor. As to the bigamy conviction, we conclude that Holm's behavior falls squarely within the terms of the "purports to marry" prong of the bigamy statute, that his conviction pursuant to that prong did not run afoul of any state or federal constitutional right, and that the trial court did not abuse its discretion by excluding expert testimony relating to the social history and health of polygamous communities.

As to the sexual-conduct-with-a-minor conviction, we conclude that Holm was properly convicted because the trial court had jurisdiction over him and because such conviction did not violate his constitutional right to equal protection. Accordingly, we affirm the judgment of the trial court.

Associate Chief Justice Wilkins and Justice Parrish concur in Justice Durrant's opinion. [...]

DURHAM, Chief Justice, concurring in part and dissenting in part:

I join the majority in upholding Holm's conviction for unlawful sexual conduct with a minor. As to the remainder of its analysis, I respectfully dissent. As interpreted by the majority, Utah Code section 76-7-101 defines "marriage" as acts undertaken for religious purposes that do not meet any other legal standard for marriage—acts that are unlicensed, unsolemnized by any civil authority, acts that are indeed entirely outside the civil law, and unrecognized as marriage for any other purpose by the state—and criminalizes those acts as "bigamy." I believe that in doing so the statute oversteps lines protecting the free exercise of religion and the privacy of intimate, personal relationships between consenting adults.

The majority upholds Holm's criminal bigamy conviction based solely on his participation in a private religious ceremony because the form of that ceremony—though not its intent—resembled what we think of as a wedding, a ritual that serves to solemnize lawful marriages and in which the parties formally undertake the legal rights, obligations, and duties that belong to that state-approved institution. In resting its conclusion on that basis, the majority, in my view, ignores the legislature's intent that the concept of marriage in Utah law be confined to a legally recognized union. I also believe that the majority's reasoning fails to distinguish between conduct that has public import of a sort that the state may legitimately regulate and conduct of the most private nature.

In particular, the majority broadly interprets the "purports to marry" prong of Utah's bigamy statute, Utah Code Ann. § 76-7-101 (2003), to include the purported entry into "marriages recognized both by law and by custom." *Supra* ¶ 25. The majority then implicitly concludes that the term "marriage" in article III, section 1 of the Utah Constitution, which declares that "polygamous and plural marriages are

forever prohibited," has the same broad meaning and, thus, that the Utah Constitution excludes even private polygamous relationships from the scope of its protections of religious freedom and individual liberty. *Supra* ¶ 47. The majority further holds that the United States Constitution's protection of individual liberty under the Fourteenth Amendment's Due Process Clause does not extend to "the type of polygamous behavior at issue in this case," *supra* ¶ 53, not only because that behavior involves a minor but also because it "implicates the public institution of marriage." *Supra* ¶ 56.

On all three points, I believe that the majority's expansive conception of marriage in Utah law is the result of a flawed analysis with problematic implications. Because I do not agree that the state can constitutionally criminalize private religiously motivated consensual relationships between adults, I believe Holm's conviction under section 76-7-101—which does not rely on the fact that Holm's partner in his alleged bigamy was a minor—must be overturned, and I therefore respectfully dissent from Part I of the majority's opinion. I explain my disagreement with the majority's reasoning below, first addressing its interpretation of the "purports to marry" prong of section 76-7-101. I then address its analysis of Holm's constitutional challenges to the bigamy statute and offer an alternative reading of our state constitution's polygamy and religious freedom provisions and of *Lawrence v. Texas*, 539 U.S. 558 (2003).

[...]

B. Religious Freedom Claim

Holm essentially argues that the State may not subject him to a criminal penalty under a generally applicable criminal law for his religiously motivated practice of polygamy because imposing that penalty is inconsistent with our constitution's protection of religious freedom. The State does not dispute the sincerity of Holm's religious motivation, and given Holm's established membership in the FLDS community, there appears to be no reason to doubt Holm's assertion that polygamy is a central tenet of his religion. Resolution of this issue therefore turns on the interpretation of the religious freedom guarantees found in the Utah Constitution.

As an initial matter, I accept the premise that our state constitution's guarantee of religious freedom encompasses religiously motivated conduct as well as belief. See, e.g., Utah Const. art. I, § 1 (recognizing right "to worship"); id. art. I, § 4 (guaranteeing "free exercise" of religion); see also Michael W. McConnell, "The Origins and Historical Understanding of Free Exercise of Religion," 103 *Harv. L. Rev.* 1409, 1459–60 (1990) [hereinafter McConnell, Origins] (concluding that the terms "exercise" and "worship" in late eighteenth century state constitutions both denoted conduct, though the term "worship" is usually limited to ritual or ceremonial acts). Thus, Holm's conduct—cohabiting with Ruth Stubbs after participating in a religious ceremony with her while legally married to another woman—qualifies as religious "exercise" within the meaning of article I, section 4.

The question remains whether, and under what circumstances, our constitution requires an exemption from generally applicable criminal laws. This court held in *Green*, 2004 UT 76, ¶ 37, that no such exemption was required under the federal constitution's Free Exercise Clause. However, as the majority states, "We have never determined whether the free exercise clause of article I, section 4 [and the other related clauses] of the Utah Constitution provide[] protection over and above that provided by the First Amendment to the United States Constitution." *Jeffs v. Stubbs*, 970 P.2d 1234, 1249 (Utah 1998). I believe that governmental burdens on religiously motivated conduct should be subject to heightened scrutiny, a proposition that a number of my colleagues, past and present, have also previously endorsed. See *Green*, 2004 UT 76, ¶ 70, 99 P.3d ¶ 20 (Durrant, J., concurring); see also *Wood v. Univ. of Utah Med. Ctr.*, 2002 UT 134, ¶ 43 n.1, 67 P.3d 436 (Durham, C.J., dissenting) (recognizing that this court employed heightened scrutiny when conducting an article I, section 4 analysis in *Soc'y of Separationists v. Whitehead*, 870 P.2d 916 (Utah 1993)).

In reaching the conclusion that the framers of our state constitution intended such an analysis, I look first to the United States Supreme Court's decision in *Reynolds v. United States*, 98 U.S. 145 (1879). In light of the fact that *Reynolds* was issued in 1879, seventeen years before the 1896 ratification of our state constitution, and the fact that the underlying controversy in *Reynolds* originated in the Utah territory, it would be disingenuous to assert that the Court's interpretation of free exercise in *Reynolds* did not inform the understanding of the framers when they inserted an identically phrased clause in article I, section 4 of the Utah Constitution. The Court has subsequently interpreted *Reynolds* as "reject[ing] the claim that criminal laws against polygamy could not be constitutionally applied to those whose religion commanded the practice." *Employment Div. v. Smith*, 494 U.S. 872, 879 (1990). However, I disagree that *Reynolds'* reasoning entirely foreclosed religion-based exemptions from criminal laws.

The *Reynolds* Court framed the issue under consideration as follows: "whether religious belief can be accepted as a justification of an overt act made criminal by the law of the land." 98 U.S. at 162. In analyzing this issue, the Court relied on Thomas Jefferson's formulations "almost as an authoritative declaration of the scope and effect" of the Free Exercise Clause. Id. at 164. The Court first quoted the 1786 Virginia Bill for Establishing Religious Freedom, drafted by Jefferson, indicating that religious freedom extends only until "principles break out into overt acts against peace and good order." Id. at 163 (internal quotation omitted). It then quoted Jefferson's 1802 letter to the Danbury Baptist Association, in which he stated that man "has no natural right in opposition to his social duties." Id. at 164 (internal quotation omitted). Summarizing these statements, the Court concluded that Congress was free, consistent with the Free Exercise Clause, "to reach actions which were in violation of social duties or subversive of good order." Id.

The Court then analyzed whether the practice of polygamy or polygamous marriage was in violation of social duties or subversive of good order. It determined that polygamy was indeed an "offence against society," and that punishing polygamy was therefore within Congress's legislative power. Id. at 165–66. Finally, reaching the question of religion-based exemption, the Court concluded that the practice of polygamy could be punished even when the practice was motivated by religious belief. Id. at 166–67. The Court observed that allowing individuals to excuse such conduct, which it compared to human sacrifice or self-immolation, because of religious motivation would effectively "permit every citizen to become a law unto himself." Id.

The essential feature of the *Reynolds* Court's analysis was its conclusion that the practice of polygamy fell within the category of conduct "in violation of social duties or subversive of good order." Id. at 164. In the *Reynolds* Court's view, polygamy was an "odious" practice that threatened to infect the surrounding society with notions of patriarchal despotism, undermining the democratic principles on which our governmental structure was founded. Id. at 164, 166. Clearly, the purpose of criminalizing polygamy, according to *Reynolds*, was to protect society and the state from such harm. Allowing individuals to engage in polygamy for religious reasons would have thus permitted them to inflict the very harm the statute was designed to prevent. The same is true in the two other examples given in *Reynolds*: (1) exempting someone engaged in religiously motivated human sacrifice from a criminal law against murder would allow that person to kill another; and (2) exempting someone wishing to burn herself on her husband's funeral pyre from a criminal law against suicide would allow that person to kill herself. Id. at 165–66.

Understood in this way, *Reynolds* is consistent with those early state constitutions that, by their express terms, guaranteed free exercise of religion to the extent such exercise was consistent with public peace and order. Indeed, when discussing its *Reynolds* decision in *Davis v. Beason*, 133 U.S. 333 (1890), the Court explicitly referred to such state constitutional provisions. Id. at 348 Note (noting that several state constitutions "have declared expressly that [religious] freedom shall not be construed to excuse acts of licentiousness, or to justify practices inconsistent with the peace and safety of the State"). Those who have studied these provisions are divided over whether their drafters contemplated a case-by-case examination in the courts of the particular conduct being criminalized, or whether the violation of any law was *per se* considered a breach of the peace. Compare McConnell, Origins, *supra* ¶ 156, at 1462 (construing these clauses to "exempt religiously motivated conduct from [generally applicable] laws up to the point that such conduct breached public peace or safety"), with Philip A. Hamburger, "A Constitutional Right of Religious Exemption: An Historical Perspective," 60 *Geo. Wash. L. Rev.* 915, 918 (1992) (indicating that the phrase "*contra pacem*," or breach of the peace, was understood in the eighteenth century to mean any criminal violation of law). Under either view, it seems clear that there is some conduct that a state may refuse to permit, regardless of its motivation.

I agree that the religious freedom provisions in our state constitution were not intended to exempt religious practitioners from criminal punishment for acts that cause injury or harm to society at large or to other individuals. Moreover, I recognize that by defining conduct as criminal, our legislature has signaled its judgment that this conduct generally does harm society or individuals to a degree that warrants criminal punishment. See Charles E. Torcia, *Wharton's Criminal Law* § 7 (15th ed. 1993) (distinguishing crime, which is "a public wrong since it implies injury to the state," from tort, which is a "private wrong since it involves injury to an individual"); Laurence H. Tribe, *American Constitutional Law* § 14–13, at 1270 (2d ed. 1988) [hereinafter Tribe, American Constitutional Law] (predicting that, "[b]eyond ... paternalistic laws, ... [free exercise] exemptions from criminal laws will be rare"). In "our role as the state's court of last resort, called upon to identify the boundaries of the constitution, [we must] giv[e] appropriate deference to the policy choices of the citizens' elected representatives."

Judd ex rel. Montgomery v. Drezga, 2004 UT 91, ¶ 22, 103 P.3d 135.

That this is generally true does not, however, foreclose close scrutiny of the circumstances of a particular case in order to determine whether a prosecution for conduct statutorily defined as criminal is truly directed against the harm the statute was intended to prevent, where the conduct in the particular case is religiously motivated. The "right to the free exercise of religion [is] a concept upon which our country was founded and a protection deeply ingrained in the hearts and minds of American citizens." *Green*, 2004 UT 76, ¶ 70 (Durrant, J., concurring). This court has recognized that this is particularly true for citizens of our state. *Soc'y of Separationists*, 870 P.2d at 935. I believe our constitution expresses this fundamental interest in protecting religious freedom. Given the fundamental nature of the constitutional interest involved and the undeniable burden that criminal penalties impose, heightened scrutiny is warranted. Cf. *Gallivan v. Walker*, 2002 UT 89, ¶ 40, 54 P.3d 1069 (recognizing that a "heightened degree of scrutiny" is required in a uniform operation-of-laws analysis where a fundamental right is implicated).

Moreover, I am cognizant of the fact that the body of criminal law has expanded over time as the state has generally expanded its reach into many areas that before went unregulated. Criminal statutes today punish conduct not only where the targeted conduct is harmful in itself, such as laws criminalizing murder, but also where the targeted conduct is closely tied to other harmful activity. Given this fact, there may be circumstances where religiously motivated conduct will not implicate the same state interests that are legitimately served by prosecuting those whose conduct was without similar motivation, simply because of the nature of the religious practice at issue. For example, the religiously motivated use of drugs defined as controlled substances may in some cases be so far removed from the context within which illegal drug use typically occurs that applying the controlled substances law to the religiously motivated use simply does not serve the government's legitimate interest in criminalizing drug use—which involves not only protecting people from the harmful physical effects of such substances, but also eliminating the harms that accompany the drug trafficking industry. Thus, the few instances in which courts have indicated that a generally applicable criminal law may not apply to a religiously motivated actor have done so on the basis that the religiously motivated conduct at issue did not create a genuine risk of harm.[1]

Applying this principle, I conclude that in some rare circumstances an individual must be exempted from the operation of a criminal law where the religiously motivated conduct at issue, while technically within the purview of the criminal prohibition, does not threaten the harm that the law was intended to prevent.

Applying heightened scrutiny, I conclude that imposing criminal penalties on Holm's religiously motivated entry into a religious union with Ruth

---

[1] *Gonzales v. O Centro Espirita Beneficente Uniao Do Vegetal*, 126 S. Ct. 1211, 1224 (2006) (recognizing in a preliminary injunction analysis of an RFRA statutory claim that the government had failed to show that its interest in protecting public health and safety was served by applying a law criminalizing use of hoasca, a hallucinogenic controlled substance, to those who use the drug in religious ceremonies); *Frank v. State*, 604 P.2d 1068, 1073–74 (Alaska 1979) (exempting the defendant under federal and state religious freedom guarantees from criminal prosecution for unlawful transportation of a moose outside hunting season because there was no evidence that the taking of the moose for ritual use in funeral potlatches would harm the moose population or cause "general lawlessness" among Alaskan citizens); *State v. Whittingham*, 504 P.2d 950, 952–53 (Ariz. Ct. App. 1973) (holding that the state could not, consistent with the Free Exercise Clause, prosecute those engaged in the religious use of peyote where such use did not cause "a substantial threat to public safety, order or peace"); *People v. Woody*, 394 P.2d 813, 818 (Cal. 1964) (explaining, when granting a Free Exercise Clause exemption from criminal prosecution to Native Americans' religious use of peyote, that "[t]he record ... does not support the state's chronicle of harmful consequences of the use of peyote"); *State v. Miller*, 549 N.W.2d 235, 242 (Wis. 1996) (exempting Amish, under the religious freedom guarantee of its state constitution, from forfeiture pursuant to a traffic law requiring a slow-moving vehicle emblem because there was no evidence that Amish horse-drawn buggies without the emblem had caused any collisions).

Stubbs is an unconstitutional burden under our constitution's religious freedom protections. This is so whether typical strict scrutiny is applied, or the standard set forth in *United States v. O'Brien*, 391 U.S. 367, 381–82 (1968) (determining whether a general law may be applied to expressive conduct consistent with the Free Speech Clause), which some have suggested provides a more suitable framework for free exercise analysis. Under either test, the burden on the religious conduct at issue must be necessary to serve a strong governmental interest unrelated to the suppression of religious freedom. I do not believe that any of the strong state interests normally served by the Utah bigamy law require that the law apply to the religiously motivated conduct at issue here—entering a religious union with more than one woman.

I note at the outset that the State has not suggested that section 76-7-101 furthers a governmental interest in preserving democratic society. I agree that no such interest is implicated here. As discussed above, the federal government's nineteenth-century criminalization of polygamy in the Utah Territory, as construed by the *Reynolds* Court, was intended to address the harm to democratic society that LDS Church polygamy was thought to embody. See *Soc'y of Separationists*, 870 P.2d at 924 (recognizing that the Morrill Act of 1862 was aimed specifically at the LDS Church's practice of polygamy in Utah); Gordon, The Mormon Question, *supra* n.9, at 30–115 (describing the nineteenth century development of the idea that the LDS Church's practice of polygamy threatened American democracy). However, I do not presume that our modern criminal bigamy statute, enacted in 1973, addresses the same fears—which have since been discounted by many as grounded more in bias than in fact—that propelled Congress' legislation a century earlier.

Indeed, this court previously set forth, in *Green*, a list of state interests served by the modern statute that omits any reference to such a concern. There, we first explained that the modern statute serves the state's interest in "regulating marriage" and in maintaining the "network of laws" that surrounds the institution of marriage. *Green*, 2004 UT 76, ¶¶ 37–38. We cited a Tenth Circuit case that described this network of laws as "'clearly establishing [Utah's] compelling state interest in and commitment to a system of domestic relations based exclusively upon the practice of monogamy as opposed to plural marriage.'" Id. ¶ 38 (quoting *Potter v. Murray City*, 760 F.2d 1065, 1070 (10th Cir. 1985)). Here, the State has emphasized its interest in "protecting" monogamous marriage as a social institution. I agree that the state has an important interest in regulating marriage, but only insofar as marriage is understood as a legal status. See *Green*, 2004 UT 76, ¶ 71 (Durrant, J., concurring) (asserting that "the State has a compelling interest in regulating and preserving the institution of marriage *as that institution has been defined by the State*" (emphasis added)). In my view, the criminal bigamy statute protects marriage, as a legal union, by criminalizing the act of purporting to enter a second legal union. Such an act defrauds the state and perhaps an innocent spouse or purported partner. It also completely disregards the network of laws that regulate entry into, and the dissolution of, the legal status of marriage, and that limit to one the number of partners with which an individual may enjoy this status. The same harm is targeted by criminalizing the act of cohabiting with a partner after purportedly entering a second legal marriage with that partner.

However, I do not believe the state's interest extends to those who enter a religious union with a second person but who do not claim to be legally married. For one thing, the cohabitation of unmarried couples, who live together "as if" they are married in the sense that they share a household and a sexually intimate relationship, is commonplace in contemporary society. See, e.g., Utah Governor's Comm'n on Marriage & Utah State Univ. Extension, Marriage in Utah Study 35–36 (2003), available at http://www.utahmarriage. org (indicating that of the 42% of Utah residents between the ages of 18 and 64 who were unmarried, 30% to 46% were currently cohabiting outside of marriage). Even outside the community of those who practice polygamy for religious reasons, such cohabitation may occur where one person is legally married to someone other than the person with whom he or she is cohabiting. Yet parties to such relationships are not prosecuted under the criminal bigamy statute, the criminal fornication statute, Utah Code Ann. § 76-7-104 (2003), or, as far as I am aware, the criminal adultery statute, id. § 76-7-103 (2003), even where their conduct violates these laws. See, e.g., *Berg v. State*, 2004 UT App 337, ¶ 15, 100 P.3d 261 (indicating that consenting adults are not prosecuted under Utah's fornication or sodomy laws).

That the state perceives no need to prosecute non-religiously motivated cohabitation, whether one of the parties to the cohabitation is married to someone else or not, demonstrates that, in the absence of any claim of legal marriage, neither participation in a religious ceremony nor cohabitation can plausibly be said to threaten marriage as a social or legal institution. The state's concern with regulating marriage, as I understand it, has to do with determining who is entitled to enter that legal status, what benefits are accorded, and what obligations and restrictions are imposed thereby. This has lately emerged as an issue of surprising complexity, with various commentators attempting to define the nexus between a couple's private relationship and the network of laws surrounding marriage as a legally recognized status. Our state's network of laws may indeed presume a particular domestic structure—whether it be that a man will live with only one woman, that a couple living together will enter a legal union, or that each household will contain a single nuclear family. However, any interest the state has in maintaining this network of laws does not logically justify its imposition of criminal penalties on those who deviate from that domestic structure, particularly when they do so for religious reasons. In my view, such criminal penalties are simply unnecessary to further the state's interest in protecting marriage.

The state's abandonment of common law marriage, and the proliferation of governmentally regulated marriage, contributes to my conclusion. As mentioned above, the state conditions entry into the legal status of marriage on the performance of certain steps beyond simply entering a marriage-like personal relationship. At the same time, the legal significance of this status has increased as federal and state governments have ventured ever further into regulating various aspects of individuals' lives. The inevitable corollary to these two facets of governmental involvement with the institution of marriage is that some will consciously choose to form relationships outside the state-delineated boundaries of that institution. At common law, the choice of entering a marriage-like personal relationship without entering the legal status of marriage was less available because a man and a woman who appeared to be married were simply considered married in the eyes of the law. As discussed above, this is no longer the case. In an important sense, then, there has been a significant social and legal divergence between the choice to enter a personal relationship and the choice to enter the legal status of marriage.

Those who choose to live together without getting married enter a personal relationship that resembles a marriage in its intimacy but claims no legal sanction. They thereby intentionally place themselves outside the framework of rights and obligations that surrounds the marriage institution. While some in society may feel that the institution of marriage is diminished when individuals consciously choose to avoid it, it is generally understood that the state is not entitled to criminally punish its citizens for making such a choice, even if they do so with multiple partners or with partners of the same sex. The only distinction in this case is that when Holm consciously chose to enter into a personal relationship that he knew would not be legally recognized as marriage, he used religious terminology to describe this relationship. The terminology that he used—"marriage" and "husband and wife"—happens to coincide with the terminology used by the state to describe the legal status of married persons. That fact, however, is not sufficient for me to conclude that criminalizing this conduct is essential in order to protect the institution of marriage.

In this regard, the case before us resembles *Spence v. Washington*, 418 U.S. 405 (1974). There, the United States Supreme Court held that a state law criminalizing the exhibition of the national flag with any extraneous material attached to it violated the defendant's First Amendment right to symbolically communicate his message through such a practice. Id. at 406. In analyzing the issue under the *O'Brien* test, mentioned above, the Court assumed without deciding that the state had valid interests "in preserving the national flag as an unalloyed symbol of our country" and "prevent[ing] the appropriation of a revered national symbol by an individual … where there was a risk that association of the symbol with a particular product or viewpoint might be taken erroneously as evidence of governmental endorsement." Id. at 412–13. The Court nevertheless held that this interest did not justify the defendant's conviction because "[t]here was no risk that [the defendant]'s acts would mislead viewers into assuming that the Government endorsed his viewpoint." Id. at 414. In other words, the defendant was free to appropriate a revered national symbol for his own communicative purposes so long as he did not thereby purport to speak for the state. I similarly conclude here that an individual is free to appropriate the terminology of marriage, a revered social and legal institution, for his own religious purposes if he does not thereby purport to have actually acquired the legal status of marriage.

The second state interest served by the bigamy law, as recognized in *Green*, is in preventing "marriage fraud," whereby an already-married individual fraudulently purports to enter a legal marriage with someone else, "or attempts to procure government benefits associated with marital status." 2004 UT 76, ¶¶ 37–39. This interest focuses on preventing the harm caused to the state, to society, and to defrauded individuals when someone purports to have entered the legal status of marriage, but in fact is not eligible to validly enter that status because of a prior legal union. This interest is simply not implicated here, where no claim to the legal status of marriage has been made.

In *Green*, the court cited "protecting vulnerable individuals from exploitation and abuse" as the third state interest served by the bigamy statute. 2004 UT 76, ¶ 40. The court concluded that this was a legitimate state interest to which the criminal bigamy statute was rationally related for purposes of our First Amendment Free Exercise Clause analysis. Id. ¶ 41. The court rested this conclusion on the idea that perpetrators of other crimes "not unusually attendant to the practice of polygamy"—such as "incest, sexual assault, statutory rape, and failure to pay child support"—could be prosecuted for bigamy in the absence of sufficient evidence to support a conviction on these other charges. Id. ¶ 40. Because the federal First Amendment analysis required only rational basis scrutiny, the court was content to rely on assertions in a student law review piece that polygamy was frequently related to other criminal conduct, together with two local cases, including the case of Green himself. Id. ¶ 40 & n.14. However, reviewing this assessment in light of the heightened scrutiny I believe is called for here, I cannot conclude that the restriction that the bigamy law places on the religious freedom of all those who, for religious reasons, live with more than one woman is necessary to further the state's interest in this regard. Upon closer review, the student Note is unconvincing. The State has provided no evidence of a causal relationship or even a strong correlation between the practice of polygamy, whether religiously motivated or not, and the offenses of "incest, sexual assault, statutory rape, and failure to pay child support," cited in *Green*, id. ¶ 40. Moreover, even assuming such a correlation did exist, neither the record nor the recent history of prosecutions of alleged polygamists warrants the conclusion that section 76-7-101 is a necessary tool for the state's attacks on such harms. For one thing, I am unaware of a single instance where the state was forced to bring a charge of bigamy in place of other narrower charges, such as incest or unlawful sexual conduct with a minor, because it was unable to gather sufficient evidence to prosecute these other crimes.[1] The State has suggested that its initial ability to file bigamy charges allows it to gather the evidence required to prosecute those engaged in more specific crimes. Even if there were support for this claim in the record, I would consider it inappropriate to let stand a criminal law simply because it enables the state to conduct a fishing expedition for evidence of other crimes. Further, the State itself has indicated that it does not prosecute those engaged in religiously motivated polygamy under the criminal bigamy statute unless the person has entered a religious union with a girl under eighteen years old. Such a policy of selective prosecution reinforces my conclusion that a blanket criminal prohibition on religious polygamous unions is not necessary to further the state's interests, and suggests that a more narrowly tailored law would be just as effective.[2]

I do not reach this conclusion lightly. I acknowledge the possibility that other criminal conduct

may accompany the act of bigamy. Such conduct may even, as was suggested in *Green*, be correlated with the practice of polygamy in a community that has isolated itself from the outside world, at least partially in fear of criminal prosecution for its religious practice. Indeed, the FLDS community in its current form has been likened to a cult, with allegations focusing on the power wielded by a single leader who exerts a high degree of control over followers, ranging from ownership of their property to the determination of persons with whom they may enter religious unions. In the latter regard, reports of forcible unions between underage girls and older men within the FLDS community have recently appeared in the media. Yet, the state does not criminalize cult membership, and for good reason. To do so would be to impose a criminal penalty based on status rather than conduct—long considered antithetical to our notion of criminal justice. See *Powell v. Texas*, 392 U.S. 514, 533 (1968); *Robinson v. California*, 370 U.S. 660, 666–67 (1962). Moreover, such a criminal law would require that the state make normative judgments distinguishing between communities that are actually "cults" and those that are voluntary associations based on common religious or other ideological beliefs. Our system of government has long eschewed this type of state interference. Rather, despite the difficulties that are always associated with gathering evidence in closed societies, the state is held to the burden of proving that individuals have engaged in conduct that is criminal because it is associated with actual harm. The State of Utah has criminal laws punishing incest, rape, unlawful sexual conduct with a minor, and domestic and child abuse. Any restrictions these laws place on the practice of religious polygamy are almost certainly justified. However, the broad criminalization of the religious practice itself as a means of attacking other criminal behavior is not. Cf. *Church of Lukumi Babalu Aye, Inc. v. City of Hialeah*, 508 U.S. 520, 538 (1993) ("The legitimate governmental interests in protecting the public health and preventing cruelty to animals could be addressed by restrictions stopping far

---

[1] The court in *Green* noted that the defendant had been convicted of criminal nonsupport and rape of a child in addition to bigamy. 2004 UT 76, ¶ 40 n.14. Similarly here, Holm has been convicted of unlawful sexual conduct with a sixteen- or seventeen-year-old in addition to bigamy. The polygamist defendant in Kingston was not charged with bigamy but was convicted of incest and unlawful sexual conduct with a sixteen- or seventeen-year-old. 2002 UT App 103, ¶ 1. It appears from these three cases that the State may be using its ability to prosecute offenders under section 76-7-101 as a means of imposing additional punishment for an already-charged offense rather than as a proxy prosecution for conduct that is otherwise unchargeable. To the extent this is true, such prosecutions may well raise double jeopardy concerns. See *Illinois v. Vitale*, 447 U.S. 410, 415 (1980) (recognizing that the Double Jeopardy Clause "protects against multiple punishments for the same offense" (internal quotation marks omitted)).

[2] The recently enacted child bigamy statute, Utah Code Ann. § 76-7-101.5 (2003), limits its criminalization to the conduct of those married individuals who purport to marry or cohabit with persons other than their legal spouse who are under the age of eighteen. As the child bigamy statute was not enacted until after Holm's prosecution, Holm was not charged with child bigamy. I express no opinion on the constitutionality of a conviction under that statute.

short of a flat prohibition of all Santeria sacrificial practice.").

Although the argument has not been raised, I note that for similar reasons I could not uphold Holm's bigamy conviction on the basis that the religiously motivated conduct at issue is inherently harmful to children who grow up in polygamous homes, and are thereby exposed to the "culture" of polygamy.[1] Our previous rulings and legislative policy support this conclusion. For example, this court has previously held that those engaged in the practice of polygamy are not automatically disqualified from petitioning for adoption of a child. *In re Adoption of W.A.T.*, 808 P.2d 1083, 1085 (Utah 1991) (plurality) ("The fact that our constitution requires the state to prohibit polygamy does not necessarily mean that the state must deny any or all civil rights and privileges to polygamists."). Rather, a trial court must hold an evidentiary hearing to consider on a case-by-case basis whether the best interests of the child would be promoted by an adoption by the prospective parents. Id. at 1086.

We have also held that a parent's custody petition could not be denied solely because she practiced polygamy. *Sanderson v. Tryon*, 739 P.2d 623, 626 (Utah 1987). Our holding in *Sanderson* was based on our recognition that the legislature's policy regarding child custody and parental rights termination issues has shifted in the past half-century, and now requires that courts focus on the "best interests of the child" rather than passing judgment on the morality of its parents. Id. at 627 (recognizing that the 1955 plurality opinion of this court in *In re Black*, 283 P.2d 887, upholding a ruling terminating the parental rights of polygamist parents, was no longer good law in light of the legislature's deletion in 1965 of moral references from the termination of parental rights statute, Utah Code Ann.

§ 78-3a-48 (1986) (current version at Utah Code Ann. § 78-3a-407 (Supp. 2005))). Given these developments, and the existence of legal mechanisms for protecting the interests of abused or neglected children apart from criminally prosecuting their parents for bigamy, I do not believe the criminalization of religiously motivated polygamous conduct is necessary to further these interests.

Thus, neither the State nor this court's prior decision in *Green* has identified an important state interest served by the criminal bigamy law that requires its application to those who enter religious unions with no claim of state legitimacy. I would therefore reverse Holm's bigamy conviction on the ground that it violates his religious freedom as guaranteed by the Utah Constitution.

III. Fourteenth Amendment Due Process Claim
Because I conclude that Holm's bigamy conviction violates the Utah Constitution's religious freedom guarantees, my dissenting vote is not based on the majority's analysis of Holm's federal constitutional claims. I do, however, wish to register my disagreement with the majority's treatment of Holm's claim that his conviction violates his Fourteenth Amendment right under the Due Process Clause to individual liberty, as recognized by the United States Supreme Court in *Lawrence v. Texas*, 539 U.S. 558 (2003). As the majority acknowledges, the Court in *Lawrence* stated the principle that "absent injury to a person or abuse of an institution the law protects," adults are free to choose the nature of their relationships "in the confines of their homes and their own private lives." Id. at 567. The majority concludes that the private consensual behavior of two individuals who did not claim legal recognition of their relationship somehow constitutes an abuse of the institution of marriage, thus rendering *Lawrence* inapplicable. On that basis,[2]

---

[1] See also *Down & Maldonado, Jr., supra* n.20, at 607 (asserting that "there are no reliable, reported data suggesting that children of polygamous families are uniquely and significantly disadvantaged from an economic or emotional standpoint").

[2] The majority could have limited its rejection of Holm's liberty claim to the fact that Holm's behavior involved a minor. That fact alone, in my view, justifies the conclusion that Holm's bigamy conviction does not violate his right to individual liberty under the Due Process Clause of the Fourteenth Amendment to the United States Constitution.

the majority summarily rejects Holm's due process claim as beyond the scope of Lawrence's holding. *Supra* ¶ 56. I disagree with this analysis.

As I have discussed extensively above, I do not believe that the conduct at issue threatens the institution of marriage, and I therefore cannot agree that it constitutes an "abuse" of that institution. The majority fails to offer a persuasive justification for its view to the contrary. It asserts that "the behavior at issue in this case" implicates "the state's ability to regulate marital relationships." *Supra* ¶ 57. According to the majority, this regulation includes the state's ability to impose a legal marriage on an individual against his or her will in order to enforce spousal support obligations or prevent welfare abuse. In regard to spousal support, I am unpersuaded that the potential interests of consenting adults who voluntarily enter legally unrecognized relationships despite the financial risks they might face in the future justify the imposition of criminal penalties on the parties to those relationships. Under the majority's rationale, the state would be justified in imposing criminal penalties on unmarried persons who enter same-sex relationships simply because the state, under the applicable constitutional and statutory provisions, is unable to hold them legally married. In regard to welfare abuse, I find it difficult to understand how those in polygamous relationships that are ineligible to receive legal sanction are committing welfare abuse when they seek benefits available to unmarried persons.

The majority also offers the view that "[t]he state must be able to … further the proliferation of social unions our society deems beneficial while discouraging those deemed harmful." *Supra* ¶ 61. The Supreme Court in *Lawrence*, however, rejected the very notion that a state can criminalize behavior merely because the majority of its citizens prefers a different form of personal relationship. Striking down Texas's criminal sodomy statute as unconstitutional, the Court in *Lawrence* recognized that the Fourteenth Amendment's individual liberty guarantee "gives substantial protection to adult persons in deciding how to conduct their private lives in matters pertaining to sex." 539 U.S. at 572. As described in *Lawrence*, this protection encompasses not merely the consensual act of sex itself but the "autonomy of the person" in making choices "relating to … family relationships." Id. at 574. The sodomy statute was thus held unconstitutional because it sought "to control a personal relationship that, whether or not entitled to formal recognition in the law, is within the liberty of persons to choose without being punished as criminals." Id. At 567.

I agree with the majority that marriage, when understood as a legal union, qualifies as "an institution the law protects." See id. at 568. However, the Court's statement in *Lawrence* that a state may interfere when such an institution is "abuse[d]," id., together with its holding that the sodomy statute was unconstitutional, leads me to infer that, in the Court's view, sexual acts between consenting adults and the private personal relationships within which these acts occur, do not "abuse" the institution of marriage simply because they take place outside its confines. See id. at 585 (O'Connor, J., concurring in the judgment) (indicating that Texas's criminal sodomy law did not implicate the state's interest in "preserving the traditional institution of marriage" but expressed "mere moral disapproval of an excluded group"). In the wake of *Lawrence*, the Virginia Supreme Court has come to the same conclusion, striking down its state law criminalizing fornication. *Martin v. Ziherl*, 607 S.E.2d 367, 371 (Va. 2005). In my opinion, these holdings correctly recognize that individuals in today's society may make varied choices regarding the organization of their family and personal relationships without fearing criminal punishment.

The majority does not adequately explain how the institution of marriage is abused or state support for monogamy threatened simply by an individual's choice to participate in a religious ritual with more than one person outside the confines of legal marriage. Rather than offering such an explanation, the majority merely proclaims that "the public nature of polygamists' attempts to extra-legally redefine the acceptable parameters of a fundamental social institution like marriage is plain." *Supra* ¶ 63. It is far from plain to me.

I am concerned that the majority's reasoning may give the impression that the state is free to criminalize any and all forms of personal relationships that occur outside the legal union of marriage. While under *Lawrence* laws criminalizing isolated acts of sodomy are void, the majority seems to suggest that the relationships within which these acts occur may still receive criminal sanction. Following such logic, non-marital cohabitation might also be considered to fall outside the scope of federal constitutional protection. Indeed, the act of living alone and unmarried could as easily be viewed as threatening social norms.

In my view, any such conclusions are foreclosed under *Lawrence*. Essentially, the Court's decision in *Lawrence* simply reformulates the longstanding principle that, in order to "secure individual liberty, ... certain kinds of highly personal relationships" must be given "a substantial measure of sanctuary from unjustified interference by the State." *Roberts v. U.S. Jaycees*, 468 U.S. 609, 618 (1984); see also Laurence H. Tribe, "*Lawrence v. Texas*: The 'Fundamental Right' That Dare Not Speak Its Name," 117 *Harv. L. Rev.* 1893, 1922 (2004) ("[T]he claim Lawrence accepted ... is that intimate relations may not be micromanaged or overtaken by the state."). Whether referred to as a right of "intimate" or "intrinsic" association, as in *Roberts*, 468 U.S. at 618, a right to "privacy," as in *Griswold v. Connecticut*, 381 U.S. 479, 485 (1965), and *Eisenstadt v. Baird*, 405 U.S. 438, 453 (1972), a right to make "choices concerning family living arrangements," as in *Moore v. City of East Cleveland*, 431 U.S. 494, 499 (1977) (plurality), or a right to choose the nature of one's personal relationships, as in *Lawrence*, 539 U.S. at 574, this individual liberty guarantee essentially draws a line around an individual's home and family and prevents governmental interference with what happens inside, as long as it does not involve injury or coercion or some other form of harm to individuals or to society.[1] As the Court in *Lawrence* recognized:

> [F]or centuries there have been powerful voices to condemn [certain private] conduct as immoral. The condemnation has been shaped by religious beliefs, conceptions of right and acceptable behavior, and respect for the traditional family. For many persons these are not trivial concerns but profound and deep convictions accepted as ethical and moral principles to which they aspire and which thus determine the course of their lives. These considerations do not answer the question before us, however. The issue is whether the majority may use the power of the State to enforce these views on the whole society through operation of the criminal law.

Id. at 571. The Court determined that when "adults ... with full and mutual consent from each other" enter into particular personal relationships with no threat of injury or coercion, a state may not criminalize the relationships themselves or the consensual intimate conduct that occurs within them. Id. at 578.

In conclusion, I agree with the majority that because Holm's conduct in this case involved a minor, he is unable to prevail on his individual liberty claim under the Due Process Clause. However, I disagree with the majority's implication that the same result would apply where an individual enters a private relationship with another adult.

---

[1] The majority treats Holm's freedom of intrinsic association claim as, in a sense, distinct from his individual liberty claim under Lawrence, while at the same time denying the association claim on the basis that no individual liberty interest had been established. Supra ¶ 72. In so doing, the majority fails to reconcile its conclusion that private relationships somehow threaten the institution of marriage, and therefore fall outside the scope of any due process protection, with the Court's recognition in Roberts that, to the contrary, private relationships can be protected. *Roberts*, 468 U.S. at 618.

UNIT II: E. Applications

Conclusion

The majority's analysis of Holm's challenges to his bigamy conviction under Utah Code section 76-7-101 relies to a large extent on its failure to distinguish between an individual's false claim to have entered the legal status of marriage and an individual's private, religiously motivated choice to enter a relationship with another person. Because I disagree with this premise, I am unpersuaded that the conclusions flowing from the majority's understanding are correct. In my view, Holm was not properly subject to prosecution under the "purports to marry" prong of section 76-7-101 because he never claimed to have entered a legally valid marriage. Moreover, I would hold Holm's conviction under the "cohabits" prong of section 76-7-101 invalid under the religious freedom provisions of the Utah Constitution. In addition, I believe the majority has erred in suggesting that the Supreme Court's decision in *Lawrence v. Texas*, 539 U.S. 558 (2003), does not recognize private relationships between consenting adults as entitled to protection under the Fourteenth Amendment's Due Process Clause. I therefore dissent from the majority's conclusion upholding Holm's bigamy conviction. I join the majority in upholding Holm's conviction for unlawful sexual conduct with a minor under section 76-5-401.2.

DISCUSSION QUESTIONS

1. Explain and evaluate the court's rejection of Holm's claim that his bigamy conviction violates his constitutional guarantee of free exercise of religion.

2. Review *Lawrence v. Texas* (reading 54), wherein the Supreme Court struck down the Texas statute outlawing homosexual sodomy. Present Holm's argument that the "liberty interest" outlined in that case ought to have applied in his. Present and evaluate the court's rejection of Holm's claim.

3. The court claims that "[o]ur state's commitment to monogamous unions is a recognition that decisions made by individuals as to how to structure even the most personal of relationships are capable of dramatically affecting public life." In what ways does the court suggest that monogamous unions affect public life? In what ways does the court suggest that polygamous unions affect public life?

4. How does the court support its assertion that it has a "substantial interest in prohibiting unlicensed marriages when there is an existing marriage"? How does the court determine whether a marriage exists? Do you agree with these criteria? Why or why not?

61

SEX, FREEDOM, AND MARRIAGE

Cheshire Calhoun, "Who's Afraid of Polygamous Marriage? Lessons for Same-Sex Marriage Advocacy from the History of Polygamy" (2005)

Cheshire Calhoun is professor in the School of Historical, Philosophical, and Religious Studies at Arizona State University. Her research interests include normative ethics and lesbian and gay studies. In this article she considers important parallels between historical debates regarding polygamous marriage and current debates surrounding the issue of same-sex marriage.

SOURCE

Calhoun, Cheshire. "Who's Afraid of Polygamous Marriage? Lessons for Same-Sex Marriage Advocacy from the History of Polygamy." *The San Diego Law Review*, Volume 42, Issue 3, August 2005, pp. 1023–42. Copyright © 2005 *San Diego Law Review*. Reprinted with the permission of the *San Diego Law Review*.

I. Introduction

In United States history, there have been four important bars to civil marriage. First, during the period of U.S. slavery, marriages between slaves, though informally celebrated, were not legally recognized.[1] The bar to civil marriage between slaves was part of slaves'[2] general legal incapacity to enter into contracts, and was not an expression of social disapproval of slave marriages. Indeed, slaveholders sometimes promoted informal marriage unions between slaves.[3] The three other marriage bars, however, specifically targeted relationships that were the subjects of intense social disapproval and were treated by lawmakers as dangerous to societal order.

Bars to marriage across racial lines—particularly between whites and blacks, but in the West, also between whites and Asians or Native Americans—were first erected in the eighteenth century and proliferated after abolition.[4] Forty-one states barred interracial marriages at some point in their history.[5]

---

[1] Nancy F. Cott, "Giving Character to Our Whole Civil Polity: Marriage and the Public Order in the Late Nineteenth Century," in Linda K. Kerber et al. (eds.), *U.S. History as Women's History: New Feminist Essays* [(Chapel Hill: University of North Carolina Press, 1995)], p. 111.

[2] Nancy F. Cott, *Public Vows: A History of Marriage and the Nation* [(Cambridge, MA: Harvard University Press, 2000)], p. 35.

[3] Cott, "Giving Character," pp. 107, 111.

[4] Cott, *Public Vows*, 99; "Giving Character," pp. 118–19.

[5] Cott, "Giving Character," p. 118.

These antimiscegenation laws were finally invalidated in 1967 in the Supreme Court case of *Loving v. Virginia*.[1]

Bars to polygamous marriages were targeted at the Mormon practice of plural marriage in the Utah territory, and were first erected under the Morrill Act of 1862 that made bigamy a federal offense.[2]

Shortly thereafter, the federal government further penalized polygamists by making cohabitation an offense, by taking away Utah women's right to vote, by making the affirmation that one is not a polygamist a condition of voter registration for men, by denying polygamists the right to serve in public office or on juries, by requiring women in polygamous marriages to testify against their husbands in court, and ultimately by seizing the assets of the Mormon church.[3] In addition, in the nineteenth century, every state made bigamy a crime.[4] The constitutionality of this marriage bar was challenged on First Amendment freedom of religion grounds in 1878, in *Reynolds v. United States*.[5] In said case, the Supreme Court upheld the bar on polygamy,[6] and that ruling still stands today.

Legal bars to same-sex marriage are of substantially more recent vintage, having largely arisen within the last decade. Bars to same-sex marriage began to proliferate at both the state and federal level only after same-sex couples began suing in court for the right to marry under marriage laws that did not specify the gender of the spouses.[7] As of November 2004, thirty-eight states explicitly defined marriage as between one man and one woman, and seventeen had incorporated those definitions into their constitutions.[8] The 1996 Defense of Marriage Act defined marriage for federal purposes as between one man and one woman.[9] It also qualified the Full Faith and Credit Clause, relieving states of the requirement to recognize marriages legally performed in another state.[10] More recently, some have advocated a Federal Marriage Amendment that would make the monogamous heterosexual nature of marriage a matter of constitutional definition.[11]

What the law recognizes as civil marriage has not, however, been determinative of how citizens understand the social institution of marriage. Slaves did marry without legal sanction.[12] Nineteenth-century members of the Latter-Day Saints (LDS) protested the federal regulation of polygamy by continuing to practice plural marriage, either openly or underground;[13] and today members of some fundamentalist offshoots of Mormonism practice polygamy in the absence of state recognition of their marriages.[14] Antimiscegenation laws did not prevent interracial couples from constructing lives together, nor do same-sex marriage bars prevent gays and lesbians from publicly celebrating their unions, or religious communities from recognizing them.

---

[1] *Loving v. Virginia*, 388 U.S. 2 (1967).

[2] Cott, *Public Vows*, p. 112.

[3] Cott, "Giving Character," pp. 118–19; Nancy Rosenblum, "Democratic Sex: *Reynolds v. U.S.*, Sexual Relations, and Community," in David M. Estlund and Martha C. Nussbaum (eds.), *Sex, Preference, and Family: Essays on Law and Nature* ([New York: Oxford University Press,] 1997), pp. 76–77.

[4] Cott, *Public Vows*, p. 112.

[5] *Reynolds v. United States*, 98 U.S. 145, 166 (1878).

[6] Ibid., pp. 166, 168.

[7] See, e.g., David Orgon Coolidge, "The Question of Marriage," in Christopher Wolfe (ed.), *Homosexuality and American Public Life* ([Dallas: Spence Publishing Company,] 1999), pp. 200, 204–08.

[8] National Gay and Lesbian Task Force Marriage Map, http://www.thetaskforce.org/community/marriagecenter. cfmn (last visited Aug. 1, 2005).

[9] Defense of Marriage Act, H.R. 3396, 104th Cong. § 3 (1996).

[10] Ibid., p. 2.

[11] The nineteenth-century antipolygamy campaign also produced (unsuccessful) demands for a constitutional amendment that would settle, with finality, the nation's commitment to heterosexual monogamy as its sole marriage form.

[12] Cott, *Public Vows*, pp. 34–35.

[13] Jessie L. Embry, *Mormon Polygamous Families: Life in the Principle*, 17–27 ([Salt Lake City: George Kofford Books, Ltd.,] 1987); Irwin Altman & Joseph Ginat, *Polygamous Families in Contemporary Society* 43–44 ([New York: Cambridge University Press,]1996).

[14] See generally Altman & Ginat, *Polygamous Families*, p. 18.

The central issue raised by marriage bars is thus not whether the state should permit nonmonogamous and nonheterosexual marriages, but whether the state should support nonmonogamous and nonheterosexual marriages by assigning them the legal status of civil marriage.[1] With the legal status of civil marriage come immigration rights, the right not to testify against one's spouse, social security survivor's benefits, inheritance without a will, and the right to give proxy consent. With the status of civil marriage also comes coverage under divorce laws and thus legal determination of property distribution, alimony payment, and child custody and support. Informally, having the status of civil marriage can also mean access to such benefits as a partner's health insurance plan, reduced membership fees for the spouse, and access to family rates.

Given that neither the polygamous marriages of some citizens nor the same-sex marriages of others are currently recognized by the state, one might have expected that advocates of same-sex marriage rights would make common cause with advocates of polygamous marriage rights. That has not been the case. With few exceptions, advocates of same-sex marriage have exercised a vigorous silence about the other marriage bar currently in effect, namely the bar to polygamy.[2] There are two main reasons for that silence. Opponents of same-sex marriage often invoke polygamy in order to make reductio arguments against expanding the definition of marriage to include same-sex couples: If the definition of marriage is treated as something that is not fixed, then what, they ask, is to prevent the definition of marriage from being expanded to include not only same-sex marriages, but also polygamous marriages (and incestuous marriages and marriages with animals, etc.)? In this way, social hostility to polygamy is invoked as a reason not to permit same-sex marriage. Thus, advocates of same-sex marriage have found it strategically unwise to press an analogy between the bars to same-sex and polygamous marriage.

The political expediency of not associating same-sex marriage with polygamous marriage explains the silence of those at the front of the political fray. It does not fully explain why academic philosophers and legal theorists have maintained a similar silence about the "other" marriage bar. The principle reason appears to be a conviction that same-sex marriages and polygamous marriages are substantially disanalogous. While same-sex marriages challenge the traditional gender structure of marriage, polygamy is more likely to exaggerate the gender hierarchy within marriage and is thus incompatible with a liberal democracy that values women's equality. Same-sex marriage advocates thus routinely dismiss the issue of polygamous marriage as irrelevant to the question of whether the bar to same-sex marriage should be lifted. In particular, they insist that polygamous marriages are sufficiently socially dangerous that extending marriage rights to same-sex couples will not put us on a slippery slope toward recognizing polygamous marriages.[3]

Despite all this, the refusal to regard the marriage bar to polygamy as a significant political issue bears closer scrutiny. In what follows, this article will be arguing that more careful attention to the historical practice of polygamy strengthens the case for same-sex marriage; and attention to the similarities between the social issues at stake in the antipolygamy campaign and the same-sex marriage campaign can productively complicate our sense of what the fundamental issues are in the same-sex marriage debate. Finally, this article will suggest that it is not

---

[1] This requires some qualification. Because cohabitation was made an offense—sometimes a felony offense, as in the 1935 Utah law—polygamy ended up not only being not supported in the law but coercively prohibited. Altman & Ginat, *Polygamous Families*, p. 46.

[2] But see Gordon Albert Babst, *Liberal Constitutionalism, Marriage, and Sexual Orientation: A Contemporary Case for Dis-Establishment* ([New York: P. Lang,] 2002), pp. 87–89 (arguing that there is a critical legal analogy between the bars to same-sex, interracial, and polygamous marriage insofar as legal reasoning in all three cases appeals to alleged Christian values and views of divine purpose).

[3] See William N. Eskridge, Jr., *The Case for Same-Sex Marriage: From Sexual Liberty to Civilized Commitment* ([New York: The Free Press,] 1996), 148–49.

altogether clear that legal recognition of polygamous marriage is incompatible with a liberal, democratic, and egalitarian society. The proper response to same-sex marriage opponents' reductio argument may instead be, "And indeed, why not also polygamy?"[1]

II. Countering Appeals to a Marriage Tradition

So let us turn first to the ways that more explicit attention to polygamy might help to build a stronger case for same-sex marriage. The same-sex marriage debate is a debate between expansionists, who argue that the traditional conception of marriage enshrined in law should be expanded to include same-sex couples, and traditionalists, who insist on the value of preserving the traditional conception of marriage as between one man and one woman. Traditionalists argue that citizens will find laws and public policies reasonable only if they are consistent with citizens' core values.[2] It is thus always relevant for the law to take into account "our" particular moral traditions and to be extremely cautious of legal innovations that might undermine core social values. In assessing the desirability of extending civil marriage to same-sex couples, traditionalists point out that it is particularly important to bear in mind the two thousand-year-old tradition of understanding marriage as the union of one man and one woman, a tradition that includes Judeo-Christian, Western European, and American cultural histories.[3] Given the extraordinary importance attached to heterosexual marriage and the absence of any comparable tradition of recognizing same-sex unions, traditionalists conclude that the state ought not expand the current legal definition of marriage.

One way of challenging the traditionalist's argument is to challenge the propriety of premising our laws on the majority's moral or religious values, no matter how longstanding, given the fact that ours is a liberal democracy designed to protect individuals' liberty to pursue a plurality of ways of life. Another way of challenging the traditionalists' argument is to challenge the truth of their claims about the Judeo-Christian marriage tradition. In this vein, one option is to observe that there has been at least a minor thread within the Judeo-Christian tradition of acknowledging same-sex unions. John Boswell's rediscovery of the union ceremonies for monks performed by the Roman Catholic Church in the Middle Ages is by now well known.[4] In the 1800s, so-called Boston marriages between two women emerged as a recognized cultural phenomenon in the U.S. which was not, at the time, regarded as incompatible with a Judeo-Christian tradition.[5] Finally, at present, a variety of religious denominations, including Unitarians, the United Church of Christ, Reform Judaism, the Society of Friends, and Episcopalians recognize same-sex unions.[6]

These facts, however, are unlikely to move traditionalists given that most of the evidence is from very recent developments within Christian and Jewish communities; and those religious communities are doing exactly what traditionalists object to the law doing—adopting policies that fly in the face of a millennia-old tradition of heterosexual monogamous marriage.[7]

A more powerful challenge might be framed by inviting traditionalists to consider whether the Judeo-Christian tradition will support both of the marriage bars they wish to sustain: the bar to same-sex marriage and the bar to polygamy. If it will not, then the Judeo-Christian "tradition" may be a dangerous tool for same-sex marriage opponents to invoke.

---

[1] See n. [2, p. 709].

[2] Carlos A. Ball, *The Morality of Gay Rights: An Exploration in Political Philosophy* ([New York: Taylor and Francis,] 2003), pp. 139–45.

[3] John Witte, Jr., "The Tradition of Traditional Marriage," in Lynn D. Wardle et al. (eds.), *Marriage and Same-Sex Unions: A Debate* (2003), pp. 47–49.

[4] John Boswell, *Same-Sex Unions in Premodern Europe* ([New York: Knopf Doubleday,] 1994), pp. 218–21.

[5] Lillian Faderman, *Surpassing The Love of Men: Romantic Friendship and Love Between Women from the Renaissance to the Present* ([New York, Morrow,] 1981), pp. 16, 190, 208–13.

[6] Babst, *Liberal Constitutionalism*, p. 83 n.14.

[7] See Witte, "The Tradition of Traditional Marriage."

Polygamy has, in fact, a lengthy history within the Judeo-Christian tradition—beginning with the polygamous marriages of the Old Testament patriarchs.[1] Nowhere in either the Hebrew Bible or the New Testament is polygamy forbidden.[2] Indeed, some European Jews practiced polygamy until the eleventh century; and even then the ban on polygamy was adopted only to avoid Christian persecution in France and Germany. Martin Luther, while not endorsing polygamy as an ideal or pervasive practice, nevertheless observed that polygamy does not contradict the Scripture and so cannot be prohibited by Christianity.[3] And within Catholicism, the question of whether polygamy was acceptable in exceptional circumstances was not finally settled until the Council of Trent in 1563.[4]

Polygamy has had an especially significant place in U.S. social life after Joseph Smith's 1843 revelation that members of the Church of Jesus Christ of Latter-day Saints (the LDS church) should begin practicing what they called "plural marriages" patterned on Old Testament patriarchal polygamy. The LDS church was an enormously powerful religious community in the nineteenth century. Occupying the Utah territory, the Church planned to expand into a territory that included parts of California, Oregon, Arizona, New Mexico, Colorado, Wyoming, and all of Nevada and Utah.[5] The Church set up its own legal system, including legally recognizing plural marriages and granting divorces and property settlements.[6] The political and economic power of the Mormon Church made credible its aim to break away from the United States and motivated a series of federal acts designed to rein in the Utah territory, including the disenfranchisement of polygamists and seizure of the Church's finances.[7] Under this federal pressure, the LDS church formally repudiated plural marriage in 1890, but fundamentalist offshoots continue to practice plural marriage today.[8] One study estimates membership at twenty to fifty thousand.[9]

In short, polygamous marriage cannot be dismissed as a negligible blip in an otherwise consistent tradition of heterosexual monogamous marriage. On the contrary, polygamy is very much part of a millennia-long pluralist Judeo-Christian tradition of marriage.[10] Traditionalists thus enter quite perilous territory when they invoke the Judeo-Christian tradition as a reason for rejecting same-sex civil marriage. The same tradition that traditionalists believe justifies limiting civil marriage to heterosexual rela-

---

[1] Altman & Ginat, *Polygamous Families*, pp. 41–42; Philip L. Kilbride, *Plural Marriage for Our Times: A Reinvented Option?* [(Westport, CT: Bergin and Garvey, 1994)], pp. 59–66.

[2] Embry, *Mormon Polygamous Families*, pp. 4–5. But note 1 Timothy 3:2, 12, where "overseers" and "deacons" in the church are to be "husband of but one wife" (personal correspondence, Steve Palmquist).

[3] "I confess, indeed, I cannot forbid anyone who wishes to marry several wives, nor is that against Holy Scripture; however, I do not want that custom introduced among Christians among whom it is proper to pass up even things that are permissible, to avoid scandal and to live respectably, which Paul everywhere enjoins." Kilbride, *Plural Marriage for Our Times*, p. 63 (quoting Luther's correspondence).

[4] Ibid., p. 64.

[5] Rosenblum, "Democratic Sex," pp. 72–73.

[6] Brigham Young issued 1,645 divorces during his presidency of the Church. Joan Smyth Iversen, *The Antipolygamy Controversy in U.S. Women's Movements, 1880–1925: A Debate on the American Home* ([New York: Garland,] 1997), p. 59.

[7] President Hayes observed that "[l]aws must be enacted which will take from the Mormon Church its temporal power. Mormonism as a sectarian idea is nothing, but as a system of government it is our duty to deal with it as an enemy of our institutions and its supporters and leaders as criminals." Rosenblum, "Democratic Sex," p. 75 (quoting Hayes).

[8] See Altman & Ginat, *Polygamous Families*, p. 18. Two prominent religious communities that accept the principle of "plural marriage" are located in Hildale, Utah, and Colorado City, Arizona (pp. 50–51).

[9] Ibid., p. 2.

[10] It is important to bear in mind that our U.S. tradition occurs within a multination state whose traditions include those of Indian nations for whom monogamy was not always the defining form of marriage and which sometimes recognized unions between same-sexed persons. See Eskridge, *The Case for Same-Sex Marriage*, pp. 27–30; Cott, *Public Vows*, p. 25.

tionships, would also justify extending civil marriage to polygamous relationships. Such an implication is likely to seriously undermine the appeal, for traditionalists, of using tradition as a guide to marriage policy. Moreover, given how pervasive appeals to tradition are in the same-sex marriage debate, marriage rights advocates stand to gain quite a lot by reminding those who would appeal to tradition that it does not support state and federal definitions of marriage as not only heterosexual, but between one man and one woman.

III. Fundamental Questions about the State Form of Marriage

More importantly, attending to the details of the nineteenth-century polygamy debate throws into relief the larger issues—both social and legal—that are at stake when marriage bars are erected and subsequently challenged. Neither the polygamy debates of the nineteenth century nor the same-sex marriage debates of today were just about a minority sexual practice. They were also debates about how to respond to the failure of heterosexual monogamous marriage to deliver the social benefits that warrant the state's legally recognizing these marriages in the first place. Should heterosexual monogamy as a marital form be protected? Or should alternative marital forms be granted social and legal standing? Both plural marriage advocates and same-sex marriage advocates argued that state support should instead be given to a different definition of marriage—polygamous or gender-neutral.

Rising divorce rates in both the late nineteenth and late twentieth centuries[1] called into question the cultural ideal of a marriage as what Karen Struening has called a "multipurpose association."[2] Marriages are supposed to satisfy a plurality of individuals' needs, including needs for sexual and emotional intimacy, reproduction, childrearing, and the care of adults' material needs. The expectation that marriages will meet individuals' sexual and emotional needs encourages individuals to dissolve their marriages when those needs are not met, and to search for new partners[3]—hence liberalization of divorce law and a rise in the divorce rate in both periods. The failure of many marriages to endure, however, is at odds with the expectation that marriages will provide stable contexts for the rearing of children and the economic support of adults—expectations that require long-term commitment to staying in the marriage.

In the nineteenth century, the polygamy debates centered on the question of what the best social response should be to the failure of conventional marriage to serve as a "multipurpose association." Moral reform movements assumed that the problem had more to do with the individuals within marriages than with the form of marriage itself.[4] Moral reformers thus argued that conventional marriage should remain the normative form of marriage but be shored up with social reform and legal regulation. They focused energy on curbing male lust, eliminating prostitution, and reducing the number of unwed mothers. Controlling the rate of divorce was also linked in the public's imagination to controlling the Mormon practice of polygamy, because relatively liberal divorce laws were condemned for permitting "serial polygamy" under conventional marriage.[5] Many called for legal steps to be taken to check both serial polygamy and Mormon plural marriage.[6] As a result, the demand for federal control of Mormon polygamy was conjoined to a request for a federal marriage law that would control the rate of divorce within monogamous marriage.[7]

---

[1] Iversen, *The Antipolygamy Controversy*, pp. 106–07; Cott, *Public Vows*, pp. 105–07, 203.

[2] Karen Struening, *New Family Values: Liberty, Equality, Diversity* ([Lanham, MD: Rowman and Littlefield,] 2002), p. 85.

[3] Ibid.

[4] Julie Dunfey, "Living the Principle of Plural Marriage: Mormon Women, Utopia, and Female Sexuality in the Nineteenth Century," *Feminist Studies* 10 (1984): 523, 527.

[5] Rosenblum, "Democratic Sex," p. 75. According to Joan Iversen, social critics charged divorce rates in New England with creating "polygamy in New England." Iversen, *The Antipolygamy Controversy*, p. 106.

[6] Iversen, *The Antipolygamy Controversy*, p. 107.

[7] Ibid., pp. 106–07, 219–20.

On the other side, polygamy advocates argued that an alternative marital form was more likely to meet with success. Mormon women, for example, argued that plural marriage promised to solve the social problems created by the failure of monogamous companionate marriage to supply both adequate sexual satisfaction for men and a stable reproductive environment for women and children.[1] Sharing their monogamous sisters' assumption that a large part of the problem was due to men's higher sex drive, Mormon women argued that if only men were allowed to have plural wives, they would not be motivated to use prostitutes (or presumably, to divorce), and thus fewer women would be degraded by work as prostitutes and fewer would suffer the hardships of bearing children out of wedlock or of being left without adequate economic support.[2] Moreover, given the scarcity of "worthy men" and the surfeit of "pure women," plural marriage would guarantee that no woman who wished to be married would have to marry beneath herself.[3]

Twentieth-century debates over same-sex marriage have been very much about the same question of what to do about conventional marriage's failure to serve all its intended purposes. Opponents of same-sex marriage see same-sex marriage as the last straw in a larger social process of decaying social commitment to committed, long-term, sexually faithful, monogamous relationships and as the culmination of a social shift toward basing relationships purely on self-indulgent personal preferences. The social consequence of this collapse of conventional marriage is a more than fifty percent divorce rate,[4] a reduction in the percentage of adults who

are married,[5] the escalation of female-headed households, and the growing number of children born to never-married women.[6] These trends are also blamed for putting pressure on the welfare system and producing a generation of children who have failed to internalize values of loyalty, commitment, and self-restraint.[7] Legal recognition of same-sex marriage, on this view, is objectionable not so much because it is same-sex, but because same-sex marriage symbolizes a kind of last straw in the social assault on the traditional conception of marriage.

Thus, in the twenty-first-century marriage debate, as in the nineteenth-century marriage debate, one side argues that conventional marriage should remain the normative form of marriage but be shored up with social and legal reforms. Proposed reforms today include conducting abstinence education in schools, reducing payments to unwed welfare mothers, reintroducing fault-based divorce, and improving tax breaks for married couples. Protecting the social status of marriage as a unique and sacred institution by withholding legal recognition of same-sex marriage becomes part of this "shoring up" strategy.

The other side argues that alternative marital and family forms are more likely to meet with success—especially if they do not burden a single relationship with meeting the full range of individuals' sexual, emotional, reproductive, childrearing, and material needs. For example, the growing practice of parenting outside of a marriage—whether as a result of divorce or of not marrying in the first place—detaches reproductive and childrearing relationships from sex and romantic love. The caretaking networks that emerged in response to the AIDS epidemic similarly detached adult caretaking relationships from those that satisfy sexual and romantic needs. Advocacy of same-sex marriage becomes part of this splitting off of the romantic and sexual

---

[1] For example, the Utah women's journal, *The Women's Exponent*, "cited stories of infanticide, alcoholic and abusive husbands, desertion, divorce, and prostitution as evidence of the corruption of the larger society." Dunfey, "Living the Principle of Plural Marriage," pp. 527–28; see also Iversen, *The Antipolygamy Controversy*, p. 63.

[2] Dunfey, "Living the Principle of Plural Marriage," pp. 528, 530.

[3] Ibid., pp. 523–26, 528–29.

[4] Cott, *Public Vows*, p. 203.

[5] The percentage of adults who are married dropped from 75% in the early 1970s to 56% in the late 1990s. Ibid., p. 203.

[6] Ibid., p. 204.

[7] Ibid.

from the reproductive and caretaking functions of conventional marriage. This is not to say that those joined via same-sex unions do not produce and rear children. It is to say that the advocacy of same-sex marriage rights has primarily invoked the importance of individuals being able to satisfy their romantic, companionate, and sexual needs.

In short, both the latter half of the nineteenth century and the past decade have been important moments in our collective social life for thinking about what sorts of relationships might best satisfy individuals' complex needs for emotional and sexual intimacy, procreation, childrearing, and adult care-taking—and for reflecting on the ways that the state should, and should not, be involved in protecting those relationships. Perhaps most crucially, these historical moments also presented the opportunity to take up fundamental political questions concerning marriage: Should there be a state supported form of marriage? If so, should there be more than one state supported form of marriage? Or should the state simply enforce whatever contracts into which individuals voluntarily enter?

Because civil marriage has always been an uneasy merging of a public status with a private contract, it is appropriate to ask these fundamental questions about whether and how the state should be involved in marriages.[1] Civil marriages are contracts insofar as they are entered into only by voluntary consent. Civil marriage is a public status insofar as individuals are not free to determine the terms of the marital contract—who may enter a marriage, what obligations spouses have, or the terms for dissolving a marriage. These features are all set by the state.

The contract and status aspects of civil marriage pull against each other.[2] To the extent that we think

of civil marriage as a private contract, voluntarily entered into for the purpose of satisfying some combination of the individual's particular sexual, emotional, caretaking, and reproductive needs, we are inevitably pulled toward the idea that if there is freedom of contract, then we should have the freedom to devise whatever marriage contract with whatever partner or partners we please and to determine the conditions of dissolution of the marriage.[3] This, one might think, is as things should be in a liberal society that permits citizens to pursue their own conception of the good so long as doing so does not infringe on others' rights, even if that conception is a minority or unpopular one. From the viewpoint of liberal theory, the state should remain neutral with respect to competing conceptions of what marriage is and of how individuals' needs for sex and emotional intimacy, material support in daily life, reproduction, and childrearing are to be met. The state fails to be neutral when it chooses one particular form of relationship to support. If we focus on the contractual, consent-based nature of marriage, the central question is: "What legal protections and supports, if any, should the state provide for the plurality of purposes that individuals might have for entering into marital contracts?"

On the other hand, to the extent that we think of marriage as a public status, like citizenship or eligibility for public office, we move in the direction of a less pluralistic definition of civil marriage. We think of civil marriage not as something that individuals define for themselves, but as a relationship that the state defines for all of us: civil marriage is state marriage. On this view, it is not up to individuals, with their varied preferences and values, to determine what will qualify as the state's form of marriage. Instead, the state must accept or reject the various candidates for the state's form of marriage—monogamous, polygamous, heterosexual, same-sex—according to whether those relationships are believed to contribute to the social good,

---

[1] See ibid., pp. 11 and 101–2, and Babst, *Liberal Constitutionalism*, pp. 16–21, for discussions of the contract and status features of civil marriage.

[2] Nancy [Rosenblum] pursues this tension as it manifests itself in liberal democratic thought. On the one hand, a privacy model of marriage pulls in a libertarian direction; on the other hand, the view that marriages and families are first schools of justice pulls in the direction of a more restrictive conception of marriage. Rosenblum, "Democratic Sex," pp. 80–81.

[3] See generally Will Kymlicka, "Rethinking the Family," *Philosophy and Public Affairs* 20 (1991): 77 (reviewing Susan Moller Okin, *Justice, Gender, and the Family* (1989)), for an elaboration of this contractual view.

not the individual's private good. That social good may be the cultivation in adults of key social virtues such as self-sacrifice, loyalty, and sexual self-restraint. Or it may be the training of adults and children in democratic virtues of equal respect. Or it may be the preservation of a foundational social tradition, such as the Judeo-Christian tradition of marriage. Monogamous, polygamous, heterosexual, and same-sex relationships then get evaluated and accepted or rejected as candidates for the state's form of marriage according to whether those relationships are believed to contribute to the social good. For example, Justice Waite, who rendered the Court's opinion in *Reynolds*,[1] assumed a status conception of marriage when he affirmed that "it is within the legitimate scope of the power of every civil government to determine whether polygamy or monogamy shall be the law of social life under its dominion."[2] He rejected polygamy as the law of social life on the grounds that it is more allied with despotism than democracy and thus is contrary to the social good.

Civil marriage's peculiar hybridization of private contract and public status means that social campaigns to revise the terms of civil marriage—by liberalizing divorce laws, offering an option of covenant marriage, or extending marriage rights to formerly excluded individuals—are often ambiguous between two claims. On the one hand, revisionist campaigns might be viewed as pressing the state toward a more genuinely contractual and pluralist conception of marriage. These campaigns might aim to disestablish a state form of marriage in order to afford individuals greater liberty to pursue their own conceptions of the good.[3] On the other hand, one might see revisionist campaigns as pressing the

state toward simply a different status conception of civil marriage.

What is striking about the pro-polygamy and pro-same-sex marriage campaigns is that neither campaign was committed to fully pluralizing marital and familial forms by insisting that the law be neutral with respect to competing conceptions of how people can best satisfy their needs for emotional and sexual intimacy, care-taking, reproduction, and childrearing. Instead the debate focused on which one of rivaling legal definitions of marriage—monogamy or polygamy, monogamous heterosexual or monogamous gender-neutral marriage—should define the state's marital form.

In the nineteenth century, polygamy advocates pursued the recognition of plural marriage as the state's marital form. Monogamous marriage had failed adequately to deliver the goods it purported to produce—to combine romantic love with a stable context for childrearing, to regulate male sexuality, and to provide women with adequate economic support and children with fathers. Polygamy was being offered up by the LDS church not just as their preferred marriage form given their particular religious beliefs, but as the marriage form that would best secure the social goods with which a state should concern itself. Justice Waite, in his *Reynolds* opinion, was exactly right to see that the question at issue was which form of marriage—monogamy or polygamy—was to be the state's marriage.[4]

In recent decades, same-sex marriage advocates have pursued recognition of non-gender-specific monogamy not just as their preferred marriage form but as the state's marital form. Heterosexual marriage has failed to prove that it can uniquely deliver important goods such as long-term commitment and satisfaction of individuals' needs for emotional intimacy. Unlike polygamy advocates, same-sex marriage advocates may not be able to argue that same-sex marriages are more likely to deliver the goods—with the one possible exception of gender equality within marriage—but advocates are positioned to argue that same-sex marriages would do at least as

---

[1] *Reynolds v. United States*, 98 U.S. 145, 153 (1878).

[2] Ibid., p. 166.

[3] Nancy F. Cott argues that an array of changes in marriage and divorce law as well as the nonprosecution of Mormon fundamentalist polygamy indicate the disestablishment of (a single form of) marriage. Cott, *Public Vows*, pp. 200–15.

[4] See *Reynolds v. United States*.

well as the currently flagging institution of hetero-sexual marriage. Thus, the state form of marriage should be redefined in gender-neutral terms. What is to be retained, however, is the existence of a singular definition of marriage, which, while gender-neutral, still presumes the monogamous and companionate form of conventional marriage. Thus, marriage rights advocates are often quick in the face of the challenge, "And what about polygamy?" to affirm their resistance to any more wide-ranging reform of marriage.[1] As Judith Butler notes, with some disenchantment, the same-sex marriage debate is not just a debate over whose relationship will be legitimated and supported by the state, but also over whose desire will become the state's desire.[2]

In short, despite their apparent radicalism, both the pro-polygamy and pro-same-sex marriage campaigns have been marked by an antipluralist and exclusionary conception of marriage. Neither debate seized the opportunity to question the desirability of defining a single form of state marriage. Both simply assumed that the state should support marriage and only one form of marriage. However, maintaining a single state definition of marriage is at odds with the fundamental premises of a liberal political society, with the private, contractual aspect of marriage, and with satisfying individuals' multiple relational needs. Thus, the state would do better to move toward a more pluralistic conception of personal relationships; and it might do so in one of two ways. On the one hand, we might adopt a fully contractual approach to emotional, sexual, child-rearing, and adult support relationships.[3] In that case, the state would simply enforce the terms of the contracts agreed upon by the contracting parties. On the other hand, the state might remain in the business of licensing marriages or other relational forms. But in a pluralist liberal society, one would expect that there would be a plurality of marriage

or relational options rather than a single state form of marriage. The U.S. is in fact moving in the direction of creating various packages of rights designed to protect and support a plurality of relational choices. On offer already are domestic partnerships (California, New Jersey), heterosexual civil marriage, same-sex civil unions (Vermont, Connecticut), same-sex marriage (Massachusetts), and covenant marriage (Arkansas, Arizona, Louisiana).[4] Same-sex marriage advocacy loses much of its radical (and plain old liberal) potential by refusing to take up the banner of disestablishing a single state form of marriage. Disestablishing a single state form of marriage would in turn, of course, open the doors to state recognition of polygamous marriages.

IV. Who's Afraid of Polygamous Marriage: Polygamy and Gender Equality

Up to this point in our discussion, polygamous marriage has remained safely in the past. If the state is to support the plurality of individuals' relational choices, and if one significant relational choice is of plural spouses, then the question of polygamy must be confronted.

Why not polygamy? John Stuart Mill famously asserted in *On Liberty* that polygamy was "a mere riveting of the chains of one half of the community [namely women], and an emancipation of the other from reciprocity of obligation towards them."[5] Antipolygamists of the nineteenth century likened husband and wives in a plural marriage to slave master and enslaved subject.[6] New England women's rights advocates of that century regarded

[1] See, e.g., Eskridge, *The Case for Same-Sex Marriage*, pp. 148–49.
[2] Judith Butler, "Is Kinship Always Already Heterosexual?" *Differences: A Journal of Feminist Cultural Studies* 13 (2002): 14, 22.
[3] See generally Kymlicka, "Rethinking the Family."

[4] See, e.g., 2000 Vt. Acts & Resolves H. 847, 3 (codified as amended at VT. STAT. ANN. tit. 15, 1201 (2002)), 2005 Conn. Acts 05–10 (Reg. Sess.) (effective Oct. 1, 2005).
[5] John Stuart Mill, *On Liberty*, In Marshall Cohen (ed.), *The Philosophy of John Stuart Mill: Ethical, Political and Religious* ([New York: Modern Library,] 1961[1863]), pp. 291–92.
[6] Iversen, *The Antipolygamy Controversy*, pp. 134–35; Sarah Barringer Gordon, *The Mormon Question: Polygamy and Constitutional Conflict in Nineteenth-Century America* ([Chapel Hill: University of North Carolina Press,] 2002), pp. 47–49.

polygamous marriages as no better than Turkish harems, a practice designed to serve male lust without women's willing consent.[1]

In marked contrast to this view, the feminist historians Joan Smyth Iversen and Julie Dunfey both offer persuasive evidence that nineteenth-century plural marriage was not a uniquely gender-inegalitarian form of marriage.[2] The Mormon women's rights advocates at the time argued, with good reason, that plural wives were in fact more liberated than their New England counterparts. In terms of educational and economic opportunities, civil and political rights, and autonomy within marriage, they rated quite well in comparison to New England women in monogamous marriages.[3] Each plural wife lived in her own house, functioning as the head of household and relying on her own judgment while her husband was away on Church missions or staying with other wives.[4] Married Mormon women had the right to own property and sometimes owned their homesteads.[5] Plural marriage was designed to free wives from some of the evils of male lust—protecting them against diseases that might be brought home from visits to prostitutes and freeing pregnant women from marital sexual duties.[6] Mormon wives were substantially more involved in economically contributing to their families than were their eastern counterparts, because their economic contribution was critical to both frontier society and their own support.[7] They were among the first women to vote in the United States,[8] and half the first enrollees in the University of Deseret (now the University

of Utah) were women.[9] They entered plural marriages as well-educated women raised originally with the expectation of monogamous marriage.[10] They were able to exit marriage through divorce, and seventy-three percent of divorce actions in Utah territory were by women.[11]

What these historical details remind us is that gender inequality is a contingent, not a conceptual, feature of polygamy. Whether or not polygamy is strongly connected to women's inequality depends on at least three sets of factors. First are the background social conditions that affect women's overall level of opportunity and self-determination. Do women have basic civil and political rights including freedom to travel and the right to own property? Do they have access to education? Do they have the means to be economically self-supporting? Is there readily available information about, and access to, alternative ways of life? Such background conditions affect women's level of genuine freedom of choice to enter into polygamous relationships as well as women's status within those relationships. One reason why Mormon women were able to mount a plausible defense of plural marriage—in spite of the patriarchal ideological underpinnings of plural marriage—was because their background conditions were favorable to women's autonomy.

Second, whether or not polygamy is strongly connected to women's inequality depends on the form that the social practice of polygamy takes. By whom are plural spouses selected and courted? Whose consent is presumed necessary? Who is presumed to have decision-making authority (and over what) within the marriage? How do participants understand their duties as a spouse? Is polygamy practiced only by heterosexuals and only as polygyny?[12] Or do lesbians, gay men, and bisexuals also practice

---

[1] Iversen, *The Antipolygamy Controversy*, pp. 142–44.

[2] Dunfey, "Living the Principle of Plural Marriage," p. 43; see also Joan Iversen, "Feminist Implications of Mormon Polygyny," *Feminist Studies* 10 (1984): 505–22; see also Iversen, *The Antipolygamy Controversy*, pp. 53–75.

[3] Iversen, "Feminist Implications," pp. 510–11, 513.

[4] Ibid., pp. 513–14.

[5] Ibid., p. 511.

[6] Dunfey, "Living the Principle of Plural Marriage," pp. 528, 530, 531; Iversen, "Feminist Implications," p. 509.

[7] Iversen, "Feminist Implications," p. 511; Rosenblum, "Democratic Sex," p. 79.

[8] Iversen, "Feminist Implications," p. 505.

[9] Iversen, *The Antipolygamy Controversy*, p. 55.

[10] Dunfey, "Living the Principle of Plural Marriage," pp. 529, 524.

[11] Iversen, *The Antipolygamy Controversy*, p. 60.

[12] Polygyny is defined as "[t]he condition or practice of having more than one wife at the same time." *Black's Law Dictionary*, 8th ed. (2004), p. 1198.

polygamy as well as heterosexual women in polyandrous relationships?[1] The customary social practices associated with polygamy help determine the degree of gender equality, mutuality, and individual autonomy versus unilateral dominance and gender inequality that is likely to occur in actual polygamous marriages. As Nancy Rosenblum observes, "There is no reason why egalitarian norms of property distribution, parenting, and the division of domestic and market labor recommended by democratic theorists could not be adjusted for plural marriage."[2]

Finally, whether or not polygamy facilitates gender inequality depends critically on the legal form it takes. To whom is polygamous civil marriage available? Same-sex groups? One woman with multiple men? Two women and two men? In a liberal political society governed by norms of gender equality, polygamous civil marriage could not be legally equated with polygyny,[3] but would have to permit a variety of gender configurations. In a society that recognizes same-sex marriages, polygamy would necessarily extend to all-male or all-female polygamous marriages. Moreover, if the idea that there is a single "head of household" is not operative in legal conceptions of monogamous marriage, it would be inconsistent to introduce that assumption into a legal conception of polygamous marriage. Of equal importance is the question, from whom is consent required? Liberal societies would not tolerate a form of civil marriage which did not assign equal importance to the consent of all spouses, and which did not offer the exit option of divorce to all spouses. What rules govern divorce and property distribution? In a liberal society that grants no-fault divorces to monogamous marriages, exit from polygamous marriages would likewise have to be on a no-fault basis. In short, the legal form of polygamous marriage determines the extent to which assumptions about gender relations and sexual orientation are encoded into marriage law. It

also determines the level of required formal consent for entrance into marriage and the availability of exit options for disaffected spouses.

The quick dismissal of polygamy on grounds that it, unlike monogamy, is distinctively gender-inegalitarian is the result of smuggling in a set of unstated assumptions about the background social conditions for women, the social practice of polygamy, and its likely legal form that would render it inegalitarian, but that are implausible assumptions about plural marriage in a liberal egalitarian democracy.

Opponents might object that, in fact, polygamy, as it is practiced worldwide, tends to take forms that are oppressive to women. Permitting polygamous civil marriage would thus open the doors to illiberal ethnic groups in the United States practicing social forms of polygamy that are oppressive to women. Two responses to this objection bear noting.

First, unless we are willing to also eliminate monogamous civil marriage because it, too, sometimes takes social forms that are oppressive to women, targeting polygamy for a special bar would involve the state in a clear failure to exercise neutrality with respect to alternative conceptions of the good. Indeed, Justice Waite's reason for rejecting polygamy in *Reynolds* was driven in part by hostility to non-European cultures.[4] "Polygamy," he noted, "has always been odious among the northern and western nations of Europe, and, until the establishment of the Mormon Church, was almost exclusively a feature of the life of Asiatic and of African people."[5] Subsequent Supreme Court Justices rejected polygamy out of hostility to non-Christian ways of life: "Bigamy and polygamy are crimes by the laws of all civilized and Christian countries,"[6] and polygamy is "a return to barbarism[;] [i]t is contrary to the spirit of Christianity

---

[1] Polyandry is defined as "[t]he condition or practice of having more than one husband at the same time." Ibid., p. 1997.

[2] Rosenblum, "Democratic Sex," p. 81.

[3] See n. [12, p. 717] for a definition of polygyny.

[4] See *Reynolds v. United States*, 98 U.S. 145, 164 (1878).

[5] Ibid.

[6] *Davis v. Beason*, 133 U.S. 333, 341 (1890); see also Babst, *Liberal Constitutionalism*, p. 96 (quoting *Davis v. Beason* and discussing the case's relevance to "shadow establishment").

and of the civilization which Christianity has produced in the Western world."[1]

Second, the existence of ethnic or religious groups in the United States that practice gender oppressive forms of polygamy is all the more reason to extend civil marriage to polygamous groups. The social and legal persecution of Mormon polygamy in the nineteenth century did not end the social practice of polygamy.[2] What it did do was to eliminate the legal status of "wife" for all but first wives.[3] As a result all secondary wives lost their legal claim for support and their children became illegitimate. Unless we are now willing to use the coercive force of the law to ensure that there simply are no polygamous relationships, some women will in fact participate in plural marriages in the United States. Failure to extend civil marriage to plural marriages leaves them unprotected by marriage and divorce law. Women who enter plural marriages without the benefit of legal divorce have substantially restricted exit options from those marriages, since they are not legally entitled to make claims for alimony or fair property distribution. For this reason, even those who are most committed to the belief that polygamy will be practiced in gender-oppressive forms should think twice about insisting on using the denial of civil marriage as a way to deter that practice.

V. Conclusion

The silence about polygamy on the part of same-sex marriage advocates is a mistake—at least in academic circles, because the historical practice of polygamy is a substantial reason for rejecting the claim that there is a millennia-long tradition of defining marriage

as between one man and one woman. In addition, reflection on the similarities between the polygamy and same-sex marriage debates helps to illuminate the larger social issue of how to satisfy individuals' multiple relational needs and whether the state should endorse a single form of marriage. Finally, the supposedly reductio force of "And why not also polygamy?" challenges to same-sex marriages are most effectively met by challenging their underlying assumptions about the nature of polygamy.

DISCUSSION QUESTIONS

1. Why does Calhoun think that the "traditionalists" ought to be wary of invoking the Judeo-Christian tradition as a reason for rejecting same-sex civil marriage?

2. Calhoun claims that "both the pro-polygamy and pro-same-sex marriage campaigns have been marked by an anti-pluralist and exclusionary conception of marriage." Explain this remark. Why does Calhoun think it would be better to advocate a pluralistic conception of personal relationships? How does doing so bring the issue of polygamy into the debate?

3. Calhoun notes that "gender inequality is a contingent, not a conceptual, feature of polygamy." Explain this remark. How does Calhoun think that recognition of this fact will demonstrate that a "liberal egalitarian democracy" can (and should) support polygamous civil marriages? Evaluate this argument.

4. Opponents of polygamy may argue that polygamy as it has traditionally been practiced in the United States has been gender-oppressive toward women. Calhoun argues that recognition of this provides all the more reason for supporting polygamous civil marriages. Explain and evaluate this argument.

---

[1] *Late Corp. of the Church of Jesus Christ of Latter-day Saints v. United States*, 136 U.S. 1, 49 (1890); see also Babst, *Liberal Constitutionalism*, p. 97 (quoting the case and discussing the case's relevance to "shadow establishment"). Babst argues that the persistent appeal to Christian values in court rulings with respect to interracial, polygamous, and same-sex marriage bars is evidence of what he calls a "shadow establishment" of religion in U.S. judicial practice.

[2] See [note 1, p. 709].

[3] Dunfey, [note 4, p. 712].

62

SEX, FREEDOM, AND MARRIAGE

James Q. Wilson, "Against Homosexual Marriage" (1996)

James Q. Wilson is the Ronald Reagan Professor of Public Policy at Pepperdine University's School of Public Policy. He has chaired the White House Task Force on Crime, the National Advisory Commission on Drug Abuse Prevention, and the Council of Academic Advisors of the American Enterprise Institute, as well as serving on numerous other commissions and boards. In this selection, Wilson criticizes Sullivan's conservative argument for gay marriage (see reading 56 above), arguing that the maintenance of society depends on preserving marriage as an institution between a man and a woman.

SOURCE

Wilson, James Q. "Against Homosexual Marriage." Reprinted from *Commentary*, March 1996, by permission of the author and *Commentary*; copyright © 1996 by Commentary Inc.

...

The second argument against homosexual marriage—Sullivan's conservative category—is based on natural law as originally set forth by Aristotle and Thomas Aquinas and more recently restated by Hadley Arkes, John Finnis, Robert George, Harry V. Jaffa, and others. How it is phrased varies a bit, but in general its advocates support a position like the following: man cannot live without the care and support of other people; natural law is the distillation of what thoughtful people have learned about the conditions of that care. The first thing they have learned is the supreme importance of marriage, for without it the newborn infant is unlikely to survive or, if he survives, to prosper. The necessary conditions of a decent family life are the acknowledgment by its members that a man will not sleep with his daughter or a woman with her son and that neither will openly choose sex outside marriage.

Now, some of these conditions are violated, but there is a penalty in each case that is supported by the moral convictions of almost all who witness the violation. On simple utilitarian grounds it may be hard to object to incest or adultery; if both parties to such an act welcome it and if it is secret, what differences [sic] does it make? But very few people, and then only ones among the overeducated, seem to care much about mounting a utilitarian assault on the family. To this assault, natural-law theorists respond much as would the average citizen—never mind "utility," what counts is what is right. In particular, homosexual uses of the repro-ductive organs violate the condition that sex serves solely as the basis of heterosexual marriage.

To Sullivan, what is defective about the natural-law thesis is that it assumes different purposes in heterosexual and homosexual love: moral consum-mation in the first case and pure utility or pleasure alone in the second. But in fact, Sullivan suggests, homosexual love can be as consummatory as het-erosexual. He notes that as the Roman Catholic Church has deepened its understanding of the invol-untary—that is, in some sense genetic—basis of homosexuality, it has attempted to keep homosex-uals in the church as objects of affection and nur-ture, while banning homosexual acts as perverse.

But this, though better than nothing, will not work, Sullivan writes. To show why, he adduces an analogy to a sterile person. Such a person is permit-ted to serve in the military or enter an unproductive marriage; why not homosexuals? If homosexuals marry without procreation, they are no different (he suggests) from a sterile man or woman who marries without hope of procreation. Yet people, I think, want the form observed even when the prac-tice varies; a sterile marriage, whether from choice or necessity, remains a marriage of a man and a woman. To this Sullivan offers essentially an aes-thetic response. Just as albinos remind us of the brilliance of color and genius teaches us about mod-eration, homosexuals are a "natural foil" to the het-erosexual union, "a variation that does not eclipse the theme." Moreover, the threat posed by the foil to the theme is slight as compared to the threats posed by adultery, divorce, and prostitution. To be consistent, Sullivan once again reminds us, society would have to ban adulterers from the military as it now bans confessed homosexuals.

But again this misses the point. It would make more sense to ask why an alternative to marriage should be invented and praised when we are having enough trouble maintaining the institution at all. Suppose that gay or lesbian marriage were autho-rized; rather than producing a "natural foil" that would "not eclipse the theme," I suspect such a move would call even more seriously into question

the role of marriage at a time when the threats to it, ranging from single-parent families to common divorces, have hit record highs. Kenneth Minogue recently wrote of Sullivan's book[1] that support for homosexual marriage would strike most people as "mere parody," one that could further weaken an already strained institution.

To me, the chief limitation of Sullivan's view is that it presupposes that marriage would have the same, domesticating, effect on homosexual members as it has on heterosexuals, while leaving the latter largely unaffected. Those are very large assumptions that no modern society has ever tested.

Nor does it seem plausible to me that a modern society resists homosexual marriages entirely out of irrational prejudice. Marriage is a union, sacred to most, that unites a man and woman together for life. It is a sacrament of the Catholic Church and central to every other faith. Is it out of misinforma-tion that every modern society has embraced this view and rejected the alternative? Societies differ greatly in their attitude toward the income people may have, the relations among their various races, and the distribution of political power. But they dif-fer scarcely at all over the distinctions between het-erosexual and homosexual couples. The former are overwhelmingly preferred over the latter. The rea-son, I believe, is that these distinctions involve the nature of marriage and thus the very meaning—even more, the very possibility—of society.

The final argument over homosexual marriage is the liberal one, based on civil rights.

... [T]he Hawaiian Supreme Court ruled that any state-imposed sexual distinction would have to meet the test of strict scrutiny, a term used by the U.S. Supreme Court only for racial and similar classifi-cations. In doing this, the Hawaiian court distanced itself from every other state court decision—there are several—in this area so far. A variant of the sus-pect-class argument, though, has been suggested by

---

[1] [*Virtually Normal: An Argument About Homosexuality* (New York: Alfred A. Knopf, Inc., 1995). The selection by Sullivan included in this text (reading 56) is from *Virtually Normal*.]

some scholars who contend that denying access to a marriage license by two people of the same sex is no different from denying access to two people of different sexes but also different races. The Hawaiian Supreme Court embraced this argument as well, explicitly comparing its decision to that of the U.S. Supreme Court when it overturned state laws banning marriages involving miscegenation.

But the comparison with black-white marriages is itself suspect. Beginning around 1964, and no doubt powerfully affected by the passage of the Civil Rights Act of that year, public attitudes toward race began to change dramatically. Even allowing for exaggerated statements to pollsters, there is little doubt that people in fact acquired a new view of blacks. Not so with homosexuals. Though the campaign to aid them has been going on vigorously for about a quarter of a century, it has produced few, if any, gains in public acceptance, and the greatest resistance, I think, has been with respect to homosexual marriages.

Consider the difference. What has been at issue in race relations is not marriage among blacks (for over a century, that right has been universally granted) or even miscegenation (long before the civil-rights movement, many Southern states had repealed such laws). Rather, it has been the routine contact between the races in schools, jobs, and neighborhoods. Our own history, in other words, has long made it clear that marriage is a different issue from the issue of social integration.

There is another way, too, in which the comparison with race is less than helpful, as Sullivan himself points out. Thanks to the changes in public attitudes I mentioned a moment ago, gradually race was held to be not central to decisions about hiring, firing, promoting, and schooling, and blacks began to make extraordinary advances in society. But then, in an effort to enforce this new view. liberals came to embrace affirmative action, a policy that said that race *was* central to just such issues, in order to ensure that *real* mixing occurred. This move created a crisis, for liberalism had always been based on the proposition that a liberal political system should encourage, as John Stuart Mill

put it, "experiments in living" free of religious or political direction. To contemporary liberals, however, being neutral about race was tantamount to being neutral about a set of human preferences that in such matters as neighborhood and schooling left groups largely (but not entirely) separate.

Sullivan, who wisely sees that hardly anybody is really prepared to ignore a political opportunity to change lives, is not disposed to have much of this either in the area of race or in that of sex. And he points out with great clarity that popular attitudes toward sexuality are anyway quite different from those about race, as is evident from the fact that wherever sexual orientation is subject to local regulations, such regulations are rarely invoked. Why? Because homosexuals can "pass" or not, as they wish; they can and do accumulate education and wealth; they exercise political power. The two things a homosexual cannot do are join the military as an avowed homosexual or marry another homosexual.

The result, Sullivan asserts, is a wrenching paradox. On the one hand, society has historically tolerated the brutalization inflicted on people because of the color of their skin, but freely allowed them to marry; on the other hand, it has given equal opportunity to homosexuals, while denying them the right to marry. This, indeed, is where Sullivan draws the line. A black or Hispanic child, if heterosexual, has many friends, he writes, but a gay child "generally has no one." And that is why the social stigma attached to homosexuality is different from that attached to race or ethnicity—"because it attacks the very heart of what makes a human being human: the ability to love and be loved." Here is the essence of Sullivan's case. It is a powerful one, even if (as I suspect) his pro-marriage sentiments are not shared by all homosexuals.

Let us assume for the moment that a chance to live openly and legally with another homosexual is desirable. To believe that, we must set aside biblical injunctions, a difficult matter in a profoundly religious nation. But suppose we manage the diversion, perhaps on the grounds that if most Americans skip church, they can as readily avoid other errors of (possibly) equal magnitude. Then we must ask on what terms the union shall be arranged. There are two alternatives—marriage or domestic partnership.

Sullivan acknowledges the choice, but disparages the domestic-partnership laws that have evolved in some foreign countries and in some American localities. His reasons, essentially conservative ones, are that domestic partnerships are too easily formed and too easily broken. Only real marriages matter. But—aside from the fact that marriage is in serious decline, and that only slightly more than half of all marriages performed in the United States this year will be between never-before-married heterosexuals—what is distinctive about marriage is that it is an institution created to sustain child-rearing. Whatever losses it has suffered in *this* respect, its function remains what it has always been.

The role of raising children is entrusted in principle to married heterosexual couples because after much experimentation—several thousand years, more or less—we have found nothing else that works as well. Neither a gay nor a lesbian couple can of its own resources produce a child; another party must be involved. What do we call this third party? A friend? A sperm or egg bank? An anonymous donor? There is no settled language for even describing, much less approving of, such persons.

Suppose we allowed homosexual couples to raise children who were created out of a prior heterosexual union or adopted from someone else's heterosexual contact. What would we think of this? There is very little research on the matter. Charlotte Patterson's famous essay, "Children of Gay and Lesbian Parents" (*Journal of Child Development*, 1992), begins by conceding that the existing studies focus on children born into a heterosexual union that ended in divorce or that was transformed when the mother or father "came out" as a homosexual. Hardly any research has been done on children acquired at the outset by a homosexual couple. We therefore have no way of knowing how they would behave. And even if we had such studies, they might tell us rather little unless they were conducted over a very long period of time.

But it is one thing to be born into an apparently heterosexual family and then many years later to learn that one of your parents is homosexual. It is quite another to be acquired as an infant from an adoption agency or a parent-for-hire and learn from the first years of life that you are, because of your family's position, radically different from almost all other children you will meet. No one can now say how grievous this would be. We know that young children tease one another unmercifully; adding this dimension does not seem to be a step in the right direction.

Of course, homosexual "families," with or without children, might be rather few in number. Just how few, it is hard to say. Perhaps Sullivan himself would marry, but, given the great tendency of homosexual males to be promiscuous, many more like him would not, or if they did, would not marry with as much seriousness....

The courts in Hawaii and in the nation's capital must struggle with all these issues under the added encumbrance of a contemporary outlook that makes law the search for rights, and responsibility the recognition of rights. Indeed, thinking of laws about marriage as documents that confer or withhold rights is itself an error of fundamental importance—one that the highest court in Hawaii has already committed. "Marriage," it wrote, "is a state-conferred legal-partnership status, the existence of which gives rise to a multiplicity of rights and benefits...." A state-conferred legal partnership? To lawyers, perhaps; to mankind, I think not. The Hawaiian court has thus set itself on the same course of action as the misguided Supreme Court in 1971 when it thought that laws about abortion were merely an assertion of the rights of a living mother and an unborn fetus.

I have few favorable things to say about the political systems of other modern nations, but on these fundamental matters—abortion, marriage, military service—they often do better by allowing legislatures to operate than we do by deferring to courts. Our challenge is to find a way of formulating a policy with respect to homosexual unions that is not the result of a reflexive act of judicial rights-conferring, but is instead a considered expression of the moral convictions of a people.

DISCUSSION QUESTIONS

1. Wilson claims that the maintenance of society depends on preserving the nature of marriage as a heterosexual union. What is his argument for this claim? Evaluate his argument.

2. Wilson claims that comparing race and sexuality is not helpful. Explain and evaluate his argument for that claim.

3. Wilson claims that "marriage is … an institution created to sustain child-rearing … [and] its function remains what it has always been." Do you agree with him? Why or why not?

UNIT III

Property and the
Distribution of Resources

Introduction

"Only two things in life are for certain: death and taxes." And these two topics have occupied the thought of philosophers to a great extent. But some political philosophers, while conceding the inevitability of death, have not been willing to concede the moral permissibility, let alone the certainty, of taxes. Taxation, by its very nature, is a form of coercive government activity, a seizing of resources currently held by some citizens so that the government can use those resources for various purposes. Is any such coercive seizing of resources permissible? Does it depend on what purposes the government intends to use the resources for? Is it relevant how the citizen came to hold the resources? Must the person from whom the resources were originally seized benefit from the government's use of such resources?

Hardly anyone would deny that private property—resources over which one or more citizens have exclusive control of one sort or another—has its dangers: the quest for wealth can make us greedy, self-centered, and blind to the needs of others. Without a doubt, wealth can corrupt. In order to guard against these effects of wealth and its pursuit, Plato, in his *Republic* (see reading 63), abolished private property among the two ruling classes, the two classes for whom the avoidance of corruption is crucial, given that they are responsible for promoting the good of the whole state. Thus, the guardians and the auxiliaries hold everything in common, living in Spartan quarters so as not to be distracted by luxury and possessiveness.

Plato seemed to regard human nature, or at least the nature of those suited for ruling, as malleable. Hobbes, on the other hand, had no such utopian optimism. He regarded the urge to accumulate property as an outgrowth of the quest for power, power being essential to human survival in the human-eat-human world of the state of nature. One important problem for each of us in the state of nature is hanging on to our resources and preventing others from simply taking them through violent means. No actions are either morally right or wrong, so it is not morally impermissible for others to take what I have collected or made for my own use. Our only rational choice is to institute a powerful sovereign who will have the task of determining who owns what and for how long: the disposal—and protection—of property, in the commonwealth, is entirely at the discretion of the sovereign.

Locke's fundamental disagreement with Hobbes concerns the status of morality in the state of nature. According to Locke (see reading 64), as opposed to Hobbes, there are moral rules, discoverable by reason, that govern our conduct even before we establish a commonwealth. Each of us has a fundamental right of property in her own person, and she can, as a result, acquire exclusive rights over resources in the natural world in so far as she mixes her labor with them and leaves enough and as good for others—this is the essence of Locke's famous labor theory of property, a theory that has greatly influenced contemporary Libertarians, most explicitly Robert

Nozick (see reading 68). For Locke, then, persons will enter the contract to form a state to protect their property rights—both in themselves and in various external resources such as land and livestock—and a state will be legitimate only as long as it does not violate natural rights in property.

With Plato, Hobbes, and Locke, then, we see three different approaches to private property: it is dangerous and corrupting and so to be avoided as far as possible (Plato), its attainment is a natural desire that we can only hope to keep within manageable bounds (Hobbes), and we have a natural right to it that constrains the state's legitimate pursuits (Locke). Hume and Smith (see readings 65 and 66) introduce a new strand into this discussion, a strand that refuses to see property as a natural right but also refuses to see its quest and accumulation as a feature of human nature to be eliminated or contained for the social good. Both Hume and Smith see the state's setting of rules for the acquisition and accumulation of property as having good consequences for the society as a whole. For Smith, famously, each individual pursuing her own good will, via the "invisible hand," maximizes the wealth of the society as a whole. Hume agrees that the correctly structured set of property rules will facilitate social cooperation, but says that the rules must be suited to the social circumstances of the society. In conditions of extreme scarcity or plenty, or of extreme altruism, rules of property would be pointless. So both Hume and Smith reject any natural right to property, but also claim that socially created property claims are useful to society as a whole.

Contemporary Libertarians, taking Locke as their model, have attempted to rebut any attempts, Marxist or otherwise, to justify the redistribution of resources from one citizen to another. Robert Nozick claims that redistributive taxation—coercive government seizing of the resources of one citizen in order to benefit another citizen—is always illegitimate. In fact, he argues, taxation is a form of enslavement. When a person is enslaved, her labor is appropriated without her consent. But, when a person is taxed, the fruit of her labor is appropriated without her con-

sent; thus, in essence, she is working without benefit, just as one does if one is enslaved.

Nozick uses his well-known Wilt Chamberlain argument to support the conclusion that no matter which distribution one starts with—choose whatever distribution one thinks is justified—as long as people are allowed to do what they choose with their resources, the favored distribution will be disrupted. And, Nozick asks, what would it come to to say that people own what they hold under the original distribution if such ownership does not entail a right to do as they choose with their holdings (barring, of course, the violation of anyone else's rights)?

Of course, this gets us right to the heart of the matter: what does it mean to say that a certain resource is my private property? We seem to understand attributions of ownership of a resource R to a person as attributions of one or more of the following rights: (i) the right to use R, (ii) the right to abuse R, (iii) the right to rent R, (iv) the right to sell R, and (v) the right to acquire benefits from R. But we do not seem to understand all attributions of ownership as involving the attribution of all of the rights (i)-(v). Consider the claim that I own my cat—we certainly do not think that such ownership involves (ii) the right to abuse my cat. But the denial of that right is not the denial of the claim that I am sole, exclusive owner of my cat, because *no one* has the right to abuse my cat. Similarly, I own my talents, but there is a great deal of disagreement as to whether such ownership involves (iv) the right to sell my talents, which would amount to the right to enslave myself, i.e., the permanent transfer to another of the ability to direct the use of my talents and labor.

Most important, however, with respect to the clash between Libertarians such as Nozick and his critics is the interpretation of (v) the right to acquire benefits from R. But which benefits does one have a right to acquire? Which benefits result from the use of one's talents is not a fact intrinsic to one's talents, but often depends on the value that other people place on one's talents. So the question then becomes, what sorts of transactions with other individuals must the state allow? We cannot appeal to ownership of self to answer this question, because the answer to this question is supposed to be part of our analysis of the concept of ownership of self.

John Rawls, in his highly influential *A Theory of Justice*, argues that claims to resources are acquired *after* the state has been established (see reading 70). In this, Rawls agrees with Hobbes as opposed to Locke and Nozick. However, unlike Hobbes, Rawls is concerned to guarantee that the rules governing property are fair. Thus, such rules will be subject to the two principles of justice that are chosen in the original position, a hypothetical bargaining situation designed to model a perfectly fair contractual situation—i.e., a situation in which all have equal status and equal ability to affect the outcome. Most important to the issue of private property is the second part of the second principle of justice, what is known as the difference principle. The difference principle states that inequalities in the distribution of resources are justified only to the extent that those inequalities work to the advantage of the worst-off class in society. Exclusive claims over resources will be structured to secure this end. But Rawls does guarantee, via the first principle of justice, a right to hold *some* personal property. Thus, while Rawls is egalitarian to a strong degree, he certainly does not aim at anything like the Marxist end state with its abolition of private property.

Suppose that, like Rawls, we understand the resources of society as the product of social cooperation, not existing prior to the creation of society. So how should these products of cooperation be distributed? Suppose that we start with an economic free market. The market sets prices in accordance with cost of production, and this is appropriate, because that cost reflects how many societal resources were diverted from the production of resources desired by other citizens. In a free market, it will cost more to purchase fine gold jewelry than to purchase plastic bead necklaces, more to purchase fine champagne than to purchase Miller Lite. So people with different preferences will receive differing amounts of goods, depending on the cost

of satisfying their preferences and what the market will pay for their talents.

People, however, differ not only in preferences, but also in abilities. If the market remains uncorrected, then people will get less due to something beyond their ability to change, namely their innate capacities or lack thereof. So the market, according to many who have been influenced by Rawls, ought not to be allowed to work unchecked: the ideal of equality demands that we redistribute, via taxation, so that those with fewer marketable skills are not completely disadvantaged.

One objection that some, including Nozick and Friedman (see reading 67), have to any kind of redistribution is that it imposes restrictions on liberty: a free-market capitalist society, it is claimed, is the society in which citizens have the most freedom. But is this really true? Cohen claims that it is manifestly not true: for every liberty gained via exclusive property rights, one is taken away; for example, in so far as Paris Hilton gains the freedom to exclude me from using her Malibu beach house, I lose the ability to use that beach house. Unless liberty is construed in some more theoretically loaded sense, Cohen claims, it is simply not true that free-market capitalism produces greater freedom than do systems in which property is, for example, jointly owned.

Let's return to the case of my cat. As I said earlier, most of us conceive of people as owning their pets. But are animals the kinds of things that can be owned? Do parents own their children? Walzer considers another sort of example: a town. He uses the real-life case of Pullman, who built a town for his workers. Anyone who wanted to work for Pullman had to live in one of the houses that Pullman owned, shop at the stores that Pullman owned, etc. Pullman controlled all of the town's government. But does his ownership of the land and buildings entitle him to govern as he sees fit? If not, then should we think that those who own factories, for example, are entitled to determine all of the rules governing the behavior of the employees?

A.
Historical
Perspectives

63

Plato, selection from
The Republic (c. 380 BCE)

In this selection, Socrates presents what is known as "the myth of the metals." He goes on to discuss the sort of life that he envisions a Guardian, or philosopher-king, living. On Plato, see reading 1 above.

SOURCE

Plato, *The Republic of Plato* (Third Edition, Volume 1. Benjamin Jowett, translator. The Clarendon Press at Oxford University Press. First published 1908; reprinted 1927).

"Citizens, we shall say to them in our tale, you are brothers, yet God has framed you differently. Some of you have the power of command, and in the composition of these he has mingled gold, wherefore also they have the greatest honour; others he has made of silver, to be auxiliaries; others again who are to be husbandmen and craftsmen he has composed of brass and iron; and the species will generally be preserved in the children. But as all are of the same original stock, a golden parent will sometimes have a silver son, or a silver parent a golden son. And God proclaims as a first principle to the rulers, and above all else, that there is nothing which should so anxiously guard, or of which they are to be such good guardians, as of the purity of the race. They should observe what elements mingle in their offspring; for if the son of a golden or silver parent has an admixture of brass and iron, then nature orders a transposition of ranks, and the eye of the ruler must not be pitiful towards the child because he has to descend in the scale and become a husbandman or artisan, just as there may be sons of artisans who having an admixture of gold or silver in them are raised to honour, and become guardians or auxiliaries. For an oracle says that when a man of brass or iron guards the State, it will be destroyed. Such is the tale; is there any possibility of making our citizens believe in it?"

"Not in the present generation," he [Glaucon] replied; "there is no way of accomplishing this; but their sons may be made to believe in the tale, and their sons' sons, and posterity after them."

"I see the difficulty," I replied; "yet the fostering of such a belief will make them care more for the city and for one another. Enough, however, of the fiction, which may now fly abroad upon the wings of rumour, while we arm our earth-born heroes, and lead them forth under the command of their rulers. Let them look round and select a spot whence they can best suppress insurrection, if any prove refractory within, and also defend themselves against enemies, who like wolves may come down on the fold from without; there let them encamp, and when they have encamped, let them sacrifice to the proper Gods and prepare their dwellings."

"Just so," he said.

"And their dwellings must be such as will shield them against the cold of winter and the heat of summer."

"I suppose that you mean houses," he replied.

"Yes," I said; "but they must be the houses of soldiers, and not of shop-keepers."

"What is the difference?" he said.

"That I will endeavour to explain," I replied. "To keep watchdogs, who, from want of discipline or hunger, or some evil habit, or evil habit or other, would turn upon the sheep and worry them, and behave not like dogs but wolves, would be a foul and monstrous thing in a shepherd?"

"Truly monstrous," he said.

"And therefore every care must be taken that our auxiliaries, being stronger than our citizens, may not grow to be too much for them and become savage tyrants instead of friends and allies?"

"Yes, great care should be taken."

"And would not a really good education furnish the best safeguard?"

"But they are well educated already," he replied.

"I cannot be so confident, my dear Glaucon," I said; "I am much certain that they ought to be, and that true education, whatever that may be, will have the greatest tendency to civilize and humanize them in their relations to one another, and to those who are under their protection."

"Very true," he replied.

"And not only their education, but their habitations, and all that belongs to them, should be such as will neither impair their virtue as guardians, nor tempt them to prey upon the other citizens. Any man of sense must acknowledge that."

"He must."

"Then let us consider what will be their way of life, if they are to realize our idea of them. In the first place, none of them should have any property of his own beyond what is absolutely necessary; neither should they have a private house or store closed against any one who has a mind to enter; their provisions should be only such as are required by trained warriors, who are men of temperance and courage; they should agree to receive from the citizens a fixed rate of pay, enough to meet the expenses of the year and no more; and they will go and live together like soldiers in a camp. Gold and silver we will tell them that they have from God; the diviner metal is within them, and they have therefore no need of the dross which is current among men, and ought not to pollute the divine by any such earthly admixture; for that commoner metal has been the source of many unholy deeds, but their own is undefiled. And they alone of all the citizens may not touch or handle silver or gold, or be under the same roof with them, or wear them, or drink from them. And this will be their salvation, and they will be the saviours of the State. But should they ever acquire homes or lands or moneys of their own, they will become housekeepers and husbandmen instead of guardians, enemies and tyrants instead of allies of the other citizens; hating and being hated, plotting and being plotted against, they will pass their whole life in much greater terror of internal than of external enemies, and the hour of ruin, both to themselves and to the rest of the State, will be at hand. For all which reasons may we not say that thus shall our State be ordered, and that these shall be the regulations appointed by us for guardians concerning their houses and all other matters?"

"Yes," said Glaucon.

Here Adeimantus interposed a question: "How would you answer, Socrates," said he, "if a person were to say that you are making these people miserable, and that they are the cause of their own unhappiness; the city in fact belongs to them, but they are none the better for it; whereas other men acquire lands, and build large and handsome houses, and have everything handsome about them, offering sacrifices to the gods on their own account, and practicing hospitality; moreover, as you were saying just now, they have gold and silver, and all that is usual among the favourites of fortune; but our poor citizens are no better than mercenaries who are quartered in the city and are always mounting guard?"

"Yes," I said; "and you may add that they are only fed, and not paid in addition to their food, like other men; and therefore they cannot, if they would, take a journey of pleasure; they have no money to spend on a mistress or any other luxurious fancy, which, as the world goes, is thought to be happiness; and many other accusations of the same nature might be added."

"But," said he, "let us suppose all this to be included in the charge."

"You mean to ask," I said, "what will be our answer?"

"Yes."

"If we proceed along the old path, my belief," I said, "is that we shall find the answer. And our answer will be that, even as they are, our guardians may very likely be the happiest of men; but that our aim in founding the State was not the disproportionate happiness of any one class, but the greatest happiness of the whole; we thought that in a State which is ordered with a view to the good of the whole we should be most likely to find Justice, and in the ill-ordered State injustice: and, having found them, we might then decide which of the two is the happier. At present, I take it, we are fashioning the happy State, not piecemeal, or with a view of making a few happy citizens, but as a whole; and by-and-by we will proceed to view the opposite kind of State. Suppose that we were painting a statue, and some one came up to us and said, 'Why do you not put the most beautiful colours on the most beautiful parts of the body—the eyes ought to

be purple, but you have made them black,'—to him we might fairly answer, 'Sir, you would not surely have us beautify the eyes to such a degree that they are no longer eyes; consider rather whether, by giving this and the other features their due proportion, we make the whole beautiful.' And so I say to you, do not compel us to assign to the guardians a sort of happiness which will make them anything but guardians; for we too can clothe our husbandmen in royal apparel, and set crowns of gold on their heads, and bid them till the ground as much as they like, and no more. Our potters also might be allowed to repose on couches, and feast by the fireside, passing round the winecup, while their wheel is conveniently at hand, and working at pottery only as much as they like; in this way we might make every class happy—and then, as you imagine, the whole State would be happy. But do not put this idea into our heads; for, if we listen to you, the husbandman will be no longer a husbandman, the potter will cease to be a potter, and no one will have the character of any distinct class in the State. Now this is not of much consequence where the corruption of society, and pretension to be what you are not, is confined to cobblers; but when the guardians of the laws and of the government are only seemingly and not real guardians, then see how they turn the State upside down; and on the other hand they alone have the power of giving order and happiness to the State. We mean our guardians to be true saviours and not the destroyers of the State, whereas our opponent is thinking of peasants at a festival, who are enjoying a life of revelry, not of citizens who are doing their duty to the State. But, if so, we mean different things, and he is speaking of something which is not a State. And therefore we must consider whether in appointing our guardians we would look to their greatest happiness individually, or whether this principle of happiness does not rather reside in the State as a whole. But the latter be the truth, then the guardians and auxiliaries, and all others equally with them, must be compelled or induced to do their own work in the best way. And thus the whole State will grow up in a noble order, and the several classes will receive the proportion of happiness which nature assigns to them."

"I think that you are quite right."

"I wonder whether you will agree with another remark which occurs to me."

"What may that be?"

"There seem to be two causes of the deterioration of the arts."

"What are they?"

"Wealth," I said, "and poverty."

"How do they act?"

"The process is as follows: When a potter becomes rich, will he, think you, any longer take the same pains with his art?"

"Certainly not."

"He will grow more and more indolent and careless?"

"Very true."

"And the result will be that he becomes a worse potter?"

"Yes; he greatly deteriorates."

"But, on the other hand, if he has no money, and cannot provide himself tools or instruments, he will not work equally well himself, nor will he teach his sons or apprentices to work equally well."

"Certainly not."

"Then, under the influence either of poverty or of wealth, workmen and their work are equally liable to degenerate?"

"That is evident."

"Here, then, is a discovery of new evils," I said, "against which the guardians will have to watch, or they will creep into the city unobserved."

"What evils?"

"Wealth," I said, "and poverty; the one is the parent of luxury and indolence, and the other of meanness and viciousness, and both of discontent."

DISCUSSION QUESTIONS

1. Why does Socrates insist that the guardian class is not to have any private property? What do you think that Socrates means by "private property"?

2. How does Socrates respond to Adeimantus' objection that he is not making the guardians happy? Do you think that Socrates is right to deny private property to the guardians? Do you think that Socrates' proposal could ever be carried out in practice?

64

John Locke, selection from *Second Treatise of Government* (1689)

In this selection, Locke explores the grounds and justification for a system of private property. On Locke, see reading 3 above.

SOURCE

Locke, John. *Two Treatises of Government*. Whitmore and Fenn, reprinted 1821.

Of Property

25. Whether we consider natural reason, which tells us, that men, being once born, have a right to their preservation, and consequently to meat and drink, and such other things as nature affords for their subsistence: or revelation, which gives us an account of those grants God made of the world to Adam, and to Noah, and his sons, it is very clear, that God, as king David says (Psalm 125:16), has given the earth to the children of men; given it to mankind in common. But this being supposed, it seems to some a very great difficulty, how any one should ever come to have a property in any thing: I will not content myself to answer, that if it be difficult to make out property, upon a supposition that God gave the world to Adam, and his posterity in common, it is impossible that any man, but one universal monarch, should have any property upon a supposition, that God gave the world to Adam, and his heirs in succession, exclusive of all the rest of his posterity. But I shall endeavour to shew, how men might come to have a property in several parts of that which God gave to mankind in common, and that without any express compact of all the commoners.

26. God, who hath given the world to men in common, hath also given them reason to make use of it to the best advantage of life, and convenience. The earth, and all that is therein, is given to men for the

support and comfort of their being. And tho' all the fruits it naturally produces, and beasts it feeds, belong to mankind in common, as they are produced by the spontaneous hand of nature; and no body has originally a private dominion, exclusive of the rest of mankind, in any of them, as they are thus in their natural state: yet being given for the use of men, there must of necessity be a means to appropriate them some way or other, before they can be of any use, or at all beneficial to any particular man. The fruit, or venison, which nourishes the wild Indian, who knows no enclosure, and is still a tenant in common, must be his, and so his, i.e., a part of him, that another can no longer have any right to it, before it can do him any good for the support of his life.

27. Though the earth, and all inferior creatures, be common to all men, yet every man has a property in his own person: this no body has any right to but himself. The labour of his body, and the work of his hands, we may say, are properly his. Whatsoever then he removes out of the state that nature hath provided, and left it in, he hath mixed his labour with, and joined to it something that is his own, and thereby makes it his property. It being by him removed from the common state nature hath placed it in, it hath by this labour something annexed to it, that excludes the common right of other men: for this labour being the unquestionable property of the labourer, no man but he can have a right to what that is once joined to, at least where there is enough, and as good, left in common for others.

28. He that is nourished by the acorns he picked up under an oak, or the apples he gathered from the trees in the wood, has certainly appropriated them to himself. No body can deny but the nourishment is his. I ask then, when did they begin to be his? when he digested? or when he eat? or when he boiled? or when he brought them home? or when he picked them up? and it is plain, if the first gathering made them not his, nothing else could. That labour put a distinction between them and common: that added something to them more than

nature, the common mother of all, had done; and so they became his private right. And will any one say, he had no right to those acorns or apples, he thus appropriated, because he had not the consent of all mankind to make them his? Was it a robbery thus to assume to himself what belonged to all in common? If such a consent as that was necessary, man had starved, notwithstanding the plenty God had given him. We see in commons, which remain so by compact, that it is the taking any part of what is common, and removing it out of the state nature leaves it in, which begins the property; without which the common is of no use. And the taking of this or that part, does not depend on the express consent of all the commoners. Thus the grass my horse has bit; the turfs my servant has cut; and the ore I have digged in any place, where I have a right to them in common with others, become my property, without the assignation or consent of any body. The labour that was mine, removing them out of that common state they were in, hath fixed my property in them.

29. By making an explicit consent of every commoner, necessary to any one's appropriating to himself any part of what is given in common, children or servants could not cut the meat, which their father or master had provided for them in common, without assigning to every one his peculiar part. Though the water running in the fountain be every one's, yet who can doubt, but that in the pitcher is his only who drew it out? His labour hath taken it out of the hands of nature, where it was common, and belonged equally to all her children, and hath thereby appropriated it to himself.

30. Thus this law of reason makes the deer that Indian's who hath killed it; it is allowed to be his goods, who hath bestowed his labour upon it, though before it was the common right of every one. And amongst those who are counted the civilized part of mankind, who have made and multiplied positive laws to determine property, this original law of nature, for the beginning of property, in what was before common, still takes place;

and by virtue thereof, what fish any one catches in the ocean, that great and still remaining common of mankind; or what ambergrise any one takes up here, is by the labour that removes it out of that common state nature left it in, made his property, who takes that pains about it. And even amongst us, the hare that any one is hunting, is thought his who pursues her during the chase: for being a beast that is still looked upon as common, and no man's private possession; whoever has employed so much labour about any of that kind, as to find and pursue her, has thereby removed her from the state of nature, wherein she was common, and hath begun a property.

31. It will perhaps be objected to this, that if gathering the acorns, or other fruits of the earth, &c. makes a right to them, then any one may ingross as much as he will. To which I answer, Not so. The same law of nature, that does by this means give us property, does also bound that property too. "God has given us all things richly" (1 Tim. 6:12), is the voice of reason confirmed by inspiration. But how far has he given it us? To enjoy. As much as any one can make use of to any advantage of life before it spoils, so much he may by his labour fix a property in: whatever is beyond this, is more than his share, and belongs to others. Nothing was made by God for man to spoil or destroy. And thus, considering the plenty of natural provisions there was a long time in the world, and the few spenders; and to how small a part of that provision the industry of one man could extend itself, and ingross it to the prejudice of others; especially keeping within the bounds, set by reason, of what might serve for his use; there could be then little room for quarrels or contentions about property so established.

32. But the chief matter of property being now not the fruits of the earth, and the beasts that subsist on it, but the earth itself; as that which takes in and carries with it all the rest; I think it is plain, that property in that too is acquired as the former. As much land as a man tills, plants, improves, cultivates, and can use the product of, so much is his

property. He by his labour does, as it were, inclose it from the common. Nor will it invalidate his right, to say every body else has an equal title to it; and therefore he cannot appropriate, he cannot inclose, without the consent of all his fellow-commoners, all mankind. God, when he gave the world in common to all mankind, commanded man also to labour, and the penury of his condition required it of him. God and his reason commanded him to subdue the earth, i.e., improve it for the benefit of life, and therein lay out something upon it that was his own, his labour. He that in obedience to this command of God, subdued, tilled and sowed any part of it, thereby annexed to it something that was his property, which another had no title to, nor could without injury take from him.

33. Nor was this appropriation of any parcel of land, by improving it, any prejudice to any other man, since there was still enough, and as good left; and more than the yet unprovided could use. So that, in effect, there was never the less left for others because of his enclosure for himself: for he that leaves as much as another can make use of, does as good as take nothing at all. No body could think himself injured by the drinking of another man, though he took a good draught, who had a whole river of the same water left him to quench his thirst: and the case of land and water, where there is enough of both, is perfectly the same.

34. God gave the world to men in common; but since he gave it them for their benefit, and the greatest conveniencies of life they were capable to draw from it, it cannot be supposed he meant it should always remain common and uncultivated. He gave it to the use of the industrious and rational, (and labour was to be his title to it;) not to the fancy or covetousness of the quarrelsome and contentious. He that had as good left for his improvement, as was already taken up, needed not complain, ought not to meddle with what was already improved by another's labour: if he did, it is plain he desired the benefit of another's pains, which he had no right to, and not the ground which God had given him

in common with others to labour on, and whereof there was as good left, as that already possessed, and more than he knew what to do with, or his industry could reach to.

35. It is true, in land that is common in England, or any other country, where there is plenty of people under government, who have money and commerce, no one can inclose or appropriate any part, without the consent of all his fellow-commoners; because this is left common by compact, i.e., by the law of the land, which is not to be violated. And though it be common, in respect of some men, it is not so to all mankind; but is the joint property of this country, or this parish. Besides, the remainder, after such enclosure, would not be as good to the rest of the commoners, as the whole was when they could all make use of the whole; whereas in the beginning and first peopling of the great common of the world, it was quite otherwise. The law man was under, was rather *for* appropriating. God commanded, and his wants forced him to labour. That was his property which could not be taken from him where-ever he had fixed it. And hence subduing or cultivating the earth, and having dominion, we see are joined together. The one gave title to the other. So that God, by commanding to subdue, gave authority so far to appropriate: and the condition of human life, which requires labour and materials to work on, necessarily introduces private possessions.

36. The measure of property nature has well set by the extent of men's labour and the conveniencies of life: no man's labour could subdue, or appropriate all; nor could his enjoyment consume more than a small part; so that it was impossible for any man, this way, to intrench upon the right of another, or acquire to himself a property, to the prejudice of his neighbour, who would still have room for as good, and as large a possession (after the other had taken out his) as before it was appropriated. This measure did confine every man's possession to a very moderate proportion, and such as he might appropriate to himself, without injury to any body, in the first

ages of the world, when men were more in danger to be lost, by wandering from their company, in the then vast wilderness of the earth, than to be straitened for want of room to plant in. And the same measure may be allowed still without prejudice to any body, as full as the world seems: for supposing a man, or family, in the state they were at first peopling of the world by the children of Adam, or Noah; let him plant in some inland, vacant places of America, we shall find that the possessions he could make himself, upon the measures we have given, would not be very large, nor, even to this day, prejudice the rest of mankind, or give them reason to complain, or think themselves injured by this man's incroachment, though the race of men have now spread themselves to all the corners of the world, and do infinitely exceed the small number [which] was at the beginning. Nay, the extent of ground is of so little value, without labour, that I have heard it affirmed, that in Spain itself a man may be permitted to plough, sow and reap, without being disturbed, upon land he has no other title to, but only his making use of it. But, on the contrary, the inhabitants think themselves beholden to him, who, by his industry on neglected, and consequently waste land, has increased the stock of corn, which they wanted. But be this as it will, which I lay no stress on; this I dare boldly affirm, that the same rule of propriety, (viz.) that every man should have as much as he could make use of, would hold still in the world, without straitening any body; since there is land enough in the world to suffice double the inhabitants, had not the invention of money, and the tacit agreement of men to put a value on it, introduced (by consent) larger possessions, and a right to them; which, how it has done, I shall by and by shew more at large.

37. This is certain, that in the beginning, before the desire of having more than man needed had altered the intrinsic value of things, which depends only on their usefulness to the life of man; or had agreed, that a little piece of yellow metal, which would keep without wasting or decay, should be worth a great piece of flesh, or a whole heap of corn; though men

had a right to appropriate, by their labour, each one of himself, as much of the things of nature, as he could use: yet this could not be much, nor to the prejudice of others, where the same plenty was still left to those who would use the same industry. To which let me add, that he who appropriates land to himself by his labour, does not lessen, but increase the common stock of mankind: for the provisions serving to the support of human life, produced by one acre of inclosed and cultivated land, are (to speak much within compass) ten times more than those which are yielded by an acre of land of an equal richness lying waste in common. And therefore he that incloses land, and has a greater plenty of the conveniencies of life from ten acres, than he could have from an hundred left to nature, may truly be said to give ninety acres to mankind: for his labour now supplies him with provisions out of ten acres, which were but the product of an hundred lying in common. I have here rated the improved land very low, in making its product but as ten to one, when it is much nearer an hundred to one: for I ask, whether in the wild woods and uncultivated waste of America, left to nature, without any improvement, tillage or husbandry, a thousand acres yield the needy and wretched inhabitants as many conveniencies of life, as ten acres of equally fertile land do in Devonshire, where they are well cultivated?

Before the appropriation of land, he who gathered as much of the wild fruit, killed, caught, or tamed, as many of the beasts, as he could; he that so imployed his pains about any of the spontaneous products of nature, as any way to alter them from the state which nature put them in, by placing any of his labour on them, did thereby acquire a propriety in them: but if they perished, in his possession, without their due use; if the fruits rotted, or the venison putrefied, before he could spend it, he offended against the common law of nature, and was liable to be punished; he invaded his neighbour's share, for he had no right, farther than his use called for any of them, and they might serve to afford him conveniencies of life.

38. The same measures governed the possession of land too: whatsoever he tilled and reaped, laid up and made use of, before it spoiled, that was his peculiar right; whatsoever he enclosed, and could feed, and make use of, the cattle and product was also his. But if either the grass of his enclosure rotted on the ground, or the fruit of his planting perished without gathering, and laying up, this part of the earth, notwithstanding his enclosure, was still to be looked on as waste, and might be the possession of any other. Thus, at the beginning, Cain might take as much ground as he could till, and make it his own land, and yet leave enough to Abel's sheep to feed on; a few acres would serve for both their possessions. But as families increased, and industry inlarged their stocks, their possessions inlarged with the need of them; but yet it was commonly without any fixed property in the ground they made use of, till they incorporated, settled themselves together, and built cities; and then, by consent, they came in time, to set out the bounds of their distinct territories, and agree on limits between them and their neighbours; and by laws within themselves, settled the properties of those of the same society: for we see, that in that part of the world which was first inhabited, and therefore like to be best peopled, even as low down as Abraham's time, they wandered with their flocks, and their herds, which was their substance, freely up and down; and this Abraham did, in a country where he was a stranger. Whence it is plain, that at least a great part of the land lay in common; that the inhabitants valued it not, nor claimed property in any more than they made use of. But when there was not room enough in the same place, for their herds to feed together, they by consent, as Abraham and Lot did (Genesis 13:5), separated and inlarged their pasture, where it best liked them. And for the same reason Esau went from his father, and his brother, and planted in Mount Seir (Genesis 36:6).

39. And thus, without supposing any private dominion, and property in Adam, over all the world, exclusive of all other men, which can no way be proved, nor any one's property be made out

from it; but supposing the world given, as it was, to the children of men in common, we see how labour could make men distinct titles to several parcels of it, for their private uses; wherein there could be no doubt of right, no room for quarrel.

40. Nor is it so strange, as perhaps before consideration it may appear, that the property of labour should be able to over-balance the community of land: for it is labour indeed that puts the difference of value on every thing; and let any one consider what the difference is between an acre of land planted with tobacco or sugar, sown with wheat or barley, and an acre of the same land lying in common, without any husbandry upon it, and he will find, that the improvement of labour makes the far greater part of the value. I think it will be but a very modest computation to say, that of the products of the earth useful to the life of man nine tenths are the effects of labour: nay, if we will rightly estimate things as they come to our use, and cast up the several expences about them, what in them is purely owing to nature, and what to labour, we shall find, that in most of them ninety-nine hundredths are wholly to be put on the account of labour.

41. There cannot be a clearer demonstration of any thing, than several nations of the Americans are of this, who are rich in land, and poor in all the comforts of life; whom nature having furnished as liberally as any other people, with the materials of plenty, i.e., a fruitful soil, apt to produce in abundance, what might serve for food, raiment, and delight; yet for want of improving it by labour, have not one hundredth part of the conveniencies we enjoy: and a king of a large and fruitful territory there, feeds, lodges, and is clad worse than a day-labourer in England.

42. To make this a little clearer, let us but trace some of the ordinary provisions of life, through their several progresses, before they come to our use, and see how much they receive of their value from human industry. Bread, wine and cloth, are things of daily use, and great plenty; yet notwithstanding, acorns, water and leaves, or skins, must be our bread, drink and cloathing, did not labour furnish us with these more useful commodities: for whatever bread is more worth than acorns, wine than water, and cloth or silk, than leaves, skins or moss, that is wholly owing to labour and industry; the one of these being the food and raiment which unassisted nature furnishes us with; the other, provisions which our industry and pains prepare for us, which how much they exceed the other in value, when any one hath computed, he will then see how much labour makes the far greatest part of the value of things we enjoy in this world: and the ground which produces the materials, is scarce to be reckoned in, as any, or at most, but a very small part of it; so little, that even amongst us, land that is left wholly to nature, that hath no improvement of pasturage, tillage, or planting, is called, as indeed it is, waste; and we shall find the benefit of it amount to little more than nothing. This shews how much numbers of men are to be preferred to largeness of dominions; and that the increase of lands, and the right employing of them, is the great art of government: and that prince, who shall be so wise and godlike, as by established laws of liberty to secure protection and encouragement to the honest industry of mankind, against the oppression of power and narrowness of party, will quickly be too hard for his neighbours: but this by the by. To return to the argument in hand,

43. An acre of land, that bears here twenty bushels of wheat, and another in America, which, with the same husbandry, would do the like, are, without doubt, of the same natural intrinsic value: but yet the benefit mankind receives from the one in a year, is worth 5 [pounds], and from the other possibly not worth a penny, if all the profit an Indian received from it were to be valued, and sold here; at least, I may truly say, not one thousandth. It is labour then which puts the greatest part of value upon land, without which it would scarcely be worth any thing: it is to that we owe the greatest part of all its useful products; for all that the straw, bran, bread, of that acre of wheat, is more

worth than the product of an acre of as good land, which lies waste, is all the effect of labour: for it is not barely the plough-man's pains, the reaper's and thresher's toil, and the baker's sweat, is to be counted into the bread we eat; the labour of those who broke the oxen, who digged and wrought the iron and stones, who felled and framed the timber employed about the plough, mill, oven, or any other utensils, which are a vast number, requisite to this corn, from its being feed to be sown to its being made bread, must all be charged on the account of labour, and received as an effect of that: nature and the earth furnished only the almost worthless materials, as in themselves. It would be a strange catalogue of things, that industry provided and made use of, about every loaf of bread, before it came to our use, if we could trace them; iron, wood, leather, bark, timber, stone, bricks, coals, lime, cloth, dying drugs, pitch, tar, masts, ropes, and all the materials made use of in the ship, that brought any of the commodities made use of by any of the workmen, to any part of the work; all which it would be almost impossible, at least too long, to reckon up.

44. From all which it is evident, that though the things of nature are given in common, yet man, by being master of himself, and proprietor of his own person, and the actions or labour of it, had still in himself the great foundation of property; and that, which made up the great part of what he applied to the support or comfort of his being, when invention and arts had improved the conveniencies of life, was perfectly his own, and did not belong in common to others.

45. Thus labour, in the beginning, gave a right of property, wherever any one was pleased to employ it upon what was common, which remained a long while the far greater part, and is yet more than mankind makes use of. Men, at first, for the most part, contented themselves with what unassisted nature offered to their necessities: and though afterwards, in some parts of the world, (where the increase of people and stock, with the use of money, had made land scarce, and so of some value) the several

communities settled the bounds of their distinct territories, and by laws within themselves regulated the properties of the private men of their society, and so, by compact and agreement, settled the property which labour and industry began; and the leagues that have been made between several states and kingdoms, either expressly or tacitly disowning all claim and right to the land in the others possession, have, by common consent, given up their pretences to their natural common right, which originally they had to those countries, and so have, by positive agreement, settled a property amongst themselves, in distinct parts and parcels of the earth; yet there are still great tracts of ground to be found, which (the inhabitants thereof not having joined with the rest of mankind, in the consent of the use of their common money) lie waste, and are more than the people who dwell on it do, or can make use of, and so still lie in common; tho' this can scarce happen amongst that part of mankind that have consented to the use of money.

46. The greatest part of things really useful to the life of man, and such as the necessity of subsisting made the first commoners of the world look after, as it doth the Americans now, are generally things of short duration; such as, if they are not consumed by use, will decay and perish of themselves: gold, silver and diamonds, are things that fancy or agreement hath put the value on, more than real use, and the necessary support of life. Now of those good things which nature hath provided in common, every one had a right (as hath been said) to as much as he could use, and property in all that he could effect with his labour; all that his industry could extend to, to alter from the state nature had put it in, was his. He that gathered a hundred bushels of acorns or apples, had thereby a property in them, they were his goods as soon as gathered. He was only to look, that he used them before they spoiled, else he took more than his share, and robbed others. And indeed it was a foolish thing, as well as dishonest, to hoard up more than he could make use of. If he gave away a part to any body else, so that it perished not uselessly in his

possession, these he also made use of. And if he also bartered away plums, that would have rotted in a week, for nuts that would last good for his eating a whole year, he did no injury; he wasted not the common stock; destroyed no part of the portion of goods that belonged to others, so long as nothing perished uselessly in his hands. Again, if he would give his nuts for a piece of metal, pleased with its colour; or exchange his sheep for shells, or wool for a sparkling pebble or a diamond, and keep those by him all his life he invaded not the right of others, he might heap up as much of these durable things as he pleased; the exceeding of the bounds of his just property not lying in the largeness of his possession, but the perishing of any thing uselessly in it.

47. And thus came in the use of money, some lasting thing that men might keep without spoiling, and that by mutual consent men would take in exchange for the truly useful, but perishable supports of life.

48. And as different degrees of industry were apt to give men possessions in different proportions, so this invention of money gave them the opportunity to continue and enlarge them: for supposing an island, separate from all possible commerce with the rest of the world, wherein there were but an hundred families, but there were sheep, horses and cows, with other useful animals, wholesome fruits, and land enough for corn for a hundred thousand times as many, but nothing in the island, either because of its commonness, or perishableness, fit to supply the place of money; what reason could any one have there to enlarge his possessions beyond the use of his family, and a plentiful supply to its consumption, either in what their own industry produced, or they could barter for like perishable, useful commodities, with others? Where there is not some thing, both lasting and scarce, and so valuable to be hoarded up, there men will not be apt to enlarge their possessions of land, were it never so rich, never so free for them to take: for I ask, what would a man value ten thousand, or an hundred

thousand acres of excellent land, ready cultivated, and well stocked too with cattle, in the middle of the inland parts of America, where he had no hopes of commerce with other parts of the world, to draw money to him by the sale of the product? It would not be worth the enclosing, and we should see him give up again to the wild common of nature, whatever was more than would supply the conveniencies of life to be had there for him and his family.

49. Thus in the beginning all the world was America, and more so than that is now; for no such thing as money was any where known. Find out something that hath the use and value of money amongst his neighbours, you shall see the same man will begin presently to enlarge his possessions.

50. But since gold and silver, being little useful to the life of man in proportion to food, raiment, and carriage, has its value only from the consent of men, whereof labour yet makes, in great part, the measure, it is plain, that men have agreed to a disproportionate and unequal possession of the earth, they having, by a tacit and voluntary consent, found out, a way how a man may fairly possess more land than he himself can use the product of, by receiving in exchange for the overplus gold and silver, which may be hoarded up without injury to any one; these metals not spoiling or decaying in the hands of the possessor. This partage of things in an inequality of private possessions, men have made practicable out of the bounds of society, and without compact, only by putting a value on gold and silver, and tacitly agreeing in the use of money: for in governments, the laws regulate the right of property, and the possession of land is determined by positive constitutions.

51. And thus, I think, it is very easy to conceive, without any difficulty, how labour could at first begin a title of property in the common things of nature, and how the spending it upon our uses bounded it. So that there could then be no reason of quarrelling about title, nor any doubt about the largeness of possession it gave. Right and conveniency went

together; for as a man had a right to all he could employ his labour upon, so he had no temptation to labour for more than he could make use of. This left no room for controversy about the title, nor for encroachment on the right of others; what portion a man carved to himself, was easily seen; and it was useless, as well as dishonest, to carve himself too much, or take more than he needed.

DISCUSSION QUESTIONS

1. What does Locke means when he says that God has given the earth to "mankind in common"? What property is not given to all in common?

2. How does one person, in the state of nature, come to have exclusive property rights in some resource? What restrictions are placed on the acquisition of resources by individual persons?

3. Locke seems to offer both a right-based and a consequence-based justification of private property. Explain. Which justification do you think is more fundamental to Locke's account? Explain.

4. Compare and contrast the accounts of property offered by Locke and Hobbes (see reading 2). Whose account do you think is more plausible? Explain.

65

David Hume, selection from *Enquiry Concerning the Principles of Morals* (1751)

In this selection, Hume argues that a system of private property is ultimately justified on the grounds of its utility. On Hume, see reading 8 above.

SOURCE

Hume, David. *Enquiries Concerning the Human Understanding and Concerning the Principles of Morals* (Second Edition). Ed. L.A. Selby-Bigge. The Clarendon Press, 1902.

That Justice is useful to society, and consequently that part of its merit, at least, must arise from that consideration, it would be a superfluous undertaking to prove. That public utility is the sole origin of justice, and that reflections on the beneficial consequences of this virtue are the sole foundation of its merit; this proposition, being more curious and important, will better deserve our examination and enquiry.

Let us suppose, that nature has bestowed on the human race such profuse abundance of all external conveniences, that, without any uncertainty in the event, without any care or industry on our part, every individual finds himself fully provided with whatever his most voracious appetites can want, or luxurious imagination wish or desire. His natural beauty, we shall suppose, surpasses all acquired ornaments: The perpetual clemency of the seasons renders useless all clothes or covering: The raw herbage affords him the most delicious fare; the clear fountain, the richest beverage. No laborious occupation required: No tillage: No navigation. Music, poetry, and contemplation form his sole business: Conversation, mirth, and friendship his sole amusement.

It seems evident, that, in such a happy state, every other social virtue would flourish, and receive tenfold encrease; but the cautious, jealous virtue of justice would never once have been dreamed of. For what purpose make a partition of goods, where every one has already more than enough? Why give rise to property, where there cannot possibly be any injury? Why call this object mine, when, upon the seizing of it by another, I need but stretch out my hand to possess myself of what is equally valuable? Justice, in that case, being totally *useless*, would be an idle ceremonial, and could never possibly have place in the catalogue of virtues.

We see, even in the present necessitous condition of mankind, that, wherever any benefit is bestowed by nature in an unlimited abundance, we leave it always in common among the whole human race, and make no subdivisions of right and property. Water and air, though the most necessary of all objects, are not challenged as the property of individuals; nor can any man commit injustice by the most lavish use and enjoyment of these blessings. In fertile extensive countries, with few inhabitants, land is regarded on the same footing. And no topic is so much insisted on by those, who defend the liberty of the seas, as the unexhausted use of them in navigation. Were the advantages, procured by navigation, as inexhaustible, these reasoners had never had any adversaries to refute; nor had any claims ever been advanced of a separate, exclusive dominion over the ocean.

It may happen, in some countries, at some periods, that there be established a property in water, none in land; if the latter be in greater abundance than can be used by the inhabitants, and the former be found, with difficulty, and in very small quantities.

Again; suppose, that, though the necessities of human race continue the same as at present, yet the mind is so enlarged, and so replete with friendship and generosity, that every man has the utmost tenderness for every man, and feels no more concern for his own interest than for that of his fellows: It seems evident, that the *use* of justice would, in this case, be suspended by such an extensive benevolence, nor would the divisions and barriers of property and obligation have ever been thought of. Why should I bind another, by a deed or promise, to do me any good office, when I know that he is already prompted, by the strongest inclination, to seek my happiness, and would, of himself, perform the desired service; except the hurt, he thereby receives, be greater than the benefit accruing to me? in which case, he knows, that, from my innate humanity and friendship, I should be the first to oppose myself to his imprudent generosity. Why raise land-marks between my neighbour's field and mine, when my heart has made no division between our interests; but shares all his joys and sorrows with the same force and vivacity as if originally my own? Every man, upon this supposition, being a second self to another, would trust all his interests to the discretion of every man; without jealousy, without partition, without distinction. And the whole human race would form only one family; where all would lie in common, and be used freely, without regard to property; but cautiously too, with as entire regard to the necessities of each individual, as if our own interests were most intimately concerned.

In the present disposition of the human heart, it would, perhaps, be difficult to find complete instances of such enlarged affections; but still we may observe, that the case of families approaches towards it; and the stronger the mutual benevolence is among the individuals, the nearer it approaches; till all distinction of property be, in a great measure, lost and confounded among them. Between married persons, the cement of friendship is by the laws supposed so strong as to abolish all division of possessions; and has often, in reality, the force ascribed to it. And it is observable, that, during the ardour of new enthusiasms, when every principle is inflamed into extravagance, the community of goods has frequently been attempted; and nothing but experience of its inconveniencies, from the returning or disguised selfishness of men, could make the imprudent fanatics adopt anew the ideas of justice and of separate property. So true is it, that this virtue derives its existence entirely from its necessary use to the intercourse and social state of mankind.

To make this truth more evident, let us reverse the foregoing suppositions; and carrying every thing to the opposite extreme, consider what would be the effect of these new situations. Suppose a society to fall into such want of all common necessaries, that the utmost frugality and industry cannot preserve the greater number from perishing, and the whole from extreme misery: It will readily, I believe, be admitted, that the strict laws of justice are suspended, in such a pressing emergence, and give place to the stronger motives of necessity and self-preservation. Is it any crime, after a shipwreck, to seize whatever means or instrument of safety one can lay hold of, without regard to former limitations of property? Or if a city besieged were perishing with hunger; can we imagine, that men will see any means of preservation before them, and lose their lives, from a scrupulous regard to what, in other situations, would be the rules of equity and justice? The *use* and *tendency* of that virtue is to procure happiness and security, by preserving order in society: But where the society is ready to perish from extreme necessity, no greater evil can be dreaded from violence and injustice; and every man may now provide for himself by all the means, which prudence can dictate, or humanity permit. The public, even in less urgent necessities, opens granaries, without the consent of proprietors; as justly supposing, that the authority of magistracy may, consistent with equity, extend so far: But were any number of men to assemble, without the tie of laws or civil jurisdiction; would an equal partition of bread in a famine, though effected by power and even violence, be regarded as criminal or injurious?

Suppose likewise, that it should be a virtuous man's fate to fall into the society of ruffians, remote from the protection of laws and government; what conduct must he embrace in that melancholy situation? He sees such a desperate rapaciousness prevail; such a disregard to equity, such contempt of order, such stupid blindness to future consequences, as must immediately have the most tragical conclusion, and must terminate in destruction to the greater number, and in a total dissolution of society to the rest. He, meanwhile, can have no other expedient than to arm himself, to whomever the sword he seizes, or the buckler, may belong: To make provision of all means of defence and security: And his particular regard to justice being no longer of use to his own safety or that of others, he must consult the dictates of self-preservation alone, without concern for those who no longer merit his care and attention.

When any man, even in political society, renders himself, by his crimes, obnoxious to the public, he is punished by the laws in his goods and person; that is, the ordinary rules of justice are, with regard to him, suspended for a moment, and it becomes equitable to inflict on him, for the benefit of society, what, otherwise, he could not suffer without wrong or injury.

The rage and violence of public war; what is it but a suspension of justice among the warring parties, who perceive, that this virtue is now no longer of any use or advantage to them? The laws of war, which then succeed to those of equity and justice, are rules calculated for the advantage and utility of that particular state, in which men are now placed. And were a civilized nation engaged with barbarians, who observed no rules even of war, the former must also suspend their observance of them, where they no longer serve to any purpose; and must render every action or re-encounter as bloody and pernicious as possible to the first aggressors.

Thus, the rules of equity or justice depend entirely on the particular state and condition, in which men are placed, and owe their origin and existence to that *utility*, which results to the public from their strict and regular observance. Reverse, in any considerable circumstance, the condition of men: Produce extreme abundance or extreme necessity: Implant in the human breast perfect moderation and humanity, or perfect rapaciousness and malice: By rendering justice totally useless, you thereby totally destroy its essence, and suspend its obligation upon mankind.

The common situation of society is a medium amidst all these extremes. We are naturally partial to ourselves, and to our friends; but are capable of learning the advantage resulting from a more equitable conduct. Few enjoyments are given us from the open and liberal hand of nature; but by art, labour, and industry, we can extract them in great abundance. Hence the ideas of property become necessary in all civil society: Hence justice derives its usefulness to the public: And hence alone arises its merit and moral obligation.

These conclusions are so natural and obvious, that they have not escaped even the poets, in their descriptions of the felicity, attending the golden age or the reign of Saturn. The seasons, in that first period of nature, were so temperate, if we credit these agreeable fictions, that there was no necessity for men to provide themselves with clothes and houses, as a security against the violence of heat and cold: The rivers flowed with wine and milk: The oaks yielded honey; and nature spontaneously produced her greatest delicacies. Nor were these the chief advantages of that happy age. Tempests were not alone removed from nature; but those more furious tempests were unknown to human breasts, which now cause such uproar, and engender such confusion. Avarice, ambition, cruelty, selfishness, were never heard of: Cordial affection, compassion, sympathy, were the only movements with which the mind was yet acquainted. Even the punctilious distinction of mine and thine was banished from among that happy race of mortals, and carried with it the very notion of property and obligation, justice and injustice.

This poetical fiction of the golden age is, in some respects, of a piece with the philosophical fiction of the state of nature; only that the former is represented as the most charming and most peaceable condition, which can possibly be imagined; whereas the latter is painted out as a state of mutual war and violence, attended with the most extreme necessity. On the first origin of mankind, we are told, their ignorance and savage nature were so prevalent, that they could give no mutual trust, but must each depend upon himself, and his own force or cunning for protection and security. No law was heard of: No rule of justice known: No distinction of property regarded: Power was the only measure of right; and a perpetual war of all against all was the result of men's untamed selfishness and barbarity.

Whether such a condition of human nature could ever exist, or if it did, could continue so long as to merit the appellation of a state, may justly be doubted. Men are necessarily born in a family-society, at least; and are trained up by their parents to some rule of conduct and behaviour. But this must be admitted, that, if such a state of mutual war and violence was ever real, the suspension of all laws of justice, from their absolute inutility, is a necessary and infallible consequence.

The more we vary our views of human life, and the newer and more unusual the lights are, in which we survey it, the more shall we be convinced, that the origin here assigned for the virtue of justice is real and satisfactory.

Were there a species of creatures, intermingled with men, which, though rational, were possessed of such inferior strength, both of body and mind, that they were incapable of all resistance, and could never, upon the highest provocation, make us feel the effects of their resentment; the necessary consequence, I think, is, that we should be bound, by the laws of humanity, to give gentle usage to these creatures, but should not, properly speaking, lie under any restraint of justice with regard to them, nor could they possess any right or property, exclusive of such arbitrary lords. Our intercourse with them could not be called society, which supposes a degree of equality; but absolute command on the one side, and servile obedience on the other. Whatever we covet, they must instantly resign: Our permission is the only tenure, by which they hold their possessions: Our compassion and kindness the only check, by which they curb our lawless will: And as no inconvenience ever results from the exercise of a power, so firmly established in nature, the restraints of justice and property, being totally useless, would never have place in so unequal a confederacy.

This is plainly the situation of men, with regard to animals; and how far these may be said to possess reason, I leave it to others to determine. The great superiority of civilized EUROPEANS above barbarous INDIANS, tempted us to imagine ourselves on the same footing with regard to them, and made us throw off all restraints of justice, and even of humanity, in our treatment of them. In many nations, the female sex are reduced to like slavery, and are rendered incapable of all property, in opposition to their lordly masters. But though the males, when united, have, in all countries, bodily force sufficient to maintain this severe tyranny, yet such are the insinuation, address, and charms of their fair companions, that women are commonly able to break the confederacy, and share with the other sex in all the rights and privileges of society.

Were the human species so framed by nature as that each individual possessed within himself every faculty, requisite both for his own preservation and for the propagation of his kind: Were all society and intercourse cut off between man and man, by the primary intention of the supreme Creator: It seems evident, that so solitary a being would be as much incapable of justice, as of social discourse and conversation. Where mutual regards and forbearance serve to no manner of purpose, they would never direct the conduct of any reasonable man. The headlong course of the passions would be checked by no reflection on future consequences. And as each man is here supposed to love himself alone, and to depend only on himself and his own activity for safety and happiness, he would, on every occasion, to the utmost of his power, challenge the preference above every other being, to none of which he is bound by any ties, either of nature or of interest.

But suppose the conjunction of the sexes to be established in nature, a family immediately arises; and particular rules being found requisite for its subsistence, these are immediately embraced; though without comprehending the rest of mankind within their prescriptions. Suppose, that several families unite together into one society, which is totally disjoined from all others, the rules, which preserve peace and order, enlarge themselves to the utmost extent of that society; but becoming then entirely useless, lose their force when carried one step farther. But again suppose, that several distinct societies maintain a kind of intercourse for mutual convenience and advantage, the boundaries of justice still grow larger, in proportion to the largeness of men's views, and the force of their mutual connexions. History, experience, reason sufficiently instruct us in this natural progress of human sentiments, and in the gradual enlargement of our regards to justice, in proportion as we become acquainted with the extensive utility of that virtue.

Part II.

If we examine the particular laws, by which justice is directed, and property determined; we shall still be presented with the same conclusion. The good of mankind is the only object of all these laws and regulations. Not only is it requisite, for the peace and interest of society, that men's possessions should be separated; but the rules, which we follow, in making the separation, are such as can best be contrived to serve farther the interests of society.

We shall suppose, that a creature, possessed of reason, but unacquainted with human nature, deliberates with himself what *rules* of justice or property would best promote public interest, and establish peace and security among mankind: His most obvious thought would be, to assign the largest possessions to the most extensive virtue, and give every one the power of doing good, proportioned to his inclination. In a perfect theocracy, where a being, infinitely intelligent, governs by particular volitions, this rule would certainly have place, and might serve to the wisest purposes: But were mankind to execute such a law; so great is the uncertainty of merit, both from its natural obscurity, and from the self-conceit of each individual, that no determinate rule of conduct would ever result from it; and the total dissolution of society must be the immediate consequence. Fanatics may suppose, that dominion is founded on grace, and that saints alone inherit the earth; but the civil magistrate very justly puts these sublime theorists on the same footing with common robbers, and teaches them by the severest discipline, that a rule, which, in speculation, may seem the most advantageous to society, may yet be found, in practice, totally pernicious and destructive.

That there were religious fanatics of this kind in ENGLAND, during the civil wars, we learn from history; though it is probable, that the obvious tendency of these principles excited such horror in mankind, as soon obliged the dangerous enthusiasts to renounce, or at least conceal their tenets. Perhaps, the levellers, who claimed an equal distribution of property, were a kind of political fanatics, which arose from the religious species, and more openly avowed their pretensions; as carrying a more plausible appearance, of being practicable in themselves, as well as useful to human society.

It must, indeed, be confessed, that nature is so liberal to mankind, that, were all her presents equally divided among the species, and improved by art and industry, every individual would enjoy all the necessaries, and even most of the comforts of life; nor would ever be liable to any ills, but such as might accidentally arise from the sickly frame and constitution of his body. It must also be confessed, that, wherever we depart from this equality, we rob the poor of more satisfaction than we add to the rich, and that the slight gratification of a frivolous vanity, in one individual, frequently costs more than bread to many families, and even provinces. It may appear withal, that the rule of equality, as it would be highly useful, is not altogether impracticable; but has taken place, at least in an imperfect degree, in some republics; particularly that of SPARTA; where it was attended, it is said, with the most beneficial consequences. Not to mention, that the AGRARIAN laws, so frequently claimed in ROME, and carried into execution in many GREEK cities, proceeded, all of them, from a general idea of the utility of this principle.

But historians, and even common sense, may inform us, that, however specious these ideas of perfect equality may seem, they are really, at bottom, impracticable; and were they not so, would be extremely pernicious to human society. Render possessions ever so equal, men's different degrees of art, care, and industry will immediately break that equality. Or if you check these virtues, you reduce society to the most extreme indigence; and instead of preventing want and beggary in a few, render it unavoidable to the whole community. The most rigorous inquisition too is requisite to watch every inequality on its first appearance; and the most severe jurisdiction, to punish and redress it. But besides, that so much authority must soon degenerate into tyranny, and be exerted with great partialities; who can possibly be possessed of it, in such a situation as is here supposed? Perfect equality of possessions, destroying all subordination, weakens extremely the authority of magistracy, and must reduce all power nearly to a level, as well as property.

We may conclude, therefore, that, in order to establish laws for the regulation of property, we must be acquainted with the nature and situation of man; must reject appearances which may be false, though specious; and must search for those rules, which are, on the whole, most useful and beneficial. Vulgar sense and slight experience are sufficient for this purpose; where men give not way to too selfish avidity, or too extensive enthusiasm.

Who sees not, for instance, that whatever is produced or improved by a man's art or industry ought, for ever, to be secured to him, in order to give encouragement to such useful habits and accomplishments? That the property ought also to descend to children and relations, for the same useful purpose? That it may be alienated by consent, in order to beget that commerce and intercourse, which is so beneficial to human society? And that all contracts and promises ought carefully to be fulfilled, in order to secure mutual trust and confidence, by which the general interest of mankind is so much promoted?

Examine the writers on the laws of nature; and you will always find, that, whatever principles they set out with, they are sure to terminate here at last, and to assign, as the ultimate reason for every rule which they establish, the convenience and necessities of mankind. A concession thus extorted, in opposition to systems, has more authority than if it had been made in prosecution of them.

What other reason, indeed, could writers ever give, why this must be mine and that yours, since uninstructed nature, surely, never made any such distinction? The objects, which receive those appellations, are, of themselves, foreign to us; they are totally disjoined and separated from us; and nothing but the general interests of society can form the connexion.

Sometimes, the interests of society may require a rule of justice in a particular case; but may not determine any particular rule, among several, which are all equally beneficial. In that case, the slightest analogies are laid hold of, in order to prevent that indifference and ambiguity, which would be the source of perpetual dissention. Thus possession alone, and first possession, is supposed to convey property, where no body else has any preceding claim and pretension. Many of the reasonings of lawyers are of this analogical nature, and depend on very slight connexions of the imagination.

Does any one scruple, in extraordinary cases, to violate all regard to the private property of individuals, and sacrifice to public interest a distinction, which had been established for the sake of that interest? The safety of the people is the supreme law: All other particular laws are subordinate to it, and dependant on it: And if, in the common course of things, they be followed and regarded; it is only because the public safety and interest commonly demand so equal and impartial an administration.

Sometimes both utility and analogy fail, and leave the laws of justice in total uncertainty. Thus, it is highly requisite, that prescription or long possession should convey property; but what number of days or months or years should be sufficient for that purpose, it is impossible for reason alone to determine. Civil laws here supply the place of the natural code, and assign different terms for prescription, according to the different utilities, proposed by the legislator. Bills of exchange and promissory notes, by the laws of most countries, prescribe sooner than bonds, and mortgages, and contracts of a more formal nature.

In general, we may observe, that all questions of property are subordinate to the authority of civil laws, which extend, restrain, modify, and alter the rules of natural justice, according to the particular convenience of each community. The laws have, or ought to have, a constant reference to the constitution of government, the manners, the climate, the religion, the commerce, the situation of each

society. A late author of genius, as well as learning, has prosecuted this subject at large, and has established, from these principles, a system of political knowledge, which abounds in ingenious and brilliant thoughts, and is not wanting in solidity.

What is a man's property? Any thing, which it is lawful for him, and for him alone, to use. But what rule have we, by which we can distinguish these objects? Here we must have recourse to statutes, customs, precedents, analogies, and a hundred other circumstances; some of which are constant and inflexible, some variable and arbitrary. But the ultimate point, in which they all professedly terminate, is, the interest and happiness of human society. Where this enters not into consideration, nothing can appear more whimsical, unnatural, and even superstitious, than all or most of the laws of justice and of property.

Those, who ridicule vulgar superstitions, and expose the folly of particular regards to meats, days, places, postures, apparel, have an easy task; while they consider all the qualities and relations of the objects, and discover no adequate cause for that affection or antipathy, veneration or horror, which have so mighty an influence over a considerable part of mankind. A SYRIAN would have starved rather than taste pigeon; an EGYPTIAN would not have approached bacon: But if these species of food be examined by the senses of sight, smell, or taste, or scrutinized by the sciences of chemistry, medicine, or physics; no difference is ever found between them and any other species, nor can that precise circumstance be pitched on, which may afford a just foundation for the religious passion. A fowl on Thursday is lawful food; on Friday abominable: Eggs, in this house, and in this diocese, are permitted during Lent; a hundred paces farther, to eat them is a damnable sin. This earth or building, yesterday was profane; to-day, by the muttering of certain words, it has become holy and sacred. Such reflections as these, in the mouth of a philosopher, one may safely say, are too obvious to have any influence; because they must always, to every man, occur at first sight; and where they prevail not, of themselves, they are surely obstructed by education, prejudice, and passion, not by ignorance or mistake.

It may appear to a careless view, or rather a too abstracted reflection, that there enters a like superstition into all the sentiments of justice; and that, if a man expose its object, or what we call property, to the same scrutiny of sense and science, he will not, by the most accurate enquiry, find any foundation for the difference made by moral sentiment. I may lawfully nourish myself from this tree; but the fruit of another of the same species, ten paces off, it is criminal for me to touch. Had I worn this apparel an hour ago, I had merited the severest punishment; but a man, by pronouncing a few magical syllables, has now rendered it fit for my use and service. Were this house placed in the neighbouring territory, it had been immoral for me to dwell in it; but being built on this side of the river, it is subject to a different municipal law, and, by its becoming mine, I incur no blame or censure. The same species of reasoning, it may be thought, which so successfully exposes superstition, is also applicable to justice; nor is it possible, in the one case more than in the other, to point out, in the object, that precise quality or circumstance, which is the foundation of the sentiment.

But there is this material difference between superstition and justice, that the former is frivolous, useless, and burdensome; the latter is absolutely requisite to the well-being of mankind and existence of society. When we abstract from this circumstance (for it is too apparent ever to be overlooked) it must be confessed, that all regards to right and property, seem entirely without foundation, as much as the grossest and most vulgar superstition. Were the interests of society no wise concerned, it is as unintelligible, why another's articulating certain sounds implying consent, should change the nature of my actions with regard to a particular object, as why the reciting of a liturgy by a priest, in a certain habit and posture, should dedicate a heap of brick and timber, and render it, thenceforth and for ever, sacred.

These reflections are far from weakening the obligations of justice, or diminishing any thing from the most sacred attention to property. On the contrary, such sentiments must acquire new force from the present reasoning. For what stronger foundation can be desired or conceived for any duty, than to observe, that human society, or even human nature could not subsist, without the establishment of it; and will still arrive at greater degrees of happiness and perfection, the more inviolable the regard is, which is paid to that duty?

The dilemma seems obvious: As justice evidently tends to promote public utility and to support civil society, the sentiment of justice is either derived from our reflecting on that tendency, or like hunger, thirst, and other appetites, resentment, love of life, attachment to offspring, and other passions, arises from a simple original instinct in the human breast, which nature has implanted for like salutary purposes. If the latter be the case, it follows, that property, which is the object of justice, is also distinguished by a simple, original instinct, and is not ascertained by any argument or reflection. But who is there that ever heard of such an instinct? Or is this a subject, in which new discoveries can be made? We may as well expect to discover, in the body, new senses, which had before escaped the observation of all mankind.

But farther, though it seems a very simple proposition to say, that nature, by an instinctive sentiment, distinguishes property, yet in reality we shall find, that there are required for that purpose ten thousand different instincts, and these employed about objects of the greatest intricacy and nicest discernment. For when a definition of property is required, that relation is found to resolve itself into any possession acquired by occupation, by industry, by prescription, by inheritance, by contract, &c. Can we think, that nature, by an original instinct, instructs us in all these methods of acquisition?

These words too, inheritance and contract, stand for ideas infinitely complicated; and to define them exactly, a hundred volumes of laws, and a thousand volumes of commentators, have not been found sufficient. Does nature, whose instincts in men are all simple, embrace such complicated and artificial objects, and create a rational creature, without trusting any thing to the operation of his reason?

But even though all this were admitted, it would not be satisfactory. Positive laws can certainly transfer property. Is it by another original instinct, that we recognize the authority of kings and senates, and mark all the boundaries of their jurisdiction? Judges too, even though their sentence be erroneous and illegal, must be allowed, for the sake of peace and order, to have decisive authority, and ultimately to determine property. Have we original, innate ideas of praetors, and chancellors and juries? Who sees not, that all these institutions arise merely from the necessities of human society?

All birds of the same species, in every age and country, build their nests alike: In this we see the force of instinct. Men, in different times and places, frame their houses differently: Here we perceive the influence of reason and custom. A like inference may be drawn from comparing the instinct of generation and the institution of property.

How great soever the variety of municipal laws, it must be confessed, that their chief out-lines pretty regularly concur; because the purposes, to which they tend, are every where exactly similar. In like manner, all houses have a roof and walls, windows and chimneys; though diversified in their shape, figure, and materials. The purposes of the latter, directed to the conveniences of human life, discover not more plainly their origin from reason and reflection, than do those of the former, which point all to a like end.

I need not mention the variations, which all the rules of property receive from the finer turns and connexions of the imagination, and from the subtleties and abstractions of law-topics and reasonings. There is no possibility of reconciling this observation to the notion of original instincts.

What alone will beget a doubt concerning the theory, on which I insist, is the influence of education and acquired habits, by which we are so accustomed to blame injustice, that we are not, in every instance, conscious of any immediate reflection on the pernicious consequences of it. The views the most familiar to us are apt, for that very reason, to escape us; and what we have very frequently performed from certain motives, we are apt likewise to continue mechanically, without recalling, on every occasion, the reflections, which first determined us. The convenience, or rather necessity, which leads to justice, is so universal, and every where points so much to the same rules, that the habit takes place in all societies; and it is not without some scrutiny, that we are able to ascertain its true origin. The matter, however, is not so obscure, but that, even in common life, we have, every moment, recourse to the principle of public utility, and ask, What must become of the world, if such practices prevail? How could society subsist under such disorders? Were the distinction or separation of possessions entirely useless, can any one conceive, that it ever should have obtained in society?

Thus we seem, upon the whole, to have attained a knowledge of the force of that principle here insisted on, and can determine what degree of esteem or moral approbation may result from reflections on public interest and utility. The necessity of justice to the support of society is the *sole* foundation of that virtue; and since no moral excellence is more highly esteemed, we may conclude, that this circumstance of usefulness has, in general, the strongest energy, and most entire command over our sentiments. It must, therefore, be the source of a considerable part of the merit ascribed to humanity, benevolence, friendship, public spirit, and other social virtues of that stamp; as it is the *sole* source of the moral approbation paid to fidelity, justice, veracity, integrity, and those other estimable and useful qualities and principles. It is entirely agreeable to the rules of philosophy, and even of common reason; where any principle has been found to have a great force and energy in one instance, to ascribe to it a like energy in all similar instances. This indeed is NEWTON's chief rule of philosophizing.

DISCUSSION QUESTIONS

1. Hume justifies the rules of property in the same way that he justifies all of the other rules of justice, by an appeal to their utility. Explain why Hume thinks that rules of private property are useful.

2. Explain how Hume uses the conditions of extreme scarcity and of extreme abundance to show that "public utility is the *sole* origin of justice." Is this appeal plausible? Explain.

3. How does Hume's account of property rules differ from that offered by Hobbes? How does it differ from that offered by Locke? Which of these three accounts do you think is most plausible? Explain.

66

Adam Smith, selection from *The Wealth of Nations* (1776)

Adam Smith (1723–90) was a Scottish moral philosopher who is widely considered the father of capitalism in particular, and modern economics more generally. In this selection from *The Wealth of Nations*, Smith presents his celebrated notion of "the invisible hand," which figures centrally into consequentialist justifications of capitalism.

SOURCE

Smith, Adam. *The Wealth of Nations* (5th Edition). Ed. E. Cannan. Methuen & Co., Ltd., 1904.

Of the Division of Labour

The greatest improvement in the productive powers of labour, and the greater part of the skill, dexterity, and judgment with which it is anywhere directed, or applied, seem to have been the effects of the division of labour.

The effects of the division of labour, in the general business of society, will be more easily understood by considering in what manner it operates in some particular manufactures. It is commonly supposed to be carried furthest in some very trifling ones; not perhaps that it really is carried further in them than in others of more importance: but in those trifling manufactures which are destined to supply the small wants of but a small number of people, the whole number of workmen must necessarily be small; and those employed in every different branch of the work can often be collected into the same workhouse, and placed at once under the view of the spectator. In those great manufactures, on the contrary, which are destined to supply the great wants of the great body of the people, every different branch of the work employs so great a number of workmen that it is impossible to collect them all into the same workhouse. We can seldom see more, at one time, than those employed in one single branch. Though in such manufactures, therefore, the work may really be divided into a much greater number of parts than in those of a more trifling nature, the division is not near so obvious, and has accordingly been much less observed.

To take an example, therefore, from a very trifling manufacture; but one in which the division of labour has been very often taken notice of, the trade of the pin-maker; a workman not educated to this business (which the division of labour has rendered a distinct trade), nor acquainted with the use of the machinery employed in it (to the invention of which the same division of labour has probably given occasion), could scarce, perhaps, with his utmost industry, make one pin in a day, and certainly could not make twenty. But in the way in which this business is now carried on, not only the whole work is a peculiar trade, but it is divided into a number of branches, of which the greater part are likewise peculiar trades. One man draws out the wire, another straights it, a third cuts it, a fourth points it, a fifth grinds it at the top for receiving the head; to make the head requires two or three distinct operations; to put it on is a peculiar business, to whiten the pins is another; it is even a trade by itself to put them into the paper; and the important business of making a pin is, in this manner, divided into about eighteen distinct operations, which, in some manufactories, are all performed by distinct hands, though in others the same man will sometimes perform two or three of them. I have seen a small manufactory of this kind where ten men only were employed, and where some of them consequently performed two or three distinct operations. But though they were very poor, and therefore but indifferently accommodated with the necessary machinery, they could, when they exerted themselves, make among them about twelve pounds of pins in a day. There are in a pound upwards of four thousand pins of a middling size. Those ten persons, therefore, could make among them upwards of forty-eight thousand pins in a day. Each person, therefore, making a tenth part of forty-eight thousand pins, might be considered as making four thousand eight hundred pins in a day. But if they had all wrought separately and independently, and without any of them having been educated to this peculiar business, they certainly could not each of them

have made twenty, perhaps not one pin in a day; that is, certainly, not the two hundred and fortieth, perhaps not the four thousand eight hundredth part of what they are at present capable of performing, in consequence of a proper division and combination of their different operations.

In every other art and manufacture, the effects of the division of labour are similar to what they are in this very trifling one; though, in many of them, the labour can neither be so much subdivided, nor reduced to so great a simplicity of operation. The division of labour, however, so far as it can be introduced, occasions, in every art, a proportionable increase of the productive powers of labour. The separation of different trades and employments from one another seems to have taken place in consequence of this advantage. This separation, too, is generally called furthest in those countries which enjoy the highest degree of industry and improvement; what is the work of one man in a rude state of society being generally that of several in an improved one. In every improved society, the farmer is generally nothing but a farmer; the manufacturer, nothing but a manufacturer. The labour, too, which is necessary to produce any one complete manufacture is almost always divided among a great number of hands. How many different trades are employed in each branch of the linen and woollen manufactures from the growers of the flax and the wool, to the bleachers and smoothers of the linen, or to the dyers and dressers of the cloth! The nature of agriculture, indeed, does not admit of so many subdivisions of labour, nor of so complete a separation of one business from another, as manufactures. It is impossible to separate so entirely the business of the grazier from that of the corn-farmer as the trade of the carpenter is commonly separated from that of the smith. The spinner is almost always a distinct person from the weaver; but the ploughman, the harrower, the sower of the seed, and the reaper of the corn, are often the same. The occasions for those different sorts of labour returning with the different seasons of the year, it is impossible that one man should be constantly employed in any one of them. This impossibility of making so complete and entire a separation of all the different branches of labour employed in agriculture is perhaps the reason why the improvement of the productive powers of labour in this art does not always keep pace with their improvement in manufactures. The most opulent nations, indeed, generally excel all their neighbours in agriculture as well as in manufactures; but they are commonly more distinguished by their superiority in the latter than in the former. Their lands are in general better cultivated, and having more labour and expense bestowed upon them, produce more in proportion to the extent and natural fertility of the ground. But this superiority of produce is seldom much more than in proportion to the superiority of labour and expense. In agriculture, the labour of the rich country is not always much more productive than that of the poor; or, at least, it is never so much more productive as it commonly is in manufactures. The corn of the rich country, therefore, will not always, in the same degree of goodness, come cheaper to market than that of the poor. The corn of Poland, in the same degree of goodness, is as cheap as that of France, notwithstanding the superior opulence and improvement of the latter country. The corn of France is, in the corn provinces, fully as good, and in most years nearly about the same price with the corn of England, though, in opulence and improvement, France is perhaps inferior to England. The corn-lands of England, however, are better cultivated than those of France, and the corn-lands of France are said to be much better cultivated than those of Poland. But though the poor country, notwithstanding the inferiority of its cultivation, can, in some measure, rival the rich in the cheapness and goodness of its corn, it can pretend to no such competition in its manufactures; at least if those manufactures suit the soil, climate, and situation of the rich country. The silks of France are better and cheaper than those of England, because the silk manufacture, at least under the present high duties upon the importation of raw silk, does not so well suit the climate of England as that of France. But the hardware and the coarse woollens of England are beyond all comparison superior to those of France, and much cheaper too in the same degree of goodness. In Poland there are said to be scarce any manufactures of any kind, a few of those coarser household manufactures excepted, without which no country can well subsist.

This great increase of the quantity of work which, in consequence of the division of labour, the same number of people are capable of performing, is owing to three different circumstances; first, to the increase of dexterity in every particular workman; secondly, to the saving of the time which is commonly lost in passing from one species of work to another; and lastly, to the invention of a great number of machines which facilitate and abridge labour, and enable one man to do the work of many.

First, the improvement of the dexterity of the workman necessarily increases the quantity of the work he can perform; and the division of labour, by reducing every man's business to some one simple operation, and by making this operation the sole employment of his life, necessarily increased very much dexterity of the workman. A common smith, who, though accustomed to handle the hammer, has never been used to make nails, if upon some particular occasion he is obliged to attempt it, will scarce, I am assured, be able to make above two or three hundred nails in a day, and those too very bad ones. A smith who has been accustomed to make nails, but whose sole or principal business has not been that of a nailer, can seldom with his utmost diligence make more than eight hundred or a thousand nails in a day. I have seen several boys under twenty years of age who had never exercised any other trade but that of making nails, and who, when they exerted themselves, could make, each of them, upwards of two thousand three hundred nails in a day. The making of a nail, however, is by no means one of the simplest operations. The same person blows the bellows, stirs or mends the fire as there is occasion, heats the iron, and forges every part of the nail: in forging the head too he is obliged to change his tools. The different operations into which the making of a pin, or of a metal button, is subdivided, are all of them much more simple, and the dexterity of the person, of whose life it has been the sole business to perform them, is usually much greater. The rapidity with which some of the operations of those manufacturers are performed, exceeds what the human hand could, by those who had never seen them, be supposed capable of acquiring.

Secondly, the advantage which is gained by saving the time commonly lost in passing from one sort of work to another is much greater than we should at first view be apt to imagine it. It is impossible to pass very quickly from one kind of work to another that is carried on in a different place and with quite different tools. A country weaver, who cultivates a small farm, must lose a good deal of time in passing from his loom to the field, and from the field to his loom. When the two trades can be carried on in the same workhouse, the loss of time is no doubt much less. It is even in this case, however, very considerable. A man commonly saunters a little in turning his hand from one sort of employment to another. When he first begins the new work he is seldom very keen and hearty; his mind, as they say, does not go to it, and for some time he rather trifles than applies to good purpose. The habit of sauntering and of indolent careless application, which is naturally, or rather necessarily acquired by every country workman who is obliged to change his work and his tools every half hour, and to apply his hand in twenty different ways almost every day of his life, renders him almost always slothful and lazy, and incapable of any vigorous application even on the most pressing occasions. Independent, therefore, of his deficiency in point of dexterity, this cause alone must always reduce considerably the quantity of work which he is capable of performing.

Thirdly, and lastly, everybody must be sensible how much labour is facilitated and abridged by the application of proper machinery. It is unnecessary to give any example. I shall only observe, therefore, that the invention of all those machines by which labour is so much facilitated and abridged seems to have been originally owing to the division of labour. Men are much more likely to discover easier and readier methods of attaining any object when the whole attention of their minds is directed towards that single object than when it is dissipated among a great variety of things. But in consequence of the division of labour, the whole of every man's attention comes naturally to be directed towards some one very simple object. It is naturally to be expected, therefore, that some one or other of those who are employed in each particular branch of labour should soon find out easier and readier methods of performing their own particular work, wherever the nature of it admits of such improvement. A great part of the machines made use of in those manufactures in which labour is most subdivided, were originally the inventions of common workmen, who, being each of them employed in some very simple operation, naturally turned their thoughts towards finding out easier and readier methods of performing it. Whoever has been much accustomed to visit such manufactures must frequently have been shown very pretty machines, which were the inventions of such workmen in order to facilitate and quicken their particular part of the work. In the first fire-engines, a boy was constantly employed to open and shut alternately the communication between the boiler and the cylinder, according as the piston either ascended or descended. One of those boys, who loved to play with his companions, observed that, by tying a string from the handle of the valve which opened this communication to another part of the machine, the valve would open and shut without his assistance, and leave him at liberty to divert himself with his playfellows. One of the greatest improvements that has been made upon this machine, since it was first invented, was in this manner the discovery of a boy who wanted to save his own labour.

All the improvements in machinery, however, have by no means been the inventions of those who had occasion to use the machines. Many improvements have been made by the ingenuity of the makers of the machines, when to make them became the business of a peculiar trade; and some by that of those who are called philosophers or men of speculation, whose trade it is not to do anything, but to observe everything; and who, upon that account, are often capable of combining together the powers of the most distant and dissimilar objects. In the progress of society, philosophy or speculation becomes, like every other employment, the principal or sole trade and occupation of a particular class of citizens. Like every other employment too, it is subdivided into a great number of different branches, each of which affords occupation to a peculiar tribe or class of philosophers; and this subdivision of employment in philosophy, as well as in every other business, improves dexterity, and saves time. Each individual becomes more expert in his own peculiar branch, more work is done upon the whole, and the quantity of science is considerably increased by it.

It is the great multiplication of the productions of all the different arts, in consequence of the division of labour, which occasions, in a well-governed society, that universal opulence which extends itself to the lowest ranks of the people. Every workman has a great quantity of his own work to dispose of beyond what he himself has occasion for; and every other workman being exactly in the same situation, he is enabled to exchange a great quantity of his own goods for a great quantity, or, what comes to the same thing, for the price of a great quantity of theirs. He supplies them abundantly with what they have occasion for, and they accommodate him as amply with what he has occasion for, and a general plenty diffuses itself through all the different ranks of the society.

Observe the accommodation of the most common artificer or day-labourer in a civilised and thriving country, and you will perceive that the number of people of whose industry a part, though but a small part, has been employed in procuring him this accommodation, exceeds all computation. The woollen coat, for example, which covers the day-labourer, as coarse and rough as it may appear, is the produce of the joint labour of a great multitude of workmen. The shepherd, the sorter of the wool, the wool-comber or carder, the dyer, the scribbler, the spinner, the weaver, the fuller, the dresser, with many others, must all join their different arts in order to complete even this homely production. How many merchants and carriers, besides, must have been employed in transporting the materials

from some of those workmen to others who often live in a very distant part of the country! How much commerce and navigation in particular, how many ship-builders, sailors, sail-makers, rope-makers, must have been employed in order to bring together the different drugs made use of by the dyer, which often come from the remotest corners of the world! What a variety of labour, too, is necessary in order to produce the tools of the meanest of those workmen! To say nothing of such complicated machines as the ship of the sailor, the mill of the fuller, or even the loom of the weaver, let us consider only what a variety of labour is requisite in order to form that very simple machine, the shears with which the shepherd clips the wool. The miner, the builder of the furnace for smelting the ore, the seller of the timber, the burner of the charcoal to be made use of in the smelting-house, the brick-maker, the brick-layer, the workmen who attend the furnace, the mill-wright, the forger, the smith, must all of them join their different arts in order to produce them. Were we to examine, in the same manner, all the different parts of his dress and household furniture, the coarse linen shirt which he wears next his skin, the shoes which cover his feet, the bed which he lies on, and all the different parts which compose it, the kitchen-grate at which he prepares his victuals, the coals which he makes use of for that purpose, dug from the bowels of the earth, and brought to him perhaps by a long sea and a long land carriage, all the other utensils of his kitchen, all the furniture of his table, the knives and forks, the earthen or pewter plates upon which he serves up and divides his victuals, the different hands employed in preparing his bread and his beer, the glass window which lets in the heat and the light, and keeps out the wind and the rain, with all the knowledge and art requisite for preparing that beautiful and happy invention, without which these northern parts of the world could scarce have afforded a very comfortable habitation, together with the tools of all the different workmen employed in producing those different conveniences; if we examine, I say, all these things, and consider what a variety of labour is employed about each of them, we shall be sensible that, without the assistance and co-operation of many thousands, the very meanest person in a civilised country could not be provided, even according to what we very falsely imagine the easy and simple manner in which he is commonly accommodated....

Of the Principle Which Gives Occasion to the Division of Labour

This division of labour, from which so many advantages are derived, is not originally the effect of any human wisdom, which foresees and intends that general opulence to which it gives occasion. It is the necessary, though very slow and gradual consequence of a certain propensity in human nature which has in view no such extensive utility; the propensity to truck, barter, and exchange one thing for another.

Whether this propensity be one of those original principles in human nature of which no further account can be given; or whether, as seems more probable, it be the necessary consequence of the faculties of reason and speech, it belongs not to our present subject to inquire. It is common to all men, and to be found in no other race of animals, which seem to know neither this nor any other species of contracts. Two greyhounds, in running down the same hare, have sometimes the appearance of acting in some sort of concert. Each turns her towards his companion, or endeavours to intercept her when his companion turns her towards himself. This, however, is not the effect of any contract, but of the accidental concurrence of their passions in the same object at that particular time. Nobody ever saw a dog make a fair and deliberate exchange of one bone for another with another dog. Nobody ever saw one animal by its gestures and natural cries signify to another, this is mine, that yours; I am willing to give this for that. When an animal wants to obtain something either of a man or of another animal, it has no other means of persuasion but to gain the favour of those whose service it requires. A puppy fawns upon its dam, and a spaniel endeavours by a thousand attractions to engage the attention of its master who is at dinner,

when it wants to be fed by him. Man sometimes uses the same arts with his brethren, and when he has no other means of engaging them to act according to his inclinations, endeavours by every servile and fawning attention to obtain their good will. He has not time, however, to do this upon every occasion. In civilised society he stands at all times in need of the cooperation and assistance of great multitudes, while his whole life is scarce sufficient to gain the friendship of a few persons. In almost every other race of animals each individual, when it is grown up to maturity, is entirely independent, and in its natural state has occasion for the assistance of no other living creature. But man has almost constant occasion for the help of his brethren, and it is in vain for him to expect it from their benevolence only. He will be more likely to prevail if he can interest their self-love in his favour, and show them that it is for their own advantage to do for him what he requires of them. Whoever offers to another a bargain of any kind, proposes to do this. Give me that which I want, and you shall have this which you want, is the meaning of every such offer; and it is in this manner that we obtain from one another the far greater part of those good offices which we stand in need of. It is not from the benevolence of the butcher, the brewer, or the baker that we expect our dinner, but from their regard to their own interest. We address ourselves, not to their humanity but to their self-love, and never talk to them of our own necessities but of their advantages. Nobody but a beggar chooses to depend chiefly upon the benevolence of his fellow-citizens. Even a beggar does not depend upon it entirely. The charity of well-disposed people, indeed, supplies him with the whole fund of his subsistence. But though this principle ultimately provides him with all the necessaries of life which he has occasion for, it neither does nor can provide him with them as he has occasion for them. The greater part of his occasional wants are supplied in the same manner as those of other people, by treaty, by barter, and by purchase. With the money which one man gives him he purchases food. The old clothes which another bestows upon him he exchanges for other old clothes which suit him better, or for lodging, or for food, or for money, with which he can buy either food, clothes, or lodging, as he has occasion.

As it is by treaty, by barter, and by purchase that we obtain from one another the greater part of those mutual good offices which we stand in need of, so it is this same trucking disposition which originally gives occasion to the division of labour. In a tribe of hunters or shepherds a particular person makes bows and arrows, for example, with more readiness and dexterity than any other. He frequently exchanges them for cattle or for venison with his companions; and he finds at last that he can in this manner get more cattle and venison than if he himself went to the field to catch them. From a regard to his own interest, therefore, the making of bows and arrows grows to be his chief business, and he becomes a sort of armourer. Another excels in making the frames and covers of their little huts or movable houses. He is accustomed to be of use in this way to his neighbours, who reward him in the same manner with cattle and with venison, till at last he finds it his interest to dedicate himself entirely to this employment, and to become a sort of house-carpenter. In the same manner a third becomes a smith or a brazier, a fourth a tanner or dresser of hides or skins, the principal part of the nothing of savages. And thus the certainty of being able to exchange all that surplus part of the produce of his own labour, which is over and above his own consumption, for such parts of the produce of other men's labour as he may have occasion for, encourages every man to apply himself to a particular occupation, and to cultivate and bring to perfection whatever talent or genius he may possess for that particular species of business.

The difference of natural talents in different men is, in reality, much less than we are aware of; and the very different genius which appears to distinguish men of different professions, when grown up to maturity, is not upon many occasions so much the cause as the effect of the division of labour. The difference between the most dissimilar characters, between a philosopher and a common street porter, for example, seems to arise not so much from nature as from habit, custom, and education. When

they came into the world, and for the first six or eight years of their existence, they were perhaps very much alike, and neither their parents nor playfellows could perceive any remarkable difference. About that age, or soon after, they come to be employed in very different occupations. The difference of talents comes then to be taken notice of, and widens by degrees, till at last the vanity of the philosopher is willing to acknowledge scarce any resemblance. But without the disposition to truck, barter, and exchange, every man must have procured to himself every necessary and conveniency of life which he wanted. All must have had the same duties to perform, and the same work to do, and there could have been no such difference of employment as could alone give occasion to any great difference of talents.

As it is this disposition which forms that difference of talents, so remarkable among men of different professions, so it is this same disposition which renders that difference useful. Many tribes of animals acknowledged to be all of the same species derive from nature a much more remarkable distinction of genius, than what, antecedent to custom and education, appears to take place among men. By nature a philosopher is not in genius and disposition half so different from a street porter, as a mastiff is from a greyhound, or a greyhound from a spaniel, or this last from a shepherd's dog. Those different tribes of animals, however, though all of the same species, are of scarce any use to one another. The strength of the mastiff is not, in the least, supported either by the swiftness of the greyhound, or by the sagacity of the spaniel, or by the docility of the shepherd's dog. The effects of those different geniuses and talents, for want of the power or disposition to barter and exchange, cannot be brought into a common stock, and do not in the least contribute to the better accommodation and conveniency of the species. Each animal is still obliged to support and defend itself, separately and independently, and derives no sort of advantage from that variety of talents with which nature has distinguished its fellows. Among men, on the contrary, the most dissimilar geniuses are of use to one another; the different produces of their respective talents, by the general disposition to truck, barter, and exchange, being brought, as it were, into a common stock, where every man may purchase whatever part of the produce of other men's talents he has occasion for.

Of Restraints Upon the Importation from Foreign Countries of Such Goods as Can Be Produced at Home

[...]

Every individual is continually exerting himself to find out the most advantageous employment for whatever capital he can command. It is his own advantage, indeed, and not that of the society, which he has in view. But the study of his own advantage naturally, or rather necessarily, leads him to prefer that employment which is most advantageous to the society.

First, every individual endeavours to employ his capital as near home as he can, and consequently as much as he can in the support of domestic industry; provided always that he can thereby obtain the ordinary, or not a great deal less than the ordinary profits of stock.

Thus, upon equal or nearly equal profits, every wholesale merchant naturally prefers the home-trade to the foreign trade of consumption, and the foreign trade of consumption to the carrying trade. In the home-trade his capital is never so long out of his sight as it frequently is in the foreign trade of consumption. He can know better the character and situation of the persons whom he trusts, and if he should happen to be deceived, he knows better the laws of the country from which he must seek redress. In the carrying trade, the capital of the merchant is, as it were, divided between two foreign countries, and no part of it is ever necessarily brought home, or placed under his own immediate view and command. The capital which an Amsterdam merchant employs in carrying corn from Konigsberg to Lisbon, and fruit and wine from Lisbon to Konigsberg, must generally be the one half of it at Konigsberg and the other half at Lisbon. No part of it need ever come to Amsterdam. The

natural residence of such a merchant should either be at Konigsberg or Lisbon, and it can only be some very particular circumstances which can make him prefer the residence of Amsterdam. The uneasiness, however, which he feels at being separated so far from his capital generally determines him to bring part both of the Konigsberg goods which he destines for the market of Lisbon, and of the Lisbon goods which he destines for that of Konigsberg, to Amsterdam: and though this necessarily subjects him to a double charge of loading and unloading, as well as to the payment of some duties and customs, yet for the sake of having some part of his capital always under his own view and command, he willingly submits to this extraordinary charge; and it is in this manner that every country which has any considerable share of the carrying trade becomes always the emporium, or general market, for the goods of all the different countries whose trade it carries on. The merchant, in order to save a second loading and unloading, endeavours always to sell in the home-market as much of the goods of all those different countries as he can, and thus, so far as he can, to convert his carrying trade into a foreign trade of consumption. A merchant, in the same manner, who is engaged in the foreign trade of consumption, when he collects goods for foreign markets, will always be glad, upon equal or nearly equal profits, to sell as great a part of them at home as he can. He saves himself the risk and trouble of exportation, when, so far as he can, he thus converts his foreign trade of consumption into a home-trade. Home is in this manner the centre, if I may say so, round which the capitals of the inhabitants of every country are continually circulating, and towards which they are always tending, though by particular causes they may sometimes be driven off and repelled from it towards more distant employments. But a capital employed in the home-trade, it has already been shown, necessarily puts into motion a greater quantity of domestic industry, and gives revenue and employment to a greater number of the inhabitants of the country, than an equal capital employed in the foreign trade of consumption: and one employed in the foreign trade of consumption has the same advantage over an equal capital employed in the carrying trade. Upon equal, or only nearly equal profits, therefore, every individual naturally inclines to employ his capital in the manner in which it is likely to afford the greatest support to domestic industry, and to give revenue and employment to the greatest number of people of his own country.

Secondly, every individual who employs his capital in the support of domestic industry, necessarily endeavours so to direct that industry that its produce may be of the greatest possible value.

The produce of industry is what it adds to the subject or materials upon which it is employed. In proportion as the value of this produce is great or small, so will likewise be the profits of the employer. But it is only for the sake of profit that any man employs a capital in the support of industry; and he will always, therefore, endeavour to employ it in the support of that industry of which the produce is likely to be of the greatest value, or to exchange for the greatest quantity either of money or of other goods.

But the annual revenue of every society is always precisely equal to the exchangeable value of the whole annual produce of its industry, or rather is precisely the same thing with that exchangeable value. As every individual, therefore, endeavours as much as he can both to employ his capital in the support of domestic industry, and so to direct that industry that its produce may be of the greatest value; every individual necessarily labours to render the annual revenue of the society as great as he can. He generally, indeed, neither intends to promote the public interest, nor knows how much he is promoting it. By preferring the support of domestic to that of foreign industry, he intends only his own security; and by directing that industry in such a manner as its produce may be of the greatest value, he intends only his own gain, and he is in this, as in many other cases, led by an invisible hand to promote an end which was no part of his intention. Nor is it always the worse for the society that it was no part of it. By pursuing his own interest he frequently promotes that of the society more effectually than when he

really intends to promote it. I have never known much good done by those who affected to trade for the public good. It is an affectation, indeed, not very common among merchants, and very few words need be employed in dissuading them from it.

What is the species of domestic industry which his capital can employ, and of which the produce is likely to be of the greatest value, every individual, it is evident, can, in his local situation, judge much better than any statesman or lawgiver can do for him. The statesman who should attempt to direct private people in what manner they ought to employ their capitals would not only load himself with a most unnecessary attention, but assume an authority which could safely be trusted, not only to no single person, but to no council or senate whatever, and which would nowhere be so dangerous as in the hands of a man who had folly and presumption enough to fancy himself fit to exercise it.

DISCUSSION QUESTIONS

1. What is the "division of labor"? How does it come about? What benefits accrue to society as a result?

2. Smith claims, "By pursuing his own interest [a person] frequently promotes [the interest of] society more effectually than when he really intends to promote it." How is this the case? What are the interests of society, which Smith has in mind?

3. Consider and explain how Smith might argue that a free-market (i.e., an economic system in which market forces are allowed to play out without governmental influence) would benefit even the worst-off members of society. How might allowing people to pursue their own interests (without conscious regard for the society's interests or other people's interest) end up benefiting everyone?

B.
Contemporary Developments

67

Milton Friedman, selection from *Capitalism and Freedom* (1962)

In this selection, Friedman considers whether the measures the government has used to alter the distribution of wealth or income in favor of greater equality have, in fact, been successful. On Friedman, see reading 35 above.

SOURCE

Friedman, Milton. Excerpts from *Capitalism and Freedom*. Copyright © 1962 by Milton Friedman. Reproduced with the permission of the University of Chicago Press.

The Distribution of Income

A central element in the development of a collectivist sentiment in this century, at least in Western countries, has been a belief in equality of income as a general goal and a willingness to use the arm of the state to promote it. Two very different questions must be asked in evaluating this egalitarian sentiment and the egalitarian measure it has produced. The first is normative and ethical: what is the justification for state intervention to promote equality? The second is positive and scientific: what has been the effect of the measures actually taken?

The Ethics of Distribution

The ethical principle that would directly justify the distribution of income in a free market society is, "To each according to what he and the instruments he owns produces." The operation of even this principle implicitly depends on state action. Property rights are matters of law and social convention. As we have seen, their definition and enforcement is one of the primary functions of the state. The final distribution of income and wealth under the full operation of this principle may well depend markedly on the rules of property adopted.

What is the relation between this principle and another that seems ethically appealing, namely, equality of treatment? In part, the two principles are not contradictory. Payment in accordance with product may be necessary to achieve true equality of treatment. Given individuals whom we are prepared to regard as alike in ability and initial resources, if some have a greater taste for leisure and others for marketable goods, inequality of return through the market is necessary to achieve equality of total return or equality of treatment. One man may prefer a routine job with much time off for basking in the sun to a more exacting job paying a higher salary; another man may prefer the opposite. If both were paid equally in money, their incomes in a more fundamental sense would be unequal. Similarly, equal treatment requires that an individual be paid more for a dirty, unattractive job than for a pleasant rewarding one. Much observed inequality is of this kind. Differences of money income offset differences in other characteristics of the occupation or trade. In the jargon of economists, they are "equalizing differences" required to make the whole of the "net advantages," pecuniary and non-pecuniary, the same.

Another kind of inequality arising through the operation of the market is also required, in a somewhat more subtle sense, to produce equality of treatment, or to put it differently to satisfy men's tastes. It can be illustrated most simply by a lottery. Consider a group of individuals who initially have equal endowments and who all agree voluntarily to enter a lottery with very unequal prizes. The resultant inequality of income is surely required to permit the individuals in question to make the most of their initial equality. Redistribution of the income after the event is equivalent to denying them the opportunity to enter the lottery. This case is far more important in practice than would appear by taking the notion of a "lottery" literally. Individuals choose occupations, investments, and the like partly in accordance with their taste for uncertainty. The girl who tries to become a movie actress rather than a civil servant is deliberately choosing to enter a lottery; so is the individual who invests in penny uranium stocks rather than government bonds. Insurance is a way of expressing a taste for certainty. Even these examples do not indicate fully the extent to which actual inequality may be the result of arrangements designed to satisfy

men's tastes. The very arrangements for paying and hiring people are affected by such preferences. If all potential movie actresses had a great dislike of uncertainty, there would tend to develop "cooperatives" of movie actresses, the members of which agreed in advance to share income receipts more or less evenly, thereby in effect providing themselves insurance through the pooling of risks. If such a preference were widespread, large diversified corporations combining risky and non-risky ventures would become the rule. The wild-cat oil prospector, the private proprietorship, the small partnership would all become rare.

Indeed, this is one way to interpret governmental measures to redistribute income through progressive taxes and the like. It can be argued that for one reason or another, costs of administration perhaps, the market cannot produce the range of lotteries or the kind of lottery desired by the members of the community, and that progressive taxation is, as it were, a government enterprise to do so. I have no doubt that this view contains an element of truth. At the same time, it can hardly justify present taxation, if only because the taxes are imposed *after* it is already largely known who have drawn the prizes and who the blanks in the lottery of life, and the taxes are voted mostly by those who think they have drawn the blanks. One might, along these lines, justify one generation's voting the tax schedules to be applied to an as yet unborn generation. Any such procedure would, I conjecture, yield income tax schedules much less highly graduated than present schedules are, at least on paper.

Though much of the inequality of income produced by payment in accordance with product reflects "equalizing" differences or the satisfaction of men's tastes for uncertainty, a large part reflects initial differences in endowment, both of human capacities and of property. This is the part that raises the really difficult ethical issue.

It is widely argued that it is essential to distinguish between inequality in personal endowments and in property, and between inequalities arising from inherited wealth and from acquired wealth.

Inequality resulting from differences in personal capacities, or from differences in wealth accumulated by the individual in question, are considered appropriate, or at least not so clearly inappropriate as differences resulting from inherited wealth.

This distinction is untenable. Is there any greater ethical justification for the high returns to the individual who inherits from his parents a peculiar voice from which there is a great demand than for the high returns to the individual who inherits property? The sons of Russian commissars surely have a higher expectation of income—perhaps also of liquidation—than the sons of peasants. Is this any more or less justifiable than the higher income expectation of the son of an American millionaire? We can look at this same question another way. A parent who has wealth that he wishes to pass on to his child can do so in different ways. He can use a given sum of money to finance his child's training as, say, a certified public accountant, or to set him up in business, or to provide a trust fund yielding him a property income. In any of these cases, the child will have a higher income than he otherwise would. But in the first case, his income will be regarded as coming from human capacities; in the second, from profits; in the third, from inherited wealth. Is there any basis for distinguishing among these categories of receipts on ethical grounds? Finally, it seems illogical to say that a man is entitled to what he has produced by personal capacities or to the produce of the wealth he has accumulated, but that he is not entitled to pass any wealth on to his children; to say that a man may use his income for riotous living but may not give it to his heirs. Surely, the latter is one way to use what he has produced.

The fact that these arguments against the so-called capitalist ethic are invalid does not of course demonstrate that the capitalist ethic is an acceptable one. I find it difficult to justify either accepting or rejecting it, or to justify any alternative principle. I am led to the view that it cannot in and of itself be regarded as an ethical principle; that it must be regarded as instrumental or a corollary of some other principle such as freedom.

Some hypothetical examples may illustrate the fundamental difficulty. Suppose there are four Robinson Crusoes, independently marooned on four islands in the same neighborhood. One happened to land on a large and fruitful island which enables him to live easily and well. The others happened to land on tiny and rather barren islands from which they can barely scratch a living. One day, they discover the existence of one another. Of course, it would be generous of the Crusoe on the large island if he invited the others to join him and share its wealth. But suppose he does not. Would the other three be justified in joining forces and compelling him to share his wealth with them? Many a reader will be tempted to say yes. But before yielding to this temptation, consider precisely the same situation in different guise. Suppose you and three friends are walking along the street and you happen to spy and retrieve a $20 bill on the pavement. It would be generous of you, of course, if you were to divide it equally with them, or at least blow them to a drink. But suppose you do not. Would the other three be justified in joining forces and compelling you to share the $20 equally with them? I suspect most readers will be tempted to say no. And on further reflection, they may even conclude that the generous course of action is not itself clearly the "right" one. Are we prepared to urge on ourselves or our fellows that any person whose wealth exceeds the average of all persons in the world should immediately dispose of the excess by distributing it equally to all the rest of the world's inhabitants? We may admire and praise such action when undertaken by a few. But a universal "potlatch" would make a civilized world impossible.

In any event, two wrongs do not make a right. The unwillingness of the rich Robinson Crusoe or the lucky finder of the $20 bill to share his wealth does not justify the use of coercion by the others. Can we justify being judges in our own case, deciding on our own when we are entitled to use force to extract what we regard as our due from others? Or what we regard as not their due? Most difference of status or position or wealth can be regarded as the product of chance at a far enough remove.

The man who is hard working and thrifty is to be regarded as "deserving"; yet these qualities owe much to the genes he was fortunate (or unfortunate?) enough to inherit.

Despite the lip service that we all pay to "merit" as compared to "chance," we are generally much readier to accept inequalities arising from chance than those clearly attributable to merit. The college professor whose colleague wins a sweepstake will envy him but is unlikely to bear him any malice or to feel unjustly treated. Let the colleague receive a trivial raise that makes his salary higher than the professor's own, and the professor is far more likely to feel aggrieved. After all, the goddess of chance, as of justice, is blind. The salary raise was a deliberate judgment of relative merit.

The Instrumental Role of Distribution According to Product

The operative function of payment in accordance with product in a market society is not primarily distributive, but allocative.... [The] central principle of a market economy is cooperation through voluntary exchange. Individuals cooperate with others because they can in this way satisfy their own wants more effectively. But unless an individual receives the whole of what he adds to the product, he will enter into exchanges on the basis of what he can receive rather than what he can produce. Exchanges will not take place that would have been mutually beneficial if each party received what he contributed to the aggregate product. Payment in accordance with product is therefore necessary in order that resources be used most effectively, at least under a system depending on voluntary cooperation. Given sufficient knowledge, it might be that compulsion could be substituted for the incentive of reward, though I doubt that it could. One can shuffle inanimate objects around; one can compel individuals to be at certain places at certain times; but one can hardly compel individuals to put forward their best efforts. Put another way, the substitution of compulsion for cooperation changes the amount of resources available.

Though the essential function of payment in accordance with product in a market society is to enable resources to be allocated efficiently without compulsion, it is unlikely to be tolerated unless it is also regarded as yielding distributive justice. No society can be stable unless there is a basic core of value judgments that are unthinkingly accepted by the great bulk of its members. Some key institutions must be accepted as "absolutes," not simply as instrumental. I believe that payment in accordance with product has been, and, in large measure, still is, one of these accepted value judgments or institutions.

One can demonstrate this by examining the grounds on which the internal opponents of the capitalist system have attacked the distribution of income resulting from it. It is a distinguishing feature of the core of central values of a society that is accepted alike by its members, whether they regard themselves as proponents or as opponents of the system of organization of the society. Even the severest internal critics of capitalism have implicitly accepted payment in accordance with product as ethically fair.

The most far-reaching criticism has come from the Marxists. Marx argued that labor was exploited. Why? Because labor produced the whole of the product but got only part of it; the rest is Marx's "surplus value." Even if the statements of fact implicit in this assertion were accepted, the value judgment follows only if one accepts the capitalist ethic. Labor is "exploited" only if labor is entitled to what it produces. If one accepts instead the socialist premise, "to each according to his need, from each according to his ability"—whatever that may mean—it is necessary to compare what labor produces, not with what it gets but with its "ability," and to compare what labor gets, not with what it produces but with its "need."

Of course, the Marxist argument is invalid on other grounds as well. There is, first, the confusion between the total product of all cooperating resources and the amount added to product—in the economist's jargon, marginal product. Even more striking, there is an unstated change in the meaning of "labor" in passing from the premise to the conclusion. Marx recognized the role of capital in producing the product but regarded capital as embodied labor. Hence, written out in full, the premises of the Marxist syllogism would run: "Present and past labor produce the whole of the product. Present labor gets only part of the product." The logical conclusion is presumably "Past labor is exploited," and the inference for action is that past labor should get more of the product, though it is by no means clear how, unless it be in elegant tombstones.

The achievement of allocation of resources without compulsion is the major instrumental role in the market place of distribution in accordance with product. We have noted [elsewhere] the role that inequality plays in providing independent foci of power to offset the centralization of political power, as well as the role that it plays in promoting civil freedom by providing "patrons" to finance the dissemination of unpopular or simply novel ideas. In addition, in the economic sphere, it provides "patrons" to finance experimentation and the development of new products—to buy the first experimental automobiles and television sets, let alone impressionist paintings. Finally, it enables distribution to occur impersonally without the need for "authority"—a special facet of the general role of the market in effecting cooperation and coordination without coercion.

Facts of Income Distribution

A capitalist system involving payment in accordance with product can be, and in practice is, characterized by considerable inequality of income and wealth. This fact is frequently misinterpreted to mean that capitalism and free enterprise produce wider inequality than alternative systems and, as a corollary, that the extension and development of capitalism has meant increased inequality. This misinterpretation is fostered by the misleading character of most published figures on the distribution of income, in particular their failure to distinguish short-run from long-run inequality. Let us look at some of the broader facts about the distribution of income.

One of the most striking facts which runs counter to many people's expectation has to do with the sources of income. The more capitalistic a country is, the smaller the fraction of income paid for the use of what is generally regarded as capital, and the larger the fraction paid for human services. In underdeveloped countries like India, Egypt, and so on, something like half of total income is property income. In the United States, roughly one-fifth is property income. And in other advanced capitalist countries, the proportion is not very different. Of course, these countries have much more capital than the primitive countries but they are even richer in the productive capacity of their residents; hence, the larger income from property is a smaller fraction of the total. The great achievement of capitalism has not been the accumulation of property, it has been the opportunities it has offered to men and women to extend and develop and improve their capacities. Yet the enemies of capitalism are fond of castigating it as materialist, and its friends all too often apologize for capitalism's materialism as a necessary cost of progress.

Another striking fact, contrary to popular conception, is that capitalism leads to less inequality than alternative systems of organization and that the development of capitalism has greatly lessened the extent of inequality. Comparisons over space and time alike confirm this view. There is surely drastically less inequality in Western capitalist societies like the Scandinavian countries, France, Britain, and the United States, than in a status society like India or a backward country like Egypt. Comparison with communist countries like Russia is more difficult because of paucity and unreliability of evidence. But if inequality is measured by differences in levels of living between the privileged and other classes, such inequality may well be decidedly less in capitalist than in communist countries. Among the Western countries alone, inequality appears to be less, in any meaningful sense, the more highly capitalist the country is: less in Britain than in France, less in the United States than in Britain—though these comparisons are rendered difficult by the problem of allowing for the intrinsic heterogeneity of populations; for a fair comparison, for example, one should perhaps compare the United States, not with the United Kingdom alone but with the United Kingdom plus the West Indies plus its African possessions.

With respect to changes over time, the economic progress achieved in the capitalist societies has been accompanied by a drastic diminution in inequality. As late as 1848, John Stuart Mill could write, "Hitherto [1848] it is questionable if all the mechanical inventions yet made have lightened the day's toil of any human being. They have enabled a greater population to live the same life of drudgery and imprisonment, and an increased number of manufacturers and others to make fortunes. They have increased the comforts of the middle classes. But they have not yet begun to effect those great changes in human destiny, which it is in their nature and in their futurity to accomplish."[1] This statement was probably not correct even for Mill's day, but certainly no one could write this today about the advanced capitalist countries. It is still true about the rest of the world.

The chief characteristic of progress and development over the past century is that it has freed the masses from backbreaking toil and has made available to them products and services that were formerly the monopoly of the upper classes, without in any corresponding way expanding the products and services available to the wealthy. Medicine aside, the advances in technology have for the most part simply made available to the masses of the people luxuries that were always available in one form or another to the truly wealthy. Modern plumbing, central heating, automobiles, television, radio, to cite just a few examples, provide conveniences to the masses equivalent to those that the wealthy could always get by the use of servants, entertainers, and so on.
[...]

---

[1] *Principles of Political Economy* (Ashley edition; London: Longmans, Green & Co., 1909), p. 751.

The Alleviation of Poverty

The extraordinary economic growth experienced by Western countries during the past two centuries and the wide distribution of the benefits of free enterprise have enormously reduced the extent of poverty in any absolute sense in the capitalistic countries of the West. But poverty is in part a relative matter, and even in these countries, there are clearly many people living under conditions that the rest of us label as poverty.

One recourse, and in many ways the most desirable, is private charity. It is noteworthy that the heyday of laissez-faire, the middle and late nineteenth century in Britain and the United States, saw an extraordinary proliferation of private eleemosynary organizations and institutions. One of the major costs of the extension of governmental welfare activities has been the corresponding decline in private charitable activities.

It can be argued that private charity is insufficient because the benefits from it accrue to people other than those who make the gifts—again, a neighborhood effect. I am distressed by the sight of poverty; I am benefited by its alleviation; but I am benefited equally whether I or someone else pays for its alleviation; the benefits of other people's charity therefore partly accrue to me. To put it differently, we might all of us be willing to contribute to the relief of poverty, *provided* everyone else did. We might not be willing to contribute the same amount without such assurance. In small communities, public pressure can suffice to realize the proviso even with private charity. In the large impersonal communities that are increasingly coming to dominate our society, it is much more difficult for it to do so.

Suppose one accepts, as I do, this line of reasoning as justifying governmental action to alleviate poverty; to set, as it were, a floor under the standard of life of every person in the community. There remain the questions, how much and how. I see no way of deciding "how much" except in terms of the amount of taxes we—by which I mean the great bulk of us—are willing to impose on ourselves for the purpose. The question, "how," affords more room for speculation.

Two things seem clear. First, if the objective is to alleviate poverty, we should have a program directed at helping the poor. There is every reason to help the poor man who happens to be a farmer, not because he is a farmer but because he is poor. The program, that is, should be designed to help people as people not as members of particular occupational groups or age groups or wage-rate groups or labor organizations or industries. This is a defect of farm programs, general old-age benefits, minimum-wage laws, pro-union legislation, tariffs, licensing provisions of crafts or professions, and so on in seemingly endless profusion. Second, so far as possible the program should, while operating through the market, not distort the market or impede its functioning. This is a defect of price supports, minimum-wage laws, tariffs and the like.

The arrangement that recommends itself on purely mechanical grounds is a negative income tax. We now have an exemption of $600 per person under the federal income tax (plus a minimum 10 per cent flat deduction). If an individual receives $100 taxable income, i.e., an income of $100 in excess of the exemption and deductions, he pays a tax. Under the proposal, if his taxable income minus $100, i.e., less than the exemption plus deductions, he would pay a negative tax, i.e., receive a subsidy. If the rate of subsidy were, say, 50 per cent, he would receive $50. If he had no income at all, and, for simplicity, no deductions, and the rate were constant, he would receive $300.... In this way, it would be possible to set a floor below which no man's net income ... could fall—in the simple example $300 per person. The precise floor set would depend on what the community could afford.

The advantages of this arrangement are clear. It is directed specifically at the problem of poverty. It gives help in the form most useful to the individual, namely, cash. It is general and could be substituted for the host of special measures now in effect. It makes explicit the cost borne by society. It operates outside the market. Like any other measures to alleviate poverty, it reduces the incentives of those

helped to help themselves, but it does not eliminate that incentive entirely, as a system of supplementing incomes up to some fixed minimum would. An extra dollar earned would always mean more money available for expenditure.
[...]

The major disadvantage of the proposed negative income tax is its political implications. It establishes a system under which taxes are imposed on some to pay subsidies to others. And presumably, these others have a vote. There is always the danger that instead of being an arrangement under which the great majority tax themselves willingly to help an unfortunate minority, it will be converted into one under which a majority imposes taxes for its own benefit on an unwilling minority. Because this proposal makes the process so explicit, the danger is perhaps greater than with other measures. I see no solution to this problem except to rely on the self-restraint and good will of the electorate.
[...]

Liberalism and Egalitarianism

The heart of the liberal philosophy is a belief in the dignity of the individual, in his freedom to make the most of his capacities and opportunities according to his own lights, subject only to the proviso that he not interfere with the freedom of other individuals to do the same. This implies a belief in the equality of men in one sense; in their inequality in another. Each man has an equal right to freedom. This is an important and fundamental right precisely because men are different, because one man will want to do different things with his freedom than another, and in the process can contribute more than another to the general culture of the society in which many men live.

The liberal will therefore distinguish sharply between equality of rights and equality of opportunity, on the one hand, and material equality or equality of outcome on the other. He may welcome the fact that a free society in fact tends toward greater material equality than any other yet tried. But he will regard this as a desirable by-product of a free society, not its major justification. He will welcome measures that promote both freedom and equality—such as measures to eliminate monopoly power and to improve the operation of the market. He will regard private charity directed at helping the less fortunate as an example of the proper use of freedom. And he may approve state action toward ameliorating poverty as a more effective way in which the great bulk of the community can achieve a common objective. He will do so with regret, however, at having to substitute compulsory for voluntary action.

The egalitarian will go this far, too. But he will want to go further. He will defend taking from some to give to others, not as a more effective means whereby the "some" can achieve an objective they want to achieve, but on grounds of "justice." At this point, equality comes sharply into conflict with freedom; one must choose. One cannot be both an egalitarian, in this sense, and a liberal.

DISCUSSION QUESTIONS

1. Consider what you take to be some of the major social and economic problems of our time. Do you think that our existing socio-economic system has any major shortcomings? Is it a *fair* system? Are there people who do not benefit from the system? In your mind, who are the worst off in the world? Why are they the worst off?

2. Explain the "capitalist ethic," which Friedman writes about. Why does he claim that the so-called capitalist ethic is not an ethical principle at all? If it is not an ethical principle, what is it?

3. Friedman provides two hypothetical situations, one regarding four Robinson Crusoes, and one involving four friends walking down the sidewalk. Explain the thought-experiment. What point does Friedman wish to draw? Do you agree with his conclusion(s)? Are the two situations strictly analogous, as Friedman suggests, or are they different in important respects?

4. What reasons does Friedman mention for favoring a capitalist system of income distribution over a non-capitalist system? Do you think these are good reasons?

68

Robert Nozick, selection from *Anarchy, State, and Utopia* (1977)

In this selection, Nozick defends his claim that the most extensive state that can be defended is actually a minimal state. The minimum state refrains from both paternalistic measures and redistributive taxation. On Nozick, see reading 6 above.

SOURCE

Nozick, Robert. *Anarchy, State, and Utopia.* Copyright © 1977 by Robert Nozick. Reprinted by permission of Basic Books, a member of the Perseus Books Group.

The minimal state is the most extensive state that can be justified. Any state more extensive violates people's rights. Yet many persons have put forth reasons purporting to justify a more extensive state. It is impossible within the compass of this book to examine all the reasons that have been put forth. Therefore, I shall focus upon those generally acknowledged to be most weighty and influential, to see precisely wherein they fail. In this chapter we consider the claim that a more extensive state is justified, because necessary (or the best instrument) to achieve distributive justice....

The term "distributive justice" is not a neutral one. Hearing the term "distribution," most people presume that some thing or mechanism uses some principle or criterion to give out a supply of things. Into this process of distributing shares some error may have crept. So it is an open question, at least, whether redistribution should take place; whether we should do again what has already been done once, though poorly. However, we are not in the position of children who have been given portions of pie by someone who now makes last minute adjustments to rectify careless cutting. There is no *central* distribution, no person or group entitled to control all the resources, jointly deciding how they are to be doled out. What each person gets, he gets from others who give to him in exchange for something, or as a gift. In a free society, diverse persons control different resources, and new holdings arise out of the voluntary exchanges and actions of persons. There is no more a distributing or distribution of shares than there is a distributing of mates in a society in which persons choose whom they shall marry. The total result is the product of many individual decisions which the different individuals involved are entitled to make. Some uses of the term "distribution," it is true, do not imply a previous distributing appropriately judged by some criterion (for example, "probability distribution"); nevertheless, despite the title of this chapter ["Distributive Justice"], it would be best to use a terminology that clearly is neutral. We shall speak of people's holdings; a principle of justice in holdings describes (part of) what justice tells us (requires) about holdings. I shall state first what I take to be the correct view about justice in holdings, and then turn to the discussion of alternate views.

The Entitlement Theory

The subject of justice in holdings consists of three major topics. The first is the *original acquisition of holdings*, the appropriation of unheld things. This includes the issues of how unheld things may come to be held, the process, or processes, by which unheld things may come to be held, the things that may come to be held by these processes, the extent of what comes to be held by a particular process, and so on. We shall refer to the complicated truth about this topic, which we shall not formulate here, as the principle of justice in acquisition. The second topic concerns the transfer of holdings from one person to another. By what processes may a person transfer holdings to another? How may a person acquire a holding from another who holds it? Under this topic come general descriptions of voluntary exchange, and gift and (on the other hand) fraud, as well as reference to particular conventional details fixed upon in a given society. The complicated truth about this subject (with placeholders for conventional details) we shall call the principle of justice in transfer. (And we shall suppose it also includes principles governing how a person may divest himself of a holding, passing it into an unheld state.)

If the world were wholly just, the following inductive definition would exhaustively cover the subject of justice in holdings.

1. A person who acquires a holding in accordance with the principle of justice in acquisition is entitled to that holding.
2. A person who acquires a holding in accordance with the principle of justice in transfer, from someone else entitled to the holding, is entitled to the holding.
3. No one is entitled to a holding except by (repeated) applications of 1 and 2.

The complete principle of distributive justice would say simply that a distribution is just if everyone is entitled to the holdings they possess under the distribution.

A distribution is just if it arises from another just distribution by legitimate means. The legitimate means of moving from one distribution to another are specified by the principle of justice in transfer. The legitimate first "moves" are specified by the principle of justice in acquisition. Whatever arises from a just situation by just steps is itself just. The means of change specified by the principle of justice in transfer preserve justice. As correct rules of inference are truth-preserving, and any conclusion deduced via repeated application of such rules from only true premises is itself true, so the means of transition from one situation to another specified by the principle of justice in transfer are justice-preserving, and any situation actually arising from repeated transitions in accordance with the principle from a just situation is itself just. The parallel between justice-preserving transformations and truth-preserving transformations illuminates where it fails as well as where it holds. That a conclusion could have been deduced by truth-preserving means from premises that are true suffices to show its truth. That from a just situation a situation *could* have arisen via justice-preserving means does *not* suffice to show its justice. The fact that a thief's victims voluntarily *could* have presented him with gifts does not entitle the thief to his ill-gotten gains. Justice in holdings is historical; it depends upon what actually has happened. We shall return to this point later.

Not all actual situations are generated in accordance with the two principles of justice in holdings: the principle of justice in acquisition and the principle of justice in transfer. Some people steal from others, or defraud them, or enslave them, seizing their product and preventing them from living as they choose, or forcibly exclude others from competing in exchanges. None of these are permissible modes of transition from one situation to another.

And some persons acquire holdings by means not sanctioned by the principle of justice in acquisition. The existence of past injustice (previous violations of the first two principles of justice in holdings) raises the third major topic under justice in holdings: the rectification of injustice in holdings. If past injustice has shaped present holdings in various ways, some identifiable and some not, what now, if anything, ought to be done to rectify these injustices? What obligations do the performers of injustice have toward those whose position is worse than it would have been had the injustice not been done? Or, than it would have been had compensation been paid promptly? How, if at all, do things change if the beneficiaries and those made worse off are not the direct parties in the act of injustice, but, for example, their descendants? Is an injustice done to someone whose holding was itself based upon an unrectified injustice? How far back must one go in wiping clean the historical slate of injustices? What may victims of injustice permissibly do in order to rectify the injustices being done to them, including the many injustices done by persons acting through their government? I do not know of a thorough or theoretically sophisticated treatment of such issues.[1] Idealizing greatly, let us suppose theoretical investigation will produce a principle of rectification. This principle uses historical information about previous situations and injustices done in them (as defined by the first two principles of justice and rights against interference),

and information about the actual course of events that flowed from these injustices, until the present, and it yields a description (or descriptions) of holdings in the society. The principle of rectification presumably will make use of its best estimate of subjunctive information about what would have occurred (or a probability distribution over what might have occurred, using the expected value) if the injustice had not taken place. If the actual description of holdings turns out not to be one of the descriptions yielded by the principle, then one of the descriptions yielded must be realized.

The general outlines of the theory of justice in holdings are that the holdings of a person are just if he is entitled to them by the principles of justice in acquisition and transfer, or by the principle of rectification of injustice (as specified by the first two principles). If each person's holdings are just, then the total set (distribution) of holdings is just. To turn these general outlines into a specific theory we would have to specify the details of each of the three principles of justice in holdings: the principle of acquisition of holdings, the principle of transfer of holdings, and the principle of rectification of violations of the first two principles. I shall not attempt that task here....

Historical Principles and End-Result Principles

The general outlines of the entitlement theory illuminate the nature and defects of other conceptions of distributive justice. The entitlement theory of justice in distribution is *historical*; whether a distribution is just depends upon how it came about. In contrast, *current time-slice principles* of justice hold that the justice of a distribution is determined by how things are distributed (who has what) as judged by some *structural* principle(s) of just distribution. A utilitarian who judges between any two distributions by seeing which has the greater sum of utility and, if the sums tie, applies some fixed equality criterion to choose the more equal distribution, would hold a current time-slice principle of justice. As would someone who had a fixed

---

[1] See, however, the useful book by Boris Bittker, *The Case for Black Reparations* (New York: Random House, 1973).

schedule of trade-offs between the sum of happiness and equality. According to a current time-slice principle, all that needs to be looked at, in judging the justice of a distribution, is who ends up with what; in comparing any two distributions one need look only at the matrix presenting the distributions. No further information need be fed into a principle of justice. It is a consequence of such principles of justice that any two structurally identical distributions are equally just. (Two distributions are structurally identical if they present the same profile, but perhaps have different persons occupying the particular slots. My having ten and your having five, and my having five and your having ten are structurally identical distributions.) Welfare economics is the theory of current time-slice principles of justice. The subject is conceived as operating on matrices representing only current information about distribution. This, as well as some of the usual conditions (for example, the choice of distribution is invariant under relabeling of columns), guarantees that welfare economics will be a current time-slice theory, with all of its inadequacies.

Most persons do not accept current time-slice principles as constituting the whole story about distributive shares. They think it relevant in assessing the justice of a situation to consider not only the distribution it embodies, but also how that distribution came about. If some persons are in prison for murder or war crimes, we do not say that to assess the justice of the distribution in the society we must look only at what this person has, and that person has, and that person has, ... at the current time. We think it relevant to ask whether someone did something so that he *deserved* to be punished, deserved to have a lower share. Most will agree to the relevance of further information with regard to punishments and penalties. Consider also desired things. One traditional socialist view is that workers are entitled to the product and full fruits of their labor; they have earned it; a distribution is unjust if it does not give the workers what they are entitled to. Such entitlements are based upon some past history. No socialist holding this view would find it comforting to be told that because the

actual distribution A happens to coincide structurally with the one he desires D, A therefore is no less just than D; it differs only in that the "parasitic" owners of capital receive under A what the workers are entitled to under D, and the workers receive under A what the owners are entitled to under D, namely very little. This socialist rightly, in my view, holds onto the notions of earning, producing, entitlement, desert, and so forth, and he rejects current time-slice principles that look only to the structure of the resulting set of holdings. (The set of holdings resulting from what? Isn't it implausible that how holdings are produced and come to exist has no effect at all on who should hold what?) His mistake lies in his view of what entitlements arise out of what sorts of productive processes.

We construe the position we discuss too narrowly by speaking of *current* time-slice principles. Nothing is changed if structural principles operate upon a time sequence of current time-slice profiles and, for example, give someone more now to counterbalance the less he has had earlier. A utilitarian or an egalitarian or any mixture of the two over time will inherit the difficulties of his more myopic comrades. He is not helped by the fact that *some* of the information others consider relevant in assessing a distribution is reflected, unrecoverably, in past matrices. Henceforth, we shall refer to such unhistorical principles of distributive justice, including the current time-slice principles, as *end-result principles* or *end-state principles*.

In contrast to end-result principles of justice, *historical principles* of justice hold that past circumstances or actions of people can create differential entitlements or differential deserts to things. An injustice can be worked by moving from one distribution to another structurally identical one, for the second, in profile the same, may violate people's entitlements or deserts; it may not fit the actual history.

Patterning

The entitlement principles of justice in holdings that we have sketched are historical principles of justice. To better understand their precise character, we shall distinguish them from another subclass of the historical principles. Consider, as an example, the principle of distribution according to moral merit. This principle requires that total distributive shares vary directly with moral merit; no person should have a greater share than anyone whose moral merit is greater. (If moral merit could be not merely ordered but measured on an interval or ratio scale, stronger principles could be formulated.) Or consider the principle that results by substituting "usefulness to society" for "moral merit" in the previous principle. Or instead of "distribute according to moral merit," or "distribute according to usefulness to society," we might consider "distribute according to the weighted sum of moral merit, usefulness to society, and need," with the weights of the different dimensions equal. Let us call a principle of distribution *patterned* if it specifies that a distribution is to vary along with some natural dimension, weighted sum of natural dimensions, or lexicographic ordering of natural dimensions. And let us say a distribution is patterned if it accords with some patterned principle. (I speak of natural dimensions, admittedly without a general criterion for them, because for any set of holdings some artificial dimensions can be gimmicked up to vary along with the distribution of the set.) The principle of distribution in accordance with moral merit is a patterned historical principle, which specifies a patterned distribution. "Distribute according to I.Q." is a patterned principle that looks to information not contained in distributional matrices. It is not historical, however, in that it does not look to any past actions creating differential entitlements to evaluate a distribution; it requires only distributional matrices whose columns are labeled by I.Q. scores. The distribution in a society, however, may be composed of such simple patterned distributions, without itself being simply patterned. Different sectors may operate different patterns, or some combination of patterns may operate in different proportions across a society. A distribution composed in this manner, from a small number of patterned distributions, we also shall term "patterned." And we extend the use of "pattern"

to include the overall designs put forth by combinations of end-state principles.

Almost every suggested principle of distributive justice is patterned: to each according to his moral merit, or needs, or marginal product, or how hard he tries, or the weighted sum of the foregoing, and so on. The principle of entitlement we have sketched is *not* patterned. There is no one natural dimension or weighted sum or combination of a small number of natural dimensions that yields the distributions generated in accordance with the principle of entitlement. The set of holdings that results when some persons receive their marginal products, others win at gambling, others receive a share of their mate's income, others receive gifts from foundations, others receive interest on loans, others receive gifts from admirers, others receive returns on investment, others make for themselves much of what they have, others find things, and so on, will not be patterned. Heavy strands of patterns will run through it; significant portions of the variance in holdings will be accounted for by pattern-variables. If most people most of the time choose to transfer some of their entitlements to others only in exchange for something from them, then a large part of what many people hold will vary with what they held that others wanted. More details are provided by the theory of marginal productivity. But gifts to relatives, charitable donations, bequests to children, and the like, are not best conceived, in the first instance, in this manner. Ignoring the strands of pattern, let us suppose for the moment that a distribution actually arrived at by the operation of the principle of entitlement is random with respect to any pattern. Though the resulting set of holdings will be unpatterned, it will not be incomprehensible, for it can be seen as arising from the operation of a small number of principles. These principles specify how an initial distribution may arise (the principle of acquisition of holdings) and how distributions may be transformed into others (the principle of transfer of holdings). The process whereby the set of holdings is generated will be intelligible, though the set of holdings itself that results from this process will be unpatterned.

The writings of F.A. Hayek focus less than is usually done upon what patterning distributive justice requires. Hayek argues that we cannot know enough about each person's situation to distribute to each according to his moral merit (but would justice demand we do so if we did have this knowledge?); and he goes on to say, "our objection is against all attempts to impress upon society a deliberately chosen pattern of distribution, whether it be an order of equality or of inequality."[1] However, Hayek concludes that in a free society there will be distribution in accordance with value rather than moral merit; that is, in accordance with the perceived value of a person's actions and services to others. Despite his rejection of a patterned conception of distributive justice, Hayek himself suggests a pattern he thinks justifiable: distribution in accordance with the perceived benefits given to others, leaving room for the complaint that a free society does not realize exactly this pattern. Stating this patterned strand of a free capitalist society more precisely, we get "To each according to how much he benefits others who have the resources for benefiting those who benefit them." This will seem arbitrary unless some acceptable initial set of holdings is specified, or unless it is held that the operation of the system over time washes out any significant effects from the initial set of holdings. As an example of the latter, if almost anyone would have bought a car from Henry Ford, the supposition that it was an arbitrary matter who held the money then (and so bought) would not place Henry Ford's earnings under a cloud. In any event, *his* coming to hold it is not arbitrary. Distribution according to benefits to others *is* a major patterned strand in a free capitalist society, as Hayek correctly points out, but it is only a strand and does not constitute the whole pattern of a system of entitlements (namely, inheritance, gifts for arbitrary reasons, charity, and so on) or a standard that one should insist a society fit. Will people tolerate for long a system yielding distributions that they believe are unpatterned?

No doubt people will not long accept a distribution they believe is *unjust*. People want their society to be and to look just. But must the look of justice reside in a resulting pattern rather than in the underlying generating principles? We are in no position to conclude that the inhabitants of a society embodying an entitlement conception of justice in holdings will find it unacceptable. Still, it must be granted that were people's reasons for transferring some of their holdings to others always irrational or arbitrary, we would find this disturbing. (Suppose people always determined what holdings they would transfer, and to whom, by using a random device.) We feel more comfortable upholding the justice of an entitlement system if most of the transfers under it are done for reasons. This does not mean necessarily that all deserve what holdings they receive. It means only that there is a purpose or point to someone's transferring a holding to one person rather than to another; that usually we can see what the transferrer thinks he's gaining, what cause he thinks he's serving, what goals he thinks he's helping to achieve, and so forth. Since in a capitalist society people often transfer holdings to others in accordance with how much they perceive these others benefiting them, the fabric constituted by the individual transactions and transfers is largely reasonable and intelligible. (Gifts to loved ones, bequests to children, charity to the needy also are nonarbitrary components of the fabric.) In stressing the large strand of distribution in accordance with benefit to others, Hayek shows the point of many transfers, and so shows that the system of transfer of entitlements is not just spinning its gears aimlessly. The system of entitlements is defensible when constituted by the individual aims of individual transactions. No overarching aim is needed, no distributional pattern is required.

To think that the task of a theory of distributive justice is to fill in the blank in "to each according to his ____" is to be predisposed to search for a pattern; and the separate treatment of "from each according to his ____" treats production and distribution as two separate and independent issues. On an entitlement view these are *not* two separate

---

[1] F.A. Hayek, *The Constitution of Liberty* (Chicago: University of Chicago Press, 1960), p. 87.

questions. Whoever makes something, having bought or contracted for all other held resources used in the process (transferring some of his holdings for these cooperating factors), is entitled to it. The situation is *not* one of something's getting made, and there being an open question of who is to get it. Things come into the world already attached to people having entitlements over them. From the point of view of the historical entitlement conception of justice in holdings, those who start afresh to complete "to each according to his ____" treat objects as if they appeared from nowhere, out of nothing. A complete theory of justice might cover this limit case as well; perhaps here is a use for the usual conceptions of distributive justice.

So entrenched are maxims of the usual form that perhaps we should present the entitlement conception as a competitor. Ignoring acquisition and rectification, we might say:

> From each according to what he chooses to do, to each according to what he does for himself (perhaps with the contracted aid of others) and what others choose to do for him and choose to give him of what they've been given previously (under this maxim) and haven't yet expended or transferred.

This, the discerning reader will have noticed, has its defects as a slogan. So as a summary and great simplification (and not as a maxim with any independent meaning) we have:

> From each as they choose, to each as they are chosen.

How Liberty Upsets Patterns

It is not clear how those holding alternative conceptions of distributive justice can reject the entitlement conception of justice in holdings. For suppose a distribution favored by one of these non-entitlement conceptions is realized. Let us suppose it is your favorite one and let us call this distribution D_1; perhaps everyone has an equal share, perhaps shares vary in accordance with some dimension you treasure. Now suppose that Wilt Chamberlain is greatly in demand by basketball teams, being a great gate attraction. (Also suppose contracts run only for a year, with players being free agents.) He signs the following sort of contract with a team: In each home game, twenty-five cents from the price of each ticket of admission goes to him. (We ignore the question of whether he is "gouging" the owners, letting them look out for themselves.) The season starts, and people cheerfully attend his team's games; they buy their tickets, each time dropping a separate twenty-five cents of their admission price into a special box with Chamberlain's name on it. They are excited about seeing him play; it is worth the total admission price to them. Let us suppose that in one season one million persons attend his home games, and Wilt Chamberlain winds up with $250,000, a much larger sum than the average income and larger even than anyone else has. Is he entitled to this income? Is this new distribution D_2, unjust? If so, why? There is *no* question about whether each of the people was entitled to the control over the resources they held in D_1; because that was the distribution (your favorite) that (for the purposes of argument) we assumed was acceptable. Each of these persons *chose* to give twenty-five cents of their money to Chamberlain. They could have spent it on going to the movies, or on candy bars, or on copies of *Dissent* magazine, or of *Monthly Review*. But they all, at least one million of them, converged on giving it to Wilt Chamberlain in exchange for watching him play basketball. If D_1 was a just distribution, and people voluntarily moved from it to D_2, transferring parts of their shares they were given under D_1 (what was it for if not to do something with?), isn't D_2 also just? If the people were entitled to dispose of the resources to which they were entitled (under D_1), didn't this include their being entitled to give it to, or exchange it with, Wilt Chamberlain? Can anyone else complain on grounds of justice? Each other person already has his legitimate share under D_1. Under D_1, there is nothing that anyone has that anyone else has a claim of justice against. After someone transfers something to Wilt Chamberlain, third parties *still* have their legitimate shares; *their* shares are not changed. By what process could such a transfer among two persons give rise to a legitimate claim of distributive justice on a portion of what was transferred, by a third party who had no claim of justice on any holding of the others *before* the transfer? To cut off objections irrelevant here, we might imagine the exchanges occurring in a socialist society, after hours. After playing whatever basketball he does in his daily work, or doing whatever other daily work he does, Wilt Chamberlain decides to put in *overtime* to earn additional money. (First his work quota is set; he works time over that.) Or imagine it is a skilled juggler people like to see, who puts on shows after hours.

Why might someone work overtime in a society in which it is assumed their needs are satisfied? Perhaps because they care about things other than needs. I like to write in books that I read, and to have easy access to books for browsing at odd hours. It would be very pleasant and convenient to have the resources of Widener Library in my back yard. No society, I assume, will provide such resources close to each person who would like them as part of his regular allotment (under D_1). Thus, persons either must do without some extra things that they want, or be allowed to do something extra to get some of these things. On what basis could the inequalities that would eventuate be forbidden? Notice also that small factories would spring up in a socialist society, unless forbidden. I melt down some of my personal possessions (under D_1) and build a machine out of the material. I offer you, and others, a philosophy lecture once a week in exchange for your cranking the handle on my machine, whose products I exchange for yet other things, and so on. (The raw materials used by the machine are given to me by others who possess them under D_1, in exchange for hearing lectures.) Each person might participate to gain things over and above their allotment under D_1. Some persons even might want to leave their job in socialist industry and work full time in this private sector.... Here I wish merely to note how private property even in means of production would occur in a socialist society that did not forbid people to use as they wished some of the resources they are given under the socialist distribution D_1.[1] The socialist society would have to forbid capitalist acts between consenting adults.

The general point illustrated by the Wilt Chamberlain example and the example of the entrepreneur in a socialist society is that no end-state principle or distributional patterned principle of justice can be continuously realized without continuous interference with people's lives. Any favored pattern would be transformed into one unfavored by the principle, by people choosing to act in various ways; for example, by people exchanging goods and services with other people, or giving things to other people, things the transferrers are entitled to under the favored distributional pattern. To maintain a pattern one must either continually interfere to stop people from transferring resources as they wish to, or continually (or periodically) interfere to take from some persons resources that others for some reason chose to transfer to them. (But if some time limit is to be set on how long people may keep resources others voluntarily transfer to them, why let them keep these resources for *any* period of time? Why not have immediate confiscation?) It might be objected that all persons voluntarily will choose to refrain from actions which would upset the pattern. This presupposes unrealistically (1) that all will most want to maintain the pattern (are those who don't, to be "re-educated" or forced to undergo "self-criticism"?), (2) that each can gather enough information about his own actions and the ongoing activities of others to discover which of his actions will upset the pattern, and (3) that diverse and far-flung persons can coordinate their actions to dovetail into the pattern. Compare the manner in which the market is neutral among persons' desires, as it reflects and

---

[1] See John Henry MacKay's novel, *The Anarchists* (New York: Doubleday Anchor Books, 1966); see also Noam Chomsky, Introduction to Daniel Guerin, *Anarchism: From Theory to Practice* (New York: Monthly Review Press, 1970), pages xiii, xv.

transmits widely scattered information via prices, and coordinates persons' activities.

It puts things perhaps a bit too strongly to say that every patterned (or end-state) principle is liable to be thwarted by the voluntary actions of the individual parties transferring some of their shares they receive under the principle. For perhaps some *very* weak patterns are not so thwarted. Any distributional pattern with any egalitarian component is overturnable by the voluntary actions of individual persons over time; as is every patterned condition with sufficient content so as actually to have been proposed as presenting the central core of distributive justice. Still, given the possibility that some weak conditions of patterns may not be unstable in this way, it would be better to formulate an explicit description of the kind of interesting and contentful patterns under discussion, and to prove a theorem about their instability. Since the weaker the patterning, the more likely it is that the entitlement system itself satisfies it, a plausible conjecture is that any patterning either is unstable or is satisfied by the entitlement system.

[...]

Redistribution and Property Rights

Apparently, patterned principles allow people to choose to expend upon themselves, but not upon others, those resources they are entitled to (or rather, receive) under some favored distributional pattern D_1. For if each of several persons chooses to expend some of his D_1 resources upon one other person, then that other person will receive more than his D_1 share, disturbing the favored distributional pattern. Maintaining a distributional pattern is individualism with a vengeance! Patterned distributional principles do not give people what entitlement principles do, only better distributed. For they do not give the right to choose what to do with what one has; they do not give the right to choose to pursue an end involving (intrinsically, or as a means) the enhancement of another's position. To such views, families are disturbing; for within a family occur transfers that upset the favored distributional pattern. Either families themselves become

units to which distribution takes place, the column occupiers (on what rationale?), or loving behavior is forbidden. We should note in passing the ambivalent position of radicals toward the family. Its loving relationships are seen as a model to be emulated and extended across the whole society, at the same time that it is denounced as a suffocating institution to be broken and condemned as a focus of parochial concerns that interfere with achieving radical goals. Need we say that it is not appropriate to enforce across the wider society the relationships of love and care appropriate within a family, relationships which are voluntarily undertaken? Incidentally, love is an interesting instance of another relationship that is historical, in that (like justice) it depends upon what actually occurred. An adult may come to love another because of the other's characteristics; but it is the other person, and not the characteristics, that is loved.[1] The love is not transferrable to someone else with the same characteristics, even to one who "scores" higher for these characteristics. And the love endures through changes of the characteristics that gave rise to it. One loves the particular person one actually encountered. Why love is historical, attaching to persons in this way and not to characteristics, is an interesting and puzzling question.

Proponents of patterned principles of distributive justice focus upon criteria for determining who is to receive holdings; they consider the reasons for which someone should have something, and also the total picture of holdings. Whether or not it is better to give than to receive, proponents of patterned principles ignore giving altogether. In considering the distribution of goods, income, and so forth, their theories are theories of recipient justice; they completely ignore any right a person might have to give something to someone. Even in exchanges where each party is simultaneously giver and recipient, patterned principles of justice focus only upon the recipient role and its supposed

---

[1] See Gregory Vlastos, "The Individual as an Object of Love in Plato," in his *Platonic Studies* (Princeton: Princeton University Press, 1973), pp. 3–34.

rights. Thus discussions tend to focus on whether people (should) have a right to inherit, rather than on whether people (should) have a right to bequeath or on whether persons who have a right to hold also have a right to choose that others hold in their place. I lack a good explanation of why the usual theories of distributive justice are so recipient oriented; ignoring givers and transferrers and their rights is of a piece with ignoring producers and their entitlements. But why is it *all* ignored?

Patterned principles of distributive justice necessitate redistributive activities. The likelihood is small that any actual freely-arrived-at set of holdings fits a given pattern; and the likelihood is nil that it will continue to fit the pattern as people exchange and give. From the point of view of an entitlement theory, redistribution is a serious matter indeed, involving, as it does, the violation of people's rights. (An exception is those things that fall under the principle of the rectification of injustices.) From other points of view, also, it is serious.

Taxation of earnings from labor is on a par with forced labor. Some persons find this claim obviously true: taking the earnings of *n* hours labor is like taking *n* hours from the person; it is like forcing the person to work *n* hours for another's purpose. Others find the claim absurd. But even these, *if* they object to forced labor, would oppose forcing unemployed hippies to work for the benefit of the needy. And they would also object to forcing each person to work five extra hours each week for the benefit of the needy. But a system that takes five hours' wages in taxes does not seem to them like one that forces someone to work five hours, since it offers the person forced a wider range of choice in activities than does taxation in kind with the particular labor specified. (But we can imagine a gradation of systems of forced labor, from one that specifies a particular activity, to one that gives a choice among two activities, to … ; and so on up.) Furthermore, people envisage a system with something like a proportional tax on everything above the amount necessary for basic needs. Some think this does not force someone to work extra hours, since there is no fixed number of

extra hours he is forced to work, and since he can avoid the tax entirely by earning only enough to cover his basic needs. This is a very uncharacteristic view of forcing for those who *also* think people are forced to do something *whenever* the alternatives they face are considerably worse. However, *neither* view is correct. The fact that others intentionally intervene, in violation of a side constraint against aggression, to threaten force to limit the alternatives, in this case to paying taxes or (presumably the worse alternative) bare subsistence, makes the taxation system one of forced labor and distinguishes it from other cases of limited choices which are not forcings.

The man who chooses to work longer to gain an income more than sufficient for his basic needs prefers some extra goods or services to the leisure and activities he could perform during the possible nonworking hours; whereas the man who chooses not to work the extra time prefers the leisure activities to the extra goods or services he could acquire by working more. Given this, if it would be illegitimate for a tax system to seize some of a man's leisure (forced labor) for the purpose of serving the needy, how can it be legitimate for a tax system to seize some of a man's goods for that purpose? Why should we treat the man whose happiness requires certain material goods or services differently from the man whose preferences and desires make such goods unnecessary for his happiness? Why should the man who prefers seeing a movie (and who has to earn money for a ticket) be open to the required call to aid the needy, while the person who prefers looking at a sunset (and hence need earn no extra money) is not? Indeed, isn't it surprising that redistributionists choose to ignore the man whose pleasures are so easily attainable without extra labor, while adding yet another burden to the poor unfortunate who must work for his pleasures? If anything, one would have expected the reverse. Why is the person with the nonmaterial or nonconsumption desire allowed to proceed unimpeded to his most favored feasible alternative, whereas the man whose pleasures or desires involve material things and who must work for extra money (thereby serving whomever considers his activities valuable enough to pay him) is constrained in what he can realize? Perhaps there is no difference in principle. And perhaps some think the answer concerns merely administrative convenience. (These questions and issues will not disturb those who think that forced labor to serve the needy or to realize some favored end-state pattern is acceptable.) In a fuller discussion we would have (and want) to extend our argument to include interest, entrepreneurial profits, and so on. Those who doubt that this extension can be carried through, and who draw the line here at taxation of income from labor, will have to state rather complicated patterned *historical* principles of distributive justice, since end-state principles would not distinguish *sources* of income in any way. It is enough for now to get away from end-state principles and to make clear how various patterned principles are dependent upon particular views about the sources or the illegitimacy or the lesser legitimacy of profits, interest, and so on; which particular views may well be mistaken.

What sort of right over others does a legally institutionalized end-state pattern give one? The central core of the notion of a property right in X, relative to which other parts of the notion are to be explained, is the right to determine what shall be done with X; the right to choose which of the constrained set of options concerning X shall be realized or attempted. The constraints are set by other principles or laws operating in the society; in our theory, by the Lockean rights people possess (under the minimal state). My property rights in my knife allow me to leave it where I will, but not in your chest. I may choose which of the acceptable options involving the knife is to be realized. This notion of property helps us to understand why earlier theorists spoke of people as having property in themselves and their labor. They viewed each person as having a right to decide what would become of himself and what he would do, and as having a right to reap the benefits of what he did.

This right of selecting the alternative to be realized from the constrained set of alternatives may be held by an *individual* or by a *group* with some procedure for reaching a joint decision; or the right may be passed back and forth, so that one year I decide what's to become of X, and the next year you do (with the alternative of destruction, perhaps, being excluded). Or, during the same time period, some types of decisions about X may be made by me, and others by you. And so on. We lack an adequate, fruitful, analytical apparatus for classifying the *types* of constraints on the set of options among which choices are to be made, and the *types* of ways decision powers can be held, divided, and amalgamated. A *theory* of property would, among other things, contain such a classification of constraints and decision modes, and from a small number of principles would follow a host of interesting statements about the *consequences* and effects of certain combinations of constraints and modes of decision.

When end-result principles of distributive justice are built into the legal structure of a society, they (as do most patterned principles) give each citizen an enforceable claim to some portion of the total social product; that is, to some portion of the sum total of the individually and jointly made products. This total product is produced by individuals laboring, using means of production others have saved to bring into existence, by people organizing production or creating means to produce new things or things in a new way. It is on this batch of individual activities that patterned distributional principles give each individual an enforceable claim. Each person has a claim to the activities and the products of other persons, independently of whether the other persons enter into particular relationships that give rise to these claims, and independently of whether they voluntarily take these claims upon themselves, in charity or in exchange for something.

Whether it is done through taxation on wages or on wages over a certain amount, or through seizure of profits, or through there being a big *social pot* so that it's not clear what's coming from where and what's going where, patterned principles of distributive justice involve appropriating the actions of other persons. Seizing the results of someone's labor is equivalent to seizing hours from him and directing him to carry on various activities. If people force you to do certain work, or unrewarded work, for a certain period of time, they decide what you are to do and what purposes your work is to serve apart from your decisions. This process whereby they take this decision from you makes them a *part-owner* of you; it gives them a property right in you. Just as having such partial control and power of decision, by right, over an animal or inanimate object would be to have a property right in it.

End-state and most patterned principles of distributive justice institute (partial) ownership by others of people and their actions and labor. These principles involve a shift from the classical liberals' notion of self-ownership to a notion of (partial) property rights in other people.

Considerations such as these confront end-state and other patterned conceptions of justice with the question of whether the actions necessary to achieve the selected pattern don't themselves violate moral side constraints. Any view holding that there are moral side constraints on actions, that not all moral considerations can be built into end states that are to be achieved … must face the possibility that some of its goals are not achievable by any morally permissible available means. An entitlement theorist will face such conflicts in a society that deviates from the principles of justice for the generation of holdings, if and only if the only actions available to realize the principles themselves violate some moral constraints. Since deviation from the first two principles of justice (in acquisition and transfer) will involve other persons' direct and aggressive intervention to violate rights, and since moral constraints will not exclude defensive or retributive action in such cases, the entitlement theorist's problem rarely will be pressing. And whatever difficulties he has in applying the principle of rectification to persons who did not themselves violate the first two principles are difficulties in balancing the conflicting considerations so as correctly to formulate the complex principle of rectification itself: he will not violate moral side constraints by applying the principle. Proponents of patterned conceptions of justice, however, often will face head-on clashes (and poignant ones if they cherish each party to the clash) between moral side constraints on how individuals may be treated and their patterned conception of justice that presents an end state or other pattern that *must* be realized.

May a person emigrate from a nation that has institutionalized some end-state or patterned distributional principle? For some principles (for example, Hayek's) emigration presents no theoretical problem. But for others it is a tricky matter. Consider a nation having a compulsoty scheme of minimal social provision to aid the neediest (or one organized so as to maximize the position of the worst-off group); no one may opt out of participating in it. (None may say, "Don't compel me to contribute to others and don't provide for me via this compulsory mechanism if I am in need.") Everyone above a certain level is forced to contribute to aid the needy. But if emigration from the country were allowed, anyone could choose to move to another country that did not have compulsory social provision but otherwise was (as much as possible) identical. In such a case, the person's *only* motive for leaving would be to avoid participating in the compulsory scheme of social provision. And if he does leave, the needy in his initial country will receive no (compelled) help from him. What rationale yields the result that the person be permitted to emigrate, yet forbidden to stay and opt out of the compulsory scheme of social provision? If providing for the needy is of overriding importance, this does militate against allowing internal opting out; but it also speaks against allowing external emigration. (Would it also support, to some extent, the kidnapping of persons living in a place without compulsory social provision, who could be forced to make a contribution to the needy in your community?) Perhaps the crucial component of the position that allows emigration solely to avoid certain arrangements, while not allowing anyone internally to opt out of them, is a concern for fraternal feelings within the country. "We don't want anyone here who doesn't contribute, who doesn't care enough about the others to contribute." That concern, in this case, would have to be tied to the view that forced aiding tends to produce fraternal feelings between the aided and the aider (or perhaps merely to the view that the knowledge that someone or other voluntarily is not aiding produces unfraternal feelings).

DISCUSSION QUESTIONS

1. Explain the distinction between Nozick's entitlement theory and what he calls historical principles and end-result principles. Explain the distinction between patterned historical principles and non-patterned historical principles.

2. Explain Nozick's Wilt Chamberlain argument against end-result and patterned historical principles. Is it a good argument? Why or why not?

3. Nozick claims that "[t]axation of earnings from labor is on a par with forced labor." Explain and evaluate his claim.

69

Gerald A. Cohen, "Illusions about Private Property and Freedom" (1981)

G.A. Cohen (1941–2009) was a political philosopher, perhaps best known for his long-time commitment to providing an analytic defense of Marxism. In the following selection, he argues that, in some circumstances, a socialist model of communal property can offer more liberty than the private property model advocated by proponents of capitalism.

SOURCE

Cohen, G.A. "Illusions About Private Property and Freedom," from Volume IV of *Issues in Marxist Philosophy*, edited by J. Mepham and D. Ruben. Sussex: Harvester Press, 1981.

1.   In capitalist societies everyone owns something, be it only his own labour power, and each is free to sell what he owns and to buy whatever the sale of it enables him to buy. Many claims made on capitalism's behalf may reasonably be doubted, but here is a freedom which it certainly bestows.

It is clear that under capitalism everyone has this freedom, unless being free to sell something is incompatible with being forced to sell it: but I do not think it is. For one is in general free to do anything which one is forced to do.

There are several reasons for affirming this possibly surprising thesis. The most direct argument in favour of it is as follows: you cannot be forced to do what you are not able to do, and you are not able to do what you are not free to do. Hence you are free to do what you are forced to do.

I am not, in the foregoing argument, equating being free to do something with being able to do it. Being free to do *A* is a necessary but not a sufficient condition of being able to do *A*. I may be unable to do something not because I am unfree to, but because I lack the relevant capacity. Thus I am no doubt free to swim across the English Channel, but I am nevertheless unable to. If I were a much better swimmer, but forbidden by well-enforced law to swim it, then, again, I would be unable to swim it. The argument of the last paragraph goes through on what is often called the "negative" or "social" conception of freedom, according to which I am free to do whatever nobody would prevent me from doing. I have no quarrel with that conception in this paper.

A second argument for the claim that I am free to do what I am forced to do is that one way of frustrating someone who would force me to do something is by rendering myself not free to do it: it follows, by contraposition, that if I am forced to do it, I am free to do it. To illustrate: I commit a crime, thereby causing myself to be gaoled, so that I cannot be forced by you to do something I abhor. If you still hope to force me to do it you will have to make me free to do it (by springing me from jail).

Look at it this way: before you are forced to do A, you are, at least in standard cases, free to do A and free not to do A. The force removes the second freedom, but why suppose that it removes the first? It puts no obstacle in the path of your doing A, and you therefore remain free to do it.

We may conclude, not only that being free to do A is compatible with being forced to do A, but that being forced to do A *entails* being free to do A. Resistance to this odd-sounding but demonstrable result reflects failure to distinguish the idea of *being free to do something* from other ideas, such as the idea of *doing something freely*. I am free to do what I am forced to do even if, as is usually true, I do not do it freely, and even though, as is always true, I am not free with respect to whether or not I do it.

I labour this truth—that one is free to do what one is forced to do—because it, and failure to perceive it, help to explain the character and the persistence of a certain ideological disagreement. Marxists say that working-class people are forced to sell their labour power. Bourgeois thinkers celebrate the freedom of contract manifest not only in the capitalist's purchase of labour power but also in the worker's sale of it. If Marxists are right, working-class people are importantly unfree: they are not free not to sell their labour power. But it remains true that (unlike chattel slaves) they are free to sell their labour power. The unfreedom asserted by Marxists is compatible with the freedom asserted by bourgeois thinkers. Indeed: if the Marxists are right the bourgeois thinkers are right, unless they

also think, as characteristically they do, that the truth they emphasise refutes the Marxist claim. The bourgeois thinkers go wrong not when they say that the worker is free to sell his labour power, but when they infer that the Marxist cannot therefore be right in his claim that the worker is forced to. And Marxists share the bourgeois thinkers' error when they think it necessary to deny what the bourgeois thinkers say. If the worker is not free to sell his labour power, of what freedom is a foreigner whose work permit is removed deprived?

2.   Freedom to buy and sell is one freedom, of which in capitalism there is a great deal. It belongs to capitalism's esssential nature. But many think that capitalism is, quite as essentially, a more comprehensively free society. Very many people, including philosophers, who try to speak carefully, use the phrase "free society" as an alternative name for societies which are capitalist.[1] And many contemporary English-speaking philosophers and economists call the doctrine which recommends a purely capitalist society "libertarianism," not, as might be thought more apt, "libertarianism with respect to buying and selling."

It is not only the libertarians themselves who think that is the right name for their party. Many who reject their aims concede the name to them: they agree that unmodified capitalism is comprehensively a realm of freedom. This applies to *some* of those who call themselves "liberals."

These liberals assert, plausibly, that liberty is a good thing, but they say that it is not the only good thing. So far, libertarians will agree. But liberals also believe that libertarians wrongly sacrifice other good things in too total defence of the one good of liberty. They agree with libertarians that pure capitalism is liberty pure and simple, or anyway *economic* liberty pure and simple, but they think

---

[1] See, for example, Jan Narveson, "A Puzzle about Economic Justice in Rawls' Theory," *Social Theory and Practice* (1976): 3; James Rachels, "What People Deserve," in J. Arthur and W. Shaw (eds.), *Justice and Economic Distribution* (Englewood Cliffs[, NJ: Prentice-Hall], 1978), p. 151.

the various good things lost when liberty pure and simple is the rule [sic] justify restraints on liberty. They want a capitalism modified by welfare legislation and state intervention in the market. They advocate, they say, not unrestrained liberty, but liberty restrained by the demands of social and economic security. They think that what they call a free economy is too damaging to those who, by nature or circumstance, are ill placed to achieve a minimally proper standard of life within it, so they favour, within limits, taxing the better off for the sake of the worse off, although they believe that such taxation reduces liberty. They also think that what they call a free economy is subject to fluctuations in productive activity and misallocations of resources which are potentially damaging to everyone, so they favour measures of interference in the market, although, again, they believe that such interventions diminish liberty. They do not question the libertarian's description of capitalism as the (economically) free society. But they believe that economic freedom may rightly and reasonably be abridged. They believe in a compromise between liberty and other values, and that what is known as the welfare state mixed economy achieves the right compromise.

I shall argue that libertarians, and liberals of the kind described, misuse the concept of freedom. This is not a comment on the attractiveness of the institutions they severally favour, but on the rhetoric they use to describe them. If, however, as I contend, they misdescribe those institutions, then that is surely because the correct description of them would make them less attractive, so my critique of the defensive rhetoric is indirectly a critique of the institutions the rhetoric defends.

My central contention is that liberals and libertarians see the freedom which is intrinsic to capitalism, but do not give proper notice to the unfreedom which necessarily accompanies it.

To expose this failure of perception, I shall criticise a description of the libertarian position provided by Antony Flew in his *Dictionary of Philosophy*. It is there said to be "wholehearted political and economic liberalism, opposed to any social or legal constraints on individual freedom."[1] Liberals of the kind I described above would avow themselves unwholehearted in the terms of this definition. For they would say that they support certain (at any rate) legal constraints on individual freedom.

Now a society in which there are *no* "social and legal constraints on individual freedom" is perhaps imaginable, at any rate by people who have highly anarchic imaginations. But, be that as it may, the Flew definition misdescribes libertarians, since it does not apply to defenders of capitalism, which is what libertarians profess to be, and are.

For consider. If the state prevents me from doing something I want to do, it evidently places a constraint on my freedom. Suppose, then, that I want to perform an action which involves a legally prohibited use of your property. I want, let us say, to pitch a tent in your large back garden, because I have no home or land of my own, but I have got hold of a tent, legitimately or otherwise. If I now try to do what I want to do, the chances are that the state will intervene on your behalf. If it does, I shall suffer a constraint on my freedom. The same goes for all unpermitted uses of a piece of private property by those who do not own it, and there are always those who do not own it, since "private ownership by one person ... presupposes nonownership on the part of other persons."[2] But the free enterprise economy advocated by libertarians rests upon private property: you can sell and buy only what you respectively own and come to own. It follows that the Flew definition is untrue to *its definiendum,* and that "libertarianism" is a questionable name for the position it now standardly denotes.

How could Flew publish the definition I have criticised? I do not think he was being dishonest. I would not accuse him of appreciating the truth of this particular matter and deliberately falsifying it. Why then is it that Flew, and libertarians like him, see the unfreedom in prospective state interference

[1] *A Dictionary of Philosophy* (London[: Routledge and Kegan Paul], 1979), p. 188.
[2] Karl Marx, *Capital, III* (Moscow[: Foreign Language Publishing House], 1970), p. 812.

with your use of your property, but do not see the unfreedom in the standing intervention against my use of it entailed by the fact that it *is* your private property? What explains their monocular vision?

One explanation is a tendency to take as part of the structure of human existence in general, and therefore as no "social or legal constraint" on freedom, any structure around which, *merely as things are,* much of our activity is organised. In capitalist society the institution of private property is such a structure. It is treated as so *given* that the obstacles it puts on freedom are not perceived, while any impingement on private property itself is immediately noticed. Yet private property pretty well is a distribution of freedom *and* unfreedom. It is necessarily associated with the liberty of private owners to do as they wish with what they own, but it no less necessarily withdraws liberty from those who do not own it. To think of capitalism as a realm of freedom is to overlook half of its nature. (I am aware that the tendency to this failure of perception is stronger, other things being equal, the more private property a person has. I do not think really poor people need to have their eyes opened to the simple conceptual truth I emphasise. I also do not claim that anyone of sound mind will for long deny that private property places restrictions on freedom, once the point has been made. What is striking is that the point so often needs to be made, against what should be *obvious* absurdities, such as Flew's definition of "libertarianism.")

I have supposed that to prevent someone from doing something he wants to do is to make him, in that respect, unfree: I am unfree whenever someone interferes, *justifiably or otherwise,* with my actions. But there is a definition of freedom which is implicit in much libertarian writing,[1] and which entails that interference is *not a* sufficient condition of unfreedom. On that definition, which I shall call the *moralised* definition, I am unfree only when someone does or *would unjustifiably* interfere with me. If one

now combines this moralised definition of freedom with a moral endorsement of private property, one reaches the result that the protection of legitimate private property cannot restrict anyone's freedom. It will follow from the moral endorsement of private property that you and the police are justified in preventing me from pitching my tent on your land, and, because of the moralised definition of freedom, it will then further follow that you and the police do not thereby restrict my freedom. So here we have another explanation of how intelligent philosophers are able to say what they do about capitalism, private property and freedom. But the characterisation of freedom which figures in the explanation is unacceptable. For it entails that a properly convicted murderer is not rendered unfree when he is justifiably imprisoned.

Even justified interference reduces freedom. But suppose for a moment that, as libertarians say or imply, it does not. On that supposition one cannot readily argue that interference with private property is wrong *because it* reduces freedom. For one can no longer take for granted, what is evident on a morally neutral account of freedom, that interference with private property *does* reduce freedom. Under a moralised account of freedom one must abstain from that assertion until one has shown that private property is morally defensible. Yet libertarians tend *both* to use a moralised definition *and* to take it for granted that interference with private property diminishes the owner's freedom. Yet they can take that for granted only on an account of freedom in which it is equally obvious that the protection of private property diminishes the freedom of nonowners, to avoid which consequence they retreat to a moralised definition of the concept.

Still, libertarians who embrace the moralised definition of freedom need not occupy this inconsistent position. They can escape it by justifying private property on grounds other than considerations of freedom. They can contrive, for example, to represent interference with rightfully held private property as unjust, and *therefore,* by virtue of the moralised definition, invasive of freedom. This is a consistent position. But it still incorporates an

---

[1] And sometimes also explicit: see Robert Nozick, *Anarchy, State, and Utopia* (New York[: Basic Books], 1974), p. 262.

unacceptable definition of freedom, and the position is improved if that is eliminated. We then have a defence of private property on grounds of justice. Freedom falls out of the picture.

3.   I now want to consider a possible response to what I said about pitching a tent on your land. It might be granted that the prohibition on my doing so restricts my freedom, but not, so it might be said, my *economic* freedom. If the connection between capitalism and freedom is overstated by libertarians and others, the possibility that capitalism is *economic* freedom still requires consideration.

The resurrected identification will survive only if the unavailability to me of your garden is no restriction on my economic freedom. I can think of only one reason for saying so. It is that I am not here restricted with respect to whether I may sell something I own, or buy something in exchange for what I own. If that is economic freedom, then my lack of access to your garden does not limit my economic freedom.

A different definition of economic freedom would include in it freedom to use goods and services. It is hard to say whether such a definition is superior to the less inclusive one just considered, since "neither the tradition of political philosophy nor common understanding provides us with a ... set of categories of economic liberty" comparable to the acknowledged set of categories of political liberty,[1] perhaps because the boundary of the economic domain is unclear.[2] A reasoned attempt to construct a clear concept of economic freedom might be a valuable exercise, but it is not one which I can report having completed. I am accordingly unable to recommend any particular characterisation of economic freedom.

I can nevertheless reply to the present claim, as follows: either economic freedom includes the freedom to use goods and services, or it does not. If it

does, then capitalism withholds economic freedom wherever it grants it, as the tent case shows. If, on the other hand, economic freedom relates only to buying and selling, then the case for identifying economic freedom and free enterprise looks better. But we have to define "economic freedom" narrowly to obtain this result. On a wide but eligible definition of economic freedom, capitalism offers a particular limited form of it. On a narrow definition, the limitations recede, but we are now talking about a much narrower freedom.

To those who do not think this freedom is narrow, I offer three comments, which may move them a little:

(i) The freedom in question is, fully described, freedom to sell what I own and to buy whatever the sale of what I own enables me to buy. Importantly, that freedom is not identical with freedom to buy and sell just anything at all, which is much broader, and which is not granted by capitalism. For first, one is evidently not free to sell what belongs to somebody else. This is, to be sure, true by definition: there logically *could* not be that freedom, in any society. But this does not diminish the importance of noticing that capitalism does not offer it. And secondly, one is free to buy, not anything at all, but only that which the sale of what one owns enables one to buy. A poor man is not free to buy a grand piano, even if one necessary condition of that freedom—he is not legally forbidden to do so—is satisfied.

(ii) It is an important fact about freedom in general, and hence about the freedom under discussion, that it comes in degrees. That I am free to do something does not say *how* free I am to do that thing, which might be more or less. To cite just one dimension in which freedom's degree varies, my freedom to do *A* is, other things equal, smaller, the greater is the cost to me of doing *A*. It might be true of both a poor man and a rich man that each is free to buy an £8 ticket to the opera, yet the rich man's freedom to do so is greater, since, unlike the poor man, he will not have to give up a few decent meals, for example, in order to buy the ticket. Since it is consistent with the capitalist character of a society that it should contain poor people, the buying and

[1] Thomas Scanlon, "Liberty, Contract and Contribution," in G. Dworkin *et al.* (eds.), *Markets and Morals* (Washington[: Hemisphere Publishing Company, 1977), p. 54; and see also p. 57.
[2] This suggestion is due to Chris Provis.

selling freedom which capitalism grants universally can be enjoyed in very limited degrees.

Now some will disagree with my claim that freedom varies in degree in the manner just described. They will deny that some people have a higher degree of a certain freedom than others (who also have that freedom), and will say, instead, that for some people it is relatively easy to exercise a freedom which others, who also have it, find it difficult to exercise. But even if they are right, the substance of my case is unweakened. For it is scarcely intelligible that one should be interested in how much freedom people have in a certain form of society without being interested in how readily they are able to exercise it.

(iii) Finally, we should consider the *point* of the freedom to buy and sell, as far as the individual who has it is concerned. For most citizens, most of the time, that point is to obtain goods and services of various sorts. When, therefore, goods and services are available independently of the market, the individual might not feel that his lack of freedom to *buy* them is a particularly significant lack. A lack of freedom to buy medical services is no serious restriction on liberty in a society which makes them publicly available on a decent scale. In a socialist society certain things will be unbuyable, and, consequently, unsellable. But, as long as they are obtainable by other means, one should not exaggerate the gravity of the resulting restrictions on freedom.

Still, restrictions on freedom do result. I may not *want* to buy a medical or an educational service, but I am nevertheless unfree to, if the transaction is forbidden. Note that I would not be unfree to if a certain popular account of freedom were correct, according to which I am unfree only when what I *want* to do is something I shall or would be prevented from doing. But that account is false.[1] There are important connections between freedom and

desire, but the straightforward one maintained in the popular account is not among them. Reference to a man's desires is irrelevant to the question "What is he free to do?" but it is, I believe, relevant to the question "How much freedom (comprehensively) does he have?" and consequently to the politically crucial question of comparing the amounts of freedom enjoyed in different societies. As far as I know, the vast philosophical literature on freedom contains no sustained attempt to formulate criteria for answering questions about quantity of freedom....

[...]

5.   I said above that capitalism and socialism offer different sets of freedoms, but I emphatically do not say that they provide freedom in two different senses of that term. To the claim that capitalism gives people freedom some socialists respond that what they get *is merely bourgeois* freedom. Good things can be meant by that response: that there are important particular liberties which capitalism does not confer; and/or that I do not have freedom, but only a necessary condition of it, when a course of action (for example, skiing) is, though not *itself* against the law, unavailable to me anyway, because other laws (for example, those of private property, which prevent a poor man from using a rich man's unused skis) forbid me the means to perform it. But when socialists suggest that there is no "real" freedom under capitalism, at any rate for the workers, or that socialism promises freedom of a higher and as yet unrealised kind, then I think their line is theoretically incorrect and politically disastrous. For there is freedom under capitalism, in a plain, good sense, and if socialism will not give us more of it, we shall rightly be disappointed. If the socialist says he is offering a new variety of freedom, the advocate of capitalism will carry the day with his reply that he prefers freedom of the known variety to an unexplained and unexemplified rival. But if, as I would recommend, the socialist argues that capitalism is, all things considered, inimical to freedom *in the very sense* of "freedom" in which, as he should concede, a person's freedom is diminished when his private property is

---

[1] See Isaiah Berlin, *Four Essays on Liberty* (Oxford[: Oxford University Press], 1969), pp. xxxviii ff., 139–40. The point was originally made by Richard Wollheim, in a review of Berlin's *Two Concepts of Liberty.* See too Hillel Steiner, "Individual Liberty," *Proceedings of the Aristotelian Society,* 1974–75, p. 34.

tampered with, then he presents a challenge which the advocate of capitalism, by virtue of his own commitment, cannot ignore.

For it is a contention of socialist thought that capitalism does not live up to its own professions. A fundamental socialist challenge to the libertarian is that pure capitalism does not protect liberty in general, but rather those liberties which are built into private property, an institution which also limits liberty. And a fundamental socialist challenge to the liberal is that the modifications of modified capitalism modify not liberty, but private property, often in the interest of liberty itself. Consequently, transformations far more revolutionary than a liberal would contemplate might be justified on the very same grounds as those which support liberal reform.

A homespun example shows how communal property offers a differently shaped liberty, in no different sense of that term, and, in certain circumstances, more liberty than the private property alternative. Neighbours A and B own sets of household tools. Each has some tools which the other lacks. If A needs tools of a kind which only B has, then, private property being what it is, he is not free to take B's one for a while, even if B does not need it during that while. Now imagine that the following rule is imposed, bringing the tools into partly common ownership: each may take and use a tool belonging to the other without permission provided that the other is not using it and that he returns it when he no longer needs it, or when the other needs it, whichever comes first. *Things being what they are* (a substantive qualification: we are talking, as often we should, about the real world, not about remote possibilities) the communising rule would, I contend, increase tool-using freedom, on any reasonable view. To be sure, some freedoms are removed by the new rule. Neither neighbour is as assured of the same easy access as before to the tools that were wholly his. Sometimes he has to go next door to retrieve one of them. Nor can either now charge the other for use of a tool he himself does not then require. But these restrictions probably count for less than the increase in the range of tools available. No one is as sovereign as before over any tool, so

the privateness of the property is reduced. But freedom is probably expanded.

It is true that each would have more freedom still if he were the sovereign owner of *all* the tools. But that is not the relevant comparison. I do not deny that full ownership of a thing gives greater freedom than shared ownership of that thing. But no one did own all the tools before the modest measure of communism was introduced. The kind of comparison we need to make is between, for example, sharing ownership with ninety-nine others in a hundred things and fully owning just one of them. I submit that which arrangement nets more freedom is a matter of cases. There is little sense in one hundred people sharing control over one hundred toothbrushes. There is an overwhelming case, from the point of view of freedom, in favour of our actual practice of public ownership of street pavements. Denationalising the pavements in favour of private ownership of each piece by the residents adjacent to it would be bad for freedom of movement.

But someone will say: ownership of private property is the only example of *full* freedom. Our practice with pavements may be a good one, but no one has full freedom with respect to any part of the pavement, since he cannot, for instance, break it up and put the result to a new use, and he cannot prevent others from using it (except, perhaps, by the costly means of indefinitely standing on it himself, and he cannot even do that when laws against obstruction are enforced). The same holds for all communal possessions. No one is fully free with respect to anything in which he enjoys a merely shared ownership. Hence even if private property entails unfreedom, and even if there is freedom without private property, *there is no case of full freedom which is not a case of private property*. The underlined thesis is unaffected by the arguments against libertarianism in sections 2 and 3 of this paper.

There are two things wrong with this fresh attempt to associate freedom and private property. First, even if it is true that every case of full freedom is a case of private property, a certain number of full freedoms need not add up to more freedom overall than a larger number of partial freedoms: so it is not clear that the underlined thesis supports any interesting conclusion.

The thesis is, moreover, questionable in itself. It is a piece of bourgeois ideology masquerading as a conceptual insight. The argument for the thesis treats freedom fetishistically, as control over *material things*. But freedom, in the central sense of the term with which we have been occupied, is freedom to *act,* and if there is a concept of full freedom in that central sense, then it is inappropriate, if we want to identify it, to focus, from the start, on control over *things*. I can be fully free to walk to your home when and because the pavement is communally owned, even though I am not free to destroy or to sell a single square inch of that pavement. To be sure, action requires the use of matter, or at least space,[1] but it does not follow that to be fully free to perform an action with certain pieces of matter in a certain portion of space I need full control over the matter and the space, since some forms of control will be unnecessary to the action in question. The rights I need over things to perform a given action depend on the nature of that action.

The thesis under examination is, then, either false, or reducible to the truism that one has full freedom *with respect to a thing* only if one privately owns that thing. But why should we be especially interested in full freedom with respect to a *thing,* unless, of course, we are already ideologically committed to the overriding importance of private property?

6. Recall the example of the tools, described above. An opponent might say: the rules of private property allow neighbours to *contract* in favour of the stated arrangement. If both would gain from the change, and they are rational, they will agree to it. No communist property rule, laid down independently of contract, is needed.

This is a good reply with respect to the case at hand. For that case my only counter is the weakish one that life under capitalism tends to generate an irrationally strong attachment to purely private use of purely private property, which can lead to neglect of mutually gainful and freedom-expanding options.

That point aside, it must be granted that contracts often establish desirably communal structures, sometimes with transaction costs which communist rules would not impose, but also without the administrative costs which often attach to public regulation.

But the stated method of achieving communism cannot be generalised. We could not by contract bring into shared ownership those non-household tools and resources which Marxists call means of production. They will never be won for socialism by contract, since they belong to a small minority, to whom the rest can offer no *quid pro quo*. Most of the rest must lease their labour power to members of that minority, in exchange for some of the proceeds of their labour on facilities in whose ownership they do not share.

So we reach, at length, a central charge with respect to freedom which Marxists lay against capitalism, and which is, in my view, well founded: that in capitalist society the great majority of people are forced, because of the character of the society, to sell their labour power to others. In properly refined form, this important claim about capitalism and liberty is, I am sure, correct....

---

[1] This fact is emphasised by Hillel Steiner in section III of his "Individual Liberty," but he goes too far when he says: "My theorem is ... that *freedom is the personal possession of physical objects*" (p. 48). I claim that the "theorem" is just bourgeois ideology. For further criticism of Steiner, see Onora O'Neill, "The Most Extensive Liberty," *Proceedings of the Aristotelian Society*, 1979–80, p. 48.

DISCUSSION QUESTIONS

1. Which freedoms does Cohen see as inherent to a capitalist system? Which denials of freedom does Cohen see as inherent in a capitalist system?

2. Explain the moralized definition of freedom. How, according to Cohen, does use of a moralized definition of freedom lead to a characterization of capitalism as a system of unrestricted freedom? Do you agree with Cohen that the moralized definition of freedom is unacceptable? Explain.

3. Does a capitalist society protect economic freedom? Explain and evaluate Cohen's response to that question.

4. Explain Cohen's example involving the household tools. Do you agree with Cohen that this example shows that sometimes communal ownership offers more freedom than does private property? Explain.

70

John Rawls, selection from *A Theory of Justice* (1971)

In the following selection, Rawls provides a detailed discussion of the principles of justice that he thinks would be selected from within the original position, a situation in which the parties know virtually nothing about themselves or their positions within society.

SOURCE

Rawls, John. Excerpts from *A Theory of Justice* by John Rawls, pp. 3–22; 65–67; 69–75; 78–80; 82–83; 111–14; 150–56. Cambridge, Mass.: The Belknap Press of Harvard University Press, Copyright © 1971, 1999 by the President and Fellows of Harvard College. Reprinted by permission of the publisher.

12. Interpretations of the Second Principle

I have already mentioned that since the phrases "everyone's advantage" and "equally open to all" are ambiguous, both parts of the second principle have two natural senses. Because these senses are independent of one another, the principle has four possible meanings. Assuming that the first principle of equal liberty has the same sense throughout, we then have four interpretations of the two principles. These are indicated in the table below.

"EQUALLY OPEN"	"EVERYONE'S ADVANTAGE"	
	Principle of efficiency	Difference principle
Equality as careers open to talents	System of Natural Liberty	Natural Aristocracy
Equality as equality of fair opportunity	Liberal Equality	Democratic Equality

I shall sketch in turn these three interpretations: the system of natural liberty, liberal equality, and democratic equality. In some respects this sequence is the more intuitive one, but the sequence via the interpretation of natural aristocracy is not without interest and I shall comment on it briefly. In working out justice as fairness, we must decide which interpretation is to be preferred. I shall adopt that of democratic equality, explaining in this chapter what this notion means. The argument for its acceptance in the original position does not begin until the next chapter [of *A Theory of Justice*].

The first interpretation (in either sequence) I shall refer to as the system of natural liberty. In this rendering the first part of the second principle is understood as the principle of efficiency adjusted so as to apply to institutions or, in this case, to the basic structure of society; and the second part is understood as an open social system in which, to use the traditional phrase, careers are open to talents. I assume in all interpretations that the first principle of equal liberty is satisfied and that the economy is roughly a free market system, although the means of production may or may not be privately owned. The system of natural liberty asserts, then, that a basic structure satisfying the principle of efficiency and in which positions are open to those able and willing to strive for them will lead to a just distribution. Assigning rights and duties in this way is thought to give a scheme which allocates wealth and income, authority and responsibility, in a fair way whatever this allocation turns out to be. The doctrine includes an important element of pure procedural justice which is carried over to the other interpretations.

At this point it is necessary to make a brief digression to explain the principle of efficiency. This principle is simply that of Pareto optimality (as economists refer to it) formulated so as to apply to the basic structure. I shall always use the term "efficiency" instead because this is literally correct and the term "optimality" suggests that the concept is much broader than it is in fact.[1] To be sure, this principle was not originally intended to apply to institutions but to particular configurations of the economic system, for example, to distributions of goods among consumers or to modes of production. The principle holds that a configuration is efficient whenever it is impossible to change it so as to make some persons (at least one) better off

without at the same time making other persons (at least one) worse off. Thus a distribution of a stock of commodities among certain individuals is efficient if there exists no redistribution of these goods that improves the circumstances of at least one of these individuals without another being disadvantaged. The organization of production is efficient if there is no way to alter inputs so as to produce more of some commodity without producing less of another. For if we could produce more of one good without having to give up some of another, the larger stock of goods could be used to better the circumstances of some persons without making that of others any worse. These applications of the principle show that it is, indeed, a principle of efficiency. A distribution of goods or a scheme of production is inefficient when there are ways of doing still better for some individuals without doing any worse for others. I shall assume that the parties in the original position accept this principle to judge the efficiency of economic and social arrangements.

The Principle of Efficiency

[...]

There are, however, many configurations which are efficient. For example, the distributions in which one person receives the entire stock of commodities is efficient, since there is no rearrangement that will make some better off and none worse off. The person who holds the whole stock must lose out. But of course not every distribution is efficient, as might be suggested by the efficiency of such disparities. As long as a distribution leaves some persons willing to swap goods with others, it cannot be efficient; for the willingness to trade shows that there is a rearrangement which improves the situation of some without hurting that of anyone else. Indeed, an efficient distribution is one in which it is not possible to find further profitable exchanges. In that sense, the allocation of goods in which one man has everything is efficient because the others have nothing to give him in return. The principle of efficiency allows then that there are many efficient configurations. Each efficient arrangement is

---

[1] On this point see T.C. Koopsman, *Three Essays on the State of Economic Science* (New York: McGraw-Hill, 1957), p. 49. Koopman remarks that a term like "allocative efficiency" would have been a more accurate name.

better than some other arrangements, but none of the efficient arrangements is better than another.

Now the principle of efficiency can be applied to the basic structure by reference to the expectations of representative men.[1] Thus we can say that an arrangement of rights and duties in the basic structure is efficient if and only if it is impossible to change the rules, to redefine the scheme of rights and duties, so as to raise the expectations of any representative man (at least one) without at the same time lowering the expectations of some (at least one) other representative man. Of course, these alterations must be consistent with the other principles. That is, in changing the basic structure we are not permitted to violate the principle of equal liberty or the requirement of open positions. What can be altered is the distribution of income and wealth and the way in which organizational powers, and various other forms of authority, regulate cooperative activities. Consistent with the constraints of liberty and accessibility, the allocation of these primary goods may be adjusted to modify the expectations of representative individuals. An arrangement of the basic structure is efficient when there is no way to change this distribution so as to raise the prospects of some without lowering the prospects of others.

There are, I shall assume, many efficient arrangements of the basic structure. Each of these specifies a particular division of advantages from social cooperation. The problem is to choose between them, to find a conception of justice that singles out one of these efficient distributions as also just. If we succeed in this, we shall have gone beyond mere efficiency yet in a way compatible with it. Now it is natural to try out the idea that as long as the social system is efficient there is no reason to be concerned with distribution. All efficient arrangements are in this case declared equally just. Of course, this suggestion would be outlandish for the allocation of particular goods to known individuals. No one would suppose that it is a matter of indifference from the standpoint of justice whether any one of a number of men happens to have everything. But the suggestion seems equally unreasonable for the basic structure. Thus it may be that under certain conditions serfdom cannot be significantly re-formed without lowering the expectations of some representative man, say that of landowners, in which case serfdom is efficient. Yet it may also happen under the same conditions that a system of free labor cannot be changed without lowering the expectations of some representative man, say that of free laborers, so this arrangement is likewise efficient. More generally, whenever a society is relevantly divided into a number of classes, it is possible, let us suppose, to maximize with respect to each one of its representative men at a time. These maxima give at least this many efficient positions, for none of them can be departed from to raise the expectations of any one representative man without lowering those of another, namely, the representative man with respect to whom the maximum is defined. Thus each of these extremes is efficient but they surely cannot be all just, and equally so. These remarks simply parallel for social systems the situation in distributing particular goods to given individuals where the distributions in which a single person has everything is efficient.

Now these reflections show only what we knew all along, that is, that the principle of efficiency cannot serve alone as a conception of justice.[2] Therefore it must be supplemented in some way. Now in the system of natural liberty the principle

---

[1] For the application of the Pareto criterion to systems of public rules, see J.M. Buchanan, "The Relevance of Pareto Optimality," *Journal of Conflict Resolution*, vol. 6 (1962), as well as his book with Gordon Tullock, *The Calculus of Consent* (Ann Arbor: The University of Michigan Press, 1962). In applying this and other principles to institutions I follow one of the points of "Two Concepts of Rules," *Philosophical Review*, vol. 64 (1955). Doing this has the advantage, among other things, of constraining the employment of principles by publicity effects....

[2] This fact is generally recognized in welfare economics, as when it is said that efficiency is to be balanced against equality. See for example Tibor Scitovsky, *Welfare and Competition* (London: George Allen and Unwin, 1952), pp. 60–69, and I.M.D. Little, *A Critique of Welfare Economics*, 2nd ed. (Oxford: The Clarendon Press, 1957), ch. VI, esp. pp. 112–16.

of efficiency is constrained by certain background institutions; when these constraints are satisfied, any resulting efficient distribution is accepted as just. The system of natural liberty selects an efficient distribution roughly as follows. Let us suppose that we know from economic theory that under the standard assumptions defining a competitive market economy, income and wealth will be distributed in an efficient way, and that the particular efficient distribution which results in any period of time is determined by the initial distribution of assets, that is, by the initial distribution of income and wealth, and of natural talents and abilities. With each initial distribution, a definite efficient outcome is arrived at. Thus it turns out that if we are to accept the outcome as just, and not merely as efficient, we must accept the basis upon which over time the initial distribution of assets is determined.

In the system of natural liberty the initial distribution is regulated by the arrangements implicit in the conception of careers open to talents (as earlier defined). These arrangements presuppose a background of equal liberty (as specified by the first principle) and a free market economy. They require a formal equality of opportunity in that all have at least the same legal rights of access to all advantaged social positions. But since there is no effort to preserve an equality, or similarity, of social conditions, except insofar as this is necessary to preserve the requisite background institutions, the initial distribution of assets for any period of time is strongly influenced by natural and social contingencies. The existing distribution of income and wealth, say, is the cumulative effect of prior distributions of natural assets—that is, natural talents and abilities—as these have been developed or left unrealized, and their use favored or disfavored over time by social circumstances and such chance contingencies as accident and good fortune. Intuitively, the most obvious injustice of the system of natural liberty is that it permits distributive shares to be improperly influenced by these factors so arbitrary from a moral point of view.

The liberal interpretation, as I shall refer to it, tries to correct for this by adding to the requirement of careers open to talents the further condition of the principle of fair equality of opportunity. The thought here is that positions are to be not only open in a formal sense, but that all should have a fair chance to attain them. Offhand it is not clear what is meant, but we might say that those with similar abilities and skills should have similar life chances. More specifically, assuming that there is a distribution of natural assets, those who are at the same level of talent and ability, and have the same willingness to use them, should have the same prospects of success regardless of their initial place in the social system, that is, irrespective of the income class into which they are born. In all sectors of society there should be roughly equal prospects of culture and achievement for everyone similarly motivated and endowed. The expectations of those with the same abilities and aspirations should not be affected by their social class.[1]

The liberal interpretation of the two principles seeks, then, to mitigate the influence of social contingencies and natural fortune on distributive shares. To accomplish this end it is necessary to impose further basic structural conditions on the social system. Free market arrangements must be set within a framework of political and legal institutions which regulates the overall trends of economic events and preserves the social conditions necessary for fair equality of opportunity. The elements of this framework are familiar enough, though it may be worthwhile to recall the importance of preventing excessive accumulations of property and wealth and of maintaining equal opportunities of education for all. Chances to acquire cultural knowledge and skills should not depend upon one's class position, and so the school system, whether public or private, should be designed to even out class barriers.

While the liberal conception seems clearly preferable to the system of natural liberty, intuitively it still

_____

[1] This definition follows Sidgwick's suggestion in *The Methods of Ethics*, 7th ed. (London: Macmillan, 1907), p. 285n. See also R.H. Tawney, *Equality* (London: George Allen and Unwin, 1931), ch. II, sec. ii; and B.A.O. Williams, "The Idea of Equality," in Peter Laslett and W.G. Runciman (eds.), *Philosophy, Politics, and Society* (Oxford: Basil Blackwell, 1962), pp. 125f.

appears defective. For one thing, even if it works to perfection in eliminating the influence of social contingencies, it still permits the distribution of wealth and income to be determined by the natural distribution of abilities and talents. Within the limits allowed by the background arrangements, distributive shares are decided by the outcome of the natural lottery; and this outcome is arbitrary from a moral perspective. There is no more reason to permit the distribution of income and wealth to be settled by the distribution of natural assets than by historical and social fortune. Furthermore, the principle of fair opportunity can be only imperfectly carried out, at least as long as the institution of the family exists. The extent to which natural capacities develop and reach fruition is affected by all kinds of social conditions and class attitudes. Even the willingness to make an effort, to try, and so to be deserving in the ordinary sense is itself dependent upon happy family and social circumstances. It is impossible in practice to secure equal chances of achievement and culture for those similarly endowed, and therefore we may want to adopt a principle which recognizes this fact and also mitigates the arbitrary effects of the natural lottery itself. That the liberal conception fails to do this encourages one to look for another interpretation of the two principles of justice.

Before turning to the conception of democratic equality, we should note that of natural aristocracy. On this view no attempt is made to regulate social contingencies beyond what is required by formal equality of opportunity, but the advantages of persons with greater natural endowments are to be limited to those that further the good of the poorer sectors of society. The aristocratic ideal is applied to a system that is open, at least from a legal point of view, and the better situation of those favored by it is regarded as just only when less would be had by those below, if less were given to those above.[1] In this way the idea of *noblesse oblige* is carried over to the conception of natural aristocracy.

Now both the liberal conception and that of natural aristocracy are unstable. For once we are troubled by the influence of either social contingencies or natural chance on the determination of distributive shares, we are bound, on reflection, to be bothered by the influence of the other. From a moral standpoint the two seem equally arbitrary. So however we move away from the system of natural liberty, we cannot be satisfied short of the democratic conception. This conception I have yet to explain. And, moreover, none of the preceding remarks are an argument for this conception, since in a contract theory all arguments, strictly speaking, are to be made in terms of what it would be rational to choose in the original position. But I am concerned here to prepare the way for the favored interpretation of the two principles so that these criteria, especially the second one, will not strike the reader as too eccentric or bizarre. I have tried to show that once we try to find a rendering of them which treats everyone equally as a moral person, and which does not weight men's share in the benefits and burdens of social cooperation according to their social fortune or their luck in the natural lottery, it is clear that the democratic interpretation is the best choice among the four alternatives. With these comments as a preface, I now turn to this conception.

Democratic Equality and the Difference Principle

[...]

To illustrate the difference principle, consider the distribution of income among social classes. Let us suppose that the various income groups correlate with representative individuals by reference to whose expectations we can judge the distribution. Now those starting out as members of the entrepreneurial class in property-owning democracy, say, have a better prospect than those who begin in the class of unskilled laborers. It seems likely that this will be true even when the social injustices which now exist are removed. What, then, can possibly justify this kind of initial inequality in life prospects? According to the difference principle, it is

---

[1] This formulation of the aristocratic ideal is derived from Santayana's account of aristocracy in ch. IV of *Reason and Society* (New York: Charles Scribner, 1905), pp. 109f.

justifiable only if the difference in expectation is to the advantage of the representative man who is worse off, in this case the representative unskilled worker. The inequality in expectation is permissible only if lowering it would make the working class even more worse off. Supposedly, given the rider in the second principle concerning open positions, and the principle of liberty generally, the greater expectations allowed to entrepreneurs encourages them to do things which raise the long-term prospects of the laboring class. Their better prospects act as incentives so that the economic process is more efficient, innovation proceeds at a faster pace, and so on. Eventually the resulting material benefits spread throughout the system and to the least advantaged. I shall not consider how far these things are true. The point is that something of this kind must be argued if these inequalities are to be just by the difference principle.

I shall now make a few remarks about this principle. First of all, in applying it, one should distinguish between two cases. The first case is that in which the expectations of the least advantaged are indeed maximized (subject, of course, to the mentioned constraints). No changes in the expectations of those better off can improve the situation of those worst off. The best arrangement obtains, what I shall call a perfectly just scheme. The second case is that in which the expectations of all those better off at least contribute to the welfare of the more unfortunate. That is, if their expectations were decreased, the prospects of the least advantaged would likewise fall. Yet the maximum is not yet achieved. Even higher expectations for the more advantaged would raise the expectations of those in the lowest position. Such a scheme is, I shall say, just throughout, but not the best just arrangement. A scheme is unjust when the higher expectations, one or more of them, are excessive. If these expectations were decreased, the situation of the least favored would be improved. How unjust an arrangement is depends on how excessive the higher expectations are and to what extent they depend upon the violation of the other principles of justice, for example, fair equality of opportunity; but I shall not attempt to measure in any exact way the degrees of injustice. The point to note here is that while the difference principle is, strictly speaking, a maximizing principle, there is a significant distinction between the cases that fall short of the best arrangement. A society should try to avoid the region where the marginal contributions of those better off are negative, since, other things equal, this seems a greater fault than falling short of the best scheme when these contributions are positive. The even larger difference between rich and poor makes the latter even worse off, and this violates the principle of mutual advantage as well as democratic equality....

A further point is this. We saw that the system of natural liberty and the liberal conception attempt to go beyond the principle of efficiency by moderating its scope of operation, by constraining it by certain background institutions and leaving the rest to pure procedural justice. The democratic conception holds that while pure procedural justice may be invoked to some extent at least, the way previous interpretations do this still leaves too much to social and natural contingency. But it should be noted that the difference principle is compatible with the principle of efficiency. For when the former is fully satisfied, it is indeed impossible to make any one representative man better off without making another worse off, namely, the least advantaged representative man whose expectations we are to maximize. Thus justice is defined so that it is consistent with efficiency, at least when the two principles are perfectly fulfilled. Of course, if the basic structure is unjust, these principles will authorize changes that may lower the expectations of some of those better off; and therefore the democratic conception is not consistent with the principle of efficiency if this principle is taken to mean that only changes which improve everyone's prospects are allowed. Justice is prior to efficiency and requires some changes that are not efficient in this sense. Consistency obtains only in the sense that a perfectly just scheme is also efficient.

Next, we may consider a certain complication regarding the meaning of the difference principle. It has been taken for granted that if the principle is satisfied, everyone is benefited. One obvious sense in which this is so is that each man's position is improved with respect to the initial arrangement of equality. But it is clear that nothing depends upon being able to identify this initial arrangement; indeed, how well off men are in this situation plays no essential role in applying the difference principle. We simply maximize the expectations of the least favored position subject to the required constraints. As long as doing this is an improvement for everyone, as we assume it is, the estimated gains from the situation of hypothetical equality are irrelevant, if not largely impossible to ascertain anyway. There may be, however, a further sense in which everyone is advantaged when the difference principle is satisfied, at least if we make certain natural assumptions. Let us suppose that inequalities in expectations are chain-connected: that is, if an advantage has the effect of raising the expectations of the lowest position, it raises the expectations of all positions in between. For example, if the greater expectations for entrepreneurs benefit the unskilled worker, they also benefit the semiskilled. Notice that chain connection says nothing about the case where the least advantaged do not gain, so that it does not mean that all effects move together. Assume further that expectations are close-knit: that is, it is impossible to raise or lower the expectation of any representative man without raising or lowering the expectation of every other representative man, especially that of the least advantaged. There is no loose-jointedness, so to speak, in the way expectations hang together. Now with these assumptions there is a sense in which everyone benefits when the difference principle is satisfied. For the representative man who is better off in any two-way comparison gains by the advantages offered him, and the man who is worse off gains from the contributions which these inequalities make. Of course, these conditions may not hold. But in this case those who are better off should not have a veto over the benefits available for the least favored. We are still to maximize the expectations of those most disadvantaged.

[...]

I shall not examine how likely it is that chain connection and close-knitness hold. The difference principle is not contingent on these relations being satisfied. However, one may note that when the contributions of the more favored positions spread generally throughout society and are not confined to particular sectors, it seems plausible that if the least advantaged benefit so do others in between. Moreover, a wide diffusion of benefits is favored by two features of institutions both exemplified by the basic structure: first, they are set up to advance certain fundamental interests which everyone has in common, and second, offices and positions are open. Thus it seems probable that if the privileges and powers of legislators and judges, say, improve the situation of the less favored, they improve that of citizens generally. Chain connection may often be true, provided the other principles of justice are fulfilled. If this is so, then we may observe that within the region of positive contributions (the region where the advantages of all those in favored positions raise the prospects of the least fortunate), any movement toward the perfectly just arrangement both increases average well-being and improves everyone's expectation. Given these special assumptions, the difference principle has the same practical consequences as the principles of average utility and efficiency. Of course, if chain connection rarely holds and these cases are unimportant, this coincidence between principles is only a curiosity. But we often suppose that within just social arrangements something like a general diffusion of gains does take place, at least in the longer run. Should this be true, these remarks indicate how the difference principle can account for these more familiar notions as special cases. It remains to be shown, though, that this principle is the more fundamental one from a moral point of view.

There is a further complication. Close-knitness is assumed in order to simplify the statement of the difference principle. It is clearly conceivable, however likely or important in practice, that the least advantaged are not affected one way or the other by some changes in expectations of the best off although these changes benefit others. In this sort

of case close-knitness fails, and to cover the situation we can express a more general principle as
follows: in a basic structure with n relevant representatives, first maximize the welfare of the worst
off representative man; second, for equal welfare
of the worst-off representative, maximize the welfare of the second worst-off representative Choice man, and
so on until the last case which is, for equal welfare
of all the preceding n-1 representatives, maximize
the welfare of the best-off representative man. We
may think of this as the lexical difference principle.[1]
However, I shall always use the difference principle
in the simpler form. And therefore, as the outcome
of the last several sections, the second principle is
to read as follows.

> Social and economic inequalities are to be
> arranged so that they are both (a) to the
> greatest benefit of the least advantaged and
> (b) attached to offices and positions open
> to all under conditions of fair equality of
> opportunity.

Finally, it should be observed that the difference principle, or the idea expressed by it, can easily be accommodated to the general conception
of justice, In fact, the general conception is simply the difference principle applied to all primary
goods including liberty and opportunity and so no
longer constrained by other parts of the special
conception....

The Reasoning Leading to the Two Principles of Justice

In this [section] I take up the choice between the
two principles of justice and the principle of average
utility. Determining the rational preference between
these two options is perhaps the central problem in
developing the conception of justice as fairness as a
viable alternative to the utilitarian tradition, I shall
begin in this section by presenting some intuitive

remarks favoring the two principles. I shall also discuss briefly the qualitative structure of the argument
that needs to be made if the case for these principles is to be conclusive.

It will be recalled that the general conception of
justice as fairness requires that all primary social
goods be distributed equally unless an unequal distribution would be to everyone's advantage. No
restrictions are placed on exchanges of these goods
and therefore a lesser liberty can be compensated
for by greater social and economic benefits. Now
looking at the situation from the standpoint of one
person selected arbitrarily, there is no way for him
to win special advantages for himself. Nor, on the
other hand, are there grounds for his acquiescing
in special disadvantages. Since it is not reasonable
for him to expect more than an equal share in the
division of social goods, and since it is not rational for him to agree to less, the sensible thing for
him to do, is to acknowledge as the first principle of justice one requiring an equal distribution.
Indeed, this principle is so obvious that we would
expect it to occur to anyone immediately.

Thus, the parties start with a principle establishing equal liberty for all, including equality of
opportunity, as well as an equal distribution of
income and wealth. But there is no reason why
this acknowledgment should be final. If there
are inequalities in the basic structure that work
to make everyone better off in comparison with
the benchmark of initial equality, why not permit
them? The immediate gain which a greater equality
might allow can be regarded as intelligently invested
in view of its future return. If, for example, these
inequalities set up various incentives which succeed
in eliciting more productive efforts, a person in the
original position may look upon them as necessary
to cover the costs of training and to encourage
effective performance. One might think that ideally individuals should want to serve one another.
But since the parties are assumed not to take an
interest in one another's interests, their acceptance
of these inequalities is only the acceptance of the
relations in which men stand in the circumstances
of justice. They have no grounds for complaining

---

[1] On this point see A.K. Sen, *Collective Choice and Social Welfare* (San Francisco: Holden-Day Inc., 1970), p. 138n.

of one another's motives. A person in the original position would, therefore, concede the justice of these inequalities. Indeed, it would be shortsighted of him not to do so. He would hesitate to agree to these regularities only if he would be dejected by the bare knowledge or perception that others were better situated; and I have assumed that the parties decide as if they are not moved by envy. In order to make the principle regulating inequalities determinate, one looks at the system from the standpoint of the least advantaged representative man. Inequalities are permissible when they maximize, or at least all contribute to, the long-term expectations of the least fortunate group in society.

Now this general conception imposes no constraints on what sorts of inequalities are allowed, whereas the special conception, by putting the two principles in serial order (with the necessary adjustments in meaning), forbids exchanges between basic liberties and economic and social benefits. I shall not try to justify this ordering here. ... But roughly, the idea underlying this ordering is that if the parties assume that their basic liberties can be effectively exercised, they will not exchange a lesser liberty for an improvement in economic well-being. It is only when social conditions do not allow the effective establishment of these rights that one can concede their limitation; and these restrictions can be granted only to the extent that they are necessary to prepare the way for a free society. The denial of equal liberty can be defended only if it is necessary to raise the level of civilization so that in due course these freedoms can be enjoyed. Thus in adopting a serial order we are in effect making a special assumption in the original position, namely, that the parties know that the conditions of their society, whatever they are, admit the effective realization of the equal liberties. The serial ordering of the two principles of justice eventually comes to be reasonable if the general conception is consistently followed. This lexical ranking is the long-run tendency of the general view. For the most part I shall assume that the requisite circumstances for the serial order obtain.

It seems clear from these remarks that the two principles are at least a plausible conception of justice. The question, though, is how one is to argue for them more systematically. Now there are several things to do. One can work out their consequences for institutions and note their implications for fundamental social policy. In this way they are tested by a comparison with our considered judgments of justice.... But one can also try to find arguments in their favor that are decisive from the standpoint of the original position. In order to see how this might be done, it is useful as a heuristic device to think of the two principles as the maximin solution to the problem of social justice. There is an analogy between the two principles and the maximin rule for choice under uncertainty.[1] This is evident from the fact that the two principles are those a person would choose for the design of a society in which his enemy is to assign him his place. The maximin rule tells us to rank alternatives by their worst possible outcomes: we are to adopt the alternative the worst outcome of which is superior to the worst outcomes of the others. The persons in the original position do not, of course, assume that their initial place in society is decided by a malevolent opponent. As I note below, they should not reason from false premises. The veil of ignorance does not violate this idea, since an absence of information is not misinformation. But that the two principles of justice would be chosen if the parties were forced to protect themselves against such a contingency explains the sense in which this conception is the maximin solution. And this analogy suggests that if the original position has been described so that it is rational for the parties to adopt the conservative attitude expressed by this rule, a conclusive argument can indeed be constructed for these principles. Clearly the maximin rule is not, in general, a suitable guide for choices under uncertainty. But it is attractive in situations marked by certain special features. My aim, then, is to show that a good case can be made for the two principles based on the fact that the original position manifests these

---

[1] [See] W.J. Baumol, *Economic Theory and Operations Analysis*, 2nd ed. (Englewood Cliffs, NJ: Prentice-Hall Inc., 1965), ch. 24....

features to the fullest possible degree, carrying them to the limit, so to speak.

Consider the gain-and-loss table below. It represents the gains and losses for a situation which is not a game of strategy. There is no one playing against the person making the decision; instead he is faced with several possible circumstances which may or may not obtain. Which circumstances happen to exist does not depend upon what the person choosing decides or whether he announces his moves in advance. The numbers in the table are monetary values (in hundreds of dollars) in comparison with some initial situation. The gain (g) depends upon the individual's decision (d) and the circumstances (c). Thus g = f (d, c). Assuming that there are three possible decisions and three possible circumstances, we might have this gain-and-loss table.

	CIRCUMSTANCES		
DECISIONS	c_1	c_2	c_3
d_1	—7	8	12
d_2	—8	7	14
d_3	5	6	8

The maximin rule requires that we make the third decision. For in this case the worst that can happen is that one gains five hundred dollars, which is better than the worst for the other actions. If we adopt one of these we may lose either eight or seven hundred dollars. Thus, the choice of d_3 maximizes f (d,c) for that value of c, which for a given d, minimizes f. The term "maximin" means the *maximum minimorum*; and the rule directs our attention to the worst that can happen under any proposed course of action, and to decide in the light of that.

Now there appear to be three chief features of situations that give plausibility to this unusual rule.[1] First, since the rule takes no account of the likelihoods of the possible circumstances, there must be

some reason for sharply discounting estimates of these probabilities. Offhand, the most natural rule of choice would seem to be to compute the expectation of monetary gain for each decision and then to adopt the course of action with the highest prospect. (This expectation is defined as follows: let us suppose that g_{ij} represent the numbers in the gain-and-loss table, where i is the row index and j is the column index; and let p_j, j = 1, 2, 3, be the likelihoods of the circumstances, with $\Sigma p_j = 1$. Then the expectation for the ith decision is equal to $\Sigma p_j g_{ij}$.) Thus it must be, for example, that the situation is one in which a knowledge of likelihoods is impossible, or at best extremely insecure. In this case it is unreasonable not to be skeptical of probabilistic calculations unless there is no other way out, particularly if the decision is a fundamental one that needs to be justified to others.

The second feature that suggests the maximin rule is the following: the person choosing has a conception of the good such that he cares very little, if anything, for what he might gain above the minimum stipend that he can, in fact, be sure of by following the maximin rule. It is not worthwhile for him to take a chance for the sake of a further advantage, especially when it may turn out that he loses much that is important to him. This last provision brings in the third feature, namely, that the rejected alternatives have outcomes that one can hardly accept. The situation involves grave risks. Of course these features work most effectively in combination. The paradigm situation for following the maximin rule is when all three features are realized to the highest degree. This rule does not, then, generally apply, nor of course is it self-evident. Rather, it is a maxim, a rule of thumb, that comes into its own in special circumstances. Its application depends upon the qualitative structure of the possible gains and losses in relation to one's conception of the good, all this against a background in which it is reasonable to discount conjectural estimates of likelihoods.

It should be noted, as the comments on the gain-and-loss table say, that the entries in the table represent monetary values and not utilities. This difference is significant since for one thing computing

---

[1] Here I borrow from William Felner, *Probability and Profit* (Homewood, IL: R.D. Irwin, Inc., 1965), pp. 140–42, where these features are noted.

expectations on the basis of such objective values is not the same thing as computing expected utility and may lead to different results. The essential point though is that in justice as fairness the parties do not know their conception of the good and cannot estimate their utility in the ordinary sense. In any case, we want to go behind de facto preferences generated by given conditions. Therefore expectations are based upon an index of primary goods and the parties make their choice accordingly. The entries in the example are in terms of money and not utility to indicate this aspect of the contract doctrine.

Now, as I have suggested, the original position has been defined so that it is a situation in which the maximin rule applies. In order to see this, let us review briefly the nature of this situation with these three special features in mind. To begin with, the veil of ignorance excludes all but the vaguest knowledge of likelihoods. The parties have no basis for determining the probable nature of their society, or their place in it. Thus they have strong reasons for being wary of probability calculations if any other course is open to them. They must also take into account the fact that their choice of principles should seem reasonable to others, in particular their descendants, whose rights will be deeply affected by it. There are further grounds for discounting that I shall mention as we go along. For the present it suffices to note that these considerations are strengthened by the fact that the parties know very little about the gain-and-loss table. Not only are they unable to conjecture the likelihoods of the various possible circumstances, they cannot say much about what the possible circumstances are, much less enumerate them and foresee the outcome of each alternative available. Those deciding are much more in the dark than the illustration by a numerical table suggests. It is for this reason that I have spoken of an analogy with the maximin rule.

Several kinds of arguments for the two principles of justice illustrate the second feature. Thus, if we can maintain that these principles provide a workable theory of social justice, and that they are compatible with reasonable demands of efficiency, then this conception guarantees a satisfactory minimum. There may be, on reflection, little reason for trying to do better. Thus much of the argument, especially in Part Two [of *A Theory of Justice*], is to show, by their application to the main questions of social justice, that the two principles are a satisfactory conception. These details have a philosophical purpose. Moreover, this line of thought is practically decisive if we can establish the priority of liberty, the lexical ordering of the two principles. For this priority implies that the persons in the original position have no desire to try for greater gains at the expense of the equal liberties. The minimum assured by the two principles in lexical order is not one that the parties wish to jeopardize for the sake of greater economic and social advantages....

Finally, the third feature holds if we can assume that other conceptions of justice may lead to institutions that the parties would find intolerable. For example, it has sometimes been held that under some conditions the utility principle (in either form) justifies, if not slavery or serfdom, at any rate serious infractions of liberty for the sake of greater social benefits. We need not consider here the truth of this claim, or the likelihood that the requisite conditions obtain. For the moment, this contention is only to illustrate the way in which conceptions of justice may allow for outcomes which the parties may not be able to accept. And having the ready alternative of the two principles of justice which secure a satisfactory minimum, it seems unwise, if not irrational, for them to take a chance that these outcomes are not realized.

[...]

DISCUSSION QUESTIONS

1. Compare and contrast the way that Rawls deals with inherited wealth vs. acquired wealth with the way that Friedman deals with it. Whose view do you think is more plausible? Explain.

2. Explain both the difference principle and the principle of fair equality of opportunity. How would Nozick respond to Rawls's second principle of justice? Evaluate Nozick's response.

3. Explain why Rawls thinks that the difference principle would be chosen in the original position. Explain the three features of the original position that make maximin the appropriate rule of choice. Evaluate Rawls's argument.

71

Henry Shue, "Security and Subsistence" (1980)

Henry Shue is the Senior Research Fellow and Professor of Political International Relations at Merton College, Oxford University. In the following selection, Shue provides an analysis of moral rights, which he claims provides the rational basis for a justified demand. He then argues that certain moral rights, including security rights and subsistence rights, are properly classified as basic rights.

SOURCE

Shue, Henry. "Security and Subsistence," from *Basic Rights: Subsistence, Affluence, and U.S. Foreign Policy*, 2nd ed., by Henry Shue. Copyright © 1980 by Princeton University Press. Reprinted by permission of Princeton University Press.

Rights

A moral right provides (1) the rational basis for a justified demand (2) that the actual enjoyment of a substance be (3) socially guaranteed against standard threats. Since this is a somewhat complicated account of rights, each of its elements deserves a brief introductory explanation. The significance of the general structure of a moral right is, however, best seen in concrete cases of rights, to which we will quickly turn.

A right provides the rational basis for a justified demand. If a person has a particular right, the demand that the enjoyment of the substance of the right be socially guaranteed is justified by good reasons, and the guarantees ought, therefore, to be provided. I do not know how to characterize in general and in the abstract what counts as a rational basis or an adequate justification. I could say that a demand for social guarantees has been justified when good enough reasons have been given for it, but this simply transfers the focus to what count as good enough reasons. This problem pervades philosophy, and I could not say anything very useful about it without saying a lot. But to have a right is to be in a position to make demands of others, and to be in such a position is, among other things, for one's situation to fall under general principles that are good reasons why one's demands ought to be granted. A person who has a right has especially compelling reasons—especially deep principles—on

808   UNIT III: B. Contemporary Developments

his or her side. People can of course have rights without being able to explain them—without being able to articulate the principles that apply to their cases and serve as the reasons for their demands. This book as a whole is intended to express a set of reasons that are good enough to justify the demands defended here. If the book is adequate, the principles it articulates are at least one specific example of how some particular demands can be justified. For now, I think, an example would be more useful than an abstract characterization.

The significance of being justified is very clear. Because a right is the basis for a justified demand, people not only may, but ought to, insist. Those who deny rights do so at their own peril. This does not mean that efforts to secure the fulfillment of the demand constituting a right ought not to observe certain constraints. It does mean that those who deny rights can have no complaint when their denial, especially if it is part of a systematic pattern of deprivation, is resisted. Exactly which counter-measures are justified by which sorts of deprivations of rights would require a separate discussion.

A right is the rational basis, then, for a justified demand. Rights do not justify merely requests, pleas, petitions. It is only because rights may lead to demands and not something weaker that having rights is tied as closely as it is to human dignity. Joel Feinberg has put this eloquently for the case of legal rights, or, in his Hohfeldian terminology, claim-rights:

> Legal claim-rights are indispensably valuable possessions. A world without claim-rights, no matter how full of benevolence and devotion to duty, would suffer an immense moral impoverishment. Persons would no longer hope for decent treatment from others on the ground of desert or rightful claim. Indeed, they would come to think of themselves as having no special claim to kindness or consideration from others, so that whenever even minimally decent treatment is forthcoming they would think themselves lucky rather than inherently deserving, and their

benefactors extraordinarily virtuous and worthy of great gratitude. The harm to individual self-esteem and character development would be incalculable.

> A claim-right, on the other hand, can be urged, pressed, or rightly demanded against other persons. In appropriate circumstances the right-holder can "urgently, peremptorily, or insistently" call for his rights, or assert them authoritatively, confidently, unabashedly. Rights are not mere gifts or favors, motivated by love or pity, for which gratitude is the sole fitting response. A right is something that can be demanded or insisted upon without embarrassment or shame. When that to which one has a right is not forthcoming, the appropriate reaction is indignation; when it is duly given there is no reason for gratitude, since it is simply one's own or one's due that one received. A world with claim-rights is one in which all persons, as actual or potential claimants, are dignified objects of respect, both in their own eyes and in the view of others. No amount of love and compassion, or obedience to higher authority, or noblesse oblige, can substitute for those values.[1]

At least as much can be said for basic moral rights, including those that ought to, but do not yet, have legal protection.

That a right provides the rational basis for a justified demand for actual enjoyment is the most neglected element of many rights. A right does not yield a demand that it should be said that people are entitled to enjoy something, or that people should be promised that they will enjoy something. A proclamation of a right is not the fulfillment of a right, any more than an airplane schedule is a flight. A proclamation may or may not be an initial step toward the fulfillment of the rights listed. It is frequently the substitute of the promise in the place of the fulfillment.

---

[1] Joel Feinberg, *Social Philosophy* (Englewood Cliffs, NJ: Prentice-Hall, Inc., 1973), pp. 58–59.

The substance of a right is whatever the right is a right to. A right is not a right to enjoy a right—it is a right to enjoy something else, like food or liberty. We do sometimes speak simply of someone's "enjoying a right," but I take this to be an elliptical way of saying that the person is enjoying something or other, which is the substance of a right, and, probably, enjoying it *as* a right. Enjoying a right to, for example, liberty normally means enjoying liberty. It may also mean enjoying liberty in the consciousness that liberty is a right. Being a right is a status that various subjects of enjoyment have. Simply to enjoy the right itself, the status, rather than to enjoy the subject of the right would have to mean something like taking satisfaction that there is such a status and that something has that status. But ordinarily when we say someone is enjoying a right, we mean the person is enjoying the substance of the right.

Being socially guaranteed is probably the single most important aspect of a standard right, because it is the aspect that necessitates correlative duties. A right is ordinarily a justified demand that some other people make some arrangements so that one will still be able to enjoy the substance of the right even if—actually, *especially* if—it is not within one's own power to arrange on one's own to enjoy the substance of the right. Suppose people have a right to physical security. Some of them may nevertheless choose to hire their own private guards, as if they had no right to social guarantees. But they would be justified, and everyone else is justified, in demanding that somebody somewhere make some effective arrangements to establish and maintain security. Whether the arrangements should be governmental or non-governmental; local, national, or international; participatory or non-participatory, are all difficult questions to which I may or may not be able to give definitive or conclusive answers here. But it is essential to a right that it is a demand upon others, however difficult it is to specify exactly which others.

And a right has been guaranteed only when arrangements have been made for people with the right to enjoy it. It is not enough that at the moment it happens that no one is violating the right. Just as a proclamation of a right is not the fulfillment of a right and may in fact be either a step toward or away from actually fulfilling the right, an undertaking to create social guarantees for the enjoyment of various subjects of rights is by no means itself the guaranteeing and may or may not lead to real guarantees. But a right has not been fulfilled until arrangements are in fact in place for people to enjoy whatever it is to which they have the right. Usually, perhaps, the arrangements will take the form of law, making the rights legal as well as moral ones. But in other cases well-entrenched customs, backed by taboos might serve better than laws—certainly better than unenforced laws.

The vague term "arrangements" is used in order to keep this general introductory explanation neutral on some controversial questions of interpretation. If the "arrangements" for fulfilling, for example, the duty to protect security are to be that every citizen is to be furnished a handgun and local neighborhoods are to elect residents to night patrols, then the right to security has not been socially guaranteed until the handguns have been distributed, the patrols elected, etc. (The right has still not been guaranteed if this arrangement will usually not work, as I would certainly assume would be the case.) On the other hand, if the "arrangements" are to have well-trained, tax-supported, professional police in adequate numbers, then the right has not been socially guaranteed until the police candidates have in fact been well-trained, enough public funds budgeted to hire an adequate force, etc.

I am not suggesting the absurd standard that a right has been fulfilled only if it is impossible for anyone to be deprived of it or only if no one is ever deprived of it. The standard can only be some reasonable level of guarantee. But if people who walk alone after dark are likely to be assaulted, or if infant mortality is 60 per 1000 live births, we would hardly say that enjoyment of, respectively, security or subsistence had yet been socially guaranteed. It is for the more precise specification of the reasonable level of social guarantees that we need the final element in the general structure of moral rights: the notion of a standard threat. This notion can be explained satisfactorily only after we look at some cases in detail, and I will take it up in the final section of this chapter.

That a right involves a rationally justified demand for social guarantees against standard threats means, in effect, that the relevant other people have a duty to create, if they do not exist, or, if they do, to preserve effective institutions for the enjoyment of what people have rights to enjoy. From no theory like the present one is it possible to deduce precisely what sort of institutions are needed, and I have no reason to think that the same institutions would be most effective in all places and at all times. On its face, such universality of social institutions is most improbable, although some threats are indeed standard. What is universal, however, is a duty to make and keep effective arrangements, and my later threefold analysis of correlative duties will suggest that these arrangements must serve at least the functions of avoiding depriving people of the substances of their rights, protecting them against deprivation, and aiding them if they are nevertheless deprived of rights. What I am now calling the duty to develop and preserve effective institutions for the fulfillment of rights is a summary of much of what is involved in performing all three of the duties correlative to typical rights, but to discuss duties now would be to jump ahead of the story.

Basic Rights

Nietzsche, who holds strong title to being the most misunderstood and most underrated philosopher of the last century, considered much of conventional morality—and not conceptions of rights only—to be an attempt by the powerless to restrain the powerful: an enormous net of fine mesh busily woven around the strong by the masses of the weak.[1]

---

[1] For his clearest single presentation of this analysis, see Friedrich Nietzsche, *On the Genealogy of Morals*, ed. Walter Kaufmann, trans. Walter Kaufmann and R.J. Hollingdale (New York: Vintage Books, 1967). Much, but not all, of what is interesting in Nietzsche's account was put into the mouth of Callicles in Plato's *Gorgias*.

And he was disgusted by it, as if fleas were pestering a magnificent leopard or ordinary ivy were weighing down a soaring oak. In recoiling from Nietzsche's *assessment* of morality, many have dismissed too quickly his insightful *analysis* of morality. Moral systems obviously serve more than one purpose, and different specific systems serve some purposes more fully or better than others, as of course Nietzsche himself also recognized. But one of the chief purposes of morality in general, and certainly of conceptions of rights, and of basic rights above all, is indeed to provide some minimal protection against utter helplessness to those too weak to protect themselves. Basic rights are a shield for the defenseless against at least some of the more devastating and more common of life's threats, which include, as we shall see, loss of security and loss of subsistence. Basic rights are a restraint upon economic and political forces that would otherwise be too strong to be resisted. They are social guarantees against actual and threatened deprivations of at least some basic needs. Basic rights are an attempt to give to the powerless a veto over some of the forces that would otherwise harm them the most.

Basic rights are the morality of the depths. They specify the line beneath which no one is to be allowed to sink. This is part of the reason that basic rights are tied as closely to self-respect as Feinberg indicates legal claim-rights are. And this helps to explain why Nietzsche found moral rights repugnant. His eye was on the heights, and he wanted to talk about how far some might soar, not about how to prevent the rest from sinking lower. It is not clear that we cannot do both.

And it is not surprising that what is in an important respect the essentially negative goal of preventing or alleviating helplessness is a central purpose of something as important as conceptions of basic rights. For everyone healthy adulthood is bordered on each side by helplessness, and it is vulnerable to interruption by helplessness, temporary or permanent, at any time. And many of the people in the world now have very little control over their fates, even over such urgent matters as whether their own children live through infancy. Nor is it surprising that, although the goal is negative, the duties correlative to rights will turn out to include positive actions. The infant and the aged do not need to be assaulted in order to be deprived of health, life, or the capacity to enjoy active rights. The classic liberal's main prescription for the good life—do not interfere with thy neighbor—is the only poison they need. To be helpless they need only to be left alone. This is why avoiding the infliction of deprivation will turn out in chapter 2 [of *Basic Rights: Subsistence, Affluence and U.S. Foreign Policy*] not to be the only kind of duty correlative to basic rights.

Basic rights, then, are everyone's minimum reasonable demands upon the rest of humanity. They are the rational basis for justified demands the denial of which no self-respecting person can reasonably be expected to accept. Why should anything be so important? The reason is that rights are basic in the sense used here only if enjoyment of them is essential to the enjoyment of all other rights. This is what is distinctive about a basic right. When a right is genuinely basic, any attempt to enjoy any other right by sacrificing the basic right would be quite literally self-defeating, cutting the ground from beneath itself. Therefore, if a right is basic, other, non-basic rights may be sacrificed, if necessary, in order to secure the basic right. But the protection of a basic right may not be sacrificed in order to secure the enjoyment of a non-basic right. It may not be sacrificed because it cannot be sacrificed successfully. If the right sacrificed is indeed basic, then no right for which it might be sacrificed can actually be enjoyed in the absence of the basic right. The sacrifice would have proven self-defeating.

In practice, what this priority for basic rights usually means is that basic rights need to be established securely before other rights can be secured. The point is that people should be able to *enjoy*, or *exercise*, their other rights. The point is simple but vital. It is not merely that people should "have" their other rights in some merely legalistic or otherwise abstract sense compatible with being unable to make any use of the substance of the right. For example, if people have rights to free association, they ought not merely to "have" the rights to free association but also to enjoy their free association itself. Their freedom of

association ought to be provided for by the relevant social institutions. This distinction between merely having a right and actually enjoying a right may seem a fine point, but it turns out later to be critical.

What is not meant by saying that a right is basic is that the right is more valuable or intrinsically more satisfying to enjoy than some other rights. For example, I shall soon suggest that rights to physical security, such as the right not to be assaulted, are basic, and I shall not include the right to publicly supported education as basic. But I do not mean by this to deny that enjoyment of the right to education is much greater and richer—more distinctively human, perhaps—than merely going through life without ever being assaulted. I mean only that, if a choice must be made, the prevention of assault ought to supersede the provision of education. Whether a right is basic is independent of whether its enjoyment is also valuable in itself. Intrinsically valuable rights may or may not also be basic rights, but intrinsically valuable rights can be enjoyed only when basic rights are enjoyed. Clearly few rights could be basic in this precise sense.

Security Rights

Our first project will be to see why people have a basic right to physical security—a right that is basic not to be subjected to murder, torture, mayhem, rape, or assault. The purpose in raising the questions why there are rights to physical security and why they are basic is not that very many people would seriously doubt either that there are rights to physical security or that they are basic. Although it is not unusual in practice for members of at least one ethnic group in a society to be physically insecure—to be, for example, much more likely than other people to be beaten by the police if arrested—few, if any, people would be prepared to defend in principle the contention that anyone lacks a basic right to physical security. Nevertheless, it can be valuable to formulate explicitly the presuppositions of even one's most firmly held beliefs, especially because these presuppositions may turn out to be general principles that will provide guidance in other areas where convictions are less firm.

Precisely because we have no real doubt that rights to physical security are basic, it can be useful to see why we may properly think so.

If we had to justify our belief that people have a basic right to physical security to someone who challenged this fundamental conviction, we could in fact give a strong argument that shows that if there are any rights (basic or not basic) at all, there are basic rights to physical security:

No one can fully enjoy any right that is supposedly protected by society if someone can credibly threaten him or her with murder, rape, beating, etc., when he or she tries to enjoy the alleged right. Such threats to physical security are among the most serious and—in much of the world—the most widespread hindrances to the enjoyment of any right. If any right is to be exercised except at great risk, physical security must be protected. In the absence of physical security people are unable to use any other rights that society may be said to be protecting without being liable to encounter many of the worst dangers they would encounter if society were not protecting the rights.

A right to full physical security belongs, then, among the basic rights—not because the enjoyment of it would be more satisfying to someone who was also enjoying a full range of other rights, but because its absence would leave available extremely effective means for others, including the government, to interfere with or prevent the actual exercise of any other rights that were supposedly protected. Regardless of whether the enjoyment of physical security is also desirable for its own sake, it is desirable as part of the enjoyment of every other right. No rights other than a right to physical security can in fact be enjoyed if a right to physical security is not protected. Being physically secure is a necessary condition for the exercise of any other right, and

guaranteeing physical security must be part of guaranteeing anything else as a right.

A person could, of course, always try to enjoy some other right even if no social provision were made to protect his or her physical safety during attempts to exercise the right. Suppose there is a right to peaceful assembly but it is not unusual for peaceful assemblies to be broken up and some of the participants beaten. Whether any given assembly is actually broken up depends largely on whether anyone else (in or out of government) is sufficiently opposed to it to bother to arrange an attack. People could still try to assemble, and they might sometimes assemble safely. But it would obviously be misleading to say that they are protected in their right to assemble if they are as vulnerable as ever to one of the most serious and general threats to enjoyment of the right, namely physical violence by other people. If they are as helpless against physical threats with the right "protected" as they would have been without the supposed protection, society is not actually protecting their exercise of the right to assembly.

So anyone who is entitled to anything as a right must be entitled to physical security as a basic right so that threats to his or her physical security cannot be used to thwart the enjoyment of the other right. This argument has two critical premises. The first is that everyone is entitled to enjoy something as a right.[1] The second, which further explains the first, is that everyone is entitled to the removal of the most serious and general conditions that would prevent or severely interfere with the exercise of whatever rights the person has. I take this second premise to be part of what is meant in saying that everyone is entitled to enjoy something as a right, as explained in the opening section of this chapter. Since this argument applies to everyone, it establishes a right that is universal.

---

[1] At considerable risk of encouraging unflattering comparisons I might as well note myself that in its general structure the argument here has the same form as the argument in H.L.A. Hart's classic, "Are There Any Natural Rights?" *Philosophical Review* 64:2 (April 1955): 175–91.... [which appears here as reading 24.]

Subsistence Rights

The main reason for discussing security rights, which are not very controversial, was to make explicit the basic assumptions that support the usual judgment that security rights are basic rights. Now that we have available an argument that supports them, we are in a position to consider whether matters other than physical security should, according to the same argument, also be basic rights. It will emerge that subsistence, or minimal economic security, which is more controversial than physical security, can also be shown to be as well justified for treatment as a basic right as physical security is—and for the same reasons.

By minimal economic security, or subsistence, I mean unpolluted air, unpolluted water, adequate food, adequate clothing, adequate shelter, and minimal preventive public health care. Many complications about exactly how to specify the boundaries of what is necessary for subsistence would be interesting to explore. But the basic idea is to have available for consumption what is needed for a decent chance at a reasonably healthy and active life of more or less normal length, barring tragic interventions. This central idea is clear enough to work with, even though disputes can occur over exactly where to draw its outer boundaries. A right to subsistence would not mean, at one extreme, that every baby born with a need for open-heart surgery has a right to have it, but it also would not count as adequate food a diet that produces a life expectancy of 55 years of fever-laden, parasite-ridden listlessness.

By a "right to subsistence" I shall always mean a right to at least subsistence. People may or may not have economic rights that go beyond subsistence rights, and I do not want to prejudge that question here. But people may have rights to subsistence even if they do not have any strict rights to economic well-being extending beyond subsistence. Subsistence rights and broader economic rights are separate questions, and I want to focus here on subsistence.

I also do not want to prejudge the issue of whether healthy adults are entitled to be provided with subsistence *only* if they cannot provide subsistence for themselves. Most of the world's malnourished, for example, are probably also diseased, since malnutrition lowers resistance to disease, and hunger and infestation normally form a tight vicious circle. Hundreds of millions of the malnourished are very young children. A large percentage of the adults, besides being ill and hungry, are also chronically unemployed, so the issue of policy toward healthy adults who refuse to work is largely irrelevant. By a "right to subsistence," then, I shall mean a right to subsistence that includes the provision of subsistence at least to those who cannot provide for themselves. I do not assume that no one else is also entitled to receive subsistence—I simply do not discuss cases of healthy adults who could support themselves but refuse to do so. If there is a right to subsistence in the sense discussed here, at least the people who cannot provide for themselves, including the children, are entitled to receive at least subsistence. Nothing follows one way or the other about anyone else.

It makes no difference whether the legally enforced system of property where a given person lives is private, state, communal, or one of the many more typical mixtures and variants. Under all systems of property people are prohibited from simply taking even what they need for survival. Whatever the property institutions and the economic system are, the question about rights to subsistence remains: if persons are forbidden by law from taking what they need to survive and they are unable within existing economic institutions and policies to provide for their own survival (and the survival of dependents for whose welfare they are responsible), are they entitled, as a last resort, to receive the essentials for survival from the remainder of humanity whose lives are not threatened?

The same considerations that support the conclusion that physical security is a basic right support the conclusion that subsistence is a basic right. Since the argument is now familiar, it can be given fairly briefly.

It is quite obvious why, if we still assume that there are some rights that society ought to protect and still mean by this the removal of the most serious and general hindrances to the actual enjoy-ment of rights, subsistence ought to be protected as a basic right:

> No one can fully, if at all, enjoy any right that is supposedly protected by society if he or she lacks the essentials for a reasonably healthy and active life. Deficiencies in the means of subsistence can be just as fatal, incapacitating, or painful as violations of physical security. The resulting damage or death can at least as decisively prevent the enjoyment of any right as can the effects of security violations. Any form of malnutrition, or fever due to expo-sure, that causes severe and irreversible brain damage, for example, can effectively pre-vent the exercise of any right requiring clear thought and may, like brain injuries caused by assault, profoundly disturb personality. And, obviously, any fatal deficiencies end all possi-bility of the enjoyment of rights as firmly as an arbitrary execution.

> Indeed, prevention of deficiencies in the essentials for survival is, if anything, more basic than prevention of violations of phys-ical security. People who lack protection against violations of their physical security can, if they are free, fight back against their attackers or flee, but people who lack essen-tials, such as food, because of forces beyond their control, often can do nothing and are on their own utterly helpless.

The scope of subsistence rights must not be taken to be broader than it is. In particular, this step of the argument does not make the following absurd claim: since death and serious illness prevent or interfere with the enjoyment of rights, everyone has a basic right not to be allowed to die or to be seriously ill. Many causes of death and illness are outside the control of society, and many deaths and illnesses are the result of very particular conjunc-tions of circumstances that general social policies cannot control. But it is not impractical to expect some level of social organization to protect the min-imal cleanliness of air and water and to oversee the adequate production, or import, and the proper dis-tribution of minimal food, clothing, shelter, and ele-mentary health care. It is not impractical, in short, to expect effective management, when necessary, of the supplies of the essentials of life. So the argu-ment is: when death and serious illness could be prevented by different social policies regarding the essentials of life, the protection of any human right involves avoidance of fatal or debilitating deficien-cies in these essential commodities. And this means fulfilling subsistence rights as basic rights. This is society's business because the problems are seri-ous and general. This is a basic right because fail-ure to deal with it would hinder the enjoyment of all other rights.

Thus, the same considerations that establish that security rights are basic for everyone also support the conclusion that subsistence rights are basic for everyone. It is not being claimed or assumed that security and subsistence are parallel in all, or even very many, respects. The only parallel being relied upon is that guarantees of security and guaran-tees of subsistence are equally essential to provid-ing for the actual exercise of any other rights. As long as security and subsistence are parallel in this respect, the argument applies equally to both cases, and other respects in which security and subsistence are not parallel are irrelevant.

It is not enough that people merely happen to be secure or happen to be subsisting. They must have a right to security and a right to subsistence—the continued enjoyment of the security and the sub-sistence must be socially guaranteed. Otherwise a person is readily open to coercion and intimida-tion through threats of the deprivation of one or the other, and credible threats can paralyze a per-son and prevent the exercise of any other right as surely as actual beatings and actual protein/calo-rie deficiencies can. Credible threats can be reduced only by the actual establishment of social arrange-ments that will bring assistance to those confronted by forces that they themselves cannot handle.

Consequently the guaranteed security and guaranteed subsistence are what we might initially be tempted to call "simultaneous necessities" for the exercise of any other right. They must be present at any time that any other right is to be exercised, or people can be prevented from enjoying the other right by deprivations or threatened deprivations of security or of subsistence. But to think in terms of simultaneity would be largely to miss the point. A better label, if any is needed, would be "inherent necessities." For it is not that security from beatings, for instance, is separate from freedom of peaceful assembly but that it always needs to accompany it. Being secure from beatings if one chooses to hold a meeting is part of being free to assemble. If one cannot safely assemble, one is not free to assemble. One is, on the contrary, being coerced not to assemble by the threat of the beatings.

The same is true if taking part in the meeting would lead to dismissal by the only available employer when employment is the only source of income for the purchase of food. Guarantees of security and subsistence are not added advantages over and above enjoyment of the right to assemble. They are essential parts of it. For this reason it would be misleading to construe security or subsistence—or the substance of any other basic right—merely as "means" to the enjoyment of all other rights. The enjoyment of security and subsistence is an essential part of the enjoyment of all other rights. Part of what it means to enjoy any other right is to be able to exercise that right without, as a consequence, suffering the actual or threatened loss of one's physical security or one's subsistence. And part of what it means to be able to enjoy any other right is not to be prevented from exercising it by lack of security or of subsistence. To claim to guarantee people a right that they are in fact unable to exercise is fraudulent, like furnishing people with meal tickets but providing no food.

What is being described as an "inherent necessity" needs to be distinguished carefully from a mere means to an end. If A is a means to end B and it is impossible to reach the end B without using the means A, it is correct to say that A is necessary for B.

But when I describe the enjoyment of physical security, for example, as necessary for the enjoyment of a right to assemble, I do not intend to say merely that enjoying security is a means to enjoying assembly. I intend to say that part of the meaning of the enjoyment of a right of assembly is that one can assemble in physical security. Being secure is an essential component of enjoying a right of assembly, so that there is no such thing as a situation in which people do have social guarantees for assembly and do not have social guarantees for security. If they do not have guarantees that they can assemble in security, they have not been provided with assembly as a right. They must assemble and merely hope for the best, because a standard threat to assembling securely has not been dealt with. The fundamental argument is that when one fully grasps what an ordinary right is, and especially which duties are correlative to a right, one can see that the guarantee of certain things (as basic rights) is part of—is a constituent of—is an essential component of—the establishment of the conditions in which the right can actually be enjoyed. These conditions include the prevention of the thwarting of the enjoyment of the right by any "standard threat," at the explanation of which we must soon look.

A final observation about the idea of subsistence rights is, however, worth making here: subsistence rights are in no way an original, new, or advanced idea. If subsistence rights seem strange, this is more than likely because Western liberalism has had a blind spot for severe economic need. Far from being new or advanced, subsistence rights are found in traditional societies that are often treated by modern societies as generally backward or primitive.

James C. Scott has shown that some of the traditional economic arrangements in Southeast Asia that were in other respects highly exploitative nevertheless were understood by both patrons and clients—to use Scott's terminology—to include rights to subsistence on the part of clients and duties on the part of patrons not only to forbear from depriving clients of subsistence but to provide assistance to any clients who were for any reason deprived:

If the need for a guaranteed minimum is a powerful motive in peasant life, one would expect to find institutionalized patterns in peasant communities which provide for this need. And, in fact, it is above all within the village—in the patterns of social control and reciprocity that structure daily conduct—where the subsistence ethic finds social expression. The principle which appears to unify a wide array of behavior is this: "All village families will be guaranteed a minimal subsistence niche insofar as the resources controlled by villagers make this possible." Village egalitarianism in this sense is conservative not radical; it claims that all should have a place, a living, not that all should be equal…. Few village studies of Southeast Asia fail to remark on the informal social controls which act to provide for the minimal needs of the village poor. The position of the better-off appears to be legitimized only to the extent that then resources are employed in ways which meet the broadly defined welfare needs of villagers.[1]

As Benedict J. Kerkvliet, also writing about an Asian society, put it: "A strong patron-client relationship was a kind of all-encompassing insurance policy whose coverage, although not total and infinitely reliable, was as comprehensive as a poor family could get."[2]

Many reasons weigh in favor of the elimination of the kind of patron—client relationships that Scott and Kerkvliet have described—no one is suggesting that they should be, or could be, preserved. The point here is only that the institutionalization of subsistence rights is in no way tied

---

[1] James C. Scott, *The Moral Economy of the Peasant: Rebellion and Subsistence in Southeast Asia* (New Haven: Yale University Press, 1976), pp. 40–41.

[2] Benedict J. Kerkvliet, *The Huk Rebellion: A Study of Peasant Revolt in the Philippines* (Berkeley: University of California Press, 1977), p. 252. On the importance for Philippine peasants of their deep belief in a right to subsistence, see pp. 252–55.

to some utopian future "advanced" society. On the contrary, the real question is whether modern nations can be as humane as, in *this* regard, many traditional villages are. If we manage, we may to a considerable extent merely have restored something of value that has for some time been lost in our theory and our practice.

Standard Threats

Before we turn over the coin of basic rights and consider the side with the duties, we need to establish two interrelated points about the rights side. One point concerns the final element in the account of the general structure of all rights, basic and nonbasic, which is the notion of standard threats as the targets of the social guarantees for the enjoyment of the substance of a right. The other point specifically concerns basic rights and the question whether the reasoning in favor of treating security and subsistence as the substances of basic rights does not generate an impractically and implausibly long list of things to which people will be said to have basic rights. The two points are interrelated because the clearest manner by which to establish that the list of basic rights must, on the contrary, be quite short is to invoke the fact that the social guarantees required by the structure of a right are guarantees, not against all possible threats, but only against what I will call standard threats. In the end we will find a supportive coherence between the account of basic rights and the account of the general structure of most moral rights. We may begin by reviewing the reasons for taking security and subsistence to be basic rights and considering whether the same reasons would support treating many other things as basic rights. Answering that question will lead us to see the role and importance of a conception of standard threats.

Why, then, according to the argument so far, are security and subsistence basic rights? Each is essential to a normal healthy life. Because the actual deprivation of either can be so very serious—potentially incapacitating, crippling, or fatal—even the threatened deprivation of either can be a powerful weapon against anyone whose security or subsistence is not in fact socially guaranteed. People who cannot provide for their own security and subsistence and who lack social guarantees for both are very weak, and possibly helpless, against any individual or institution in a position to deprive them of anything else they value by means of threatening their security or subsistence. A fundamental purpose of acknowledging any basic rights at all is to prevent, or to eliminate, insofar as possible, the degree of vulnerability that leaves people at the mercy of others. Social guarantees of security and subsistence would go a long way toward accomplishing this purpose.

Security and subsistence are basic rights, then, because of the roles they play in both the enjoyment and the protection of all other rights. Other rights could not be enjoyed in the absence of security or subsistence, even if the other rights were somehow miraculously protected in such a situation. And other rights could in any case not be protected if security or subsistence could credibly be threatened. The enjoyment of the other rights requires a certain degree of physical integrity, which is temporarily undermined, or eliminated, by deprivations of security or of subsistence. Someone who has suffered exposure or a beating is incapable of enjoying the substances of other rights, although only temporarily, provided he or she receives good enough care to recover the use of all essential faculties.

But as our earlier discussion of helplessness made clear, either the actual or the credibly threatened loss of security or subsistence leaves a person vulnerable to any other deprivations the source of the threat has in mind. Without security or subsistence one is helpless, and consequently one may also be helpless to protect whatever can be protected only at the risk of security or subsistence. Therefore, security and subsistence must be socially guaranteed, if any rights are to be enjoyed. This makes them basic rights.

In the construction of any philosophical argument, a principal challenge is to establish what needs to be established without slipping into the assertion of too much. By "too much" I mean a conclusion so inflated that, even if it is not a

reduction to absurdity in the strict sense, it nevertheless strains credulity. The argument for security rights and subsistence rights may seem to suffer this malady, which might be called the weakness of too much strength. Specifically, the argument may be feared to have implicit implications that people have rights to an unlimited number of things, in addition to security and subsistence, that it is difficult to believe that people actually could justifiably demand of others.

Now it is true that we have no reason to believe that security and subsistence are the only basic rights, and chapter 3 [of *Basic Rights: Subsistence, Affluence and U.S. Foreign Policy*] is devoted to the question of whether some kinds of liberties are also basic rights. But as we shall see in that chapter, it is quite difficult to extend the list of basic rights, and we face little danger that the catalogue of basic rights will turn out to be excessively long. Before it becomes perhaps painfully obvious from the case of liberty, it may be helpful to see why in the abstract the list of basic rights is sharply limited even if it may have some members not considered here.

The structure of the argument that a specific right is basic may be outlined as follows, provided we are careful about what is meant by "necessary":

1. Everyone has a right to something.
2. Some other things are necessary for enjoying the first thing as a right, whatever the first thing is.
3. Therefore, everyone also has rights to the other things that are necessary for enjoying the first as a right.

Since this argument abstracts from the substance of the right assumed in the first premise, it is based upon what it normally means for anything to be a right or, in other words, upon the concept of a right. So, if the argument to establish the substances of basic rights is summarized by saying that these substances are the "other things ... necessary" for enjoying any other right, it is essential to interpret "necessary" in the restricted sense of "made essential by the very concept of a right." The "other things" include not whatever would be convenient or useful, but only what is indispensable to anything else's being enjoyed as a right. Nothing will turn out to be necessary, in this sense, for the enjoyment of any right unless it is also necessary for the enjoyment of every right and is, for precisely this reason, qualified to be the substance of a basic right.

Since the concept of a right is a profoundly Janus-faced concept, this conceptual necessity can be explained both from the side of the bearer of the right and ... from the side of the bearers of the correlative duties. The content of the basic rights is such that for the bearer of any right (basic or non-basic) to pursue its fulfillment by means of the trade-off of the fulfillment of a basic right is self-defeating, and such that for the bearer of duties to claim to be fulfilling the duties correlative to any right in spite of not fulfilling the duties correlative to a basic right is fraudulent. But both perspectives can be captured more concretely by the notion of common, or ordinary, and serious but remediable threats or "standard threats," which was introduced earlier as the final element in the explanation of the structure of a right.[1] Certainly from the viewpoint of the bearer of a right it would be false or misleading to assert that a right had been fulfilled unless in the enjoyment of the substance of that right, a person also enjoyed protection against the threats that could ordinarily be expected to prevent, or hinder to a major degree, the enjoyment of the initial right assumed. And certainly from the viewpoint of the bearers of the correlative duties it would be false or misleading to assert that a right had been honored unless social guarantees had been established that would prevent the most common and serious threats from preventing or acutely hindering the enjoyment of the substance of the right. On the side of duties this places

especially heavy emphasis upon preventing standard threats, which ... is the joint function of the fulfillment of duties to avoid depriving and duties to protect against deprivation.

But the measure of successful prevention of thwarting by ordinary and serious but remediable threats is not utopian. People are neither entitled to social guarantees against every conceivable threat, nor entitled to guarantees against ineradicable threats like eventual serious illness, accident, or death. Another way to indicate the restricted scope of the argument, then, is as follows. The argument rests upon what might be called a transitivity principle for rights: If everyone has a right to y, and the enjoyment of x is necessary for the enjoyment of y, then everyone also has a right to x. But the necessity in question is analytic. People also have rights—according to this argument—only to the additional substances made necessary by the paired concepts of a right and its correlative duties. It is analytically necessary that if people are to be provided with a right, their enjoyment of the substance of the right must be protected against the typical major threats. If people are as helpless against ordinary threats as they would be on their own, duties correlative to a right are not being performed. Precisely what those threats are, and which it is feasible to counter, are of course largely empirical questions, and the answers to both questions will change as the situation changes. In the argument for acknowledging security and subsistence as basic rights I have taken it to be fairly evident that the erosion of the enjoyment of any assumed right by deficiencies in subsistence is as common, as serious, and as remediable at present as the destruction of the enjoyment of any assumed right by assaults upon security.

What is, for example, eradicable changes, of course, over time. Today, we have very little excuse for allowing so many poor people to die of malaria and more excuse probably for allowing people to die of cancer. Later perhaps we will have equally little excuse to allow deaths by many kinds of cancer, or perhaps not. In any case, the measure is a realistic, not a utopian, one, and what is realistic can change. Chapter 4 [of *Basic Rights: Subsistence, Affluence*

---

[1] I am grateful to Douglas MacLean for emphasizing the similarity between the notion toward which I am groping here and the one in Thomas M. Scanlon, "Human Rights as a Neutral Concern," in Peter G. Brown and Douglas MacLean (eds.), *Human Rights and U.S. Foreign Policy: Principles and Applications* (Lexington, MA: Lexington Books, 1979), pp. 83–92.

and U.S. Foreign Policy] returns to the question of what is realistic now in the realm of subsistence, and consideration of this concrete case will probably also provide the clearest understanding of what constitutes an ordinary and serious but remediable threat.

We noticed in an earlier section that one fundamental purpose served by acknowledging basic rights at all is, in Camus's phrase, that we "take the victim's side," and the side of the potential victims. The honoring of basic rights is an active alliance with those who would otherwise be helpless against natural and social forces too strong for them. A basic right has, accordingly, not been honored until people have been provided rather firm protection—what I am calling "social guarantees"—for enjoying the substance of their basic rights. What I am now stressing is that this protection need neither be ironclad nor include the prevention of every imaginable threat.

But the opposite extreme is to offer such weak social guarantees that people are virtually as vulnerable with their basic rights "fulfilled" as they are without them. The social guarantees that are part of any typical right need not provide impregnable protection against every imaginable threat, but they must provide effective defenses against predictable remediable threats. To try to count a situation of unrelieved vulnerability to standard threats as the enjoyment of basic rights by their bearers or the fulfillment of these rights by the bearers of the correlative duties is to engage in double-speak, or to try to behave as if concepts have no boundaries at all. To allow such practices to continue is to acquiesce in not only the violation of rights but also the destruction of the concept of rights.

Insofar as it is true that moral rights generally, and not basic rights only, include justified demands for social guarantees against standard threats, we have an interesting theoretical result. The fulfillment of both basic and non-basic moral rights consists of effective, but not infallible, social arrangements to guard against standard threats like threats to physical security and threats to economic security or subsistence. One way to characterize the substances of basic rights, which ties the account of basic rights tightly to the account of the structure of moral rights generally, is this: the substance of a basic right is something the deprivation of which is one standard threat to rights generally. The fulfillment of a basic right is a successful defense against a standard threat to rights generally. This is precisely why basic rights are basic. That to which they are rights is needed for the fulfillment of all other rights. If the substance of a basic right is not socially guaranteed, attempts actually to enjoy the substance of other rights remain open to a standard threat like the deprivation of security or subsistence. The social guarantees against standard threats that are part of moral rights generally *are the same as* the fulfillment of basic rights. This is why giving less priority to any basic right than to normal non-basic rights is literally impossible.

DISCUSSION QUESTIONS

1. How does Shue explain the notion of a "moral right"? (When may we say that we have a "right to *x*"?) How does Shue's analysis of this term differ from those offered by the philosophers in Unit II?

2. How does Shue define a "basic right"? According to Shue, on what grounds are security rights and subsistence rights properly classified as being basic rights?

3. Shue notes that a discussion of security rights is not very controversial, yet he recognizes that more resistance might be met when attempting to grant subsistence rights the status of being "basic." Why do you think this is? Do you think that Shue's argument regarding the status of subsistence rights is successful? Why or why not?

4. Within a community, who becomes responsible for shouldering the burden of ensuring the protection of basic rights (particularly subsistence rights)? Do you think that this is fair or justified? Defend your answer.

C.
Applications

72

Michael Walzer, selection from *Spheres of Justice* (1984)

Michael Walzer (b.1935) is professor emeritus at the Institute for Advanced Study, the editor of *Dissent*, and a contributing editor to *The New Republic*. Along with Alasdair MacIntyre and Michael Sandel, Walzer is one of the principal figures associated with the "communitarian" position in political theory. In this selection he considers the relationship between property and powers, devoting particular attention to the case of Pullman, Illinois, a town that was once entirely owned and governed by the train-car magnate George Pullman.

SOURCE

Walzer, Michael, from *Spheres of Justice: A Defense of Pluralism and Equality*. Copyright © 1984 Michael Walzer. Reprinted by permission of Basic Books, a member of the Perseus Books Group.

Property/Power

Ownership is properly understood as a certain sort of power over things. Like political power, it consists in the capacity to determine destinations and risks—that is, to give things away or to exchange them (within limits) and also to keep them and use or abuse them, freely deciding on the costs in wear and tear. But ownership can also bring with it various sorts and degrees of power over people. The extreme case is slavery, which far exceeds the usual forms of political rule. I am concerned here, however, not with the actual possession, but only with the control, of people—mediated by the possession of things; this is a kind of power closely analogous to that which the state exercises over its subjects and disciplinary institutions over their inmates. Ownership also has effects well short of subjection. People engage with one another, and with institutions too, in all sorts of ways that reflect the momentary inequality of their economic positions. I own such-and-such book, for example, and you would like to have it; I am free to decide whether to sell or lend or give it to you or keep it for myself. We organize a factory commune and conclude that so-and-so's skills do not suit him for membership. You gather your supporters and defeat me in the competition for a hospital directorship. Their company squeezes out ours in intense bidding for a city contract. These are examples of brief encounters. I see no way to avoid them except through a political arrangement that systematically replaces the encounters of men and women with what Engels once called "the administration of things"—a harsh response to what are, after all, normal events in the spheres of money and office. But what sovereignty entails, and what ownership sometimes achieves (outside its sphere), is sustained control over the destinations and risks of other people; and that is a more serious matter.

It's not easy to make out just when the free use of property converts into the exercise of power. There are difficult issues here, and much political and academic controversy. Two further examples, very much of the kind that figure in the literature, will illuminate some of the problems.

1. Beset by market failures, we decide to close down or relocate our cooperatively owned factory, thereby causing considerable harm to local merchants. Are we exercising power over the merchants? Not in any sustained way, I think, though our decision may well have serious effects on their lives. We certainly don't control their response to the new conditions we have created (nor are the new conditions entirely our creation: we didn't decide to fail on the market). Still, given our commitment to democratic politics, it might be argued that we should have included the merchants in our decision making. Inclusion is suggested by the medieval maxim, much favored by modern democrats, *What touches all should be decided by all*. But once one begins including all the people who are touched or affected by a given decision, and not just those whose daily activities are directed by it, it is hard to know where to stop. Surely the merchants in the various towns where the factory might relocate must be included as well. And all the people affected by the well-being of all the merchants, and so on. So power is drained away from local associations and communities and comes more and more to reside in the one association that includes all the affected people—namely, the state (and ultimately, if we pursue the logic of "touching," the global state). But this argument only suggests that affecting others cannot be a sufficient basis for distribut-

ing inclusion rights. It doesn't amount to exercising power in the relevant political sense.

By contrast, the state's decision to relocate the district offices of one of its bureaucracies must, if challenged, be fought through the political process. These are public offices, paid for out of public funds, providing public services. Hence the decision is clearly an exercise of power over the men and women who are taxed to make up the funds and who depend upon the services. A private firm, whether individually or collectively owned, is different. Its relations with its customers are more like brief encounters. If we tried to control these relations, insisting, for example, that every decision to locate or relocate had to be fought out politically, the sphere of money and commodities would effectively be eliminated, together with its attendant freedoms. All such attempts lie beyond the rightful range of (limited) government. But what if our factory is the only one, or by far the largest one, in town? Then our decision to close down or relocate might well have devastating effects; and in any genuine democracy, the political authorities would be pressed to step in. They might seek to alter market conditions (by subsidizing the factory, for example), or they might buy us out, or they might look for some way to attract new industry to the town. These choices, however, are a matter more of political prudence than of distributive justice.

2. We run our factory in such a way as to pollute the air over much of the town in which we are located and so to endanger the health of its inhabitants. Day after day, we impose risks on our fellow citizens, and we decide, for technical and commercial reasons, what degree of risk to impose. But to impose risks, or at least risks of this sort, is precisely to exercise power in the political sense of the phrase. Now the authorities will have to step in, defending the health of their constituents or insisting on the right to determine, on behalf of those constituents, the degree of risk they will accept. Even here, however, the authorities won't involve themselves in any sustained way in factory decision making. They will simply set or reset the limits within which decisions are made. If we (the

members of the factory commune) were able to stop them from doing that—by threatening to relocate, for example—and so maintain an unlimited ability to pollute, then it would make sense to call us tyrants. We would be exercising power in violation of the common (democratic) understanding of what power is and how it is to be distributed. Would it make a difference if we weren't aiming to maintain our profit margins but just struggling to keep the factory afloat? I am not sure; probably we would be bound, either way, to inform the local authorities of our financial condition and to accept their view of acceptable risks.

These are hard cases, the second more so than the first; and I shall not attempt any detailed resolution of them here. In a democratic society, the boundary of the sphere of money and commodities is likely to be drawn, roughly, between the two, so as to include the first but not the second. I have, however, radically simplified my accounts of the cases by assuming a cooperatively owned factory; and I need now to consider, at rather greater length, the more common example of private ownership. Now the workers in the factory are no longer economic agents, licensed to make a set of decisions; only the owners are agents of that sort, and the workers, like the townspeople, are threatened by the factory's failures and by its pollution. But they aren't merely "touched," more or less seriously. Unlike the townspeople, they are participants in the enterprise that causes the effects; they are bound by its rules. Ownership constitutes a "private government," and the workers are its subjects. So I must take up again, as in my earlier discussion of wage determination, the character of economic agency.

The classic setting for private government was the feudal system, where property in land was conceived to entitle the owner to exercise direct disciplinary (judicial and police) powers over the men and women who lived on the land—and who were, moreover, barred from leaving. These people were not slaves, but neither were they tenants. They are best called "subjects"; their landlord was also their lord, who taxed them and even conscripted them for his private army. It took many years of local

resistance, royal aggrandizement, and revolutionary activity before a clear boundary was drawn between the estate and the realm, between property and polity. Not until 1789 was the formal structure of feudal rights abolished and the disciplinary power of the lords effectively socialized. Taxation, adjudication, and conscription: all these dropped out of our conception of what property means. The state was emancipated, as Marx wrote, from the economy.[1] The entailments of ownership were redefined so as to exclude certain sorts of decision making that, it was thought, could only be authorized by the political community as a whole. This redefinition established one of the crucial divisions along which social life is organized today. On one side are activities called "political," involving the control of destinations and risks; on the other side are activities called "economic," involving the exchange of money and commodities. But though this division shapes our understanding of the two spheres, it does not itself determine what goes on within them. Indeed, private government survives in the post-feudal economy. Capitalist ownership still generates political power, if not in the market, where blocked exchanges set limits at least on the legitimate uses of property, then in the factory itself, where work seems to require a certain discipline. Who disciplines whom? It is a central feature of a capitalist economy that owners discipline non-owners.

What justifies this arrangement, we are commonly told, is the risk taking that ownership requires, and the entrepreneurial zeal, the inventiveness, and the capital investment through which economic firms are founded, sustained, and expanded. Whereas feudal property was founded on armed force and sustained and expanded through the power of the sword (though it was also traded and inherited), capitalist property rests upon forms of activity that are intrinsically non-coercive and non-political. The modern factory is distinguished from the feudal manor because men and women

---

[1] Karl Marx, "On the Jewish Question," in *Early Writings*, trans. T.B. Bottomore (London[: Watts], 1963), pp. 12–14.

come willingly to work in the factory, drawn by the wages, working conditions, prospects for the future, and so on that the owner offers, while the workers on the manor are serfs, prisoners of their noble lords. All this is true enough, at least sometimes, but it doesn't satisfactorily mark off property rights from political power. For everything that I have just said of firms and factories might also be said of cities and towns, if not always of states. They, too, are created by entrepreneurial energy, enterprise, and risk taking; and they, too, recruit and hold their citizens, who are free to come and go, by offering them an attractive place to live. Yet we should be uneasy about any claim to own a city or a town; nor is ownership an acceptable basis for political power within cities and towns. If we consider deeply why this is so, we shall have to conclude, I think, that it shouldn't be acceptable in firms or factories either. What we need is a story about a capitalist entrepreneur who is also a political founder and who tries to build his power on his property.

The Case of Pullman, Illinois

George Pullman was one of the most successful entrepreneurs of late nineteenth century America. His sleeping, dining, and parlor cars made train travel a great deal more comfortable than it had been, and only somewhat more expensive; and on this difference of degree, Pullman established a company and a fortune. When he decided to build a new set of factories and a town around them, he insisted that this was only another business venture. But he clearly had larger hopes; he dreamed of a community without political or economic unrest—happy workers and a strike-free plant.[1] He clearly belongs, then, to the great tradition of the political founder, even though, unlike Solon of Athens, he didn't enact his plans and then go off to Egypt, but stayed on

to run the town he had designed. What else could he do, given that he owned the town?

Pullman, Illinois, was built on a little over four thousand acres of land along Lake Calumet just south of Chicago, purchased (in seventy-five individual transactions) at a cost of eight hundred thousand dollars. The town was founded in 1880 and substantially completed, according to a single unified design, within two years. Pullman (the owner) didn't just put up factories and dormitories, as had been done in Lowell, Massachusetts,[2] some fifty years earlier. He built private homes, row houses, and tenements for some seven to eight thousand people, shops and offices (in an elaborate arcade), schools, stables, playgrounds, a market, a hotel, a library, a theater, even a church: in short, a model town, a planned community. And every bit of it belonged to him.

> A stranger arriving at Pullman puts up at a hotel managed by one of Mr. Pullman's employees, visits a theater where all the attendants are in Mr. Pullman's service, drinks water and burns gas which Mr. Pullman's water and gas works supply, hires one of his outfits from the manager of Mr. Pullman's livery stable, visits a school in which the children of Mr. Pullman's employees are taught by other employees, gets a bill charged at Mr. Pullman's bank, is unable to make a purchase of any kind save from some tenant of Mr. Pullman's, and at night he is guarded by a fire department every member of which from the chief down is in Mr. Pullman's service.[3]

This account is from an article in the *New York Sun* (the model town attracted a lot of attention), and it is entirely accurate except for the line about the school. In fact, the schools of Pullman were at

---

[1] Stanley Buder, *Pullman: An Experiment in Industrial Order and Community Planning, 1880–1930* (New York[: Oxford University Press], 1967).

[2] [Lowell, Massachusetts, was a nineteenth-century factory town. Workers were housed in dormitories owned by the mill-owners.]

[3] Ibid., pp. 98–99.

least nominally run by the elected school board of Hyde Park Township. The town was also subject to the political jurisdiction of Cook County and the State of Illinois. But there was no municipal government. Asked by a visiting journalist how he "governed" the people of Pullman, Pullman replied, "We govern them in the same way a man governs his house, his store, or his workshop. It is all simple enough."[1] Government was, in his conception, a property right; and despite the editorial "we," this was a right singly held and singly exercised. In his town, Pullman was an autocrat. He had a firm sense of how its inhabitants should live, and he never doubted his right to give that sense practical force. His concern, I should stress, was with the appearance and the behavior of the people, not with their beliefs. "No one was required to subscribe to any set of ideals before moving to [Pullman]." Once there, however, they were required to live in a certain way. Newcomers might be seen "lounging on their doorsteps, the husband in his shirtsleeves, smoking a pipe, his untidy wife darning, and half-dressed children playing about them." They were soon made aware that this sort of thing was unacceptable. And if they did not mend their ways, "company inspectors visited to threaten fines."[2]

Pullman refused to sell either land or houses—so as to maintain "the harmony of the town's design" and also, presumably, his control over the inhabitants. Everyone who lived in Pullman (Illinois) was a tenant of Pullman (George). Home renovation was strictly controlled; leases were terminable on ten days' notice. Pullman even refused to allow Catholics and Swedish Lutherans to build churches of their own, not because he opposed their worship (they were permitted to rent rooms), but because his conception of the town called for one rather splendid church, whose rent only the Presbyterians could afford. For somewhat different reasons, though with a similar zeal for order, liquor was available only in

the town's one hotel, at a rather splendid bar, where ordinary workers were unlikely to feel comfortable.

I have stressed Pullman's autocracy; I could also stress his benevolence. The housing he provided was considerably better than that generally available to American workers in the 1880s; rents were not unreasonable (his profit margins were in fact quite low); the buildings were kept in repair; and so on. But the crucial point is that all decisions, benevolent or not, rested with a man, governor as well as owner, who had not been chosen by the people he governed. Richard Ely, who visited the town in 1885 and wrote an article about it for *Harper's Monthly*, called it "unAmerican ... benevolent, well-wishing feudalism."[3] But that description wasn't quite accurate, for the men and women of Pullman were entirely free to come and go. They were also free to live outside the town and commute to work in its factories, though in hard times Pullman's tenants were apparently the last to be laid off. These tenants are best regarded as the subjects of a capitalist enterprise that has simply extended itself from manufacturing to real estate and duplicated in the town the discipline of the shop. What's wrong with that?

I mean the question to be rhetorical, but it is perhaps worthwhile spelling out the answer. The inhabitants of Pullman were guest workers, and that is not a status compatible with democratic politics. George Pullman hired himself a metic[4] population in a political community where self-respect was closely tied to citizenship and where decisions about destinations and risks, even (or especially) local destinations and risks, were supposed to be shared. He was, then, more like a dictator than a feudal lord; he ruled by force. The badgering of the townspeople by his inspectors was intrusive and tyrannical and can hardly have been experienced in any other way.

Ely argued that Pullman's ownership of the town made its inhabitants into something less than

[1] Ibid., p. 107.
[2] Ibid., p. 95; see also William M. Carwardine, *The Pullman Strike*, intro. Virgil J. Vogel, (Chicago[: H. Kerr], 1973), chaps. 8, 9, 10.

[3] Richard Ely, quoted in Buder, *Pullman*, p. 103.
[4] [In ancient Greece metics were persons who did not have the same rights as citizens in their place of residence.]

American citizens: "One feels that one is mingling with a dependent, servile people." Apparently, Ely caught no intimations of the great strike of 1894 or of the courage and discipline of the strikers.[1] He wrote his article early on in the history of the town; perhaps the people needed time to settle in and learn to trust one another before they dared oppose themselves to Pullman's power. But when they did strike, it was as much against his factory power as against his town power. Indeed, Pullman's foremen were even more tyrannical than his agents and inspectors. It seems odd to study the duplicated discipline of the model town and condemn only one half of it. Yet this was the conventional understanding of the time. When the Illinois Supreme Court in 1898 ordered the Pullman Company (George Pullman had died a year earlier) to divest itself of all property not used for manufacturing purposes, it argued that the ownership of a town, but not of a company, "was incompatible with the theory and spirit of our institutions."[2] The town had to be governed democratically—not so much because ownership made the inhabitants servile, but because it forced them to fight for rights they already possessed as American citizens.

It is true that the struggle for rights in the factory was a newer struggle, if only because factories were newer institutions than cities and towns. I want to argue, however, that with regard to political power democratic institutions can't stop at the factory gates. The deep principles are the same for both sorts of institution. This identity is the moral basis of the labor movement—not of "business unionism," which has another basis, but of every demand for progress toward industrial democracy. It doesn't follow from these demands that factories can't be owned; nor did opponents of feudalism say that land couldn't be owned. It's even conceivable that all the inhabitants of a (small) town might pay rent, but not homage, to the same landlord. The issue in all these cases is not the existence but the entailments of property. What democracy requires is that property should have no political currency, that it shouldn't convert into anything like sovereignty, authoritative command, sustained control over men and women. After 1894, at least, the town was undemocratic. But was his ownership of the company any different? The unusual juxtaposition of the two makes for a nice comparison.

They are not different because of the entrepreneurial vision, energy, inventiveness, and so on that went into the making of Pullman sleepers, diners, and parlor cars. For these same qualities went into the making of the town. This, indeed, was Pullman's boast: that his "'system' which had succeeded in railroad travel, was now being applied to the problems of labor and housing."[3] And if the application does not give rise to political power in the one case, why should it do so in the other?

Nor are the two different because of the investment of private capital in the company. Pullman invested in the town, too, without thereby acquiring the right to govern its inhabitants. The case is the same with men and women who buy municipal bonds: they don't come to own the municipality. Unless they live and vote in the town, they cannot even share in decisions about how their money is to be spent. They have no political rights, whereas residents do have rights, whether they are investors or not. There seems no reason not to make the same distinction in economic associations, marking off investors from participants, a just return from political power.

Finally, the factory and the town are not different because men and women come willingly to work in the factory with full knowledge of its rules and regulations. They also come willingly to live in the town, and in neither case do they have full knowledge of the rules until they have some experience of them. Anyway, residence does not constitute an agreement to despotic rules even if the rules are known in advance; nor is prompt departure the only way of expressing opposition. There are, in fact, some associations for which these last propositions might plausibly be reversed. A man who joins

---

[1] Ibid; see also Carwardine, *Pullman Strike*, chap. 4.
[2] Carwardine, *Pullman Strike*, p. XXXIII.

[3] Buder, *Pullman*, p. 44.

a monastic order requiring strict and unquestioning obedience, for example, seems to be choosing a way of life rather than a place to live (or a place to work). We would not pay him proper respect if we refused to recognize the efficacy of his choice. Its purpose and its moral effect are precisely to authorize his superior's decisions, and he can't withdraw that authority without himself withdrawing from the common life it makes possible. But the same thing can't be said of a man or a woman who joins a company or comes to work in a factory. Here the common life is not so all-encompassing and it does not require the unquestioning acceptance of authority. We respect the new worker only if we assume that he has not sought out political subjection. Of course, he encounters foremen and company police, as he knew he would; and it may be that the success of the enterprise requires his obedience, just as the success of a city or a town requires that citizens obey public officials. But in neither case would we want to say (what we might say to the novice monk): if you don't like these officials and the orders they give, you can always leave. It's important that there be options short of leaving, connected with the appointment of the officials and the making of the rules they enforce.

Other sorts of organizations raise more difficult questions. Consider an example that Marx used in the third volume of *Capital* to illustrate the nature of authority in a communist factory. Cooperative labor requires, he wrote, "one commanding will," and he compared this will to that of an orchestra conductor.[1] The conductor presides over a harmony of sounds and also, Marx seems to have thought, over a harmony of musicians. It is a disturbing comparison, for conductors have often been despots. Should their will be commanding? Perhaps it should, since an orchestra must express a single interpretation of the music it plays. But patterns of work in a factory are more readily negotiated. Nor is it the case that the members of an orchestra must yield to the conductor with regard to every aspect of the life they share. They might claim a considerable voice in the orchestra's affairs, even if they accept when they play the conductor's commanding will.

But the members of an orchestra, like the workers in a factory, while they spend a great deal of time with one another, don't live with one another. Perhaps the line between politics and economics has to do with the difference between residence and work. Pullman brought the two together, submitted residents and workers to the same rule. Is it enough if residents rule themselves while only workers are submitted to the power of property, if the residents are citizens and the workers metics? Certainly the self-rule of residents is commonly thought to be a matter of the first importance. That's why a landlord has so much less power over his tenants than a factory owner over his workers. Men and women must collectively control the place where they live in order to be safe in their own homes. *A man's home is his castle.* I will assume that this ancient maxim expresses a genuine moral imperative. But what the maxim requires is not political self-rule so much as the legal protection of the domestic sphere—and not only from economic but also from political interventions. We need a space for withdrawal, rest, intimacy, and (sometimes) solitude. As a feudal baron retired to his castle to brood over public slights, so I retire to my home. But the political community is not a collection of brooding places, or not only that. It is also a common enterprise, a public place where we argue together over the public interest, where we decide on goals and debate acceptable risks. All this was missing in Pullman's model town, until the American Railway Union provided a forum for workers and residents alike.

From this perspective, an economic enterprise seems very much like a town, even though—or, in part, because—it is so unlike a home. It is a place not of rest and intimacy but of cooperative action. It is a place not of withdrawal but of decision. If landlords possessing political power are likely to be intrusive on families, so owners possessing

---

[1] Karl Marx, *Capital* (New York, 1967), vol. III, pp. 383, 386. Lenin repeats the argument, suggesting "the mild leadership of a conductor of an orchestra" as an example of communist authority; see "The Immediate Tasks of the Soviet Government," in *Selected Works* (New York, n.d.), vol. VII, p. 342.

political power are likely to be coercive of individuals. Conceivably the first of these is worse than the second, but this comparison doesn't distinguish the two in any fundamental way; it merely grades them. Intrusiveness and coercion are alike made possible by a deeper reality—the usurpation of a common enterprise, the displacement of collective decision making, by the power of property. And for this, none of the standard justifications seems adequate. Pullman exposed their weaknesses by claiming to rule the town he owned exactly as he ruled the factories he owned. Indeed, the two sorts of rule are similar to one another, and both of them resemble what we commonly understand as authoritarian politics. The right to impose fines does the work of taxation; the right to evict tenants or discharge workers does (some of) the work of punishment. Rules are issued and enforced without public debate by appointed rather than by elected officials. There are no established judicial procedures, no legitimate forms of opposition, no channels for participation or even for protest. If this sort of thing is wrong for towns, then it is wrong for companies and factories, too.

Imagine now a decision by Pullman or his heirs to relocate their factory/town. Having paid off the initial investment, they see richer ground elsewhere; or, they are taken with a new design, a better model for a model town, and want to try it out. The decision, they claim, is theirs alone since the factory/town is theirs alone; neither the inhabitants nor the workers have anything to say. But how can this be right? Surely to uproot a community, to require large-scale migration, to deprive people of homes they have lived in for many years; these are political acts, and acts of a rather extreme sort. The decision is an exercise of power; and were the townspeople simply to submit, we would think they were not self-respecting citizens. What about the workers?

What political arrangements should the workers seek? Political rule implies a certain degree of autonomy, but it's not clear that autonomy is possible in a single factory or even in a group of factories. The citizens of a town are also the consumers of the goods and services the town provides; and

except for occasional visitors, they are the only consumers. But workers in a factory are producers of goods and services; they are only sometimes consumers, and they are never the only consumers. Moreover, they are locked into close economic relationships with other factories that they supply or on whose products they depend. Private owners relate to one another through the market. In theory, economic decisions are non-political, and they are coordinated without the interventions of authority. Insofar as this theory is true, worker cooperatives would simply locate themselves within the network of market relations. In fact, however, the theory misses both the collusions of owners among themselves and their collective ability to call upon the support of state officials. Now the appropriate replacement is an industrial democracy organized at national as well as local levels. But how, precisely, can power be distributed so as to take into account both the necessary autonomy and the practical linkage of companies and factories? The question is often raised and variously answered in the literature on workers' control. I shall not attempt to answer it again, nor do I mean to deny its difficulties; I only want to insist that the sorts of arrangements required in an industrial democracy are not all that different from those required in a political democracy. Unless they are independent states, cities and towns are never fully autonomous; they have no absolute authority even over the goods and services they produce for internal consumption. In the United States today, we enmesh them in a federal structure and regulate what they can do in the areas of education, criminal justice, environmental use, and so on. Factories and companies would have to be similarly enmeshed and similarly regulated (and they would also be taxed). In a developed economy, as in a developed polity, different decisions would be made by different groups of people at different levels of organization. The division of power in both these cases is only partly a matter of principle; it is also a matter of circumstance and expediency.

The argument is similar with regard to the constitutional arrangements within factories and companies. There will be many difficulties working these out; there will be false starts and failed experiments exactly as there have been in the history of cities and towns. Nor should we expect to find a single appropriate arrangement. Direct democracy, proportional representation, single-member constituencies, mandated and independent representatives, bicameral and unicameral legislatures, city managers, regulatory commissions, public corporations—political decision making is organized and will continue to be organized in many different ways. What is important is that we know it to be political, the exercise of power, not the free use of property. Today, there are many men and women who preside over enterprises in which hundreds and thousands of their fellow citizens are involved, who direct and control the working lives of their fellows, and who explain themselves exactly as George Pullman did. I govern these people, they say, in the same way a man governs the things he owns. People who talk this way are wrong. They misunderstand the prerogatives of ownership (and of foundation, investment, and risk taking). They claim a kind of power to which they have no right.

To say this is not to deny the importance of entrepreneurial activity. In both companies and towns, one looks for people like Pullman, full of energy and ideas, willing to innovate and take risks, capable of organizing large projects. It would be foolish to create a system that did not bring them forward. They are of no use to us if they just brood in their castles. But there is nothing they do that gives them a right to rule over the rest of us, unless they can win our agreement. At a certain point in the development of an enterprise, then, it must pass

out of entrepreneurial control; it must be organized or reorganized in some political way, according to the prevailing (democratic) conception of how power ought to be distributed. It is often said that economic entrepreneurs won't come forward if they cannot hope to own the companies they found. But this is like saying that no one would seek divine grace or knowledge who did not hope to come into hereditary possession of a church or "holy commonwealth," or that no one would found new hospitals or experimental schools who did not intend to pass them on to his children, or that no one would sponsor political innovation and reform unless it were possible to own the state. But ownership is not the goal of political or religious life, and there are still attractive and even compelling goals. Indeed, had Pullman founded a better town, he might have earned for himself the sort of public honor that men and women have sometimes taken as the highest end of human action. If he wanted power as well, he should have run for mayor.

DISCUSSION QUESTIONS

1. Explain the case of Pullman, Illinois. Walzer claims that the issue in this case "is not the existence but the entailments of property." Explain what he means.

2. Do you think that government and workplace are analogous in the ways that Walzer claims that they are? Why or why not?

73

Milton Friedman, selection from *Capitalism and Freedom* (1962)

In this selection, Friedman distinguishes between what he takes to be the legitimate and illegitimate functions of government. On Friedman, see reading 35 above.

SOURCE

Friedman, Milton. Excerpts from *Capitalism and Freedom*. Copyright © 1962 by Milton Friedman. Reproduced with the permission of the University of Chicago Press.

Government Measures Used to Alter the Distribution of Income

The methods that governments have used most widely to alter the distribution of income have been graduated income and inheritance taxation. Before considering their desirability, it is worth asking whether they have succeeded in their aim.

No conclusive answer can be given to this question with our present knowledge. The judgment that follows is a personal, though I hope not utterly uninformed, opinion, stated, for sake of brevity, more dogmatically than the nature of the evidence justifies. My impression is that these tax measures have had a relatively minor, though not negligible, effect in the direction of narrowing the differences between the average position of groups of families classified by some statistical measures of income. However, they have also introduced essentially arbitrary inequalities of comparable magnitude between persons within such income classes. As a result, it is by no means clear whether the net effect in terms of the basic objective of equality of treatment or equality of outcome has been to increase or decrease equality.

The tax rates are on paper both high and highly graduated. But their effect has been dissipated in two different ways. First, part of their effect has been simply to make the pre-tax distribution more unequal. This is the usual incidence effect of taxation. By discouraging entry into activities highly taxed—in this case activities with large risk and non-pecuniary disadvantages—they raise returns in those activities. Second, they have stimulated both legislative and other provisions to evade the tax—so-called "loopholes" in the law such as percentage depletion, exemption of interest on state and municipal bonds, specially favorable treatment of capital gains, expense accounts, other indirect ways of payment, conversion of ordinary income to capital gains, and so on in bewildering number and kind. The effect has been to make the actual rates imposed far lower than the nominal rates and, perhaps more important, to make the incidence of the taxes capricious and unequal. People at the same economic level pay very different taxes depending on the accident of the source of their income and the opportunities they have to evade the tax. If present rates were made fully effective, the effect on incentives and the like might well be so serious as to cause a radical loss in the productivity of the society. Tax avoidance may therefore have been essential for economic wellbeing. If so, the gain has been bought at the cost of a great waste of resources, and of the introduction of widespread inequity. A much lower set of nominal rates, plus a more comprehensive base through more equal taxation of all sources of income could be both more progressive in average incidence, more equitable in detail, and less wasteful of resources.

This judgment that the personal income tax has been arbitrary in its impact and of limited effectiveness in reducing inequality is widely shared by students of the subject, including many who strongly favor the use of graduated taxation to reduce inequality. They too urge that the top bracket rates be drastically reduced and the base broadened.

A further factor that has reduced the impact of the graduated tax structure on inequality of income and wealth is that these taxes are much less taxes on being wealthy than on becoming wealthy. While they limit the use of the income from existing wealth, they impede even more strikingly—so far as they are effective—the accumulation of wealth. The taxation of the income from the wealth does nothing to reduce the wealth itself; it simply reduces the level of consumption and additions to wealth that the owners can support. The tax measures give an incentive to avoid risk and to embody existing wealth in relatively stable forms, which reduces the likelihood that existing accumulations of wealth will be dissipated. On the other side, the major route to new accumulations is through large current incomes of which a large fraction is saved and invested in risky activities, some of which will yield high returns. If the income tax were effective, it would close this route. In consequence, its effect would be to protect existing holders of wealth from the competition of newcomers. In practice, this effect is largely dissipated by the avoidance devices already referred to. It is notable how large a fraction of the new accumulations have been in oil, where the percentage depletion allowances provide a particularly easy route to the receipt of tax-free income.

In judging the desirability of graduated income taxation it seems to me important to distinguish two problems, even though the distinction cannot be precise in application: first, the raising of funds to finance the expenses of those governmental activities it is decided to undertake (including perhaps measures to eliminate poverty ...); second, the imposition of taxes for redistributive purposes alone. The former might well call for some measure of graduation, both on grounds of assessing costs in accordance with benefits and on grounds of social standards of equity. But the present high nominal rates on top brackets of income and inheritance can hardly be justified on this ground—if only because their yield is so low.

I find it hard, as a liberal, to see any justification for graduated taxation solely to redistribute income. This seems a clear case of using coercion to take from some in order to give to others and thus to conflict head-on with individual freedom.

All things considered, the personal income tax structure that seems to me best is a flat-rate tax on income above an exemption, with income defined very broadly and deductions allowed only for strictly defined expenses of earning income. As already suggested in chapter v [of *Capitalism and*

Freedom], I would combine this program with the abolition of the corporate income tax, and with the requirement that corporations be required to attribute their income to stockholders, and that stockholders be required to include such sums on their tax returns. The most important other desirable changes are the elimination of percentage depletion on oil and other raw materials, the elimination of tax exemption of interest on state and local securities, the elimination of special treatment of capital gains, the co-ordination of income, estate, and gift taxes, and the elimination of numerous deductions now allowed.

An exemption, it seems to me, can be a justified degree of graduation.... It is very different for 90 per cent of the population to vote taxes on themselves and an exemption for 10 per cent than for 90 per cent to vote punitive taxes on the other 10 per cent—which is in effect what has been done in the United States. A proportional flat-rate tax would involve higher absolute payments by persons with higher incomes for governmental services, which is not clearly inappropriate on grounds of benefits conferred. Yet it would avoid a situation where any large numbers could vote to impose on others taxes that did not also affect their own tax burden.

The proposal to substitute a flat-rate income tax for the present graduated rate structure will strike many a reader as a radical proposal. And so it is in terms of concept. For this very reason, it cannot be too strongly emphasized that it is not radical in terms of revenue yield, redistribution of income, or any other relevant criterion. Our present income tax rates range from 20 per cent to 91 per cent, with the rate reaching 50 per cent on the excess of taxable incomes over $18,000 for single taxpayers or $36,000 for married taxpayers filing joint returns. Yet a flat rate of 23½ per cent on taxable income as presently reported and presently defined, that is, above present exemptions and after all presently allowable deductions, would yield as much revenue as the present highly graduated rate. In fact, such a flat rate, even with no change whatsoever in other features of the law, would yield a higher revenue because a larger amount of taxable income

would be reported for three reasons: there would be less incentive than now to adopt legal but costly schemes that reduce the amount of taxable income reported (so called tax avoidance); there would be less incentive to fail to report income that legally should be reported (tax evasion); the removal of the disincentive effects of the present structure of rates would produce a more efficient use of present resources and a higher income.

If the yield of the present highly graduated rates is so low, so also must be their redistributive effects. This does not mean that they do no harm. On the contrary. The yield is so low partly because some of the most competent men in the country devote their energies to devising ways to keep it so low; and because many other men shape their activities with one eye on tax effects. All this is sheer waste. And what do we get for it? At most, a feeling of satisfaction on the part of some that the state is redistributing income. And even this feeling is founded on ignorance of the actual effects of the graduated tax structure, and would surely evaporate if the facts were known.

To return to the distribution of income, there is a clear justification for social action of a very different kind than taxation to affect the distribution of income. Much of the actual inequality derives from imperfections of the market. Many of these have themselves been created by government action or could be removed by government action. There is every reason to adjust the rules of the game so as to eliminate these sources of inequality. For example, special monopoly privileges granted by government, tariffs, and other legal enactments benefiting particular groups, are a source of inequality. The removal of these, the liberal will welcome. The extension and widening of educational opportunities has been a major factor tending to reduce inequalities. Measures such as these have the operational virtue that they strike at the sources of inequality rather than simply alleviating the symptoms.

The distribution of income is still another area in which government has been doing more harm by one set of measures than it has been able to undo by others. It is another example of the justification of government intervention in terms of alleged defects of the private enterprise system when many of the phenomena of which champions of big government complain are themselves the creation of government, big and small.

DISCUSSION QUESTIONS

1. What is it about a graduated tax scheme that Friedman finds morally objectionable? What does he take to be the morally significant distinction between graduated taxation and flat-rate taxation? Do you agree with his view? Explain.

2. Friedman writes, "the personal income tax structure that seems to me best is a flat-rate tax on income above an exemption...." What justification(s) might be provided for this "exemption" clause, which would presumably exempt those with an extremely low income from paying taxes?

74

Karl Marx and Friedrich Engels, selection from *The Communist Manifesto*[1] (1848)

Karl Marx (1818–83) was a German philosopher, economist, historian, and political revolutionary. Marx's philosophy and theories were famously—or perhaps infamously—adapted by a number of controversial political figures, most notably Vladimir Lenin, Leon Trotsky, and Mao Tse Tung. Friedrich Engels (1820–95) was also a German philosopher, author, and political theorist. He and Marx met in Paris in 1844. During the years 1845–48, Engels and Marx joined and worked for the German Communist League in Brussels. *The Communist Manifesto* lays out the central principles and aims of the Communist League, an international political party that brought together representatives of socialist workers' groups and Christian communist organizations.

SOURCE

http://www.anu.edu.au/polsci/marx/
classics/manifesto.html.

I. Bourgeois and Proletarians

The history of all hitherto existing society is the history of class struggles.

Freeman and slave, patrician and plebian, lord and serf, guild-master and journeyman, in a word, oppressor and oppressed, stood in constant opposition to one another, carried on an uninterrupted, now hidden, now open fight, a fight that each time ended, either in a revolutionary reconstitution of society at large, or in the common ruin of the contending classes.

In the earlier epochs of history, we find almost everywhere a complicated arrangement of society into various orders, a manifold gradation of social rank. In ancient Rome we have patricians, knights, plebians, slaves; in the Middle Ages, feudal lords, vassals, guild-masters, journeymen, apprentices, serfs; in almost all of these classes, again, subordinate gradations.

The modern bourgeois society that has sprouted from the ruins of feudal society has not done away with class antagonisms. It has but established new classes, new conditions of oppression, new forms of struggle in place of the old ones.

Our epoch, the epoch of the bourgeoisie, possesses, however, this distinct feature: it has simplified class antagonisms. Society as a whole is more and more splitting up into two great hostile camps,

---

[1] [Original notes have been omitted.]

into two great classes directly facing each other—bourgeoisie and proletariat.

From the serfs of the Middle Ages sprang the chartered burghers of the earliest towns. From these burgesses the first elements of the bourgeoisie were developed.

The discovery of America, the rounding of the Cape, opened up fresh ground for the rising bourgeoisie. The East-Indian and Chinese markets, the colonisation of America, trade with the colonies, the increase in the means of exchange and in commodities generally, gave to commerce, to navigation, to industry, an impulse never before known, and thereby, to the revolutionary element in the tottering feudal society, a rapid development.

The feudal system of industry, in which industrial production was monopolized by closed guilds, now no longer suffices for the growing wants of the new markets. The manufacturing system took its place. The guild-masters were pushed aside by the manufacturing middle class; division of labor between the different corporate guilds vanished in the face of division of labor in each single workshop.

Meantime, the markets kept ever growing, the demand ever rising. Even manufacturers no longer sufficed. Thereupon, steam and machinery revolutionized industrial production. The place of manufacture was taken by the giant, MODERN INDUSTRY; the place of the industrial middle class by industrial millionaires, the leaders of the whole industrial armies, the modern bourgeois.

Modern industry has established the world market, for which the discovery of America paved the way. This market has given an immense development to commerce, to navigation, to communication by land. This development has, in turn, reacted on the extension of industry; and in proportion as industry, commerce, navigation, railways extended, in the same proportion the bourgeoisie developed, increased its capital, and pushed into the background every class handed down from the Middle Ages.

We see, therefore, how the modern bourgeoisie is itself the product of a long course of development, of a series of revolutions in the modes of production and of exchange.

Each step in the development of the bourgeoisie was accompanied by a corresponding political advance in that class. An oppressed class under the sway of the feudal nobility, an armed and self-governing association of medieval commune: here independent urban republic (as in Italy and Germany); there taxable "third estate" of the monarchy (as in France); afterward, in the period of manufacturing proper, serving either the semi-feudal or the absolute monarchy as a counterpoise against the nobility, and, in fact, cornerstone of the great monarchies in general—the bourgeoisie has at last, since the establishment of Modern Industry and of the world market, conquered for itself, in the modern representative state, exclusive political sway. The executive of the modern state is but a committee for managing the common affairs of the whole bourgeoisie.

The bourgeoisie, historically, has played a most revolutionary part.

The bourgeoisie, wherever it has got the upper hand, has put an end to all feudal, patriarchal, idyllic relations. It has pitilessly torn asunder the motley feudal ties that bound man to his "natural superiors," and has left no other nexus between people than naked self-interest, than callous "cash payment." It has drowned out the most heavenly ecstasies of religious fervor, of chivalrous enthusiasm, of philistine sentimentalism, in the icy water of egotistical calculation. It has resolved personal worth into exchange value, and in place of the numberless indefeasible chartered freedoms, has set up that single, unconscionable freedom—Free Trade. In one word, for exploitation, veiled by religious and political illusions, it has substituted naked, shameless, direct, brutal exploitation.

The bourgeoisie has stripped of its halo every occupation hitherto honored and looked up to with reverent awe. It has converted the physician, the lawyer, the priest, the poet, the man of science, into its paid wage laborers.

The bourgeoisie has torn away from the family its sentimental veil, and has reduced the family relation into a mere money relation.

The bourgeoisie has disclosed how it came to pass that the brutal display of vigor in the Middle Ages, which reactionaries so much admire, found its fitting complement in the most slothful indolence. It has been the first to show what man's activity can bring about. It has accomplished wonders far surpassing Egyptian pyramids, Roman aqueducts, and Gothic cathedrals; it has conducted expeditions that put in the shade all former exoduses of nations and crusades.

The bourgeoisie cannot exist without constantly revolutionizing the instruments of production, and thereby the relations of production, and with them the whole relations of society. Conservation of the old modes of production in unaltered form, was, on the contrary, the first condition of existence for all earlier industrial classes. Constant revolutionizing of production, uninterrupted disturbance of all social conditions, everlasting uncertainty and agitation distinguish the bourgeois epoch from all earlier ones. All fixed, fast frozen relations, with their train of ancient and venerable prejudices and opinions, are swept away, all new-formed ones become antiquated before they can ossify. All that is solid melts into air, all that is holy is profaned, and man is at last compelled to face with sober senses his real condition of life and his relations with his kind.

The need of a constantly expanding market for its products chases the bourgeoisie over the entire surface of the globe. It must nestle everywhere, settle everywhere, establish connections everywhere.

The bourgeoisie has, through its exploitation of the world market, given a cosmopolitan character to production and consumption in every country. To the great chagrin of reactionaries, it has drawn from under the feet of industry the national ground on which it stood. All old-established national industries have been destroyed or are daily being destroyed. They are dislodged by new industries, whose introduction becomes a life and death question for all civilized nations, by industries that no longer work up indigenous raw material, but raw material drawn from the remotest zones; industries whose products are consumed, not only at home, but in every quarter of the globe. In place of the old wants, satisfied by the production of the country, we find new wants, requiring for their satisfaction the products of distant lands and climes. In place of the old local and national seclusion and self-sufficiency, we have intercourse in every direction, universal inter-dependence of nations. And as in material, so also in intellectual production. The intellectual creations of individual nations become common property. National one-sidedness and narrow-mindedness become more and more impossible, and from the numerous national and local literatures, there arises a world literature.

The bourgeoisie, by the rapid improvement of all instruments of production, by the immensely facilitated means of communication, draws all, even the most barbarian, nations into civilization. The cheap prices of commodities are the heavy artillery with which it forces the barbarians' intensely obstinate hatred of foreigners to capitulate. It compels all nations, on pain of extinction, to adopt the bourgeois mode of production; it compels them to introduce what it calls civilization into their midst, i.e., to become bourgeois themselves. In one word, it creates a world after its own image.

The bourgeoisie has subjected the country to the rule of the towns. It has created enormous cities, has greatly increased the urban population as compared with the rural, and has thus rescued a considerable part of the population from the idiocy of rural life. Just as it has made the country dependent on the towns, so it has made barbarian and semi-barbarian countries dependent on the civilized ones, nations of peasants on nations of bourgeois, the East on the West.

The bourgeoisie keeps more and more doing away with the scattered state of the population, of the means of production, and of property. It has agglomerated population, centralized the means of production, and has concentrated property in a few hands. The necessary consequence of this was political centralization. Independent, or but loosely connected provinces, with separate interests, laws, governments, and systems of taxation, became lumped together into one nation, with one government, one code of laws, one national class interest, one frontier, and one customs tariff.

The bourgeoisie, during its rule of scarce one hundred years, has created more massive and more colossal productive forces than have all preceding generations together. Subjection of nature's forces to man, machinery, application of chemistry to industry and agriculture, steam navigation, railways, electric telegraphs, clearing of whole continents for cultivation, canalization of rivers, whole populations conjured out of the ground—what earlier century had even a presentiment that such productive forces slumbered in the lap of social labor?

We see then: the means of production and of exchange, on whose foundation the bourgeoisie built itself up, were generated in feudal society. At a certain stage in the development of these means of production and of exchange, the conditions under which feudal society produced and exchanged, the feudal organization of agriculture and manufacturing industry, in one word, the feudal relations of property became no longer compatible with the already developed productive forces; they became so many fetters. They had to be burst asunder; they were burst asunder.

Into their place stepped free competition, accompanied by a social and political constitution adapted in it, and the economic and political sway of the bourgeois class.

A similar movement is going on before our own eyes. Modern bourgeois society, with its relations of production, of exchange and of property, a society that has conjured up such gigantic means of production and of exchange, is like the sorcerer who is no longer able to control the powers of the nether world whom he has called up by his spells. For many a decade past, the history of industry and commerce is but the history of the revolt of modern productive forces against modern conditions of production, against the property relations that are the conditions for the existence of the bourgeois and of its rule. It is enough to mention the commercial crises that, by their periodical return, put the existence of the entire bourgeois society on its trial, each time more threateningly. In these crises, a great part not only of the existing products, but also of the previously created productive forces, are periodically destroyed. In these crises, there breaks out an epidemic that, in all earlier epochs, would have seemed an absurdity—the epidemic of overproduction. Society suddenly finds itself put back into a state of momentary barbarism; it appears as if a famine, a universal war of devastation, had cut off the supply of every means of subsistence; industry and commerce seem to be destroyed. And why? Because there is too much civilization, too much means of subsistence, too much industry, too much commerce. The productive forces at the disposal of society no longer tend to further the development of the conditions of bourgeois property; on the contrary, they have become too powerful for these conditions, by which they are fettered, and so soon as they overcome these fetters, they bring disorder into the whole of bourgeois society, endanger the existence of bourgeois property. The conditions of bourgeois society are too narrow to comprise the wealth created by them. And how does the bourgeoisie get over these crises? On the one hand, by enforced destruction of a mass of productive forces; on the other, by the conquest of new markets, and by the more thorough exploitation of the old ones. That is to say, by paving the way for more extensive and more destructive crises, and by diminishing the means whereby crises are prevented.

The weapons with which the bourgeoisie felled feudalism to the ground are now turned against the bourgeoisie itself.

But not only has the bourgeoisie forged the weapons that bring death to itself; it has also called into existence the men who are to wield those weapons—the modern working class—the proletarians.

In proportion as the bourgeoisie, i.e., capital, is developed, in the same proportion is the proletariat, the modern working class, developed—a class of laborers, who live only so long as they find work, and who find work only so long as their labor increases capital. These laborers, who must sell themselves piecemeal, are a commodity, like every other article of commerce, and are consequently exposed to all the vicissitudes of competition, to all the fluctuations of the market.

Owing to the extensive use of machinery, and to the division of labor, the work of the proletarians has lost all individual character, and, consequently, all charm for the workman. He becomes an appendage of the machine, and it is only the most simple, most monotonous, and most easily acquired knack, that is required of him. Hence, the cost of production of a workman is restricted, almost entirely, to the means of subsistence that he requires for maintenance, and for the propagation of his race. But the price of a commodity, and therefore also of labor, is equal to its cost of production. In proportion, therefore, as the repulsiveness of the work increases, the wage decreases. What is more, in proportion as the use of machinery and division of labor increases, in the same proportion the burden of toil also increases, whether by prolongation of the working hours, by the increase of the work exacted in a given time, or by increased speed of machinery, etc.

Modern Industry has converted the little workshop of the patriarchal master into the great factory of the industrial capitalist. Masses of laborers, crowded into the factory, are organized like soldiers. As privates of the industrial army, they are placed under the command of a perfect hierarchy of officers and sergeants. Not only are they slaves of the bourgeois class, and of the bourgeois state; they are daily and hourly enslaved by the machine, by the overlooker, and, above all, in the individual bourgeois manufacturer himself. The more openly this despotism proclaims gain to be its end and aim, the more petty, the more hateful and the more embittering it is.

The less the skill and exertion of strength implied in manual labor, in other words, the more modern industry becomes developed, the more is the labor of men superseded by that of women. Differences of age and sex have no longer any distinctive social validity for the working class. All are instruments of labor, more or less expensive to use, according to their age and sex.

No sooner is the exploitation of the laborer by the manufacturer, so far at an end, that he receives his wages in cash, than he is set upon by the other portion of the bourgeoisie, the landlord, the shopkeeper, the pawnbroker, etc.

The lower strata of the middle class—the small tradespeople, shopkeepers, and retired tradesmen generally, the handicraftsmen and peasants—all these sink gradually into the proletariat, partly because their diminutive capital does not suffice for the scale on which Modern Industry is carried on, and is swamped in the competition with the large capitalists, partly because their specialized skill is rendered worthless by new methods of production. Thus, the proletariat is recruited from all classes of the population. The proletariat goes through various stages of development. With its birth begins its struggle with the bourgeoisie. At first, the contest is carried on by individual laborers, then by the work of people of a factory, then by the operative of one trade, in one locality, against the individual bourgeois who directly exploits them. They direct their attacks not against the bourgeois condition of production, but against the instruments of production themselves; they destroy imported wares that compete with their labor, they smash to pieces machinery, they set factories ablaze, they seek to restore by force the vanished status of the workman of the Middle Ages.

At this stage, the laborers still form an incoherent mass scattered over the whole country, and broken up by their mutual competition. If anywhere they unite to form more compact bodies, this is not yet the consequence of their own active union, but of the union of the bourgeoisie, which class, in order to attain its own political ends, is compelled to set the whole proletariat in motion, and is moreover yet, for a time, able to do so. At this stage, therefore, the proletarians do not fight their enemies, but the enemies of their enemies, the remnants of absolute monarchy, the landowners, the non-industrial bourgeois, the petty bourgeois. Thus, the whole historical movement is concentrated in the hands of the bourgeoisie; every victory so obtained is a victory for the bourgeoisie.

But with the development of industry, the proletariat not only increases in number; it becomes concentrated in greater masses, its strength grows, and it feels that strength more. The various interests and conditions of life within the ranks of the proletariat are more and more equalized, in proportion as machinery obliterates all distinctions of labor, and nearly everywhere reduces wages to the same low level. The growing competition among the bourgeois, and the resulting commercial crises, make the wages of the workers ever more fluctuating. The increasing improvement of machinery, ever more rapidly developing, makes their livelihood more and more precarious; the collisions between individual workmen and individual bourgeois take more and more the character of collisions between two classes. Thereupon, the workers begin to form combinations (trade unions) against the bourgeois; they club together in order to keep up the rate of wages; they found permanent associations in order to make provision beforehand for these occasional revolts. Here and there, the contest breaks out into riots.

Now and then the workers are victorious, but only for a time. The real fruit of their battles lies not in the immediate result, but in the ever expanding union of the workers. This union is helped on by the improved means of communication that are created by Modern Industry, and that place the workers of different localities in contact with one another. It was just this contact that was needed to centralize the numerous local struggles, all of the same character, into one national struggle between classes. But every class struggle is a political struggle. And that union, to attain which the burghers of the Middle Ages, with their miserable highways, required centuries, the modern proletarians, thanks to railways, achieve in a few years.

This organization of the proletarians into a class, and, consequently, into a political party, is continually being upset again by the competition between the workers themselves. But it ever rises up again, stronger, firmer, mightier. It compels legislative recognition of particular interests of the workers, by taking advantage of the divisions among the bourgeoisie itself. Thus, the Ten-Hours Bill in England was carried.[1]

Altogether, collisions between the classes of the old society further in many ways the course of development of the proletariat. The bourgeoisie finds itself involved in a constant battle. At first with the aristocracy; later on, with those portions of the bourgeoisie itself, whose interests have become antagonistic to the progress of industry; at all time with the bourgeoisie of foreign countries. In all these battles, it sees itself compelled to appeal to the proletariat, to ask for help, and thus to drag it into the political arena. The bourgeoisie itself, therefore, supplies the proletariat with its own elements of political and general education; in other words, it furnishes the proletariat with weapons for fighting the bourgeoisie.

Further, as we have already seen, entire sections of the ruling class are, by the advance of industry, precipitated into the proletariat, or are at least threatened in their conditions of existence. These also supply the proletariat with fresh elements of enlightenment and progress.

Finally, in times when the class struggle nears the decisive hour, the progress of dissolution going on within the ruling class, in fact within the whole range of old society, assumes such a violent, glaring character, that a small section of the ruling class cuts itself adrift, and joins the revolutionary class, the class that holds the future in its hands. Just as, therefore, at an earlier period, a section of the nobility went over to the bourgeoisie, so now a portion of the bourgeoisie goes over to the proletariat, and in particular, a portion of the bourgeois ideologists, who have raised themselves to the level of comprehending theoretically the historical movement as a whole.

Of all the classes that stand face to face with the bourgeoisie today, the proletariat alone is a genuinely revolutionary class. The other classes decay and finally disappear in the face of Modern

---

[1] [This law was passed by the British Parliament in 1847 and limited the working days of women and children to ten hours.]

Industry; the proletariat is its special and essential product.

The lower middle class, the small manufacturer, the shopkeeper, the artisan, the peasant, all these fight against the bourgeoisie, to save from extinction their existence as fractions of the middle class. They are therefore not revolutionary, but conservative. Nay, more, they are reactionary, for they try to roll back the wheel of history. If, by chance, they are revolutionary, they are only so in view of their impending transfer into the proletariat; they thus defend not their present, but their future interests; they desert their own standpoint to place themselves at that of the proletariat.

The "dangerous class," the social scum, that passively rotting mass thrown off by the lowest layers of the old society, may, here and there, be swept into the movement by a proletarian revolution; its conditions of life, however, prepare it far more for the part of a bribed tool of reactionary intrigue.

In the condition of the proletariat, those of old society at large are already virtually swamped. The proletarian is without property; his relation to his wife and children has no longer anything in common with the bourgeois family relations; modern industry labor, modern subjection to capital, the same in England as in France, in America as in Germany, has stripped him of every trace of national character. Law, morality, religion, are to him so many bourgeois prejudices, behind which lurk in ambush just as many bourgeois interests.

All the preceding classes that got the upper hand sought to fortify their already acquired status by subjecting society at large to their conditions of appropriation. The proletarians cannot become masters of the productive forces of society, except by abolishing their own previous mode of appropriation, and thereby also every other previous mode of appropriation. They have nothing of their own to secure and to fortify; their mission is to destroy all previous securities for, and insurances of, individual property.

All previous historical movements were movements of minorities, or in the interest of minorities. The proletarian movement is the self-conscious, independent movement of the immense majority, in the interest of the immense majority. The proletariat, the lowest stratum of our present society, cannot stir, cannot raise itself up, without the whole superincumbent strata of official society being sprung into the air.

Though not in substance, yet in form, the struggle of the proletariat with the bourgeoisie is at first a national struggle. The proletariat of each country must, of course, first of all settle matters with its own bourgeoisie.

In depicting the most general phases of the development of the proletariat, we traced the more or less veiled civil war, raging within existing society, up to the point where that war breaks out into open revolution, and where the violent overthrow of the bourgeoisie lays the foundation for the sway of the proletariat.

Hitherto, every form of society has been based, as we have already seen, on the antagonism of oppressing and oppressed classes. But in order to oppress a class, certain conditions must be assured to it under which it can, at least, continue its slavish existence. The serf, in the period of serfdom, raised himself to membership in the commune, just as the petty bourgeois, under the yoke of the feudal absolutism, managed to develop into a bourgeois. The modern laborer, on the contrary, instead of rising with the process of industry, sinks deeper and deeper below the conditions of existence of his own class. He becomes a pauper, and pauperism develops more rapidly than population and wealth. And here it becomes evident that the bourgeoisie is unfit any longer to be the ruling class in society, and to impose its conditions of existence upon society as an overriding law. It is unfit to rule because it is incompetent to assure an existence to its slave within his slavery, because it cannot help letting him sink into such a state, that it has to feed him, instead of being fed by him. Society can no longer live under this bourgeoisie; in other words, its existence is no longer compatible with society.

The essential conditions for the existence and for the sway of the bourgeois class is the formation and augmentation of capital; the condition for capital is wage labor. Wage labor rests exclusively on competition between the laborers. The advance of industry, whose involuntary promoter is the bourgeoisie, replaces the isolation of the laborers, due to competition, by the revolutionary combination, due to association. The development of Modern Industry, therefore, cuts from under its feet the very foundation on which the bourgeoisie produces and appropriates products. What the bourgeoisie therefore produces, above all, are its own grave-diggers. Its fall and the victory of the proletariat are equally inevitable.

II. Proletarians and Communists

In what relation do the Communists stand to the proletarians as a whole? The Communists do not form a separate party opposed to the other working-class parties.

They have no interests separate and apart from those of the proletariat as a whole.

They do not set up any sectarian principles of their own, by which to shape and mold the proletarian movement.

The Communists are distinguished from the other working-class parties by this only:

(1) In the national struggles of the proletarians of the different countries, they point out and bring to the front the common interests of the entire proletariat, independently of all nationality.

(2) In the various stages of development which the struggle of the working class against the bourgeoisie has to pass through, they always and everywhere represent the interests of the movement as a whole.

The Communists, therefore, are on the one hand, practically, the most advanced and resolute section of the working-class parties of every country, that section which pushes forward all others; on the other hand, theoretically, they have over the great mass of the proletariat the advantage of clearly understanding the lines of march, the conditions, and the ultimate general results of the proletarian movement.

The immediate aim of the Communists is the same as that of all other proletarian parties: Formation of the proletariat into a class, overthrow of the bourgeois supremacy, conquest of political power by the proletariat.

The theoretical conclusions of the Communists are in no way based on ideas or principles that have been invented, or discovered, by this or that would-be universal reformer.

They merely express, in general terms, actual relations springing from an existing class struggle, from a historical movement going on under our very eyes. The abolition of existing property relations is not at all a distinctive feature of communism.

All property relations in the past have continually been subject to historical change consequent upon the change in historical conditions.

The French Revolution, for example, abolished feudal property in favor of bourgeois property.

The distinguishing feature of communism is not the abolition of property generally, but the abolition of bourgeois property. But modern bourgeois private property is the final and most complete expression of the system of producing and appropriating products that is based on class antagonisms, on the exploitation of the many by the few.

In this sense, the theory of the Communists may be summed up in the single sentence: Abolition of private property.

We Communists have been reproached with the desire of abolishing the right of personally acquiring property as the fruit of a man's own labor, which property is alleged to be the groundwork of all personal freedom, activity and independence.

Hard-won, self-acquired, self-earned property! Do you mean the property of petty artisan and of the small peasant, a form of property that preceded the bourgeois form? There is no need to abolish that; the development of industry has to a great extent already destroyed it, and is still destroying it daily.

Or do you mean the modern bourgeois private property?

But does wage labor create any property for the laborer? Not a bit. It creates capital, i.e., that kind of property which exploits wage labor, and which cannot increase except upon conditions of begetting a new supply of wage labor for fresh exploitation. Property, in its present form, is based on the antagonism of capital and wage labor. Let us examine both sides of this antagonism.

To be a capitalist, is to have not only a purely personal, but a social STATUS in production. Capital is a collective product, and only by the united action of many members, nay, in the last resort, only by the united action of all members of society, can it be set in motion.

Capital is therefore not only personal; it is a social power.

When, therefore, capital is converted into common property, into the property of all members of society, personal property is not thereby transformed into social property. It is only the social character of the property that is changed. It loses its class character.

Let us now take wage labor.

The average price of wage labor is the minimum wage, i.e., that quantum of the means of subsistence which is absolutely requisite to keep the laborer in bare existence as a laborer. What, therefore, the wage laborer appropriates by means of his labor merely suffices to prolong and reproduce a bare existence. We by no means intend to abolish this personal appropriation of the products of labor, an appropriation that is made for the maintenance and reproduction of human life, and that leaves no surplus wherewith to command the labor of others. All that we want to do away with is the miserable character of this appropriation, under which the laborer lives merely to increase capital, and is allowed to live only in so far as the interest of the ruling class requires it.

In bourgeois society, living labor is but a means to increase accumulated labor. In communist society, accumulated labor is but a means to widen, to enrich, to promote the existence of the laborer.

In bourgeois society, therefore, the past dominates the present; in communist society, the present dominates the past. In bourgeois society, capital is independent and has individuality, while the living person is dependent and has no individuality.

And the abolition of this state of things is called by the bourgeois, abolition of individuality and freedom! And rightly so. The abolition of bourgeois individuality, bourgeois independence, and bourgeois freedom is undoubtedly aimed at.

By freedom is meant, under the present bourgeois conditions of production, free trade, free selling and buying.

But if selling and buying disappears, free selling and buying disappears also. This talk about free selling and buying, and all the other "brave words" of our bourgeois about freedom in general, have a meaning, if any, only in contrast with restricted selling and buying, with the fettered traders of the Middle Ages, but have no meaning when opposed to the communist abolition of buying and selling, or the bourgeois conditions of production, and of the bourgeoisie itself.

You are horrified at our intending to do away with private property. But in your existing society, private property is already done away with for nine-tenths of the population; its existence for the few is solely due to its non-existence in the hands of those nine-tenths. You reproach us, therefore, with intending to do away with a form of property, the necessary condition for whose existence is the non-existence of any property for the immense majority of society.

In one word, you reproach us with intending to do away with your property. Precisely so; that is just what we intend.

From the moment when labor can no longer be converted into capital, money, or rent, into a social power capable of being monopolized, i.e., from the moment when individual property can no longer be transformed into bourgeois property, into capital, from that moment, you say, individuality vanishes.

You must, therefore, confess that by "individual" you mean no other person than the bourgeois, than the middle-class owner of property. This person must, indeed, be swept out of the way, and made impossible.

Communism deprives no man of the power to appropriate the products of society; all that it does is to deprive him of the power to subjugate the labor of others by means of such appropriations.

It has been objected that upon the abolition of private property, all work will cease, and universal laziness will overtake us.

According to this, bourgeois society ought long ago to have gone to the dogs through sheer idleness; for those who acquire anything, do not work. The whole of this objection is but another expression of the tautology: There can no longer be any wage labor when there is no longer any capital.

All objections urged against the communistic mode of producing and appropriating material products, have, in the same way, been urged against the communistic mode of producing and appropriating intellectual products. Just as to the bourgeois, the disappearance of class property is the disappearance of production itself, so the disappearance of class culture is to him identical with the disappearance of all culture.

That culture, the loss of which he laments, is, for the enormous majority, a mere training to act as a machine.

But don't wrangle with us so long as you apply, to our intended abolition of bourgeois property, the standard of your bourgeois notions of freedom, culture, law, etc. Your very ideas are but the outgrowth of the conditions of your bourgeois production and bourgeois property, just as your jurisprudence is but the will of your class made into a law for all, a will whose essential character and direction are determined by the economical conditions of existence of your class.

The selfish misconception that induces you to transform into eternal laws of nature and of reason the social forms stringing from your present mode of production and form of property—historical relations that rise and disappear in the progress of production—this misconception you share with every ruling class that has preceded you. What you see clearly in the case of ancient property, what you admit in the case of feudal property, you are of course forbidden to admit in the case of your own bourgeois form of property.

Abolition of the family! Even the most radical flare up at this infamous proposal. On what foundation is the present family, the bourgeois family, based? On capital, on private gain. In its completely developed form, this family exists only among the bourgeoisie. But this state of things finds its complement in the practical absence of the family among proletarians, and in public prostitution.

The bourgeois family will vanish as a matter of course when its complement vanishes, and both will vanish with the vanishing of capital.

Do you charge us with wanting to stop the exploitation of children by their parents? To this crime we plead guilty.

But, you say, we destroy the most hallowed of relations, when we replace home education by social.

And your education! Is not that also social, and determined by the social conditions under which you educate, by the intervention direct or indirect, of society, by means of schools, etc.? The Communists have not invented the intervention of society in education; they do but seek to alter the character of that intervention, and to rescue education from the influence of the ruling class.

The bourgeois claptrap about the family and education, about the hallowed correlation of parents and child, becomes all the more disgusting, the more, by the action of Modern Industry, all the family ties among the proletarians are torn asunder, and their children transformed into simple articles of commerce and instruments of labor.

But you Communists would introduce community of women, screams the bourgeoisie in chorus.

The bourgeois sees his wife a mere instrument of production. He hears that the instruments of production are to be exploited in common, and, naturally, can come to no other conclusion that the lot of being common to all will likewise fall to the women.

He has not even a suspicion that the real point aimed at is to do away with the status of women as mere instruments of production.

For the rest, nothing is more ridiculous than the virtuous indignation of our bourgeois at the community of women which, they pretend, is to be openly and officially established by the Communists. The Communists have no need to introduce free love; it has existed almost from time immemorial.

Our bourgeois, not content with having wives and daughters of their proletarians at their disposal, not to speak of common prostitutes, take the greatest pleasure in seducing each other's wives. (Ah, those were the days!)

Bourgeois marriage is, in reality, a system of wives in common and thus, at the most, what the Communists might possibly be reproached with is that they desire to introduce, in substitution for a hypocritically concealed, an openly legalized system of free love. For the rest, it is self-evident that the abolition of the present system of production must bring with it the abolition of free love springing from that system, i.e., of prostitution both public and private.

The Communists are further reproached with desiring to abolish countries and nationality.

The workers have no country. We cannot take from them what they have not got. Since the proletariat must first of all acquire political supremacy, must rise to be the leading class of the nation, must constitute itself *the* nation, it is, so far, itself national, though not in the bourgeois sense of the word.

National differences and antagonism between peoples are daily more and more vanishing, owing to the development of the bourgeoisie, to freedom of commerce, to the world market, to uniformity in the mode of production and in the conditions of life corresponding thereto.

The supremacy of the proletariat will cause them to vanish still faster. United action of the leading civilized countries at least is one of the first conditions for the emancipation of the proletariat.

In proportion as the exploitation of one individual by another will also be put an end to, the exploitation of one nation by another will also be put an end to. In proportion as the antagonism between classes within the nation vanishes, the hostility of one nation to another will come to an end.

The charges against communism made from a religious, a philosophical and, generally, from an ideological standpoint, are not deserving of serious examination.

Does it require deep intuition to comprehend that man's ideas, views, and conception, in one word, man's consciousness, changes with every change in the conditions of his material existence, in his social relations and in his social life?

What else does the history of ideas prove, than that intellectual production changes its character in proportion as material production is changed? The ruling ideas of each age have ever been the ideas of its ruling class.

When people speak of the ideas that revolutionize society, they do but express that fact that within the old society the elements of a new one have been created, and that the dissolution of the old ideas keeps even pace with the dissolution of the old conditions of existence.

When the ancient world was in its last throes, the ancient religions were overcome by Christianity. When Christian ideas succumbed in the eighteenth century to rationalist ideas, feudal society fought its death battle with the then revolutionary bourgeoisie. The ideas of religious liberty and freedom of conscience merely gave expression to the sway of free competition within the domain of knowledge.

"Undoubtedly," it will be said, "religious, moral, philosophical, and juridical ideas have been modified in the course of historical development. But religion, morality, philosophy, political science, and law, constantly survived this change."

"There are, besides, eternal truths, such as Freedom, Justice, etc., that are common to all states of society. But communism abolishes eternal truths, it abolishes all religion, and all morality, instead of constituting them on a new basis; it therefore acts in contradiction to all past historical experience."

What does this accusation reduce itself to? The history of all past society has consisted in the development of class antagonisms, antagonisms that assumed different forms at different epochs.

But whatever form they may have taken, one fact is common to all past ages, viz., the exploitation of one part of society by the other. No wonder, then, that the social consciousness of past ages, despite all the multiplicity and variety it displays, moves within certain common forms, or general ideas, which cannot completely vanish except with the total disappearance of class antagonisms.

The communist revolution is the most radical rupture with traditional relations; no wonder that its development involved the most radical rupture with traditional ideas.

But let us have done with the bourgeois objections to communism.

We have seen above that the first step in the revolution by the working class is to raise the proletariat to the position of ruling class to win the battle of democracy.

The proletariat will use its political supremacy to wrest, by degree, all capital from the bourgeoisie, to centralize all instruments of production in the hands of the state, i.e., of the proletariat organized as the ruling class; and to increase the total productive forces as rapidly as possible.

Of course, in the beginning, this cannot be effected except by means of despotic inroads on the rights of property, and on the conditions of bourgeois production; by means of measures, therefore, which appear economically insufficient and untenable, but which, in the course of the movement, outstrip themselves, necessitate further inroads upon the old social order, and are unavoidable as a means of entirely revolutionizing the mode of production.

These measures will, of course, be different in different countries.

Nevertheless, in most advanced countries, the following will be pretty generally applicable.

1. Abolition of property in land and application of all rents of land to public purposes.

2. A heavy progressive or graduated income tax.

3. Abolition of all rights of inheritance.

4. Confiscation of the property of all emigrants and rebels.

5. Centralization of credit in the banks of the state, by means of a national bank with state capital and an exclusive monopoly.

6. Centralization of the means of communication and transport in the hands of the state.

7. Extension of factories and instruments of production owned by the state; the bringing into cultivation of waste lands, and the improvement of the soil generally in accordance with a common plan.

8. Equal obligation of all to work. Establishment of industrial armies, especially for agriculture.

9. Combination of agriculture with manufacturing industries; gradual abolition of all the distinction between town and country by a more equable distribution of the populace over the country.

10. Free education for all children in public schools. Abolition of children's factory labor in its present form. Combination of education with industrial production, etc.

When, in the course of development, class distinctions have disappeared, and all production has been concentrated in the hands of a vast association of the whole nation, the public power will lose its political character. Political power, properly so called, is merely the organized power of one class for oppressing another. If the proletariat during its contest with the bourgeoisie is compelled, by the force of circumstances, to organize itself as a class; if, by means of a revolution, it makes itself the ruling class, and, as such, sweeps away by force the old conditions of production, then it will, along with these conditions, have swept away the conditions for the existence of class antagonisms and of classes generally, and will thereby have abolished its own supremacy as a class.

In place of the old bourgeois society, with its classes and class antagonisms, we shall have an association in which the free development of each is the condition for the free development of all.

DISCUSSION QUESTIONS

1. Marx and Engels write, "To be a capitalist, is to have not only a purely personal, but a social STATUS in production." What do they mean by this?

2. Explain what is meant by "bourgeois private property." Why do Marx and Engels favor the abolishment of bourgeois private property? Is personal private property possible under communism? Explain.

3. What do Marx and Engels mean when they write about bourgeois individuality and freedom? Why do they think that the abolishment of bourgeois individuality and freedom is a good thing? In what sense would abolishing these things constitute progress?

4. Compare and contrast Milton Friedman's view of private property and capital with that of Marx and Engels.

75

Kelo v. New London[1]
(2005)

This case arose as a result of the city of New London condemning privately owned real estate for use in a redevelopment project. It was estimated that the development of the land would have created thousands of jobs and millions of dollars of tax revenue. The case was unique because the township exercised its power of eminent domain to transfer land from one private party to another. The court held that such taking and transferring of property for the purposes of bringing about economic growth constituted a "public use" of the land and was thus permitted by the Fifth Amendment, so long as the owners were appropriately compensated.

SOURCE
545 U.S. 469 U.S. Supreme Court.

ON WRIT OF CERTIORARI TO THE SUPREME COURT OF CONNECTICUT [June 23, 2005]

Justice Stevens delivered the opinion of the Court.

In 2000, the city of New London approved a development plan that, in the words of the Supreme Court of Connecticut, was "projected to create in excess of 1,000 jobs, to increase tax and other revenues, and to revitalize an economically distressed city, including its downtown and waterfront areas." 268 Conn. 1, 5, 843 A. 2d 500, 507 (2004). In assembling the land needed for this project, the city's development agent has purchased property from willing sellers and proposes to use the power of eminent domain to acquire the remainder of the property from unwilling owners in exchange for just compensation. The question presented is whether the city's proposed disposition of this property qualifies as a "public use" within the meaning of the Takings Clause of the Fifth Amendment to the Constitution.

I

The city of New London (hereinafter City) sits at the junction of the Thames River and the Long Island Sound in southeastern Connecticut. Decades of economic decline led a state agency in 1990 to designate the City a "distressed municipality." In 1996, the Federal Government closed the Naval Undersea

---

[1] [Original notes have been omitted.]

848

UNIT III: C. Applications

Warfare Center, which had been located in the Fort Trumbull area of the City and had employed over 1,500 people. In 1998, the City's unemployment rate was nearly double that of the State, and its population of just under 24,000 residents was at its lowest since 1920.

These conditions prompted state and local officials to target New London, and particularly its Fort Trumbull area, for economic revitalization. To this end, respondent New London Development Corporation (NLDC), a private nonprofit entity established some years earlier to assist the City in planning economic development, was reactivated. In January 1998, the State authorized a $5.35 million bond issue to support the NLDC's planning activities and a $10 million bond issue toward the creation of a Fort Trumbull State Park. In February, the pharmaceutical company Pfizer Inc. announced that it would build a $300 million research facility on a site immediately adjacent to Fort Trumbull; local planners hoped that Pfizer would draw new business to the area, thereby serving as a catalyst to the area's rejuvenation. After receiving initial approval from the city council, the NLDC continued its planning activities and held a series of neighborhood meetings to educate the public about the process. In May, the city council authorized the NLDC to formally submit its plans to the relevant state agencies for review. Upon obtaining state-level approval, the NLDC finalized an integrated development plan focused on 90 acres of the Fort Trumbull area.

The Fort Trumbull area is situated on a peninsula that juts into the Thames River. The area comprises approximately 115 privately owned properties, as well as the 32 acres of land formerly occupied by the naval facility (Trumbull State Park now occupies 18 of those 32 acres). The development plan encompasses seven parcels. Parcel 1 is designated for a waterfront conference hotel at the center of a "small urban village" that will include restaurants and shopping. This parcel will also have marinas for both recreational and commercial uses. A pedestrian "riverwalk" will originate here and continue down the coast, connecting the waterfront areas of the development. Parcel 2 will be the site of

approximately 80 new residences organized into an urban neighborhood and linked by public walkway to the remainder of the development, including the state park. This parcel also includes space reserved for a new U.S. Coast Guard Museum. Parcel 3, which is located immediately north of the Pfizer facility, will contain at least 90,000 square feet of research and development office space. Parcel 4A is a 2.4-acre site that will be used either to support the adjacent state park, by providing parking or retail services for visitors, or to support the nearby marina. Parcel 4B will include a renovated marina, as well as the final stretch of the riverwalk. Parcels 5, 6, and 7 will provide land for office and retail space, parking, and water-dependent commercial uses. 1 App. 109–113.

The NLDC intended the development plan to capitalize on the arrival of the Pfizer facility and the new commerce it was expected to attract. In addition to creating jobs, generating tax revenue, and helping to "build momentum for the revitalization of downtown New London," id., at 92, the plan was also designed to make the City more attractive and to create leisure and recreational opportunities on the waterfront and in the park.

The city council approved the plan in January 2000, and designated the NLDC as its development agent in charge of implementation. See Conn. Gen. Stat. §8–188 (2005). The city council also authorized the NLDC to purchase property or to acquire property by exercising eminent domain in the City's name. §8–193. The NLDC successfully negotiated the purchase of most of the real estate in the 90-acre area, but its negotiations with petitioners failed. As a consequence, in November 2000, the NLDC initiated the condemnation proceedings that gave rise to this case.

II

Petitioner Susette Kelo has lived in the Fort Trumbull area since 1997. She has made extensive improvements to her house, which she prizes for its water view. Petitioner Wilhelmina Dery was born in her Fort Trumbull house in 1918 and has lived there her entire life. Her husband Charles (also a petitioner) has lived in the house since they married some 60 years ago. In all, the nine petitioners own 15 properties in Fort Trumbull—4 in parcel 3 of the development plan and 11 in parcel 4A. Ten of the parcels are occupied by the owner or a family member; the other five are held as investment properties. There is no allegation that any of these properties is blighted or otherwise in poor condition; rather, they were condemned only because they happen to be located in the development area.

In December 2000, petitioners brought this action in the New London Superior Court. They claimed, among other things, that the taking of their properties would violate the "public use" restriction in the Fifth Amendment. After a 7-day bench trial, the Superior Court granted a permanent restraining order prohibiting the taking of the properties located in parcel 4A (park or marina support). It, however, denied petitioners relief as to the properties located in parcel 3 (office space). 2 App. to Pet. for Cert. 343–350.

After the Superior Court ruled, both sides took appeals to the Supreme Court of Connecticut. That court held, over a dissent, that all of the City's proposed takings were valid. It began by upholding the lower court's determination that the takings were authorized by chapter 132, the State's municipal development statute. See Conn. Gen. Stat. §8–186 *et seq.* (2005). That statute expresses a legislative determination that the taking of land, even developed land, as part of an economic development project is a "public use" and in the "public interest." 268 Conn., at 18–28, 843 A. 2d, at 515–521. Next, relying on cases such as *Hawaii Housing Authority* v. *Midkiff,* 467 U.S. 229 (1984), and *Berman* v. *Parker,* 348 U.S. 26 (1954), the court held that such economic development qualified as a valid public use under both the Federal and State Constitutions. 268 Conn., at 40, 843 A. 2d, at 527.

Finally, adhering to its precedents, the court went on to determine, first, whether the takings of the particular properties at issue were "reasonably necessary" to achieving the City's intended public use, id., at 82, 843 A. 2d, at 552–553, and, second, whether the takings were for "reasonably

foreseeable needs," id., at 93, 843 A. 2d, at 558–559. The court upheld the trial court's factual findings as to parcel 3, but reversed the trial court as to parcel 4A, agreeing with the City that the intended use of this land was sufficiently definite and had been given "reasonable attention" during the planning process. Id., at 120–121, 843 A. 2d, at 574.

The three dissenting justices would have imposed a "heightened" standard of judicial review for takings justified by economic development. Although they agreed that the plan was intended to serve a valid public use, they would have found all the takings unconstitutional because the City had failed to adduce "clear and convincing evidence" that the economic benefits of the plan would in fact come to pass. Id., at 144, 146, 843 A. 2d, at 587, 588 (Zarella, J., joined by Sullivan, C. J., and Katz, J., concurring in part and dissenting in part).

We granted *certiorari* to determine whether a city's decision to take property for the purpose of economic development satisfies the "public use" requirement of the Fifth Amendment. 542 U.S. (2004).

III

Two polar propositions are perfectly clear. On the one hand, it has long been accepted that the sovereign may not take the property of *A* for the sole purpose of transferring it to another private party *B,* even though *A* is paid just compensation. On the other hand, it is equally clear that a State may transfer property from one private party to another if future "use by the public" is the purpose of the taking; the condemnation of land for a railroad with common-carrier duties is a familiar example. Neither of these propositions, however, determines the disposition of this case.

As for the first proposition, the City would no doubt be forbidden from taking petitioners' land for the purpose of conferring a private benefit on a particular private party. See *Midkiff,* 467 U.S., at 245 ("A purely private taking could not withstand the scrutiny of the public use requirement; it would serve no legitimate purpose of government and would thus be void"); *Missouri Pacific R. Co.*

v. Nebraska, 164 U.S. 403 (1896). Nor would the City be allowed to take property under the mere pretext of a public purpose, when its actual purpose was to bestow a private benefit. The takings before us, however, would be executed pursuant to a "carefully considered" development plan. 268 Conn., at 54, 843 A. 2d, at 536. The trial judge and all the members of the Supreme Court of Connecticut agreed that there was no evidence of an illegitimate purpose in this case. Therefore, as was true of the statute challenged in *Midkiff,* 467 U.S., at 245, the City's development plan was not adopted "to benefit a particular class of identifiable individuals."

On the other hand, this is not a case in which the City is planning to open the condemned land—at least not in its entirety—to use by the general public. Nor will the private lessees of the land in any sense be required to operate like common carriers, making their services available to all comers. But although such a projected use would be sufficient to satisfy the public use requirement, this "Court long ago rejected any literal requirement that condemned property be put into use for the general public." Id., at 244. Indeed, while many state courts in the mid-19th century endorsed "use by the public" as the proper definition of public use, that narrow view steadily eroded over time. Not only was the "use by the public" test difficult to administer (e.g., what proportion of the public need have access to the property? at what price?), but it proved to be impractical given the diverse and always evolving needs of society. Accordingly, when this Court began applying the Fifth Amendment to the States at the close of the 19th century, it embraced the broader and more natural interpretation of public use as "public purpose." See, e.g., *Fallbrook Irrigation Dist. v. Bradley,* 164 U.S. 112, 158–164 (1896). Thus, in a case upholding a mining company's use of an aerial bucket line to transport ore over property it did not own, Justice Holmes' opinion for the Court stressed "the inadequacy of use by the general public as a universal test." *Strickley v. Highland Boy Gold Mining Co.,* 200 U.S. 527, 531 (1906).

We have repeatedly and consistently rejected that narrow test ever since.

The disposition of this case therefore turns on the question whether the City's development plan serves a "public purpose." Without exception, our cases have defined that concept broadly, reflecting our longstanding policy of deference to legislative judgments in this field.

In *Berman v. Parker,* 348 U.S. 26 (1954), this Court upheld a redevelopment plan targeting a blighted area of Washington, DC, in which most of the housing for the area's 5,000 inhabitants was beyond repair. Under the plan, the area would be condemned and part of it utilized for the construction of streets, schools, and other public facilities. The remainder of the land would be leased or sold to private parties for the purpose of redevelopment, including the construction of low-cost housing.

The owner of a department store located in the area challenged the condemnation, pointing out that his store was not itself blighted and arguing that the creation of a "better balanced, more attractive community" was not a valid public use. Id., at 31. Writing for a unanimous Court, Justice Douglas refused to evaluate this claim in isolation, deferring instead to the legislative and agency judgment that the area "must be planned as a whole" for the plan to be successful. Id., at 34. The Court explained that "community redevelopment programs need not, by force of the Constitution, be on a piecemeal basis-lot by lot, building by building." Id., at 35. The public use underlying the taking was unequivocally affirmed:

> We do not sit to determine whether a particular housing project is or is not desirable. The concept of the public welfare is broad and inclusive.... The values it represents are spiritual as well as physical, aesthetic as well as monetary. It is within the power of the legislature to determine that the community should be beautiful as well as healthy, spacious as well as clean, well-balanced as well as carefully patrolled. In the present case, the Congress and its authorized agencies have

made determinations that take into account a wide variety of values. It is not for us to reappraise them. If those who govern the District of Columbia decide that the Nation's Capital should be beautiful as well as sanitary, there is nothing in the Fifth Amendment that stands in the way. Id., at 33.

In *Hawaii Housing Authority v. Midkiff*, 467 U.S. 229 (1984), the Court considered a Hawaii statute whereby fee title was taken from lessors and transferred to lessees (for just compensation) in order to reduce the concentration of land ownership. We unanimously upheld the statute and rejected the Ninth Circuit's view that it was "a naked attempt on the part of the state of Hawaii to take the property of A and transfer it to B solely for B's private use and benefit." Id., at 235 (internal quotation marks omitted). Reaffirming *Berman*'s deferential approach to legislative judgments in this field, we concluded that the State's purpose of eliminating the "social and economic evils of a land oligopoly" qualified as a valid public use. 467 U.S., at 241–242. Our opinion also rejected the contention that the mere fact that the State immediately transferred the properties to private individuals upon condemnation somehow diminished the public character of the taking. "[I]t is only the taking's purpose, and not its mechanics," we explained, that matters in determining public use. Id., at 244.

In that same Term we decided another public use case that arose in a purely economic context. In *Ruckelshaus v. Monsanto, Co.*, 467 U.S. 986 (1984), the Court dealt with provisions of the Federal Insecticide, Fungicide, and Rodenticide Act under which the Environmental Protection Agency could consider the data (including trade secrets) submitted by a prior pesticide applicant in evaluating a subsequent application, so long as the second applicant paid just compensation for the data. We acknowledged that the "most direct beneficiaries" of these provisions were the subsequent applicants, id., at 1014, but we nevertheless upheld the statute under *Berman* and *Midkiff*. We found sufficient Congress' belief that sparing applicants the cost of time-consuming research eliminated a significant barrier to entry in the pesticide market and thereby enhanced competition. 467 U.S., at 1015.

Viewed as a whole, our jurisprudence has recognized that the needs of society have varied between different parts of the Nation, just as they have evolved over time in response to changed circumstances. Our earliest cases in particular embodied a strong theme of federalism, emphasizing the "great respect" that we owe to state legislatures and state courts in discerning local public needs. See *Hairston v. Danville & Western R. Co.*, 208 U.S. 598, 606–607 (1908) (noting that these needs were likely to vary depending on a State's "resources, the capacity of the soil, the relative importance of industries to the general public welfare, and the long-established methods and habits of the people"). For more than a century, our public use jurisprudence has wisely eschewed rigid formulas and intrusive scrutiny in favor of affording legislatures broad latitude in determining what public needs justify the use of the takings power.

IV

Those who govern the City were not confronted with the need to remove blight in the Fort Trumbull area, but their determination that the area was sufficiently distressed to justify a program of economic rejuvenation is entitled to our deference. The City has carefully formulated an economic development plan that it believes will provide appreciable benefits to the community, including—but by no means limited to—new jobs and increased tax revenue. As with other exercises in urban planning and development, the City is endeavoring to coordinate a variety of commercial, residential, and recreational uses of land, with the hope that they will form a whole greater than the sum of its parts. To effectuate this plan, the City has invoked a state statute that specifically authorizes the use of eminent domain to promote economic development. Given the comprehensive character of the plan, the thorough deliberation that preceded its adoption, and the limited scope of our review, it is appropriate for us, as it was in *Berman*, to resolve the challenges of the individual owners, not on a piecemeal basis, but rather in light of the entire plan. Because that plan unquestionably serves a public purpose, the takings challenged here satisfy the public use requirement of the Fifth Amendment.

To avoid this result, petitioners urge us to adopt a new bright-line rule that economic development does not qualify as a public use. Putting aside the unpersuasive suggestion that the City's plan will provide only purely economic benefits, neither precedent nor logic supports petitioners' proposal. Promoting economic development is a traditional and long accepted function of government. There is, moreover, no principled way of distinguishing economic development from the other public purposes that we have recognized. In our cases upholding takings that facilitated agriculture and mining, for example, we emphasized the importance of those industries to the welfare of the States in question, see, e.g., *Strickley,* 200 U.S. 527; in *Berman,* we endorsed the purpose of transforming a blighted area into a "well-balanced" community through redevelopment, 348 U.S., at 33; in *Midkiff,* we upheld the interest in breaking up a land oligopoly that "created artificial deterrents to the normal functioning of the State's residential land market," 467 U.S., at 242; and in *Monsanto,* we accepted Congress' purpose of eliminating a "significant barrier to entry in the pesticide market," 467 U.S., at 1014–1015. It would be incongruous to hold that the City's interest in the economic benefits to be derived from the development of the Fort Trumbull area has less of a public character than any of those other interests. Clearly, there is no basis for exempting economic development from our traditionally broad understanding of public purpose.

Petitioners contend that using eminent domain for economic development impermissibly blurs the boundary between public and private takings. Again, our cases foreclose this objection. Quite simply, the government's pursuit of a public purpose will often benefit individual private parties. For example, in *Midkiff,* the forced transfer of property conferred a direct and significant benefit on those lessees who were previously unable to purchase their homes. In *Monsanto,* we recognized that the "most direct beneficiaries" of the data-sharing provisions were the subsequent pesticide applicants, but benefiting them in this way was necessary to promoting competition in the pesticide market. 467 U.S., at 1014. The owner of the department store in *Berman* objected to "taking from one businessman for the benefit of another businessman," 348 U.S., at 33, referring to the fact that under the redevelopment plan land would be leased or sold to private developers for redevelopment. Our rejection of that contention has particular relevance to the instant case: "The public end may be as well or better served through an agency of private enterprise than through a department of government—or so the Congress might conclude. We cannot say that public ownership is the sole method of promoting the public purposes of community redevelopment projects." Id., at 34.

It is further argued that without a bright-line rule nothing would stop a city from transferring citizen A's property to citizen B for the sole reason that citizen B will put the property to a more productive use and thus pay more taxes. Such a one-to-one transfer of property, executed outside the confines of an integrated development plan, is not presented in this case. While such an unusual exercise of government power would certainly raise a suspicion that a private purpose was afoot, the hypothetical cases posited by petitioners can be confronted if and when they arise. They do not warrant the crafting of an artificial restriction on the concept of public use.

Alternatively, petitioners maintain that for takings of this kind we should require a "reasonable certainty" that the expected public benefits will actually accrue. Such a rule, however, would represent an even greater departure from our precedent. "When the legislature's purpose is legitimate and its means are not irrational, our cases make clear that empirical debates over the wisdom of takings—no less than debates over the wisdom of other kinds of socioeconomic legislation—are not to be carried out in the federal courts." *Midkiff,* 467 U.S., at 242. Indeed, earlier this Term we explained why similar practical concerns (among others) undermined the use of the "substantially advances" formula in our regulatory takings doctrine. See *Lingle v. Chevron U.S.A. Inc....* (2005) (slip op., at 14–15) (noting that this formula "would empower—and might often require—courts to substitute their predictive judgments for those of elected legislatures and expert agencies"). The disadvantages of a heightened form of review are especially pronounced in this type of case. Orderly implementation of a comprehensive redevelopment plan obviously requires that the legal rights of all interested parties be established before new construction can be commenced. A constitutional rule that required postponement of the judicial approval of every condemnation until the likelihood of success of the plan had been assured would unquestionably impose a significant impediment to the successful consummation of many such plans.

Just as we decline to second-guess the City's considered judgments about the efficacy of its development plan, we also decline to second-guess the City's determinations as to what lands it needs to acquire in order to effectuate the project. "It is not for the courts to oversee the choice of the boundary line nor to sit in review on the size of a particular project area. Once the question of the public purpose has been decided, the amount and character of land to be taken for the project and the need for a particular tract to complete the integrated plan rests in the discretion of the legislative branch." *Berman*, 348 U.S., at 35–36.

In affirming the City's authority to take petitioners' properties, we do not minimize the hardship that condemnations may entail, notwithstanding the payment of just compensation. We emphasize that nothing in our opinion precludes any State from placing further restrictions on its exercise of the takings power. Indeed, many States already impose "public use" requirements that are stricter than the federal baseline. Some of these requirements have been established as a matter of state constitutional law, while others are expressed in state eminent domain statutes that carefully limit the grounds upon which takings may be exercised. As the submissions of the parties and their *amici* make clear, the necessity and wisdom of using eminent domain to promote economic development are certainly matters of legitimate public debate. This Court's authority, however, extends only to determining whether the City's proposed condemnations are for a "public use" within the meaning of the Fifth Amendment to the Federal Constitution. Because over a century of our case law interpreting that provision dictates an affirmative answer to that question, we may not grant petitioners the relief that they seek.

The judgment of the Supreme Court of Connecticut is affirmed.

DISCUSSION QUESTIONS

1. Why did the Court affirm the city's right to seize Kelo's land? Do you agree with the Court's decision? Explain.

2. The Court affirmed the city's right to condemn property, so long as the owners were provided "just compensation." How could we go about determining whether a compensatory package was "just"? In other contexts, how does one determine a "fair" price for a product or service, and what would lead us to conclude that a price was unfair or unjust?

3. If we can justify the city's right to seize property in the form of land, could we also extend this to include a right to seize other property (e.g., cars, labor, inventions, or even bodily organs/blood)?

UNIT IV
Responses to Injustice

Introduction

In one way or another many of the selections in this anthology try to identify various kinds of unjust behavior. It is one thing to recognize examples of injustice (actions that are wrong, people doing what they shouldn't have done); it is another to figure out precisely what our reaction should be to the injustice we discover. One obvious issue concerns the role of punishment in responding to injustice.

Punishment

Hobbes famously suggested that when punishing people one should look to the future. One should punish someone for acting in some way only when the world will be better, all things considered, from doing so. Hobbes was particularly worried about punishing merely for the sake of getting even—something that he thought would often lead to an endless cycle of violence—S2 harms S1 for some perceived injustice, but S3 who is an ally of S1 then proceeds to exact revenge on S2, and so on, until we have the Hatfields and the McCoys (or the Israelis and the Palestinians, the Sunni Iraqis and the Shiite Iraqis).

In earlier introductions we've talked about consequentialist approaches to morality. On such views, what we ought to do depends on the consequences (actual, probable, or possible) of one's actions. If one were a consequentialist, it is not even clear that one should tie "punishment" to wrongdoing. We might, for example, think that some vigilante

was perfectly justified in taking justice into his own hands, but also think that for the greater future good of society, we ought to make an example of the vigilante. (Perhaps we think that failure to do so would encourage too many others to act in a similar fashion where we are relatively confident that many would-be vigilantes would act inappropriately.) To be sure, one can quarrel over the use of the term "punishment" when one employs institutions to inflict some harm on an individual who has done nothing wrong. It is not implausible to suppose that one meaning of the term requires that one think of the harm inflicted as *punishment* only if it is a response to a perceived injustice. But there is no need to argue about the meaning of a word. Whether the incarceration is punishment or something one does for some consequentialist reason unrelated to a judgment that the person has acted wrongly, the person in jail is still behind bars.

We suspect that the Hobbesian conception of the role of punishment is implicitly rejected by many, if not most, ordinary people. To be sure, when one listens to debates about capital punishment, for example, the participants might argue for some time about various consequences of the practice. The opponent of capital punishment will often argue, for example, that the practice is unacceptably dangerous (because we will kill too many innocents), too costly, ineffective as a deterrent, and so on. The proponent of capital punishment will often deny some of these claims, but it is not unusual for the debate to shift course dramatically when the impatient supporter of the death penalty declares that it doesn't really matter what happens as a result of inflicting the ultimate penalty on someone who takes another's life. Those who take a life, the argument goes, deserve to lose theirs. An eye for an eye—a tooth for a tooth: so states (a simplified version of) the *retributive* theory of punishment. Retributivists typically reject consequentialism, although if one allows that harm befalling the perpetrator of wrongdoing is something that is itself intrinsically good, a consequentialist can factor that in among the other consequences of punishment. The debate between consequentialists and retributivists is one that clearly involves deep underlying metaethical controversies.

Rectifying Injustice

Punishment is only one response to perceived injustice. Often, we are more concerned with repairing a harm resulting from the injustice. In applying tort law, for example, we might require a person who negligently caused damage to another's property to replace or repair that which was damaged. Things get considerably more complicated, however, when an injustice was committed long ago but has lasting negative consequences. Suppose, for example, that I found out that your great-great-grandfather swindled my great-great-grandfather out of land. Oil was subsequently found on that land and as a descendent you have inherited the fabulous wealth that accrued to your ancestor as a result of his unjust behavior. Do you owe me money? Should society force you to compensate me for an injustice that you had no part in, but from which you indirectly benefited? If so, how precisely should we "make things right"?

If we decide that in the above example reparations are owed to descendents of the person originally victimized by unjust behavior, we might try to model a defense of affirmative action (or even more dramatic reparations) as part of a social policy designed to mitigate past injustice done to the ancestors of slaves ripped from their homes in Africa, or Native Americans whose land was appropriated by European settlers. To be sure, contemporary Caucasians may have had no part in those historical injustices, but they are still, arguably, benefiting from them.

The devil is in the details of a theory of reparation. In one approach, the ideal might seem to be to imagine hypothetically how the world would have been had the unjust behavior not taken place. We then try to bring about as closely as possible that very state of affairs—we return the world to the state it would be in without the unjust behavior. One might, however, get some rather odd, and counterintuitive, results. Suppose, for example, that when your ancestor swindled mine out of the land, he went bankrupt attempting to find oil on the property. My ancestor would have done the same, but because of the unjust appropriation decided to invest in railroads, an investment that made him billions. If we correct the injustice by returning the world to the state it would have been in had the injustice not occurred, the billions I inherited should probably go to you! You would then profit from your ancestor's injustice. A similar sort of odd outcome might occur if we tried to correct the injustice of slavery in the manner envisioned above. Had the ancestors of African Americans not been kidnapped from their homeland, contemporary African Americans might be living in war-torn, impoverished countries in Africa. Would anyone think that we would be acting correctly in requiring them to return to that situation?

The utilitarian, of course, is always lurking in the background ready to offer a consequentialist justification for programs that others justify in terms of reparations. As long as people are suffering in ways that can be ameliorated, the programs that reduce that suffering will presumably have a presumptive utilitarian justification, though attempts to prevent harm can often have unintended effects that result in even more harm than the harm that we are trying to prevent.

Revolution and Secession

Most of the above discussion is implicitly confined to a state attempting to respond to injustice that occurs within its borders. But individuals who live within a state may also conclude that the government is acting unjustly. Although a state may have institutionalized ways in which citizens might respond to perceived injustice, one needn't search long to find societies in which the only practical recourse for citizens victimized by unjust institutions is force—violent revolution designed either to overthrow existing authority or secede from existing authority by forming another state. Under Saddam Hussein, the Kurds were obviously interested in using force to escape the oppression of the central government of Iraq. In the history of the United States, the South concluded that the central government was attempting to impose illegitimate restrictions on individual states and attempted to use force to escape control of that government. Under what circumstances are individuals who live within a state entitled to use force to overthrow or escape the control of that state? And assuming that the attempt to escape is legitimate, what methods can the rebels legitimately use in effecting their goals? Is terrorism ever justified? How, in fact, should we distinguish acts of terrorism from legitimate violence against those who support the injustice that made legitimate the attempts at rebellion?

War

Many of the considerations that arise in attempting to determine what legitimizes rebellion and secession might also seem to arise concerning the circumstances under which one nation may legitimately use force against another. To be sure, we live in a world in which such bodies as the United Nations seem to place enormous importance on territorial integrity. It is only supposed to be under extreme conditions that one nation may legitimately attempt to overthow the government of another.

The most obvious circumstance in which use of such force is justified is self-defense. Almost everyone concedes that when one is attacked by another nation one may use force in self-defense, and that such self-defense might extend to removing from power through force the governing bodies that initiated the threat. In the modern world, the concept of self-defense gets more complicated. After the U.S. invasion of Iraq, for example, we are all familiar with the notion of pre-emptive strikes that are still nevertheless justified by the goal of self-defense. If an openly hostile nation is developing nuclear weapons and a system to deliver them, may those verbally threatened take pre-emptive action to eliminate the threat? May such pre-emptive action extend to the removal of the very *system* of government which "bred" the threatening situation?

While self-defense is perhaps the most universally recognized legitimate use of force, one can also raise questions about more altruistic efforts to interfere with force in the internal affairs of other countries. When we see the government of another nation acting in grotesquely unjust ways toward its citizens, may another country use violence to stop the injustice? Does it depend on whether the citizens of that country explicitly seek help? How would we discover such a desire for aid given that tyranny is often quite successful in silencing dissent? And furthermore can we sometimes legitimately conclude on paternalistic grounds that as a result of years of propaganda supported by violence, the victims are no longer able to recognize how unjust their situation is? (Perhaps, for example, mistreatment of women in a given culture can occur for so long that the victims of such mistreatment no longer are capable of seeing it for what it is.)

However reluctant one is to interfere in the affairs of another country, it is difficult to avoid the conclusion that in the most extreme cases such intervention may not only be permissible, but required. The most obvious example is, perhaps, the behavior of the Third Reich. Suppose that Germany began to engage in the systematic racism that endangered the lives and property of millions of people, but did so without attempting to spread its control beyond its borders. Should the rest of the world have felt some obligation to do *something*?

When we see potential genocide taking place in the Balkans or in parts of Africa, should we at least consider using force to end it? Once one concedes that force can be used to correct injustice occurring in states other than one's own, is there any principled way to limit the circumstances in which such intervention should occur, or must it be taken (as the utilitarian would no doubt argue) on a case-by-case basis, taking into account, among other things, the likelihood and cost of success?

As always, once one decides that one is entitled to use force, questions arise concerning what principled limits, if any, should be placed on the kind of force used. We often make a distinction between combatants and noncombatants, for example. In fighting a just war we are urged to make every effort to avoid harming noncombatants. But the distinction is hardly clear. Who should we include among the combatants? Soldiers, of course. But should we also include those who work in munitions factories, or those who work in factories that make the uniforms that clothe the soldiers? But come to that, the farmers who feed the soldiers are just as obviously playing a critical supporting role. Indeed, one might argue that anyone who supported through some sort of political process the perpetrators of injustice are indirectly contributing to that very injustice we are trying to correct. If we conclude that by "demoralizing" civilian support through massive attacks on cities, we can more quickly end a war, would that justify such action, or is this just a clearly illegitimate form of terrorism under a different name? In fact, is the label "terrorism" just used to describe various forms of violence used in causes of which we disapprove? These and related questions lie at the heart of many contemporary controversies, controversies that are unlikely to disappear in the foreseeable future.

The State's Regulation of Itself: Theories of Punishment and Restitution

76

Thomas Hobbes, selection from *Leviathan* (1651)

In this selection, Hobbes considers the nature, justification, and limits of public punishment and reward. On Hobbes, see reading 2 above.

SOURCE

Hobbes, Thomas. *Leviathan* (Second Edition). George Routledge and Sons, 1886.

Of Punishment and Rewards

A punishment is an evil inflicted by public authority on him that hath done or omitted that which is judged by the same authority to be a transgression of the law, to the end that the will of men may thereby the better be disposed to obedience.

Before I infer anything from this definition, there is a question to be answered of much importance; which is, by what door the right or authority of punishing, in any case, came in. For by that which has been said before, no man is supposed bound by covenant not to resist violence; and consequently it cannot be intended that he gave any right to another to lay violent hands upon his person. In the making of a Commonwealth every man giveth away the right of defending another, but not of defending himself. Also he obligeth himself to assist him that hath the sovereignty in the punishing of another, but of himself not. But to covenant to assist the sovereign in doing hurt to another, unless he that so covenanteth have a right to do it himself, is not to give him a right to punish. It is manifest therefore that the right which the Commonwealth (that is, he or they that represent it) hath to punish is not grounded on any concession or gift of the subjects. But I have also shown formerly that before the institution of Commonwealth, every man had a right to everything, and to do whatsoever he thought necessary to his own preservation; subduing, hurting, or killing any man in order thereunto. And this is the foundation of that right of punishing which is exercised in every Commonwealth. For the subjects did not give the sovereign that right; but only, in laying down theirs, strengthened him to use his own as he should think fit for the preservation of them all: so that it was not given, but left to him, and to him only; and, excepting the limits set him by natural law, as entire as in the condition of mere nature, and of war of every one against his neighbour.

From the definition of punishment, I infer, first, that neither private revenges nor injuries of private men can properly be styled punishment, because they proceed not from public authority.

Secondly, that to be neglected and unpreferred by the public favour is not a punishment, because no new evil is thereby on any man inflicted; he is only left in the estate he was in before.

Thirdly, that the evil inflicted by public authority, without precedent public condemnation, is not to be styled by the name of punishment, but of a hostile act, because the fact for which a man is punished ought first to be judged by public authority to be a transgression of the law.

Fourthly, that the evil inflicted by usurped power, and judges without authority from the sovereign, is not punishment, but an act of hostility, because the acts of power usurped have not for author the person condemned, and therefore are not acts of public authority.

Fifthly, that all evil which is inflicted without intention or possibility of disposing the delinquent or, by his example, other men to obey the laws is not punishment, but an act of hostility, because without such an end no hurt done is contained under that name.

Sixthly, whereas to certain actions there be annexed by nature diverse hurtful consequences; as when a man in assaulting another is himself slain or wounded; or when he falleth into sickness by the doing of some unlawful act; such hurt, though in respect of God, who is the author of nature, it may be said to be inflicted, and therefore a punishment divine; yet it is not contained in the name

of punishment in respect of men, because it is not inflicted by the authority of man.

Seventhly, if the harm inflicted be less than the benefit of contentment that naturally followeth the crime committed, that harm is not within the definition and is rather the price or redemption than the punishment of a crime: because it is of the nature of punishment to have for end the disposing of men to obey the law; which end (if it be less than the benefit of the transgression) it attaineth not, but worketh a contrary effect.

Eighthly, if a punishment be determined and prescribed in the law itself, and after the crime committed there be a greater punishment inflicted, the excess is not punishment, but an act of hostility. For seeing the aim of punishment is not a revenge, but terror; and the terror of a great punishment unknown is taken away by the declaration of a less, the unexpected addition is no part of the punishment. But where there is no punishment at all determined by the law, there whatsoever is inflicted hath the nature of punishment. For he that goes about the violation of a law, wherein no penalty is determined, expecteth an indeterminate, that is to say, an arbitrary punishment.

Ninthly, harm inflicted for a fact done before there was a law that forbade it is not punishment, but an act of hostility: for before the law, there is no transgression of the law: but punishment supposeth a fact judged to have been a transgression of the law; therefore harm inflicted before the law made is not punishment, but an act of hostility.

Tenthly, hurt inflicted on the representative of the Commonwealth is not punishment, but an act of hostility: because it is of the nature of punishment to be inflicted by public authority, which is the authority only of the representative itself.

Lastly, harm inflicted upon one that is a declared enemy falls not under the name of punishment: because seeing they were either never subject to the law, and therefore cannot transgress it; or having been subject to it, and professing to be no longer so, by consequence deny they can transgress it, all the harms that can be done them must be taken as acts of hostility. But in declared hostility all infliction of evil is lawful. From whence it followeth that if a subject shall by fact or word wittingly and deliberately deny the authority of the representative of the Commonwealth (whatsoever penalty hath been formerly ordained for treason), he may lawfully be made to suffer whatsoever the representative will: for in denying subjection, he denies such punishment as by the law hath been ordained, and therefore suffers as an enemy of the Commonwealth; that is, according to the will of the representative. For the punishments set down in the law are to subjects, not to enemies; such as are they that, having been by their own act subjects, deliberately revolting, deny the sovereign power.

The first and most general distribution of punishments is into *divine* and *human*. Of the former I shall have occasion to speak in a more convenient place hereafter.

Human are those punishments that be inflicted by the commandment of man; and are either *corporal*, or *pecuniary*, or *ignominy*, or *imprisonment*, or *exile*, or mixed of these.

Corporal punishment is that which is inflicted on the body directly, and according to the intention of him that inflicteth it: such as are stripes, or wounds, or deprivation of such pleasures of the body as were before lawfully enjoyed.

And of these, some be *capital*, some *less* than *capital*. Capital is the infliction of death; and that either simply or with torment. Less than capital are stripes, wounds, chains, and any other corporal pain not in its own nature mortal. For if upon the infliction of a punishment death follow, not in the intention of the inflicter, the punishment is not to be esteemed capital, though the harm prove mortal by an accident not to be foreseen; in which case death is not inflicted, but hastened.

Pecuniary punishment is that which consisteth not only in the deprivation of a sum of money, but also of lands, or any other goods which are usually bought and sold for money. And in case the law that ordaineth such a punishment be made with design to gather money from such as shall transgress the same, it is not properly a punishment, but the price of privilege and exemption from the law, which doth not absolutely forbid the fact but only to those that are not able to pay the money: except where the law is natural, or part of religion; for in that case it is not an exemption from the law, but a transgression of it. As where a law exacteth a pecuniary mulct of them that take the name of God in vain, the payment of the mulct is not the price of a dispensation to swear, but the punishment of the transgression of a law indispensable. In like manner if the law impose a sum of money to be paid to him that has been injured, this is but a satisfaction for the hurt done him, and extinguisheth the accusation of the party injured, not the crime of the offender.

Ignominy is the infliction of such evil as is made dishonourable; or the deprivation of such good as is made honourable by the Commonwealth. For there be some things honourable by nature; as the effects of courage, magnanimity, strength, wisdom, and other abilities of body and mind: others made honourable by the Commonwealth; as badges, titles, offices, or any other singular mark of the sovereign's favour. The former, though they may fail by nature or accident, cannot be taken away by a law; and therefore the loss of them is not punishment. But the latter may be taken away by the public authority that made them honourable, and are properly punishments: such are, degrading men condemned, of their badges, titles, and offices; or declaring them incapable of the like in time to come.

Imprisonment is when a man is by public authority deprived of liberty, and may happen from two diverse ends; whereof one is the safe custody of a man accused; the other is the inflicting of pain on a man condemned. The former is not punishment, because no man is supposed to be punished before he be judicially heard and declared guilty. And therefore whatsoever hurt a man is made to suffer by bonds or restraint before his cause be heard, over and above that which is necessary to assure his custody, is against the law of nature. But the latter is punishment because evil, and inflicted by public authority for somewhat that has by the same authority been judged a transgression of the law. Under this word *imprisonment*, I comprehend all restraint of motion caused by an external obstacle, be it a house, which is called by the general name of a prison; or an island, as when men are said to be confined to it; or a place where men are set to work, as in old time men have been condemned to quarries, and in these times to galleys; or be it a chain or any other such impediment.

Exile (banishment) is when a man is for a crime condemned to depart out of the dominion of the Commonwealth, or out of a certain part thereof, and during a prefixed time, or for ever, not to return into it; and seemeth not in its own nature, without other circumstances, to be a punishment, but rather an escape, or a public commandment to avoid punishment by flight. And Cicero says there was never any such punishment ordained in the city of Rome; but calls it a refuge of men in danger.[1] For if a man banished be nevertheless permitted to enjoy his goods, and the revenue of his lands, the mere change of air is no punishment; nor does it tend to that benefit of the Commonwealth for which all punishments are ordained, that is to say, to the forming of men's wills to the observation of the law; but many times to the damage of the Commonwealth. For a banished man is a lawful enemy of the Commonwealth that banished him, as being no more a member of the same. But if he be withal deprived of his lands, or goods, then the punishment lieth not in the exile, but is to be reckoned amongst punishments pecuniary.

All punishments of innocent subjects, be they great or little, are against the law of nature: for punishment is only for transgression of the law, and therefore there can be no punishment of the innocent. It is therefore a violation, first, of that law of nature which forbiddeth all men, in their revenges, to look at anything but some future good: for there can arrive no good to the Commonwealth by punishing the innocent. Secondly, of that which forbiddeth ingratitude: for seeing all sovereign power is originally given by the consent of every one of the subjects, to the end they should as long as they are

obedient be protected thereby, the punishment of the innocent is a rendering of evil for good. And thirdly, of the law that commandeth equity; that is to say, an equal distribution of justice, which in punishing the innocent is not observed.

But the infliction of what evil soever on an innocent man that is not a subject, if it be for the benefit of the Commonwealth, and without violation of any former covenant, is no breach of the law of nature. For all men that are not subjects are either enemies, or else they have ceased from being so by some precedent covenants. But against enemies, whom the Commonwealth judgeth capable to do them hurt, it is lawful by the original right of nature to make war; wherein the sword judgeth not, nor doth the victor make distinction of nocent and innocent as to the time past, nor has other respect of mercy than as it conduceth to the good of his own people. And upon this ground it is that also in subjects who deliberately deny the authority of the Commonwealth established, the vengeance is lawfully extended, not only to the fathers, but also to the third and fourth generation not yet in being, and consequently innocent of the fact for which they are afflicted: because the nature of this offence consisteth in the renouncing of subjection, which is a relapse into the condition of war commonly called rebellion; and they that so offend, suffer not as subjects, but as enemies. For rebellion is but war renewed.

Reward is either of *gift* or by *contract*. When by contract, it is called *salary* and *wages*; which is benefit due for service performed or promised. When of gift, it is benefit proceeding from the *grace* of them that bestow it, to encourage or enable men to do them service. And therefore when the sovereign of a Commonwealth appointeth a salary to any public office, he that receiveth it is bound in justice to perform his office; otherwise, he is bound only in honour to acknowledgement and an endeavour of requital. For though men have no lawful remedy when they be commanded to quit their private business to serve the public, without reward or salary, yet they are not bound thereto by the law of nature, nor by the institution of the Commonwealth, unless the service cannot otherwise be done; because it is

---

[1] [From a speech by Cicero made in 69 BCE in defense of Aulus Caecina, who had been banished for publishing a work denouncing Caesar.]

supposed the sovereign may make use of all their means, insomuch as the most common soldier may demand the wages of his warfare as a debt.

The benefits which a sovereign bestoweth on a subject, for fear of some power and ability he hath to do hurt to the Commonwealth, are not properly rewards: for they are not salaries, because there is in this case no contract supposed, every man being obliged already not to do the Commonwealth disservice: nor are they graces, because they be extorted by fear, which ought not to be incident to the sovereign power: but are rather sacrifices, which the sovereign, considered in his natural person, and not in the person of the Commonwealth, makes for the appeasing the discontent of him he thinks more potent than himself; and encourage not to obedience, but, on the contrary, to the continuance and increasing of further extortion.

And whereas some salaries are certain, and proceed from the public treasury; and others uncertain and casual, proceeding from the execution of the office for which the salary is ordained; the latter is in some cases hurtful to the Commonwealth, as in the case of judicature. For where the benefit of the judges, and ministers of a court of justice, ariseth for the multitude of causes that are brought to their cognizance, there must needs follow two inconveniences: one is the nourishing of suits; for the more suits, the greater benefit: and another that depends on that, which is contention which is about jurisdiction; each court drawing to itself as many causes as it can. But in offices of execution there are not those inconveniences, because their employment cannot be increased by any endeavour of their own. And thus much shall suffice for the nature of punishment and reward; which are, as it were, the nerves and tendons that move the limbs and joints of a Commonwealth.

Hitherto I have set forth the nature of man, whose pride and other passions have compelled him to submit himself to government; together with the great power of his governor, whom I compared to *Leviathan*, taking that comparison out of the two last verses of the one-and-fortieth of Job; where God, having set forth the great power of Leviathan, calleth him king of the proud. "There is nothing," saith he, "on earth to be compared with him. He is made so as not to be afraid. He seeth every high thing below him; and is king of all the children of pride." But because he is mortal, and subject to decay, as all other earthly creatures are; and because there is that in heaven, though not on earth, that he should stand in fear of, and whose laws he ought to obey; I shall in the next following chapters speak of his diseases and the causes of his mortality, and of what laws of nature he is bound to obey.

DISCUSSION QUESTIONS

1. What is the ultimate justification for the "rights of sovereigns"? Give examples of some of the rights that Hobbes grants to the sovereign and the justification that he offers for each right.

2. Explain Hobbes's theory of legitimate punishment, and explain how it fits into his general theory of the rights of sovereigns.

3. Hobbes imagines a critic objecting "that the condition of subjects is very miserable" (see reading 32). Explain why someone might make such an objection after reading this chapter on rights of sovereigns, with particular reference to Hobbes's theory of punishment. How does Hobbes respond to the objection? Is his response adequate? Why or why not?

77

Jeremy Bentham, selection from *The Principles of Morals and Legislation* (1780)

In this selection, Bentham provides a utilitarian account of the functions of punishment and blame. On Bentham, see reading 22 above.

SOURCE

Bentham, Jeremy. *An Introduction to the Principles of Morals and Legislation* (Second Edition). The Clarendon Press. Reprinted 1879.

Of the Consequences of a Mischievous Act

§1. Shapes in which the mischief of an act may show itself.

I. Hitherto we have been speaking of the various articles or objects on which the consequences or tendency of an act may depend: of the bare act itself: of the circumstances it may have been, or may have been supposed to be, accompanied with: of the consciousness a man may have had with respect to any such circumstances: of the intentions that may have preceded the act: of the motives that may have given birth to those intentions: and of the disposition that may have been indicated by the connexion between such intentions and such motives. We now come to speak of consequences or tendency: an article which forms the concluding link in all this chain of causes and effects, involving in it the materiality of the whole. Now, such part of this tendency as is of a mischievous nature, is all that we have any direct concern with; to that, therefore, we shall here confine ourselves.

II. The tendency of an act is mischievous when the consequences of it are mischievous; that is to say, either the certain consequences or the probable. The consequences, how many and whatsoever they may be, of an act, of which the tendency is mischievous, may, such of them as are mischievous, be conceived to constitute one aggregate body, which may be termed the mischief of the act.

III. This mischief may frequently be distinguished, as it were, into two shares or parcels: the one containing what may be called the primary mischief; the other, what may be called the secondary. That share may be termed the primary, which is sustained by an assignable individual, or a multitude of assignable individuals. That share may be termed the secondary, which, taking its origin from the former, extends itself either over the whole community, or over some other multitude of unassignable individuals.

IV. The primary mischief of an act may again be distinguished into two branches: 1. The original: and, 2. The derivative. By the original branch, I mean that which alights upon and is confined to any person who is a sufferer in the first instance, and on his own account: the person, for instance, who is beaten, robbed, or murdered. By the derivative branch, I mean any share of mischief which may befall any other assignable persons in consequence of his being a sufferer, and no otherwise. These persons must, of course, be persons who in some way or other are connected with him. Now the ways in which one person may be connected with another, have been already seen: they may be connected in the way of interest (meaning self-regarding interest) or merely in the way of sympathy. And again, persons connected with a given person, in the way of interest, may be connected with him either by affording support to him, or by deriving it from him.

V. The secondary mischief, again, may frequently be seen to consist of two other shares or parcels: the first consisting of pain; the other of danger. The pain which it produces is a pain of apprehension: a pain grounded on the apprehension of suffering such mischiefs or inconveniences, whatever they may be, as it is the nature of the primary mischief to produce. It may be styled, in one word, the alarm. The danger is the chance, whatever it may be, which the multitude it concerns may in consequence of the primary mischief stand exposed to, of suffering such mischiefs or inconveniences. For danger is nothing but the chance of pain, or, what comes to the same thing, of loss of pleasure.

VI. An example may serve to make this clear. A man attacks you on the road, and robs you. You suffer a pain on the occasion of losing so much money: you also suffered a pain at the thoughts of the personal ill-treatment you apprehended he might give you, in case of your not happening to satisfy his demands. These together constitute the original branch of the primary mischief, resulting from the act of robbery. A creditor of yours, who expected you to pay him with part of that money, and a son of yours, who expected you to have given him another part, are in consequence disappointed. You are obliged to have recourse to the bounty of your father, to make good part of the deficiency. These mischiefs together make up the derivative branch. The report of this robbery circulates from hand to hand, and spreads itself in the neighbourhood. It finds its way into the newspapers, and is propagated over the whole country. Various people, on this occasion, call to mind the danger which they and their friends, as it appears from this example, stand exposed to in travelling; especially such as may have occasion to travel the same road. On this occasion they naturally feel a certain degree of pain: slighter or heavier, according to the degree of ill-treatment they may understand you to have received; the frequency of the occasion each person may have to travel in that same road, or its neighbourhood; the vicinity of each person to the spot; his personal courage; the quantity of money he may have occasion to carry about with him; and a variety of other circumstances. This constitutes the first part of the secondary mischief, resulting from the act of robbery; viz. the alarm. But people of one description or other, not only are disposed to conceive themselves to incur a chance of being robbed, in consequence of the robbery committed upon you, but (as will be shown presently) they do really incur such a chance. And it is this chance which constitutes the remaining part of the secondary mischief of the act of robbery; viz. the danger.

VII. Let us see what this chance amounts to; and whence it comes. How is it, for instance, that one robbery can contribute to produce another? In the first place, it is certain that: it cannot create any direct motive. A motive must be the prospect of some pleasure, or other advantage, to be enjoyed in future: but the robbery in question is past: nor would it furnish any such prospect were it to come: for it is not one robbery that will furnish pleasure to him who may be about to commit another robbery. The consideration that is to operate upon a man, as a motive or inducement to commit a robbery, must be the idea of the pleasure he expects to derive from the fruits of that very robbery: but this pleasure exists independently of any other robbery.

VIII. The means, then, by which one robbery tends, as it should seem, to produce another robbery, are two. 1. By suggesting to a person exposed to the temptation, the idea of committing such another robbery (accompanied, perhaps, with the belief of its facility). In this case the influence it exerts applies itself, in the first place, to the understanding. 2. By weakening the force of the tutelary motives which tend to restrain him from such an action, and thereby adding to the strength of the temptation. In this case the influence applies itself to the will. These forces are, 1. The motive of benevolence, which acts as a branch of the physical sanction 2. The motive of self-preservation, as against the punishment that may stand provided by the political sanction. 3. The fear of shame; a motive belonging to the moral sanction. 4. The fear of the divine displeasure; a motive belonging to the religious sanction. On the first and last of these forces it has, perhaps, no influence worth insisting on: but it has on the other two.

IX. The way in which a past robbery may weaken the force with which the political sanction tends to prevent a future robbery, may be thus conceived. The way in which this sanction tends to prevent a robbery, is by denouncing some particular kind of punishment against any who shall be guilty of it: the real value of which punishment will of course be diminished by the real uncertainty: as also, if there be any difference, the apparent value by the apparent uncertainty. Now this uncertainty is proportionably increased by every instance in which a man is known to commit the offence, without undergoing the punishment. This, of course, will

be the case with every offence for a certain time; in short, until the punishment allotted to it takes place. If punishment takes place at last, this branch of the mischief of the offence is then at last, but not till then, put a stop to.

X. The way in which a past robbery may weaken the force with which the moral sanction tends to prevent a future robbery, may be thus conceived. The way in which the moral sanction tends to prevent a robbery, is by holding forth the indignation of mankind as ready to fall upon him who shall be guilty of it. Now this indignation will be the more formidable, according to the number of those who join in it: it will be the less so, the fewer they are who join in it. But there cannot be a stronger way of showing that a man does not join in whatever indignation may be entertained against a practice, than the engaging in it himself. It shows not only that he himself feels no indignation against it, but that it seems to him there is no sufficient reason for apprehending what indignation may be felt against it by others. Accordingly, where robberies are frequent, and unpunished, robberies are committed without shame. It was thus amongst the Grecians formerly. It is thus among the Arabs still.

XI. In whichever way then a past offence tends to pave the way for the commission of a future. Hence, whether by suggesting the idea of committing it, or by adding to the strength of the temptation, in both cases it may be said to operate by the force or influence of example.

XII. The two branches of the secondary mischief of an act, the alarm and the danger, must not be confounded: though intimately connected, they are perfectly distinct: either may subsist without the other. The neighbourhood may be alarmed with the report of a robbery, when, in fact, no robbery either has been committed or is in a way to be committed: a neighbourhood may be on the point of being disturbed by robberies, without knowing any thing of the matter. Accordingly, we shall soon perceive, that some acts produce alarm without danger: others, danger without alarm.

XIII. As well the danger as the alarm may again be divided, each of them, into two branches: the first, consisting of so much of the alarm or danger as may be apt to result from the future behaviour of the same agent: the second, consisting of so much as may be apt to result from the behaviour of other persons: such others, to wit, as may come to engage in acts of the same sort and tendency.

XIV. The distinction between the primary and the secondary consequences of an act must be carefully attended to. It is so just, that the latter may often be of a directly opposite nature to be the former. In some cases, where the primary consequences of the act are attended with a mischief, the secondary consequences may be beneficial, and that to such a degree, as even greatly to outweigh the mischief of the primary. This is the case, for instance, with all acts of punishment, when properly applied. Of these, the primary mischief being never intended to fall but upon such persons as may happen to have committed some act which it is expedient to prevent, the secondary mischief, that is, the alarm and the danger, extends no farther than to such persons as are under temptation to commit it: in which case, in as far as it tends to restrain them from committing such acts, it is of a beneficial nature.

XV. Thus much with regard to acts that produce positive pain, and that immediately. This case, by reason of its simplicity, seemed the fittest to take the lead. But acts may produce mischief in various other ways; which, together with those already specified, may all be comprised by the following abridged analysis.

Mischief may admit of a division in any one of three points of view. 1. According to its own nature. 2. According to its cause. 3. According to the person, or other party, who is the object of it. With regard to its nature, it may be either simple or complex: when simple, it may either be positive or negative: positive, consisting of actual pain: negative, consisting of the loss of pleasure. Whether simple or complex, and whether positive or negative, it may be either certain or contingent. When it is negative, it consists of the loss of some benefit or advantage: this benefit may be material in both or either of two ways: 1. By affording actual

pleasure: or, 2. By averting pain or danger, which is the chance of pain: that is, by affording security. In as far, then, as the benefit which a mischief tends to avert, is productive of security, the tendency of such mischief is to produce insecurity. 2. With regard to its cause, mischief may be produced either by one single action, or not without the concurrence of other actions: if not without the concurrence of other actions, these others may be the actions either of the same person, or of other persons: in either case, they may be either acts of the same kind as that in question, or of other kinds. 3. Lastly, with regard to the party who is the object of the mischief, or, in other words, who is in a way to be affected by it, such party may be either an assignable individual, or assemblage of individuals, or else a multitude of unassignable individuals. When the object is an assignable individual, this individual may either be the person himself who is the author of the mischief, or some other person. When the individuals who are the objects of it, are an unassignable multitude, this multitude may be either the whole political community or state, or some subordinate division of it. Now when the object of the mischief is the author himself, it may be styled self-regarding: when any other party is the object, extra-regarding: when such other party is an individual, it may be styled private: when a subordinate branch of the community, semi-public: when the whole community, public. Here, for the present, we must stop. To pursue the subject through its inferior distinctions, will be the business of the chapter which exhibits the division of offences.

The cases which have been already illustrated, are those in which the primary mischief is not necessarily otherwise than a simple one, and that positive: present, and therefore certain: producible by a single action, without any necessity of the concurrence of any other action, either on the part of the same agent, or of others; and having for its object an assignable individual, or, by accident an assemblage of assignable individuals: extra-regarding therefore, and private. This primary mischief is accompanied by a secondary: the first branch of which is sometimes contingent and sometimes certain, the other never otherwise than contingent: both extra-regarding and semi-public: in other respects, pretty much upon a par with the primary mischief: except that the first branch, viz. the alarm, though inferior in magnitude to the primary, is, in point of extent, and therefore, upon the whole, in point of magnitude, much superior.

XVI. Two instances more will be sufficient to illustrate the most material of the modifications above exhibited.

A man drinks a certain quantity of liquor, and intoxicates himself. The intoxication in this particular instance does him no sort of harm: or, what comes to the same thing, none that is perceptible. But it is probable, and indeed next to certain, that a given number of acts of the same kind would do him a very considerable degree of harm: more or less according to his constitution and other circumstances: for this is no more than what experience manifests every day. It is also certain, that one act of this sort, by one means or other, tends considerably to increase the disposition a man may be in to practise other acts of the same sort: for this also is verified by experience. This, therefore, is one instance where the mischief producible by the act is contingent in other words, in which the tendency of the act is no otherwise mischievous than in virtue of its producing a chance of mischief. This chance depends upon the concurrence of other acts of the same kind; and those such as must be practiced by the same person. The object of the mischief is that very person himself who is the author of it, and he only, unless by accident. The mischief is therefore private and self-regarding.

As to its secondary mischief, alarm, it produces none: it produces indeed a certain quantity of danger by the influence of example: but it is not often that this danger will amount to a quantity worth regarding.

XVII. Again. A man omits paying his share to a public tax. This we see is an act of the negative kind. Is this then to be placed upon the list of mischievous acts? Yes, certainly. Upon what grounds? Upon the following. To defend the community against its external as well as its internal adversaries are

tasks, not to mention others of a less indispensable nature which cannot be fulfilled but at a considerable expense. But whence is the money for defraying this expense to come? It can be obtained in no other manner than by contributions to be collected from individuals; in a word, by taxes. The produce then of these taxes is to be looked upon as a kind of benefit which it is necessary the governing part of the community should receive for the use of the whole. This produce, before it can be applied to its destination, requires that there should be certain persons commissioned to receive and to apply it. Now if these persons, had they received it, would have applied it to its proper destination, it would have been a benefit: the not putting them in a way to receive it, is then a mischief. But it is possible, that if received, it might not have been applied to its proper destination; or that the services, in consideration of which it was bestowed, might not have been performed. It is possible, that the under-officer, who collected the produce of the tax, might not have paid it over to his principal: it is possible that the principal might not have forwarded it on according to its farther destination; to the judge, for instance, who is to protect the community against its clandestine enemies from within, or the soldier, who is to protect it against its open enemies from without: it is possible that the judge, or the soldier, had they received it, would not however have been induced by it to fulfil their respective duties: it is possible, that the judge would not have sat for the punishment of criminals, and the decision of controversies: it is possible that the soldier would not have drawn his sword in the defense of the community. These, together with an infinity of other intermediate acts, which for the sake of brevity I pass over, form a connected chain of duties, the discharge of which is necessary to the preservation of the community. They must every one of them be discharged, ere the benefit to which they are contributory can be produced. If they are all discharged, in that case the benefit subsists, and any act, by tending to intercept that benefit, may produce a mischief. But if any of them are not, the benefit fails: it fails of itself: it would not have subsisted, although the act in question (the act of non-payment) had not been committed. The benefit is therefore contingent; and, accordingly, upon a certain supposition, the act which consists in the averting of it is not a mischievous one. But this supposition, in any tolerably-ordered government, will rarely indeed be verified. In the very worst ordered government that exists, the greatest part of the duties that are levied are paid over according to their destination: and, with regard to any particular sum, that is attempted to be levied upon any particular person upon any particular occasion, it is therefore manifest, that, unless it be certain that it will not be so disposed of, the act of withholding it is a mischievous one.

The act of payment, when referable to any particular sum, especially if it be a small one, might also have failed of proving beneficial on another ground: and, consequently, the act of nonpayment, of proving mischievous. It is possible that the same services, precisely, might have been rendered without the money as with it. If, then, speaking of any small limited sum, such as the greatest which any one person is called upon to pay at a time, a man were to say, that the non-payment of it would be attended with mischievous consequences; this would be far from certain: but what comes to the same thing as if it were, it is perfectly certain when applied to the whole. It is certain, that if all of a sudden the payment of all taxes was to cease, there would no longer be anything effectual done, either for the maintenance of justice, or for the defence of the community against its foreign adversaries: that therefore the weak would presently be oppressed and injured in all manner of ways, by the strong at home, and both together overwhelmed by oppressors abroad. Upon the whole, therefore, it is manifest, that in this case, though the mischief is remote and contingent, though in its first appearance it consists of nothing more than the interception of a benefit, and though the individuals, in whose favour that benefit would have been reduced into the explicit form of pleasure or security, are altogether unassignable, yet the mischievous tendency of the act is not on all these accounts the less indisputable. The mischief, in point of intensity and

duration, is indeed unknown: it is uncertain: it is remote. But in point of extent it is immense; and in point of fecundity, pregnant to a degree that baffles calculation.

XVIII. It may now be time to observe, that it is only in the case where the mischief is extra-regarding, and has an assignable person or persons for its object, that so much of the secondary branch of it as consists in alarm can have place. When the individuals it affects are uncertain, and altogether out of sight, no alarm can be produced: as there is nobody whose sufferings you can see, there is nobody whose sufferings you can be alarmed at. No alarm, for instance, is produced by nonpayment to a tax. If at any distant and uncertain period of time such offence should chance to be productive of any kind of alarm, it would appear to proceed, as indeed immediately it would proceed, from a very different cause. It might be immediately referable, for example, to the act of a legislator, who should deem it necessary to lay on a new tax, in order to make up for the deficiency occasioned in the produce of the old one. Or it might be referable to the act of an enemy, who, under favour of a deficiency thus created in the fund allotted for defense, might invade the country, and exact from it much heavier contributions than those which had been thus withholden from the sovereign.

As to any alarm which such an offence might raise among the few who might chance to regard the matter with the eyes of statesmen, it is of too slight and uncertain a nature to be worth taking into the account.

§ 2. How intentionality, &c. may influence the mischief of an act.

XIX. We have seen the nature of the secondary mischief, which is apt to be reflected, as it were, from the primary, in the cases where the individuals who are the objects of the mischief are assignable. It is now time to examine into the circumstances upon which the production of such secondary mischief depends. These circumstances are no others than the four articles which have formed the subjects of the four last preceding chapters: viz. 1. The intentionality.

2. The consciousness. 3. The motive. 4. The disposition. It is to be observed all along, that it is only the danger that is immediately governed by the real state of the mind in respect to those articles: it is by the apparent state of it that the alarm is governed. It is governed by the real only in as far as the apparent happens, as in most cases it may be expected to do, to quadrate with the real. The different influences of the articles of intentionality and consciousness may be represented in the several cases following.

XX. Case 1. Where the act is so completely unintentional, as to be altogether involuntary. In this case it is attended with no secondary mischief at all.

A bricklayer is at work upon a house: a passenger is walking in the street below. A fellow-workman comes and gives the bricklayer a violent push, in consequence of which he falls upon the passenger, and hurts him. It is plain there is nothing in this event that can give other people, who may happen to be in the street, the least reason to apprehend any thing in future on the part of the man who fell, whatever there may be with regard to the man who pushed him.

XXI. Case 2. Where the act, though not unintentional, is unadvised, insomuch that the mischievous part of the consequences is unintentional, but the unadvisedness is attended with heedlessness. In this case the act is attended with some small degree of secondary mischief, in proportion to the degree of heedlessness.

A groom being on horseback, and riding through a frequented street, turns a corner at a full pace, and rides over a passenger, who happens to be going by. It is plain, by this behaviour of the groom, some degree of alarm may be produced, less or greater, according to the degree of heedlessness betrayed by him: according to the quickness of his pace, the fullness of the street, and so forth. He has done mischief, it may be said, by his carelessness, already: who knows but that on other occasions the like cause may produce the like effect.

XXII. Case 3. Where the act is misadvised with respect to a circumstance, which, had it existed, would fully have excluded or (what comes to the same thing) outweighed the primary mischief: and

there is no rashness in the case. In this case the act attended with no secondary mischief at all.

It is needless to multiply examples any farther.

XXIII. Case 4. Where the act is misadvised with respect to a circumstance which would have excluded or counterbalanced the primary mischief in part, but not entirely: and still there is no rashness. In this case the set is attended with some degree of secondary mischief, in proportion to that part of the primary which remains unexcluded or uncounterbalanced.

XXIV. Case 5. Where the act is misadvised with respect to a circumstance, which, had it existed, would have excluded or counterbalanced the primary mischief entirely, or in part: and there is a degree of rashness in the supposal. In this case, the act is also attended with a farther degree of secondary mischief, in proportion to the degree of rashness.

XXV. Case 6. Where the consequences are completely intentional, and there is no mis-supposal in the case. In this case the secondary mischief is at the highest.

XXVI. Thus much with regard to intentionality and consciousness. We now come to consider in what manner the secondary mischief is affected by the nature of the motive.

Where an act is pernicious in its primary consequences, the secondary mischief is not obliterated by the goodness of the motive; though the motive be of the best kind. For, notwithstanding the goodness of the motive, an act of which the primary consequences are pernicious, is produced by it in the instance in question, by the supposition. It may, therefore, in other instances: although this is not so likely to happen from a good motive as from a bad one.

XXVII. An act, which, though pernicious in its primary consequences, is rendered in other respects beneficial upon the whole, by virtue of its secondary consequences, is not changed back again, and rendered pernicious upon the whole by the badness of the motive: although the motive be of the worst kind.

XXVIII. But when not only the primary consequences of an act are pernicious, but, in other respects, the secondary likewise, the secondary mischief may be aggravated by the nature of the motive: so much of that mischief, to wit, as respects the future behaviour of the same person.

XXIX. It is not from the worst kind of motive, however, that the secondary mischief of an act receives its greatest aggravation.

XXX. The aggravation which the secondary mischief of an act, in as far as it respects the future behaviour of the same person, receives from the nature of a motive in an individual case, is as the tendency of the motive to produce, on the part of the same person, acts of the like bad tendency with that of the act in question.

XXXI. The tendency of a motive to produce acts of the like kind, on the part of any given person, is as the strength and constancy of its influence on that person, as applied to the production of such effects.

XXXII. The tendency of a species of motive to give birth to acts of any kind, among persons in general, is as the strength, constancy, and extensiveness of its influence, as applied to the production of such effects.

XXXIII. Now the motives, whereof the influence is at once most powerful, most constant, and most extensive, are the motives of physical desire, the love of wealth, the love of ease, the love of life, and the fear of pain: all of them self-regarding motives. The motive of displeasure, whatever it may be in point of strength and extensiveness, is not near so constant in its influence (the case of mere antipathy excepted) as any of the other three. A pernicious act, therefore, when committed through vengeance, or otherwise through displeasure, is not near so mischievous as the same pernicious act, when committed by force of any one of those other motives.

XXXIV. As to the motive of religion, whatever it may sometimes prove to be in point of strength and constancy, it is not in point of extent so universal, especially in its application to acts of a mischievous nature, as any of the three preceding motives. It may, however, be as universal in a particular state, or in a particular district of a particular state. It is liable indeed to be very irregular in its operations. It is apt, however, to be frequently as powerful as the motive of vengeance, or indeed any other motive whatsoever. It will sometimes even be more powerful than any other motive. It is, at any rate, much more constant. A pernicious act, therefore, when committed through the motive of religion, is more mischievous than when committed through the motive of ill-will.

XXXV. Lastly, The secondary mischief, to wit, so much of it as hath respect to the future behaviour of the same person, is aggravated or lessened by the apparent depravity or beneficence of his disposition: and that in the proportion of such apparent depravity or beneficence.

XXXVI. The consequences we have hitherto been speaking of, are the natural consequences, of which the act, and the other articles we have been considering, are the causes: consequences that result from the behaviour of the individual, who is the offending agent, without the interference of political authority. We now come to speak of punishment: which, in the sense in which it is here considered, is an artificial consequence, annexed by political authority to an offensive act, in one instance, in the view of putting a stop to the production of events similar to the obnoxious part of its natural consequences, in other instances.

Cases Unmeet for Punishment

§ 1. General view of cases unmeet for punishment.

I. The general object which all laws have, or ought to have, in common, is to augment the total happiness of the community; and therefore, in the first place, to exclude, as far as may be, every thing that tends to subtract from that happiness: in other words, to exclude mischief.

II. But all punishment is mischief: all punishment in itself is evil. Upon the principle of utility, if it ought at all to be admitted, it ought only to be admitted in as far as it promises to exclude some greater evil.

III. It is plain, therefore, that in the following cases punishment ought not to be inflicted.

1. Where it is groundless: where there is no mischief for it to prevent; the act not being mischievous upon the whole.

2. Where it must be inefficacious: where it cannot act so as to prevent the mischief.

3. Where it is unprofitable, or too expensive: where the mischief it would produce would be greater than what it prevented.

4. Where it is needless: where the mischief may be prevented, or cease of itself, without it: that is, at a cheaper rate.

§ 2. Cases in which punishment is groundless.

These are,

IV. 1. Where there has never been any mischief: where no mischief has been produced to any body by the act in question. Of this number are those in which the act was such as might, on some occasions, be mischievous or disagreeable, but the person whose interest it concerns gave his consent to the performance of it. This consent, provided it be free, and fairly obtained, is the best proof that can be produced, that, to the person who gives it, no mischief, at least no immediate mischief, upon the whole, is done. For no man can be so good a judge as the man himself, what it is gives him pleasure or displeasure.

V. 2. Where the mischief was outweighed: although a mischief was produced by that act, yet the same act was necessary to the production of a benefit which was of greater value than the mischief. This may be the case with any thing that is done in the way of precaution against instant calamity, as also with any thing that is done in the exercise of the several sorts of powers necessary to be established in every community, to wit, domestic, judicial, military, and supreme.

VI. 3. Where there is a certainty of an adequate compensation: and that in all cases where the offence can be committed. This supposes two things: 1. That the offence is such as admits of an adequate compensation: 2. That such a compensation is sure to be forthcoming. Of these suppositions, the latter will be found to be a merely ideal one: a supposition that cannot, in the universality here given to it, be verified by fact. It cannot,

therefore, in practice, be numbered amongst the grounds of absolute impunity. It may, however, be admitted as a ground for an abatement of that punishment, which other considerations, standing by themselves, would seem to dictate.

§ 3. Cases in which punishment must be inefficacious.

These are,

VII. 1. Where the penal provision is not established until after the act is done. Such are the cases, 1. Of an ex-post-facto law; where the legislator himself appoints not a punishment till after the act is done. 2. Of a sentence beyond the law; where the judge, of his own authority, appoints a punishment which the legislator had not appointed.

VIII. 2. Where the penal provision, though established, is not conveyed to the notice of the person on whom it seems intended that it should operate. Such is the case where the law has omitted to employ any of the expedients which are necessary, to make sure that every person whatsoever, who is within the reach of the law, be apprised of all the cases whatsoever, in which (being in the station of life he is in) he can be subjected to the penalties of the law.

IX. 3. Where the penal provision, though it were conveyed to a man's notice, could produce no effect on him, with respect to the preventing him from engaging in any act of the sort in question. Such is the case, 1. In extreme infancy; where a man has not yet attained that state or disposition of mind in which the prospect of evils so distant as those which are held forth by the law, has the effect of influencing his conduct. 2. In insanity; where the person, if he has attained to that disposition, has since been deprived of it through the influence of some permanent though unseen cause. 3. In intoxication; where he has been deprived of it by the transient influence of a visible cause: such as the use of wine, or opium, or other drugs, that act in this manner on the nervous system: which condition is indeed neither more nor less than a temporary insanity produced by an assignable cause.

X. 4. Where the penal provision (although, being conveyed to the party's notice, it might very well prevent his engaging in acts of the sort in question, provided he knew that it related to those acts) could not have this effect, with regard to the individual act he is about to engage in: to wit, because he knows not that it is of the number of those to which the penal provision relates. This may happen, 1. In the case of unintentionality; where he intends not to engage, and thereby knows not that he is about to engage, in the act in which eventually he is about to engage, 2. In the case of unconsciousness; where, although he may know that he is about to engage in the act itself, yet, from not knowing all the material circumstances attending it, he knows not of the tendency it has to produce that mischief, in contemplation of which it has been made penal in most instances, 3. In the case of missupposal; where, although he may know of the tendency the act has to produce that degree of mischief, he supposes it, though mistakenly, to be attended with some circumstance, or set of circumstances, which, if it had been attended with, it would either not have been productive of that mischief, or have been productive of such a greater degree of good, as has determined the legislator in such a case not to make it penal.

XI. 5. Where, though the penal clause might exercise a full and prevailing influence, were it to act alone, yet by the predominant influence of some opposite cause upon the will, it must necessarily be ineffectual; because the evil which he sets himself about to undergo, in the case of his not engaging in the act, is so great, that the evil denounced by the penal clause, in case of his engaging in it, cannot appear greater. This may happen, 1. In the case of physical danger; where the evil is such as appears likely to be brought about by the unassisted powers of nature. 2. In the case of a threatened mischief; where it is such as appears likely to be brought about through the intentional and conscious agency of man.

XII. 6. Where (though the penal clause may exert a full and prevailing influence over the will of the party) yet his physical faculties (owing to the predominant influence of some physical cause) are not in a condition to follow the determination of the will: insomuch that the act is absolutely involuntary. Such is the case of physical compulsion or restraint, by whatever means brought about; where the man's hand, for instance, is pushed against some object which his will disposes him not to touch; or tied down from touching some object which his will disposes him to touch.

§ 4. Cases where punishment is unprofitable.

These are,

XIII. 1. Where, on the one hand, the nature of the offence, on the other hand, that of the punishment, are, in the ordinary state of things, such, that when compared together, the evil of the latter will turn out to be greater than that of the former.

XIV. Now the evil of the punishment divides itself into four branches, by which so many different sets of persons are affected. 1. The evil of coercion or restraint: or the pain which it gives a man not to be able to do the act, whatever it be, which by the apprehension of the punishment he is deterred from doing. This is felt by those by whom the law is observed. 2. The evil of apprehension: or the pain which a man, who has exposed himself to punishment, feels at the thoughts of undergoing it. This is felt by those by whom the law has been broken, and who feel themselves in danger of its being executed upon them. 3. The evil of sufferance: or the pain which a man feels, in virtue of the punishment itself, from the time when he begins to undergo it. This is felt by those by whom the law is broken, and upon whom it comes actually to be executed. 4. The pain of sympathy, and the other derivative evils resulting to the persons who are in connection with the several classes of original sufferers just mentioned. Now of these four lots of evil, the first will be greater or less, according to the nature of the act from which the party is restrained: the second and third according to the nature of the punishment which stands annexed to that offence.

XV. On the other hand, as to the evil of the offence, this will also, of course, be greater or less, according to the nature of each offence. The proportion between the one evil and the other will therefore be different in the case of each particular offence. The cases, therefore, where punishment is unprofitable on this ground, can by no other means be discovered, than by an examination of each particular offence; which is what will be the business of the body of the work.

XVI. 2. Where, although in the ordinary state of things, the evil resulting from the punishment is not greater than the benefit which is likely to result from the force with which it operates, during the same space of time, towards the excluding the evil of the offences, yet it may have been rendered so by the influence of some occasional circumstances. In the number of these circumstances may be, 1. The multitude of delinquents at a particular juncture; being such as would increase, beyond the ordinary measure, the quantum of the second and third lots, and thereby also of a part of the fourth lot, in the evil of the punishment. 2. The extraordinary value of the services of some one delinquent; in the case where the effect of the punishment would be to deprive the community of the benefit of those services. 3. The displeasure of the people; that is, of an indefinite number of the members of the same community, in cases where (owing to the influence of some occasional incident) they happen to conceive, that the offence or the offender ought not to be punished at all, or at least ought not to be punished in the way in question. 4. The displeasure of foreign powers; that is, of the governing body, or a considerable number of the members of some foreign community or communities, with which the community in question is connected.

§ 5. Cases where punishment is needless.
These are,

XVII. 1. Where the purpose of putting an end to the practice may be attained as effectually at a cheaper rate: by instruction, for instance, as well as by terror: by informing the understanding, as well as by exercising an immediate influence on the will. This seems to be the case with respect to all those offences which consist in the disseminating pernicious principles in matters of duty; of whatever kind the duty be; whether political, or moral, or religious. And this, whether such principles be disseminated under, or even without, a sincere persuasion of their being beneficial. I say, even without: for

though in such a case it is not instruction that can prevent the writer from endeavouring to inculcate his principles, yet it may the readers from adopting them: without which, his endeavouring to inculcate them will do no harm. In such a case, the sovereign will commonly have little need to take an active part: if it be the interest of one individual to inculcate principles that are pernicious, it will as surely be the interest of other individuals to expose them. But if the sovereign must needs take a part in the controversy, the pen is the proper weapon to combat error with, not the sword.

Of the Proportion between Punishments and Offences

I. We have seen that the general object of all laws is to prevent mischief; that is to say, when it is worth while; but that, where there are no other means of doing this than punishment, there are four cases in which it is not worth while.

II. When it is worth while, there are four subordinate designs or objects, which, in the course of his endeavours to compass, as far as may be, that one general object, a legislator, whose views are governed by the principle of utility, comes naturally to propose to himself.

III. 1. His first, most extensive, and most eligible object, is to prevent, in as far as it is possible, and worth while, all sorts of offences whatsoever: in other words, so to manage, that no offence whatsoever may be committed.

IV. 2. But if a man must needs commit an offence of some kind or other, the next object is to induce him to commit an offence less mischievous, rather than one more mischievous: in other words, to choose always the least mischievous, of two offences that will either of them suit his purpose.

V. 3. When a man has resolved upon a particular offence, the next object is to dispose him to do no more mischief than is necessary to his purpose: in other words, to do as little mischief as is consistent with the benefit he has in view.

VI. 4. The last object is, whatever the mischief be, which it is proposed to prevent, to prevent it at as cheap a rate as possible.

VII. Subservient to these four objects, or purposes, must be the rules or canons by which the proportion of punishments to offences is to be governed.

VIII. Rule 1. The first object, it has been seen, is to prevent, in as far as it is worth while, all sorts of offences; therefore,

The value of the punishment must not be less in any case than what is sufficient to outweigh that of the profit of the offence.

If it be, the offence (unless some other considerations, independent of the punishment should intervene and operate efficaciously in the character of tutelary motives) will be sure to be committed notwithstanding: the whole lot of punishment will be thrown away: it will be altogether inefficacious.

IX. The above rule has been often objected to, on account of its seeming harshness: but this can only have happened for want of its being properly understood. The strength of the temptation, *cæteris paribus*, is as the profit of the offence: the quantum of the punishment must rise with the profit of the offence: *cæteris paribus*, it must therefore rise with the strength of the temptation. This there is no disputing. True it is, that the stronger the temptation, the less conclusive is the indication which the act of delinquency affords of the depravity of the offender's disposition. So far then as the absence of any aggravation, arising from extraordinary depravity of disposition, may operate, or at the utmost, so far as the presence of a ground of extenuation, resulting from the innocence or beneficence of the offender's disposition, can operate, the strength of the temptation may operate in abatement of the demand for punishment. But it can never operate so far as to indicate the propriety of making the punishment ineffectual, which it is sure to be when brought below the level of the apparent profit of the offence.

The partial benevolence which should prevail for the reduction of it below this level, would counteract as well those purposes which such a motive would actually have in view, as those more extensive purposes which benevolence ought to have in view: it would be cruelty not only to the public, but to the very persons in whose behalf it pleads:

in its effects, I mean, however opposite in its intention. Cruelty to the public, that is cruelty to the innocent, by suffering them, for want of an adequate protection, to lie exposed to the mischief of the offence: cruelty even to the offender himself, by punishing him to no purpose, and without the chance of compassing that beneficial end, by which alone the introduction of the evil of punishment is to be justified.

X. Rule 2. But whether a given offence shall be prevented in a given degree by a given quantity of punishment, is never any thing better than a chance; for the purchasing of which, whatever punishment is employed, is so much expended into advance. However, for the sake of giving it the better chance of outweighing the profit of the offence,

The greater the mischief of the offence, the greater is the expense which it may be worth while to be at, in the way of punishment.

XI. Rule 3. The next object is, to induce a man to choose always the least mischievous of two offences; therefore,

Where two offences come in competition, the punishment for the greater offence must be sufficient to induce a man to prefer the less.

XII. Rule 4. When a man has resolved upon a particular offence, the next object is, to induce him to do no more mischief than what is necessary for his purpose: therefore

The punishment should be adjusted in such manner to each particular offence, that for every part of the mischief there may be a motive to restrain the offender from giving birth to it.

XIII. Rule 5. The last object is, whatever mischief is guarded against, to guard against it at as cheap a rate as possible: therefore

The punishment ought in no case to be more than what is necessary to bring it into conformity with the rules here given.

XIV. Rule 6. It is further to be observed, that owing to the different manners and degrees in which persons under different circumstances are affected by the same exciting cause, a punishment which is the same in name will not always either really produce, or even so much as appear to others to produce, in two different persons the same degree of pain: therefore

That the quantity actually indicted on each individual offender may correspond to the quantity intended for similar offenders in general, the several circumstances influencing sensibility ought always to be taken into account.

XV. Of the above rules of proportion, the first four, we may perceive serve to mark out limits on the side of diminution; the limits below which a punishment ought not to be diminished: the fifth the limits on the side of increase; the limits above which it ought not to be increased. The five first are calculated to serve as guides to the legislator: the sixth is calculated in some measure, indeed, to the same purpose; but principally for guiding the judge in his endeavours to conform, on both sides, to the intentions of the legislator.

XVI. Let us look back a little. The first rule, in order to render it more conveniently applicable to practice, may need perhaps to be a little more particularly unfolded. It is to be observed, then, that for the sake of accuracy, it was necessary, instead of the word quantity to make use of the less perspicuous term value. For the word quantity will not properly include the circumstances either of certainty or proximity: circumstances which, in estimating the value of a lot of pain or pleasure, must always be taken into the account. Now, on the one hand, a lot of punishment is a lot of pain; on the other hand, the profit of an offence is a lot of pleasure, or what is equivalent to it. But the profit of the offence is commonly more certain than the punishment, or, what comes to the same thing, appears so at least to the offender. It is at any rate commonly more immediate. It follows, therefore, that, in order to maintain its superiority over the profit of the offence, the punishment must have its value made up in some other way, in proportion to that whereby it falls short in the two points of certainty and proximity. Now there is no other way in which it can receive any addition to its value, but by receiving an addition in point of magnitude. Wherever then the value of the punishment falls short, either in point of certainty, or of proximity, of that of the profit of the offence, it must receive a proportionable addition in point of magnitude.

XVII. Yet farther. To make sure of giving the value of the punishment the superiority over that of the offence, it may be necessary, in some cases, to take into account the profit not only of the individual offence to which the punishment is to be annexed, but also of such other offences of the same sort as the offender is likely to have already committed without detection. This random mode of calculation, severe as it is, it will be impossible to avoid having recourse to, in certain cases: in such, to wit, in which the profit is pecuniary, the chance of detection very small, and the obnoxious act of such a nature as indicates a habit: for example, in the case of frauds against the coin. If it be not recurred to, the practice of committing the offence will be sure to be, upon the balance of the account, a gainful practice. That being the case, the legislator will be absolutely sure of not being able to suppress it, and the whole punishment that is bestowed upon it will be thrown away. In a word (to keep to the same expressions we set out with) that whole quantity of punishment will be inefficacious.

XVIII. Rule 7. These things being considered, the three following rules may be laid down by way of supplement and explanation to Rule 1.

To enable the value of the punishment to outweigh that of the profit of the offence, it must be increased, in point of magnitude, in proportion as it falls short in point of certainty.

XIX. Rule 8. Punishment must be further increased in point of magnitude, in proportion as it falls short in point of proximity.

XX. Rule 9. Where the act is conclusively indicative of a habit, such an increase must be given to the punishment as may enable it to outweigh the profit not only of the individual offence, but of such other like offences as are likely to have been committed with impunity by the same offender.

XXI. There may be a few other circumstances or considerations which may influence, in some small degree, the demand for punishment: but as the propriety of these is either not so demonstrable, or not so constant, or the application of them not so determinate, as that of the foregoing, it may be doubted whether they be worth putting on a level with the others.

XXII. Rule 10. When a punishment, which in point of quality is particularly well calculated to answer its intention cannot exist in less than a certain quantity, it may sometimes be of use, for the sake of employing it, to stretch a little beyond that quantity which, on other accounts, would be strictly necessary.

XXIII. Rule 11. In particular, this may sometimes be the case, where the punishment proposed is of such a nature as to be particularly well calculated to answer the purpose of a moral lesson.

XXIV. Rule 12. The tendency of the above considerations is to dictate an augmentation in the punishment: the following rule operates in the way of diminution. There are certain cases (it has been seen) in which, by the influence of accidental circumstances, punishment may be rendered unprofitable in the whole: in the same cases it may chance to be rendered unprofitable as to a part only. Accordingly,

In adjusting the quantum of punishment, the circumstances, by which all punishment may be rendered unprofitable, ought to be attended to.

XXV. Rule 13. It is to be observed, that the more various and minute any set of provisions are, the greater the chance is that any given article in them will not be borne in mind: without which, no benefit can ensue from it. Distinctions, which are more complex than what the conceptions of those whose conduct it is designed to influence can take in, will even be worse than useless. The whole system will present a confused appearance: and thus the effect, not only of the proportions established by the articles in question, but of whatever is connected with them, will be destroyed. To draw a precise line of direction in such case seems impossible. However, by way of memento, it may be of some use to subjoin the following rule.

Among provisions designed to perfect the proportion between punishments and offences, if any occur, which, by their own particular good effects, would not make up for the harm they would do

by adding to the intricacy of the Code, they should be omitted.

XXVI. It may be remembered, that the political sanction, being that to which the sort of punishment belongs, which in this chapter is all along in view, is but one of four sanctions, which may all of them contribute their share towards producing the same effects. It may be expected, therefore, that in adjusting the quantity of political punishment, allowance should be made for the assistance it may meet with from those other controlling powers. True it is, that from each of these several sources a very powerful assistance may sometimes be derived. But the case is, that (setting aside the moral sanction, in the case where the force of it is expressly adopted into and modified by the political) the force of those other powers is never determinate enough to be depended upon. It can never be reduced, like political punishment, into exact lots, nor meted out in number, quantity, and value. The legislator is therefore obliged to provide the full complement of punishment, as if he were sure of not receiving any assistance whatever from any of those quarters. If he does, so much the better: but lest he should not, it is necessary he should, at all events, make that provision which depends upon himself.

XXVII. It may be of use, in this place, to recapitulate the several circumstances, which, in establishing the proportion betwixt punishments and offences, are to be attended to. These seem to be as follows:

I. On the part of the offence:
1. The profit of the offence;
2. The mischief of the offence;
3. The profit and mischief of other greater or lesser offences, of different sorts, which the offender may have to choose out of;
4. The profit and mischief of other offences, of the same sort, which the same offender may probably have been guilty of already.

II. On the part of the punishment:
5. The magnitude of the punishment: composed of its intensity and duration;

6. The deficiency of the punishment in point of certainty;

7. The deficiency of the punishment in point of proximity;

8. The quality of the punishment;

9. The accidental advantage in point of quality of a punishment, not strictly needed in point of quantity;

10. The use of a punishment of a particular quality, in the character of a moral lesson.

III. On the part of the offender:

11. The responsibility of the class of persons in a way to offend;

12. The sensibility of each particular offender;

13. The particular merits or useful qualities of any particular offender, in case of a punishment which might deprive the community of the benefit of them;

14. The multitude of offenders on any particular occasion.

IV. On the part of the public, at any particular conjuncture:

15. The inclinations of the people, for or against any quantity or mode of punishment;

16. The inclinations of foreign powers.

V. On the part of the law: that is, of the public for a continuance:

17. The necessity of making small sacrifices, in point of proportionality, for the sake of simplicity.

XXVIII. There are some, perhaps, who, at first sight, may look upon the nicety employed in the adjustment of such rules, as so much labour lost: for gross ignorance, they will say, never troubles itself about laws, and passion does not calculate. But, the evil of ignorance admits of cure: and as to the proposition that passion does not calculate, this, like most of these very general and oracular propositions, is not true. When matters of such importance as pain and pleasure are at stake, and these in the highest degree (the only matters, in short, that can be of importance) who is there that does not calculate? Men calculate, some with less exactness, indeed, some with more: but all men calculate. I would not say, that even a madman does not calculate. Passion calculates, more or less, in every man: in different men, according to the warmth or coolness of their dispositions: according to the firmness or irritability of their minds: according to the nature of the motives by which they are acted upon. Happily, of all passions, that is the most given to calculation, from the excesses of which, by reason of its strength, constancy, and universality, society has most to apprehend: I mean that which corresponds to the motive of pecuniary interest: so that these niceties, if such they are to be called, have the best chance of being efficacious, where efficacy is of the most importance.

Of the Properties to Be Given to a Lot of Punishment

I. It has been shown what the rules are, which ought to be observed in adjusting the proportion between the punishments and the offence. The properties to be given to a lot of punishment, in every instance, will of course be such as it stands in need of, in order to be capable of being applied, in conformity to those rules: the quality will be regulated by the quantity.

II. The first of those rules, we may remember, was, that the quantity of punishment must not be less, in any case, than what is sufficient to outweigh the profit of the offence: since, as often as it is less, the whole lot (unless by accident the deficiency should be supplied from some of the other sanctions) is thrown away: it is inefficacious. The fifth was, that the punishment ought in no case to be more than what is required by the several other rules: since, if it be, all that is above that quantity is needless. The fourth was, that the punishment should be adjusted in such manner to each individual offence, that every part of the mischief of that offence may have a penalty (that is, a tutelary motive) to encounter it: otherwise, with respect to so much of the offence as has not a penalty to correspond to it, it is as if there were no punishment in the case. Now to none of those rules can a lot of punishment be conformable, unless, for every variation in point of quantity, in the mischief of the species of offence to which it is annexed, such lot of punishment admits of a correspondent variation. To prove this, let the profit of the offence admit of a multitude of degrees. Suppose it, then, at any one of these degrees: if the punishment be less than what is suitable to that degree, it will be inefficacious; it will be so much thrown away: if it be more, as far as the difference extends, it will be needless; it will therefore be thrown away also in that case.

The first property, therefore, that ought to be given to a lot of punishment, is that of being variable in point of quantity, in conformity to every variation which can take place in either the profit or mischief of the offence. This property might, perhaps, be termed, in a single word, variability.

III. A second property, intimately connected with the former, may be styled equability. It will avail but little, that a mode of punishment (proper in all other respects) has been established by the legislator; and that capable of being screwed up or let down to any degree that can be required; if, after all, whatever degree of it be pitched upon, that same degree shall be liable, according to circumstances, to produce a very heavy degree of pain, or a very slight one, or even none at all. In this case, as in the former, if circumstances happen one way, there will be a great deal of pain produced which will be needless: if the other way, there will be no pain at all applied, or none that will be efficacious. A punishment, when liable to this irregularity, may be styled an unequable one: when free from it, an equable one. The quantity of pain produced by the punishment will, it is true, depend in a considerable degree upon circumstances distinct from the nature of the punishment itself: upon the condition which the offender is in, with respect to the circumstances by which a man's sensibility is liable to be influenced. But the influence of these very circumstances will in many cases be reciprocally influenced by the nature of the punishment: in other words, the pain which is produced by any mode of punishment, will be the joint effect of the punishment which is applied to him, and the circumstances in which he is exposed to it. Now there are some punishments, of which the effect may be liable to undergo a greater alteration by the influence of such foreign circumstances, than the effect of other punishments is liable to undergo. So far, then, as this is the case, equability or unequability may be regarded as properties belonging to the punishment itself.

IV. An example of a mode of punishment which is apt to be unequable, is that of banishment, when the locus a quo (or place the party is banished from) is some determinate place appointed by the law, which perhaps the offender cares not whether he ever see or no. This is also the case with pecuniary, or quasi-pecuniary punishment, when it respects some particular species of property, which the offender may have been possessed of, or not, as it may happen. All these punishments may be split down into parcels, and measured out with the utmost nicety: being divisible by time, at least, if by nothing else. They are not, therefore, any of them defective in point of variability: and yet, in many cases, this defect in point of equability may make them as unfit for use as if they were.

V. The third rule of proportion was, that where two offences come in competition, the punishment for the greater offences must be sufficient to induce a man to prefer the less. Now, to be sufficient for this purpose, it must be evidently and uniformly greater: greater, not in the eyes of some men only, but of all men who are liable to be in a situation to take their choice between the two offences; that is, in effect, of all mankind. In other words, the two punishments must be perfectly commensurable. Hence arises a third property, which may be termed commensurability: to wit, with reference to other punishments.

VI. But punishments of different kinds are in very few instances uniformly greater one than another; especially when the lowest degrees of that which is ordinarily the greater, are compared with the highest degrees of that which is ordinarily the less: in other words, punishments of different kinds are in few instances uniformly commensurable. The only certain and universal means of making two lots of punishment perfectly commensurable, is by making the lesser an ingredient in the composition of the greater. This may be done in either of two ways. 1. By adding to the lesser punishment another quantity of punishment of the same kind. 2. By adding to it another quantity of a different kind. The latter mode is not less certain than the former: for though one cannot always be absolutely sure, that to the same person a given punishment will appear greater than another given punishment; yet one may be always absolutely sure, that any given punishment, so as it does but come into contemplation, will appear greater than none at all.

VII. Again: Punishment cannot act any farther than in as far as the idea of it, and of its connection with the offence, is present in the mind. The idea of it, if not present, cannot act at all; and then the punishment itself must be inefficacious. Now, to be present, it must be remembered, and to be remembered it must have been learnt. But of all punishments that can be imagined, there are none of which the connection with the offence is either so easily learnt, or so efficaciously remembered, as those of which the idea is already in part associated with some part of the idea of the offence: which is the case when the one and the other have some circumstance that belongs to them in common. When this is the case with a punishment and an offence, the punishment is said to bear an analogy to, or to be characteristic of, the offence. Characteristicalness is, therefore, a fourth property, which on this account ought to be given, whenever it can conveniently be given, to a lot of punishment.

VIII. It is obvious, that the effect of this contrivance will be the greater, as the analogy is the closer. The analogy will be the closer, the more material that circumstance is, which is in common. Now the most material circumstance that can belong to an offence and a punishment in common, is the hurt or damage which they produce. The closest analogy, therefore, that can subsist between an offence and the punishment annexed to it, is that which subsists between them when the hurt or damage they produce is of the same nature: in other words, that which is constituted by the circumstance of identity in point of damage. Accordingly, the mode of punishment, which of all others bears the closest

analogy to the offence, is that which in the proper and exact sense of the word is termed retaliation. Retaliation, therefore, in the few cases in which it is practicable, and not too expensive, will have one great advantage over every other mode of punishment.

IX. Again: It is the idea only of the punishment (or, in other words, the apparent punishment) that really acts upon the mind; the punishment itself (the real punishment) acts not any farther than as giving rise to that idea. It is the apparent punishment, therefore, that does all the service, I mean in the way of example, which is the principal object. It is the real punishment that does all the mischief. Now the ordinary and obvious way of increasing the magnitude of the apparent punishment, is by increasing the magnitude of the real. The apparent magnitude, however, may to a certain degree be increased by other less expensive means: whenever, therefore, at the same time that these less expensive means would have answered that purpose, an additional real punishment is employed, this additional real punishment is needless. As to these less expensive means, they consist, 1. In the choice of a particular mode of punishment, a punishment of a particular quality, independent of the quantity. 2. In a particular set of solemnities distinct from the punishment itself, and accompanying the execution of it.

X. A mode of punishment, according as the appearance of it bears a greater proportion to the reality, may be said to be the more exemplary. Now as to what concerns the choice of the punishment itself, there is not any means by which a given quantity of punishment can be rendered more exemplary, than by choosing it of such a sort as shall bear an analogy to the offence. Hence another reason for rendering the punishment analogous to, or in other words characteristic of, the offence.

XI. Punishment, it is still to be remembered, is in itself an expense: it is in itself an evil. Accordingly the fifth rule of proportion is, not to produce more of it than what is demanded by the other rules. But this is the case as often as any particle of pain is produced, which contributes nothing to the effect proposed. Now if any mode of punishment is more apt than another to produce any such superfluous and needless pain, it may be styled unfrugal; if less, it may be styled frugal. Frugality, therefore, is a sixth property to be wished for in a mode of punishment.

XII. The perfection of frugality, in a mode of punishment, is where not only no superfluous pain is produced on the part of the person punished, but even that same operation, by which he is subjected to pain, is made to answer the purpose of producing pleasure on the part of some other person. Understand a profit or stock of pleasure of the self-regarding kind: for a pleasure of the dissocial kind is produced almost of course, on the part of all persons in whose breasts the offence has excited the sentiment of ill-will. Now this is the case with pecuniary punishment, as also with such punishments of the quasi-pecuniary kind as consist in the subtraction of such a species of possession as is transferable from one party to another. The pleasure, indeed, produced by such an operation, is not in general equal to the pain: it may, however, be so in particular circumstances, as where he, from whom the thing is taken, is very rich, and he, to whom it is given, very poor: and, be it what it will, it is always so much more than can be produced by any other mode of punishment.

XIII. The properties of exemplarity and frugality seem to pursue the same immediate end, though by different courses. Both are occupied in diminishing the ratio of the real suffering to the apparent: but exemplarity tends to increase the apparent; frugality to reduce the real.

XIV. Thus much concerning the properties to be given to punishments in general, to whatsoever offences they are to be applied. Those which follow are of less importance, either as referring only to certain offences in particular, or depending upon the influence of transitory and local circumstances.

In the first place, the four distinct ends into which the main and general end of punishment is divisible, may give rise to so many distinct properties, according as any particular mode of punishment appear to be more particularly adapted to the compassing of one or of another of those ends. To that of example, as being the principal one, a particular property has already been adapted. There remain the three inferior ones of reformation, disablement, and compensation.

XV. A seventh property, therefore, to be wished for in a mode of punishment, is that of subserviency to reformation, or reforming tendency. Now any punishment is subservient to reformation in proportion to its quantity: since the greater the punishment a man has experienced, the stronger is the tendency it has to create in him an aversion towards the offence which was the cause of it: and that with respect to all offences alike. But there are certain punishments which, with regard to certain offences, have a particular tendency to produce that effect by reason of their quality: and where this is the case, the punishments in question, as applied to the offences in question, will *pro tanto* have the advantage over all others. This influence will depend upon the nature of the motive which is the cause of the offence: the punishment most subservient to reformation will be the sort of punishment that is best calculated to invalidate the force of that motive.

XVI. Thus, in offences originating from the motive of ill-will, that punishment has the strongest reforming tendency, which is best calculated to weaken the force of the irascible affections. And more particularly, in that sort of offence which consists in an obstinate refusal, on the part of the offender, to do something which is lawfully required of him, and in which the obstinacy is in great measure kept up by his resentment against those who have an interest in forcing him to compliance, the most efficacious punishment seems to be that of confinement to spare diet.

XVII. Thus, also, in offences which owe their birth to the joint influence of indolence and pecuniary interest, that punishment seems to possess the strongest reforming tendency, which is best calculated to weaken the force of the former of those dispositions. And more particularly, in the cases of theft, embezzlement, and every species of defraudment, the mode of punishment best adapted to this purpose seems, in most cases, to be that of penal labour.

XVIII. An eighth property to be given to a lot of punishment in certain cases, is that of efficacy with respect to disablement, or, as it might be styled more briefly, disabling efficacy. This is a property which may be given in perfection to a lot of punishment; and that with much greater certainty than the property of subserviency to reformation. The inconvenience is, that this property is apt, in general, to run counter to that of frugality: there being, in most cases, no certain way of disabling a man from doing mischief, without, at the same time, disabling him, in a great measure, from doing good, either to himself or others. The mischief therefore of the offence must be so great as to demand a very considerable lot of punishment, for the purpose of example, before it can warrant the application of a punishment equal to that which is necessary for the purpose of disablement.

XIX. The punishment, of which the efficacy in this way is the greatest, is evidently that of death. In this case the efficacy of it is certain. This accordingly is the punishment peculiarly adapted to those cases in which the name of the offender, so long as he lives, may be sufficient to keep a whole nation in a flame. This will now and then be the case with competitors for the sovereignty, and leaders of the factions in civil wars: though, when applied to offences of so questionable a nature, in which the question concerning criminality turns more upon success than any thing else, an infliction of this sort may seem more to savour of hostility than punishment. At the same time this punishment, it is evident, is in an eminent degree unfrugal; which forms one among the many objections there are against the use of it, in any but very extraordinary cases.

XX. In ordinary cases the purpose may be sufficiently answered by one or other of the various kinds of confinement and banishment: of which, imprisonment is the most strict and efficacious. For when an offence is so circumstanced that it cannot be committed but in a certain place, as is the case, for the most part, with offences against the person, all the law has to do, in order to disable the offender from committing it, is to prevent his being in that place. In any of the offences which consist in the breach or the abuse of any kind of trust, the purpose may be compassed at a still cheaper rate, merely by forfeiture of the trust: and in general, in any of those offences which can only be committed under favour of some relation in which the offender stands with reference to any person, or sets of persons, merely by forfeiture of that relation: that is, of the right of continuing to reap the advantages belonging to it. This is the case, for instance, with any of those offences which consist in an abuse of the privileges of marriage, or of the liberty of carrying on any lucrative or other occupation.

XXI. The ninth property is that of subserviency to compensation. This property of punishment, if it be vindictive compensation that is in view, will, with little variation, be in proportion to the quantity: if lucrative, it is the peculiar and characteristic property of pecuniary punishment.

XXII. In the rear of all these properties may be introduced that of popularity; a very fleeting and indeterminate kind of property, which may belong to a lot of punishment one moment, and be lost by it the next. By popularity is meant the property of being acceptable, or rather not unacceptable, to the bulk of the people, among whom it is proposed to be established. In strictness of speech, it should rather be called absence of unpopularity: for it cannot be expected, in regard to such a matter as punishment, that any species or lot of it should be positively acceptable and grateful to the people: it is sufficient, for the most part, if they have no decided aversion to the thoughts of it. Now the property of characteristicalness, above noticed, seems to go as far towards conciliating the approbation of the people to a mode of punishment, as any; insomuch that popularity may be regarded as a kind of secondary quality, depending upon that of characteristicalness. The use of inserting this property in the catalogue, is chiefly to make it serve by way of memento to the legislator not to introduce, without a cogent necessity, any mode or lot of punishment, towards which he happens to perceive any violent aversion entertained by the body of the people.

XXIII. The effects of unpopularity in a mode of punishment are analogous to those of unfrugality.

The unnecessary pain which denominates a punishment unfrugal, is most apt to be that which is produced on the part of the offender. A portion of superfluous pain is in like manner produced when the punishment is unpopular: but in this case it is produced on the part of persons altogether innocent, the people at large. This is already one mischief; and another is, the weakness which it is apt to introduce into the law. When the people are satisfied with the law, they voluntarily lend their assistance in the execution: when they are dissatisfied, they will naturally withhold that assistance; it is well if they do not take a positive part in raising impediments. This contributes greatly to the uncertainty of the punishment; by which, in the first instance, the frequency of the offence receives an increase. In process of time that deficiency, as usual, is apt to draw on an increase in magnitude: an addition of a certain quantity which otherwise would be needless.

XXIV. This property, it is to be observed, necessarily supposes, on the part of the people, some prejudice or other, which it is the business of the legislator to endeavour to correct. For if the aversion to the punishment in question were grounded on the principle of utility, the punishment would be such as, on other accounts, ought not to be employed: in which case its popularity or unpopularity would never be worth drawing into question. It is properly therefore a property not so much of the punishment as of the people: a disposition to entertain an unreasonable dislike against an object which merits their approbation. It is the sign also of another property, to wit, indolence or weakness, on the part of the legislator: in suffering the people for the want of some instruction, which ought to be and might be given them, to quarrel with their own interest. Be this as it may, so long as any such dissatisfaction subsists, it behooves the legislator to have an eye to it, as much as if it were ever so well grounded. Every nation is liable to have its prejudices and its caprices which it is the business of the legislator to look out for, to study, and to cure.

XXV. The eleventh and last of all the properties that seem to be requisite in a lot of punishment, is that of remissibility. The general presumption is, that when punishment is applied, punishment is needful: that it ought to be applied, and therefore cannot want to be remitted. But in very particular, and those always very deplorable cases, it may by accident happen otherwise. It may happen that punishment shall have been inflicted, where, according to the intention of the law itself, it ought not to have been inflicted: that is, where the sufferer is innocent of the offence. At the time of the sentence passed he appeared guilty: but since then, accident has brought his innocence to light. This being the case, so much of the destined punishment as he has suffered already, there is no help for. The business is then to free him from as much as is yet to come. But is there any yet to come? There is very little chance of there being any, unless it be so much as consists of chronical punishment: such as imprisonment, banishment, penal labour, and the like. So much as consists of acute punishment, to wit where the penal process itself is over presently, however permanent the punishment may be in its effects, may be considered as irremissible. This is the case, for example, with whipping, branding, mutilation, and capital punishment. The most perfectly irremissible of any is capital punishment. For though other punishments cannot, when they are over, be remitted, they may be compensated for; and although the unfortunate victim cannot be put into the same condition, yet possibly means may be found of putting him into as good a condition, as he would have been in if he had never suffered. This may in general be done very effectually where the punishment has been no other than pecuniary.

There is another case in which the property of remissibility may appear to be of use: this is, where, although the offender has been justly punished, yet on account of some good behaviour of his, displayed at a time subsequent to that of the commencement of the punishment, it may seem expedient to remit a part of it. But this it can scarcely be, if the proportion of the punishment is, in other respects, what it ought to be. The purpose of example is the more important object, in comparison of that of reformation. It is not very likely, that less punishment should be required for the former purpose than for the latter.

For it must be rather an extraordinary case, if a punishment, which is sufficient to deter a man who has only thought of it for a few moments, should not be sufficient to deter a man who has been feeling it all the time. Whatever, then, is required for the purpose of example, must abide at all events: it is not any reformation on the part of the offender, that can warrant the remitting of any part of it: if it could, a man would have nothing to do but to reform immediately, and so free himself from the greatest part of that punishment which was deemed necessary. In order, then, to warrant the remitting of any part of a punishment upon this ground, it must first be supposed that the punishment at first appointed was more than was necessary for the purpose of example, and consequently that a part of it was needless upon the whole. This, indeed, is apt enough to be the case, under the imperfect systems that are as yet on foot: and therefore, during the continuance of those systems, the property of remissibility may, on this second ground likewise, as well as on the former, be deemed a useful one. But this would not be the case in any new-constructed system, in which the rules of proportion above laid down should be observed. In such a system, therefore, the utility of this property would rest solely on the former ground.

XXVI. Upon taking a survey of the various possible modes of punishment, it will appear evidently, that there is not any one of them that possesses all the above properties in perfection. To do the best that can be done in the way of punishment, it will therefore be necessary, upon most occasions, to compound them, and make them into complex lots, each consisting of a number of different modes of punishment put together: the nature and proportions of the constituent parts of each lot being different, according to the nature of the offence which it is designed to combat.

XXVII. It may not be amiss to bring together, and exhibit in one view, the eleven properties above established. They are as follows:

Two of them are concerned in establishing a proper proportion between a single offence and its punishment; viz.

1. Variability.
2. Equability.

One, in establishing a proportion, between more offences than one, and more punishments than one; viz.

3. Commensurability.

A fourth contributes to place the punishment in that situation in which alone it can be efficacious; and at the same time to be bestowing on it the two farther properties of exemplarity and popularity; viz.

4. Characteristicalness.

Two others are concerned in excluding all useless punishment; the one indirectly, by heightening the efficacy of what is useful; the other in a direct way; viz.

5. Exemplarity.
6. Frugality.

Three others contribute severally to the three inferior ends of punishment; viz.

7. Subserviency to reformation.
8. Efficacy in disabling.
9. Subserviency to compensation.

Another property tends to exclude a collateral mischief, which a particular mode of punishment is liable accidentally to produce; viz.

10. Popularity.

The remaining property tends to palliate a mischief, which all punishment, as such, is liable accidentally to produce; viz.

11. Remissibility.

The properties of commensurability, characteristicalness, exemplarity, subserviency to reformation, and efficacy in disabling, are more particularly calculated to augment the profit which is to be made by punishment: frugality, subserviency to compensation, popularity, and remissibility, to diminish the expense: variability and equability are alike subservient to both those purposes.

XXVIII. We now come to take a general survey of the system of offences: that is, of such acts to which, on account of the mischievous consequences they have a natural tendency to produce, and in the view of putting a stop to those consequences, it may be proper to annex a certain artificial consequence, consisting of punishment, to be inflicted on the authors of such acts according to the principles just established.

DISCUSSION QUESTIONS

1. Explain why, given Bentham's commitment to utilitarianism, he views punishment as in need of justification. What, given his utilitarian position, could provide a justification of punishment?

2. Give an example of each of the following: (i) a case in which punishment is groundless, (ii) a case in which punishment would be inefficacious, (iii) a case in which punishment is unprofitable, and (iv) a case in which punishment is needless. Explain each case in terms of Bentham's utilitarianism.

3. Explain how, according to Bentham, we are to determine what punishment is proportionate to each crime. Do you think that his account of the proportionality of punishment to crime is plausible? Why or why not?

Michael S. Moore holds the Charles R. Walgreen, Jr., university-wide chair for all three of the University of Illinois's campuses. He is also a professor of law in the College of Law at the University of Illinois and is jointly appointed as a professor of philosophy in the College of Liberal Arts and Sciences. Additionally, he is a professor with the Center for Advanced Studies at the same university. Moore has written extensively on legal and philosophical topics; in the piece selected below, he provides a careful analysis of the concepts of punishment and retribution.

SOURCE

Moore, Michael S. *Law and Psychiatry: Rethinking the Relationship*. Cambridge University Press, 1985. Copyright © 1985 by Michael S. Moore. Reprinted with permission of the author.

A Taxonomy of Purposes of Punishment

The Prima Facie Justifications of Punishment
[...]
Retributivism ... is the view that punishment is justified by the desert of the offender. The good that is achieved by punishing, in this view, has nothing to do with future states of affairs, such as the prevention of crime or the maintenance of social cohesion. Rather, the good that punishment achieves is that someone who deserves it gets it.

Retributivism is quite distinct from a view that urges that punishment is justified because a majority of citizens feel that offenders should be punished. Rather, retributivism is a species of objectivism in ethics that asserts that there is such a thing as desert and that the presence of such a (real) moral quality in a person justifies punishment of that person. What a populace may think or feel about vengeance on an offender is one thing; what treatment an offender deserves is another. And it is only this last notion that is relevant to retributivism.

Retributivism is also distinct from what is sometimes called "revenge utilitarianism." This is the view that the state must punish because private citizens otherwise will take the law into their own hands and that such private vengeance leads to chaos and disorder. Punishment in such a view is justified by its ability to prevent these bad things. Retributivism has nothing to do with this essentially forward-looking justification. Moreover, this "prevention of private vengeance" theory is to my mind not even a prima facie justifying reason for punishment. The obvious thing to do if citizens are going to violate the law by taking it into their own hands, is to deter those citizens by punishing them, not by punishing someone else. It places retributivism in an unnecessarily bad light to think that it justifies punishment only because of the shadow cast by a threat of illegal violence by vengeful citizens.

The Two Pure Theories of Punishment

It is common to reduce the survivors on this list of prima facie justifications of punishment to two general theories, the utilitarian theory and the retributive theory. To see how this is done, one need only consider the good state of affairs that is to be achieved by incarceration, special deterrence, general deterrence, and rehabilitation (to the extent that it is of the first sort of rehabilitative theory, and not the second). For all four of these rationales for punishment share the prevention of crime as the beneficial end that justifies punishment. In each case, the ultimate justification for inflicting the harm of punishment is that it is outweighed by the good to be achieved, namely, the prevention of future crimes by that offender or by others. This justification of an institution by the social welfare it will enhance makes all such theories instances of the utilitarian theory of punishment.

Thus, the denunciation theory of punishment is a second kind of utilitarian theory of punishment, insofar as the good it seeks to achieve is not simply the prevention of crime. To the extent one grants intrinsic value to social cohesion, and does not regard that as a value only because it contributes to the maintenance of public order, the denunciation theory can be distinguished from the other utilitarian theories just considered by the differing social good it seeks to achieve. Nonetheless, it is still a utilitarian theory, since it outweighs the harm that is punishment by some form of net social gain that punishment achieves.

Both crime prevention and the maintenance of social cohesion are types of collective good. The general utilitarian theory of punishment is one that combines these and other forms of collective good that punishment might achieve, and calls them all a "social gain." Whenever the social gain outweighs the harm punishment causes to offenders or their families, such a theory would say that there is a net social gain. Such a vocabulary allows us a succinct definition of any form of utilitarian theory: Punishment is justified if and only if some net social gain is achieved by it.

A retributivist theory is necessarily nonutilitarian in character, for it eschews justifying punishment by its tendency to achieve any form of net social gain. Rather, retributivism asserts that punishment is properly inflicted because, and only because, the person deserves it. That some people deserve punishment in such a theory is both a necessary and a sufficient condition justifying criminal sanctions. A succinct definition of the retributivist theory of punishment, paralleling that given of the utilitarian theory, is that punishment is justified if and only if the persons receiving it deserve it.

The Mixed Theory of Punishment

Once one grants that there are two sorts of prima facie justifications of punishment—effecting a net social gain (utilitarian) and giving just deserts (retributivist)—one can also see that in addition to the two pure theories of punishment there can also be mixed theories. There are two logically possible mixed theories, although only one of these merits any serious attention. There is first of all the popular form of mixed theory that asserts that punishment is justified if and only if it achieves a net social gain *and* is given to offenders who deserve it. Giving just deserts and achieving a net social gain, in such a case, are each individually necessary but only jointly sufficient conditions justifying punishment. The second logically possible mixed theory would be one asserting that punishment is justified if and only if it achieves a net social gain, or if it is given to offenders who deserve it. Such a theory has no name, because there is no one, to my knowledge, who has ever adopted it. Such a theory is unnamed and unclaimed because it shares the defects of each of the pure theories, utilitarianism and retributivism.

I shall accordingly put this "mixed theory" aside from further consideration.

The first kind of mixed theory itself has two branches. By far the most usual and popular form of the theory asserts that we do not punish people *because* they deserve it. Desert enters in, this theory further asserts, only as a limit on punishment: We punish offenders *because* some net social gain is achieved, such as the prevention of crime, but only if such offenders deserve it. It is, in other words, the achieving of a net social gain that justifies punishment, whereas the desert of offenders serves as a limiting condition on punishment but as not part of its justification. The alternative branch of the mixed theory is just the converse: One would urge that we punish *because* offenders deserve it, but *only if* some net social gain is achieved by doing so. In such a case, the roles of net social gain and desert are simply reversed: Giving offenders their just deserts serves as the justification of punishment, and the achieving of a net social gain as the limiting condition.

A cynic might view these two branches of the mixed theory as nothing more than an uncomfortable shuffle by mixed theorists. When accused of barbarism for punishing persons for retributivist reasons, they assert the first branch of the theory (they punish not because some persons deserve it, but because of a collective good that is achieved). When accused of immorality for imposing harsh treatment on someone as a means of making everyone else better off, such theorists shift to the other foot, and claim they do not punish someone to achieve a net social gain, but only to give offenders their just deserts. The cynic has a point here, because there is a sense in which the two branches of the theory are the same, namely, the sense that they justify exactly the same kinds of treatment for all cases. The only difference in theories is in the motivations of those who hold them. And while that may make a difference in our moral judgments of those who hold the different branches of the mixed theory of punishment, it does not make a difference in terms of the actual social institutions and judgments such theories will justify. I shall accordingly lump both of these branches together and call them the mixed theory of punishment.

The Argument for Retributivism

The argument against the Pure Utilitarian Theory
In exploring one's thoughts about punishment, it is perhaps easiest to start with some standard kinds of thought experiments directed against a pure utilitarian theory of punishment. A thought experiment is essentially a device allowing one to sort out one's true reasons for believing that certain propositions are true. To be successful, such a thought experiment need not involve any actual case or state of affairs, nor need the cases envisioned even be very likely; they only need be conceivable in order to test our own thoughts.

It is standard fare in the philosophy of punishment to assert, by way of several thought experiments, counterexamples to the utilitarian thesis that punishment is justified if and only if some net social gain is achieved. I mention only two such counterexamples: scapegoating and preventive detention. With regard to the first, it might be recalled that D.B. Cooper successfully skyjacked an aircraft some years ago, and that this successful, unsolved crime apparently encouraged the mass of skyjackings that have cost so much in terms of dollars, lives, and convenience. Cooper wore large sunglasses in his escapade, and there was accordingly only a very limited description available of him. Imagine that shortly after his skyjacking we had the benefit of the knowledge we now have by hindsight, and we decided that it would be better to punish someone who looked like Cooper (and who had no good alibi) in order to convince others that skyjacking did not pay. For a consistent utilitarian, there is a net social gain that would be achieved by punishing such an innocent person, and there is no a priori reason that the net social gain in such a case might not outweigh the harm that is achieved by punishing an innocent person.

The preventive detention kind of counterexample is very similar: Imagine that a psychiatrist discovers that a patient has extremely dangerous propensities. The patient is also the accused in a criminal trial. It turns out, however, that the accused is not guilty of the crime for which he is charged and in fact has committed no crime whatsoever. Should a judge who, we may suppose, is the only one who knows that the man is both dangerous and innocent find the accused guilty? Doing so will prevent the defendant's predicted criminal behavior because he will be incarcerated. In a utilitarian theory, it is difficult to see why such a judgment would not be perfectly appropriate, as long as the prediction is reliable enough, and as long as the crimes predicted are sufficiently serious that the good of their prevention outweighs the harm of punishing that person, even though he has committed no crime as yet.

The general form of the argument arising from these kinds of thought experiments is that of a *reductio ad absurdum* argument. The argument has three premises:

1. Punishment should be inflicted if and only if doing so achieves a net social gain.
2. A net social gain would be achieved in this case by the infliction of punishment.
3. Punishment should not be inflicted in this case.

Each of these premises corresponds to steps in both of the foregoing thought experiments. The first premise is simply a restatement of the utilitarian theory of punishment. The second premise presupposes that there are some cases where a net social gain can be achieved by punishing an innocent person and asserts that this is such a case. The third premise asserts our intuition that such persons ought not to be punished.

All three premises together yield a contradiction:

4. Punishment should not be inflicted and punishment should be inflicted.

The first two premises have as their joint conclusion that the person should be punished; this conclusion, when conjoined with the third premise, produces the contradictory conclusion.

The strongest possible form of a *reductio ad absurdum* argument is one that ends in a formal contradiction. To avoid the contradiction, there are only three possibilities, corresponding to each of the three premises. One could give up the third premise and simply admit that in such cases the persons should be punished, despite their innocence. This move is a rather implausible one, inasmuch as it commits one to admitting that one will punish an entirely innocent person. The second possibility is to deny that there will be cases where there will be a net social gain from punishing an innocent person. This move is usually associated with the name of rule utilitarianism and involves the idea that one cannot make a general practice of punishing the innocent, because then the harm of so doing (in terms of demoralization costs in society and the like) will outweigh any possible good to be achieved, even the prevention of skyjacking. The problem with this response, popular as it is, is that it fails to deal fairly with the nature of the thought experiment. That is, suppose there are some risks of detection of punishment of innocent persons, and, thus, some risks of demoralization costs; such risk will only allow utilitarians to say that the number of cases in which punishment of the innocent will maximize utility is somewhat diminished. It does not foreclose as somehow impossible that there are such cases. Such cases are conceivable, and if in them one is still not willing to punish, one thereby shows oneself not to be a utilitarian about punishment.

This brings us to the third possibility: One can simply give up the first premise, that is, one can repudiate the utilitarian theory of punishment. Such thought experiments, I think, when clearly conceived and executed, show almost all of us that we are not pure utilitarians about punishment.

Arguments against the Mixed Theory of Punishment

The arguments against the pure utilitarian theory of punishment do not by themselves drive one into retributivism. For one can alleviate the injustice of the pure utilitarian theory of punishment by adopting the mixed theory. Since under the mixed theory the desert of the offender is a necessary condition of punishment, it will follow from the mixed theory that in each of the kinds of counterexamples considered (where punishment is not deserved), punishment should not be given. No contradictions will be generated, because the premises are consistent:

1.   Punishment should be inflicted if and only if doing so achieves both a net social gain and gives an offender his just deserts.
2.   A net social gain would be achieved in this case by the infliction of punishment.
3.   It is not the case that punishment would give an offender his just deserts in this case.
4.   Punishment should not be inflicted.

From the first three of these premises, the conclusion is deducible that there should be no punishment. This is also what the fourth premise asserts, so that there is no contradiction when one substitutes the mixed theory for the utilitarian theory of punishment.

There is, nonetheless, another sort of thought experiment that tests whether one truly believes the mixed theory, or is in fact a pure retributivist. Such thought experiments are the kind that fill the editorial pages where outrage is expressed at the lightness of sentence in a particular case, or the lightness of sentencing generally in the courts of some communities. An example is provided by *State v. Chaney* wherein the defendant was tried and convicted of two counts of forcible rape and one count of robbery. The defendant and a companion had picked up the prostitute at a downtown location in Anchorage. After driving the victim around in their car, the defendant and his companion beat her and forcibly raped her four times, also forcing her to perform an act of fellatio with the defendant's companion. During this same period of time, the victim's money was removed from her purse, and she only then was allowed to leave the vehicle after dire threats of reprisals if she attempted to report the incident to the police. Despite this horrendous

series of events, the trial judge imposed the minimum sentence on the defendant for each of the three counts and went out of his way to remark that he (the trial judge) was "sorry that the [military] regulations would not permit keeping [defendant] in the service if he wanted to stay because it seems to me that is a better setup for everybody concerned than putting him in the penitentiary." The trial judge also mentioned that as far as he was concerned, there would be no problem for the defendant to be paroled on the very first day of his sentence, if the parole board should so decide. The sentence was appealed by the state under a special Alaska procedure, and the attorney general urged the Alaska Supreme Court to disapprove the sentence.

The thought experiment such a case begins to pose for us is as follows: Imagine in such a case that after the rape but before sentencing the defendant has gotten into an accident so that his sexual desires are dampened to such an extent that he presents no further danger of rape; if money is also one of his problems, suppose further that he has inherited a great deal of money, so that he no longer needs to rob. Suppose, because of both of these facts, we are reasonably certain that he does not present a danger of either forcible assault, rape, robbery, or related crimes in the future. Since Chaney is (by hypothesis) not dangerous, he does not need to be incapacitated, specially deterred, or reformed. Suppose further that we could successfully pretend to punish Chaney, instead of actually punishing him, and that no one is at all likely to find out. Our pretending to punish him will thus serve the needs of general deterrence and maintain social cohesion, and the cost to the state will be less than if it actually did punish him. Is there anything in the mixed theory of punishment that would urge that Chaney nonetheless should really be punished? I think not, so that if one's conclusion is that Chaney and people like him nonetheless should be punished, one will have to give up the mixed theory of punishment.

The argument structure is again that of a *reductio* and is as follows:

1.   Punishment should be inflicted if and only if doing so both achieves a net social gain and gives an offender his just deserts.
2.   A net social gain would not be achieved in this case by the infliction of punishment.
3.   Punishment should be inflicted.

Again, these three premises generate a contradiction:

4.   Punishment should not be inflicted and punishment should be inflicted.

From the first two premises, it follows that there should be no punishment; this contradicts the third premise that there nonetheless should be punishment.

One again has the choice of giving up one of the three premises of the argument. To give up the third premise is very unappealing to most people; doing so requires that people like Chaney should not be punished at all. Again, the tempting move is to assert that there will be no cases in which one will be sure enough that the danger is removed, or the ends of general deterrence served, that one can never successfully assert the second premise. But as in the earlier case, this is simply to misunderstand the nature of the thought experiment. One only need think it conceivable that such dangers could be removed, or such ends of deterrence served, in order to test one's theory of punishment. And nothing in utilitarianism can guarantee that utility is always maximized by the punishment of the guilty. The only other way to avoid the contradiction is to give up the first premise. Yet this means that one would have to give up the mixed theory of punishment.

The Argument for Retributivism
If one follows the predicted paths through these thought experiments, the end result is that one finds oneself, perhaps surprisingly, to be a retributivist.

We might call this an argument through the back door for retributivism, because the argument does not assert in any positive way the correctness of retributivism. It only asserts that the two theories of punishment truly competitive with retributivism, namely, the pure utilitarian theory and the mixed theory, are each unacceptable to us. That leaves retributivism as the only remaining theory of punishment we can accept.

It has seemed to some theorists that there is a limited amount of positive argument that can be given in favor of a retributivist theory and still have the theory remain truly retributivist. Hugo Bedau has recently reminded us, for example, that the retributivist faces a familiar dilemma:

> Either he appeals to something else—
> some good end—that is accomplished by
> the practice of punishment, in which case
> he is open to the criticism that he has a
> nonretributivist, consequentialist justification
> for the practice of punishment. Or his
> justification does not appeal to something
> else, in which case it is open to the criticism
> that is circular and futile.[1]

In this respect, however, retributivism is no worse off than any other nonutilitarian theories in ethics, each of which seeks to justify an institution or practice not by the good consequences it may engender, but rather by the inherent rightness of the practice. The justification for any such theories is one that appeals to both our particular judgments and our more general principles, in order to show that the theory fits judgments that on reflection we are sure of, and principles that on reflection we are proud of. [...]

---

[1] Hugo Bedau, "Retribution and the Theory of Punishment," *Journal of Philosophy* 75 (1978): 601–20.

DISCUSSION QUESTIONS

1. What is a retributivist theory of punishment? What is the view that Moore calls "revenge utilitarianism," and how does it differ from retributivism? What does Moore mean when he talks about a "forward-looking justification" of punishment?

2. Explain the theory of punishment that Moore calls "the popular form of mixed theory." Explain the two versions of that popular version of a mixed theory.

3. Explain the two counterexamples to the utilitarian theory, scapegoating and preventive detention, that Moore discusses. Do you think that these cases provide a good argument against the utilitarian theory? Why or why not?

4. Explain Moore's modified version of *State v. Chaney*. Why does Moore think that it provides a counterexample to the mixed theory of punishment? Evaluate his argument.

79

Joel Feinberg, selection from *Doing and Deserving* (1970)

In this selection, Feinberg provides a careful analysis and discussion of the concepts of "penalty" and "punishment." On Feinberg, see reading 39 above.

SOURCE

Feinberg, Joel. *Doing and Deserving: Essays in the Theory of Responsibility*, pp. 95–105, 110–13. Princeton, NJ: Princeton University Press, 1970. Reprinted with the permission of Betty Feinberg.

It might well appear to a moral philosopher absorbed in the classical literature of his discipline, or to a moralist sensitive to injustice and suffering, that recent philosophical discussions of the problem of punishment have somehow missed the point of his interest. Recent influential articles[1] have quite sensibly distinguished between questions of definition and justification, between justifying general rules and particular decisions, between moral and legal guilt. So much is all to the good. When these articles go on to *define* "punishment," however, it seems to many that they leave out of their ken altogether the very element that makes punishment theoretically puzzling and morally disquieting. Punishment is defined in effect as the infliction of hard treatment by an authority on a person for his prior failing in some respect (usually an infraction of a rule or command).[2] There may be a

---

[1] See esp. the following: A.G.N. Flew, "The Justification of Punishment," *Philosophy* 29 (1954): 291–307; S.I. Benn, "An Approach to the Problems of Punishment," *Philosophy* 33 (1958): 325–41; and H.L.A. Hart, "Prolegomenon to the Principles of Punishment," *Proceedings of the Aristotelian Society* 60 (1959/60): 1–26.

[2] Hart and Benn both borrow Flew's definition. In Hart's paraphrase (op. cit., 4), punishment "(i) ... must involve pain or other consequences normally considered unpleasant. (ii) It must be for an offense against legal rules. (iii) It must be of an actual or supposed offender for his offense. (iv) It must be intentionally administered by human beings other than the offender. (v) It must be imposed and administered by an authority constituted by a legal system against which the offense is committed."

very general sense of the word "punishment" which is well expressed by this definition; but even if that is so, we can distinguish a narrower, more emphatic sense that slips through its meshes. Imprisonment at hard labor for committing a felony is a clear case of punishment in the emphatic sense. But I think we would be less willing to apply that term to parking tickets, offside penalties, sackings, flunkings, and disqualifications. Examples of the latter sort I propose to call *penalties* (merely), so that I may inquire further what distinguishes punishment, in the strict and narrow sense that interests the moralist, from other kinds of penalties.[1]

One method of answering this question is to focus one's attention on the class of nonpunitive penalties in an effort to discover some clearly identifiable characteristic common to them all, and absent from all punishments, on which the distinction between the two might be grounded. The hypotheses yielded by this approach, however, are not likely to survive close scrutiny. One might conclude, for example, that mere penalties are less severe than punishments, but although this is generally true, it is not necessarily and universally so. Again, we might be tempted to interpret penalties as mere "pricetags" attached to certain types of behavior that are generally undesirable, so that only those with especially strong motivation will be willing to pay the price. In this way deliberate efforts on the part of some Western states to keep roads from urban centers to wilderness areas few in number and poor in quality would be viewed as essentially no different from various parking fines and football penalties. In each case a certain kind of conduct is discouraged without being absolutely prohibited: anyone who desires strongly enough to get to the wilderness (or park overtime, or interfere with a pass) may do so provided he is willing to pay the penalty (price). On this view, penalties are in effect licensing fees, different from other purchased permits in that the price is often paid afterward rather than in advance. Since a similar interpretation of punishments seems implausible, it might be alleged that this is the basis of the distinction between penalties and punishments. However, even though a great number of penalties can no doubt plausibly be treated as retroactive licensing fees, it is hardly possible to view all of them as such. It is certainly not true, for example, of most demotions, firings, and flunking that they are "prices" paid for some already consumed benefit; and even parking fines are sanctions for rules "meant to be taken seriously as ... standard[s] of behavior"[2] and thus are more than mere public parking fees.

Rather than look for a characteristic common and peculiar to the penalties on which to ground the distinction between penalties and punishments, we would be better advised, I think, to turn our attention to the examples of punishments. Both penalties and punishments are authoritative deprivations for failures; but, apart from these common features, penalties have a miscellaneous character, whereas punishments have an important additional characteristic in common. That characteristic, or specific difference, I shall argue, is a certain expressive function: punishment is a conventional device for the expression of attitudes of resentment and indignation, and of judgments of disapproval and reprobation, on the part either of the punishing authority himself or of those "in whose name" the punishment is inflicted. Punishment, in short, has a *symbolic significance* largely missing from other kinds of penalties.

The reprobative symbolism of punishment and its character as "hard treatment," though never separate in reality, must be carefully distinguished for purposes of analysis. Reprobation is itself painful, whether or not it is accompanied by further "hard treatment," and hard treatment, such as fine or imprisonment, because of its conventional symbolism, can itself be reprobatory. Still, we can conceive of ritualistic condemnation unaccompanied by any *further* hard treatment, and of inflictions and deprivations which, because of different symbolic

---

[1] The distinction between punishments and penalties was first called to my attention by Dr. Anita Fritz of the University of Connecticut....

[2] Hart, loc. cit.

conventions, have no reprobative force. It will be my thesis in this essay that (1) both the "hard treatment" aspect of punishment and its reprobative function must be part of the *definition* of legal punishment, and that (2) each of these aspects raises its own kind of question about the *justification* of legal punishment as a general practice. I shall argue that some of the jobs punishment does, and some of the conceptual problems it raises, cannot be intelligibly described unless (1) is true, and that the incoherence of a familiar form of the retributive theory results from failure to appreciate the force of (2).

I.

That the expression of the community's condemnation is an essential ingredient in legal punishment is widely acknowledged by legal writers. Henry M. Hart, for example, gives eloquent emphasis to the point:

> What distinguishes a criminal from a civil sanction and all that distinguishes it, it is ventured, is the judgment of community condemnation which accompanies ... its imposition. As Professor Gardner wrote not long ago, in a distinct but cognate connection:

> The essence of punishment for moral delinquency lies in the criminal conviction itself. One may lose more money on the stock market than in a court-room; a prisoner of war camp may well provide a harsher environment than a state prison; death on the field of battle has the same physical characteristics as death by sentence of law. It is the expression of the community's hatred, fear, or contempt for the convict which alone characterizes physical hardship as punishment.

> If this is what a "criminal" penalty is, then we can say readily enough what a "crime" is.... It is conduct which, if duly shown to have taken place, will incur a formal and

solemn pronouncement of the moral condemnation of the community.... Indeed the condemnation plus the added [unpleasant physical] consequences may well be considered, compendiously, as constituting the punishment.[1]

Professor Hart's compendious definition needs qualification in one respect. The moral condemnation and the "unpleasant consequences" that he rightly identifies as essential elements of punishment are not as distinct and separate as he suggests. It does not always happen that the convicted prisoner is first solemnly condemned and then subjected to unpleasant physical treatment. It would be more accurate in many cases to say that the unpleasant treatment itself expresses the condemnation, and that this expressive aspect of his incarceration is precisely the element by reason of which it is properly characterized as punishment and not mere penalty. The administrator who regretfully suspends the license of a conscientious but accident-prone driver can inflict a deprivation without any scolding, express or implied; but the reckless motorist who is sent to prison for six months is thereby inevitably subject to shame and ignominy—the very walls of his cell condemn him, and his record becomes a stigma.

To say that the very physical treatment itself expresses condemnation is to say simply that certain forms of hard treatment have become the conventional symbols of public reprobation. This is neither more nor less paradoxical than to say that certain words have become conventional vehicles in our language for the expression of certain attitudes, or that champagne is the alcoholic beverage traditionally used in celebration of great events, or that black is the color of mourning. Moreover, particular kinds of punishment are often used to express quite specific attitudes (loosely speaking, this is part of their "meaning"); note the differences, for example, between beheading a nobleman and

---

[1] Henry M. Hart, "The Aims of the Criminal Law," *Law and Contemporary Problems* 23 (1958): II, A, 4.

hanging a yeoman, burning a heretic and hanging a traitor, hanging an enemy soldier and executing him by firing squad.

It is much easier to show that punishment has a symbolic significance than to state exactly what it is that punishment expresses. At its best, in civilized and democratic countries, punishment surely expresses the community's strong *disapproval* of what the criminal did. Indeed, it can be said that punishment expresses the *judgment* (as distinct from any emotion) of the community that what the criminal did was wrong. I think it is fair to say of our community, however, that punishment generally expresses more than judgments of disapproval; it is also a symbolic way of getting back at the criminal, of expressing a kind of vindictive resentment. To any reader who has in fact spent time in a prison, I venture to say, even Professor Gardner's strong terms—"hatred, fear, or contempt for the convict"—will not seem too strong an account of what imprisonment is universally taken to express. Not only does the criminal feel the naked hostility of his guards and the outside world—that would be fierce enough—but that hostility is self-righteous as well. His punishment bears the aspect of legitimized vengefulness. Hence there is much truth in J.F. Stephen's celebrated remark that "The criminal law stands to the passion of revenge in much the same relation as marriage to the sexual appetite."[1]

If we reserve the less dramatic term "resentment" for the various vengeful attitudes and the term "reprobation" for the stern judgment of disapproval, then perhaps we can characterize *condemnation* (or denunciation) as a kind of fusing of resentment and reprobation. That these two elements are generally to be found in legal punishment was well understood by the authors of the *Report of the Royal Commission on Capital Punishment*:

> Discussion of the principle of *retribution* is apt to be confused because the word is not always used in the same sense. Sometimes it

is intended to mean vengeance, sometimes reprobation. In the first sense the idea is that of satisfaction by the State of a wronged individual's desire to be avenged; in the second it is that of the State's *marking its disapproval* of the breaking of its laws by a punishment proportionate to the gravity of the offense.[2]

II.

The relation of the expressive function of punishment to its various central purposes is not always easy to trace. Symbolic public condemnation added to deprivation may help or hinder deterrence, reform, and rehabilitation—the evidence is not clear. On the other hand, there are other functions of punishment, often lost sight of in the preoccupation with deterrence and reform, that presuppose the expressive function and would be difficult or impossible without it.

Authoritative disavowal. Consider the standard international practice of demanding that a nation whose agent has unlawfully violated the complaining nation's rights should punish the offending agent. For example, suppose that an airplane of nation *A* fires on an airplane of nation *B* while the latter is flying over international waters. Very likely high authorities in nation *B* will send a note of protest to their counterparts in nation *A* demanding, among other things, that the transgressive pilot be punished. Punishing the pilot is an emphatic, dramatic, and well-understood way of *condemning* and thereby *disavowing* his act. It tells the world that the pilot had no right to do what he did, that he was on his own in doing it, that his government does not condone that sort of thing. It testifies thereby to government *A*'s recognition of the violated rights of government *B* in the affected area and, therefore, to the wrongfulness of the pilot's act. Failure to punish the pilot tells the world that government *A* does not consider him to have been personally at fault. That in turn is to claim responsibility for the act, which in effect labels that act

---

[1] *General View of the Criminal Law of England* (London: Macmillan & Co., 1863), 99.

[2] (London, 1953), 17–18; my italics.

as an "instrument of deliberate national policy" and hence an act of war. In that case either formal hostilities or humiliating loss of face by one side or the other almost certainly will follow. None of this scenario makes any sense without the clearly understood reprobative symbolism of punishment. In quite parallel ways punishment enables employers to disavow the acts of their employees (though not civil liability for those acts), and fathers the destructive acts of their sons.

Symbolic nonacquiescence: "Speaking in the name of the people." The symbolic function of punishment also explains why even those sophisticated persons who abjure resentment of criminals and look with small favor generally on the penal law are likely to demand that certain kinds of conduct be punished when or if the law lets them go by. In the state of Texas, so-called paramour killings were regarded by the law as not merely mitigated, but completely justifiable. Many humanitarians, I believe, will feel quite spontaneously that a great injustice is done when such killings are left unpunished. The sense of violated justice, moreover, might be distinct and unaccompanied by any frustrated *Schadenfreude* toward the killer, lust for blood or vengeance, or metaphysical concern lest the universe stay "out of joint." The demand for punishment in cases of this sort may instead represent the feeling that paramour killings deserve to be *condemned*, that the law in condoning, even approving of them, speaks for all citizens in expressing a wholly inappropriate attitude toward them. For in effect the law expresses the judgment of the "people of Texas," in whose name it speaks, that the vindictive satisfaction in the mind of a cuckolded husband is a thing of greater value than the very life of his wife's lover. The demand that paramour killings be punished may simply be the demand that this lopsided value judgment be withdrawn and that the state *go on record* against paramour killings and the law *testify to the recognition* that such killings are wrongful. Punishment no doubt would also help deter killers. This too is a desideratum and a closely related one, but it is not to be identified with reprobation; for deterrence might be

achieved by a dozen other techniques, from simple penalties and forfeitures to exhortation and propaganda; but effective public denunciation and, through it, symbolic nonacquiescence in the crime seem virtually to require punishment.

This symbolic function of punishment was given great emphasis by Kant, who, characteristically, proceeded to exaggerate its importance. Even if a desert island community were to disband, Kant argued, its members should first execute the last murderer left in its jails, "for otherwise they might all be regarded as participators in the [unpunished] murder...."[1] This Kantian idea that in failing to punish wicked acts society endorses them and thus becomes *particeps criminis* does seem to reflect, however dimly, something embedded in common sense. A similar notion underlies whatever is intelligible in the widespread notion that all citizens share the responsibility for political atrocities. Insofar as there is a coherent argument behind the extravagant distributions of guilt made by existentialists and other literary figures, it can be reconstructed in some such way as this: to whatever extent a political act is done "in one's name," to that extent one is responsible for it; a citizen can avoid responsibility in advance by explicitly disowning the government as his spokesman, or after the fact through open protest, resistance, and so on; otherwise, by "acquiescing" in what is done in one's name, one incurs the responsibility for it. The root notion here is a kind of "power of attorney" a government has for its citizens.

Vindication of the law. Sometimes the state goes on record through its statutes, in a way that might well please a conscientious citizen in whose name it speaks, but then owing to official evasion and unreliable enforcement gives rise to doubts that the law really means what it says. It is murder in Mississippi, as elsewhere, for a white man intentionally to kill a Negro; but if grand juries refuse to issue indictments or if trial juries refuse to convict, and this fact is clearly recognized by most

---

[1] *The Philosophy of Law*, tr. W. Hastie (Edinburgh: T. & T. Clark, 1887), 198.

citizens, then it is in a purely formal and empty sense indeed that killings of Negroes by whites are illegal in Mississippi. Yet the law stays on the books, to give ever less convincing lip service to a noble moral judgment. A statute honored mainly in the breach begins to lose its character as law, unless, as we say, it is *vindicated* (emphatically reaffirmed); and clearly the way to do this (indeed the only way) is to punish those who violate it.

Similarly, *punitive damages*, so called, are sometimes awarded the plaintiff in a civil action, as a supplement to compensation for his injuries. What more dramatic way of vindicating his violated right can be imagined than to have a court thus forcibly condemn its violation through the symbolic machinery of punishment?

Absolution of others. When something scandalous has occurred and it is clear that the wrongdoer must be one of a small number of suspects, then the state, by punishing one of these parties, thereby relieves the others of suspicion and informally absolves them of blame. Moreover, quite often the absolution of an accuser hangs as much in the balance at a criminal trial as the inculpation of the accused. A good example of this point can be found in James Gould Cozzens's novel *By Love Possessed*. A young girl, after an evening of illicit sexual activity with her boy friend, is found out by her bullying mother, who then insists that she clear her name by bringing criminal charges against the boy. He used physical force, the girl charges; she freely consented, he replies. If the jury finds him guilty of rape, it will by the same token absolve her from (moral) guilt; and her reputation as well as his rides on the outcome. Could not the state do this job without punishment? Perhaps, but when it speaks by punishing, its message is loud and sure of getting across.

[...]

IV.

The distinction between punishments and mere penalties, and the essentially reprobative function of the former, can also help clarify the controversy among writers on the criminal law about the propriety of so-called strict liability offenses—offenses for the conviction of which there need be no proof of "fault" or "culpability" on the part of the accused. If it can be shown that he committed an act proscribed by statute, then he is guilty irrespective of whether he had any justification or excuse for what he did. Perhaps the most familiar examples come from the traffic laws: leaving a car parked beyond the permitted time in a restricted zone is automatically to violate the law, and penalties will be imposed however good the excuse. Many strict liability statutes do not even require an overt act; these proscribe not certain conduct, but certain *results*. Some make mere unconscious possession of contraband, firearms, or narcotics a crime, others the sale of misbranded articles or impure foods. The liability for so-called public welfare offenses may seem especially severe:

> ... with rare exceptions, it became definitely established that *mens rea* is not essential in the public welfare offenses, indeed that even a very high degree of care is irrelevant. Thus a seller of cattle feed was convicted of violating a statute forbidding misrepresentation of the percentage of oil in the product, despite the fact that he had employed a reputable chemist to make the analysis and had even understated the chemist's findings.[1]

The rationale of strict liability in public welfare statutes is that violation of the public interest is more likely to be prevented by unconditional liability than by liability that can be defeated by some kind of excuse; that, even though liability without "fault" is severe, it is one of the known risks incurred by businessmen; and that, besides, the sanctions are *only fines*, hence not really "punitive" in character. On the other hand, strict liability to *imprisonment* (or "punishment proper") "has been held by many to be incompatible with the basic

---

[1] [Jerome] Hall, [*General Principles of Criminal Law*, 2nd edition (Indianapolis: The Bobbs-Merrill Co., 1960)], 329.

requirements of our Anglo-American, and indeed, any civilized jurisprudence."[1] What accounts for this difference in attitude? In both kinds of case, defendants may have sanctions inflicted upon them even though they are acknowledged to be without fault; and the difference cannot be merely that imprisonment is always and necessarily a greater harm than a fine, for this is not always so. Rather, the reason why strict liability to imprisonment (punishment) is so much more repugnant to our sense of justice than is strict liability to fine (penalty) is simply that imprisonment in modern times has taken on the symbolism of public reprobation. In the words of Justice Brandeis, "It is ... imprisonment in a penitentiary, which now renders a crime infamous."[2] We are familiar with the practice of penalizing persons for "offenses" they could not help. It happens every day in football games, business firms, traffic courts, and the like. But there is something very odd and offensive in *punishing* people for admittedly faultless conduct; for not only is it arbitrary and cruel to *condemn* someone for something he did (admittedly) without fault, it is also self-defeating and irrational.

[...]

---

[1] Richard A. Wasserstrom, "Strict Liability in the Criminal Law," *Stanford Law Review* 12 (1960): 730.

[2] *United States v. Moreland*, 258 U.S. 433, 447–448 (1922). Quoted in Hall, op. cit., 327.

DISCUSSION QUESTIONS

1. Explain what Feinberg means when he says that "[p]unishment ... has a *symbolic significance* largely missing from other kinds of penalties."

2. Feinberg claims that the following functions of punishment can only be explained by appeal to the expressive function of punishment: (i) authoritative disavowal, (ii) symbolic nonacquiescence, (iii) vindication of the law, and (iv) absolution of others. Explain and evaluate his claims.

3. Explain how Feinberg explains "why strict liability to imprisonment (punishment) is so much more repugnant to our sense of justice than is strict liability to fine (penalty)." Do you think that he is right? Why or why not?

80

Randy Barnett, "Restitution: A New Paradigm of Criminal Justice" (1977)

Randy E. Barnett (b.1952) is the Carmack Waterhouse Professor of Legal Theory at the Georgetown University Law Center. In the following piece, Barnett argues that our current legal paradigm is in its "death throes."

He argues that our legal system understands the primary focus of the criminal justice system as the meting out of punishment and that we ought to shift the focus away from punishment and onto restitution for victims.

SOURCE

Barnett, Randy. "Restitution: A New Paradigm of Criminal Justice." *Ethics*, Volume 87, No. 4, July 1977. Copyright © 1977 by The University of Chicago Press.

[...]

The problems which the paradigm of punishment is supposed to solve are many and varied. A whole literature on the philosophy of punishment has arisen in an effort to justify or reject the institution of punishment. For our purposes the following definition from the *Encyclopedia of Philosophy* should suffice: "Characteristically punishment is unpleasant. It is inflicted on an offender because of an offense he has committed; it is deliberately imposed, not just the natural consequence of a person's action (like a hangover), and the unpleasantness is *essential* to it, not an accompaniment to some other treatment (like the pain of the dentist's drill)."[1]

Two types of arguments are commonly made in defense of punishment. The first is that punishment is an appropriate means to some justifiable end such as, for example, deterrence of crime. The second type of argument is that punishment is justified as an end in itself. On this view, whatever ill effects it might engender, punishment for its own sake is good.

The first type of argument might be called the *political* justification of punishment, for the end which justifies its use is one which a political order is presumably dedicated to serve: the maintenance of peaceful interactions between individuals and groups in a society. There are at least three ways

---

[1] Stanley I. Benn, "Punishment," in Paul Edwards (ed.), *The Encyclopedia of Philosophy* (New York: Macmillan Publishing Co., 1967), 7:29 (emphasis added).

that deliberate infliction of harm on an offender is said to be politically justified.

1. One motive for punishment, especially capital punishment and imprisonment, is the "intention to deprive offenders of the power of doing future mischief."[1] Although it is true that an offender cannot continue to harm society while incarcerated, a strategy of punishment based on disablement has several drawbacks.

Imprisonment is enormously expensive. This means that a double burden is placed on the innocent who must suffer the crime and, in addition, pay through taxation for the support of the offender and his family if they are forced onto welfare. Also, any benefit of imprisonment is temporary; eventually, most offenders will be released. If their outlook has not improved—and especially if it has worsened—the benefits of incarceration are obviously limited. Finally, when disablement is permanent, as with capital punishment or psychosurgery, it is this very permanence, in light of the possibility of error, which is frightening. For these reasons, "where disablement enters as an element into penal theories, it occupies, as a rule, a subordinate place and is looked upon as an object subsidiary to some other end which is regarded as paramount...."[2]

2. Rehabilitation of a criminal means a change in his mental *habitus* so that he will not offend again. It is unclear whether the so-called treatment model which views criminals as a doctor would view a patient is truly a "retributive" concept. Certainly it does not conform to the above definition characterizing punishment as deliberately and essentially unpleasant. It is an open question whether any end justifies the intentional, forceful manipulation of an individual's thought processes by anyone, much less the state. To say that an otherwise just system has incidentally rehabilitative effects which may be desirable is one thing, but it is quite another to argue that these effects themselves justify the system. The horrors to which such reasoning can lead are obvious from abundant examples in history and contemporary society.[3]

Rehabilitation as a reaction against the punishment paradigm will be considered below, but one aspect is particularly relevant to punishment as defined here. On this view, the visiting of unpleasantness itself will cause the offender to see the error of his ways; by having "justice" done him, the criminal will come to appreciate his error and will change his moral outlook. This end, best labeled "reformation," is speculative at best and counterfactual at worst. On the contrary, "it has been observed that, as a rule ... ruthless punishments, far from mollifying men's ways, corrupt them and stir them to violence."[4]

3. The final justification to be treated here—deterrence—actually has two aspects. The first is the deterrent effect that past demonstrations of punishment have on the future conduct of others; the second is the effect that threats of future punishment have on the conduct of others. The distinction assumes importance when some advocates argue that future threats lose their deterrent effect when there is a lack of past demonstrations. Past punishment, then, serves as an educational tool. It is a substitute for or reinforcement of threats of future punishment.

As with the goals mentioned above, the empirical question of whether punishment has this effect is a disputed one.[5] I shall not attempt to resolve this question here, but will assume *arguendo* that punishment even as presently administered has some deterrent effect. It is the moral question which is disturbing. Can an argument from deterrence alone "justify" in any sense the infliction of pain on a criminal? It is particularly disquieting that the actual levying of punishment is done not for the

[1] Heinrich Oppenheimer, *The Rationale of Punishment* (London: University of London Press, 1913), p. 255.
[2] Ibid.

[3] See Thomas Szasz, *Law, Liberty, and Psychiatry* (New York: Macmillan Co., 1963).

[4] Giorgio del Vecchio, "The Stuggle against Crime," in H.B. Acton (ed.), *The Philosophy of Punishment* (London: Macmillan Co., 1969), p. 199.

[5] See, e.g., Samuel Yochlson and Stanton E. Samenow, *The Criminal Personality*, vol. 1, *A Profile for Change* (New York: Jason Aronson, Inc., 1976), pp. 411–16.

criminal himself, but for the educational impact it will have on the community. The criminal act becomes the occasion of, but not the reason for, the punishment. In this way, the actual crime becomes little more than an excuse for punishing.

Surely this distorts the proper functioning of the judicial process. For if deterrence is the end it is unimportant whether the individual actually committed the crime. Since the public's perception of guilt is the prerequisite of the deterrent effect, all that is required for deterrence is that the individual is "proved" to have committed the crime. The actual occurrence would have no relevance except insofar as a truly guilty person is easier to prove guilty. The judicial process becomes, not a truth-seeking device, but solely a means to legitimate the use of force. To treat criminals as means to the ends of others in this way raises serious moral problems. This is not to argue that men may never use others as means but rather to question the use of force against the individual because of the effect such use will have on others. It was this that concerned del Vecchio when he stated that "the human person always bears in himself something sacred, and it is therefore not permissible to treat him merely as a means towards an end outside of himself."[1]

Finally, deterrence as the ultimate justification of punishment cannot rationally limit its use. It "provides *no* guidance until we're told *how much* commission of it is to be deterred."[2] Since there are always some who commit crimes, one can always argue for more punishment. Robert Nozick points out that there must be criteria by which one decides how much deterrence may be inflicted.[3] One is forced therefore to employ "higher" principles to evaluate the legitimacy of punishment.

It is not my thesis that deterrence, reformation, and disablement are undesirable goals. On the contrary, any criminal justice system should be critically examined to see if it is having these and other beneficial effects. The view advanced here is simply that these utilitarian benefits must be incidental to a just system; they cannot, alone or in combination, justify a criminal justice system. Something more is needed. There is another more antiquated strain of punishment theory which seeks to address this problem. The *moral* justifications of punishment view punishment as an end in itself. This approach has taken many forms.[4] On this view, whatever ill or beneficial results it might have, punishment of lawbreakers is good for its own sake. This proposition can be analyzed on several levels.

… Even assuming that it would be good if, in the nature of things, the wicked got their "come-uppance," what behavior does this moral fact justify? Does it justify the victim authoring the punishment of his offender? Does it justify the same action by the victim's family, his friends, his neighbors, the state? If so what punishment should be imposed and who should decide?

It might be argued that the natural punishment for the violation of natural rights is the deserved hatred and scorn of the community, the resultant ostracism, and the existential hell of *being* an evil person. The question then is not whether we have the right to inflict some "harm" or unpleasantness on a morally contemptible person—surely, we do; the question is not whether such a punishment is "good"—arguably, it is. The issue is whether the "virtue of some punishment" justifies the *forceful* imposition of unpleasantness on a *rights violator* as distinguished from the morally imperfect. Any *moral* theory of punishment must recognize and deal with this distinction. Finally, it must be established that the state is the legitimate author of punishment, a proposition which further assumes the moral and legal legitimacy of the state. To raise these issues is not to resolve them, but it would seem that the burden of proof is on those seeking to justify the use of force against the individual. Suffice it to say that I am skeptical of finding any theory which justifies the deliberate, forceful

---

[1] Del Vecchio, "The Struggle against Crime," p. 199.

[2] Robert Nozick, *Anarchy, State, and Utopia* (New York: Basic Books, 1974), p. 61.

[3] Ibid., pp. 59–63.

[4] For a concise summary, see Oppenheimer, *The Rationale for Punishment*, p. 31.

imposition of punishment within or without a system of criminal justice.

The final consideration in dealing with punishment as an end in itself is the possibility that the current crisis in the criminal justice system is in fact a crisis of the paradigm of punishment. While this, if true, does not resolve the philosophical issues, it does cast doubt on the punishment paradigm's vitality as the motive force behind a system of criminal justice. Many advocates of punishment argue that its apparent practical failings exist because we are not punishing enough. All that is needed, they say, is a crackdown on criminals and those victims and witnesses who shun participation in the criminal justice system; the only problem with the paradigm of punishment is that we are not following it.[1] This response fails to consider *why* the system doggedly refuses to punish to the degree required to yield beneficial results and instead punishes in such a way as to yield harmful results. The answer may be that the paradigm of punishment is in eclipse, that the public lacks the requisite will to apply it in anything but the prevailing way.

[...]

[If] the paradigm of punishment is in a "crisis period" it is as much because of its practical drawbacks as the uncertainty of its moral status. The infliction of suffering on a criminal tends to cause a general feeling of sympathy for him. There is no rational connection between a term of imprisonment and the harm caused the victim. Since the prison term is supposed to be unpleasant, at least a part of the public comes to see the criminal as a victim, and the lack of rationality also causes the offender to feel victimized. This reaction is magnified by the knowledge that most crimes go unpunished and that even if the offender is caught the judicial process is long, arduous, and far removed from the criminal act. While this is obvious to most, it is perhaps less obvious that the punishment paradigm is largely at fault. The slow, ponderous nature of our system of justice is largely due to a fear of an unjust infliction

of punishment on the innocent (or even the guilty). The more awful the sanction, the more elaborate need be the safeguards. The more the system is perceived as arbitrary and unfair, the more incentive there is for defendants and their counsel to thwart the truth-finding process. Acquittal becomes desirable at all costs. As the punitive aspect of a sanction is diminished, so too would be the perceived need for procedural protections.

A system of punishment, furthermore, offers no incentive for the victim to involve himself in the criminal justice process other than to satisfy his feelings of duty or revenge. The victim stands to gain little if at all by the conviction and punishment of the person who caused his loss. This is true even of those systems discussed below which dispense state compensation based on the victim's need. The system of justice itself imposes uncompensated costs by requiring a further loss of time and money by the victim and witnesses and by increasing the perceived risk of retaliation.

Finally, punishment which seeks to change an offender's moral outlook, or at least to scare him, can do nothing to provide him with the skills needed to survive in the outside world. In prison, he learns the advanced state of the criminal arts and vows not to repeat the mistake that led to his capture. The convict emerges better trained and highly motivated to continue a criminal career.

[...]

Outline of a New Paradigm

The idea of restitution is actually quite simple. It views crime as an offense by one individual against the rights of another. The victim has suffered a loss. Justice consists of the culpable offender making good the loss he has caused. It calls for a complete refocusing of our image of crime. Kuhn would call it a "shift of world-view." Where we once saw an offense against society, we now see an offense against an individual victim. In a way, it is a common sense view of crime. *The armed robber did not rob society; he robbed the victim.* His debt, therefore, is not to society; it is to the victim. There

---

[1] See, e.g., "Crime: A Case for More Punishment," *Business Week*, September 15, 1975: 92–97.

are really two types of restitution proposals: a system of "punitive" restitution and a "pure" restitutional system.

1. Punitive restitution. "Since rehabilitation was admitted to the aims of penal law two centuries ago, the number of penological aims has remained virtually constant. Restitution is waiting to come in."[1] Given this view, restitution should merely be added to the paradigm of punishment. Stephen Schafer outlines the proposal: "[Punitive] restitution, like punishment, must always be the subject of judicial consideration. Without exception it must be carried out by personal performance by the wrong-doer, and should even then be equally burdensome and just for all criminals, irrespective of their means, whether they be millionaires or labourers."[2]

There are many ways by which such a goal might be reached. The offender might be forced to compensate the victim by his own work, either in prison or out. If it came out of his pocket or from the sale of his property this would compensate the victim, but it would not be sufficiently unpleasant for the offender. Another proposal would be that the fines be proportionate to the earning power of the criminal. Thus, "A poor man would pay in days of work, a rich man by an equal number of days' income or salary."[3] Herbert Spencer made a proposal along similar lines in his excellent "Prison-Ethics," which is well worth examining.[4] Murray N. Rothbard and others have proposed a system of "double payments" in cases of criminal behavior.[5] While closer to pure restitution than other proposals, the "double damages" concept preserves a punitive aspect.

Punitive restitution is an attempt to gain the benefits of pure restitution, which will be considered shortly, while retaining the perceived advantages of the paradigm of punishment. Thus, the prisoner is still "sentenced" to some unpleasantness—prison labor or loss of x number of days' income. That the intention is to preserve the "hurt" is indicated by the hesitation to accept an out-of-pocket payment or sale of assets. This is considered too "easy" for the criminal and takes none of his time. The amount of payment is determined not by the *actual harm* but by the *ability of the offender to pay*. Of course, by retaining the paradigm of punishment this proposal involves many of the problems we raised earlier. In this sense it can be considered another attempt to salvage the old paradigm.

2. Pure restitution. "Recompense or restitution is scarcely a punishment as long as it is merely a matter of returning stolen goods or money.... The point is not that the offender deserves to suffer; it is rather that the offended party desires compensation."[6] This represents the complete overthrow of the paradigm of punishment. No longer would the deterrence, reformation, disablement, or rehabilitation of the criminal be the guiding principle of the judicial system. The attainment of these goals would be incidental to, and as a result of, reparations paid to the victim. No longer would the criminal deliberately be made to suffer for his mistake. Making good that mistake is all that would be required. What follows is a possible scenario of such a system.

When a crime occurred and a suspect was apprehended, a trial court would attempt to determine his guilt or innocence. If found guilty, the criminal would be sentenced to make restitution to the victim. If a criminal is able to make restitution immediately, he may do so. This would discharge his liability. If he were unable to make restitution, but were found by the court to be trustworthy, he would be permitted to remain at his job (or find a new one) while paying restitution out of his future wages. This would entail a legal claim against future

[1] Gerhard O.W. Mueller, "Compensation for Victims of Crime: Thought before Action," *Minnesota Law Review* 50 (1965): 221.

[2] Steven Schafer, *Compensation and Restitution to Victims of Crime*, 2nd ed., enl. (Montclair, NJ: Patterson Smith Publishing Corp., 1970), p. 127.

[3] Ibid.

[4] Herbert Spencer, "Prison-Ethics," in *Essays: Scientific, Political and Speculative* (New York: D. Appleton & Co., 1907), 3: 152–91.

[5] Murray N. Rothbard, *Libertarian Forum* 14.1 (January 1972): 7–8.

[6] Walter Kaufman, *Without Guilt and Justice* (New York: Peter H. Wyden, Inc., 1973), esp. chap. 2.

wages. Failure to pay could result in garnishment or a new type of confinement.

If it is found that the criminal is not trustworthy, or that he is unable to gain employment, he would be confined to an employment project.[1] This would be an industrial enterprise, preferably run by a private concern, which would produce actual goods or services. The level of security at each employment project would vary according to the behavior of the offenders. Since the costs would be lower, inmates at a lower-security project would receive higher wages. There is no reason why many workers could not be permitted to live with their families inside or outside the facility, depending, again, on the trustworthiness of the offender. Room and board would be deducted from the wages first, then a certain amount for restitution. Anything over that amount the worker could keep or apply toward further restitution, thus hastening his release. If a worker refused to work, he would be unable to pay for his maintenance, and therefore would not in principle be entitled to it. If he did not make restitution he could not be released. The exact arrangement which would best provide for high productivity, minimal security, and maximum incentive to work and repay the victim cannot be determined in advance. Experience is bound to yield some plans superior to others....

While this might be the basic system, all sorts of refinements are conceivable, and certainly many more will be invented as needs arise. A few examples might be illuminating. With such a system of repayment, victim *crime insurance* would be more economically feasible than at present and highly desirable. The cost of awards would be offset by the insurance company's right to restitution in place of the victim (right of subrogation). The insurance company would be better suited to

supervise the offender and mark his progress than would the victim. To obtain an earlier recovery, it could be expected to innovate so as to enable the worker to repay more quickly (and, as a result, be released that much sooner). The insurance companies might even underwrite the employment projects themselves as well as related industries which would employ the skilled worker after his release. Any successful effort on their part to reduce crime and recidivism would result in fewer claims and lower premiums. The benefit of this insurance scheme for the victim is immediate compensation, conditional on the victim's continued cooperation with the authorities for the arrest and conviction of the suspect. In addition, the centralization of victim claims would, arguably, lead to efficiencies which would permit the pooling of small claims against a common offender.

Another highly useful refinement would be *direct arbitration* between victim and criminal. This would serve as a sort of healthy substitute for plea bargaining. By allowing the guilty criminal to negotiate a reduced payment in return for a guilty plea, the victim (or his insurance company) would be saved the risk of an adverse finding at trial and any possible additional expense that might result. This would also allow an indigent criminal to substitute personal services for monetary payments if all parties agreed.

Arbitration is argued for by John M. Greacen, deputy director of the National Institute for Law Enforcement and Criminal Justice. He sees the possible advantages of such reform as the

> ... development of more creative dispositions for most criminal cases; for criminal victims the increased use of restitution, the knowledge that their interests were considered in the criminal process; and an increased satisfaction with the outcome; increased awareness in the part of the offender that his crime was committed against another human being, and not against society in general; increased possibility that the criminal process will

---

[1] Such a plan (with some significant differences) has been suggested by Kathleen J. Smith in *A Cure for Crime: The Case for the Self-determinate Prison Sentence* (London: Gerald, Duckworth & Co., 1965), pp. 13–29; see also Morris and Linda Tannehill, *The Market for Liberty* (Lansing, MI: Privately printed, 1970), pp. 44–108.

cause the offender to acknowledge responsibility for his acts.[1]

Greacen notes several places where such a system has been tried with great success, most notably Tucson, Arizona, and Columbus, Ohio.[2]

Something analogous to the medieval Irish system of *sureties* might be employed as well.[3] Such a system would allow a concerned person, group, or company to make restitution (provided the offender agrees to this). The worker might then be released in the custody of the surety. If the surety had made restitution, the offender would owe restitution to the surety who might enforce the whole claim or show mercy. Of course, the more violent and unreliable the offender, the more serious and costly the offense, the less likely it would be that anyone would take the risk. But for first offenders, good workers, or others that charitable interests found deserving (or perhaps unjustly convicted) this would provide an avenue of respite.

Restitution and Rights

These three possible refinements clearly illustrate the flexibility of a restitutional system. It may be less apparent that this flexibility is *inherent* to the restitutional paradigm. Restitution recognizes rights in the victim, and this is a principal source of its strength. The nature and limit of the victim's right to restitution at the same time defines the nature and limit of the criminal liability. In this way, the aggressive action of the criminal creates a *debt* to the victim. The recognition of rights and obligations makes possible many innovative arrangements. Subrogation, arbitration, and suretyship are three examples mentioned above. They are possible because this right to compensation is considered the property of the victim and can therefore be delegated, assigned, inherited, or bestowed. One could determine in advance who would acquire the right to any restitution which he himself might be unable to collect.

The natural owner of an unenforced death claim would be an insurance company that had insured the deceased. The suggestion has been made that a person might thus increase his personal safety by insuring with a company well known for tracking down those who injure its policy holders. In fact, the partial purpose of some insurance schemes might be to provide the funds with which to track down the malefactor. The insurance company, having paid the beneficiaries, would "stand in their shoes." It would remain possible, of course, to simply assign or devise the right directly to the beneficiaries, but this would put the burden of enforcement on persons likely to be unsuited to the task.

If one accepts the Lockean trichotomy of property ownership,[4] that is, acquiring property via exchange, gifts, and *homesteading* (mixing one's labor with previously unowned land or objects), the possibility arises that upon a person's wrongful death, in the absence of any heirs or assignees, his right to compensation becomes unowned property. The right could then be claimed (homesteaded) by anyone willing to go to the trouble of catching and prosecuting the criminal. Firms might specialize in this sort of activity, or large insurance

---

[1] John M. Greacen, "Arbitration: A Tool for Criminal Cases?" *Barrister* (Winter 1975): 53; see also [Burt] Galaway and [Joe] Hudson, [*Considering the Victim: Readings in Restitution and Victim Compensation* (Springfield, IL: Charles C. Thomas, 1975)], pp. 352–55; "Conclusions and Recommendations, International Study Institute on Victimology, Bellagio, Italy, July 1–12, 1975," *Victimology* 1 (1976): 150–51; Ronald Goldfarb, *Jails: The Ultimate Ghetto* (Garden City, NY: Anchor Press/ Doubleday, 1976), p. 480.

[2] Greacen, "Arbitration," p. 53.

[3] For a description of the Irish system, see Joseph R. Peden, "Property Rights in Medieval Ireland: Celtic Law versus Church and State" (paper presented at the Symposium on the Origins and Development of Property Rights, University of San Francisco, January 1973); for a theoretical discussion of a similar proposal, see Spencer, "Prison-Ethics," pp. 182–86.

[4] For a brief explanation of this concept and several of its applications, see Murray N. Rothbard, "Justice and Property Rights," in Samuel L. Blumenfeld (ed.), *Property in a Humane Economy* (La Salle, IL: Open Court Publishing Co., 1974), pp. 101–22.

companies might make the effort as a kind of "loss leader" for public relations purposes.

This does, however, lead to a potentially serious problem with the restitutional paradigm: what exactly constitutes "restitution"? What is the *standard* by which compensation is to be made? Earlier we asserted that any such problem facing the restitutional paradigm faces civil damage suits as well. The method by which this problem is dealt with in civil cases could be applied to restitution cases. But while this is certainly true, it may be that this problem has not been adequately handled in civil damage suits either.

Restitution in cases of crimes against property is a manageable problem. Modern contract and tort doctrines of restitution are adequate. The difficulty lies in cases of personal injury or death. How can you put a price on life or limb, pain or suffering? Is not any attempt to do so of necessity arbitrary? It must be admitted that a fully satisfactory solution to this problem is lacking, but it should also be stressed that this dilemma, though serious, has little impact on the bulk of our case in favor of a restitutional paradigm. It is possible that no paradigm of criminal justice can solve every problem, yet the restitutional approach remains far superior to the paradigm of punishment or any other conceivable rival.

This difficulty arises because certain property is unique and irreplaceable. As a result, it is impossible to approximate a "market" or "exchange" value expressed in monetary terms. Just as there is no rational relationship between a wrongfully taken life and ten years in prison, there is little relationship between that same life and $20,000. Still, the nature of this possibly insoluble puzzle reveals a restitutional approach theoretically superior to punishment. For it must be acknowledged that a real, tangible loss *has* occurred. The problem is only one of incommensurability. Restitution provides *some* tangible, albeit inadequate, compensation for personal injury. Punishment provides none at all.

It might be objected that to establish some "pay scale" for personal injury is not only somewhat arbitrary but also a disguised reimplementation of punishment. Unable to accept the inevitable consequences of restitutional punishment, the argument continues, I have retreated to a pseudorestitutional award. Such a criticism is unfair. The true test in this instance is one of primacy of intentions. Is the purpose of a system to compensate victims for their losses (and perhaps, as a consequence, punish the criminals), or is its purpose to punish the criminals (and perhaps, as a consequence, compensate the victims for their losses)? The true ends of a criminal justice system will determine its nature. In short, arbitrariness *alone* does not imply a retributive motive. And while arbitrariness remains to some extent a problem for the restitutional paradigm, it is less of a problem for restitution than for punishment, since compensation has *some* rational relationship to damages and costs.

Advantages of a Restitutional System

1. The first and most obvious advantage is the assistance provided to victims of crime. They may have suffered an emotional, physical, or financial loss. Restitution would not change the fact that a possibly traumatic crime has occurred (just as the award of damages does not undo tortuous conduct). Restitution, however, would make the resulting loss easier to bear for both victims and their families. At the same time, restitution would avoid a major pitfall of victim compensation/welfare plans: Since it is the criminal who must pay, the possibility of collusion between victim and criminal to collect "damages" from the state would be all but eliminated.

2. The possibility of receiving compensation would encourage victims to report crimes and to appear at trial. This is particularly true if there were a crime insurance scheme which contractually committed the policyholder to testify as a condition for payment, thus rendering unnecessary oppressive and potentially tyrannical subpoenas and contempt citations. Even the actual reporting of the crime to police is likely to be a prerequisite for compensation. Such a requirement in auto theft insurance policies has made car thefts the most fully

reported crime in the United States. Furthermore, insurance companies which paid the claim would have a strong incentive to see that the criminal was apprehended and convicted. Their pressure and assistance would make the proper functioning of law enforcement officials all the more likely.

3. Psychologist Albert Eglash has long argued that restitution would aid in the rehabilitation of criminals. "Restitution is something an inmate does, not something done for or to him…. Being reparative, restitution can alleviate guilt and anxiety, which can otherwise precipitate further offenses."[1] Restitution, says Eglash, is an active effortful role on the part of the offender. It is socially constructive, thereby contributing to the offender's self-esteem. It is related to the offense and may thereby redirect the thoughts which motivated the offense. It is reparative, restorative, and may actually leave the situation better than it was before the crime, both for the criminal and victim.[2]

4. This is a genuinely "self-determinative" sentence.[3] The worker would know that the length of his confinement was in his own hands. The harder he worked, the faster he would make restitution. He would be the master of his fate and would have to face that responsibility. This would encourage useful, productive activity and instill a conception of reward for good behavior and hard work. Compare this with the current probationary system and "indeterminate sentencing" where the decision for release is made by the prison bureaucracy, based only (if fairly administered) on "good behavior"; that is, passive acquiescence to prison discipline. Also, the fact that the worker would be acquiring *marketable* skills rather than more skillful methods of crime should help to reduce the shocking rate of recidivism.

5. The savings to taxpayers would be enormous. No longer would the innocent taxpayer pay for the apprehension and internment of the guilty. The cost of arrest, trial, and internment would be borne by the criminal himself. In addition, since now-idle inmates would become productive workers (able, perhaps, to support their families), the entire economy would benefit from the increase in overall production.

6. Crime would no longer pay. Criminals, particularly shrewd white-collar criminals, would know that they could not dispose of the proceeds of their crime and, if caught, simply serve time. They would have to make full restitution plus enforcement and legal costs, thereby greatly increasing the incentive to prosecute. While this would not eliminate such crime it would make it rougher on certain types of criminals, like bank and corporation officials, who harm many by their acts with a virtual assurance of lenient legal sanctions.[4] It might also encourage such criminals to keep the money around for a while so that, if caught, they could repay more easily. This would make a full recovery more likely.

Objections to Restitution

1. Practical criticisms of restitution. It might be objected that "crimes disturb and offend not only those who are directly their victim, but also the whole social order."[5] Because of this, society, that is, individuals other than the victim, deserves some satisfaction from the offender. Restitution, it is argued, will not satisfy the lust for revenge felt by the victim or the "community's sense of justice." This criticism appears to be overdrawn. Today most members of the community are mere spectators of the criminal justice system, and this is largely true even of

[1] Albert Eglash, "Creative Restitution: Some Suggestions for Prison Rehabilitation Programs," *American Journal of Correction* 40 (November–December 1958): 20.

[2] Ibid.; see also Eglash's "Creative Restitution: A Broader Meaning for an Old Term," *Journal of Criminal Law and Criminology* 48 (1958): 619–22; Burt Galaway and Joe Hudson, "Restitution and Rehabilitation—Some Central Issues," *Crime and Delinquency* 18 (1972): 403–10.

[3] Smith, *A Cure for Crime*, pp. 13–29.

[4] This point is also made by Minocher Jehangirji Sethna in his paper, "Treatment and Atonement for Crime," in [Emilo C. Viano, ed.,] *Victims and Society* [(Washington, DC: Visage Press, 1976)], p. 538.

[5] Del Vecchio, "The Struggle against Crime," p. 198.

the victim.[1] One major reform being urged presently is more victim involvement in the criminal justice process.[2] The restitution proposal would necessitate this involvement. And while the public generally takes the view that officials should be tougher on criminals, with "tougher" taken by nearly everyone to mean more severe in punishing, one must view this "social fact" in light of the lack of a known alternative. The real test of public sympathies would be to see which sanction people would choose: incarceration of the criminal for a given number of years or the criminal's being compelled to make restitution to the victim. While the public's choice is not clearly predictable, neither can it be assumed that it would reject restitution…

This brings us to a second practical objection: that monetary sanctions are insufficient deterrents to crime. Again, this is something to be discovered, not something to be assumed. There are a number of reasons to believe that our *current* system of punishment does not adequately deter, and for the reasons discussed earlier an increase in the level of punishment is unlikely. In fact, many have argued that the deterrent value of sanctions has less to do with *severity* than with *certainty*,[3] and the preceding considerations indicate that law enforcement would be more certain under a restitutional system. In the final analysis, however, it is irrelevant to argue that more crimes may be committed if

our proposal leaves the victim better off. It must be remembered: *Our goal is not the suppression of crime; it is doing justice to victims.*

A practical consideration which merits considerable future attention is the feasibility of the employment project proposal. A number of questions can be raised. At first blush, it seems naively optimistic to suppose that offenders will be able or willing to work at all, much less earn their keep and pay reparations as well. On the contrary, this argument continues, individuals turn to crime precisely because they lack the skills which the restitutional plan assumes they have. Even if these workers have the skills, but refuse to work, what could be done? Would not the use of force to compel compliance be tantamount to slavery? This criticism results in part from my attempt to sketch an "ideal" restitution system; that is, I have attempted to outline the type toward which every criminal justice system governed by the restitution paradigm should strive. This is not to say that every aspect of the hypothetical system would, upon implementation, function smoothly. Rather, such a system could only operate ideally once the paradigm had been fully accepted and substantially articulated.

With this in mind, one can advance several responses. First, the problem as usually posed assumes the offender to be highly irrational and possibly mentally unbalanced. There is no denying that some segment of the criminal population fits the former description. What this approach neglects, however, is the possibility that many criminals are making rational choices within an irrational and unjust political system. Specifically I refer to the myriad laws and regulations which make it difficult for the unskilled or persons of transitory outlook to find legal employment. I refer also to the laws which deny legality to the types of services which are in particular demand in economically impoverished communities. Is it "irrational" to choose to steal or rob when one is virtually foreclosed from the legal opportunity to do otherwise? Another possibility is that the criminal chooses crime not because of foreclosure, but because he enjoys and obtains satisfaction from

[1] William F. McDonald, "Towards a Bicentennial Revolution in Criminal Justice: The Return of the Victim," *American Criminal Law Review* 13 (1976): 659; see also his paper, "Notes on the Victim's Role in the Prosecutional and Dispositional Stages of the Criminal Justice Process" (paper presented at the Second International Symposium on Victimology, Boston, September 1976); Jack M. Kress, "The Role of the Victim at Sentencing" (paper presented at the Second International Symposium on Victimology, Boston, September 1976).

[2] McDonald, "Towards a Bicentennial Revolution," pp. 669–73; Kress, "The Role of the Victim," pp. 11–15. Kress specifically analyzes restitution as a means for achieving victim involvement.

[3] [Samuel] Yochelson and [Stanton E.] Samenow [*The Criminal Personality*, vol. 1, *A Profile for Change* (New York: Jason Aronson, Inc., 1996)], pp. 453–57.

a criminal way of life. Though morally repugnant, this is hardly irrational.

Furthermore, it no longer can be denied that contact with the current criminal justice system is itself especially damaging among juveniles.[1] The offenders who are hopelessly committed to criminal behavior are not usually the newcomers to crime but those who have had repeated exposure to the penal system.... While a restitutionary system might not change these hard-core offenders, it could, by the early implementation of sanctions perceived by the criminal to be just, break the vicious circle which in large part accounts for their existence.

Finally, if offenders could not or would not make restitution, then the logical and just result of their refusal would be confinement until they could or would. Such an outcome would be entirely in their hands. While this "solution" does not suggest who should justly pay for this confinement, the problem is not unique to a restitutionary system. In this and other areas of possible difficulty we must seek guidance from existing pilot programs as well as from the burgeoning research in this area and in victimology in general.

2. Distributionary criticisms of restitution. There remains one criticism of restitution which is the most obvious and the most difficult with which to deal. Simply stated, it takes the following form: "Doesn't this mean that rich people will be able to commit crimes with impunity if they can afford it? Isn't this unfair?" The *practical* aspect of this objection is that whatever deterrent effect restitution payments may have, they will be less for those most able to pay. The *moral* aspect is that whatever retributive or penal effect restitution payments may have they will be less for those who are well off. Some concept of equality of justice underlies both considerations.

Critics of restitution fail to realize that the "cost" of crime will be quite high. In addition to compensation for pain and suffering, the criminal must pay for the cost of his apprehension, the cost of the trial, and the legal expenditures of *both* sides. This should make even an unscrupulous wealthy person think twice about committing a crime. The response to this is that we cannot have it both ways. If the fines would be high enough to bother the rich, then they would be so high that a project worker would have no chance of earning that much and would, therefore, have no incentive to work at all. If, on the other hand, you lower the price of crime by ignoring all its costs, you fail to deter the rich or fully compensate the victim.

This is where the option of arbitration and victim crime insurance becomes of practical importance. If the victim is uninsured, he is unlikely to recover for all costs of a very severe crime from a poor, unskilled criminal, since even in an employment project the criminal might be unable to earn enough. If he had no hope of earning his release, he would have little incentive to work very hard beyond paying for his own maintenance. The victim would end up with less than if he had "settled" the case for the lesser amount which a project worker could reasonably be expected to earn. If, however, the victim had full-coverage criminal insurance, he would recover his damages in full, and the insurance company would absorb any disparity between full compensation and maximal employment project worker's output. This cost would be reflected in premium prices, enabling the insurance company which settled cases at an amount which increased the recovery from the criminal to offer the lowest rates. Eventually a "maximum" feasible fine for project workers would be determined based on these considerations. The "rich," on the other hand, would naturally have to pay in full. This arrangement would solve the practical problem, but it should not be thought of as an imperative of the restitutional paradigm.

The same procedure of varying the payments according to ability to pay would answer the moral considerations as well (that the rich are not hurt enough) and this is the prime motive behind *punitive* restitution proposals. However, we reject the moral consideration outright. The paradigm of restitution calls not for the (equal) hurting of

---

[1] See, e.g., Edwin M. Schur, *Radical Noninterventionism, Rethinking the Deliquency Problem* (Englewood Cliffs, NJ: Prentice-Hall, Inc., 1973).

criminals, but for restitution to victims. Any appeal to "inadequate suffering" is a reversion to the paradigm of punishment, and by varying the sanction for crimes of the same magnitude according to the economic status of the offender it reveals its own inequity. *Equality of justice means equal treatment of victims.* It should not matter to the victim if his attacker was rich or poor. His plight is the same regardless. Any reduction of criminal liability because of reduced earning power would be for practical, not moral, reasons.

Equality of justice derives from the fact that the rights of men should be equally enforced and respected. Restitution recognizes a victim's right to compensation for damages from the party responsible. Equality of justice, therefore, calls for equal enforcement of each victim's right to restitution. *Even if necessary or expedient, any lessening of payment to the victim because of the qualities of the criminal is a violation of that victim's rights and an inequality of justice.* Any such expedient settlement is only a recognition that an imperfect world may make possible only imperfect justice. As a practical matter, a restitutional standard gives victims an enormous incentive to pursue wealthy criminals since they can afford quick, full compensation. Contrast this with the present system where the preference given the wealthy is so prevalent that most victims simply assume that nothing will be done.

The paradigm of restitution, to reiterate, is neither a panacea for crime nor a blueprint for utopia. Panaceas and utopias are not for humankind.

We must live in a less than perfect world with less than perfect people. Restitution opens the possibility of an improved and more just society. The old paradigm of punishment, even reformed, simply cannot offer this promise.

[...]

DISCUSSION QUESTIONS

1. Explain the two types of argument that Barnett claims have been made in defense of punishment. Explain and evaluate his responses to these two types of arguments.

2. Explain how restitution differs from punishment, and how punitive restitution differs from pure restitution. Explain and evaluate what Barnett views as the six advantages of a system of restitution as opposed to a system of punishment.

3. Explain what Barnett calls the distributionary criticism of restitution. Do you think that he adequately responds to this criticism? Why or why not?

4. How would a retributivist like Moore respond to Barnett's restitution paradigm? How would a utilitarian like Bentham respond to it? Which of the three theories do you think is most plausible? Explain.

81
Thomas E. Hill, Jr., "The Message of Affirmative Action" (1991)

Thomas E. Hill Jr. is the Kenan Professor in the Philosophy Department at the University of North Carolina, Chapel Hill. Hill's work is focused in ethics, the history of ethics, and political philosophy. In this selection, Hill discusses what he takes to be the "messages" that are sent by various defenses of affirmative action. Hill offers his own proposal for how affirmative action policies ought to be defended, one that he thinks sends the right message.

SOURCE

Hill, Thomas E., Jr. "The Message of Affirmative Action." *Social Philosophy and Policy 8*, Issue 2, 1991. pp. 108–29. Reprinted with the permission of Cambridge University Press.

Affirmative action programs remain controversial, I suspect, partly because the familiar arguments for and against them start from significantly different moral perspectives. Thus I want to step back for a while from the details of debate about particular programs and give attention to the moral viewpoints presupposed in different *types* of argument. My aim, more specifically, is to compare the "messages" expressed when affirmative action is defended from different moral perspectives. Exclusively forward-looking (for example, utilitarian) arguments, I suggest, tend to express the wrong message, but this is also true of exclusively backward-looking (for example, reparation-based) arguments. However, a moral outlook that focuses on cross-temporal narrative values (such as mutually respectful social relations) suggests a more appropriate account of what affirmative action should try to express. Assessment of the message, admittedly, is only one aspect of a complex issue, but it is a relatively neglected one. My discussion takes for granted some common-sense ideas about the communicative function of action, and so I begin with these.

Actions, as the saying goes, often *speak* louder than words. There are times, too, when only actions can effectively communicate the message we want to convey and times when giving a message is a central part of the purpose of action. What our actions say to others depends largely, though not entirely, upon our avowed reasons for acting; and this is a matter for reflective decision, not something we discover later by looking back at what we did and its effects. The decision is important because "the same act" can have very different consequences, depending upon how we choose to justify it. In a sense, acts done for different reasons are not "the same act" even if they are otherwise similar, and so not merely the consequences but also the moral nature of our acts depends in part on our decisions about the reasons for doing them.

Unfortunately, the message actually conveyed by our actions does not depend only on our intentions and reasons, for our acts may have a meaning for others quite at odds with what we hoped to express. Others may misunderstand our intentions, doubt our sincerity, or discern a subtext that undermines the primary message. Even if sincere, well-intended, and successfully conveyed, the message of an act or policy does not by itself justify the means by which it is conveyed; it is almost always a relevant factor, however, in the moral assessment of an act or policy.

These remarks may strike you as too obvious to be worth mentioning; for, even if we do not usually express the ideas so abstractly, we are all familiar with them in our daily interactions with our friends, families, and colleagues. Who, for example, does not know the importance of the message expressed in offering money to another person, as well as the dangers of misunderstanding? What is superficially the same "act" can be an offer to buy, an admission of guilt, an expression of gratitude, a contribution to a common cause, a condescending display of superiority, or an outrageous insult. Since all this is so familiar, the extent to which these elementary points are ignored in discussions of the pros and cons of social policies such as affirmative action is surprising. The usual presumption is that social policies can be settled entirely by debating the rights involved or by estimating the consequences, narrowly conceived of as separate from the messages that we want to give and those that are likely to be received.

I shall focus attention for a while upon this relatively neglected issue of the message of affirmative action. In particular, I want to consider what message we *should try* to give with affirmative action programs and what messages we should try to avoid. What is the best way to convey the intended message, and indeed whether it is likely to be heard, are empirical questions that I cannot settle; but the question I propose to consider is nonetheless important, and it is *a prior* question. What do we want to say with our affirmative action programs, and why? Since the message that is received and its consequences are likely to depend to some extent on what we decide, in all sincerity, to be the rationale for such programs, it would be premature and foolish to try to infer or predict these outcomes without adequate reflection on what the message and rationale should be. Also, for those who accept the historical/narrative perspective described in Section IV, there is additional reason to focus first on the desired message; for that perspective treats the message of affirmative action not merely as a minor side effect to be weighed in, for or against, but rather as an important part of the legitimate purpose of affirmative action.

Much useful discussion has been devoted to the constitutionality of affirmative action programs, to the relative moral rights involved, and to the advantages and disadvantages of specific types of programs. By deemphasizing these matters here, I do not mean to suggest that they are unimportant. Even more, my remarks are not meant to convey the message, "It doesn't matter what we do or achieve, all that matters is what we say." To the contrary, I believe that mere gestures are insufficient and that universities cannot even communicate what they should by affirmative action policies unless these are sincerely designed to result in increased opportunities for those disadvantaged and insulted by racism and sexism.

I divide my discussion as follows. *First,* I describe briefly two affirmative action programs with which I am acquainted, so that we can have in mind some concrete examples before we turn to controversial principles. *Second,* I summarize why I think that affirmative action programs need not be illegitimate forms of "reverse discrimination" that violate the rights of non-minority males. This is a large issue, well discussed by others, but it must be considered at least briefly in order to open the way for more positive considerations. *Third,* I discuss two familiar strategies for justifying affirmative action and give some reasons for thinking that these should not be considered the whole story. One strategy, the "forward-looking," appeals exclusively to the good results expected from such programs; the other, the "backward-looking," focuses on past injustice and demands reparation. One of my main points is that this very division leads us to overlook some other important considerations. *Fourth,* in a brief philosophical interlude, I sketch a mode of evaluation that seems to provide a helpful alternative or supplement to the traditional sorts of evaluation that have dominated discussions of affirmative action. This suggestion draws from recent work in ethical theory that stresses the importance of historical context, narrative unity, and interpersonal relations. *Fifth,* combining these ideas with my proposal to consider the message of affirmative action, I present some analogies that point to an alternative perspective on the aims of affirmative action programs. Seen from this perspective, programs that stress outreach, encouragement, and development opportunities appear in a more favorable light than those that simply alter standards to meet quotas.

I. Samples of Affirmative Action Programs

Affirmative action programs take various forms and are used in many different contexts. Here, however, I shall concentrate on hiring and admission policies in universities and colleges. Even in this area there are many complexities that must be taken into account in the assessment of particular programs. It may matter, for example, whether the program is voluntary or government-mandated, quota-based or flexible, fixed-term or indefinite, in a formerly segregated institution or not, and so on. Obviously it is impossible to examine all these variations here. It is also unnecessary, for my project is not to defend or criticize specific programs but to raise general questions about how we should approach the issue. Nonetheless, though a full range

of cases is not needed for this purpose, it may prove useful to sketch some sample programs that at least illustrate what the more abstract debate is about.

A common feature of affirmative action programs is that they make use of the categories of race and gender (more specifically, blacks and women) in their admissions and hiring policies, and they do so in a way that gives positive weight to being in one or the other of these latter categories. Policies use these classifications in different ways, as is evident in the cases described below.

When I taught at Pomona College in 1966–68, for example, the faculty/student Admissions Committee was blessed, or cursed, with applications numbering several times the number of places for new students. After a careful study of the correlation between grade-point averages of graduating seniors and data available in their initial application dossiers, a professor had devised a formula for predicting "success" at the college, where success was measured by the student's academic average at graduation from college. The predictive factors included high school grades, national test scores, and a ranking of the high school according to the grades its previous graduates received at the college. All applicants were then ranked according to this formula, which was supposed purely to reflect academic promise. The top ten percent were automatically admitted; a cut-off point was established below which candidates were deemed incapable of handling the college curriculum. Then committee members made a "subjective" evaluation of the remaining (middle) candidates in which the members were supposed to give weight to special talents, high-minded ambition, community service, intriguing personality, and (more generally) the likelihood of contributing to the sort of college community that the evaluators thought desirable. Another cut was made, reflecting both the "pure academic" criteria and the subjective evaluations. Next (as I recall) the football coach, the drama instructor, the orchestra leader, and others were invited to pick a specified number from those above the minimum cut-off if they needed a quarterback, a lead actor, a tuba player, or whatever. Then those identified as minorities but above the minimum cut-off line were admitted, if they had not been already, by a procedure that started with the most qualified academically, moving down the list until the minority applicants to be admitted made up at least a certain percentage of the final number of students to be admitted (10 percent, as I recall). The rest were admitted by their place on the academic list.

Pomona College is a private institution, but some state colleges and universities have adopted policies that are similar in important respects. At the University of California at Los Angeles in the 1970s, I became familiar with a significantly different kind of affirmative action regarding graduate student admissions and faculty hiring and promotion. The emphasis here was on positive efforts to seek out and encourage qualified minority applicants—for example, through recruitment letters, calls, and campus visits. Special funds were allocated to create new faculty positions for qualified minority candidates, and special fellowships were made available to release minority faculty from some teaching duties prior to tenure. Teaching and research interests in race and gender problems were officially recognized as relevant to hiring and promotion decisions in certain departments, provided the usual academic standards were maintained. Guidelines and watchdog committees were established to require departments to prove that, each time they hired a non-minority male, they did so only after a thorough search for and examination of minority and female candidates. Since decisions to hire and promote were still determined by the judgments of diverse individuals, I suspect that some deans, department heads, and voting faculty members carried affirmative action beyond the guidelines, some countered this effect by negative bias, and some simply refused to deviate from what they perceived as "color-blind" and "sex-blind" criteria.

II. Affirmative Action or Reverse Discrimination?

Is affirmative action *necessarily* a morally illegitimate form of "reverse discrimination" that violates the rights of white male applicants?

The question here is not whether some particular affirmative action program is illegitimate, for example, because it uses quotas or causes the deliberate hiring of less qualified teachers; the question, rather, is whether making gender and race a relevant category in university policy is *in itself* unjust. If so, we need not go further with our discussion of the message of affirmative action and its advantages and disadvantages: for however important the need is to communicate and promote social benefits, we should not do so by unjust means.

Some think that the injustice of all affirmative action programs is obvious or easily demonstrated. Two facile but confused arguments seem to have an especially popular appeal. The first goes this way: "Affirmative action, by definition, gives preferential treatment to minorities and women. This is discrimination in their favor and against non-minority males. All discrimination by public institutions is unjust, no matter whether it is the old kind or the newer 'reverse discrimination.' So all affirmative action programs in public institutions are unjust."

This deceptively simple argument, of course, trades on an ambiguity. In one sense, to "discriminate" means to "make a distinction," to pay attention to a difference. In this evaluatively neutral sense, of course, affirmative action programs do discriminate. But public institutions must, and justifiably do, "discriminate" in this sense—for example, between citizens and non-citizens, freshmen and seniors, the talented and the retarded, and those who pay their bills and those who do not. Whether it is unjust to note and make use of a certain distinction in a given context depends upon many factors: the nature of the institution, the relevant rights of the parties involved, the purposes and effects of making that distinction, and so on.

All this would be obvious except for the fact that the word "discrimination" is also used in a pejorative sense, meaning (roughly) "making use of a distinction in an unjust or illegitimate way." To discriminate in this sense is obviously wrong; but now it remains an open question whether the use of race and gender distinctions in affirmative action programs is really "discrimination" in this sense. The simplistic argument uses the evaluatively neutral sense of "discrimination" to show that affirmative action discriminates; it then shifts to the pejorative sense when it asserts that discrimination is always wrong. Although one may, in the end, *conclude* that all public use of racial and gender distinctions is unjust, to do so requires more of an *argument* than the simple one (just given) that merely exploits an ambiguity of the word "discrimination."

A slightly more sophisticated argument runs as follows: "Affirmative action programs give special benefits to certain individuals 'simply because they are women or blacks.' But one's color and gender are morally irrelevant features of a person. It is unjust for public institutions to give special benefits to individuals solely because they happen to have certain morally irrelevant characteristics. Hence affirmative action programs are always unjust."

A special twist is often added to this argument, as follows: "What was wrong with Jim Crow laws, denial of the vote to women and blacks, and segregation in schools and public facilities was just the fact that such practices treated people differently simply because they happened to have certain morally irrelevant characteristics. Affirmative action programs, however well-intentioned, are doing exactly the same thing. So they are wrong for the same reason."

Now people who argue in this way may well be trying to express something important, which should not be dismissed; but, as it stands, the argument is confused, unfair, and historically inaccurate. The confusion and unfairness lie in the misleading use of the expression "*simply* because they are women or blacks." It is true that typical affirmative action programs, such as those I described earlier, use the categories of "black" (or "minority") and "female" as an instrumental part of a complex policy. This does not mean, however, that the fundamental reason, purpose, or justification of the policy is nothing more than "this individual is black (or female)." To say that someone favors a person "*simply because* that person is black (or female)" implies that there is no further reason, purpose, or

justification, as if one merely had an utterly arbitrary preference for dark skin as opposed to light or female anatomy over male anatomy. But no serious advocate of affirmative action thinks the program is justified by such personal preferences. On the contrary, advocates argue that, given our historical situation, quite general principles of justice or utility justify the temporary classificatory use of race and gender. That being black or white, male or female, does not in itself make anyone morally better or more deserving is acknowledged on all sides.

Thus even if one should conclude that the attempts to justify affirmative action fail, the fair and clear way to express this would be to say that the grounds that have been offered for using race and gender categories as affirmative action programs are unconvincing. Unlike the rhetorical claim that they favor individuals "merely because they are black (or female)," this does not insinuate unfairly that the programs were instituted for no reason other than personal taste. And, of course, those of us who believe that there are good reasons for affirmative action policies, with their sorting by gender and race, have even more reason to reject the misleading and insulting description that we advocate special treatment for individuals *merely because* they are blacks or women.

The argument we have been considering is objectionable in another way as well. As Richard Wasserstrom points out, the moral wrongs against blacks and women in the past were not wrong just because people were classified and treated differently according to the morally irrelevant features of gender and color.[1] There was this sort of arbitrary treatment, of course, but the main problem was not that women and blacks were treated differently *somehow* but that they were *treated as no human being should be treated.* Segregation, for example, was in practice not merely a pointless

---

[1] See Richard Wasserstrom, "Racism and Sexism," "Preferential Treatment," in his *Philosophy and Social Issues* (Notre Dame, IN: University of Notre Dame Press, 1980).

sorting of individuals, like separating people according to the number of letters in their names. It was a way of expressing and perpetuating white contempt for blacks and preserving social structures that kept blacks from taking full advantage of their basic human rights. The mistreatment of women was not merely that they were arbitrarily selected for the more burdensome but still legitimate social roles. It was, in large part, that the practices expressed an attitude towards women that subtly undermined their chances of making use of even the limited opportunities they had. The proper conclusion, then, is not that any current program that makes use of race and gender categories is simply committing the same old wrongs in reverse. The worst wrongs of the past went far beyond merely the arbitrary use of these categories; moreover, it has yet to be established that the new use of these categories in affirmative action is in fact arbitrary (like the old use). An arbitrary category is one used without good justification; the charge that affirmative action programs use race and gender categories unjustifiably is just what is at issue, not something we can assume at the start.

Another argument to show that affirmative action is unjust is that it violates the rights of white males who apply for admission or jobs in the university. This is a complex issue, discussed at length in journals and before the Supreme Court; rather than review that debate, I will just mention a few of the considerations that lead me to think that, though certain *types* of affirmative action may violate the rights of white males, appropriately designed affirmative action programs do not.

First, no individual, white male or otherwise, has an absolute right to a place in a public university—that is, a right independent of complex considerations of the functions of the university, the reasonable expectations of actual and potential taxpayers and other supporters, the number of places available, the relative merits of other candidates, and so on. What rights does an applicant have? Few would dispute that each individual has

a right to "formal justice."[1] That is, one should not be arbitrarily denied a place to which one is entitled under the existing and publicly-declared rules and regulations. Any university must have rules concerning residency, prior education, submission of application forms, taking of entrance tests, and the like, as well as more substantive standards and policies for selecting among those who satisfy these minimal requirements. Formal justice requires that individual administrators do not deviate from the pre-established rules and standards currently in effect, whether from personal preference or high-minded social ideals. But this is not to say that old policies cannot reasonably be changed. One does not, for example, necessarily have a right to be treated by the rules and standards in force when one was born or when one first thought about going to college.

Formal justice is quite limited, however, for it is compatible with substantively unjust rules and standards. In addition to formal justice, each individual citizen has a right that the rules and standards of the university to which he or she applies be made (and, when necessary, changed) only for good reasons, consistent with the purposes of the university and the ideals of justice and basic human equality. This is a more stringent standard; it does establish a *presumption* against using race and gender categories in policies which affect the distribution of opportunities, such as jobs and student status. This is because race and gender, like height and musculature, are not *in themselves* morally relevant characteristics. Considered in isolation from their connections with other matters, they do not make anyone more, or less, deserving of anything. As the Supreme Court

---

[1] William K. Frankena, "The Concept of Social Justice," in Richard B. Brandt (ed.), *Social Justice* (Englewood Cliffs, NJ: Prentice Hall, Inc., 1962), pp. 8–9; Henry Sidgwick, *Methods of Ethics*, 7th ed. (London: Macmillan, 1907), pp. 379, 386ff; John Rawls, *A Theory of Justice* (Cambridge, MA: Harvard University Press, 1971), pp. 56–60, 180, 235–39, 504ff.

says, they are classifications that are "suspect."[1] But this does not mean that it is always unjust to use them, but only that their use stands in need of justification. What counts as a justification depends crucially upon our assessment of the legitimate purposes of the institution that uses the categories.

No one denies that the education of citizens and the pursuit of knowledge are central among the purposes of public universities. But, when resources are limited, decisions must be made as to what knowledge is to be pursued and who is to be offered education in each institution. Here we must consider the roles that universities play as parts of a complex network of public institutions (of many kinds) in a country committed to democratic ideals and faced with deep social problems. It has never been the practice of universities to disregard their social roles in the name of "purely academic" concerns; given current social problems, few would morally defend such disregard now. The more serious issue is not whether this role should be considered but rather whether the role is better served by affirmative action or by admission and hiring policies that admit only classification by test scores, grades, and past achievements. To decide this, we must look more closely at the purposes that affirmative action is supposed to serve.

III. Strategies of Justification: Consequences and Reparations

Some arguments for affirmative action look exclusively to its future benefits. The idea is that what has happened in the past is not in itself relevant to what we should do; at most, it provides clues as to what acts and policies are likely to bring about the best future. The philosophical tradition associated with this approach is utilitarianism, which declares that the morally right act is whatever produces the best consequences. Traditionally, utilitarianism evaluated consequences in terms of happiness

and unhappiness, but the anticipated consequences of affirmative action are often described more specifically. For example, some argue that affirmative action will ease racial tensions, prevent riots, improve services in minority neighborhoods, reduce unemployment, remove inequities in income distribution, eliminate racial and sexual prejudice, and enhance the self-esteem of blacks and women. Some have called attention to the fact that women and minorities provide alternative perspectives on history, literature, philosophy, and politics, and that this has beneficial effects for both education and research.

These are important considerations, not irrelevant to the larger responsibilities of universities. For several reasons, however, I think it is a mistake for advocates of affirmative action to rest their case exclusively on such forward-looking arguments. First, critics raise reasonable doubts about whether affirmative action is necessary to achieve these admirable results. The economist Thomas Sowell argues that a free-market economy can achieve the same results more efficiently; his view is therefore that even if affirmative action has beneficial results (which he denies), it is not necessary for the purpose.[2] Though Sowell's position can be contested, the controversy itself tends to weaken confidence in the entirely forward-looking defense of affirmative action.

An even more obvious reason why affirmative action advocates should explore other avenues for its defense is that the exclusively forward-looking approach must give equal consideration to possible negative consequences of affirmative action. It may be, for example, that affirmative action will temporarily increase racial tensions, especially if its message is misunderstood. Even legitimate use of race and sex categories may encourage others to abuse the categories for unjust purposes. If applied without sensitive regard to the educational and research purposes of the university, affirmative action might severely undermine its efforts to fulfill these primary

---

[1] *Regents of the University of California v. Allen Bakke*, 98 S.Ct. 2733, 46 L.W. 4896 (1978). [Reprinted in this volume, reading 85.]

[2] Thomas Sowell, *Race and Economics* (New York: David McKay Co., 1975), ch. 6; *Markets and Minorities* (New York: Basic Books, Inc., 1981), pp. 114–15.

responsibilities. *If* affirmative action programs were to lower academic standards for blacks and women, they would run the risk of damaging the respect that highly qualified blacks and women have earned by leading others to suspect that these highly qualified people lack the merits of white males in the same positions. This could also be damaging to the self-respect of those who accept affirmative action positions. Even programs that disavow "lower standards" unfortunately arouse the suspicion that they don't really do so, and this by itself can cause problems. Although I believe that well-designed affirmative action programs can minimize these negative effects, the fact that they are a risk is a reason for not resting the case for affirmative action on a delicate balance of costs and benefits.

Reflection on the *message* of affirmative action also leads me to move beyond entirely forward-looking arguments. For if the sole purpose is to bring about a brighter future, then we give the wrong message to both the white males who are rejected and to the women and blacks who are benefited. To the latter what we say, in effect, is this: "Never mind how you have been treated. Forget about the fact that your race or sex has in the past been actively excluded and discouraged, and that you yourself may have had handicaps due to prejudice. Our sole concern is to bring about certain good results in the future, and giving you a break happens to be a useful means for doing this. Don't think this is a recognition of your rights as an individual or your disadvantages as a member of a group. Nor does it mean that we have confidence in your abilities. We would do the same for those who are privileged and academically inferior if it would have the same socially beneficial results."

To the white male who would have had a university position but for affirmative action, the exclusively forward-looking approach says: "We deny you the place you otherwise would have had simply as a means to produce certain socially desirable outcomes. We have not judged that others are more deserving, or have a right, to the place we are giving them instead of you. Past racism and sexism are irrelevant. The point is just that the sacrifice of

your concerns is a useful means to the larger end of the future welfare of others."

This, I think, is the wrong message to give. It is also unnecessary. The proper alternative, however, is not to ignore the possible future benefits of affirmative action but rather to take them into account as a part of a larger picture.

A radically different strategy for justifying affirmative action is to rely on backward-looking arguments. Such arguments call our attention to certain events in the past and assert that *because* these past events occurred, we have certain duties now. The modern philosopher who most influentially endorsed such arguments was W.D. Ross.[1] He argued that there are duties of fidelity, justice, gratitude, and reparation that have a moral force independent of any tendency these may have to promote good consequences. The fact that you have made a promise, for example, gives you a strong moral reason to do what you promised, whether or not doing so will on balance have more beneficial consequences. The Rossian principle that is often invoked in affirmative action debates is a principle of reparation. This says that those who wrongfully injure others have a (*prima facie*) duty to apologize and make restitution. Those who have wronged others owe reparation.

James Forman dramatically expressed this idea in New York in 1969 when he presented "The Black Manifesto," which demanded five hundred million dollars in reparation to American blacks from white churches and synagogues.[2] Such organizations, the

---

[1] W.D. Ross, *The Right and the Good* (Oxford: Clarendon Press, 1930).

[2] James Forman was at the time director of international affairs for SNCC (Student Nonviolent Coordinating Committee). The "Black Manifesto" stems from an economic development conference sponsored by the Interreligious Foundation for Community Organizations, April 26, 1969, and presented by Forman at the New York Interdenominational Riverside Church on May 4, 1969. Later the demand was raised to three billion dollars. See Robert S. Lecky and H. Elliot Wright, *Black Manifesto* (New York: Sheed and Ward Publishers, 1969), pp. vii, 114–26.

Manifesto contends, contributed to our history of slavery and racial injustice; as a result, they incurred a debt to the black community that still suffers from its effects. Objections were immediately raised: for example, both slaves and slave-owners are no longer alive; not every American white is guilty of racial oppression; and not every black in America was a victim of slavery and its aftermath.

Bernard Boxill, author of *Blacks and Social Justice,* developed a more sophisticated version of the backward-looking argument with a view to meeting these objections.[1] Let us admit, he says, that both the perpetrators and the primary victims of slavery are gone, and let us not insist that contemporary whites are guilty of perpetrating further injustices. Some do, and some do not, and public administrators cannot be expected to sort out the guilty from the non-guilty. However, reparation, or at least some "compensation,"[2] is still owed, because contemporary whites have reaped the profits of past injustice to blacks. He asks us to consider the analogy with a stolen bicycle. Suppose my parent stole your parent's bicycle some time ago, both have since died, and I "inherited" the bike from my parent, the thief. Though I may be innocent of any wrongdoing (so far), I am in possession of stolen goods rightfully belonging to you, the person who would have inherited the bike if it had not been stolen. For me to keep the bike and declare that I owe you nothing would be wrong, even if I was not the cause of your being deprived. By analogy, present-day whites owe reparations to contemporary blacks, not because they are themselves guilty of causing the disadvantages of blacks,

but because they are in possession of advantages that fell to them as a result of the gross injustices of their ancestors. Special advantages continue to fall even to innocent whites because of the ongoing prejudice of their white neighbors.

Although it raises many questions, this line of argument acknowledges some important points missing in most exclusively forward-looking arguments: for example, it stresses the (intrinsic) relevance of past injustice and it calls attention to the rights and current disadvantages of blacks (in contrast with future benefits for others). When developed as an argument for affirmative action, it does not accuse all white males of prejudice and wrongdoing; at the same time, however, it sees the fundamental value as justice. As a result, it avoids giving the message to either rejected white males or reluctant affirmative action applicants that they are "mere means" to a social goal that is largely independent of their rights and interests as individuals.

There are, however, serious problems in trying to justify affirmative action by this backward-looking argument, especially if it is treated as the exclusive or central argument. Degrees of being advantaged and disadvantaged are notoriously hard to measure. New immigrants have not shared our history of past injustices, and so the argument may not apply to them in any straightforward way. The argument appeals to controversial ideas about property rights, inheritance, and group responsibilities. Some argue that affirmative action tends to benefit the least disadvantaged blacks and women; though this does not mean that they are owed nothing, their claims would seem to have lower priority than the needs of the most disadvantaged. Some highly qualified blacks and women object that affirmative action is damaging to their reputations and self-esteem, whereas the reparation argument seems to assume that it is a welcome benefit to all blacks and women.

If we focus on the message that the backward-looking argument sends, there are also some potential problems. Though rightly acknowledging past injustice, the argument (by itself) seems to convey the message that racial and sexual oppression consisted primarily in the loss of tangible goods, or the

---

[1] Bernard Boxill, "The Morality of Reparation," *Social Theory and Practice* 2.1 (1972): 113–22, and *Blacks and Social Justice* [(Lanham, MD: Rowman and Littlefield, 1992)], ch. 7.

[2] In the article cited above, Boxill calls what is owed "reparations," but in the book (above) he calls it "compensation." ... We could describe the backward-looking arguments presented here as demands for "compensation" rather than "reparation," so long as we keep in mind that the compensation is supposed to be due as the morally appropriate response to past wrongdoing.

deprivation of specific rights and opportunities, that can be "paid back" in kind. The background idea, which goes back at least to Aristotle, is that persons wrongfully deprived of their "due" can justly demand an "equivalent" to what they have lost.[1] But, while specific deprivations were an important part of our racist and sexist past, they are far from the whole story. Among the worst wrongs then, as now, were humiliations and contemptuous treatment of a type that cannot, strictly, be "paid back." The problem was, and is, not just that specific rights and advantages were denied, but that prejudicial attitudes damaged self-esteem, undermined motivations, limited realistic options, and made even "officially open" opportunities seem undesirable. Racism and sexism were (and are) *insults*, not merely tangible *injuries*.[2] These are not the sort of thing that can be adequately measured and repaid with equivalents. The trouble with treating insulting racist and sexist practices on a pure reparation model is not merely the practical difficulty of identifying the offenders, determining the degree of guilt, assessing the amount of payment due, etc. It is also that penalty payments and compensation for lost benefits are not the only, or primary, moral responses that are called for. When affirmative action is defended exclusively by analogy with reparation, it tends to express the misleading message that the evils of racism and sexism are all tangible losses that can be "paid off"; by being silent on the insulting nature of racism and sexism, it tends to add insult to insult.

The message suggested by the reparation argument, by itself, also seems objectionable because it conveys the idea that higher education, teaching, and doing research are mainly benefits awarded in response to self-centered demands. The underlying picture too easily suggested is that applicants are a group of self-interested, bickering people, each grasping for limited "goodies" and insisting on a right to them. When a university grants an opportunity through affirmative action, its message would seem to be this. "We concede that you have a valid claim to this benefit and we yield to your demand, though this is not to suggest that we have confidence in your abilities or any desire to have you here." This invitation seems too concessive, the atmosphere too adversarial, and the emphasis too much on the benefits rather than the responsibilities of being a part of the university.

IV. Philosophical Interlude: An Alternative Perspective

Here I want to digress from the explicit consideration of affirmative action in order to consider more abstract philosophical questions about the ways we evaluate acts and policies. At the risk of oversimplifying, I want to contrast some assumptions that have, until recently, been dominant in ethical theory with alternatives suggested by contemporary philosophers who emphasize historical context, narrative unity, and community values.[3] Although these alternatives, in my opinion, have not yet been adequately developed, there seem to be at least four distinguishable themes worth considering.

First, when we reflect on what we deeply value, we find that we care not merely about the present moment and each future moment in isolation but also about how our past, present, and future cohere or fit together into a life and a piece of history. Some of our values, we might say, are cross-time wholes, with past, present, and future parts united in certain ways. Thus, for example, the commitments I have made, the projects I have begun, what I have shared with those I love, the injuries I have caused, and the hopes I have encouraged importantly affect

---

[1] Aristotle, *Nicomachean Ethics*, tr. A.K. Thomson (Baltimore: Penguin Books, Inc., 1955), bk. V, esp. pp. 143–55.

[2] See Boxill, *Blacks and Social Justice*, pp. 132ff., and Ronald Dworkin, "Reverse Discrimination," in *Taking Rights Seriously* (Cambridge, MA: Harvard University Press, 1978), pp. 231ff.

[3] See, for example, Alasdair MacIntyre, *After Virtue* (Notre Dame, IN: Notre Dame University Press, 1981). Similar themes are found in Carol Gilligan's *In a Different Voice* (Cambridge, MA: Harvard University Press, 1982) and in Lawrence Blum, *Friendship, Altruism, and Morality* (Boston: Routledge and Kegan Paul, 1980).

both whether I am satisfied with my present and how I want the future to go.

Second, in reflecting on stretches of our lives and histories, we frequently use evaluative concepts drawn more from narrative literature than from accounting. Thus, for example, we think of our lives as having significant beginnings, crises, turning points, dramatic tension, character development, climaxes, resolutions, comic interludes, tragic disruptions, and eventually fitting (or unfitting) endings. The value of any moment often depends on what came before and what we anticipate to follow. And since our lives are intertwined with others in a common history, we also care about how our moments cohere with others' life stories. The past is seen as more than a time of accumulated debts and assets, and the future is valued as more than an opportunity for reinvesting and cashing in assets.

Third, evaluation must take into account one's particular historical context, including one's cultural, national, and ethnic traditions, and the actual individuals in one's life. Sometimes this point is exaggerated, I think, to suggest a dubious cultural relativism or "particularism" in ethics: for example, the thesis that what is valuable for a person is defined by the person's culture or that evaluations imply no general reasons beyond particular judgments, such as "That's *our* way" and "John is *my* son." But, construed modestly as a practical or epistemological point, it seems obvious enough, on reflection, that we should take into account the historical context of our acts and that we are often in a better position to judge what is appropriate in particular cases than we are to articulate universally valid premises supporting the judgment. We can sometimes be reasonably confident about what is right in a particular context without being sure about whether or not there are relevant differences blocking the same judgment in seemingly similar but less familiar contexts. We know, as a truism, that the same judgment applies if there are no relevant differences, but in practice the particular judgment may be more evident than the exact scope of the moral generalizations that hold across many cases. Thus, though giving reasons for our

judgments in particular contexts commits us to acknowledging their potential relevance in other contexts, moral judgment cannot be aptly represented simply as deducing specific conclusions from clear and evident general principles.

Fourth, when we evaluate particular acts and policies as parts of lives and histories, what is often most important is the value of the whole, which cannot always be determined by "summing up" the values of the parts. Lives, histories, and interpersonal relations over time are what G.E. Moore called "organic unities"—that is, wholes the value of which is not necessarily the sum of the values of the parts.[1] The point here is not merely the obvious practical limitation that we cannot measure and quantify values in this area. More fundamentally, the idea is that it would be a mistake even to try to evaluate certain unities by assessing different parts in isolation from one another, then adding up all their values. Suppose, for example, a woman with terminal cancer considered two quite different ways of spending her last days. One way, perhaps taking a world cruise, might seem best when evaluated in terms of the quality of each future moment, in isolation from her past and her present ties; but another way, perhaps seeking closure in projects and with estranged family members, might seem more valuable when seen as a part of her whole life.

Taken together, these ideas cast doubt on both the exclusively forward-looking method of assessment and the standard backward-looking alternative. Consequentialism, or the exclusively forward-looking method, attempts to determine what ought to be done at present by fixing attention entirely on future results. To be sure, any sensible consequentialist will consult the past for lessons and clues helpful in predicting future outcomes: for example, recalling that you offended someone yesterday may enable you to predict that the person will be cool to you tomorrow unless you apologize. But beyond this, consequentialists have no concern with the past, for their "bottom line" is always

---

[1] G.E. Moore, *Principia Ethica* (Cambridge: Cambridge University Press, 1912), pp. 27ff.

"what happens from now on," evaluated independently of the earlier chapters of our lives and histories. For the consequentialist, assessing a life or history from a narrative perspective becomes impossible or at least bizarre, as what must be evaluated at each shifting moment is "the story from now on" independently of what has already been written.

The standard Rossian alternative to this exclusively forward-looking perspective is to introduce certain (*prima facie*) *duties* to respond to certain past events in specified ways—for example, pay debts, keep promises, pay reparation for injuries. These duties are supposed to be self-evident and universal (though they are *prima facie*), and they do not hold because they tend to promote anything good or valuable. Apart from aspects of the acts mentioned in the principles (for example, fulfilling a promise, returning favors, not injuring, etc.), details of historical and personal context are considered irrelevant.

By contrast, the narrative perspective sketched above considers the past as an integral part of the valued unities that we aim to bring about, not merely as a source of duties. If one has negligently wronged another, Ross regards this past event as generating a duty to pay reparations even if doing so will result in nothing good. But from the narrative perspective, the past becomes relevant in a further way. One may say, for example, that the *whole* consisting of your life and your relationship with that person from the time of the injury into the future will be a better thing if you acknowledge the wrong and make efforts to restore what you have damaged. For Ross, the duty is generated by the past and unrelated to bringing about anything good; from the narrative perspective, however, the requirement is just what is required to bring about a valuable connected whole with past, present, and future parts—the best way to complete a chapter, so to speak, in two intersecting life-stories.

So far, neither the Rossian nor the narrative account has told us much about the ultimate reasons for their evaluations, but they reveal ways to consider the matter. The Rossian asks us to judge particular cases in the light of "self-evident" general principles asserting that certain past events tend to generate present (or future) duties. The alternative perspective calls for examining lives and relationships, over time, in context, as organic unities evaluated (partly) in narrative terms.

To illustrate, consider two persons, John and Mary. John values having Mary's trust and respect, and conversely Mary values having John's; moreover, John values the fact that Mary values being trusted and respected by him, and conversely Mary values the same about John.

Now suppose that other people have been abusive and insulting to Mary, and that John is worried that Mary may take things he had said and done as similarly insulting, even though he does not think that he consciously meant them this way. Though he is worried, Mary does not seem to suspect him; he fears that he may only make matters worse if he raises the issue, creating suspicions she did not have or focusing on doubts that he cannot allay. Perhaps, he thinks, their future relationship would be better served if he just remained silent, hoping that the trouble, if any, will fade in time. If so, consequentialist thinking would recommend silence. Acknowledging this, he might nonetheless feel that duties of friendship and fidelity demand that he raise the issue, regardless of whether or not the result will be worse. Then he would be thinking as a Rossian.

But, instead, he might look at the problem from an alternative perspective, asking himself what response best affirms and contributes to the sort of ongoing relationship he has and wants to continue with Mary. Given their history together, it is important to him to do his part towards restoring the relationship if it indeed has been marred by perceived insults or suspicions. To be sure, he wants *future* relations of mutual trust and respect, but not at any price and not by just any means. Their history together is not irrelevant, for what he values is not merely a future of a certain kind, but that their relationship over time be of the sort he values. He values an ongoing history of mutual trust and respect that *calls for* an explicit response in this current situation, not merely as a means to a brighter future but as a present affirmation of what they value together. Even if unsure which course will be best for the future, he may be reasonably confident that the act that best expresses his respect and trust (and his valuing hers, etc.) is to confront the problem, express his regrets, reaffirm his respect, ask for her trust, be patient with her doubts, and welcome an open dialogue. If the insults were deep and it is not entirely clear whether or not he really associated himself with them, then mere words may not be enough to convey the message or even to assure himself of his own sincerity. Positive efforts, even at considerable cost, may be needed to express appropriately and convincingly what needs to be said. How the next chapter unfolds is not entirely up to him, and he would not be respectful if he presumed otherwise by trying to manipulate the best future unilaterally.

The example concerns only two persons and their personal values, but it illustrates a perspective that one can also take regarding moral problems involving many persons.

V. Mutual Respect, Fair Opportunity, and Affirmative Action

Turning back to our main subject, I suggest that some of the values that give affirmative action its point are best seen as cross-time values that fall outside the exclusively forward-looking and backward-looking perspectives. They include having a history of racial and gender relations governed, so far as possible, by the ideals of mutual respect, trust, and fair opportunity for all.

Our national history provides a context of increasing recognition and broader interpretation of the democratic ideal of the equal dignity of all human beings—an ideal that has been flagrantly abused from the outset, partially affirmed in the bloody Civil War, and increasingly extended in the civil rights movement, but is still far from being fully respected. More specifically, blacks and women were systematically treated in an unfair and demeaning way by public institutions, including universities, until quite recently, and few could confidently claim to have rooted out racism and sexism even now. The historical context is not what

grounds or legitimates democratic values, but it is the background of the current problem, the sometimes admirable and often ugly way the chapters up until now have been written.

Consider first the social ideal of mutual respect and trust among citizens. The problem of implementing this in the current context is different from the problem in the two-person example discussed above, for the history of our racial and gender relations is obviously not an idyllic story of mutual respect and trust momentarily interrupted by a crisis. Even so, the question to ask is not merely, "What will promote respectful and trusting racial and gender relations in future generations?" but rather, "Given our checkered past, how can we appropriately express the social value of mutual respect and trust that we want, so far as possible, to characterize our history?" We cannot change our racist and sexist past, but we also cannot express full respect for those present individuals who live in its aftermath if we ignore it. What is called for is not merely repayment of tangible debts incurred by past injuries, but also a message to counter the deep insult inherent in racism and sexism.

Recognizing that problems of this kind are not amenable to easy solutions deduced from self-evident moral generalizations, we may find it helpful instead to reflect on an analogy. Suppose you return to the hometown you left in childhood, remembering with pride its Fourth of July speeches about the values of community, equality, and fairness for all. You discover, however, that the community was never as perfect as you thought. In fact, for years—until quite recently—certain families, who had been disdainfully labeled "the Barefeet," had not only been shunned by most folk but had also been quietly terrorized by a few well-placed citizens. The Barefeet had been arrested on false charges, beaten, raped, and blackmailed into silent submission. The majority, perhaps, would never have done these things, but their contempt for the Barefeet was such that most would have regarded these crimes less important than if they had been done to insiders. Fortunately, the worst offenders have died, and so have the victims of the most outrageous crimes.

Majority attitudes have changed somewhat, though often only from open contempt to passive disregard. Some new citizens have come to town, and a few of the Barefeet (now more politely called "Cross-towners") have managed to become successful. Nonetheless, the older Cross-towners are still fearful and resigned, and the younger generation is openly resentful and distrustful when officials proclaim a new commitment to democratic ideals. It is no surprise, then, that few Cross-towners take full advantage of available opportunities and that the two groups tend to isolate themselves from each other.

Now suppose you, as one of the majority, could persuade the rest to give a message to the Cross-towners, a message appropriate to the majority's professed value of being a community committed to mutual respect and trust. What would you propose? And, assuming that doing so would violate no one's rights, what means would you think best to convey that message sincerely and effectively? Some would no doubt suggest simply forgetting about the past and hoping that time will heal the wounds. But, whether effective in the future or not, this plan fails to express full respect for the Cross-towners now. Others might suggest a more legalistic approach, trying to determine exactly who has been the disadvantaged, the degree of loss, which citizens are most responsible, etc., in order to pay off the debt. But this, taken by itself, faces the sorts of disadvantages we have already considered. If, instead, the value of mutual respect and trust is the governing ideal, the appropriate message would be to acknowledge and deplore the past openly, to affirm a commitment to promote mutual respect and trust in the future, to welcome full interchange and participation with the Cross-towners, and to urge them to undertake the risks of overcoming their understandable suspicions by joining in a common effort to work towards fulfilling the ideal. This would address not merely the injury but also the insult implicit in the town's history.

The more difficult question, however, is how we might express such a message effectively and with evident sincerity in an atmosphere already poisoned by the past. Mere words will be taken as mere words; they may in fact turn out to be just that. What is needed is more positive action—concrete steps to prove commitment, to resist backsliding, and to overcome reluctance on both sides. The sort of affirmative action taken in the U.C.L.A. program described in Section I seems especially appropriate for this purpose. Here the emphasis was on outreach, increasing awareness of opportunities, accountability and proof of fairness in procedures, and allocating resources (fellowships, release time, etc.) in a way that showed trust that, if given an adequate chance, those formerly excluded would enrich the university by fully appropriate standards. These seem the most natural way to give force to the message, though arguably other methods may serve the purpose as well.

There is another historical value that is also relevant and seems to favor even more radical steps in affirmative action. The issue is too complex to address adequately here, but it should at least be mentioned. What I have in mind might be called "fair opportunity." That is, implicit in our democratic ideals is the idea that our public institutions should be so arranged that they afford to each person, over time, more or less equal opportunities to develop and make use of his or her natural talents and to participate and contribute to those institutions. The idea is hard to make precise, but it clearly does not mean that all should have equal chances to have a desirable position, regardless of effort and natural aptitude. The physically handicapped and the mentally retarded suffer from natural misfortunes; though society should not ignore them, they cannot expect standards to be rigged to ensure the former equal odds at making the basketball team or the latter equal odds of being appointed to the faculty. Similarly, those who choose not to make the effort to develop their capacities have no right to expect public institutions to include them in a pool from which candidates are selected by lot. But when persons have been disadvantaged by social injustice, having had their initial chances diminished by the network of public institutions themselves, then positive steps are needed to equalize their opportunities over time.

This ideal calls for something more than efforts to ensure that future generations do not suffer from the same disadvantages, for those efforts fail to respond to the unfairness to the present individuals. But, for obvious practical reasons, legal efforts to remedy precisely identifiable disadvantages incurred by individuals are bound to be quite inadequate to address the many subtle losses of opportunity caused by past institutional racism and sexism. Since no perfect solution is possible, we need to choose between this inadequate response and policies that address the problem in a less fine-grained way. Affirmative action programs that employ a working presumption that women and minorities generally have had their opportunities restricted to some degree by institutional racism and sexism will admittedly risk compensating a few who have actually had, on balance, as much opportunity as white males. But the practical alternatives, it seems, are to accept this risk or to refuse to respond at all to the innumerable ways that institutional racism and sexism have undermined opportunities too subtly for the courts to remedy.

Given these options, what would be the message of choosing to limit redress to precisely identifiable losses? This would say, in effect, to women and minorities, "We cannot find a way to ensure *precisely* that each talented and hard-working person has an equal opportunity over time; and, given our options, we count it more important to see that *none* of you women and minorities are over-compensated than to try to see that the *majority* of you have more nearly equal opportunities over your life-time. Your grievances are too subtle and difficult to measure, and your group may be harboring some who were not disadvantaged. We would rather let the majority of white males enjoy the advantages of their unfair head start than risk compensating one of you who does not deserve it."

Now *if* it had been established on antecedent grounds that the affirmative action measures in question would violate the *rights* of white male applicants, then one could argue that these coarse-grained efforts to honor the ideal of fair opportunity are illegitimate. But that premise, I think, has not been established. Affirmative action programs would violate the rights of white males only if, all things considered, their guidelines temporarily favoring women and minorities were arbitrary, not serving the legitimate social role of universities or fulfilling the ideals of fairness and respect for all. The considerations offered here, however, point to the conclusion that some affirmative action programs, even those involving a degree of preferential treatment, are legitimated by ideals of mutual respect, trust, and fair opportunity.

Conclusion

All this, I know, is too brief, loose, and incomplete. I hope it is worth considering nonetheless. The main suggestion is that, ideally, a central purpose of affirmative action would be to communicate a much-needed message, sincerely and effectively. The message is called for not just as a means to future good relations or a dutiful payment of a debt incurred by our past. It is called for by the ideal of being related to other human beings over time, so that our histories and biographies reflect the responses of those who deeply care about fair opportunity, mutual trust, and respect for all.

If so, what should public universities try to say to those offered opportunities through affirmative action? Perhaps something like this: "Whether we individually are among the guilty or not, we acknowledge that you have been wronged—if not by specific injuries which could be named and repaid, at least by the humiliating and debilitating attitudes prevalent in our country and our institutions. We deplore and denounce these attitudes and the wrongs that spring from them. We acknowledge that, so far, most of you have had your opportunities in life diminished by the effects of these attitudes, and we want no one's prospects to be diminished by injustice. We recognize your understandable grounds for suspicion and mistrust when we express these high-minded sentiments, and we want not only to ask respectfully for your trust but also to give concrete evidence of our sincerity. We welcome you respectfully into the university community and ask you to take a full share of the responsibilities as well as the benefits. By creating special opportunities, we recognize the disadvantages you have probably suffered; we show our respect for your talents and our commitment to the ideals of the university, however, by not faking grades and honors for you. Given current attitudes about affirmative action, accepting this position will probably have drawbacks as well as advantages. It is an opportunity and a responsibility offered neither as charity nor as entitlement, but rather as part of a special effort to welcome and encourage minorities and women to participate more fully in the university at all levels. We believe that this program affirms some of the best ideals implicit in our history without violating the rights of any applicants. We hope that you will choose to accept the position in this spirit as well as for your own benefit."

The appropriate message is no doubt harder to communicate to those who stand to lose some traditional advantages under a legitimate affirmative action program. But if we set aside practical difficulties and suppose that the proper message could be sincerely given and accepted as such, what would it say? Ideally, it would convey an understanding of the moral reasoning for the program; perhaps, in conclusion, it would say something like the following.

"These are the concerns that we felt made necessary the policy under which the university is temporarily giving special attention to women and minorities. We respect your rights to formal justice and to a policy guided by the university's education and research mission as well as its social responsibilities. Our policy in no way implies the view that your opportunities are less important than others', but we estimate (roughly, as we must) that

as a white male you have probably had advantages and encouragement that for a long time have been systematically, unfairly, insultingly unavailable to most women and minorities. We deplore invidious race and gender distinctions; we hope that no misunderstanding of our program will prolong them. Unfortunately, nearly all blacks and women have been disadvantaged to some degree by bias against their groups, and it is impractical for universities to undertake the detailed investigations that would be needed to assess how much particular individuals have suffered or gained from racism and sexism. We appeal to you to share the historical values of fair opportunity and mutual respect that underlie this policy; we hope that, even though its effects may be personally disappointing, you can see the policy as an appropriate response to the current situation."

Unfortunately, as interests conflict and tempers rise, it is difficult to convey this idea without giving an unintended message as well. White males unhappy about the immediate effects of affirmative action may read the policy as saying that "justice" is the official word for giving preferential treatment to whatever group one happens to favor. Some may see a subtext insinuating that blacks and women are naturally inferior and "cannot make it on their own." Such cynical readings reveal either misunderstanding or the willful refusal to take the moral reasoning underlying affirmative action seriously. They pose serious obstacles to the success of affirmative action—practical problems that may be more intractable than respectful moral disagreement and counter-argument. But some types of affirmative action invite misunderstanding and suspicion more than others. For this reason, anyone who accepts the general case for affirmative action suggested here would do well to reexamine in detail the means by which they hope to communicate its message.

DISCUSSION QUESTIONS

1. Hill mentions that candidates to a university have a right to "formal justice." What is formal justice? Why does Hill claim that formal justice is "compatible with substantively unjust rules and standards"?

2. What "message" does Hill think is sent by the "forward-looking" approach of providing justification for affirmative action policies? Why does he think this is the wrong message to give? Do you agree with Hill's characterization of the received message? Even if you do, do you agree that it is the "wrong" message? Defend your answer. What other reasons does Hill give for rejecting this "forward-looking" approach? Evaluate.

3. How does Hill characterize "backward-looking" arguments which attempt to justify affirmative action? While Hill notes that such arguments "acknowledg[e] some important points missing in most exclusively forward-looking arguments," he nonetheless maintains that this strategy is vulnerable to serious problems. What are they? Do you agree? Why or why not? As with the "forward-looking" arguments, Hill also criticizes the message sent by "backward-looking" arguments. Explain and evaluate his objection.

4. Explain why Hill rejects both the consequentialist and Rossian perspectives which are commonly used to evaluate acts and policies. What sort of perspective does Hill himself advocate that we adopt? How does this relate to the issue of affirmative action?

5. On what grounds does Hill think we would be able to correctly claim that a white male applicant's rights have been violated by affirmative action programs? How does Hill argue that affirmative action programs which adhere to the ideals of mutual respect, trust, and fair opportunity may be called legitimate? Evaluate. Additionally, characterize (in your own words) the "message" that Hill thinks such programs would send. Do you think that it is possible (in a practical sense) for an affirmative action program to be designed such that it would be able to send such a message? Why or why not?

B.
Applications

82

Furman v. Georgia (1972)

The Supreme Court case of *Furman v. Georgia* (decided in 1972) brought to the country's attention important questions about the role of the death penalty within the system of criminal justice. Defendant William Henry Furman was convicted of shooting and killing a homeowner while burglarizing the home. Sentenced to the death penalty, Furman argued that this punishment was "cruel and unusual." The 5/4 decision of the court led to a temporary *de facto* moratorium on the death penalty in the US for several years.

SOURCE

408 U.S. 238 (U.S. Supreme Court).

[...]

The Court holds that the imposition and carrying out of the death penalty in these cases constitute cruel and unusual punishment in violation of the Eighth and Fourteenth Amendments. The judgment in each case is therefore reversed insofar as it leaves undisturbed the death sentence imposed, and the cases are remanded for further proceedings.

Justice Douglas's Concurring Opinion

In these three cases the death penalty was imposed, one of them for murder, and two for rape. In each the determination of whether the penalty should be death or a lighter punishment was left by the State to the discretion of the judge or of the jury. In each of the three cases the trial was to a jury. They are here on petitions for *certiorari* which we granted limited to the question whether the imposition and execution of the death penalty constitute "cruel and unusual punishment" within the meaning of the Eighth Amendment as applied to the States by the Fourteenth. I vote to vacate each judgment, believing that the exaction of the death penalty does violate the Eighth and Fourteenth Amendments....

It has been assumed in our decisions that punishment by death is not cruel, unless the manner of execution can be said to be inhuman and barbarous. It is also said in our opinions that the proscription of cruel and unusual punishments "is not fastened to the obsolete but may acquire meaning as public opinion becomes enlightened by a humane justice." *Weems v. United States*. A like statement was made in *Trop v. Dulles*, that the Eighth Amendment "must draw its meaning from the evolving standards of decency that mark the progress of a maturing society."

The generality of a law inflicting capital punishment is one thing. What may be said of the validity of a law on the books and what may be done with the law in its application do, or may, lead to quite different conclusions.

It would seem to be incontestable that the death penalty inflicted on one defendant is "unusual" if it discriminates against him by reason of his race, religion, wealth, social position, or class, or if it is imposed under a procedure that gives room for the play of such prejudices....

But the debates of the First Congress on the Bill of Rights throw little light on its intended meaning. All that appears is the following:

> Mr. Smith, of South Carolina, objected to the words 'nor cruel and unusual punishments;' the import of them being too indefinite.

> Mr. Livermore: The clause seems to express a great deal of humanity, on which account I have no objection to it; but as it seems to have no meaning in it, I do not think it necessary. What is meant by the terms excessive bail? Who are to be the judges? What is understood by excessive fines? It lies with the court to determine. No cruel and unusual punishment is to be inflicted; it is sometimes necessary to hang a man, villains often deserve whipping, and perhaps having their ears cut off; but are we in future to be prevented from inflicting these punishments because they are cruel? If a more lenient mode of correcting vice and deterring others from the commission of it could be invented, it would be very prudent in the Legislature to adopt it; but until we have some security that this will be done, we ought not to be restrained from making necessary laws by any declaration of this kind.

The words "cruel and unusual" certainly include penalties that are barbaric. But the words, at least when read in light of the English proscription against selective and irregular use of penalties, suggest that it is "cruel and unusual" to apply the death penalty—or any other penalty—selectively to minorities whose numbers are few, who are outcasts of society, and who are unpopular, but whom society is willing to see suffer though it would not countenance general application of the same penalty across the board.

There is increasing recognition of the fact that the basic theme of equal protection is implicit in "cruel and unusual" punishments. "A penalty ... should be considered 'unusually' imposed if it is administered arbitrarily or discriminatorily." The same authors add that "the extreme rarity with which applicable death penalty provisions are put to use raises a strong inference of arbitrariness." The President's Commission on Law Enforcement and Administration of Justice recently concluded:

> Finally there is evidence that the imposition of the death sentence and the exercise of dispensing power by the courts and the executive follow discriminatory patterns. The death sentence is disproportionately imposed and carried out on the poor, the Negro, and the members of unpopular groups.

Those who wrote the Eighth Amendment knew what price their forebears had paid for a system based, not on equal justice, but on discrimination. In those days the target was not the blacks or the poor, but the dissenters, those who opposed absolutism in government, who struggled for a parliamentary regime, and who opposed governments' recurring efforts to foist a particular religion on the people. But the tool of capital punishment was used with vengeance against the opposition and those unpopular with the regime. One cannot read this history without realizing that the desire for equality was reflected in the ban against "cruel and unusual punishments" contained in the Eighth Amendment.

In a Nation committed to equal protection of the laws there is no permissible "caste" aspect of law enforcement. Yet we know that the discretion of judges and juries in imposing the death penalty enables the penalty to be selectively applied, feeding prejudices against the accused if he is poor and despised, and lacking political clout, or if he is a member of a suspect or unpopular minority, and saving those who by social position may be in a more protected position. In ancient Hindu law a Brahman was exempt from capital punishment, and under that law, "generally, in the law books, punishment increased in severity as social status diminished." We have, I fear, taken in practice the same position, partially as a result of making the death penalty discretionary and partially as a result of the ability of the rich to purchase the services of the most respected and most resourceful legal talent in the Nation.

The high service rendered by the "cruel and unusual" punishment clause of the Eighth Amendment is to require legislatures to write penal laws that are evenhanded, nonselective, and nonarbitrary, and to require judges to see to it that general laws are not applied sparsely, selectively, and spottily to unpopular groups.

A law that stated that anyone making more than $50,000 would be exempt from the death penalty would plainly fall, as would a law that in terms said that blacks, those who never went beyond the fifth grade in school, those who made less than $3,000 a year, or those who were unpopular or unstable should be the only people executed. A law which in the overall view reaches that result in practice has no more sanctity than a law which in terms provides the same.

Thus, these discretionary statutes are unconstitutional in their operation. They are pregnant with discrimination and discrimination is an ingredient not compatible with the idea of equal protection of the laws that is implicit in the ban on "cruel and unusual" punishments.

I concur in the judgments of the Court.

Justice Brennan's Concurring Opinion

III

The punishment challenged in these cases is death. Death, of course, is a "traditional" punishment, *Trop v. Dulles*, one that "has been employed throughout our history," and its constitutional background is accordingly an appropriate subject of inquiry.

There is, first, a textual consideration raised by the Bill of Rights itself. The Fifth Amendment declares that if a particular crime is punishable by death, a person charged with that crime is entitled to certain procedural protections. We can thus infer that the Framers recognized the existence of what was then a common punishment. We cannot, however, make the further inference that they intended to exempt this particular punishment from the express prohibition of the Cruel and Unusual Punishments Clause. Nor is there any indication in the debates on the Clause that a special exception was to be made for death. If anything, the indication is to the contrary, for *Livermore* specifically mentioned death as a candidate for future proscription under the Clause. Finally, it does not advance analysis to insist that the Framers did not believe that adoption of the Bill of Rights would immediately prevent the infliction of the punishment of death; neither did they believe that it would immediately prevent the infliction of other corporal punishments that, although common at the time, see n. 6, *supra*, are now acknowledged to be impermissible.

There is also the consideration that this Court has decided three cases involving constitutional challenges to particular methods of inflicting this punishment. In *Wilkerson v. Utah* and *In re Kemmler*, the Court, expressing in both cases the since-rejected "historical" view of the Clause, approved death by shooting and death by electrocution. In *Wilkerson*, the Court concluded that shooting was a common method of execution … in *Kemmler*, the Court held that the Clause did not apply to the States. In *Louisiana ex rel. Francis v. Resweber*, the Court approved a second attempt at electrocution after the first had failed. It was said that "the Fourteenth

[Amendment] would prohibit by its due process clause execution by a state in a cruel manner," but that the abortive attempt did not make the "subsequent execution any more cruel in the constitutional sense than any other execution." These three decisions thus reveal that the Court, while ruling upon various methods of inflicting death, has assumed in the past that death was a constitutionally permissible punishment. Past assumptions, however, are not sufficient to limit the scope of our examination of this punishment today. The constitutionality of death itself under the Cruel and Unusual Punishments Clause is before this Court for the first time; we cannot avoid the question by recalling past cases that never directly considered it.

The question, then, is whether the deliberate infliction of death is today consistent with the command of the Clause that the State may not inflict punishments that do not comport with human dignity. I will analyze the punishment of death in terms of the principles set out above and the cumulative test to which they lead: It is a denial of human dignity for the State arbitrarily to subject a person to an unusually severe punishment that society has indicated it does not regard as acceptable, and that cannot be shown to serve any penal purpose more effectively than a significantly less drastic punishment. Under these principles and this test, death is today a "cruel and unusual" punishment.

Death is a unique punishment in the United States. In a society that so strongly affirms the sanctity of life, not surprisingly the common view is that death is the ultimate sanction. This natural human feeling appears all about us. There has been no national debate about punishment, in general or by imprisonment, comparable to the debate about the punishment of death. No other punishment has been so continuously restricted, nor has any State yet abolished prisons, as some have abolished this punishment. And those States that still inflict death reserve it for the most heinous crimes. Juries, of course, have always treated death cases differently, as have governors exercising their commutation powers. Criminal defendants are of the same view. "As all practicing lawyers know, who have defended persons charged

with capital offenses, often the only goal possible is to avoid the death penalty" (*Griffin v. Illinois*). Some legislatures have required particular procedures, such as two-stage trials and automatic appeals, applicable only in death cases. "It is the universal experience in the administration of criminal justice that those charged with capital offenses are granted special considerations." This Court, too, almost always treats death cases as a class apart. And the unfortunate effect of this punishment upon the functioning of the judicial process is well known; no other punishment has a similar effect.

The only explanation for the uniqueness of death is its extreme severity. Death is today an unusually severe punishment, unusual in its pain, in its finality, and in its enormity. No other existing punishment is comparable to death in terms of physical and mental suffering. Although our information is not conclusive, it appears that there is no method available that guarantees an immediate and painless death. Since the discontinuance of flogging as a constitutionally permissible punishment, death remains as the only punishment that may involve the conscious infliction of physical pain. In addition, we know that mental pain is an inseparable part of our practice of punishing criminals by death, for the prospect of pending execution exacts a frightful toll during the inevitable long wait between the imposition of sentence and the actual infliction of death. As the California Supreme Court pointed out, "the process of carrying out a verdict of death is often so degrading and brutalizing to the human spirit as to constitute psychological torture." Indeed, as Mr. Justice Frankfurter noted, "the onset of insanity while awaiting execution of a death sentence is not a rare phenomenon."

The unusual severity of death is manifested most clearly in its finality and enormity. Death, in these respects, is in a class by itself. Expatriation, for example, is a punishment that "destroys for the individual the political existence that was centuries in the development," that "strips the citizen of his status in the national and international political community," and that puts "his very existence" in jeopardy. Expatriation thus inherently entails "the total destruction of the individual's status in organized society." "In short, the expatriate has lost the right to have rights." Yet, demonstrably, expatriation is not "a fate worse than death." Although death, like expatriation, destroys the individual's "political existence" and his "status in organized society," it does more, for, unlike expatriation, death also destroys "his very existence." There is, too, at least the possibility that the expatriate will in the future regain "the right to have rights." Death forecloses even that possibility.

Death is truly an awesome punishment. The calculated killing of a human being by the State involves, by its very nature, a denial of the executed person's humanity. The contrast with the plight of a person punished by imprisonment is evident. An individual in prison does not lose "the right to have rights." A prisoner retains, for example, the constitutional rights to the free exercise of religion, to be free of cruel and unusual punishments, and to treatment as a "person" for purposes of due process of law and the equal protection of the laws. A prisoner remains a member of the human family. Moreover, he retains the right of access to the courts. His punishment is not irrevocable. Apart from the common charge, grounded upon the recognition of human fallibility, that the punishment of death must inevitably be inflicted upon innocent men, we know that death has been the lot of men whose convictions were unconstitutionally secured in view of later, retroactively applied, holdings of this Court. The punishment itself may have been unconstitutionally inflicted, see *Witherspoon v. Illinois*, yet the finality of death precludes relief. An executed person has indeed "lost the right to have rights." As one 19th-century proponent of punishing criminals by death declared, "When a man is hung, there is an end of our relations with him. His execution is a way of saying, 'You are not fit for this world, take your chance elsewhere.'"

In comparison to all other punishments today, then, the deliberate extinguishment of human life by the State is uniquely degrading to human dignity. I would not hesitate to hold, on that ground alone, that death is today a "cruel and unusual" punishment, were it not that death is a punishment of longstanding usage and acceptance in this country. I therefore turn to the second principle—that the State may not arbitrarily inflict an unusually severe punishment.

The outstanding characteristic of our present practice of punishing criminals by death is the infrequency with which we resort to it. The evidence is conclusive that death is not the ordinary punishment for any crime....

When a country of over 200 million people inflicts an unusually severe punishment no more than 50 times a year, the inference is strong that the punishment is not being regularly and fairly applied. To dispel it would indeed require a clear showing of nonarbitrary infliction.

Although there are no exact figures available, we know that thousands of murders and rapes are committed annually in States where death is an authorized punishment for those crimes. However the rate of infliction is characterized—as "freakishly" or "spectacularly" rare, or simply as rare—it would take the purest sophistry to deny that death is inflicted in only a minute fraction of these cases. How much rarer, after all, could the infliction of death be?

When the punishment of death is inflicted in a trivial number of the cases in which it is legally available, the conclusion is virtually inescapable that it is being inflicted arbitrarily. Indeed, it smacks of little more than a lottery system. The States claim, however, that this rarity is evidence not of arbitrariness, but of informed selectivity: Death is inflicted, they say, only in "extreme" cases.

Informed selectivity, of course, is a value not to be denigrated. Yet presumably the States could make precisely the same claim if there were 10 executions per year, or five, or even if there were but one. That there may be as many as 50 per year does not strengthen the claim. When the rate of infliction is at this low level, it is highly implausible that only the worst criminals or the criminals who commit the worst crimes are selected for this punishment. No one has yet suggested a rational basis that could differentiate in those terms the few who die from the many who go to prison. Crimes and criminals simply do not admit of a distinction that can be drawn so finely as to explain, on that ground, the execution of such a tiny sample of those eligible. Certainly the laws that provide for this punishment do not attempt to draw that distinction; all cases to which the laws apply are necessarily "extreme."

Although it is difficult to imagine what further facts would be necessary in order to prove that death is, as my Brother Stewart [from Justice Stewart's concurring opinion in this case] puts it, "wantonly and ... freakishly" inflicted, I need not conclude that arbitrary infliction is patently obvious. I am not considering this punishment by the isolated light of one principle. The probability of arbitrariness is sufficiently substantial that it can be relied upon, in combination with the other principles, in reaching a judgment on the constitutionality of this punishment.

When there is a strong probability that an unusually severe and degrading punishment is being inflicted arbitrarily, we may well expect that society will disapprove of its infliction. I turn, therefore, to the third principle. An examination of the history and present operation of the American practice of punishing criminals by death reveals that this punishment has been almost totally rejected by contemporary society.

... I emphasize, however, one significant conclusion that emerges from that history. From the beginning of our Nation, the punishment of death has stirred acute public controversy. Although pragmatic arguments for and against the punishment have been frequently advanced, this longstanding and heated controversy cannot be explained solely as the result of differences over the practical wisdom of a particular government policy. At bottom, the battle has been waged on moral grounds. The country has debated whether a society for which the dignity of the individual is the supreme value can, without a fundamental inconsistency, follow the practice of deliberately putting some of its members to death. In the United States, as in other nations of the western world, "the struggle about this punishment has been one between ancient and deeply rooted beliefs in retribution, atonement or vengeance on the one hand, and, on

the other, beliefs in the personal value and dignity of the common man that were born of the democratic movement of the eighteenth century, as well as beliefs in the scientific approach to an understanding of the motive forces of human conduct, which are the result of the growth of the sciences of behavior during the nineteenth and twentieth centuries."[1] It is this essentially moral conflict that forms the backdrop for the past changes in and the present operation of our system of imposing death as a punishment for crime....

Thus, although "the death penalty has been employed throughout our history," in fact the history of this punishment is one of successive restriction. What was once a common punishment has become, in the context of a continuing moral debate, increasingly rare. The evolution of this punishment evidences, not that it is an inevitable part of the American scene, but that it has proved progressively more troublesome to the national conscience. The result of this movement is our current system of administering the punishment, under which death sentences are rarely imposed.

The progressive decline in, and the current rarity of, the infliction of death demonstrate that our society seriously questions the appropriateness of this punishment today. The States point out that many legislatures authorize death as the punishment for certain crimes and that substantial segments of the public, as reflected in opinion polls and referendum votes, continue to support it. Yet the availability of this punishment through statutory authorization, as well as the polls and referenda, which amount simply to approval of that authorization, simply underscores the extent to which our society has in fact rejected this punishment. When an unusually severe punishment is authorized for wide-scale application but not, because of society's refusal, inflicted save in a few instances, the inference is compelling that there is a deep-seated reluctance to inflict it. Indeed, the likelihood is great that the punishment is tolerated

---

[1] [T. Sellin, *The Death Penalty: A Report for the Moral Penal Code Project of the American Law Institute* 15 (1959).]

only because of its disuse. The objective indicator of society's view of an unusually severe punishment is what society does with it, and today society will inflict death upon only a small sample of the eligible criminals. Rejection could hardly be more complete without becoming absolute. At the very least, I must conclude that contemporary society views this punishment with substantial doubt.

The final principle to be considered is that an unusually severe and degrading punishment may not be excessive in view of the purposes for which it is inflicted. This principle, too, is related to the others. When there is a strong probability that the State is arbitrarily inflicting an unusually severe punishment that is subject to grave societal doubts, it is likely also that the punishment cannot be shown to be serving any penal purpose that could not be served equally well by some less severe punishment.

The States' primary claim is that death is a necessary punishment because it prevents the commission of capital crimes more effectively than any less severe punishment. The first part of this claim is that the infliction of death is necessary to stop the individuals executed from committing further crimes. The sufficient answer to this is that if a criminal convicted of a capital crime poses a danger to society, effective administration of the State's pardon and parole laws can delay or deny his release from prison, and techniques of isolation can eliminate or minimize the danger while he remains confined.

The more significant argument is that the threat of death prevents the commission of capital crimes because it deters potential criminals who would not be deterred by the threat of imprisonment. The argument is not based upon evidence that the threat of death is a superior deterrent. Indeed, ... the available evidence uniformly indicates, although it does not conclusively prove, that the threat of death has no greater deterrent effect than the threat of imprisonment. The States argue, however, that they are entitled to rely upon common human experience, and that experience, they say, supports the conclusion that death must be a more effective deterrent than any less severe punishment. Because people fear death the most, the argument runs, the threat of death must be the greatest deterrent.

It is important to focus upon the precise import of this argument. It is not denied that many, and probably most, capital crimes cannot be deterred by the threat of punishment. Thus the argument can apply only to those who think rationally about the commission of capital crimes. Particularly is that true when the potential criminal, under this argument, must not only consider the risk of punishment, but also distinguish between two possible punishments. The concern, then, is with a particular type of potential criminal, the rational person who will commit a capital crime knowing that the punishment is long-term imprisonment, which may well be for the rest of his life, but will not commit the crime knowing that the punishment is death. On the face of it, the assumption that such persons exist is implausible.

In any event, this argument cannot be appraised in the abstract. We are not presented with the theoretical question whether under any imaginable circumstances the threat of death might be a greater deterrent to the commission of capital crimes than the threat of imprisonment. We are concerned with the practice of punishing criminals by death as it exists in the United States today. Proponents of this argument necessarily admit that its validity depends upon the existence of a system in which the punishment of death is invariably and swiftly imposed. Our system, of course, satisfies neither condition. A rational person contemplating a murder or rape is confronted, not with the certainty of a speedy death, but with the slightest possibility that he will be executed in the distant future. The risk of death is remote and improbable; in contrast, the risk of longterm imprisonment is near and great. In short, whatever the speculative validity of the assumption that the threat of death is a superior deterrent, there is no reason to believe that as currently administered the punishment of death is necessary to deter the commission of capital crimes. Whatever might be the case were all or substantially all eligible criminals quickly put to death, unverifiable possibilities are an insufficient basis upon which to conclude that the threat of death today has any greater deterrent efficacy than the threat of imprisonment.

There is, however, another aspect to the argument that the punishment of death is necessary for the protection of society. The infliction of death, the States urge, serves to manifest the community's outrage at the commission of the crime. It is, they say, a concrete public expression of moral indignation that inculcates respect for the law and helps assure a more peaceful community. Moreover, we are told, not only does the punishment of death exert this widespread moralizing influence upon community values, it also satisfies the popular demand for grievous condemnation of abhorrent crimes and thus prevents disorder, lynching, and attempts by private citizens to take the law into their own hands.

The question, however, is not whether death serves these supposed purposes of punishment, but whether death serves them more effectively than imprisonment. There is no evidence whatever that utilization of imprisonment rather than death encourages private blood feuds and other disorders. Surely if there were such a danger, the execution of a handful of criminals each year would not prevent it. The assertion that death alone is a sufficiently emphatic denunciation for capital crimes suffers from the same defect. If capital crimes require the punishment of death in order to provide moral reinforcement for the basic values of the community, those values can only be undermined when death is so rarely inflicted upon the criminals who commit the crimes. Furthermore, it is certainly doubtful that the infliction of death by the State does in fact strengthen the community's moral code; if the deliberate extinguishment of human life has any effect at all, it more likely tends to lower our respect for life and brutalize our values. That, after all, is why we no longer carry out public executions. In any event, this claim simply means that one purpose of punishment is to indicate social disapproval of crime. To serve that purpose our laws distribute punishments according to the gravity of crimes and punish more severely the crimes society regards as more serious. That

purpose cannot justify any particular punishment as the upper limit of severity.

There is, then, no substantial reason to believe that the punishment of death, as currently administered, is necessary for the protection of society. The only other purpose suggested, one that is independent of protection for society, is retribution. Shortly stated, retribution in this context means that criminals are put to death because they deserve it.

Although it is difficult to believe that any State today wishes to proclaim adherence to "naked vengeance," the States claim, in reliance upon its statutory authorization, that death is the only fit punishment for capital crimes and that this retributive purpose justifies its infliction. In the past, judged by its statutory authorization, death was considered the only fit punishment for the crime of forgery, for the first federal criminal statute provided a mandatory death penalty for that crime. Obviously, concepts of justice change; no immutable moral order requires death for murderers and rapists. The claim that death is a just punishment necessarily refers to the existence of certain public beliefs. The claim must be that for capital crimes death alone comports with society's notion of proper punishment. As administered today, however, the punishment of death cannot be justified as a necessary means of exacting retribution from criminals. When the overwhelming number of criminals who commit capital crimes go to prison, it cannot be concluded that death serves the purpose of retribution more effectively than imprisonment. The asserted public belief that murderers and rapists deserve to die is flatly inconsistent with the execution of a random few. As the history of the punishment of death in this country shows, our society wishes to prevent crime; we have no desire to kill criminals simply to get even with them.

In sum, the punishment of death is inconsistent with all four principles: Death is an unusually severe and degrading punishment; there is a strong probability that it is inflicted arbitrarily; its rejection by contemporary society is virtually total; and there is no reason to believe that it serves any penal purpose more effectively than the less severe punishment of imprisonment. The function of these principles is to enable a court to determine whether a punishment comports with human dignity. Death, quite simply, does not.

[...]

When this country was founded, memories of the Stuart horrors[1] were fresh and severe corporal punishments were common. Death was not then a unique punishment. The practice of punishing criminals by death, moreover, was widespread and by and large acceptable to society. Indeed, without developed prison systems, there was frequently no workable alternative. Since that time, successive restrictions, imposed against the background of a continuing moral controversy, have drastically curtailed the use of this punishment. Today death is a uniquely and unusually severe punishment. When examined by the principles applicable under the Cruel and Unusual Punishments Clause, death stands condemned as fatally offensive to human dignity. The punishment of death is therefore "cruel and unusual," and the States may no longer inflict it as a punishment for crimes. Rather than kill an arbitrary handful of criminals each year, the States will confine them in prison. "The State thereby suffers nothing and loses no power. The purpose of punishment is fulfilled, crime is repressed by penalties of just, not tormenting, severity, its repetition is prevented, and hope is given for the reformation of the criminal" (*Weems v. United States*).

I concur in the judgments of the Court.

Justice White's Concurring Opinion

The facial constitutionality of statutes requiring the imposition of the death penalty for first-degree murder, for more narrowly defined categories of murder, or for rape would present quite different issues under the Eighth Amendment than are posed by the cases before us. In joining the Court's judgments,

therefore, I do not at all intimate that the death penalty is unconstitutional *per se* or that there is no system of capital punishment that would comport with the Eighth Amendment. That question, ably argued by several of my Brethren, is not presented by these cases and need not be decided.

The narrower question to which I address myself concerns the constitutionality of capital punishment statutes under which (1) the legislature authorizes the imposition of the death penalty for murder or rape; (2) the legislature does not itself mandate the penalty in any particular class or kind of case (that is, legislative will is not frustrated if the penalty is never imposed), but delegates to judges or juries the decisions as to those cases, if any, in which the penalty will be utilized; and (3) judges and juries have ordered the death penalty with such infrequency that the odds are now very much against imposition and execution of the penalty with respect to any convicted murderer or rapist. It is in this context that we must consider whether the execution of these petitioners would violate the Eighth Amendment.

I begin with what I consider a near truism: that the death penalty could so seldom be imposed that it would cease to be a credible deterrent or measurably to contribute to any other end of punishment in the criminal justice system. It is perhaps true that no matter how infrequently those convicted of rape or murder are executed, the penalty so imposed is not disproportionate to the crime and those executed may deserve exactly what they received. It would also be clear that executed defendants are finally and completely incapacitated from again committing rape or murder or any other crime. But when imposition of the penalty reaches a certain degree of infrequency, it would be very doubtful that any existing general need for retribution would be measurably satisfied. Nor could it be said with confidence that society's need for specific deterrence justifies death for so few when for so many in like circumstances life imprisonment or shorter prison terms are judged sufficient, or that community values are measurably reinforced by authorizing a penalty so rarely invoked.

---

[1] [During the Stuart period in England (1603–1714), torture was used to extract confessions or names of co-conspirators, famously so in the case of the rebel Guy Fawkes (1570–1606).]

Most important, a major goal of the criminal law—to deter others by punishing the convicted criminal—would not be substantially served where the penalty is so seldom invoked that it ceases to be the credible threat essential to influence the conduct of others. For present purposes I accept the morality and utility of punishing one person to influence another. I accept also the effectiveness of punishment generally and need not reject the death penalty as a more effective deterrent than a lesser punishment. But common sense and experience tell us that seldom-enforced laws become ineffective measures for controlling human conduct and that the death penalty, unless imposed with sufficient frequency, will make little contribution to deterring those crimes for which it may be exacted.

The imposition and execution of the death penalty are obviously cruel in the dictionary sense. But the penalty has not been considered cruel and unusual punishment in the constitutional sense because it was thought justified by the social ends it was deemed to serve. At the moment that it ceases realistically to further these purposes, however, the emerging question is whether its imposition in such circumstances would violate the Eighth Amendment. It is my view that it would, for its imposition would then be the pointless and needless extinction of life with only marginal contributions to any discernible social or public purposes. A penalty with such negligible returns to the State would be patently excessive and cruel and unusual punishment violative of the Eighth Amendment.

It is also my judgment that this point has been reached with respect to capital punishment as it is presently administered under the statutes involved in these cases. Concededly, it is difficult to prove as a general proposition that capital punishment, however administered, more effectively serves the ends of the criminal law than does imprisonment. But however that may be, I cannot avoid the conclusion that as the statutes before us are now administered, the penalty is so infrequently imposed that the threat of execution is too attenuated to be of substantial service to criminal justice.

I concur in the judgments of the Court.

Chief Justice Burger's Dissenting Opinion

If we were possessed of legislative power, I would either join with Mr. Justice Brennan and Mr. Justice Marshall or, at the very least, restrict the use of capital punishment to a small category of the most heinous crimes. Our constitutional inquiry, however, must be divorced from personal feelings as to the morality and efficacy of the death penalty, and be confined to the meaning and applicability of the uncertain language of the Eighth Amendment. There is no novelty in being called upon to interpret a constitutional provision that is less than self-defining, but, of all our fundamental guarantees, the ban on "cruel and unusual punishments" is one of the most difficult to translate into judicially manageable terms. The widely divergent views of the Amendment expressed in today's opinions reveal the haze that surrounds this constitutional command. Yet it is essential to our role as a court that we not seize upon the enigmatic character of the guarantee as an invitation to enact our personal predilections into law.

Although the Eighth Amendment literally reads as prohibiting only those punishments that are both "cruel" and "unusual," history compels the conclusion that the Constitution prohibits all punishments of extreme and barbarous cruelty, regardless of how frequently or infrequently imposed.

II

Counsel for petitioners properly concede that capital punishment was not impermissibly cruel at the time of the adoption of the Eighth Amendment. Not only do the records of the debates indicate that the Founding Fathers were limited in their concern to the prevention of torture, but it is also clear from the language of the Constitution itself that there was no thought whatever of the elimination of capital punishment. The opening sentence of the Fifth Amendment is a guarantee that the death penalty not be imposed "unless on a presentment or indictment of a Grand Jury." The Double Jeopardy Clause of the Fifth Amendment is a prohibition against being "twice put in jeopardy of life" for the same offense. Similarly, the Due Process Clause commands "due process of law" before an accused can be "deprived of life, liberty, or property." Thus, the explicit language of the Constitution affirmatively acknowledges the legal power to impose capital punishment; it does not expressly or by implication acknowledge the legal power to impose any of the various punishments that have been banned as cruel since 1791. Since the Eighth Amendment was adopted on the same day in 1791 as the Fifth Amendment, it hardly needs more to establish that the death penalty was not "cruel" in the constitutional sense at that time.

In the 181 years since the enactment of the Eighth Amendment, not a single decision of this Court has cast the slightest shadow of a doubt on the constitutionality of capital punishment. In rejecting Eighth Amendment attacks on particular modes of execution, the Court has more than once implicitly denied that capital punishment is impermissibly "cruel" in the constitutional sense [see *Wilkerson v. Utah, Louisiana ex rel. Francis v. Resweber, In re Kemmler*]. "The Eighth Amendment forbids 'cruel and unusual punishments.' In my view, these words cannot be read to outlaw capital punishment because that penalty was in common use and authorized by law here and in the countries from which our ancestors came at the time the Amendment was adopted. It is inconceivable to me that the framers intended to end capital punishment by the Amendment." (*McGautha v. California*) (separate opinion).

DISCUSSION QUESTIONS

1. Douglas (for the majority) and Burger (for the dissent) disagree as to whether jury discretion with respect to sentencing in capital cases violates the Eighth Amendment. Explain their dispute. With whom do you agree? Explain.

2. How does Brennan (for the majority) understand what it is for a punishment to meet the requirements of the Eighth Amendment? Explain the four principles that he claims should guide the application of that amendment.

3. Explain what White (for the majority) takes the primary goal of punishment to be. Does he think that the death penalty serves that goal? Explain.

83

Woodson v. North Carolina (1976)

Petitioners James Tyrone Woodson and Luby Waxton were found guilty of first-degree murder in the shooting death of a convenience-store clerk. North Carolina's law at the time mandated an automatic assignment of the death penalty to any first-degree murder conviction. The defendants appealed their sentencing, arguing that the death penalty constituted cruel and unusual punishment in violation of the Eighth and Fourteenth Amendments. The majority opinion of the Court concluded that a mandatory death sentence was indeed unconstitutional, arguing that the North Carolina law failed to meet the Constitution's requirement that punishment be "exercised within the limits of civilized standards."

SOURCE

428 U.S. 280 U.S. Supreme Court.

Following this Court's decision in *Furman v. Georgia* the North Carolina law that previously had provided that in cases of first-degree murder the jury in its unbridled discretion could choose whether the convicted defendant should be sentenced to death or life imprisonment was changed to make the death penalty mandatory for that crime. Petitioners, whose convictions of first-degree murder and whose death sentences under the new statute were upheld by the Supreme Court of North Carolina, have challenged the statute's constitutionality.

Held: The judgment is reversed insofar as it upheld the death sentences, and the case is remanded.

Opinion of the Court
… The question in this case is whether the imposition of a death sentence for the crime of first-degree murder under the law of North Carolina violates the Eighth and Fourteenth Amendments.

I

The petitioners were convicted of first-degree murder as the result of their participation in an armed robbery of a convenience food store, in the course of which the cashier was killed and a customer was seriously wounded. There were four participants in the robbery: the petitioners James Tyrone Woodson and Luby Waxton and two others, Leonard Tucker and Johnnie Lee Carroll. At the petitioners' trial Tucker and Carroll testified for the prosecution after having been permitted to plead guilty to lesser offenses; the petitioners testified to plead own defense.

The evidence for the prosecution established that the four men had been discussing a possible robbery for some time. On the fatal day Woodson had been drinking heavily. About 9:30 p.m., Waxton and Tucker came to the trailer where Woodson was staying. When Woodson came out of the trailer, Waxton struck him in the face and threatened to kill him in an effort to make him sober up and come along on the robbery. The three proceeded to Waxton's trailer where they met Carroll. Waxton armed himself with a nickel-plated derringer, and Tucker handed Woodson a rifle. The four then set out by automobile to rob the store. Upon arriving at their destination Tucker and Waxton went into the store while Carroll and Woodson remained in the car as lookouts. Once inside the store, Tucker purchased a package of cigarettes from the woman cashier. Waxton then also asked for a package of cigarettes, but as the cashier approached him he pulled the derringer out of his hip pocket and fatally shot her at point-blank range. Waxton then took the money tray from the cash register and gave it to Tucker, who carried it out of the store, pushing past an entering customer as he reached the door. After he was outside, Tucker heard a second shot from inside the store, and shortly thereafter Waxton emerged, carrying a handful of paper money. Tucker and Waxton got in the car and the four drove away.

The petitioners' testimony agreed in large part with this version of the circumstances of the robbery. It differed diametrically in one important respect: Waxton claimed that he never had a gun, and that Tucker had shot both the cashier and the customer.

During the trial Waxton asked to be allowed to plead guilty to the same lesser offenses to which Tucker had pleaded guilty, but the solicitor refused to accept the pleas. Woodson, by contrast, maintained throughout the trial that he had been coerced by Waxton, that he was therefore innocent, and that he would not consider pleading guilty to any offense.

The petitioners were found guilty on all charges, and, as was required by statute, sentenced to death.

The Supreme Court of North Carolina affirmed. We granted *certiorari* to consider whether the imposition of the death penalties in this case comports with the Eighth and Fourteenth Amendments to the United States Constitution.

II

The petitioners argue that the imposition of the death penalty under any circumstances is cruel and unusual punishment in violation of the Eighth and Fourteenth Amendments. We reject this argument for the reasons stated today in *Gregg v. Georgia.*

III

At the time of this Court's decision in *Furman v. Georgia,* North Carolina law provided that in cases of first-degree murder, the jury in its unbridled discretion could choose whether the convicted defendant should be sentenced to death or to life imprisonment. After the Furman decision the Supreme Court of North Carolina in *State v. Waddell,* held unconstitutional the provision of the death penalty statute that gave the jury the option of returning a verdict of guilty without capital punishment, but held further that this provision was severable so that the statute survived as a mandatory death penalty law.

The North Carolina General Assembly in 1974 followed the court's lead and enacted a new statute that was essentially unchanged from the old one except that it made the death penalty mandatory. The statute now reads as follows:

> Murder in the first and second degree
> defined; punishment.—A murder which shall
> be perpetrated by means of poison, lying
> in wait, imprisonment, starving, torture,
> or by any other kind of willful, deliberate
> and premeditated killing, or which shall be
> committed in the perpetration or attempt
> to perpetrate any arson, rape, robbery,
> kidnapping, burglary or other felony, shall
> be deemed to be murder in the first degree
> and shall be punished with death. All other
> kinds of murder shall be deemed murder in

the second degree, and shall be punished by imprisonment for a term of not less than two years nor more than life imprisonment in the State's prison.

It was under this statute that the petitioners, who committed their crime on June 3, 1974, were tried, convicted, and sentenced to death.

North Carolina, unlike Florida, Georgia, and Texas, has thus responded to the Furman decision by making death the mandatory sentence for all persons convicted of first-degree murder. In ruling on the constitutionality of the sentences imposed on the petitioners under this North Carolina statute, the Court now addresses for the first time the question whether a death sentence returned pursuant to a law imposing a mandatory death penalty for a broad category of homicidal offenses constitutes cruel and unusual punishment within the meaning of the Eighth and Fourteenth Amendments. The issue, like that explored in *Furman*, involves the procedure employed by the State to select persons for the unique and irreversible penalty of death.

A
The Eighth Amendment stands to assure that the State's power to punish is "exercised within the limits of civilized standards." Central to the application of the Amendment is a determination of contemporary standards regarding the infliction of punishment. As discussed in *Gregg v. Georgia*, indicia of societal values identified in prior opinions include history and traditional usage, legislative enactments, and jury determinations.

In order to provide a frame for assessing the relevancy of these factors in this case we begin by sketching the history of mandatory death penalty statutes in the United States. At the time the Eighth Amendment was adopted in 1791, the States uniformly followed the common-law practice of making death the exclusive and mandatory sentence for certain specified offenses. Although the range of capital offenses in the American Colonies was quite limited in comparison to the more than 200 offenses then punishable by death in England, the

Colonies at the time of the Revolution imposed death sentences on all persons convicted of any of a considerable number of crimes, typically including at a minimum, murder, treason, piracy, arson, rape, robbery, burglary, and sodomy. As at common law, all homicides that were not involuntary, provoked, justified, or excused constituted murder and were automatically punished by death. Almost from the outset jurors reacted unfavorably to the harshness of mandatory death sentences. The States initially responded to this expression of public dissatisfaction with mandatory statutes by limiting the classes of capital offenses.

This reform, however, left unresolved the problem posed by the not infrequent refusal of juries to convict murderers rather than subject them to automatic death sentences. In 1794, Pennsylvania attempted to alleviate the undue severity of the law by confining the mandatory death penalty to "murder of the first degree" encompassing all "wilful, deliberate and premeditated" killings. Other jurisdictions, including Virginia and Ohio, soon enacted similar measures, and within a generation the practice spread to most of the States.

Despite the broad acceptance of the division of murder into degrees, the reform proved to be an unsatisfactory means of identifying persons appropriately punishable by death. Although its failure was due in part to the amorphous nature of the controlling concepts of willfulness, deliberateness, and premeditation, a more fundamental weakness of the reform soon became apparent. Juries continued to find the death penalty inappropriate in a significant number of first-degree murder cases and refused to return guilty verdicts for that crime.

The inadequacy of distinguishing between murderers solely on the basis of legislative criteria narrowing the definition of the capital offense led the States to grant juries sentencing discretion in capital cases. Tennessee in 1838, followed by Alabama in 1841, and Louisiana in 1846, were the first States to abandon mandatory death sentences in favor of discretionary death penalty statutes. This flexibility remedied the harshness of mandatory statutes by permitting the jury to respond to mitigating factors by withholding the death penalty. By the turn of the century, 23 States and the Federal Government had made death sentences discretionary for first-degree murder and other capital offenses. During the next two decades 14 additional States replaced their mandatory death penalty statutes. Thus, by the end of World War I, all but eight States, Hawaii, and the District of Columbia either had adopted discretionary death penalty schemes or abolished the death penalty altogether. By 1963, all of these remaining jurisdictions had replaced their automatic death penalty statutes with discretionary jury sentencing.

The history of mandatory death penalty statutes in the United States thus reveals that the practice of sentencing to death all persons convicted of a particular offense has been rejected as unduly harsh and unworkably rigid. The two crucial indicators of evolving standards of decency respecting the imposition of punishment in our society—jury determinations and legislative enactments—both point conclusively to the repudiation of automatic death sentences. At least since the Revolution, American jurors have, with some regularity, disregarded their oaths and refused to convict defendants where a death sentence was the automatic consequence of a guilty verdict. As we have seen, the initial movement to reduce the number of capital offenses and to separate murder into degrees was prompted in part by the reaction of jurors as well as by reformers who objected to the imposition of death as the penalty for any crime. Nineteenth-century journalists, statesmen, and jurists repeatedly observed that jurors were often deterred from convicting palpably guilty men of first-degree murder under mandatory statutes. Thereafter, continuing evidence of jury reluctance to convict persons of capital offenses in mandatory death penalty jurisdictions resulted in legislative authorization of discretionary jury sentencing by Congress for federal crimes in 1897, by North Carolina in 1949, and by Congress for the District of Columbia in 1962.

As we have noted today in *Gregg v. Georgia*, legislative measures adopted by the people's chosen representatives weigh heavily in ascertaining contemporary standards of decency. The consistent course charted by the state legislatures and by Congress since the middle of the past century demonstrates that the aversion of jurors to mandatory death penalty statutes is shared by society at large.

Still further evidence of the incompatibility of mandatory death penalties with contemporary values is provided by the results of jury sentencing under discretionary statutes. In *Witherspoon v. Illinois*, the Court observed that "one of the most important functions any jury can perform" in exercising its discretion to choose "between life imprisonment and capital punishment" is "to maintain a link between contemporary community values and the penal system." Various studies indicate that even in first-degree murder cases juries with sentencing discretion do not impose the death penalty "with any great frequency." The actions of sentencing juries suggest that under contemporary standards of decency death is viewed as an inappropriate punishment for a substantial portion of convicted first-degree murderers.

Although the Court has never ruled on the constitutionality of mandatory death penalty statutes, on several occasions dating back to 1899 it has commented upon our society's aversion to automatic death sentences. In *Winston v. United States*, the Court noted that the "hardship of punishing with death every crime coming within the definition of murder at common law, and the reluctance of jurors to concur in a capital conviction, have induced American legislatures, in modern times, to allow some cases of murder to be punished by imprisonment, instead of by death." Fifty years after *Winston*, the Court underscored the marked transformation in our attitudes toward mandatory sentences: "The belief no longer prevails that every offense in a like legal category calls for an identical punishment without regard to the past life and habits of a particular offender. This whole country has traveled far from the period in which the death sentence was an automatic and commonplace result of convictions...."

More recently, the Court in *McGautha v. California*, detailed the evolution of discretionary imposition of death sentences in this country, prompted by what it termed the American "rebellion against the common-law rule imposing a mandatory death sentence on all convicted murderers." Perhaps the one important factor about evolving social values regarding capital punishment upon which the Members of the *Furman* Court agreed was the accuracy of *McGautha*'s assessment of our Nation's rejection of mandatory death sentences. Mr. Justice Blackmun, for example, emphasized that legislation requiring an automatic death sentence for specified crimes would be "regressive and of an antique mold" and would mark a return to a "point in our criminology [passed beyond] long ago." The Chief Justice, speaking for the four dissenting Justices in *Furman*, discussed the question of mandatory death sentences at some length:

> I had thought that nothing was clearer
> in history, as we noted in *McGautha* one
> year ago, than the American abhorrence
> of 'the common-law rule imposing a man-
> datory death sentence on all convicted
> murderers.' ... [T]he 19th century move-
> ment away from mandatory death sen-
> tences marked an enlightened introduction
> of flexibility into the sentencing process.
> It recognized that individual culpability is
> not always measured by the category of the
> crime committed. This change in sentenc-
> ing practice was greeted by the Court as a
> humanizing development.

Although it seems beyond dispute that, at the time of the *Furman* decision in 1972, mandatory death penalty statutes had been renounced by American juries and legislatures, there remains the question whether the mandatory statutes adopted by North Carolina and a number of other States following *Furman* evince a sudden reversal of societal values regarding the imposition of capital punishment. In view of the persistent and unswerving legislative rejection of mandatory death penalty statutes beginning in 1838 and continuing for more than 130 years until Furman, it seems evident that

the post-*Furman* enactments reflect attempts by the States to retain the death penalty in a form consistent with the Constitution, rather than a renewed societal acceptance of mandatory death sentencing. The fact that some States have adopted mandatory measures following *Furman* while others have legislated standards to guide jury discretion appears attributable to diverse readings of this Court's multi-opinioned decision in that case.

A brief examination of the background of the current North Carolina statute serves to reaffirm our assessment of its limited utility as an indicator of contemporary values regarding mandatory death sentences. Before 1949, North Carolina imposed a mandatory death sentence on any person convicted of rape or first-degree murder. That year, a study commission created by the state legislature recommended that juries be granted discretion to recommend life sentences in all capital cases:

> We propose that a recommendation of mercy
> by the jury in capital cases automatically
> carry with it a life sentence. Only three
> other states now have the mandatory death
> penalty and we believe its retention will be
> definitely harmful. Quite frequently, juries
> refuse to convict for rape or first degree
> murder because, from all the circumstances,
> they do not believe the defendant, although
> guilty, should suffer death. The result is that
> verdicts are returned hardly in harmony with
> evidence. Our proposal is already in effect in
> respect to the crimes of burglary and arson.
> There is much testimony that it has proved
> beneficial in such cases. We think the law
> can now be broadened to include all capital
> crimes. (Report of the Special Commission
> For the Improvement of the Administration
> of Justice, North Carolina, Popular
> Government 13 [Jan. 1949])

The 1949 session of the General Assembly of North Carolina adopted the proposed modifications of its rape and murder statutes. Although in subsequent years numerous bills were introduced in the legislature to limit further or abolish the death penalty in North Carolina, they were rejected as were two 1969 proposals to return to mandatory death sentences for all capital offenses.

... [W]hen the Supreme Court of North Carolina analyzed the constitutionality of the State's death penalty statute following this Court's decision in *Furman*, it severed the 1949 proviso authorizing jury sentencing discretion and held that "the remainder of the statute with death as the mandatory punishment ... remains in full force and effect." The North Carolina General Assembly then followed the course found constitutional in Waddell and enacted a first-degree murder provision identical to the mandatory statute in operation prior to the authorization of jury discretion. The State's brief in this case relates that the legislature sought to remove "all sentencing discretion [so that] there could be no successful Furman based attack on the North Carolina statute."

It is now well established that the Eighth Amendment draws much of its meaning from "the evolving standards of decency that mark the progress of a maturing society." As the above discussion makes clear, one of the most significant developments in our society's treatment of capital punishment has been the rejection of the common-law practice of inexorably imposing a death sentence upon every person convicted of a specified offense. North Carolina's mandatory death penalty statute for first-degree murder departs markedly from contemporary standards respecting the imposition of the punishment of death and thus cannot be applied consistently with the Eighth and Fourteenth Amendments' requirement that the State's power to punish "be exercised within the limits of civilized standards."

B

A separate deficiency of North Carolina's mandatory death sentence statute is its failure to provide a constitutionally tolerable response to *Furman*'s rejection of unbridled jury discretion in the imposition of capital sentences. Central to the limited holding in *Furman* was the conviction that the vesting of standardless sentencing power in the jury violated the Eighth and Fourteenth Amendments. It is argued that North Carolina has remedied the inadequacies of the death penalty statutes held unconstitutional in *Furman* by withdrawing all sentencing discretion from juries in capital cases. But when one considers the long and consistent American experience with the death penalty in first-degree murder cases, it becomes evident that mandatory statutes enacted in response to Furman have simply papered over the problem of unguided and unchecked jury discretion.

As we have noted in Part III-A, *supra*, there is general agreement that American juries have persistently refused to convict a significant portion of persons charged with first-degree murder of that offense under mandatory death penalty statutes. The North Carolina study commission reported that juries in that State "[q]uite frequently" were deterred from rendering guilty verdicts of first-degree murder because of the enormity of the sentence automatically imposed. Moreover, as a matter of historic fact, juries operating under discretionary sentencing statutes have consistently returned death sentences in only a minority of first-degree murder cases. In view of the historic record, it is only reasonable to assume that many juries under mandatory statutes will continue to consider the grave consequences of a conviction in reaching a verdict. North Carolina's mandatory death penalty statute provides no standards to guide the jury in its inevitable exercise of the power to determine which first-degree murderers shall live and which shall die. And there is no way under the North Carolina law for the judiciary to check arbitrary and capricious exercise of that power through a review of death sentences. Instead of rationalizing the sentencing process, a mandatory scheme may well exacerbate the problem identified in Furman by resting the penalty determination on the particular jury's willingness to act lawlessly. While a mandatory death penalty statute may reasonably be expected to increase the number of persons sentenced to death, it does not fulfill *Furman*'s basic requirement by replacing arbitrary and wanton jury discretion with objective standards to guide, regularize, and make rationally reviewable the process for imposing a sentence of death.

C

A third constitutional shortcoming of the North Carolina statute is its failure to allow the particularized consideration of relevant aspects of the character and record of each convicted defendant before the imposition upon him of a sentence of death. In *Furman*, members of the Court acknowledged what cannot fairly be denied—that death is a punishment different from all other sanctions in kind rather than degree. A process that accords no significance to relevant facets of the character and record of the individual offender or the circumstances of the particular offense excludes from consideration in fixing the ultimate punishment of death the possibility of compassionate or mitigating factors stemming from the diverse frailties of humankind. It treats all persons convicted of a designated offense not as uniquely individual human beings, but as members of a faceless, undifferentiated mass to be subjected to the blind infliction of the penalty of death.

This Court has previously recognized that "[f]or the determination of sentences, justice generally requires consideration of more than the particular acts by which the crime was committed and that there be taken into account the circumstances of the offense together with the character and propensities of the offender." Consideration of both the offender and the offense in order to arrive at a just and appropriate sentence has been viewed as a progressive and humanizing development. While the prevailing practice of individualizing sentencing determinations generally reflects simply enlightened policy rather than a constitutional imperative, we believe that in capital cases the fundamental respect for humanity underlying the Eighth Amendment requires consideration of the character and record of the individual offender and the circumstances of the particular offense as a constitutionally indispensable part of the process of inflicting the penalty of death.

This conclusion rests squarely on the predicate that the penalty of death is qualitatively different from a sentence of imprisonment, however long. Death, in its finality, differs more from life imprisonment than a 100-year prison term difference from one of only a year or two. Because of that qualitative difference, there is a corresponding difference in the need for reliability in the determination that death is the appropriate punishment in a specific case.

For the reasons stated, we conclude that the death sentences imposed upon the petitioners under North Carolina's mandatory death sentence statute violated the Eighth and Fourteenth Amendments and therefore must be set aside. The judgment of the Supreme Court of North Carolina is reversed insofar as it upheld the death sentences imposed upon the petitioners, and the case is remanded for further proceedings not inconsistent with this opinion.

It is so ordered.

DISCUSSION QUESTIONS

1. The majority claims that mandatory death sentences are unconstitutional. Explain and evaluate their argument for that claim.

2. The majority claims that the Eighth Amendment must be applied by an appeal to "contemporary standards." Explain what they mean and how they think that the court is to get evidence about such standards. Do you think that contemporary standards are relevant? Why or why not?

84

Kindler v. Canada (1991)

Kindler v. Canada was the historic decision of the Supreme Court of Canada in which it was decided that it was constitutional for the government to allow for the extradition of convicted criminals to a country where the defendant could face the death penalty. Kindler argued that the policy violated the Canadian Charter of Rights and Freedoms guarantee of a right to life, liberty, and security of person, as well as allegedly violating the Charter's protection against cruel and unusual punishment. The Court, however, rejected these arguments.

SOURCE

[1991] 2 S.C.R. 779 Supreme Court of Canada.

Kindler *v.* Canada (Minister of Justice), [1991] 2 S.C.R. 779
Joseph John Kindler *Appellant*
v.
Mr. John Crosbie, Minister of Justice and Attorney General of Canada

Respondent

and
Amnesty International *Intervener*
Indexed as: Kindler *v.* Canada (Minister of Justice)
File No.: 21321.
1991: February 21; 1991: September 26.
Present: Lamer C.J. and La Forest, L'Heureux-Dubé, Sopinka, Gonthier, Cory and McLachlin JJ.
on appeal from the federal court of appeal.
[...]

The appellant was found guilty of first degree murder, conspiracy to commit murder and kidnapping in the State of Pennsylvania and the jury recommended the imposition of the death penalty. Before he was sentenced, the appellant escaped from prison and fled to Canada where he was arrested. After a hearing, the extradition judge allowed the U.S.'s application for his extradition and committed the appellant to custody. The Minister of Justice of Canada, after reviewing the material supplied by the appellant, ordered his extradition pursuant to s. 25 of the *Extradition Act* without seeking assurances from the U.S., under Art. 6 of the Extradition Treaty between the two countries, that the death penalty would not be imposed or, if imposed, not carried out. Both the Trial Division and the Court of Appeal of the Federal Court dismissed appellant's application to review the Minister's decision. This appeal is to determine whether the Minister's decision to surrender the appellant to the U.S., without first seeking assurances that the death penalty will not be imposed or executed, violates the appellant's rights under s. 7 or s. 12 of the *Canadian Charter of Rights and Freedoms*. In addition, this Court stated the following two constitutional questions: whether s. 25 of the *Extradition Act* infringes s. 7 or s. 12 of the *Charter*; and, if so, whether such infringement is justified under s. 1.

Held (Lamer C.J. and Sopinka and Cory JJ. dissenting): The appeal should be dismissed. The extradition order is confirmed. Section 25 of the *Extradition Act* does not infringe s. 7 or s. 12 of the *Charter*.

Per La Forest, L'Heureux-Dubé and Gonthier JJ.: Section 7 of the *Charter*, and not s. 12, is the appropriate provision under which the actions of the Minister are to be assessed. The Minister's actions do not constitute cruel and unusual punishment. The execution, if it ultimately takes place, will be in the U.S. under American law against an American citizen in respect of an offence that took place in the U.S. It does not result from any initiative taken by the Canadian Government. The real question is whether the action of the Canadian Government in returning the appellant to his own country infringes his liberty and security in an impermissible way.

The unconditional surrender of the appellant seriously affects his right to liberty and security of the person. The issue is whether the surrender violates the principles of fundamental justice in the circumstances of this case. The values emanating from s. 12 play an important role in defining fundamental justice in this context. The Court has held that extradition must be refused if the circumstances facing the accused on surrender are such as to "shock the conscience." There are situations where the punishment imposed following surrender—torture, for example—would be so outrageous as to shock the conscience of Canadians, but that is not so of the death penalty in all cases. While there is strong ground that, barring

exceptional cases, the death penalty could not be justified in Canada having regard to the limited extent to which it advances any penological objectives and its serious invasion of human dignity, that is not the issue in this case. The issue is whether the extradition to the U.S. of a person who may face the death penalty there shocks the conscience.

In considering whether such surrender may constitutionally take place, the global setting where the vast majority of the nations of the world retain the death penalty must be kept in mind. While there has been a welcome trend in Western nations to abolish the death penalty, some nations have resisted the trend, notably the U.S. whose relatively open borders and cultural affinity with Canada make the escape of criminals to this country a pressing problem. While there are a number of major international instruments supporting the trend, all except one fall short of actually prohibiting the death penalty. More directly reflective of international attitudes is the recent *Model Treaty on Extradition* prepared under the United Nations' auspices, which like the Canada-U.S. Extradition Treaty, gives a state discretion to decide whether it should demand assurances against the imposition of the death penalty.

The Government has a right and duty to keep criminals out of Canada and to expel them by deportation. Otherwise Canada could become a haven for criminals. The issue has arisen in several recent cases in relation to persons facing the death penalty for murder. Similar policy concerns apply to extradition. It would be strange if Canada could keep out lesser offenders but be obliged to grant sanctuary to those accused or convicted of the worst types of crimes.

In summary, the extradition of an individual who has been accused of the worst form of murder in the U.S., which has a system of justice similar to our own, could not be said to shock the conscience of Canadians or to violate any international norm. The extradition did not go beyond what was necessary to serve the legitimate and compelling social purpose of preventing Canada from becoming an attractive haven for fugitives. The Minister determined, in the interests of protecting the security of Canadians, that he should not, in this case, seek assurances regarding the penalty to be imposed. On the evidence before the Court, the Minister's determination was not unreasonable and this Court should not interfere with his decision to extradite without restrictions.

The procedure followed by the Minister in reaching his decision to surrender the appellant did not offend the principles of fundamental justice. Nor did the subsidiary grounds—the alleged arbitrariness, the "death row" phenomenon and the mode of execution—lead to a different result.

Per L'Heureux-Dubé and Gonthier and McLachlin JJ.: While the *Charter* applies to extradition matters, including the executive decision of the Minister that effects the fugitive's surrender, the guarantee against cruel and unusual punishment found in s. 12 of the *Charter* has no application to s. 25 of the *Extradition Act* or to ministerial acts done pursuant to that section. The decision to surrender a fugitive under s. 25 does not constitute the imposition of cruel and unusual punishment by a Canadian government. The purpose and effect of s. 25 is to permit the fugitive to be extradited to face the consequences of the judicial process elsewhere. The punishment, if any, to which the fugitive is ultimately subject will be punishment imposed, not by the Government of Canada, but by the foreign state. The fact that the Minister may seek assurances that the death penalty will not be demanded or enforced in the foreign jurisdiction does not change this situation. Since the *Charter*'s reach is confined to the legislative and executive acts of Canadian governments, to apply s. 12 directly to the act of surrender to a foreign country where a particular penalty may be imposed would be to give the section extraterritorial effect. Effective relations between different states require that Canada respects the differences of its neighbours and that it refrains from imposing its constitutional guarantees on other states.

Section 25 of the *Extradition Act*, which permits the extradition of fugitives without assurances that the death penalty will not be applied in the requesting states, does not offend the fundamental principles of justice enshrined in s. 7 of the *Charter*. Section 25 is consistent with extradition practices, viewed historically and in light of current conditions, and is consonant with the fundamental conceptions of what is fair and right in Canadian society. Bearing in mind the nature of the offence and the penalty, the justice system of the requesting state including the safeguards and guarantees it affords the fugitive, the considerations of comity and of security, and according due latitude to the Minister to balance the competing interests involved in particular extradition cases, the extradition of a fugitive to a state where he may face capital punishment, if convicted, is not a situation which is shocking and fundamentally unacceptable in our society. There is no clear consensus in this country that capital punishment is morally abhorrent and absolutely unacceptable. Further, while in some cases it may be mandatory for the Minister to seek death penalty assurances, the variance between cases supports legislation which accords to the Minister a measure of discretion on the question of whether such assurances should be demanded. If such assurances were mandatory, Canada might become a safe haven for criminals in the U.S. seeking to avoid the death penalty. Finally, the importance of maintaining effective extradition arrangements with other countries, in a world where law enforcement is increasingly international in scope, also supports the ministerial discretion found in s. 25. An effective extradition process is founded on respect for sovereignty and differences in the judicial systems among various nations.

The Minister's decision to extradite without seeking death penalty assurances from the U.S. did not infringe s. 7 of the *Charter*. The reasons for extradition were compelling and the procedural guarantees in the reciprocating state high. The sole fact that at the end of the process, the appellant could face the death penalty was insufficient in the context of the extradition system of this country to render the decision unconstitutional. The courts should not lightly interfere with executive decisions on extradition matters.

[...]

Per Lamer C.J. and Sopinka J. (dissenting): While capital punishment *per se* constitutes cruel and unusual punishment, it is preferable not to decide whether s. 12 of the *Charter* applies because s. 7 is the appropriate provision for the determination of this appeal.

The surrender order infringes s. 7 of the *Charter*. Extradition to face the potential imposition of capital punishment deprives the appellant of liberty and security of the person. The circumstances in which extradition constitutes a breach of the principles of fundamental justice are not limited to situations which "shock the conscience." The protection afforded by s. 7 extends to individuals who face situations that are "simply unacceptable." This requirement entails more than a simple consideration of majority opinion. It must be interpreted in light of the values underlying s. 7. Here, the Minister's decision to surrender the appellant without seeking the assurances against the imposition of what would be a violation of s. 12 of the *Charter*, were it carried out in Canada, offends the principles of fundamental justice. Indeed, the extradition of the fugitive to face the death penalty without seeking assurances that it would not be imposed or carried out shocks the conscience. The Minister did not even ask the U.S. to give such assurances. It is quite possible that they would have been given. With the cooperation of the requesting state, it is possible to achieve the goals of an effective extradition system in a manner that does not deprive the fugitive of the protection of the *Charter*. To refuse to seek such assurances is to give an official blessing to the death penalty, despite the fact that Canadian public policy stands firmly opposed to its use. The surrender order is not justifiable under s. 1 of the *Charter*.

Per Lamer C.J. and Cory J. (dissenting): Capital punishment for murder is prohibited in Canada. As the ultimate desecration of human dignity, the death penalty is *per se* a cruel and unusual punishment and violates s. 12 of the *Charter*. The decision of the Minister to surrender a fugitive who may be subject to execution without obtaining an assurance pursuant to Art. 6 of the Extradition Treaty is one which can be reviewed under s. 12. Although the *Charter* has no extraterritorial application, persons in Canada who are subject to extradition proceedings must be accorded all the rights which flow from the *Charter*. Notwithstanding the fact that it is the U.S. and not Canada which would impose the death penalty, Canada has the obligation not to extradite a person to face a cruel and unusual treatment or punishment. Indeed, to surrender a fugitive who may be subject to the death penalty violates s. 12 of the *Charter* just as surely as would the execution of the fugitive in Canada. Canada, as the extraditing state, must accept responsibility for the ultimate consequence of the extradition. It follows that the Minister must not surrender the appellant without obtaining the undertaking described in Art. 6 of the Treaty. To do so would render s. 25 of the *Extradition Act* inconsistent with the *Charter* in its application to fugitives who would be subject to the death penalty.

This conclusion is based upon the historical reluctance displayed by jurors over the centuries to impose the death penalty, the provisions of s. 12 of the *Charter* and the decisions of this Court pertaining to that section. It is also based upon the pronouncements of this Court emphasizing the fundamental importance of human dignity, and upon the international statements and commitments made by Canada stressing the importance of the dignity of the individual and urging the abolition of the death penalty.

In the absence of obtaining an Art. 6 assurance, the surrender order would contravene s. 12 of the *Charter* and could not be justified under s. 1. There is simply no evidence that the existence of Art. 6 has led to a flood of American murderers into Canada. Nor is there any reason to believe that this would occur if Ministers of Justice uniformly sought Art. 6 assurances. Further, Canada has committed itself in the international community to the recognition and support of human dignity and to the abolition of the death penalty. These commitments, like the *Charter* and this Court's judicial pronouncements, reflect Canadian values and principles. The preservation of Canada's integrity and reputation in the international community require that extradition be refused unless an undertaking is obtained pursuant to Art. 6. To take this position does not constitute an absolute refusal to extradite. It simply requires the requesting state to undertake that it will substitute a penalty of life imprisonment for the execution of the prisoner if that prisoner is found to be guilty of the crime.

[...]

VII The Canadian Position

A consideration of the place of the death penalty in Canadian society must now take place in the context of the *Charter*. In particular, it must be determined whether the death penalty violates the *Charter* proscription against cruel and unusual punishment. Section 12 of the *Charter* provides:

> 12. Everyone has the right not to be subjected to any cruel and unusual treatment or punishment.

The constitutional status of capital punishment under s. 12 of the *Charter* is to be derived from the Canadian experience with respect to both the death penalty and the broader concept of cruel and unusual punishment.

[...]

The House of Commons Votes to Abolish the Death Penalty

In free votes in both 1976 and 1987, a majority of the members of the House of Commons supported the abolition of the death penalty. These votes, held after extensive and thorough debate, demonstrate that the elected representatives of the Canadian people found the death penalty for civil crimes to be an affront to human dignity which cannot be tolerated in Canadian society. These votes are a clear indication that capital punishment is considered to be contrary to basic Canadian values.

The rejection of the death penalty by the majority of the members of the House of Commons on two occasions can be taken as reflecting a basic abhorrence of the infliction of capital punishment either directly, within Canada, or through Canadian complicity in the actions of a foreign state.

The Position under the Charter

What then is the constitutional status of the death penalty under s. 12 of the *Charter*?

The American experience provides no guidance. Cases dealing with the constitutional validity of the death penalty were decided on very narrow bases unique to the wording of the American Constitution and rooted in early holdings of the United States Supreme Court. Canadian courts should articulate a distinct Canadian approach with respect to cruel and unusual punishment based on Canadian traditions and values.

The approach to be taken by this Court in determining whether capital punishment contravenes s. 12 of the *Charter* should, in my view, be guided by two central considerations. First is the principle of human dignity which lies at the heart of s. 12. It is the dignity and importance of the individual which is the essence and the cornerstone of democratic government. Second is the decision of this Court in *Smith, supra*.

1. Human Dignity under the Charter

The fundamental importance of human dignity in Canadian society has been recognized in numerous cases. In *R. v. Oakes*, [1986] 1 S.C.R. 103, Dickson C.J. at p. 136 referred to the basic principles and values which are enshrined in the *Charter*. He wrote:

> The Court must be guided by the values and principles essential to a free and democratic society which I believe embody, to name but a few, respect for the inherent dignity of the human person, commitment to social justice and equality, accommodation of a wide variety of beliefs, respect for cultural and group identity, and faith in social and political institutions which enhance the participation of individuals and groups in society. The underlying values and principles of a free and democratic society are the genesis of the rights and freedoms guaranteed by the *Charter* and

the ultimate standard against which a limit on a right or freedom must be shown, despite its effect, to be reasonable and demonstrably justified.

In her reasons in *R. v. Morgentaler*, [1988] 1 S.C.R. 30, at p. 166, Wilson J. stressed the importance of human dignity in understanding the protections afforded by the *Charter*. She wrote:

> The idea of human dignity finds expression in almost every right and freedom guaranteed in the *Charter*. Individuals are afforded the right to choose their own religion and their own philosophy of life, the right to choose with whom they will associate and how they will express themselves, the right to choose where they will live and what occupation they will pursue.

Again, in *Andrews v. Law Society of British Columbia*, [1989] 1 S.C.R. 143, this Court emphasized the importance of human dignity. McIntyre J. wrote at p. 171:

> It is clear that the purpose of s. 15 is to ensure equality in the formulation and application of the law. The promotion of equality entails the promotion of a society in which all are secure in the knowledge that they are recognized at law as human beings equally deserving of concern, respect and consideration.

In *Re B.C. Motor Vehicle Act*, *supra*, the Court once again noted the fundamental importance of human dignity to the provisions of the *Charter*. Lamer J., as he then was, stated at p. 512:

> Sections 8 to 14 address specific deprivations of the "right" to life, liberty and security of the person in breach of the principles of fundamental justice, and as such, violations of s. 7. They are therefore illustrative of the meaning, in criminal or penal law, of "principles of fundamental justice"; they represent principles which have been recognized by the common law, the international conventions and by the very fact of entrenchment in the *Charter*, as essential elements of a system for the administration of justice which is founded upon the belief in the dignity and worth of the human person and the rule of law.

Let us now turn to consider the second guiding consideration, the decision of this Court in *Smith*.

2. Section 12 and the Smith Case

In *Smith*, *supra*, this Court considered a challenge to the minimum sentencing provision of the *Narcotic Control Act*, R.S.C. 1970, c. N-1. The penalty prescribed by the *Narcotic Control Act* for importing a narcotic into Canada was imprisonment for a minimum of seven years up to life. The minimum term was challenged on the ground that it constituted cruel and unusual punishment contrary to s. 12 of the *Charter*. It was argued that the punishment was unduly severe and disproportionate to the offence committed. The decision focused upon the element of proportionality.

Lamer J., as he then was, carefully considered the nature of the protection afforded by s. 12 of the *Charter*. In giving a broad interpretation to the s. 12 right, Lamer J., at p. 1072, held that punishments "must not be grossly disproportionate to what would have been appropriate." He later held, at pp. 1073–74, that certain punishments will by their very nature always be grossly disproportionate:

> Finally, I should add that some punishments or treatments will always be grossly disproportionate and will always outrage our standards of decency: for example, the infliction of corporal punishment, such as the lash, irrespective of the number of lashes imposed, or, to give examples of treatment, the lobotomisation of certain dangerous offenders or the castration of sexual offenders.

From this decision two principles emerge. First, punishments must never be grossly disproportionate to that which would have been appropriate to punish, rehabilitate or deter the particular offender or to protect the public from that offender. Second, and more importantly for the purposes of this case, punishments must not in themselves be unacceptable no matter what the crime, no matter what the offender. Although any form of punishment may be a blow to human dignity, some form of punishment is essential for the orderly functioning of society. However, when a punishment becomes so demeaning that all human dignity is lost, then the punishment must be considered cruel and unusual. At a minimum, the infliction of corporal punishment, lobotomisation of dangerous offenders and the castration of sexual offenders will not be tolerated.

3. Does the Death Penalty Violate Section 12 of the Charter?

In light of both the decisions stressing the importance of human dignity under the *Charter* and the principles espoused in the *Smith* case, it remains to be determined whether the death penalty violates s. 12 of the *Charter*. In my view, there can be no doubt that it does.

A consideration of the effect of the imposition of the death penalty on human dignity is enlightening. Descriptions of executions demonstrate that it is state-imposed death which is so repugnant to any belief in the importance of human dignity. The methods utilized to carry out the execution serve only to compound the indignities inflicted upon the individual.

In his book *Condemned to Die: Life Under Sentence of Death* (1981), at pp. 86–87, Johnson makes this reference to executions in the electric chair:

> Electrocution has been described by one medical doctor as "a form of torture [that] rivals burning at the stake." Electrocutions have been known to drag on interminably, literally cooking the prisoners. In one

instance, a man's brain "was found to be 'baked hard,' the blood in his head had turned to charcoal, and his entire back was burnt black." One man somehow survived electrocution and was returned months later, with the approval of the Supreme Court, for a second (and unsuccessful) encounter with the chair. More recently, John Spenkelink's electrocution lasted over six minutes and required three massive surges of electricity before he finally died. Although we have no accounts of the damage to Spenkelink's body caused by his execution, allegations that Florida prison officials stuffed his anus with cotton and taped his mouth shut suggest that they may have anticipated the forbidding spectacle typically provided by electrocution, and made every effort to make the sanction cosmetically acceptable.

This description of the imposition of the death penalty clearly indicates that persons executed by the state are deprived of all semblance of human dignity. The stuffing of the anus with cotton wool and the taping shut of the mouth suggest that even the authorities carrying out the execution were not only insensitive to human dignity but fully expected a horrible reaction to a dreadful punishment. Even so, these indignities are simply adjuncts to the ultimate attack on human dignity, the destruction of life by the state.

The following description by the Reverend Myer Tobey of the execution by lethal gas of Eddie Daniels is to similar effect:

> In the chamber now, he was strapped to the chair. The cyanide had been prepared, and was placed beneath his chair, over a pan of acid that would later react with the cyanide to form the deadly gas. Electrocardiographic wires were attached to Daniels' forearms and legs, and connected to a monitor in the observation area. This lets the doctor know when the heart stops beating.

This done, the prison guards left the room, shutting the thick door, and sealing it to prevent the gas from leaking. I took my place at one of the windows, and looked at Eddie, and he looked at me. We said the prayer together, over and over.

At a motion of the warden, a prison guard then pulled a lever releasing the cyanide crystals beneath the chair. Eddie heard the chemical pellets drop, and he braced himself. We did not take our eyes off each other.

In an instant, puffs of light white smoke began to rise. Daniels saw the smoke, and moved his head to try to avoid breathing it in. As the gas continued to rise he moved his head this way and that way, thrashing as much as his straps would allow still in an attempt to avoid breathing. He was like an animal in a trap, with no escape, all the time being watched by his fellow humans in the windows that lined the chamber. He could steal only glimpses of me in his panic, but I continued to repeat "My Jesus I Love You," and he too would try to mouth it.

Then the convulsions began. His body strained as much as the straps would allow. He had inhaled the deadly gas, and it seemed as if every muscle in his body was straining in reaction. His eyes looked as if they were bulging, much as a choking man with a rope cutting off his windpipe. But he could get no air in the chamber.

Then his head dropped forward. The doctor in the observation room said that that was it for Daniels. This was within the first few minutes after the pellets had dropped. His head was down for several seconds. Then, as we had thought it was over, he again lifted his head in another convulsion. His eyes were open, he strained and he looked at me. I said one more time, automatically, "My Jesus I Love You." And he went with me, mouthing the prayer. He was still alive after those several minutes, and I was horrified. He was in great agony. Then he

strained and began the words with me again. I knew he was conscious, this was not an automatic response of an unconscious man. But he did not finish. His head fell forward again.

There were several more convulsions after this, but his eyes were closed. I could not tell if he were conscious or not at that point. Then he stopped moving, approximately ten minutes after the gas began to rise, and was officially pronounced dead.

The death penalty not only deprives the prisoner of all vestiges of human dignity, it is the ultimate desecration of the individual as a human being. It is the annihilation of the very essence of human dignity.

Let us now consider the principles set out in *Smith* to determine whether the death penalty is of the same nature as corporal punishment, lobotomy or castration which were designated as cruel and unusual punishment.

What is acceptable as punishment to a society will vary with the nature of that society, its degree of stability and its level of maturity. The punishments of lashing with the cat-o-nine tails and keel-hauling were accepted forms of punishment in the 19th century in the British navy. Both of those punishments could, and not infrequently did, result in death to the recipient. By the end of the 19th century, however, it was unthinkable that such penalties would be inflicted. A more sensitive society had made such penalties abhorrent.

Similarly, corporal punishment is now considered cruel and unusual yet it was an accepted form of punishment in Canada until it was abolished in 1973. The explanation, it seems to me, is that a maturing society has recognized that the imposition of the lash would now be a cruel and intolerable punishment.

If corporal punishment, lobotomy and castration are no longer acceptable and contravene s. 12 then the death penalty cannot be considered to be anything other than cruel and unusual punishment. It is the supreme indignity to the individual, the ultimate corporal punishment, the final and complete lobotomy and the absolute and irrevocable castration.

As the ultimate desecration of human dignity, the imposition of the death penalty in Canada is a clear violation of the protection afforded by s. 12 of the *Charter*. Capital punishment is *per se* cruel and unusual.

If Kindler had committed the murder in Canada, then not simply the abolition of the death penalty in this country but, more importantly, the provisions of s. 12 of the *Charter* would prevent his execution. The next question is whether the fact that American, not Canadian, authorities would carry out the execution is fatal to Kindler's s. 12 claim. That is, does the Minister's decision to surrender Kindler to American authorities who may impose the death penalty "subject" him, within the meaning of s. 12, to cruel and unusual punishment?

VIII The Relevance of the Fact That the Death Penalty Would Be Inflicted by the United States and Not Canada

The respondent contends that even if it is assumed that the death penalty constitutes cruel punishment, the *Charter* protections should not apply to a fugitive. In support of this position it was said that the surrender of Kindler did not mean that the Government of Canada would be subjecting the fugitive to cruel and unusual punishment, since the punishment would be inflicted by the requesting state. It was argued that so long as the trial procedure the fugitive had undergone or would undergo in the requesting state was fair, the punishment that followed a finding of guilt was not something which could be subject to the provisions of the *Charter*. Based on the *Charter* jurisprudence of this Court, this argument must be rejected.

The Approach That Should Be Taken in Applying the Charter

Although the *Charter* has no extraterritorial application, persons in Canada who are subject to extradition proceedings must be accorded all the rights which flow from the *Charter*. The approach to be taken is indicated by this Court in *Singh v. Minister of Employment and Immigration*, [1985] 1 S.C.R. 177. In that case the refugee claimants contended that Canada's decision not to extend convention refugee status to them placed them at risk that they would be prosecuted in their home country for their political beliefs. Wilson J., for the plurality, found that this decision deprived the claimants of their s. 7 right to security of the person and that this was sufficient to trigger the protection of the *Charter*. Specifically, Wilson J. stressed that the *Charter* affords freedom not only from actual punishment but also from the threat of punishment.

The *Singh* principle was applied in the extradition context in *Schmidt, supra*, where La Forest J. held that the manner in which the foreign state will deal with the fugitive upon surrender may, in some situations, violate the *Charter*. When such a likelihood arises, Canada, as the extraditing state, must accept responsibility for the ultimate consequence of the extradition. This, I believe, is the conclusion to be drawn from the reasons of La Forest J., at p. 522:

> I have no doubt either that in some circumstances the manner in which the foreign state will deal with the fugitive on surrender, whether that course of conduct is justifiable or not under the law of that country, may be such that it would violate the principles of fundamental justice to surrender an accused under those circumstances. To make the point, I need only refer to a case that arose before the European Commission on Human Rights, *Altun v. Germany* (1983), 5 E.H.R.R. 611, where it was established that prosecution in the requesting country might involve the infliction of torture. *Situations falling far short of this may well arise where the nature of the criminal procedures or penalties in a foreign country sufficiently shocks the conscience as to make a decision to surrender a fugitive for trial there one that breaches the principles of fundamental justice enshrined in s. 7.* [Emphasis added.]

This position was reiterated in *Argentina v. Mellino*, [1987] 1 S.C.R. 536, and *United States v. Allard*, [1987] 1 S.C.R. 564. While true that these cases were based upon a consideration of s. 7 of the *Charter*, the same principles of *Charter* application must apply to s. 12. The same conclusion has been reached in Europe, where arguments similar to those of the respondent have been firmly rejected.

[...]

DISCUSSION QUESTIONS

1. The court claims that the extradition of Kindler to the United States "was necessary to serve the legitimate and compelling social purpose of preventing Canada from becoming an attractive haven for fugitives." Do you think that this goal should outweigh Canada's moral objections to the death penalty? Why or why not?

2. Do you think that it is relevant that it will not be the Government of Canada imposing the death penalty? If one thinks that the death penalty is morally wrong, should it matter to the evaluation of one's actions whether one is carrying out the penalty oneself or merely turning a criminal over to those who may carry out the penalty?

3. In one dissenting opinion it is claimed that the death penalty is incompatible with human dignity. Explain and evaluate this claim and the arguments in support of that claim.

85

Regents of the University of California v. Bakke (1978)

In 1973 and 1974, Allan Bakke, a white male, was denied admission to the University of California, Davis, School of Medicine. During this same time, other candidates with lower academic scores were admitted under special admissions programs for members of minority and economically/educationally disadvantaged groups. Bakke sued UC Davis Medical School as a means of compelling his admission to their program. He alleged that the special admissions programs discriminated against him on the basis of his race and thus constituted a violation of the Equal Protection Clause of the Fourteenth Amendment.

The trial court found that the school's special admissions programs violated, among other things, Title VI of the Civil Rights Act. However, they did not compel the University to admit Bakke. On appeal, the California Supreme Court ruled that the special admissions programs violated the Equal Protection Clause, and it ordered Bakke's admission on the grounds that the school could not prove that he wouldn't have been admitted even if the programs had not been in place.

The U.S. Supreme Court offered a pluralizing opinion with Justice Powell holding the determining vote.

SOURCE

438 U.S. 265 U.S. Supreme Court.

The Medical School of the University of California at Davis (hereinafter Davis) had two admissions programs for the entering class of 100 students—the regular admissions program and the special admissions program. Under the regular procedure, candidates whose overall under-graduate grade point averages fell below 2.5 on a scale of 4.0 were summarily rejected. About one out of six applicants was then given an interview, following which he was rated on a scale of 1 to 100 by each of the committee members (five in 1973 and six in 1974), his rating being based on the interviewers' summaries, his overall grade point average, his science courses grade point average, his Medical College Admissions Test (MCAT) scores, letters of recommendation, extracurricular activities, and other biographical data, all of which resulted in a total "benchmark score." The full admissions committee then made offers of admission on the basis of their review of the applicant's file and his score, considering and acting upon applications as they were received. The committee chairman was responsible for placing names on the waiting list and had discretion to include persons with "special skills." A separate committee, a majority of whom were members of minority groups, operated the special admissions program. The 1973 and 1974 application forms, respectively, asked candidates whether they wished to be considered as "economically and/or educationally disadvantaged" applicants and members of a "minority group" (blacks, Chicanos, Asians,

American Indians). If an applicant of a minority group was found to be "disadvantaged," he would be rated in a manner similar to the one employed by the general admissions committee. Special candidates, however, did not have to meet the 2.5 grade point cutoff and were not ranked against candidates in the general admissions process. About one-fifth of the special applicants were invited for interviews in 1973 and 1974, following which they were given benchmark scores, and the top choices were then given to the general admissions committee, which could reject special candidates for failure to meet course requirements or other specific deficiencies. The special committee continued to recommend candidates until 16 special admission selections had been made. During a four-year period 63 minority students were admitted to Davis under the special program and 44 under the general program. No disadvantaged whites were admitted under the special program, though many applied. Respondent, a white male, applied to Davis in 1973 and 1974, in both years being considered only under the general admissions program. Though he had a 468 out of 500 score in 1973, he was rejected since no general applicants with scores less than 470 were being accepted after respondent's application, which was filed late in the year, had been processed and completed. At that time four special admission slots were still unfilled. In 1974 respondent applied early, and though he had a total score of 549 out of 600, he was again rejected. In neither year was his name placed on the discretionary waiting list. In both years special applicants were admitted with significantly lower scores than respondent's. After his second rejection, respondent filed this action in state court for mandatory, injunctive, and declaratory relief to compel his admission to Davis, alleging that the special admissions program operated to exclude him on the basis of his race in violation of the Equal Protection Clause of the Fourteenth Amendment, a provision of the California Constitution, and 601 of Title VI of the Civil Rights Act of 1964, which provides, *inter alia*, that no person shall on the ground of race or color be excluded from participating in any program receiving federal financial assistance. Petitioner cross-claimed for a declaration that its special admissions program was lawful. The trial court found that the special program operated as a racial quota, because minority applicants in that program were rated only against one another, and 16 places in the class of 100 were reserved for them. Declaring that petitioner could not take race into account in making admissions decisions, the program was held to violate the Federal and State Constitutions and Title VI. Respondent's admission was not ordered, however, for lack of proof that he would have been admitted but for the special program. The California Supreme Court, applying a strict-scrutiny standard, concluded that the special admissions program was not the least intrusive means of achieving the goals of the admittedly compelling state interests of integrating the medical profession and increasing the number of doctors willing to serve minority patients. Without passing on the state constitutional or federal statutory grounds the court held that petitioner's special admissions program violated the Equal Protection Clause. Since petitioner could not satisfy its burden of demonstrating that respondent, absent the special program, would not have been admitted, the court ordered his admission to Davis.

Held:

The judgment below is affirmed insofar as it orders respondent's admission to Davis and invalidates petitioner's special admissions program, but is reversed insofar as it prohibits petitioner from taking race into account as a factor in its future admissions decisions.

[...]

MR. JUSTICE POWELL, concluded:

1. Title VI proscribes only those racial classifications that would violate the Equal Protection Clause if employed by a State or its agencies.

2. Racial and ethnic classifications of any sort are inherently suspect and call for the most exacting judicial scrutiny. While the goal of achieving a diverse student body is sufficiently compelling to justify consideration of race in admissions decisions

under some circumstances, petitioner's special admissions program, which forecloses consideration to persons like respondent, is unnecessary to the achievement of this compelling goal and therefore invalid under the Equal Protection Clause.

3. Since petitioner could not satisfy its burden of proving that respondent would not have been admitted even if there had been no special admissions program, he must be admitted.

Mr. Justice Brennan, Mr. Justice White, Mr. Justice Marshall, and Mr. Justice Blackmun concluded:

1. Title VI proscribes only those racial classifications that would violate the Equal Protection Clause if employed by a State or its agencies.

2. Racial classifications call for strict judicial scrutiny. Nonetheless, the purpose of overcoming substantial, chronic minority underrepresentation in the medical profession is sufficiently important to justify petitioner's remedial use of race. Thus, the judgment below must be reversed in that it prohibits race from being used as a factor in university admissions.

Mr. Justice Stevens, joined by the Chief Justice, Mr. Justice Stewart, and Mr. Justice Rehnquist, being of the view that whether race can ever be a factor in an admissions policy is not an issue here; that Title VI applies; and that respondent was excluded from Davis in violation of Title VI, concurs in the Court's judgment insofar as it affirms the judgment of the court below ordering respondent admitted to Davis.

Mr. Justice Powell announced the judgment of the Court.

This case presents a challenge to the special admissions program of the petitioner, the Medical School of the University of California at Davis, which is designed to assure the admission of a specified number of students from certain minority groups. The Superior Court of California sustained respondent's challenge, holding that petitioner's program violated the California Constitution, Title VI of the Civil Rights Act of 1964, and the Equal Protection Clause of the

Fourteenth Amendment. The court enjoined petitioner from considering respondent's race or the race of any other applicant in making admissions decisions. It refused, however, to order respondent's admission to the Medical School, holding that he had not carried his burden of proving that he would have been admitted but for the constitutional and statutory violations. The Supreme Court of California affirmed those portions of the trial court's judgment declaring the special admissions program unlawful and enjoining petitioner from considering the race of any applicant. It modified that portion of the judgment denying respondent's requested injunction and directed the trial court to order his admission.

For the reasons stated in the following opinion, I believe that so much of the judgment of the California court as holds petitioner's special admissions program unlawful and directs that respondent be admitted to the Medical School must be affirmed. For the reasons expressed in a separate opinion, my Brothers the Chief Justice, Mr. Justice Stewart, Mr. Justice Rehnquist, and Mr. Justice Stevens concur in this judgment.

I also conclude for the reasons stated in the following opinion that the portion of the court's judgment enjoining petitioner from according any consideration to race in its admissions process must be reversed. For reasons expressed in separate opinions, my Brothers Mr. Justice Brennan, Mr. Justice White, Mr. Justice Marshall, and Mr. Justice Blackmun concur in this judgment.

Affirmed in part and reversed in part.

I

The Medical School of the University of California at Davis opened in 1968 with an entering class of 50 students. In 1971, the size of the entering class was increased to 100 students, a level at which it remains. No admissions program for disadvantaged or minority students existed when the school opened, and the first class contained three Asians but no blacks, no Mexican-Americans, and no American Indians. Over the next two years, the faculty devised a special admissions program to increase the representation of "disadvantaged" students in each Medical School class. The special program consisted of a separate admissions system operating in coordination with the regular admissions process.

Under the regular admissions procedure, a candidate could submit his application to the Medical School beginning in July of the year preceding the academic year for which admission was sought. Record 149. Because of the large number of applications, the admissions committee screened each one to select candidates for further consideration. Candidates whose overall undergraduate grade point averages fell below 2.5 on a scale of 4.0 were summarily rejected. About one out of six applicants was invited for a personal interview. Ibid. Following the interviews, each candidate was rated on a scale of 1 to 100 by his interviewers and four other members of the admissions committee. The rating embraced the interviewers' summaries, the candidate's overall grade point average, grade point average in science courses, scores on the Medical College Admissions Test (MCAT), letters of recommendation, extracurricular activities, and other biographical data. The ratings were added together to arrive at each candidate's "benchmark" score. Since five committee members rated each candidate in 1973, a perfect score was 500; in 1974, six members rated each candidate, so that a perfect score was 600. The full committee then reviewed the file and scores of each applicant and made offers of admission on a "rolling" basis. The chairman was responsible for placing names on the waiting list. They were not placed in strict numerical order; instead, the chairman had discretion to include persons with "special skills."

The special admissions program operated with a separate committee, a majority of whom were members of minority groups. On the 1973 application form, candidates were asked to indicate whether they wished to be considered as "economically and/or educationally disadvantaged" applicants; on the 1974 form the question was whether they wished to be considered as members of a "minority group,"

which the Medical School apparently viewed as "Blacks," "Chicanos," "Asians," and "American Indians." If these questions were answered affirmatively, the application was forwarded to the special admissions committee. No formal definition of "disadvantaged" was ever produced, but the chairman of the special committee screened each application to see whether it reflected economic or educational deprivation. Having passed this initial hurdle, the applications then were rated by the special committee in a fashion similar to that used by the general admissions committee, except that special candidates did not have to meet the 2.5 grade point average cutoff applied to regular applicants. About one-fifth of the total number of special applicants were invited for interviews in 1973 and 1974. Following each interview, the special committee assigned each special applicant a benchmark score. The special committee then presented its top choices to the general admissions committee. The latter did not rate or compare the special candidates against the general applicants, id., at 388, but could reject recommended special candidates for failure to meet course requirements or other specific deficiencies. The special committee continued to recommend special applicants until a number prescribed by faculty vote were admitted. While the overall class size was still 50, the prescribed number was 8; in 1973 and 1974, when the class size had doubled to 100, the prescribed number of special admissions also doubled, to 16.

From the year of the increase in class size—1971—through 1974, the special program resulted in the admission of 21 black students, 30 Mexican-Americans, and 12 Asians, for a total of 63 minority students. Over the same period, the regular admissions program produced 1 black, 6 Mexican-Americans, and 37 Asians, for a total of 44 minority students. Although disadvantaged whites applied to the special program in large numbers, none received an offer of admission through that process. Indeed, in 1974, at least, the special committee explicitly considered only "disadvantaged" special applicants who were members of one of the designated minority groups.

Allan Bakke is a white male who applied to the Davis Medical School in both 1973 and 1974. In both years Bakke's application was considered under the general admissions program, and he received an interview. His 1973 interview was with Dr. Theodore C. West, who considered Bakke "a very desirable applicant to [the] medical school." Despite a strong benchmark score of 468 out of 500, Bakke was rejected. His application had come late in the year, and no applicants in the general admissions process with scores below 470 were accepted after Bakke's application was completed. There were four special admissions slots unfilled at that time, however, for which Bakke was not considered. After his 1973 rejection, Bakke wrote to Dr. George H. Lowrey, Associate Dean and Chairman of the Admissions Committee, protesting that the special admissions program operated as a racial and ethnic quota.

Bakke's 1974 application was completed early in the year. His student interviewer gave him an overall rating of 94, finding him "friendly, well tempered, conscientious and delightful to speak with." His faculty interviewer was, by coincidence, the same Dr. Lowrey to whom he had written in protest of the special admissions program. Dr. Lowrey found Bakke "rather limited in his approach" to the problems of the medical profession and found disturbing Bakke's "very definite opinions which were based more on his personal viewpoints than upon a study of the total problem." Dr. Lowrey gave Bakke the lowest of his six ratings, an 86; his total was 549 out of 600. Again, Bakke's application was rejected. In neither year did the chairman of the admissions committee, Dr. Lowrey, exercise his discretion to place Bakke on the waiting list. In both years, applicants were admitted under the special program with grade point averages, MCAT scores, and benchmark scores significantly lower than Bakke's.

After the second rejection, Bakke filed the instant suit in the Superior Court of California. He sought mandatory, injunctive, and declaratory relief compelling his admission to the Medical School. He alleged that the Medical School's special admissions program operated to exclude him from the [438 U.S. 265, 278] school on the basis of his race, in violation of his rights under the Equal Protection Clause of the Fourteenth Amendment, Art. I, 21, of the California Constitution, and 601 of Title VI of the Civil Rights Act of 1964, 78 Stat. 252, 42 U.S.C. 2000d. The University cross-complained for a declaration that its special admissions program was lawful. The trial court found that the special program operated as a racial quota, because minority applicants in the special program were rated only against one another, Record 388, and 16 places in the class of 100 were reserved for them. Declaring that the University could not take race into account in making admissions decisions, the trial court held the challenged program violative of the Federal Constitution, the State Constitution, and Title VI. The court refused to order Bakke's admission, however, holding that he had failed to carry his burden of proving that he would have been admitted but for the existence of the special program.

Bakke appealed from the portion of the trial court judgment denying him admission, and the University appealed from the decision that its special admissions program was unlawful and the order enjoining it from considering race in the processing of applications. The Supreme Court of California transferred the case directly from the trial court, "because of the importance of the issues involved." The California court accepted the findings of the trial court with respect to the University's program. Because the special admissions program involved a racial classification, the Supreme Court held itself bound to apply strict scrutiny. It then turned to the goals the University presented as justifying the special program. Although the court agreed that the goals of integrating the medical profession and increasing the number of physicians willing to serve members of minority groups were compelling state interests, it concluded that the special admissions program was not the least intrusive means of achieving those goals. Without passing on the state constitutional or the federal statutory grounds cited in the trial court's judgment, the California court held that the Equal Protection

Clause of the Fourteenth Amendment required that "no applicant may be rejected because of his race, in favor of another who is less qualified, as measured by standards applied without regard to race."

Turning to Bakke's appeal, the court ruled that since Bakke had established that the University had discriminated against him on the basis of his race, the burden of proof shifted to the University to demonstrate that he would not have been admitted even in the absence of the special admissions program. The court analogized Bakke's situation to that of a plaintiff under Title VII of the Civil Rights Act of 1964, 42 U.S.C. 2000e-17. On this basis, the court initially ordered a remand for the purpose of determining whether, under the newly allocated burden of proof, Bakke would have been admitted to either the 1973 or the 1974 entering class in the absence of the special admissions program. In its petition for rehearing... however, the University conceded its inability to carry that burden. California court thereupon amended its opinion to direct that the trial court enter judgment ordering Bakke's admission to the Medical School. That order was stayed pending review in this Court. We granted *certiorari* to consider the important constitutional issue.

II

In this Court the parties neither briefed nor argued the applicability of Title VI of the Civil Rights Act of 1964. Rather, as had the California court, they focused exclusively upon the validity of the special admissions program under the Equal Protection Clause. Because it was possible, however, that a decision on Title VI might obviate resort to constitutional interpretation, see *Ashwander v. TVA*, 297 U.S. 288, 346–348 (1936) (concurring opinion), we requested supplementary briefing on the statutory issue.

A

At the outset we face the question whether a right of action for private parties exists under Title VI. Respondent argues that there is a private right of

action, invoking the test set forth in *Cort v. Ash*, 422 U.S. 66, 78 (1975). He contends that the statute creates a federal right in his favor, that legislative history reveals an intent to permit private actions, that such actions would further the remedial purposes of the statute, and that enforcement of federal rights under the Civil Rights Act generally is not relegated to the States. In addition, he cites several lower court decisions which have recognized or assumed the existence of a private right of action. Petitioner denies the existence of a private right of action, arguing that the sole function of 601 was to establish a predicate for administrative action under 602, 78 Stat. 252, 42 U.S.C. 2000d-1. In its view, administrative curtailment of federal funds under that section was the only sanction to be imposed upon recipients that violated 601. Petitioner also points out that Title VI contains no explicit grant of a private right of action, in contrast to Titles II, III, IV, and VII, of the same statute....

We find it unnecessary to resolve this question in the instant case. The question of respondent's right to bring an action under Title VI was neither argued nor decided in either of the courts below, and this Court has been hesitant to review questions not addressed below. We therefore do not address this difficult issue. Similarly, we need not pass upon petitioner's claim that private plaintiffs under Title VI must exhaust administrative remedies. We assume, only for the purposes of this case, that respondent has a right of action under Title VI.

B

The language of 601, 78 Stat. 252, like that of the Equal Protection Clause, is majestic in its sweep: "No person in the United States shall, on the ground of race, color, or national origin, be excluded from participation in, be denied the benefits of, or be subjected to discrimination under any program or activity receiving Federal financial assistance."

The concept of "discrimination," like the phrase "equal protection of the laws," is susceptible of varying interpretations, for as Mr. Justice Holmes declared, "[a] word is not a crystal, transparent and unchanged, it is the skin of a living thought and may vary greatly in color and content according to the circumstances and the time in which it is used." We must, therefore, seek whatever aid is available in determining the precise meaning of the statute before us. Examination of the voluminous legislative history of Title VI reveals a congressional intent to halt federal funding of entities that violate a prohibition of racial discrimination similar to that of the Constitution. Although isolated statements of various legislators, taken out of context, can be marshaled in support of the proposition that 601 enacted a purely color-blind scheme, without regard to the reach of the Equal Protection Clause, these comments must be read against the background of both the problem that Congress was addressing and the broader view of the statute that emerges from a full examination of the legislative debates.

The problem confronting Congress was discrimination against Negro citizens at the hands of recipients of federal moneys. Indeed, the color blindness pronouncements ... generally occur in the midst of extended remarks dealing with the evils of segregation in federally funded programs. Over and over again, proponents of the bill detailed the plight of Negroes seeking equal treatment in such programs. There simply was no reason for Congress to consider the validity of hypothetical preferences that might be accorded minority citizens; the legislators were dealing with the real and pressing problem of how to guarantee those citizens equal treatment.

In addressing that problem, supporters of Title VI repeatedly declared that the bill enacted constitutional principles. For example, Representative Celler, the Chairman of the House Judiciary Committee and floor manager of the legislation in the House, emphasized this in introducing the bill:

> The bill would offer assurance that hospitals financed by Federal money would not deny adequate care to Negroes. It would prevent abuse of food distribution programs whereby Negroes have been known to be denied food [438 U.S. 265, 286] surplus supplies when white persons were given such food. It would assure Negroes the benefits now accorded only white students in programs of high[er] education financed by Federal funds. It would, in short, assure the existing right to equal treatment in the enjoyment of Federal funds. It would not destroy any rights of private property or freedom of association.

Other sponsors shared Representative Celler's view that Title VI embodied constitutional principles.

In the Senate, Senator Humphrey declared that the purpose of Title VI was "to insure that Federal funds are spent in accordance with the Constitution and the moral sense of the Nation." Senator Ribicoff agreed that Title VI embraced the constitutional standard: "Basically, there is a constitutional restriction against discrimination in the use of federal funds; and title VI simply spells out the procedure to be used in enforcing that restriction." Other Senators expressed similar views.

Further evidence of the incorporation of a constitutional standard into Title VI appears in the repeated refusals of the legislation's supporters precisely to define the term "discrimination." Opponents sharply criticized this failure, but proponents of the bill merely replied that the meaning of "discrimination" would be made clear by reference to the Constitution or other existing law. For example, Senator Humphrey noted the relevance of the Constitution:

> As I have said, the bill has a simple purpose. That purpose is to give fellow citizens— Negroes—the same rights and opportunities that white people take for granted. This is no more than what was preached by the prophets, and by Christ Himself. It is no more than what our Constitution guarantees.

In view of the clear legislative intent, Title VI must be held to proscribe only those racial classifications that would violate the Equal Protection Clause or the Fifth Amendment.

III

A

Petitioner does not deny that decisions based on race or ethnic origin by faculties and administrations of state universities are reviewable under the Fourteenth Amendment. The parties do disagree as to the level of judicial scrutiny to be applied to the special admissions program. Petitioner argues that the court below erred in applying strict scrutiny, as this inexact term has been applied in our cases. That level of review, petitioner asserts, should be reserved for classifications that disadvantage "discrete and insular minorities." Respondent, on the other hand, contends that the California court correctly rejected the notion that the degree of judicial scrutiny accorded a particular racial or ethnic classification hinges upon membership in a discrete and insular minority and duly recognized that the "rights established [by the Fourteenth Amendment] are personal rights."

En route to this crucial battle over the scope of judicial review, the parties fight a sharp preliminary action over the proper characterization of the special admissions program. Petitioner prefers to view it as establishing a "goal" of minority representation in the Medical School. Respondent, echoing the courts below, labels it a racial quota.

This semantic distinction is beside the point: The special admissions program is undeniably a classification based on race and ethnic background. To the extent that there existed a pool of at least minimally qualified minority applicants to fill the 16 special admissions seats, white applicants could compete only for 84 seats in the entering class, rather than the 100 open to minority applicants. Whether this limitation is described as a quota or a goal, it is a line drawn on the basis of race and ethnic status.

The guarantees of the Fourteenth Amendment extend to all persons. Its language is explicit: "No State shall . . . deny to any person within its jurisdiction the equal protection of the laws." It is settled beyond question that the "rights created by the first section of the Fourteenth Amendment are, by its terms, guaranteed to the individual. The rights established are personal rights." The guarantee of equal protection cannot mean one thing when applied to one individual and something else when applied to a person of another color. If both are not accorded the same protection, then it is not equal.

Nevertheless, petitioner argues that the court below erred in applying strict scrutiny to the special admissions program because white males, such as respondent, are not a "discrete and insular minority" requiring extraordinary protection from the majoritarian political process. This rationale, however, has never been invoked in our decisions as a prerequisite to subjecting racial or ethnic distinctions to strict scrutiny. Nor has this Court held that discreteness and insularity constitute necessary preconditions to a holding that a particular classification is invidious. These characteristics may be relevant in deciding whether or not to add new types of classifications to the list of "suspect" categories or whether a particular classification survives close examination. Racial and ethnic classifications, however, are subject to stringent examination without regard to these additional characteristics. We declared as much in the first cases explicitly to recognize racial distinctions as suspect: "Distinctions between citizens solely because of their ancestry are by their very nature odious to a free people whose institutions are founded upon the doctrine of equality."

"[A]ll legal restrictions which curtail the civil rights of a single racial group are immediately suspect. That is not to say that all such restrictions are unconstitutional. It is to say that courts must subject them to the most rigid scrutiny."

The Court has never questioned the validity of those pronouncements. Racial and ethnic distinctions of any sort are inherently suspect and thus call for the most exacting judicial examination.

B

This perception of racial and ethnic distinctions is rooted in our Nation's constitutional and demographic history. The Court's initial view of the Fourteenth Amendment was that its "one pervading purpose" was "the freedom of the slave race, the security and firm establishment of that freedom, and the protection of the newly-made freeman and citizen from the oppressions of those who had formerly exercised dominion over him." The Equal Protection Clause, however, was "[v]irtually strangled in infancy by post-civil-war judicial reactionism." It was relegated to decades of relative desuetude while the Due Process Clause of the Fourteenth Amendment, after a short germinal period, flourished as a cornerstone in the Court's defense of property and liberty of contract. In that cause, the Fourteenth Amendment's "one pervading purpose" was displaced. It was only as the era of substantive due process came to a close, that the Equal Protection Clause began to attain a genuine measure of vitality.

By that time it was no longer possible to peg the guarantees of the Fourteenth Amendment to the struggle for equality of one racial minority. During the dormancy of the Equal Protection Clause, the United States had become a Nation of minorities. Each had to struggle—and to some extent struggles still—to overcome the prejudices not of a monolithic majority, but of a "majority" composed of various minority groups of whom it was said—perhaps unfairly in many cases—that a shared characteristic was a willingness to disadvantage other groups. As the Nation filled with the stock of many lands, the reach of the Clause was gradually extended to all ethnic groups seeking protection from official discrimination. The guarantees of equal protection, said the Court in *Yick Wo*, "are universal in their application, to all persons within the territorial jurisdiction, without regard to any differences of race, of color, or of nationality; and the equal protection of the laws is a pledge of the protection of equal laws."

Although many of the Framers of the Fourteenth Amendment conceived of its primary function as bridging the vast distance between members of the Negro race and the white "majority," the Amendment itself was framed in universal terms, without reference to color, ethnic origin, or condition of prior servitude. As this Court recently remarked in interpreting the 1866 Civil Rights Act to extend to claims of racial discrimination against white persons, "the 39th Congress was intent upon establishing in the federal law a broader principle than would have been necessary simply to meet the particular and immediate plight of the newly freed Negro slaves." And that legislation was specifically broadened in 1870 to ensure that "all persons," not merely "citizens," would enjoy equal rights under the law. Indeed, it is not unlikely that among the Framers were many who would have applauded a reading of the Equal Protection Clause that states a principle of universal application and is responsive to the racial, ethnic, and cultural diversity of the Nation.

Over the past 30 years, this Court has embarked upon the crucial mission of interpreting the Equal Protection Clause with the view of assuring to all persons "the protection of equal laws," in a Nation confronting a legacy of slavery and racial discrimination. Because the landmark decisions in this area arose in response to the continued exclusion of Negroes from the mainstream of American society, they could be characterized as involving discrimination by the "majority" white race against the Negro minority. But they need not be read as depending upon that characterization for their results. It suffices to say that "[o]ver the years, this Court has consistently repudiated '[d]istinctions between citizens solely because of their ancestry' as being 'odious to a free people whose institutions are founded upon the doctrine of equality.'"

Petitioner urges us to adopt for the first time a more restrictive view of the Equal Protection Clause and hold that discrimination against members of the white "majority" cannot be suspect if its purpose can be characterized as "benign." The clock of our liberties, however, cannot be turned back to 1868. It is far too late to argue that the guarantee of equal protection to all persons permits the recognition of special wards entitled to a degree of protection greater than that accorded others. "The Fourteenth Amendment is not directed solely against discrimination due to a 'two-class theory'—that is, based upon differences between 'white' and Negro."

Once the artificial line of a "two-class theory" of the Fourteenth Amendment is put aside, the difficulties entailed in varying the level of judicial review according to a perceived "preferred" status of a particular racial or ethnic minority are intractable. The concepts of "majority" and "minority" necessarily reflect temporary arrangements and political judgments. As observed above, the white "majority" itself is composed of various minority groups, most of which can lay claim to a history of prior discrimination at the hands of the State and private individuals. Not all of these groups can receive preferential treatment and corresponding judicial tolerance of distinctions drawn in terms of race and nationality, for then the only "majority" left would be a new minority of white Anglo-Saxon Protestants. There is no principled basis for deciding which groups would merit "heightened judicial solicitude" and which would not. Courts would be asked to evaluate the extent of the prejudice and consequent harm suffered by various minority groups. Those whose societal injury is thought to exceed some arbitrary level of tolerability then would be entitled to preferential classifications at the expense of individuals belonging to other groups. Those classifications would be free from exacting judicial scrutiny. As these preferences began to have their desired effect, and the consequences of past discrimination were undone, new judicial rankings would be necessary. The kind of variable sociological and political analysis necessary to produce such rankings simply does not lie within the judicial competence—even if they otherwise were politically feasible and socially desirable.

Moreover, there are serious problems of justice connected with the idea of preference itself. First, it may not always be clear that a so-called preference is in fact benign. Courts may be asked to validate burdens imposed upon individual members of a particular group in order to advance the group's general interest. Nothing in the Constitution supports the notion that individuals may be asked to suffer otherwise impermissible burdens in order to enhance the societal standing of their ethnic groups. Second, preferential programs may only reinforce common stereotypes holding that certain groups are unable to achieve success without special protection

based on a factor having no relationship to individual worth. Third, there is a measure of inequity in forcing innocent persons in respondent's position to bear the burdens of redressing grievances not of their making.

By hitching the meaning of the Equal Protection Clause to these transitory considerations, we would be holding, as a constitutional principle, that judicial scrutiny of classifications touching on racial and ethnic background may vary with the ebb and flow of political forces. Disparate constitutional tolerance of such classifications well may serve to exacerbate racial and ethnic antagonisms rather than alleviate them. Also, the mutability of a constitutional principle, based upon shifting political and social judgments, undermines the chances for consistent application of the Constitution from one generation to the next, a critical feature of its coherent interpretation. In expounding the Constitution, the Court's role is to discern "principles sufficiently absolute to give them roots throughout the community and continuity over significant periods of time, and to lift them above the level of the pragmatic political judgments of a particular time and place" (A. Cox, *The Role of the Supreme Court in American Government* 114, 1976).

If it is the individual who is entitled to judicial protection against classifications based upon his racial or ethnic background because such distinctions impinge upon personal rights, rather than the individual only because of his membership in a particular group, then constitutional standards may be applied consistently. Political judgments regarding the necessity for the particular classification may be weighed in the constitutional balance, but the standard of justification will remain constant. This is as it should be, since those political judgments are the product of rough compromise struck by contending groups within the democratic process. When they touch upon an individual's race or ethnic background, he is entitled to a judicial determination that the burden he is asked to bear on that basis is precisely tailored to serve a compelling governmental interest. The Constitution guarantees that right to every person regardless of his background.

C

Petitioner contends that on several occasions this Court has approved preferential classifications without applying the most exacting scrutiny. Most of the cases upon which petitioner relies are drawn from three areas: school desegregation, employment discrimination, and sex discrimination. Each of the cases cited presented a situation materially different from the facts of this case.

The school desegregation cases are inapposite. Each involved remedies for clearly determined constitutional violations. Racial classifications thus were designed as remedies for the vindication of constitutional entitlement. Moreover, the scope of the remedies was not permitted to exceed the extent of the violations. Here, there was no judicial determination of constitutional violation as a predicate for the formulation of a remedial classification.

The employment discrimination cases also do not advance petitioner's cause. For example, in *Franks v. Bowman Transportation Co.*, 424 U.S. 747 (1976), we approved a retroactive award of seniority to a class of Negro truckdrivers who had been the victims of discrimination—not just by society at large, but by the respondent in that case. While this relief imposed some burdens on other employees, it was held necessary "to make [the victims] whole for injuries suffered on account of unlawful employment discrimination." The Courts of Appeals have fashioned various types of racial preferences as remedies for constitutional or statutory violations resulting in identified, race-based injuries to individuals held entitled to the preference. Such preferences also have been upheld where a legislative or administrative body charged with the responsibility made determinations of past discrimination by the industries affected, and fashioned remedies deemed appropriate to rectify the discrimination. But we have never approved preferential classifications in the absence of proved constitutional or statutory violations.

Nor is petitioner's view as to the applicable standard supported by the fact that gender-based classifications are not subjected to this level of scrutiny. Gender-based distinctions are less likely to create

the analytical and practical problems present in preferential programs premised on racial or ethnic criteria. With respect to gender there are only two possible classifications. The incidence of the burdens imposed by preferential classifications is clear. There are no rival groups which can claim that they, too, are entitled to preferential treatment. Classwide questions as to the group suffering previous injury and groups which fairly can be burdened are relatively manageable for reviewing courts. The resolution of these same questions in the context of racial and ethnic preferences presents far more complex and intractable problems than gender-based classifications. More importantly, the perception of racial classifications as inherently odious stems from a lengthy and tragic history that gender-based classifications do not share. In sum, the Court has never viewed such classification as inherently suspect or as comparable to racial or ethnic classifications for the purpose of equal protection analysis.

Petitioner also cites *Lau v. Nichols* in support of the proposition that discrimination favoring racial or ethnic minorities has received judicial approval without the exacting inquiry ordinarily accorded "suspect" classifications. In *Lau*, we held that the failure of the San Francisco school system to provide remedial English instruction for some 1,800 students of oriental ancestry who spoke no English amounted to a violation of Title VI of the Civil Rights Act of 1964, and the regulations promulgated thereunder. Those regulations required remedial instruction where inability to understand English excluded children of foreign ancestry from participation in educational programs. Because we found that the students in *Lau* were denied "a meaningful opportunity to participate in the educational program," we remanded for the fashioning of a remedial order.

Lau provides little support for petitioner's argument. The decision rested solely on the statute, which had been construed by the responsible administrative agency to reach educational practices "which have the effect of subjecting individuals to discrimination," We stated: "Under these state-imposed standards there is no equality of treatment merely by providing students with the same facilities, textbooks, teachers, and curriculum; for students who do not understand English are effectively foreclosed from any meaningful education." Moreover, the "preference" approved did not result in the denial of the relevant benefit—"meaningful opportunity to participate in the educational program"—to anyone else. No other student was deprived by that preference of the ability to participate in San Francisco's school system, and the applicable regulations required similar assistance for all students who suffered similar linguistic deficiencies.

In a similar vein, petitioner contends that our recent decision in *United Jewish Organizations v. Carey*, indicates a willingness to approve racial classifications designed to benefit certain minorities, without denominating the classifications as "suspect." The State of New York had redrawn its reapportionment plan to meet objections of the Department of Justice under ... the Voting Rights Act of 1965. Specifically, voting districts were redrawn to enhance the electoral power of certain "nonwhite" voters found to have been the victims of unlawful "dilution" under the original reapportionment plan. *United Jewish Organizations*, like *Lau*, properly is viewed as a case in which the remedy for an administrative finding of discrimination encompassed measures to improve the previously disadvantaged group's ability to participate, without excluding individuals belonging to any other group from enjoyment of the relevant opportunity—meaningful participation in the electoral process.

In this case, unlike *Lau* and *United Jewish Organizations*, there has been no determination by the legislature or a responsible administrative agency that the University engaged in a discriminatory practice requiring remedial efforts. Moreover, the operation of petitioner's special admissions program is quite different from the remedial measures approved in those cases. It prefers the designated minority groups at the expense of other individuals who are totally foreclosed from competition for the 16 special admissions seats in every Medical School class. Because of that foreclosure,

some individuals are excluded from enjoyment of a state-provided benefit—admission to the Medical School—they otherwise would receive. When a classification denies an individual opportunities or benefits enjoyed by others solely because of his race or ethnic background, it must be regarded as suspect.

IV

We have held that in "order to justify the use of a suspect classification, a State must show that its purpose or interest is both constitutionally permissible and substantial, and that its use of the classification is 'necessary ... to the accomplishment' of its purpose or the safeguarding of its interest." The special admissions program purports to serve the purposes of: (i) "reducing the historic deficit of traditionally disfavored minorities in medical schools and in the medical profession"; (ii) countering the effects of societal discrimination; (iii) increasing the number of physicians who will practice in communities currently underserved; and (iv) obtaining the educational benefits that flow from an ethnically diverse student body. It is necessary to decide which, if any, of these purposes is substantial enough to support the use of a suspect classification.

A

If petitioner's purpose is to assure within its student body some specified percentage of a particular group merely because of its race or ethnic origin, such a preferential purpose must be rejected not as insubstantial but as facially invalid. Preferring members of any one group for no reason other than race or ethnic origin is discrimination for its own sake. This the Constitution forbids.

B

The State certainly has a legitimate and substantial interest in ameliorating, or eliminating where feasible, the disabling effects of identified discrimination. The line of school desegregation cases, commencing with Brown, attests to the importance of this state goal and the commitment of the judiciary to affirm all lawful means toward its attainment. In the school cases, the States were required by court order to redress the wrongs worked by specific instances of racial discrimination. That goal was far more focused than the remedying of the effects of "societal discrimination," an amorphous concept of injury that may be ageless in its reach into the past.

We have never approved a classification that aids persons perceived as members of relatively victimized groups at the expense of other innocent individuals in the absence of judicial, legislative, or administrative findings of constitutional or statutory violations. After such findings have been made, the governmental interest in preferring members of the injured groups at the expense of others is substantial, since the legal rights of the victims must be vindicated. In such a case, the extent of the injury and the consequent remedy will have been judicially, legislatively, or administratively defined. Also, the remedial action usually remains subject to continuing oversight to assure that it will work the least harm possible to other innocent persons competing for the benefit. Without such findings of constitutional or statutory violations, it cannot be said that the government has any greater interest in helping one individual than in refraining from harming another. Thus, the government has no compelling justification for inflicting such harm.

Petitioner does not purport to have made, and is in no position to make, such findings. Its broad mission is education, not the formulation of any legislative policy or the adjudication of particular claims of illegality. For reasons similar to those stated in Part III of this opinion, isolated segments of our vast governmental structures are not competent to make those decisions, at least in the absence of legislative mandates and legislatively determined criteria. Before relying upon these sorts of findings in establishing a racial classification, a governmental body must have the authority and capability to establish, in the record, that the classification is responsive to identified discrimination. Lacking this capability, petitioner has not carried its burden of justification on this issue.

Hence, the purpose of helping certain groups whom the faculty of the Davis Medical School perceived as victims of "societal discrimination" does not justify a classification that imposes disadvantages upon persons like respondent, who bear no responsibility for whatever harm the beneficiaries of the special admissions program are thought to have suffered. To hold otherwise would be to convert a remedy heretofore reserved for violations of legal rights into a privilege that all institutions throughout the Nation could grant at their pleasure to whatever groups are perceived as victims of societal discrimination. That is a step we have never approved.

C

Petitioner identifies, as another purpose of its program, improving the delivery of health-care services to communities currently underserved. It may be assumed that in some situations a State's interest in facilitating the health care of its citizens is sufficiently compelling to support the use of a suspect classification. But there is virtually no evidence in the record indicating that petitioner's special admissions program is either needed or geared to promote that goal. The court below addressed this failure of proof:

> The University concedes it cannot assure that minority doctors who entered under the program, all of whom expressed an 'interest' in practicing in a disadvantaged community, will actually do so. It may be correct to assume that some of them will carry out this intention, and that it is more likely they will practice in minority communities than the average white doctor. (See Sandalow, *Racial Preferences in Higher Education: Political Responsibility and the Judicial Role,* 1975, 42 U. Chi. L. Rev. 653, 688.) Nevertheless, there are more precise and reliable ways to identify applicants who are genuinely interested in the medical problems of minorities than by race. An applicant of whatever race who has demonstrated his concern for

disadvantaged minorities in the past and who declares that practice in such a community is his primary professional goal would be more likely to contribute to alleviation of the medical shortage than one who is chosen entirely on the basis of race and disadvantage. In short, there is no empirical data to demonstrate that any one race is more selflessly socially oriented or by contrast that another is more selfishly acquisitive.

Petitioner simply has not carried its burden of demonstrating that it must prefer members of particular ethnic groups over all other individuals in order to promote better health-care delivery to deprived citizens. Indeed, petitioner has not shown that its preferential classification is likely to have any significant effect on the problem.

D

The fourth goal asserted by petitioner is the attainment of a diverse student body. This clearly is a constitutionally permissible goal for an institution of higher education. Academic freedom, though not a specifically enumerated constitutional right, long has been viewed as a special concern of the First Amendment. The freedom of a university to make its own judgments as to education includes the selection of its student body. Mr. Justice Frankfurter summarized the "four essential freedoms" that constitute academic freedom:

> It is the business of a university to provide that atmosphere which is most conductive to speculation, experiment and creation. It is an atmosphere in which there prevail "the four essential freedoms" of a university—to determine for itself on academic grounds who may teach, what may be taught, how it shall be taught, and who may be admitted to study.

Our national commitment to the safeguarding of these freedoms within university communities was emphasized in *Keyishian v. Board of Regents.*

Our Nation is deeply committed to safeguarding academic freedom which is of transcendent value to all of us and not merely to the teachers concerned. That freedom is therefore a special concern of the First Amendment.... The Nation's future depends upon leaders trained through wide exposure to that robust exchange of ideas which discovers truth 'out of a multitude of tongues, [rather] than through any kind of authoritative selection.'

The atmosphere of "speculation, experiment and creation"—so essential to the quality of higher education—is widely believed to be promoted by a diverse student body. As the Court noted in *Keyishian*, it is not too much to say that the "nation's future depends upon leaders trained through wide exposure" to the ideas and mores of students as diverse as this Nation of many peoples.

Thus, in arguing that its universities must be accorded the right to select those students who will contribute the most to the "robust exchange of ideas," petitioner invokes a countervailing constitutional interest, that of the First Amendment. In this light, petitioner must be viewed as seeking to achieve a goal that is of paramount importance in the fulfillment of its mission.

It may be argued that there is greater force to these views at the undergraduate level than in a medical school where the training is centered primarily on professional competency. But even at the graduate level, our tradition and experience lend support to the view that the contribution of diversity is substantial. In *Sweatt v. Painter*, the Court made a similar point with specific reference to legal education:

> The law school, the proving ground for legal learning and practice, cannot be effective in isolation from the individuals and institutions with which the law interacts. Few students and no one who has practiced law would choose to study in an academic vacuum, removed from the interplay of ideas

and the exchange of views with which the law is concerned.

Physicians serve a heterogeneous population. An otherwise qualified medical student with a particular background—whether it be ethnic, geographic, culturally advantaged or disadvantaged—may bring to a professional school of medicine experiences, outlooks, and ideas that enrich the training of its student body and better equip its graduates to render with understanding their vital service to humanity.

Ethnic diversity, however, is only one element in a range of factors a university properly may consider in attaining the goal of a heterogeneous student body. Although a university must have wide discretion in making the sensitive judgments as to who should be admitted, constitutional limitations protecting individual rights may not be disregarded. Respondent urges—and the courts below have held—that petitioner's dual admissions program is a racial classification that impermissibly infringes his rights under the Fourteenth Amendment. As the interest of diversity is compelling in the context of a university's admissions program, the question remains whether the program's racial classification is necessary to promote this interest.

V

A

It may be assumed that the reservation of a specified number of seats in each class for individuals from the preferred ethnic groups would contribute to the attainment of considerable ethnic diversity in the student body. But petitioner's argument that this is the only effective means of serving the interest of diversity is seriously flawed. In a most fundamental sense the argument misconceives the nature of the state interest that would justify consideration of race or ethnic background. It is not an interest in simple ethnic diversity, in which a specified percentage of the student body is in effect guaranteed to be members of selected ethnic groups, with the remaining percentage an undifferentiated aggregation of students. The diversity that furthers a compelling state interest encompasses a far broader array of qualifications and characteristics of which racial or ethnic origin is but a single though important element. Petitioner's special admissions program, focused solely on ethnic diversity, would hinder rather than further attainment of genuine diversity.

Nor would the state interest in genuine diversity be served by expanding petitioner's two-track system into a multitrack program with a prescribed number of seats set aside for each identifiable category of applicants. Indeed, it is inconceivable that a university would thus pursue the logic of petitioner's two-track program to the illogical end of insulating each category of applicants with certain desired qualifications from competition with all other applicants.

The experience of other university admissions programs, which take race into account in achieving the educational diversity valued by the First Amendment, demonstrates that the assignment of a fixed number of places to a minority group is not a necessary means toward that end. An illuminating example is found in the Harvard College program:

In recent years Harvard College has expanded the concept of diversity to include students from disadvantaged economic, racial and ethnic groups. Harvard College now recruits not only Californians or Louisianans but also blacks and Chicanos and other minority students....

In practice, this new definition of diversity has meant that race has been a factor in some admission decisions. When the Committee on Admissions reviews the large middle group of applicants who are 'admissible' and deemed capable of doing good work in their courses, the race of an applicant may tip the balance in his favor just as geographic origin or a life spent on a farm may tip the balance in other candidates' cases. A farm boy from Idaho can bring something to Harvard College that a Bostonian cannot offer. Similarly, a black student can usually bring something that a white person cannot offer....

In Harvard College admissions the Committee has not set target-quotas for the number of blacks, or of musicians, football players, physicists or Californians to be admitted in a given year.... But that awareness [of the necessity of including more than a token number of black students] does not mean that the Committee sets a minimum number of blacks or of people from west of the Mississippi who are to be admitted. It means only that in choosing among thousands of applicants who are not only 'admissible' academically but have other strong qualities, the Committee, with a number of criteria in mind, pays some attention to distribution among many types and categories of students. (App. to Brief for Columbia University, Harvard University, Stanford University, and the University of Pennsylvania, as *Amici Curiae* 2–3).

In such an admissions program, race or ethnic background may be deemed a "plus" in a particular applicant's file, yet it does not insulate the individual from comparison with all other candidates for the available seats. The file of a particular black applicant may be examined for his potential contribution to diversity without the factor of race being decisive when compared, for example, with that of an applicant identified as an Italian-American if the latter is thought to exhibit qualities more likely to promote beneficial educational pluralism. Such qualities could include exceptional personal talents, unique work or service experience, leadership potential, maturity, demonstrated compassion, a history of overcoming disadvantage, ability to communicate with the poor, or other qualifications deemed important. In short, an admissions program operated in this way is flexible enough to consider all pertinent elements of diversity in light of the particular qualifications of each applicant, and to place them on the same footing for consideration, although not necessarily according them the same weight. Indeed, the weight attributed to a particular quality may vary from year to year depending upon the "mix" both of the student body and the applicants for the incoming class.

This kind of program treats each applicant as an individual in the admissions process. The applicant who loses out on the last available seat to another candidate receiving a "plus" on the basis of ethnic background will not have been foreclosed from all consideration for that seat simply because he was not the right color or had the wrong surname. It would mean only that his combined qualifications, which may have included similar nonobjective factors, did not outweigh those of the other applicant. His qualifications would have been weighed fairly and competitively, and he would have no basis to complain of unequal treatment under the Fourteenth Amendment.

It has been suggested that an admissions program which considers race only as one factor is simply a subtle and more sophisticated—but no less effective—means of according racial preference than the Davis program. A facial intent to discriminate, however, is evident in petitioner's preference program and not denied in this case. No such facial infirmity exists in an admissions program where race or ethnic background is simply one element—to be weighed fairly against other elements—in the selection process. "A boundary line," as Mr. Justice Frankfurter remarked in another connection, "is none the worse for being narrow." And a court would not assume that a university, professing to employ a facially nondiscriminatory admissions policy, would operate it as a cover for the functional equivalent of a quota system. In short, good faith would be presumed in the absence of a showing to the contrary in the manner permitted by our cases.

B

In summary, it is evident that the Davis special admissions program involves the use of an explicit racial classification never before countenanced by this Court. It tells applicants who are not Negro, Asian, or Chicano that they are totally excluded from a specific percentage of the seats in an entering class. No matter how strong their qualifications, quantitative and extracurricular, including their own potential for contribution to educational diversity, they are never afforded the chance to compete with applicants from the preferred groups for the special admissions seats. At the same time, the preferred applicants have the opportunity to compete for every seat in the class.

The fatal flaw in petitioner's preferential program is its disregard of individual rights as guaranteed by the Fourteenth Amendment. Such rights are not absolute. But when a State's distribution of benefits or imposition of burdens hinges on ancestry or the color of a person's skin, that individual is entitled to a demonstration that the challenged classification is necessary to promote a substantial state interest. Petitioner has failed to carry this burden. For this reason, that portion of the California court's judgment holding petitioner's special admissions program invalid under the Fourteenth Amendment must be affirmed.

C

In enjoining petitioner from ever considering the race of any applicant, however, the courts below failed to recognize that the State has a substantial interest that legitimately may be served by a properly devised admissions program involving the competitive consideration of race and ethnic origin. For this reason, so much of the California court's judgment as enjoins petitioner from any consideration of the race of any applicant must be reversed.

VI

With respect to respondent's entitlement to an injunction directing his admission to the Medical School, petitioner has conceded that it could not carry its burden of proving that, but for the existence of its unlawful special admissions program, respondent still would not have been admitted. Hence, respondent is entitled to the injunction, and that portion of the judgment must be affirmed.

DISCUSSION QUESTIONS

1. Setting aside possible constitutional (i.e., legal) issues, how might one defend an affirmative action policy? What principles might one employ if one is to make a moral (not legal) case for affirmative action?

2. How might a defender of affirmative action respond to Bakke's claim that "the special admissions program operated to exclude him on the basis of his race"?

3. Was the intent of the UC Davis affirmative action policy to exclude qualified non-minorities? To what extent is the *intent* of the policy morally significant?

4. On appeal, the California Supreme Court noted that the state had a compelling interest in promoting diversity in the medical profession. For what reasons would the state have such an interest? What principles would one appeal to in claiming that such an interest obtains?

86

Gratz v. Bollinger and *Grutter v. Bollinger* (2003)

In 2003, the US Supreme Court heard joint arguments in the cases of *Gratz v. Bollinger* and *Grutter v. Bollinger*. Both were cases involving the University of Michigan's affirmative action policies. In *Gratz*, the white petitioners who were denied admission to the university argued that their rights to equal protection guaranteed by the Fourteenth Amendment had been violated. The case of *Grutter* likewise argued that the University of Michigan Law School's admissions policy granted members of minority groups unfair advantages, thus resulting in the discrimination of the white petitioner. The Court's decisions—wherein the University of Michigan's policy was deemed to be too "rigid," yet wherein the Law School's policy was allowed to stand—sparked debate about the role of affirmative action policies.

SOURCE

539 U.S. 244, 539 U.S. 306 (U.S. Supreme Court).

Gratz v. Bollinger—Argued April 1, 2003; Decided June 23, 2003

Petitioners Gratz and Hamacher, both of whom are Michigan residents and Caucasian, applied for admission to the University of Michigan's (University) College of Literature, Science, and the Arts (LSA) in 1995 and 1997, respectively. Although the LSA considered Gratz to be well qualified and Hamacher to be within the qualified range, both were denied early admission and were ultimately denied admission. In order to promote consistency in the review of the many applications received, the University's Office of Undergraduate Admissions (OUA) uses written guidelines for each academic year. The guidelines have changed a number of times during the period relevant to this litigation. The OUA considers a number of factors in making admissions decisions, including high school grades, standardized test scores, high school quality, curriculum strength, geography, alumni relationships, leadership, and race. During all relevant periods, the University has considered African-Americans, Hispanics, and Native Americans to be "underrepresented minorities," and it is undisputed that the University admits virtually every qualified applicant from these groups. The current guidelines use a selection method under which every applicant from an underrepresented racial or ethnic minority group is automatically awarded 20 points of the 100 needed to guarantee admission.

Petitioners filed this class action alleging that the University's use of racial preferences in undergraduate admissions violated the Equal Protection Clause of the Fourteenth Amendment. They sought compensatory and punitive damages for past violations, declaratory relief finding that respondents violated their rights to nondiscriminatory treatment, an injunction prohibiting respondents from continuing to discriminate on the basis of race, and an order requiring the LSA to offer Hamacher admission as a transfer student. The District Court granted petitioners' motion to certify a class consisting of individuals who applied for and were denied admission to the LSA for academic year 1995 and forward and who are members of racial or ethnic groups that respondents treated less favorably on the basis of race. Hamacher, whose claim was found to challenge racial discrimination on a classwide basis, was designated as the class representative. On cross-motions for summary judgment, respondents relied on Justice Powell's principal opinion in *Regents of Univ. of Cal. v. Bakke*, which expressed the view that the consideration of race as a factor in admissions might in some cases serve a compelling government interest. Respondents contended that the LSA has just such an interest in the educational benefits that result from having a racially and ethnically diverse student body and that its program is narrowly tailored to serve that interest. The court agreed with respondents as to the LSA's current admissions guidelines and granted them summary judgment in that respect. However, the court also found that the LSA's admissions guidelines for 1995 through 1998 operated as the functional equivalent of a quota running afoul of Justice Powell's *Bakke* opinion, and thus granted petitioners summary judgment with respect to respondents' admissions programs for those years. While interlocutory appeals were pending in the Sixth Circuit, that court issued an opinion in *Grutter v. Bollinger*, *post*, upholding the admissions program used by the University's Law School. This Court granted *certiorari* in both cases, even though the Sixth Circuit had not yet rendered judgment in this one.

Held:

Petitioners have standing to seek declaratory and injunctive relief. The Court rejects Justice Stevens' contention that, because Hamacher did not actually apply for admission as a transfer student, his future injury claim is at best conjectural or hypothetical rather than real and immediate. The "injury in fact" necessary to establish standing in this type of case is the denial of equal treatment resulting from the imposition of the barrier, not the ultimate inability to obtain the benefit. In the face of such a barrier, to establish standing, a party need only demonstrate that it is able and ready to perform and that a discriminatory policy prevents it from doing so on an equal basis. Ibid. In bringing his equal protection challenge against the University's use of race in undergraduate admissions, Hamacher alleged that the University had denied him the opportunity to compete for admission on an equal basis. Hamacher was denied admission to the University as a freshman applicant even though an underrepresented minority applicant with his qualifications would have been admitted. After being denied admission, Hamacher demonstrated that he was "able and ready" to apply as a transfer student should the University cease to use race in undergraduate admissions. He therefore has standing to seek prospective relief with respect to the University's continued use of race. Also rejected is Justice Stevens' contention that such use in undergraduate transfer admissions differs from the University's use of race in undergraduate freshman admissions, so that Hamacher lacks standing to represent absent class members challenging the latter. Each year the OUA produces a document setting forth guidelines for those seeking admission to the LSA, including freshman and transfer applicants. The transfer applicant guidelines specifically cross-reference factors and qualifications considered in assessing freshman applicants. In fact, the criteria used to determine whether a transfer applicant will contribute to diversity are identical to those used to evaluate freshman applicants. The only difference is that all underrepresented minority freshman applicants receive 20 points and "virtually" all who are minimally qualified are admitted, while "generally" all minimally qualified minority transfer applicants are admitted outright. While this difference might be relevant to a narrow tailoring analysis, it clearly has no effect on petitioners' standing to challenge the University's use of race in undergraduate admissions and its assertion that diversity is a compelling state interest justifying its consideration of the race of its undergraduate applicants. The District Court's carefully considered decision to certify this class action is correct. Hamacher's personal stake, in view of both his past injury and the potential injury he faced at the time of certification, demonstrates that he may maintain the action.

Because the University's use of race in its current freshman admissions policy is not narrowly tailored to achieve respondents' asserted interest in diversity, the policy violates the Equal Protection Clause. For the reasons set forth in *Grutter v. Bollinger*, the Court has today rejected petitioners' argument that diversity cannot constitute a compelling state interest. However, the Court finds that the University's current policy, which automatically distributes 20 points, or one-fifth of the points needed to guarantee admission, to every single "underrepresented minority" applicant solely because of race, is not narrowly tailored to achieve educational diversity. In *Bakke*, Justice Powell explained his view that it would be permissible for a university to employ an admissions program in which "race or ethnic background may be deemed a 'plus' in a particular applicant's file." He emphasized, however, the importance of considering each particular applicant as an individual, assessing all of the qualities that individual possesses, and in turn, evaluating that individual's ability to contribute to the unique setting of higher education. The admissions program Justice Powell described did not contemplate that any single characteristic automatically ensured a specific and identifiable contribution to a university's diversity. The current LSA policy does not provide the individualized consideration Justice Powell contemplated. The only consideration that accompanies the 20-point automatic distribution to all applicants from underrepresented minorities is a factual review

to determine whether an individual is a member of one of these minority groups. Moreover, unlike Justice Powell's example, where the race of a "particular black applicant" could be considered without being decisive, the LSA's 20-point distribution has the effect of making "the factor of race ... decisive" for virtually every minimally qualified underrepresented minority applicant. The fact that the LSA has created the possibility of an applicant's file being flagged for individualized consideration only emphasizes the flaws of the University's system as a whole when compared to that described by Justice Powell. The record does not reveal precisely how many applications are flagged, but it is undisputed that such consideration is the exception and not the rule in the LSA's program. Also, this individualized review is only provided after admissions counselors automatically distribute the University's version of a "plus" that makes race a decisive factor for virtually every minimally qualified underrepresented minority applicant. The Court rejects respondents' contention that the volume of applications and the presentation of applicant information make it impractical for the LSA to use the admissions system upheld today in *Grutter*. The fact that the implementation of a program capable of providing individualized consideration might present administrative challenges does not render constitutional an otherwise problematic system. Nothing in Justice Powell's *Bakke* opinion signaled that a university may employ whatever means it desires to achieve diversity without regard to the limits imposed by strict scrutiny.

[...]

Reversed in part and remanded.

Grutter v. Bollinger—Argued April 1, 2003; Decided June 23, 2003

The University of Michigan Law School (Law School), one of the Nation's top law schools, follows an official admissions policy that seeks to achieve student body diversity through compliance with *Regents of Univ. of Cal. v. Bakke*. Focusing on students' academic ability coupled with a flexible assessment of their talents, experiences, and potential, the policy requires admissions officials to evaluate each applicant based on all the information available in the file, including a personal statement, letters of recommendation, an essay describing how the applicant will contribute to Law School life and diversity, and the applicant's undergraduate grade point average (GPA) and Law School Admissions Test (LSAT) score. Additionally, officials must look beyond grades and scores to so-called "soft variables," such as recommenders' enthusiasm, the quality of the undergraduate institution and the applicant's essay, and the areas and difficulty of undergraduate course selection. The policy does not define diversity solely in terms of racial and ethnic status and does not restrict the types of diversity contributions eligible for "substantial weight," but it does reaffirm the Law School's commitment to diversity with special reference to the inclusion of African-American, Hispanic, and Native-American students, who otherwise might not be represented in the student body in meaningful numbers. By enrolling a "critical mass" of underrepresented minority students, the policy seeks to ensure their ability to contribute to the Law School's character and to the legal profession.

When the Law School denied admission to petitioner Grutter, a white Michigan resident with a 3.8 GPA and 161 LSAT score, she filed this suit, alleging that respondents had discriminated against her on the basis of race in violation of the Fourteenth Amendment, Title VI of the Civil Rights Act of 1964, and 42 U.S.C. § 1981; that she was rejected because the Law School uses race as a "predominant" factor, giving applicants belonging to certain minority groups a significantly greater chance of admission than students with similar credentials from disfavored racial groups; and that respondents had no compelling interest to justify that use of race. The District Court found the Law School's use of race as an admissions factor unlawful. The Sixth Circuit reversed, holding that Justice Powell's opinion in Bakke was binding precedent establishing diversity as a compelling state interest, and that the Law School's use of race was narrowly tailored

because race was merely a "potential 'plus' factor" and because the Law School's program was virtually identical to the Harvard admissions program described approvingly by Justice Powell and appended to his *Bakke* opinion.

Held:

The Law School's narrowly tailored use of race in admissions decisions to further a compelling interest in obtaining the educational benefits that flow from a diverse student body is not prohibited by the Equal Protection Clause, Title VI, or §1981.

(a) In the landmark *Bakke* case, this Court reviewed a medical school's racial set-aside program that reserved 16 out of 100 seats for members of certain minority groups. The decision produced six separate opinions, none of which commanded a majority. Four Justices would have upheld the program on the ground that the government can use race to remedy disadvantages cast on minorities by past racial prejudice. Four other Justices would have struck the program down on statutory grounds. Justice Powell, announcing the Court's judgment, provided a fifth vote not only for invalidating the program, but also for reversing the state court's injunction against any use of race whatsoever. In a part of his opinion that was joined by no other Justice, Justice Powell expressed his view that attaining a diverse student body was the only interest asserted by the university that survived scrutiny. Grounding his analysis in the academic freedom that "long has been viewed as a special concern of the First Amendment," Justice Powell emphasized that the "'nation's future depends upon leaders trained through wide exposure' to the ideas and mores of students as diverse as this Nation." However, he also emphasized that "[i]t is not an interest in simple ethnic diversity, in which a specified percentage of the student body is in effect guaranteed to be members of selected ethnic groups," that can justify using race. Rather, "[t]he diversity that furthers a compelling state interest encompasses a far broader array of qualifications and characteristics of which racial or ethnic origin is but a single though important element." Since *Bakke*,

Justice Powell's opinion has been the touchstone for constitutional analysis of race-conscious admissions policies. Public and private universities across the Nation have modeled their own admissions programs on Justice Powell's views. Courts, however, have struggled to discern whether Justice Powell's diversity rationale is binding precedent. The Court finds it unnecessary to decide this issue because the Court endorses Justice Powell's view that student body diversity is a compelling state interest in the context of university admissions.

(b) All government racial classifications must be analyzed by a reviewing court under strict scrutiny. But not all such uses are invalidated by strict scrutiny. Race-based action necessary to further a compelling governmental interest does not violate the Equal Protection Clause so long as it is narrowly tailored to further that interest. Context matters when reviewing such action. Not every decision influenced by race is equally objectionable, and strict scrutiny is designed to provide a framework for carefully examining the importance and the sincerity of the government's reasons for using race in a particular context.

(c) The Court endorses Justice Powell's view that student body diversity is a compelling state interest that can justify using race in university admissions. The Court defers to the Law School's educational judgment that diversity is essential to its educational mission. The Court's scrutiny of that interest is no less strict for taking into account complex educational judgments in an area that lies primarily within the university's expertise. See, e.g., *Bakke*. Attaining a diverse student body is at the heart of the Law School's proper institutional mission, and its "good faith" is "presumed" absent "a showing to the contrary." Enrolling a "critical mass" of minority students simply to assure some specified percentage of a particular group merely because of its race or ethnic origin would be patently unconstitutional. But the Law School defines its critical mass concept by reference to the substantial, important, and laudable educational benefits that diversity is designed to produce, including cross-racial understanding and the breaking down of racial stereotypes. The

Law School's claim is further bolstered by numerous expert studies and reports showing that such diversity promotes learning outcomes and better prepares students for an increasingly diverse workforce, for society, and for the legal profession. Major American businesses have made clear that the skills needed in today's increasingly global marketplace can only be developed through exposure to widely diverse people, cultures, ideas, and viewpoints. High-ranking retired officers and civilian military leaders assert that a highly qualified, racially diverse officer corps is essential to national security. Moreover, because universities, and in particular, law schools, represent the training ground for a large number of the Nation's leaders, the path to leadership must be visibly open to talented and qualified individuals of every race and ethnicity. Thus, the Law School has a compelling interest in attaining a diverse student body.

(d) The Law School's admissions program bears the hallmarks of a narrowly tailored plan. To be narrowly tailored, a race-conscious admissions program cannot "insulat[e] each category of applicants with certain desired qualifications from competition with all other applicants." Instead, it may consider race or ethnicity only as a "'plus' in a particular applicant's file"; i.e., it must be "flexible enough to consider all pertinent elements of diversity in light of the particular qualifications of each applicant, and to place them on the same footing for consideration, although not necessarily according them the same weight." It follows that universities cannot establish quotas for members of certain racial or ethnic groups or put them on separate admissions tracks. The Law School's admissions program, like the Harvard plan approved by Justice Powell, satisfies these requirements. Moreover, the program is flexible enough to ensure that each applicant is evaluated as an individual and not in a way that makes race or ethnicity the defining feature of the application. See *Bakke*. The Law School engages in a highly individualized, holistic review of each applicant's file, giving serious consideration to all the ways an applicant might contribute to a diverse educational environment. There is no policy, either *de jure* or *de facto*, of automatic acceptance or rejection based on any single "soft" variable. Also, the program adequately ensures that all factors that may contribute to diversity are meaningfully considered alongside race. Moreover, the Law School frequently accepts nonminority applicants with grades and test scores lower than underrepresented minority applicants (and other nonminority applicants) who are rejected. The Court rejects the argument that the Law School should have used other race-neutral means to obtain the educational benefits of student body diversity, e.g., a lottery system or decreasing the emphasis on GPA and LSAT scores. Narrow tailoring does not require exhaustion of every conceivable race-neutral alternative or mandate that a university choose between maintaining a reputation for excellence or fulfilling a commitment to provide educational opportunities to members of all racial groups. The Court is satisfied that the Law School adequately considered the available alternatives. The Court is also satisfied that, in the context of individualized consideration of the possible diversity contributions of each applicant, the Law School's race-conscious admissions program does not unduly harm nonminority applicants. Finally, race-conscious admissions policies must be limited in time. The Court takes the Law School at its word that it would like nothing better than to find a race-neutral admissions formula and will terminate its use of racial preferences as soon as practicable. The Court expects that 25 years from now, the use of racial preferences will no longer be necessary to further the interest approved today.

(e) Because the Law School's use of race in admissions decisions is not prohibited by the Equal Protection Clause, petitioner's statutory claims based on Title VI and §1981 also fail.

DISCUSSION QUESTIONS

1. On what grounds did the University argue it had a compelling interest in accepting minority applicants? That is, what were the University's stated reasons in instituting the policy? Do you think these are good (i.e., overriding) reasons to take race into consideration? Why or why not?

2. What other reasons (aside those offered by the University) might be offered in support of an affirmative action program like the one the University employed?

87

Tuneen E. Chisolm, "Sweep Around Your Own Front Door: Examining the Argument for Legislative African American Reparations"[1] (1999)

Tuneen Chisolm is an attorney practicing in Atlanta, Georgia. She received her J.D. from the University of Pennsylvania Law School where she was a senior editor for the Law Review. In this article she considers whether and on what grounds legislative reparations for African Americans are justified.

SOURCE

Chisolm, Tuneen. "Sweep Around Your Own Front Door: Examining the Argument for Legislative African American Reparations." *University of Pennsylvania Law Review* 147, April 1999, pp. 677–727. Copyright © 1999. Reproduced with permission of the *University of Pennsylvania Law Review.*

As a world leader emphasizing the need for international relations grounded upon democracy and human rights, the United States has yet to face the dilemma of how to deal with its own past and its most egregious historical injustices, an obvious example being the legacy of slavery.

Introduction

The current state of race relations in America is charged with vigorous debates over the utility of a formal apology for slavery and the appropriate fate of affirmative action, as well as vivid reminders of past civil- and government-sanctioned transgressions against African Americans. The enslavement of Africans in America from 1619 to 1865 is one of the most callous, vexatious, near-genocidal violations of human rights in world history; that history is buried in the conscience of this Nation. The legacy of slavery in America is marked by the continued marginalization of African Americans within the firmly rooted, self-perpetuating economic caste system that is this Nation's foundation.

President Clinton has a vision of America becoming "the world's first truly multiracial, multiethnic, multireligious democracy," so that we as a Nation will be "better positioned ... to lead the world toward peace and freedom and prosperity" in the twenty-first century. To that end, the President has

---

[1] [The original notes have been omitted.]

commissioned the "President's Advisory Board on Race" to examine how we can end the racial divide that still pervades the Nation more than three decades after the end of overt, systemic discrimination and Jim Crow laws. The order provides that the board shall advise the President on matters involving race and racial reconciliation, including ways in which the President can: (1) promote a constructive national dialogue to confront and work through challenging issues that surround race; (2) increase the Nation's understanding of our recent history of race relations and the course our Nation is charting on issues of race relations and racial diversity; (3) bridge racial divides by encouraging leaders in communities throughout the Nation to develop and implement innovative approaches to calming racial tensions; [and] (4) identify, develop, and implement solutions to problems in areas in which race has a substantial impact, such as education, economic opportunity, housing, health care, and the administration of justice.

That agenda echoes the famous I Have A Dream speech in which Martin Luther King, Jr. painted his vision for a harmonious multiracial, multiethnic, and multireligious American democracy. That was three and one-half decades ago, and still, America is far from reaching a true equal-access democracy in which every individual enjoys full citizenship and equal opportunity. "If we can finally achieve [that] multicultural balance, America would unquestionably be perceived as the moral leader of a world characterized by intranational ethnic dissension and oppression."

In recent years, however, many have interpreted the very protections that were enacted to alleviate systemic racial discrimination against disadvantaged minority groups—namely, the Fourteenth Amendment and Title VII—in a way that threatens to eradicate progress. California's Proposition 209, which succeeded in amending the California Constitution, is spawning "copycat" legislation that ultimately may result in the demise of government affirmative action. Some affirmative-action opponents justify their position by suggesting that the elimination of all race-preferential policies in favor of a strict meritocracy reflects King's ideal. Against the backdrop of race-neutral policy reasoning, President Clinton's vision conjures up images of the utopian America that we have not been able to achieve—images of an America where people are judged by the "content of their character" and where we truly can all just get along. A discussion of whether colorblindness is a necessary step to achieve equality, or whether colorblindness is even desirable as an end objective, is beyond the scope of this Comment. However, "assum[ing] that our goal is a color-blind society, whatever that really means," the question is whether "requiring that people act in a color-blind manner [will] hasten the day when people actually think in a color-blind way in their socially and economically significant dealings with others." The evidence suggests not. Despite some progress, "[e]conomic and social disadvantages remain powerfully linked with color, and this linkage exacts an enormous toll on the perception and reality of opportunity in America. Racial discrimination and race-based exclusion remain significant forces."

Therefore, I submit that at least one prerequisite to resolving the dilemma of race relations in America is reparations for African Americans. The issue addressed in this Comment is whether legislative reparations are a justifiable remedy for African Americans, particularly in light of the imminent dismantling of affirmative action with Proposition 209 and the decisions that have followed. Part I gives a brief overview of the quest for African American reparations since the end of slavery. Part II focuses on the continuing effects of slavery and systemic discrimination, and on the argument that continuing black and white inequities are rooted in such institutions. This Part discusses wealth as a measure of inequity to set the stage for determining damages and the appropriate compensation. Part III discusses why reparations are a prerequisite to an equitable society. In addition, Part III reflects on the "moral economy" incentive for granting reparations to African Americans. Part IV presents the rationale for a legislative remedy in the context of distributive justice. This section reviews the Civil

Liberties Act as a precedent for race-based reparations, and discusses the arguments reconciling African American reparations and the Equal Protection Clause. Finally, Part V offers suggestions in answer to the who, what, and how of implementing an African American reparations scheme.

I. History of the Quest

Five major waves of political activism have promoted the idea of reparations for African Americans since the emancipation of slaves: (1) the Civil War Reconstruction Era, (2) the turn of the twentieth century, (3) the Garvey movement, (4) the Civil Rights movement, and (5) the resurgence of efforts following the Civil Liberties Act of 1988, which, most recently, has been fueled by the trend toward an official dismantling of affirmative-action policies. The redress sought has included claims for back pay of slave wages; land acquisition and educational benefits; monetary compensation for abuse, indignities suffered, forced indoctrination into a foreign culture, and/or destruction of the family unit; relocation to Africa or designated lands; relief from income tax obligations; and forty acres and a mule, or the equivalent value. For purposes of this Comment, the focus is narrowed to only that compensation necessary to enable slave descendants to function in an America with race-neutral policies. Consequently, exodus and other separatist options are not considered.

Early reparations measures were legislative remedies which Congress promoted not only to aid the transition of freed Africans from slavery to freedom, but also to gain leverage during the Civil War through confiscation of land from rebels. According to Foner, the "Confiscation Act, of August 1861, was directed only against property used in aid of the rebellion." The 1862 Confiscation Act authorized the taking of all rebel property, amassing thousands of acres of land; however, "President Lincoln, who strongly opposed widespread confiscation, forced Congress to … limit[] the seizure of land to the lifetime of the owner." The Lincoln administration did little to enforce the 1862 Act, which was eventually repealed to make way for a measure authorizing permanent seizure. Nevertheless, freedmen were permitted to settle on thousands of acres of abandoned land in South Carolina and Georgia pursuant to General Sherman's field order.

The Freedmen's Bureau Act of 1865 created the Bureau of Freedmen's Affairs to provide special assistance to refugees and persons of African descent. The 1865 Act, effective for one year, authorized the lease and sale of confiscated land to refugees and Africans and was broad enough to enable the Bureau to supply basic necessities and medical assistance. The 1866 Freedmen's Bureau bill, in turn, proposed to extend the 1865 Act indefinitely, to authorize Congress's appropriation of funds to purchase school buildings for refugees and freedmen, and to empower the President to "reserve up to three million acres of 'good' public land," for lease and sale "to freedmen and refugees in parcels not exceeding forty acres." The 1866 bill passed in both the House and the Senate, but President Johnson unexpectedly vetoed the bill, and it failed to garner enough votes to override the veto. The bill was modified to exclude the land reservation—no forty acres—and to extend the Bureau Act for only two years; however, the new bill "provided special aid and protection" for African Americans that was "substantially more explicit than the vetoed bill or the 1865 Freedmen's Bureau Act."

First, the modified 1866 Act authorized the Bureau to assist freed African Americans as necessary to ensure that their freedom was "'available to them and beneficial to the Republic,'" but limited the authorized assistance to white refugees to "that assistance necessary to make them self-supporting." Second, the modified bill limited educational programs to freed African Americans, whereas the vetoed bill had authorized "construction of schools 'for refugees and freedmen dependent on the Government for support.'" Third, the modified bill provided protections to free African Americans who were already occupying certain abandoned land pursuant to General Sherman's field order. Fourth, the modified bill prohibited only discrimination on the basis of race or color or previous condition of slavery, instead of also protecting refugees from discriminatory administration of civil and criminal law. Again Johnson vetoed the bill, but Congress voted to enact the 1866 Act nonetheless. The Act went into effect in 1868, and for two years, the Freedmen's Bureau enacted legislation for the education of freed African Americans. In 1870, however, a bill proposing indefinite continuation of education benefits passed in the House but died in the Senate, ending the Freedmen's Bureau activity.

Since the Freedmen's Bureau Acts, there has been no consistent measure of reparations for African Americans. In 1989 and in every session of Congress since 1993, the African American Reparations Commissions Act ("H.R. 40") has been introduced, calling for the establishment of a Commission to Study Reparations Proposals for African Americans. To date, the bill has not gone past the Committee on the Judiciary.

II. The Legacy of Slavery: Defining the Harm

Disparities in wealth between blacks and whites are not the product of haphazard events, inborn traits, isolated incidents or solely contemporary individual accomplishments. Rather, wealth inequality has been structured over many generations through the same systemic barriers that have hampered blacks throughout their history in American society: slavery, Jim Crow, so-called de jure discrimination, and institutionalized racism.

Simply put, reparations for African Americans is a touchy subject. The inequalities between blacks and whites in America often manifest themselves, and are therefore expressed, in terms that do not clearly relate back to slavery and the ensuing discrimination. For example, African Americans represent approximately 12% of the population, but account for 45% of prisoners nationwide; African Americans are 6.8 times more likely than whites to be homicide victims; African American families are 4.3 times more likely to live below the poverty level than whites; African Americans are only 65% as likely as whites to own their own home; and

the teenage pregnancy rate of African Americans is twice that for whites. Moreover, the unemployment rate of African Americans is more than twice than that of whites; whites are at least two times more likely to have completed four or more years of college than African Americans; and while the median income for whites increased by 11% from 1970 to 1992, that of African Americans decreased by 1%.

The connection between historical race bias and these statistics—particularly those for teenage pregnancy, imprisonment, and homicide—is not readily apparent. To assume that the statistics reflecting black and white inequities have no relation to past patterns of discrimination is to accept an argument that these statistics reflect the true inherent abilities or disabilities of African Americans. As the ensuing discussion will show, however, and as other studies have shown, this is not the case. The result of this apparent disconnection is often a reflexive denial of the relationship between slavery and the Jim Crow era to any racism that exists today. The need for a more concrete way of assessing the injury to African Americans is answered, in part, by considering wealth.

A. Wealth as the Measure

As Oliver and Shapiro argue in *Black Wealth/White Wealth*, private wealth is a more appropriate indicator of inequality than income, education, or occupation, because "the command over resources that wealth entails is … closer in meaning and theoretical significance to our traditional notions of economic well-being and access to life chances." According to Oliver and Shapiro, although "resources theoretically imply both income and wealth, the reality for most families is that income supplies the necessities of life, while wealth represents a kind of 'surplus' resource available for … securing prestige, passing status along to one's family, and influencing the political process." If, for instance, wealth affords an individual the opportunity to acquire controlling ownership of a production facility, that individual is freed from authority structures and can enjoy occupational autonomy. Transfer of that wealth from generation to generation assures that the position of authority and opportunity remain in the same family; thus wealth enables one to account for cumulative advantage and disadvantage. Some who dispute the relation between wealth and economic power argue that the two do not equate because "individuals with relatively little wealth may ... nonetheless exercise considerable economic power because of their institutional positions." This argument, however, presumes that those with power based on institutional positions are secure and bear no risk to their position regardless of the choices made in exercising their authority and influence. Such security is usually guaranteed by financial independence; thus the significance of wealth is inevitable.

Oliver and Shapiro demonstrate that income alone does not predict wealth. A comparison of income, net worth, and net financial assets for black and white, middle-class workers shows that, although blacks in the sample earned 70–85% of the income that whites earned, their net worth was only 16–31% of whites' net worth, and their net financial assets were zero. Further, a comparison of black and white net worth for various scenarios shows that there is a 74% differential in net worth between similar white and black households that cannot be explained by age, work experience, household size, or level of education. More importantly, because wealth encompasses resources and material assets that are transferred from generation to generation, thus having "historic origins," a wealth-based analysis of racial inequalities underscores the justice in reparations for a historic wrong.

B. Beneath the Surface Status Quo

"[African American] conservatives and liberals alike ... contend that land and man's own self-contained sense of industry serve as the greatest emancipators and equalizers of people in America." As key routes to wealth, control of land and labor are cornerstones in a capitalistic society, where political empowerment is closely tied to economic empowerment. This connection between land/labor control and political voice manifests itself in voter districting and lobbying, both of which directly impact state and federal legislative and executive powers,

which in turn control the appointment of judicial power. In areas where state and local judges are elected, the ramifications of land/labor control extend directly to the state judicial power. Thus, it is instructive to explore the connection between historical race biases against African Americans and the status quo of black/white inequalities by focusing on land ownership and entrepreneurship.

1. Early Disenfranchisement

At the close of the Civil War, four million former slaves emerged from "two and a half centuries of legalized oppression ... [to enter] Southern society with little or no material assets." The majority of slaves had been agricultural workers. An estimated half million had experience in mining, lumbering, railroad building, construction, and various craft occupations, and of these, about 50,000 were engaged in manufacturing. As previously discussed, the Confiscation Act failed to help the majority of freed slaves to secure land. However, in 1866, the Southern Homestead Act "did provide part of the basis for the fact that by 1900 one-quarter of Southern black farmers owned their own farms." Those that had not secured their own land entered the labor market; the competition was not welcomed by white laborers, who were unwilling to admit African American workers to their unions. African Americans without land or alternative means were forced to return to white-owned farms for meager monthly wages or a share of the crop. (...)

The enactment of Black Codes throughout various southern states effectively suppressed the free labor market. In response, Congress passed the 1866 Civil Rights Act, which provided that freed slaves born in the United States were citizens entitled to the same rights and privileges as white citizens. The Fourteenth Amendment, ratified in 1868, was designed in part to validate the Civil Rights Act of 1866. Once overt legislative discrimination was outlawed, African American workers were able to command wages more in line with the value of their labor. African American workers began to migrate in search of better work and life opportunities.

Group migrations were significant for several reasons. First, such migrations were sometimes a form of political protest, one of the few forms of protest in which disenfranchised African Americans could engage. African Americans frequently deserted regions in response to lynchings and other forms of white lawlessness, or in response to unfavorable legislation. African Americans would move to places where they were relatively well treated or had relatively good economic prospects.

White employers lobbied for facially neutral laws in an effort to stop these migrations, because the ability to migrate gave great leverage to African American workers. Although some state supreme courts ruled that these statutes were unconstitutional, the U.S. Supreme Court held that they were constitutional, thereby "negatively affect[ing] the lives of millions of African-Americans."

2. Entrepreneurship

Self-employment or entrepreneurship is a means of social mobility that has become almost synonymous with the "American Dream." African American men are only 38% as likely as white men to be self-employed, and small businesses owned by African Americans account for approximately 2.4% of the Nation's corporations, partnerships, and sole proprietorships. In an effort to bolster arguments that any disadvantage African Americans now suffer is of their own making, affirmative-action opponents are apt to point to the success of other non-European ethnic groups—especially the Japanese, Korean, and Jewish communities—in using self-employment as a means to social and economic progression. The problem with such a surface-level comparison is that it ignores the unique historic and still prevailing frustrations of African American entrepreneurial efforts.

"'Between 1867 and 1917 the number of [African] American enterprises increased from four thousand to fifty thousand.'" Three powerful illustrations of early frustration thwarting that remarkable growth trend are the race riots of Tulsa, Rosewood, and Wilmington. The Tulsa riot took place in the Greenwood district known as "Black Wall Street," an area in which African Americans owned the land and independently operated the district's businesses, schools, and banks. The "district encompassed forty-one grocers and meat markets, thirty restaurants, fifteen physicians, five hotels, two theaters, and two newspapers. The black community also included many wealthy blacks who had invested in and profited from oil leases." Reportedly, the 1921 Tulsa race riot lasted for three days, as whites "rampaged through the Greenwood district breaking into homes, looting businesses and attacking any black person they saw." "At the height of the melee, bundles of dynamite were dropped from an airplane[,] ... destroying everything." The resulting damage, in addition to fatalities, was the destruction of thirty-five city blocks, including 18,000 African American homes, businesses, and churches. "Afterward, more than 4000 blacks were interned on fairgrounds in cattle and hog pens." Many of the district's members left the area, but some stayed and attempted to rebuild.

Rosewood, a relatively prosperous logging town of about 200 African Americans in western Levy County, Florida, was destroyed by a mob of white men who looted and killed, eventually burning down every home belonging to the blacks in the town. In Wilmington, North Carolina, according to one account, "'there was grumbling among white professional classes' because ... 'black entrepreneurs, located conspicuously downtown, deprived white businessmen of legitimate sources of income to which they thought they were entitled.'" The Wilmington Riot of 1898 "created an 'economic diaspora' in which black businessmen were forced to steal away in the night," eventually relocating "to Northern and Southeastern cities." These riots, all of which proceeded for days with no prohibitive state action, caused the demise of entire cities and business districts that were owned and populated by African Americans. The damage was not only the loss of life and property, but also the loss of opportunity to prosper in a networked environment, and the lost inheritance of future generations. Thus, although African Americans have enjoyed some success despite the odds, the instability of that success resulting from racist state policy, Jim Crow segregation, systemic discrimination, and outright violence has had a significant impact on efforts toward the economic empowerment of African Americans.

3. The Plight of African American Farmers

Post-reconstruction efforts toward entrepreneurship and land acquisition have been largely thwarted by lack of capital and access to financing, as well as by limited access to information. In 1920, African Americans owned fifteen million acres of land and 17.4% of farm operators were black. Today, however, African American farmers account for only 3% of American farmers. As of 1991, African Americans owned less than four million acres of land, and, reportedly, face a possible annual average loss of fifty thousand acres resulting in a projected net loss of $2.5 million. The decline is attributed to a "lack of capital needed to expand production capabilities through the purchase of increased acreage and new forms of technology."

Recently, the National Black Farmers' Association launched a "grassroots battle against more than three decades of documented discrimination by the U.S. Department of Agriculture ("USDA") and its employees." Programs designed fifty to sixty years ago, "to provide technical assistance to improve farm production, financial aid to help rural families acquire decent housing and economically viable farms, and price supports to protect farmers from the hazards of the market" have benefited white farmers to the detriment of African American farmers. Prior to the USDA's establishment of a nondiscriminatory policy for federal programs in 1964, African American farmers were largely unaware of these farm support programs and opportunities. Subsequently, although access to information has improved, access to available loan dollars has still been hindered by widespread discrimination. Based on investigations of the Farmers Home Administration ("FHA"), the USDA concluded that the FHA lending practices were influenced by "politics and racism." The USDA has "frozen foreclosures on farms where the owner has filed a discrimination complaint" and legislation has been introduced "to prevent similar discrimination practices ... in the future."

4. Houses and Land

"Housing is ... intimately connected with the quality of life since it is closely linked with education," health, and welfare—all social components of citizenship—as well as employment opportunities and income. Varied forms of racial discrimination in housing often exist in combination. They include more structurally substandard housing among blacks than whites; higher rent for black ghetto residents for equal or poorer facilities; three to four times more "overcrowding in the ghetto ... which has been intensified rather than lessened by urban renewal"; higher prices for merchandise sold to ghetto residents "caught in a captive market"; compromised access to employment opportunities in expanding suburban industrial parks, as a result of barriers to acquiring suburban housing; and premiums charged to black homeowners seeking to buy into white or mixed areas. In addition, a disproportionate share of hazardous waste landfills and facilities are located in areas predominately populated by African Americans.

Another prevalent form of housing discrimination against African Americans is banking discrimination and redlining. "A 1991 Federal Reserve study of 6.4 million home mortgage applications by race and income confirmed suspicions of bias in lending by reporting a widespread and systemic pattern of institutional discrimination in the nation's banking system." This study showed that African American applicants are denied loans two to three times more often than white applicants; high-income African Americans are declined loans more often that low-income whites; mortgage rates for African Americans are 5.4 points higher for federal program loans, and 9.2 points higher for conventional loans compared to whites; and these trends are present regardless of the area in which African Americans seek to buy homes.

C. The Effect on Full Citizenship

"The essence of equal [or full] citizenship is the dignity of full membership in the society." This membership necessarily entails a civil or legal component, a political component, and a social component. The civil component refers to an individual's security in the basic rights and liberties derived from the societal values reflected in the Bill of Rights and the Fifth and Fourteenth Amendments: the right to secure one's self and property; freedom of speech, religion, assembly, and association; and "both substantive and procedural equality before the law." The political component is essentially democratic enfranchisement—participation in the governmental process through the right to a "formal voice in the selection of leadership" and the right to "attempt to influence policy." The social component concerns welfare and general well-being, or those resources and capacities required to secure the "opportunity to express and implement the [civil and political] rights derived from ... societal values."

The social component includes health, education, and welfare, and "presumptively forbids the organized society to treat an individual ... as a member of an inferior or dependent caste or as a nonparticipant." Thus, the social component addresses social status. Theoretically, "the societal community defines and presents standards for the allocation of resources to the community as a whole." That allocation translates into "the definition of the terms on which capacities, as matched with opportunities, can be involved in the process of inclusion."

In practice, white males with wealth and influence have controlled this process. Consequently, the creation and protection of full citizenship depends on not only the formal equality of legal and political rights, but also on the prohibition of the subtle disenfranchisement that would render those rights moot. Underlying the concept of full membership in a societal community is the notion of "solidarity or mutual loyalty of its members" and a sense of "commitment of the members to the collectivity in which they are associated." For Americans, this notion translates into a national patriotism that supersedes state and local affiliations, as well

as a mutual respect and priority for each individual's rights, regardless of the individual's race, ethnicity, or gender.

The prevailing condition for African Americans, however, is one of exclusion, not inclusion. Illustrations in the context of education alone include the proven bias of standardized tests used in university admissions; the poor quality of public education in predominately African American communities; and the monocultural emphasis in educational materials that neglects the African American presence and contribution. Statistics reflecting disproportionate numbers of African American prisoners, disparate sentencing, and lingering blatant discrimination in the private and government sectors call into question even the surety of the civil component of full citizenship, substantive and procedural equality before the law. Further, the political component has been and still is retarded by the nullifying effects of various voting practices on the African American vote and a stifled African American participation in the lobbying process. Thus, African Americans as a group still do not enjoy the dignity of full membership in the American community.

III. Why Reparations?

You do not take a person who, for years, has been hobbled by chains and liberate him, bring him up to the starting line of a race and then say, "you are free to compete with all the others," and still justly believe that you have been completely fair.

President Clinton's charge to the Race Advisory Board narrows the focus to "recent ... race relations," suggesting that the racial tensions that exist today have little to do with American history that is not "recent." Affirmative action is preferred over revisiting the past. Affirmative action has been helpful in forcing access for a small number of individuals to certain educational and economic venues, but it does not effectively level the playing field for African Americans as a collective race. Indeed, one general justification for affirmative action, as a "corrective for the continuing effects of past discrimination," is that, "against the backdrop of a terrible history of oppressive color conscious discrimination[,] ... immediate colorblindness would perpetuate exclusion and be unfair." Given the historical severity of the black-white relationship, is it really feasible to move forward without looking back? Or is healing the racial divide, without addressing the underlying sources of racial animosities, as unlikely as healing a festering wound by applying bandages, without first cleaning away the infectious pus? Seemingly, these questions are rhetorical. Nevertheless, although apologies and reparations have been extended for lesser atrocities, the idea of extending the same to African Americans for slavery and the related continuing discrimination is still met with resistance, despite President Clinton's acknowledgment and informal apology to sub-Saharan Africa for America's part in the slave trade. One articulation of the reluctance is that "'[i]t's been so long, and we're so many generations removed'"; another expressed reluctance, which has also been stated in opposition to affirmative action, is that African American reparations would do more to incite racial tensions than to resolve them. Both excuses ignore the equitable rationale for the continuing-wrongs doctrine—"when [wrongful] conduct continues[,] ... repose is outweighed by the interest in securing compensation for serious harm." The latter "public popular consensus" rationale ignores the power of Congress and the judiciary to rectify even that which the majority population seeks to uphold—the very power that the Supreme Court confirmed in the racial context in *Brown v. Board of Education*.

A. Race-Neutrality, Meritocracy, and Remediation

Presumably, merit is understood as achievement based on functional capacity—or intellect and hard work. Three elements at the core of the "moral claim for the merit principle" are: maximization of efficiency and social welfare; entitlement to decisions based on "individual desert" and "personal qualities," rather than "social or political conventions tied to group identity"; and alignment of "incentives so as to promote and reinforce both autonomy and personal responsibility." This argument, however, is flawed in several respects. Two problems with the meritocratic argument are that: first, it wrongly assumes that merit is something that can be consistently measured between individuals under any circumstances; and second, it assumes that all have fair access to opportunity, dismissing the evidence that, as a collective, African Americans continue to suffer harms of past and present discriminations. A third problem is that the meritocratic argument ignores the relation between economic empowerment and political empowerment, and thus fails to address the problem of access to full citizenry. In actuality, each individual's access to success and well-being in a capitalistic economy is tied to the accumulated wealth and opportunities enjoyed by past generations, both of which directly impact political influence.

A clear warning of the inevitable failure of meritocracy in a society still prone to racial discrimination comes from tester studies in which black and white applicants are given identical fabricated credentials and sent on interviews seeking employment, loans, or housing. Studies showed that, even for blue-collar jobs, black applicants were 20–25% less likely to advance in the hiring process. Black applicants also faced discrimination in contacts with realtors, and are declined for loan approvals at disparate rates. Despite any claim to the contrary, white Americans simply have an unfair advantage over African Americans that bears no relation to their individual character or qualifications.

Thus, a true meritocracy cannot be achieved unless everyone starts with a clean slate or, at least, a fair allocation of the basic resources that ensure full citizenship. "Affirmative action is not the most important issue for [African American] progress in America, but it is part of a redistributive chain that must be strengthened if we are to confront and eliminate black poverty [and disenfranchisement]."

B. The Moral Economy Incentive

If "the success of the moral economy of restitution" is measured "by the degree to which it enables the victims to claim a share of the economic pie ...

and legitimize their side of history," then America cannot achieve an equitable multicultural society without granting reparations to African Americans.

Whether through active military involvement, international trade sanctions, or diplomatic mediation, the U.S. government has a history of actively advocating human rights and democracy in the international arena. Increasingly, the principle of restitution is forming the "basis for a new worldwide moral economy," in which the empowered global market supports restitution as moral atonement for "wrongs of one people against another." A familiar example of the global trend toward nations compensating victims because of political pressure is the German grant of reparations to Jewish Holocaust survivors. A more recent example is Japanese reparations to Korean "comfort women." There has also been a rash of public apologies: from President Clinton to native Hawaiians; from Poland to Jews for a massacre in 1946; from Canada to Canadian-Ukrainians for maltreatment during World War I.

Quite significant is President Clinton's apology to sub-Saharan African nations for the role of the United States in the slave trade. The timing of this apology and the African Growth and Opportunity Act is reminiscent of the circumstances surrounding the reparations for Japanese Americans and "pro-Japan trade policies." "For Congress, lingering animosity over the [internment] of Japanese-Americans during World War II may have been viewed by some as a barrier to effective economic relations between Japan and the United States." Similarly, the coincidence of President Clinton's apology with the African Growth and Opportunity Act is, perhaps, the epitome of bartering guilt for economic gain because the Act provides for a "new trade and investment policy for sub-Saharan Africa." Furthermore, the African Growth and Opportunity Act includes a provision deeming ineligible those countries that are "determined by the President to engage in a consistent pattern of gross violations of internationally recognized human rights." Absent at least a symbolic atonement for slavery, the United States could not seek to impose such a moral provision regarding trade with Africa without appearing hypocritical. The apology to Africa, however, is meaningless without redress for African Americans. It would be a double standard if America does not grant reparations to African Americans who have suffered through the many dehumanizing experiences that litter the African American experience.

IV. In Support of Legislation

"While [African Americans] may be justified in seeking redress for past and present injustices, it is not within the jurisdiction of this Court to grant the requested relief. The legislature, rather than the judiciary, is the appropriate forum for plaintiffs' grievances."

A. Procedural Barriers to Individual Suits

As there is no statutory ground for pursuing African American reparations through the courts, the alternative lies in tort. In theory, there are several potential tort suit scenarios. The plaintiff could be an individual African American or a class of African Americans. The defendant could be an individual white American, a class of white Americans, the government as a surrogate for white Americans, or the government as a wrongdoer in its own right. A suit in tort for African American reparations, however, is plagued with procedural problems that have proven dispositive. Some of the problems were illustrated by the first federal appellate court case to be heard on African American reparations—*Cato v. United States*. In *Cato*, the plaintiffs sued the United States seeking damages for past and present injustices related to ancestral slavery. They also sought an acknowledgment of and apology for discrimination against freed slaves and their descendants from the end of the Civil War to the present. The Ninth Circuit affirmed the district court's dismissal, finding that the complaint did not state a legally cognizable claim and could not be cured by amendment.

Without consent to suit in an action to which the federal government is a party, federal jurisdiction is limited to those claims "arising under the

Constitution, laws, or treaties of the United States." Moreover, sovereign immunity bars any suit against the United States, unless a waiver is "'unequivocally expressed,'" Even under the Federal Tort Claims Act, which gives federal courts jurisdiction over civil actions against the United States "for money damages, accruing on and after January 1, 1945," a tort claim based on slavery would be barred unless the plaintiff could show: (1) that the continuing violations doctrine applies because African Americans are still impacted by the legacy of slavery and subsequent systemic discrimination; and (2) continuing wrongful acts by the government.

Without the government as a defendant, "rights theory has made traditional remedies law a virtual obstacle course for racial remedies theorists." Generally, we believe group responsibility and group entitlement are not appropriate when "individuals are defined and treated as part of a group whose behavior they do not necessarily endorse or have significant control over." This is especially so when the group is defined by an immutable characteristic such as race.

Verdun's analysis of the rights theory in terms of the dominant (white American) perspective versus the African American consciousness provides an interesting synopsis of why the standing doctrine and causation doctrine are barriers to African American reparations suits in tort. The dominant group embraces the rights theory and "perceives that each individual is responsible for his or her own behavior." From their perspective, vicarious liability for the actions of others is only applicable where the person assuming responsibility has control over the offender; if no such control relationship exists, then there is no legal or moral responsibility for the actions of others. In contrast, Verdun posits that, "African American consciousness emphasizes the significance of group identification.... Cooperation through collective efforts is the accepted means of achieving culturally prescribed goals." Verdun argues that society at large is the appropriate wrongdoer, because "[s]ociety, propelled by a set of values that were manifested in the laws, allowed the injury to take place and remain uncompensated

for generations." The African American consciousness justifies society as the appropriate wrongdoer because "[s]ociety, unlike individuals, does not have a natural life," and "[t]he society that committed the wrong is still thriving."

For reparation suits, the rights theory affects the ability to establish standing, as well as causation. Although past affirmative-action cases have not required plaintiffs to prove that they were the ones actually harmed by the wrongful act, the courts, in alignment with the dominant perspective, have shown an unwillingness to let anyone other than the actual wrongdoer assume or accept responsibility for compensation. Accordingly, the death of the last slave and slaveholder made reparations through judicial relief moot. One could imagine the courtroom argument: "To hold that descendants of the millions of blacks harmed throughout our history are entitled to compensation for the long-past injury of their ancestors" violates the principle that the parties compensated should be the parties harmed; likewise, to hold that the "current generations of whites should pay for the sins of earlier generations of whites" necessarily violates the principle that only those parties that caused the harm should compensate the plaintiffs. Thus, cases based in tort necessarily fail for lack of standing and/or causation. Therefore, the tort suit as a vehicle for African American reparations is not a viable option.

B. Distributive Justice

As happens with affirmative action, any legislative reparations scheme would at least indirectly impact the white American population. The tax dollars from all citizens fund the government, and government resources—such as land, employment, and education accommodations—must be shared. Outside the litigation context, however, "[g]roup responsibility and group entitlement are appropriate when the characteristic defining the group is of primary relevance to the reward or punishment in question, and when the group behavior can be said to be the product of voluntary effort by the individuals who comprise it." "Individuals who have not personally harmed minorities may nevertheless be prevented from reaping the benefits of the harm inflicted by the society at large."

This is the nature of distributive justice. According to rights theorist Robert Nozick, "If the world were wholly just…. [t]he complete principle of distributive justice would say simply that a distribution is just if everyone is entitled to the holdings they possess under the distribution." The determination results from a three-step induction:

(1)   A person who acquires a holding in accordance with the principle of justice in acquisition is entitled to that holding.

(2)   A person who acquires a holding in accordance with the principle of justice in transfer, from someone else entitled to the holding, is entitled to the holding.

(3)   No one is entitled to a holding except by (repeated) applications of 1 and 2.

The relevance of this entitlement theory to reparations for African Americans is the inherent use of historical information, which extends the analysis to the intergenerational transfer of wealth and opportunity. Redistribution in the context of reparations does not mean a radical redistribution of wealth from the rich to the poor; rather, it is more a legitimate reallocation of that which has been unrightfully gained at the expense of African Americans. Under this analysis, the issue of unfair assignment of group responsibility is replaced by the notion of entitlement only to justly acquired holdings, and disgorgement of unjustly acquired holdings.

C. American Precedent: The Civil Liberties Act

1. Japanese American Reparations

Apart from the Freedmen's Bureau Acts, the key federal precedent for reparations as compensation for racially motivated government acts is the Civil Liberties Act (the "Act"), which provided restitution for the World War II internment of Japanese Americans and Aleuts.

During World War II, all individuals of Japanese ancestry living in the United States were excluded from military zones and subject to forced evacuation and relocation to detention centers, without regard for their citizenship, pursuant to Executive Order 9066. The Supreme Court upheld enforcement of the order.

Four decades later, Congress established the Commission on Wartime Relocation and Internment of Civilians to study and document the impact of Executive Order 9066 on Japanese American citizens and permanent resident aliens. The Commission found that:

> The excluded individuals of Japanese ancestry suffered enormous damages, both material and intangible, and there were incalculable losses in education and job training, all of which resulted in significant human suffering for which appropriate compensation has not been made…. [T]hese [were] fundamental violations of the basic civil liberties and constitutional rights….

Along with an acknowledgment and apology for the "grave injustice … done," the Act provided for: (1) compensation in the amount of $20,000 to individuals of Japanese ancestry who were interned, and living on the date of the enactment of the Act (or to their living heirs); and (2) a public education fund to facilitate public awareness of the internment and prevent a recurrence. The entitlement to compensation now extends to all children of excluded individuals eligible under the Act who were deprived of liberty by exclusion from their families' domiciles.

2. Reparations to the Aleuts

According to the statement of Congress:

> [T]he Aleut civilian residents of the Pribilof Islands and the Aleutian Islands west of Unimak Island were relocated to temporary camps in isolated regions of southeast Alaska where they remained, under United States control and in the care of the United States, until long after any potential danger to their home villages had passed.

The grant to Aleuts is often overlooked when the Act is discussed in relation to reparations for African Americans. The Commission's findings with respect to the Aleuts, however, are instructive in establishing governmental liability for misfeasance:

> The United States failed to provide reasonable care for the Aleuts, and this resulted in widespread illness, disease, and death among the residents of the camps; and the United States further failed to protect Aleut personal and community property while such property was in its possession or under its control.

The Act granted compensation to Aleut residents for property taken or destroyed by the United States during World War II and "for injustices and unreasonable hardships endured" while the Aleuts were under United States control during the war.

3. An Analogy to African Americans

The monetary reparations paid to Japanese Americans were funded by the tax dollars of United States citizens. Obviously, the broad group that shouldered responsibility for payment of the compensation included at least "four groups of 'innocents'": "1) people who were not born in 1941; 2) people who were alive but objected strenuously to the internment; 3) people who immigrated to the United States after the internment was over; and 4) a host of other people who just had nothing whatsoever to do with it." One way in which the African American case is more complex than that of the Japanese Americans and Aleuts is that African Americans have suffered from not one, but many harmful acts by both private citizens and state and federal governments. Ironically, the existence of private actors should make the argument for legislative reparations stronger in the case of African Americans, because it clouds the innocence of the so-called "innocents." If tax dollars were used to fund reparations to African Americans, the group responsible for payment would include the parallel "innocent" groups to the Japanese American reparations scenario: "1) people who were born

after slavery ended …; 2) abolitionists; 3) people who immigrated after slavery ended; and 4) people who are not descendants of slaveholders." The difference between the African American and the Japanese American scenario is that most, if not all, of the "innocents" in the African American case have benefited from many of the wrongs giving rise to the reparations.

In sum, the Civil Liberties Act recognized tangible and intangible harms caused by federal action and inaction. The Act established a precedent for legislative compensation to a particular racial group that suffered unique injuries due to racially motivated law enforcement. Based on a comparison of the "victim" experiences, it is difficult to fathom a reasonable justification for not enacting the African American Reparations bill. Simple substitutions in the language of the congressional findings for the Japanese Americans and the Aleuts could easily provide a starting point to summarize the case for African Americans:

> The [enslaved] individuals of [African] ancestry [and their descendants] suffered enormous damages, both material and intangible, and there were incalculable losses in education and job training, all of which resulted in significant human suffering for which appropriate compensation has not been made.… [T]hese [were] fundamental violations of the basic civil liberties and constitutional rights.…

The United States failed to provide reasonable care for the [Africans and their descendants], and this resulted in widespread illness, disease, and death among the [African American population]; and the United States further failed to protect [African Americans and their] personal and community property [by uniform enforcement of the law].

B. Reconciling African American Reparations and the Equal Protection Clause

In the wake of *Adarand Contractors, Inc. v. Pena*, race-based congressional legislation must now withstand the same strict scrutiny standard that has been applied to the states since *City of Richmond v. J.A. Croson Co.*, and that standard applies whether or not the measure benefits or burdens the affected race.

In his extensive analysis of Reconstruction Era legislation, Eric Schnapper argues that the legislative intent behind the Fourteenth Amendment confirms the constitutionality of certain race-based remedies. Schnapper bases his argument on the contemporaneous consideration of the Fourteenth Amendment and the Freedmen's Bureau Acts. He argues that:

> The framers of the fourteenth amendment cannot have intended it to nullify remedial legislation of the sort Congress simultaneously adopted.... [The legislative debates] provide clear examples of the kinds of reasons and circumstances that would justify the use of race-conscious remedies in the eyes of [the framers]. Conversely, the arguments made unsuccessfully against those programs by the legislators who also opposed the fourteenth amendment cannot represent the standards embodied in the amendment.

Schnapper's analysis has not been 100% persuasive before federal courts in refuting the argument that race-preferential remedies violate the Fourteenth Amendment per se by discriminating against those not targeted by the remedy. His argument, however, is particularly relevant to the reparations issue, when the objectives and ideologies behind the Reconstruction Acts and Amendments are understood.

Congress specifically enacted the Freedmen's Bureau Acts and the Civil Rights Act of 1866 to ensure the citizenship rights of African Americans. Thus, "[t]here is no violation of equal protection when society acts to restore the equilibrium that would have naturally occurred under nonracist conditions. Indeed, to fail to maintain the equilibrium by using final-stage measures of merit is to allow the processes of racism to culminate in their inevitable inequities." Foner notes that the major Reconstruction legislation resulted from a "complex series of legislative compromises and maneuvers" sponsored by senators and congressmen with significant influence. According to Schnapper's discussion of the legislative history, two dominant motivations drove supporters of the Freedmen's Acts. The first was that the Acts would aid the freedmen's transition from slavery to freedom, and thus alleviate the social burden associated with the four million Africans who were uneducated and without land or assets. The second was to give the freed slaves the opportunity to establish their economic independence.

Thaddeus Stevens, Speaker of the House, argued for redistribution of the land to enable the emergence of a "new class of black and white yeomen," who would replace the planter class of the south, serve as the basis for future southern political and social power, and ally themselves with the northern Republican middle class. Stevens was a proponent of enabling the economic independence of freedmen, so as to prepare them for full citizenry which would eventually include voting rights. The sponsors of the Fourteenth Amendment were Congressman Stevens, Senator Wade, and Congressman Bingham, who authored the Amendment. The sponsors of the Bureau Act were Senator Trumbull and Congressman Eliot. The proponents of the Bureau Acts and the Fourteenth Amendment subscribed to the promotion of self-sufficiency, so as to preclude an indefinite dependence on public assistance. They supported special assistance for freedmen in view of the freedmen's lack of "political influence of whites to advance their own interests" and for the "'safety of the nation.'"

Given that the motivation behind reparations to African Americans is to provide the means to enfranchise a group that has been intentionally denied the social status, resources, and well-being required to enjoy the civil and political rights to which every United States citizen is entitled, legislative reparations follow the precedents for allowing race-based remedies.

V. Anticipating the Obstacles to Implementation

The African-American Reparations Commissions Act is closely patterned after the precursor to the Civil Liberties Act. The purposes of H.R. 40 are: (1) to acknowledge the fundamental injustice, cruelty, brutality, and inhumanity of slavery in the United States and the thirteen American colonies between 1619 and 1865; and (2) to establish a commission to examine the institution of slavery, subsequent de jure and de facto racial and economic discrimination against African Americans, and the impact of these forces on living African Americans, and to make recommendations to the Congress for appropriate remedies.

Representative Conyers, author of H.R. 40, has not yet specified what form of reparations should be pursued in the event of a positive finding by the commission. The question of implementation for an African American reparations scheme, however, is not only what should the compensation be, but who are the appropriate beneficiaries. As previously stated, it is beyond the scope of this Comment to exhaustively state the types and extent of harms suffered by African Americans as a result of slavery and ensuing private and government discriminatory action. Accordingly, it is not this author's intention to assume the formidable task of definitively stating what reparations for African Americans should be. Rather, this is an attempt to address some of the problems that have been or may be posed as obstacles to the implementation of reparations for African Americans.

A. Who?

Unlike the injured group in the case for Japanese American reparations, the African Americans injured from slavery and the ensuing systemic discrimination number in the millions. Considering the pool of black Americans, it is safe to concede that not all black people in America are descendants of African slaves. Moreover, individuals who are descendants of slaves may not necessarily have descended from African American slaves.

Despite these uncertainties, there are several possible approaches to answering the "who" question to identify the appropriate beneficiaries of African American reparations.

One approach is to adjust the degree of eligibility according to the number of generations an individual's family has resided in America. Such an approach could reasonably limit entitlements and avoid overburdening those who are not African American. Eligibility based on generational considerations would also be consistent with the argument that black/white inequities are partially due to the intergenerational transfer of wealth among white Americans.

The distinction of origin and generational citizenship, however, loses some of its significance in some relation to the length of time an African American family has been in America. An immigrant of African descent will suffer the same discrimination and advantages as indigenous African Americans regardless of his actual citizenship. In time, the cumulative harm to that immigrant's generation residing in America will approach the harm caused to indigenous African Americans. Furthermore, by reason of the slave experience in the Caribbean, England, South America, and other regions whence blacks have migrated to this country, the entitlement to remediation might be considered absolute. Thus, an alternative approach is to require only that beneficiaries have American citizenship.

Ultimately, the appropriate beneficiary of a remedial measure will depend upon the particular remediation. The difficulty in identifying beneficiaries—and which beneficiaries have suffered which particular injuries—can be alleviated by applying the fluid recovery mechanism sometimes used in class action suits. "In a fluid recovery the money is either distributed through a market system in the way of reduced charges or is used to fund a project which will likely benefit the members of the class." The use of this mechanism would be appropriate, because legislative reparations—as this Comment justifies them—would embody policies of disgorgement, compensation, and deterrence. The population of African American citizens should be treated as the class of injured parties, and divided into subclasses as necessary to determine eligibility for specific remedies.

B. What and How?

If the overall goal of reparations for African Americans is to eventually enable a harmonious and diverse democracy, then the remedies and compensation must necessarily target areas critical to social well-being and economic empowerment. That, in turn, should ensure the opportunity to enjoy civil rights and enable political empowerment.

1. Non-Specific Reparations

A logical starting point for African American reparations is to extend an acknowledgment and apology for the grave injustices done, and at least provide: (1) some amount of monetary compensation for individuals (or their living heirs) who were either slaves or alive during the Jim Crow era, and living on the date of the enactment of the Reparations Act; and (2) a public education fund to facilitate public awareness of slavery, the Jim Crow era, and systemic discrimination, and to prevent their recurrence. Although no amount of money can compensate for the injuries suffered, governments have issued some form of monetary compensation to many groups whose fundamental human rights have been violated. Yet, even assuming an arbitrary sum set at an amount of only $20,000 per individual, some would argue that the total monetary award to African American beneficiaries would approach unfeasible and excessive sums.

An alternative to issuing actual monetary awards is to allow a comparable tax exemption over a period of years. This approach essentially results in the African American beneficiaries paying themselves, because the result is theoretically the same as if the beneficiaries' tax dollars were pooled and then redistributed. Arguably, such an exemption for African Americans increases the tax burden on nonreparee taxpayers, particularly if the tax burden of nonreparees is increased specifically to cover what would otherwise be contributed absent the exemption. Even with an increased tax obligation, nonreparee taxpayers might consider the exemption a substantial subsidization because reparees would still be entitled to all the benefits enjoyed by the average citizen. Nevertheless, this potential subsidization should not be a barrier to monetary compensation because such compensation has been afforded to Japanese Americans and Aleuts.

A "public education fund to increase awareness" is a non-specific remedy that would provide redress for the gross historical understatement of the African American contribution to the development of the United States. Instead of reserving one month out of the year to acknowledge the various histories of non-white, non-male American groups, the education curriculum must move away from its current monocultural, Eurocentric focus, toward a more inclusive reflection of American culture and history. African Americans as a group, as well as American society as a whole, would eventually benefit as fallacies of inferiority and social irresponsibility are replaced by a true understanding of how integral the African American presence has been to the success of our capitalist foundation.

2. Specific Reparations

It is simply unrealistic to think that relief from the effects of deep-rooted inequities and discrimination can be resolved by a lump sum payment. Therefore, reparations must include specific remedies that address the specific harms suffered. Areas for reparation measures include housing and land ownership, education, employment, and loans.

To the extent that non-specific and specific remedies can be accommodated by affirmative action, reparations and affirmative action must not be mutually exclusive. We should, however, revisit the construct of affirmative action and resolve the misconceptions that hinder the effectiveness of these programs. One drawback that makes affirmative action susceptible to attack is that there are no clear goals that indicate progress and mark the point at which affirmative action is no longer necessary. In the context of reparations, the goals are to ensure full citizenship and to correct past wrongs, where the measure of success is a tangible metric.

a. Housing Discrimination Remedies

A brief analysis of the two remedies currently used for systemic housing discrimination in federally subsidized housing programs—"mobility relief" and "equalization relief"—provides a useful illustration of how specific remedies should be used. "Mobility relief attempts to alleviate the isolation caused by segregation by moving victims of discrimination closer to better schools and a better supply of jobs in safer areas." This is accomplished via one of two methods. Either the victim is transferred to a unit or project within a development in which the victim's race does not predominate, or the victim receives Section Eight certificates to enable "federally assisted housing in nonracially impacted areas." In contrast, equalization relief includes such remedies as "housing rehabilitation and modernization, the submission of [detailed] equalization plans.... housing code enforcement, provision of certain amenities and tenant services, demolition of dilapidated housing with one-for-one unit replacement, and real community redevelopment addressing neighborhood conditions, municipal services, and exposure to environmental hazards." Equalization relief has generally been more difficult to obtain than mobility relief. From the perspective of a reparations advocate, equalization is a better remedy because it remedies the discrimination in a way that empowers the victim.

Most often, victims of housing discrimination live in racially segregated areas. These areas become undesirable not because of the purely social aspect of segregation, but because of the consequential impact of discrimination on services, job availability, and safety in the areas. Equalization accommodates the right to choose by allowing the affected individuals to remain in an area that would be desirable, but for the effects of discrimination. When municipal services, school facilities, crime deterrence, and protection from environmental hazard exposure are brought on a par with nonsegregated areas, the civil and social aspects of full citizenship

are restored. Equalization relief also enables political empowerment by allowing African Americans to remain in a concentrated area. This is significant for strengthening the political voice—dilution of political strength occurs when mobility is the sole relief option.

b. Education Remedies

Another drawback of affirmative action is that the term is simultaneously used to describe programs that are (1) vehicles to correct past discrimination; (2) vehicles to diversify (based on gender, race and class); as well as (3) vehicles to give candidates who lack the traditional qualifications the opportunity to prove themselves. The implications of the latter two stigmatize the first because whites (particularly, males) feel excluded or "discriminated against" when all three initiatives are thought to be one and the same. In the context of reparations, uncertainties and ambiguities can be eliminated because the initiative is to compensate for harm suffered. The measure of progress is equalization.

As applied to education, this may call for short-term remediation, in which affirmative action is taken to level the playing field for the next three school-aged generations. A hypothetical scenario might be as follows: Phase one: For the next three generations (or at least for the next thirty-six years), any pre-college educational institution that is heavily populated by African American students from historically disadvantaged areas, for the express purpose of providing remedial education, could be government funded and/or receive government contracts. Such schools would be geared toward college preparatory programs at the high school level. Phase two: Then, for the following two generations (or at least over the following twenty-four years), implement proactive recruiting and financial assistance for minority applicants that meet the "standard" entrance criteria to public and private colleges. Simultaneously, create college access programs for disadvantaged students who show academic potential but do not meet the current standard entrance criteria due to prior discrimination in education. The objective of such a scenario would be to level the playing field in preparation for the removal of race and ethnicity indications from all college application materials starting twelve years after the end of Phase two; and removal of the same from all pre-college applications starting at the end of Phase one, thus achieving a race-neutral meritocracy in education.

c. Other Remedies

Discrimination in areas such as loans and employment are more difficult to address, because these involve more subjective evaluations on the part of private individuals. To the extent that fair loan qualification can be monitored, reparations could grant lower loan rates for a specific period of time to African Americans who have suffered discrimination as compensation for the loss in equity and economic opportunity. Where such subjective evaluations are involved, however, non-specific reparations—such as the above-mentioned "public education fund to increase awareness"—can only attempt to sway individual attitudes.

Conclusion

In sum, I have argued that providing reparations for African Americans is not only a justifiable remedy, but a prerequisite to racial harmony and any movement toward race neutrality. I have shown—though by no means is the illustration exhaustive—that current inequalities between African Americans and white Americans are rooted in historic patterns of discrimination by federal, state, and private actors. Reparations for African Americans must come in the form of legislation, because the courts provide no available recourse, given the procedural barriers of sovereign immunity, statutes of limitations, causation, and standing. In addition to general relief that would benefit this multicultural nation as a whole, specific remedies and compensation can be targeted to rectify specific inequities. Thus, legislative reparations to African Americans would not be unlike previous race-based remedies that were deemed constitutional.

There is an old saying that applies here: Sweep around your own front door before you sweep around mine. It is time for America to ensure the citizenry rights of African Americans with the same commitment and zeal that America has demonstrated in protecting human rights abroad.

DISCUSSION QUESTIONS

1. Chisholm indicates that a failure to provide reparations to African Americans would constitute a failure to ensure the "citizenry rights" of such people. Explain what she means. Do you agree? Why or why not?

2. In section IV.B., Chisholm references Robert Nozick's discussion of distributive justice (see reading 68). Do you think Nozick would support a program of reparations such as Chisholm advocates? Support your answer by referencing Nozick's arguments in reading 68 and elsewhere.

C.
Radical Solutions at Home and Abroad: Secession, Revolution, and War

88

Thomas Hobbes, selection from *Leviathan* (1651)

In this selection, Hobbes considers the causes and justifications for civil unrest and the dissolution of states. On Hobbes, see reading 2 above.

SOURCE

Hobbes, Thomas. *Leviathan* (Second Edition). George Routledge and Sons, 1886.

Of Those Things That Weaken or Tend to the Dissolution of a Commonwealth

Though nothing can be immortal which mortals make; yet, if men had the use of reason they pretend to, their Commonwealths might be secured, at least, from perishing by internal diseases. For by the nature of their institution, they are designed to live as long as mankind, or as the laws of nature, or as justice itself, which gives them life. Therefore when they come to be dissolved, not by external violence, but intestine disorder, the fault is not in men as they are the matter, but as they are the makers and orderers of them. For men, as they become at last weary of irregular jostling and hewing one another, and desire with all their hearts to conform themselves into one firm and lasting edifice; so for want both of the art of making fit laws to square their actions by, and also of humility and patience to suffer the rude and cumbersome points of their present greatness to be taken off, they cannot without the help of a very able architect be compiled into any other than a crazy building, such as, hardly lasting out their own time, must assuredly fall upon the heads of their posterity.

Amongst the infirmities therefore of a Commonwealth, I will reckon in the first place those that arise from an imperfect institution, and resemble the diseases of a natural body, which proceed from a defectuous procreation.

Of which this is one: that a man to obtain a kingdom is sometimes content with less power than to the peace and defence of the Commonwealth is necessarily required. From whence it cometh to pass that when the exercise of the power laid by is for the public safety to be resumed, it hath the resemblance of an unjust act, which disposeth great numbers of men, when occasion is presented, to rebel; in the same manner as the bodies of children gotten by diseased parents are subject either to untimely death, or to purge the ill quality derived from their vicious conception, by breaking out into biles and scabs. And when kings deny themselves some such necessary power, it is not always (though sometimes) out of ignorance of what is necessary to the office they undertake, but many times out of a hope to recover the same again at their pleasure: wherein they reason not well; because such as will hold them to their promises shall be maintained against them by foreign Commonwealths; who in order to the good of their own subjects let slip few occasions to weaken the estate of their neighbours. So was Thomas Becket, Archbishop of Canterbury, supported against Henry the Second by the Pope; the subjection of ecclesiastics to the Commonwealth having been dispensed with by William the Conqueror at his reception, when he took an oath not to infringe the liberty of the Church. And so were the barons, whose power was by William Rufus, to have their help in transferring the succession from his elder brother to himself, increased to a degree inconsistent with the sovereign power, maintained in their rebellion against King John by the French.

Nor does this happen in monarchy only. For whereas the style of the ancient Roman Commonwealth was, "The Senate and People of Rome"; neither senate nor people pretended to the whole power; which first caused the seditions of Tiberius Gracchus, Caius Gracchus, Lucius Saturninus, and others; and afterwards the wars between the senate and the people under Marius and Sylla; and again under Pompey and Caesar to the extinction of their democracy and the setting up of monarchy.

The people of Athens bound themselves but from one only action, which was that no man on pain of death should propound the renewing of the war for the island of Salamis; and yet thereby, if Solon had not caused to be given out he was mad, and afterwards in gesture and habit of a madman, and in verse, propounded it to the people that flocked about him, they had had an enemy perpetually in readiness, even at the gates of their city: such damage, or shifts, are all Commonwealths forced to that have their power never so little limited.

In the second place, I observe the diseases of a Commonwealth that proceed from the poison of seditious doctrines, whereof one is that every private man is judge of good and evil actions. This is true in the condition of mere nature, where there are no civil laws; and also under civil government in such cases as are not determined by the law. But otherwise, it is manifest that the measure of good and evil actions is the civil law; and the judge the legislator, who is always representative of the Commonwealth. From this false doctrine, men are disposed to debate with themselves and dispute the commands of the Commonwealth, and afterwards to obey or disobey them as in their private judgments they shall think fit; whereby the Commonwealth is distracted and weakened.

Another doctrine repugnant to civil society is that whatsoever a man does against his conscience is sin; and it dependeth on the presumption of making himself judge of good and evil. For a man's conscience and his judgement is the same thing; and as the judgement, so also the conscience may be erroneous. Therefore, though he that is subject to no civil law sinneth in all he does against his conscience, because he has no other rule to follow but his own reason, yet it is not so with him that lives in a Commonwealth, because the law is the public conscience by which he hath already undertaken to be guided. Otherwise in such diversity as there is of private consciences, which are but private opinions, the Commonwealth must needs be distracted, and no man dare to obey the sovereign power farther than it shall seem good in his own eyes.

It hath been also commonly taught that faith and sanctity are not to be attained by study and reason, but by supernatural inspiration or infusion. Which granted, I see not why any man should render a reason of his faith; or why every Christian should not be also a prophet; or why any man should take the law of his country rather than his own inspiration for the rule of his action. And thus we fall again into the fault of taking upon us to judge of good and evil; or to make judges of it such private men as pretend to be supernaturally inspired, to the dissolution of all civil government. Faith comes by hearing, and hearing by those accidents which guide us into the presence of them that speak to us; which accidents are all contrived by God Almighty, and yet are not supernatural, but only, for the great number of them that concur to every effect, unobservable. Faith and sanctity are indeed not very frequent; but yet they are not miracles, but brought to pass by education, discipline, correction, and other natural ways by which God worketh them in His elect, at such time as He thinketh fit. And these three opinions, pernicious to peace and government, have in this part of the world proceeded chiefly from tongues and pens of unlearned divines; who, joining the words of Holy Scripture together otherwise than is agreeable to reason, do what they can to make men think that sanctity and natural reason cannot stand together.

A fourth opinion repugnant to the nature of a Commonwealth is this: that he that hath the sovereign power is subject to the civil laws. It is true that sovereigns are all subject to the laws of nature, because such laws be divine and cannot by any man or Commonwealth be abrogated. But to those laws which the sovereign himself, that is, which the Commonwealth, maketh, he is not subject. For to be subject to laws is to be subject to the Commonwealth, that is, to the sovereign representative, that is, to himself which is not subjection, but freedom from the laws. Which error, because it setteth the laws above the sovereign, setteth also a judge above him, and a power to punish him; which is to make a new sovereign; and again for the same reason a third to punish the second; and

so continually without end, to the confusion and dissolution of the Commonwealth.

A fifth doctrine that tendeth to the dissolution of a Commonwealth is that every private man has an absolute propriety in his goods, such as excludeth the right of the sovereign. Every man has indeed a propriety that excludes the right of every other subject: and he has it only from the sovereign power, without the protection whereof every other man should have right to the same. But if the right of the sovereign also be excluded, he cannot perform the office they have put him into, which is to defend them both from foreign enemies and from the injuries of one another; and consequently there is no longer a Commonwealth.

And if the propriety of subjects exclude not the right of the sovereign representative to their goods; much less, to their offices of judicature or execution in which they represent the sovereign himself.

There is a sixth doctrine, plainly and directly against the essence of a Commonwealth, and it is this: that the sovereign power may be divided. For what is it to divide the power of a Commonwealth, but to dissolve it; for powers divided mutually destroy each other. And for these doctrines men are chiefly beholding to some of those that, making profession of the laws, endeavour to make them depend upon their own learning, and not upon the legislative power.

And as false doctrine, so also oftentimes the example of different government in a neighbouring nation disposeth men to alteration of the form already settled. So the people of the Jews were stirred up to reject God, and to call upon the prophet Samuel for a king after the manner of the nations: so also the lesser cities of Greece were continually disturbed with seditions of the aristocratical and democratical factions; one part of almost every Commonwealth desiring to imitate the Lacedaemonians; the other, the Athenians. And I doubt not but many men have been contented to see the late troubles in England out of an imitation of the Low Countries, supposing there needed no more to grow rich than to change, as they had done, the form of their government. For the constitution of man's nature is of itself subject to desire novelty: when therefore they are provoked to the same by the neighbourhood also of those that have been enriched by it, it is almost impossible to be content with those that solicit them to change; and love the first beginnings, though they be grieved with the continuance of disorder; like hot bloods that, having gotten the itch, tear themselves with their own nails till they can endure the smart no longer.

And as to rebellion in particular against monarchy, one of the most frequent causes of it is the reading of the books of policy and histories of the ancient Greeks and Romans; from which young men, and all others that are unprovided of the antidote of solid reason, receiving a strong and delightful impression of the great exploits of war achieved by the conductors of their armies, receive withal a pleasing idea of all they have done besides; and imagine their great prosperity not to have proceeded from the emulation of párticular men, but from the virtue of their popular form of government not considering the frequent seditions and civil wars produced by the imperfection of their policy. From the reading, I say, of such books, men have undertaken to kill their kings, because the Greek and Latin writers in their books and discourses of policy make it lawful and laudable for any man so to do, provided before he do it he call him tyrant. For they say not regicide, that is, killing of a king, but tyrannicide, that is, killing of a tyrant, is lawful. From the same books they that live under a monarch conceive the opinion that the subjects in a popular Commonwealth enjoy liberty, but that in a monarchy they are all slaves. I say, they that live under a monarchy conceive such an opinion; not that they live under a popular government: for they find no such matter. In sum, I cannot imagine how anything can be more prejudicial to a monarchy than the allowing of such books to be publicly read, without present applying such correctives of discreet masters as are fit to take away their venom: which venom I will not doubt to compare to the biting of a mad dog, which is a disease that physicians call hydrophobia, or fear of water. For as he that is so bitten has a continual torment of thirst,

and yet abhorreth water; and is in such an estate as if the poison endeavoured to convert him into a dog; so when a monarchy is once bitten to the quick by those democratical writers that continually snarl at that estate, it wanteth nothing more than a strong monarch, which nevertheless out of a certain tyrannophobia, or fear of being strongly governed, when they have him, they abhor.

As there have been doctors that hold there be three souls in a man; so there be also that think there may be more souls, that is, more sovereigns, than one in a Commonwealth; and set up a supremacy against the sovereignty; canons against laws; and a ghostly authority against the civil; working on men's minds with words and distinctions that of themselves signify nothing, but bewray, by their obscurity, that there walketh (as some think invisibly) another kingdom, as it were a kingdom of fairies, in the dark. Now seeing it is manifest that the civil power and the power of the Commonwealth is the same thing; and that supremacy, and the power of making canons, and granting faculties, implieth a Commonwealth; it followeth that where one is sovereign, another supreme; where one can make laws, and another make canons; there must needs be two Commonwealths, of one and the same subjects; which is a kingdom divided in itself, and cannot stand. For notwithstanding the insignificant distinction of temporal and ghostly, they are still two kingdoms, and every subject is subject to two masters. For seeing the ghostly power challengeth the right to declare what is sin, it challengeth by consequence to declare what is law, sin being nothing but the transgression of the law; and again, the civil power challenging to declare what is law, every subject must obey two masters, who both will have their commands be observed as law, which is impossible. Or, if it be but one kingdom, either the civil, which is the power of the Commonwealth, must be subordinate to the ghostly, and then there is no sovereignty but the ghostly; or the ghostly must be subordinate to the temporal, and then there is no supremacy but the temporal. When therefore these two powers oppose one another, the Commonwealth cannot but be in great danger of civil war and dissolution. For the civil authority being more visible, and standing in the clearer light of natural reason, cannot choose but draw to it in all times a very considerable part of the people: and the spiritual, though it stand in the darkness of School distinctions and hard words; yet, because the fear of darkness and ghosts is greater than other fears, cannot want a party sufficient to trouble, and sometimes to destroy, a Commonwealth. And this is a disease which not unfitly may be compared to the epilepsy, or falling sickness (which the Jews took to be one kind of possession by spirits), in the body natural. For as in this disease there is an unnatural spirit or wind in the head that obstructeth the roots of the nerves and, moving them violently, taketh the motion which naturally they should have from the power of the soul in the brain; thereby causeth violent and irregular motions, which men call convulsions, in the parts; insomuch as he that is seized therewith falleth down sometimes into the water, and sometimes into the fire, as a man deprived of his senses: so also in the body politic, when the spiritual power moveth the members of a Commonwealth by the terror of punishments and hope of rewards, which are the nerves of it, otherwise than by the civil power, which is the soul of the Commonwealth, they ought to be moved; and by strange and hard words suffocates their understanding; it must needs thereby distract the people, and either overwhelm the Commonwealth with oppression, or cast it into the fire of a civil war.

Sometimes also in the merely civil government there be more than one soul: as when the power of levying money, which is the nutritive faculty, has depended on a general assembly; the power of conduct and command, which is the motive faculty, on one man; and the power of making laws, which is the rational faculty, on the accidental consent, not only of those two, but also of a third: this endangereth the Commonwealth, sometimes for want of consent to good laws, but most often for want of such nourishment as is necessary to life and motion. For although few perceive that such government is not government, but division of the Commonwealth into three factions, and call it mixed monarchy; yet the truth is that it is not one independent Commonwealth, but three independent factions; nor one representative person, but three. In the kingdom of God there may be three persons independent, without breach of unity in God that reigneth; but where men reign, that be subject to diversity of opinions, it cannot be so. And therefore if the king bear the person of the people, and the general assembly bear also the person of the people, and another assembly bear the person of a part of the people, they are not one person, nor one sovereign; but three persons, and three sovereigns.

To what disease in the natural body of man I may exactly compare this irregularity of a Commonwealth, I know not. But I have seen a man that had another man growing out of his side, with a head, arms, breast, and stomach of his own: if he had had another man growing out of his other side, the comparison might then have been exact.

Hitherto I have named such diseases of a Commonwealth as are of the greatest and most present danger. There be other, not so great, which nevertheless are not unfit to be observed. As first, the difficulty of raising money for the necessary uses of the Commonwealth, especially in the approach of war. This difficulty ariseth from the opinion that every subject hath of a propriety in his lands and goods exclusive of the sovereign's right to the use of the same. From whence it cometh to pass that the sovereign power, which foreseeth the necessities and dangers of the Commonwealth, finding the passage of money to the public treasury obstructed by the tenacity of the people, whereas it ought to extend itself, to encounter and prevent such dangers in their beginnings, contracteth itself as long as it can, and when it cannot longer, struggles with the people by stratagems of law to obtain little sums, which, not sufficing, he is fain at last violently to open the way for present supply or perish; and, being put often to these extremities, at last reduceth the people to their due temper, or else the Commonwealth must perish. Insomuch as we may compare this distemper very aptly to an ague; wherein, the fleshy parts being congealed, or by venomous matter obstructed, the veins which by their natural course empty themselves into the heart, are not (as they ought to be) supplied from the arteries, whereby there succeedeth at first a cold contraction and trembling of the limbs; and afterwards a hot and strong endeavour of the heart to force a passage for the blood; and before it can do that, contenteth itself with the small refreshments of such things as cool for a time, till, if nature be strong enough, it break at last the contumacy of the parts obstructed, and dissipateth the venom into sweat; or, if nature be too weak, the patient dieth.

Again, there is sometimes in a Commonwealth a disease which resembleth the pleurisy; and that is when the treasury of the Commonwealth, flowing out of its due course, is gathered together in too much abundance in one or a few private men, by monopolies or by farms of the public revenues; in the same manner as the blood in a pleurisy, getting into the membrane of the breast, breedeth there an inflammation, accompanied with a fever and painful stitches.

Also, the popularity of a potent subject, unless the Commonwealth have very good caution of his fidelity, is a dangerous disease; because the people, which should receive their motion from the authority of the sovereign, by the flattery and by the reputation of an ambitious man, are drawn away from their obedience to the laws to follow a man of whose virtues and designs they have no knowledge. And this is commonly of more danger in a popular government than in a monarchy, because an army is of so great force and multitude as it may easily be made believe they are the people. By this means it was that Julius Caesar, who was set up by the people against the senate, having won to himself the affections of his army, made himself master both of senate and people. And this proceeding of popular and ambitious men is plain rebellion, and may be resembled to the effects of witchcraft.

Another infirmity of a Commonwealth is the immoderate greatness of a town, when it is able to furnish out of its own circuit the number and expense of a great army; as also the great number of corporations, which are as it were many lesser Commonwealths in the bowels of a greater, like worms in the entrails of a natural man. To which may be added, liberty of disputing against absolute power by pretenders to political prudence; which though bred for the most part in the lees of the people, yet animated by false doctrines are perpetually meddling with the fundamental laws, to the molestation of the Commonwealth, like the little worms which physicians call ascarides.

We may further add the insatiable appetite, or bulimia, of enlarging dominion, with the incurable wounds thereby many times received from the enemy; and the wens, of ununited conquests, which are many times a burden, and with less danger lost than kept; as also the lethargy of ease, and consumption of riot and vain expense.

Lastly, when in a war, foreign or intestine, the enemies get a final victory, so as, the forces of the Commonwealth keeping the field no longer, there is no further protection of subjects in their loyalty, then is the Commonwealth dissolved, and every man at liberty to protect himself by such courses as his own discretion shall suggest unto him. For the sovereign is the public soul, giving life and motion to the Commonwealth, which expiring, the members are governed by it no more than the carcass of a man by his departed, though immortal, soul. For though the right of a sovereign monarch cannot be extinguished by the act of another, yet the obligation of the members may. For he that wants protection may seek it anywhere; and, when he hath it, is obliged (without fraudulent pretence of having submitted himself out of fear) to protect his protection as long as he is able. But when the power of an assembly is once suppressed, the right of the same perisheth utterly, because the assembly itself is extinct; and consequently, there is no possibility for sovereignty to re-enter.

DISCUSSION QUESTIONS

1. When discussing the various ways by which a commonwealth may become weakened to the point of dissolution, Hobbes notes that the blame of internal disorder is not to be placed upon the governed, but rather upon the sovereign. Why does he say this?

2. Why does Hobbes think that it is detrimental to the health of a commonwealth for the sovereign to tolerate the attitude that each person may be the judge of good and evil? We often think that it is wise for us to follow our own conscience, even if our conscience dictates that we act against common law. What is Hobbes's argument against this claim? Do you agree with him?

3. Hobbes criticizes the "repugnant opinion" that the sovereign is subject to the civil laws. Do you agree that a sovereign is—or should be—"above the law"? Why or why not?

4. Why does Hobbes think that it is dangerous to allow the power of the sovereign to be divided? How might this apply to the practice of dividing a government into different branches?

5. It may be argued that, even if we are for the most part satisfied with our particular governmental arrangement, if we see or read about a different form of government which somehow seems better or more efficient, then we should consider revising our system. What would Hobbes say about this?

89

John Locke, selection from *Second Treatise of Government* (1689)

In this selection from his *Second Treatise of Government*, Locke explores the justification for dissolving or overthrowing a government. On Locke, see reading 3 above.

SOURCE
Locke, John. *Two Treatises of Government*. Whitmore and Fenn, reprinted 1821.

Of the Dissolution of Government

211. He that will with any clearness speak of the dissolution of government, ought in the first place to distinguish between the dissolution of the society and the dissolution of the government. That which makes the community, and brings men out of the loose state of nature, into one politic society, is the agreement which every one has with the rest to incorporate, and act as one body, and so be one distinct commonwealth. The usual, and almost only way whereby this union is dissolved, is the inroad of foreign force making a conquest upon them: for in that case, (not being able to maintain and support themselves, as one entire and independent body) the union belonging to that body which consisted therein, must necessarily cease, and so every one return to the state he was in before, with a liberty to shift for himself, and provide for his own safety, as he thinks fit, in some other society. Whenever the society is dissolved, it is certain the government of that society cannot remain. Thus conquerors' swords often cut up governments by the roots, and mangle societies to pieces, separating the subdued or scattered multitude from the protection of, and dependence on, that society which ought to have preserved them from violence. The world is too well instructed in, and too forward to allow of, this way of dissolving of governments, to need any more to be said of it; and there wants not much argument to prove, that where the society is dissolved, the

government cannot remain; that being as impossible, as for the frame of an house to subsist when the materials of it are scattered and dissipated by a whirl-wind, or jumbled into a confused heap by an earthquake.

212. Besides this over-turning from without, governments are dissolved from within.

First, when the legislative is altered. Civil society being a state of peace, amongst those who are of it, from whom the state of war is excluded by the umpirage, which they have provided in their legislative, for the ending all differences that may arise amongst any of them, it is in their legislative, that the members of a commonwealth are united, and combined together into one coherent living body. This is the soul that gives form, life, and unity, to the commonwealth: from hence the several members have their mutual influence, sympathy, and connexion: and therefore, when the legislative is broken, or dissolved, dissolution and death follows: for the essence and union of the society consisting in having one will, the legislative, when once established by the majority, has the declaring, and as it were keeping of that will. The constitution of the legislative is the first and fundamental act of society, whereby provision is made for the continuation of their union, under the direction of persons, and bonds of laws, made by persons authorized thereunto, by the consent and appointment of the people, without which no one man, or number of men, amongst them, can have authority of making laws that shall be binding to the rest. When any one, or more, shall take upon them to make laws, whom the people have not appointed so to do, they make laws without authority, which the people are not therefore bound to obey; by which means they come again to be out of subjection, and may constitute to themselves a new legislative, as they think best, being in full liberty to resist the force of those, who without authority would impose any thing upon them. Every one is at the disposure of his own will, when those who had, by the delegation of the society, the declaring of the public will, are excluded

from it, and others usurp the place, who have no such authority or delegation.

213. This being usually brought about by such in the commonwealth who misuse the power they have; it is hard to consider it aright, and know at whose door to lay it, without knowing the form of government in which it happens. Let us suppose then the legislative placed in the concurrence of three distinct persons.

1. A single hereditary person, having the constant, supreme, executive power, and with it the power of convoking and dissolving the other two within certain periods of time.

2. An assembly of hereditary nobility.

3. An assembly of representatives chosen, pro tempore, by the people. Such a form of government supposed, it is evident,

214. First, That when such a single person, or prince, sets up his own arbitrary will in place of the laws, which are the will of the society, declared by the legislative, then the legislative is changed: for that being in effect the legislative, whose rules and laws are put in execution, and required to be obeyed; when other laws are set up, and other rules pretended, and inforced, than what the legislative, constituted by the society, have enacted, it is plain that the legislative is changed. Whoever introduces new laws, not being thereunto authorized by the fundamental appointment of the society, or subverts the old, disowns and overturns the power by which they were made, and so sets up a new legislative.

215. Secondly, When the prince hinders the legislative from assembling in its due time, or from acting freely, pursuant to those ends for which it was constituted, the legislative is altered: for it is not a certain number of men, no, nor their meeting, unless they have also freedom of debating, and leisure of perfecting, what is for the good of the society, wherein the legislative consists: when these are taken away or altered, so as to deprive the society of the due exercise of their power, the legislative is truly altered; for it is not names that constitute

governments, but the use and exercise of those pow-ers that were intended to accompany them; so that he, who takes away the freedom, or hinders the acting of the legislative in its due seasons, in effect takes away the legislative, and puts an end to the government.

216. Thirdly, When, by the arbitrary power of the prince, the electors, or ways of election, are altered, without the consent, and contrary to the common interest of the people, there also the legislative is altered: for, if others than those whom the soci-ety hath authorized thereunto, do choose, or in another way, than what the society hath prescribed, those chosen are not the legislative appointed by the people.

217. Fourthly, The delivery also of the people into the subjection of a foreign power, either by the prince, or by the legislative, is certainly a change of the legislative, and so a dissolution of the govern-ment: for the end why people entered into society being to be preserved one entire, free, indepen-dent society, to be governed by its own laws; this is lost, whenever they are given up into the power of another.

218. Why, in such a constitution as this, the dis-solution of the government in these cases is to be imputed to the prince, is evident; because he, having the force, treasure and offices of the state to employ, and often persuading himself, or being flattered by others, that as supreme magistrate he is uncapable of control; he alone is in a condition to make great advances toward such changes, under pretence of lawful authority, and has it in his hands to terrify or suppress opposers, as factious, seditious, and ene-mies to the government: whereas no other part of the legislative, or people, is capable by themselves to attempt any alteration of the legislative, with-out open and visible rebellion, apt enough to be taken notice of, which, when it prevails, produces effects very little different from foreign conquest. Besides, the prince in such a form of government, having the power of dissolving the other parts of

the legislative, and thereby rendering them private persons, they can never in opposition to him, or without his concurrence, alter the legislative by a law, his consent being necessary to give any of their decrees that sanction. But yet so far as the other parts of the legislative any way contribute to any attempt upon the government, and do either pro-mote, or not (what lies in them) hinder such designs, they are guilty, and partake in this which is cer-tainly the greatest crime men can be guilty of one towards another.

219. There is one way more whereby such a gov-ernment may be dissolved, and that is: When he who has the supreme executive power neglects and abandons that charge, so that the laws already made can no longer be put in execution; this is demon-stratively to reduce all to anarchy, and so effec-tively to dissolve the government. For laws not being made for themselves, but to be, by their exe-cution, the bonds of the society to keep every part of the body politic in its due place and function, when that totally ceases, the government visibly ceases, and the people become a confused multi-tude without order or connection. Where there is no longer the administration of justice for the securing of men's rights, nor any remaining power within the community to direct the force, or provide for the necessities of the public, there certainly is no government left. Where the laws cannot be exe-cuted it is all one as if there were no laws, and a government without laws is, I suppose, a mystery in politics inconceivable to human capacity, and inconsistent with human society.

220. In these and the like cases, when the govern-ment is dissolved, the people are at liberty to pro-vide for themselves, by erecting a new legislative, differing from the other, by the change of persons, or form, or both, as they shall find it most for their safety and good: for the society can never, by the fault of another, lose the native and original right it has to preserve itself, which can only be done by a settled legislative, and a fair and impartial execution of the laws made by it. But the state of mankind is

not so miserable that they are not capable of using this remedy, till it be too late to look for any. To tell people they may provide for themselves, by erecting a new legislative, when by oppression, artifice, or being delivered over to a foreign power, their old one is gone, is only to tell them, they may expect relief when it is too late, and the evil is past cure. This is in effect no more than to bid them first be slaves, and then to take care of their liberty; and when their chains are on, tell them, they may act like freemen. This, if barely so, is rather mockery than relief; and men can never be secure from tyranny, if there be no means to escape it till they are perfectly under it: and therefore it is, that they have not only a right to get out of it, but to prevent it.

221. There is therefore, secondly, another way whereby governments are dissolved, and that is, when the legislative, or the prince, either of them, act contrary to their trust.

First, The legislative acts against the trust reposed in them, when they endeavour to invade the property of the subject, and to make themselves, or any part of the community, masters, or arbitrary disposers of the lives, liberties, or fortunes of the people.

222. The reason why men enter into society, is the preservation of their property; and the end why they choose and authorize a legislative, is, that there may be laws made, and rules set, as guards and fences to the properties of all the members of the society, to limit the power, and moderate the dominion, of every part and member of the society: for since it can never be supposed to be the will of the society, that the legislative should have a power to destroy that which every one designs to secure, by entering into society, and for which the people submitted themselves to legislators of their own making; whenever the legislators endeavour to take away, and destroy the property of the people, or to reduce them to slavery under arbitrary power, they put themselves into a state of war with the people, who are thereupon absolved from any farther obedience, and are left to the common refuge, which God hath provided for all

men, against force and violence. Whensoever therefore the legislative shall transgress this fundamental rule of society; and either by ambition, fear, folly or corruption, endeavour to grasp themselves, or put into the hands of any other, an absolute power over the lives, liberties, and estates of the people; by this breach of trust they forfeit the power the people had put into their hands for quite contrary ends, and it devolves to the people, who have a right to resume their original liberty, and, by the establishment of a new legislative, (such as they shall think fit) provide for their own safety and security, which is the end for which they are in society. What I have said here, concerning the legislative in general, holds true also concerning the supreme executor, who having a double trust put in him, both to have a part in the legislative, and the supreme execution of the law, acts against both, when he goes about to set up his own arbitrary will as the law of the society. He acts also contrary to his trust, when he either employs the force, treasure, and offices of the society, to corrupt the representatives, and gain them to his purposes; or openly pre-engages the electors, and prescribes to their choice, such, whom he has, by solicitations, threats, promises, or otherwise, won to his designs; and employs them to bring in such, who have promised before-hand what to vote, and what to enact. Thus to regulate candidates and electors, and new-model the ways of election, what is it but to cut up the government by the roots, and poison the very fountain of public security? for the people having reserved to themselves the choice of their representatives, as the fence to their properties, could do it for no other end, but that they might always be freely chosen, and so chosen, freely act, and advise, as the necessity of the commonwealth, and the public good should, upon examination, and mature debate, be judged to require. This, those who give their votes before they hear the debate, and have weighed the reasons on all sides, are not capable of doing. To prepare such an assembly as this, and endeavour to set up the declared abettors of his own will, for the true representatives of the people, and the lawmakers of the society, is certainly as great a breach of trust, and as perfect a declaration of a design to subvert the government, as is possible to be met with. To which, if one shall add rewards and punishments visibly employed to the same end, and all the arts of perverted law made use of, to take off and destroy all that stand in the way of such a design, and will not comply and consent to betray the liberties of their country, it will be past doubt what is doing. What power they ought to have in the society, who thus employ it contrary to the trust went along with it in its first institution, is easy to determine; and one cannot but see, that he, who has once attempted any such thing as this, cannot any longer be trusted.

223. To this perhaps it will be said, that the people being ignorant, and always discontented, to lay the foundation of government in the unsteady opinion and uncertain humour of the people, is to expose it to certain ruin; and no government will be able long to subsist, if the people may set up a new legislative, whenever they take offence at the old one. To this I answer, Quite the contrary. People are not so easily got out of their old forms, as some are apt to suggest. They are hardly to be prevailed with to amend the acknowledged faults in the frame they have been accustomed to. And if there be any original defects, or adventitious ones introduced by time, or corruption; it is not an easy thing to get them changed, even when all the world sees there is an opportunity for it. This slowness and aversion in the people to quit their old constitutions, has, in the many revolutions which have been seen in this kingdom, in this and former ages, still kept us to, or, after some interval of fruitless attempts, still brought us back again to our old legislative of king, lords and commons: and whatever provocations have made the crown be taken from some of our princes' heads, they never carried the people so far as to place it in another line.

224. But it will be said, this hypothesis lays a ferment for frequent rebellion. To which I answer,

First, No more than any other hypothesis: for when the people are made miserable, and find themselves exposed to the ill usage of arbitrary power, cry up their governors, as much as you will, for sons of Jupiter; let them be sacred and divine, descended, or authorized from heaven; give them out for whom or what you please, the same will happen. The people generally ill treated, and contrary to right, will be ready upon any occasion to ease themselves of a burden that sits heavy upon them. They will wish, and seek for the opportunity, which in the change, weakness and accidents of human affairs, seldom delays long to offer itself. He must have lived but a little while in the world, who has not seen examples of this in his time; and he must have read very little, who cannot produce examples of it in all sorts of governments in the world.

225. Secondly, I answer, such revolutions happen not upon every little mismanagement in public affairs. Great mistakes in the ruling part, many wrong and inconvenient laws, and all the slips of human frailty, will be borne by the people without mutiny or murmur. But if a long train of abuses, prevarications and artifices, all tending the same way, make the design visible to the people, and they cannot but feel what they lie under, and see whither they are going; it is not to be wondered, that they should then rouse themselves, and endeavour to put the rule into such hands which may secure to them the ends for which government was at first erected; and without which, ancient names, and specious forms, are so far from being better, that they are much worse, than the state of nature, or pure anarchy; the inconveniencies being all as great and as near, but the remedy farther off and more difficult.

226. Thirdly, I answer, that this doctrine of a power in the people of providing for their safety a-new, by a new legislative, when their legislators have acted contrary to their trust, by invading their property, is the best fence against rebellion, and the probablest means to hinder it: for rebellion being an opposition, not to persons, but authority, which is founded only in the constitutions and laws of the government; those, whoever they be, who by force break through, and by force justify their violation of them, are truly and properly rebels: for when men, by entering into

society and civil-government, have excluded force, and introduced laws for the preservation of property, peace, and unity amongst themselves, those who set up force again in opposition to the laws, do *rebellare*, that is, bring back again the state of war, and are properly rebels: which they who are in power, (by the pretence they have to authority, the temptation of force they have in their hands, and the flattery of those about them) being likeliest to do; the properest way to prevent the evil, is to shew them the danger and injustice of it, who are under the greatest temptation to run into it.

227. In both the fore-mentioned cases, when either the legislative is changed, or the legislators act contrary to the end for which they were constituted; those who are guilty are guilty of rebellion: for if any one by force takes away the established legislative of any society, and the laws by them made, pursuant to their trust, he thereby takes away the umpirage, which every one had consented to, for a peaceable decision of all their controversies, and a bar to the state of war amongst them. They, who remove, or change the legislative, take away this decisive power, which no body can have, but by the appointment and consent of the people; and so destroying the authority which the people did, and no body else can set up, and introducing a power which the people hath not authorized, they actually introduce a state of war, which is that of force without authority: and thus, by removing the legislative established by the society, (in whose decisions the people acquiesced and united, as to that of their own will) they untie the knot, and expose the people a-new to the state of war, And if those, who by force take away the legislative, are rebels, the legislators themselves, as has been shewn, can be no less esteemed so; when they, who were set up for the protection, and preservation of the people, their liberties and properties, shall by force invade and endeavour to take them away; and so they putting themselves into a state of war with those who made them the protectors and guardians of their peace, are properly, and with the greatest aggravation, *rebellantes*, rebels.

228. But if they, who say it lays a foundation for rebellion, mean that it may occasion civil wars, or intestine broils, to tell the people they are absolved from obedience when illegal attempts are made upon their liberties or properties, and may oppose the unlawful violence of those who were their magistrates, when they invade their properties contrary to the trust put in them; and that therefore this doctrine is not to be allowed, being so destructive to the peace of the world: they may as well say, upon the same ground, that honest men may not oppose robbers or pirates, because this may occasion disorder or bloodshed. If any mischief come in such cases, it is not to be charged upon him who defends his own right, but on him that invades his neighbours. If the innocent honest man must quietly quit all he has, for peace sake, to him who will lay violent hands upon it, I desire it may be considered, what a kind of peace there will be in the world, which consists only in violence and rapine; and which is to be maintained only for the benefit of robbers and oppressors. Who would not think it an admirable peace betwix the mighty and the mean, when the lamb, without resistance, yielded his throat to be torn by the imperious wolf? Polyphemus's den[1] gives us a perfect pattern of such a peace, and such a government, wherein Ulysses and his companions had nothing to do, but quietly to suffer themselves to be devoured. And no doubt Ulysses, who was a prudent man, preached up passive obedience, and exhorted them to a quiet submission, by representing to them of what concernment peace was to mankind; and by shewing the inconveniences might happen, if they should offer to resist Polyphemus, who had now the power over them.

229. The end of government is the good of mankind; and which is best for mankind, that the people should be always exposed to the boundless will of tyranny, or that the rulers should be sometimes liable to be opposed, when they grow exorbitant

---

[1] [Polyphemus, in ancient Greek mythology, was a Cyclops—a giant one-eyed monster. In Homer's *Odyssey*, he traps and eats some of Odysseus' men.]

in the use of their power, and employ it for the destruction, and not the preservation of the properties of their people?

230. Nor let any one say, that mischief can arise from hence, as often as it shall please a busy head, or turbulent spirit, to desire the alteration of the government. It is true, such men may stir, whenever they please; but it will be only to their own just ruin and perdition: for till the mischief be grown general, and the ill designs of the rulers become visible, or their attempts sensible to the greater part, the people, who are more disposed to suffer than right themselves by resistance, are not apt to stir. The examples of particular injustice, or oppression of here and there an unfortunate man, moves them not. But if they universally have a persuasion, grounded upon manifest evidence, that designs are carrying on against their liberties, and the general course and tendency of things cannot but give them strong suspicions of the evil intention of their governors, who is to be blamed for it? Who can help it, if they, who might avoid it, bring themselves into this suspicion? Are the people to be blamed, if they have the sense of rational creatures, and can think of things no otherwise than as they find and feel them? And is it not rather their fault, who put things into such a posture, that they would not have them thought to be as they are? I grant, that the pride, ambition, and turbulency of private men have sometimes caused great disorders in commonwealths, and factions have been fatal to states and kingdoms. But whether the mischief hath oftener begun in the people's wantonness, and a desire to cast off the lawful authority of their rulers, or in the ruler's insolence, and endeavours to get and exercise an arbitrary power over their people; whether oppression, or disobedience, gave the first rise to the disorder, I leave it to impartial history to determine. This I am sure, whoever, either ruler or subject, by force goes about to invade the rights of either prince or people, and lays the foundation for overturning the constitution and frame of any just government, is highly guilty of the greatest crime, I think, a man is capable of, being to answer for

all those mischiefs of blood, rapine, and desolation, which the breaking to pieces of governments bring on a country. And he who does it, is justly to be esteemed the common enemy and pest of mankind, and is to be treated accordingly.

231. That subjects or foreigners, attempting by force on the properties of any people, may be resisted with force, is agreed on all hands. But that magistrates, doing the same thing, may be resisted, hath of late been denied: as if those who had the greatest privileges and advantages by the law, had thereby a power to break those laws, by which alone they were set in a better place than their brethren: whereas their offence is thereby the greater, both as being ungrateful for the greater share they have by the law, and breaking also that trust, which is put into their hands by their brethren.

232. Whosoever uses force without right, as every one does in society, who does it without law, puts himself into a state of war with those against whom he so uses it; and in that state all former ties are cancelled, all other rights cease, and every one has a right to defend himself, and to resist the aggressor. This is so evident, that Barclay[1] himself, that great assertor of the power and sacredness of kings, is forced to confess, That it is lawful for the people, in some cases, to resist their king; and that too in a chapter, wherein he pretends to shew, that the divine law shuts up the people from all manner of rebellion. Whereby it is evident, even by his own doctrine, that, since they may in some cases resist, all resisting of princes is not rebellion. His words are these:

233. But if any one should ask, Must the people then always lay themselves open to the cruelty and rage of tyranny? Must they see their cities pillaged, and laid in ashes, their wives and children exposed to the tyrant's lust and fury, and themselves and families

---

1 [William Barclay (1546–1608) was a Scottish jurist who, in 1600, published a monumental defense of the divine right of kings entitled "De Regno et Ragali potestate."]

reduced by their king to ruin, and all the miseries of want and oppression, and yet sit still? Must men alone be debarred the common privilege of opposing force with force, which nature allows so freely to all other creatures for their preservation from injury? I answer: Self-defence is a part of the law of nature; nor can it be denied the community, even against the king himself: but to revenge themselves upon him, must by no means be allowed them; it being not agreeable to that law. Wherefore if the king shall shew an hatred, not only to some particular persons, but sets himself against the body of the commonwealth, whereof he is the head, and shall, with intolerable ill usage, cruelly tyrannize over the whole, or a considerable part of the people, in this case the people have a right to resist and defend themselves from injury: but it must be with this caution, that they only defend themselves, but do not attack their prince: they may repair the damages received, but must not for any provocation exceed the bounds of due reverence and respect. They may repulse the present attempt, but must not revenge past violences: for it is natural for us to defend life and limb, but that an inferior should punish a superior, is against nature. The mischief which is designed them, the people may prevent before it be done; but when it is done, they must not revenge it on the king, though author of the villainy. This therefore is the privilege of the people in general, above what any private person hath; that particular men are allowed by our adversaries themselves (Buchanan[1] only excepted) to have no other remedy but patience; but the body of the people may with respect resist intolerable tyranny; for when it is but moderate, they ought to endure it. (Barclay, *Contra Monarchomachos*, lib. 3, c. 8)

234. Thus far that great advocate of monarchical power allows of resistance.

235. It is true, he has annexed two limitations to it, to no purpose:

First, He says, it must be with reverence.

Secondly, It must be without retribution, or punishment; and the reason he gives is, because an inferior cannot punish a superior.

First, How to resist force without striking again, or how to strike with reverence, will need some skill to make intelligible. He that shall oppose an assault only with a shield to receive the blows, or in any more respectful posture, without a sword in his hand, to abate the confidence and force of the assailant, will quickly be at an end of his resistance, and will find such a defence serve only to draw on himself the worse usage. This is as ridiculous a way of resisting, as Juvenal thought it of fighting; *ubi tu pulsas, ego vapulo tantum.*[2] And the success of the combat will be unavoidably the same he there describes it:

> *Libertas pauperis haec est:*
> *Pulsatus rogat, & pugnis concisus, adorat,*
> *Ut liceat paucis cum dentibus inde reverti.*[3]

This will always be the event of such an imaginary resistance, where men may not strike again. He therefore who may resist, must be allowed to strike. And then let our author, or any body else, join a knock on the head, or a cut on the face, with as much reverence and respect as he thinks fit. He that can reconcile blows and reverence, may, for aught I know, desire for his pains, a civil, respectful cudgeling where-ever he can meet with it.

Secondly, as to his second, an inferior cannot punish a superior; that is true, generally speaking, whilst he is his superior. But to resist force with force, being the state of war that levels the parties, cancels all former relation of reverence, respect, and

---

[1] [George Buchanan was instrumental in removing Queen Mary from the throne of England via his attacks on her moral character.]

[2] [Where you hit only am I beaten.]

[3] [This is a poor man's freedom: when he is beaten, he begs, when he is knocked down, he kneels, for his goal is to escape with some of his teeth remaining.]

superiority: and then the odds that remains, is, that he, who opposes the unjust aggressor, has this superiority over him, that he has a right, when he prevails, to punish the offender, both for the breach of the peace, and all the evils that followed upon it. Barclay therefore, in another place, more coherently to himself, denies it to be lawful to resist a king in any case. But he there assigns two cases, whereby a king may un-king himself.
[…]

237. What then, can there no case happen wherein the people may of right, and by their own authority, help themselves, take arms, and set upon their king, imperiously domineering over them? None at all, whilst he remains a king. Honour the king, and he that resists the power, resists the ordinance of God; are divine oracles that will never permit it. The people therefore can never come by a power over him, unless he does something that makes him cease to be a king: for then he divests himself of his crown and dignity, and returns to the state of a private man, and the people become free and superior, the power which they had in the interregnum, before they crowned him king, devolving to them again. But there are but few miscarriages which bring the matter to this state. After considering it well on all sides, I can find but two. Two cases there are, I say, whereby a king, *ipso facto*, becomes no king, and loses all power and regal authority over his people; which are also taken notice of by Winzerus.[1]

The first is, If he endeavour to overturn the government, that is, if he have a purpose and design to ruin the kingdom and commonwealth, as it is recorded of Nero, that he resolved to cut off the senate and people of Rome, lay the city waste with fire and sword, and then remove to some other place. And of Caligula, that he openly declared, that he would be no longer a head to the people or senate, and that he had it in his thoughts to cut off the worthiest men of both ranks, and then retire to Alexandria: and he wisht that the people had but one neck, that he might dispatch them all at a blow.

Such designs as these, when any king harbours in his thoughts, and seriously promotes, he immediately gives up all care and thought of the commonwealth; and consequently forfeits the power of governing his subjects, as a master does the dominion over his slaves whom he hath abandoned.

238. The other case is, When a king makes himself the dependent of another, and subjects his kingdom which his ancestors left him, and the people put free into his hands, to the dominion of another: for however perhaps it may not be his intention to prejudice the people; yet because he has hereby lost the principal part of regal dignity, viz. to be next and immediately under God, supreme in his kingdom; and also because he betrayed or forced his people, whose liberty he ought to have carefully preserved, into the power and dominion of a foreign nation. By this, as it were, alienation of his kingdom, he himself loses the power he had in it before, without transferring any the least right to those on whom he would have bestowed it; and so by this act sets the people free, and leaves them at their own disposal. One example of this is to be found in the Scotch Annals[2] (lib. 3, c.16).

239. In these cases Barclay, the great champion of absolute monarchy, is forced to allow, that a king may be resisted, and ceases to be a king. That is, in short, not to multiply cases, in whatsoever he has no authority, there he is no king, and may be resisted: for wheresoever the authority ceases, the king ceases too, and becomes like other men who have no authority. And these two cases he instances in, differ little from those above mentioned, to be destructive to governments, only that he has omitted the principle from which his doctrine flows: and that is, the breach of trust, in not preserving the form of government agreed on, and in not intending the end of government itself, which is the public good and preservation of property. When a king has dethroned himself, and put himself in a state of war with his people, what shall hinder them from

---

[1] [There is dispute and uncertainty among historians as to which author Locke is here referring to.]

[2] [Early works on Irish and Scottish history.]

prosecuting him who is no king, as they would any other man, who has put himself into a state of war with them, Barclay, and those of his opinion, would do well to tell us. This farther I desire may be taken notice of out of Barclay, that he says, The mischief that is designed them, the people may prevent before it be done: whereby he allows resistance when tyranny is but in design. Such designs as these (says he) when any king harbours in his thoughts and seriously promotes, he immediately gives up all care and thought of the commonwealth; so that, according to him, the neglect of the public good is to be taken as an evidence of such design, or at least for a sufficient cause of resistance. And the reason of all, he gives in these words, because he betrayed or forced his people, whose liberty he ought carefully to have preserved. What he adds, into the power and dominion of a foreign nation, signifies nothing, the fault and forfeiture lying in the loss of their liberty, which he ought to have preserved, and not in any distinction of the persons to whose dominion they were subjected. The people's right is equally invaded, and their liberty lost, whether they are made slaves to any of their own, or a foreign nation; and in this lies the injury, and against this only have they the right of defence. And there are instances to be found in all countries, which shew, that it is not the change of nations in the persons of their governors, but the change of government, that gives the offence. Bilson,[1] a bishop of our church, and a great stickler for the power and prerogative of princes, does, if I mistake not, in his *Treatise of Christian Subjection*, acknowledge, that princes may forfeit their power, and their title to the obedience of their subjects; and if there needed authority in a case where reason is so plain, I could send my reader to Bracton, Fortescue, and the author of the *Mirrour*,[2] and others, writers that

cannot be suspected to be ignorant of our government, or enemies to it. But I thought Hooker alone might be enough to satisfy those men, who relying on him for their ecclesiastical polity, are by a strange fate carried to deny those principles upon which he builds it. Whether they are herein made the tools of cunninger workmen, to pull down their own fabric, they were best look. This I am sure, their civil policy is so new, so dangerous, and so destructive to both rulers and people, that as former ages never could bear the broaching of it; so it may be hoped, those to come, redeemed from the impositions of these Egyptian under-task-masters, will abhor the memory of such servile flatterers, who, whilst it seemed to serve their turn, resolved all government into absolute tyranny, and would have all men born to, what their mean souls fitted them for, slavery.

240. Here, it is like, the common question will be made, Who shall be judge, whether the prince or legislative act contrary to their trust? This, perhaps, ill-affected and factious men may spread amongst the people, when the prince only makes use of his due prerogative. To this I reply, The people shall be judge; for who shall be judge whether his trustee or deputy acts well, and according to the trust reposed in him, but he who deputes him, and must, by having deputed him, have still a power to discard him, when he fails in his trust? If this be reasonable in particular cases of private men, why should it be otherwise in that of the greatest moment, where the welfare of millions is concerned, and also where the evil, if not prevented, is greater, and the redress very difficult, dear, and dangerous?

241. But farther, this question, (Who shall be judge?) cannot mean, that there is no judge at all: for where there is no judicature on earth, to decide controversies amongst men, God in heaven is judge. He alone, it is true, is judge of the right. But every man is judge for himself, as in all other cases, so in this, whether another hath put himself into a state of war with him, and whether he should appeal to the Supreme Judge, as Jeptha[3] did.

---

[1] [Thomas Bilson (1547–1616) was an Anglican bishop who was one of the overseers of the printing of the King James Bible.]

[2] [Henry of Bracton (1210–68) was an English jurist. Sir John Fortescue (1395–1477) became lord chief justice in 1442 but was exiled in 1461. *Mirrour* here probably refers to *Mirror of Justices*, possibly written by Andrew Horn around 1640.]

---

[3] [A judge of Israel, mentioned in the *Book of Judges*.]

242. If a controversy arise betwixt a prince and some of the people, in a matter where the law is silent, or doubtful, and the thing be of great consequence, I should think the proper umpire, in such a case, should be the body of the people: for in cases where the prince hath a trust reposed in him, and is dispensed from the common ordinary rules of the law; there, if any men find themselves aggrieved, and think the prince acts contrary to, or beyond that trust, who so proper to judge as the body of the people, (who, at first, lodged that trust in him) how far they meant it should extend? But if the prince, or whoever they be in the administration, decline that way of determination, the appeal then lies no where but to heaven; force between either persons, who have no known superior on earth, or which permits no appeal to a judge on earth, being properly a state of war, wherein the appeal lies only to heaven; and in that state the injured party must judge for himself, when he will think fit to make use of that appeal, and put himself upon it.

243. To conclude, The power that every individual gave the society, when he entered into it, can never revert to the individuals again, as long as the society lasts, but will always remain in the community; because without this there can be no community, no commonwealth, which is contrary to the original agreement: so also when the society hath placed the legislative in any assembly of men, to continue in them and their successors, with direction and authority for providing such successors, the legislative can never revert to the people whilst that government lasts; because having provided a legislative with power to continue for ever, they have given up their political power to the legislative, and cannot resume it. But if they have set limits to the duration of their legislative, and made this supreme power in any person, or assembly, only temporary; or else, when by the miscarriages of those in authority, it is forfeited; upon the forfeiture, or at the determination of the time set, it reverts to the society, and the people have a right to act as supreme, and continue the legislative in themselves; or erect a new form, or under the old form place it in new hands, as they think good.

DISCUSSION QUESTIONS

1. What rights does Locke think the people have once their government has been dissolved? Compare and contrast this with what Hobbes says on the matter.

2. Explain the role that trust plays between the people and the prince and/or legislators. What does Locke think the people are justified in doing if their trust is violated by any of these figures? How does his response compare to what Hobbes would say on the matter?

3. Locke argues that the foundation of government ought to lie in the hands of the people, and that they likewise have the right to revise and alter their governmental structure. He recognizes the objection that this opinion may lead to ruin or provide a setting for rebellion, yet he rejects such an objection. What are his reasons?

4. Locke argues that magistrates do not have the power to break the laws; they are not "above the law." How does Locke defend this opinion, and how does his argument compare with that offered by Hobbes on the same subject? In your opinion, whose argument is better?

90

Allen Buchanan, "Secession and Nationalism" (1995)

Allen Buchanan is the James B. Duke Professor of Philosophy at Duke University. In addition to his scholarship pertaining to international law and political philosophy, he regularly writes on issues in bioethics. He has served in a number of advisory positions, including as a consultant to the President's Council on Bioethics in 2007. In this selection he considers various justifications that may be given in defense of a group's right to secede.

SOURCE
Buchanan, Allen. "Secession and Nationalism," from *A Companion to Contemporary Political Philosophy*, edited by R. Goodin, P. Pettit, and T. Pogge. Copyright © 1995 by Blackwell Publishing Ltd. Reproduced with permission of Blackwell Publishing Ltd.

Secession, Autonomy and the Modern State

From Croatia to Azerbaijan to Quebec, secessionist movements are breaking states apart. In some cases, as with Lithuania, a formerly subordinate unit seeks to become and remain a fully sovereign state in its own right. In others, such as Ukraine, one of the first exercises of new-found sovereignty is to forge ties with other units to create new forms of political association—ties which immediately limit the sovereignty of their components. These momentous events call into question not only the legitimacy of particular states and their boundaries, but also the nature of sovereignty and the purposes of political association.

Less publicized and less dramatic movements for greater self-determination of groups within the framework of existing states are also becoming pervasive. The indigenous peoples' rights movement, pursued with vigour in the United Nations and other arenas of international law, embraces Indians in North, Central and South America, Southeast Asian Hill Tribes, the Saami (Lapps) in a number of countries touched by the Arctic Circle, and Native Hawaiians, among others. Self-determination movements among Flemings in Belgium and Scots in the United Kingdom appear to be building as well. In most of these cases the groups in question do not seek full sovereignty, but rather greater autonomy through the achievement of limited rights of self-government as distinct subunits within the state.

The proper analysis of the concept of sovereignty is, of course, a matter of dispute. However, the root idea is that of a supreme authority—one whose powers are unrestricted by those of other entities. It is useful to distinguish between *internal* and *external* sovereignty (McCallum, 1987, pp. 36–45). Internal sovereignty is the state's supremacy with respect to all affairs within its borders. External sovereignty is the state's supremacy with respect to its relations with other political units beyond its borders; in particular, its right to the integrity of its territory, and to control crossings of its borders, as well as the right to enter as an independent party into economic agreements or military alliances or treaties with other states,

No state enjoys literally unrestricted external sovereignty. International law imposes a number of restrictions on every state's dealings with other states, the most fundamental of which is that each is to recognize the others' territorial integrity. In addition, virtually all modern states acknowledge (in principle if not in practice) that their internal sovereignty is limited by *individual rights*, in particular the human rights recognized in international law.

Autonomy movements seek to impose further limitations on internal sovereignty through the recognition of various *group rights*. These include not only so-called minority cultural rights, such as the right to speak one's own language or to wear cultural dress, but also collective property rights for the group, rights of internal self-government, and in some cases rights to participate in joint decision-making concerning the development and exploitation of resources in the area occupied by the group (Quebec, 1991).

Autonomy movements may appear to be less radical than outright bids for secession. After all, what they demand is not the dismemberment of the state into two or more new states, but only a reallocation of certain powers within the state. This appearance, however, is misleading. If a state recognizes substantial powers of self-determination for groups within its borders, it thereby acknowledges limits on its own sovereignty. And if the modern state is defined as a political authority which (credibly) claims full sovereignty over the entire area within its borders, then a state that recognizes rights of self-determination for minorities within its borders thereby transforms itself into something less than a fully sovereign state. (For example, American Indian law in conferring significant powers of self-government upon Indian tribes, uses the term "Indian Nation," and is increasingly regarded as approaching the status of *inter*national law; Williams, 1990, pp. 74–103.)

Thus, secession movements only threaten the myth of the permanence of the state; autonomy movements assault the concept of state sovereignty itself. Successful and frequent secession would certainly shatter the international order; but it would not challenge the basic conceptual framework that has governed international law for over 300 years, since the rise of the modern state. What is fundamental to that framework is the assumption that international law concerns relations among sovereign states. If successful, autonomy movements within existing states may make the case of sovereign states the exception rather than the rule (Hannum, 1990, pp. 14–26, 453–77).

Even though secession is in this sense a phenomenon which the traditional framework of international law and relations can in principle accommodate, it is the most extreme and radical response to the problems of group conflict within the state. For this reason, a consideration of the case for and against secession puts the moral issues of group conflict in bold relief. In what follows, we will explore the morality of secession, while bearing in mind that it is only the most extreme point on a continuum of phenomena involving the struggles of groups within existing political units to gain greater autonomy.

Nationalism and the Justification of Secession

Some see the spate of secessionist movements now appearing around the globe as the expression of an unpredicted and profoundly disturbing resurgence of *nationalism*, which many rightly regard as one of the most dangerous phenomena of the modern era (Buchanan, 1991, pp. 2, 48–52). And indeed one of the most familiar and stirring justifications offered for secession appeals to *the right of self-determination for "peoples,"* interpreted such that it is equivalent to what is sometimes called the *normative nationalist principle*. It is also one of the least plausible justifications.

The normative nationalist principle states that every "people" is entitled to its own state, that is, that political and cultural (or ethnic) boundaries must coincide (Gellner, 1983, pp. 1–3). In other words, according to the normative nationalist principle, the right of self-determination is to be understood in a very strong way, as requiring complete political independence—that is, full sovereignty.

An immediate difficulty, of course, is the meaning of "peoples." Presumably a "people" is a distinct ethnic group, the identifying marks of which are a common language, shared tradition and a common culture. Each of these criteria has its own difficulties. The question of what count as different dialects of the same language, as opposed to two or more distinct languages, raises complex theoretical and metatheoretical issues in linguistics. The histories of many groups exhibit frequent discontinuities, infusion of new cultural elements from outside, and alternating degrees of assimilation to and separation from other groups.

More disturbingly, if "people" is interpreted broadly enough, then the normative nationalist principle denies the legitimacy of any state containing more than one cultural group (unless all "peoples" within it freely waive their rights to their own states). Yet cultural pluralism is often taken to be a distinguishing feature of the modern state, or at least of the modern liberal state. Moreover, if the number of ethnic or cultural groups or peoples is not fixed but may increase, then the normative nationalist principle is a recipe for limitless political fragmentation.

Nor is this all. Even aside from the instability and economic costs of the repeated fragmentation which it endorses, there is a more serious objection to the normative nationalist principle, forcefully formulated by Ernest Gellner.

> To put it in the simplest terms: there is a very large number of potential nations on earth. Our planet also contains room for a certain number of independent or autonomous political units. On any reasonable calculation, the former number (of potential nations) is probably much, much larger than that of possible viable states. If this argument or calculation is correct, not all nationalisms can be satisfied, at any rate not at the same time. The satisfaction of some spells the frustration of others. This argument is furthered and immeasurably strengthened by the fact that very many of the potential nations of this world live, or until recently have lived, not in compact territorial units but intermixed with each other in complex patterns. It follows that a territorial political unit can only become ethnically homogenous, in such cases, if it either kills, or expels, or assimilates all non-nationals. (Gellner, 1983, p. 2)

With arch understatement, Gellner concludes that the unwillingness of people to suffer such fates "may make the implementation of the nationalist principle difficult." Thus, to say that the normative nationalist principle must be rejected because it is too *impractical* or *economically costly* would be grossly misleading. It ought to be abandoned because the *moral costs* of even attempting to implement it would be prohibitive.

It is important to see that this criticism of the principle of self-determination is decisive *only* against the strong version of that principle that makes it equivalent to the normative nationalist principle, which states that each people (or ethnic group) is to have its own fully sovereign state. For the objection focuses on the unacceptable implications of granting a right of self-determination to all "peoples" *on the assumption that self-determination means complete political independence, that is, full sovereignty.*

However, as we have already suggested, the notion of self-determination is vague or, rather, multiply ambiguous, inasmuch as there are numerous forms and a range of degrees of political independence or autonomy that a group might attain. Instead of asserting an ambiguous right to self-determination, it might be better to acknowledge that many if not most groups have a legitimate interest in self-determination and that this interest can best be served in different circumstances by a range of more specific rights or combinations of rights, including a number of distinct group rights to varying forms and degrees of political autonomy, with the right to secede being only the most extreme of these.

I have argued elsewhere that there is a moral right to secede, though it is a highly qualified, limited right. It is not a right which all "peoples" or ethnic or cultural groups have simply by virtue of their being distinct groups. Instead, only those groups whose predicament satisfies the conditions laid out in any of several sound justifications for secession have this right. In this sense the right to secede, as I conceive it, is not a general right of groups, but rather a special or selective right that obtains only under certain conditions (Buchanan, 1991, pp. 151–62).

Among the strongest justifications that can be given for the claim that a group has a right to secede under certain circumstances are (1) the argument from the rectification of past unjust takings; (2) the self-defence argument; and (3) the argument from discriminatory redistribution (Buchanan, 1991, pp. 27–81). Since secession involves the taking of territory, not just the severing of bonds of political obligation, each prosecession argument must be construed as including the establishment of a valid claim to the territory on the part of the seceding group.

Rectifying Past Unjust Takings

This first justification is the simplest and most intuitively appealing argument for secession. It has obvious application to many actual secessionist movements, including some of those which completed the dissolution of the Soviet Union. The claim is that a region has a right to secede if it was unjustly incorporated into the larger unit from which its members seek to separate.

The argument's power stems from the assumption that secession is simply the reappropriation, by the legitimate owner, of stolen property. The right to secede, under these circumstances, is just the right to reclaim what is one's own. This simple interpretation is most plausible, of course, in situations in which the people attempting to secede are literally the same people who held legitimate title to the territory at the time of the unjust annexation, or at least are the indisputable descendants of those people (their legitimate political heirs, so to speak). But matters are considerably more complex if the seceding group is not closely or clearly related to the group whose territory was unjustly taken, or if the group that was wrongly dispossessed did not itself have clear, unambiguous title to it. But at least in the paradigm case, the argument from rectificatory justice is a convincing argument for a moral right to secede. The right of the Baltic Republics to secede from the Soviet Union, which forcibly and unjustly annexed them in 1940, is well supported by this first justification.

It is one thing to say that a group has the right to secede because in so doing they will simply be reclaiming what was unjustly taken from them. The *terms* of secession are another question. In some cases secession will adversely affect individuals who had no part in the unjust acquisition of the territory. Whether, or under what conditions, they are owed compensation or other special consideration is a complex matter (Buchanan, 1991, pp. 87–91).

The Self-Defence Argument

The common law, common-sense morality and the great majority of ethical systems, religious and secular, acknowledge a right of self-defence against an aggressor who threatens lethal force. For good reason this is not thought to be an unlimited right.

Among the more obvious restrictions on it are (1) that only that degree of force necessary to avert the threat be used, and (2) that the attack against which one defends oneself not be provoked by one's own actions. If such restrictions are acknowledged, the assertion that there is a right of self-defence is highly plausible. Each of these restrictions is pertinent to the right of groups to defend themselves. There are two quite different types of situations in which a group might invoke the right of self-defence to justify secession.

In the first, a group wishes to secede from a state in order to protect its members from extermination by that state itself. Under such conditions the group may either attempt to overthrow the government, that is, to engage in revolution; or, if strategy requires it, the group may secede in order to organize a defensible territory, forcibly appropriating the needed territory from the aggressor, creating the political and military machinery required for its survival, and seeking recognition and aid from other sovereign states and international bodies. Whatever moral title to the seceding territory the aggressor state previously held is *invalidated* by the gross injustice of its genocidal efforts. Or, at the very least, we can say that whatever legitimate claims to the seceding territory the state had are *outweighed* by the claims of its innocent victims. We may think of the aggressor's right to the territory, in the former case, as dissolving in the acid of his own iniquities, and, in the latter, as being pushed down in the scales of the balance by the greater weight of the victim's right of self-defence. Whether we say that the evil state's right to territory is invalidated (and disappears entirely) or merely is outweighed, it is clear enough that in these circumstances its claim to the territory should not be an insurmountable bar to the victim group's seceding, if this is the only way to avoid its wrongful destruction. Unfortunately, this type of case is far from fanciful. One of the strongest arguments for recognizing an independent Kurdish state, for example, is that only this status, with the control over territory it includes, will ensure the survival of this group in the face of genocidal threats from Turkey, Iran and Iraq.

There is a second situation in which secessionists might invoke the right of self-defence, but in a more controversial manner. They could argue that in order to defend itself against a lethal aggressor a group may secede from a state that is not itself that aggressor. This amounts to the claim that the need to defend itself against genocide can generate a claim to territory of sufficient moral weight to override the claims of those who until now held valid title to it and who, unlike the aggressor in the first version of the argument, have not forfeited their claim to it by lethal aggression.

Suppose the year is 1939. Germany has inaugurated a policy of genocide against the Jews. Jewish pleas to the democracies for protection have fallen on deaf ears (in part because the Jews are not regarded as a *nation*—nationhood carrying a strong presumption of territory, which they do not possess). Leaders of Jewish populations in Germany, Eastern Europe and the Soviet Union agree that the only hope for the survival of their people is to create a Jewish state, a sovereign territory to serve as a last refuge for European Jewry. Suppose further that the logical choice for its location—the only choice with the prospect of any success in saving large numbers of Jews—is a portion of Poland. Polish Jews, who are not being protected from the Nazis by the government of Poland, therefore occupy a portion of Poland and invite other Jews to join them there in a Jewish sanctuary state. They do not expel non-Jewish Poles who already reside in that area but, instead, treat them as equal citizens. (From 1941 until 1945 something like this actually occurred on a smaller scale. Jewish partisans, who proved to be heroic and ferocious fighters, occupied and defended an area in the forests of Poland, in effect creating their own mini-state, for purposes of defending themselves and others from annihilation by the Germans.)

The force of this second application of the self-defence argument derives in part from the assumption that the Polish Jews who create the sanctuary state *are not being protected by their own state, Poland*. The idea is that a *state's authority over territory is based at least in part in its providing protection to all its citizens*—and that its retaining that authority is conditional on its continuing to do so. In the circumstances described, the Polish state is not providing protection to its Jewish citizens, and this fact voids the state's title to the territory in question. The Jews may rightly claim the territory, if doing so is necessary for their protection against extermination.

Escaping Discriminatory Redistribution

The idea here is that a group may secede if this is the only way for them to escape discriminatory redistribution. Discriminatory redistribution, also called regional exploitation and internal colonization, occurs whenever the state implements economic policies that systematically work to the disadvantage of some groups, while benefiting others, in morally arbitrary ways. A clear example of discriminatory redistribution would be the state imposing higher taxes on one group while spending less on it, or placing economic restrictions on one region, without any sound moral justification for this unequal treatment.

Charges of discriminatory redistribution abound in actual secessionist movements. Indeed, it would be hard to find cases in which this charge does not play a central role in justification for secession, even though other reasons are often given as well. Here are only a few illustrations:

1. American Southerners complained that the federal tariff laws were discriminatory in intent and effect—that they served to foster the growth of infant industries in the North by protecting them from European and especially British competition, at the expense of the South's import-dependent economy. The Southern statesman John C. Calhoun and others argued that the amount of money the South was contributing to the federal government, once the effects of the tariff were taken into account, far exceeded what that region was receiving from it.

2. Basque secessionists have noted that the percentage of total tax revenues in Spain paid by those in their region is more than three times the percentage of state expenditures there (a popular Basque protest song expresses this point vividly, saying that "the cow of the state has its mouth in the Basque country but its udder elsewhere") (Horowitz, 1985, pp. 249–54).

3. Biafra, which unsuccessfully attempted to become independent from Nigeria in 1967, while containing only 22 per cent of the Nigerian population, contributed 38 per cent of total revenues, and received back from the government only 14 per cent of those revenues (Nwanko and Ifejika, 1970, p. 229).

4. Secessionists in the Baltic Republics and in Soviet Central Asia protested that the government in Moscow for many years implemented economic policies that benefited the rest of the country at the expense of staggering environmental damage in their regions. To support this allegation of discriminatory redistribution, they cited reports of abnormally high rates of birth defects in Estonia, Latvia and Lithuania, apparently due to chemical pollutants from the heavy industry which Soviet economic policy concentrated there, and contamination of ground water in Central Asia due to massive use of pesticides and herbicides at the order of planners in Moscow whose goal it was to make that area a major cotton producer.

An implicit premise of the argument from discriminatory redistribution is that *failure to satisfy this fundamental condition of non-discrimination voids the state's claim to the territory in which the victims reside*, whereas the fact that they have no other recourse to avoid this fundamental injustice *gives them a valid title to it*. This premise forges the needed connection between the grounds for seceding (discriminatory redistribution) and the territorial claim that every sound justification for secession must include (since secession involves the taking of territory). One good reason for accepting this premiss is that it explains our intuitions about the justifiability of secession in certain central and relatively uncontroversial cases.

In other words, unless this premiss is acceptable, the argument from discriminatory redistribution is not sound; and unless the argument from discriminatory redistribution is sound, it is hard to see how secession is justifiable in certain cases in which there is widespread agreement that it is justified. Consider, for example, the secession of the thirteen American Colonies from the British Empire. (Strictly speaking this was secession, not revolution. The aim of the American colonists was not to overthrow the British government, but only to remove a part of the North American territory from the Empire.) The chief justification for American independence was discriminatory redistribution: Britain's mercantilist policies systematically worked to the disadvantage of the colonies for the benefit of the mother country. Lacking representation in the British Parliament, the colonists reasonably concluded that this injustice would persist. It seems, then, that if the American "Revolution" was justified, then there are cases in which the state's persistence in the injustice of discriminatory redistribution, together with the lack of alternatives to secession for remedying it, *generates* a valid claim to territory on the part of the secessionists.

The force of the argument from discriminatory redistribution does not rest solely, however, on brute moral intuitions about particular cases such as that of American independence. We can *explain* our responses to such cases by a simple but powerful principle: the legitimacy of the state—including its rightful jurisdiction over territory—depends upon its providing a framework for cooperation that does not systematically discriminate against any group.

The self-defence argument and the argument from discriminatory redistribution share an underlying assumption, namely, that the justification for a state's control over territory is at least in part *functional*. Generally speaking, what entitles a state to exercise exclusive jurisdiction ("territorial sovereignty") over a territory is the state's provision of a regime that enforces basic rights in a nondiscriminatory way. If the state fails to fulfill these legitimating jurisdictional functions with respect to a group, and if there is no other way for the group to protect itself from the ensuing injustices, then it can rightfully claim the jurisdictional authority for itself.

Attempts to justify secession on grounds of discriminatory redistribution are more complicated than might first appear. The mere fact that there is a net flow of revenue out of one region does not show that discriminatory redistribution is occurring. Instead, the state may simply be implementing policies designed to satisfy the demands of distributive justice. (Theories of distributive justice attempt to formulate and defend principles that specify the proper distribution of the burdens and benefits of social cooperation.) The problem is that distributive justice is a highly controversial matter and that different theories will yield different and in some cases directly opposing assessments of distributive patterns across regions of a country. A policy which redistributes wealth from one region to others may be a case of discriminatory redistribution according to one theory of distributive justice, but a case of just redistribution according to another. Even if there is fairly widespread agreement that the better-off owe something to the worse-off, there can be and is disagreement as to how much is owed. To this extent, the theory of secession is derivative upon the theory of distributive justice and subject to its uncertainties.

Justifications for Forcible Resistance to Secession

An adequate moral theory of secession must consider not only arguments to justify secession but justifications for resisting it as well. Here I will concentrate on only two of the more influential and plausible of the latter (Buchanan, 1991, pp. 87–125).

Avoiding Anarchy

From Lincoln to Gorbachev, leaders of states have opposed secession, warning that recognition of a right to secede would result in chaos. The *reductio ad absurdum* of the right to secede is the prospect of the most extreme anarchy: not every man's home his castle; rather, every man's yard his country. Even if political fragmentation stops short of this, recognition of a right to secede is likely to produce more fragmentation than is tolerable.

This argument would be much more plausible if recognizing a right to secede meant recognizing an *unlimited* right to secede. But as we have argued, the right to secede is a special or selective right that exists only when one or more of a limited set of justifying conditions is satisfied; it is not a general right of all peoples. Nor, as we have also seen, can it reasonably be understood to be included in or derivable from an alleged right of all peoples to self-determination. At most, the threat of anarchy could create a rebuttable presumption against secession, so that secessionists would, generally speaking, have to make a case for seceding.

The theory of the right to secede sketched above can be seen as including such a presumption: a sound justification for secession is to include a justification for the secessionists' claim to the territory. In a sense, this requirement constitutes a presumption in favour of the status quo and to that extent addresses the worry about anarchy. And since, as I have also noted, secession involves not only the severing of bonds of political obligation but also the taking of territory, this requirement seems reasonable.

Some might argue that by requiring secessionists to offer grounds for their claim to the territory, the theory proposed here stacks the deck against them (Kymlicka, 1992). Especially from the standpoint of liberal political philosophy, which prizes liberty and self-determination, why should there not be a presumption that secession is justified, or at the very least, why should not secessionists and anti-secessionists start out on level ground in the process of justification?

There are, I believe, two sound reasons for a presumption that secessionists must make a case for taking the territory. First, a moral theory of secession should be viewed as a branch of *institutional* ethics. One relevant consideration for evaluating proposed principles for institutional ethics is the consequences of their general acceptance. So long as it is recognized that the presumption against secession can be rebutted by any of the arguments stated above in favour of a right to secede, such a presumption seems superior to the alternatives.

Given the gravity of secession—and the predictable and unpredictable disruptions and violence which it may produce—legitimate interests in the stability of the international order speak in favour of the presumption.

Another consideration in favour of assigning the burden of argument where I have is that such a presumption—which gives some weight to the status quo—is much more likely to contribute to general acceptance of a right to secede in the international community. Other things being equal, a moral theory which is more likely to gain acceptance is to be preferred, especially if it is a theory of how institutions, in this case, the institutions of international law and diplomacy, ought to operate. It is often remarked that the one principle of international law that has gained almost universal acceptance is a strong presumption against violations of the territorial integrity of existing states. Requiring that secessionists be able to justify secession and in such a way as to establish their claim to the territory in question, serves to give appropriate weight to this fundamental principle, while at the same time recognizing that the state's claim to control over its territory is not absolute and can be overridden under certain conditions.

Avoiding Strategic Bargaining That Undermines Majority Rule

It could be argued that if the right to secede is recognized, then a minority may use the threat of secession to undermine majority rule. In conditions in which the majority views secession a prohibitive cost, a group's threat to secede can function as a veto over the majority's decisions. Consideration of this risk might lead one to conclude that the only adequate way to protect democracy is to refuse to acknowledge a right to secede.

However, as we have seen, there can be compelling justifications for secession under certain conditions. Accordingly, a more appropriate response than denying the right to secede is to devise constitutional mechanisms or processes of international law that give some weight both to legitimate interests in secession and to the equally legitimate interest in preserving the integrity of majority rule (and in political stability). The most obvious way to do this would be to allow secession under certain circumstances, but to minimize the risk of strategic bargaining with the threat of secession by erecting inconvenient but surmountable procedural hurdles to secession. For example a constitution might recognize a right to secede, but require a strong majority—say three-quarters—of those in the potentially seceding area to endorse secession in a referendum. This type of hurdle is the analogue of an obstacle to constitutional amendment which the US Constitution's Amendment Clause itself establishes: any proposed amendment must receive a two-thirds vote in Congress and be ratified by three-quarters of the states.

The purpose of allowing amendment while erecting these two strong (that is, non-simple) majority requirements is to strike an appropriate balance between two legitimate interests: the interest in providing flexibility for needed change and the interest in securing stability. Similarly, the point of erecting inconvenient but surmountable barriers to secession (either in a constitution or in international law) would be not to make secession impossible but to avoid making it too easy. A second approach would be to levy special exit costs, a secession tax (Buchanan, 1991). Once these possibilities are recognized, the objection that acknowledgment of a right to secede necessarily undermines democracy is seen to be less than compelling.

Secession and the Problem of Group Conflict in the Modern State

Secession is only the most extreme—and in some cases the least desirable—response to problems of group conflict. A comprehensive moral theory of international relations would include an account of the scope and limits of the right to secede; but it would also formulate and support principles to guide the establishment of a wider range of rights of self-determination. Such a theory, if it gained wide acceptance, would undoubtedly produce fundamental changes in our conceptions of the state, of sovereignty, and of the basic categories of international law.

References

Buchanan, A.: *Secession: The Morality of Political Divorce: From Fort Sumter to Lithuania and Quebec* (Boulder, CO: Westview Press, 1991).

Gellner, E.: *Nations and Nationalism* (Oxford: Blackwell, 1983).

Hannum, H.: *Autonomy, Sovereignty, and Self Determination* (Philadelphia: University of Pennsylvania Press, 1990).

Horowitz, D.: *Ethnic Groups in Conflict* (Berkeley: University of California Press, 1985).

Kymlicka, W.: "Review of *Secession: The Morality of Political Divorce: From Fort Sumter to Lithuania and Quebec*," *Political Theory*, 20 (1992), 527–32.

McCallum, G.C.: *Political Philosophy* (Englewood Cliffs, NJ: Prentice-Hall, 1987).

Nwanko, A., and Ifejika, S.: *The Making of a Nation: Biafra* (London: C. Hurst and Co., 1970).

Quebec, Province of: *James Bay and Northern Quebec Agreement and Complementary Agreements* (Quebec: Les Publications du Québec, 1991).

Williams, R.A., Jr: *The American Indian in Western Legal Thought: The Discourses of Conquest* (New York: Oxford University Press, 1990).

DISCUSSION QUESTIONS

1. Buchanan writes that "[a]utonomous movements may appear to be less radical than outright bids for secession," yet he continues to argue that this is actually not the case; i.e., he claims that "autonomy movements assault the concept of state sovereignty itself." Explain and evaluate his argument.

2. What is the normative nationalist principle, and why does Buchanan argue that it is "one of the least plausible justifications" for secessionist movements? Evaluate.

3. Buchanan claims that the right to secede is a "special" or "selective" right which obtains only under certain conditions. He outlines three arguments which he takes to provide the strongest justification for secession under certain conditions. What are the arguments, and what conditions must be met in order for the arguments to be applicable? Can you think of any other circumstances which you feel would result in a group's right to secede? Defend your answer.

4. Under what conditions does Buchanan think that forcible resistance to secessionist movements is justified? Do you agree? Why or why not?

91

Niccolò Machiavelli, selection from *The Prince* (1513/1532)

Niccolò Machiavelli (1469–1527) was an Italian diplomat and political thinker. In *The Prince*, which was published posthumously, Machiavelli presents what has become known as a Realist conception of political power and authority.

SOURCE

Machiavelli, Niccolò. *The Prince, and Other Pieces* (Second Edition). Ed. H. Morley. George Routledge and Sons, 1886.

That Which Concerns A Prince on the Subject of the Art of War

A prince ought to have no other aim or thought, nor select anything else for his study, than war and its rules and discipline; for this is the sole art that belongs to him who rules, and it is of such force that it not only upholds those who are born princes, but it often enables men to rise from a private station to that rank. And, on the contrary, it is seen that when princes have thought more of ease than of arms they have lost their states. And the first cause of your losing it is to neglect this art; and what enables you to acquire a state is to be master of the art. Francesco Sforza,[1] through being martial, from a private person became Duke of Milan; and the sons, through avoiding the hardships and troubles of arms, from dukes became private persons. For among other evils which being unarmed brings you, it causes you to be despised, and this is one of those ignominies against which a prince ought to guard himself, as is shown later on. Because there is nothing proportionate between the armed and the unarmed; and it is not reasonable that he who is armed should yield obedience willingly to him who is unarmed, or that the unarmed man should be secure among armed servants. Because, there being in the one disdain and in the other suspicion, it is not possible for

---

[1] [Francesco Sforza (1401–66) was the founder of the Sforza dynasty in Milan, Italy.]

them to work well together. And therefore a prince who does not understand the art of war, over and above the other misfortunes already mentioned, cannot be respected by his soldiers, nor can he rely on them. He ought never, therefore, to have out of his thoughts this subject of war, and in peace he should addict himself more to its exercise than in war; this he can do in two ways, the one by action, the other by study.

As regards action, he ought above all things to keep his men well organized and drilled, to follow incessantly the chase, by which he accustoms his body to hardships, and learns something of the nature of localities, and gets to find out how the mountains rise, how the valleys open out, how the plains lie, and to understand the nature of rivers and marshes, and in all this to take the greatest care. Which knowledge is useful in two ways. Firstly, he learns to know his country, and is better able to undertake its defence; afterwards, by means of the knowledge and observation of that locality, he understands with ease any other which it may be necessary for him to study hereafter; because the hills, valleys, and plains, and rivers and marshes that are, for instance, in Tuscany, have a certain resemblance to those of other countries, so that with a knowledge of the aspect of one country one can easily arrive at a knowledge of others. And the prince that lacks this skill lacks the essential which it is desirable that a captain should possess, for it teaches him to surprise his enemy, to select quarters, to lead armies, to array the battle, to besiege towns to advantage.

Philopoemen,[1] Prince of the Achaeans, among other praises which writers have bestowed on him,

is commended because in time of peace he never had anything in his mind but the rules of war; and when he was in the country with friends, he often stopped and reasoned with them: "If the enemy should be upon that hill, and we should find ourselves here with our army, with whom would be the advantage? How should one best advance to meet him, keeping the ranks? If we should wish to retreat, how ought we to set about it? If they should retreat, how ought we to pursue?" And he would set forth to them, as he went, all the chances that could befall an army; he would listen to their opinion and state his, confirming it with reasons, so that by these continual discussions there could never arise, in time of war, any unexpected circumstances that he could deal with.

But to exercise the intellect the prince should read histories, and study there the actions of illustrious men, to see how they have borne themselves in war, to examine the causes of their victories and defeat, so as to avoid the latter and imitate the former; and above all do as an illustrious man did, who took as an exemplar one who had been praised and famous before him, and whose achievements and deeds he always kept in his mind, as it is said Alexander the Great imitated Achilles, Caesar Alexander, Scipio Cyrus. And whoever reads the life of Cyrus, written by Xenophon, will recognize afterwards in the life of Scipio how that imitation was his glory, and how in chastity, affability, humanity, and liberality Scipio conformed to those things which have been written of Cyrus by Xenophon. A wise prince ought to observe some such rules, and never in peaceful times stand idle, but increase his resources with industry in such a way that they may be available to him in adversity, so that if fortune changes it may find him prepared to resist her blows.

---

[1] [Philopoemen (253–183 BCE) was a Greek general and statesman.]

DISCUSSION QUESTIONS

1. In Machiavelli's view, what is the primary purpose of war? Is Machiavelli describing how princes do *in fact* act, or how they *ought* to act?

2. How (if at all) could Machiavelli's suggestions be adopted for modern states or leaders? Should they be adopted?

3. Does Machiavelli seem to presuppose either the thesis of psychological egoism or some rationality thesis of egoism (see introduction to Unit I)?

4. Given Machiavelli's view of war, would he endorse pre-emptive war (e.g., the U.S. invading Iran to prevent the development of nuclear weapons)? Would he endorse an invasion for the purposes of securing important natural resources, such as oil?

92

Hugo Grotius, selections from *On the Law of War and Peace* (1625)

Hugo Grotius (1583–1645) was a Dutch jurist, philosopher, and theologian. He is credited with formulating the doctrine of *mare liberum*—i.e., the notion that the seas are international territory, free for use by all nations. In this selection, Grotius considers the conditions under which the use of force is or is not permissible between nations.

SOURCE

Grotius, Hugo. *On the Law of War and Peace*. Trans. A.C. Campbell. London (1814).

On the Unjust Causes of War

[...]

By having before examined and established the principles of just and necessary war, we may form a better idea of what goes to constitute the injustice of the same. As the nature of things is best seen by contrast, and we judge of what is crooked by comparing it with what is straight. But for the sake of perspicuity, it will be necessary to treat upon the leading points.

… [A]pprehensions from a neighbouring power are not a sufficient ground for war. For to authorize hostilities as a defensive measure, they must arise from the necessity, which just apprehensions create; apprehensions not only of the power, but of the intentions of a formidable state, and such apprehensions as amount to a moral certainty. For which reason the opinion of those is by no means to be approved of, who lay down as a just ground of war, the construction of fortifications in a neighbouring country, with whom there is no existing treaty to prohibit such constructions, or the securing of a strong hold, which may at some future period prove a means of annoyance. For as a guard or against such apprehensions, every power may construct, in its own territory, strong works, and other military securities of the same kind, without having recourse to actual war. One cannot but admire the character, which Tacitus has drawn of the Chauci, a noble and high-spirited people of Germany, "who, he says, were desirous of maintaining their greatness by justice, rather than by acts of ungovernable rapacity and ambition—provoking no wars, invading no countries, spoiling no neighbours to aggrandize themselves,—yet, when necessity prompted, able to raise men with arms in their hands at a moment's warning—a great population with a numerous breed of horses to form a well mounted cavalry—and, with all these advantages, upholding their reputation in the midst of peace."[1]

VI. Nor can the advantage to be gained by a war be ever pleaded as a motive of equal weight and justice with necessity.

[...]

VII. and VIII. Neither can the desire of emigrating to a more favourable soil and climate justify an attack upon a neighbouring power. This, as we are informed by Tacitus, was a frequent cause of war among the ancient Germans.

IX. There is no less injustice in setting up claims, under the pretence of newly discovered titles, to what belongs to another.

Neither can the wickedness, and impiety, nor any other incapacity of the original owner justify such a claim. For the title and right by discovery can apply only to countries and places that have no owner.

X. Neither moral nor religious virtue, nor any intellectual excellence is requisite to form a good title to property. Only where a race of men is so destitute of reason as to be incapable of exercising any act of ownership, they can hold no property, nor will the law of charity require that they should have more than the necessaries of life. For the rules of the law of nations can only be applied to those, who are capable of political or commercial intercourse: but not to a people entirely destitute of reason, though it is a matter of just doubt, whether any such is to be found.

It was an absurdity therefore in the Greeks to suppose, that difference of manners, or inferiority of intellect made those, whom they were pleased to call barbarians, their natural enemies. But as to atrocious crimes striking at the very root and existence of society, the forfeiture of property ensuing from thence is a question of a different nature, belonging to punishments, under the head of which it was discussed.

XI. But neither the independence of individuals, nor that of states, is a motive that can at all times justify recourse to arms, as if all persons *indiscriminately* had a natural right to do so. For where liberty is said to be a natural right belonging to all men and states, by that expression is understood a right of nature, antecedent to every human obligation or contract. But in that case, liberty is spoken of in a negative sense, and not by way of contrast to independence, the meaning of which is, that no one is by the law of nature doomed to servitude, though he is not forbidden by that law to enter into such a condition. For in this sense no one can be called free, if nature leaves him not the privilege of choosing his own condition: as Albutius[2] pertinently remarks, "the terms, freedom and servitude are not founded in the principles of nature, but are names subsequently applied to men according to the dispositions of fortune." And Aristotle defines the relations of master and servant to be the result of political and not of natural appointment. Whenever therefore the condition of servitude, either personal or political, subsists, from lawful causes, men should be contented with that state, according to the injunction of the Apostle, "Art thou called, being a servant, let not that be an anxious concern?"[3]

XII. And there is equal injustice in the desire of reducing, by force of arms, any people to a state of servitude, under the pretext of its being the condition for which they are best qualified by nature. It does not follow that, because any one is fitted for a particular condition, another has a right to impose it upon him. For every reasonable creature ought

---

[1] [Publius Cornelius Tacitus (56–117 CE) was a Roman historian and senator. This quotation is from his work *Germania* (98 CE).]

[2] [Titus Albucius (second to first century BCE) was a well-known Roman orator. This quotation is from his orations.]

[3] [From Paul's First Letter to the Corinthians 7:21.]

to be left free in the choice of what may be deemed useful or prejudicial to him, provided another has no just right to a control over him.

[...]

As to the argument in favor of universal dominion from its being so beneficial to mankind, it may be observed that all its advantages are counterbalanced by still greater disadvantages. For as a ship may be built too large to be conveniently managed, so an empire may be too extensive in population and territory to be directed and governed by one head. But granting the expediency of universal empire, that expediency can not give such a right, as can be acquired only by treaty or conquest. There were many places formerly belonging to the Roman Empire, over which the Emperor has at present no control. For war, treaty, or cession have made many changes, by which the rights of territory have passed to other states or sovereign princes, and the standards of different communities, whether kingdoms or commonwealths, now wave in places, which the Roman Eagle once overshadowed with his wings. These are losses and changes, that have been experienced by other powers no less than that, which was once mistress of the world.

[...]

XVI. As the imperfect obligations of charity, and other virtues of the same kind are not cognizable in a court of justice, so neither can the performance of them be compelled by force of arms. For it is not the moral nature of a duty that can enforce its fulfillment, but there must be some legal right in one of the parties to exact the obligation. For the moral obligation receives an additional weight from such a right. This obligation therefore must be united to the former to give a war the character of a just war. Thus a person who has conferred a favour, has not, strictly speaking, a *right* to demand a return, for that would be converting an act of kindness into a contract.

XVII. It is necessary to observe that a war may be just in its origin, and yet the intentions of its authors may become unjust in the course of its prosecution. For some other motive, not unlawful *in itself*, may actuate them more powerfully than the original right, for the attainment of which the war was begun. It is laudable, for instance, to maintain national honour; it is laudable to pursue a public or a private interest, and yet those objects may not form the justifiable grounds of the war in question. A war may gradually change its nature and its object from the prosecution of a right to the desire of seconding or supporting the aggrandizement of some other power. But such motives, though blamable, when even connected with a just war, do not render the war *itself* unjust, nor invalidate its conquests.

On Doubtful Causes

I. There is much truth in Aristotle's observation that moral reasonings can never amount to the certainty of mathematical demonstration. Because in mathematical reasoning, all the figures are considered in the abstract, purely by themselves, and without relation to the circumstances of time or place, so that there is nothing to warp the judgment from the object immediately under consideration. Besides the figures in general form a direct contrast to each other. Thus, for instance, there is no intermediate line between a straight line and a curve.

But it is not so in morals, where the least circumstances vary the subject, and admit a latitude of interpretation, settling the points of truth and justice between two extremes. So that between what is right and what is unlawful there is a middle space, where it is easy to incline to the one side, or to the other. This occasions an ambiguity somewhat like the difficulty of deciding the precise moment, where the twilight begins, and where it ends. From hence Aristotle concludes that it is sometimes difficult to determine, between two extremes, what line of conduct ought to be chosen or rejected.

II. But it must be laid down as a necessary principle, that although an action may in reality be just, yet if the party doing it, after weighing every circumstance, cannot reconcile the act to his conscience, he incurs some degree of guilt. "For whatever is not of faith," says the Apostle, "is sin;"[1] where, by the term faith he means a deliberate judgment of the mind. For God has given conscience a judicial power to be the sovereign guide of human actions, by despising whose admonitions the mind is stupefied into brutal hardness. For it often happens that judgment can point out nothing certain, but hesitates; and when such doubts and hesitations cannot satisfactorily be cleared up, the rule of Cicero is a safe one to follow, who says, that it is an excellent injunction, which forbids us to do a thing of the rectitude or impropriety of which we entertain a doubt.

But this rule cannot be applied, where of two things, in the choice of which there is equal doubt, the one must be done, in which case that must be selected, which seems to be the least unjust. For on all occasions, where a choice cannot be avoided, the less of two evils assumes the appearance of a virtue.

III. But in doubtful cases, after examination, the mind seldom remains neuter, but inclines to one side, or the other, persuaded either by the merits of the case, or by respect for the judgment of those, who have delivered an opinion upon the question. Now the merits of the case are derived either from the causes, the effects, or other concomitant circumstances.

IV. To apprehend such distinctions properly, practice and penetration are necessary, and where men have not in themselves a capacity for the active exercise of judgment it behooves them to follow the maxims of others, who are distinguished by their wisdom and experience. For, in the opinion of Aristotle, those things are probably just, or true, which seem so to all, or to the greater part of men of worth. And this is the method of judging pursued by Sovereign Princes, whose engagements in the affairs of life allow them but little leisure for study and deliberation Thus the ancient Romans never undertook wars, till they had consulted the sacred college, established for that purpose, and the Christian Emperors scarcely ever did so without

advising with the Bishops, in order to be apprized of any thing therein that might affect religion.

V. It may happen in many disputed points, that the intrinsic merits of the case, or the opinions of the learned, are equal on both sides. When that happens, if the matters in discussion are of no great importance, there is nothing to blame in the person, that makes his choice either way. But in matters of moment, where the lives of men are at stake, the decision should incline to the safer side, according to the proverbial maxim, which pronounces it better to acquit the guilty than to condemn the innocent.

VI. War then being an object of such weighty magnitude, in which the innocent must often be involved in the sufferings of the guilty, between wavering opinions the balance should incline in favour of peace.

There are three methods, by which independent nations may settle their disputed rights without coming to the decision of the sword.

VII. The first method is that of conference. For, in the words of Cicero, "there being two methods of deciding quarrels, the one by discussion and the other by force, the former, a peculiar characteristic of man, and the latter, of the brute creation: when the first of these methods fails, men are obliged to have recourse to the latter."[2] Mardonius, in the Polyhymnia of Herodotus,[3] blames the Grecians, who, being united in one language, might settle their quarrels by messengers of peace, by heralds, and negotiations, rather than by war.

VIII. The other method is that of compromise, which takes place between those, who have no common judge. Among innumerable instances of this kind in ancient history, we may select that given by Xenophon in his account of Cyrus, where that prince takes the king of the Indians for arbitrator between himself and the king of Assyria. The

---

[1] [From Paul's Letter to the Romans 14:23.]

[2] [From his *Epistles*.]

[3] [Herodotus was an ancient Greek historian who lived in the fifth century BCE. Mardonius (d.479 BCE) was a Persian military commander in the Persian wars with Greece.]

Carthaginians in their disputes with Masinissa[1] prefer a settlement of this kind before a decision of war. Livy too informs us that the Romans themselves, in a dispute with the Samnites, made an appeal to the common allies of both.

The office of deciding wars and putting an end to the contentions of armies was assigned, according to Strabo,[2] to the Druids of the Gauls, and upon the testimony of the same writer, it formed a part of the priestly functions among the Iberians.

Surely then it is a mode of terminating their disputes, balancing their powers, and settling their pretensions worthy to be adopted by Christian Kings and States. For if, in order to avoid trials before judges who were strangers to the true religion, the Jews and Christians appointed arbitrators of their own, and it was a practice recommended and enjoined by St. Paul, how much more ought such a practice to be recommended and enforced, to gain the still nobler end of preventing the calamities of war.

These and many other reasons of no less importance might be advanced for recommending to Christian powers general congresses for the adjustment of their various interests, and for compelling the refractory to submit to equitable terms of peace.

IX. A third method of terminating disputes, without hostilities, was by lot, a practice commended by Dion Chrysostom[3] in his speech on the interposition of fortune in directing affairs, and it was commended long before him by Solomon in the xviii. chapter of his Proverbs.

X. Nearly related to the last named method is that of single combat, a practice recommended

under the idea that by the risque of two lives a quarrel might be decided, which would otherwise have cost the blood of thousands. In Livy we find Metius addressing Tullus in the following terms, "let us try some method of determining to whom the pre-eminence shall belong, without wasting the blood of each people." Strabo says it was the practice of the ancient Greeks, and Aeneas proposed it to Turnus [in Virgil's *Aeneid*], as the most equitable way of settling their pretensions. It is described too as the custom of the ancient Franks.

XI. Although in doubtful cases, both sides are bound to devise every means of avoiding hostilities, yet it is a duty more incumbent upon the claimant than upon the immediate possessor of whatever may be the subject of dispute. For it is a rule not only of civil, but of natural law, that, where the pretensions are equal, those of the possessor are to be preferred.

To the foregoing remarks an additional observation may be made, that if any one, knowing his pretensions to be just, cannot produce sufficient proofs to convict the intruder of injustice, he cannot lawfully have recourse to arms, because he has no *ostensible right*, by which he can compel the intruder to relinquish the possession.

XII. But where the right is ambiguous, and neither party has possession, the pretender, who refuses to divide the claims, may reasonably be charged with injustice.

XIII. From what has been said it will not be difficult to settle a much agitated question, whether, with respect to those, who are the principal movers of a war, there can be justice on both sides. For there are distinctions proper to be made in the various acceptations of the word *just*.

A thing is said to be just, either as to its causes, or its effects. The causes too may be confined either to justice in a *particular* acceptation, or they may be extended so as to include under that name every kind of rectitude. Again, a particular acceptation may be divided into two kinds, one relating to the *action*, and the other to the agent. An agent may be said to act justly, when, in what he does, he com-

---

[1] [Masinissa (third to second century BCE) was a Numidian who fought on the side of Carthage at the beginning of the Second Punic War. However, in 206 BCE he switched sides and played a crucial role on the side of the Romans in the battle of Zama, which led to the Roman victory in the Second Punic War.]

[2] [Strabo (63 BCE-24 CE) was a Greek historian and geographer. The reference is most likely to his monumental 17-volume work *Geographica*.]

[3] [Dion Chrysostom was a Greek historian, orator, and philosopher in the first century CE.]

mits no breach of *strict law*, though his conduct may not be conformable to equity.

In a *particular* acceptation of the word justice, with regard to a matter in dispute, it cannot in war, any more than in legal proceedings, apply to both sides. For there can be no moral principle, commanding us, under the same circumstances, both to do, and to *abstain* from a particular action. It may happen indeed that neither of two belligerent powers may act unjustly. For no one can be charged with acting unjustly unless he knows that he is doing so; but there are many, who are not aware of the nature, extent, and consequences of their measures. Thus in a law-suit, both parties may sincerely believe that they have justice on their side. For many things both in law and fact, which would establish a right, may escape the notice of men.

In a *general* acceptation, an action may be called just, where the agent is free from every kind of blame. Yet in many cases an agent may deviate from the strict rules of legal justice, and be liable to no blame, when that deviation is owing to unavoidable ignorance, there having been neither time nor opportunity sufficient for him to know the substance, or perhaps existence of the law. So it may happen in law-suits, that both parties are free not only from the imputation of injustice, but from all blame, especially where either of them is litigating a matter not on his own, but on another's account; as for instance where a guardian is acting for his ward, he would not be authorized in abandoning even a doubted right. Aristotle says that in matters of disputed right neither side can be charged with injustice; conformably to which opinion Quintilian[1] observes that an upright pleader may be engaged on either side of the question. Aristotle further observes that passing a just judgment is an ambiguous term, signifying that a judge determines either according to the strict letter of the law, or according to the dictates of his own conscience. And, in another place, he has said that giving a wrong judgment through ignorance is no act of injustice.[2]

But in matters of war and peace, where such weighty and varied interests on all sides are concerned, it would be difficult to obtain a judgment purely impartial, and abstracted from all personal motives, unless there be the most clear and undeniable evidence on the points in question.

If we denominate a thing to be just, from its effect in conferring certain rights, in this sense it is plain that in war there may be justice on both sides. In the same manner, a sentence not strictly legal, or a possession not perfectly just may nevertheless confer certain rights.

[...]

Precautions against Rashly Engaging in War, Even upon Just Grounds

1. Although it seems not to fall within the immediate province of a treatise, entitled the *rights of war*, to enter into an investigation of other moral duties, which the relations of war and peace prescribe, yet it may not be improper slightly to touch upon certain errors, which it is necessary to obviate, in order to prevent any one from supposing, that, after establishing the right of war, he is authorized, *instantly* or at *all times*, to carry his principles into action, and to reduce his theory to practice. So far from this, it frequently happens that it is an act of greater piety and rectitude to yield a right than to enforce it.

It was before shewn, in its proper place how honourable it is to be regardless of our own lives, where we can preserve the lives, and promote the lasting welfare of others. A duty that should operate with greater force upon Christians, who have before their eyes continually the example of him, who died to save us, while we were enemies and ungodly. An example which calls upon us, in the most affecting manner, not to insist upon the rigorous prosecution of our justest rights, where it cannot be done but by the calamities, which war occasions.

---

[1] [Marcus Fabius Quintilianus (first century CE) was a Roman rhetorician.]

[2] [In Aristotle's *Rhetoric*.]

If arguments and motives like these wanted authorities, abundance of authorities might be adduced for their support.

II. Many reasons might be brought to dissuade us from urging the full infliction of a punishment. There is an obvious instance in the conduct of fathers, who connive at many faults in their children. But whoever is authorized to punish another, assumes the character of a sovereign ruler, that is, of a father; in allusion to which St. Augustine, addressing Count Marcellinus, says, "O Christian judge, fulfil the office of a pious father."[1]

Sometimes indeed men are so circumstanced, that to relinquish a right becomes not only a laudable act, but a debt of respect to that law, which commands us to love our enemies: a law to be respected and obeyed not only for its intrinsic value, but as being a precept of the gospel. By the same law, and for the same reasons, we are commanded to pray for and to promote the welfare and safety of Christian Princes and Kings, because their welfare and safety are so essential to the order, peace, and happiness of society.

III. With respect to the pardon of offences committed against ourselves, little need be said, as it is known to be a leading clause in the code of a Christian's duty, to which he readily and freely submits, knowing that God for Christ's sake has forgiven him. Thus revealed law adds a sanction to what was known by heathens to be an amiable precept. Cicero has drawn a fine character of Caesar, in which he commends the excellence of his memory that could recollect every thing but injuries. We find many noble examples of this excellent virtue in the writings of Moses and in various other parts of scripture. These, and these motives *alone*, when they can safely be complied with are sufficient to keep the sword within its scabbard. For the debt of love and forbearance to our enemies is an obligation, which it is honourable to discharge.

IV. It is often a duty, which we owe to our country and ourselves, to forbear having recourse to arms. After the college of heralds had pronounced a war to be just we are informed by Plutarch in the life of Numa, that the Senate further deliberated, whether it was expedient to undertake it. According to our Saviour's beautiful and instructive parable, a king, when he is obliged to go to war with another king, should first sit down, an expression implying an act of deliberation, and consider within himself, whether, with ten thousand men he is able to encounter one who is coming against him with twenty times that number: and if he finds himself unequal to the contest, before the enemy has entered his territories he will send an embassy to him offering terms of peace.

V. In all cases of deliberation, not only the ultimate but the intermediate objects leading to the principal ends are to be considered. The final object is always some good, or at least the evasion of some evil, which amounts to the same. The means are never to be considered by *themselves*, but only as they have a tendency to the proposed end. Wherefore in all cases of deliberation, the proportion, which the means and the end bear to each other, is to be duly weighed, by comparing them together: a mode of comparison, in which there are three rules necessary to be observed.

The first thing, in a moral point of view, to be considered is, what tendency the desired object has to produce good or evil; and, if the former has the preponderancy, we are then at liberty to choose it.— In the second place, if it appears difficult to decide, whether the good or the evil predominates, we may choose the object, if, in the choice and use of our means, we can give a turn to affairs, that may throw the preponderance into the scale of advantage—or lastly if the good and the evil bear no proportion to each other, nor the means, *at the first view*, appear adequate to the end, if, in pursuing an object, the tendency to good, compared with the tendency to evil be greater than the evil itself when compared

---

[1] [Marcellinus was a Christian saint and martyr who was executed in 413 CE. Around 412 or 413, Augustine wrote to his good friend Marcellinus, counseling the latter to be just as he sat in judgment on the Donatists whom Marcellinus had denounced as heretics.]

with the good; or if the good, in comparison of the evil, be greater than the tendency to evil, in comparison of the tendency to good, we may decide in favour of it.

Cicero has treated these abstruse points in a more popular and pleasing manner than abstract reasoning would allow. Applying all the beauties of eloquence to elucidate moral truth, he says, "it is the height of folly and presumption *unnecessarily* to expose ourselves to dangers. In encountering calamities we must imitate the conduct of physicians who use gentle remedies with weakly constitutions. But in constitutions of a stronger cast, especially, in virulent disorders, they must have recourse to more powerful, though more dangerous expedients. In the same manner, a skilful pilot would not attempt to face the wind directly, but would tack about in order to avoid its fury."[1]

VI. An example of evils, that ought by all possible means to be avoided, is furnished by the consultations among the states of Gaul, who, according to the account of Tacitus, deliberated, whether they should make choice of liberty or peace. By liberty is here meant civil liberty, that is, the right of governing themselves, and remaining independent states; and by peace is meant such a peace, as would prevent the whole people from being exterminated, a calamity like that which befell the Jews, when their city was besieged by Titus.

In such cases reason itself dictates the choice of peace, as the only means of preserving life, which is the immediate gift of God, and the foundation of every blessing. So that the Almighty, as we read in his sacred volume, deems it a kindness, when instead of destroying a people, he permits them to be reduced to slavery. Therefore: he admonishes the Hebrews, by the mouth of his prophet, to surrender to the Babylonians, rather than to die by pestilence and famine.

What has been said of submitting to disadvantages, and some calamities for the preservation of life or liberty, may be applied to every object of dear value. As Aristides[2] says, it is a moral duty in a storm, to save the ship by casting overboard the goods, but not the crew.

VII. In exacting punishment it is necessary to use the precaution of avoiding hostilities with a power of equal strength. For to avenge a wrong, or to assert a right by force of arms requires a superiority of strength. So that not only prudence, but a regard for their subjects will at all times deter rulers from involving their people in the calamities of war. A principle of justice too, the sole directress of human affairs, binding sovereigns and subjects to each other by their mutual interests, will teach this lesson of precaution. For reparation must be looked for at the hands of those, who bring on the calamities of wanton and unnecessary war. Livy calls that a just, which is a necessary war, and it is a pious cause, when no hope is left, but in recourse to arms.

VIII. It is but now and then a cause of such imperious necessity occurs, as to demand the decision of the sword, and that is, when, as Florus[3] says, the desertion of a right will be followed by calamities far more cruel, than the fiercest wars. Seneca[4] says, "that it is right to meet danger, when equal harm would result from acquiescing in an injury," and in this, he is supported by Tacitus, who calls "war a happy exchange for a miserable and insecure peace," and the same animated writer in another place observes, that "an oppressed people may recover their liberty by daring enterprize, and, if defeated they cannot be reduced to greater subjection than before"; a sentiment, with which Livy accords, in naming "peace, when coupled with servitude, a far more grievous calamity, than all the horrors of war."[5] But it is not so, as Cicero says, where defeat will be attended with proscription, and victory with bondage.

---

[1] [From Cicero's *On Duty*.]

[2] [Aristides (530–468 BCE) was a Greek statesman.]

[3] [A Roman historian who published, in the first half of the second century CE, a history of the Roman Empire.]

[4] [Seneca (d.65 CE) was a Roman stoic philosopher and statesman.]

[5] [From Book X of his *History of Rome*.]

IX. Another necessary precaution relates to the *time*, when it is proper to undertake a war, which depends upon a due calculation, whether there are resources and strength, sufficient to support our just pretensions. This is conformable to what was said by Augustus, that no war should be undertaken, but where the hopes of advantage could be shewn to overbalance the apprehensions of ruin. Scipio Africanus, and Lucius Aemilius Paulus[1] used to speak in terms not inapplicable to this subject, for they said "it was never right to try the event of battle, but under extreme necessity, or favourable circumstances."

The above precautions are of great use, where we hope by the dread and fame of our preparations to accomplish our object with little or no danger.

---

[1] [Scipio Africanus (235–183 BCE was a Roman general who defeated Hannibal at the final battle of the Second Punic War. Aemilius Paulus (229–160 BCE) was a Roman general and statesman.]

DISCUSSION QUESTIONS

1. How do you think Grotius would respond to the concept of pre-emptive warfare, which was used in the United States' invasion of Iraq? That is to say, do you think Grotius would support pre-emptive attacks justified by concerns for self-defense? Explain.

2. Suppose a powerful, well-armed aggressor attacks a country with very limited resources, which is primarily populated by people under the age of eighteen, many of whom are sick or malnourished. What course of action would Grotius suggest to the leaders of this weak country? What does this tell us about Grotius' conception of the grounds (justification) for warfare?

93

Michael Walzer, selection from *Obligations: Essays on Disobedience, War, and Citizenship* (1970)

In this selection, Walzer considers whether an individual can ever be obligated to die for his or her country or state. On Walzer, see reading 72 above.

SOURCE

Walzer, Michael. "The Obligation to Die for the State," from *Obligations: Essays on Disobedience, War, and Citizenship*, by Michael Walzer, pp. 80–98. Cambridge, Mass.: Harvard University Press, Copyright © 1970 by the President and Fellows of Harvard College. Reprinted by permission of the publisher.

The question then is: can an individual citizen be obligated to make the safety of the state the motive of his voluntary death? Can a prisoner be obligated to wait quietly for his executioner or a soldier to stand in the breach or march up to the cannon's mouth, when neither man has any conceivable reason for waiting, standing, or marching except the safety of the state? Or rather, except the *alleged* safety of the state, for this proviso must be added to what has so far been said: if any obligation exists, the prisoner and soldier are obligated (within certain limits) to accept public definitions of public safety and danger and to die when they are commanded. One cannot be obligated to die sometimes, at one's own discretion. No more can one be obligated to die a little bit. The question must be answered with a yes or a no. One may want to qualify the answer by referring it to a particular state or kind of state, or to a particular group—or kind—of citizens. But the situation of a given man in a given society is necessarily simple: he is either obligated or not. Afterwards, he is either dead or not. As to the obligation, all sorts of equivocations are possible in practice: public authorities may grant that no obligations exist and then presume upon their subjects' sense of obligation, as a captain does when he asks for volunteers; or they may insist upon the obligation, but never presume upon it, as when they load a prisoner with chains or encourage religious fervor among soldiers. These are practical and perhaps necessary confusions, but theorists must try to clear them up and offer one or the other answer. I want now to describe and comment upon two of the answers that have been proposed by two of the major theorists of consent: Hobbes's no and Rousseau's yes.

Hobbes begins by examining one of the practical equivocations. In chapter 14 of *Leviathan*, "Of the First and Second Natural Laws and of Contracts," he writes:

> A covenant not to defend myself from force, by force, is always void. For … no man can transfer or lay down his right to save himself from death, wounds or imprisonment (the avoiding whereof is the only end of laying down any right).… For though a man may covenant thus, *Unless I do so, or so, kill me*; he cannot covenant thus, *Unless I do so, or so, I will not resist you when you come to kill me*. For men by nature chooseth the lesser evil, which is death in resisting, rather than the greater, which is certain and present death in not resisting. And this is granted to be true by all men, in that they lead criminals to execution and prison, with armed men, notwithstanding that such criminals have consented to the law, by which they are condemned.

Now Hobbes's illustration does not really make his point, for the prison authorities need not admit that criminals necessarily and by nature will fight or escape if they can; they only presume that some of them will do so and that it is not possible to know which ones. Nor are prison authorities likely to grant Hobbes's argument that criminals have a right to try to escape. They would surely be uncomfortable with that idea, for their claim to be "authorities" implies that right is on their side alone. But that is not Hobbes's view. He would argue both that the prisoner has a right to escape if he can and that the guards have a right to stop him if they can. Prisoner and guard are simply at war with one another; they are no longer members of the same state. The decision to punish a criminal is, for

Hobbes, his effective expulsion from the political community; he is no longer protected but actively endangered; hence he is free from his contract and under no obligations whatsoever. More than this, he is not merely free to resist or escape, he is physically or psychically bound to do so. Given Hobbes's theory, the behavior of Socrates is literally inexplicable; Hobbes would have to say that the man was mad. That is not at all the view of prison authorities. When they find a passive, resigned, quiet, and obedient prisoner, they do not call him mad, they call him good—which suggests, I think, both the inappropriateness of Hobbes's example and the radicalism of his theory.

The foundations of the theory can be briefly described. For Hobbes, the end of the state is individual life. That is both its primary purpose as an institution and the primary aim of each and every man who participates in its foundation and preservation. The brief moment of political creativity and the subsequent eternity of obedience both have a purely instrumental significance: the goal toward which both are directed is survival, or rather, security, which is survival along with freedom from the terrible fear of violent death. A man who dies for the state defeats his only purpose in forming the state: death is the contradiction of politics. A man who risks his life for the state accepts the insecurity which it was the only end of his political obedience to avoid: war is the failure of politics. Hence there can be no political obligation either to die or to fight. Obligation disappears in the presence of death or of the fear of death.[1]

Fighting, however, is not the same as dying and therefore Hobbes's discussion of the obligation of soldiers poses difficulties not present in the discussion of prisoners—difficulties which need to be examined in some detail. When war begins, the political authorities, instead of protecting their subjects, invite their subjects, in Hobbes's words,

---

[1] These negative assertions can be sustained, I believe, whatever positive view one takes as to the place of moral obligation in Hobbes's philosophy.

"to protect their protection."[1] This request is an admission of failure and can best be described by paraphrasing a line from Brecht's *Mother Courage*: only a bad sovereign needs brave subjects. Nevertheless, Hobbes argues that subjects are obligated to defend their society as long as they are able. They may not be "able" for very long, of course, since "by nature" they will choose to defend themselves first. Indeed, when they protect their protection they are doing nothing more than defending themselves, and so they cannot protect their protection after their protection ceases to protect them. At that point, it ceases to be their protection. The state has no value over and above the value of the lives of the concrete individuals whose safety it provides. No man has a common life to defend, but only an individual life. And so Hobbes's injunction has very narrow limits and obligates men to a very narrow range of actions. An individual can be obligated to contribute financially to the defense of the state; he may be obligated to engage in military exercises and demonstrations for the sake of deterrence, or even to march bravely off to battle, still hoping to frighten the enemy by his stalwart and resplendent appearance. But it is difficult to see how, in Hobbes's terms, he can be obligated actually to fight. For, if he loses his life while protecting his protection, he loses everything there is to lose and saves nothing.

Once again, however, risking one's life is not the same as losing it, and it might be said even of Hobbesian men that they can be bound (can bind themselves) to take certain limited and foreknown risks for the sake of a secure social life. The difficulty here is that the limits of such risks, expressed as the statistical probability of dying or of facing death in battle, have a timeless and general application: they describe the individual as a nameless member of society living at no particular moment. But then there comes a more precise time when a particular man finds himself or thinks he finds himself face-to-face with death. Hobbes insists that whatever the commitments made earlier such a man

at such a time is morally free to do whatever he is driven to do by his fear. He cannot foreswear that freedom (in any degree) because he cannot know in advance the point at which the fear of death will strike him. Now many of us in everyday life and discourse make "special allowances" for individuals who run or hide or surrender under the strain of battle and imminent death. Soldiers normally are expected to surrender rather than be killed. But Hobbes makes this "special allowance" into the central theme of his philosophical system. Recognizing the power of the fear of death (or of physical pain) is not for him a way of excusing actions that violate previous commitments; it is a way of delimiting the moral world: beyond this point there are no commitments. Still, the practical consequences of the two positions are not so different, and the extent to which "special allowance" has become a cultural imperative suggests the triumph of Hobbesianism in the modem world.

When a frightened man refuses to fight or runs away when battle begins, then, he does not break faith with the state; he does nothing unjust. The crucial passage is this one:

> A man that is commanded as a soldier to fight against the enemy, though his sovereign have right enough to punish his refusal with death, may nevertheless in many cases refuse, without injustice.... When armies fight, there is on one side, or both, a running away, yet when they do it, not out of treachery, but fear, they are not esteemed to do it unjustly, but dishonorably.[2]

It is important to stress immediately that Hobbes does not say that all men will run away. Only some men ("of feminine courage") will do so. The others are presumably bound to fight since they have not been moved by their fear to refuse. This is the only difference I have been able to discover in Hobbes's theory between the acceptance of death and the acceptance of the risk of death: the first is auto-

---

[1] Thomas Hobbes, *Leviathan*, pt. II, chap. 29.

[2] Hobbes, *Leviathan*, chap. 21.

matically void; the second is subject to private re-evaluation of the risks involved and to unilateral annulment. Such an annulment may in fact be morally wrong if it has any other reason than the fear of death. Only God, however, can know its reasons; men must grant the rights of the fearful to all who claim them. The use of the word "punish" is therefore technically incorrect, for a man cannot be punished for acting "without injustice." As in the case of the prison guard and the escaped prisoner, the cowardly soldier and his sovereign are simply returned to the state of nature. This is the radical argument that Hobbes makes: faced with death or with the spectre of death, any man may reclaim his natural rights.

He immediately suggests two exceptions to this far-reaching assertion, however. First, he argues that individuals who have enlisted in an army or accepted press money (a kind of enlistment after the fact) are obligated to fight. The obligation here is not really political, since the individual is presumably bound by his military oath, and this is an ordinary contract, subsequent to and different from the social contract. Nor is the mercenary or impressed soldier obligated by Hobbes to make his oath the motive of his fighting. Plunder and pay, presumably his original motives, will suffice to motivate the fighting. Nevertheless, this first exception does not seem consistent with Hobbes's general theory, and it is worth suggesting just why it is not. If a soldier admitted that the acceptance of money or even the taking of an oath obligated him to kill and be killed, he would be turning himself into a mere instrument of the state or of the mercenary captain who hires him and utterly destroying himself as a Hobbesian person, that is, as a man who fears death. An individual can sell his labor to another, and a soldier can also, but he can neither sell nor give away his right of self-defense. That is an inalienable right, and it must include the right, under certain circumstances, to run away. Individual bodily security is the only ultimate in Hobbes's system and the search for that security can never be forsaken or transcended. In fact, then, for Hobbes there can be no obligation to die of any sort. The critique of

political obligation is also a critique of all forms of ultimate obligation, though by no means, as we have just seen, an unequivocal critique.

Hobbes's second exception is more precisely political in character and brings us to the very heart of the whole problem of political dying. After asserting the obligation of enlisted soldiers, he writes (chapter 21):

> when the defense of the commonwealth requires at once the help of all that are able to bear arms, everyone is obliged; because otherwise the institution of the commonwealth, which they have not the purpose or the courage to preserve, was in vain.

The most obvious, the most Hobbesian, response to this is simply: if a man dies defending the commonwealth, its institution, from his point of view, was equally in vain. Only if the destruction of the commonwealth involves the certain death of all its citizens could it be said that those citizens should (or perhaps better, must) risk their lives in its defense. Hobbes, however, seems to say more than this; he seems to say that unless men are actually willing to fight, even when defeat would not involve certain death, the commonwealth will not long survive. Either a man obligates himself to risk his life when contracting to form society or in the act of contracting he contradicts himself. Society must be an agreement to die if necessary in order to live together in safety as long as possible, for otherwise it is not possible to live in safety at all. Now that is palpably not what the Hobbesian contract is. Instead, it is an agreement to live together in safety as long as possible and to disband whenever group safety is no longer possible and allow each individual to face the risks of nature alone. Hobbes's second exception is so obviously inconsistent with his general theory that it would hardly be worth considering if it did not raise, indirectly, a very crucial question: can a man be morally bound to take into account the possible long-term consequences of such an act as running away? More important, can a man be morally bound to consider what would happen if every other man acted as he did?

Hobbes is here very close, I think, to a more explicit argument of Spinoza's, put forward in *The Ethics* as proof of the proposition: "The free man never acts fraudulently, but always in good faith."[1] Spinoza goes on:

> If it be asked: What should a man's conduct be in a case where he could by breaking faith free himself from the danger of present death? Would not his plan of self-preservation completely persuade him to deceive? This may be answered by pointing out that, if reason persuaded him to act thus, it would persuade all men to act in a similar manner, in which case reason would persuade men not to agree in good faith to unite their forces, or to have laws in common, that is, not to have any general laws, which is absurd.

If one man breaks faith, all will do so, and the commonwealth will collapse. Hobbes's argument is weaker, since he is really not talking about breaking faith. His argument would go like this: one man's cowardice leads to cowardly behavior on the part of all men, and so destroys the commonwealth. Therefore, a man ought to control his fearfulness and so maintain his obligations and preserve the commonwealth which he helped to found, and if he is unwilling or unable to do this, he has no business founding commonwealths in the first place. It is not, perhaps, a moral argument (given Hobbes's psychology it is barely a comprehensible argument), yet it is common enough in the history of theory and may well have a point. In any case, it suggests the great difficulty of Hobbes's political philosophy. One man's cowardice kills society, and yet, by virtue of the instinct for self-preservation and the fundamental law of nature, all men have a right to be cowards. The very existence of the state seems to require some limit upon the right of self-preservation, and yet the state is nothing more than an instrument designed to fulfill that right.

"The essence of the contradiction inherent in patriotism," writes Simone Weil, "is that one's country is something limited whose demands are unlimited."[2] But not all states are limited in the same way or to the same degree. The contradiction so apparent in Hobbes is missing entirely in the *Crito*, chiefly, I think, because the Athenian state had other, more extensive purposes than the preservation of individual life. Socrates was asked to die for the common life, or rather, he was told to die because he had no right to do any damage whatsoever to the common life: "are you going ... to overturn us ... *as far as in you lies*?" His escape would be criminal even if the overthrow of the Athenian state did not lie within his power—as it certainly did not. But Hobbes and Spinoza cannot say that citizens are forbidden to damage the common life; they are driven to the logically extremist argument that any individual's breach of faith or cowardly flight in some sense entails everyone else's breach of faith and cowardly flight and then the collapse of society: and therefore contradicts his own previous political acts and endangers his own life. The breach and the flight, motivated presumably by terrible fear of death, are wrong because they eventually lead to death or to terrible fear. But the obvious reply to this is Hobbes's own: "for man by nature chooseth the lesser evil, which is danger of death ... rather than the greater, which is certain and present death."

If society is indeed an agreement to die, then Hobbesian men can form society only through a kind of mutual deceit. The commonwealth may not endure if its citizens all run away in battle, but that only means that it would be irrational for them to tell one another that they are likely to run away. Kant's requirement of publicity might well turn the Hobbesian contract into an absurd contradiction. Nevertheless, in a moment of personal crisis, faced

---

[1] Baruch Spinoza, *The Ethics* (trans. R.H.M. Elwes, [(London: George Bell and Sons, 1901)]), pt. IV, proposition lxxii, proof.

[2] Simone Weil, *The Need for Roots*, trans. Arthur Wills [(London: Routledge and Kegan Paul, 1952)], p. 157.

with the danger of violent death, each individual legitimately makes his own decision, without consulting either the public authorities or his fellow citizens, since neither government nor society offers him any salvation. There is no reason for him to assume, he is in fact most unlikely to assume, that his cowardly flight entails the cowardly flight of all other men. But what if it does? What fears can the breakdown of society hold for an individual faced with immediate danger—an individual moreover who came into society only to avoid such danger? The empirical fact (I am not at the moment questioning it) that society will not endure unless men risk their lives on its behalf cannot obligate a particular man to risk his life at a particular time. Only if something more is said than either Hobbes or Spinoza say about the nature of political society will the obligation conceivably follow.

Much of what I have just argued about Hobbes is true also of all those later liberal theorists who retain his individualist foundations—even when they give up, as Spinoza had already given up, his narrow emphasis upon bodily security and the fear of violent death. John Locke, because of the peculiarly collectivist formulation he gives to the fundamental law of nature, is able to reassert an obligation to die, but the reassertion seems inconsistent with the general pattern of his political thought.[1] For any theory which, like Locke's, begins with the absolute independence of freely willing individuals and goes on to treat politics and the state as instrumental to the achievement of individual purposes would seem by its very nature incapable of describing ultimate obligation. This is certainly true when individual purposes reach no further than bodily safety or physical welfare or the appropriation and enjoyment of physical objects. Then "the preservation of the city," as the young Hegel wrote, "can only be important to [its citizens] as a means to the preservation of their property and its enjoyment. Therefore, to expose themselves to the danger of death would be to do something ridiculous, since the means, death, would forthwith annul the end, property and enjoyment."[2]

Once they have freed themselves from Hobbesian fearfulness, liberal writers can, of course, describe various kinds of ethical (not political) dying. Moved by love, sympathy, or friendship, men in liberal society can and obviously do incur ultimate obligations. They may even find themselves in situations where they are or think they are obligated to risk their lives to defend the state which defends in its turn the property and enjoyment of their friends or families. But if they then actually risk their lives or die, they do so because they have incurred private obligations which have nothing to do with politics. The state may shape the environment within which these obligations are freely incurred, and it may provide the occasions and the means for their fulfillment. But this is only to say that, when states make war and men fight, the reasons of the two often are and ought to be profoundly different. Indeed, the great advantage of liberal society may simply be this: that no one can be asked to die for public reasons or on behalf of the state.

A good society might, however, be defined in precisely opposite terms: as one worth dying for, whose citizens actually are obligated to risk their lives for public reasons. This, I think, is Rousseau's definition, and it represents a return to the argument of the *Crito*. At first glance, however, Rousseau seems to offer only a rather obtuse version of the Hobbesian position.

The social treaty has for its end the preservation of the contracting parties. He who wills the end wills the means also, and the means must involve some risks, and even some losses. He who wishes to preserve his life at others' expense should also, when it is necessary, be ready to give it up for their sake. Furthermore, the citizen is no longer the judge of the dangers to which the law desires

---

[1] John Locke, *The Second Treatise of Government*, pars. 6 and 139. The argument is by no means clear.

[2] G.W.F. Hegel, *Early Theological Writings*, trans. T.M. Knot (Chicago[: University of Chicago Press], 1948), p. 165 (*The Positivity of the Christian Religion*).

him to expose himself, and when the prince says to him: "It is expedient for the State that you should die," he ought to die, because it is only on that condition that he has been living in security up to the present, and because his life is no longer a mere bounty of nature, but a gift made conditionally by the state.[1]

This is surely untenable as it stands, for several reasons. First, a man fundamentally interested in self-preservation can never give up the right to judge the peril to which he is exposed, for that would be to surrender his interest in self-preservation. Second, men who associate solely to preserve their individual lives cannot then be obligated to die on each other's behalf. What a man does when he signs the social contract is to turn the others into means to his own safety. If he makes any moral commitment at all, it is simply to obey the sovereign as long as they do and as long as his life is not endangered. Finally, by his contract the citizen has exchanged his natural freedom for his security in society. His obedience is now the price of his security, and he pays, so to speak, as he goes. He cannot be obligated to make a further exchange and give his life for such security as he has already enjoyed—and already paid for.

But Rousseau's politics is not really based upon self-preservation or upon any absolute interest in security, property, welfare, or happiness. Indeed, he rejects interests of this sort precisely because they cannot serve as the basis of an obligation to die.

> Self-interest, so they say, induces each of us to agree for the common good. But ... does a man go to death from self-interest? No doubt each man acts for his own good, but if there is no such thing as moral good to be taken into consideration, self-interest will

only enable you to account for the deeds of the wicked.[2]

Nor is Rousseau's politics in any simple sense contractualist. What he calls the social contract represents less an exchange than a moral transformation, and this transformation depends less on the separate wills of the individuals involved than on the quality of the collective will that they together create. All this is suggested, I think, by the words with which Rousseau concludes the long defense of voluntary death which I quoted above: "because his life is no longer a mere bounty of nature, but a gift made conditionally by the state." The reference here might be to nothing more than that Hobbesian security that the state provides, but in the light of the body of Rousseau's work, it is more plausible to argue that the words "bounty" and "gift" refer to two different kinds of life and that a qualitative change has occurred in the transition from nature to the state. Into the state, according to this interpretation, a man brings the life which he has received from the bounty of nature and which is wholly his own. From the state, that is, from the shared experiences and general will of the political community, he receives a second life, a moral life, which is not his sole possession, but whose reality depends upon the continued existence of his fellow-citizens and of their association. Thus Rousseau: "At once, in place of the individual personality of each contracting party, [the] act of association creates a moral and collective body."[3] And again:

> The passage from the state of nature to the civil state produces a very remarkable change in man by substituting justice for instinct in his conduct [that is, the obligation to die for self-preservation] and giving his actions the morality they had previously lacked.[4]

[1] Jean-Jacques Rousseau, *The Social Contract*, bk. 11, chap. 5. (All quotations from *The Social Contract* are from the G.D.H. Cole translation [(London: J.M. Dent, 1913)].

[2] Jean-Jacques Rousseau, *Emile*, trans. Barbara Foxley (London: J.M. Dent, 1911), p. 252.

[3] Rousseau, *Social Contract*, bk. 1, chap. 6.

[4] Ibid., chap. 8.

A good society is one in which the new man, a moral member of a moral body, achieves his fullest development. The very instincts of pre-social man are overwhelmed and above all the instinct for self-preservation. When the state is in danger, its citizens rush to its defense, forgetful of all personal danger. They die willingly for the sake of the state, not because the state protects their lives—which would be, as Hegel argued, absurd—but because the state is their common life. So long as the state survives, something of the citizen lives on, even after the natural man is dead. The state, or rather, the common life of the citizens, generates those "moral goods" for which, according to Rousseau, men can in fact be obligated to die. The character of the political community obligates the citizen who participates in it to die on its behalf and it simultaneously provides him with a motive for dying. Once again, Hegel has stated the point most clearly: in the society of egotists, he argued,

> death, the phenomenon which demolishes the whole structure of [the individual's] purposes and the activity of his entire life, must ... become something terrifying....
> But the republican's whole soul was in the republic; the republic survived him, and there hovered before his mind the thought of its immortality.[1]

I want to stress those last three words: of *its* immortality—and not his own. The republican citizen may well dream of glory and eternal renown, but that is not his most important dream. Many of Rousseau's contemporaries among the *philosophes* were as eager as he was to produce citizens loyal unto death, patriotic soldiers on the model of the Spartans at Thermopylae or the Roman Horatio. But since they believed that society had been formed, to quote Diderot's friend, Paul Holbach, only in order to maintain its members "in the advantages of their nature," they could not admit an obligation they thought so obviously against

nature. "To overcome the instinct for self-preservation," wrote Holbach, "... a special courage is necessary, and not all citizens are capable of such courage." The state must seek to persuade its soldiers to risk their lives by "feeding the ardor" of its young men and promising glory to its heroes. But it cannot with justice force men into the army or soldiers into battle.[2] As I suggested earlier, the hope for glory generates no obligation. Men cannot be bound to seek a secular immortality, nor would such a search necessarily lead them to serve the state. The Rousseauian republic does not claim, then, to be an eternal shrine to the memory of its heroes; it claims something more: to be the totality of their present existence. Its collapse does not merely deprive them of glory, nor of bodily security, nor even of life itself; it is literally a fate worse than death, a fate undreamt of in Hobbes's philosophy. "If the citizen is alone," writes Rousseau, "he is nothing; if he has no more country, he has no existence; and if he is not dead, he is worse than dead."[3]

Now this is, even in Rousseau's terms, overstated. For Rousseau knew very well that the transformation of natural man into citizen is never complete. Instinct and nature survive; the ego defends and aggrandizes itself. The general will of the community, which speaks for the common life, is always in conflict with the particular wills of the individual members. Rousseau's political theory is designed to give the communal being supremacy over the natural egotist, while recognizing that in fact a tension always exists between the two. This supremacy is most dramatically manifest when the state says to the natural man: die! He ought then to die, and if he does not, he can be forced to die, just as he can be "forced to be free." Obviously, however, he cannot be forced to die, though he can be put to death, *for the sake of the state.* The resort to

---

[1] Hegel, *Early Theological Writings*, p. 157.

[2] Paul Holbach, *La Politique naturelle* (London, 1773), I, 190.

[3] Jean-Jacques Rousseau, *Considerations on the Government of Poland*, chap. 4, in *Political Writings*, trans. Frederick Watkins (Edinburgh[: Thomas Nelson and Sons], 1953).

punishment is an admission of the failure of political transformation: "in putting the guilty to death we slay not so much a citizen as an enemy."[1]

Hobbes might have said the same thing, but there is a crucial and revealing difference here between the two theorists. For Hobbes, the guilty man would be killed as an enemy of the sovereign and of the sovereign only, and he would be killed by natural right, that is, by the right of self-defense. There is no political right to punish in Hobbes, no right generated by the social contract, no right of collective defense vested in the community as a whole.[2] In Rousseau, on the other hand, a guilty man is an enemy of the state, an enemy of the people. But perhaps "enemy" is not the best word for Rousseau's purposes. The domestic criminal and the wartime deserter were once citizens of the state, themselves committed to its preservation. They have "broken the social treaty," they are "rebels" and "traitors," fallen members. They can now be put to death (as enemies cannot be) by virtue of their own previous consent, and they can only rightfully be put to death because they have previously consented.[3] The right to punish derives from the universally recognized need to defend the common life. This, at any rate, is Rousseau's claim, and I think it suggests the great difficulty of his theory of ultimate obligation. Let me approach that difficulty cautiously.

In general, the political obligation to die implies the political right to punish, though it need not imply the vesting of that right in any man or group of men. One can imagine a society so confident of the moral transformation of its members that it leaves their punishment to themselves: it patiently awaits the suicide of its criminals and traitors, certain that their actions are only temporary aberrations and that they will return to reason and then die by their own hand. In his study of crime in primitive Melanesia, Malinowski describes such a society. There individuals publicly accused of certain crimes, chiefly violations of the sexual taboos, and knowing themselves to be guilty, actually commit suicide. They do so, however, only if they have been publicly accused, and their suicide is more a socially expected response to personal dishonor than it is an example of political obligation—though Malinowski does insist upon the element of self-punishment in the act.[4] In a way, the Greeks with their hemlock were closer to that primitive society than to us with our guillotines and gas-chambers. Here Rousseau is a modern. He anticipates that there will be traitors and rebels who will have to be put to death, and this is to admit that the moral transformation of the citizens is not entirely successful. If we go just a step further and imagine a case where it is not successful at all, then there is a very obvious defense that a man might offer when he refuses to die at the state's command.

"Look at me," he might say, "an unreconstructed egotist. I have lived among you, but never shared in your common life. I do not attend your meetings; I do not rejoice at your festivals. The image of the immortality of your state never dances before my eyes. If this state should collapse, I am certain that I will make out well enough in the next; but I am less sure about this world and the next, and so I have determined to save my skin at all costs. I shall not fight in your wars, and if I am driven into battle, I shall hide or run away. If you come to kill me, I shall struggle against you with all the force at my command."

Now Rousseau argues at one point in *The Social Contract* that any man who lives in the state must be regarded as a member.[5] But this seems a woefully inadequate criterion for moral membership; it is surely not obvious that every resident shares

[1] Rousseau, *Social Contract*, bk. 11, chap. 7.

[2] See *Leviathan*, pt. 11, chap. 28: "For the subjects did not give the sovereign that right; but only in laying down theirs, strengthened him to use his own."

[3] Captured enemies cannot be put to death; they are "merely men, whose life no one has any right to take" (*Social Contract*, bk. 1, chap. 4).

[4] Bronislaw Malinowski, *Crime and Custom in Savage Society* (London[: Routledge and Kegan Paul], 1926), pp. 85–100.

[5] Bk. 1, chap. 5.

in the "moral goods" of the political community, even if he shares in the material goods that the state provides. If we insist upon anything more than residence, however, then the unreconstructed egotist that I have just quoted must be called a noncitizen (a resident alien, perhaps, though not necessarily in the strict legal sense), and it follows necessarily that he cannot be called a traitor or rebel if he refuses to die on behalf of the state. Since he has never shared in civic life, the state has no right to kill him (unless the political authorities claim a natural right to do so) and he has no obligation to die. He is, so to speak, a Hobbesian man loose in a Rousseauian society.

This will surely be the condition of many men in Rousseau's or in any other society and especially of many of those who refuse to defend the political community in time of war. They are not fallen members, but political strangers. Such men are not necessarily without any obligations at all. They need not be *moral* strangers, like the anti-hero of Camus's novel, for it may be that they are egotists only with regard to the political community, not with regard to every other community. They may share in some other common life. Insofar as Hobbes is describing an association of such men (loyal, perhaps, to their families, but literally devoid of any more extensive commitment, self-consciously exchanging limited obedience for benefits received in the political world), he is perfectly correct to insist that there can be no ultimate obligation. A political stranger can never be morally bound, or rightly forced, to risk his life for the state.

How, then, do men cease to be strangers? How do they create and recognize those moral goods for which political dying is conceivable? I am not sure, but I am sure that no man can be obligated to die unless he admits or has at some time in the past admitted that such moral goods actually exist. There is a crucially important sense in which the obligation to die can only be stated in the first person singular. For this reason, both Plato in the *Crito* and Rousseau in all his major works are driven to contractualist arguments. The individual's contract is obviously not a founding act; nor, I think, is it

simply a solemn promise upon which all subsequent obligation is based—for that would not meet Hobbes's argument that the promise to die is different from all other promises. Rather, the contract must involve some acknowledgment of the reality of the common life and of the moral transformation which it makes possible. I think, also, that the contract must be acted out, the common life must be lived, before it can be said to generate ultimate obligation. Consent must be given over time. Thus Socrates' contract includes all his politically relevant actions right up to the moment of his condemnation, and these actions are listed by the Laws: born in the city and educated there, when he came of age he chose to stay; he married and raised children in the city; he fought in the army, participated in the assembly, argued in the streets, held public office. At any point he could have left, renouncing his accumulating obligations. Even after his condemnation, he could have chosen exile as his punishment. Now he can no longer choose, now he is bound to die, but his whole life has been a choice.

All this comes dangerously near to suggesting that a man is obligated to die only if he feels or thinks himself obligated. That seems to be the consequence of arguing first, with Rousseau, that there are moral goods for which a man might well be bound to die, and arguing secondly, against Rousseau, that it is never possible to say that a particular man is bound to die for a particular moral good (unless he has said so himself). But it is surely not the case that being and feeling obligated are the same. It is not enough that a common life be felt or thought to exist; there must be a common life. I do not mean to defend all those nationalistic or ideological mystifications that lead men to believe they are living in a community when in fact they are not. Men are bound by their significant actions, not by their feelings or thoughts; action is the crucial language of moral commitment. Socrates is bound because he chose to act like a citizen in a world where citizenship was morally significant. Up to some point in the history of his actions, he might have changed his mind. After that, he had "spoken" and egotism was no longer his right. This suggests that, when men are called upon to face death for the state, an assertion is always being made, and when young men are called a presumption is being made (both of which are subject to critical examination) about the very character and quality of their lives. The assertion or presumption is that they have chosen or will choose, and also that they can choose, to live like citizens.

DISCUSSION QUESTIONS

1. It is D-Day. You are on a transport about to be unloaded on to Normandy Beach. However, you see a way of escaping to a boat in the rear that does not contain landing forces. According to Hobbes, as presented by Walzer, are you obligated to charge onto the beach? Explain.

2. Same scenario as in (1). According to Rousseau, as presented by Walzer, are you obligated to charge onto the beach? Explain.

3. Same scenario as in (1). Do *you* think that you are obligated to charge on to the beach? Explain.

94

Thomas Nagel, "War and Massacre" (1979)

Thomas Nagel (b.1937) is a University Professor of Philosophy and Law at New York University. His work in philosophy of mind, ethics, and political philosophy is well known. In the following selection, Nagel argues that there are what he calls "absolutist" moral restrictions on the conduct of warfare.

SOURCE

Nagel, Thomas. *Mortal Questions*, excerpt from Chapter 10, "War and Massacre." Copyright © 1979 Cambridge University Press. Reprinted with the permission of Cambridge University Press.

From the apathetic reaction to atrocities committed in Vietnam by the United States and its allies, one may conclude that moral restrictions on the conduct of war command almost as little sympathy among the general public as they do among those charged with the formation of U.S. military policy.[1] Even when restrictions on the conduct of warfare are defended, it is usually on legal grounds alone: their moral basis is often poorly understood. I wish to argue that certain restrictions are neither arbitrary nor merely conventional, and that their validity does not depend simply on their usefulness. There is, in other words, a moral basis for the rules of war, even though the conventions now officially in force are far from giving it perfect expression.

I

No elaborate moral theory is required to account for what is wrong in cases like the Mylai massacre, since it did not serve, and was not intended to serve, any strategic purpose. Moreover, if the participation of the United States in the Indo-Chinese war is entirely wrong to begin with, then that engagement is incapable of providing a justification for *any* measures taken in its pursuit—not only for the measures which are atrocities in every war, however just its aims.

---

[1] This essay was completed in 1971. Direct U.S. involvement in the Vietnam War lasted from 1961 to 1973. Hence the present tense.

But this war has revealed attitudes of a more general kind, that influenced the conduct of earlier wars as well. After it has ended, we shall still be faced with the problem of how warfare may be conducted, and the attitudes that have resulted in the specific conduct of this war will not have disappeared. Moreover, similar problems can arise in wars or rebellions fought for very different reasons, and against very different opponents. It is not easy to keep a firm grip on the idea of what is not permissible in warfare, because while some military actions are obvious atrocities, other cases are more difficult to assess, and the general principles underlying these judgments remain obscure. Such obscurity can lead to the abandonment of sound intuitions in favor of criteria whose rationale may be more obvious. If such a tendency is to be resisted, it will require a better understanding of the restrictions than we now have.

I propose to discuss the most general moral problem raised by the conduct of warfare: the problem of means and ends. In one view, there are limits on what may be done even in the service of an end worth pursuing—and even when adherence to the restriction may be very costly. A person who acknowledges the force of such restrictions can find himself in acute moral dilemmas. He may believe, for example, that by torturing a prisoner he can obtain information necessary to prevent a disaster, or that by obliterating one village with bombs he can halt a campaign of terrorism. If he believes that the gains from a certain measure will clearly outweigh its costs, yet still suspects that he ought not to adopt it, then he is in a dilemma produced by the conflict between two disparate categories of moral reason: categories that may be called *utilitarian* and *absolutist*.

Utilitarianism gives primacy to a concern with what will *happen*. Absolutism gives primacy to a concern with what one is *doing*. The conflict between them arises because the alternatives we face are rarely just choices between *total outcomes*: they are also choices between alternative pathways or measures to be taken. When one of the choices is to do terrible things to another person, the problem is

altered fundamentally; it is no longer merely a question of which outcome would be worse.

Few of us are completely immune to either of these types of moral intuition, though in some people, either naturally or for doctrinal reasons, one type will be dominant and the other suppressed or weak. But it is perfectly possible to feel the force of both types of reason very strongly; in that case the moral dilemma in certain situations of crisis will be acute, and it may appear that every possible course of action or inaction is unacceptable for one reason or another.

II

Although it is this dilemma that I propose to explore, most of the discussion will be devoted to its absolutist component. The utilitarian component is straightforward by comparison, and has a natural appeal to anyone who is not a complete skeptic about ethics. Utilitarianism says that one should try, either individually or through institutions, to maximize good and minimize evil (the definition of these categories need not enter into the schematic formulation of the view), and that if faced with the possibility of preventing a great evil by producing a lesser, one should choose the lesser evil. There are certainly problems about the formulation of utilitarianism, and much has been written about it, but its intent is morally transparent. Nevertheless, despite the addition of various refinements, it continues to leave large portions of ethics unaccounted for. I do not suggest that some form of absolutism can account for them all, only that an examination of absolutism will lead us to see the complexity, and perhaps the incoherence, of our moral ideas.

Utilitarianism certainly justifies *some* restrictions on the conduct of warfare. There are strong utilitarian reasons for adhering to any limitation which seems natural to most people—particularly if the limitation is widely accepted already. An exceptional measure which seems to be justified by its results in a particular conflict may create a precedent with disastrous long-term effects. It may even be argued that war involves violence on such a scale that it is never justified on utilitarian grounds—the consequences of refusing to go to war will never be as bad as the war itself would be, even if atrocities were not committed. Or in a more sophisticated vein it might be claimed that a uniform policy of never resorting to military force would do less harm in the long run, if followed consistently, than a policy of deciding each case on utilitarian grounds (even though on occasion particular applications of the pacifist policy might have worse results than a specific utilitarian decision). But I shall not consider these arguments, for my concern is with reasons of a different kind, which may remain when reasons of utility and interest fail.

In the final analysis, I believe that the dilemma cannot always be resolved. While not every conflict between absolutism and utilitarianism creates an insoluble dilemma, and while it is certainly right to adhere to absolutist restrictions unless the utilitarian considerations favoring violation are overpoweringly weighty and extremely certain—nevertheless, when that special condition is met, it may become impossible to adhere to an absolutist position. What I shall offer, therefore, is a somewhat qualified defense of absolutism. I believe it underlies a valid and fundamental type of moral judgment—which cannot be reduced to or overridden by other principles. And while there may be other principles just as fundamental, it is particularly important not to lose confidence in our absolutist intuitions, for they are often the only barrier before the abyss of utilitarian apologetics for large-scale murder.

III
One absolutist position that creates no problems of interpretation is pacifism: the view that one may not kill another person under any circumstances, no matter what good would be achieved or evil averted thereby. The type of absolutist position that I am going to discuss is different. Pacifism draws the conflict with utilitarian considerations very starkly. But there are other views according to which violence may be undertaken, even on a large scale, in a clearly just cause, so long as certain absolute restrictions on the character and direction of that

violence are observed. The line is drawn somewhat closer to the bone, but it exists.

The philosopher who has done most to advance contemporary philosophical discussion of such a view, and to explain it to those unfamiliar with its extensive treatment in Roman Catholic moral theology, is G.E.M. Anscombe. In 1958 Miss Anscombe published a pamphlet entitled *Mr. Truman's Degree*,[1] on the occasion of the award by Oxford University of an honorary doctorate to Harry Truman. The pamphlet explained why she had opposed the decision to award that degree, recounted the story of her unsuccessful opposition, and offered some reflections on the history of Truman's decision to drop atom bombs on Hiroshima and Nagasaki, and on the difference between murder and allowable killing in warfare. She pointed out that the policy of deliberately killing large numbers of civilians either as a means or as an end in itself did not originate with Truman, and was common practice among all parties during World War II for some time before Hiroshima. The Allied area bombings of German cities by conventional explosives included raids which killed more civilians than did the atomic attacks; the same is true of certain fire-bomb raids on Japan.

The policy of attacking the civilian population in order to induce an enemy to surrender, or to damage his morale, seems to have been widely accepted in the civilized world, and seems to be accepted still, at least if the stakes are high enough. It gives evidence of a moral conviction that the deliberate killing of noncombatants—women, children, old people—is permissible if enough can be gained by it. This follows from the more general position that any means can in principle be justified if it leads to a sufficiently worthy end. Such an attitude is evident not only in the more spectacular current weapons systems but also in the day-to-day conduct of the nonglobal war in Indo-China: the indiscriminate

---

[1] (Privately printed.) See also her essay "War and Murder," in *Nuclear Weapons and Christian Conscience*, ed. Walter Stein (London: The Merlin Press, 1961). The present paper is much indebted to these two essays throughout.

destructiveness of antipersonnel weapons, napalm, and aerial bombardment; cruelty to prisoners; massive relocation of civilians; destruction of crops; and so forth. An absolutist position opposes to this the view that certain acts cannot be justified no matter what the consequences. Among those acts is murder—the deliberate killing of the harmless: civilians, prisoners of war, and medical personnel.

In the present war such measures are sometimes said to be regrettable, but they are generally defended by reference to military necessity and the importance of the long-term consequences of success or failure in the war. I shall pass over the inadequacy of this consequentialist defense in its own terms. (That is the dominant form of moral criticism of the war, for it is part of what people mean when they ask, "Is it worth it?") I am concerned rather to account for the inappropriateness of offering any defense of that kind for such actions.

Many people feel, without being able to say much more about it, that something has gone seriously wrong when certain measures are admitted into consideration in the first place. The fundamental mistake is made there, rather than at the point where the overall benefit of some monstrous measure is judged to outweigh its disadvantages, and it is adopted. An account of absolutism might help us to understand this. If it is not allowable to *do* certain things, such as killing unarmed prisoners or civilians, then no argument about what will happen if one doesn't do them can show that doing them would be all right.

Absolutism does not, of course, require one to ignore the consequences of one's acts. It operates as a limitation on utilitarian reasoning, not as a substitute for it. An absolutist can be expected to try to maximize good and minimize evil, so long as this does not require him to transgress an absolute prohibition like that against murder. But when such a conflict occurs, the prohibition takes complete precedence over any consideration of consequences. Some of the results of this view are clear enough. It requires us to forgo certain potentially useful military measures, such as the slaughter of hostages and prisoners or indiscriminate attempts

to reduce the enemy civilian population by starvation, epidemic infectious diseases like anthrax and bubonic plague, or mass incineration. It means that we cannot deliberate on whether such measures are justified by the fact that they will avert still greater evils, for as intentional measures they cannot be justified in terms of any consequences whatever.

Someone unfamiliar with the events of this century might imagine that utilitarian arguments, or arguments of national interest, would suffice to deter measures of this sort. But it has become evident that such considerations are insufficient to prevent the adoption and employment of enormous antipopulation weapons once their use is considered a serious moral possibility. The same is true of the piecemeal wiping out of rural civilian populations in airborne antiguerrilla warfare. Once the door is opened to calculations of utility and national interest, the usual speculations about the future of freedom, peace, and economic prosperity can be brought to bear to ease the consciences of those responsible for a certain number of charred babies.

For this reason alone it is important to decide what is wrong with the frame of mind which allows such arguments to begin. But it is also important to understand absolutism in the cases where it genuinely conflicts with utility. Despite its appeal, it is a paradoxical position, for it can require that one refrain from choosing the lesser of two evils when that is the only choice one has. And it is additionally paradoxical because, unlike pacifism, it permits one to do horrible things to people in some circumstances but not in others.

IV

Before going on to say what, if anything, lies behind the position, there remain a few relatively technical matters which are best discussed at this point.

First, it is important to specify as clearly as possible the kind of thing to which absolutist prohibitions can apply. We must take seriously the proviso that they concern what we deliberately do to people. There could not, for example, without incoherence, be an absolute prohibition against *bringing about* the death of an innocent person. For one may find oneself in a situation in which, no matter what one does, some innocent people will die as a result. I do not mean just that there are cases in which someone will die no matter what one does, because one is not in a position to affect the outcome one way or the other. That, it is to be hoped, is one's relation to the deaths of most innocent people. I have in mind, rather, a case in which someone is bound to die, but who it is will depend on what one does. Sometimes these situations have natural causes, as when too few resources (medicine, lifeboats) are available to rescue everyone threatened with a certain catastrophe. Sometimes the situations are man-made, as when the only way to control a campaign of terrorism is to employ terrorist tactics against the community from which it has arisen. Whatever one does in cases such as these, some innocent people will die as a result. If the absolutist prohibition forbade doing what would result in the deaths of innocent people, it would have the consequence that in such cases nothing one could do would be morally permissible.

This problem is avoided, however, because what absolutism forbids is *doing* certain things to people, rather than bringing about certain *results*. Not everything that happens to others as a result of what one does is something that one has *done* to them. Catholic moral theology seeks to make this distinction precise in a doctrine known as the law of double effect, which asserts that there is a morally relevant distinction between bringing about the death of an innocent person deliberately, either as an end in itself or as a means, and bringing it about as a side effect of something else one does deliberately. In the latter case, even if the outcome is foreseen, it is not murder, and does not fall under the absolute prohibition, though of course it may still be wrong for other reasons (reasons of utility, for example). Briefly, the principle states that one is sometimes permitted knowingly to bring about as a side effect of one's actions something which it would be absolutely impermissible to bring about deliberately as an end or as a means. In application to war or revolution, the law of double effect permits a certain amount of civilian carnage as a side effect of

bombing munitions plants or attacking enemy soldiers. And even this is permissible only if the cost is not too great to be justified by one's objectives.

However, despite its importance and its usefulness in accounting for certain plausible moral judgments, I do not believe that the law of double effect is a generally applicable test for the consequences of an absolutist position. Its own application is not always clear, so that it introduces uncertainty where there need not be uncertainty.

In Indo-China, for example, there is a great deal of aerial bombardment, strafing, spraying of napalm, and employment of pellet- or needle-spraying antipersonnel weapons against rural villages in which guerrillas are suspected to be hiding, or from which small-arms fire has been received. The majority of those killed and wounded in these aerial attacks are reported to be women and children, even when some combatants are caught as well. However, the government regards these civilian casualties as a regrettable side effect of what is a legitimate attack against an armed enemy.

It might be thought easy to dismiss this as sophistry: if one bombs, burns, or strafes a village containing a hundred people, twenty of whom one believes to be guerrillas, so that by killing most of them one will be statistically likely to kill most of the guerrillas, then isn't one's attack on the group of one hundred a *means* of destroying the guerrillas, pure and simple? If one makes no attempt to discriminate between guerrillas and civilians, as is impossible in an aerial attack on a small village, then one cannot regard as a mere side effect the deaths of those in the group that one would not have bothered to kill if more selective means had been available.

The difficulty is that this argument depends on one particular description of the act, and the reply might be that the means used against the guerrillas is not: killing everybody in the village—but rather: obliteration bombing of the *area* in which the twenty guerrillas are known to be located. If there are civilians in the area as well, they will be killed as a side effect of such action.[1]

---

[1] This counter-argument was suggested by Rogers Albritton.

Because of casuistical problems like this, I prefer to stay with the original, unanalyzed distinction between what one does to people and what merely happens to them as a result of what one does. The law of double effect provides an approximation to that distinction in many cases, and perhaps it can be sharpened to the point where it does better than that. Certainly the original distinction itself needs clarification, particularly since some of the things we do to people involve things happening to them as a result of other things we do. In a case like the one discussed, however, it is clear that by bombing the village one slaughters and maims the civilians in it. Whereas by giving the only available medicine to one of two sufferers from a disease, one does not kill the other, even if he dies as a result.

The second technical point to take up concerns a possible misinterpretation of this feature of the position. The absolutist focus on actions rather than outcomes does not merely introduce a new, outstanding item into the catalogue of evils. That is, it does not say that the worst thing in the world is the deliberate murder of an innocent person. For if that were all, then one could presumably justify one such murder on the ground that it would prevent several others, or ten thousand on the ground that they would prevent a hundred thousand more. That is a familiar argument. But if this is allowable, then there is no absolute prohibition against murder after all. Absolutism requires that we *avoid* murder at all costs, not that we *prevent* it at all costs. [...]

... [L]et me remark on a frequent criticism of absolutism that depends on a misunderstanding. It is sometimes suggested that such prohibitions depend on a kind of moral self-interest, a primary obligation to preserve one's own moral purity, to keep one's hands clean no matter what happens to the rest of the world. If this were the position, it might be exposed to the charge of self-indulgence. After all, what gives one man a right to put the purity of his soul or the cleanness of his hands above the lives or welfare of large numbers of other people? It might be argued that a public servant like Truman has no right to put himself first in that way;

therefore if he is convinced that the alternatives would be worse, he must give the order to drop the bombs, and take the burden of those deaths on himself, as he must do other distasteful things for the general good.

But there are two confusions behind the view that moral self-interest underlies moral absolutism. First, it is a confusion to suggest that the need to preserve one's moral purity might be the *source* of an obligation. For if by committing murder one sacrifices one's moral purity or integrity, that can only be because there is *already* something wrong with murder. The general reason against committing murder cannot therefore be merely that it makes one an immoral person. Secondly, the notion that one might sacrifice one's moral integrity justifiably, in the service of a sufficiently worthy end, is an incoherent notion. For if one were justified in making such a sacrifice (or even morally required to make it), then one would not be sacrificing one's moral integrity by adopting that course: one would be preserving it.

Moral absolutism is not unique among moral theories in requiring each person to do what will preserve his own moral purity in all circumstances. This is equally true of utilitarianism, or of any other theory which distinguishes between right and wrong. Any theory which defines the right course of action in various circumstances and asserts that one should adopt that course, *ipso facto* asserts that one should do what will preserve one's moral purity, simply because the right course of action is what will preserve one's moral purity in those circumstances. Of course utilitarianism does not assert that this is *why* one should adopt that course, but we have seen that the same is true of absolutism.

V

It is easier to dispose of false explanations of absolutism than to produce a true one. A positive account of the matter must begin with the observation that war, conflict, and aggression are relations between persons. The view that it can be wrong to consider merely the overall effect of one's actions on the general welfare comes into prominence when those actions involve relations with others. A man's acts usually affect more people than he deals with directly, and those effects must naturally be considered in his decisions. But if there are special principles governing the manner in which he should *treat* people, that will require special attention to the particular persons toward whom the act is directed, rather than just to its total effect.

Absolutist restrictions in warfare appear to be of two types: restrictions on the class of persons at whom aggression or violence may be directed and restrictions on the manner of attack, given that the object falls within that class. These can be combined, however, under the principle that hostile treatment of any person must be justified in terms of something *about that person* which makes the treatment appropriate. Hostility is a personal relation, and it must be suited to its target. One consequence of this condition will be that certain persons may not be subjected to hostile treatment in war at all, since nothing about them justifies such treatment. Others will be proper objects of hostility only in certain circumstances, or when they are engaged in certain pursuits. And the appropriate manner and extent of hostile treatment will depend on what is justified by the particular case.

A coherent view of this type will hold that extremely hostile behavior toward another is compatible with treating him as a person—even perhaps as an end in himself. This is possible only if one has not automatically stopped treating him as a person as soon as one starts to fight with him. If hostile, aggressive, or combative treatment of others always violated the condition that they be treated as human beings, it would be difficult to make further distinctions on that score *within* the class of hostile actions. That point of view, on the level of international relations, leads to the position that if complete pacifism is not accepted, no holds need be barred at all, and we may slaughter and massacre to our hearts' content, if it seems advisable. Such a position is often expressed in discussions of war crimes.

But the fact is that ordinary people do not believe this about conflicts, physical or otherwise,

between individuals, and there is no more reason why it should be true of conflicts between nations. There seems to be a perfectly natural conception of the distinction between fighting clean and fighting dirty. To fight dirty is to direct one's hostility or aggression not at its proper object, but at a peripheral target which may be more vulnerable, and through which the proper object can be attacked indirectly. This applies in a fist fight, an election campaign, a duel, or a philosophical argument. If the concept is general enough to apply to all these matters, it should apply to war—both to the conduct of individual soldiers and to the conduct of nations.

Suppose that you are a candidate for public office, convinced that the election of your opponent would be a disaster, that he is an unscrupulous demagogue who will serve a narrow range of interests and seriously infringe the rights of those who disagree with him; and suppose you are convinced that you cannot defeat him by conventional means. Now imagine that various unconventional means present themselves as possibilities: you possess information about his sex life which would scandalize the electorate if made public; or you learn that his wife is an alcoholic or that in his youth he was associated for a brief period with a proscribed political party, and you believe that this information could be used to blackmail him into withdrawing his candidacy; or you can have a team of your supporters flatten the tires of a crucial subset of his supporters on election day; or you are in a position to stuff the ballot boxes; or, more simply, you can have him assassinated. What is wrong with these methods, given that they will achieve an overwhelmingly desirable result?

There are, of course, many things wrong with them: some are against the law; some infringe the procedures of an electoral process to which you are presumably committed by taking part in it; very importantly, some may backfire, and it is in the interest of all political candidates to adhere to an unspoken agreement not to allow certain personal matters to intrude into a campaign. But that is not all. We have in addition the feeling that these measures, these methods of attack are *irrelevant* to the issue between you and your opponent, that in taking them up you would not be directing yourself to that which makes him an object of your opposition. You would be directing your attack not at the true target of your hostility, but at peripheral targets that happen to be vulnerable.

The same is true of a fight or argument outside the framework of any system of regulations or law. In an altercation with a taxi driver over an excessive fare, it is inappropriate to taunt him about his accent, flatten one of his tires, or smear chewing gum on his windshield; and it remains inappropriate even if he casts aspersions on your race, politics, or religion, or dumps the contents of your suitcase into the street.

The importance of such restrictions may vary with the seriousness of the case; and what is unjustifiable in one case may be justified in a more extreme one. But they all derive from a single principle: that hostility or aggression should be directed at its true object. This means both that it should be directed at the person or persons who provoke it and that it should aim more specifically at what is provocative about them. The second condition will determine what form the hostility may appropriately take.

It is evident that some idea of the relation in which one should stand to other people underlies this principle, but the idea is difficult to state. I believe it is roughly this: whatever one does to another person intentionally must be aimed at him as a subject, with the intention that he receive it as a subject. It should manifest an attitude to *him* rather than just to the situation, and he should be able to recognize it and identify himself as its object. The procedures by which such an attitude is manifested need not be addressed to the person directly. Surgery, for example, is not a form of personal confrontation but part of a medical treatment that can be offered to a patient face to face and received by him as a response to his needs and the natural outcome of an attitude toward *him*.

Hostile treatment, unlike surgery, is already addressed *to* a person, and does not take its interpersonal meaning from a wider context. But hostile acts can serve as the expression or implementation of only a limited range of attitudes to the person who is attacked. Those attitudes in turn have as objects certain real or presumed characteristics or activities of the person which are thought to justify them. When this background is absent, hostile or aggressive behavior can no longer be intended for the reception of the victim as a subject. Instead it takes on the character of a purely bureaucratic operation. This occurs when one attacks someone who is not the true object of one's hostility—the true object may be someone else, who can be attacked through the victim; or one may not be manifesting a hostile attitude toward anyone, but merely using the easiest available path to some desired goal. One finds oneself not facing or addressing the victim at all, but operating on him—without the larger context of personal interaction that surrounds a surgical operation.

If absolutism is to defend its claim to priority over considerations of utility, it must hold that the maintenance of a direct interpersonal response to the people one deals with is a requirement which no advantages can justify one in abandoning. The requirement is absolute only if it rules out any calculation of what would justify its violation. I have said earlier that there may be circumstances so extreme that they render an absolutist position untenable. One may find then that one has no choice but to do something terrible. Nevertheless, even in such cases absolutism retains its force in that one cannot claim *justification* for the violation. It does not become *all right*.

As a tentative effort to explain this, let me try to connect absolutist limitations with the possibility of justifying *to the victim* what is being done to him. If one abandons a person in the course of rescuing several others from a fire or a sinking ship, one *could* say to him, "You understand, I have to leave you to save the others." Similarly, if one subjects an unwilling child to a painful surgical procedure, one can say to him, "If you could understand, you would realize that I am doing this to help you." One could *even* say, as one bayonets an enemy soldier, "It's either you or me." But one cannot really say while torturing a prisoner, "You understand, I have to pull out your fingernails because it is absolutely essential that we have the names of your confederates"; nor can one say to the victims of Hiroshima, "You understand, we have to incinerate you to provide the Japanese government with an incentive to surrender."

This does not take us very far, of course, since a utilitarian would presumably be willing to offer justifications of the latter sort to his victims, in cases where he thought they were sufficient. They are really justifications to the world at large, which the victim, as a reasonable man, would be expected to appreciate. However, there seems to me something wrong with this view, for it ignores the possibility that to treat someone else horribly puts you in a special relation to him, which may have to be defended in terms of other features of your relation to him. The suggestion needs much more development; but it may help us to understand how there may be requirements which are absolute in the sense that there can be no justification for violating them. If the justification for what one did to another person had to be such that it could be offered to him specifically, rather than just to the world at large, that would be a significant source of restraint.

If the account is to be deepened, I would hope for some results along the following lines. Absolutism is associated with a view of oneself as a small being interacting with others in a large world. The justifications it requires are primarily interpersonal. Utilitarianism is associated with a view of oneself as a benevolent bureaucrat distributing such benefits as one can control to countless other beings, with whom one may have various relations or none. The justifications it requires are primarily administrative. The argument between the two moral attitudes may depend on the relative priority of these two conceptions.

VI

Some of the restrictions on methods of warfare which have been adhered to from time to time are to be explained by the mutual interests of the involved parties: restrictions on weaponry, treatment of prisoners, etc. But that is not all there is to it. The conditions of directness and relevance which I have argued apply to relations of conflict and aggression apply to war as well. I have said that there are two types of absolutist restrictions on the conduct of war: those that limit the legitimate targets of hostility and those that limit its character, even when the target is acceptable. I shall say something about each of these. As will become clear, the principle I have sketched does not yield an unambiguous answer in every case.

First let us see how it implies that attacks on some people are allowed, but not attacks on others. It may seem paradoxical to assert that to fire a machine gun at someone who is throwing hand grenades at your emplacement is to treat him as a human being. Yet the relation with him is direct and straightforward. The attack is aimed specifically against the threat presented by a dangerous adversary, and not against a peripheral target through which he happens to be vulnerable but which has nothing to do with that threat. For example, you might stop him by machine-gunning his wife and children, who are standing nearby, thus distracting him from his aim of blowing you up and enabling you to capture him. But if his wife and children are not threatening your life, that would be to treat them as means with a vengeance.

This, however, is just Hiroshima on a smaller scale. One objection to weapons of mass annihilation—nuclear, thermonuclear, biological, or chemical—is that their indiscriminateness disqualifies them as direct instruments for the expression of hostile relations. In attacking the civilian population, one treats neither the military enemy nor the civilians with that minimal respect which is owed to them as human beings. This is clearly true of the direct attack on people who present no threat at all. But it is also true of the character of the attack on those who *are* threatening you, viz., the government and military forces of the enemy. Your aggression is directed against an area of vulnerability quite distinct from any threat presented by them which you may be justified in meeting. You are taking aim at them through the mundane life and survival of their countrymen, instead of aiming at the destruction of their military capacity. And of course it does not require hydrogen bombs to commit such crimes.

This way of looking at the matter also helps us to understand the importance of the distinction between combatants and noncombatants, and the irrelevance of much of the criticism offered against its intelligibility and moral significance, According to an absolutist position, deliberate killing of the innocent is murder, and in warfare the role of the innocent is filled by noncombatants. This has been thought to raise two sorts of problems: first, the widely imagined difficulty of making a division, in modern warfare, between combatants and noncombatants; second, problems deriving from the connotation of the word "innocence."

Let me take up the latter question first.[1] In the absolutist position, the operative notion of innocence is not moral innocence, and it is not opposed to moral guilt. If it were, then we would be justified in killing a wicked but noncombatant hairdresser in an enemy city who supported the evil policies of his government, and unjustified in killing a morally pure conscript who was driving a tank toward us with the profoundest regrets and nothing but love in his heart. But moral innocence has very little to do with it, for in the definition of murder "innocent" means "currently harmless," and it is opposed not to "guilty" but to "doing harm." It should be noted that such an analysis has the consequence that in war we may often be justified in killing people who do not deserve to die, and unjustified in killing people who do deserve to die, if anyone does.

So we must distinguish combatants from noncombatants on the basis of their immediate threat or harmfulness. I do not claim that the line is a sharp one, but it is not so difficult as is often supposed to place individuals on one side of it or the other. Children are not combatants even though they may join the armed forces if they are allowed to grow up. Women are not combatants just because

they bear children or offer comfort to the soldiers. More problematic are the supporting personnel, whether in or out of uniform, from drivers of munitions trucks and army cooks to civilian munitions workers and farmers. I believe they can be plausibly classified by applying the condition that the prosecution of conflict must direct itself to the cause of danger, and not to what is peripheral. The threat presented by an army and its members does not consist merely in the fact that they are men, but in the fact that they are armed and are using their arms in the pursuit of certain objectives. Contributions to their arms and logistics are contributions to this threat; contributions to their mere existence as men are not. It is therefore wrong to direct an attack against those who merely serve the combatants' needs as human beings, such as farmers and food suppliers, even though survival as a human being is a necessary condition of efficient functioning as a soldier.

This brings us to the second group of restrictions: those that limit what may be done even to combatants. These limits are harder to explain clearly. Some of them may be arbitrary or conventional, and some may have to be derived from other sources; but I believe that the condition of directness and relevance in hostile relations accounts for them to a considerable extent.

Consider first a case which involves both a protected class of noncombatants and a restriction on the measures that may be used against combatants. One provision of the rules of war which is universally recognized, though it seems to be turning into a dead letter in Vietnam, is the special status of medical personnel and the wounded in warfare. It might be more efficient to shoot medical officers on sight and to let the enemy wounded die rather than be patched up to fight another day. But someone with medical insignia is supposed to be left alone and permitted to tend and retrieve the wounded. I believe this is because medical attention is a species of attention to completely general human needs, not specifically the needs of a combat soldier, and our conflict with the soldier is not with his existence as a human being.

[1] What I say on this subject derives from [G.E.M.] Anscombe.

By extending the application of this idea, one can justify prohibitions against certain particularly cruel weapons: starvation, poisoning, infectious diseases (supposing they could be inflicted on combatants only), weapons designed to maim or disfigure or torture the opponent rather than merely to stop him. It is not, I think, mere casuistry to claim that such weapons attack the men, not the soldiers. The effect of dum-dum bullets, for example, is much more extended than necessary to cope with the combat situation in which they are used. They abandon any attempt to discriminate in their effects between the combatant and the human being. For this reason the use of flame-throwers and napalm is an atrocity in all circumstances that I can imagine, whoever the target may be. Burns are both extremely painful and extremely disfiguring—far more than any other category of wound. That this well-known fact plays no (inhibiting) part in the determination of U.S. weapons policy suggests that moral sensitivity among public officials has not increased markedly since the Spanish Inquisition.

Finally, the same condition of appropriateness to the true object of hostility should limit the scope of attacks on an enemy country: its economy, agriculture, transportation system, and so forth. Even if the parties to a military conflict are considered to be not armies or governments but entire nations (which is usually a grave error), that does not justify one nation in warring against every aspect or element of another nation. That is not justified in a conflict between individuals, and nations are even more complex than individuals, so the same reasons apply. Like a human being, a nation is engaged in countless other pursuits while waging war, and it is not in those respects that it is an enemy.

The burden of the argument has been that absolutism about murder has a foundation in principles governing all one's relations to other persons, whether aggressive or amiable, and that these principles, and that absolutism, apply to warfare as well, with the result that certain measures are impermissible no matter what the consequences. I do not mean to romanticize war. It is sufficiently

utopian to suggest that when nations conflict they might rise to the level of limited barbarity that typically characterizes violent conflict between individuals, rather than wallowing in the moral pit where they appear to have settled, surrounded by enormous arsenals.

VII

Having described the elements of the absolutist position, we must now return to the conflict between it and utilitarianism. Even if certain types of dirty tactics become acceptable when the stakes are high enough, the most serious of the prohibited acts, like murder and torture, are not just supposed to require unusually strong justification. They are supposed *never* to be done, because no quantity of resulting benefit is thought capable of *justifying* such treatment of a person.

The fact remains that when an absolutist knows or believes that the utilitarian cost of refusing to adopt a prohibited course will be very high, he may hold to his refusal to adopt it, but he will find it difficult to feel that a moral dilemma has been satisfactorily resolved. The same may be true of someone who rejects an absolutist requirement and adopts instead the course yielding the most acceptable consequences. In either case, it is possible to feel that one has acted for reasons insufficient to justify violation of the opposing principle. In situations of deadly conflict, particularly where a weaker party is threatened with annihilation or enslavement by a stronger one, the argument for resorting to atrocities can be powerful, and the dilemma acute.

There may exist principles, not yet codified, which would enable us to resolve such dilemmas. But then again there may not. We must face the pessimistic alternative that these two forms of moral intuition are not capable of being brought together into a single, coherent moral system, and that the world can present us with situations in which there is no honorable or moral course for a man to take, no course free of guilt and responsibility for evil.

The idea of a moral blind alley is a perfectly intelligible one. It is possible to get into such a situation by one's own fault, and people do it all the time. If, for example, one makes two incompatible promises or commitments—becomes engaged to two people, for example—then there is no course one can take which is not wrong, for one must break one's promise to at least one of them. Making a clean breast of the whole thing will not be enough to remove one's reprehensibility. The existence of such cases is not morally disturbing, however, because we feel that the situation was not unavoidable: one had to do something wrong in the first place to get into it. But what if the world itself, or someone else's actions, could face a previously innocent person with a choice between morally abominable courses of action, and leave him no way to escape with his honor? Our intuitions rebel at the idea, for we feel that the constructibility of such a case must show a contradiction in our moral views. But it is not in itself a contradiction to say that someone can do X or not do X, and that for him to take either course would be wrong. It merely contradicts the supposition that *ought* implies *can*—since presumably one ought to refrain from what is wrong, and in such a case it is impossible to do so.[1] Given the limitations on human action, it is naïve to suppose that there is a solution to every moral problem with which the world can face us. We have always known that the world is a bad place. It appears that it may be an evil place as well.

---

[1] This was first pointed out to me by Christopher Boorse. The point is also made in E.J. Lemmon's "Moral Dilemmas," *Philosophical Review* LXXI (April 1962): 150.

DISCUSSION QUESTIONS

1. Nagel says that the absolutist, as opposed to the utilitarian, forbids "*doing* certain things to people, rather than bringing about certain *results*." Explain what he means.

2. Explain the two types of restriction in warfare. How, according to Nagel, must either of these two types of restriction be justified? Explain. How does this connect to the distinction between fighting clean and fighting dirty? Illustrate with Nagel's example of the election campaign.

3. Clearly state and explain Nagel's absolutist principle. How does this principle apply to the bombing of Hiroshima? Explain. How does Nagel attempt to defend this principle? Do you find his defense compelling? Why or why not?

4. Nagel claims that the deliberate killing of noncombatants in war is wrong. How does he distinguish combatants from noncombatants? How does he justify his claim that killing noncombatants is wrong? Evaluate his argument.

5. Nagel claims that there are absolutist restrictions on how we may treat even those who are combatants. Explain his claim and how he tries to defend it. Evaluate his argument.

95

Tomis Kapitan, "Can Terrorism Be Justified?" (2009)

Tomis Kapitan is professor of philosophy at Northern Illinois University. In addition to his work on international ethics, he has published in the areas of metaphysics and philosophy of language. He is the author (along with Raja Halwani) of *The Israeli-Palestinian Conflict: Philosophical Essays on Self-Determination, Terrorism, and the One-State Solution*. Here Kapitan addresses the question of whether the use of terrorist violence is ever justified.

SOURCE

Kapitan, Tomis. "Can Terrorism Be Justified?" Unpublished manuscript, copyright © 2009 by Tomis Kapitan. Reprinted by permission of the author.

1. The Difficulty in Posing the Question

To justify terrorism seems an impossible task. The dominant view is that acts of terrorism are wrong, a presumption that is virtually unquestioned within the mainstream media, governmental agencies, and scholarly studies around the world. There is ample reason to concur. As usually understood, terrorism is violence directed against those who are not themselves directly involved in carrying out military operations, notably, civilians. Extending the familiar moral guidelines of just war theory to all political violence, terrorism appears to directly violate one of its central norms, namely, the *jus in bello* principle of discrimination according to which attacks on noncombatants are prohibited.

Yet, there are at least two reasons to pause before embracing this conclusion. In the first place, terrorism is as ancient as organized warfare itself, emerging as soon as one society, pitted against another in the quest for land, resources, or domination, was moved by a desire for vengeance, or found advantages in military operations against noncombatants or other "soft" targets. It is sanctioned within holy scriptures,[1] and has been part of the genesis of independent states and the expansion of empires from the inception of recorded history. The United States itself emerged through the

[1] In the Bible, for example, such violence is mandated in Numbers 33:50–56 and 1 Samuel 15:1–3.

systematic ethnic cleansing of native Americans, a nearly 300-year campaign that featured the destruction of homes and crops, the theft of land, forced expulsions, massacres, and tears.[1] In the past 70 years, U.S. politicians have sanctioned bombings in Japan, Germany, Korea, Vietnam, Cambodia, Iraq, and Afghanistan that have knowingly taken the lives of hundreds of thousands of civilians, actions that have been supported by substantial numbers of U.S. citizens.

Such violence is not always called "terrorism," nor are its perpetrators identified as "terrorists," and this brings me to the second reason for hesitating before condemning terrorism, namely, the fact that a rhetoric of "terror" has emerged which has obscured serious philosophical thought about this mode of violence. Within it, the terms "terrorism" and "terrorist" have acquired an intensely negative connotation as well as an egocentric character whereby they are used to describe actions and persons to whom the speaker is politically opposed but never the actions of oneself and one's allies. So, few people will admit to supporting, planning, or committing terrorism, preferring to use other terms to describe the violence in question. Of course, neither feature is grounds for moral opprobrium; terms like "enemy," "stranger," "foreigner" also harbor a degree of negativity and egocentrism, but they apply to everyone, saint and sinner alike.

Yet, even when these points are understood, they do little to reduce the powerful impact that the rhetoric of "terror" has had upon our thinking. The negative connotation runs so deep that affixing the "terrorist" label to individuals or groups automatically places them outside the norms of acceptable social and political behavior, portraying them

as "evil" people that cannot be reasoned with. As a consequence, the rhetoric of "terror" serves not only to discredit those who are charged with terrorism but also, to

- dehumanize any individuals or groups described as "terrorist";
- erase any incentive an audience might have to understand their point of view so that questions about the nature and origins of their grievances and the possible legitimacy of their demands are never raised;
- deflect attention away from one's own policies that might have contributed to their grievances;
- erase the distinction between national liberation movements and fringe fanatics;
- repudiate any calls to negotiate with those labeled "terrorist" and, instead, pave the way for the use of force and violence in dealing with them.[2]

While some might think that terrorists deserve to be so discredited, the problem is that the rhetoric is effective enough to preclude a more patient discussion of the historical circumstances from which

---

[1] See the descriptions in Brown (1970), Churchill (1997), and Mann (2005). Holy scriptures were not far from the minds of those Americans who supported atrocities against native Americans. In 1794, George Henry Loskiel wrote that the American settlers "represented the Indians as Canaanites who without mercy ought to be destroyed from the face of the earth, and considered America as the land of promise given to the Christians" (cited in Mann 2005, 151).

[2] Noam Chomsky has made the point vividly: "... the term 'terrorism' is commonly used as a term of abuse, not accurate description. It is close to a historical universal that our terrorism against them is right and just (whoever we happen to be), while their terrorism against us is an outrage. As long as that practice is adopted, discussion of terrorism is not serious. It is no more than a form of propaganda and apologetics" (interview Number 5 with Chomsky on Znet at www.znet.com, accessed on September 7, 2005). Elsewhere (Kapitan 2003), I have advocated a stronger thesis: namely, that the rhetoric of "terror" is itself a terrorist tool that states avail themselves of. The "terrorist" label is a means of characterizing a certain group so as to dehumanize them, portray them as irrational beings devoid of any moral sense and beyond all norms. In so doing, governments find it easier to deflect criticisms of their own policies, and to justify military responses that deface the distinction between agents of terrorist actions and the populations from which they emerge. The logic of the strategy is simple: *to get away with a crime, demonize your victims.*

acts of terrorism have arisen, much less to raise the difficult issues of appropriate response and possible justification.[1]

To complicate matters, the semantically unwarranted perspectivalism of the "terrorist" label means that it is not consistently employed. Just ask yourself: who gets described as a "terrorist"? All and only those who commit violence against civilians to achieve political ends? Guess again. In fact, the answer depends on where you are and to whom you are listening. If you are tuned into the mainstream U.S. media, or into the various agencies of the U.S. government, or, for that matter, into the statements of virtually any government and their associated media, it quickly becomes apparent that the term "terrorism" is ascribed selectively. When our political opponents commit acts such as those mentioned we readily label it "terrorism" and the perpetrators "terrorists," but if we or our allies engage in similar sorts of activity we use different terms, e.g., "retaliation" or "counter-terrorism" to describe their acts. If the agents are a sub-national group we approve of, then we use "freedom-fighters" to describe them.

A few examples should suffice to make the point. Some of the violence directed against civilians that were committed by sub-national groups include attacks upon civilians in Nicaragua by the U.S. financed "contra" rebels of the 1980s that claimed several thousand civilian lives, the massacre of over 2,000 Palestinian civilians by the Israeli-supported members of Lebanese militias in the Sabra and Shatilla refugee camps in Beirut in 1982, and the massacre of Bosnian civilians in the mid-1990s. None of these atrocities were labeled as acts of "terrorism" by the mainstream media or by western governments.

If we broaden our scope and examine overt actions committed by states, there are numerous examples that are not usually labeled as "terrorist" even though they qualify as such under definitions that allow for state terrorism. These include Israel's invasion of the Gaza Strip in December 2008-January 2009, its massive incursions into the West Bank in the spring of 2002, and its bombardment of Lebanon in the summers of 1982 and 2006.[2] Other governmental armed forces have engaged in similar actions, for example, the U.S.

---

[1] In a detailed study of eighteen suicide terrorism campaigns and 315 attacks from 1980–2003, Robert Pape concluded that desires for national self-determination and an end to military occupation were at the root of every instance of this form of terrorism (Pape 2005, 79). In chapter 5, Pape wrote that groups such as Hamas, Islamic Jihad, Hezbollah, and the Tamil Tigers, began with more conventional guerrilla operations against military targets, but after these operations proved ineffective, they resorted to suicide attacks which proved successful in coercing governments to negotiate.

[2] According to Palestinian estimates, 1434 Palestinians were killed during Israel's invasion of Gaza, 960 of whom were civilians, including at least 121 women and 288 children. The Israeli military contests this figure but has not made its own analysis available for review. UN investigators gave the total number of dead as 1,440, saying of these 431 were children and 114 women. In a filmed testimony and written statements, more than two dozen soldiers told an Israeli army veterans' group that they forced Palestinian civilians to serve as human shields, needlessly killed unarmed Gazans and improperly used white phosphorus shells to burn down buildings as part of Israel's three-week military offensive in the Gaza Strip last winter [2009] (see http://www.reuters.com/article/middleeast-Crisis/idUSLN537222, accessed on July 15, 2009). Again, the first three years of the Israeli crackdown during the Al Aqsa Intifada claimed the lives of 2600 Palestinians, three-quarters of whom were noncombatants. These figures have been compiled from various sources, including the Israeli Ministry of Defense at www.israel-mfa.gov.il, the Israeli human rights group, B'tselem, at www.btselem.org, the Palestine Monitor at www.palestinemonitor.org, and Miftah at www.miftah.org. In the 1982 Israeli invasion of Lebanon, between 17,000–20,000 Lebanese and Palestinians lost their lives, the majority of whom were civilians (Hirst 2003, 569; Fisk 2005, 268). The Reagan Administration, despite its support of the Israeli invasion, imposed a six-year ban on cluster-weapon sales to Israel in 1982, after a Congressional investigation found that Israel had used the weapons in civilian areas. Despite this, Israel employed cluster bombs again in southern Lebanon in the summer of 2006, "pretty much everywhere—in villages, at road junctions, in olive groves and on banana plantations" ("Israel May Have Violated Arms Pact, Officials Say," *The New York Times*, January 28, 2007).

bombing of Fallujah and other Iraqi cities in 2004,[1] the destruction of Grozny by Russian forces during the Chechnya war in 1999, the Syrian army's attack on the city of Hama in the spring of 1982, and the Indonesian invasion and occupation of East Timor from 1975–1998. This violence pales in comparison to more large-scale campaigns such as the U.S. bombing of North Vietnam and Cambodia during the Vietnam War, or the Allied bombing of German and Japanese cities near the end of WWII. From March to August 1945, for example, nearly 800,000 Japanese civilians were killed in U.S. air raids against Japan's 62 largest cities, with about 85,000 of these dying on March 9, 1945, the first day of the bombing in Tokyo. Again, the word "terrorism" is rarely applied to violence against civilians on this scale.

The inconsistencies of usage and the politically-charged rhetoric of "terror" aside, the fact remains that there is a peculiar mode of political violence

that has come to be referred to as "terrorism" in scholarly discussions as well as in mainstream media and political rhetoric. Whether its perpetrators are non-state agents or governmental militias, questions about its legitimacy are vitally important to moral discussions about violence and war. Other terms could be used in its place, but given the precedence, I will not shy away from using the terms "terrorism" and "terrorist" in what follows. As long as we fix our terminology, employ it consistently, and remain aware of the politically-charged rhetorical uses of the terms "terrorist" and "terrorism," we can confront the ethical questions about the justification of terrorism in a more rational manner.

2. What Is Terrorism?

Despite the danger of being misled by the rhetoric of "terror," there is a real phenomenon of terrorism that merits our attention. Among the various questions that can be asked about it are the following:

> What is terrorism?
> Why would anyone engage in terrorism?
> Are any terrorist actions justifiable?

My concern here is with the last of these questions, though it is nearly impossible to answer it apart from addressing the first two.

There is a surprising amount of disagreement about the very meaning of the term "terrorism." It is sometimes used so broadly as to become synonymous with "coercion" or "coercive intimidation," hence, no different from "violence" (Wilkinson 1986, 51; Primoratz 2004a, 16). Often, an explicit definition is not even attempted—perhaps deliberately, to conceal inconsistency—and even a cursory glance at the relevant literature reveals that there is no single universally accepted definition of the term. Even the various agencies of the U.S.

---

[1] In January 2005, the Iraq Body Count Database website at http://www.iraqbodycount.org/database/ reported that up to 31,676 Iraqi civilians were killed in the first two years of the American invasion, actions by the U.S. military forces accounting for a sizeable percentage of this total. John Pilger reports that in May 2004, American forces killed approximately 600 civilians in Fallujah, "a figure far greater than the total number of civilians killed by the 'insurgents' during the past year. The generals were candid; this futile slaughter was an act of revenge for the killing of three American mercenaries" (Pilger 2004). See also Pilger's "What is the Difference Between Their 'Terrorism' and our 'War'?" at www.axisoflogic.com/artman/publish/article_19213.shtml, which reports that after the American siege of Fallujah in November 2004, 60–70 percent of all buildings had been damaged enough to render them uninhabitable. The full force of America's arsenal, including F-16s, C-130s, Abrams tanks, and Apache Helicopters were unleashed on a few thousand rebels in a civilian enclave that contained at least 50,000 residents according to Red Cross estimates at the time. Among the 1,200 Iraqis killed in the first week of the siege, at least 800 were civilians (Jamail 2004), and some estimate that the final total of Iraqis killed in Fallujah was 6,000 (see www.dahrjamailiraq.com, and www.afsc.org/pwork/0412/041204.htm).

Government are not united.[1] While lack of a clear definition need not be a problem for rhetorical purposes, policy-making, legislation, and scholarship about terrorism require greater clarity in order to identify the phenomenon, justify ascriptions, and motivate moral judgments. Otherwise, how can we determine which actions and agents are "terrorist" and which are not? How else can we fashion policies and statutes to deal with what some regard as a fundamental challenge to world peace? How else could proponents of a "war on terror" identify the enemy and justify their actions?

While it is to some extent arbitrary how we define terms that we choose to use in our arguments, we cannot make much headway without some agreed-upon definition, and it is helpful to respect ordinary usage in such a way that secures the label for widely acknowledged instances of terrorism. Most writers on the topic agree that terrorism is,

(i) a deliberate use or threat of violence,
(ii) politically-motivated, and
(iii) directed against non-military personnel, that is, against civilians or noncombatants.

Taking these as the only essential features of terrorism, perhaps the simplest and most accurate reportive definition is this:

Terrorism is deliberate politically-motivated violence, or the threat of such, directed against civilians.[2]

Several points must be addressed to clarify this standard definition of "terrorism."

First, where "violence" refers to any coercive action or policy that causes physical or mental harm, then violence is politically-motivated if caused by desires to achieve political goals, where those desires might be those of the agent *or* those of others whose actions have moved the agent to react. This allows that action born out of frustration over a political situation, brought about by others pursuing their political agendas, is politically-motivated even if the agent does not act from a plan within which terrorism is a means to a definite political goal.

Second, there are different types of terrorism depending on facts about the agents and about the modes and mechanisms whereby harm is carried out. One contrast is that terrorism is *strategic* if employed to achieve a political goal, but *reactive* if it derives from an emotional response to politically induced grievances, e.g., anger, outrage, desire

---

[1] The U.S. State Department (www.state.gov) takes its definition from Title 22 of the *United States Code*, Section 2656f(d): "The term 'terrorism' means premeditated, politically motivated violence perpetrated against noncombatant targets by sub-national groups or clandestine agents, usually intended to influence an audience. (The term 'noncombatant' is interpreted to include, in addition to civilians, military personnel who at the time of the incident are unarmed or not on duty.)" The FBI (www.fbi.gov/publish/terror/terrusa.html) offers this definition: "Terrorism is the unlawful use of force and violence against person or property to intimidate or coerce a government, the civilian population, or any segment thereof, in further of political or social objectives." The U.S. Defense Department (www.periscope.usni.com/demo/termst0000282.html) says something similar: "Terrorism is the unlawful use or threatened use of force or violence against individuals or property to coerce or intimidate governments or societies, often to achieve political, religious, or ideological objectives."

[2] Compare *Wikipedia* : "Terrorism is the intentional use or threat to use violence against civilians and non-combatants 'in order to achieve political goals'" (accessed July 9, 2009). Similar definitions can be found in several sources, e.g., Garnor (2001), Coady (2004c), and Netanyahu (2001). In Article 2(b) of its *International Convention for the Suppression of the Financing of Terrorism* (May 5, 2004), the United Nations provided this definition of terrorism: "any act intended to cause death or serious bodily harm to a civilian or non-combatants, or to any other person not taking an active part in the hostilities in a situation of armed conflict, when the purpose of such an act by its nature or context, is to intimidate a population, or to compel a government or an international organization to do or to abstain from doing any act." An interesting list of definitions of "terrorism" appears in Best and Nocella (2004, 9–13).

for vengeance, despair. Since strategy and emotion can be jointly operative, and actions can have multiple agents, a given act might manifest both modes of violence. A second contrast concerns the causal route whereby harm is inflicted. *Direct terrorism* consists in assault or an immediate threat to do so, for example, killing someone or giving the orders to do so. But violence can also be committed by other means, say, by imprisoning people, depriving them of clean water, food, or necessary medical supplies, destroying their shelters, or damaging the institutional fabric of their society, e.g., hospitals, schools, factories and businesses. States, in particular, accomplish such *structural terrorism* by forcibly implementing—or impeding—institutions, laws, policies, and practices that result in harm to noncombatants.

Third, the term "civilian" is ambiguous. In the widest sense, "civilian" designates any person who is not a member of a state's military organizations. In a narrower sense, "civilian" applies to all and only those who are not members of any militia, be it a state militia or a non-state militia. Terrorism is also defined in terms of the broader notion of noncombatant, where a combatant is someone who is actively engaged in carrying out military operations—as distinct from the cooks and medics that might also serve in a military organization, or soldiers home on furlough. I will use "civilian" in the narrower sense—those who play no role in a military organization—but my argument applies even if "terrorism" is defined in terms of violence directed against noncombatants.

Fourth, the occurrence of "deliberate" implies that the perpetrator is intentionally using or threatening violence to achieve political objectives *and* is identifying the victims *as* civilians. But while the combination of "deliberate" with the phrase "directed against" suggests that actual or threatened violence is *intentional*, harm to civilians might be incidental to the main aim of a terrorist action, say, to destroy property, to gain attention, or to provoke a government's response. For example, if the attacks on the World Trade Center towers were aimed solely at provoking an American military action, as some contend, then, while harm to civilians was foreseen and deliberate, it might not have been viewed as essential to the action plan intended, and if so, it was not itself intentional. What was intentional was destroying those buildings in order to engage the U.S. militarily in the Middle East, not killing civilians, though the latter was a foreseen consequence of what was intended. This is why I do not want to define "terrorism" in terms of *targeting* civilians where targeting implies intentionally harming. But even if one insists that intentional harm to civilians is essential to terrorism, it need not be the primary objective of the act. Some distinguish the *primary targets* of terrorism, viz., those whom the perpetrators wish to move in some way, typically, governments, from the *secondary targets*, namely, the civilians, harm to whom is viewed as a means of moving the primary targets.

Fifth, it might be thought that etymology demands that terrorism involve the creation of terror, fear, and alarm. While several writers speak of such psychological effects as essential to terrorism, the use of "deliberate" in the definiens of the standard definition once again requires care. Fear and alarm are typically the byproducts of actions that deliberately expose civilians to violence, and certainly many instances of terrorism have had such effects, especially since they are unexpected and unpredictable. But if the perpetrator's aim is simply to cause outrage and thereby provoke a response in order to achieve political objectives, then fear and alarm may very well be unintended and inessential. In this way, also, terrorists might carefully choose their secondary targets, making it erroneous to require that an act of terrorism be "random," "indiscriminate," or "irrational."

Sixth, the standard definition does not *imply* that terrorism is unjustifiable. It might seem to have that implication given the use of "deliberate" and "civilians," but a separate argument is needed to establish that a given act of violence directed against such persons is morally unjustifiable. Definitions that *explicitly* make terrorism illegitimate through such adjectives as "illegal," "unlawful," "random," "indiscriminate," etc. make it more contentious to classify a given action as a terrorist act. A definition that avoids this implication, by contrast, has the advantage that a moral assessment can be defended upon an examination of the case rather than being settled by arbitrary stipulation. Moreover, it makes it less difficult to classify an action as "terrorist."

Seventh, the standard definition excludes no kind of person or organization—including a government or state—from being an agent of terrorism. There are several reasons to resist the U.S. Code's stipulation that terrorism is practiced only by non-state agents or clandestine state agencies, never *states*. For one thing, there are no semantic grounds for restricting "terrorism" to non-state agents, if we are to judge from the most recent editions of the *Oxford English Dictionary, Webster's Dictionary of the English Language*, the *Encyclopedia Britannica*, and the *Encyclopedia Americana*. Etymologically, "terror" and, hence, "terrorism" imply nothing about the identity of the agent. The *Oxford English Dictionary* (OED) does not restrict the definition of "terrorism" to non-state agents, and the 15th edition of the *Encyclopedia Britannica* (vol. 11, pp. 650–651), explicitly allows that governments can be the agents of terrorism when it speaks of "establishment terrorism."[1]

The restriction of terrorism to actions by non-state agents is ultimately disingenuous. The term "terrorism" has become the term of art in labeling illegitimate methods of political violence.

Exempting states from being agents of terrorism yields an unfair rhetorical advantage to established governments, especially since the weaponry and organization that modern states have brought to bear in pursuing their ends through violence against civilians consistently dwarfs any amount of harm achieved by non-state actors engaged in terrorist activity. That states can commit criminal acts of warfare has long been recognized in international law, for example, by the Hague Conventions and the Geneva Conventions. But, not to be unduly stubborn, we may speak of what non-state groups do as *ordinary terrorism* and what states do as *state-terrorism*. Interestingly, the argument I am about to present concerning the justification of terrorism can easily be restricted to ordinary terrorism.

3. An Argument for Justified Terrorism

As mentioned at the outset of this paper, attempts to justify terrorist actions on moral grounds are likely to be met with expressions of incredulity, at both the scholarly and popular levels. Robespierre's ominous "virtue without terror is powerless" lost whatever credibility it might have appeared to have long ago, at least as a moral maxim. It is more common to hear sweeping denunciations of terrorism on the grounds that it is a brutal violation of human rights, fails to treat people as "moral persons" (Katchadourian 1998), does not differ from murder (French 2003), indiscriminately attacks the innocent (Walzer 1988, 238), targets those who are innocent of the grievances from which it stems (Primoratz 2004a, 21; Jaggar 2005, 212), or, simply, is a violation of the *jus in bello* discrimination rule.

Terrorism is also likely to generate disgust, hatred, and vengeance, not only within the targeted community, but also among the external audience with little understanding of the relevant history, rendering it a strategy that backfires by increasing the determination and volume of one's enemies. Michael Walzer contends that no sort of "apologetic descriptions and explanations," e.g., that it is effective, a last resort,

---

[1] The OED describes terrorism as "a policy intended to strike with terror those against whom it is adopted; the employment of methods of intimidation; the fact of terrorizing or condition of being terrorised." The Encyclopedia Britannica Online defines terrorism generally as "the systematic use of violence to create a general climate of fear in a population and thereby to bring about a particular political objective," and adds that terrorism has been practiced by "state institutions such as armies, intelligence services, and police." For example, the terms "terroriste" and "le terreur" were initially applied by the Jacobin leaders to refer to the actions by their own revolutionary government in eradicating its enemies. During Robespierre's Reign of Terror, for example, it is estimated that some 400,000 men, women, and children were imprisoned by government authorities, and some writers estimate that the number executed was as high as 40,000.

the only alternative, or not distinct from other forms of political struggle, provide an excuse for terrorism (Walzer 1988, 239–42). Recalling Kant's insistence that war can be justified only if it is expected to contribute to future peace, it is precisely because terrorism is capable of generating intense feelings of hatred and vengeance that it threatens to undermine trust and the possibility of future coexistence (Katchadourian 1998). As Kant realized, criminal stratagems raise the frightening possibility that genocidal annihilation of one or both parties might be the only way to end a conflict.[1]

Yet, it is not obvious that these considerations trump all others *if* terrorism is the only means available to secure an *overridingly justifiable end*, that is, when *not* committing terrorism would have morally worse consequences than engaging in terrorism. Can such a scenario ever exist? We have already noted that history is replete with defenses of terrorism as a necessary means of conquering territory, or as a mechanism for advancing the interests and safety of "the people." Apart from such dubious identifications of the public good or glorifications of territorial theft, some have justified state terrorism on defensive grounds, say, in the case of "supreme emergency," and others have added that terrorism by communities other than states might be justified in similar cases of self-defense.[2]

Let us employ a generalized notion of *community* to include any society of persons having some level of geographical and political unity and containing entire families that ensure its continued existence through the usual reproduction of individuals who *ipso facto* become members. States are communities possessing sovereignty over territory, but there are various levels of non-state communities as well, e.g., those constituting political or regional divisions within a state, local municipalities, religious communities, ethnic minorities, etc. Any community can be subjected to threats and attacks stemming from civil disorder, government oppression, foreign invasions and occupations. Normally, the job of defending a community is vested in the sovereign power, but the sovereign might not deliver, especially if it is too weak, has been decimated or destroyed, or is itself the aggressor. Just as individuals have a right of self-defense in the absence of police protection, so too, a community has the right to collective self-defense when state protection is unavailable—at least when it is legitimately constituted within the territory where the aggression occurs. If so, the constraints imposed by just war theory can be considered in relation to nonstate agents (Valls 2000), for refusing to apply the considerations of *jus ad bellum* and *jus in bello* to violence waged by non-state agents would be to delegitimize any resistance to repression by a non-state community, including all revolutions, national liberation movements, and resistance to tyrannical government. That is an implausible conclusion.

We must set forth, then, the generalized rules for justified violence by all communities, non-state as well as state. In brief, the generalized correlates of the familiar *jus ad bellum* criteria are the following:

---

[1] See Kant's sixth preliminary article in his 1795 essay "To Perpetual Peace" (Kant 1983, 109–10).

[2] Walzer (1977, 255–61) and Rawls (1999a, 98–99; 1999b, 568) have defended a state's recourse to terrorism by means of this supreme emergency exemption to the discrimination rule. As for non-state terrorism, Hare (1979) suggests that the terrorism practiced by the European Resistance during WWII was morally justified, and Wilkins (1992, 26–28) similarly argues that Jews would have been justified in using terrorism against the Germans at that time. More recent defenses can be found in Valls (2000a), Honderich (2006), Young (2004), Held (2004a, 2005), and Dahbour (2005). Both C.A.J. Coady (2004b) and Christopher Toner (2004) point out that the justification Walzer and Rawls provide for state terrorism under supreme emergency implies that individuals and non-state groups may also engage in terrorism against "innocents" in supreme emergencies, and for this reason, both reject the supreme emergency exemption.

1076   UNIT IV: C. Radical Solutions at Home and Abroad: Secession, Revolution, and War

1. *Just Cause.* Violence may be launched only for the right reason. The just causes most frequently mentioned include: self-defense from external attack, the defense of others from such, and the protection of innocents from brutal, aggressive regimes.
2. *Right Intention.* Agents must intend to fight the war only for the sake of its just cause(s).
3. *Competent Authority and Public Declaration.* A community may use violence only if the decision has been made by the appropriate authorities, according to the proper process, and made public, notably to its own citizens and to the enemy state(s) or communities.
4. *Last Resort.* A community may resort to violence only if it has exhausted all plausible, peaceful alternatives to resolving the conflict in question, in particular diplomatic negotiation.
5. *Proportionality.* A community must, prior to initiating a war, weigh the total goods expected to result from it, such as securing the just cause, against the total evils expected to result, notably casualties. Only if the benefits are proportional to, or "worth," the costs may the war action proceed.
6. *Probability of Success.* A community may not resort to war if it can reasonably predict that doing so will have no measurable impact upon achieving the goal of the just cause.

Similarly, the relevant criteria of *jus in bello* are these:

1. *Discrimination*: Noncombatants should be immune from attack.
2. *Proportionality*: Use no more force than is necessary to achieve just military objectives.
3. *Legitimate Means* (No means *mala in se*): There should be no use of weapons or methods "evil in themselves," e.g., rape, genocide, poison, treachery, use of human shields, forcing captured soldiers to fight against their own side, and using weapons whose effects cannot be controlled, like biological agents.
4. *Benevolent Quarantine*: Prisoners of conflict must be treated humanely.

Let us now apply these provisions to the case where a community faces an aggressive threat to its very existence. This can take different forms (Gilbert 2003, 26), with attempted extermination of its members being the clearest threat warranting a community's recourse to self-defense. But even where extermination is not at issue, an aggressor might try to destroy a community in other ways, say, by enslavement or forced conversions of its members, destruction of its vital institutions (economic, agricultural, political, cultural), appropriation of its natural resources, seizure of its territory and dispersion of its members. Each of these threats to a community's survival is an *existential* threat and, typically, will be viewed as unjustifiable from that community's perspective. Such a situation is a paradigmatic case where a community may exercise its right of collective self-defense, though the right may also be exercised in other instances, say, when there are threats to a society's political independence, territory, resources, technological and military capabilities, or "basic freedoms of its citizens and its constitutionally democratic political institutions" (Rawls 1999a, 91).

When a community faces such an existential threat, the *jus ad bellum* criterion of just cause is readily satisfied. Without a protective sovereign, a community is justified in taking self-defense into its own hands through strategies that it judges will best end or abate the threat, whether these involve acquiescence, surrender, flight, or resistance. The situation is similar to what we, as individuals, encounter when assaulted or threatened with assault in the absence of police protection; we have a right of active self-defense. However, for a community to justifiably defend itself, its chosen courses of action must also satisfy the requirement of *competent authority*, either through endorsement by the acknowledged leadership of the community or by the community itself through the best available means of determining consent. Moreover, if the goal of the agents of that contemplated action is to end or reduce the existential threat, then they act with *right intent*. These conditions can be readily satisfied.[1]

What methods might a community use for self-defense when confronted with what it takes to be an unjustifiable existential threat? Obviously, this depends upon the broader legal and political orders that the community exists under, but the following are what might be called the *standard measures* of self-defense that a community may take when threatened by an aggressor:

- Offers of direct negotiation with the aggressor to resolve the problem.
- Appeals to external agencies, institutions, and laws in order to arbitrate and work towards a peaceful solution of the problem.
- Appeals to a recognized sovereign, or to external powers to forcibly intervene to stop the aggression.
- Resort to non-violent resistance to halt or retard the aggression.

If these measures fail, then the community has the right to

- Resort to military resistance, whether through conventional or guerrilla warfare, against the aggressor's military forces.

---

[1] Andrew Valls writes: "if an organization claims to act on behalf of a people and is widely seen by that people as legitimately doing so, then the rest of us should look on that organization as the legitimate authority of the people for the purpose of assessing its entitlement to engage in violence on their behalf" (Valls 2000, 71). Virginia Held (2005, 185–88) points out that while democratic authorization of a leadership is not always possible when democratic mechanisms are inhibited, this does not preclude the requirement of legitimate authority from being satisfied for acts of terrorism by non-state groups.

While this latter measure is usually accorded to organized states, if a community is not being protected by a state then it has the right to direct its members to take up arms in pursuit of collective self-defense. This is not a surprising allowance given that the government of a state might persecute its own population or a segment thereof.

Suppose, now, that the leadership of the community under threat has resorted to each of the standard measures for self-defense against the aggression. In particular, this leadership has appealed to the aggressor for direct negotiations, publicly argued its case by appeal to international law, requested assistance from international organizations (say, the United Nations), regional alliances, and major world powers, resorted to non-violent methods of protest, and confronted the aggressor's military within the standard *jus in bello* guidelines. Suppose, furthermore, that repeated efforts of these sorts have proved unsuccessful. In such circumstances, the targeted community faces a *radical* existential threat, namely, a situation when it is subject to an unjustifiable existential threat, and its recourse to the standard measures of self-defense have failed to end or abate that threat. A situation of radical existential threat qualifies as a "supreme emergency" and a paradigmatic *just cause*—namely, to eliminate or reduce the threat—if anything does.

Would terrorism be a justifiable option when a community faces a radical existential threat? If so, then either the *jus in bello* principle of discrimination can be overridden or it must be suitably refined; otherwise we would step outside the bounds of generalized just war theory. I am going to favor the refinement option herein, but before articulating it, let me first observe how the other criteria of generalized just war theory can be satisfied by communities contemplating a campaign of terrorism.

By the very way a radical existential threat is described, recourse to terrorism can easily satisfy the *jus ad bellum* requirements of *proportionality* and *last resort* given that the aggression is unjustified and that standard measures of self-defense have been tried and have failed. Terrorism would then be a *Machiavellian* course of action since it would violate widely shared standards for the sake of an overridingly just goal, namely, to reduce or end an unwarranted existential threat. Machiavelli's allowance for occasional cruelty was offered as a "last resort" strategy for the sovereign, but in a situation of radical existential threat a community is its own sovereign. In plain fact, communities have and still do face radical existential threats, and some have tried the standard measures of self-defense before resorting to terrorism. It is precisely because of gross disparities in economic and military resources between oppressor and oppressed, and because of the continual technological improvements in protection of military personnel, that terrorism might be the only means of resistance available. Suicide terrorism, in particular, is viewed by its agents as a strategy of last resort when embroiled with a zero-sum conflict (Pape 2005, 89–94).

If a proposed act or campaign of terrorism is to satisfy the last resort condition, not only must it be assumed that terrorist acts can be carried out, but its proponents must have evidence that there is a *reasonable hope of success* that they might enable the community to reach the goals related to the just cause. This is often the most difficult *jus ad bellum* condition to satisfy (Fotion 2004, 49–53), but a few points should be kept in mind. First, although some argue that terrorism never works to advance a community's political goals (thus, Walzer 1988, 240; Katchadourian 1998, 27), there are a number of counterexamples. It has already been mentioned that state terrorism has sometimes achieved desired goals; the American "manifest destiny" was partly achieved through terrorism against native Americans, and it has been argued that the terror bombing of Japanese cities in 1945 was a least one factor hastening the end of WWII (though see Tanaka & Young 2009). Non-state terrorism has also been effective (see Wilkins 1992, 39; Pape 2005, 61–76), notably, in achieving both short-term

and long-term goals by non-state groups in the struggle over Palestine.[1]

Second, in the case of a radical existential threat, it is not difficult to understand how a threatened community's resort to terrorism against powerful unwarranted aggression *could* be successful in advancing its goal of self-preservation.

1. The aggressor concludes that the price of its aggression is too high and, to avoid the effects

---

[1] Both sides in the Israeli/Palestinian conflict have achieved some of their goals through terrorism. One of the objectives of Jewish terrorists in the late 1940s was to make the cost of governing Palestine too great for a war-weary Great Britain. Another objective during the 1947–49 war between Jews and Arabs was to induce as many Palestinian Arabs to flee from their homes in Palestine as was possible. Through a few well-timed massacres, notably of some 250 civilians in the Palestinian village of Deir Yassin in April 1948, over 300,000 Palestinians fled from their homes, villages, and lands in the areas that eventually became part of Israel, paving the way for the establishment of a decisive Jewish majority in these areas (Childers 1961; Morris 1987; Flapan 1987). Chaim Weizmann, Israel's first president, described this flight of Palestinians, and the forced removal of some 400,000 others, as "a miraculous clearing of the land: the miraculous simplification of Israel's task" (Hirst 2003, 268–69). Menachem Begin, head of the Jewish terrorist group, Irgun, wrote, "Of the about 800,000 Arabs who lived on the present territory of the State of Israel, only some 165,000 are still there. The political and economic significance of this development can hardly be overestimated" (Begin 1977: 164). One effect of Palestinian terrorism of the early 1970s is that it drew attention to the grievances of dispossessed Palestinians, grievances that had been largely ignored in the first two decades after the loss of their homeland and the crushing of their quest for self-determination. For example, after the kidnappings and killings at the Munich Olympics in 1972, the Palestinian leader, Abu Iyad, said the following: "The sacrifices made by the Munich heroes were not entirely in vain. They didn't bring about the liberation of any of their comrades imprisoned in Israel . . . but they did obtain the operation's other two objectives; world opinion was forced to take note of the Palestinian drama, and the Palestinian people imposed their presence on an international gathering that had sought to exclude them" (Abou Iyad 1981: 111–12).

of terrorism upon its own civilian population, decides to desist from that aggression.[1]

2. External states and alliances are caused to intervene to bring an end to the aggression.[2]

3. By retaliating against aggression, the threatened community gains credibility and recognition, both from external parties and from other members of its own community who might thereby become more confident, more hopeful, and more committed to joining a resistance whose likelihood of success is increased with greater participation and unity.[3]

The probability of success is enhanced if the aggressor has itself used terrorism in either its direct or structural modes. Such *parity of means* in the method of violence might strengthen the conviction in external parties, as well as in the aggressor's own population, either that it is appropriate to return terrorism for terrorism or that tit-for-tat violence has escalated out of proportion. An asymmetrical use of terrorism, by contrast, runs the risk of evoking contempt for the threatened community among external parties and in alienating members of the threatened community who would normally be opposed to such tactics.

Up to this point, the argument has been consequentialist; communities have a right to defend themselves against radical existential threats by terrorist means because the consequences of failing to act in this way are worse. Barring a pure utilitarian consequentialism, however, concern for a *just* distribution of the value of the expected consequences must also be factored in, and here we come to a direct challenge to any attempt to justify terrorism. If one party is innocent of an aggression against another, then the latter's violence against the former in pursuit of redress would be a gross violation of justice (Primoratz 2004a, 20–21). So, how could violence against civilians be justified if they are innocent of the terrorists' grievances?

Answer? Violence directed against an innocent person *cannot* be justified, but it is incorrect to suppose that civilians are automatically "innocent" of their community's aggression against another community. They might be culpable of that aggression in a number of ways and in varying degrees (Holmes 1989, 187). For one thing, civilians might participate by voluntarily paying taxes or by publicly supporting political, economic, or national policies and activities that generate and sustain that aggression. For another, the aggressor might have a representative political system that operates under the principle of popular sovereignty, namely, that ultimate political power is vested in the citizenry and exercised by the governing institutions through the consent of that citizenry. Popular sovereignty entails *shared responsibility* for the laws, policies, and actions of the state insofar as these represent the consent of the collective of which each individual is a member. Those who voluntarily join *any* association or institution share in responsibility for its actions, and

---

[1] Pape (2005, chapter 5), addresses the issue whether suicide terrorists calculate the benefits of their policies. He says that groups such as Hamas, Islamic Jihad, Hezbollah, and the Tamil Tigers began with more conventional guerrilla operations but after these operations proved ineffective, they resorted to suicide attacks with an initial confidence that they would yield more positive results. Governments have entered into negotiations with these groups after the suicide campaigns began (pp. 64–65), and in some cases, governments have been coerced, as with the U.S. and France in Lebanon in 1983, Israel in Lebanon in 2000, and Sri Lanka in 2001 (p. 55). Pape conjectures that the government of Israel was coerced by Hamas in 1994–95 (pp. 66–73).

[2] The motivation of intervening parties can vary. Some might see intervention as a means of either harming or defeating the aggressor or as an opportunity to extend influence over the threatened community. Again, the intervener might be caused to act because it is alarmed that the violence between the two communities has reached such proportions and poses greater threats to future peace and stability. Such intervention has repeatedly taken place since WWII, especially in Africa. The intervention by Western powers in the Balkans in the 1990s was partly caused by a desire to halt the continued aggression and atrocities in Bosnia and Kosovo. It is likely that the PLO adopted this strategy by provoking Israel into an extreme reaction that would bring Israel into conflict with neighboring states and discredit it in the eyes of the world community (O'Brien 1991, 13).

[3] The positive effects of violence as a confidence building measure and as a means of unity among members of an oppressed community were argued for by Frantz Fanon (1963, 38). Pape (2005, chapter 6) provides further evidence in support of this strategy.

citizenship in a representative system is voluntary; it can be renounced, even if there are dramatic consequences for so doing such as imprisonment or exile. Responsibility in a representative system is not avoided by belonging to the political opposition or having been critical of the government's policies and acts, even though, in such cases, one's culpability might be of a lesser degree. In sum, terrorism is justified only if a further *culpability condition* is satisfied, namely, that those who would direct violence against civilians within the aggressor community must have evidence that those civilians share in the responsibility for that aggression.[1]

While this might seem a brute tossing of the *jus in bello* rules to the wind, the departure is less dra-

matic than might appear. The *jus in bello* demand of proportionality can continue to be respected; not every imagined act of terrorism by the threatened community could be justified, and no more should be used than is necessary to end or reduce the existential threat. Further, the prohibition on using illegitimate means can be respected; the weapons used by terrorists, bombs, guns, knives, etc., are more primitive forms of the weapons in the arsenals of state militaries; that *some* terrorism is justified does not imply that terrorism through any means, for example, nuclear weapons, nerve gas, etc., would also be justified. Similarly, the requirement of treating prisoners of war humanely is satisfiable; even though the weaker parties in asymmetric conflicts usually do not have the resources to take prisoners of war, when they do, there is no reason they could not respect the standard conventions on prisoners of war. Finally, and perhaps most importantly, while the principle of noncombatant immunity is abandoned in the case of a radical existential threat, a modified principle of discrimination, remains: *in redressing a grievance, those innocent of that grievance are to be immune from harm.* In yet other words, there is no reason why terrorism cannot discriminate, targeting only those members of the aggressor community who are guilty of that aggression (Valls 2000, 76). The truly non-culpable, e.g., children, the mentally ill, and so forth, should be immune from attack.[2]

Let me now bring this to a head. I have argued that where various conditions are met, then ter-

---

[1] Similar reasoning can be found in Wilkins (1992), who cites Karl Jaspers' distinction between the *political guilt* that people within a community harbor when their state commits crimes, and the *moral guilt* of an individual who participates in, supports, or favors those crimes (Wilkins 1992, 21–22). Wilkins finds that political guilt is both collective and distributive, and only individuals who completely sever their ties to the political community are exempt from moral guilt (p. 25). On these grounds, he argues that terrorism is justified as a form of self-defense when all other political and legal remedies have been exhausted or are inapplicable and the terrorism is directed against guilty members of the aggressor (1992, 28). See also Virginia Held, who writes that "*If* a government's policies are *unjustifiable* and *if* political violence to resist them is *justifiable* (these are very large 'ifs,' but not at all unimaginable), then it is not clear why the political violence should not be directed at those responsible for these policies" (Held 2004b, 6; emphasis in original). Some writers are skeptical of using "collective responsibility" as a way of widening the range of legitimate targets; for example, Coady (2004a, 55–57) and Miller (2005), who argue that one shares in collective responsibility for a rights violation only if one "intentionally contributed" to that violation, and, thus, where intention is lacking, so is the responsibility. However, the "consent" one gives through membership in a voluntary association is a *general* intention to abide by, and accept responsibilities for, that association's policies and acts, whatever these might be. But, quite apart from this, it is doubtful that moral responsibility for a situation requires an intention to bring about or sustain that situation. Criminal law typically allows that one can be responsible for what one rationally foresees will happen as a result of one's action or inaction.

[2] It should be mentioned that two main reasons are usually used in defense of the principle of discrimination. First, targeting civilians is not essential towards achieving the military end of victory, for as civilians are unarmed, they do not constitute an impediment towards the prosecution of military strategy and violence against them is gratuitous. Second, targeting civilians is targeting those who are innocent of the terrorists' grievances. So, violence against civilians cannot be justified. I think it should be clear from what has been said above that while gratuitous violence directed against an innocent person *cannot* be justified, it is both incorrect to suppose that violence against civilians need be gratuitous and incorrect to suppose that civilians are automatically "innocent" of their community's aggression against another community.

rorism against an aggressor can be justified. More precisely, *if* the members of a community have adequate evidence that

- their community is subjected to an unjustifiable radical existential threat from an identifiable aggressor (hence, that the *jus ad bellum* just cause and last resort conditions are met);
- a projected campaign of terrorism would satisfy the *jus ad bellum* conditions of competent authority, proportionality, right intent, and reasonable hope of success;
- the aggressor is using terrorism against their community (parity of means condition);
- the adult civilians of the aggressor are culpable of the aggression that constitutes the existential threat (the culpability condition); and
- the *jus in bello* demands of proportionality, legitimate means, humane treatment of captives, and modified discrimination (do not target innocents) are to be respected;

then their recourse to terrorism against the aggressor community for the purposes of ending or reducing that threat is morally justifiable.

It should be noted that this provides only a sufficient condition for terrorism, not a necessary condition. Nothing I have said precludes defenses of terrorism on yet other grounds.

4. Case Study: The Israeli-Palestinian Conflict

It might be thought that the scenario of a radical existential threat is highly contrived and that the conditions for justified terrorism never actually materialize. This is plainly mistaken. During the 16th-19th centuries, the societies of indigenous peoples in North and South America were systematically obliterated by European invaders. Closer to our own time, there are communities in Africa, southern Asia, and China that feel that they are similarly threatened. There is one case of a radical existential threat that has consumed a good deal of diplomatic attention for the past century, namely, the threat that the Arab community of Palestine has faced from the Zionist movement and the state of Israel. Terrorism has been practiced by both sides in this conflict, often with devastating results that are almost impossible to justify. But using the argument from radical self-defense presented above, there is a *prima facie* case for the legitimacy of both past and current Palestinian terrorism directed against Israelis. Let's look at the situation.

First, the Palestinian community throughout Palestine, and the Palestinian communities in various regions within Palestine, have faced, and still face, an existential threat from Zionism. This threat has been demonstrated by

- the forcible imposition of a Jewish state in Palestine in 1947–48, engineered by the Zionist movement, against the wishes of the vast majority of the population in Palestine and throughout the entire Islamic world;
- Israel's expulsion of Palestinians from Palestine in 1948 and again in 1967, and its refusal to repatriate Palestinian refugees;
- Israel's colonization, land confiscation, and other forms of structural terrorism in the occupied West Bank that began in 1967 and have continued until the present, including throughout the period of the Oslo Accords 1993–2000;
- Israel's systematic violation of the human rights of Palestinians in the occupied territories, including the use of lethal force (see note 5);
- Israel's refusal to comply with international resolutions calling for its withdrawal from the territories occupied in the 1967 war;
- Israel's opposition to peace initiatives, e.g., repeated calls for an international peace conference on the Middle East, the Rogers Plan of 1969–70, the Reagan Plan of 1982, Prince Fahd's peace plan of 1982, the PLO's offer of peace in 1988, and the Arab League's proposals of 2002;
- Israel's deliberate efforts to destroy the Palestinians' capacity to establish and

maintain an independent state in the occupied territories;

- Israel's assassinations of Palestinian political leaders, extending from the 1970s to the first decade of the 21st century;
- the expressed intention by the dominant Israeli political parties to retain control of the West Bank or large segments thereof;
- the refusal by Israel's leadership to permit a viable Palestinian state to be established in the occupied territories, extending from Moshe Sharett's agreements with Abdullah (Rogan and Shlaim 2001), to Ehud Barak's breaking off talks at Taba in Jan. 2001 (Reinhart 2002, chap. II), to Ariel Sharon's rejection of the Arab League's peace overtures in spring 2002, the 2002 Geneva Accords between moderate Israelis and Palestinians (Shuman 2003), and the Bush Administration's 2002 "Road Map" for peace;
- the almost unquestioned support for Israeli policies by the government of the world's most powerful country, the United States.[1]

---

[1] See Kapitan (2008b, 160–64). American support for Israel is well-documented (see, for example, Lilienthal 1982, Christison 1999, Chomsky 1999, Aruri 2003, Swisher 2004, Mearsheimer and Walt 2005, Petras 2006). Opposition to Israeli settlements moved from "illegal" under the Carter Administration, to "obstacles" under Reagan, to "unhelpful" under Clinton. A letter from President Bush to Ariel Sharon dated April 14, 2004, stated that "it is unrealistic to expect that the outcome of the final status negotiations will be a full and complete return to the armistice lines" (www.whitehouse.gov), and in June 2004, the House of Representatives voted 407–9 to endorse the text of Bush's letter. The statements by some Congressional leaders have been truly astounding. For example, the House Majority Whip in 2002, Dick Armey, publicly advocated Israel's confiscation of the entire West Bank and the expulsion of the Palestinian population (Abunimah 2006, 102). Again, Senator Hillary Clinton called for "total U.S. support of Israeli policy" while visiting Israel in February 2002. When a reporter asked Clinton whether Palestinians also deserve U.S. sympathy, she replied: "The United States' role is to support Israel's decisions" (Chicago Tribune, February 26, 2002).

That this existential threat is unjustifiable is due to its violation of the human rights of Palestinians including the right of self-determination (see Halwani and Kapitan 2008, chapter 1, section 10).

Second, in light of this threat, the Palestinians have a just cause for resorting to self-defensive measures, but the just cause in this case is that of survival, not solely that of achieving political independence. A group's goal of self-determination is not always overriding and cannot, by itself, justify a campaign of terrorism, for not every impediment to a national group's quest for political independence poses a radical existential threat. The Palestinians' quest is for their survival as a community *in* their home territory, and in this sense their case is arguably different from the situation faced by Kurds, Tamils, Basques, Irish, etc., however legitimate the demands for self-determination for these groups might be.

Third, the Palestinians have attempted the standard measures of self-defense noted above (Holmes 1995, Saleh 2003). (a) The major Palestinian political organization, the PLO, has tried diplomacy by entering into direct negotiations with Israelis. The Palestine National Council ratified the two-state solution in 1988 thereby explicitly recognizing Israel's right to exist. The Palestinian Authority in the occupied territories has repeatedly stressed its acceptance of the two-state solution. Yet Israel has not reciprocated, since it has steadfastly refused to negotiate any deal with the Palestinians that would grant them a viable state in Palestine. Only the most naive or deceptive would claim that Israel's leadership has been interested in a meaningful compromise with the Palestinians. If they were, they would not have initiated the direct and structural terrorism in territories occupied since 1967 or persisted in its vilification and dehumanization of Palestinians (Kapitan 2008b, 142–54 and 160–64). (b) The Palestinians have also appealed to external agencies for assistance (for example, the League of Nations, the United Nations, the Arab League) and to external powers, they have supported international resolutions calling for a two-state solution to the conflict and they endorsed the Bush

Administration's Road Map. (c) Palestinians have repeatedly used techniques of non-violence in combating the Israeli occupation, and have sought and received the help of like-minded Israelis, but to no avail. (d) The Palestinians have resisted established militaries, viz., the British military in 1936–39, the Zionist forces in 1947–48, and the Israeli military since the establishment of the Jewish state. None of these measures have been successful in ending or abating the existential threat they face, much less in securing their self-determination. In the atmosphere of ongoing hostilities accompanying the American occupation of the Middle East, there is even less likelihood that availing themselves of these standard measures of self-defense will be successful. By emasculating Palestinian diplomacy, intensifying the control over the West Bank, Israel has deprived young Palestinians of hope, leaving terrorism one of the few avenues of active resistance left. Thus, there is good reason to conclude that the Palestinians in the West Bank face a *radical* existential threat, in which case terrorism presents itself as a last resort strategy for that community.[1]

Fourth, there is evidence that recourse to terrorism has produced at least some desired results for the Palestinians, even though it has not yet secured Palestinian self-determination nor ended the existential threat posed by Israel. In plain fact,

Palestinian terrorism has succeeded in perpetuating the cycle of violence that Israelis and Palestinians have been locked in for over eighty years. One result is that considerable attention is kept riveted upon the conflict and, thus, upon Palestinian suffering and Palestinian demands. As indicated in section 4 above, the result is that not only have many people pressed for answers to questions about why this sort of violence is occurring, but many people throughout the world have become more sympathetic and supportive of the Palestinians. For over eighty years, beginning with the British commissions of the 1920s, extreme violence *has* caused external players to play a more active role in resolving the Israeli-Palestinian conflict. It has led some Israelis to question policies of the Israeli government in the occupied territories, and, in a few instances, it has caused the Israeli government to make some concessions to the Palestinians (Pape 2005, chap. 5). Given the intentions of the Israeli leadership, quiet acquiescence on the part of Palestinians would have resulted in slow strangulation. Further, striking back against their oppressors has also reduced the Palestinians' sense of impotence against a powerful adversary and, thereby, strengthened the confidence, resolve and unity among their communities.[2]

Fifth, the remaining conditions for justifying the Palestinian's campaign of terrorism appear to be satisfied. Palestinian militancy has received enough

---

[1] See section 6 above, and also, Pape (2005, 64–74). The Hamas leader, Dr. Abd al-Aziz Rantisi, assassinated by Israel in April of 2004, justified suicide bombings against Israel saying they were the "weapons of last resort" because "Israel is offering us two choices, either to die a meek lamb's death at the slaughter house or as martyr-bombers" (www.infoimagination.org/islamnm/second_intifada.html). Smilansky (2004) claims that the Palestinians have not availed themselves of viable alternatives to terrorism. However, he gives a historically skewed summary of the choices Palestinians made and did not make (pp. 794–95), for example, that they could have had a state in 1948 alongside Israel, that they did not attempt a campaign of nonviolent resistance in the territories, that they, rather than Israel, derailed the progress towards a Palestinian state called for in the Oslo Accords, and that they rejected a "generous offer" by Prime Minister Barak in the summer of 2000 (see Kapitan 2008a and 2008b, *passim*).

[2] Igor Primoratz (2006), while acknowledging that the Palestinian community faces a "true moral disaster" (37), argues that terrorism "does not seem to have brought the Palestinians any closer to liberation, self-determination, and repatriation" and, therefore, cannot be justified since it fails to meet the condition of effectiveness (40). This judgment seems premature. He underestimates Fanon's emphasis upon the role of violence in strengthening determination to combat a much more powerful adversary. The Palestinian cause is at the forefront of ever-widening Islamic resistance to U.S.-Israeli hegemony over the Middle East. The so-called "war on terrorism" may well strengthen the willingness of Muslims to support the Palestinians and confront this hegemony as they see their own fate as increasingly linked to the Israeli-Palestinian conflict, something that would likely not have happened had not tensions between Israelis and Palestinians been kept before the public eye.

popular support from the Palestinian residents of the territories to sanction at least the general strategy of violence against Israeli civilians. This kind of support intensifies whenever the Israeli military increases the amount of terrorism it employs against the Palestinians (sections 3–5 above). Not only is the *parity of means condition* satisfied, thereby, but since Israel is a representative democracy with large percentages of its adult citizens publicly supporting the measures that constitute the existential threat to the Palestinians, then the *culpability condition* is also met. Indeed, the election of Ariel Sharon—arguably, the most aggressive and violent man towards Palestinians in the past 50 years—in 2001 and his re-election in 2004 provide concrete evidence that the Israel public supports Israeli state terrorism against Palestinians.

While these factors certainly do not justify every act of terrorism committed by Palestinians, they constitute a strong *prima facie* case that the Palestinians have been justified in resorting to terrorism against Israelis.

References

Abou Iyad, with Eric Rouleau. 1981. *My Home, My Land: A Narrative of the Palestinian Struggle*. New York: Times Books.

Abunimah, Ali. 2006. *One Country: A Bold Proposal to End the Israeli-Palestinian Impasse*. New York: Metropolitan Books.

Aruri, Naseer, 2003. *Dishonest Broker: The U.S. Role in Israel and Palestine*. Cambridge, MA: South End Press.

Begin, Menachem. 1977. *The Revolt*. Rev. ed. New York: Nash Publishing.

Best, Steven, and Anthony J. Nocella II. 2004. "Defining Terrorism." *Animal Liberation Philosophy and Policy Journal* 2: 1–18.

Brown, Dee. 1970. *Bury My Heart at Wounded Knee*. New York: Bantam Books.

Childers, Erskine. 1961. "The Other Exodus." *The Spectator*, May 12, 1961: 672–75.

Chomsky, Noam. 1999. *The Fateful Triangle: The United States, Israel, and the Palestinians*. Cambridge, MA: South End Press.

Christison, Kathleen. 1999. *Perceptions of Palestine: Their Influence on U.S. Middle East Policy*. Berkeley: University of California Press.

Churchill, Ward. 1997. *A Little Matter of Genocide: Holocaust and Denial in the Americas, 1492 to the Present*. San Francisco: City Lights Books.

Coady, C.A.J. 2004a. "Terrorism and Innocence." *The Journal of Ethics* 8: 37–58.

Coady, C.A.J. 2004b. "Terrorism, Morality, and Supreme Emergency." *Ethics* 114: 772–89.

Coady, C.A.J. 2004c. "Defining Terrorism." In Primoratz, ed. (2004c): 3–14.

Dahbour, Omar. 2005. "The Response to Terrorism: Moral Condemnation or Ethical Judgment?" *The Philosophical Forum* 36: 87–95.

Fanon, Frantz. 1963. *The Wretched of the Earth*. New York: Grove Press.

Fisk, Robert. 2005. *The Great War for Civilisation*. New York: Alfred A. Knopf.

Flapan, Simha. 1987. *The Birth of Israel*. New York: Pantheon.

Fotion, Nick. 2004. "The Burdens of Terrorism." In Primoratz (ed.) (2004c): 44–54.

French, Shannon. 2003. "Murderers, Not Warriors: The Moral Distinction between Terrorists and Legitimate Fighters in Asymmetric Conflicts." In James Sterba (ed.), *Terrorism and International Justice*. New York: Oxford University Press.

Garnor, Boaz. 2001, "Defining terrorism: is one man's terrorist another man's freedom fighter?" Institute for Counter-Terrorism: www.ict.org.il 25 June 2001 (accessed on 15 November 2006).

Gilbert, Paul. 2003. *New Terror, New Wars*. Washington, DC: Georgetown University Press.

Glover, J. 1991. "State Terrorism." In R.G. Frey and C. Morris (eds.), *Violence, Terrorism, and Justice*. Cambridge: Cambridge University Press. 256–75.

Halwani, Raja, and Tomis Kapitan. 2008. *The Israeli-Palestinian Conflict: Philosophical Essays on Self-Determination, Terrorism, and the One-State Solution*. London: Palgrave-Macmillan.

Hare, R.M. 1979. "On Terrorism." *Journal of Value Inquiry* 13: 240–49.

Held, Virginia. 2004a. "Terrorism, Rights, and Political Goals." In Primoratz (2004c): 65–79.

Held, Virginia. 2004b. "Terrorism and War." *The Journal of Ethics* 8: 59–75.

Held, Virginia. 2005. "Legitimate Authority in Non-state Groups Using Violence." *Journal of Social Philosophy* 36: 175–93.

Hirst, D. 2003. *The Gun and the Olive Branch: The Roots of Violence in the Middle East.* 3rd ed. London: Faber and Faber.

Holmes, Robert. 1989. *On War and Morality.* Princeton, NJ: Princeton University Press.

Holmes, Robert. 1995. "Nonviolence and the Intifada." In L.F. Bove and L.D. Kaplan (eds.), *From the Eye of the Storm.* Amsterdam: Rodopi.

Honderich, Ted. 2006. *Right and Wrong, and Palestine, 9–11, Iraq, 7–7…* Boston: Seven Stories Press.

Jaggar, Allison. 2005. "What is terrorism, why is it wrong, and could it ever be morally permissible?" *Journal of Social Philosophy* 36(2): 202–17.

Kant, Immanuel. 1983. *Perpetual Peace and Other Essays.* Trans. T. Humphrey. Indianapolis: Hackett.

Kapitan, Tomis. 2003. "The Terrorism of 'Terrorism.'" In J. Sterba (ed.), *Terrorism and International Justice.* Oxford: Oxford University Press. 47–66.

Kapitan, Tomis. 2008a. "Self-Determination." In R. Halwani and T. Kapitan (eds.), *The Israeli-Palestinian Conflict.* London: Palgrave Macmillan. 13–71.

Kapitan, Tomis. 2008b. "Terrorism." In R. Halwani and T. Kapitan (eds.), *The Israeli-Palestinian Conflict.* London: Palgrave Macmillan. 132–97.

Katchadourian, Haig. 1998. *The Morality of Terrorism.* New York: Peter Lang.

Lilienthal, Alfred. 1982. *The Zionist Connection II.* New Brunswick, NJ: North American Publishers.

Mann, Barbara. 2005. *George Washington's War against Native Americans.* Westport, CT: Praeger.

Mearsheimer, John, and Stephen Walt. 2005. *The Israel Lobby and U.S. Foreign Policy.* New York: Farrar, Straus, and Giroux.

Miller, Seumas. 2005. "Terrorism and Collective Responsibility." In Georg Meggle (ed.), *Ethics of Terrorism and Counter-Terrorism.* Frankfurt: Ontos Verlag.

Morris, Benny. 1987. *The Birth of the Palestinian Refugee Problem, 1947–1949.* Cambridge: Cambridge University Press.

Morris, Benny. 2001. "Revisiting the Palestinian exodus of 1948." In Rogan and Shlaim (2001): 37–59.

Netanyahu, Benjamin. 2001. *Fighting Terrorism: How the West Can Defeat the International Terrorist Network.* New York: Farrar, Straus, and Giroux.

O'Brien, William. 1991. *Law and Morality in Israel's War with the PLO.* New York: Routledge.

Pape, Robert. 2005. *Dying to Win: The Strategic Logic of Suicide Terrorism.* New York: Random House.

Pappe, Ilan. 2006. *The Ethnic Cleansing of Palestine.* Oxford: Oxford University Press.

Petras, James. 2006. *The Power of Israel in the United States.* Atlanta: Clarity Press.

Pilger, John. 2004. "The Most Important Terrorism Is Ours." *The New Statesman*, September 16, 2004.

Primoratz, Igor. 2004a. "What Is Terrorism?" In Primoratz (2004c): 15–27.

Primoratz, Igor. 2004b. "State Terrorism and Counter-terrorism." In Primoratz (2004c): 113–27.

Primoratz, Igor (ed.). 2004c. *Terrorism: The Philosophical Issues.* Houndmills, UK: Palgrave Macmillan.

Primoratz, Igor. 2006. "Terrorism in the Israeli-Palestinian Conflict." *Iyyun: The Jerusalem Philosophical Quarterly* 55: 27–48.

Rawls, John. 1999a. *The Law of Peoples.* Cambridge, MA: Harvard University Press.

Rawls, John. 1999b. "Fifty Years after Hiroshima." In S. Freeman (ed.), *Collected Papers.* Cambridge, MA: Harvard University Press.

Reinhart, Tanya. 2002. *Israel/Palestine: How to End the War of 1948.* New York: Seven Stories Press.

Rogan, Eugene L., and Avi Shlaim (eds.). 2001. *The War for Palestine: Rewriting the History of 1948.* Cambridge: Cambridge University Press.

Saleh, Abdul Jawad. 2003. "The Palestinian nonviolent resistance movement." Alternative Palestinian Agenda, http://www.ap-agenda.org/11–02/overview.htm.

Shuman, Ellis. 2003. "Sharon: 'Geneva Accord' Is Most Historic, Tragic Mistake Since Oslo." *Israelinsider*, October 13, 2003. www.israelinsider.com.

Smilansky, Saul. 2004. "Terrorism, Justification, and Illusion." *Ethics* 114: 790–805.

Swisher, Clayton. 2004. *The Truth About Camp David: The Untold Story About the Collapse of the Middle East Peace Process*. New York: Nation Books.

Tanaka, Yuki, and Marilyn B. Young. 2009. *Bombing Civilians*. New York: The New Press.

Toner, Christopher. 2004. "Just War and Graduated Discrimination." *The American Catholic Philosophical Quarterly* 78: 649–65.

Valls, Andrew. 2000. "Can terrorism be justified?" In A. Valls (ed.), *Ethics in International Affairs*. Lanham, MD: Rowman & Littlefield, pp. 65–79.

Walzer, Michael. 1977. *Just and Unjust Wars: A Moral Argument with Historical Illustrations*. New York: Basic Books.

Walzer, Michael. 1988. "Terrorism: A Critique of Excuses." In S. Luper-Foy (ed.), *Problems of International Justice*. Boulder, CO: Westview Press.

Wilkins, Burleigh Taylor. 1992. *Terrorism and Collective Responsibility*. New York: Routledge.

Wilkinson, Paul. 1986. *Terrorism and the Liberal State*. 2nd ed. New York: New York University Press.

Young, Iris Marion. 2005. "Self-Determination as Non-Domination: Ideals Applied to Palestine/Israel." *Ethnicities* 5: 139–59.

DISCUSSION QUESTIONS

1. Why does Kapitan claim that the "rhetoric of 'terror' ... has obscured serious philosophical thought about this mode of violence"? How does Kapitan define and use the term "terrorism" in this piece? Do you think that this is an acceptable definition? Why or why not?

2. Given Kapitan's definition of "terrorism," could any United States military actions be deemed terrorist acts? If so, is this problematic? Explain your answers. Explain and discuss Kapitan's sufficient conditions for justified terrorism. Given these criteria, have any United States military actions been justified acts of terror? Explain.

3. Kapitan argues that civilians may share in the responsibility for their community's aggression towards another community. Explain and evaluate the various ways in which Kapitan thinks civilians may be culpable.

4. Kapitan claims that he has outlined a list of conditions which are jointly sufficient for justified terrorism. He does not claim that these are necessary conditions. Can you think of any other sufficient conditions which would justify one's involvement in terrorism?

D.
Applications

96

David Gauthier,
"Breaking Up: An Essay on
Secession" (1994)

In this essay, Gauthier presents what he takes to be the necessary conditions for a secession movement to be considered legitimate or justified. Gauthier applies his theory to prominent cases in world history. On Gauthier, see reading 5 above.

SOURCE

Gauthier, David. "Breaking Up: An Essay on Secession." *Canadian Journal of Philosophy*, Volume 24 (1994), pp. 357–71. Reprinted with permission of the University of Calgary Press.

I

Current discussion of the normative issues surrounding secession is both helped and hindered by the existence of but one philosophic treatment of these issues sufficiently systematic and comprehensive to qualify as a *theory* of secession—Allen Buchanan's.[1] He provides the unique focal point, and so simplifies the task of those who seek to begin from the present state of the art. But in providing the unique focal point, Buchanan complicates the task of those who view, or think they view, secession rather differently than he does. He defends "a moral right to secede" but a very qualified right, focusing on state-perpetrated injustice, the preservation of group culture and, in extreme cases, the literal survival of group members (152–53). And Buchanan further

[1] See Allen Buchanan, *Secession* (Boulder, CO: Westview Press, 1991). This paper was first presented at a symposium of the American Philosophical Association, Pacific Division, with Buchanan as lead symposiast. Buchanan notes a very few philosophic discussions that touch on secession; perhaps the most important is by Harry Beran, who defends a right to secede in *The Consent Theory of Political Obligation* (London: Croom Helm, 1987), 37–42. One of the referees for this journal drew my attention to what, so far as I know, is the only book-length work on secession other than Buchanan's: Lee C. Buchheit, *Secession: The Legitimacy of Self-Determination* (New Haven: Yale University Press, 1978). Buchheit focuses on the claim to secede within the framework of international law and includes several case studies, but deals only briefly with moral and philosophic issues.

insists that where preservation of group culture is at stake, "Neither the state nor any third party has a valid claim to the seceding territory"—or such a claim is waived so that "secession in order to preserve a culture is permissible if both parties consent to it"—a condition that he thinks may come to apply to the situation of Québec.

I want to sketch a rather more permissive view of secession. And I want to undermine the idea that territorial claims by existing states are significant blocks to secession. But I have no structure in any way comparable to Buchanan's within which I can defend this more permissive view. All that I can hope to do is to sketch; if the sketch has some appeal then it might seem promising to attempt to construct the theory that will be conspicuously lacking from my account.

In developing my position, I shall have, as surely any Canadian at this time must have, one particular application always in mind. For Canada's existence is threatened by a secessionist movement. Not all secessionist movements constitute such threats. The success of Baltic secessionism was not what doomed the Soviet Union. Should the secessionist Catholics of Northern Ireland succeed in their aims (and I shall argue later that however permissive my view of secession may be, it does not support their cause), the United Kingdom would continue largely as before. But if Québec secedes, what will remain will be a country very different from the one that I know and love. And so I have constantly to ask myself: "What are the implications of my sketch of the rights and wrongs of secession for my native land?"

In discussing secession, I propose largely to ignore all of those cases in which the existing political order is illegitimate. To be sure, one wants an account of political legitimacy to decide which these cases are, but I shall not produce one. Instead, I shall simply share what I hope will seem some plausible judgments of cases. The Baltic states were not legitimately incorporated into the Soviet Union; the effective basis of their incorporation was force and their appearance of consent was fraud. Putting Ireland to one side for later consideration, the United Kingdom, conceived as including

England, Scotland, and Wales, is a legitimate political order; the thirty-three states of the United States of America in 1860 comprised a legitimate political order; the ten provinces of Canada today comprise a legitimate political order.[1] Each of these three has or had a valid claim on the obedience of the inhabitants of its several parts—a claim that I should want to relate to the recognition it gives or gave to the rights of participation of those inhabitants. But this claim, which is at the core of legitimacy, does not in my view undermine the possibility of making a case for secession.

Buchanan compares political dissolution to divorce (7, and frequently thereafter). Divorce is not annulment; divorce does not call into question the legitimacy of the marriage that it ends. I want to say that metaphorically, Lithuania sought annulment, whereas South Carolina sought divorce. But even within the framework of divorce, I want to distinguish situations in which the political union has in effect broken down and lost its legitimacy—a fact that is then recognized in secession—from situations in which the political union loses its legitimacy only through secession. And of course these distinctions—between annulment and divorce, breakdown and dissolution—become matters of degree and interpretation when applied. For example, how shall we interpret secession in Croatia and Slovenia: annulment of a union that was coercively formed after the First World War and was never legitimate, or divorce from a union that had acquired but then lost legitimacy?

In restricting my attention to legitimate political orders, I want to exclude situations central to Buchanan's account, both those that involve state-perpetrated injustice, at least of a serious kind, and those in which the existing state is unable or unwilling to assure the literal survival of the prospective secessionists. I take significant injustice to deprive the state of legitimacy in relation to those treated

---

[1] I leave also to one side the existence of groups who fall outside the legitimate order—certainly Blacks in the ante-bellum United States, conceivably the first peoples—Amerindians and Inuit—today in Canada.

unjustly; hence I deny that Blacks in ante-bellum America had any obligation to accept the political and legal order. (Compulsion is of course another matter.) And if literal survival is at stake, then, as Hobbes (for example) acknowledges, persons are free to make whatever arrangements for themselves they can, whatever their prior political obligations may have been.[1] So I can agree with Buchanan that Jews in pre-WW II Europe would have been entitled to secede from existing states to create their own if that had been a feasible option for them (66).

II

In what follows, I shall suppose that neither injustice nor literal survival is involved. I shall suppose a secessionist movement that may have cultural or other aims, but that for whatever reason wants to redraw the political map by creating a new and distinct sovereign community—or less frequently, perhaps, by separating from one political community and joining another existing one, as I interpret the case of secessionist Catholics in Northern Ireland.

To discuss secession in these contexts, I shall appeal to what might be thought of as weak rights of association and non-association. I shall treat these as strictly individual rights; I have no place for group rights in my account. I begin from the simple idea of interaction. Familiar arguments exhibit the costs of unconstrained interaction in which each person directly seeks to realize his or her concerns; the deep contractarian idea is that each person is morally bound by terms of interaction that it would have been rational for her to agree to in a suitably characterized *ex ante* situation. It is then natural to suppose that these terms will favor social institutions and practices that provide for an extensive although not unlimited freedom of contract and association. Although each person will be constrained in the unilateral costs she may impose on her fellows in the pursuit of her concerns, decisions to associate or not, to contract or not, will be left to be decided by free consent and so, given rationality,

mutual benefit, where such decisions are not associated with significant negative externalities.

What I have just said is advanced as a supposition, not a conclusive argument. A contractarian justification of political association, in terms of a rational *ex ante* agreement, need not in principle justify a contractual society—a society in which the freedom to relate to others by contract is central. For present purposes I am simply assuming that there is such a justification; I do not deny the size and significance of the assumption.

Consent applies directly to decisions to contract or not, given the bilateral character of the activity, but it must apply less directly to decisions to associate or not, given the multilateral character of many forms of association. I find it helpful to think of each person as having a weak right to enter into and continue political association with those with whom she wishes to associate and who wish to associate with her, and to avoid or exit from association with those with whom she wishes not to associate. By a "weak right" I intend one whose exercise must be coordinated with that of other persons in such a way that, other things equal, as many persons as possible will find themselves in mutually desirable association. Of course, other things often are not equal, and I shall have at least to indicate some of the relevant inequalities.

Let me underline the mutuality that is involved in the weak right of association. I do not have a right to enter into or continue in association with those who do not want to associate with me, however much I may think such association desirable. There are of course circumstances in which persons may be held to political associations with those whom they would avoid, but not because those whom they would avoid want them as political associates. Just as secession may be compared to divorce, so political association may be compared to marriage. I may have the right to marry the woman of my choice who also chooses me, but not the woman of my choice who rejects me.

It may be helpful to apply the idea of a weak right of association directly to the Irish situation. We may reasonably suppose that a significant majority

---

[1] Thomas Hobbes, *Leviathan* (London: Andrew Crooke, 1651), 114.

of the Catholic inhabitants of Northern Ireland (the Six Counties) do not want to continue in political association with the United Kingdom, and do want to enter political association with the Republic of Ireland,[1] a majority of whose inhabitants reciprocally want to enter into association with the North. But we must also suppose that a substantial majority of the Protestant inhabitants of Northern Ireland do want to continue in political association with the UK, and want not to enter political association with the Irish Republic.[2] Given that there are significantly more Protestants in Northern Ireland than Catholics (the ratio is about 5:3), if the Six Counties were to be united with the Republic, more persons would find themselves in association with those with whom they did not want to be in association than at present. And this would be contrary to the *prima facie* requirements of the weak right—the number of persons whose right of association was effectively exercised would diminish.

It may well be the case that if a referendum were held in the whole of Ireland, a substantial majority would support unification. But the desire for unification has in itself no weight insofar as it fails to be mutual. Consider the situation prior to the establishment of the then Irish Free State (i.e., what is now the Republic) in 1922. If a referendum had been held in what was then the United Kingdom—i.e., in the British Isles as a whole—almost certainly a majority would have opposed Irish secession. But the desire to maintain the British Isles as a single political association had no normative weight insofar as it failed to be mutual—that Englishmen wanted an association that included the Irish was in itself no reason for continuing such association, given that the Irish did not want association with the English. However, in accepting the

Free State, the United Kingdom nevertheless recognized that in the largest part of Ulster, most of the inhabitants preferred continued association with the UK than entry into association with the Free State, and so partitioned Ireland in such a way that more Irishmen were associated with those who were willing to associate with them, than would have occurred without partition.

To be sure, one might argue that the boundary between the Free State and Northern Ireland might have been drawn to accommodate the exercise of right of association by even more persons. Indeed, someone might argue that in principle the boundary could be drawn—by permitting enclaves of one state surrounded by another (compare Llivia, or Campione d'Italia)[3]—so that almost everyone could be accommodated in the association of his or her choice. But in the drawing of boundaries there are factors other than the right of association to consider, such as the provision of public services and the character of local economic relations. I merely gesture at these matters—my only claim is that some partition of Ireland seems clearly justified by the right of association, and that the actual partition is better justified than no partition.

I have dwelt on Ireland partly because I think that the reasons that lead me to reject the claims of the Catholic secessionists require me to accept the secession of Québec, should it be supported by a significant majority of Québécois. For even if the overwhelming majority of other Canadians opposed secession, our desire to continue association with Québec would have no more weight than the desire of the inhabitants of the Irish Republic to incorporate the Six Counties. For in both cases, this would be a desire to impose association on persons the majority of whom did not want it. If the Québécois come or have come to wish to be, in a fully sovereign sense, "Maîtres chez Nous,"[4] then the secession of Québec would lead to more persons being

---

[1] But perhaps not an overwhelming majority. A study reported in the British press in the autumn of 1992 suggested only 53% of Northern Irish Catholics preferred a united Ireland, while 38% preferred association with the United Kingdom.

[2] Indeed an overwhelming majority. The study referred to in n. [1, above] suggested that 92% of Northern Irish Protestants preferred association with the United Kingdom.

[3] Llivia is a Spanish enclave surrounded by France, Campione d'Italia an Italian enclave surrounded by Switzerland.

[4] ["Masters of our own house."]

in mutually acceptable association, in accordance with the requirements of the weak right.

III

But the weak right is certainly not the only consideration relevant to the justification of secession. By returning to the Irish situation I can introduce another fundamentally important factor. Suppose that the majority of the inhabitants of Great Britain, fed up with Irish squabbling, the IRA planting bombs in railway stations, blowing up military and police posts, Protestant extremists gunning down elderly Catholics in betting shops, and so on and on, decide that they no longer want to be in political association with the Six Counties. Then it may seem that the Northern Irish Protestants could no longer plead a weak right of association as justification for the continued incorporation of the Six Counties in the United Kingdom. For they would no longer be seeking to maintain association with those who reciprocally wanted to be associated with them.

As I have been interpreting the Irish situation, the Protestant majority of the Six Counties has been acting within the rights of its individual members in seeking to maintain association with the United Kingdom, and some members of the Catholic minority have wrongfully been seeking to deny members of the majority this exercise of their rights. (That the Catholics have themselves been wrongfully and unjustly treated in certain ways is no doubt true, but that mistreatment does not, at least in my view, justify them in trying to impose their desire to unite with the Irish Republic on a majority that prefers to be part of the United Kingdom.) To suppose that the inhabitants of Great Britain would be, in these circumstances, entitled to cut off the Six Counties is to suppose them entitled to terminate an existing political association because of the costs of defending it against an initially wrongful attempt to disrupt it. In effect the British would be saying to the Northern Irish, "Your right to be associated with us depends, not only on your wishing such an association, but also on our wishing it. But because of the costs of maintaining that right, we no longer wish it. And so you no longer have a right to association." The

British would be claiming that they were not acquiescing in the wrongful attempt of the Catholics to deny the Protestants exercise of their right of association, but merely terminating the conditions for the existence of the right that the Protestants were seeking to exercise.

Were the British to do this, the old label "Perfidious Albion" would be amply justified. A state that would refuse to defend one of its hitherto accepted and welcome parts against an attempt at dismemberment because the costs of defense made the part no longer welcome, would clearly not be fulfilling an essential part of the role for which political association exists. Thus I deny that the inhabitants of Great Britain have the right of majority secession, as it were—the right to cut off the Six Counties from the United Kingdom. They may not plead the cost of defending the association against an attempt to disrupt it as adequate normative ground for withdrawing their own consent to it.

Underlying my argument here is a more general principle. As I see it, the revised Lockean proviso, in the form I present it in *Morals by Agreement*—the requirement that one not better oneself by worsening another—is the core moral requirement.[1] Or, one might say, morality requires that one justify unilaterally imposing costs on or worsening the position of another, and admissible justifications must appeal either to an underlying expectation that particular unilateral impositions lead overall to mutual bettering, or to the necessity of the imposition in order to avoid worsening one's own position. The key problem in applying the proviso is to determine the background conditions against which bettering and worsening are to be measured. Now I take existing normative relationships, including those involved in political association, to be among these conditions. Thus given an existing political association between members of two groups, A and B, on terms that do not incorporate significant injustice, the members of A would violate the proviso were they to secede or exclude the members of B in a

---

[1] David Gauthier, *Morals by Agreement* (Oxford: Clarendon Press, 1986), 201–05.

way that increased their benefits (or lessened their costs) by reducing the benefits of the members of B (or increasing their costs). But this needs qualification: in particular, the intrinsic benefit derived from the desire to be part of the particular association itself is not to be included in the calculation. (Thus if A and B divorce at A's behest, B may not appeal to the loss of satisfaction of her desire to be married to A as a loss of benefit entitling her to compensation to avoid a proviso violation.)

Note that appeal to existing normative relationships must assume the justifiability of those relationships. That Lithuania's secession from the then Soviet Union might benefit Lithuanians at the expense of Russians and others provided no basis for alleging a proviso violation, given the coercive incorporation of Lithuania into the Soviet Union. But the proviso does have clear application to the prospect of the British seeking to exclude Northern Ireland from the United Kingdom. For it is evident that such exclusion would be intended to benefit the British—no more IRA bombings in London, no more defense forces in Northern Ireland—while making it more difficult for the Protestant Irish to protect themselves against the use of force by Catholics in the endeavor to create a single Irish state. And the inhabitants of Great Britain clearly may not complain that their existing political association with Northern Ireland has been coercively imposed on them, or that its terms discriminate against them.

I began with an appeal to a weak right of association that might seem to provide a much broader justification for secession than Buchanan is willing to accept. But now I have invoked a proviso that may seem to narrow that justification even more than he might wish. For will not almost any proposed secession benefit the seceding party and impose costs on the other, so that in the absence of injustice in the existing association that would nullify appeal to the proviso, the secession will be unjustifiable? In the case of Québec, is it not the case that the rest of Canada would be left poorer—culturally if not materially—were Québec to secede, so that the proviso could be invoked as a normative ground against it?

To answer this, I must argue that the scope of the proviso should be limited in a non-arbitrary, non-ad hoc way. I shall propose two limitations. The first relates directly to what I have just said about the Canadian situation. When different groups unite in political association, the members of each may expect to benefit from characteristics peculiar to and distinctive of the others, in ways that they would not benefit either from uniting with equal numbers of persons but with characteristics similar to their own, or from the existence of the others outside of the association. Secession necessarily ends those benefits. But I want to insist that their loss cannot justify any claim either against secession or for compensation. These benefits are not necessary to achieve the fundamental purposes of political association. They are best thought of as akin to the goods achieved through friendship, which depend on the truly voluntary and affectionate character of the relationship. To suppose that when friendship ceases, the parties may have claims against each other for the withdrawal of the goods that arose because of their friendly relationship, would be to misunderstand that relationship and its distinctive goods. I take the same to be true in the case of political association. We may see a parallel between the withdrawal of personal affection and that of political affection.

And so if the Québécois lose political affection for us, their fellow Canadians, they owe us no compensation and violate no obligation if we no longer enjoy the goods of that affection. But, it may be urged, the secession of Québec will deprive the rest of Canada of other goods. Perhaps there need be no direct material cost, but there may be, and there will indeed be, a political cost in that the Canada that remains will have a diminished capacity to advance its interests, particularly in relation to that nation which is at once our historic enemy and closest friend.[1]

---

[1] The second stanza of "The Maple Leaf," which in my youth rivalled "O Canada" as the national song, begins "At Queenston Heights and Lundy's Lane / Our brave fathers fought and died"—it was the United States they fought.

Here then I come to the second limitation on the scope of the proviso in relation to secession. I want to distinguish the productive consequences of secession from the distributive. A political community may achieve certain economies of scale—not only in the production of material goods, but also, as I have suggested, in advancing the interests of its members vis-à-vis the members of other political communities—that are lost if it divides. This loss is a productive consequence of secession. A political community also realizes a certain distribution of goods among its parts, and this distribution may be altered if it divides. Now I want to place the latter, but not the former, within the scope of the proviso. In the absence of existing injustice, the members of a group are not entitled to secede from an existing political community in a way that redistributes the goods achieved in that community in their favor, and at the expense of the other members. On the other hand, they are entitled to secede even if this eliminates certain economies of scale and therefore reduces the capacity of each successor or residual community to produce or provide certain goods for its members, so long as this reduction is shared among the successor or residual communities. Presumably those seceding expect other benefits—perhaps cultural—that outweigh the productive losses; my claim then is that they may secede to secure such goods without compensating the others for a shared productive loss.

Before attempting to defend this distinction, let me suggest some of the applications of the redistributive prohibition to our Canadian situation. Suppose Québec were to propose to secede, leaving the remainder with the entire national debt (this, I should emphasize, is not what Québécois separatists do propose). This would clearly be redistributive, and would obviously violate the proviso—per capita public debt would diminish to $0 in Québec and increase elsewhere. On the other hand, suppose the rest of Canada were to demand that Québec were to pay for all federal property in the province that would come into its possession, even though such property, in Québec and elsewhere, had been paid for by tax monies collected equitably in all parts of Canada, and the location of such property had been equitably and reasonably located in the various parts of Canada. This would then also be redistributive, and would be a proviso violation on the part of those opposing secession. Redistributive violations may occur in both directions, making the terms of secession either too permissive or too restrictive. Québec should not be permitted to secede without taking its fair share of the national debt, but it should be permitted to secede taking its fair share of what is presently federal property.

Or consider a very different type of situation. Suppose that the United Kingdom were to propose to cut St Helena loose, not in response to a demand for independence from St Helenans, but simply to save the annual subsidy. The subsidy is in itself redistributive; St Helena consumes more than it produces. It might then be alleged that the subsidy constitutes an existing proviso violation that would be eliminated were the UK to "secede" from it. But this, according to my account, is mistaken. The UK chose to acquire and subsidize St Helena; it can have then no grievance in justice against the existing arrangement. The subsidy is part of the background normative considerations against which violations of the proviso are to be determined; were the UK to seek to cut St Helena loose it would therefore be bettering the lot of its inhabitants (by eliminating the subsidy) and worsening the lot of the St Helenans. A state is not entitled to divest itself of colonies that it has ceased to want if such divestiture is not wanted by and would be at the expense of the inhabitants of the colony.

We are, I think, disposed to reject redistributive secession (in the absence of existing injustice). But precisely what is the case against it? And is there a principled distinction between distributive and productive considerations, such that a secession that diminishes production by eliminating certain economies of scale is nevertheless justifiable? Before proceeding, let me qualify the case for what might be called unproductive secession by setting aside the possibility of eliminating economies of scale on such a level that one of the successor communities would not be politically or economically viable. It seems to me that loss of viability would in practice involve a redistributive violation of the proviso; in any event, I think the possibility of loss of viability without such a violation sufficiently unlikely that I shall not attempt to deal with it.[1]

The proviso is intended to rule out the taking of advantage. It may seem evident that redistributive secession involves such taking. The secessionist party seeks to alter the character of an ongoing relationship, in which the several participants have coordinated their activities on the basis of shared expectations about the distribution of benefits each will receive from the outcome. And the secessionist party seeks to do this, not because the relationship has ceased to be advantageous or the distribution has ceased to conform to agreed terms, but merely in order to improve its relative position. We may suppose that the participants have invested in their relationship, expecting a continuing return on this investment, which the secessionist party proposes to deny them. A particular allocation of resources and pattern of mutual complementarity in economic development has been rationalized in part by the existence of boundaries that the secessionist party proposes to alter. One might deny that any of this involves the taking of advantage by arguing that if each participant envisages the possibility of unilateral secession, it will rationally take advance precautions to prevent being disadvantaged. Thus advantage would be taken only if some participant irrationally failed to anticipate this possibility, and one should not appeal to such a failure to argue that secession is unjustified. But precautions need not always be feasible, and in any event constitute unproductive costs; the potential value of association is therefore diminished by the prospect of redistributive secession. And so the character and form of political association will be affected adversely if each party thinks of itself as entitled to terminate it by secession merely in order to improve its relative position vis-à-vis the others.

But if the value and effectiveness of political association would be undermined by the use of

secession as an essentially strategic tool, it would be undermined in a very different way were secession to be unavailable to the members of those groups that seek to express and realize shared values through political association. Now I want to be very careful in the endorsement I offer here. I want to endorse only groups whose members themselves endorse both the weak right of association and the proviso. If you like, I want to legitimate secession only by those groups whose members accept the standards I am proposing for legitimating secession. But I want to hold that acceptance of the weak right of association is incompatible with applying the proviso to constrain unproductive secession. The weak right of association expresses the value we place on an individual being free to associate with whom he wishes to associate provided they wish to associate with him, and being equally free not to associate with those with whom he wishes not to associate, whether or not they wish to associate with him. Although, as I have noted, the effective exercise of this right must be limited in several ways, it would be totally undermined were persons not free to withdraw from existing political associations even when economies of scale would thereby be sacrificed.

And so I must be prepared to acquiesce, should the Québécois express a clear wish to secede from Canada. But there are terms and conditions—and boundaries. It will, I hope, prove illuminating to explore some of these, if only to apply and illustrate the more abstract ideas about secession that I have sketched.

IV

I want very briefly to introduce three particular issues. First, if Québec were to secede, then Canada would no longer be geographically contiguous; there would be the problem of access between Atlantic Canada and Ontario. Second, if the large majority of francophone Québécois were to wish to secede, there would be anglophone regions, especially the western part of the island of Montréal, whose inhabitants would be opposed to secession. And third, there would also be the enormous region of northern

---

[1] But see n. [2, p. 1097].

Québec, not part of the original French colony or of the province at the time of Confederation, much of which is inhabited largely by Cree and Inuit who may well not favor secession, and also the site of the power projects that many Québécois see as an essential part of their future well-being.

All of these issues have a territorial dimension. And I have said nothing, or almost nothing, about territoriality. The technology of political association is strongly territorial; whether this gives territoriality the appearance of being a value, or whether it reveals territoriality as an underlying human value, I shall not speculate. But let me say that I regard the territorial claims of political communities as strictly derivative from what might be called claims of habitation by individuals. If most of the persons actually inhabiting a particular territory wish to establish a political community among and restricted to themselves, then their claims of habitation provide a basis for the territorial claim of the community they establish—and a basis that normally overrides any other territorial claims.[1]

If Québec were to secede, then the terms of secession should guarantee free access between what would become non-contiguous regions of Canada. If the Atlantic provinces, Québec, and, say, Ontario formed three separate states, and if the Atlantic provinces and Ontario were to wish to unite, they would have no special right of mutual access that Québec (or alternatively the United States) would have a duty to recognize. But the right to secede from an existing state is not the right to disrupt what remains, or to prevent it from functioning as a single community. Access between the parts of a legitimate political community constitutes part of the background conditions against which benefits and costs are to be measured. And so failure to ensure effective access and communication between the newly non-contiguous parts of a state from which one seceded would constitute a unilateral imposition of cost on the remaining

inhabitants of that state. The seceding party should be expected to internalize the cost of providing such access in determining the benefits and costs of secession.[2]

My second issue addresses the situation of the anglophone majority in the western part of the island of Montréal, assuming that most of these persons would be strongly opposed to secession from Canada. The territorial claim—that the island of Montréal was part of the original French colony, and of the province of Québec as recognized at the time of Confederation—carries little weight in my argument. At most I can allow an appeal to historical considerations in seeking to establish salient boundaries in areas that might reasonably be disputed between different political communities. Of greater importance, in my view, is the extent to which the economic and social relations among parts of the island of Montréal and between Montréal and other parts of Québec, make the political division of the island infeasible. To be sure, one can divide a single urban community if one is sufficiently determined; the example of Berlin is fresh in memory. But it is hardly an example to be emulated.

My third and final issue addresses the situation of northern Québec. Let us assume that the Cree and Inuit inhabitants of that region do not wish to be part of an independent Québec, but prefer to

---

[1] I say "normally" because, for example, it might be the case that the actual inhabitants had recently and unjustly expelled other persons.

[2] One of the referees for this journal suggested that the secession of Québec might undermine the economic viability of the Atlantic provinces even if their access to the rest of Canada were assured. Since secession would not be overtly redistributive, this questions my claim that any loss of viability resulting from secession would in practice involve a redistributive violation of the proviso. However, the referee suggests, plausibly, that the most adverse effects for the Atlantic region would arise should the secession of Québec precipitate the break-up of the remainder of Canada. Certainly were that to occur, Ontario and the Western provinces, seeking to better their own situation, would have the obligation to avoid any redistribution costly to the Atlantic region. If honoring this obligation would permit the continuing viability of the Atlantic provinces, then the referee's real worry should be that the obligation would be ignored. While this is a legitimate political concern, it would not tell against my claim.

remain related to Canada.[1] The territory in question was not part of the original province of Québec, but was acquired by Canada from the Hudson's Bay Company in 1869, and was later transferred, part in 1898 and the remainder in 1912, by the Canadian government to Québec, reserving the federal government's rights and responsibilities in relation to the native peoples. Here considerations of economic and social feasibility do not speak strongly against the exercise of the weak right of association by the Cree and Inuit. To be sure, given the investment by the province of Québec in the development of hydro-electric power in the James Bay region, compensation for what would otherwise be a loss of capital and use at favorable rates of much of the electricity generated, would have to be provided by Canada.

But there is a further issue that does illustrate one way in which territorial considerations may be relevant to secession. Suppose that the land was uninhabited, or inhabited only by workers on the power projects. Would a seceding Québec have the right to this territory, given that it had come to jurisdiction over it only by transfer from the Canadian government? I think not. We may assume that the territory was transferred to the jurisdiction of Québec in the general interests of Canada. For Québec now to claim the territory would be to claim a benefit that the Québécois would not have attained on their own, since had Québec not been part of Canada it would not have gained jurisdiction over the territory of an English company, and to impose a cost on the inhabitants of the rest of Canada, who would no longer be members of the overall political community sharing in the products and wealth of that region. Against the background constituted by the way in which northern Québec was acquired by Canada and later placed under the jurisdiction of Québec, for an independent Québec to claim the area would be for it to seek to benefit itself at the expense of the remainder of Canada, in violation of the proviso.

The weak right to associate with those with whom you want to associate provided they want to associate with you, and the proviso against bettering yourself by worsening your fellows, have provided what normative framework there has been to my discussion. I have argued that these ground a broad right for the members of a group to bring about the secession of that group from the political community of which it has been a part, even if that community has been fully legitimate. Just as there is a moral case for no-fault divorce, so there is a moral case for no-fault secession. And just as no-fault divorce may be emotionally agonizing for those who experience it, so may no-fault secession. I do not want that agony, and so I can only conclude with the hope that my country will not prove to be one of the first states in which the theory of no-fault secession is put into political practice.

---

[1] I say "related to" because there are complications here arising from the demands of first peoples for some form of autonomy.

DISCUSSION QUESTIONS

1. Explain Gauthier's notion of a weak right of association and how it bears on the issue of secession. What conditions must be met for secession to be legitimate or justified?

2. Compare and contrast the case of possible secession on the part of Québec, which Gauthier discusses, with the secession of the South from the United States in the nineteenth century. Should the South's secession be viewed as legitimate or illegitimate under Gauthier's theory? Is there a significant moral difference between the South's desire to secede and the desire of the American colonists to secede from Britain?

97

Abraham Lincoln, First Inaugural Address (1861)

Abraham Lincoln (1809–65) served as the sixteenth president of the United States from March of 1861 until his assassination in April of 1865. The following is the text of Lincoln's first inaugural address to the nation, delivered on March 4, 1861, as Lincoln was sworn into office. The speech is aimed primarily at the South, as the nation was on the verge of Civil War. Indeed, at the time of Lincoln's inauguration, seven states had already seceded from the Union to form the Confederate States of America. Here, Lincoln informs the nation of his intentions as president, explains why he thinks the nation is indissoluble, and presents his argument against secession.

SOURCE

Lincoln, Abraham. *Abraham Lincoln: Complete Works*, vol. II. Ed. J.G. Nicolay and J. Hay. The Century Co., 1922.

Fellow citizens of the United States: in compliance with a custom as old as the government itself, I appear before you to address you briefly and to take, in your presence, the oath prescribed by the Constitution of the United States, to be taken by the President "before he enters on the execution of his office."

I do not consider it necessary, at present, for me to discuss those matters of administration about which there is no special anxiety, or excitement.

Apprehension seems to exist among the people of the Southern States that by the accession of a Republican administration their property and their peace and personal security are to be endangered. There has never been any reasonable cause for such apprehension. Indeed, the most ample evidence to the contrary has all the while existed and been open to their inspection. It is found in nearly all the published speeches of him who now addresses you. I do but quote from one of those speeches when I declare that "I have no purpose, directly or indirectly, to interfere with the institution of slavery where it exists. I believe I have no lawful right to do so, and I have no inclination to do so." Those who nominated and elected me did so with full knowledge that I had made this and many similar declarations, and had never recanted them. And, more than this, they placed in the platform for my acceptance, and as a law to themselves and to me, the clear and emphatic resolution which I now read:

Resolved: that the maintenance inviolate of the rights of the States, and especially the right of each State to order and control its own domestic institutions according to its own judgment exclusively, is essential to that balance of power on which the perfection and endurance of our political fabric depend, and we denounce the lawless invasion by armed force of the soil of any State or Territory, no matter under what pretext, as among the gravest of crimes.

I now reiterate these sentiments; and, in doing so, I only press upon the public attention the most conclusive evidence of which the case is susceptible, that the property, peace, and security of no section are to be in any wise endangered by the now incoming administration. I add, too, that all the protection which, consistently with the Constitution and the laws, can be given, will be cheerfully given to all the States when lawfully demanded, for whatever cause—as cheerfully to one section as to another.

There is much controversy about the delivering up of fugitives from service or labor. The clause I now read is as plainly written in the Constitution as any other of its provisions:

No person held to service or labor in one State, under the laws thereof, escaping into another, shall in consequence of any law or regulation therein be discharged from such service or labor, but shall be delivered up on claim of the party to whom such service or labor may be due.

It is scarcely questioned that this provision was intended by those who made it for the reclaiming of what we call fugitive slaves; and the intention of the lawgiver is the law. All members of Congress swear their support to the whole Constitution—to this provision as much as to any other. To the proposition, then, that slaves whose cases come within the terms of this clause "shall be delivered up," their oaths are unanimous. Now, if they would make the effort in good temper, could they not with nearly

equal unanimity frame and pass a law by means of which to keep good that unanimous oath?

There is some difference of opinion whether this clause should be enforced by national or by State authority; but surely that difference is not a very material one. If the slave is to be surrendered, it can be of but little consequence to him or to others by which authority it is done. And should any one in any case be content that his oath shall go unkept on a merely unsubstantial controversy as to *how* it shall be kept? Again, in any law upon this subject, ought not all the safeguards of liberty known in civilized and humane jurisprudence to be introduced, so that a free man be not, in any case, surrendered as a slave? And might it not be well at the same time to provide by law for the enforcement of that clause in the Constitution which guarantees that "the citizen of each State shall be entitled to all privileges and immunities of citizens in the several States"?

I take the official oath today with no mental reservations, and with no purpose to construe the Constitution or laws by any hypercritical rules. And while I do not choose now to specify particular acts of Congress as proper to be enforced, I do suggest that it will be much safer for all, both in official and private stations, to conform to and abide by all those acts which stand unrepealed, than to violate any of them, trusting to find impunity in having them held to be unConstitutional.

It is seventy-two years since the first inauguration of a President under our national Constitution. During that period fifteen different and greatly distinguished citizens have, in succession, administered the executive branch of the government. They have conducted it through many perils, and generally with great success. Yet, with all this scope of precedent, I now enter upon the same task for the brief Constitutional term of four years under great and peculiar difficulty. A disruption of the Federal Union, heretofore only menaced, is now formidably attempted.

I hold that, in contemplation of universal law and of the Constitution, the Union of these States is perpetual. Perpetuity is implied, if not expressed, in the fundamental law of all national governments.

It is safe to assert that no government proper ever had a provision in its organic law for its own termination. Continue to execute all the express provisions of our National Constitution, and the Union will endure forever—it being impossible to destroy it except by some action not provided for in the instrument itself.

Again, if the United States be not a government proper, but an association of States in the nature of contract merely, can it, as a contract, be peaceably unmade by less than all the parties who made it? One party to a contract may violate it—break it, so to speak; but does it not require all to lawfully rescind it?

Descending from these general principles, we find the proposition that in legal contemplation the Union is perpetual confirmed by the history of the Union itself. The Union is much older than the Constitution. It was formed, in fact, by the Articles of Association in 1774. It was matured and continued by the Declaration of Independence in 1776. It was further matured, and the faith of all the then thirteen States expressly plighted and engaged that it should be perpetual, by the Articles of Confederation in 1778. And, finally, in 1787 one of the declared objects for ordaining and establishing the Constitution was "*to form a more perfect union.*"

But if the destruction of the Union by one or by a part only of the States be lawfully possible, the Union is *less* perfect than before the Constitution, having lost the vital element of perpetuity.

It follows from these views that no State upon its own mere motion can lawfully get out of the Union; that Resolves and Ordinances to that effect are legally void; and that acts of violence, within any State or States, against the authority of the United States, are insurrectionary or revolutionary, according to circumstances.

I therefore consider that, in view of the Constitution and the laws, the Union is unbroken; and to the extent of my ability I shall take care, as the Constitution itself expressly enjoins upon me, that the laws of the Union be faithfully executed in all the States. Doing this I deem to be only a simple duty on my part; and I shall perform it so far as practicable, unless my rightful masters, the American people, shall withhold the requisite means, or in some authoritative manner direct the contrary. I trust this will not be regarded as a menace, but only as the declared purpose of the Union that it *will* Constitutionally defend and maintain itself.

In doing this there needs to be no bloodshed or violence; and there shall be none, unless it be forced upon the national authority. The power confided to me will be used to hold, occupy, and possess the property and places belonging to the government, and to collect the duties and imposts; but beyond what may be necessary for these objects, there will be no invasion, no using of force against or among the people anywhere. Where hostility to the United States, in any interior locality, shall be so great and universal as to prevent competent resident citizens from holding the Federal offices, there will be no attempt to force obnoxious strangers among the people for that object. While the strict legal right may exist in the government to enforce the exercise of these offices, the attempt to do so would be so irritating, and so nearly impracticable withal, that I deem it better to forego for the time the uses of such offices.

The mails, unless repelled, will continue to be furnished in all parts of the Union. So far as possible, the people everywhere shall have that sense of perfect security which is most favorable to calm thought and reflection. The course here indicated will be followed unless current events and experience shall show a modification or change to be proper, and in every case and exigency my best discretion will be exercised according to circumstances actually existing, and with a view and a hope of a peaceful solution of the national troubles and the restoration of fraternal sympathies and affections.

That there are persons in one section or another who seek to destroy the Union at all events, and are glad of any pretext to do it, I will neither affirm nor deny; but if there be such, I need address no word to them. To those, however, who really love the Union may I not speak?

Before entering upon so grave a matter as the destruction of our national fabric, with all its benefits, its memories, and its hopes, would it not be wise to ascertain precisely why we do it? Will you hazard so desperate a step while there is any possibility that any portion of the ills you fly from have no real existence? Will you, while the certain ills you fly to are greater than all the real ones you fly from—will you risk the commission of so fearful a mistake?

All profess to be content in the Union if all Constitutional rights can be maintained. Is it true, then, that any right, plainly written in the Constitution, has been denied? I think not. Happily the human mind is so constituted that no party can reach to the audacity of doing this. Think, if you can, of a single instance in which a plainly written provision of the Constitution has ever been denied. If by the mere force of numbers a majority should deprive a minority of any clearly written Constitutional right, it might, in a moral point of view, justify revolution—certainly would if such a right were a vital one. But such is not our case. All the vital rights of minorities and of individuals are so plainly assured to them by affirmations and negations, guaranties and prohibitions, in the Constitution, that controversies never arise concerning them. But no organic law can ever be framed with a provision specifically applicable to every question which may occur in practical administration. No foresight can anticipate, nor any document of reasonable length contain, express provisions for all possible questions. Shall fugitives from labor be surrendered by national or State authority? The Constitution does not expressly say. May Congress prohibit slavery in the Territories? The Constitution does not expressly say. *Must* Congress protect slavery in the Territories? The Constitution does not expressly say.

From questions of this class spring all our Constitutional controversies, and we divide upon them into majorities and minorities. If the minority will not acquiesce, the majority must, or the government must cease. There is no other alternative; for continuing the government is acquiescence on one side or the other.

If a minority in such case will secede rather than acquiesce, they make a precedent which in turn will divide and ruin them; for a minority of their own will secede from them whenever a majority refuses to be controlled by such minority. For instance, why may not any portion of a new confederacy a year or two hence arbitrarily secede again, precisely as portions of the present Union now claim to secede from it? All who cherish disunion sentiments are now being educated to the exact temper of doing this.

Is there such perfect identity of interests among the States to compose a new Union, as to produce harmony only, and prevent renewed secession?

Plainly, the central idea of secession is the essence of anarchy. A majority held in restraint by Constitutional checks and limitations, and always changing easily with deliberate changes of popular opinions and sentiments, is the only true sovereign of a free people. Whoever rejects it does, of necessity, fly to anarchy or to despotism. Unanimity is impossible; the rule of a minority, as a permanent arrangement, is wholly inadmissible; so that, rejecting the majority principle, anarchy or despotism in some form is all that is left.

I do not forget the position, assumed by some, that Constitutional questions are to be decided by the Supreme Court; nor do I deny that such decisions must be binding, in any case, upon the parties to a suit, as to the object of that suit, while they are also entitled to very high respect and consideration in all parallel cases by all other departments of the government. And while it is obviously possible that such decision may be erroneous in any given case, still the evil effect following it, being limited to that particular case, with the chance that it may be overruled and never become a precedent for other cases, can better be borne than could the evils of a different practice. At the same time, the candid citizen must confess that if the policy of the government, upon vital questions affecting the whole people, is to be irrevocably fixed by decisions of the Supreme Court, the instant they are made, in ordinary litigation between parties in personal actions, the people will have ceased to be their own rulers, having to that extent practically resigned their government into the hands of that eminent tribunal. Nor is there in this view any assault upon the court or the judges. It is a duty from which they may not shrink to decide cases properly brought before them, and it is no fault of theirs if others seek to turn their decisions to political purposes.

One section of our country believes slavery is *right*, and ought to be extended, while the other believes it is *wrong*, and ought not to be extended. This is the only substantial dispute. The fugitive-slave clause of the Constitution, and the law for the suppression of the foreign slave-trade, are each as well enforced, perhaps, as any law can ever be in a community where the moral sense of the people imperfectly supports the law itself. The great body of the people abide by the dry legal obligation in both cases, and a few break over in each. This, I think, cannot be perfectly cured; and it would be worse in both cases *after* the separation of the sections than *before*. The foreign slave-trade, now imperfectly suppressed, would be ultimately revived, without restriction, in one section, while fugitive slaves, now only partially surrendered, would not be surrendered at all by the other.

Physically speaking, we cannot separate. We cannot remove our respective sections from each other, nor build an impassable wall between them. A husband and wife may be divorced, and go out of the presence and beyond the reach of each other; but the different parts of our country cannot do this. They cannot but remain face to face, and intercourse, either amicable or hostile, must continue between them. Is it possible, then, to make that intercourse more advantageous or more satisfactory after separation than before? Can aliens make treaties easier than friends can make laws? Can treaties be more faithfully enforced between aliens than laws can among friends? Suppose you go to war, you cannot fight always; and when, after much loss on both sides, and no gain on either, you cease fighting, the identical old questions as to terms of intercourse are again upon you.

This country, with its institutions, belongs to the people who inhabit it. Whenever they shall grow weary of the existing government, they can exercise their *Constitutional* right of amending it, or their *revolutionary* right to dismember or overthrow it. I cannot be ignorant of the fact that many worthy and patriotic citizens are desirous of having the national Constitution amended. While I make no recommendation of amendments, I fully recognize the rightful authority of the people over the whole subject, to be exercised in either of the modes prescribed in the instrument itself; and I should, under existing circumstances, favor rather than oppose a fair opportunity being afforded the people to act upon it. I will venture to add that to me the convention mode seems preferable, in that it allows amendments to originate with the people themselves, instead of only permitting them to take or reject propositions originated by others not especially chosen for the purpose, and which might not be precisely such as they would wish to either accept or refuse. I understand a proposed amendment to the Constitution—which amendment, however, I have not seen—has passed Congress, to the effect that the Federal Government shall never interfere with the domestic institutions of the States, including that of persons held to service. To avoid misconstruction of what I have said, I depart from my purpose not to speak of particular amendments so far as to say that, holding such a provision to now be implied Constitutional law, I have no objection to its being made express and irrevocable.

The chief magistrate derives all his authority from the people, and they have conferred none upon him to fix terms for the separation of the states. The people themselves can do this also if they choose; but the executive, as such, has nothing to do with it. His duty is to administer the present government, as it came to his hands, and to transmit it, unimpaired by him, to his successor.

Why should there not be a patient confidence in the ultimate justice of the people? Is there any better or equal hope in the world? In our present differences is either party without faith of being in the right? If the Almighty Ruler of Nations, with his eternal truth and justice, be on your side of the North, or on yours of the South, that truth and that justice will surely prevail, by the judgment of this great tribunal, the American people.

By the frame of the government under which we live, this same people have wisely given their public servants but little power for mischief; and have, with equal wisdom, provided for the return of that little to their own hands at very short intervals. While the people retain their virtue and vigilance, no administration, by any extreme of wickedness or folly, can very seriously injure the government in the short space of four years.

My countrymen, one and all, think calmly and *well* upon this whole subject. Nothing valuable can be lost by taking time. If there be an object to *hurry* any of you in hot haste to a step which you would never take *deliberately*, that object will be frustrated by taking time; but no good object can be frustrated by it. Such of you as are now dissatisfied, still have the old Constitution unimpaired, and, on the sensitive point, the laws of your own framing under it; while the new administration will have no immediate power, if it would, to change either. If it were admitted that you who are dissatisfied hold the right side in the dispute, there still is no single good reason for precipitate action. Intelligence, patriotism, Christianity, and a firm reliance on him who has never yet forsaken this favored land, are still competent to adjust in the best way all our present difficulty.

In *your* hands, my dissatisfied fellow-countrymen, and not in *mine*, is the momentous issue of civil war. The government will not assail *you*. You can have no conflict without being yourselves the aggressors. *You* have no oath registered in heaven to destroy the government, while *I* shall have the most solemn one to "preserve, protect, and defend it."

I am loath to close. We are not enemies, but friends. We must not be enemies. Though passion may have strained, it must not break our bonds of affection. The mystic chords of memory, stretching from every battlefield and patriot grave to every living heart and hearthstone all over this broad land, will yet swell the chorus of the Union when again touched, as surely they will be, by the better angels of our nature.

DISCUSSION QUESTIONS

1. Lincoln writes, "the Union of these States is perpetual," and "no government proper even had a provision in its organic law for its own termination." What does he mean by this? How does this bear on the issue of secession? Does this provide reasons for supposing secession is wrong? Is there any reason why a state *couldn't* have a provision of this sort?

2. What reasons or arguments does Lincoln provide against secession? Do you think these are good reasons? Why or why not?

3. Would Lincoln largely agree or largely disagree with Gauthier's theory of secession? Cite specific passages from the readings to support your case.

4. Lincoln claims, "The central idea of secession is the essence of anarchy." What does he mean by this? Would Lincoln be able to recognize the legitimacy of the American Revolution, or must he view it as he views the possibility of Southern secession—i.e., as unjustified and misdirected? Explain.

98

G.E.M. Anscombe, "Mr. Truman's Degree" (1981)

G.E.M. Anscombe (1919–2001) was a British analytic philosopher. She is perhaps best known for her translation of Ludwig Wittgenstein's *Philosophical Investigations*. Following 24 years at Oxford, she served as professor of philosophy at Cambridge University from 1970 until her retirement in 1986. In 1956, while at Oxford, Anscombe wrote the following pamphlet as an act of protest against the university's decision to award an honorary doctorate to Harry Truman.

SOURCE

Anscombe, G.E.M. "Mr. Truman's Degree," from *The Collected Philosophical Papers of G.E.M. Anscombe*, Vol. III (Ethics, Religion and Politics). Copyright © 1981 by Blackwell Publishing Ltd. Reproduced with permission of Blackwell Publishing Ltd.

In 1939, on the outbreak of war, the President of the United States asked for assurances from the belligerent nations that civil populations would not be attacked.

In 1945, when the Japanese enemy was known by him to have made two attempts toward a negotiated peace, the President of the United States gave the order for dropping an atom bomb on a Japanese city; three days later a second bomb, of a different type, was dropped on another city. No ultimatum was delivered before the second bomb was dropped.

Set side by side, these events provide enough of a contrast to provoke enquiry. Evidently development has taken place; one would like to see its course plotted. It is not, I think, difficult to give an intelligible account:—

(1) The British Government gave President Roosevelt the required assurance, with a reservation which meant "If the Germans do it we shall do it too." You don't promise to abide by the Queensbury Rules even if your opponent abandons them.

(2) The only condition for ending the war was announced to be unconditional surrender. Apart from the "liberation of the subject peoples," the objectives were vague in character. Now the demand for unconditional surrender was mixed up with a determination to make no peace with Hitler's government. In view of the character of Hitler's regime that attitude was very intelligible. Nevertheless some people have doubts about it now. It is suggested that defeat of itself would have resulted in the rapid

discredit and downfall of that government. On this I can form no strong opinion. The important question to my mind is whether the intention of making no peace with Hitler's government necessarily entailed the objective of unconditional surrender. If, as may not be impossible, we could have formulated a pretty definite objective, a rough outline of the terms which we were willing to make with Germany, while at the same time indicating that we would not make terms with *Hitler's* government, then the question of the wisdom of this latter demand seems to me a minor one; but if not, then that settles it. It was the insistence on unconditional surrender that was the root of all evil. The connection between such a demand and the need to use the most ferocious methods of warfare will be obvious. And in itself the proposal of an unlimited objective in war is stupid and barbarous.

(3) The Germans did a good deal of indiscriminate bombing in this country. It is impossible for an uninformed person to know how much, in its first beginnings, was due to indifference on the part of pilots to using their loads only on military targets, and how much to actual policy on the part of those who sent them. Nor do I know what we were doing at the same time. But certainly anyone would have been stupid who had thought in 1939 that there would not be such bombing, developing into definite raids on cities.

(4) For some time before war broke out, and more intensely afterwards, there was propaganda in this country on the subject of the "indivisibility" of modern war. The civilian population, we were told, is really as much combatant as the fighting forces. The military strength of a nation includes its whole economic and social strength. Therefore the distinction between the people engaged in prosecuting the war and the population at large is unreal. There is no such thing as a non-participator; you cannot buy a postage stamp or any taxed article, or grow a potato or cook a meal, without contributing to the "war effort." War indeed is a "ghastly evil," but once it has broken out no one can "contract out" of it. "Wrong" indeed must be being done if war is waged, but you cannot help being involved in it.

There was a doctrine of "collective responsibility" with a lugubriously elevated moral tone about it. The upshot was that it was senseless to draw any line between legitimate and illegitimate objects of attack.—Thus the court chaplains of democracy. I am not sure how children and the aged fitted into this story: probably they cheered the soldiers and munitions workers up.

(5) The Japanese attacked Pearl Harbor and there was war between America and Japan. Some American (Republican) historians now claim that the acknowledged fact that the American Government knew an attack was impending some hours before it occurred, but did not alert the people in local command, can only be explained by a purpose of arousing the passions of American people. However that may be, those passions were suitably aroused and the war was entered on with the same vague and hence limitless objectives; and once more unconditional surrender was the only condition on which the war was going to end.

(6) Then came the great change: we adopted the system of "area bombing" as opposed to "target bombing." This differed from even big raids on cities, such as had previously taken place in the course of the war, by being far more extensive and devastating and much less random; the whole of a city area would be systematically plotted out and dotted with bombs. "Attila was a Sissy," as the *Chicago Tribune* headed an article on this subject.

(7) In 1945, at the Postdam conference in July, Stalin informed the American and British statesmen that he had received two requests from the Japanese to act as a mediator with a view to ending the war. He had refused. The Allies agreed on the "general principle"—marvellous phrase!—of using the new type of weapon that the Americans now possessed. The Japanese were given a chance in the form of the Potsdam Declaration, calling for unconditional surrender in face of overwhelming force soon to be arrayed against them. The historian of the Survey of International Affairs considers that this phrase was rendered meaningless by the statement of a series of terms; but of these the ones incorporating the Allies' demands were mostly of so vague and

sweeping a nature as to be rather a declaration of what unconditional surrender would be like than to constitute conditions. It seems to be generally agreed that the Japanese were desperate enough to have accepted the Declaration but for their loyalty to their Emperor: the "terms" would certainly have permitted the Allies to get rid of him if they chose. The Japanese refused the Declaration. In consequence, the bombs were dropped on Hiroshima and Nagasaki. The decision to use them on people was Mr. Truman's.

[...]

For men to choose to kill the innocent as a means to their ends is always murder, and murder is one of the worst of human actions. So the prohibition on deliberately killing prisoners of war or the civilian population is not like the Queensbury Rules: its force does not depend on its promulgation as part of positive law, written down, agreed upon, and adhered to by the parties concerned.

When I say that to choose to kill the innocent as a means to one's ends is murder, I am saying what would generally be accepted as correct. But I shall be asked for my definition of "the innocent." I will give it, but later. Here, it is not necessary; for with Hiroshima and Nagasaki we are not confronted with a borderline case. In the bombing of these cities it was certainly decided to kill the innocent as a means to an end. And a very large number of them, all at once, without warning, without the interstices of escape or the chance to take shelter, which existed even in the "area bombing" of the German cities.

I have long been puzzled by the common cant about President Truman's courage in making this decision. Of course, I know that you can be cowardly without having reason to think you are in danger. But how can you be courageous? Light has come to me lately: the term is an acknowledgement of the truth. Mr. Truman was brave because, and only because, what he did was so bad. But I think the judgement unsound. Given the right circumstances (e.g., that no one whose opinion matters will disapprove), a quite mediocre person can do spectacularly wicked things without thereby becoming impressive.

I determined to oppose the proposal to give Mr. Truman an honorary degree here at Oxford. Now, an honorary degree is not a reward of merit: it is, as it were, a reward for being a very distinguished person, and it would be foolish to enquire whether a candidate deserves to be as distinguished as he is. That is why, in general, the question whether so-and-so should have an honorary degree is devoid of interest. A very distinguished person will hardly be also a notorious criminal, and if he should chance to be a non-notorious criminal it would, in my opinion, be improper to bring the matter up. It is only in the rather rare case in which a man is known everywhere for an action, in fact of which it is sycophancy to honor him, that the question can be of the slightest interest.

I have been accused of being "high-minded." I must be saying "You may not do evil that good may come," which is a disagreeably high-minded doctrine. The action was necessary, or at any rate it was thought by competent, expert military opinion to be necessary; it probably saved more lives than it sacrificed; it had a good result, it ended the war. Come now: if you had to choose between boiling one baby and letting some frightful disaster befall a thousand people—or a million people, if a thousand is not enough—what would you do? Are you going to strike an attitude and say "You may not do evil that good may come"? (People who never hear such arguments will hardly believe they take place, and will pass this rapidly by.)

"It pretty certainly saved a huge number of lives." Given the conditions, I agree. That is to say, if those bombs had not been dropped the Allies would have had to invade Japan to achieve their aim, and they would have done so. Very many soldiers on both sides would have been killed; the Japanese, it is said—and it may well be true—would have massacred the prisoners of war; and large numbers of their civilian population would have been killed by "ordinary" bombing.

I do not dispute it. Given the conditions, that was probably what was averted by that action. But what were the conditions? The unlimited objective, the fixation on unconditional surrender. The disregard of the fact that the Japanese were desirous of negotiating peace. The character of the Potsdam Declaration—their "chance." I will not suggest, as some would like to do, that there was an exultant itch to use the new weapons, but it seems plausible to think that the consciousness of the possession of such instruments had its effect on the manner in which the Japanese were offered their "chance."

We can now reformulate the principle of "doing evil that good may come." Every fool can be as much of a knave as suits him.

I recommend this history to undergraduates reading Greats as throwing a glaring light on Aristotle's thesis that you cannot be or do any good where you are stupid.

I informed the Senior Proctor of my intention to oppose Mr. Truman's degree. He consulted the Registrar to get me informed on procedure. The Vice-Chancellor was informed; I was cautiously asked if I had got up a party. I had not; but a fine House was whipped up to vote for the honour. The dons at St. John's were simply told "The women are up to something in Convocation; we have to go and vote them down." In Worcester, in All Souls, in New College, however, consciences were greatly exercised, as I have heard. A reason was found to satisfy them: *It would be wrong to try to PUNISH Mr. Truman!* I must say I rather like St. John's.

The Censor of St. Catherine's had an odious task. He must make a speech which should pretend to show that a couple of massacres to a man's credit are not exactly a reason for not showing him honour. He had, however, one great advantage: he did not have to persuade his audience, who were already perfectly convinced of that proposition. But at any rate he had to make a show.

The defence, I think, would not have been well received at Nuremberg.

We do not approve the action; no, we think it was a *mistake*. (That is how communists now talk about Stalin's more murderous proceedings.) Further, Mr. Truman did not make the bombs by himself, and decide to drop them without consulting anybody; no, he was only responsible for the decision. Hang it all, you can't make a man responsible just because "his is the signature at the foot of the order." Or was he not even responsible for the decision? It was not quite clear whether Mr. Bullock was saying that or not; but I never heard anyone else seem to give the lie to Mr. Truman's boasts. Finally, an action of this sort is, after all, only one episode: an incident, as it were, in a career. Mr. Truman has done some good.

I know that in one way such a speech does not deserve scrutiny; after all, it was just something to say on its occasion. And he had to say something. One must not suppose that one can glean anything a man actually thinks from what he says in such circumstances. Professor Stebbing exposing the logical fallacies in politicians' speeches is a comic spectacle.

II.

Choosing to kill the innocent as a means to your ends is always murder. Naturally, killing the innocent as an end in itself is murder too; but that is no more than a possible future development for us:[1] In our part of the globe it is a practice that has so far been confined to the Nazis. I intend my formulation to be taken strictly; each term in it is necessary. For killing the innocent, even if you know as a matter of statistical certainty that the things you do involve it, is not necessarily murder. I mean that if you attack a lot of military targets, such as munitions factories and naval dockyards, as carefully as you can, you will be certain to kill a number of innocent people; but that is not murder. On the other hand, unscrupulousness in considering the possibilities turns it into murder. I here print as a case in point a letter which I received lately from Holland:

We read in our paper about your opposition to Truman. I do not like him either, but do you know that in the war the English bombed the dykes of our province Zeeland,

---

[1] This will seem a preposterous assertion; but we are certainly on the way, and I can think of no reasons for confidence that it will not happen.

an island where nobody could escape anywhere to. Where the whole population was drowned, children, women, farmers working in the field, all the cattle, everything, hundreds and hundreds, and we were your allies! Nobody ever speaks about that. Perhaps it were well to know this. Or, to remember.

That was to trap some fleeing German military. I think my correspondent has something.

It may be impossible to take the thing (or people) you want to destroy as your target; it may be possible to attack it only by taking as the object of your attack what includes large numbers of innocent people. Then you cannot very well say they died by accident. Here, your action is murder.

"But where will you draw the line? It is impossible to draw an exact line." This is a common and absurd argument against drawing any line; it may be very difficult, and there are obviously borderline cases. But we have fallen into the way of drawing no line and offering as justifications what an uncaptive mind will find only a bad joke. Wherever the line is, certain things are certainly well to one side or the other of it.

Now who are "the innocent" in war? They are all those who are not fighting and not engaged in supply those who are with the means of fighting. A farmer growing wheat which may be eaten by the troops is not "supplying them with the means of fighting." Over this, too, the line may be difficult to draw. But that does not mean that no line should be drawn, or that, even if one is in doubt just where to draw the line, one cannot be crystal clear that this or that is well over the line.

"But the people fighting are probably just conscripts! In that case they are just as innocent as anyone else." "Innocent" here is not a term referring to personal responsibility at all. It means rather "not harming." But the people fighting are "harming," so they can be attacked; but if they surrender they become in this sense innocent and so may not be maltreated or killed. Nor is there ground for trying them on a criminal charge; not, indeed, because a man has no personal responsibility for fighting, but because they were not the subjects of the state whose prisoners they are.

There is an argument which I know from experience it is necessary to forestall at this point, though I think it is visibly captious. It is this: on my theory, would it not follow that a soldier can only be killed when he is actually attacking? Then, *e.g.*, it would be impossible to attack a sleeping camp. The answer is that "what someone is doing" can refer to what he is doing at the moment or to his rôle in a situation. A soldier under arms is "harming" in the latter sense even if he is asleep. But it is true that the enemy should not be attacked more ferociously than is necessary to put them *hors de combat*.

These conceptions are distinct and intelligible ones; they would formerly have been said to belong to the Law of Nations. Anyone can see that they are good, and we pay tribute to them by our moral indignation when our enemies violate them. But in fact they are going, and only fragments of them are left. General Eisenhower, for example, is reported to have spoken slightingly once of the notion of chivalry towards prisoners—as if that were based on respect for their virtue or for the nation from which they come, and not on the fact that they are now defenceless.

It is characteristic of nowadays to talk with horror of killing rather than of murder, and hence, since in war, since you have committed yourself to killing—*i.e.*, "accepted an evil"—not to mind whom you kill. This seems largely to be the work of the devil; but I also suspect that it is in part an effect of the existence of pacifism, as a doctrine which many people respect though they would not adopt it. This effect would not exist if people had a distinct notion of what makes pacifism a false doctrine.

It therefore seems to me important to show that for one human being deliberately to kill another is not inevitably wrong. I may seem to be wasting my time, as most people do reject pacifism. But it is nevertheless important to argue the point because if one does so one sees that there are pretty severe restrictions on legitimate killing. Of course, people accept this within the state, but when it comes to war they have the idea that any restrictions are something like the Queensbury Rules—instead of making the difference between being guilty and not guilty of murder.

I will not discuss the self-defence of a private person. If he kills the man who attacks him […], it ought to be accidental. To aim at killing, even when one is defending oneself, is murderous. (I fear even this idea is going. A man was acquitted recently who had successfully set a lethal booby trap to kill a thief in his absence.)

But the state actually has the authority to order deliberate killing in order to protect its people or to put frightful injustices right. (For example, the plight of the Jews under Hitler would have been a reasonable cause of war.) The reason for this is pretty simple: it stands out most clearly if we first consider the state's right to order such killing within its confines. I am not referring to the death penalty, but to what happens when there is rioting or when violent malefactors have to be caught. Rioters can sometimes only be restrained, or malefactors seized, by force. Law without force is ineffectual, and human beings without laws miserable (though we, who have too many and too changeable laws, may easily not feel this very distinctly). So much is indeed fairly obvious, though the more peaceful the society the less obvious it is that the force in the hands of the servants of the law has to be force up to the point of killing. It would become perfectly obvious any time there was rioting or gangsterism which had to be dealt with by the servants of the law fighting.

The death penalty itself is a completely different matter. The state is not fighting the criminal who is condemned to death. That is why the death penalty is not indispensable. People keep on discussing whether the point of it is deterrence or vengeance; it is neither. Not deterrence, because nobody has proved anything about that, and people think what they think in accordance with their prejudices. And not vengeance, because that's nobody's business. Confusion arises on this subject because the state is said, and correctly said, to *punish* the criminal, and "punishment" suggests "vengeance." Therefore many humane people dislike the idea and prefer such notions as "correction" and "rehabilitation."

But the action of the state in depriving a man of his rights, up to his very life, has to be considered from two sides. First, from that of the man himself. If he could say "Why have you done this to me? I have not deserved it," then the state would be acting with injustice. Therefore he must be proved guilty, and only as punishment has the state the right to inflict anything on him. The concept of punishment is our one safeguard against being done "good" to, in ways involving a deprivation of rights, by impudent powerful people. Second, from the side of the state, divine retributive justice is not its affair: it only has to protect its people and restrain malefactors. The ground of its right to deprive of liberty and even life is only that the malefactor is a nuisance, like a gangrenous limb. Therefore it can cut him off entirely, if his crime is so bad that he could not justly protest "I have not deserved *this*." But when I say that the sole ground of state's right to kill him is that he is a nuisance, I only mean that he is a nuisance *qua* malefactor. The lives of the innocent are the actual point of society, so the fact that in some other way they may be a nuisance (troublesome to look after, for example) does not justify the state in getting rid of them. Though that is another thing we may yet come to. But the blood of the innocent cries to heaven for vengeance.

Thus the malefactor who has been found guilty is the only defenceless person whom the state may put to death. It need not; it can choose more merciful laws. (I have no prejudice in favour of the death penalty.) Any other defenceless person is as such innocent, in the sense of "not harming." And so the state can only order to kill others of its subjects besides convicted criminals if they are rioting or doing something that has to be stopped, and can only be stopped by the servants of the law fighting them.

Now, this is also the ground of the state's right to order people to fight external enemies who are unjustly attacking them or something of theirs. The right to order to fight for the sake of other people's wrongs, to put right something affecting people who are not actually under the protection of the state, is a rather more dubious thing obviously, but it exists because of the common sympathy of human beings whereby one feels for one's neighbour if he is attacked. So in an attenuated sense it can be said that something that belongs to, or concerns, one is attacked if anybody is unjustly attacked or maltreated.

Pacifism, then, is a false doctrine. Now, no doubt, it is bad just for that reason, because it is always bad to have a false conscience. In this way the doctrine that it is a bad act to lay a bet is bad: it is all right to bet what it is all right to risk or drop in the sea. But I want to maintain that pacifism is a harmful doctrine in a far stronger sense than this. Even the prevalence of the idea that it was wrong to bet would have no particularly bad consequences; a false doctrine which merely forbids what is not actually bad need not encourage people in anything bad. But with pacifism it is quite otherwise. It is a factor in the loss of the conception of murder which is my chief interest in this pamphlet.

I have very often heard people say something like this: "It is all very well to say 'Don't do evil that good may come.' But *war* is evil. We all know that. Now, of course, it is possible to be an Absolute Pacifist. I can respect that, but I can't be one myself, and most other people won't be either. So we have to accept the evil. It is not that we do not see the evil. And once you are in for it, you have to go the whole hog."

This is much as if I were defrauding someone, and when someone tried to stop me I said: "Absolute honesty! I respect that. But of course absolute honesty really means having no property at all...." Having offered the sacrifice of a few sighs and tears to absolute honesty, I go on as before.

The correct answer to the statement that "war is evil" is that it is bad—*i.e.*, a misfortune—to be at war. And no doubt if two nations are at war at least one is unjust. But that does not show that it is wrong to fight or that if one does fight one can also commit murder.

Naturally my claim that pacifism is a very harmful doctrine is contingent on its being a false one. If it were a true doctrine, its encouragement of this nonsensical "hypocrisy of the ideal standard" would

not count against it. But given that it is false, I am inclined to think it is also very bad, unusually so for an idea which seems as it were to err on the noble side.

When I consider the history of the events from 1939 to 1945, I am not surprised that Mr. Truman is made the recipient of honours. But when I consider his actions by themselves, I am surprised again.

Some people actually praise the bombings and commend the stockpiling of atomic weapons on the ground that they are so horrible that nations will be afraid ever again to make war. "We have made a covenant with death, and with hell we are at an agreement." There does not seem to be good ground for such a hope for any long period of time.

Pacifists have for long made it a point in their propaganda that men must grow more murderous as their techniques of destruction improve, and those who defend murder eagerly seize on this point, so that I imagine by now it is pretty well accepted by the whole world. Of course, it is not true. In Napoleon's time, for example, the means of destruction had much improved since the time of Henry V; but Henry, not Napoleon, was a great massacrer of civilians, saying when he did particularly atrocious things that the French were a sinful nation and that he had a mission from God to punish them. And, of course, really large scale massacre up to now has belonged to times with completely primitive methods of killing. Weapons are now manufactured whose sole point is to be used in massacre of cities. But the people responsible are not murderous because they have these weapons; they have them because they are murderous. Deprived of atomic bombs, they would commit massacres by means of other bombs.

Protests by people who have not power are a waste of time. I was not seizing an opportunity to make a "gesture of protest" at atomic bombs; I vehemently object to *our* action in offering Mr. Truman honours, because one can share in the guilt of a bad action by praise and flattery, as also by defending it. When I puzzle myself over the attitude of the Vice-Chancellor and the Hebdomadal Council, I look round to see if any explanation is available why so many Oxford people should be willing to flatter such a man.

I get some small light on the subject when I consider the productions of Oxford moral philosophy since the first world war, which I have lately had occasion to read. Its character can easily be briefly demonstrated. Up to the second world war the prevailing moral philosophy in Oxford taught that an action can be "morally good" no matter how objectionable the thing done may be. An instance would be Himmler's efforts at exterminating the Jews: he did it from the "motive of duty" which has "supreme value." In the same philosophy—which has much pretence of moral seriousness, claiming that "rightness" is an objective character in acts, that can be discerned by a moral sense—it is also held that it might be right to kill the innocent for the good of the people, since the "prima facie duty" of securing some advantage might outweigh the "prima facie duty" of not killing the innocent. This sort of philosophy is less prevalent now, and in its place I find another, whose cardinal principle is that "good" is not a "descriptive" term, but one expressive of a favourable attitude on the part of the speaker. Hand in hand with this, though I do not know if there is any logical connection, goes a doctrine that it is impossible to have any quite general moral laws; such laws as "It's wrong to lie" or "Never commit sodomy" are rules of thumb which an experienced person knows when to break. Further, both his selection of these as the rules on which to proceed, and his tactful adjustments of them in particular cases, are based on their fitting together with the "way of life" which is his preference. Both these philosophies, then, contain a repudiation of the idea that any class of actions, such as murder, may be absolutely excluded. I do not know how influential they may have been or

be; they are perhaps rather symptomatic. Whether influential or symptomatic, they throw some light on the situation.

It is possible still to withdraw from this shameful business in some slight degree; it is possible not to go to Encaenia; if it should be embarrassing to someone who would normally go to plead other business, he could take to his bed. I, indeed, should fear to go, in case God's patience suddenly ends.

DISCUSSION QUESTIONS

1. Do you think the bombings of Hiroshima and Nagasaki were justified or unjustified? Explain your response.

2. Anscombe argues, "Choosing to kill the innocent as a means to your own end is always murder." In her view, which people are "innocent" people? Do you agree with her? Why or why not?

3. Anscombe is prepared to grant that if Truman had not authorized the bombings, many people would have died as a result of the continuation of the war. Why shouldn't we think of Truman as being morally guilty of allowing these people to die if he had failed to authorize the bombings?

4. Anscombe distinguishes between bombing civilian targets on the one hand, and military targets that will inevitably lead to the deaths of civilians, on the other. Do you think this is a morally significant distinction?

99

David Mellow, "Iraq: A Morally Justified Resort to War" (2006)

David Mellow received his Ph.D. in philosophy from the University of Calgary in 2003. In this article, he argues that the controversial US-led war in Iraq is morally justified according to just war theory. Mellow argues that this moral justification remains even when various claims made by the critics of the war are granted.

SOURCE

Mellow, David. "Iraq: A Morally Justified Resort to War." *Journal of Applied Philosophy* 23, Issue 3, August 2006, pp. 293–310.

For argument's sake, let us assume the following in regards to the US-led war in Iraq:

1. Saddam Hussein's regime neither possessed weapons of mass destruction (WMD) nor was actively engaged in developing or intending to develop such weapons.
2. Given a further amount of time, the UN inspectors would have gathered sufficient information to confirm the first assumption.
3. The Bush and Blair governments intentionally deceived their citizens regarding the likelihood that Saddam Hussein's regime possessed weapons of mass destruction.
4. Based on international law, the war represented an illegal act of aggression against the state of Iraq, and furthermore, was not justified in light of the negotiated agreement reached at the end of the earlier Gulf War.

Admittedly many of these assumptions are debatable. Nonetheless, I propose we grant all these assumptions to the opponent of the war. In this paper I will argue that even if all these assumptions are true, the resort to war was still morally justified.

My argument will proceed on the assumption that the just war tradition (so called "just war theory") provides the correct understanding of the morality of war.[1] I begin by offering the following list of criteria that must be met for the resort to war to be morally justified:

1. There must be a sufficient just cause.
2. Only a legitimate authority may undertake the war.
3. The war must be undertaken with the right intention.
4. The war must be undertaken as a last resort.
5. The war must pass the test of proportionality.[2]

While different just war theorists may propose different lists of criteria, the list presented here encapsulates the criteria that most commonly and consistently appear in such lists. Furthermore, it is in the context of the criteria listed that most of the moral criticisms of the resort to war in Iraq have been raised. It is, therefore, in reference to these criteria that I will make the case that the resort to war in Iraq was morally justified.[3]

---

[1] Consequently my argument will not speak directly to either those who take a principled pacifist position regarding the morality of war or those who adopt an act utilitarian view of morality—though the discussion will, tangentially, raise moral issues which both the pacifist and utilitarian need to address. The argument could speak to a rule utilitarian who adopts a set of rules regarding war that are sympathetic to those found in the just war tradition.

[2] My list focuses on *ad bellum* criteria—those criteria that must be met for the resort to war to be fully justified. In this paper I will not consider *in bello* questions about whether particular acts in the war were morally justified.

[3] As part of that process, I will raise questions about how the criteria should be defined and whether, in particular, the right intention criterion should be included in the list of criteria. This should not, however, be viewed as questioning my commitment to the just war tradition. Central to that tradition has been an ongoing debate both about which criteria must be met for a war to be justified and about how to define those criteria. Over time, and at any given time, the list of criteria proposed by just war theorists has varied in important ways. Admittedly, in questioning the relevance of the right intention criterion I am going against a long tradition, but this it is entirely in keeping with the spirit of just war theory. Furthermore, it was in large part my reflecting on the appropriateness of including the right intention criterion that led me to see the importance of writing a paper on the morality of the war in Iraq.

Sufficient Just Cause

According to just war theory, a morally justified decision to go to war requires the presence of a just cause of sufficient moral importance. The crucial task is to identify precisely what counts as "sufficient." More precisely, we need some account of what sorts of causes are not only just, but also of sufficient importance to defeat the prima facie presumption against the use of direct, forceful, and violent military means that intervene in the cultural and political affairs of another people, nation or state.

With respect to Iraq, at least three considerations have been offered as constituting (individually or collectively) a possible sufficient just cause. The first, which was arguably the main focus prior to the war, was removing the threat posed to other nations by Iraq's possession of, or attempts to acquire, WMD. The second was that Iraq, by failing to fully cooperate with the inspectors, was violating the legal terms agreed to at the end of the earlier Gulf War. The third was putting an end to the ongoing grave humanitarian injustices suffered by the Iraqi people.

While the first two considerations lead to some much discussed questions regarding if and when wars of prevention are justified, I will, in light of the assumptions granted at the start of the paper, accept for argument's sake that neither of the first two considerations provides a sufficient just cause, and instead, will argue that the humanitarian injustices provided such a cause. I begin by describing the two general moral considerations that ground humanitarian sufficient just causes.[4]

First, there is the value attached to a people being self-determining. This value lies both in the *collective right* that a people have to be politically and culturally self-determining and in the *basic good* of a people engaging in a collective process of self-determination. When a people's ability to be self-determining is ruthlessly suppressed, with

---

[4] Elsewhere (D. Mellow, *A Critique of Just War Theory*, PhD dissertation, The University of Calgary, 2003) I argue that all sufficient just causes are grounded in these two general moral values.

no reasonable hope that the people themselves can overthrow the tyranny, this generally provides third party states with a sufficient just cause.

The claim that a sufficient just cause may be grounded (in part) in violations of a people's prima facie right of collective self-determination is not uncontroversial.[1] In particular, Richard Norman rejects this claim. Norman contends that that "[n]ations do not have an automatic right to be defended" and that "we cannot escape the need to make *qualitative* judgements about its [a nation's] cultural and political life."[2]

While I agree with Norman that we do need to make qualitative judgements about a nation's cultural and political life, this recognition is, *contra* Norman, compatible with nations having a prima facie right of self-determination that is often a central consideration in determining whether there is a sufficient just cause. A comparison with individual autonomy rights should help.

In the case of individuals, the generally held view is that each and every individual possesses prima facie autonomy rights. Autonomy rights are intimately tied to our concept of what it is to be a person. One does not have to do anything to earn either those autonomy rights or the right to defend them. Though one can do things that, in certain situations, will undermine the moral case for exercising and defending autonomy rights—and which might even, in a hard to define sense, result in the forfeiture of those rights—autonomy rights exist and carry moral weight prior to any qualitative judgements regarding a person's actions, plans and character.

Similarly, the collective right of self-determination is intimately tied to our concept of what it is to be a nation or a people. Each nation or state possesses the prima facie right of collective self-determination. A nation or people is not required to do certain things, or act in certain ways, to gain either that right or the right to defend it. While certain actions or political and cultural features may, in certain contexts, undermine the moral case for exercising that right, and even result in the forfeiture of the right, the right exists and carries moral weight prior to any judgement about such actions and features. In other words, one starts with the presumption that a people or a nation has the right to be self-determining.

A common argument raised against some or all humanitarian military interventions is that even if such interventions are grounded in just causes, those just causes are usually not sufficient to justify interfering in a people's process of self-determination. However, this argument loses much (and arguably all) of its force when a people are *severely* oppressed because they are then not engaged, or are engaged only very minimally in a process of self-determination. To put this last observation in slightly different terms, when people are severely oppressed there is a significant lowering of the bar with respect to what just causes count as sufficient.

The second set of moral considerations that underlie humanitarian sufficient just causes are systematic violations of *individual* human rights and the existence of widespread *individual* human suffering. Sometimes the violations of individual rights or the experiences of human suffering are on such a scale and of such a degree that they provide third parties with a sufficient just cause. While this consideration has historically not always been given its due, there is now widespread recognition that it is an important moral consideration in determining whether military intervention is justified.

In summary, there are both collective and individual grounds for the use of military force. Furthermore, such grounds may justify not only first party but also third party use of military force.

What then about the people of Iraq? In Iraq, the ruling regime clearly was repressive. The severity and systematic nature of the oppression was, perhaps, most obvious in the case of the Shiites and Kurds, but even amongst the Sunnis there

---

[1] Though both the United Nations' *International Covenant on Civil and Political Rights* and the United Nations' *International Covenant on Economic, Social and Cultural Rights* recognize that: "All peoples have the right of self-determination."

[2] R. Norman, *Ethics, Killing and War* (Cambridge: Cambridge University Press, 1995), p. 153 (bracketed text added, italics in the original).

was a systematic reign of terror that made any significant assertion of collective will a practical impossibility. Thus it is clear that the peoples of Iraq could only very minimally exercise a process of collective self-determination. Furthermore, the oppression involved massive systematic individual human rights violations—killing, gassing, torture, rape, forced displacement, campaigns of terror, and severe religious restrictions. The numbers killed, maimed, tortured and displaced, though imprecise, are staggering—at the very minimum involving hundreds of thousands in a population of twenty-two million.

While it is sometimes contended that the large-scale human rights violations mainly occurred prior to and immediately after the 1991 Gulf War, this is not the case. First, the severe oppression of any meaningful collective process of self-determination was clearly an ongoing reality. Furthermore, even in regards to individual human rights violations there was strong evidence of ongoing systematic violations. In January 2003 Human Rights Watch documented the "ongoing campaign ... against the Ma'dan or so-called Marsh Arabs whose numbers, at the time of writing had been reduced from some 250,000 people as recently as 1991 ... to ... fewer than 40,000 in their ancestral homeland."

Additionally, reports and statements presented throughout the 1990s by Max Van Der Stoel, Special U.N. Rapporteur of the Commission on Human Rights on the Situation of Human Rights in Iraq, indicate ongoing large-scale and systematic violations of human rights. As recently as March 1999, he addressed the U.N. Commission on Human Rights stating that it is his "sad duty yet again to report: allegations of numerous and systematic arbitrary executions, interferences with the independent religious practice of the Shi'ite community, continuing internal deportations of ethnic Kurds, violations of the rights to food and health, violations of the rights of the child...." The Special Rapporteur also goes on to document the assassination of religious leaders and the broader humanitarian suffering and deaths caused by the government's unwillingness to either work with the U.N. de-mining program or take full advantage of the food-for-oil program. Of course, one may have

hoped that the future under Saddam Hussein and his likely successors (i.e., his sons) would not continue past practices, but the serial ongoing actions of the regime give us no reason to think this likely. Again quoting the Special Rapporteur: "Regrettably, the situation of human rights has not improved in Iraq, nor does it show any sign of improving."[1]

The crucial question, of course, is whether the oppression, suffering and rights violations were systematic and grave enough to ground a sufficient just cause. There is (rightly) now substantial agreement that stopping an act of genocide against a people represents a sufficient just cause. But surely if stopping a genocide represents a sufficient just cause, then there are massive cases of systematic oppression, killing, and terror that, while not quite a genocide, also ground a sufficient just cause.[2]

---

[1] The quotes are found at: http://www.unhchr.ch/huricane/huricane.nsf/0/9792F0662148A0648025674B00551A95?opendocument. Also see the Human Rights Watch Briefing Paper (January 2003), "The Iraqi Government Assault on the Marsh Arabs," which also contains additional references to reports made by the Special Rapporteur. The Human Rights Watch Policy Paper (December 2002), "Justice for Iraq" documents atrocities carried out by the Iraq regime in the 1980s and 1990s.

[2] The implausibility, and even the offensiveness, of drawing a stark moral line, *for purposes of humanitarian interventions,* between genocides and something slightly less is highlighted by the recent *Report of the International Commission of Inquiry on Darfur to the United Nations Secretary General* (www.ohchr.org/english/darfur.htm). The authors of that report conclude that "no genocidal policy has been pursued and implemented in Darfur by the Government authorities, directly or through the militias under their control...." Yet surely, regardless of the legal implications drawn on the basis of that conclusion, the slaughter and displacement of the people in Darfur is so widespread, grave and systematic that, assuming all the other just war conditions are met, military intervention to stop the slaughter would be permissible. (The authors go on to say that that their conclusion "... should not be taken in any way as detracting from the gravity of the crimes perpetrated in that region. International offences such as the crimes against humanity and war crimes that have been committed in Darfur may be no less serious and heinous than genocide." In contrast with this claim, I contend that if there truly is not a genocide in Darfur, then what is taking place is, while morally less heinous than genocide, still so heinous that it represents a sufficient just cause.)

For example, if one could stop the ruthless ethnic cleansing of one hundred thousand people through a military intervention that would cost a few dozen lives, surely the prevention of that ethnic cleansing would represent a sufficient just cause.[1] In the case of Iraq, the gravity of atrocities (whether considered from a serial or ongoing perspective) was even greater than this. Therefore, *setting aside for now questions of proportionality,* there was a sufficient just cause. Furthermore, remember the crucial point made earlier, that when a people are severely oppressed, the sufficiency threshold is significantly lowered because the central moral concern that one would be interfering in and undermining a people's process of self-determination carries little, if any, weight.

Some may contend that despite the oppression, it is important that the people themselves be left to overthrow their oppressor, and therefore this oppression does not provide third parties with a sufficient just cause. This position, however, is morally untenable. First, there was no strong evidence that the Iraqi people themselves would have been able, in the foreseeable future, to overthrow the current regime and replace it with a more benevolent one, let alone a more democratic form of government and a just legal system.[2] Second,

a similar contention made about a domestic case involving individuals would be morally absurd and even offensive. Imagine that a family is being ruthlessly oppressed by the father/husband under threats—often carried out—of grave beatings if they speak out against any of his commands or attempt to leave the house without him. The moral offensiveness of someone saying that it is not society's place to, if necessary, physically intervene is obvious.[3]

A critic might protest that, unlike the domestic case, it is important or even vital for a people themselves to overthrow the oppressor if they are to ultimately engage in a flourishing process of self-determination. Michael Walzer, in his discussion of self determination, approvingly refers to Mill's "stern doctrine of self-help" and quotes Mill's claim that "[i]t is during an arduous struggle to become free by their own efforts that these virtues [the virtues needed for maintaining freedom] have the best chance of springing up." Walzer also goes on to say: "revolutionary activity is an exercise in self determination, while foreign interfer-

---

[1] In the broader international community there is clearly growing recognition that humanitarian interventions are justified in cases other than genocides. For example, see the report by the International Commission on Intervention and State Sovereignty (December 2001), *The Responsibility to Protect* (Ottawa: International Development Research Centre), p. 32, in which the commission contends a just cause exists when there is either or both: (a) *"large scale loss of life, actual or apprehended, with genocidal intent or not, which is the product either of deliberate state action, or state neglect or inability to act, or a failed state situation; or"* (b) *"large scale 'ethnic cleansing,' actual or apprehended, whether carried out by killing, forced expulsion, acts of terror or rape."* See also A. Bellamy, "Motives, outcomes, intent and the legitimacy of humanitarian intervention," *Journal of Military Ethics* 3.3 (2004).

[2] The horrific consequences of the Shia uprising in 1991 provide evidence of just how unlikely it is that a domestic uprising could succeed.

[3] It is worth noting that I will often make use of domestic analogies to test a claim or principle that I assert. I have found these examples helpful in testing out my own judgements about international issues, and I offer them in the hopes that they will help readers test their judgements. Some may be concerned that such domestic examples differ substantially from international examples. Elsewhere, I have discussed the ways in which those examples do and do not differ from the international cases (Mellow, 2003). For the purposes of this paper, let me simply point out that using examples quite different from the context under discussion to test a principle or claim is well established in the field of applied ethics. Of course once an example is presented, it becomes appropriate to question whether there are any morally relevant differences between the example and the case under consideration. I use the examples in this spirit, and often, after presenting the examples, I attempt to anticipate the differences that a critic may contend are morally relevant. At a minimum, I believe such examples are useful in making progress in thinking ethically, and once presented they shift the onus onto one's critics to explain why they think the example is not morally analogous—thereby entering into a dialogue that is very useful philosophically.

UNIT IV: D. Applications

ence denies to a people those political capacities that only such exercise can bring."[1]

The correct response to Walzer and Mill is to simply observe that it is not true that the virtues or political capacities needed for maintaining freedom and exercising the right of self-determination can only arise through "arduous struggle." Surely people can learn to value freedom and develop the capacity to exercise it through, for example, education, learning of and empathizing with the positive and negative examples set by other peoples, and robustly engaging in a "post-oppression" political environment. It may be true that people who have "struggled" to exercise their right of self-determination will, for a period of time, have a heightened appreciation of the value of that right and of their freedom. But the heightened appreciation, even if it cannot be acquired except through an arduous struggle (a doubtful premise) is not an indispensable "political capacity." Even without such a heightened appreciation, people can grow to value and effectively exercise their right of self-determination and their freedom.

Another possible objection is that for humanitarian military intervention to be justified, it must have the support of those who are oppressed. For example, Jeff McMahan tells us that "[f]or humanitarian intervention to be justified, it must be consistent with the will of the supposed beneficiaries" and in the case of Iraq "there was no indication that the people whom the US claimed to be saving actually welcomed American intervention."[2] While I agree that the desires of the people sometimes do matter in determining whether there is a sufficient just cause, one must be careful in this regard.

First, the approval of the people is arguably not always necessary to justify humanitarian intervention. In particular, if systematic large-scale killing

and torture is occurring, one may still be justified in interfering, even if the victimized people express a desire that others not interfere. While this last claim will be controversial, support for it can be found in an example of individual self-defence. Imagine that a group of armed attackers are torturing and killing a nearby family. You are part of an armed group (for example, you and your hunting buddies) who happen to pass the scene. You have no way of stopping the attackers other than using your guns, so you prepare to shoot. However, just at that moment the family yells at you to stop, explaining that they are committed pacifists and have chosen to suffer and die. Must you defer to their request and simply let the torture and killing proceed? Surely you need not. The act of torture and murder is a great evil—so great that you are permitted to stop the act even if the victims of the evil would rather you didn't do so. While the victims' personal convictions and autonomy rights do carry moral weight, they do not carry enough weight to make it wrong for you to intervene to stop such an immoral act. (This would be especially true if the family includes children on whose behalf the parents are making decisions.) Similarly, in a case of systematic large-scale government oppression, killing and torture, military intervention represents a sufficient just cause even if the vast majority of the victims are opposed to that intervention.

Second, even if expressed wishes carry some weight, when large-scale oppression and rights violations are occurring it is surely the wishes of the terrorized and oppressed populations that should be the central consideration, rather than the wishes of the entire population—many of whom may be beneficiaries of that oppression.

Third, there is reason to think that the people suffering under Saddam Hussein's rule did welcome the US action to remove his regime. In a Gallup Poll conducted in Baghdad between August 28 and September 4, 2003, 62 percent of citizens surveyed did "think ousting Saddam Hussein was worth any hardships they have personally endured since the invasion" (*The Globe and Mail,* Thursday, September 25, 2003). And in a second country-wide

---

[1] M. Walzer, *Just and Unjust Wars*, 2nd ed. (New York: Basic Books, 1992), pp. 87, 89 (bracketed text added).

[2] J. McMahan, "Unjust war in Iraq," Leiter Reports, 2004; http://leiterreports.typepad.com/blog/2004/09/the_moral_case_.html.

Gallup Poll conducted for *USA Today* in March and April 2004, a clear majority of Iraqis (61 percent) answered "Worth It" when asked: "Thinking about any hardships you might have suffered since the US/British invasion, do you personally think that ousting Saddam Hussein was worth it or not?" Furthermore, and importantly given the observations in the last paragraph, in Shia and Kurdish areas the corresponding percentages were 74 and 97 percent respectively. (Poll results found on the *USA Today* website.)

In response, some people may contend that the current resentment regarding the ongoing occupation and the significant support for the actions of the insurgents both provide evidence that the invasion was unwelcome. Such a conclusion, however, would not be justified. First, it is doubtful that a majority of the Iraqi people support the acts of the insurgents. When asked in the *USA Today* poll: "To what extent can you personally justify the following actions morally … Current attacks against US forces in Iraq," 25 percent said "Cannot at all," 22 percent said "Cannot somewhat," 22 percent said "Sometime can/can't," 17 percent said "Can somewhat," and 13 percent said "Can completely."

Second, even if a majority of Iraqis support the insurgents' actions, or support the immediate withdrawal of American troops from Iraqi territory, this does not demonstrate that the people of Iraq were, or are, opposed to the invasion and overthrow of Saddam Hussein's regime. There is nothing inconsistent in a people welcoming their liberators, but objecting to their ongoing occupation. Furthermore, support for the insurgents' acts may not even indicate opposition to short-term occupation. It rather could be grounded in: opposition to certain aspects of that occupation, or a desire to ensure that the occupation is only short-term, or anger based upon, for example, the perception (whether right or wrong) that America played a significant role in earlier injustices that the Iraqis and peoples of the Middle East experienced.

In summary, the humanitarian imperative provided a sufficient just cause. There were both collective and individual considerations that when combined, and probably even when considered separately, were of sufficient moral importance to justify third party military intervention.

Right Intention

Even if there is a sufficient humanitarian just cause, many will contend that the war was immoral because the US and British governments' actual motivation for going to war was something other than the humanitarian cause. It has, for example, been contended that the "true" intentions were one or more of the following: a concern for oil security, a (misguided) desire to rid Iraq of its WMD, a desire to establish a strong American base or hegemony in the Middle East, and even a desire on the part of George W. Bush to complete the war his father had begun.

In supporting this claim, however, some very difficult problems arise:

1. Whose intention is the relevant one? Is the relevant intention that of President Bush himself, that of the larger administration, or that of the relevant legislative bodies?
2. If the relevant intention is that of a group, how do you identify the group's intention?[1]
3. Should the right intention criterion require a *right* intention (for example, one appropriately connected to the sufficient just cause) or, instead, only require that certain bad intentions not be present?[2]
4. If there must be a *right* intention, is it sufficient that the intention simply be present or must it also carry motivational force? If the latter, must the motivational force meet some minimal threshold? And should that threshold be defined in some counterfactual way? For example, perhaps the right intention

[1] G. Kavka, "Was the Gulf War a just war?" *Journal of Social Philosophy* 22.1 (1991).

[2] The latter suggestion is found in Augustine's work—see D. Lackey, *The Ethics of War and Peace* (Englewood Cliffs, NJ: Prentice Hall, 1989), p. 32.

must be sufficient to motivate the relevant agent's actual decision even if there were no other motive. Or perhaps the counterfactual requirement is that the agent would not have gone to war in the absence of the belief that there was a just cause.[1]

Unless these questions are satisfactorily answered, the criticism based on wrong intention is problematic. But even if these questions can be satisfactorily answered, there is a deeper problem with the criticism. There are strong grounds for questioning the inclusion of the right intention criterion among the just war criteria.

Its inclusion suggests that an act of resorting to war should be judged not only on the basis of external features, but also on the basis of the internal motives, desires, and intentions of the agents. This suggestion, however, confuses two separate judgements. One judgement has to do with the moral character of the person or nation carrying out the act. The second judgement has to do with the morality of the act itself. The content of individuals' intentions, desires and motives are, for the most part, relevant to making judgements of character, but not to making judgements about the rightness or wrongness of an act. For example, stopping a murderer from assaulting and killing a victim is the right thing to do even if the person who intervenes does so solely in the hope that there will be a reward, and not out of any concern for the victim. Of course the motivation of the intervener is central to our judgement of the intervener's character, but it in no way influences the judgement about the correctness of the action. Similarly, it is sensible to talk about a person who, throughout her life, continuously does the right thing, but with the wrong motives. Such a person has a flawed moral character, and we would likely describe that person's life as morally flawed. Nonetheless, it still remains the case that the acts the person committed were the right acts.

The focus of just war theory is on the rightness or wrongness of *the act* of resorting to war, not the moral character of the interveners. Therefore, even untoward motives, desires, and intentions are permissible as long as the military declaration or intervention meets the other criteria—though such motives may be important when making judgements about the moral character of a nation or its leaders. Consider, for example, a case in which a junta is asked by another country to help it repel an unjust aggressor. That junta decides to assist that third party, not because there is a sufficient just cause (which there is) but because it will arouse a sense of patriotism in the people the junta rule—a sense of patriotism that the junta hopes will undermine any opposition to its rule. While such a cynical undertaking of a military campaign would comment heavily on the moral character of the junta's members, it would not undermine the justness of the military intervention itself.

A critic may suggest that while some immoral motives, desires and intentions are permissible, there are, nonetheless, a set of immoral motives, desires or intentions that go beyond the pale (for example, action done purely on the basis of hatred or racist sentiments[2]) and which make an action unjust. In response, consider the following modification to the earlier example of preventing a murder.

This time imagine that the individual's sole motivation for acting to prevent the assault and murder is something more heinous than a desire for the reward. Perhaps the individual takes pleasure in killing members of a certain race. Seeing that the attacker is of that race, he engages the attacker solely in the hope that the attacker will resist and need to be killed.

Of course there is a terribly offensive element in the intervener's motivation, and we are right to express revulsion regarding his character; nonetheless, surely we would not contend that he was

---

[1] Mellow, *A Critique of Just War Theory*.

[2] See footnote [2, p. 1119].

wrong to intervene.[1] In short, there are no intentions, desires or motives that are "beyond the pale" because such internal considerations are not determining factors in judging the rightness or wrongness of the act. One can do the right thing for horrifically wrong reasons.

In the international context then, what a nation must defend is not its intentions or motives, but rather the claim that its declaration of war or decision to use military force represents the undertaking of a sufficient just cause. That is to say, what needs satisfying is not the right intention criterion, but rather, the sufficient just cause criterion. What is of concern is not evidence per se of self-interested or even immoral motives or intentions, but rather evidence that a nation's military action is not systematically structured so as to achieve a sufficient just cause. Evidence of immoral intentions may well be a red flag to warn us that the military action is not so structured, but such intentions do not *in and of themselves* make the military action immoral.[2]

In summary, it is inappropriate to include the right intention criterion among the just war criteria. We should not give intentions and motives separate standing in the pantheon of just war criteria. The intentions of the leaders in the Iraq war might not have always been virtuous, but this, in itself, does not make the resort to war morally unjustified.

---

[1] Furthermore, if a third party arrived on the scene—a party that had a good idea of our intervener's mental state—the third party should not prevent the intervener from acting. This is because stopping or preventing the act of rape is the right thing to do, *regardless* of the motivations of the intervener. While admittedly this last suggestion does not necessarily follow from the fact that the third party should not stop the intervener, it does seem to be the most compelling explanation of the fact. Furthermore, even if, in the face of my arguments, one continues to contend that while the intervener should not be stopped, by either the murderer or a third party, the intervener is still acting wrongly (a very odd position); notice that much of the moral importance of the right intention criterion, and hence reason for its inclusion, has been lost. For surely most people, in pointing to violations of the right intention criterion are not merely making assertions about the wrongness of an act, but are contending, on the basis of that violation, that the act (e.g. the resort to war) should not be undertaken. Also see J. Thomson, "Self-defense," *Philosophy and Public Affairs* 20.4 (1991) where she makes arguments parallel to mine against the "… very odd idea … that a person's intentions play a role in fixing what he may or may not do" (p. 293).

[2] In an excellent article by Fernando Tesón, which was published after my first draft of this paper, he makes important points that support and echo some of what I have said about the right intention criterion (F. Tesón, "Ending tyranny in Iraq," *Ethics & International Affairs* 19.2 (2005)). Ultimately, however, he contends, contrary to what I have proposed here, that intentions (when properly defined and distinguished from motives) still "ought to be retained" when characterizing an action (e.g., of resorting to war). To support his position, he considers the example of the Falkland Islands war and, in particular, the role the defeat of Argentina played in replacing the country's illegitimate leaders with democratic institutions. Unlike Iraq, however, Tesón rightly observes we would not, as a result of the liberation of the Argentines, think it appropriate to describe the Falkland Islands war as a humanitarian intervention. According to Tesón, the reason for the difference is one which requires an appeal to intentions, namely that "[w]hile the restoration of democracy and human rights in Argentina was a humanitarian outcome, *neither the motive nor the intention* of Prime Minister Margaret Thatcher included freeing the Argentines. The liberation of Argentina was a relatively remote consequence of the war" (p. 8, italics in the original). I, however, don't see why we need to appeal to intentions to explain why the Falkland Islands war does not count as a humanitarian intervention. The reason it does not count as a humanitarian intervention, either prospectively or retrospectively, is precisely and simply because the war was so structured that *the liberation of Argentina was a relatively remote consequence of the war.* Full stop. There is no need to invoke the intention of Prime Minister Thatcher. Expressed slightly differently, it is not Margaret Thatcher's intention that determines whether the war was humanitarian, but whether the military action was structured so as to plausibly or directly achieve a humanitarian just cause. In the case of the Falkland Islands war, there was no such structure.

Last Resort

Some may contend that in resorting to war to thwart Iraqi possession or development of WMD, the last resort criterion was not satisfied because there was another alternative that had a reasonable hope of succeeding, namely letting the UN inspectors, backed by international pressure, continue their work. Let us, for argument's sake, accept this criticism. This does not affect my argument, since I have claimed that the humanitarian imperative provided a sufficient just cause. Thus the question that needs answering is whether or not resorting to war to achieve the humanitarian aims met the last resort criterion.

The answer arguably hinges on whether or not there were other ways of substantially improving the humanitarian situation in the near term.[1] I see no reason to think that any "other ways" could have been expected to succeed. It was not plausible to think (especially given the ineffectiveness of sanctions) that further economic and political pressure could be expected to substantially moderate the ruthless behaviour of the regime. Furthermore, there was little cooperation among members of the UN Security Council, and little reason to think that US and British diplomatic efforts would lead the Security Council to collectively act militarily, even if they had focused their appeal on the humanitarian injustices.[2] Finally, the chances of an internal uprising being successful in the near term were minimal given the regime's ability and willingness (as demonstrated, for example, by its actions against the Shiites and Kurds) to brutally crush any potential opposition and systematically terrorize and divide the population. As a general rule, brutal ruthless dictatorships are not readily defeated by minimally armed populations.[3]

Perhaps some would contend that rather than a massive military action, a more selective targeting of force could have been used to remove Saddam Hussein and institute a more humanitarian government. The problem with this suggestion is that there is no evidence that such an approach was feasible. In fact, in the early days of the war the US did make attempts to target the high-ranking officials, including Saddam Hussein himself, but this proved to be in practice very difficult. And to the extent that such targeting did succeed, it did not seriously weaken the regime or its resolve. So there seems to be no basis for thinking that the alternative of more selective targeting prior to the war would have led to the institution of a more benevolent regime, let alone a democratic government. Also, if the US military and government thought such an alternative was available, surely they would have pursued it, rather than risk the lives of large numbers of civilians and US soldiers and incur the huge expense of fighting the war.

The war, combined with those early attempts to target and destabilize the regime, was the only approach that could reasonably be expected to, in the foreseeable future, overthrow the Iraqi regime. Therefore, the last resort criterion was satisfied.

Legitimate Authority

There has been much discussion of legitimacy based on: 1) questions of international law, and 2) questions about the extent to which the Blair and Bush governments were not fully forthcoming regarding what they knew about Iraq's possession of WMD.[4]

---

[1] I say arguably because some may question whether, in the face of ongoing grave systematic human suffering and injustices, the last resort test even applies (cf. J. McKenna, "The just war," in J. Rachels (ed.), *Moral Problems,* 3rd ed. (New York: Harper and Row, 1979). Though I will not pursue the point here, I do think the last resort criterion, properly interpreted (Mellow, *A Critique of Just War Theory*), still applies in such cases.

[2] Even though it surely would not have been successful, it is legitimate to criticize the US and British governments for not, prior to the war, more forcefully emphasizing and considering the humanitarian injustices.

[3] Interestingly, in the *USA Today* poll when the Iraqis were asked "Would Saddam Hussein have been removed from power by Iraqis if US/British forces had not taken direct military action?" 89 percent said "No" and only 4 percent said "Yes."

[4] Some may also argue that the determination of legitimacy hinges on the issue of whether the Iraqi people supported the invasion. I have dealt with this issue in my discussion of the sufficient just cause criterion.

With respect to international law, for argument's sake let us grant that the resort to war was illegal. Does this make the resort to war immoral? I contend that it does not. As a general rule, laws that are reasonably motivated and are not clearly unjust do carry moral weight. However, when that law demands that we not intervene to stop a wide-scale humanitarian catastrophe or moral injustice, it is not plausible, when the legal authorities will not take the needed action, to claim that the law carries sufficient moral force to make it morally wrong for others to intervene and prevent the catastrophe or injustice. Interestingly, I suspect that most of us recognize the truth of this claim in the domestic realm.

Imagine that your next-door neighbour was brutally beating his family and threatening to kill them. You have called the police, but they are unwilling to intervene—perhaps they claim no officers are available. If there were a law stating that only the police and not ordinary citizens could use lethal force against other citizens, surely the law would carry very little (or even no) moral force in deciding whether you are morally permitted to act. Despite the law, you would clearly be morally justified, if necessary, in killing the neighbour in order to save the family.

In contrast, in the international realm many have contended that due to international law it is not morally permissible for individual third party states to intervene in the affairs of fellow states, even when there are grave, systematic, and ongoing humanitarian catastrophes and injustices. However, this simply demonstrates an inconsistency in moral thinking rather than being grounded in some morally important difference between the domestic and international cases. It is true, as was indicated earlier, that there is value and even an associated right in a people engaging in a process of self-determination. However, it is important to recognize that the political state and the people are not one and the same. Furthermore, the moral rights of the state are ultimately grounded in the rights of the people. Thus when the state is engaged in grievous systematic activities that violate the individual and collective rights of the people, the oppressive political state may not, in objecting to possible military intervention, appeal to the people's collective right of self-determination since the state is not, as it stands, a plausible vehicle for exercising and protecting those collective rights. Such an appeal is no more plausible than the brutalizing family member claiming that outsiders may not intervene to stop him since the family has a collective right to privacy or non-interference.

It is sometimes suggested that if individual states violate international law, especially with respect to the third party use of military force, this will undermine the willingness of other states to respect the demands of international law. While there may be some truth here, we must remember that there are cases and there are cases.[1] When the violation of international law serves an important humanitarian purpose, it seems just as likely that this violation, rather than undermining international law, may well force the law makers to confront the moral failings in their laws and create new laws and structures which better reflect the moral imperatives. In the long-term this may actually increase respect for the law.

Furthermore, even if there is some risk that the violation of international law may undermine the respect others show for the law (and associated international organizations) this does not obviously undermine the morality of the act. Consider again the domestic example. If just prior to shooting your violent neighbour, someone pointed out that your doing so (given some strange scenario) would cause a degree of breakdown in general respect for law and authority, this does not entail that you should not act to save the family. It is unfortunate that others will use this opportunity to more generally disregard or undermine authority, but this does not make your action immoral. A similar line of reasoning applies in the international realm.[2]

In addition to concerns with international law, there have been post-war concerns raised regarding what undisclosed information the Blair and Bush

---

[1] Echoing, in a different context, Judith Jarvis Thomson.

[2] It is for reasons similar to these that when turning to the question of proportionality I will not entertain as a relevant harm the possibility that the war undermined respect for international law or international institutions.

governments had regarding Iraq's WMD program (or lack thereof) and to what extent those governments intentionally exaggerated the threat. Again, for argument's sake, let us assume that the Blair and Bush governments were deceptive in their presentation of the facts. Should we then conclude that the war to overthrow the Iraqi regime was immoral? The answer is, in an important sense, no.

It is certainly true that the act of deception, if it occurred, would be morally wrong, and those deceived would be right to express moral outrage. Also, it is possible that a moral or legal case could be made that because of this deception the culpable parties should resign or be impeached. Nonetheless, this does not make the resort to war immoral. Put very roughly, the deception is a moral matter internal to the deceiver and the deceived and can be separated from the question of the morality of the war. In slightly different terms, the deception provides no basis for Saddam Hussein (nor you or I) to claim that the resort to war was, *in itself*, immoral.

In hopes of making this point more compelling, I return once more to the violent neighbour case. This time, just as you head out the door to stop the neighbour, your spouse, out of concern for your safety and that of your family, demands that you not go. In response, and in order to get your spouse to concur with your decision, you lie, telling him or her that the neighbour has, in fact, explicitly told you that after killing his family, he is going to come next door and kill your family. Now your spouse agrees that despite the risk you should go next door and, if necessary, kill the neighbour.

If, after the fact, your spouse learns about your deception, she or he would be justified in taking offence. However, notice that the immorality of that deception did not make it immoral for you to proceed next door and stop the neighbour. There is an important moral line to be drawn between the act of deception and the act of stopping the neighbour. And a similar line exists between any deception carried out by the Blair and Bush governments and the moral judgement we make about the resort to war to overthrow Saddam Hussein's regime.

Proportionality

Finally, we turn to the issue of whether the war in Iraq was a proportional war. That is, did the relevant good effects outweigh the relevant bad effects?[1] Admittedly, this is a difficult question to answer. In part, this is because it relies on empirical claims that are open to dispute. But it also reflects vagueness in the criterion. In particular, what precisely count as *relevant* good effects and *relevant* bad effects? I contend that the obvious relevant good effect consists in the achievement of the sufficient just cause. Furthermore, the achievement of that cause has these features: (a) preventing systematic oppression, killings, harms, and injustices that the Iraqi people would have incurred under current and future Iraqi regimes, and (b) providing the people with a chance to both engage in a process of political and cultural self-determination and live in a country that is respectful of fundamental individual and collective human rights. As for the relevant bad effects, these, I suggest, are the injuries, deaths, and injustices that were caused (or expected to be caused) by the war—including the risks of civil or a broader Middle East war.[2]

On the assumption that these are the relevant effects, the question remains whether the relevant good effects outweigh the relevant bad effects. An

---

[1] J. McMahan and R. McKim, "The just war and the Gulf War," *Canadian Journal of Philosophy* 23.4 (1993).

[2] That not all good and bad effects count in the proportionality calculation is compellingly argued for by Thomas Hurka, "Proportionality in the morality of war," *Philosophy and Public Affairs* 33.1 (2005). To give one of his examples, imagine that our nation is in an economic recession and that fighting a war (for a just cause) will lift our nation and the world out of that recession. Hurka says: "Although the economic benefits of war are real, they surely cannot count toward its proportionality or make an otherwise disproportionate war proportionate" (p. 40). For discussion of which good and bad effects are relevant see also McMahan and McKim, "The just war and the Gulf War," and Mellow, *A Critique of Just War Theory.* By claiming that only relevant good and bad effects count in the proportionality calculation, I am not "stacking the deck" in favour of the war in Iraq. My view of what count as relevant good and bad effects closely parallels that of McMahan who has written in opposition to the war.

answer to this question may appear to require very difficult evaluations of the values that attach to goods and harms of very different kinds. For example, how does one weigh the value of providing a people an opportunity to be politically self-determining against the loss of civilian and military lives? Assuming there is some "objective truth" about such values, I am unsure how to argue for particular evaluations. I suspect assigning values, even relative ones, will usually need to rely on considered judgements of individuals. And perhaps we can use some thought experiments to make progress on that count.

Imagine, for example, that you and your children are living under a ruthless regime similar to that of pre-war Iraq. You live in constant fear that you will be arrested and tortured, either for speaking out against the government or simply because someone reports you to the authorities. In the past, tens of thousands of your people have been killed in ruthless campaigns of oppression, and you do not know if or when another such campaign may be mounted. Finally, you fear for the future of your children. Not only will they likely experience the same oppression and systematic terror you face (including the risk of being forced to serve the military or oppressive apparatus of the state), they will also be subject to the harm of being indoctrinated by state propaganda.

If, under this scenario, a foreign power were considering an invasion to overthrow the current regime, with the promise to help the people institute more democratic institutions and a just rule-of-law, I suspect most people would agree that this opportunity would be worth the risks of war—even though those risks include death, horrible maiming and other severe hardships, and even if, as was surely true among Iraqis, there is some doubt about the intentions of the foreign powers.[1]

Even though some would be compelled by such thought experiments, especially if buttressed by further considerations that those oppressed in Iraq likely would share a similar view (see the earlier references to polls in Iraq in which a majority of Iraqis thought removing Saddam Hussein was worth the hardships they suffered), others would object that using such intuitive judgements as a criterion for deciding the (relative) value of certain goods and harms is at best doubtful. In particular, they would point to the possibility of divergence between individuals' "considered" value judgements of moral worth (or the use of thought experiments to arrive at such judgements) and the "truth" of those judgements. While I do not share such scepticism,[2] I do, fortunately, think there is another way of considering the proportionality of *this particular war* that does not rely on the sort of thought experiment and judgements employed so far.

This approach requires recognizing that applying the proportionality criterion involves comparing the relevant goods and harms that the war causes against those relevant goods and harms that would have occurred if the US (and others) had "done nothing" to affect any reduction in the relevant harms and injustices that underlay the humanitarian sufficient just cause.

At first glance, the comparative use of the "doing nothing" alternative may appear to be much too weak an interpretation of the proportionality test, as there are often many alternatives to war that involve more than doing nothing. This objection, however, misses the point of the proportionality test, which is precisely to test the war against such a base case. In contrast, it is in applying the last resort criterion, something I have already done, that one compares the particular "war option" against the "do something else" alternatives. Given this, one may be tempted to draw the conclusion that the proportionality criterion is redundant given the presence of the last resort criterion. This would be a mistake. To see the necessary role played by the proportionality test, one simply needs to recognize

---

[1] For further discussion regarding why a people's capacity and right to be self-determining holds substantial value in proportionality calculations see Hurka, "Proportionality in the morality of war," pp. 52–56. Though Hurka is considering the issue in the context of a military aggressor who is threatening a people's right to be self-determining, what he has to say also speaks to the question of what value legitimately attches to an oppressed people's right and ability to be self-determining.

[2] I do, however, recognize the difficulties that one faces in trying to provide a compelling response to the sceptic.

that the military option can have better relevant consequences than all the other alternatives that have some likelihood of achieving the sufficient just causes and yet still not satisfy the baseline test—i.e. still not be better than "doing nothing."[1]

Once we recognize that the proportionality test requires a comparison between the relevant goods and harms the war caused and those that could reasonably be expected to occur if nothing was done, we are able to show that the war was proportional without relying on comparisons of goods and harms of very different kinds. Instead, we can restrict ourselves to comparisons between similar kinds and show that each such comparison favours the war over doing nothing. This uniformity in results enables us to conclude that the proportionality criterion is satisfied.

Consider first the harm of civilian deaths, injuries and suffering. It is admittedly hard to be precise regarding the extent of suffering that would have occurred if the US had not led an invasion, but a credible argument can be made that the experience would have been much worse without the invasion. Under the roughly twenty years of Saddam Hussein's rule, it is widely agreed that the numbers killed, tortured and displaced was in the hundreds of thousands. Without military action it is very likely that Saddam Hussein and his successors would have continued to carry out large numbers of killings and continued an organized campaign of using torture, fear and displacement of peoples.[2] Even if the numbers only amounted to a fraction of those killed, tortured or terrorized in Saddam Hussein's first twenty years, this would eventually surpass all the civilian and military deaths that have occurred both in the war and in post-war attacks by insurgents and the invading forces. Furthermore,

even if there was a chance that the people themselves (likely far in the future) could have overthrown the regime of Saddam Hussein and his successors, there is no reason to expect that such an event would not itself result in civilian deaths in numbers equal to or much greater than those that resulted, or could have been expected to result, from the invasion and its aftermath.

In response, some may contend that the pre- and post-war risk of the situation deteriorating into a civil war or long-term terrorist campaign by the insurgents must be considered, and that this makes the war, both prospectively and retrospectively (at the time of writing) disproportionate. While the risk of a civil war was and remains significant, I do not, *contra* the suggestion, think this negatively impacts the proportionality calculation. This is because the risk of civil war now or prior to the war was also present in the "do nothing" alternative, in the eventuality that the Iraqi people would be able to overthrow the regime. In fact, it is arguable that if the people themselves overthrew the regime, there would be even less post-war structure and, therefore, even a greater risk that the situation would deteriorate into civil war or wars of succession. The "do nothing" alternative must either, like the war, include the eventual risk of civil war or, on the assumption that the people would not be able to overthrow the regime, include a close to endless litany of acts of killing, torture, terror and oppression that, at some point, would amount to more harm than would likely occur in a civil war. Either way, the proportionality calculation is not negatively affected if we recognize the ongoing risk of civil war.

Consider next the major relevant good of enabling the people to both engage in a collective process of self-determination and establish a rule-of-law that respects human rights. The post-war US help in facilitating elections and in establishing a constitution gives more hope for realizing these goods than if the invasion had not taken place. If, without the US invasion, the people themselves had somehow managed to overthrow the regime, the chances of that regime being replaced with another totalitarian regime or repressive fundamentalist

---

[1] The idea of viewing the "doing nothing" counterfactual as the appropriate baseline comes from Kavka, "Was the Gulf War a just war?," though he suggests there are difficulties with this suggestion—difficulties which I resolve elsewhere (Mellow, *A Critique of Just War Theory*).

[2] A point made earlier in the paper when discussing sufficient just cause, in part by demonstrating the ongoing nature of the large-scale human rights violations.

theocracy would be greater than they are under the US occupation. Furthermore, the war provided the opportunity to realize the above goods years and probably decades sooner than if nothing had been done—a benefit that carries substantial value for the people currently living in Iraq and which, therefore, significantly increases the value of relevant goods resulting from the war. In response, some may point to doubts they had (and continue to have) regarding the intentions of the Bush administration. Given, however, the pre- and post-war rhetoric of the Blair and Bush governments, and the scrutiny provided by the international community and the media, it is (and was) reasonable to conclude that the US and British would be "forced" to move towards more democratic institutions and, ultimately, self-rule.

Thus whether considering harms to civilians and soldiers or the good of enabling the people to engage in a process of self-determination, the US led invasion is on balance substantially better than the alternative of doing nothing. Furthermore, arguably such a conclusion can be made not only post-war, but prospectively as well.[1] Therefore, both prospectively and retrospectively the war meets the proportionality criterion. In making this determination, I have attempted to reason in a way that side-steps the need to undertake precise calculations of the costs and benefits of the war. However, some may remain unconvinced and still contend, at least retrospectively, that the proportionality issue cannot be decided without such calculations. In reply, I have three comments. First, at minimum my principled reasons for counting the war as proportional put the onus on those who demand more precise numbers to explain why those numbers are required in the face of my arguments.

Second, the initial burden to provide the detailed calculations, if required, may also rest on the opponents of the war. Whether this is the case will depend on where one thinks the onus to demonstrate proportionality, or a lack thereof, lies. For example, if just war theory carries a presumption against war that extends to proportionality, then the onus will arguably lie on the supporter of the war to reasonably demonstrate the war's proportionality. However, if there is no such presumption against war, or if that presumption does not extend to the proportionality criterion, then the burden to determine the war's proportionality arguably lies at least as much on opponents of the war as the supporters. For example, in describing the proportionality requirement many contend that the war is unjust if the costs entailed are disproportionate to the expected benefits. In the face of the war meeting the other *(ad bellum)* just war criteria, this could be interpreted as requiring the war's opponent to demonstrate that it is disproportionate.[2]

Finally, for those who contend there is a need for detailed numbers, they must face the reality that there are a range of very complex factual and counterfactual issues in just war theory that have yet to be satisfactorily resolved. Until those issues are resolved, if they can be, any requirement to provide relevant hard numbers in most wars, including the war in Iraq, may well have to remain unanswered.

---

[1] It may be important to have determined that the invasion is "substantially better" than doing nothing, because it may be that the proportionality criterion requires more than mere "on-balance better." Though this possibility is not adequately addressed in the just war literature, it seems plausible that the relevant good effects could slightly outweigh the relevant bad effects and yet not satisfy the proportionality criterion. Imagine, for example, that you could militarily stop a mass killing of a million people, but in doing so would kill, as a side-effect, all but one thousand of those people. My intuition, which may be shared by others, is that such an intervention may not satisfy the proportionality criterion. This intuition may reflect the belief that when third party interveners do the killing, even as a side-effect, this is somehow worse than a ruthless regime doing the killing, something I doubt, or it may reflect the thought that the proportionality criterion is more than an "on-balance" test. If the latter, there remains the difficult question of the precise extent to which the relevant good effects must exceed the relevant bad effects. I am not sure what to say in this regard, and I suspect that an argument for any sort of precise ratio is not likely to be found. Instead, it is plausible that ultimately there will be a large grey area in which the proportionality of a military intervention is open to dispute and where the only arguments available will involve appeals to (intuitive) considered judgements.

---

[2] I am indebted to David Rodin for the points made in this paragraph.

Summary

In summary, I have argued that even if we accept the central claims of the opponents of the war, the resort to war in Iraq was morally justified, both prospectively and retrospectively. I have argued that it meets the sufficient just cause, last resort, and proportionality criteria, and that any failings in terms of legitimate authority and right intention do not undermine the morality of the act of resorting to war. In fact, we have discovered grounds for questioning the inclusion of the right intention criterion in the set of just war criteria.

At the same time it is important to acknowledge that horrific suffering, death and injustices occurred in the war and continue to occur post-war, and also to recognize that grave risks remain. The suffering and death is, of course, to be regretted; the perpetrators of the injustices should, to the extent possible, be punished; and as invaders and occupiers the Americans and the British are obligated to do much to improve the lives of the Iraqis and cooperate with them to help avoid or overcome the future perils they face. Nonetheless, even at this early post-war stage, the morality of resorting to war is clear.

Postscript[1]

Since this article was published a number of reports have come out that underline the magnitude of death and violence that the Iraqis have incurred in the aftermath of the US-led invasion of Iraq. For example, *The Lancet* recently published a study in which the authors estimate that as of July 2006 there were 654,965 excess deaths as a result of the war.[2] And the UN recently reported that over 34,000 Iraqis were killed in 2006.[3] Given these staggering numbers and the real possibility that large scale violence and killing will continue in the months and years ahead, one may reasonably ask if and how these figures, assuming their accuracy, impact on the morality of US-led forces resorting to war.

In writing the original article, I strongly believed (for reasons spelled out in the article) that the most credible debate over the morality of resorting to war in Iraq lay in the debate over the war's proportionality. Given that I still believe this, I suggest the key question is as follows. Does the horrific extent of ongoing violence and killing give us reason to conclude that the resort to war was, retrospectively, not proportionate?

I still contend, for the reasons argued in the original article, that the answer to this question will crucially turn on whether the level of post-invasion violence is worse than the level of violence that one could reasonably expect to have occurred if the invasion had not taken place and, instead, Saddam's regime had, after some uncertain further period of repression, somehow been overthrown or transformed in some other way. On the assumption that this contention is right, I still—even in the face of the horrific violence in Iraq—see no compelling reason to believe that the "other route" to transformation would have, after some further period of terrible oppression under Saddam and the Ba'ath Party, had a better likelihood of avoiding the level of violence we see today. (For more on why this counterfactual comparison is the appropriate one—and not, for example, a mere comparison of the state of affairs before the war with the state of affairs after the intervention—see my article "Counterfactuals and the Proportionality Criterion," *Ethics and International Affairs* 20.4 (2006).)

However, in opposition to my contention others may assert that other paths would have led to the overthrow or transformation of the Iraqi government in ways that would likely have caused much less civil strife. It is hard to know how one

---

[1] [This article was originally published in 2006 in *Journal of Applied Philosophy* 23:3: 293–310. The original article did not have this postscript.]

[2] G. Burnham, R. Lafta, S. Doocy and L. Roberts, "Mortality after the 2003 invasion of Iraq: a cross-sectional cluster sample survey," *The Lancet* 368 (2006). This article is a follow-up to an earlier article: L. Roberts, R. Lafta, R. Garfield, J. Khudhairi and G. Burnham, "Mortality before and after the 2003 invasion of Iraq: cluster sample survey," *The Lancet* 364 (2004).

[3] *The New York Times*, January 17, 2007.

can definitively settle such a debate—a debate that involves a variety of controversial empirical claims and counterfactual assertions. Given this difficulty, let me simply reiterate a point made in the original article, namely that a crucial factor in deciding the morality of the resort to war may well involve determining on whom, and to what extent, the onus lies to demonstrate whether or not the proportionality criterion is satisfied. Making the latter determination is not simply a problem in the current war in Iraq, but also more generally is a significant principled challenge facing just war theorists. Since I see no prospect for a resolution to this nettlesome problem in the near future, I must admit, upon further reflection and in light of the large scale violence, to being less certain about the extent to which, in the context of proportionality, *either side* can make a definitive case that, in retrospect, the proportionality criterion has or has not been adequately satisfied.

Finally, let me use this opportunity to finish with a few additional comments.

Firstly, I see no reason to contend that the current magnitude of violence was anything near inevitable. The twists and turns of war, societies, and governments are notoriously difficult to predict. So just as it would have been a mistake, prior to the war, to contend that there would almost certainly be a straightforward transition to a flourishing and fairly liberal democracy in Iraq, it is equally implausible to contend post-invasion that the current level of strife was inevitable and that the coalition leaders should have realized this. The vast majority of the Iraqi people have always desired a better life with security, basic infrastructure, and self-rule. For one to claim that the desire for a better life was, in hindsight, *inevitably* to be thwarted post-invasion is simply not credible. Instead, I still contend that prospectively there was reason to expect, with some significant likelihood, an outcome better than has transpired. (One must also acknowledge that for many Iraqis things are better than under Saddam and that in certain areas of Iraq there are still reasonable expectations of improvement as we move

forward.[1]) Based on these observations, it is worth emphasizing that even if, *for argument's sake*, one were to accept (contrary to my view) that the war retrospectively fails the proportionality criterion, it does not follow that those who made the original decision to go to war are, on that basis, morally culpable for making the (prospective) decision to resort to war. (However, any discussion of prospective proportionality must, like retrospective discussions, face the existence of the unresolved "onus" problem highlighted in the previous paragraph.)

Secondly, even if the resort to war is morally justified, there may well still be substantial room for morally or strategically criticizing *in bello* or *post bellum* actions of the United States and other coalition members. With respect to moral criticisms, there may, of course, be certain *in bello* or *post bellum* actions that are in themselves immoral and for which those responsible deserve moral condemnation and punishment. This must be decided on a case-by-case basis. With respect to strategic criticisms one may also argue that certain *in bello* or *post bellum* actions or strategies have made the situation worse than it otherwise could have been. Such criticism or questioning represents crucial and appropriate follow-up to all the complexity that is inherent in undertaking a war and *post bellum* activities. However, even if such criticism highlights legitimate flaws, this need not entail that those responsible for the flawed strategies have acted in ways that make them deserving of moral condemnation. This would only be the case if there were further evidence of negligence. Again, the possibility of such negligence (or other immoral activities) would have to be explored on a case-by-case basis.

Finally, even if the resort to war was morally justified, this does not entail that the American and British peoples may not have cause to debate or question whether the resources used in war and post-intervention activities could not have been used more

---

[1] Obviously conditions are shifting fairly quickly in Iraq, but I refer the reader to the following poll carried out by a number of media organizations: http://news.bbc.co.uk/l/hi/world/middle_east/4514414.stm.

effectively elsewhere and without the terrible cost in terms of military lives. With the financial cost of the war being measured in the hundreds of billions of dollars, Americans should reflect upon and ask if that money (based on either prospective or retrospective estimates) would not have been better spent both domestically and internationally in ways that would have improved the plight of the world's poor and suffering, provided better schooling for America's youth, reduced the level of America's growing government debt, and so on. Such a debate is both appropriate and healthy for the simple reason that doing what is morally permissible or morally justifiable is not the same as doing what is best.

Acknowledgements

My gratitude goes out to Dennis McKerlie, Thomas Hurka, Jeff McMahan, members of the Ethics and Political Philosophy Research Group at the University of Calgary, and readers for the *Journal of Applied Philosophy,* all of whom provided helpful comments on earlier drafts of this paper.

Index